T0189891

Lecture Notes in Computer Science   12352

More information about this series at http://www.springer.com/series/7412

Andrea Vedaldi · Horst Bischof ·
Thomas Brox · Jan-Michael Frahm (Eds.)

Computer Vision – ECCV 2020

16th European Conference
Glasgow, UK, August 23–28, 2020
Proceedings, Part VII

Springer

Editors
Andrea Vedaldi (iD)
University of Oxford
Oxford, UK

Horst Bischof (iD)
Graz University of Technology
Graz, Austria

Thomas Brox (iD)
University of Freiburg
Freiburg im Breisgau, Germany

Jan-Michael Frahm
University of North Carolina at Chapel Hill
Chapel Hill, NC, USA

ISSN 0302-9743   ISSN 1611-3349 (electronic)
Lecture Notes in Computer Science
ISBN 978-3-030-58570-9   ISBN 978-3-030-58571-6 (eBook)
https://doi.org/10.1007/978-3-030-58571-6

LNCS Sublibrary: SL6 – Image Processing, Computer Vision, Pattern Recognition, and Graphics

This Springer imprint is published by the registered company Springer Nature Switzerland AG
The registered company address is: Gewerbestrasse 11, 6330 Cham, Switzerland

Foreword

Hosting the European Conference on Computer Vision (ECCV 2020) was certainly an exciting journey. From the 2016 plan to hold it at the Edinburgh International Conference Centre (hosting 1,800 delegates) to the 2018 plan to hold it at Glasgow's Scottish Exhibition Centre (up to 6,000 delegates), we finally ended with moving online because of the COVID-19 outbreak. While possibly having fewer delegates than expected because of the online format, ECCV 2020 still had over 3,100 registered participants.

Although online, the conference delivered most of the activities expected at a face-to-face conference: peer-reviewed papers, industrial exhibitors, demonstrations, and messaging between delegates. In addition to the main technical sessions, the conference included a strong program of satellite events with 16 tutorials and 44 workshops.

Furthermore, the online conference format enabled new conference features. Every paper had an associated teaser video and a longer full presentation video. Along with the papers and slides from the videos, all these materials were available the week before the conference. This allowed delegates to become familiar with the paper content and be ready for the live interaction with the authors during the conference week. The live event consisted of brief presentations by the oral and spotlight authors and industrial sponsors. Question and answer sessions for all papers were timed to occur twice so delegates from around the world had convenient access to the authors.

As with ECCV 2018, authors' draft versions of the papers appeared online with open access, now on both the Computer Vision Foundation (CVF) and the European Computer Vision Association (ECVA) websites. An archival publication arrangement was put in place with the cooperation of Springer. SpringerLink hosts the final version of the papers with further improvements, such as activating reference links and supplementary materials. These two approaches benefit all potential readers: a version available freely for all researchers, and an authoritative and citable version with additional benefits for SpringerLink subscribers. We thank Alfred Hofmann and Aliaksandr Birukou from Springer for helping to negotiate this agreement, which we expect will continue for future versions of ECCV.

August 2020

Vittorio Ferrari
Bob Fisher
Cordelia Schmid
Emanuele Trucco

Preface

Welcome to the proceedings of the European Conference on Computer Vision (ECCV 2020). This is a unique edition of ECCV in many ways. Due to the COVID-19 pandemic, this is the first time the conference was held online, in a virtual format. This was also the first time the conference relied exclusively on the Open Review platform to manage the review process. Despite these challenges ECCV is thriving. The conference received 5,150 valid paper submissions, of which 1,360 were accepted for publication (27%) and, of those, 160 were presented as spotlights (3%) and 104 as orals (2%). This amounts to more than twice the number of submissions to ECCV 2018 (2,439). Furthermore, CVPR, the largest conference on computer vision, received 5,850 submissions this year, meaning that ECCV is now 87% the size of CVPR in terms of submissions. By comparison, in 2018 the size of ECCV was only 73% of CVPR.

The review model was similar to previous editions of ECCV; in particular, it was double blind in the sense that the authors did not know the name of the reviewers and vice versa. Furthermore, each conference submission was held confidentially, and was only publicly revealed if and once accepted for publication. Each paper received at least three reviews, totalling more than 15,000 reviews. Handling the review process at this scale was a significant challenge. In order to ensure that each submission received as fair and high-quality reviews as possible, we recruited 2,830 reviewers (a 130% increase with reference to 2018) and 207 area chairs (a 60% increase). The area chairs were selected based on their technical expertise and reputation, largely among people that served as area chair in previous top computer vision and machine learning conferences (ECCV, ICCV, CVPR, NeurIPS, etc.). Reviewers were similarly invited from previous conferences. We also encouraged experienced area chairs to suggest additional chairs and reviewers in the initial phase of recruiting.

Despite doubling the number of submissions, the reviewer load was slightly reduced from 2018, from a maximum of 8 papers down to 7 (with some reviewers offering to handle 6 papers plus an emergency review). The area chair load increased slightly, from 18 papers on average to 22 papers on average.

Conflicts of interest between authors, area chairs, and reviewers were handled largely automatically by the Open Review platform via their curated list of user profiles. Many authors submitting to ECCV already had a profile in Open Review. We set a paper registration deadline one week before the paper submission deadline in order to encourage all missing authors to register and create their Open Review profiles well on time (in practice, we allowed authors to create/change papers arbitrarily until the submission deadline). Except for minor issues with users creating duplicate profiles, this allowed us to easily and quickly identify institutional conflicts, and avoid them, while matching papers to area chairs and reviewers.

Papers were matched to area chairs based on: an affinity score computed by the Open Review platform, which is based on paper titles and abstracts, and an affinity score computed by the Toronto Paper Matching System (TPMS), which is based on the paper's full text, the area chair bids for individual papers, load balancing, and conflict avoidance. Open Review provides the program chairs a convenient web interface to experiment with different configurations of the matching algorithm. The chosen configuration resulted in about 50% of the assigned papers to be highly ranked by the area chair bids, and 50% to be ranked in the middle, with very few low bids assigned.

Assignments to reviewers were similar, with two differences. First, there was a maximum of 7 papers assigned to each reviewer. Second, area chairs recommended up to seven reviewers per paper, providing another highly-weighed term to the affinity scores used for matching.

The assignment of papers to area chairs was smooth. However, it was more difficult to find suitable reviewers for all papers. Having a ratio of 5.6 papers per reviewer with a maximum load of 7 (due to emergency reviewer commitment), which did not allow for much wiggle room in order to also satisfy conflict and expertise constraints. We received some complaints from reviewers who did not feel qualified to review specific papers and we reassigned them wherever possible. However, the large scale of the conference, the many constraints, and the fact that a large fraction of such complaints arrived very late in the review process made this process very difficult and not all complaints could be addressed.

Reviewers had six weeks to complete their assignments. Possibly due to COVID-19 or the fact that the NeurIPS deadline was moved closer to the review deadline, a record 30% of the reviews were still missing after the deadline. By comparison, ECCV 2018 experienced only 10% missing reviews at this stage of the process. In the subsequent week, area chairs chased the missing reviews intensely, found replacement reviewers in their own team, and managed to reach 10% missing reviews. Eventually, we could provide almost all reviews (more than 99.9%) with a delay of only a couple of days on the initial schedule by a significant use of emergency reviews. If this trend is confirmed, it might be a major challenge to run a smooth review process in future editions of ECCV. The community must reconsider prioritization of the time spent on paper writing (the number of submissions increased a lot despite COVID-19) and time spent on paper reviewing (the number of reviews delivered in time decreased a lot presumably due to COVID-19 or NeurIPS deadline). With this imbalance the peer-review system that ensures the quality of our top conferences may break soon.

Reviewers submitted their reviews independently. In the reviews, they had the opportunity to ask questions to the authors to be addressed in the rebuttal. However, reviewers were told not to request any significant new experiment. Using the Open Review interface, authors could provide an answer to each individual review, but were also allowed to cross-reference reviews and responses in their answers. Rather than PDF files, we allowed the use of formatted text for the rebuttal. The rebuttal and initial reviews were then made visible to all reviewers and the primary area chair for a given paper. The area chair encouraged and moderated the reviewer discussion. During the discussions, reviewers were invited to reach a consensus and possibly adjust their ratings as a result of the discussion and of the evidence in the rebuttal.

After the discussion period ended, most reviewers entered a final rating and recommendation, although in many cases this did not differ from their initial recommendation. Based on the updated reviews and discussion, the primary area chair then made a preliminary decision to accept or reject the paper and wrote a justification for it (meta-review). Except for cases where the outcome of this process was absolutely clear (as indicated by the three reviewers and primary area chairs all recommending clear rejection), the decision was then examined and potentially challenged by a secondary area chair. This led to further discussion and overturning a small number of preliminary decisions. Needless to say, there was no in-person area chair meeting, which would have been impossible due to COVID-19.

Area chairs were invited to observe the consensus of the reviewers whenever possible and use extreme caution in overturning a clear consensus to accept or reject a paper. If an area chair still decided to do so, she/he was asked to clearly justify it in the meta-review and to explicitly obtain the agreement of the secondary area chair. In practice, very few papers were rejected after being confidently accepted by the reviewers.

This was the first time Open Review was used as the main platform to run ECCV. In 2018, the program chairs used CMT3 for the user-facing interface and Open Review internally, for matching and conflict resolution. Since it is clearly preferable to only use a single platform, this year we switched to using Open Review in full. The experience was largely positive. The platform is highly-configurable, scalable, and open source. Being written in Python, it is easy to write scripts to extract data programmatically. The paper matching and conflict resolution algorithms and interfaces are top-notch, also due to the excellent author profiles in the platform. Naturally, there were a few kinks along the way due to the fact that the ECCV Open Review configuration was created from scratch for this event and it differs in substantial ways from many other Open Review conferences. However, the Open Review development and support team did a fantastic job in helping us to get the configuration right and to address issues in a timely manner as they unavoidably occurred. We cannot thank them enough for the tremendous effort they put into this project.

Finally, we would like to thank everyone involved in making ECCV 2020 possible in these very strange and difficult times. This starts with our authors, followed by the area chairs and reviewers, who ran the review process at an unprecedented scale. The whole Open Review team (and in particular Melisa Bok, Mohit Unyal, Carlos Mondragon Chapa, and Celeste Martinez Gomez) worked incredibly hard for the entire duration of the process. We would also like to thank René Vidal for contributing to the adoption of Open Review. Our thanks also go to Laurent Charling for TPMS and to the program chairs of ICML, ICLR, and NeurIPS for cross checking double submissions. We thank the website chair, Giovanni Farinella, and the CPI team (in particular Ashley Cook, Miriam Verdon, Nicola McGrane, and Sharon Kerr) for promptly adding material to the website as needed in the various phases of the process. Finally, we thank the publication chairs, Albert Ali Salah, Hamdi Dibeklioglu, Metehan Doyran, Henry Howard-Jenkins, Victor Prisacariu, Siyu Tang, and Gul Varol, who managed to compile these substantial proceedings in an exceedingly compressed schedule. We express our thanks to the ECVA team, in particular Kristina Scherbaum for allowing open access of the proceedings. We thank Alfred Hofmann from Springer who again serve as the publisher. Finally, we thank the other chairs of ECCV 2020, including in particular the general chairs for very useful feedback with the handling of the program.

August 2020   Andrea Vedaldi
                                                                        Horst Bischof
                                                                        Thomas Brox
                                                                        Jan-Michael Frahm

Organization

General Chairs

Vittorio Ferrari	Google Research, Switzerland
Bob Fisher	University of Edinburgh, UK
Cordelia Schmid	Google and Inria, France
Emanuele Trucco	University of Dundee, UK

Program Chairs

Andrea Vedaldi	University of Oxford, UK
Horst Bischof	Graz University of Technology, Austria
Thomas Brox	University of Freiburg, Germany
Jan-Michael Frahm	University of North Carolina, USA

Industrial Liaison Chairs

Jim Ashe	University of Edinburgh, UK
Helmut Grabner	Zurich University of Applied Sciences, Switzerland
Diane Larlus	NAVER LABS Europe, France
Cristian Novotny	University of Edinburgh, UK

Local Arrangement Chairs

Yvan Petillot	Heriot-Watt University, UK
Paul Siebert	University of Glasgow, UK

Academic Demonstration Chair

Thomas Mensink	Google Research and University of Amsterdam, The Netherlands

Poster Chair

Stephen Mckenna	University of Dundee, UK

Technology Chair

Gerardo Aragon Camarasa	University of Glasgow, UK

Tutorial Chairs

Carlo Colombo   University of Florence, Italy
Sotirios Tsaftaris   University of Edinburgh, UK

Publication Chairs

Albert Ali Salah   Utrecht University, The Netherlands
Hamdi Dibeklioglu   Bilkent University, Turkey
Metehan Doyran   Utrecht University, The Netherlands
Henry Howard-Jenkins   University of Oxford, UK
Victor Adrian Prisacariu University of Oxford, UK
Siyu Tang   ETH Zurich, Switzerland
Gul Varol   University of Oxford, UK

Website Chair

Giovanni Maria Farinella University of Catania, Italy

Workshops Chairs

Adrien Bartoli   University of Clermont Auvergne, France
Andrea Fusiello   University of Udine, Italy

Area Chairs

Lourdes Agapito   University College London, UK
Zeynep Akata   University of Tübingen, Germany
Karteek Alahari   Inria, France
Antonis Argyros   University of Crete, Greece
Hossein Azizpour   KTH Royal Institute of Technology, Sweden
Joao P. Barreto   Universidade de Coimbra, Portugal
Alexander C. Berg   University of North Carolina at Chapel Hill, USA
Matthew B. Blaschko   KU Leuven, Belgium
Lubomir D. Bourdev   WaveOne, Inc., USA
Edmond Boyer   Inria, France
Yuri Boykov   University of Waterloo, Canada
Gabriel Brostow   University College London, UK
Michael S. Brown   National University of Singapore, Singapore
Jianfei Cai   Monash University, Australia
Barbara Caputo   Politecnico di Torino, Italy
Ayan Chakrabarti   Washington University, St. Louis, USA
Tat-Jen Cham   Nanyang Technological University, Singapore
Manmohan Chandraker   University of California, San Diego, USA
Rama Chellappa   Johns Hopkins University, USA
Liang-Chieh Chen   Google, USA

Haibin Ling	Stony Brooks, State University of New York, USA
Jiaying Liu	Peking University, China
Ming-Yu Liu	NVIDIA, USA
Si Liu	Beihang University, China
Xiaoming Liu	Michigan State University, USA
Huchuan Lu	Dalian University of Technology, China
Simon Lucey	Carnegie Mellon University, USA
Jiebo Luo	University of Rochester, USA
Julien Mairal	Inria, France
Michael Maire	University of Chicago, USA
Subhransu Maji	University of Massachusetts, Amherst, USA
Yasushi Makihara	Osaka University, Japan
Jiri Matas	Czech Technical University in Prague, Czech Republic
Yasuyuki Matsushita	Osaka University, Japan
Philippos Mordohai	Stevens Institute of Technology, USA
Vittorio Murino	University of Verona, Italy
Naila Murray	NAVER LABS Europe, France
Hajime Nagahara	Osaka University, Japan
P. J. Narayanan	International Institute of Information Technology (IIIT), Hyderabad, India
Nassir Navab	Technical University of Munich, Germany
Natalia Neverova	Facebook AI Research, France
Matthias Niessner	Technical University of Munich, Germany
Jean-Marc Odobez	Idiap Research Institute and Swiss Federal Institute of Technology Lausanne, Switzerland
Francesca Odone	Università di Genova, Italy
Takeshi Oishi	The University of Tokyo, Tokyo Institute of Technology, Japan
Vicente Ordonez	University of Virginia, USA
Manohar Paluri	Facebook AI Research, USA
Maja Pantic	Imperial College London, UK
In Kyu Park	Inha University, South Korea
Ioannis Patras	Queen Mary University of London, UK
Patrick Perez	Valeo, France
Bryan A. Plummer	Boston University, USA
Thomas Pock	Graz University of Technology, Austria
Marc Pollefeys	ETH Zurich and Microsoft MR & AI Zurich Lab, Switzerland
Jean Ponce	Inria, France
Gerard Pons-Moll	MPII, Saarland Informatics Campus, Germany
Jordi Pont-Tuset	Google, Switzerland
James Matthew Rehg	Georgia Institute of Technology, USA
Ian Reid	University of Adelaide, Australia
Olaf Ronneberger	DeepMind London, UK
Stefan Roth	TU Darmstadt, Germany
Bryan Russell	Adobe Research, USA

Kwang Moo Yi	University of Victoria, Canada
Zhaozheng Yin	Stony Brook, State University of New York, USA
Chang D. Yoo	Korea Advanced Institute of Science and Technology, South Korea
Shaodi You	University of Amsterdam, The Netherlands
Jingyi Yu	ShanghaiTech University, China
Stella Yu	University of California, Berkeley, and ICSI, USA
Stefanos Zafeiriou	Imperial College London, UK
Hongbin Zha	Peking University, China
Tianzhu Zhang	University of Science and Technology of China, China
Liang Zheng	Australian National University, Australia
Todd E. Zickler	Harvard University, USA
Andrew Zisserman	University of Oxford, UK

Technical Program Committee

Sathyanarayanan N. Aakur	Samuel Albanie	Pablo Arbelaez
Wael Abd Almgaeed	Shadi Albarqouni	Shervin Ardeshir
Abdelrahman Abdelhamed	Cenek Albl	Sercan O. Arik
Abdullah Abuolaim	Hassan Abu Alhaija	Anil Armagan
Supreeth Achar	Daniel Aliaga	Anurag Arnab
Hanno Ackermann	Mohammad S. Aliakbarian	Chetan Arora
Ehsan Adeli	Rahaf Aljundi	Federica Arrigoni
Triantafyllos Afouras	Thiemo Alldieck	Mathieu Aubry
Sameer Agarwal	Jon Almazan	Shai Avidan
Aishwarya Agrawal	Jose M. Alvarez	Angelica I. Aviles-Rivero
Harsh Agrawal	Senjian An	Yannis Avrithis
Pulkit Agrawal	Saket Anand	Ismail Ben Ayed
Antonio Agudo	Codruta Ancuti	Shekoofeh Azizi
Eirikur Agustsson	Cosmin Ancuti	Ioan Andrei Bârsan
Karim Ahmed	Peter Anderson	Artem Babenko
Byeongjoo Ahn	Juan Andrade-Cetto	Deepak Babu Sam
Unaiza Ahsan	Alexander Andreopoulos	Seung-Hwan Baek
Thalaiyasingam Ajanthan	Misha Andriluka	Seungryul Baek
Kenan E. Ak	Dragomir Anguelov	Andrew D. Bagdanov
Emre Akbas	Rushil Anirudh	Shai Bagon
Naveed Akhtar	Michel Antunes	Yuval Bahat
Derya Akkaynak	Oisin Mac Aodha	Junjie Bai
Yagiz Aksoy	Srikar Appalaraju	Song Bai
Ziad Al-Halah	Relja Arandjelovic	Xiang Bai
Xavier Alameda-Pineda	Nikita Araslanov	Yalong Bai
Jean-Baptiste Alayrac	Andre Araujo	Yancheng Bai
	Helder Araujo	Peter Bajcsy
		Slawomir Bak

Mahsa Baktashmotlagh
Kavita Bala
Yogesh Balaji
Guha Balakrishnan
V. N. Balasubramanian
Federico Baldassarre
Vassileios Balntas
Shurjo Banerjee
Aayush Bansal
Ankan Bansal
Jianmin Bao
Linchao Bao
Wenbo Bao
Yingze Bao
Akash Bapat
Md Jawadul Hasan Bappy
Fabien Baradel
Lorenzo Baraldi
Daniel Barath
Adrian Barbu
Kobus Barnard
Nick Barnes
Francisco Barranco
Jonathan T. Barron
Arslan Basharat
Chaim Baskin
Anil S. Baslamisli
Jorge Batista
Kayhan Batmanghelich
Konstantinos Batsos
David Bau
Luis Baumela
Christoph Baur
Eduardo
  Bayro-Corrochano
Paul Beardsley
Jan Bednavr'ik
Oscar Beijbom
Philippe Bekaert
Esube Bekele
Vasileios Belagiannis
Ohad Ben-Shahar
Abhijit Bendale
Róger Bermúdez-Chacón
Maxim Berman
Jesus Bermudez-cameo

Florian Bernard
Stefano Berretti
Marcelo Bertalmio
Gedas Bertasius
Cigdem Beyan
Lucas Beyer
Vijayakumar Bhagavatula
Arjun Nitin Bhagoji
Apratim Bhattacharyya
Binod Bhattarai
Sai Bi
Jia-Wang Bian
Simone Bianco
Adel Bibi
Tolga Birdal
Tom Bishop
Soma Biswas
Mårten Björkman
Volker Blanz
Vishnu Boddeti
Navaneeth Bodla
Simion-Vlad Bogolin
Xavier Boix
Piotr Bojanowski
Timo Bolkart
Guido Borghi
Larbi Boubchir
Guillaume Bourmaud
Adrien Bousseau
Thierry Bouwmans
Richard Bowden
Hakan Boyraz
Mathieu Brédif
Samarth Brahmbhatt
Steve Branson
Nikolas Brasch
Biagio Brattoli
Ernesto Brau
Toby P. Breckon
Francois Bremond
Jesus Briales
Sofia Broomé
Marcus A. Brubaker
Luc Brun
Silvia Bucci
Shyamal Buch

Pradeep Buddharaju
Uta Buechler
Mai Bui
Tu Bui
Adrian Bulat
Giedrius T. Burachas
Elena Burceanu
Xavier P. Burgos-Artizzu
Kaylee Burns
Andrei Bursuc
Benjamin Busam
Wonmin Byeon
Zoya Bylinskii
Sergi Caelles
Jianrui Cai
Minjie Cai
Yujun Cai
Zhaowei Cai
Zhipeng Cai
Juan C. Caicedo
Simone Calderara
Necati Cihan Camgoz
Dylan Campbell
Octavia Camps
Jiale Cao
Kaidi Cao
Liangliang Cao
Xiangyong Cao
Xiaochun Cao
Yang Cao
Yu Cao
Yue Cao
Zhangjie Cao
Luca Carlone
Mathilde Caron
Dan Casas
Thomas J. Cashman
Umberto Castellani
Lluis Castrejon
Jacopo Cavazza
Fabio Cermelli
Hakan Cevikalp
Menglei Chai
Ishani Chakraborty
Rudrasis Chakraborty
Antoni B. Chan

Kwok-Ping Chan
Siddhartha Chandra
Sharat Chandran
Arjun Chandrasekaran
Angel X. Chang
Che-Han Chang
Hong Chang
Hyun Sung Chang
Hyung Jin Chang
Jianlong Chang
Ju Yong Chang
Ming-Ching Chang
Simyung Chang
Xiaojun Chang
Yu-Wei Chao
Devendra S. Chaplot
Arslan Chaudhry
Rizwan A. Chaudhry
Can Chen
Chang Chen
Chao Chen
Chen Chen
Chu-Song Chen
Dapeng Chen
Dong Chen
Dongdong Chen
Guanying Chen
Hongge Chen
Hsin-yi Chen
Huaijin Chen
Hwann-Tzong Chen
Jianbo Chen
Jianhui Chen
Jiansheng Chen
Jiaxin Chen
Jie Chen
Jun-Cheng Chen
Kan Chen
Kevin Chen
Lin Chen
Long Chen
Min-Hung Chen
Qifeng Chen
Shi Chen
Shixing Chen
Tianshui Chen

Weifeng Chen
Weikai Chen
Xi Chen
Xiaohan Chen
Xiaozhi Chen
Xilin Chen
Xingyu Chen
Xinlei Chen
Xinyun Chen
Yi-Ting Chen
Yilun Chen
Ying-Cong Chen
Yinpeng Chen
Yiran Chen
Yu Chen
Yu-Sheng Chen
Yuhua Chen
Yun-Chun Chen
Yunpeng Chen
Yuntao Chen
Zhuoyuan Chen
Zitian Chen
Anchieh Cheng
Bowen Cheng
Erkang Cheng
Gong Cheng
Guangliang Cheng
Jingchun Cheng
Jun Cheng
Li Cheng
Ming-Ming Cheng
Yu Cheng
Ziang Cheng
Anoop Cherian
Dmitry Chetverikov
Ngai-man Cheung
William Cheung
Ajad Chhatkuli
Naoki Chiba
Benjamin Chidester
Han-pang Chiu
Mang Tik Chiu
Wei-Chen Chiu
Donghyeon Cho
Hojin Cho
Minsu Cho

Nam Ik Cho
Tim Cho
Tae Eun Choe
Chiho Choi
Edward Choi
Inchang Choi
Jinsoo Choi
Jonghyun Choi
Jongwon Choi
Yukyung Choi
Hisham Cholakkal
Eunji Chong
Jaegul Choo
Christopher Choy
Hang Chu
Peng Chu
Wen-Sheng Chu
Albert Chung
Joon Son Chung
Hai Ci
Safa Cicek
Ramazan G. Cinbis
Arridhana Ciptadi
Javier Civera
James J. Clark
Ronald Clark
Felipe Codevilla
Michael Cogswell
Andrea Cohen
Maxwell D. Collins
Carlo Colombo
Yang Cong
Adria R. Continente
Marcella Cornia
John Richard Corring
Darren Cosker
Dragos Costea
Garrison W. Cottrell
Florent Couzinie-Devy
Marco Cristani
Ioana Croitoru
James L. Crowley
Jiequan Cui
Zhaopeng Cui
Ross Cutler
Antonio D'Innocente

Rozenn Dahyot
Bo Dai
Dengxin Dai
Hang Dai
Longquan Dai
Shuyang Dai
Xiyang Dai
Yuchao Dai
Adrian V. Dalca
Dima Damen
Bharath B. Damodaran
Kristin Dana
Martin Danelljan
Zheng Dang
Zachary Alan Daniels
Donald G. Dansereau
Abhishek Das
Samyak Datta
Achal Dave
Titas De
Rodrigo de Bem
Teo de Campos
Raoul de Charette
Shalini De Mello
Joseph DeGol
Herve Delingette
Haowen Deng
Jiankang Deng
Weijian Deng
Zhiwei Deng
Joachim Denzler
Konstantinos G. Derpanis
Aditya Deshpande
Frederic Devernay
Somdip Dey
Arturo Deza
Abhinav Dhall
Helisa Dhamo
Vikas Dhiman
Fillipe Dias Moreira
de Souza
Ali Diba
Ferran Diego
Guiguang Ding
Henghui Ding
Jian Ding

Mingyu Ding
Xinghao Ding
Zhengming Ding
Robert DiPietro
Cosimo Distante
Ajay Divakaran
Mandar Dixit
Abdelaziz Djelouah
Thanh-Toan Do
Jose Dolz
Bo Dong
Chao Dong
Jiangxin Dong
Weiming Dong
Weisheng Dong
Xingping Dong
Xuanyi Dong
Yinpeng Dong
Gianfranco Doretto
Hazel Doughty
Hassen Drira
Bertram Drost
Dawei Du
Ye Duan
Yueqi Duan
Abhimanyu Dubey
Anastasia Dubrovina
Stefan Duffner
Chi Nhan Duong
Thibaut Durand
Zoran Duric
Iulia Duta
Debidatta Dwibedi
Benjamin Eckart
Marc Eder
Marzieh Edraki
Alexei A. Efros
Kiana Ehsani
Hazm Kemal Ekenel
James H. Elder
Mohamed Elgharib
Shireen Elhabian
Ehsan Elhamifar
Mohamed Elhoseiny
Ian Endres
N. Benjamin Erichson

Jan Ernst
Sergio Escalera
Francisco Escolano
Victor Escorcia
Carlos Esteves
Francisco J. Estrada
Bin Fan
Chenyou Fan
Deng-Ping Fan
Haoqi Fan
Hehe Fan
Heng Fan
Kai Fan
Lijie Fan
Linxi Fan
Quanfu Fan
Shaojing Fan
Xiaochuan Fan
Xin Fan
Yuchen Fan
Sean Fanello
Hao-Shu Fang
Haoyang Fang
Kuan Fang
Yi Fang
Yuming Fang
Azade Farshad
Alireza Fathi
Raanan Fattal
Joao Fayad
Xiaohan Fei
Christoph Feichtenhofer
Michael Felsberg
Chen Feng
Jiashi Feng
Junyi Feng
Mengyang Feng
Qianli Feng
Zhenhua Feng
Michele Fenzi
Andras Ferencz
Martin Fergie
Basura Fernando
Ethan Fetaya
Michael Firman
John W. Fisher

Matthew Fisher
Boris Flach
Corneliu Florea
Wolfgang Foerstner
David Fofi
Gian Luca Foresti
Per-Erik Forssen
David Fouhey
Katerina Fragkiadaki
Victor Fragoso
Jean-Sébastien Franco
Ohad Fried
Iuri Frosio
Cheng-Yang Fu
Huazhu Fu
Jianlong Fu
Jingjing Fu
Xueyang Fu
Yanwei Fu
Ying Fu
Yun Fu
Olac Fuentes
Kent Fujiwara
Takuya Funatomi
Christopher Funk
Thomas Funkhouser
Antonino Furnari
Ryo Furukawa
Erik Gärtner
Raghudeep Gadde
Matheus Gadelha
Vandit Gajjar
Trevor Gale
Juergen Gall
Mathias Gallardo
Guillermo Gallego
Orazio Gallo
Chuang Gan
Zhe Gan
Madan Ravi Ganesh
Aditya Ganeshan
Siddha Ganju
Bin-Bin Gao
Changxin Gao
Feng Gao
Hongchang Gao

Jin Gao
Jiyang Gao
Junbin Gao
Katelyn Gao
Lin Gao
Mingfei Gao
Ruiqi Gao
Ruohan Gao
Shenghua Gao
Yuan Gao
Yue Gao
Noa Garcia
Alberto Garcia-Garcia
Guillermo
    Garcia-Hernando
Jacob R. Gardner
Animesh Garg
Kshitiz Garg
Rahul Garg
Ravi Garg
Philip N. Garner
Kirill Gavrilyuk
Paul Gay
Shiming Ge
Weifeng Ge
Baris Gecer
Xin Geng
Kyle Genova
Stamatios Georgoulis
Bernard Ghanem
Michael Gharbi
Kamran Ghasedi
Golnaz Ghiasi
Arnab Ghosh
Partha Ghosh
Silvio Giancola
Andrew Gilbert
Rohit Girdhar
Xavier Giro-i-Nieto
Thomas Gittings
Ioannis Gkioulekas
Clement Godard
Vaibhava Goel
Bastian Goldluecke
Lluis Gomez
Nuno Gonçalves

Dong Gong
Ke Gong
Mingming Gong
Abel Gonzalez-Garcia
Ariel Gordon
Daniel Gordon
Paulo Gotardo
Venu Madhav Govindu
Ankit Goyal
Priya Goyal
Raghav Goyal
Benjamin Graham
Douglas Gray
Brent A. Griffin
Etienne Grossmann
David Gu
Jiayuan Gu
Jiuxiang Gu
Lin Gu
Qiao Gu
Shuhang Gu
Jose J. Guerrero
Paul Guerrero
Jie Gui
Jean-Yves Guillemaut
Riza Alp Guler
Erhan Gundogdu
Fatma Guney
Guodong Guo
Kaiwen Guo
Qi Guo
Sheng Guo
Shi Guo
Tiantong Guo
Xiaojie Guo
Yijie Guo
Yiluan Guo
Yuanfang Guo
Yulan Guo
Agrim Gupta
Ankush Gupta
Mohit Gupta
Saurabh Gupta
Tanmay Gupta
Danna Gurari
Abner Guzman-Rivera

JunYoung Gwak
Michael Gygli
Jung-Woo Ha
Simon Hadfield
Isma Hadji
Bjoern Haefner
Taeyoung Hahn
Levente Hajder
Peter Hall
Emanuela Haller
Stefan Haller
Bumsub Ham
Abdullah Hamdi
Dongyoon Han
Hu Han
Jungong Han
Junwei Han
Kai Han
Tian Han
Xiaoguang Han
Xintong Han
Yahong Han
Ankur Handa
Zekun Hao
Albert Haque
Tatsuya Harada
Mehrtash Harandi
Adam W. Harley
Mahmudul Hasan
Atsushi Hashimoto
Ali Hatamizadeh
Munawar Hayat
Dongliang He
Jingrui He
Junfeng He
Kaiming He
Kun He
Lei He
Pan He
Ran He
Shengfeng He
Tong He
Weipeng He
Xuming He
Yang He
Yihui He

Zhihai He
Chinmay Hegde
Janne Heikkila
Mattias P. Heinrich
Stéphane Herbin
Alexander Hermans
Luis Herranz
John R. Hershey
Aaron Hertzmann
Roei Herzig
Anders Heyden
Steven Hickson
Otmar Hilliges
Tomas Hodan
Judy Hoffman
Michael Hofmann
Yannick Hold-Geoffroy
Namdar Homayounfar
Sina Honari
Richang Hong
Seunghoon Hong
Xiaopeng Hong
Yi Hong
Hidekata Hontani
Anthony Hoogs
Yedid Hoshen
Mir Rayat Imtiaz Hossain
Junhui Hou
Le Hou
Lu Hou
Tingbo Hou
Wei-Lin Hsiao
Cheng-Chun Hsu
Gee-Sern Jison Hsu
Kuang-jui Hsu
Changbo Hu
Di Hu
Guosheng Hu
Han Hu
Hao Hu
Hexiang Hu
Hou-Ning Hu
Jie Hu
Junlin Hu
Nan Hu
Ping Hu

Ronghang Hu
Xiaowei Hu
Yinlin Hu
Yuan-Ting Hu
Zhe Hu
Binh-Son Hua
Yang Hua
Bingyao Huang
Di Huang
Dong Huang
Fay Huang
Haibin Huang
Haozhi Huang
Heng Huang
Huaibo Huang
Jia-Bin Huang
Jing Huang
Jingwei Huang
Kaizhu Huang
Lei Huang
Qiangui Huang
Qiaoying Huang
Qingqiu Huang
Qixing Huang
Shaoli Huang
Sheng Huang
Siyuan Huang
Weilin Huang
Wenbing Huang
Xiangru Huang
Xun Huang
Yan Huang
Yifei Huang
Yue Huang
Zhiwu Huang
Zilong Huang
Minyoung Huh
Zhuo Hui
Matthias B. Hullin
Martin Humenberger
Wei-Chih Hung
Zhouyuan Huo
Junhwa Hur
Noureldien Hussein
Jyh-Jing Hwang
Seong Jae Hwang

Sung Ju Hwang
Ichiro Ide
Ivo Ihrke
Daiki Ikami
Satoshi Ikehata
Nazli Ikizler-Cinbis
Sunghoon Im
Yani Ioannou
Radu Tudor Ionescu
Umar Iqbal
Go Irie
Ahmet Iscen
Md Amirul Islam
Vamsi Ithapu
Nathan Jacobs
Arpit Jain
Himalaya Jain
Suyog Jain
Stuart James
Won-Dong Jang
Yunseok Jang
Ronnachai Jaroensri
Dinesh Jayaraman
Sadeep Jayasumana
Suren Jayasuriya
Herve Jegou
Simon Jenni
Hae-Gon Jeon
Yunho Jeon
Koteswar R. Jerripothula
Hueihan Jhuang
I-hong Jhuo
Dinghuang Ji
Hui Ji
Jingwei Ji
Pan Ji
Yanli Ji
Baoxiong Jia
Kui Jia
Xu Jia
Chiyu Max Jiang
Haiyong Jiang
Hao Jiang
Huaizu Jiang
Huajie Jiang
Ke Jiang

Lai Jiang
Li Jiang
Lu Jiang
Ming Jiang
Peng Jiang
Shuqiang Jiang
Wei Jiang
Xudong Jiang
Zhuolin Jiang
Jianbo Jiao
Zequn Jie
Dakai Jin
Kyong Hwan Jin
Lianwen Jin
SouYoung Jin
Xiaojie Jin
Xin Jin
Nebojsa Jojic
Alexis Joly
Michael Jeffrey Jones
Hanbyul Joo
Jungseock Joo
Kyungdon Joo
Ajjen Joshi
Shantanu H. Joshi
Da-Cheng Juan
Marco Körner
Kevin Köscr
Asim Kadav
Christine Kaeser-Chen
Kushal Kafle
Dagmar Kainmueller
Ioannis A. Kakadiaris
Zdenek Kalal
Nima Kalantari
Yannis Kalantidis
Mahdi M. Kalayeh
Anmol Kalia
Sinan Kalkan
Vicky Kalogeiton
Ashwin Kalyan
Joni-kristian Kamarainen
Gerda Kamberova
Chandra Kambhamettu
Martin Kampel
Meina Kan

Christopher Kanan
Kenichi Kanatani
Angjoo Kanazawa
Atsushi Kanehira
Takuhiro Kaneko
Asako Kanezaki
Bingyi Kang
Di Kang
Sunghun Kang
Zhao Kang
Vadim Kantorov
Abhishek Kar
Amlan Kar
Theofanis Karaletsos
Leonid Karlinsky
Kevin Karsch
Angelos Katharopoulos
Isinsu Katircioglu
Hiroharu Kato
Zoltan Kato
Dotan Kaufman
Jan Kautz
Rei Kawakami
Qiuhong Ke
Wadim Kehl
Petr Kellnhofer
Aniruddha Kembhavi
Cem Keskin
Margret Kcuper
Daniel Keysers
Ashkan Khakzar
Fahad Khan
Naeemullah Khan
Salman Khan
Siddhesh Khandelwal
Rawal Khirodkar
Anna Khoreva
Tejas Khot
Parmeshwar Khurd
Hadi Kiapour
Joe Kileel
Chanho Kim
Dahun Kim
Edward Kim
Eunwoo Kim
Han-ul Kim

Gil Levi
Evgeny Levinkov
Aviad Levis
Jose Lezama
Ang Li
Bin Li
Bing Li
Boyi Li
Changsheng Li
Chao Li
Chen Li
Cheng Li
Chenglong Li
Chi Li
Chun-Guang Li
Chun-Liang Li
Chunyuan Li
Dong Li
Guanbin Li
Hao Li
Haoxiang Li
Hongsheng Li
Hongyang Li
Houqiang Li
Huibin Li
Jia Li
Jianan Li
Jianguo Li
Junnan Li
Junxuan Li
Kai Li
Ke Li
Kejie Li
Kunpeng Li
Lerenhan Li
Li Erran Li
Mengtian Li
Mu Li
Peihua Li
Peiyi Li
Ping Li
Qi Li
Qing Li
Ruiyu Li
Ruoteng Li
Shaozi Li

Sheng Li
Shiwei Li
Shuang Li
Siyang Li
Stan Z. Li
Tianye Li
Wei Li
Weixin Li
Wen Li
Wenbo Li
Xiaomeng Li
Xin Li
Xiu Li
Xuelong Li
Xueting Li
Yan Li
Yandong Li
Yanghao Li
Yehao Li
Yi Li
Yijun Li
Yikang LI
Yining Li
Yongjie Li
Yu Li
Yu-Jhe Li
Yunpeng Li
Yunsheng Li
Yunzhu Li
Zhe Li
Zhen Li
Zhengqi Li
Zhenyang Li
Zhuwen Li
Dongze Lian
Xiaochen Lian
Zhouhui Lian
Chen Liang
Jie Liang
Ming Liang
Paul Pu Liang
Pengpeng Liang
Shu Liang
Wei Liang
Jing Liao
Minghui Liao

Renjie Liao
Shengcai Liao
Shuai Liao
Yiyi Liao
Ser-Nam Lim
Chen-Hsuan Lin
Chung-Ching Lin
Dahua Lin
Ji Lin
Kevin Lin
Tianwei Lin
Tsung-Yi Lin
Tsung-Yu Lin
Wei-An Lin
Weiyao Lin
Yen-Chen Lin
Yuewei Lin
David B. Lindell
Drew Linsley
Krzysztof Lis
Roee Litman
Jim Little
An-An Liu
Bo Liu
Buyu Liu
Chao Liu
Chen Liu
Cheng-lin Liu
Chenxi Liu
Dong Liu
Feng Liu
Guilin Liu
Haomiao Liu
Heshan Liu
Hong Liu
Ji Liu
Jingen Liu
Jun Liu
Lanlan Liu
Li Liu
Liu Liu
Mengyuan Liu
Miaomiao Liu
Nian Liu
Ping Liu
Risheng Liu

Helmut Mayer
Amir Mazaheri
David McAllester
Steven McDonagh
Stephen J. Mckenna
Roey Mechrez
Prakhar Mehrotra
Christopher Mei
Xue Mei
Paulo R. S. Mendonca
Lili Meng
Zibo Meng
Thomas Mensink
Bjoern Menze
Michele Merler
Kourosh Meshgi
Pascal Mettes
Christopher Metzler
Liang Mi
Qiguang Miao
Xin Miao
Tomer Michaeli
Frank Michel
Antoine Miech
Krystian Mikolajczyk
Peyman Milanfar
Ben Mildenhall
Gregor Miller
Fausto Milletari
Dongbo Min
Kyle Min
Pedro Miraldo
Dmytro Mishkin
Anand Mishra
Ashish Mishra
Ishan Misra
Niluthpol C. Mithun
Kaushik Mitra
Niloy Mitra
Anton Mitrokhin
Ikuhisa Mitsugami
Anurag Mittal
Kaichun Mo
Zhipeng Mo
Davide Modolo
Michael Moeller

Pritish Mohapatra
Pavlo Molchanov
Davide Moltisanti
Pascal Monasse
Mathew Monfort
Aron Monszpart
Sean Moran
Vlad I. Morariu
Francesc Moreno-Noguer
Pietro Morerio
Stylianos Moschoglou
Yael Moses
Roozbeh Mottaghi
Pierre Moulon
Arsalan Mousavian
Yadong Mu
Yasuhiro Mukaigawa
Lopamudra Mukherjee
Yusuke Mukuta
Ravi Teja Mullapudi
Mario Enrique Munich
Zachary Murez
Ana C. Murillo
J. Krishna Murthy
Damien Muselet
Armin Mustafa
Siva Karthik Mustikovela
Carlo Dal Mutto
Moin Nabi
Varun K. Nagaraja
Tushar Nagarajan
Arsha Nagrani
Seungjun Nah
Nikhil Naik
Yoshikatsu Nakajima
Yuta Nakashima
Atsushi Nakazawa
Seonghyeon Nam
Vinay P. Namboodiri
Medhini Narasimhan
Srinivasa Narasimhan
Sanath Narayan
Erickson Rangel
Nascimento
Jacinto Nascimento
Tayyab Naseer

Lakshmanan Nataraj
Neda Nategh
Nelson Isao Nauata
Fernando Navarro
Shah Nawaz
Lukas Neumann
Ram Nevatia
Alejandro Newell
Shawn Newsam
Joe Yue-Hei Ng
Trung Thanh Ngo
Duc Thanh Nguyen
Lam M. Nguyen
Phuc Xuan Nguyen
Thuong Nguyen Canh
Mihalis Nicolaou
Andrei Liviu Nicolicioiu
Xuecheng Nie
Michael Niemeyer
Simon Niklaus
Christophoros Nikou
David Nilsson
Jifeng Ning
Yuval Nirkin
Li Niu
Yuzhen Niu
Zhenxing Niu
Shohei Nobuhara
Nicoletta Noceti
Hyeonwoo Noh
Junhyug Noh
Mehdi Noroozi
Sotiris Nousias
Valsamis Ntouskos
Matthew O'Toole
Peter Ochs
Ferda Ofli
Seong Joon Oh
Seoung Wug Oh
Iason Oikonomidis
Utkarsh Ojha
Takahiro Okabe
Takayuki Okatani
Fumio Okura
Aude Oliva
Kyle Olszewski

Björn Ommer
Mohamed Omran
Elisabeta Oneata
Michael Opitz
Jose Oramas
Tribhuvanesh Orekondy
Shaul Oron
Sergio Orts-Escolano
Ivan Oseledets
Aljosa Osep
Magnus Oskarsson
Anton Osokin
Martin R. Oswald
Wanli Ouyang
Andrew Owens
Mete Ozay
Mustafa Ozuysal
Eduardo Pérez-Pellitero
Gautam Pai
Dipan Kumar Pal
P. H. Pamplona Savarese
Jinshan Pan
Junting Pan
Xingang Pan
Yingwei Pan
Yannis Panagakis
Rameswar Panda
Guan Pang
Jiahao Pang
Jiangmiao Pang
Tianyu Pang
Sharath Pankanti
Nicolas Papadakis
Dim Papadopoulos
George Papandreou
Toufiq Parag
Shaifali Parashar
Sarah Parisot
Eunhyeok Park
Hyun Soo Park
Jaesik Park
Min-Gyu Park
Taesung Park
Alvaro Parra
C. Alejandro Parraga
Despoina Paschalidou

Nikolaos Passalis
Vishal Patel
Viorica Patraucean
Badri Narayana Patro
Danda Pani Paudel
Sujoy Paul
Georgios Pavlakos
Ioannis Pavlidis
Vladimir Pavlovic
Nick Pears
Kim Steenstrup Pedersen
Selen Pehlivan
Shmuel Peleg
Chao Peng
Houwen Peng
Wen-Hsiao Peng
Xi Peng
Xiaojiang Peng
Xingchao Peng
Yuxin Peng
Federico Perazzi
Juan Camilo Perez
Vishwanath Peri
Federico Pernici
Luca Del Pero
Florent Perronnin
Stavros Petridis
Henning Petzka
Patrick Peursum
Michael Pfeiffer
Hanspeter Pfister
Roman Pflugfelder
Minh Tri Pham
Yongri Piao
David Picard
Tomasz Pieciak
A. J. Piergiovanni
Andrea Pilzer
Pedro O. Pinheiro
Silvia Laura Pintea
Lerrel Pinto
Axel Pinz
Robinson Piramuthu
Fiora Pirri
Leonid Pishchulin
Francesco Pittaluga

Daniel Pizarro
Tobias Plötz
Mirco Planamente
Matteo Poggi
Moacir A. Ponti
Parita Pooj
Fatih Porikli
Horst Possegger
Omid Poursaeed
Ameya Prabhu
Viraj Uday Prabhu
Dilip Prasad
Brian L. Price
True Price
Maria Priisalu
Veronique Prinet
Victor Adrian Prisacariu
Jan Prokaj
Sergey Prokudin
Nicolas Pugeault
Xavier Puig
Albert Pumarola
Pulak Purkait
Senthil Purushwalkam
Charles R. Qi
Hang Qi
Haozhi Qi
Lu Qi
Mengshi Qi
Siyuan Qi
Xiaojuan Qi
Yuankai Qi
Shengju Qian
Xuelin Qian
Siyuan Qiao
Yu Qiao
Jie Qin
Qiang Qiu
Weichao Qiu
Zhaofan Qiu
Kha Gia Quach
Yuhui Quan
Yvain Queau
Julian Quiroga
Faisal Qureshi
Mahdi Rad

Filip Radenovic
Petia Radeva
Venkatesh
  B. Radhakrishnan
Ilija Radosavovic
Noha Radwan
Rahul Raguram
Tanzila Rahman
Amit Raj
Ajit Rajwade
Kandan Ramakrishnan
Santhosh
  K. Ramakrishnan
Srikumar Ramalingam
Ravi Ramamoorthi
Vasili Ramanishka
Ramprasaath R. Selvaraju
Francois Rameau
Visvanathan Ramesh
Santu Rana
Rene Ranftl
Anand Rangarajan
Anurag Ranjan
Viresh Ranjan
Yongming Rao
Carolina Raposo
Vivek Rathod
Sathya N. Ravi
Avinash Ravichandran
Tammy Riklin Raviv
Daniel Rebain
Sylvestre-Alvise Rebuffi
N. Dinesh Reddy
Timo Rehfeld
Paolo Remagnino
Konstantinos Rematas
Edoardo Remelli
Dongwei Ren
Haibing Ren
Jian Ren
Jimmy Ren
Mengye Ren
Weihong Ren
Wenqi Ren
Zhile Ren
Zhongzheng Ren

Zhou Ren
Vijay Rengarajan
Md A. Reza
Farzaneh Rezaeianaran
Hamed R. Tavakoli
Nicholas Rhinehart
Helge Rhodin
Elisa Ricci
Alexander Richard
Eitan Richardson
Elad Richardson
Christian Richardt
Stephan Richter
Gernot Riegler
Daniel Ritchie
Tobias Ritschel
Samuel Rivera
Yong Man Ro
Richard Roberts
Joseph Robinson
Ignacio Rocco
Mrigank Rochan
Emanuele Rodolà
Mikel D. Rodriguez
Giorgio Roffo
Grégory Rogez
Gemma Roig
Javier Romero
Xuejian Rong
Yu Rong
Amir Rosenfeld
Bodo Rosenhahn
Guy Rosman
Arun Ross
Paolo Rota
Peter M. Roth
Anastasios Roussos
Anirban Roy
Sebastien Roy
Aruni RoyChowdhury
Artem Rozantsev
Ognjen Rudovic
Daniel Rueckert
Adria Ruiz
Javier Ruiz-del-solar
Christian Rupprecht

Chris Russell
Dan Ruta
Jongbin Ryu
Ömer Sümer
Alexandre Sablayrolles
Faraz Saeedan
Ryusuke Sagawa
Christos Sagonas
Tonmoy Saikia
Hideo Saito
Kuniaki Saito
Shunsuke Saito
Shunta Saito
Ken Sakurada
Joaquin Salas
Fatemeh Sadat Saleh
Mahdi Saleh
Pouya Samangouei
Leo Sampaio
  Ferraz Ribeiro
Artsiom Olegovich
  Sanakoyeu
Enrique Sanchez
Patsorn Sangkloy
Anush Sankaran
Aswin Sankaranarayanan
Swami Sankaranarayanan
Rodrigo Santa Cruz
Amartya Sanyal
Archana Sapkota
Nikolaos Sarafianos
Jun Sato
Shin'ichi Satoh
Hosnieh Sattar
Arman Savran
Manolis Savva
Alexander Sax
Hanno Scharr
Simone Schaub-Meyer
Konrad Schindler
Dmitrij Schlesinger
Uwe Schmidt
Dirk Schnieders
Björn Schuller
Samuel Schulter
Idan Schwartz

William Robson Schwartz
Alex Schwing
Sinisa Segvic
Lorenzo Seidenari
Pradeep Sen
Ozan Sener
Soumyadip Sengupta
Arda Senocak
Mojtaba Seyedhosseini
Shishir Shah
Shital Shah
Sohil Atul Shah
Tamar Rott Shaham
Huasong Shan
Qi Shan
Shiguang Shan
Jing Shao
Roman Shapovalov
Gaurav Sharma
Vivek Sharma
Viktoriia Sharmanska
Dongyu She
Sumit Shekhar
Evan Shelhamer
Chengyao Shen
Chunhua Shen
Falong Shen
Jie Shen
Li Shen
Liyue Shen
Shuhan Shen
Tianwei Shen
Wei Shen
William B. Shen
Yantao Shen
Ying Shen
Yiru Shen
Yujun Shen
Yuming Shen
Zhiqiang Shen
Ziyi Shen
Lu Sheng
Yu Sheng
Rakshith Shetty
Baoguang Shi
Guangming Shi

Hailin Shi
Miaojing Shi
Yemin Shi
Zhenmei Shi
Zhiyuan Shi
Kevin Jonathan Shih
Shiliang Shiliang
Hyunjung Shim
Atsushi Shimada
Nobutaka Shimada
Daeyun Shin
Young Min Shin
Koichi Shinoda
Konstantin Shmelkov
Michael Zheng Shou
Abhinav Shrivastava
Tianmin Shu
Zhixin Shu
Hong-Han Shuai
Pushkar Shukla
Christian Siagian
Mennatullah M. Siam
Kaleem Siddiqi
Karan Sikka
Jae-Young Sim
Christian Simon
Martin Simonovsky
Dheeraj Singaraju
Bharat Singh
Gurkirt Singh
Krishna Kumar Singh
Maneesh Kumar Singh
Richa Singh
Saurabh Singh
Suriya Singh
Vikas Singh
Sudipta N. Sinha
Vincent Sitzmann
Josef Sivic
Gregory Slabaugh
Miroslava Slavcheva
Ron Slossberg
Brandon Smith
Kevin Smith
Vladimir Smutny
Noah Snavely

Roger
   D. Soberanis-Mukul
Kihyuk Sohn
Francesco Solera
Eric Sommerlade
Sanghyun Son
Byung Cheol Song
Chunfeng Song
Dongjin Song
Jiaming Song
Jie Song
Jifei Song
Jingkuan Song
Mingli Song
Shiyu Song
Shuran Song
Xiao Song
Yafei Song
Yale Song
Yang Song
Yi-Zhe Song
Yibing Song
Humberto Sossa
Cesar de Souza
Adrian Spurr
Srinath Sridhar
Suraj Srinivas
Pratul P. Srinivasan
Anuj Srivastava
Tania Stathaki
Christopher Stauffer
Simon Stent
Rainer Stiefelhagen
Pierre Stock
Julian Straub
Jonathan C. Stroud
Joerg Stueckler
Jan Stuehmer
David Stutz
Chi Su
Hang Su
Jong-Chyi Su
Shuochen Su
Yu-Chuan Su
Ramanathan Subramanian
Yusuke Sugano

Masanori Suganuma
Yumin Suh
Mohammed Suhail
Yao Sui
Heung-Il Suk
Josephine Sullivan
Baochen Sun
Chen Sun
Chong Sun
Deqing Sun
Jin Sun
Liang Sun
Lin Sun
Qianru Sun
Shao-Hua Sun
Shuyang Sun
Weiwei Sun
Wenxiu Sun
Xiaoshuai Sun
Xiaoxiao Sun
Xingyuan Sun
Yifan Sun
Zhun Sun
Sabine Susstrunk
David Suter
Supasorn Suwajanakorn
Tomas Svoboda
Eran Swears
Paul Swoboda
Attila Szabo
Richard Szeliski
Duy-Nguyen Ta
Andrea Tagliasacchi
Yuichi Taguchi
Ying Tai
Keita Takahashi
Kouske Takahashi
Jun Takamatsu
Hugues Talbot
Toru Tamaki
Chaowei Tan
Fuwen Tan
Mingkui Tan
Mingxing Tan
Qingyang Tan
Robby T. Tan

Xiaoyang Tan
Kenichiro Tanaka
Masayuki Tanaka
Chang Tang
Chengzhou Tang
Danhang Tang
Ming Tang
Peng Tang
Qingming Tang
Wei Tang
Xu Tang
Yansong Tang
Youbao Tang
Yuxing Tang
Zhiqiang Tang
Tatsunori Taniai
Junli Tao
Xin Tao
Makarand Tapaswi
Jean-Philippe Tarel
Lyne Tchapmi
Zachary Teed
Bugra Tekin
Damien Teney
Ayush Tewari
Christian Theobalt
Christopher Thomas
Diego Thomas
Jim Thomas
Rajat Mani Thomas
Xinmei Tian
Yapeng Tian
Yingli Tian
Yonglong Tian
Zhi Tian
Zhuotao Tian
Kinh Tieu
Joseph Tighe
Massimo Tistarelli
Matthew Toews
Carl Toft
Pavel Tokmakov
Federico Tombari
Chetan Tonde
Yan Tong
Alessio Tonioni

Andrea Torsello
Fabio Tosi
Du Tran
Luan Tran
Ngoc-Trung Tran
Quan Hung Tran
Truyen Tran
Rudolph Triebel
Martin Trimmel
Shashank Tripathi
Subarna Tripathi
Leonardo Trujillo
Eduard Trulls
Tomasz Trzcinski
Sam Tsai
Yi-Hsuan Tsai
Hung-Yu Tseng
Stavros Tsogkas
Aggeliki Tsoli
Devis Tuia
Shubham Tulsiani
Sergey Tulyakov
Frederick Tung
Tony Tung
Daniyar Turmukhambetov
Ambrish Tyagi
Radim Tylecek
Christos Tzelepis
Georgios Tzimiropoulos
Dimitrios Tzionas
Seiichi Uchida
Norimichi Ukita
Dmitry Ulyanov
Martin Urschler
Yoshitaka Ushiku
Ben Usman
Alexander Vakhitov
Julien P. C. Valentin
Jack Valmadre
Ernest Valveny
Joost van de Weijer
Jan van Gemert
Koen Van Leemput
Gul Varol
Sebastiano Vascon
M. Alex O. Vasilescu

Subeesh Vasu
Mayank Vatsa
David Vazquez
Javier Vazquez-Corral
Ashok Veeraraghavan
Erik Velasco-Salido
Raviteja Vemulapalli
Jonathan Ventura
Manisha Verma
Roberto Vezzani
Ruben Villegas
Minh Vo
MinhDuc Vo
Nam Vo
Michele Volpi
Riccardo Volpi
Carl Vondrick
Konstantinos Vougioukas
Tuan-Hung Vu
Sven Wachsmuth
Neal Wadhwa
Catherine Wah
Jacob C. Walker
Thomas S. A. Wallis
Chengde Wan
Jun Wan
Liang Wan
Renjie Wan
Baoyuan Wang
Boyu Wang
Cheng Wang
Chu Wang
Chuan Wang
Chunyu Wang
Dequan Wang
Di Wang
Dilin Wang
Dong Wang
Fang Wang
Guanzhi Wang
Guoyin Wang
Hanzi Wang
Hao Wang
He Wang
Heng Wang
Hongcheng Wang

Hongxing Wang
Hua Wang
Jian Wang
Jingbo Wang
Jinglu Wang
Jingya Wang
Jinjun Wang
Jinqiao Wang
Jue Wang
Ke Wang
Keze Wang
Le Wang
Lei Wang
Lezi Wang
Li Wang
Liang Wang
Lijun Wang
Limin Wang
Linwei Wang
Lizhi Wang
Mengjiao Wang
Mingzhe Wang
Minsi Wang
Naiyan Wang
Nannan Wang
Ning Wang
Oliver Wang
Pei Wang
Peng Wang
Pichao Wang
Qi Wang
Qian Wang
Qiaosong Wang
Qifei Wang
Qilong Wang
Qing Wang
Qingzhong Wang
Quan Wang
Rui Wang
Ruiping Wang
Ruixing Wang
Shangfei Wang
Shenlong Wang
Shiyao Wang
Shuhui Wang
Song Wang

Tao Wang
Tianlu Wang
Tiantian Wang
Ting-chun Wang
Tingwu Wang
Wei Wang
Weiyue Wang
Wenguan Wang
Wenlin Wang
Wenqi Wang
Xiang Wang
Xiaobo Wang
Xiaofang Wang
Xiaoling Wang
Xiaolong Wang
Xiaosong Wang
Xiaoyu Wang
Xin Eric Wang
Xinchao Wang
Xinggang Wang
Xintao Wang
Yali Wang
Yan Wang
Yang Wang
Yangang Wang
Yaxing Wang
Yi Wang
Yida Wang
Yilin Wang
Yiming Wang
Yisen Wang
Yongtao Wang
Yu-Xiong Wang
Yue Wang
Yujiang Wang
Yunbo Wang
Yunhe Wang
Zengmao Wang
Zhangyang Wang
Zhaowen Wang
Zhe Wang
Zhecan Wang
Zheng Wang
Zhixiang Wang
Zilei Wang
Jianqiao Wangni

Anne S. Wannenwetsch
Jan Dirk Wegner
Scott Wehrwein
Donglai Wei
Kaixuan Wei
Longhui Wei
Pengxu Wei
Ping Wei
Qi Wei
Shih-En Wei
Xing Wei
Yunchao Wei
Zijun Wei
Jerod Weinman
Michael Weinmann
Philippe Weinzaepfel
Yair Weiss
Bihan Wen
Longyin Wen
Wei Wen
Junwu Weng
Tsui-Wei Weng
Xinshuo Weng
Eric Wengrowski
Tomas Werner
Gordon Wetzstein
Tobias Weyand
Patrick Wieschollek
Maggie Wigness
Erik Wijmans
Richard Wildes
Olivia Wiles
Chris Williams
Williem Williem
Kyle Wilson
Calden Wloka
Nicolai Wojke
Christian Wolf
Yongkang Wong
Sanghyun Woo
Scott Workman
Baoyuan Wu
Bichen Wu
Chao-Yuan Wu
Huikai Wu
Jiajun Wu

Jialin Wu
Jiaxiang Wu
Jiqing Wu
Jonathan Wu
Lifang Wu
Qi Wu
Qiang Wu
Ruizheng Wu
Shangzhe Wu
Shun-Cheng Wu
Tianfu Wu
Wayne Wu
Wenxuan Wu
Xiao Wu
Xiaohe Wu
Xinxiao Wu
Yang Wu
Yi Wu
Yiming Wu
Ying Nian Wu
Yue Wu
Zheng Wu
Zhenyu Wu
Zhirong Wu
Zuxuan Wu
Stefanie Wuhrer
Jonas Wulff
Changqun Xia
Fangting Xia
Fei Xia
Gui-Song Xia
Lu Xia
Xide Xia
Yin Xia
Yingce Xia
Yongqin Xian
Lei Xiang
Shiming Xiang
Bin Xiao
Fanyi Xiao
Guobao Xiao
Huaxin Xiao
Taihong Xiao
Tete Xiao
Tong Xiao
Wang Xiao

Yang Xiao
Cihang Xie
Guosen Xie
Jianwen Xie
Lingxi Xie
Sirui Xie
Weidi Xie
Wenxuan Xie
Xiaohua Xie
Fuyong Xing
Jun Xing
Junliang Xing
Bo Xiong
Peixi Xiong
Yu Xiong
Yuanjun Xiong
Zhiwei Xiong
Chang Xu
Chenliang Xu
Dan Xu
Danfei Xu
Hang Xu
Hongteng Xu
Huijuan Xu
Jingwei Xu
Jun Xu
Kai Xu
Mengmeng Xu
Mingze Xu
Qianqian Xu
Ran Xu
Weijian Xu
Xiangyu Xu
Xiaogang Xu
Xing Xu
Xun Xu
Yanyu Xu
Yichao Xu
Yong Xu
Yongchao Xu
Yuanlu Xu
Zenglin Xu
Zheng Xu
Chuhui Xue
Jia Xue
Nan Xue

Tianfan Xue
Xiangyang Xue
Abhay Yadav
Yasushi Yagi
I. Zeki Yalniz
Kota Yamaguchi
Toshihiko Yamasaki
Takayoshi Yamashita
Junchi Yan
Ke Yan
Qingan Yan
Sijie Yan
Xinchen Yan
Yan Yan
Yichao Yan
Zhicheng Yan
Keiji Yanai
Bin Yang
Ceyuan Yang
Dawei Yang
Dong Yang
Fan Yang
Guandao Yang
Guorun Yang
Haichuan Yang
Hao Yang
Jianwei Yang
Jiaolong Yang
Jie Yang
Jing Yang
Kaiyu Yang
Linjie Yang
Meng Yang
Michael Ying Yang
Nan Yang
Shuai Yang
Shuo Yang
Tianyu Yang
Tien-Ju Yang
Tsun-Yi Yang
Wei Yang
Wenhan Yang
Xiao Yang
Xiaodong Yang
Xin Yang
Yan Yang

Yanchao Yang
Yee Hong Yang
Yezhou Yang
Zhenheng Yang
Anbang Yao
Angela Yao
Cong Yao
Jian Yao
Li Yao
Ting Yao
Yao Yao
Zhewei Yao
Chengxi Ye
Jianbo Ye
Keren Ye
Linwei Ye
Mang Ye
Mao Ye
Qi Ye
Qixiang Ye
Mei-Chen Yeh
Raymond Yeh
Yu-Ying Yeh
Sai-Kit Yeung
Serena Yeung
Kwang Moo Yi
Li Yi
Renjiao Yi
Alper Yilmaz
Junho Yim
Lijun Yin
Weidong Yin
Xi Yin
Zhichao Yin
Tatsuya Yokota
Ryo Yonetani
Donggeun Yoo
Jae Shin Yoon
Ju Hong Yoon
Sung-eui Yoon
Laurent Younes
Changqian Yu
Fisher Yu
Gang Yu
Jiahui Yu
Kaicheng Yu

Ke Yu
Lequan Yu
Ning Yu
Qian Yu
Ronald Yu
Ruichi Yu
Shoou-I Yu
Tao Yu
Tianshu Yu
Xiang Yu
Xin Yu
Xiyu Yu
Youngjae Yu
Yu Yu
Zhiding Yu
Chunfeng Yuan
Ganzhao Yuan
Jinwei Yuan
Lu Yuan
Quan Yuan
Shanxin Yuan
Tongtong Yuan
Wenjia Yuan
Ye Yuan
Yuan Yuan
Yuhui Yuan
Huanjing Yue
Xiangyu Yue
Ersin Yumer
Sergey Zagoruyko
Egor Zakharov
Amir Zamir
Andrei Zanfir
Mihai Zanfir
Pablo Zegers
Bernhard Zeisl
John S. Zelek
Niclas Zeller
Huayi Zeng
Jiabei Zeng
Wenjun Zeng
Yu Zeng
Xiaohua Zhai
Fangneng Zhan
Huangying Zhan
Kun Zhan

Xiaohang Zhan
Baochang Zhang
Bowen Zhang
Cecilia Zhang
Changqing Zhang
Chao Zhang
Chengquan Zhang
Chi Zhang
Chongyang Zhang
Dingwen Zhang
Dong Zhang
Feihu Zhang
Hang Zhang
Hanwang Zhang
Hao Zhang
He Zhang
Hongguang Zhang
Hua Zhang
Ji Zhang
Jianguo Zhang
Jianming Zhang
Jiawei Zhang
Jie Zhang
Jing Zhang
Juyong Zhang
Kai Zhang
Kaipeng Zhang
Ke Zhang
Le Zhang
Lei Zhang
Li Zhang
Lihe Zhang
Linguang Zhang
Lu Zhang
Mi Zhang
Mingda Zhang
Peng Zhang
Pingping Zhang
Qian Zhang
Qilin Zhang
Quanshi Zhang
Richard Zhang
Rui Zhang
Runze Zhang
Shengping Zhang
Shifeng Zhang

Shuai Zhang
Songyang Zhang
Tao Zhang
Ting Zhang
Tong Zhang
Wayne Zhang
Wei Zhang
Weizhong Zhang
Wenwei Zhang
Xiangyu Zhang
Xiaolin Zhang
Xiaopeng Zhang
Xiaoqin Zhang
Xiuming Zhang
Ya Zhang
Yang Zhang
Yimin Zhang
Yinda Zhang
Ying Zhang
Yongfei Zhang
Yu Zhang
Yulun Zhang
Yunhua Zhang
Yuting Zhang
Zhanpeng Zhang
Zhao Zhang
Zhaoxiang Zhang
Zhen Zhang
Zheng Zhang
Zhifei Zhang
Zhijin Zhang
Zhishuai Zhang
Ziming Zhang
Bo Zhao
Chen Zhao
Fang Zhao
Haiyu Zhao
Han Zhao
Hang Zhao
Hengshuang Zhao
Jian Zhao
Kai Zhao
Liang Zhao
Long Zhao
Qian Zhao
Qibin Zhao

Qijun Zhao
Rui Zhao
Shenglin Zhao
Sicheng Zhao
Tianyi Zhao
Wenda Zhao
Xiangyun Zhao
Xin Zhao
Yang Zhao
Yue Zhao
Zhichen Zhao
Zijing Zhao
Xiantong Zhen
Chuanxia Zheng
Feng Zheng
Haiyong Zheng
Jia Zheng
Kang Zheng
Shuai Kyle Zheng
Wei-Shi Zheng
Yinqiang Zheng
Zerong Zheng
Zhedong Zheng
Zilong Zheng
Bineng Zhong
Fangwei Zhong
Guangyu Zhong
Yiran Zhong
Yujie Zhong
Zhun Zhong
Chunluan Zhou
Huiyu Zhou
Jiahuan Zhou
Jun Zhou
Lei Zhou
Luowei Zhou
Luping Zhou
Mo Zhou
Ning Zhou
Pan Zhou
Peng Zhou
Qianyi Zhou
S. Kevin Zhou
Sanping Zhou
Wengang Zhou
Xingyi Zhou

Yanzhao Zhou
Yi Zhou
Yin Zhou
Yipin Zhou
Yuyin Zhou
Zihan Zhou
Alex Zihao Zhu
Chenchen Zhu
Feng Zhu
Guangming Zhu
Ji Zhu
Jun-Yan Zhu
Lei Zhu
Linchao Zhu
Rui Zhu
Shizhan Zhu
Tyler Lixuan Zhu

Wei Zhu
Xiangyu Zhu
Xinge Zhu
Xizhou Zhu
Yanjun Zhu
Yi Zhu
Yixin Zhu
Yizhe Zhu
Yousong Zhu
Zhe Zhu
Zhen Zhu
Zheng Zhu
Zhenyao Zhu
Zhihui Zhu
Zhuotun Zhu
Bingbing Zhuang
Wei Zhuo

Christian Zimmermann
Karel Zimmermann
Larry Zitnick
Mohammadreza
  Zolfaghari
Maria Zontak
Daniel Zoran
Changqing Zou
Chuhang Zou
Danping Zou
Qi Zou
Yang Zou
Yuliang Zou
Georgios Zoumpourlis
Wangmeng Zuo
Xinxin Zuo

Additional Reviewers

Victoria Fernandez
  Abrevaya
Maya Aghaei
Allam Allam
Christine
  Allen-Blanchette
Nicolas Aziere
Assia Benbihi
Neha Bhargava
Bharat Lal Bhatnagar
Joanna Bitton
Judy Borowski
Amine Bourki
Romain Brégier
Tali Brayer
Sebastian Bujwid
Andrea Burns
Yun-Hao Cao
Yuning Chai
Xiaojun Chang
Bo Chen
Shuo Chen
Zhixiang Chen
Junsuk Choe
Hung-Kuo Chu

Jonathan P. Crall
Kenan Dai
Lucas Deecke
Karan Desai
Prithviraj Dhar
Jing Dong
Wei Dong
Turan Kaan Elgin
Francis Engelmann
Erik Englesson
Fartash Faghri
Zicong Fan
Yang Fu
Risheek Garrepalli
Yifan Ge
Marco Godi
Helmut Grabner
Shuxuan Guo
Jianfeng He
Zhezhi He
Samitha Herath
Chih-Hui Ho
Yicong Hong
Vincent Tao Hu
Julio Hurtado

Jaedong Hwang
Andrey Ignatov
Muhammad
  Abdullah Jamal
Saumya Jetley
Meiguang Jin
Jeff Johnson
Minsoo Kang
Saeed Khorram
Mohammad Rami Koujan
Nilesh Kulkarni
Sudhakar Kumawat
Abdelhak Lemkhenter
Alexander Levine
Jiachen Li
Jing Li
Jun Li
Yi Li
Liang Liao
Ruochen Liao
Tzu-Heng Lin
Phillip Lippe
Bao-di Liu
Bo Liu
Fangchen Liu

Hanxiao Liu
Hongyu Liu
Huidong Liu
Miao Liu
Xinxin Liu
Yongfei Liu
Yu-Lun Liu
Amir Livne
Tiange Luo
Wei Ma
Xiaoxuan Ma
Ioannis Marras
Georg Martius
Effrosyni Mavroudi
Tim Meinhardt
Givi Meishvili
Meng Meng
Zihang Meng
Zhongqi Miao
Gyeongsik Moon
Khoi Nguyen
Yung-Kyun Noh
Antonio Norelli
Jaeyoo Park
Alexander Pashevich
Mandela Patrick
Mary Phuong
Bingqiao Qian
Yu Qiao
Zhen Qiao
Sai Saketh Rambhatla
Aniket Roy
Amelie Royer
Parikshit Vishwas
  Sakurikar
Mark Sandler
Mert Bülent Sarıyıldız
Tanner Schmidt
Anshul B. Shah

Ketul Shah
Rajvi Shah
Hengcan Shi
Xiangxi Shi
Yujiao Shi
William A. P. Smith
Guoxian Song
Robin Strudel
Abby Stylianou
Xinwei Sun
Reuben Tan
Qingyi Tao
Kedar S. Tatwawadi
Anh Tuan Tran
Son Dinh Tran
Eleni Triantafillou
Aristeidis Tsitiridis
Md Zasim Uddin
Andrea Vedaldi
Evangelos Ververas
Vidit Vidit
Paul Voigtlaender
Bo Wan
Huanyu Wang
Huiyu Wang
Junqiu Wang
Pengxiao Wang
Tai Wang
Xinyao Wang
Tomoki Watanabe
Mark Weber
Xi Wei
Botong Wu
James Wu
Jiamin Wu
Rujie Wu
Yu Wu
Rongchang Xie
Wei Xiong

Yunyang Xiong
An Xu
Chi Xu
Yinghao Xu
Fei Xue
Tingyun Yan
Zike Yan
Chao Yang
Heran Yang
Ren Yang
Wenfei Yang
Xu Yang
Rajeev Yasarla
Shaokai Ye
Yufei Ye
Kun Yi
Haichao Yu
Hanchao Yu
Ruixuan Yu
Liangzhe Yuan
Chen-Lin Zhang
Fandong Zhang
Tianyi Zhang
Yang Zhang
Yiyi Zhang
Yongshun Zhang
Yu Zhang
Zhiwei Zhang
Jiaojiao Zhao
Yipu Zhao
Xingjian Zhen
Haizhong Zheng
Tiancheng Zhi
Chengju Zhou
Hao Zhou
Hao Zhu
Alexander Zimin

Contents – Part VII

Multiview Detection with Feature Perspective Transformation

Yunzhong Hou, Liang Zheng[✉], and Stephen Gould

Australian Centre for Robotic Vision, Australian National University,
Canberra, Australia
{yunzhong.hou,liang.zheng,stephen.gould}@anu.edu.au

Abstract. Incorporating multiple camera views for detection alleviates the impact of occlusions in crowded scenes. In a multiview detection system, we need to answer two important questions. First, how should we aggregate cues from multiple views? Second, how should we aggregate information from spatially neighboring locations? To address these questions, we introduce a novel multiview detector, MVDet. During multiview aggregation, for each location on the ground, existing methods use multiview anchor box features as representation, which potentially limits performance as pre-defined anchor boxes can be inaccurate. In contrast, via feature map perspective transformation, MVDet employs anchor-free representations with feature vectors directly sampled from corresponding pixels in multiple views. For spatial aggregation, different from previous methods that require design and operations outside of neural networks, MVDet takes a fully convolutional approach with large convolutional kernels on the multiview aggregated feature map. The proposed model is end-to-end learnable and achieves 88.2% MODA on Wildtrack dataset, outperforming the state-of-the-art by 14.1%. We also provide detailed analysis of MVDet on a newly introduced synthetic dataset, MultiviewX, which allows us to control the level of occlusion. Code and MultiviewX dataset are available at https://github.com/hou-yz/MVDet.

Keywords: Multiview detection · Anchor-free · Perspective transformation · Fully convolutional · Synthetic data

1 Introduction

Occlusion is a fundamental issue that confronts many computer vision tasks. Specifically, in detection problems, occlusion introduces great difficulties and many methods have been proposed to address it. Some methods focus on the single view detection problem, *e.g.*, part-based detection [25,35,48], loss design [39,46], and learning non-maximum suppression [13]. Other methods jointly infer objects from multiple cues, *e.g.*, RGB-D [10,12,27], LIDAR point cloud [6], and multiple RGB camera views [3,8]. In this paper, we focus on pedestrian detection from multiple RGB camera views (multiview).

Electronic supplementary material The online version of this chapter (https://doi.org/10.1007/978-3-030-58571-6_1) contains supplementary material, which is available to authorized users.

© Springer Nature Switzerland AG 2020
A. Vedaldi et al. (Eds.): ECCV 2020, LNCS 12352, pp. 1–18, 2020.
https://doi.org/10.1007/978-3-030-58571-6_1

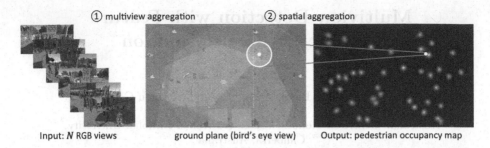

① multiview aggregation   ② spatial aggregation

Input: N RGB views   ground plane (bird's eye view)   Output: pedestrian occupancy map

Fig. 1. Overview of the multiview pedestrian detection system. **Left**: the system takes synchronized frames from N cameras as input. **Middle**: the camera field-of-views overlap on the ground plane, where the multiview cues can be aggregated. **Right**: the system outputs a pedestrian occupancy map (POM). There are two important questions here. **First**, how can we aggregate multiple cues. **Second**, how can we aggregate spatial neighbor information for joint consideration (large white circle), and make a comprehensive decision for pedestrian occupancy (small white circle). (Color figure online)

Multiview pedestrian detections usually have synchronized frames from multiple calibrated cameras as input [3,8,29]. These cameras focus on the same area, and have overlapping field-of-view (see Fig. 1). Camera calibrations provide the matching between 2D image coordinate (u, v) and 3D world location (x, y, z). We refer to points with $z = 0$ in the 3D world as being on the ground plane (bird's eye view). For each point on the ground plane, based on 3D human width and height assumption, its corresponding bounding box in multiple views can be calculated via projection and then stored. Since the bounding boxes can be retrieved via table lookup, multiview pedestrian detection tasks usually evaluate pedestrian occupancy on the ground plane [3,8].

Addressing the ambiguities from occlusions and crowdedness is the main challenge for multiview pedestrian detection. Under occlusion, it is difficult to determine if a person exists in a certain location, or how many people exist and where they are. To solve this, one must focus on two important aspects of multiview detection: first, *multiview aggregation* and, second, *spatial aggregation* (Fig. 1). Aggregation of multiview information is essential since having multiple views is the main difference between monocular-view detection and multiview detection. Previously, for a given ground plane location, multiview systems usually choose an anchor-based multiview aggregation approach and represent certain ground plane location with multiview anchor box features [1,4,17]. However, researchers find the performance of anchor-based methods might be limited by pre-defined anchor boxes in monocular view systems [16,43,49], while multiview anchor boxes calculated from pre-defined human 3D height and width might also be inaccurate. Aggregation of spatial neighbors is also vital for occlusion reasoning. Previous methods [1,8,29] usually adopt conditional random field (CRF) or mean-field inference to jointly consider the spatial neighbors. These methods usually requires specific potential terms design or additional operations outside of convolutional neural networks (CNNs).

In this paper, we propose a simple yet effective method, MVDet, that has heretofore not been explored in the literature for multiview detection. First, for *multiview aggregation*, as representation based on inaccurate anchor boxes can limit system performance, rather than anchor-based approaches [1,4,17], MVDet choose an anchor-free representation with feature vectors sampled at corresponding pixels in multiple views. Specifically, MVDet projects the convolution feature map via perspective transformation and concatenates the multiple projected feature maps. Second, for *spatial aggregation*, to minimize human design and operations outside of CNN, instead of CRF or mean-field inference [1,8,29], MVDet adopts an fully convolutional solution. It applies (learned) convolutions on the aggregated ground plane feature map, and use the large receptive field to jointly consider ground plane neighboring locations. The proposed fully convolutional MVDet can be trained in an end-to-end manner.

We demonstrate the effectiveness of MVDet on two large scale datasets. On Wildtrack, a real-world dataset, MVDet achieved 88.2% MODA [15], a 14.1% increase over previous state-of-the-art. On MultiviewX, a synthetic dataset, MVDet also achieves competitive results under multiple levels of occlusions.

2   Related Work

Monocular View Detection. Detection is one of the most important problems in computer vision. Anchor-based methods like faster R-CNN [28] and SSD [21] achieve great performance. Recently, finding pre-defined anchors might limit performance, many anchor-free methods are proposed [7,16,18,36,43,49]. On pedestrian detection, some researchers detect pedestrian bounding boxes through head-foot point detection [32] or center and scale detection [22]. Occlusion handling in pedestrian detection draws great attention from the research community. Part-based detectors are very popular [24,25,35,46] since the occluded people are only partially observable. Hosang *et al.* [13] learn non-maximal suppression for occluded pedestrians. Repulsion loss [39] is proposed to repulse bounding boxes.

3D Object Understanding with Multiple Information Sources. Incorporating multiple information sources, such as depth, point cloud, and other RGB camera views is studied for 3D object understanding. For multiple view 3D object classification, Su *et al.* [33] use maximum pooling to aggregate the features from different 2D views. For 3D object detection, aggregating information from RGB image and LIDAR point cloud are widely studied. Chen *et al.* [5] investigate 3D object detection with stereo image. View aggregation for 3D anchors is studied in [17], where the researchers extract features for every 3D anchor from RGB camera and LIDAR bird's eye view. Liang *et al.* [19] calculate the feature for each point from bird's eye view as multi-layer perceptron output from camera view features of K nearest neighbor LIDAR points. Frustum PointNets [27] first generate 2D bounding boxes proposal from RGB image, then extrude them to 3D viewing frustums. Yao *et al.* edit attributes of 3D vehicle models to create content consistent vehicle dataset [44].

Multiview Pedestrian Detection. In multiview pedestrian detections, first, aggregating information from multiple RGB cameras is essential. In [1,4], researchers fuse multiple information source for multiview 2D anchors. Given fixed assumption of human width and height, all ground plane locations and their corresponding multiview 2D anchor boxes are first calculated. Then, researchers in [1,4] represent ground plane position with corresponding anchor box features. In [8,29,41], single view detection results are fused instead. Second, in order to aggregate spatial neighbor information, mean-field inference [1,8] and conditional random field (CRF) [1,29] are exploited. In [1,8], the overall occupancy in the scenario is cast as an energy minimization problem and solved with CRF. Fleuret *et al.* [8] first estimate ideal 2D images under certain occupancy, and then compare them with the real multiview inputs. Baque *et al.* [1] construct higher-order potentials as consistency between CNN estimations and generated ideal images, and train the CRF with CNN in a combined manner, and achieve state-of-the-art performance on Wildtrack dataset [3].

Geometric Transformation in Deep Learning. Geometric transformations such as affine transformation and perspective transformation can model many phenomena in computer vision, and can be explicitly calculated with a fixed set of parameters. Jaderberg *et al.* [14] propose Spatial Transformer Network that learns the affine transformation parameters for translation and rotation on the 2D RGB input image. Wu *et al.* [40] estimate the projection parameters and project 2D key points from the 3D skeleton. Yan *et al.* [42] translate one 3D volume to 2D silhouette via perspective transformation. Geometry-aware scene text detection is studied in [38] through estimating instance-level affine transformation. For cross-view image retrieval, Shi *et al.* [30] apply polar transformation to bring the representations closer in feature space. Lv *et al.* propose a perspective-aware generative model for novel view synthesis for vehicles [23].

3   Methodology

In this work, we focus on the occluded pedestrian detection problem in an multiview scenario and design MVDet for dealing with ambiguities. MVDet features anchor-free *multiview aggregation* that alleviate the influence from inaccurate anchor boxes in previous works [1,4,6,17], and fully convolutional *spatial aggregation* that does not rely on CRF or mean-field inference [1,8,29]. As shown in Fig. 2, MVDet takes multiple RGB images as input, and outputs the pedestrian occupancy map (POM) estimation. In the following sections, we will introduce the proposed multiview aggregation (Sect. 3.1), spatial aggregation (Sect. 3.2), and training and testing configurations (Sect. 3.3).

3.1   Multiview Aggregation

Multiview aggregation is a very important part of multiview systems. In this section, we explain the anchor-free aggregation method in MVDet that alleviate influence from inaccurate anchor boxes, and compare it with several alternatives.

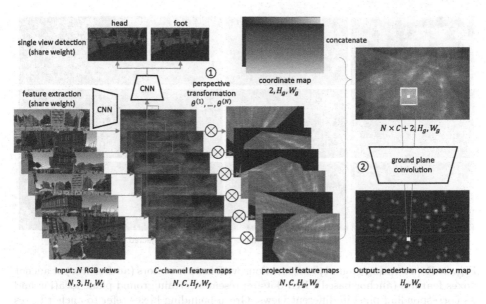

Fig. 2. MVDet architecture. First, given input images of shape $[3, H_i, W_i]$ from N cameras, the proposed network uses a CNN to extract C-channel feature maps for each input image. The CNN feature extractor here shares weight among N inputs. Next, we reshape the C-channel feature maps into the size of $[H_f, W_f]$, and run single view detection by detecting the head-foot pairs. Then, for **multiview aggregation** (circled 1), we take an anchor-free approach and combine the perspective transformation of N feature maps based on their camera calibrations $\theta^{(1)}, \ldots, \theta^{(N)}$, which results in N feature maps of shape $[C, H_g, W_g]$. For each ground plane location, we store its X-Y coordinates in a 2-channel coordinate map [20]. Through concatenating N projected feature maps with a coordinate map, we aggregate the ground plane feature map for the whole scenario (of shape $[N \times C + 2, H_g, W_g]$). At last, we apply large kernel convolutions on the ground plane feature map, so as to **aggregate spatial neighbor information** (circled 2) for a joint and comprehensive final occupancy decision.

Feature Map Extraction. In MVDet, first, given N images of shape $[H_i, W_i]$ as input (H_i and W_i denote the image height and width), the proposed architecture uses a CNN to extract N C-channel feature maps (Fig. 2). Here, we choose ResNet-18 [11] for its strong performance and light-weight. This CNN calculates C-channel feature maps separately for N input images, while sharing weight among all calculations. In order to maintain a relatively high spatial resolution for the feature maps, we replace the last 3 strided convolutions with dilated convolutions [45]. Before projection, we resize N feature maps into a fixed size $[H_f, W_f]$ (H_f and W_f denote the feature map height and width). In each view, similar to [18,32], we then detect pedestrians as a pair of head-foot points with a shared weight single view detector.

Anchor-Free Representation. Previously, in detection tasks that have multiple cues, *e.g.*, 3D object detection and multiview pedestrian detection,

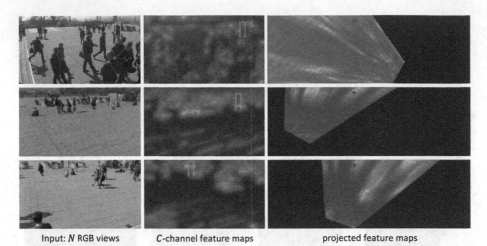

Input: *N* RGB views   *C*-channel feature maps   projected feature maps

Fig. 3. Representing ground plane locations with feature vectors (anchor-free) or anchor boxes features (anchor-based). Red dots represent a certain ground plane location and its corresponding pixel in different views. Green bounding boxes refer to anchor boxes corresponding to that ground plane location. As human targets might not be the same size as assumed (*e.g.*, sitting lady in white coat), ROI-pooling for multiview anchor boxes might fail to provide the most accurate feature representation for that location. On the contrary, being anchor-free, feature vectors retrieved from corresponding points avoids the impact of inaccurate anchor boxes. (Color figure online)

anchor-based representation is commonly adopted [1,4,6,17]. Specifically, one can represent a ground plane location (red points in Fig. 3) with anchor box (green boxes in Fig. 3) features via ROI-pooling [9]. As the size and shape of anchor boxes are calculated from assumed 3D human height and width [1,4], these anchor boxes might *not* be accurate, which potentially limits system performance [16,43,49]. As in Fig. 3, the lady in the white coat is sitting and only takes up half of the anchor box. As a result, ROI pooling will result in feature representation that describes the background to a large extent and causes confusion.

In contrast, being anchor-free, the proposed method represents ground plane locations with feature vectors sampled from feature maps at corresponding points, which avoids the impact of inaccurate anchor boxes. Given camera calibrations, the corresponding points can be retrieved accurately. With learnable convolution kernels, these feature vectors can represent information from an adaptive region in its receptive field. As a result, ground plane feature maps constructed via anchor-free feature representation avoid pooling from inaccurate anchor boxes, and still contains sufficient information from 2D images for detection.

Perspective Transformation. To retrieve anchor-free representations, we project feature maps with perspective transformation. Translation between 3D locations (x, y, z) and 2D image pixel coordinates (u, v) is done via

Fig. 4. Illustration of perspective transformation. Assuming all pixels are on the ground plane ($z = 0$), we can use a parameterized sampling grid (green dots) to project a 2D image (left) to the ground plane (right). The remaining locations are padded with 0. (Color figure online)

$$s \begin{pmatrix} u \\ v \\ 1 \end{pmatrix} = P_\theta \begin{pmatrix} x \\ y \\ z \\ 1 \end{pmatrix} = A\,[R|\mathbf{t}] \begin{pmatrix} x \\ y \\ z \\ 1 \end{pmatrix} = \begin{bmatrix} \theta_{11} & \theta_{12} & \theta_{13} & \theta_{14} \\ \theta_{21} & \theta_{22} & \theta_{23} & \theta_{24} \\ \theta_{31} & \theta_{32} & \theta_{33} & \theta_{34} \end{bmatrix} \begin{pmatrix} x \\ y \\ z \\ 1 \end{pmatrix}, \qquad (1)$$

where s is a real-valued scaling factor, and P_θ is a 3×4 perspective transformation matrix. Specifically, A is the 3×3 intrinsic parameter matrix. $[R|\mathbf{t}]$ is the 3×4 joint rotation-translation matrix, or extrinsic parameter matrix, where R specifies the rotation and $\mathbf{t}$ specifies the translation.

A point (pixel) from an image lies on a line in the 3D world. To determine exact 3D locations of image pixels, we consider a common reference plane: the ground plane, $z = 0$. For all 3D location $(x, y, 0)$ on the ground plane, the point-wise transformation can be written as

$$s \begin{pmatrix} u \\ v \\ 1 \end{pmatrix} = P_{\theta,0} \begin{pmatrix} x \\ y \\ 1 \end{pmatrix} = \begin{bmatrix} \theta_{11} & \theta_{12} & \theta_{14} \\ \theta_{21} & \theta_{22} & \theta_{24} \\ \theta_{31} & \theta_{32} & \theta_{34} \end{bmatrix} \begin{pmatrix} x \\ y \\ 1 \end{pmatrix}, \qquad (2)$$

where $P_{\theta,0}$ denotes the 3×3 perspective transformation matrix that have the third column canceled from P_θ.

To implement this within neural networks, we quantize the ground plane locations into a grid of shape $[H_g, W_g]$. For camera $n \in \{1, \dots, N\}$ with calibration $\theta^{(n)}$, we can project the image onto the $z = 0$ ground plane by applying a parameterized sampling grid of shape $[H_g, W_g]$ based on Eq. 2. These sampling grids generate projected feature maps on the ground plane, where the remaining (out-of-view) locations are padded with zero (Fig. 4). We concatenate a 2-channel coordinate map [20] to specify the X-Y coordinates for ground plane locations (Fig. 2). Together with projected C-channel feature maps from N cameras, we have a $(N \times C + 2)$ channel ground plane feature map.

Different Projection Choices. For multiview aggregation, there are multiple choices for projection: we can project the RGB images, feature maps, or single view results (Fig. 5). First, RGB pixels on its own contains relatively little information, and much information is preserved in the spatial structures. However, projection breaks the spatial relationship between neighboring RGB pixels.

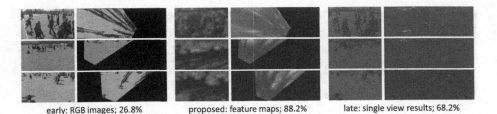

early: RGB images; 26.8%   proposed: feature maps; 88.2%   late: single view results; 68.2%

Fig. 5. Different projection choices and their performances (MODA [15]). **Left:** early projection of RGB images breaks the spatial relationship between RGB pixels, which introduces great difficulties to the convolutions. **Right:** late projection of single view detection results (foot) limits the information to be aggregated. **Middle:** the proposed projection of feature maps not only are more robust to the pixel structure break (high-level semantic feature can represent information by itself, thus suffer less from structure break), but also contain more information.

As a result, this limits the performance of the multiview detector. Second, projecting the single view results (detected foot points) limits the information to be aggregated. In fact, in this setup, the system has no access to cues other than the single view detection results. Since single view results might not be accurate under occlusion (which is the reason for introducing multiple views), this setup can also limit the overall performance. In this paper, we propose to project the feature map. Compared to other choices, feature maps not only suffer less from the spatial structure break (since 2D spatial information have already been concentrated into individual pixels in feature maps), but also contain more information. As shown in Fig. 5, aggregation via feature maps projection achieves highest MODA [15] performance.

3.2 Spatial Aggregation

In the previous section, we show that multiview information can be aggregated in an anchor-free manner through perspective transformation and concatenation. One remaining problem is how to aggregate information from spatial neighbors.

Occlusion are generated by human crowd within a certain area. To deal with the ambiguities, one can consider the certain area and the human crowd in that area jointly for an overall informed decision. Previously, CRFs and mean-field inference are adopted, but requires design and operations besides CNN. In this work, we propose an fully convolutional alternative with large kernel convolutions on the ground plane feature map. In fact, Zheng *et al.* [47] find that CNN can model some behavior and characteristics of CRFs. And Peng *et al.* [26] outperform CRFs with large kernel convolutions for semantic segmentation. In MVDet, we feed the $(N \times C + 2)$ channel ground plane feature map to convolution layers that have a relatively large receptive field, so as to jointly consider the ground plane neighbors. Here, we use three layers of dilated convolution for having minimal parameters while still keeping a larger ground plane receptive field. The last layer outputs an 1-channel $[H_g, W_g]$ pedestrian occupancy map (POM) $\tilde{\mathbf{g}}$ with no activation.

3.3 Training and Testing

In Training, we train MVDet as a regression problem. Given ground truth pedestrian occupancy $\mathbf{g}$, similar to landmark detection [2], we use a Gaussian kernel $f(\cdot)$ to generate a "*soft*" ground truth target $f(\mathbf{g})$. In order to train the whole network, we use Euclidean distance $\|\cdot\|_2$ between network output $\tilde{\mathbf{g}}$ and "*soft*" target $f(\mathbf{g})$ as loss function,

$$\mathcal{L}_{\text{ground}} = \|\tilde{\mathbf{g}} - f(\mathbf{g})\|_2. \tag{3}$$

We also include bounding box regression loss from N camera inputs as another supervision. The single view head-foot detection is also trained as a regression problem. For single view detection results $\tilde{\mathbf{s}}_{\text{head}}^{(n)}, \tilde{\mathbf{s}}_{\text{foot}}^{(n)}$ and the corresponding ground truth $\mathbf{s}_{\text{head}}^{(n)}, \mathbf{s}_{\text{foot}}^{(n)}$ in view $n \in \{1, ..., N\}$, the loss is computed as,

$$\mathcal{L}_{\text{single}}^{(n)} = \left\|\tilde{\mathbf{s}}_{\text{head}}^{(n)} - f\left(\mathbf{s}_{\text{head}}^{(n)}\right)\right\|_2 + \left\|\tilde{\mathbf{s}}_{\text{foot}}^{(n)} - f\left(\mathbf{s}_{\text{foot}}^{(n)}\right)\right\|_2. \tag{4}$$

Combining ground plane loss $\mathcal{L}_{\text{ground}}$ and N single view losses $\mathcal{L}_{\text{single}}^{(n)}$, we have the overall loss for training MVDet,

$$\mathcal{L}_{\text{combined}} = \mathcal{L}_{\text{ground}} + \alpha \times \frac{1}{N} \sum_{n=1}^{N} \mathcal{L}_{\text{single}}^{(n)}, \tag{5}$$

where α is a hyper-parameter for singe view loss weight.

During Testing, MVDet outputs a single-channel occupancy probability map $\tilde{\mathbf{g}}$. We filter the occupancy map with a minimum probability of 0.4, and then apply non-maximum suppression (NMS) on the proposals. This NMS uses a Euclidean distance threshold of 0.5 meters, which is the same threshold for considering this location proposal as true positive in evaluation [3].

4 Experiment

4.1 Experiment Setup

Datasets. We test on two multiview pedestrian detection datasets (Table 1).

The *Wildtrack* dataset includes 400 synchronized frames from 7 cameras, covering a 12 m by 36 m region. For annotation, the ground plane is quantized into a 480 × 1440 grid, where each grid cell is a 2.5-centimeter square. The 7 cameras capture images with a 1080 × 1920 resolution, and are annotated at 2 frames per second (fps). On average, there are 20 persons per frame in Wildtrack dataset and each locations in the scene is covered by 3.74 cameras.

The *MultiviewX* dataset is a new synthetic dataset collected for multiview pedestrian detection. We use Unity engine [37] to create the scenario. As for pedestrians, we use human models from PersonX [34]. MultiviewX dataset covers a slightly smaller area of 16 m by 25 m. Using the same 2.5-centimeter square

Table 1. Datasets comparison for multiview pedestrian detection

	#camera	Resolution	Frames	Area	Crowdedness	Avg. coverage
Wildtrack	7	1080×1920	400	12×36 m^2	20 person/frame	3.74 cameras
MultiviewX	6	1080×1920	400	16×25 m^2	40 person/frame	4.41 cameras

grid cell, we quantize the ground plane into a 640×1000 grid. There are 6 cameras with overlapping field-of-view in MultiviewX dataset, each of which outputs a 1080×1920 resolution image. We also generate annotations for 400 frames in MultiviewX at 2 fps (same as Wildtrack). On average, 4.41 cameras cover the same location. Being a synthetic dataset, there are various potential configurations for the scenario with free annotations. Under the default setting, MultiviewX has 40 persons per frame, doubling the crowdedness in Wildtrack. If not specified, MultiviewX refers to this default setting.

Evaluation Metrics. Following [3], we use the first 90% frames in both datasets for training, and the last 10% frames for testing. We report precision, recall, MODA, and MODP. MODP evaluates the localization precision, whereas MODA accounts for both the false positives and false negatives [15]. We use MODA as the primary performance indicator, as it considers both false positives and false negatives. A threshold of 0.5 meters is used to determine true positives.

4.2   Implementation Details

For memory usage concerns, we downsample the 1080×1920 RGB images to $H_i = 720, W_i = 1280$. We remove the last two layers (global average pooling; classification output) in ResNet-18 [11] for $C = 512$ channel feature extraction, and use dilated convolution to replace the strided convolution. This results in a $8\times$ downsample from the 720×1280 input. Before projection, we bilinearly interpolate the feature maps into shape of $H_f = 270, W_f = 480$. With $4\times$ down sample, for Wildtrack and MultiviewX, the ground plane grid sizes are set as $H_g = 120, W_g = 360$ and $H_g = 160, W_g = 250$, respectively, where each cell represents a 10 cm square. For spatial aggregation, we use 3 convolutional layers with 3×3 kernels and dilation of $1, 2, 4$. This will increase the receptive field for each ground plane location (cell) to 15×15 square cells, or 1.5×1.5 square meters. In order to train MVDet, we use an SGD optimizer with a momentum of 0.5, L2-normalization of 5×10^{-4}. The weight α for single view loss is set to 1. We use the one-cycle learning rate scheduler [31] with the max learning rate set to 0.1, and train for 10 epochs with batch size set to 1. We finish all experiments on two RTX-2080Ti GPUs.

4.3   Method Comparisons

In Table 2, we compare multiview aggregation and spatial aggregation in different methods. For multiview aggregation, previous methods either project

Table 2. Multiview aggregation and spatial aggregation in different methods

Method	Multiview aggregation	Spatial aggregation
RCNN & Clustering [41]	Detection results	Clustering
POM-CNN [8]	Detection results	Mean-field inference
DeepMCD [4]	Anchor box features	N/A
Deep-Occlusion [1]	Anchor box features	CRF + mean-field inference
MVDet (project images)	RGB image pixels	Large kernel convolution
MVDet (project results)	Detection results	Large kernel convolution
MVDet (w/o large kernel)	Feature maps	N/A
MVDet	Feature maps	Large kernel convolution

Table 3. Performance comparison with state-of-the-art methods on multiview pedestrian detection datasets. *indicates that the results are from our implementation

Method	Wildtrack				MultiviewX			
	MODA	MODP	Prec	Recall	MODA	MODP	Prec	Recall
RCNN & Clustering	11.3	18.4	68	43	18.7*	46.4*	63.5*	43.9*
POM-CNN	23.2	30.5	75	55	-	-	-	-
DeepMCD	67.8	64.2	85	82	70.0*	73.0*	85.7*	83.3*
Deep-Occlusion	74.1	53.8	**95**	80	75.2*	54.7*	**97.8***	80.2*
MVDet (project images)	26.8	45.6	84.2	33.0	19.5	51.0	84.4	24.0
MVDet (project results)	68.2	71.9	85.9	81.2	73.2	79.7	87.6	85.0
MVDet (w/o large kernel)	76.9	71.6	84.5	93.5	77.2	76.3	89.5	85.9
MVDet	**88.2**	**75.7**	94.7	**93.6**	**83.9**	79.6	96.8	**86.7**

single view detection results [8,41] or use multiview anchor box features [1,4]. For spatial aggregation, clustering [41], mean-field inference [1,8], and CRF [1,29] are investigated. In order to compare against previous methods, we create the following variants for MVDet. To compare anchor-free aggregation with anchor-based methods, we create "MVDet (w/o large kernel)", which remove the large kernel convolutions. This variant is created as a direct comparison against DeepMCD [4], both of which do not include spatial aggregation. To compare different projection choices (Sect. 3.1), we include two variants that either project RGB image pixels "MVDet (project images)" or single view detection results "MVDet (project results)". "MVDet (w/o large kernel)" also show the effectiveness of spatial aggregation. All variants follow the same training protocol as original MVDet.

4.4 Evaluation of MVDet

Comparison Against State-of-the-Art Methods. In Table 3, we compare the performance of MVDet against multiple state-of-the-art methods on multiview pedestrian detection. Since there are no available codes for some of the

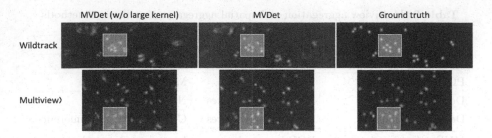

Fig. 6. Effectiveness of spatial aggregation via large kernel convolution. Compared to "MVDet (w/o large kernel)", MVDet outputs occupancy probabilities more similar to the ground truth, especially in highlighted areas.

methods, for a fair comparison on MultiviewX, we re-implement these methods to the best as we can. On Wildtrack dataset, MVDet achieves 88.2% MODA, a +14.1% increase over previous state-of-the-art. On MultiviewX dataset, MVDet achieves 83.9% MODA, an 8.7% increase over our implementation of Deep-Occlusion [1]. MVDet also achieves highest MODP and recall on both datasets, but slightly falls behind Deep-Occlusion in terms of precision. It is worth mentioning that Deep-Occlusion outperforms MVDet in terms of precision, but falls behind in terms of recall. This shows that their CNN-CRF method is very good at suppressing the false positives, but sometimes has a tendency to miss a few targets.

Effectiveness of Anchor-Free Multiview Aggregation. Even without spatial aggregation, "MVDet (w/o large kernel)" achieves 76.9% MODA on Wildtrack dataset and 77.2% MODA on MultiviewX dataset. In fact, it slightly outperforms current state-of-the-art by +2.8% and +2.0% on two datasets. The high performance proves the effectiveness of our anchor-free aggregation via feature map projection. In Sect. 3.1, we hypothesize that inaccurate anchor boxes could possibly result in less accurate aggregated features and thus proposed an anchor-free approach. In Table 3, we prove the effectiveness of our anchor-free approach by comparing anchor-based DeepMCD [4] against anchor-free "MVDet (w/o large kernel)", both of which do not include spatial aggregation. The variant of MVDet outperforms DeepMCD by 9.1% on Wildtrack dataset, and 7.2% MODA on MultiviewX dataset, which demonstrates anchor-free feature maps projection can be a better choice for multiview aggregation in multiview pedestrian detection when the anchor boxes are not accurate.

Feature map projection brings less improvement over multiview anchor box features on MultiviewX dataset (+7.2% on MultiviewX compared to +9.1% on Wildtrack). This is because MultiviewX dataset has synthetic humans, whereas Wildtrack captures real-world pedestrians. Naturally, the variances of human height and width are higher in the real-world scenario, as synthetic humans are of very similar sizes. This suggests less accurate anchor boxes on average for the real-world dataset, Wildtrack. As a result, aggregation via feature map projection brings larger improvement on Wildtrack dataset.

Comparison Between Different Projection Choices. We claim that projecting the feature maps is a better choice than projecting the RGB images or single view results in Sect. 3.1. Projecting the RGB images breaks the spatial relationship between pixels, and a single RGB pixel represents little information. As a result, in Table 3, we find "MVDet (project images)" leads to largely inferior performance on both datasets (26.8% and 19.5% MODA). Although single view results are robust to spatial patter break from projection, the information contained in them is limited. Due to crowdedness and occlusion, single view detection might lose many true positives. As such, clustering these projected single view results as in "RCNN & clustering" [41] are proven to be extremely difficult (11.3% and 18.7% MODA). Replacing the clustering with large kernel convolution "MVDet (project results)" increases the performance by a large margin (68.2% and 73.2% MODA), as it alleviates the problem of formulating 1-size clusters (clusters that have only one component, as the detections are missing from occlusion) and can be trained in an end-to-end manner. Still, the restricted information in detection results prevents the variant from higher performance.

Effectiveness of Spatial Aggregation via Large Kernel Convolution. Spatial aggregation with large kernel convolutions brings forward a +11.3% MODA increase on Wildtrack dataset, and a +6.7% performance increase on MultiviewX dataset. In comparison, spatial aggregation with CRF and mean-field inference brings forward increases of +6.3% and +5.2% on the two datasets, going from DeepMCD to Deep-Occlusion. We do not assert superiority of either the CRF-based or CNN-based methods. We only argue that the proposed CNN-based method can effectively aggregate spatial neighbor information to address the ambiguities from crowdedness or occlusion while need no design or operations besides CNN. As shown in Fig. 6, large kernel convolutions manages to output results that are more similar to the ground truth.

For spatial aggregation, both the proposed large kernel convolution and CRF bring less improvement on MultiviewX dataset. As mentioned in Table 1, even though there are fewer cameras in MultiviewX dataset, each ground plane location in MultiviewX dataset is covered by more cameras on average. Each location is covered by 4.41 cameras (field-of-view) on average for MultiviewX dataset, as opposed to 3.74 in Wildtrack. More camera coverage usually introduces more information and reduces the ambiguities, which also limits the performance increase from addressing ambiguities via spatial aggregation.

Influence of Different Crowdedness and Occlusion Levels. Being a synthetic dataset, there are multiple available configurations for MultiviewX. In Fig. 7 (left), we show the camera views under multiple levels of crowdedness. As the crowdedness of the scenario increases, the occlusion also increases. In Fig. 7 (right), we show the MVDet performance under multiple levels of occlusions. As crowdedness and occlusions increase (more difficult), MODA of both MVDet and MVDet "MVDet (w/o large kernel)" decrease. In addition, performance increases from spatial aggregation also drop, due to the task being more challenging and heavy occlusion also affecting the spatial neighbors.

20 person/frame   40 person/frame (default)   60 person/frame   80 person/frame

Fig. 7. MultiviewX dataset under different crowdedness configuration (left), and corresponding MVDet performance (right).

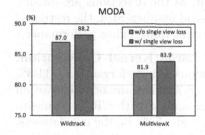

Fig. 8. MODA performance of MVDet with ($\alpha = 1$) or without ($\alpha = 0$) single view detection loss.

Influence of Single View Detection Loss. In our default setting of MVDet, for the combined loss in Eq. 5, the ratio α is set to 1. In Fig. 8, we investigate the influence of removing the single view loss. Without single view detection loss, we find a -1.2% and a -2.0% performance loss on both datasets, which are still very competitive. In fact, we believe single view foot detection loss does not further benefit the system, as the foot points are already supervised on the ground plane. The head point detection loss, on the other hand, can produce heterogeneous supervision, thus further improving system performance. As discussed in Sects. 3.1 and 4.4, less accurate bounding box annotations limit the performance gain from single view loss on Wildtrack dataset.

5   Conclusion

In this paper, we investigate pedestrian detection in a crowded scene, through incorporating multiple camera views. Specifically, we focus on addressing the ambiguities that arise from occlusion with multiview aggregation and spatial aggregation, two core aspects of multiview pedestrian detection. For multiview aggregation, rather than anchor-based approach in previous methods, we take an anchor-free approach by combining the projected feature maps. For spatial aggregation, different from previous methods that need design and operations aside from CNN, we apply large kernels in our fully convolutional approach. The proposed system, MVDet, achieves 88.2% MODA on Wildtrack dataset, outperforming previous state-of-the-art by 14.1%. On MultiviewX, a new synthetic dataset for multiview pedestrian detection, MVDet also achieves very competitive results. We believe the proposed MVDet can serve as a strong baseline for multiview pedestrian detection, encouraging further studies in related fields.

Acknowledgement. Dr. Liang Zheng is the recipient of Australian Research Council Discovery Early Career Award (DE200101283) funded by the Australian Government. The authors thank all anonymous reviewers and ACs for their constructive comments.

References

1. Baqué, P., Fleuret, F., Fua, P.: Deep occlusion reasoning for multi-camera multi-target detection. In: Proceedings of the IEEE International Conference on Computer Vision, pp. 271–279 (2017)
2. Cao, Z., Simon, T., Wei, S.E., Sheikh, Y.: Realtime multi-person 2D pose estimation using part affinity fields. In: Proceedings of the IEEE Conference on Computer Vision and Pattern Recognition, pp. 7291–7299 (2017)
3. Chavdarova, T., et al.: WILDTRACK: a multi-camera hd dataset for dense unscripted pedestrian detection. In: Proceedings of the IEEE Conference on Computer Vision and Pattern Recognition, pp. 5030–5039 (2018)
4. Chavdarova, T., et al.: Deep multi-camera people detection. In: 2017 16th IEEE International Conference on Machine Learning and Applications (ICMLA), pp. 848–853. IEEE (2017)
5. Chen, X., et al.: 3D object proposals for accurate object class detection. In: Advances in Neural Information Processing Systems, pp. 424–432 (2015)
6. Chen, X., Ma, H., Wan, J., Li, B., Xia, T.: Multi-view 3D object detection network for autonomous driving. In: Proceedings of the IEEE Conference on Computer Vision and Pattern Recognition, pp. 1907–1915 (2017)
7. Duan, K., Bai, S., Xie, L., Qi, H., Huang, Q., Tian, Q.: CenterNet: keypoint triplets for object detection. In: Proceedings of the IEEE International Conference on Computer Vision, pp. 6569–6578 (2019)
8. Fleuret, F., Berclaz, J., Lengagne, R., Fua, P.: Multicamera people tracking with a probabilistic occupancy map. IEEE Trans. Pattern Anal. Mach. Intell. **30**(2), 267–282 (2007)
9. Girshick, R.: Fast R-CNN object detection with caffe. Microsoft Research (2015)
10. Gupta, S., Girshick, R., Arbeláez, P., Malik, J.: Learning rich features from RGB-D images for object detection and segmentation. In: Fleet, D., Pajdla, T., Schiele, B., Tuytelaars, T. (eds.) Computer Vision – ECCV 2014. Lecture Notes in Computer Science, vol. 8695, pp. 345–360. Springer, Cham (2014). https://doi.org/10.1007/978-3-319-10584-0_23
11. He, K., Zhang, X., Ren, S., Sun, J.: Deep residual learning for image recognition. In: Proceedings of the IEEE Conference on Computer Vision and Pattern Recognition, pp. 770–778 (2016)
12. Hoffman, J., Gupta, S., Leong, J., Guadarrama, S., Darrell, T.: Cross-modal adaptation for RGB-D detection. In: 2016 IEEE International Conference on Robotics and Automation (ICRA), pp. 5032–5039. IEEE (2016)
13. Hosang, J., Benenson, R., Schiele, B.: Learning non-maximum suppression. In: Proceedings of the IEEE Conference on Computer Vision and Pattern Recognition, pp. 4507–4515 (2017)
14. Jaderberg, M., Simonyan, K., Zisserman, A., et al.: Spatial transformer networks. In: Advances in Neural Information Processing Systems, pp. 2017–2025 (2015)
15. Kasturi, R., Goldgof, D., Soundararajan, P., Manohar, V., Garofolo, J., Bowers, R., Boonstra, M., Korzhova, V., Zhang, J.: Framework for performance evaluation of face, text, and vehicle detection and tracking in video: data, metrics, and protocol. IEEE Trans. Pattern Anal. Mach. Intell. **31**(2), 319–336 (2008)

16. Kong, T., Sun, F., Liu, H., Jiang, Y., Shi, J.: FoveaBox: beyond anchor-based object detector. arXiv preprint arXiv:1904.03797 (2019)
17. Ku, J., Mozifian, M., Lee, J., Harakeh, A., Waslander, S.L.: Joint 3D proposal generation and object detection from view aggregation. In: 2018 IEEE/RSJ International Conference on Intelligent Robots and Systems (IROS), pp. 1–8. IEEE (2018)
18. Law, H., Deng, J.: CornerNet: Detecting objects as paired keypoints. In: Ferrari, V., Sminchisescu, C., Weiss, Y., Hebert, M. (eds.) Proceedings of the European Conference on Computer Vision (ECCV-2018). Lecture Notes in Computer Science, vol. 11218, pp. 765–781. Springer, Munich (2018). https://doi.org/10.1007/978-3-030-01264-9_45
19. Liang, M., Yang, B., Wang, S., Urtasun, R.: Deep continuous fusion for multi-sensor 3D object detection. In: Ferrari, V., Hebert, M., Sminchisescu, C., Weiss, Y. (eds.) Computer Vision – ECCV 2018. Lecture Notes in Computer Science, vol. 11220, pp. 663–678. Springer, Cham (2018). https://doi.org/10.1007/978-3-030-01270-0_39
20. Liu, R., et al.: An intriguing failing of convolutional neural networks and the Coord-Conv solution. In: Advances in Neural Information Processing Systems, pp. 9605–9616 (2018)
21. Liu, W., et al.: SSD: single shot multibox detector. In: Leibe, B., Matas, J., Sebe, N., Welling, M. (eds.) Computer Vision – ECCV 2016. Lecture Notes in Computer Science, vol. 9905, pp. 21–37. Springer, Cham (2016). https://doi.org/10.1007/978-3-319-46448-0_2
22. Liu, W., Liao, S., Ren, W., Hu, W., Yu, Y.: High-level semantic feature detection: a new perspective for pedestrian detection. In: Proceedings of the IEEE Conference on Computer Vision and Pattern Recognition, pp. 5187–5196 (2019)
23. Lv, K., Sheng, H., Xiong, Z., Li, W., Zheng, L.: Pose-based view synthesis for vehicles: a perspective aware method. IEEE Trans. Image Process. 29, 5163–5174 (2020)
24. Noh, J., Lee, S., Kim, B., Kim, G.: Improving occlusion and hard negative handling for single-stage pedestrian detectors. In: Proceedings of the IEEE Conference on Computer Vision and Pattern Recognition, pp. 966–974 (2018)
25. Ouyang, W., Zeng, X., Wang, X.: Partial occlusion handling in pedestrian detection with a deep model. IEEE Trans. Circ. Syst. Video Technol. 26(11), 2123–2137 (2015)
26. Peng, C., Zhang, X., Yu, G., Luo, G., Sun, J.: Large kernel matters-improve semantic segmentation by global convolutional network. In: Proceedings of the IEEE Conference on Computer Vision and Pattern Recognition, pp. 4353–4361 (2017)
27. Qi, C.R., Liu, W., Wu, C., Su, H., Guibas, L.J.: Frustum pointnets for 3D object detection from RGB-D data. In: Proceedings of the IEEE Conference on Computer Vision and Pattern Recognition, pp. 918–927 (2018)
28. Ren, S., He, K., Girshick, R., Sun, J.: Faster R-CNN: towards real-time object detection with region proposal networks. In: Advances in Neural Information Processing Systems, pp. 91–99 (2015)
29. Roig, G., Boix, X., Shitrit, H.B., Fua, P.: Conditional random fields for multi-camera object detection. In: 2011 International Conference on Computer Vision, pp. 563–570. IEEE (2011)
30. Shi, Y., Liu, L., Yu, X., Li, H.: Spatial-aware feature aggregation for image based cross-view geo-localization. In: Advances in Neural Information Processing Systems, pp. 10090–10100 (2019)

31. Smith, L.N., Topin, N.: Super-convergence: very fast training of neural networks using large learning rates. In: Artificial Intelligence and Machine Learning for Multi-Domain Operations Applications, vol. 11006, p. 1100612. International Society for Optics and Photonics (2019)
32. Song, T., Sun, L., Xie, D., Sun, H., Pu, S.: Small-scale pedestrian detection based on topological line localization and temporal feature aggregation. In: Ferrari, V., Hebert, M., Sminchisescu, C., Weiss, Y. (eds.) Computer Vision – ECCV 2018. Lecture Notes in Computer Science, vol. 11211, pp. 554–569. Springer, Cham (2018). https://doi.org/10.1007/978-3-030-01234-2_33
33. Su, H., Maji, S., Kalogerakis, E., Learned-Miller, E.: Multi-view convolutional neural networks for 3D shape recognition. In: Proceedings of the IEEE International Conference on Computer Vision, pp. 945–953 (2015)
34. Sun, X., Zheng, L.: Dissecting person re-identification from the viewpoint of viewpoint. In: Proceedings of the IEEE Conference on Computer Vision and Pattern Recognition, pp. 608–617 (2019)
35. Tian, Y., Luo, P., Wang, X., Tang, X.: Deep learning strong parts for pedestrian detection. In: Proceedings of the IEEE International Conference on Computer Vision, pp. 1904–1912 (2015)
36. Tian, Z., Shen, C., Chen, H., He, T.: FCOS: fully convolutional one-stage object detection. In: Proceedings of the IEEE International Conference on Computer Vision, pp. 9627–9636 (2019)
37. Unity: Unity technologies. https://unity.com/
38. Wang, F., Zhao, L., Li, X., Wang, X., Tao, D.: Geometry-aware scene text detection with instance transformation network. In: Proceedings of the IEEE Conference on Computer Vision and Pattern Recognition, pp. 1381–1389 (2018)
39. Wang, X., Xiao, T., Jiang, Y., Shao, S., Sun, J., Shen, C.: Repulsion loss: detecting pedestrians in a crowd. In: Proceedings of the IEEE Conference on Computer Vision and Pattern Recognition, pp. 7774–7783 (2018)
40. Wu, J., et al.: Single image 3D interpreter network. In: Leibe, B., Matas, J., Sebe, N., Welling, M. (eds.) Computer Vision – ECCV 2016. Lecture Notes in Computer Science, vol. 9910, pp. 365–382. Springer, Cham (2016). https://doi.org/10.1007/978-3-319-46466-4_22
41. Xu, Y., Liu, X., Liu, Y., Zhu, S.C.: Multi-view people tracking via hierarchical trajectory composition. In: Proceedings of the IEEE Conference on Computer Vision and Pattern Recognition, pp. 4256–4265 (2016)
42. Yan, X., Yang, J., Yumer, E., Guo, Y., Lee, H.: Perspective transformer nets: learning single-view 3D object reconstruction without 3d supervision. In: Advances in Neural Information Processing Systems, pp. 1696–1704 (2016)
43. Yang, T., Zhang, X., Li, Z., Zhang, W., Sun, J.: Metaanchor: learning to detect objects with customized anchors. In: Advances in Neural Information Processing Systems, pp. 320–330 (2018)
44. Yao, Y., Zheng, L., Yang, X., Naphade, M., Gedeon, T.: Simulating content consistent vehicle datasets with attribute descent. arXiv preprint arXiv:1912.08855 (2019)
45. Yu, F., Koltun, V.: Multi-scale context aggregation by dilated convolutions. arXiv preprint arXiv:1511.07122 (2015)
46. Zhang, S., Wen, L., Bian, X., Lei, Z., Li, S.Z.: Occlusion-aware R-CNN: detecting pedestrians in a crowd. In: Ferrari, V., Hebert, M., Sminchisescu, C., Weiss, Y. (eds.) Computer Vision – ECCV 2018. Lecture Notes in Computer Science, vol. 11207, pp. 357–374. Springer, Cham (2018). https://doi.org/10.1007/978-3-030-01219-9_39

47. Zheng, S., et al.: Conditional random fields as recurrent neural networks. In: Proceedings of the IEEE International Conference on Computer Vision, pp. 1529–1537 (2015)
48. Zhou, C., Yuan, J.: Multi-label learning of part detectors for heavily occluded pedestrian detection. In: Proceedings of the IEEE International Conference on Computer Vision, pp. 3486–3495 (2017)
49. Zhu, C., He, Y., Savvides, M.: Feature selective anchor-free module for single-shot object detection. In: Proceedings of the IEEE Conference on Computer Vision and Pattern Recognition, pp. 840–849 (2019)

Learning Object Relation Graph and Tentative Policy for Visual Navigation

Heming Du[1], Xin Yu[1,2(✉)], and Liang Zheng[1]

[1] Australian National University, Canberra, Australia
{heming.du,liang.zheng}@anu.edu.au
[2] University of Technology Sydney, Ultimo, Australia
xin.yu@uts.edu.au

Abstract. Target-driven visual navigation aims at navigating an agent towards a given target based on the observation of the agent. In this task, it is critical to learn informative visual representation and robust navigation policy. Aiming to improve these two components, this paper proposes three complementary techniques, object relation graph (ORG), trial-driven imitation learning (IL), and a memory-augmented tentative policy network (TPN). ORG improves visual representation learning by integrating object relationships, including category closeness and spatial correlations, *e.g.*, a TV usually co-occurs with a remote spatially. Both Trial-driven IL and TPN underlie robust navigation policy, instructing the agent to escape from deadlock states, such as looping or being stuck. Specifically, trial-driven IL is a type of supervision used in policy network training, while TPN, mimicking the IL supervision in unseen environment, is applied in testing. Experiment in the artificial environment AI2-Thor validates that each of the techniques is effective. When combined, the techniques bring significantly improvement over baseline methods in navigation effectiveness and efficiency in unseen environments. We report 22.8% and 23.5% increase in success rate and Success weighted by Path Length (SPL), respectively. The code is available at https://github.com/xiaobaishu0097/ECCV-VN.git.

Keywords: Graph · Imitation learning · Tentative policy learning · Visual navigation

1 Introduction

Visual navigation aims to steer an agent towards a target object based on its first-view visual observations. To achieve this goal, a mapping from visual observations to agent actions is expected to be established. Thus, representing visual observations and designing navigation policy are the two key components in navigation systems. For example, to "grab the TV remote", an agent needs to

Electronic supplementary material The online version of this chapter (https://doi.org/10.1007/978-3-030-58571-6_2) contains supplementary material, which is available to authorized users.

© Springer Nature Switzerland AG 2020
A. Vedaldi et al. (Eds.): ECCV 2020, LNCS 12352, pp. 19–34, 2020.
https://doi.org/10.1007/978-3-030-58571-6_2

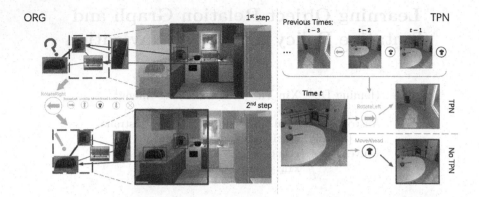

Fig. 1. Illustration of our proposed ORG and TPN in unseen testing environments. Right: Looking for a toaster. The agent first sights the coffee machine and our ORG advises that the coffee machine is usually close to the toaster. Given that the agent has not detected the toaster (on the right side of the coffee machine), the agent will turn left to find it. Left: illustration of escaping deadlock by TPN. Based on the current observation, the agent repeats action MoveAhead and falls in deadlock. However, our TPN lets the agent select action RotateRight, thus breaking the deadlock state.

know what a remote looks like and then searches it in an environment. Due to the small size of the target object, an agent might fail to find it within allowed search steps. Furthermore, an agent may also fail to move towards the target because of the complexity of the environments. Therefore, learning informative visual representation and failure-aware navigation policy is highly desirable.

We observe that common objects often exhibit very high concurrence relationships. For instance, cushions often lie on a sofa, or a mouse is next to a laptop. The concurrence not only indicates the closeness of object categories but also provides important spatial clues for agents to approach to target objects effectively and efficiently, especially when targets are too small or invisible in the current view, as illustrated in Fig. 1. Leveraging the concurrence relationships, an agent can narrow down the search area and then find small targets, thus increasing the effectiveness and efficiency of navigation.

Regarding there are various object categories and different environments, it is difficult to manually design concurrence relationships covering different situations comprehensively [25]. Instead, in this paper, we propose an object relation graph (ORG) to learn concurrence relationships among object classes from different environments. Different from traditional graph convolutional networks (GCN) [25] in which a category adjacent matrix is pre-defined or learned from an external knowledge database, our ORG does not need to resort to external knowledge but learns the category closeness and spatial correlations simultaneously from the object detection information from the training dataset. The object detection also provides stronger association between object concepts and their appearances in comparison to previous works [27, 29] that only employ word embedding to establish the association. To let an agent focus on moving towards targets without being distracted, we develop a graph attention layer. Our graph attention layer emphasizes target related object features while suppressing irrelevant ones via our ORG. In this manner, our extracted local features are more discriminative, thus facilitating object localization.

Due to the complexity of an environment, an agent might fail to reach the target and is stuck in a deadlock state, *e.g.*, repeating the same actions. Only using reinforcement learning in training cannot solve this problem since the reward does not provide explicit guidance of leaving deadlock states to an agent. Thus, an explicit instruction is required to provide when an agent is trapped in the deadlock. Inspired by human trial-and-practice behaviors, we propose a trial-driven imitation learning (IL) supervision to guide the agent with the expert experience to avoid deadlock. In this manner, we can continue training our policy network, improving the effectiveness of our navigation policy network. However, if we clone the expert experience at every step, the policy network will overfit to the seen training environment.

In unseen testing environments, the IL supervision is not available to an agent and it may fall in deadlock in testing. In order to enable an agent to avoid deadlock states in testing, we develop a memory-augmented tentative policy network (TPN). Our TPN firstly employs an external memory to record visual representations for detecting deadlock states. When the visual representations are repeated, it implies that an agent may fall in deadlock states. Then, TPN utilizes an internal memory that stores the past state and action pairs to generate explicit instructions for the agent, allowing it to leave deadlock in testing, as visible in Fig. 1. Unlike the work [27] that provides a scalar reward at every step in testing, our TPN provides explicit action instructions at failure steps to update our navigation network. Therefore, our method obtains a failure-aware navigation policy.

We adopt the standard A3C architecture [17] to learn our navigation policy in the artificial environment AI2-Thor [15]. Experiments in *unseen* scenes demonstrate that our method achieves superior navigation performance to the baseline methods. Remarkably, we improve the success rate from 56.4% to 69.3% and Success weighted by Path Length (SPL) from 0.319 to 0.394.

Overall, our major contributions are summarized as follows:

- We propose a novel object representation graph (ORG) to learn a category concurrence graph including category closeness and spatial correlations among different classes. Benefiting from our learned ORG, navigation agents are able to find targets more effectively and efficiently.
- We introduce trial-driven imitation learning to provide expert experience to an agent in training, thus preventing the navigation network from being trapped in deadlock and improving its training effectiveness.
- To the best of our knowledge, we are the first to propose a memory-augmented tentative policy network (TPN) to provide deadlock breaking policy in the *testing* phase. By exploiting our TPN, an agent is able to notice deadlock states and obtains an escape policy in unseen testing environment.

- Experimental results demonstrate that our method significantly improves the baseline visual navigation systems in unseen environments by a large margin of 22.8% in terms of the success rate.

2   Related Work

Visual navigation, as a fundamental task in robotic and artificial intelligence, has attracted great attention in the past decades. Prior works often require an entire map of an environment before navigation and have been divided into three parts: mapping, localization and path planning. The works employ a given map to obviate obstruction [3,4] while others use a map for navigation [19]. Dissanayke et al. [8] infer positions from the techniques of simultaneous localization and mapping [8] (SLAM). However, a map of an environment is not always available and those methods are not applicable in unseen environments.

Benefitting from the significant progress of the Deep neural networks (DNN), Gupta et al. [10] introduce cognitive mapping and planning (CMP) to build a map and then plan a route through deep neural network. Recently, reinforcement learning (RL) based visual navigation approaches aim at taking the current visual observation as input and predicting an action for the next step without intermediate steps, i.e., mapping and planning.

Mirowski et al. [16] adapt two auxiliary tasks, namely predict depth and loop closure classification, to improve navigation performance in complex 3D mazes environment. The methods [6,9] adopt a collision reward and collision detector to avoid collisions. Several works exploit more information from environments to improve navigation performance. Natural-language instruction are available in [1,26] to guide the agent actions. The methods [5,22,23] propose to use both visual observation features and the topological guidance of scenes. Furthermore, Kahn et al. [13] purpose a self-supervised approach to build a model of an environment through reinforcement learning. Wu et al. [28] propose a Bayesian relational memory to build room correlations. Meanwhile, Shen et al. [24] produce a robust action based on multiple actions from different visual representations.

Recently, target-oriented visual navigation methods have been proposed to search different kinds of object in an environment. Zhu et al. [30] employ reinforcement learning to generate an action for the next step based on the current visual observation and a given destination image instead of a specific target class. Mousavian et al. [18] fuse semantic segmentation and detection masks and then feed the fused features into their policy network for navigation. Furthermore, Wortsman et al. [27] adopt Glove embedding to represent target objects and a network to simulate the reward function in reinforcement learning for navigation in unseen environments. Similar to the works [2,9], Yang et al. [29] propose a graph convolutional network [25] to exploit relationships among object categories, but they need to resort to an external knowledge database and do not explore the category spatial correlations. However, those works may suffer semantic ambiguity or non-discriminative representations of the visual information, and thus navigate an agent to contextually similar objects instead of targets or fail to recognize targets.

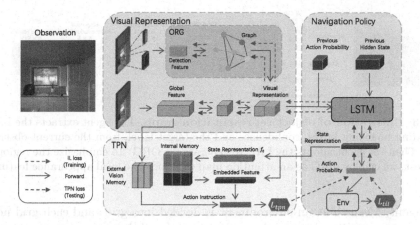

Fig. 2. Overview of our proposed framework. The visual representation is combined by the global feature and local feature encoded by our ORG. The navigation network adopts A3C model but trained with both the reinforcement learning reward and our trial-driven IL supervision. TPN is trained in the deadlock states. In training TPN, our navigation network is fixed. In testing, TPN updates our navigation network.

In contrast, our method exploits the detection results and thus significantly alleviates the semantic ambiguity. Moreover, our memory augmented TPN is the first attempt to enable an agent to escape from deadlock states in the testing phase among reinforcement learning based navigation systems.

3   Proposed Method

Our goal is to introduce an informative visual representation and a failure-aware navigation policy for a target-driven visual navigation system. To achieve this goal, our navigation system contains three major components, as illustrated in Fig. 2: (i) learning visual representation from RGB observations; In this component, we introduce an object representation graph (ORG) to extract informative visual representation for objects of interest. (ii) learning navigation policy based on our visual representation; To prevent an agent from being trapped in local minima, such as deadlock states, in training, we propose trial-driven imitation learning. (iii) learning a tentative policy network; This allows an agent to receive policy instruction in order to break deadlock during testing.

3.1   Task Definition

Given a target object category, *e.g.*, remote control, our task is to navigate an agent to an instance of this class using visual information. During navigation, RGB images in an egocentric view are the only available source for an agent and the agent predicts its actions based on the current view. Information about the entire environment, *i.e.* topological map and 3D meshes, is not available to

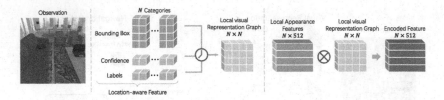

Fig. 3. Illustration of object representation graph. The agent extracts the LAF, including bounding boxes, confidences and the target label, from the current observation. Then the agent adopts the LAF to generate the ORG. To emphasize the region of interest, we employ ORG as an attention map to encode the local appearance features.

the agent. Meanwhile, an environment is divided into grids and each grid node represents one unique state in the environment. In all the environments, an agent is able to move between nodes with 6 different actions, including `MoveAhead`, `RotateLeft`, `RotateRight`, `LookUp`, `LookDown`, `Done`.

One successful episode is defined as: an agent selects the termination action `Done` when the distance between the agent and the target is less than a threshold (*i.e.*, 1.5 meters) and the target is in its field of view. If a termination action is executed at any other time, the agent fails and the episode ends.

At the beginning of each episode, an agent is given a random target class word $T \in \{\text{Sink}, \dots, \text{Microwave}\}$ and starts from a random state $s = \{x, y, \theta_r, \theta_h\}$ in a random room to maintain the uniqueness of each episode, where x and y represent the position of the agent, θ_r and θ_h indicate the point of view of the agent. At each timestamp t, an agent captures the current observation O_t in the first-person perspective. Based on the visual representation extracted from O_t and the T, the agent generates a policy $\pi(a_t|O_t, T)$, where a_t represents the distribution of actions, and the action with the highest probability is selected for the next step. The agent will continue moving until the action `Done` is issued.

3.2 Object Representation Graph

Regarding the agent observes an environment in an egocentric view instead of a bird's-eye view, how to design an effective exploration method plays a critical role in visual navigation. Inspired by the human searching behaviors, we aim to fully explore the relationship among categories as well as their spatial correlations for navigation. Therefore, we introduce an object representation graph network to explore such concurrence information.

Detection and Location-Aware Feature. In order to learn the relationship among classes and their spatial correlations, we need to find all the objects in an image first. Thus, we train an object detector, *i.e.*, Faster RCNN [21], to achieve this goal. Given an input image, we first perform object detection to localize all the objects of interest. If there are multiple instances of an object class, we only choose the one with the highest confidence score. We record the bounding box positions and detection confidence for each category and then concatenate them as our local detection feature. It is likely that some category objects do not appear in the current view. Therefore, we record the bounding box positions and confidence of those categories as 0. In order to provide the target information during navigation, we concatenate a one-hot encoded target vector with our local detection feature as our location-aware feature (LAF), as seen in Fig. 3. Moreover, we extract not only the location feature but also appearance feature for the object. We project the bounding boxes to the same layer in the backbone network of the detector and then extract our location-aware appearance features, as seen in Fig. 3. Due to the small resolution of input images [15], we extract appearance features from the second ResBlock layer in the backbone network to preserve spatial details of local regions.

Learning Object Representation Graph. After obtaining our extracted LAF, we introduce our graph convolutional network to learn our object representation graph (ORG). We first define a graph by $G = (N, A)$, where N and A denote the nodes and the edges between nodes respectively. To be specific, each node $n \in N$ denotes the concatenated vector of the bounding box position, confidence and label (see Fig. 3), and each edge $a \in A$ denotes the relationships among different classes. Our graph convolutional network (GCN) takes all the nodes as inputs $X \in \mathbb{R}^{|N| \times D}$ and then embeds each input node by a matrix $W \in \mathbb{R}^{D \times N}$, where D indicates the dimension of our LAF. After encoding each node, our GCN embeds, regarded as convolution, all the nodes according to the adjacent relationship $A \in \mathbb{R}^{|N| \times N}$ and outputs a new encoding $Z \in \mathbb{R}^{|N| \times N}$. Our graph convolutional layer is expressed as:

$$Z = f(A \cdot X \cdot W), \tag{1}$$

where $f(\cdot)$ denotes the ReLU activation function. Different from traditional GCNs in which an adjacent matrix A is often pre-defined, our ORG network learns the node embedding W as well as the adjacent matrix A. The process of learning A actually can be regarded as encoding the spatial correlations among categories as well as their relationships since A encodes the embedded LAF across different categories. The output Z (i.e., ORG) encodes the location information among objects and their closeness. Moreover, since our object representation graph is learned in accordance with environments rather than a graph learned from external databases, such as FastText [12], our ORG is able to adapt to different environments.

Graph Attention Layer. To let the agent focus on moving towards the target or the areas where the target is likely placed, we adopt an attention mechanism in our network. Specifically, we employ our Z as our attention map to the location-aware appearance feature. Denote our location-aware appearance feature as $F \in \mathbb{R}^{|N| \times d}$, where d represents the dimension of our location-aware appearance feature. Our graph attention layer is expressed as:

$$\hat{F} = f(Z \cdot F), \tag{2}$$

where $\hat{F} \in \mathbb{R}^{|N| \times d}$ is our attended location-aware appearance feature. Note that, there is no learnable parameters in our graph attention layer. Then we concatenate our attentive location-aware appearance feature with LAF for explicit target location information.

Another advantage of our graph attention module is that our concatenated location-aware appearance feature is more robust than X. For instance, when our detector fails to localize targets or produces false positives, our model is still able to exploit target related information for navigation. In contrast, X does not provide such concurrence relationships among objects and an agent needs more steps to re-discover target objects. This also implies that using concatenated location-aware appearance feature we can achieve a more efficient navigation system. When the category relationships may not follow our learned ORG, our LAF (from our detector) is still valid for navigation and ensures the effectiveness of our navigation system in those cases.

3.3   Navigation Driven by Visual Features

Besides the task-specific visual representations, such as our concatenated location-aware appearance feature, an agent requires a global feature to describe the surroundings of an environment. Similar to [27], we employ ResNet18 [11] pretrained on ImageNet [7] to extract the global feature of the current view. We then fuse the global visual feature as well as our concatenated location-aware appearance feature as our final visual representation.

We adopt the standard Asynchronous Advantage Actor-Critic (A3C) architecture [17] to predict policy at each step. The input of our A3C model is the concatenation of our visual representation, the previous action and state embedding. Recall that the representation of previous actions and state embedding are feature vectors while our visual representation is a feature volume. Thus, we repeat them along the spatial dimensions so as to fit the size of our visual representation, and then feed the concatenated features to our A3C model. Our A3C model produces two outputs, *i.e.*, policy and value. We sample the action from the predicted policy with the highest probability and the output value is used to train our policy network.

3.4   Trial-Driven Imitation Learning

Concerning the complexity of the simulation environment, an agent may be trapped into deadlock states. Since the reinforcement reward cannot provide detailed action instruction for deadlock breaking, agents are difficult to learn escape policy without explicit supervision. Therefore, we propose trial-driven imitation learning (IL) to advise agents through explicit action instructions. To learn optimal action instructions, we employ expert experience acting as the policy guidance for an agent. We use Dijkstra's Shortest Path First algorithm to generate the expert experience. Under the supervision of policy guidance, an agent is able to imitate the optimal deadlock breaking solution. The IL loss L_{il} is given by the cross-entropy $L_{il} = CE(a_t, \hat{a})$, where a_t is the action predicted by our navigation policy, $\hat{a}$ represents the action instruction and CE indicates the

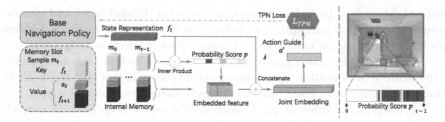

Fig. 4. Illustration of memory-argumented tentative policy network. Right: Agent compares the state representation with the key of the internal memory and then generates a weight to encode the past state and action pairs. The embedded feature and the state are concatenated to learning an action for breaking deadlock. The supervision of TPN comes from expert experience of IL. Left: visualization of the probability score p when TPN guides the agent to escape from the deadlock states. The darker color indicates which previous state will be more likely used for learning policy.

cross-entropy loss. The total training loss L for training our navigation policy network is formulated as:

$$L = L_{nav} + L_{il}, \tag{3}$$

where L_{nav} represents our navigation loss from reinforcement learning.

Due to the limited training data, imitation learning may lead navigation policy to overfitting seen environments after millions of episode training. In order to maintain the generalization ability of agents to unseen environments, we need to balance imitation learning and reinforcement learning. Inspired by human trial-and-practice behaviors, we utilize the policy guidance in deadlock states instead of every state. In doing so, we can continue the episode instead of staying in deadlock states till termination, thus improving our training effectiveness. For instance, when the target object is in the corner of the room, using our imitate learning supervision, our agent is able to escape from deadlock and reach the target after a few turns. In contrast, without IL supervision, the agent traps in a position far away from the target till the episode ends.

3.5 Memory-Augmented Tentative Policy Network

External Memory. Unlike in the training stage, instructions from an environment, such as expert experience and validation information of actions, are not available to agents in testing. Therefore, we propose a memory-augmented tentative policy network to assist an agent to break deadlock. In order to detect the deadlock states, we employ an external vision memory. Our external vision memory is designed to record visual features from an off-the-shelf feature extractor. Once there is at least one visual feature as the same as those recorded in memory, we assume an agent is stuck in deadlock states. Denoted an episode by $\{s_0, s_1, \ldots, s_t\}$, where s_t represents a states of an agent at time t. We define s_t as a deadlock if the visual features extracted from s_t and another previous state s_t' are similar.

Internal Memory. In order to capture long-term dependencies and generate instructions based on past states, we present an internal state memory. Different from the external vision memory, our internal state memory is designed to store state and action pairs. Each memory slot m_t at time t includes two components: (i) the state representation f_t at time t serving as a key of m_t; (ii) both the action distribution a_t at time t and the transformed state representation f_{t+1} at time $t + 1$ serving as value of m_t. In each step, a newly-generated memory slot will be inserted at the end of the internal state memory.

Tentative Policy Network (TPN). To fully utilize the previous adventures, our TPN first employs a soft attention mechanism to generate pseudo expert experience from our internal memory. Given the preceding actions and state transformation, TPN computes the probability score p between keys k of each memory slot and current state representation f_t by taking the inner product followed by a softmax,

$$p = \sigma(f_t^T \cdot k), \tag{4}$$

where $\sigma(x_i) = \frac{e^{x_i}}{\sum_j e^{x_j}}$. Then, the embedded memory feature is the weighted sum over the value of memory slots by the probability score, as illustrated in Fig. 4.

To obtain informative representation, we concatenate the embedded memory feature with the current state and then encode them as a joint feature embedding. After that, TPN exploits the joint feature embedding to generate the action guidance for our base navigation policy network. In this manner, TPN will provide deadlock breaking policy based on previous action and state pairs.

In order to train TPN, we use our trained base navigation network to navigate in an environment. When the agent falls into deadlock, we use our imitation learning supervision to train our TPN. In this fashion, our TPN learns how to provide deadlock breaking actions in the deadlock situation. In testing, our TPN is fixed and an agent will update its base navigation policy by the cross-entropy $L_{tpn} = CE(a_t, a')$, where a_t is the action predicted by the base navigation policy and a' indicates the action from the expert experience. Overall, our trial-driven imitation learning supervision and TPN facilitate an agent to establish a failure-aware navigation policy in both training and testing.

3.6   Training Details

We train our model in two stages: (i) training navigation policy for 6M episodes in total with 12 asynchronous agents; In this stage, we use trial-driven imitation learning and reinforcement learning rewards as our objective. (ii) training our TPN for 2M episodes in total with 12 asynchronous agents; We select the navigation model performing the best on the *validation set* in terms of success rate as the fixed backbone to train our TPN. Both training stages are performed on the training set. Similar to [27], in learning navigation policy we penalize each action step with -0.001. When an agent reaches a target and sends the termination signal **Done**, we will reward the agent with a large value 5. In our experiments, we employ Adam optimizer [14] to update the parameters of our networks with a learning rate 10^{-4}.

We employ Faster RCNN as our detector and re-train it on the training dataset, (*i.e.*, AI2-Thor environment [15]). We employ half of the training dataset and data augmentation to train our detector to avoid overfitting. We will release our training protocols and codes for reproducibility.

4   Experiments

4.1   Dataset and Evaluation

Dataset. We choose AI2-Thor [15] environment to evaluate our method. AI2thor dataset contains four types of scenes, including kitchen, living room, bedroom and bathroom, and each scene includes 30 rooms, where each room is unique in terms of furniture placement and item types. Following [27], we select 22 categories from those four types of scenes. In each scene, there are more than four target classes, and an agent randomly starts navigation at over 2000 states.

Evaluation. We use the success rate and Success Weighted by Path Length (SPL) for performance evaluation. The success rate measures the effectiveness of trajectories and is formulated as $\frac{1}{N}\sum_{n=0}^{N} S_n$, where N stands for the total number of episodes, and S_n is the binary indicator of n-th episode. SPL evaluates the efficiency of the model through $\frac{1}{N}\sum_{n=0}^{N} \frac{Len_n}{max(Len_n,Len_{opt})}$, where Len_n and Len_{opt} represent the length of the n-th episode and its optimal path, respectively.

4.2   Task Setup and Comparison Methods

We use the evaluation protocol in [27]. To ensure the generalization of our method, there is no overlap between our training rooms and testing ones. We select 25 out of 30 rooms per scene as the training and validation set. We test our method only in the remaining 20 **unseen** rooms. During the evaluation, each model performs 250 episodes per scene from the validation set. The model with the highest success rate will be performed on the test set as the reported results.

Baseline. We feed the detection results to A3C for navigation as our baseline, on top of which we build our model.

Random policy. An agent navigates based on a uniform action probability. Thus, the agent will randomly walk in the scene or randomly stop.

Scene Priors (SP). [29] exploits a category relation graph learned from an external database, FastText [12]. We replace its original WE with detection results for fair comparison, dubbed **D-SP**.

Word Embedding (WE). An agent uses Glove embedding to associate target concepts and appearances.

Self-adaptive Visual Navigation method (SAVN). [27] introduces a meta reinforcement learning method in unseen environments. Furthermore, SAVN employs WE to associate target concepts and appearances. We replace its original WE with detection results to achieve a stronger baseline, dubbed **D-SAVN**.

Table 1. Comparisons of navigation results. We report the success rate (%), denoted by Success, and SPL. $L > 5$ indicates the optimal path is larger than 5 steps

Method	ALL		$L \geq 5$	
	Success	SPL	Success	SPL
Random	8.0	0.036	0.3	0.001
WE	33.0	0.147	21.4	0.117
SP [29]	35.1	0.155	22.2	0.114
D-SP [29]	59.6	0.303	47.9	0.273
SAVN [27]	40.8	0.161	28.7	0.139
D-SAVN [27]	62.3	0.264	53.3	0.254
Baseline	56.4	0.319	42.5	0.270
Baseline + TPN	58.7	0.316	45.8	0.274
Baseline + IL	63.6	0.354	52.8	0.326
Baseline + ORG	65.3	0.375	54.8	0.361
Ours (TPN + ORG + IL)	**69.3**	**0.394**	**60.7**	**0.386**

4.3   Results

Quantitative Results. We demonstrate the results of four comparison methods and our baseline model in Table 1. For fair comparisons, we also follow the setup and protocols in [27] when measuring the performance of our method.

As indicated in Table 1, our method outperforms our baseline significantly in terms of the success rate and SPL. Meanwhile, each module of our method is able to improve navigation performance. Since the baseline does not exploit category concurrence relation, it needs to search the target object only based on detection. This experiment indicates that our ORG encodes informative visual representation for agents, thus significantly increasing efficiency and effectiveness of navigation. Furthermore, both our trial-driven imitation learning and TPN are able to predict advisable instructions to guide agent escape from local minima, and thus those two models achieve better performance than our baseline. Note that, our baseline does not have any mechanism to avoid deadlock states.

SP [29] also aims at utilizing category relationships and leverages external knowledge to encode the category relationship. However, SP also employs WE to associate object appearances and concepts, while our ORG encodes object locations and appearances directly from our detector. Therefore, our method achieves superior performance to SP on both the success rate and SPL. Unlike D-SP that concatenates a graph representation with detection features from different modalities, our model fuses detection results via a learned graph and thus achieves better performance.

Although state-of-the-art model SAVN employs meta reinforcement learning to improve navigation performance, SAVN uses word embedding [20] to represent targets, thus suffering the ambiguity when objects often appear together, such as

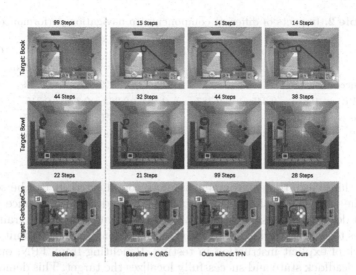

Fig. 5. Visual results of different models in testing environments. We compare our proposed model with our proposed model without TPN and our baseline with/without ORG. The target objects are highlighted by the yellow bounding boxes. Green and red lines represent success cases and failure cases, respectively. First row: the target is *book*. Second row: the target is *bowl*. Third row: the target is *Garbage Can*.

a TV set and a remote. We replace the word embedding with our detection module, named D-SAVN. The experiment indicates that the detection information significantly improves the performance of SAVN. Compared to D-SAVN that improves navigation effectiveness by simulating a reward in testing, our model explicitly provides instructions to escape from deadlock states and thus achieves better performance on both metrics, as indicated in Table 1.

Case Study. Fig. 5 illustrates trajectories of three navigation tasks proceeded by four models, *i.e.*, the baseline, the baseline with ORG, our model without TPN and our full model, in *unseen* testing environments.

In the first case, the baseline fails to find the target and is stuck in the environment, since it reaches the maximum step limit *i.e.*, 99 steps. On the contrary, the baseline with ORG finds the target object successfully. This implies that using our ORG, we can improve the navigation effectiveness. Moreover, the navigation system with ORG only uses 15 steps to localize the object. This indicates our ORG improves the navigation efficiency.

In the second case, the baseline and the baseline with ORG repeat the same actions until the agents terminate. It can be seen that both the baseline and the baseline with ORG are trapped in deadlock states. In contrast, the navigation system trained with IL supervision overcomes the deadlock and reaches the target. This demonstrates the importance of our trial-driven IL supervision. Furthermore, our model escapes the deadlock using the least steps, demonstrating TPN improves the navigation effectiveness in testing.

Table 2. Impacts of different components on navigation performances

Method		w/o IL	w/o ORG	w/o TPN	IL		TPN		Ours
					Failed	All	All	Random	
ALL	Success	66.8%	67.5%	66.6%	63.6%	47.7%	66.2%	62.3%	**69.3%**
	SPL	0.375	0.345	0.387	0.354	0.284	0.325	0.315	**0.394**
$L \geq 5$	Success	57.2%	57.8%	57.4%	52.8%	35.3%	56.4%	49.5%	**60.7%**
	SPL	0.364	0.327	0.374	0.326	0.218	0.295	0.266	**0.386**

In the third case, the environment is more complicated. It can be seen that the baseline with and without ORG both fail to find the target since they are trapped in deadlock states. As seen in the third column, the model trained with IL manages to escape the deadlock, but reaches the maximum step limit and fails for the lack of explicit instruction in testing. Benefiting from TPN, our model leaves the deadlock state and successfully localizes the target. This demonstrates that TPN is very helpful for breaking the deadlock states in testing and improves the navigation effectiveness.

4.4 Ablation Study

Our method has three major contributions, *i.e.* ORG, trial-driven IL supervision and TPN. We dissect their impacts as follows.

Impact of Trial-Driven IL. As seen in Table 2, our trial-driven IL improves the navigation policy compared to the model without using IL supervision to train our navigation network (w/o IL). This manifests that involving clear action guidance in deadlock states improves the navigation results compare to naviga- tion rewards. Furthermore, to study the influence of IL on generalization, we train our baseline model with IL at every step, marked all in IL. Table 2 implies that providing IL supervision at every step will overfit to the training data, thus undermining the generalization of navigation systems to unseen environments.

Impact of ORG. Our ORG improves the performance of navigation systems compared with the model without ORG (w/o ORG), as indicated in Table 2. Note that the significant SPL improvements demonstrate ORG improves the efficiency of navigation systems.

Impact of TPN. As indicated in Tab. 2, our TPN improves the success rate and SPL for our navigation system compared to the model without TPN (w/o TPN). It implies that our TPN helps agents to break deadlock in testing. Since our TPN focuses on learning deadlock avoidance policy, using TPN updates our based navigation network at every state will harm the navigation performance, marked all in TPN. As seen in Tab. 2, using random actions to solve deadlock states (random in TPN) suffers performance degradation. This indicates that our TPN predicts reasonable escape policy rather than random walking.

5   Conclusions

In this paper, we proposed an effective and robust target-driven visual navigation system. Benefiting from our proposed object representation graph, our navigation agent can localize targets effectively and efficiently even when targets are invisible in the current view. Furthermore, our proposed trial-driven imitation learning empowers our agent to escape from deadlock states in training, while our tentative policy network allows our navigation system to leave deadlock states in unseen testing environments, thus further promoting navigation effectiveness and achieving better navigation performance. Experiments demonstrate that our method achieves state-of-the-art performance.

Acknowledgements. Dr. Liang Zheng is the recipient of Australian Research Council Discovery Early Career Award (DE200101283) funded by the Australian Government. This research was also supported by the Australia Research Council Centre of Excellence for Robotics Vision (CE140100016).

References

1. Anderson, P., et al.: Vision-and-language navigation: interpreting visually-grounded navigation instructions in real environments. In: Proceedings of the IEEE Conference on Computer Vision and Pattern Recognition, pp. 3674–3683 (2018)
2. Battaglia, P., Pascanu, R., Lai, M., Rezende, D.J., et al.: Interaction networks for learning about objects, relations and physics. In: Advances in Neural Information Processing Systems, pp. 4502–4510 (2016)
3. Borenstein, J., Koren, Y.: Real-time obstacle avoidance for fast mobile robots. IEEE Trans. Syst. Man Cybern. **19**(5), 1179–1187 (1989)
4. Borenstein, J., Koren, Y.: The vector field histogram-fast obstacle avoidance for mobile robots. IEEE Trans. Robot. Autom. **7**(3), 278–288 (1991)
5. Chen, K., et al.: A behavioral approach to visual navigation with graph localization networks. arXiv preprint arXiv:1903.00445 (2019)
6. Chen, T., Gupta, S., Gupta, A.: Learning exploration policies for navigation. arXiv preprint arXiv:1903.01959 (2019)
7. Deng, J., Dong, W., Socher, R., Li, L.J., Li, K., Fei-Fei, L.: ImageNet: a large-scale hierarchical image database. In: 2009 IEEE Conference on Computer Vision and Pattern Recognition, pp. 248–255. IEEE (2009)
8. Dissanayake, M.G., Newman, P., Clark, S., Durrant-Whyte, H.F., Csorba, M.: A solution to the simultaneous localization and map building (slam) problem. IEEE Trans. Robot. Autom. **17**(3), 229–241 (2001)
9. Fang, K., Toshev, A., Fei-Fei, L., Savarese, S.: Scene memory transformer for embodied agents in long-horizon tasks. In: Proceedings of the IEEE Conference on Computer Vision and Pattern Recognition, pp. 538–547 (2019)
10. Gupta, S., Davidson, J., Levine, S., Sukthankar, R., Malik, J.: Cognitive mapping and planning for visual navigation. In: Proceedings of the IEEE Conference on Computer Vision and Pattern Recognition, pp. 2616–2625 (2017)
11. He, K., Zhang, X., Ren, S., Sun, J.: Deep residual learning for image recognition. In: Proceedings of the IEEE Conference on Computer Vision and Pattern Recognition, pp. 770–778 (2016)

12. Joulin, A., Grave, E., Bojanowski, P., Mikolov, T.: Bag of tricks for efficient text classification. arXiv preprint arXiv:1607.01759 (2016)
13. Kahn, G., Villaflor, A., Ding, B., Abbeel, P., Levine, S.: Self-supervised deep reinforcement learning with generalized computation graphs for robot navigation. In: 2018 IEEE International Conference on Robotics and Automation (ICRA), pp. 1–8. IEEE (2018)
14. Kingma, D.P., Ba, J.: Adam: a method for stochastic optimization. arXiv preprint arXiv:1412.6980 (2014)
15. Kolve, E., et al.: AI2-THOR: An Interactive 3D Environment for Visual AI. arXiv (2017)
16. Mirowski, P., et al.: Learning to navigate in complex environments. arXiv preprint arXiv:1611.03673 (2016)
17. Mnih, V., et al.: Asynchronous methods for deep reinforcement learning. In: International Conference on Machine Learning, pp. 1928–1937 (2016)
18. Mousavian, A., Toshev, A., Fišer, M., Košecká, J., Wahid, A., Davidson, J.: Visual representations for semantic target driven navigation. In: 2019 International Conference on Robotics and Automation (ICRA), pp. 8846–8852. IEEE (2019)
19. Oriolo, G., Vendittelli, M., Ulivi, G.: On-line map building and navigation for autonomous mobile robots. In: Proceedings of 1995 IEEE International Conference on Robotics and Automation, vol. 3, pp. 2900–2906. IEEE (1995)
20. Pennington, J., Socher, R., Manning, C.: Glove: Global vectors for word representation. In: Proceedings of the 2014 Cence on Empirical Methods in Natural Language Processing (EMNLP), pp. 1532–1543 (2014)
21. Ren, S., He, K., Girshick, R., Sun, J.: Faster R-CNN: towards real-time object detection with region proposal networks. In: Advances in Neural Information Processing Systems, pp. 91–99 (2015)
22. Savinov, N., Dosovitskiy, A., Koltun, V.: Semi-parametric topological memory for navigation. arXiv preprint arXiv:1803.00653 (2018)
23. Sepulveda, G., Niebles, J.C., Soto, A.: A deep learning based behavioral approach to indoor autonomous navigation. In: 2018 IEEE International Conference on Robotics and Automation (ICRA), pp. 4646–4653. IEEE (2018)
24. Shen, W.B., Xu, D., Zhu, Y., Guibas, L.J., Fei-Fei, L., Savarese, S.: Situational fusion of visual representation for visual navigation. arXiv preprint arXiv:1908.09073 (2019)
25. Veličković, P., Cucurull, G., Casanova, A., Romero, A., Lio, P., Bengio, Y.: Graph attention networks. arXiv preprint arXiv:1710.10903 (2017)
26. Wang, X., et al.: Reinforced cross-modal matching and self-supervised imitation learning for vision-language navigation. In: Proceedings of the IEEE Conference on Computer Vision and Pattern Recognition, pp. 6629–6638 (2019)
27. Wortsman, M., Ehsani, K., Rastegari, M., Farhadi, A., Mottaghi, R.: Learning to learn how to learn: self-adaptive visual navigation using meta-learning. In: Proceedings of the IEEE Conference on Computer Vision and Pattern Recognition, pp. 6750–6759 (2019)
28. Wu, Y., Wu, Y., Tamar, A., Russell, S., Gkioxari, G., Tian, Y.: Bayesian relational memory for semantic visual navigation. In: Proceedings of the IEEE International Conference on Computer Vision, pp. 2769–2779 (2019)
29. Yang, W., Wang, X., Farhadi, A., Gupta, A., Mottaghi, R.: Visual semantic navigation using scene priors. arXiv preprint arXiv:1810.06543 (2018)
30. Zhu, Y., et al.: Target-driven visual navigation in indoor scenes using deep reinforcement learning. In: 2017 IEEE International Conference on Robotics and Automation (ICRA), pp. 3357–3364. IEEE (2017)

Adversarial Self-supervised Learning for Semi-supervised 3D Action Recognition

Chenyang Si[1,2,3]($\boxtimes$) (iD), Xuecheng Nie[3], Wei Wang[1,2], Liang Wang[1,2], Tieniu Tan[1,2], and Jiashi Feng[3]

[1] University of Chinese Academy of Sciences, Beijing, China
[2] CRIPAC & NLPR, Institute of Automation, Chinese Academy of Sciences, Beijing, China
{wangwei,wangliang,tnt}@nlpr.ia.ac.cn, chenyang.si@cripac.ia.ac.cn
[3] Department of ECE, National University of Singapore, Singapore, Singapore
niexuecheng@u.nus.edu, elefjia@nus.edu.sg

Abstract. We consider the problem of semi-supervised 3D action recognition which has been rarely explored before. Its major challenge lies in how to effectively learn motion representations from unlabeled data. Self-supervised learning (SSL) has been proved very effective at learning representations from unlabeled data in the image domain. However, few effective self-supervised approaches exist for 3D action recognition, and directly applying SSL for semi-supervised learning suffers from misalignment of representations learned from SSL and supervised learning tasks. To address these issues, we present Adversarial Self-Supervised Learning (ASSL), a novel framework that tightly couples SSL and the semi-supervised scheme via neighbor relation exploration and adversarial learning. Specifically, we design an effective SSL scheme to improve the discrimination capability of learned representations for 3D action recognition, through exploring the data relations within a neighborhood. We further propose an adversarial regularization to align the feature distributions of labeled and unlabeled samples. To demonstrate effectiveness of the proposed ASSL in semi-supervised 3D action recognition, we conduct extensive experiments on NTU and N-UCLA datasets. The results confirm its advantageous performance over state-of-the-art semi-supervised methods in the few label regime for 3D action recognition.

Keywords: Semi-supervised 3D action recognition · Self-supervised learning · Neighborhood consistency · Adversarial learning

1 Introduction

Recently, 3D action recognition (a.k.a. skeleton-based action recognition) has made remarkable progress through learning discriminative features with effective networks [7,12,18,29,30,44,47]. However, these methods heavily rely on the available manual annotations that are costly to acquire. Techniques requiring less or no manual annotations are therefore developed, and among them a

© Springer Nature Switzerland AG 2020
A. Vedaldi et al. (Eds.): ECCV 2020, LNCS 12352, pp. 35–51, 2020.
https://doi.org/10.1007/978-3-030-58571-6_3

powerful approach is semi-supervised learning. It is aimed at leveraging unlabeled data to enhance the model's capability of learning and generalization such that the requirement for labeled data can be alleviated. It has been widely applied in the image domain [14–16,24,25,27,34]. Compared with these methods, [45] has recently proposed a more efficient way of feature learning from unlabeled data, namely self-supervised semi-supervised learning (S^4L), that couples self-supervision with a semi-supervised learning algorithm. It employs the self-supervised technique to learn representations of unlabeled data to benefit semi-supervised learning tasks. Self-supervised learning is very advantageous in making full use of unlabeled data, which learns the representations of unlabeled data via defining and solving various pretext tasks. Thus in this work we exploit its application to semi-supervised 3D action recognition, which has little previous investigation.

As images contain rich information that is beneficial to feature extraction, many effective SSL techniques [5,37, 42] are image-based. Comparatively, for tasks over skeleton data which represent a person by 3D coordinate positions of key joints, it becomes very challenging to leverage SSL techniques to learn discriminative motion representation. Therefore, how to learn motion representation with SSL technique is an urgent problem for this task. Recently, [48] proposes a SSL method to learn temporal information of unlabeled sequence via skeleton inpainting. This SSL treats each sample as an *individual* such that it ignores the shared information among samples with the same action class. As a result, semi-supervised 3D action recognition has derived little benefit from the representations learned by skeleton inpainting.

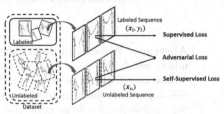

Fig. 1. Illustration of our main idea. We design an effective SSL scheme to capture the discriminative motion representations of unlabeled skeleton sequences for 3D action recognition. Since directly applying SSL to semi-supervised learning suffers from misalignment of representations learned from SSL and supervised learning tasks, we further pioneer to align their feature distributions via adversarial learning

Moreover, we also find that, directly applying SSL for semi-supervised learning suffers from misalignment of representations learned from self-supervised and supervised learning tasks. As shown in Fig. 1, labeled and unlabeled samples are enforced with supervised and self-supervised optimization objectives respectively. Though both sampled from the same data distribution, their feature distributions are misaligned. This misalignment would weaken the generalization of semi-supervised 3D action recognition models to unseen samples. A task with similar problem as ours is unsupervised domain adaptation (UDA) that matches the feature distributions from *different domains*. While their problem is quite similar to ours, there exist important differences between UDA and our task. In UDA, the discrepancy of feature distributions is caused by different domains. Our problem is the misalignment of representations learned from SSL and supervised learning tasks in semi-supervised 3D action recognition. One line of research in UDA is adversarial-based adaptation methods [9,20,35] that have shown promising results in domain adaptation. These methods seek to minimize an approximate domain discrepancy distance through an adversarial objective with respect to a domain discriminator. Hence, inspired by the alignment effect of adversarial learning in UDA, we exploit its application to couple the self-supervision method into a semi-supervised learning algorithm.

In this work, we propose an Adversarial Self-Supervised Learning (ASSL) Network for semi-supervised 3D action recognition. As shown in Fig. 1, our model leverages (i) self-supervised learning to capture discriminative motion representation of unlabeled skeleton sequences, and (ii) adversarial regularization that allows to align feature distributions of labeled and unlabeled sequences. More specifically, in addition to a self-inpainting constraint [48] for learning temporal information of each *individual* unlabeled sample, we propose a new perspective of consistency regularization within the neighborhood to explore the data relationships. Neighborhoods can be considered as tiny sample-anchored clusters with high compactness and class consistency. Consistency regularization within the neighborhood further reveals the underlying class concept of the self-supervised motion representation. Such discriminative motion representations significantly improve the performance of semi-supervised 3D action recognition. Moreover, considering that adversarial learning can minimize the discrepancy between two distributions, we also propose a novel adversarial learning strategy to couple the self-supervision method and a semi-supervised algorithm. The adversarial regularization allows the model to align the feature distributions of labeled and unlabeled data, which boosts the capability of generalization to unseen samples for semi-supervised 3D action recognition.

We perform extensive studies for semi-supervised 3D action recognition on two benchmark datasets: NTU RGB+D [28] and N-UCLA [39] datasets. With the proposed ASSL network, we establish new state-of-the-art performances of semi-supervised 3D action recognition. Summarily, our main contributions are in three folds:

1. We present an Adversarial Self-Supervised Learning (ASSL) framework for semi-supervised 3D action recognition, which tightly couples SSL and a semi-supervised scheme via adversarial learning and neighbor relation exploration.
2. We offer a new self-supervised strategy, *i.e.*, neighborhood consistency, for semi-supervised 3D action recognition. By exploring data relationships within the neighborhood, our model can learn discriminative motion representations that significantly improve the performance of semi-supervised 3D action recognition.
3. We identify that directly applying SSL for semi-supervised learning suffers from the representation misalignment of labeled and unlabeled samples. A novel adversarial regularization is pioneered to couple SSL into a semi-supervised algorithm to align their feature distributions, which further boosts the capability of generalization.

2   Related Work

2.1   3D Action Recognition

Human action recognition is one of important computer vision tasks. Due to the informative representation for the action, skeleton-based action recognition has been examined thoroughly in past literature. Previously, the traditional approaches [11,36–38] try to design various hand-crafted features from skeleton sequences to represent human motion, e.g., relative 3D geometry between all pairs of body parts [36]. Recently, deep learning has also been applied to this task due to its wide success. To model temporal dependencies, many methods leverage and extend the recurrent neural networks (RNNs) to capture the motion features for skeleton-based action recognition, e.g., HBRNN [7] and VA-LSTM [47]. Based on Convolutional Neural Networks (CNNs) that are powerful at learning hierarchical representations, spatio-temporal representations are extracted for action recognition in [6,12,18,41]. For graph-structured data, graph-based approaches [19,31,32] are popularly adopted for skeleton-based action recognition, e.g., ST-GCN [44] and AGC-LSTM [30]. Though successful, these supervised methods highly rely on massive data samples with annotated action labels, which are expensive to obtain. Semi-supervised approaches are thus developed to alleviate this data annotation limitation, and in this paper, we apply it to learning motion representation for 3D action recognition.

2.2   Semi-supervised Learning

Semi-supervised learning algorithms learn from a data set that includes both labeled and unlabeled data, usually mostly unlabeled. For a comprehensive review of semi-supervised methods, we refer readers to [3]. Recently, there is increasing interest in deep learning based semi-supervised algorithms. One group of these methods is based on generative models, e.g., denoising autoencoders [26], variational autoencoders [14] and generative adversarial networks [25,27]. Some semi-supervised methods add small perturbations to unlabeled data, and require similar outputs between them by enforcing a consistency regularization, e.g., Π-Model [15], Temporal Ensembling [15], Mean Teacher [34] and Virtual Adversarial Training [24]. There are also some other works. To name a few, Lee et al. [16] pick up the class with maximum predicted probability as pseudo-labels for unlabeled data, and use them to train the models. [10] presents a conditional entropy minimization for unlabeled data, which encourages their predicted probability to bias some class. The work most related to ours is [45] which proposes a new technique for semi-supervised learning by leveraging SSL techniques to learn representation of unlabeled images. Their work enlarges the generalization of semi-supervised learning methods. In this work, we exploit effective SSL to learn discriminative motion representation for semi-supervised 3D action recognition. Moreover, we further propose a novel adversarial regularization to couple SSL into the semi-supervised algorithm.

2.3   Self-supervised Learning for Action Recognition

Self-supervised learning for action recognition aims to learn motion representations from the unlabeled data by solving the pretext tasks. Recently, a stream of studies [1,8,17,23,33,43] design various temporal-related tasks to learn the temporal pattern from the unlabeled RGB videos. For example, a sequence sorting task is introduced in [17]. [21,40] propose to learn the video representation by predicting motion flows. Note that, these methods are for learning representations from RGB videos and not applicable to long-term skeleton sequences. For 3D action recognition, Zheng *et al.* [48] propose a conditional skeleton inpainting architecture to learn the long-term dynamics from unlabeled skeleton data. However, this SSL ignores the shared information among samples with the same action class and therefore may yield less discriminative feature representations. Hence, we propose an effective self-supervised strategy to learn discriminative representation that is beneficial for semi-supervised 3D action recognition.

3   Method

3.1   Problem Formulation

Instead of relying on massive labels in existing methods, we use only a few labeling data in semi-supervised 3D action recognition. Formally, let $\mathcal{X}$ be the training set. The training samples $x_i \in \mathcal{X}$ are skeleton sequences with T frames, and $x_i = \{x_{i,1}, \ldots, x_{i,T}\}$. At each time t, the $x_{i,t}$ is a set of 3D coordinates of body joints, which can be obtained by the Microsoft Kinect and the advanced human pose estimation algorithms [2,46]. In contrast to supervised 3D action classification, training samples are split to two subsets in our task here: a labeled training set denoted as $\mathcal{X}_L = \{x_1, \ldots, x_L\}$ and an unlabeled training set denoted as $\mathcal{X}_U = \{x_1, \ldots, x_U\}$. The training samples $x_l \in \mathcal{X}_L$ have annotated labels $\{y_1, \ldots, y_L\}$ with $y_l \in \mathcal{C}$, where $\mathcal{C} = \{1, \ldots, C\}$ is a discrete label set for C action classes. The training samples $x_u \in \mathcal{X}_U$ are unlabeled. Usually, L is smaller than U ($L \ll U$).

Inspired by S^4L [45], we propose an Adversarial Self-Supervised Learning framework to learn discriminative motion representations from $\mathcal{X}_L$ and $\mathcal{X}_U$. It couples self-supervised techniques into the semi-supervised scheme via adversarial learning and neighbor relation exploration. Detailed descriptions of ASSL are described in the following subsections.

3.2   Neighborhood Consistency for Semi-supervised 3D Action Recognition

Semi-supervised 3D action recognition aims to learn discriminative motion representation from massive unlabeled sequences. However, this is difficult over succinct 3D human poses. To tackle this challenge, we propose an effective SSL strategy, neighborhood consistency, that enhances the underlying class semantics

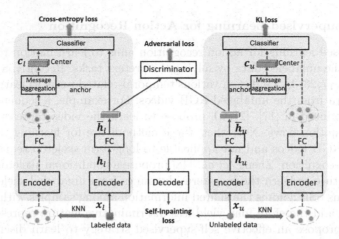

Fig. 2. Framework of Adversarial Self-Supervised Learning (ASSL). The ASSL leverages SSL and adversarial regularization for semi-supervised 3D action recognition. For SSL techniques, in addition to a self-inpainting constraint [48] for learning temporal information of each individual unlabeled sample, we propose to apply a new consistency regularization within the neighborhood to explore data relations. The adversarial training with a feature discriminator is used to align feature distributions of labeled and unlabeled samples, which further boosts generalization of semi-supervised models to unseen samples

of motion representation by exploring data relations within the neighborhoods, so as to improve recognition performance.

As shown in Fig. 2, we first employ skeleton inpainting [48] to learn temporal information for each unlabeled sequence. Specifically, an encoder network Enc takes an input skeleton sequence $\boldsymbol{x}_u$ from training set $\mathcal{X}_U$ and produces a vector as the temporal features $\boldsymbol{h}_u \in \mathbb{R}^d$. Conditioned on the learned representation $\boldsymbol{h}_u$, a decoder network Dec aims to fill the masked regions in the input sequence. Due to the difference between the action classification (discrimination) and skeleton inpainting (regression) tasks, we use a translation layer *i.e.*, a linear layer, to bridge the gap between the feature spaces of both tasks. The output of linear layer is denoted as $\bar{\boldsymbol{h}}_u$ for the sample $\boldsymbol{x}_u$. Then, in this feature space, we employ K-nearest neighbor [4] to select K nearest neighbors from unlabeled training set $\mathcal{X}_U$. The neighbor set of $\boldsymbol{x}_u$ is denoted as $\Omega_{\boldsymbol{x}_u} = \{\boldsymbol{x}_u^1, \ldots, \boldsymbol{x}_u^K\}$. A message aggregation module is proposed to produce the local center vector. We use a multilayer perceptron to assign a weight for each neighbor sample, which evaluates their similarities as the anchor. The weights α_k are computed as follows:

$$\alpha_k = \frac{\exp\left(MLP\left(|\bar{\boldsymbol{h}}_u - \bar{\boldsymbol{h}}_u^k|\right)\right)}{\sum_{k=1}^{K} \exp\left(MLP\left(|\bar{\boldsymbol{h}}_u - \bar{\boldsymbol{h}}_u^k|\right)\right)}, \tag{1}$$

where $\bar{\boldsymbol{h}}_u^k$ is the translated feature of neighbor sample $\boldsymbol{x}_u^k \in \Omega_{\boldsymbol{x}_u}$, $MLP(\cdot)$ denotes the multilayer perceptron in message aggregation module. According to the computed weights $\{\alpha_1, \ldots, \alpha_K\}$, the local class center c_u can be aggregated with the neighbor set Ω_{x_u} as follows:

$$c_u = \sum_{k=1}^{K} \alpha_k \bar{h}_u^k. \tag{2}$$

Considering the high compactness and class consistency within neighborhoods, we require that the samples within neighborhoods achieve a similar prediction with the local center c_u. However, for a sample x_u, its neighbor samples either share the class label (positive) with x_u or not (negative). To minimize the impact of negative neighbors, we introduce a simple selecting criterion: we get the 1-nearest labeled neighbor from the labeled training set $\mathcal{X}_L$ for the anchor x_u and the neighbor x_u^k. If the labeled neighbors of the anchor x_u and the neighbor x_u^k have the same label, x_u^k is regarded as the positive neighbor. The set of selected positive neighbor for sample x_u is denoted as $\Omega_{x_u}^p$. Finally, the loss of consistency regularization within neighborhood is defined as follows:

$$\mathcal{L}_{KL} = \sum_{x_u \in \mathcal{X}_U} \left(KL\left(f_c(c_u), f_c(\bar{h}_u)\right) + \sum_{x_u^K \in \Omega_{x_u}^P} KL\left(f_c(c_u), f_c(\bar{h}_u^k)\right) \right), \tag{3}$$

where $f_c(\cdot)$ is the classifier that outputs the predictions, $KL(\cdot)$ denotes Kullback-Leibler divergence.

Like consistency regularization for unlabeled samples $x_u \in \mathcal{X}_U$, the neighbor sets of labeled examples $x_l \in \mathcal{X}_L$ are also selected from the unlabeled set $\mathcal{X}_U$. which are denoted as Ω_{x_l}. Similarly, we use the feature $\bar{h}_l$ of x_l as the anchor to estimate its local center representation c_l with its neighbors set Ω_{x_l} as the Eq. (1)–(2) (shown in Fig. 2). Under the assumption that the anchor shares the same class semantic with the local center, we use a cross-entropy loss $CE(\cdot)$ for the center c_l:

$$\mathcal{L}_{CE}^c = \sum_{x_l \in \mathcal{X}_L} \left(CE\left(f_c(c_l), y_l\right) \right), \tag{4}$$

where y_l is the class label of x_l.

Overall, the optimization objectives of unlabeled samples can be formulated as follows:

$$\mathcal{L}_U = \mathcal{L}_{KL} + \mathcal{L}_{CE}^c + \mathcal{L}_{inp}, \tag{5}$$

where $\mathcal{L}_{inp}$ denotes the skeleton inpainting loss that is the L_2 distance between the inpainted sequence and the original input sequence. Minimizing this optimization objective $\mathcal{L}_U$ encourages the model to enhance the underlying class concept of the self-supervised motion representation and yield discriminative feature representations.

3.3 Adversarial Learning for Aligning Self-supervised and Semi-supervised Representations

According to the training of existing semi-supervised learning methods, the labeled and unlabeled samples are enforced with supervised and
SSL objectives, respectively. In this
work, Eq. (5) is used for the unlabeled
samples. Although our proposed SSL
technique is quite effective for semi-
supervised 3D action recognition, we
identify that the representations learned
with supervised and SSL task are misaligned. As shown in the Fig. 3, with
the benefit of SSL technique, the features of *Sup. + Sel.* present a more compact distribution than *Sup.*. However, in
contrast to the intra-class compactness
of labeled data (the squares with black
border), there are scattering distributions for the unlabeled data in Fig. 3(b).

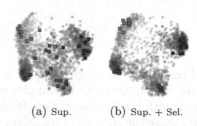

(a) Sup.   (b) Sup. + Sel.

Fig. 3. The t-SNE visualization of
motion features learned by *Sup.* and *Sup.
+ Sel.*. (a) *Sup.* is trained with the supervised objective for the labeled samples.
(b) *Sup. + Sel.* is trained through optimizing the supervised and SSL objectives (Eq. (5)) for the labeled and unlabeled samples, respectively. Different colors indicate different classes. Best viewed
in color. The squares with black border
denote the labeled data, and others are
unlabeled data (Color figure online)

Thus, although both sequences are sam-
pled from the same data distribution, their feature distributions are misaligned
due to different optimization objectives. To tackle this problem, we propose
a novel adversarial training strategy to couple SSL method with the semi-
supervised 3D action recognition. Specifically, a discriminator Dis is trained to
distinguish the unlabeled features from the labeled features. And the model is
trained simultaneously to confuse the discriminator Dis. Hence, the adversarial
loss is defined as follows:

$$\mathcal{L}_{adv} = \frac{1}{L} \sum_{x_l \in \mathcal{X}_L} \left(\log\left(Dis(\bar{h}_l) \right) \right) + \frac{1}{U} \sum_{x_u \in \mathcal{X}_U} \left(\log\left(1 - Dis(\bar{h}_u) \right) \right). \quad (6)$$

The adversarial regularization allows the model to align the feature distributions of labeled and unlabeled data. Therefore, like the labeled data, the feature distribution of unlabeled data becomes more intra-class compactness, which
boosts the capability of generalization to unseen samples. More analyses about
adversarial regularization are reported in Sect. 4.3.

3.4 Model Architecture and Optimization

Unlike the existing 3D action recognition method [7,12,18,29,30,44,47] learning
the discriminative features through the designed effective networks, the goal of
this work is to explore effective semi-supervised scheme for 3D action recognition. Therefore, this work adopts a universal architecture. In order to effectively
capture the motion dynamics, we use three bidirectional GRU layers to encode

the input skeleton sequence in the *Enc.* The decoder consists of two unidirectional GRU layers. We use 4 linear layers and 3 linear layers in the discriminator and the multilayer perceptron of message aggregation, respectively. The classifier is a two-layer perceptron.

During training, our ASSL network is learned by minimizing the following loss on the training data:

$$\mathcal{L} = \mathcal{L}_L + \lambda_1 \mathcal{L}_U + \lambda_2 \mathcal{L}_{adv}. \tag{7}$$

where $\mathcal{L}_L$ is a cross-entropy loss of all labeled examples in $\mathcal{X}_L$, λ_1 and λ_2 are nonnegative scalar weights. Note that, we always sample the same number labeled and unlabeled samples in mini-bathes.

4 Experiments

In this section, we evaluate and compare our work with previous semi-supervised methods and also conduct detailed component analysis.

4.1 Experimental Setup

Datasets. Two popular benchmark datasets, NTU RGB+D dataset [28] and Northwestern-UCLA dataset [39], are used for our experiments.

NTU RGB+D dataset [28] contains 56,880 samples covering 60 different classes of human actions performed by 40 distinct subjects. These videos are collected with three cameras simultaneously in different horizontal views. Two evaluation protocols are provided: Cross-Subject (CS) and Cross-View (CV). For CS protocol, skeleton sequences performed by 20 subjects are used for training, and the rest for testing. For CV protocol, all videos from Camera 2 and 3 are used for training while those from Camera 1 are used for testing. For semi-supervised 3D action recognition, 5%, 10%, 20% and 40% of training sequences of each class are labeled on the training set.

Northwestern-UCLA dataset [39] has 1,494 samples performed by 10 different subjects belonging to 10 action classes. Each action sample is captured by three Kinect cameras simultaneously from a variety of viewpoints. Its training set consists of samples from the first two cameras and the rest from the third camera form the testing set. For semi-supervised 3D action recognition, we use 5%, 15%, 30% and 40% labels of training sequences of each class on the training set.

Baselines. There is no available semi-supervised baseline for 3D action recognition, so we use following methods as baselines that achieve state-of-the-art performances in the RGB domain:

1) Supervised-only (Sup.), training with labeled skeleton sequences only.
2) Pseudo labels [16], leveraging the idea that the predicted labels of unlabeled samples are used for training. First, train a model with the labeled data, then predict the classes of unlabeled samples. These pseudo labels are used to retrain the network in a supervised fashion with labeled and unlabeled data simultaneously.

3) Virtual Adversarial Training (VAT) [24], training with unlabeled data to make the model robust around input data point against local perturbation. It generates small adversarial perturbations for unlabeled samples, which greatly alter the output distribution; then consistency loss is applied over unlabeled training data to encourage consistency of predictions for input data and its adversarially perturbed version.

4) Conditional Entropy Minimization (EntMin) [10], minimizing the entropy of prediction over unlabeled training data as a regularization for model training. Predicted class probabilities are encouraged to be near a one-hot vector via training with unlabeled data.

5) Self-Supervised Semi-Supervised Learning (S^4L) [45], the most related method to ours. It trains the model on self-supervised and semi-supervised tasks in a multi-task fashion. For 3D action recognition, we use the skeleton inpainting framework [48] as the pretext task for self-supervised learning.

Implementation. All comparisons with semi-supervised baselines are made under the same setting to be fair. In all experiments, the dimension of hidden states in the GRU and bidirectional GRU is set to 512. On both datasets, we randomly sample $T = 40$ frames from each skeleton sequence as input during training and testing. We train all networks by the ADAM optimizer [13]. The learning rate, initiated with 0.0005, is reduced by multiplying it by 0.5 every 30 epochs. We set $\lambda_1 = 1$ and $\lambda_2 = 0.1$ in Eq. (7). Our experiments are all implemented with PyTorch and 1 Titan Xp GPU.

4.2   Comparison with Semi-supervised Methods

We evaluate our method by comparing it with baselines for semi-supervised 3D action recognition and show results on NTU and N-UCLA datasets respectively in Tables 1 and 2.

Table 1. Test accuracy (%) on NTU dataset (Cross-Subject (CS) and Cross-View protocols (CV)) with 5%, 10%, 20 and 40% labels of training set. *v./c.* denotes the number of labeled videos per class

Method	5%		10%		20%		40%	
	CS (33 *v./c.*)	CV (31 *v./c.*)	CS (66 *v./c.*)	CV (62 *v./c.*)	CS (132 *v./c.*)	CV (124 *v./c.*)	CS (264 *v./c.*)	CV (248 *v./c.*)
Supervised-only	47.2	53.7	57.2	63.1	62.4	70.4	68.0	76.8
Pseudolabels [16]	50.9	56.3	58.4	65.8	63.9	71.2	69.5	77.7
VAT [24]	51.3	57.9	60.3	66.3	65.6	72.6	70.4	78.6
VAT + EntMin [10]	51.7	58.3	61.4	67.5	65.9	73.3	70.8	78.9
S^4L (Inpainting) [45]	48.4	55.1	58.1	63.6	63.1	71.1	68.2	76.9
ASSL (ours)	**57.3**	**63.6**	**64.3**	**69.8**	**68.0**	**74.7**	**72.3**	**80.0**

As seen from tables, with the proposed ASSL network, we establish new state-of-the-art performances of semi-supervised 3D action recognition. To be specific, S^4L *(Inpainting)* performs worse than *Pseudolabels*, *VAT* and *VAT + EntMin*, suggesting it is inefficient to learn discriminative representation via

Table 2. Test accuracy (%) on N-UCLA dataset with 5%, 15%, 30% and 40% labels of training set. $v./c.$ denotes the number of labeled videos per class

Method	5% (5 $v./c.$)	15% (15 $v./c.$)	30% (30 $v./c.$)	40% (40 $v./c.$)
Supervised-only	34.1	37.9	48.9	58.8
Pseudolabels [16]	35.6	48.9	60.6	65.7
VAT [24]	44.8	63.8	73.7	73.9
VAT + EntMin [10]	46.8	66.2	75.4	75.6
S^4L (Inpainting) [45]	35.3	46.6	54.5	60.6
ASSL (ours)	**52.6**	**74.8**	**78.0**	**78.4**

skeleton inpainting and thus semi-supervised 3D action recognition has derived little benefit from self-supervised representations. S^4L *(Inpainting)*, though a advanced semi-supervised approach, requires an effective self-supervised representations that are difficult to learn in this task. Compared with these semi-supervised methods, our benefit is larger when the number of labels is reduced. For example, with 5% labels of training set on NTU dataset, the results of our ASSL present greater improvement compared with *VAT + EntMin*. This clearly demonstrates the power of the proposed ASSL.

4.3   Ablation Study

We then investigate effectiveness of the neighborhood consistency and adversarial training in our proposed ASSL on NTU and N-UCLA datasets. We also analyze effects of different neighborhood sizes and Neighborhood quality.

Neighborhood Consistency. We evaluate the effects of the proposed self-supervised strategy, neighborhood consistency, upon the discriminativeness of motion representations that is shown in final performance of semi-supervised 3D action recognition. In Table 3, the model *Sup. + Inp.* is trained with a cross-entropy loss for labeled data and a self-inpainting loss $\mathcal{L}_{inp}$ for unlabeled data. Instead of self-inpainting loss, *Sup. + Nei.* explores the data relations within neighborhoods by enforcing the consistency regularization (Eq. (3), (4)) for unlabeled data. We can see that *Sup. + Nei.* significantly outperforms the *Sup. + Inp.*. The comparison results justify that our neighborhood consistency can learn more discriminative motion representations that are more beneficial for semi-supervised 3D action recognition.

Moreover, the self-inpainting constraint [48] aims at learning temporal information of each *individual* unlabeled sequence. The goal of our neighborhood consistency regularization is to explore inter-sample relations within neighborhoods. We jointly learn the two features in *Sup. + Inp. + Nei.*. It can be seen compared with *Sup. + Inp.* and *Sup. + Nei.*, *Sup. + Inp. + Nei.* achieves better performance on both datasets for semi-supervised 3D action recognition. This illustrates that the representations learned by our neighborhood consistency are complementary to those learned with self-inpainting. Therefore, the benefits of

Table 3. Ablation study on self-supervised learning methods, skeleton inpainting (*Inp.*) [48] and neighbor consistency (*Nei.*). Classification accuracy (%) is reported on NTU with 5% labels and N-UCLA with 15% labels.

Methods	NTU 5%		N-UCLA 15%
	CS (33 *v./c.*)	CV (31 *v./c.*)	(15 *v./c.*)
Supervised-only (Sup.)	47.2	53.7	37.9
Sup. + Inp	48.4	55.1	46.6
Sup. + Nei	52.1	57.8	60.0
Sup. + Inp. + Nei	55.2	61.1	66.4
ASSL	**57.3**	**63.6**	**74.8**

combining these two SSL techniques to capture discriminative representation from unlabeled sequences in our final model are verified (seen Eq. (5)).

Neighborhood Size. We assume that the larger neighborhood size imposes stronger regularization and gives better performance. In order to justify this hypothesis, we investigate the effects of different neighborhood sizes in Fig. 4. As neighborhood size increases, the performance is improved and then becomes saturated. This implies that more discriminative representations can be learned with a larger size. But, if using too large a size, the model will cover distant data points that have weak semantic consistency within the neighborhood, and hence the performance becomes saturated.

Neighborhood Quality. We further examine effects of the class consistency of anchor Neighborhood, *i.e.*, Neighborhood quality. In Fig. 5, we report the progress of the ratio of neighbor samples sharing the same action label as the anchor throughout training. We can observe the ratio of class consistent neighborhoods increases, and then becomes saturated. This indicates exploring data relations is helpful to inferring underlying class semantics, thus facilitating the clustering of samples with the same action labels.

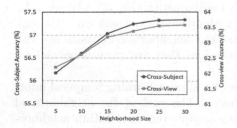

Fig. 4. Classification accuracy (%) with different neighborhood size on NTU dataset with 5% labels

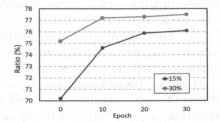

Fig. 5. The ratio of neighbor samples sharing the same action label as the anchor throughout training on N-UCLA dataset

Table 4. Ablation study on adversarial training. Classification accuracy (%) is reported on NTU with 5% labels and N-UCLA with 15% labels.

Methods		NTU 5%		N-UCLA 15%
		CS (33 *v./c.*)	CV (31 *v./c.*)	(15 *v./c.*)
Sup. + Inp.	*w/o* adv	48.4	55.1	46.6
	w/ adv	51.2	57.1	52.4
Sup. + Nei.	*w/o* adv	52.1	57.8	60.0
	w/ adv	53.4	59.1	68.5
ASSL	*w/o* adv	55.2	61.1	66.4
(Sup. + Inp. + Nei.)	*w/* adv	57.3	63.6	74.8

Adversarial Training. The adversarial alignment is proposed to mitigate the gap between representations learned from supervised and self-supervised tasks. To evaluate effectiveness of adversarial training for coupling self-supervision methods with the semi-supervised 3D action recognition, we train several self-supervised models with or without adversarial regularization. The results are reported in Table 4. It is obvious that all models with adversarial regularization achieve better performances than those without. For example, on N-UCLA dataset, the result of *ASSL w/adv* is 74.8%, outperforming *ASSL w/o adv* by 8.4%. The improved performance in Table 4 demonstrates that it is an effective strategy to couple self-supervision with semi-supervised algorithms by adversarial training.

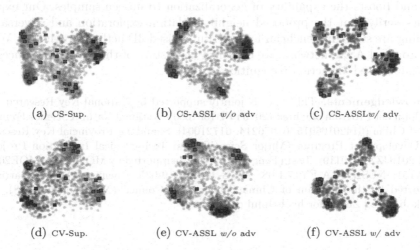

(a) CS-Sup.   (b) CS-ASSL *w/o* adv   (c) CS-ASSL *w/* adv

(d) CV-Sup.   (e) CV-ASSL *w/o* adv   (f) CV-ASSL *w/* adv

Fig. 6. The t-SNE visualization of motion features learned by *Supervised Baseline* (Sup.), *ASSL w/o adv* and *ASSL w/adv* (ours) on NTU dataset. Different colors indicate different classes. Best viewed in color. The squares with black border denote the labeled data, and others are unlabeled data (Color figure online)

To further explore this scheme, we visualize the feature distributions of *Sup.*, *ASSL w/o adv* and *ASSL w/adv* by using t-SNE [22] in Fig. 6. For the model *Sup.* trained with only supervised objective on labeled data, the decision boundaries of its feature distributions are very ambiguous. The model *ASSL w/o adv* is trained with supervised and self-supervised objectives for labeled and unlabeled data, respectively. Compared with *Sup.*, the features of *ASSL w/o adv* present tighter distributions, which benefit from self-supervised learning. But, long-tail distributions still exist for unlabeled samples (circles). Figure 6(c) and (f) show clearly the alignment between feature distributions of labeled and unlabeled data for *ASSL w/adv*, *i.e.*, the proposed ASSL. Overall, the comparison results prove the effectiveness of adversarial training for coupling self-supervision with semi-supervised action recognition. And this drives our model to learn more discriminative features that have desired intra-class compactness and inter-class separability.

5   Conclusions

In this paper, we consider the semi-supervised learning scheme for 3D action recognition task. The proposed ASSL effectively couples SSL into semi-supervised algorithm via neighbor relation exploration and adversarial learning. Exploring data relations with neighborhood consistency regularization encourages the model to learn discriminative motion representations that significantly improve the performance of this task. Moreover, we introduce a novel adversarial regularization to couple SSL method into a semi-supervised algorithm. This allows the model to align the feature distributions of labeled and unlabeled samples and boosts the capability of generalization to unseen samples. Our experiments verify that the proposed neighbor relation exploration and adversarial learning are strongly beneficial for semi-supervised 3D action recognition. With the proposed ASSL network, we establish news state-of-the-art performances of semi-supervised 3D action recognition.

Acknowledgements. This work is jointly supported by National Key Research and Development Program of China (2016YFB1001000), National Natural Science Foundation of China (61420106015, 61976214, 61721004), Shandong Provincial Key Research and Development Program (Major Scientific and Technological Innovation Project) (NO. 2019JZZY010119). Jiashi Feng was partially supported by MOE Tier 2 MOE2017-T2-2-151, NUS_ECRA_FY17_P08, AISG-100E-2019-035. Chenyang Si was partially supported by the program of China Scholarships Council (No. 201904910608). We thank Jianfeng Zhang for his helpful comments.

References

1. Büchler, U., Brattoli, B., Ommer, B.: Improving spatiotemporal self-supervision by deep reinforcement learning. In: Ferrari, V., Hebert, M., Sminchisescu, C., Weiss, Y. (eds.) ECCV 2018. LNCS, vol. 11219, pp. 797–814. Springer, Cham (2018). https://doi.org/10.1007/978-3-030-01267-0_47
2. Cao, Z., Simon, T., Wei, S.E., Sheikh, Y.: Realtime multi-person 2D pose estimation using part affinity fields. In: CVPR (2017)
3. Chapelle, O., Scholkopf, B., Zien, A.: Semi-supervised Learning. MIT Press, Cambridge (2006)
4. Cover, T., Hart, P.: Nearest neighbor pattern classification. IEEE Trans. Inf. Theor. **13**, 21–27 (1967)
5. Dosovitskiy, A., Springenberg, J.T., Riedmiller, M., Brox, T.: Discriminative unsupervised feature learning with convolutional neural networks. In: NIPS (2014)
6. Du, Y., Fu, Y., Wang, L.: Skeleton based action recognition with convolutional neural network. In: ACPR (2015)
7. Du, Y., Wang, W., Wang, L.: Hierarchical recurrent neural network for skeleton based action recognition. In: CVPR (2015)
8. Fernando, B., Bilen, H., Gavves, E., Gould, S.: Self-supervised video representation learning with odd-one-out networks. In: CVPR (2017)
9. Ganin, Y., Lempitsky, V.: Unsupervised domain adaptation by backpropagation. In: ICML (2015)
10. Grandvalet, Y., Bengio, Y.: Semi-supervised learning by entropy minimization. In: NIPS (2005)
11. Hussein, M.E., Torki, M., Gowayyed, M.A., El-Saban, M.: Human action recognition using a temporal hierarchy of covariance descriptors on 3D joint locations. In: IJCAI (2013)
12. Ke, Q., Bennamoun, M., An, S., Sohel, F., Boussaid, F.: A new representation of skeleton sequences for 3D action recognition. In: CVPR (2017)
13. Kingma, D.P., Ba, J.: Adam: a method for stochastic optimization. In: ICLR (2015)
14. Kingma, D.P., Mohamed, S., Rezende, D.J., Welling, M.: Semi-supervised learning with deep generative models. In: NIPS (2014)
15. Laine, S., Aila, T.: Temporal ensembling for semi-supervised learning. In: ICLR (2017)
16. Lee, D.H.: Pseudo-label: the simple and efficient semi-supervised learning method for deep neural networks. In: ICML (2013)
17. Lee, H.Y., Huang, J.B., Singh, M., Yang, M.H.: Unsupervised representation learning by sorting sequences. In: ICCV (2017)
18. Li, C., Zhong, Q., Xie, D., Pu, S.: Co-occurrence feature learning from skeleton data for action recognition and detection with hierarchical aggregation. In: IJCAI (2018)
19. Li, M., Chen, S., Chen, X., Zhang, Y., Wang, Y., Tian, Q.: Actional-structural graph convolutional networks for skeleton-based action recognition. In: CVPR (2019)
20. Long, M., Cao, Z., Wang, J., Jordan, M.I.: Conditional adversarial domain adaptation. In: NIPS (2018)
21. Luo, Z., Peng, B., Huang, D.A., Alahi, A., Fei-Fei, L.: Unsupervised learning of long-term motion dynamics for videos. In: CVPR (2017)
22. van der Maaten, L., Hinton, G.: Visualizing data using t-SNE. J. Mach. Learn. Res. **9**, 2579–2605 (2008)

23. Misra, I., Zitnick, C.L., Hebert, M.: Shuffle and learn: unsupervised learning using temporal order verification. In: Leibe, B., Matas, J., Sebe, N., Welling, M. (eds.) ECCV 2016. LNCS, vol. 9905, pp. 527–544. Springer, Cham (2016). https://doi.org/10.1007/978-3-319-46448-0_32
24. Miyato, T., Maeda, S., Koyama, M., Ishii, S.: Virtual adversarial training: a regularization method for supervised and semi-supervised learning. IEEE Trans. Pattern Anal. Mach. Intell. **41**, 1979–1993 (2018)
25. Odena, A.: Semi-supervised learning with generative adversarial networks. arXiv preprint arXiv:1606.01583 (2016)
26. Rasmus, A., Berglund, M., Honkala, M., Valpola, H., Raiko, T.: Semi-supervised learning with ladder networks. In: NIPS (2015)
27. Salimans, T., Goodfellow, I., Zaremba, W., Cheung, V., Radford, A., Chen, X.: Improved techniques for training GANs. In: NIPS (2016)
28. Shahroudy, A., Liu, J., Ng, T.T., Wang, G.: NTU RGB+D: a large scale dataset for 3D human activity analysis. In: CVPR (2016)
29. Shi, L., Zhang, Y., Cheng, J., Lu, H.: Two-stream adaptive graph convolutional networks for skeleton-based action recognition. In: CVPR (2019)
30. Si, C., Chen, W., Wang, W., Wang, L., Tan, T.: An attention enhanced graph convolutional LSTM network for skeleton-based action recognition. In: CVPR (2019)
31. Si, C., Jing, Y., Wang, W., Wang, L., Tan, T.: Skeleton-based action recognition with spatial reasoning and temporal stack learning. In: Ferrari, V., Hebert, M., Sminchisescu, C., Weiss, Y. (eds.) ECCV 2018. LNCS, vol. 11205, pp. 106–121. Springer, Cham (2018). https://doi.org/10.1007/978-3-030-01246-5_7
32. Si, C., Jing, Y., Wang, W., Wang, L., Tan, T.: Skeleton-based action recognition with hierarchical spatial reasoning and temporal stack learning network. Pattern Recogn. **107**, 107511 (2020)
33. Srivastava, N., Mansimov, E., Salakhudinov, R.: Unsupervised learning of video representations using LSTMs. In: ICML (2015)
34. Tarvainen, A., Valpola, H.: Mean teachers are better role models: weight-averaged consistency targets improve semi-supervised deep learning results. In: NIPS (2017)
35. Tzeng, E., Hoffman, J., Saenko, K., Darrell, T.: Adversarial discriminative domain adaptation. In: CVPR (2017)
36. Vemulapalli, R., Arrate, F., Chellappa, R.: Human action recognition by representing 3D skeletons as points in a lie group. In: CVPR (2014)
37. Vemulapalli, R., Chellappa, R.: Rolling rotations for recognizing human actions from 3D skeletal data. In: CVPR (2016)
38. Wang, J., Liu, Z., Wu, Y., Yuan, J.: Mining actionlet ensemble for action recognition with depth cameras. In: CVPR (2012)
39. Wang, J., Nie, X., Xia, Y., Wu, Y., Zhu, S.C.: Cross-view action modeling, learning, and recognition. In: CVPR (2014)
40. Wang, J., Jiao, J., Bao, L., He, S., Liu, Y., Liu, W.: Self-supervised spatio-temporal representation learning for videos by predicting motion and appearance statistics. In: CVPR (2019)
41. Wang, P., Li, Z., Hou, Y., Li, W.: Action recognition based on joint trajectory maps using convolutional neural networks. In: ACM MM (2016)
42. Wu, Z., Xiong, Y., Yu, S.X., Lin, D.: Unsupervised feature learning via nonparametric instance discrimination. In: CVPR (2018)
43. Xu, D., Xiao, J., Zhao, Z., Shao, J., Xie, D., Zhuang, Y.: Self-supervised spatiotemporal learning via video clip order prediction. In: CVPR (2019)
44. Yan, S., Xiong, Y., Lin, D., xiaoou Tang: Spatial temporal graph convolutional networks for skeleton-based action recognition. In: AAAI (2018)

45. Zhai, X., Oliver, A., Kolesnikov, A., Beyer, L.: S4L: self-supervised semi-supervised learning. In: ICCV (2019)
46. Zhang, J., Nie, X., Feng, J.: Inference stage optimization for cross-scenario 3D human pose estimation. arXiv preprint arXiv:2007.02054 (2020)
47. Zhang, P., Lan, C., Xing, J., Zeng, W., Xue, J., Zheng, N.: View adaptive recurrent neural networks for high performance human action recognition from skeleton data. In: ICCV (2017)
48. Zheng, N., Wen, J., Liu, R., Long, L., Dai, J., Gong, Z.: Unsupervised representation learning with long-term dynamics for skeleton based action recognition. In: AAAI (2018)

Across Scales and Across Dimensions: Temporal Super-Resolution Using Deep Internal Learning

Liad Pollak Zuckerman[1], Eyal Naor[1], George Pisha[3], Shai Bagon[2(✉)], and Michal Irani[1]

[1] Department of Computer Science and Applied Math, The Weizmann Institute of Science, Rehovot, Israel
[2] Weizmann Artificial Intelligence Center (WAIC), Rehovot, Israel
shai.bagon@weizmann.ac.il
[3] Technion, Israel Institute of Technology, Haifa, Israel
http://www.wisdom.weizmann.ac.il/~vision/DeepTemporalSR

Abstract. When a very fast dynamic event is recorded with a low-framerate camera, the resulting video suffers from severe motion blur (due to exposure time) and motion aliasing (due to low sampling rate in time). True Temporal Super-Resolution (TSR) is more than just Temporal-Interpolation (increasing framerate). It can also recover new high temporal frequencies beyond the temporal Nyquist limit of the input video, thus *resolving both motion-blur and motion-aliasing* – effects that temporal frame interpolation (as sophisticated as it may be) cannot undo. In this paper we propose a "Deep Internal Learning" approach for true TSR. We train a video-specific CNN on examples extracted directly from the low-framerate input video. Our method exploits the strong recurrence of small space-time patches inside a single video sequence, both within and across different spatio-temporal scales of the video. We further observe (for the first time) that small space-time patches recur also *across-dimensions* of the video sequence – i.e., by swapping the spatial and temporal dimensions. In particular, the higher spatial resolution of video frames provides strong examples as to how to increase the temporal resolution of that video. Such internal video-specific examples give rise to strong self-supervision, requiring no data but the input video itself. This results in **Zero-Shot Temporal-SR** of complex videos, which removes both motion blur and motion aliasing, outperforming previous supervised methods trained on external video datasets.

E. Naor and G. Pisha—joint first authors.

Electronic supplementary material The online version of this chapter (https://doi.org/10.1007/978-3-030-58571-6_4) contains supplementary material, which is available to authorized users.

1   Introduction

The problem of upsampling video framerate has recently attracted much attention [2,9,14–16,24]. These methods perform high-quality Temporal Interpolation on *sharp videos* (no motion blur or motion aliasing). However, temporal-interpolation methods cannot undo motion blur nor aliasing. This is a fundamental difference between Temporal Interpolation and Temporal Super-Resolution.

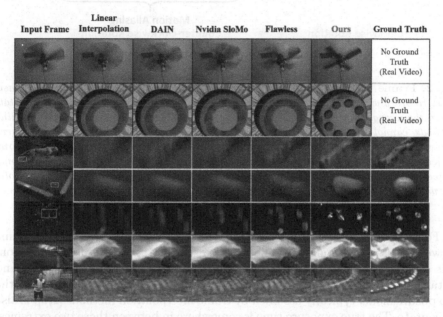

Fig. 1. Visual Comparison on TS×8. *We compared our method to state-of-the-art methods (DAIN [2], NVIDIA SloMo [9], Flawless [10]). Blurs of highly non-rigid objects (fire, water) pose a challenge to all methods. None of the competitors can resolve the motion blur or aliasing induced by the fast rotating fans. Our unsupervised TSR handles these better.* **View videos in our** *project website* **to see the strong aliasing effects.**

What is Temporal Super-Resolution (TSR)? The *temporal resolution* of a video camera is determined by the frame-rate and exposure-time of the camera. These limit the maximal speed of dynamic events that can be captured correctly in a video. *Temporal Super-Resolution* (TSR) aims to increase the framerate in order to unveil rapid dynamic events that occur *faster than the video-frame rate*, and are therefore invisible, or else seen incorrectly in the video sequence [19].

A low-temporal-resolution **(LTR)** video L, and its corresponding high-temporal-resolution **(HTR)** video H, are related by blur and subsampling in time:

$$L = (H * rect) \downarrow_{s_{temporal}}$$

where *rect* is a rectangular temporal blur kernel induced by the exposure time.

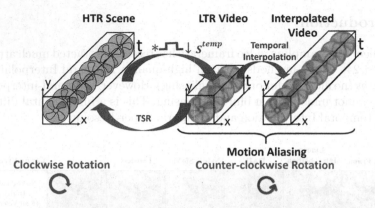

Fig. 2. Frame interpolation vs. Temporal-SR. *A fan is rotating* <u>*clockwise*</u> *fast, while recorded with a 'slow' camera. The resulting LTR video shows a blurry fan rotating in the wrong* <u>*counter-clockwise*</u> *direction. Temporal frame interpolation/upsampling methods cannot undo motion blur nor motion aliasing. They only add new blurry frames, while preserving the wrong aliased counter-clockwise motion.* **Please see our** project website **to view these dynamic effects.** *In contrast, true TSR not only increases the framerate, but also recovers the lost high temporal frequencies, thus resolving motion aliasing and blur (restoring the correct fan motion).*

For simplicity, we will assume here that the exposure time is equal to the time between consecutive frames. While this is a simplifying inaccurate assumption, it is still a useful one, as can be seen in our real video results (Fan video and Rotating-Disk video on our project website). Note that the other extreme – the δ exposure model typically assumed by frame interpolation methods [2,9], is also inaccurate. The true exposure time is somewhere in between those two extremes.

When a very fast dynamic event is recorded with a "slow" camera, the resulting video suffers from severe motion blur and motion aliasing. Motion blur results from very large motions during exposure time (while the shutter is open), often resulting in distorted or unrecognizable shapes. Motion aliasing occurs when the recorded dynamic events have temporal frequencies beyond the Nyquist limit of the temporal sampling (framerate). Such an illustrative example is shown in Fig. 2. A fan rotating fast *clockwise*, is recorded with a "slow" camera. The resulting LTR video shows a *blurry fan* moving in the *wrong direction* – counter-clockwise.

Frame-interpolation methods [2,9,14–16,24] cannot undo motion blur nor motion aliasing. They only add new blurry frames, while preserving the wrong aliased counter-clockwise motion (illustrated in Fig. 2, and shown for real videos of a fan and a dotted wheel in Fig. 1 & full videos in the project website).

Methods for Video Deblurring (e.g., [7,23]) were proposed for removing motion blur from video sequences. These, however, do not increase the framerate, hence cannot resolve motion aliasing.

In contrast, true Temporal Super-Resolution (TSR) aims not only to increase the framerate and/or deblur the frames, but also to recover the lost high temporal

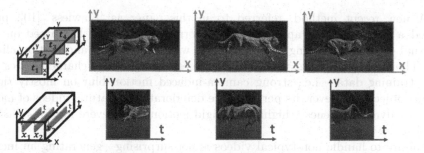

Fig. 3. Slices of the space-time video volume. *(Top:) xy slices = frames, (Bottom:) ty slices. The xy slices (video frames) provide high-resolution patch examples for the patches in the low-resolution ty slices. (See text for more details)* (Color figure online)

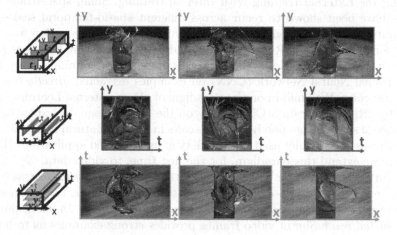

Fig. 4. Slices of the space-time video volume of a complex motion. *(Top to bottom:) xy slices, ty slices, xt slices. Note that patch similarities across-dimensions hold even for highly complex non-linear motions. See project website for videos of slices across different dimensions.* (Color figure online)

frequencies beyond the Nyquist limit of the original framerate. "Defying" the Nyquist limit in the *temporal* domain is possible due to the motion blur in the *spatial* domain. Consider two cases: (i) A fan rotating clockwise fast, which due to temporal aliasing appears to rotate slowly counter-clockwise; and (ii) A fan rotating slowly counter-clockwise. When the exposure time is long (not δ), the fan in (i) has severe motion blur, while the fan in (ii) exhibits the same motion with no blur. Hence, while temporally (i) and (ii) are indistinguishable, spatially they are. Therefore, TSR can resolve both motion-aliasing and motion-blur, producing sharper frames, as well as the true motion of the fan/wheel (clockwise rotation, at correct speed). See results in Fig. 1, and full videos in the project website (motion aliasing is impossible to display in a still figure).

A new recent method, referred to in this paper as 'Flawless' [10], presented a Deep-Learning approach for performing *true TSR*. It trained on an external dataset containing video examples with motion blur and motion aliasing. Their method works very well on videos with similar characteristics to their training data – i.e., strong camera-induced motion blur on mostly rigid scenes/objects. However, its performance deteriorates on natural videos of more complex dynamic scenes – highly non-rigid motions and severe motion-aliasing (see Fig. 1).

Failure to handle non-typical videos is not surprising—generating an inclusive video dataset containing all possible combinations of spatial appearances, scene dynamics, different motion speeds, different framerates, different blurs and different motion aliasing, is combinatorially infeasible.

In this work we propose to overcome these dataset-dependant limitations by replacing the External training with Internal training. Small space-time video patches have been shown to recur across different spatio-temporal scales of a single natural video sequence [18]. This strong internal video-prior was used by [18] for performing TSR from a single video (using Nearest-Neighbor patch search within the video). Here we exploit this property for training a Deep Fully Convolutional Neural Network (CNN) on examples extracted *directly from the LTR input video*. We build upon the paradigm of "Deep Internal Learning", first coined by [21]. They train a CNN solely on the input image, by exploiting the recurrence of small image-patches across scales in a single natural image [5]. This paradigm was successfully used for a variety of image-based applications [17,20, 21]. Here we extend this paradigm, for the first time, to video data.

We further observe (for the first time) that *small space-time patches (ST-patches) recur also across-dimensions of the video sequence*, i.e., when swapping between the spatial and temporal dimensions (see Fig. 3). In particular, the higher *spatial resolution* of video frames provides strong examples as to how to increase the *temporal resolution* of that video (see Fig. 7.b). We exploit this recurrence of ST-patches across-dimensions (in addition to their traditional recurrence across video scales), to generate *video-specific training examples*, extracted directly from the input video. These are used to train a video-specific CNN, resulting in *Zero-Shot Temporal-SR* of complex videos, which resolves both motion blur and motion aliasing. It can handle videos with complex dynamics and highly non-rigid scenes (flickering fire, splashing water, etc.), that supervised methods trained on external video datasets cannot handle well.

Our contributions are several-fold:

- Extending "Deep Internal Learning" to video data.
- Observing the recurrence of data *across video dimensions* (by swapping space and time), and its implications to TSR.
- Zero-Shot TSR (no training examples are needed other than the input video).
- We show that internal training resolves motion blur and motion aliasing of complex dynamic scenes, better than externally-trained supervised methods.

2 Patch Recurrence Across Dimensions

It was shown [18] that small Space-Time (ST) patches tend to repeat abundantly inside a video sequence, both within the input scale, as well as across coarser spatio-temporal video scales. Here we present a new observation *ST-patches recur also across video dimensions*, i.e., when the spatial and temporal dimensions are swapped. Figure 3 displays the space-time video volume (x-y-t) of a running cheetah. The video frames are the *spatial* x-y slices of this volume (marked in magenta). Each frame corresponds to the plane (slice) of the video volume at time $t = t_i$. Swapping the spatial and the temporal dimensions, we can observe "frames" that capture the information in y-t slices ($x = x_i$ plane) or x-t slices ($y = y_i$ plane). Examples of such slices appear in Figs. 3 and 4 (green and blue slices). These slices can also be viewed dynamically, by flipping the video volume (turning the x-axis (or y-axis) to be the new t-axis), and then playing as a video. Such examples are found in the project website.

When an object moves fast, patches in x-t and y-t slices appear to be *low-resolution versions* of the higher-resolution x-y slices (traditional frames). Increasing the resolution of these x-t and y-t slices in t direction is the same as increasing the temporal resolution of the video. The *spatial* x-y video frames thus provide examples as to how to increase the *temporal* resolution of the x-t and y-t slices within the same video. Interestingly, when the object moves very slowly, patches in x-t and y-t slices appear as stretc.hed versions of the patches in x-y frames, indicating that these temporal slices may provide examples as to how to increase the *spatial* resolution of the video frames. This however, is beyond the scope of the current paper.

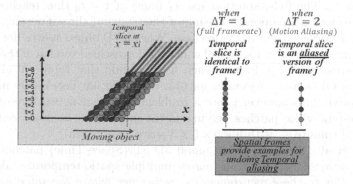

Fig. 5. 1D illustration of "across dimension" recurrence. *A 1D object moves to the right. When properly sampled in time ($\Delta T = 1$), temporal slices are similar to spatial slices (1D "frames"). However, when the temporal sampling rate is too low ($\Delta T = 2$), temporal slices are undersampled (aliased) versions of the spatial slices. Thus, spatial frames provide examples for undoing the temporal aliasing. (See text for more details.)*

Fig. 6. Similarity Across-Dimensions: *Nearest-Neighbor (NN) heat map indicating the percent of best patch matches (out of 10), found "across-dimensions" vs. "within the same dimension". Red color indicates patches for which all 10 best matches were found "across dimension"; Blue indicates patches for which all 10 best matches were found "within the same dimension". As can be seen, a significant portion of the ST-patches found their best matches across dimensions.* (Color figure online)

Figure 5 explains this phenomenon in a simplified "flat" world. A 1D object moves horizontally to the right with constant speed. The 2D space-time plane here (xt), is equivalent to the 3D space-time video volume (xyt) in the general case. If we look at a specific point $x = x_i$, the entire object passes through this location over time. Hence looking at the temporal slice through $x = x_i$ (here the slices are 1D lines), we can see the entire object emerging in that temporal slice. The resolution of the 1D temporal slice depends on the object's speed compared to the framerate. For example, if the object's speed is 1 pixel/s, then taking frames every 1 s ($\Delta t = 1$) will show the entire object in the 1D temporal slice at $x = x_i$. However, if we sample slower in time (which is equivalent to a faster motion with the same framerate), the temporal slice at $x = x_i$ will now display an <u>aliased</u> version of the object (Fig. 5, on the right). In other words, the spatial frame at $t = t_0$ is a high-resolution version of the aliased temporal slice at $x = x_i$. The full-resolution *spatial* frame at $t = t_0$ thus teaches us how to *undo* the motion (temporal) aliasing of the *temporal* slice at $x = x_i$.

The same applies to the 3D video case. When a 2D object moves horizontally with constant speed, the y-t slice will contain a downscaled version of that object. The higher-resolution x-y frames teach how to undo that temporal aliasing in the y-t slice. Obviously, objects in natural videos do not necessarily move in a constant speed. This however is not a problem, since our network resolves only small space-time video patches, relying on the speed being constant only *locally* in space and time (e.g., within a $5 \times 5 \times 3$ space-time patch).

Shahar et al. [18] showed that small 3D ST (Space-Time) patches tend to recur in a video sequence, within/across multiple spatio-temporal scales of the video. We refer to these recurrences as *'recurrence within the same dimension'* (i.e., no swap between the axes of the video volume). Patch *'recurrence across dimensions'* provides additional high-quality internal examples for temporal-SR. This is used *in addition* to the patch recurrence within the same dimension.

Figure 6 visually conveys the strength of 'recurrence across dimensions' of small ST-patches in the Cheetah video, compared to their recurrence within the same dimension. Each $5 \times 5 \times 3$ patch in the original video searched for its top 10 approximate nearest-neighbors (using Patch-Match [4]). These best matches were searched in various scales, both within the same dimension (in the original video orientation, xyt), and across dimensions (tyx, by flipping the video volume so that the x-axis becomes the new t-axis). The colors indicate how many of these best matches were found across-dimension. Red color (100%) indicates patches for which all 10 best matches were found *across dimension*; Blue (0%) indicates patches for which all 10 best matches were found *within the same dimension*. The figure illustrates that a significant portion of the ST-patches found their best matches across dimensions (showing here one slice of the video volume). These tend to be patches with large motions – the background in this video (note that the background moves very fast, due to the fast camera motion which tracks the cheetah). Indeed, as explained above, patches with large motions can benefit the most from using the cross-dimension examples.

Both of these types of patch recurrences (within and across dimensions) are used to perform *Zero-Shot Temporal-SR* from a single video. Sect. 3 explains how to exploit these internal ST-patch recurrences to generate training examples from the input video alone. This allows to increase the framerate while undoing both motion blur and motion aliasing, by training a light *video-specific CNN*.

Figure 4 shows that patch recurrence across dimensions applies not only to simple linear motions, but also in videos with very complex motions. A ball falling into a liquid filled glass was recorded with a circuiting slow-motion (high framerate) camera. We can see x-t and y-t slices from that video contain similar patches as in the original x-y frames. Had this scene been recorded with a regular (low-framerate) camera, the video frames would have provided high-resolution examples for the lower temporal resolution of the x-t and y-t slices.

3   Generating an Internal Training Set

Low-temporal-resolution (LTR) & *High-temporal-resolution* (HTR) pairs of examples are extracted directly from the input video, giving rise to self-supervised training. These example pairs are used to train a relatively shallow fully convolutional network, which learns to increase the temporal resolution of the ST-patches *of this specific video*. Once trained, this video-specific CNN is applied to the input video, to generate a HTR output.

The rationale is: Small ST-patches in the input video recur in different space-time scales and different dimensions of the input video. Therefore, the same network that is trained to increase the temporal resolution of these ST-patches in other scales/dimensions of the video, will also be good for increasing their temporal-resolution in the *input* video itself (analogous to ZSSR in images [21]).

The creation of relevant training examples is thus crucial to the success of the learning process. In order for the CNN to generalize well to the input video, the LTR-HTR training examples should *bear resemblance* and have similar statistics of ST-patches as in the input video and its (unknown) HTR version. This process is explained next.

3.1 Example Pairs from "Same Dimension"
The first type of training examples makes use of similarity of small ST-patches

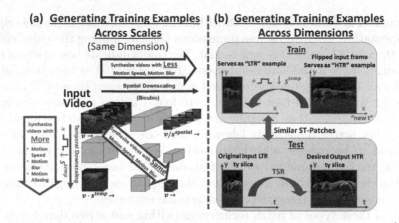

Fig. 7. Generating Internal Training Set. *(a) Different combinations of spatio-temporal scales provide a variety of speeds, sizes, different degrees of motion blur & aliasing. This generates a variety of LTR example videos, for which their corresponding ground-truth HTR videos are known (the space-time volumes just above them). (b) The xy video frames provide high-resolution examples for the ty and xt slices. Training examples can therefore be generated from these spatial frames, showing how to increase the temporal resolution.* **Please see the video in our** *project website* **for a visual explanation and demonstration of those internal augmentations.**

across spatio-temporal scales of the video. As was observed in [18], and shown in Fig. 7.a:

- Downscaling the video frames spatially (e.g., using bicubic downscaling), causes edges to appear sharper and move slower (in pixels/frame). This generates ST-patches with *higher temporal resolution.*
- Blurring and sub-sampling a video in time (i.e., reducing the framerate and increasing the "exposure-time" by averaging frames), causes an increase in speed, blur, and motion aliasing. This generates ST-patches with *lower temporal resolution.* Since the "exposure-time" is a highly **non-ideal LPF** (its temporal support is ≤ than the gap between 2 frames), such temporal coarsening introduces additional motion aliasing.
- Donwscaling by the same scale-factor both in space and in time (the diagonal arrow in Fig. 7.a), preserves the same amount of speed and blur. This generates ST-patches with *same temporal resolution.*

Different combinations of spatio-temporal scales provide a variety of speeds, sizes, different degrees of motion blur and different degrees of motion aliasing. In particular, downscaling by the same scale-factor in space and in time (the diagonal arrow in Fig. 7.a), generates a variety of LTR videos, whose ST-patches are similar to those in the LTR input video, but for which their corresponding ground-truth HTR videos are known (the corresponding space-time volumes just above them in the space-time pyramid of Fig. 7.a).

Moreover, if the same object moves at different speeds in different parts of the video (such as in the rotating fan/wheel videos in project website), the slow part of the motion provides examples how to undo the motion blur and aliasing in faster parts of the video. Such LTR-HTR example pairs are obtained from the bottom-left part of the space-time pyramid (below the diagonal in Fig. 7.a).

To further enrich the training-set with a variety of examples, we apply additional augmentations to the input video. These include mirror flips, rotations by $90°, 180°, 270°$, as well as flipping the video in time. This is useful especially in the presence of chaotic non-rigid motions.

3.2 Example Pairs "Across Dimensions"

In order to make use of the similarity between small ST-patches across dimensions (see Sect. 2), we create additional training examples by rotating the 3D video volume – i.e., swapping the spatial and temporal dimensions of the video. Such swaps are applied to a variety of spatially (bicubically) downscaled versions of the input video. Once swapped, a variety of 1D temporal-downscalings (temporal rect) are applied to the *new* "temporal" dimension (originally the x-axis or y-axis). The pair of volumes before and after such "temporal" downscaling form our training pairs.

While at test time the network is applied to the input video in its original orientation (i.e., TSR is performed along the original t-axis), training the network on ST-patches with similarity across dimensions creates a richer training set and improves our results. Here too, data augmentations are helpful (mirror flips, rotations, etc.). For example, if an object moves to the right (as in the Cheetah video), the y-t slices will bare resemblance to *mirror-reflected* versions of the original x-y frames (e.g., see the cheetah slices in Fig. 3).

In our current implementation, we use both types of training examples ('within-dimension' and 'across-dimensions'), typically with equal probability. Our experiments have shown that in most videos, using both types of training examples is superior to using only one type (see also ablation study in Sect. 5).

4   'Zero-Shot' Temporal-SR – The Algorithm

The repetition of small ST-patches inside the input video (aross scales and across dimensions), provide ample data for training. Such an internal training-set concisely captures the characteristic statistics of the given input video: its local spatial appearances, scene dynamics, motion speeds, etc. Moreover, such an internal training-set has relatively few "distracting" examples which are irrelevant to the specific task at hand. This is in stark contrast to the external training paradigm, where the vast majority of the training examples are irrelevant, and may even be harmful, for performing inference on a specific given video. This high quality training allows us to perform true TSR using a simple conv net without any bells and whistles; our model has no motion estimation nor optical flow components, nor does it use any complicated building blocks.

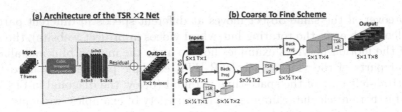

Fig. 8. Coarse to fine scheme and Architecture. (see text for details).

4.1 Architecture

A fully Convolutional Neural Network (CNN) efficiently calculates its output patch by patch. Each output pixel is a result of a calculation over a patch in the input video. The size of that patch is determined by the effective receptive field of the net [13]. Patch recurrence across scales and dimensions holds best for relatively small patches, hence we need to ascertain that the receptive field of our model is relatively small in size. Keeping our network and filters small (eight 3D conv layers, some with $3 \times 3 \times 3$ filters and some with $1 \times 3 \times 3$, all with stride 1), we ensure working on small patches as required. Each of our 8 conv layers has 128 channels, followed by a ReLU activation. The input to the network is a temporally interpolated video (simple cubic interpolation), and the network learns only the residual between the interpolated LTR video to the target HTR video. Figure 8.a provides a detailed description of our model.

At each iteration, a $36 \times 36 \times 16$ space-time video crop is randomly selected from the various internal augmentations (Sect. 3). A crop is selected with probability proportional to its mean intensity gradient magnitude. This crop forms a HTR (High Temporal Resolution) example. It is then blurred and subsampled by a factor of 2 *in time*, to generate an internal LTR-HTR training pair.

An ℓ_2 loss is computed on the recovered space-time outputs. We use an ADAM optimizer [12]. The learning rate is initially set to 10^{-4}, and is adaptively decreased according to the training procedure proposed in [21]. The training stops when the learning rate reaches 10^{-6}.

The advantage of *video-specific* internal training is the adaptation of the network to the specific data at hand. The downside of such Internal-Learning is that it requires training the network from scratch for each new input video. Our network requires ~2 h training time per video on a single Nvidia V100 GPU. Once trained, inference time at 720×1280 spatial resolution is ~1.7 s/frame.

4.2 Coarse-to-Fine Scheme (in Space and in Time)

Temporal-SR becomes complex when there are large motions and severe blur. As shown in Fig. 7.a, spatially downscaling the video results in smaller motions and less motion blur. Denoting the input video resolution by $S_{\times 1}T_{\times 1}$, our goal is to recover a video with $\times 8$ higher temporal resolution: $S_{\times 1}T_{\times 8}$. To perform our temporal-SR we use a coarse-to-fine approach (Fig. 8.b).

We start by training our network on a spatially downscaled version of the input video (typically $S_{\times 1/8}T_{\times 1}$, or $S_{\times 1/4}T_{\times 1}$ for spatially small videos).

Figure 8.b details a coarse-to-fine upscaling scheme from $S_{\times 1/4}T_{\times 1}$. The scheme to upscale from $S_{\times 1/8}T_{\times 1}$ includes an additional "Back-Projection" stage at the end. The network trains on this small video, learning to increase its temporal resolution by a factor of 2. Once trained, the network is applied to $S_{\times 1/8}T_{\times 1}$ to generate $S_{\times 1/8}T_{\times 2}$. We then use "Back-Projection" [1] [8] (both spatially and temporally), to increase the spatial resolution of the video by a factor of 2, resulting in $S_{\times 1/4}T_{\times 2}$. The spatial Back-Projection guarantees the *spatial* (bicubic) consistency of the resulting $S_{\times 1/4}T_{\times 2}$ with the spatially smaller $S_{\times 1/8}T_{\times 2}$, and its *temporal* (rect) consistency with the temporally coarser $S_{\times 1/4}T_{\times 1}$.

Now, since we increased both the spatial and temporal resolutions by the same factor ($\times 2$), the motion sizes and blurs in $S_{\times 1/4}T_{\times 2}$ remain similar in their characteristics to those in $S_{\times 1/8}T_{\times 1}$. This allows us to apply the same network again, as-is, to reach a higher temporal resolution: $S_{\times 1/4}T_{\times 4}$. We iterate through these two steps: increasing temporal resolution using our network, and subsequently increasing the spatial resolution via spatio-temporal Back-Projection, going up the diagonal in Fig. 7.a, until we reach the goal resolution of $S_{\times 1}T_{\times 8}$.

The recurring use of TSRx2 and "Back-Projection" accumulates errors. Fine-tuning at each scale is likely to improve our results, and also provide a richer set of training examples as we go up the coarse-to-fine scales. However, fine-tuning was not used in our current reported results due to the tradeoff in runtime.

5   Experiments and Results

True TSR (as opposed to simple frame interpolation) is mostly in-need when temporal information in the video is severely under-sampled and lost, resulting in motion aliasing. Similarly, very fast stochastic motions recorded within a long exposure time result in unrecognizable objects. To the best of our knowledge, a dataset of such low-quality (LTR) videos of complex dynamic scenes, along with their "ground truth" HTR videos, is not publicly available. Note that these are very different from datasets used by frame-interpolation methods (e.g., [1,3,11,22,24]), since these do not exhibit motion blur or motion aliasing, and hence are irrelevant for the task of TSR.

We therefore curated a challenging dataset of 25 LTR videos of very complex fast dynamic scenes, "recorded" with a 'slow' (30 fps) video camera *with full inter-frame exposure time*. The dataset was generated from real complex videos recorded with high speed cameras (mostly 240 fps). The LTR videos were generated from our HTR 'ground-truth' videos by *blurring and sub-sampling them in time* (averaging every 8 frames). Since these 25 videos are quite long, they provide ample data (a very large number of frames) to compare and evaluate on. We further split our LTR dataset into 2 groups: (i) 13 extremely challenging videos, not only with severe motion blur, but also with severe motion aliasing and/or complex highly non-rigid motions (e.g., splashing water, flickerig fire); (ii) 12 less challenging videos, still with sever motion blur, but mostly rigid motions.

---

[1] Don't confuse "Back-Projection" [8] with "backpropagation" [6].

Table 1. Comparing TSR×8 results on our dataset. *When applied to challenging videos with severe motion blur and motion aliasing, sophisticated frame upsampling methods (Nvidia SlowMo and DAIN) score significantly lower. However, even methods trained to overcome such challenges (e.g., Flawless), but were pre-trained on an external dataset, struggle to compete on videos that deviate from the typical motions and dynamic behaviors they were trained on.*

		Ours	Flawless [10]	DAIN [2]	Nvidia SloMo [9]	linear interp.
Entire dataset	PSNR [dB]	**28.27**	28.22	27.29	27.23	26.79
	SSIM	0.913	**0.918**	0.903	0.901	0.895
	LPIPS^a[25]	0.194	**0.174**	0.214	0.214	0.231
Challenging videos	PSNR [dB]	**28.05**	27.58	27.09	27.03	26.99
	SSIM	**0.922**	0.918	0.909	0.906	0.907
	LPIPS^a[25]	**0.184**	0.188	0.208	0.205	0.212

^{a} LPIPS (perceptual *distance*) – lower is better. PSNR and SSIM – higher is better.

Figure 1 displays a few such examples for TSR×8. We compared our results (both visually and numerically) to the leading methods in the field (DAIN [2], NVIDIA SloMo [9], Flawless [10]). As can be seen, complex dynamic scenes pose a challenge to all methods. Moreover, the rotating fan/wheel, which induce severe motion blur and severe motion aliasing, cannot be resolved by any of these methods. Not only are the recovered frames extremely distorted and blurry (as seen in Fig. 1), they all recover a false direction of motion (counter-clockwise rotation), and with a wrong rotation speed. *The reader is urged to view the videos in our* project website *in order to see these strong aliasing effects.* Table 1 provides quantitative comparisons of all methods on our dataset – compared using PSNR, structural similarity (SSIM), and a perceptual measure (LPIPS [25]). The full table of all 25 videos is found in the project website. Since Flawless is restricted to ×10 temporal expansion (as opposed to the ×8 of all other methods), we ran it in a slightly different setting, so that their results could be compared to the same ground truth. Although most closely related to our work, we could not compare to [18], due to its outdated software. Moreover, our end-to-end method is currently adapted to TSRx8, whereas their few published results are TSRx2 and TSRx4, hence we could not visually compare to them either (our TSRx2 network can currently train only on small (coarse) spatial video scales, whereas [18] applies SRx2 to their fine spatial scale.

The results in Table 1 indicate that sophisticated frame-interpolation methods (DAIN [2], NVIDIA SloMo [9]) are not adequate for the task of TSR, and are significantly inferior (−1 dB) on LTR videos compared to dedicated TSR methods (Ours and Flawless [10]). In fact, they are not much better (+0.5 dB) than plain intensity-based linear interpolation on those videos. Flawless and Ours provide comparable quantitative results on the dataset, even though Flawless is a pre-trained supervised method, whereas Ours is *unsupervised* and requires

Table 2. Ablation study: 'Within' vs. 'Across' examples. *Average results of our atomic TSRx2 network, when trained on examples extracted from: (i) same-dimension only ('Within'); (ii) across-dimensions only ('Across'); (iii) best configuration for each video ('within', 'across', or both). The ablation results indicate that on average, the cross-dimension augmentations are more informative than the within (same-dimension) augmentations, leading to an overall improvement in PSNR, SSIM and LPIPS (improvements shown in blue parentheses). However, since different videos have different preferences, training each video with its best 'within' and/or 'across' configuration can provide an additional overall improvement in all 3 measures.*

	Only within	Only across	Best of all configurations
PSNR [dB]	33.96	34.25 (✓0.28)	34.33 (✓0.37)
SSIM	0.962	0.964 (✓0.002)	0.965 (✓0.003)
LPIPS[a] [25]	0.035	0.033 (✓0.002)	0.032 (✓0.003)

[a] LPIPS (perceptual *distance*) – lower is better. PSNR and SSIM – higher is better.

no prior training examples. Moreover, on the subset of extremely challenging videos (highly complex non-rigid motions), our Zero-Shot TSR outperforms the externally trained Flawless [10]. We attribute this to the fact that it is practically infeasible to generate an exhaustive enough external training set to cover the variety of all possible *non-rigid* motions. In contrast, highly relevant *video-specific* training examples are found internally, inside the LTR input video itself.

Since rigid motions are easier to model and capture in an external training set, Flawless provided high-quality results (better than ours) on the videos which are dominated by rigid motions. However, even in those videos, when focusing on the areas with non-rigid motions, our method visually outperforms the externally trained Flawless. While these non-rigid areas are smaller in those videos (hence have negligible effect on PSNR), they often tend to be the salient and more interesting regions in the frame. Such examples are found in Fig. 1 (e.g., the billiard-ball and hoola-hoop examples), and in the videos in project website.

Ablation Study: One of the important findings of this paper is the strong patch recurrence *across-dimensions*, and its implication on extracting useful internal training examples for TSR. To examine the power of such cross-dimension augmentations, we conducted an ablation study. Table 2 compares the performance of our network when: (i) Training only on examples from *same-dimension* ('Within'); (ii) Training only on examples *across-dimensions* ('Across'); (iii) Training each video on its best configuration – 'within', 'across', or on both.

Since our atomic TSRx2 network is trained only on a coarse spatial scale of the video, we performed the ablation study at that scale (hence the differences between the values in Tables 1 and 2). This allowed us to isolate purely the effects of the choice of augmentations on the training, without the distracting effects of the subsequent spatial and temporal Back-Projection steps. Table 2 indicates that, on the average, the cross-dimension augmentations are more informative than the within (same-dimension) augmentations. However, since different videos have different preferences, training each video with its best within and/or across configuration provides an additional overall improvement in PSNR, SSIM and LPIPS (improvements are shown in blue parentheses in Table 2).

This suggests that each video should ideally be paired with its best training configuration – a viable option with Internal training. For example, our video-specific ablation study indicated that videos with large uniform motions tend to benefit significantly more from cross-dimension training examples (e.g., the falling diamonds video in Fig. 1 and in the project website). In contrast, videos with gradually varying speeds or with rotating motions tend to benefit from within-dimension examples (e.g., the rotating fan video in Fig. 1 and in the project website). Such general video-specific preferences can be estimated per video by using very crude (even inaccurate) optical-flow estimation at very coarse spatial scales of the video. This is part of our future work. In the meantime, our default configuration randomly samples augmentations from both 'within' (same-dimension) and 'across-dimensions'.

6. Conclusion

We present an approach for Zero-Shot Temporal-SR, which requires no training examples other than the input test video. Training examples are extracted from coarser spatio-temporal scales of the input video, as well as from other video dimensions (by swapping space and time). Internal-Training adapts to the data-specific statistics of the input data. It is therefore more adapted to cope with new challenging (never-before-seen) data. Our approach can resolve motion blur and motion aliasing in very complex dynamic scenes, surpassing previous supervised methods trained on external video datasets.

Acknowledgments. Thanks to Ben Feinstein for his invaluable help in getting the GPUs to run smoothly and efficiently. This project received funding from the European Research Council (ERC) Horizon 2020, grant No. 788535, and from the Carolito Stiftung. Dr Bagon is a Robin Chemers Neustein AI Fellow.

References

1. Baker, S., Scharstein, D., Lewis, J., Roth, S., Black, M.J., Szeliski, R.: A database and evaluation methodology for optical flow. Int. J. Comput. Vis. **92**(1), 1–31 (2011)
2. Bao, W., Lai, W.S., Ma, C., Zhang, X., Gao, Z., Yang, M.H.: Depth-aware video frame interpolation. In: Proceedings of the IEEE Conference on Computer Vision and Pattern Recognition (CVPR), pp. 3703–3712 (2019)
3. Bao, W., Lai, W.S., Zhang, X., Gao, Z., Yang, M.H.: MEMC-Net: motion estimation and motion compensation driven neural network for video interpolation and enhancement. IEEE Trans. Pattern Anal. Mach. Intell. **12**, 1–16 (2019)
4. Barnes, C., Shechtman, E., Goldman, D.B., Finkelstein, A.: The generalized Patch-Match correspondence algorithm. In: Daniilidis, K., Maragos, P., Paragios, N. (eds.) ECCV 2010. LNCS, vol. 6313, pp. 29–43. Springer, Heidelberg (2010). https://doi.org/10.1007/978-3-642-15558-1_3

5. Glasner, D., Bagon, S., Irani, M.: Super-resolution from a single image. In: 2009 IEEE 12th International Conference on Computer Vision (ICCV) (2009)
6. Goodfellow, I., Bengio, Y., Courville, A.: Deep Learning, vol. 11. MIT Press, Cambridge (2016)
7. Hyun Kim, T., Mu Lee, K.: Generalized video deblurring for dynamic scenes. In: Proceedings of the IEEE Conference on Computer Vision and Pattern Recognition (CVPR) (2015)
8. Irani, M., Peleg, S.: Improving resolution by image registration. CVGIP Graph. Models Image Process. **53**, 231–239 (1991)
9. Jiang, H., Sun, D., Jampani, V., Yang, M.H., Learned-Miller, E., Kautz, J.: Super SloMo: high quality estimation of multiple intermediate frames for video interpolation. In: Proceedings of the IEEE Conference on Computer Vision and Pattern Recognition (CVPR) (2018)
10. Jin, M., Hu, Z., Favaro, P.: Learning to extract flawless slow motion from blurry videos. In: The IEEE Conference on Computer Vision and Pattern Recognition (CVPR) (2019)
11. Kiani Galoogahi, H., Fagg, A., Huang, C., Ramanan, D., Lucey, S.: Need for speed: a benchmark for higher frame rate object tracking. In: Proceedings of the IEEE International Conference on Computer Vision (CVPR) (2017)
12. Kingma, D.P., Ba, J.: Adam: A method for stochastic optimization. arXiv preprint arXiv:1412.6980 (2014)
13. Luo, W., Li, Y., Urtasun, R., Zemel, R.: Understanding the effective receptive field in deep convolutional neural networks. In: Advances in Neural Information Processing Systems (NeurIPS) (2016)
14. Meyer, S., Djelouah, A., McWilliams, B., Sorkine-Hornung, A., Gross, M., Schroers, C.: PhaseNet for video frame interpolation. In: The IEEE Conference on Computer Vision and Pattern Recognition (CVPR) (June 2018)
15. Niklaus, S., Mai, L., Liu, F.: Video frame interpolation via adaptive separable convolution. In: Proceedings of the IEEE International Conference on Computer Vision (ICCV) (2017)
16. Peleg, T., Szekely, P., Sabo, D., Sendik, O.: IM-Net for high resolution video frame interpolation. In: The IEEE Conference on Computer Vision and Pattern Recognition (CVPR) (June 2019)
17. Shaham, T.R., Dekel, T., Michaeli, T.: SinGAN: learning a generative model from a single natural image. In: The IEEE Conference on Computer Vision and Pattern Recognition (CVPR) (2019)
18. Shahar, O., Faktor, A., Irani, M.: Super-resolution from a single video. In: Proceedings of the IEEE Conference on Computer Vision and Pattern Recognition (CVPR) (2011)
19. Shechtman, E., Caspi, Y., Irani, M.: Increasing space-time resolution in video. In: Heyden, A., Sparr, G., Nielsen, M., Johansen, P. (eds.) ECCV 2002. LNCS, vol. 2350, pp. 753–768. Springer, Heidelberg (2002). https://doi.org/10.1007/3-540-47969-4_50
20. Shocher, A., Bagon, S., Isola, P., Irani, M.: InGAN: capturing and remapping the "DNA" of a natural image. In: The IEEE Conference on Computer Vision and Pattern Recognition (CVPR) (2019)
21. Shocher, A., Cohen, N., Irani, M.: "zero-shot" super-resolution using deep internal learning. Proceedings of the IEEE Conference on Computer Vision and Pattern Recognition (CVPR), vol. 5, no. 8, p. 10 (2018)
22. Soomro, K., Zamir, A.R., Shah, M.: A dataset of 101 human action classes from videos in the wild. Center for Research in Computer Vision (2012)

23. Su, S., Delbracio, M., Wang, J., Sapiro, G., Heidrich, W., Wang, O.: Deep video deblurring for hand-held cameras. In: Proceedings of the IEEE Conference on Computer Vision and Pattern Recognition, pp. 1279–1288 (2017)
24. Xue, T., Chen, B., Wu, J., Wei, D., Freeman, W.T.: Video enhancement with task-oriented flow. Int. J. Comput. Vis. (IJCV) **127**(8), 1106–1125 (2019)
25. Zhang, R., Isola, P., Efros, A.A., Shechtman, E., Wang, O.: The unreasonable effectiveness of deep features as a perceptual metric. In: The IEEE Conference on Computer Vision and Pattern Recognition (CVPR), vol. 12, no. 13, p. 14 (2018)

Inducing Optimal Attribute Representations for Conditional GANs

Binod Bhattarai[1(✉)] and Tae-Kyun Kim[1,2]

[1] Imperial College London, London, UK
{b.bhattarai,tk.kim}@imperial.ac.uk
[2] KAIST, Daejeon, South Korea

Abstract. Conditional GANs (cGANs) are widely used in translating an image from one category to another. Meaningful conditions on GANs provide greater flexibility and control over the nature of the target domain synthetic data. Existing conditional GANs commonly encode target domain label information as hard-coded categorical vectors in the form of 0s and 1s. The major drawbacks of such representations are inability to encode the high-order semantic information of target categories and their relative dependencies. We propose a novel end-to-end learning framework based on Graph Convolutional Networks to learn the attribute representations to condition the generator. The GAN losses, the discriminator and attribute classification loss, are fed back to the graph resulting in the synthetic images that are more natural and clearer with respect to the attributes generation. Moreover, prior-arts are mostly given priorities to condition on the generator side, not on the discriminator side of GANs. We apply the conditions on the discriminator side as well via multi-task learning. We enhanced four state-of-the-art cGANs architectures: Stargan, Stargan-JNT, AttGAN and STGAN. Our extensive qualitative and quantitative evaluations on challenging face attributes manipulation data set, CelebA, LFWA, and RaFD, show that the cGANs enhanced by our methods outperform by a large margin, compared to their counter-parts and other conditioning methods, in terms of both target attributes recognition rates and quality measures such as PSNR and SSIM.

Keywords: Conditional GAN · Graph Convolutional Network · Multi-task learning · Face attributes

1 Introduction

Someone buying bread is likely to buy butter, blue sky comes with a sunny day. Similarly, some of the attributes of the faces co-occur more frequently than others. Figure 2 shows co-occurring probabilities of facial attributes. We see some set of attributes such as *wearing lipsticks* and *male* are least co-occurring (0.01) and *male* and *bald* are highly co-related (1.0).

Electronic supplementary material The online version of this chapter (https://doi.org/10.1007/978-3-030-58571-6_5) contains supplementary material, which is available to authorized users.

© Springer Nature Switzerland AG 2020
A. Vedaldi et al. (Eds.): ECCV 2020, LNCS 12352, pp. 69–85, 2020.
https://doi.org/10.1007/978-3-030-58571-6_5

Fig. 1. Simultaneous manipulation of target facial attributes along with their auxiliary. From left to right, in each pair, original images change to Old (along with negate of black hair), Female (lipstick/makeup), and Bald (wrinkles). The attribute representations embedding relations are automatically learnt and applied to condition the generator.

Face attribute manipulation using GAN [3,7,9,16,23,26,42,46,48] is one of the challenging and popular research problem. Since the advent of conditional GAN [31], several variants of conditional GANs (cGANs) have been proposed. For conditioning the GAN, existing methods rely on target domain one-hot vectors [9,16,25,33], synthetic model parameters of target attributes [11], facial action units [39], or key point landmarks [31], to mention a few of them. Recently, [26] proposed to use the difference of one-hot vectors corresponding to the target and source attributes. This trick *alone* boosts Target Attributes Recognition Rate (TARR) on synthetic data compared to [9] by a large margin. Another recent study on GAN's [35] identified conditioning on GAN is co-related with its performance. The major limitation of existing cGANs for arbitrary multiple face attributes manipulation is [9,16,25,26,37] are: hard coded 1 and 0 form, treating every attribute equally different and ignoring the co-existence of the attributes. In reality, as we can see in Fig. 2, some attributes are more co-related than others. Moreover, the existing methods are giving less attention to conditioning on the discriminator side except minimising the cross-entropy loss of target attributes.

Another recent work [28] identified the problem of artefacts on synthetic examples due to unnatural transition from source to target. This problem arises due to the ignorance of existing GANs regarding the co-existence of certain sub set of attributes. To overcome this, they propose a hard-coded method to condition both target attribute (aging) and its associated attributes (gender, race) on generator and also on discriminator in order to faithfully retain them after translation. However, this approach is limited to a single attribute and infeasible to hard code such rules in the case like ours where multiple arbitrary attributes are manipulated simultaneously. Recent study on GAN [5] identifies the forgetting problem of discriminator due to the non-stationary nature of the data from the generator. Applying a simple structural identification loss (rotation angle) helps to improve the performance and stability of GAN (Fig. 1).

To address the above mentioned challenges of cGANs, we investigate few continuous representations including semantic label embedding (word2vec) [30], attributes model parameters (attrbs-weights) (see Sect. 4). The advantages of conditioning with such representations instead of 0s and 1s form are mainly two

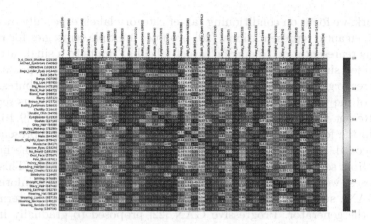

Fig. 2. Co-occurrence matrix of facial attributes (zoom in the view).

folds: i) carries high-order semantic information, ii) establishes relative relationship between the attributes. These representations are, however, still sub-optimal and less natural as these are computed offline and also do not capture simultaneous existing tendency of different face attributes. Thus, we propose a novel conditioning method for cGAN to induce higher order semantic representations of target attributes, automatically embedding inter-attributes co-occurrence and also sharing the information based on degree of interaction. Towards this goal, we propose to exploit the attributes co-occurrence probability and apply Graph Convolutional Network (GCN) [24] to condition GAN. GCN is capable of generating dense vectors, distilling the higher dimensional data and also capable of convolving the un-ordered data [15]. The conditioning parameters i.e. GCN are optimised via the discriminator and attribute classification losses of GAN in an end-to-end fashion. In order to maintain such semantic structural relationship of the attributes at the discriminator side as well, we adapted on-line multitask learning objectives [4] constrained by the same co-occurrence matrix. The experiments show that the proposed method substantially improve state-of-the-art cGAN methods and other conditioning methods in terms of target attributes classification rates and PSNR/SSIM. The synthesised images by our method exhibit associated multi-attributes and clearer target attributes. Details of the method are explained in Sect. 3, following the literature review in Sect. 2, and experimental results and conclusions are shown in Sect. 4 and Sect. 5.

2 Related Works

Conditional GANs. After the seminal work from Mirza et al. [31] on Conditional GANs (cGANs), several variants such as, conditioning target category labels in addition to the input [6,9,16,26,35,50], semantic text or layout representations conditioning [17,40,49,51], image conditioning [18,19,27], facial landmarks [47], have been proposed to solve different vision tasks. These works highlight the importance of semantic representations of target domain as a condition.

In this work, we focus on conditioning target category labels especially by continuous and semantic representations. [20] proposes multiple strategies for random continuous representation to encode target label but limits to a single attribute. [10] extended similar approaches for arbitrary attributes. [21] proposes to use decision tree to generate hierarchical codes to control the target attributes. These are some of the works related to ours in terms of inducing continuous representations. Recent works on cGANs for face attribute manipulations [9,16,25,37] encodes in the form of 0s and 1s or their difference [26]. These representations are hard-coded. STGAN [26] also proposes conditional control of the information flow from source to target in the intermediate layers of GANs. This is one of the closest works in terms of the adaptive conditioning target information. Other cGANs, such as StyleGAN [23] propose to condition on the intermediate layers of the generator. Progressive GAN [22] proposed to gradually increase the parameters of the generator and discriminator successively to generate high quality images. Our method is orthogonal to this line of methods, and can be extended to these works for a higher quality. Recently, attribute aware age progression GAN [28] proposes to condition both associated attributes and target attributes at both generator and discriminator side. This work is closest in terms of conditioning at both the sides and retaining the auxiliary attributes in addition to target attribute. This approach limits to single attribute manipulation i'e aging, whereas, our method supports multiple attributes. Also their method is hard-coded whereas our method is automatic and directly inferred from the co-occurrence matrix.

Graph Convolutional Network (GCN). Frameworks similar to [24] are popular for several tasks including link prediction [12], clustering [38], node classification [45]. Recent works on image classification [8] and face attributes classification [34] propose to use GCN to induce more discriminative representations of attributes by sharing information between the co-occurring attributes. Unlike these works, we propose to apply GCN to induce such higher-order representations of target categories for the generative neural networks and optimise it via end-to-end adversarial learning. To the best of our knowledge, this is the first work to use such embedding as conditions in cGANS. For more details on the work based on Graph Convolutional Networks, we suggest reader to refer to [52].

Regularizing/Conditioning the Discriminator. Conditioning on the discriminator side has been shown useful in generating more realistic and diverse images [5,32,33,36]. [35] maximises the distribution of target label in addition to source distribution to improve the quality of synthetic images. [5] introduced rotation loss on the discriminator side to mitigate the forgetting problem of the discriminator. Projecting the target conditional vector to the penultimate representation of the input at discriminator side [33] substantially improved the quality of synthetic images. Another work on Spectral normalisation of weight parameters [32] of every layer of the discriminator stabilises the training of GANs. Recent works on face attribute manipulations [9,16,26] minimise the target label cross entropy loss on discriminator. In this work, we introduce conditioning of the discriminator with multi-task learning framework while minimising the target attributes cross entropy loss.

3   Proposed Method

3.1   Overview on the Pipeline

Figure 3 shows the schematic diagram of the proposed method, where both the generator G and discriminator D are conditioned. As mentioned in Sect. 1, existing cGANs arts such as Stargan [9], AttGAN [16] or STGAN [26] condition the generator, which can be done either at the encoder or the decoder part of G, to synthesise the image with intended attributes. But the problem with their conditions is that they ignore the intrinsic properties of the attributes and their relationships. They use single digit (0 or 1) for an attribute, and treat every attributes are equally similar to each other. In Fig. 3, the graph on the generator side represents the attributes and their relationships. Each node in the graph represents higher-order semantic representations of attributes, and the edges between them represent their relationship. We propose to induce the attribute representations which encode attribute properties including their relations, based on how they co-occur in the real world scenario. To induce such representations, we propose to apply GCN [24] with convolutional layers on the generator side. The graph is optimised via end-to-end learning of the entire system of networks. The discriminator and the attribute classifier guide the graph learning such that the learnt conditional representations help the generator synthesise more realistic images and preserve target attributes. Such semantically rich and higher-order conditional representations of the target attributes play an important role in the natural transitioning to the target attribute. This helps to synthesise images with less artefacts, improved quality and better contrast, as also partially observed in StackGAN [49].

We also condition the parameters of attributes on the discriminator side using multi-task learning framework, similar to [4], based on the co-occurrence matrix. Using the learnt representation i.e. the graph to condition the discriminator might also be possible via EM-like alternating optimisation, however due to the complexity and instability, is not considered in this work. Conditioning both target and its associated attributes on generator and on discriminator enabled GAN to retain the target as well as the associated attributes faithfully [28]. Unlike [28] which is hard-coded, limited to a single attribute, our method is automatic, and supports arbitrary multiple attributes. See Sect. 3.3 for more details. Before diving into in the details of the proposed method, we first introduce attributes co-occurrence matrix which is exploited in both the generator and discriminator of the proposed method.

Co-occurrence Matrix: To capture the relationship between the attributes based on how frequently they go together, we constructed a co-occurrence matrix, $C \in \mathbb{R}^{k \times k}$, where k is the total number of attributes. The value at position (i, j) in the matrix gives us an idea about probability of attributes a_j

occurring given the attribute a_i. Figure 2 shows the co-occurrence matrix. We approximate this probability from the training data set as in Eq. 1.

$$P(a_i|a_j) = \frac{\#\text{images with } a_i \cap a_j}{\#\text{images with attribute } a_j} \tag{1}$$

3.2   Graph Convolution and Generator

As stated before, we propose to learn the representations via GCN [24], which we simultaneously use to condition the generator. They are in the form of a Graph, $\mathcal{G} = (V, E)$. In our case there are k different facial attributes, thus total nodes in the graph will be k. We represent each node, also called a vertex V of the graph, by their initial representations of the attributes and the edges between the graph encode their relationship. In our case, this is the co-occurrence probability. Since $P(a_i|a_j) \neq P(a_j|a_i)$, the co-occurrence matrix, C is asymmetric in nature. The graph is constructed from co-occurrence information encoded on C and initial continuous representations of the attributes $X \in \mathbb{R}^{k \times d}$. In Fig. 3, we show a single un-directed edge between the two nodes for clarity. The thickness of edges is proportional to the probability of co-occurrence.

The goal of GCN [24,52] is to learn a function $f(\cdot, \cdot)$ on a graph $\mathcal{G}$, which takes initial node representations X and an adjacency matrix $(\widehat{C})$, which we derive from co-occurrence matrix $C \in \mathbb{R}^{k \times k}$ as inputs. And, it updates the node features as $X^{l+1} \in \mathbb{R}^{k \times d'}$ after passing them through every convolutional layer. Every GCN layer can be formulated as

$$X^{l+1} = f(X^l, \widehat{C}) = \sigma(\widehat{C} X^l \theta^l) \tag{2}$$

where $\theta^l \in \mathbb{R}^{d \times d'}$ is a transformation matrix learned during training and $\widehat{C} = D^{-1}C \in \mathbb{R}^{k \times k}$, $D^{ii} = \sum_{ij} C$ is a diagonal matrix and σ denotes a non-linear operation, which is LeakyReLU [29] for our purpose. The induced representations of the attributes from the final convolutional layer of GCN, denoted as $Z \in \mathbb{R}^{k \times d'}$ are the condition at the generator side as a cue to synthesise new synthetic images. Graph convolutions enable combining and averaging information from first-order neighbourhood [14,24] to generate higher-order representations of the attributes. From Eq. 2, we can see that the node representations at layer $l + 1$ is induced by adding and averaging the representations of a node itself and its neighbours from layer l. The sharing of information from the neighbouring nodes are controlled by the co-occurrence matrix.

Generator. The higher-order representations of the target attributes induced by graph convolution operations are fed into the generator along with the input image. Recent study [26] has shown that the difference of target and source one-hot vector of attributes helps to generate synthetic images with higher rate of target attributes preservation in comparison to the standard target one-hot vectors [9,16]. We propose to feed the generator with the graph induced representations of attributes scaled by the difference of target, t and source, s attributes one-hot vectors as: $Z_t = Z \odot (t - s)$, where, $Z_t \in \mathbb{R}^{k \times d'}$ is a matrix containing

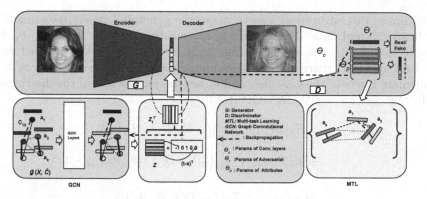

Fig. 3. Schematic diagram showing the pipeline of the proposed method. Each node of the Graph $\mathcal{G}$ represents an attribute and the edge between them encode their co-occurrence defined on $\widehat{C}$. GCN induces the higher-order representations of the attributes (Z) which are further scaled by (t-s) to generate Z_t. We concatenate Z_t with the latent representations of input image and feed to the decoder of (G). At discriminator, we apply Multi-Task Learning (MTL) to share the weights between the tasks constrained on C. During end-to-end learning, we back-propagate the error to the induced representations (Z) to fine-tune their representations. We maintain the color codes among the attributes (best viewed in color). (Color figure online)

the final representations of the target attributes which we feed to the generator as shown in Fig. 3. Given an input image x and the matrix containing continuous representations of target attributes Z_t, we learn the parameters, θ_g of the generator G to generate a new image $\hat{x}$ in an adversarial manner. The generator usually consists of both encoder and decoder or only decoder with few convolutional layers. Also conditions are either concatenated with image at encoder side or concatenated with the image latent representations on the input of decoder side. As we mentioned, our approach is agnostic to the architectures of GANs. Hence, the induced representations from our approach can be fed into the encoder [9] or decoder [16,26] of the generator. In Fig. 3 we present a diagram where target attributes conditioning representations are fed from the decoder part of the generator similar to that of Attgan [16] and STGAN [26]. We flatten Z_t and concatenate it with the latent representations of the input image generated from the encoder and feed it to the decoder. In contrast, in Stargan [9] case, each of the columns in Z_t is duplicated separately and overlaid to match the dimension $128 \times 128 \times 3$ of input RGB image and concatenated with RGB channels.

$$\hat{x} = G(x, Z_t; \theta_g)$$

Loss Functions and End-to-End Learning. The overall loss for the generator is

$$\mathcal{L} = \alpha_1 \mathcal{L}_{G_{adv}} + \alpha_2 \mathcal{L}_{cls} + \alpha_3 \mathcal{L}_{rec}$$

where $\mathcal{L}_{G_{adv}}, \mathcal{L}_{cls}, \mathcal{L}_{rec}$ are the adversarial loss, the classification loss and the reconstruction loss respectively and $\alpha_1, \alpha_2, \alpha_3$ represent the hyper-parameters.

We minimise the adversarial loss to make the generated image indistinguishable from the real data. The generator θ_g and discriminator $\theta_d = \{\theta_c, \theta_p, \theta_r\}$ compete to each other in an adversarial manner. Here, θ_c are the parameters of convolutional layers shared by the discriminator and attribute classifier, θ_p is of penultimate layers of the classifier, and θ_r are the parameters of the discriminator. In our case, we use WGAN-GP [1,13]:

$$\max_{[\theta_c;\theta_r]} \mathcal{L}_{D_{adv}} = \mathbb{E}_x[D(x; [\theta_c, \theta_r])] - \mathbb{E}_{\hat{x}}[D(\hat{x}; [\theta_c, \theta_r])]$$
$$+ \lambda \mathbb{E}_{x'=\beta x+(1-\beta)\hat{x}}[(||\nabla_{x'} D(x'; [\theta_c, \theta_r])||_2 - 1)^2]$$

$$\min_{\theta_g} \mathcal{L}_{G_{adv}} = \mathbb{E}_{\hat{x}}[1 - D(\hat{x}; [\theta_c, \theta_r])]$$

where $\hat{x} = G(x, Z_t; \theta_g)$.

The classification loss here is the standard binary cross-entropy loss in target category label: $\mathcal{L}_{cls} = \sum_k \mathcal{L}^k([\theta_c, \theta_p])$, where θ_c and θ_p form the attribute classifier. The reconstruction loss is computed setting the target attributes equal to that of the source. This results $(t - s)$ into zero vector and ultimately, Z_t turns to the zero matrix.

$$\mathcal{L}_{rec} = ||x - G(x, O; \theta_g)||_1$$

The above combined loss, $\mathcal{L}$ trains the generator G, the discriminator D, and the graph CNN in an end-to-end fashion. The optimal attribute representations are learnt to help generate realistic images (by the discriminator loss), and preserve target attributes (by the classification loss). In the process, multi-attribute relations are also embedded to the representations. The networks would consider more natural i.e. realistic when the output image has the presence of associated other attributes as well as the target attribute.

3.3   Online Multitask Learning for Discriminator

While minimising the target attribute classification loss on the discriminator side, we propose to share weights between the co-occurring attributes model parameters. We adapted online multitask learning for training multiple linear classifiers [4] to achieve this. The rate of the weights shared between the model parameters of attributes is constrained by the attributes interaction matrix. We derive the interaction matrix from the co-occurrence matrix C.

As before, θ_c are the parameters of convolutional layers and θ_p is of the penultimate layers of the classifier. We minimize the objective given in Eq. 3 for target attribute classification with respect to discriminator. The first term in Eq. 3 is the standard binary cross entropy loss. The second term is a regularizer which enforces to maintain similar model parameters of frequently co-occurring attributes by sharing the weights. During training, if prediction for any attribute k is wrong, we update not only the parameters of the particular attribute but also the parameters of related attributes. Rate is determined by the co-relation defined on $\widehat{C}$. For more details on regularizer, we suggest to refer the original paper [4].

$$\mathcal{L}_{cls}^{real} = \sum_k \mathcal{L}^k([\theta_c, \theta_p]) + \lambda \mathcal{R}(\theta_p, \widehat{C}) \tag{3}$$

Note that the multi-task loss is computed on real data. Such updates induce similar model parameters of the attributes which are frequently co-occurring as defined in the co-occurrence matrix.

The multitask attribute classification loss in the above is exploited instead of the conventional single task loss without sharing the parameters. The sharing of parameters between the tasks has advantages over conventional methods: it enforces the discriminator to remember the semantic structural relationship between the attributes defined on the co-occurrence matrix. Such kind of constrains on the discriminator also helps to minimize the risk of forgetting [5] and also retain associated attributes [28]. We can also draw analogy between our method and Label Smoothing. Our difference from one-sided Label Smoothing [41] is randomly softening the labels while our approach is constrained with the meaningful co-occurrence matrix and regularises the parameters of the attributes by sharing the weights. We train the whole system i.e. G, D, and the graph in end-to-end as in the previous section, by replacing the binary classification loss with the multitask loss. Conditioning at the discriminator side also helps improve the generator.

4 Experiments

Data Sets and Evaluation Metrics: To evaluate the proposed method we carried out our major experiments on **CelebA** which has around $200K$ images annotated with 40 different attributes. In our experiments, we took 13 attributes similar to that of [26] on face attribute editing. Similarly, **LFWA** is another benchmark. This data set contains around $13,233$ images and each image is annotated with the same 40 different attributes as CelebA. We took $12K$ images to train the model and report the performance on the remaining examples. Finally, we use **RaFD** data set annotated with the expressions to do attributes transfer from **CelebA**. This data set consists of $4,824$ images annotated with 8 different facial expressions.

For quantitative evaluations, we employed **Target Attributes Recognition Rate (TARR), PSNR, SSIM** which are commonly used quantitative metrics for conditional GANs [9,16,26,43]. For cGANs, it is not sufficient just to have synthetic realistic images, these being recognisable as the target class is also highly important [43]. Thus we choose to compute TARR similar to that of existing works [9,16,26]. TARR measures the generation of conditioned attributes on synthetic data by a model trained on real data. We took a publicly available pre-trained attribute prediction network [26] with a mean accuracy of 94.2% on 13 different attributes on test set of CelebA. Similarly, we employ PSNR (Peak Signal to Noise Ratio) and SSIM (Structural Similarity) to assess the quality of the synthetic examples.

Compared Methods: To validate our idea, we compare the performance of our GCN induced representations (*gcn-reprs*) with wide ranges of both categorical and continuous types of target attributes encoding methods.

- *One-hot vector:* As mentioned from the beginning, this is the most commonly and widely used conditioning technique for cGANs [9,16,25,26]. Here, the presence and absence of a *target attribute* (*t*) is encoded by i.e. 1 and 0 respectively.
- *Latent Representations (latent-reprs):* [10] proposed to represent presence/absence of a target expression by a positive/negative *d*-dimensional normal random vector for expression manipulation.
- *Word2Vec:* Words embedding [30] to encode target domain information are successfully applied to synthesise image from text [40]. We represented target attributes by the embedding of the attributes labels.
- *Co-occurrence:* We use co-occurrence vectors as representations of target label attributes to obtain an approximate performance comparison to [28]. As, [28] rules were hard coded which is not feasible in our arbitrary attributes manipulation case.
- *Attrbs-weights:* We use attribute model parameters obtained from [26] to represent the target attributes.

As [26] demonstrated the effectiveness of conditioning the difference of target and source attributes one-hot vector (t-s) compared to target attributes one-hot vector (t) alone, we mostly perform our experiments on the difference set up. We call conditioning difference of target and source as Difference (**Diff**) mode and conditioning target only as Standard (**Std**) mode. We employed several *types* of attribute encoding on both the *modes* and report their performances on multiple state-of-the-art GAN architectures (***GAN Archs***): Stargan [9], Attgan [16], STGAN [26], Stargan-JNT [9]. In addition to these conditioning on the generator side, we also proposed to apply Multi-task Learning (**MTL**) on the discriminator side.

Implementation Details: We initialise the nodes of the graph with model parameters of attributes (weight vectors) obtained from pre-trained attribute classifiers [26]. The dimensions of input and output nodes of the graph are 1024 and 128 respectively. GCN has 2 convolution layers. For all the data sets in our experiment, we pre-process and crop image to the size of $128 \times 128 \times 3$.

Quantitative Evaluations

Ablation Studies: We train Stargan [9] on both Std and Diff mode with various types of attribute encodings. We computed TARR on 5 different target attributes viz. hair color *(black, blond, brown)*, gender *(male/female)*, and age *(young/old)* on CelebA, similar to the original paper. Table 1 summarises the performance comparison. Among the four compared condition types (*one-hot vec, co-occurrence, word2vec, attrbs-weights*), *attrbs-weights* obtain the best performance. Thus, we chose *attrb-weights* to initialise nodes of GCN. Please note, nodes can be initialised with any other type of representations. Referring

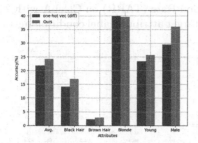

Fig. 4. Perf. comparison on LFWA

Table 1. Avg. TARR due to various types of attribute representations

Condition type	Condition mode		Average
	Std	Diff	
one-hot vec	✓		78.6
one-hot vec		✓	80.2
co-occurrence		✓	78.6
word2vec		✓	81.3
attrbs-weights		✓	81.9
gcn-reprs		✓	**84.0**

to the same Table, we observe GCN induced representations (*gcn-reprs*) out-performing all other compared methods.

Discussion: Semantic representations of attributes: *word2vec* and *attrbs-weights* outperformed *one-hot vec*. *Co-occurrence* also lagged behind the semantic representations as it has no visual information and not optimised for arbitrary attribute manipulations. Please note, [28] designed similar representation for single target attribute. As we know, *word2vec* are learned from the large corpus and bears syntactic and semantic relationships between the words [30]. These are also being useful for attributes classification [2]. *Attrbs-weights* are equipped with higher-order visual information including the spatial location of the attributes (See Fig. 4 from [44]). Finally, *gcn-reprs* benefited from both semantic representations and co-occurrence relationship. Thus, it is essential that conditions hold semantically rich higher-order target attributes characteristics.

MTL at Discriminator: We compare our idea to apply MTL at discriminator side. It is evident that, in MTL, interaction between the tasks is important. Thus, we extend the number of target attributes to 13 for this experiments. First two rows from the second block of Table 2 shows the performance comparison between the baseline w/ and w/o MTL. We observe an overall increase of +1.1% in performance over the baseline. On category level, MTL on the discriminator is outperforming in 9 different attributes out of 13 attributes.

Comparison With Existing Arts: To further validate our idea, we compare our method with multiple state-of-the-art GAN architectures to date in three different quantitative measurements viz. TARR, PSNR and SSIM on three different benchmarks.

Target Attribute Recognition Rate (TARR): Table 2 compares the TARR on CelebA. In the Table, the top block shows the performance of two earlier works: IcGAN [37] and FaderNet [25]. These figures are as reported on [26]. These methods relied on *one-hot vec* type of the target attributes in Std mode as their conditions. The TARR of these methods are modest. In the Second block, we compare the performance of *attrbs-weights, latent-reprs,gcn-repres* with the

Table 2. Comparison of Target Attributes Recognition Rate (TARR) on CelebA with different existing cGANs architectures with different target attribute label conditioning.

GAN Arch.	Condition type	C. mode		Attributes													Average
		Std	Diff	Bald	Bangs	Black hair	Blonde hair	Brown hair	B. eyebrows	Eyeglasses	Mth. Slt. open	Mustache	No beard	Pale skin	Male	Young	
IcGAN [37]	one-hot vec	✓		19.4	74.2	40.6	34.6	19.7	14.7	82.4	78.8	5.5	22.6	41.8	89	37.6	43.2
FaderNet[25]	one-hot vec	✓		1.5	5	27	20.9	15.6	24.2	87.4	44	10	27.2	11.1	48.3	20.3	29.8
Stargan [9] + MTL	one-hot vec	✓		24.4	92.3	59.4	68.9	55.7	50.1	95.7	96.1	18.8	66.6	84	77.1	83.9	67.2
	one-hot vec		✓	22.7	95.4	63	62.3	51.9	58	99.2	98.7	24	52.2	90.5	83.7	86.8	68.3
	one-hot vec		✓	41.9	93.6	74.7	75.2	67.4	65.9	99	95.3	26.8	64.3	86.2	89	89.3	74.5
	latent-reprs	✓		18.4	93.8	68.5	60.9	62.5	69.4	97.0	97.7	14.0	34.4	91.3	78.5	76.7	66.4
	latent-reprs		✓	32.5	93.2	68.9	79.5	71.5	55.3	97.2	98.4	30.0	58.5	85.1	84.0	75.1	71.4
	attrbs-weights		✓	32.7	96.0	74.4	77.5	74.1	66.7	98.8	32.2	78.2	90.9	81.6	98.5	86.7	76.0
+ MTL + MTL + End2End	gcn-reprs		✓	28.2	**99.4**	**76.5**	77.1	70.9	74.2	**99.5**	99.4	37.3	89.6	92	93.4	94.9	79.4
	gcn-reprs		✓	34.4	98.4	73.3	78.6	70.8	**85.5**	**99.5**	99.1	44.2	**90**	92.3	**95.6**	91.7	81.0
	gcn-reprs		✓	**56.6**	98.2	76	**81.1**	**80**	73.4	99.4	**99.5**	50.9	89.1	**94.2**	92	**95**	**83.4**
STGAN [26]	one-hot vec	✓		40.7	92.5	69.5	69.7	59.4	65.2	99.2	95	26.8	69.7	90.8	70	52.8	69.3
	one-hot vec		✓	59.9	**97.7**	93	79	89.9	88.3	99.7	96.7	38.9	93.4	97.0	**98.5**	86.7	86.1
+ MTL + End2End	gcn-reprs		✓	**82.0**	95.5	92.6	**85.4**	82.0	86.2	**99.9**	**99.4**	**55.3**	**98.4**	96.0	98.1	**86.9**	**89.1**
AttGAN [16]	one-hot vec	✓		22.5	93	46.3	40.4	51	49.2	98.6	97	30.3	81.3	84.4	83.3	67.9	65
	one-hot vec		✓	69.1	97.5	78.8	84.4	76.5	73.4	99.6	95.8	34.2	85.8	96.8	95.8	92.9	83
+ MTL + End2End	gcn-reprs		✓	**72.8**	**97.9**	**93.9**	**94.4**	**92.3**	**86.8**	99.8	98.6	48.4	**97.1**	**97.1**	98.5	**96.4**	**90.3**

default conditioning type of Stargan [9] on both the conditioning modes. Simply switching the default type from Std mode to Diff mode improves the TARR from 67.2% to 74.5%. This is the best performance of Stargan reported by [26]. The encoding principle of *latent-reprs* [10] is similar to that of *one hot vec*, as positive and negative random vectors are used instead of 1 and 0. Attribute-specific information rich *attrbs-weights* out-performs these representations. We observe the performance of these representations similar to that of *one-hot vec*. We trained our GCN network to induce *gcn-reprs* and replaced the default conditioning on the generator of Stargan [9] by *gcn-reprs*, the performance improved to 79.4%(+4.9%). Another experiment with the same set-up on the generator and MTL on the discriminator improves the performance to 81.0%(+6.5%). Training GCN and GAN on multi-stage fashion make the representations sub-optimal. Thus, we train GCN and GAN and apply MTL simultaneously and attained an average accuracy of 83.4%, the highest performance reported on Stargan [9]. We also applied our method to two other best performing GAN architecture [16,26] for face attribute manipulations. Last two blocks of the Table 2 compares the performance on these architectures. Similar to that with Stargan [9], instead of existing method of conditioning target attributes and applied ours to both the generator and discriminator and train the model from scratch in an end-to-end fashion. After we applied our method on STGAN [26], which is the state-of-the-art method to date, we improve the mean average performance from 86.1% to 89.1%. Similarly, on Attgan [16] we outperformed the best reported performance by +7.3% and attain the new state-of-the-art performance on CelebA. This is +4.2% above the current state-of-the-art [26]. These results show that our method is agnostic to the cGAN architecture. We also evaluated our method on LFWA. We applied our method to Stargan and compared it to the default conditioning type, *one-hot vec* on Diff mode. Figure 4 shows the TARR. From this figure, we can see our approach outperforming the baseline. If we carefully check the performance of individual attributes on both the benchmarks (Table 2, Fig. 4), our method is substantially outperforming existing arts in attributes such

Table 3. Comparison of PSNR and SSIM with existing arts

GAN Arch.	PSNR ↑		SSIM ↑		Data set
	Before	After	Before	After	
Stargan-JNT [9]	23.82	**28.0**	0.867	**0.944**	RaFD+CelebA
StarGAN [9]	22.80	**27.20**	0.819	**0.897**	CelebA
StarGAN [9]	24.65	**27.96**	0.856	**0.912**	LFWA
AttGAN [16]	24.07	**26.68**	0.841	**0.858**	CelebA

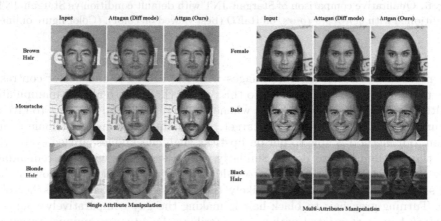

Fig. 5. Qualitative comparison of Attgan [16] (default conditioned with *one-hot vector*) trained on diff mode vs Attgan trained with *gcn-reprs (ours)* trained on diff-mode on CelebA (best viewed on color). (Color figure online)

as *bald, moustache, young, male*. These attributes follows law of nature and it is essential to make natural transition to better retain the target label.

PSNR/SSIM: We compute PSNR and SSIM scores between real and synthetic images and compare the performance between with the counter-parts. In Table 3, the two columns `Before` and `After` show the scores of GANs before and after applying our method respectively. Our approach consistently improves the performance of the counter-parts.

Qualitative Evaluations: To further validate our idea, we performed extensive qualitative analysis. We compare our method over the existing arts on two different scenarios i'e in and across data set attributes transfer.

In Data Set Attribute Transfer: In this scenario, we train a model on train set and evaluate the performance on the test set of the same data set. Figure 5 compares the qualitative outcomes of Attgan [16] conditioned with *one-hot vec* on Diff mode with *gcn-reprs* on the same mode. The left block in the figure shows the result of single target attribute manipulation whereas the right block shows that of multi-attributes manipulation. From the results, we can clearly see that

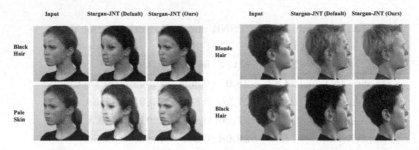

Fig. 6. Qualitative comparison of Stargan-JNT with default condition vs Stargan-JNT conditioned with *gcn-reprs (ours)* on RaFD (best viewed on color). (Color figure online)

our method is able to generate images with less artefacts and better contrast (see the background). In addition to this, our method is also able to manipulate multiple attributes simultaneously, whenever it is meaningful to do so, to give a natural transition from source to target. For example, for male-to-female transition, our method is able to put on lipsticks, high cheekbones, arched eyebrows but the baseline fails to do so. Similarly, wrinkles on face with few remaining grey hair gives natural transition to bald instead just completely removing the hairs from head. As it is highly likely that a person gets bald in his/her old age. Turning grey hair to black hair is making the guy comparatively younger as *black hair* is associated with *young* attribute. Due to such unique strengths of our method, enabled by GCN on the generator and MTL on the discriminator, we observe substantial improvements over the baselines especially in the recognition of certain attributes: *Young, Male, Bald, Moustache* where a natural transition is essential as these are naturally occurring attributes associated with different factors.

Cross Data Set Attributes Transfer: Stargan-JNT [9] propose to train a GAN with multiple data sets having disjoint sets of attributes simultaneously to improve the quality of the cross-data set attribute transfer. We applied our conditioning method to train the network on CelebA and RaFD simultaneously.

And, we compare the performance with their default conditioning method which is *one-hot vec*. Figure 6 shows a few test examples from RaFD and their synthetic images when target attributes are from CelebA. Please note attribute annotations such as *Black Hair, Blonde Hair, Pale Skin* are absent on RaFD train set. From the same figure, we can clearly see that the synthetic images generated by our method are with less artefacts, better contrast and better preservation of the target attributes.

5   Conclusions

We propose a Graph Convolutional Network enabled novel method to induce target attributes embeddings for Conditional GANs on the Generator part. Similarly, we proposed a MTL based structural regularisation mechanism on the discriminator of the GAN. For both of these, we exploit the co-occurrences of the attributes. Finally, we propose a framework to learn them in an end-to-end fashion. We applied our method on multiple existing target label conditioned GANs and evaluated on multiple benchmarks for face attribute manipulations. From our both extensive quantitative and qualitative evaluations, we observed a substantial improvement over the existing arts, attaining new state-of-the-art performance. As a future work, we plan to design a framework to dynamically adjust the co-occurrence distribution of the attributes to synthesize naturally realistic attributes manipulated images.

Acknowledgements. Authors would like to thank EPSRC Programme Grant 'FACER2VM'(EP/N007743/1) for generous support. We would also like to thank Prateek Manocha, undergraduate student from IIT Guwahati for some of the baseline experiments during his summer internship at Imperial College London.

References

1. Arjovsky, M., Chintala, S., Bottou, L.: Wasserstein GAN. arXiv preprint arXiv:1701.07875 (2017)
2. Bhattarai, B., Bodur, R., Kim, T.K.: AugLabel: exploiting word representations to augment labels for face attribute classification. In: ICASSP (2020)
3. Cao, J., Huang, H., Li, Y., Liu, J., He, R., Sun, Z.: Biphasic learning of GANs for high-resolution image-to-image translation. In: CVPR (2019)
4. Cavallanti, G., Cesa-Bianchi, N., Gentile, C.: Linear algorithms for online multitask classification. JMLR **11**, 2901–2934 (2010)
5. Chen, T., Zhai, X., Ritter, M., Lucic, M., Houlsby, N.: Self-supervised GANs via auxiliary rotation loss. In: CVPR (2019)
6. Chen, X., Duan, Y., Houthooft, R., Schulman, J., Sutskever, I., Abbeel, P.: Info-GAN: interpretable representation learning by information maximizing generative adversarial nets. In: NIPS (2016)
7. Chen, Y.C., et al.: Facelet-bank for fast portrait manipulation. In: CVPR (2018)
8. Chen, Z.M., Wei, X.S., Wang, P., Guo, Y.: Multi-label image recognition with graph convolutional networks. In: CVPR (2019)
9. Choi, Y., Choi, M., Kim, M., Ha, J.W., Kim, S., Choo, J.: StarGAN: unified generative adversarial networks for multi-domain image-to-image translation. In: CVPR (2018)
10. Ding, H., Sricharan, K., Chellappa, R.: ExprGAN: facial expression editing with controllable expression intensity. In: AAAI (2018)
11. Gecer, B., Bhattarai, B., Kittler, J., Kim, T.-K.: Semi-supervised adversarial learning to generate photorealistic face images of new identities from 3D morphable model. In: Ferrari, V., Hebert, M., Sminchisescu, C., Weiss, Y. (eds.) ECCV 2018. LNCS, vol. 11215, pp. 230–248. Springer, Cham (2018). https://doi.org/10.1007/978-3-030-01252-6_14
12. Grover, A., Leskovec, J.: Node2vec: scalable feature learning for networks. In: SIGKDD (2016)
13. Gulrajani, I., Ahmed, F., Arjovsky, M., Dumoulin, V., Courville, A.C.: Improved training of Wasserstein GANs. In: NIPS (2017)
14. Hamilton, W., Ying, Z., Leskovec, J.: Inductive representation learning on large graphs. In: NIPS (2017)

15. Hamilton, W.L., Ying, R., Leskovec, J.: Representation learning on graphs: Methods and applications. arXiv preprint arXiv:1709.05584 (2017)
16. He, Z., Zuo, W., Kan, M., Shan, S., Chen, X.: AttGAN: facial attribute editing by only changing what you want. IEEE TIP **28**, 5464–5478 (2019)
17. Hong, S., Yang, D., Choi, J., Lee, H.: Inferring semantic layout for hierarchical text-to-image synthesis. In: CVPR (2018)
18. Huang, X., Liu, M.-Y., Belongie, S., Kautz, J.: Multimodal unsupervised image-to-image translation. In: Ferrari, V., Hebert, M., Sminchisescu, C., Weiss, Y. (eds.) ECCV 2018. LNCS, vol. 11207, pp. 179–196. Springer, Cham (2018). https://doi.org/10.1007/978-3-030-01219-9_11
19. Isola, P., Zhu, J.Y., Zhou, T., Efros, A.A.: Image-to-image translation with conditional adversarial networks. In: CVPR (2017)
20. Kaneko, T., Hiramatsu, K., Kashino, K.: Generative attribute controller with conditional filtered generative adversarial networks. In: CVPR (2017)
21. Kaneko, T., Hiramatsu, K., Kashino, K.: Generative adversarial image synthesis with decision tree latent controller. In: CVPR (2018)
22. Karras, T., Aila, T., Laine, S., Lehtinen, J.: Progressive growing of GANs for improved quality, stability, and variation. In: ICLR (2018)
23. Karras, T., Laine, S., Aila, T.: A style-based generator architecture for generative adversarial networks. In: CVPR (2019)
24. Kipf, T.N., Welling, M.: Semi-supervised classification with graph convolutional networks. In: ICLR (2016)
25. Lample, G., Zeghidour, N., Usunier, N., Bordes, A., Denoyer, L., et al.: Fader networks: manipulating images by sliding attributes. In: NIPS (2017)
26. Liu, M., et al.: STGAN: a unified selective transfer network for arbitrary image attribute editing. In: CVPR (2019)
27. Liu, M.Y., Breuel, T., Kautz, J.: Unsupervised image-to-image translation networks. In: NeurIPS (2017)
28. Liu, Y., Li, Q., Sun, Z.: Attribute-aware face aging with wavelet-based generative adversarial networks. In: CVPR (2019)
29. Maas, A.L., Hannun, A.Y., Ng, A.Y.: Rectifier nonlinearities improve neural network acoustic models. In: ICML (2013)
30. Mikolov, T., Sutskever, I., Chen, K., Corrado, G.S., Dean, J.: Distributed representations of words and phrases and their compositionality. In: NurIPS (2013)
31. Mirza, M., Osindero, S.: Conditional generative adversarial nets. arXiv preprint arXiv:1411.1784 (2014)
32. Miyato, T., Kataoka, T., Koyama, M., Yoshida, Y.: Spectral normalization for generative adversarial networks. In: ICLR (2018)
33. Miyato, T., Koyama, M.: cGANs with projection discriminator. In: ICLR (2018)
34. Nian, F., Chen, X., Yang, S., Lv, G.: Facial attribute recognition with feature decoupling and graph convolutional networks. IEEE Access **7**, 85500–85512 (2019)
35. Odena, A., et al.: Is generator conditioning causally related to GAN performance? In: ICML (2018)
36. Odena, A., Olah, C., Shlens, J.: Conditional image synthesis with auxiliary classifier GANs. In: ICML (2017)
37. Perarnau, G., Van De Weijer, J., Raducanu, B., Álvarez, J.M.: Invertible conditional GANs for image editing. In: NIPSW (2016)
38. Perozzi, B., Al-Rfou, R., Skiena, S.: DeepWalk: online learning of social representations. In: SIGKDD (2014)

39. Pumarola, A., Agudo, A., Martinez, A.M., Sanfeliu, A., Moreno-Noguer, F.: GAN-imation: anatomically-aware facial animation from a single image. In: Ferrari, V., Hebert, M., Sminchisescu, C., Weiss, Y. (eds.) ECCV 2018. LNCS, vol. 11214, pp. 835–851. Springer, Cham (2018). https://doi.org/10.1007/978-3-030-01249-6_50
40. Reed, S., Akata, Z., Yan, X., Logeswaran, L., Schiele, B., Lee, H.: Generative adversarial text to image synthesis (2016)
41. Salimans, T., Goodfellow, I., Zaremba, W., Cheung, V., Radford, A., Chen, X.: Improved techniques for training GANs. In: NIPS (2016)
42. Shen, W., Liu, R.: Learning residual images for face attribute manipulation. In: CVPR (2017)
43. Shmelkov, K., Schmid, C., Alahari, K.: How good is my GAN? In: Ferrari, V., Hebert, M., Sminchisescu, C., Weiss, Y. (eds.) ECCV 2018. LNCS, vol. 11206, pp. 218–234. Springer, Cham (2018). https://doi.org/10.1007/978-3-030-01216-8_14
44. Taherkhani, F., Nasrabadi, N.M., Dawson, J.: A deep face identification network enhanced by facial attributes prediction. In: CVPRW (2018)
45. Tang, J., Qu, M., Wang, M., Zhang, M., Yan, J., Mei, Q.: Line: large-scale information network embedding. In: WWW (2015)
46. Xiao, T., Hong, J., Ma, J.: ELEGANT: exchanging latent encodings with GAN for transferring multiple face attributes. In: Ferrari, V., Hebert, M., Sminchisescu, C., Weiss, Y. (eds.) ECCV 2018. LNCS, vol. 11214, pp. 172–187. Springer, Cham (2018). https://doi.org/10.1007/978-3-030-01249-6_11
47. Zakharov, E., Shysheya, A., Burkov, E., Lempitsky, V.: Few-shot adversarial learning of realistic neural talking head models. arXiv preprint arXiv:1905.08233 (2019)
48. Zhang, G., Kan, M., Shan, S., Chen, X.: Generative adversarial network with spatial attention for face attribute editing. In: Ferrari, V., Hebert, M., Sminchisescu, C., Weiss, Y. (eds.) ECCV 2018. LNCS, vol. 11210, pp. 422–437. Springer, Cham (2018). https://doi.org/10.1007/978-3-030-01231-1_26
49. Zhang, H., et al.: StackGAN: text to photo-realistic image synthesis with stacked generative adversarial networks. In: CVPR (2017)
50. Zhang, Z., Song, Y., Qi, H.: Age progression/regression by conditional adversarial autoencoder. In: CVPR (2017)
51. Zhao, B., Meng, L., Yin, W., Sigal, L.: Image generation from layout. In: CVPR (2019)
52. Zhou, J., Cui, G., Zhang, Z., Yang, C., Liu, Z., Sun, M.: Graph neural networks: A review of methods and applications. arXiv:1812.08434 (2018)

AR-Net: Adaptive Frame Resolution
for Efficient Action Recognition

Yue Meng[1]([✉]), Chung-Ching Lin[1], Rameswar Panda[1], Prasanna Sattigeri[1],
Leonid Karlinsky[1], Aude Oliva[1,3], Kate Saenko[1,2], and Rogerio Feris[1]

[1] MIT-IBM Watson AI Lab, IBM Research, New York, USA
mengyue@ibm.com
[2] Boston University, Boston, USA
[3] Massachusetts Institute of Technology, Cambridge, USA

Abstract. Action recognition is an open and challenging problem in computer vision. While current state-of-the-art models offer excellent recognition results, their computational expense limits their impact for many real-world applications. In this paper, we propose a novel approach, called AR-Net (Adaptive Resolution Network), that selects on-the-fly the optimal resolution for each frame conditioned on the input for efficient action recognition in long untrimmed videos. Specifically, given a video frame, a policy network is used to decide what input resolution should be used for processing by the action recognition model, with the goal of improving both accuracy and efficiency. We efficiently train the policy network jointly with the recognition model using standard back-propagation. Extensive experiments on several challenging action recognition benchmark datasets well demonstrate the efficacy of our proposed approach over state-of-the-art methods. The project page can be found at https://mengyuest.github.io/AR-Net.

Keywords: Efficient action recognition · Multi-resolution processing · Adaptive learning

1 Introduction

Action recognition has attracted intense attention in recent years. Much progress has been made in developing a variety of ways to recognize complex actions, by either applying 2D-CNNs with additional temporal modeling [15,31,54] or 3D-CNNs that model the space and time dimensions jointly [7,25,49]. Despite impressive results on commonly used benchmark datasets, the accuracy obtained by most of these models usually grows proportionally with their complexity and computational cost. This poses an issue for deploying these models in many resource-limited applications such as autonomous vehicles and mobile platforms.

Electronic supplementary material The online version of this chapter (https://doi.org/10.1007/978-3-030-58571-6_6) contains supplementary material, which is available to authorized users.

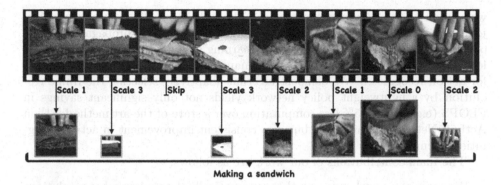

Fig. 1. A conceptual overview of our approach. Rather than processing all the frames at the same resolution, our approach learns a policy to select the optimal resolution (or skip) per frame, that is needed to correctly recognize an action in a given video. As can be seen from the figure, the seventh frame is the most useful frame for recognition, therefore could be processed only with the highest resolution, while the rest of the frames could be processed at lower resolutions or even skipped without losing any accuracy. Best viewed in color. (Color figure online)

Motivated by these applications, extensive studies have been recently conducted for designing compact architectures [2,27,28,44,64] or compressing models [9,13,35,57]. However, most of the existing methods process all the frames in a given video at the same resolution. In particular, orthogonal to the design of compact models, the computational cost of a CNN model also has much to do with the input frame size. To illustrate this, let us consider the video in Fig. 1, represented by eight uniformly sampled frames. We ask, *Do all the frames need to be processed at the highest resolution (e.g., 224 × 224) to recognize the action as "Making a sandwich" in this video?* The answer is clear: No, the seventh frame is the most useful frame for recognition, therefore we could process only this frame at the highest resolution, while the rest of the frames could be processed at lower resolutions or even skipped (i.e., resolution set to zero) without losing any accuracy, resulting in large computational savings compared to processing all the frames with the same 224 × 224 resolution. Thus, in contrast to the commonly used one-size-fits-all scheme, we would like these decisions to be made individually per input frame, leading to different amounts of computation for different videos. Based on this intuition, we present a new perspective for efficient action recognition by adaptively selecting input resolutions, on a per frame basis, for recognizing complex actions.

In this paper, we propose AR-Net, a novel and differentiable approach to learn a decision policy that selects optimal frame resolution conditioned on inputs for efficient action recognition. The policy is sampled from a discrete distribution parameterized by the output of a lightweight neural network (referred to as the policy network), which decides on-the-fly what input resolution should be used on a per frame basis. As these decision functions are discrete and non-differentiable, we rely on a recent Gumbel Softmax sampling approach [29] to learn the policy jointly with the network parameters through standard back-propagation, without resorting to complex reinforcement learning as in [14,62,63]. We design the loss to achieve both competitive performance and resource efficiency required for action recognition. We demonstrate that adaptively selecting the frame resolution by a lightweight policy network yields not only significant savings in FLOPS (e.g., about 45% less computation over a state-of-the-art method [61] on ActivityNet-v1.3 dataset [5]), but also consistent improvement in action recognition accuracy.

The main contributions of our work are as follows:

- We propose a novel approach that automatically determines what resolutions to use per target instance for efficient action recognition.
- We train the policy network jointly with the recognition models using back-propagation through Gumbel Softmax sampling, making it highly efficient.
- We conduct extensive experiments on three benchmark datasets (ActivityNet-V1.3 [5], FCVID [30] and Mini-Kinetics [7]) to demonstrate the superiority of our proposed approach over state-of-the-art methods.

2   Related Works

Efficient Action Recognition. Action recognition has made rapid progress with the introduction of a number of large-scale datasets such as Kinetics [7] and Moments-In-Time [39,40]. Early methods have studied action recognition using shallow classification models such as SVM on top of local visual features extracted from a video [34,53]. In the context of deep neural networks, it is typically performed by either 2D-CNNs [10,17,21,31,46] or 3D-CNNs [7,25,49]. A straightforward but popular approach is the use of 2D-CNNs to extract frame-level features and then model the temporal causality across frames using different aggregation modules such as temporal averaging in TSN [54], a bag of features scheme in TRN [65], channel shifting in TSM [36], depthwise convolutions in TAM [15], non-local neural networks [55], and LSTMs [12]. Many variants of 3D-CNNs such as C3D [49], I3D [7] and ResNet3D [25], that use 3D convolutions to model space and time jointly, have also been introduced for action recognition.

While extensive studies have been conducted in the last few years, limited efforts have been made towards *efficient* action recognition [20,61,62]. Specifically, methods for efficient recognition focus on either designing new lightweight architectures (e.g., R(2+1)D [51], Tiny Video Networks [44], channel-separated CNNs [50]) or selecting salient frames/clips conditioned on the input [20,33,62,63]. Our approach is most related to the latter which focuses on adaptive data sampling and is agnostic to the network architecture used for recognizing actions. Representative methods typically use Reinforcement Learning (RL) where an agent [14,62,63] or multiple agents [59] are trained with policy gradient methods to select relevant video frames, without deciding frame resolution as in our approach. More recently, audio has also been used as an efficient way to select salient frames for action recognition [20,33]. Unlike existing works, our framework requires neither complex RL policy gradients nor additional modalities such as audio. LiteEval [61] proposes a coarse-to-fine framework for resource efficient action recognition that uses a binary gate for selecting either coarse or fine features. In contrast, we address both the selection of optimal frame resolutions and skipping in an unified framework and jointly learn the selection and recognition mechanisms in a fully differentiable manner. Moreover, unlike binary sequential decision being made at every step in LiteEval, our proposed approach has the flexibility in deciding multiple actions in a single step and also the scalability towards long untrimmed videos via multi-step skipping operations. We include a comprehensive comparison to LiteEval in our experiments.

Adaptive Computation. Many adaptive computation methods have been recently proposed with the goal of improving computational efficiency [3,4,23, 52,56]. Several works have been proposed that add decision branches to different layers of CNNs to learn whether to exit the network for faster inference [18,38]. BlockDrop [60] effectively reduces the inference time by learning to dynamically select which layers to execute per sample during inference. Adaptive computation time for recurrent neural networks is also presented in [23]. SpotTune [24] learns to adaptively route information through finetuned or pre-trained layers. Reinforcement learning has been used to adaptively select different regions for fast object detection in large images [19,41]. While our approach is inspired by these methods, in this paper, we focus on adaptive computation in videos, where our goal is to adaptively select optimal frame resolutions for efficient action recognition.

Multi-resolution Processing. Multi-resolution feature representations have a long history in computer vision. Traditional methods include image pyramids [1], scale-space representations [43], and coarse-to-fine approaches [42]. More recently, in the context of deep learning, multi-scale feature representations have been used for detection and recognition of objects at multiple scales [6,37], as well as to speed up deep neural networks [8,37]. Very few approaches have explored multi-scale recognition for efficient video understanding. A two-branch network that fuses the information of high-resolution and low-resolution video frames is proposed in [31]. bLVNet-TAM [15] also uses a two-branch multi-resolution architecture based on the Big-Little Net model [8], while learning long-term temporal dependencies across frames. SlowFast Networks [16] rely on a similar two-branch model, but each branch encodes different frame rates (i.e., different temporal resolutions), as opposed to frames with different spatial resolutions. Unlike these methods, rather than processing video frames at multiple resolutions with specialized network branches, our approach determines optimal resolution for each frame, with the goal of improving accuracy and efficiency.

3   Proposed Method

Given a video dataset $\mathcal{D} = \{(V_i, y_i)\}_{i=1}^{N}$, where each video V_i contains frames with spatial resolution $3 \times H_0 \times W_0$ and is labelled from the predefined classes:

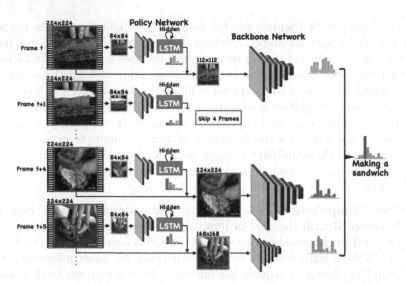

Fig. 2. Illustration of Our Approach. AR-Net consists of a policy network and different backbone networks corresponding to different resolutions. The policy network decides what resolution (or skip) to use on a per frame basis to achieve accuracy and efficiency. In training, policies are sampled from a Gumbel Softmax distribution, which allows to optimize the policy network via backpropagation. During inference, input frames are first fed into the policy network to decide the proper resolutions, then the rescaled frames are routed to corresponding backbones to generate predictions. Finally the network averages all the predictions for action classification. Best viewed in color. (Color figure online)

$y_i \in \mathbb{Y} = \{0, 1, \ldots, C - 1\}$, our goal is to create an adaptive selection strategy that decides, per input frame, which resolution to use for processing by the classifier $\mathcal{F} : \mathbb{V} \rightarrow \mathbb{Y}$ with the goal of improving accuracy and efficiency. To this end, we first present an overview of our approach in Sect. 3.1. Then, we show how we learn the decision policy using Gumbel Softmax sampling in Sect. 3.2. Finally, we discuss the loss functions used for learning the decision policy in Sect. 3.3.

3.1   Approach Overview

Figure 2 illustrates an overview of our approach, which consists of a policy network and backbone networks for classifying actions. The policy network contains a lightweight feature extractor and an LSTM module that decides what resolutions (or skipping) to use per input frame, for efficient action recognition. Inspired by the compound scaling method [48], we adopt different network sizes to handle different resolutions, as a frame with a higher resolution should be processed by a heavier network because of its capability to handle the detailed visual information and vice versa. Furthermore, it is often unnecessary and inefficient to process every frame in a video due to large redundancy coming from static scenes or the frame quality being very low (blur, low-light condition, etc.). Thus, we design a skipping mechanism in addition to the adaptive selection of frame resolutions in an unified framework to skip frames (i.e., resolution set to zero) whenever necessary to further improve the efficiency in action recognition.

During training, the policy network is jointly trained with the recognition models using Gumbel Softmax sampling, as we will describe next. At test time, an input frame is first fed into a policy network, whose output decides the proper resolutions, and then the resized frames are routed to the corresponding models to generate the predictions. Finally, the network averages all the predictions as the action classification result. Note that the additional computational cost is incurred by resizing operations and the policy network, which are negligible in comparison to the original recognition models (the policy network is designed to be very lightweight, e.g., MobileNetv2 in our case).

3.2   Learning the Adaptive Resolution Policy

Adaptive Resolution. AR-Net adaptively chooses different frame scales to achieve efficiency. Denote a sequence of resolutions in descending order as $\{s_i\}_{i=0}^{L-1}$, where $s_0 = (H_0, W_0)$ stands for the original (also the highest) frame resolution, and $s_{L-1} = (H_{L-1}, W_{L-1})$ is the lowest resolution. The frame at time t in the lth scale (resolution $s_l = (H_l, W_l)$) is denoted as I_t^l. We consider skipping frames as a special case "choosing resolutions s_∞". We define the skippings sequence (ascending order) as $\{F_i\}_{i=0}^{M-1}$, where the ith operation means to skip the current frame and the following $(F_i - 1)$ frames from predictions. The choices for resolutions and skippings formulate our action space Ω.

Policy Network. The policy network contains a lightweight feature extractor $\Phi(\cdot; \theta_\Phi)$ and an LSTM module. At time step $t < T$ we resize the frame I_t to the lowest resolution I_t^{L-1} (for efficiency) and send it to the feature extractor,

$$f_t = \Phi(I_t^{L-1}; \theta_\Phi) \tag{1}$$

where f_t is a feature vector and θ_Φ denotes learnable parameters (we use θ_{name} for the learnable parameters in the rest of this section). The LSTM updates hidden state h_t and outputs o_t using the extracted feature and previous states,

$$h_t, o_t = \text{LSTM}(f_t, h_{t-1}, o_{t-1}; \theta_{LSTM}) \tag{2}$$

Given the hidden state, the policy network estimates the policy distribution and samples the action $a_t \in \Omega = \{0, 1, \ldots, L + M - 1\}$ via the Gumbel Softmax operation (will be discussed in the next section),

$$a_t \sim \text{GUMBEL}(h_t, \theta_G) \tag{3}$$

If $a_t < L$, we resize the frame to spatial resolution $3 \times H_{a_t} \times W_{a_t}$ and forward it to the corresponding backbone network $\Psi_{a_t}(\cdot; \theta_{\Psi_{a_t}})$ to get a frame-level prediction,

$$y_t^{a_t} = \Psi_{a_t}(I_t^{a_t}; \theta_{\Psi_{a_t}}) \tag{4}$$

where $I_t^{a_t} \in \mathbb{R}^{3 \times H_{a_t} \times W_{a_t}}$ is the resized frame and $y_t^{a_t} \in \mathbb{R}^C$ is the prediction. Finally, all the frame-level predictions are averaged to generate the video-level prediction y for the given video V.

When the action $a_t >= L$, the backbone networks will skip the current frame for prediction, and the following $(F_{a_t - L} - 1)$ frames will be skipped by the policy network. Moreover, to save the computation, we share the policy network for generating both policy and predictions for the lowest resolution, i.e., $\Psi_{L-1} = \Phi^1$.

Training Using Gumbel Softmax Sampling. AR-Net makes decisions about which resolutions (or skipping) to use per training example. However, the fact that the decision policy is discrete makes the network non-differentiable and therefore difficult to optimize via backpropagation. One common practice is to use a score function estimator (e.g., REINFORCE [22,58]) to avoid back-propagating through the discrete samples. However, due to the undesirable fact that the variance of the score function estimator scales linearly with the discrete variable dimension (even when a variance reduction method is adopted), it is slow to converge in many applications [29,61]. As an alternative, in this paper, we adopt Gumbel-Softmax Sampling [29] to resolve this non-differentiability and enable direct optimization of the discrete policy in an efficient way.

The Gumbel Softmax trick [29] is a simple and effective way to substitute the original non-differentiable sample from a discrete distribution with a differentiable sample from a corresponding Gumbel-Softmax distribution. Specifically, at each time step t, we first generate the logits $z \in \mathbb{R}^{L+M-1}$ from hidden states h_t by a fully-connected layer $z = \text{FC}(h_t, \theta_{FC})$. Then we use Softmax to generate a categorical distribution π_t,

$$\pi_t = \left\{ p_i \;\middle|\; p_i = \frac{\exp(z_i)}{\sum_{j=0}^{L+M-1} \exp(z_j)} \right\} \tag{5}$$

With the Gumbel-Max trick [29], the discrete samples from a categorical distribution are drawn as follows:

$$\hat{p} = \arg\max_i (\log p_i + G_i), \tag{6}$$

where $G_i = -\log(-\log U_i)$ is a standard Gumbel distribution with U_i sampled from a uniform i.i.d distribution $Unif(0,1)$. Due to the non-differentiable property of arg max operation in Eq. 6, the Gumbel Softmax distribution [29] is thus used as a continuous relaxation to arg max. Accordingly, sampling from a Gumbel Softmax distribution allows us to backpropagate from the discrete samples to the policy network. Let $\hat{P}$ be a one hot vector $[\hat{P}_0, \ldots, \hat{P}_{L+M-1}]$:

$$\hat{P}_i = \begin{cases} 1, & \text{if } i = \hat{p} \\ 0, & \text{otherwise} \end{cases} \tag{7}$$

---

[1] The notation here is for brevity. Actually, the output for Φ is a feature vector, whereas the output for Ψ_{L-1} is a prediction. In implementation, we use a fully connected layer after the feature vector to get the prediction.

The one-hot coding of vector $\hat{P}$ is relaxed to a real-valued vector P using softmax:

$$P_i = \frac{\exp((\log p_i + G_i)/\tau)}{\sum_{j=0}^{L+M-1} \exp((\log p_j + G_j)/\tau)}, \qquad i \in [0, \ldots, L+M-1] \qquad (8)$$

where τ is a temperature parameter, which controls the 'smoothness' of the distribution P, as $\lim_{\tau \to +\infty} P$ converges to a uniform distribution and $\lim_{\tau \to 0} P$ becomes a one-hot vector. We set $\tau = 5$ as the initial value and gradually anneal it down to 0 during the training, as in [24].

To summarize, during the forward pass, we sample the decision policy using Eq. 6 (this is equivalent to the process mentioned in Eq. 3 and $\theta_{FC} = \theta_G$) and during the backward pass, we approximate the gradient of the discrete samples by computing the gradient of the continuous softmax relaxation in Eq. 8.

3.3 Loss Functions

During training, we use the standard cross-entropy loss to measure the classification quality as:

$$\mathcal{L}_{acc} = \mathbb{E}_{(V,y) \sim \mathcal{D}_{train}} \left[-y \log(\mathcal{F}(V; \Theta)) \right] \qquad (9)$$

where $\Theta = \{\theta_\Phi, \theta_{LSTM}, \theta_G, \theta_{\Psi_0}, \ldots, \theta_{\Psi_{L-2}}\}$ and (V, y) is the training video sample with associated one-hot encoded label vector. The above loss only optimizes for accuracy without taking efficiency into account. To address computational efficiency, we compute the GFLOPS for each individual module (and specific resolution of frames) offline and formulate a lookup table. We estimate the overall runtime GFLOPS for our network based on the offline lookup table $\text{GFLOPS}_{\mathcal{F}} : \Omega \to \mathbb{R}^+$ and online policy $a_{V,t}$ for each training video $(V, y) \sim \mathcal{D}_{train}$. We use the GFLOPS per frame as a loss term to punish for high-computation operations,

$$\mathcal{L}_{flops} = \mathbb{E}_{(V,y) \sim \mathcal{D}_{train}} \left[\frac{1}{T} \sum_{t=0}^{T-1} \text{FLOPS}_{\mathcal{F}}(a_{V,t}) \right] \qquad (10)$$

Furthermore, to encourage the policy learning to choose more frames for skipping, we add an additional regularization term to enforce a balanced policy usage,

$$\mathcal{L}_{uni} = \sum_{i=0}^{L+M-1} \left(\mathbb{E}_{(V,y) \sim \mathcal{D}_{train}} \left[\frac{1}{T} \sum_{t=0}^{T-1} \mathbb{1}(a_{V,t} = i) \right] - \frac{1}{L+M} \right)^2 \qquad (11)$$

where $\mathbb{1}(\cdot)$ is the indicator function. Here $\mathbb{E}_{(V,y) \sim \mathcal{D}_{train}} \left[\frac{1}{T} \sum_{t=0}^{T-1} \mathbb{1}(a_{V,t} = i) \right]$ represents the frequency of action i being made through the dataset. Intuitively, this loss function term drives the network to balance the policy usage in order to obtain a high entropy for the action distribution. To sum up, our final loss function for the training becomes:

$$\mathcal{L} = (1 - \alpha) \cdot \mathcal{L}_{acc} + \alpha \cdot \mathcal{L}_{flops} + \beta \cdot \mathcal{L}_{uni} \qquad (12)$$

where α denotes respective loss weight for the computing efficiency, and β controls the weight for the regularization term.

4   Experiments

In this section, we conduct extensive experiments to show that our model outperforms many strong baselines while significantly reducing the computation budget. We first show that our model-agnostic AR-Net boosts the performance of existing 2D CNN architectures (ResNet [26], EfficientNet [48]) and then show our method outperforms the State-of-the-art approaches for efficient video understanding. Finally, we conduct comprehensive experiments on ablation studies and qualitative analysis to verify the effectiveness of our policy learning.

4.1   Experimental Setup

Datasets. We evaluate our approach on three large-scale action recognition datasets: ActivityNet-v1.3 [5], FCVID(Fudan-Columbia Video Dataset) [30] and Mini-Kinetics [32]. ActivityNet [5] is labelled with 200 action categories and contains 10,024 videos for training and 4,926 videos for validation with an average duration of 117 s. FCVID [30] has 91,223 videos (45,611 videos for training and 45,612 videos for testing) with 239 label classes and the average length is 167 s. Mini-Kinetics dataset contains randomly selected 200 classes and 131,082 videos from Kinetics dataset [32]. We use 121,215 videos for training and 9,867 videos for testing. The average duration is 10 s.

Implementation Details. We uniformly sample $T = 16$ frames from each video. During training, images are randomly cropped to 224×224 patches with augmentation. At the inference stage, the images are rescaled to 256×256 and center-cropped to 224×224. We use four different frame resolutions ($L = 4$) and three skipping strategies ($M = 3$) as the action space. Our backbones network consists of ResNet-50 [26], ResNet-34 [26], ResNet-18 [26], and MobileNetv2 [45], corresponding to the input resolutions 224×224, 168×168, 112×112, and 84×84 respectively. The MobileNetv2 [45] is re-used and combined with a single-layer LSTM (with 512 hidden units) to serve as the policy network. The policy network can choose to skip 1, 2 or 4 frames.

Policy learning in the first stage is extremely sensitive to initialization of the policy. We observe that optimizing for both accuracy and efficiency is not effective with a randomly initialized policy. Thus, we divide The training process into 3 stages: warm-up, joint-training and fine-tuning. For warm-up, we fix the policy network and only train the backbones network (pretrained from ImageNet [11]) for 10 epochs with learning rate 0.02. Then the whole pipeline is jointly trained for 50 epochs with learning rate 0.001. After that, we fix the policy network parameters and fine-tune the backbones networks for 50 epochs with a lower learning rate of 0.0005. We set the initial temperature τ to 5, and gradually anneal it with an exponential decay factor of -0.045 in every epoch [29]. We choose $\alpha = 0.1$ and $\beta = 0.3$ for the loss function and use SGD [47] with momentum 0.9 for optimization. We will make our source code and models publicly available.

Baselines. We compare with the following baselines and existing approaches:

- UNIFORM: averages the frame-level predictions at the highest resolution 224×224 from ResNet-50 as the video-level prediction.
- LSTM: updates ResNet-50 predictions at the highest resolution 224×224 by hidden states and averages all predictions as the video-level prediction.
- RANDOM: uses our backbone framework but randomly samples policy actions from uniform distribution (instead of using learned policy distribution).
- Multi-Scale: gathers the frame-level predictions by processing different resolutions through our backbone framework (instead of selecting an optimal resolution with one corresponding backbone at each time step). This serves as a very strong baseline for classification, at the cost of heavy computation.
- AdaFrame [62]: uses MobileNetV2/ResNet-101 as lightweight CNN/backbone.
- LiteEval [61]: uses MobileNetV2/ResNet-101 as Policy Network/backbone.
- ListenToLook(Image) [20]: we compared with a variant of their approach with only the visual modality (MobileNetv2|ResNet-101). We also report other results obtained by using audio data as an extra modality in Fig. 3.
- SCSampler [33]: as official code is not available, we re-implemented the SCSampler using AC loss as mentioned in [33]. We choose MobileNetv2 as the sampler network and use ResNet-50 as the backbone. We select 10 frames out of 16 frames for prediction, as in [33].

Metrics. We compute the mAP (mean average precision) and estimate the GFLOPS(gigabyte floating point operations per second) to reflect the performance for efficient video understanding. Ideally, a good system should have a high mAP with only a small amount of GFLOPS used during the inference stage. Since different baseline methods use different number of frames for classification, we calculate both GFLOPS per frame (denoted as GFLOPS/f) and GFLOPS per video (denoted as GFLOPS/V) in the following experiments.

4.2 Main Results

Adaptive Resolution Policy improves 2D CNN. We first compare our AR-Net with several simple baselines on ActivityNet and FCVID datasets to show how much performance our adaptive approach can boost in 2D convolution networks. We verify our method on both ResNet [26] and EfficientNet [48] to show the improvement is not limited to model architectures. As shown in Table 1,

Table 1. Action recognition results (in mAP and GFLOPS) on ActivityNet-v1.3 and FCVID. Our method consistently outperforms all simple baselines

Approach	Arch	ActivityNet-v1.3			FCVID		
		mAP(%)	GFLOPS/f	GFLOPS/V	mAP(%)	GFLOPS/f	GFLOPS/V
Uniform	ResNet	72.5	4.11	65.76	81.0	4.11	65.76
LSTM		71.2	4.12	65.89	81.1	4.12	65.89
Random policy		65.0	**1.04**	**16.57**	75.3	**1.03**	**16.49**
Multi-Scale		<u>73.5</u>	6.90	110.43	**81.3**	6.90	110.43
AR-Net		**73.8**	<u>2.09</u>	<u>33.47</u>	**81.3**	<u>2.19</u>	<u>35.12</u>
Uniform	Efficient Net	78.8	1.80	28.80	83.5	1.80	28.80
LSTM		78.0	1.81	28.88	83.7	1.81	28.88
Random policy		72.5	**0.38**	**6.11**	79.7	**0.38**	**6.11**
Multi-Scale		<u>79.5</u>	2.35	37.56	<u>84.2</u>	2.35	37.56
AR-Net		**79.7**	<u>0.96</u>	<u>15.29</u>	**84.4**	<u>0.88</u>	<u>14.06</u>

Table 2. SOTA efficient methods comparison on ActivityNet-v1.3 and FCVID

Approach	ActivityNet-v1.3			FCVID		
	mAP(%)	GFLOPS/f	GFLOPS/V	mAP(%)	GFLOPS/f	GFLOPS/V
AdaFrame [62]	71.5	3.16	78.97	80.2	3.01	75.13
LiteEval [61]	72.7	3.80	95.10	80.0	3.77	94.30
ListenToLook(Image) [20]	72.3	5.09	81.36	-	-	-
SCSampler [33]	72.9	2.62	41.95	81.0	2.62	41.95
AR-Net(ResNet)	**73.8**	**2.09**	**33.47**	**81.3**	**2.19**	**35.12**
AR-Net(EfficientNet)	**79.7**	**0.96**	**15.29**	**84.4**	**0.88**	**14.06**

comparing to traditional "Uniform" and "LSTM" methods, we save 50% of the computation while getting a better classification performance.

We further show that it is the adaptively choosing resolutions and skippings that helps the most for efficient video understanding tasks. Taking ResNet architecture as an example, "Random Policy" can only reach 65.0% mAP on ActivityNet and 75.3% on FCVID, whereas AR-Net using learned policy can reach 73.8% and 81.3% respectively. Specifically, "Multi-Scale" can be a very strong baseline because it gathers all the predictions from multi-scale inputs through multiple backbones. It is noticeable that AR-Net's classification performance is comparable to the "Multi-Scale" baseline, while using 70% less computation. One possible explanation is that there exist noisy and misleading frames in the videos, and AR-Net learns to skip those frames and uses the rest of the frames for prediction. Similar conclusion can also be drawn from using EfficientNet architectures, which shows our approach is model-agnostic.

Adaptive Resolution Policy Outperforms State-of-the-Art Methods. We compare the performance of AR-Net with several state-of-the-art methods on ActivityNet and FCVID in Table 2. The result section of the table is divided into two parts. The upper part contains all the methods using Residual Network architecture, whereas the lower part shows the best result we have achieved by using the latest EfficientNet [48] architecture. Usually it is hard to improve

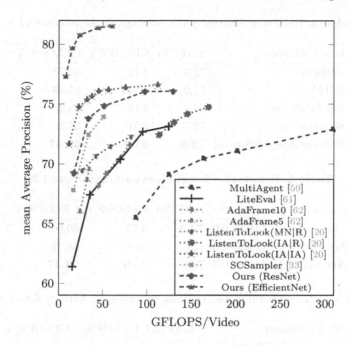

Fig. 3. Comparisons with state-of-the-art alternatives on ActivityNet dataset. Our proposed AR-Net obtains the best recognition accuracy with much fewer GFLOPS than the compared methods. We directly quote the numbers reported in published papers when possible and compare the mAP against the average GFLOPs per test video. See text for more details.

Table 3. Results for video classification on Mini-Kinetics dataset

Approach	Mini-Kinetics		
	Top1(%)	GFLOPS/f	GFLOPS/V
LiteEval [61]	61.0	3.96	99.00
SCSampler [33]	70.8	2.62	41.95
AR-Net(ResNet)	**71.7**	**2.00**	**32.00**
AR-Net(EfficientNet)	**74.8**	**1.02**	**16.32**

the classification accuracy while maintaining a low computation cost, but our "AR-Net(ResNet)" outperforms all the state-of-the-art methods in terms of mAP scores, frame-level GFLOPS and video-level GFLOPS. Our method achieves 73.8% mAP on ActivityNet and 81.3% mAP on FCVID while using 17%–64% less computation budgets compared with other approaches. This shows the power of our adaptive resolution learning approach in efficient video understanding tasks. When integrated with EfficientNet [48], our "AR-Net(EfficientNet)" further gains 5.9% in mAP on ActivityNet and 3.1% on FCVID, with 54%–60% less computation compared to "AR-Net(ResNet)". Since

Table 4. Results of different policy settings on ActivityNet-v1.3

Policy settings	mAP(%)	GFLOPS/f	GFLOPS/V
Uniform	72.5	4.11	65.76
LSTM	71.2	4.12	65.89
Resolution only	73.4	2.13	34.08
Skipping only	72.7	2.21	34.90
Resolution+Skipping	**73.8**	**2.09**	**33.47**

Table 5. Results of different losses on ActivityNet-v1.3

Losses	α	β	mAP(%)	GFLOPS/f	GFLOPS/V
Acc	0.0	0.0	**74.5**	3.75	60.06
Acc+Eff	0.1	0.0	73.8	2.28	36.48
Acc+Eff+Uni	0.1	0.3	73.8	**2.09**	**33.47**

Table 6. Results of different training strategies on ActivityNet-v1.3

Training strategy			mAP(%)	GFLOPS/f	GFLOPS/V
Warm-up	Joint	Finetuning			
✗	✓	✗	67.1	1.16	17.86
✓	✓	✗	73.3	2.03	32.40
✓	✓	✓	73.8	2.09	33.47

there is no published result using EfficientNet for efficient video understanding, these results can serve as the new baselines for future research.

Figure 3 illustrates the GFLOPS-mAP curve on ActivityNet dataset, where our AR-Net obtains significant computational efficiency and action recognition accuracy with much fewer GFLOPS than other baseline methods. We quote the reported results on MultiAgent [59], AdaFrame[62] and ListenToLook[20] (here "(IA|R)" and "(MN|R)" are short for "(Image-Audio|ResNet-101)" and "(MobileNetV2|ResNet-101)" mentioned in [20]). The results of LiteEval [61] are generated through the codes shared by the authors, and the results of SCSampler [33] are obtained by our re-implementation following their reported details. ListenToLook (IA|R) denotes models using both visual and audio data as inputs. Given the same ResNet architectural family, our approach achieves substantial improvement compared to the best competitors, demonstrating the superiority of our method. Additionally, our best performing model, which employs EfficientNet [48] architecture, yields more than 5% improvement in mAP at the same computation budgets. It shows that our approach of adaptively selecting proper resolutions on a per frame basis is able to yield significant savings in computation budget and to improve recognition precision.

Further Experiment on Mini-Kinetics. To further test the capability of our method, we conduct experiments on Mini-Kinetics dataset. Compared with the recent methods LiteEval [61] and SCSampler [33], our method achieves better Top-1 accuracy and the computation cost is reduced with noticeable margin. In brief, our method consistently outperform the existing methods in terms of accuracy and speed on different datasets, which implies our AR-Net provides an effective framework for various action recognition applications (Table 3).

4.3   Ablation Studies

Effectiveness of Choosing Resolution and Skipping. Here we inspect how each type of operation enhances the efficient video understanding. We define three different action spaces: "Resolution Only" (the policy network can only choose different resolutions), "Skipping Only" (the policy network can only decide how many frames to skip) and "Resolution+Skipping". We follow the same training procedures as illustrated in Sect. 4.1 and evaluate each approach on ActivityNet dataset. We adjust the training loss to keep their GFLOPS at the same level and we only compare the differences in classification performances. As shown in Table 4, comparing with baseline methods ("Uniform" and "LSTM"), they all improve the performance, and the best strategy is to combine skippings and choosing resolutions. Intuitively, skipping can be seen as "choosing zero resolution" for the current frame, hence gives more flexibility in decision-making.

Trade-off Between Accuracy and Efficiency. As discussed in Sect. 3.3, hyper-parameters α and β in Eq. 12 affect the classification performance, efficiency and policy distribution. Here we train our model using 3 different weighted combinations: "Acc" (only using accuracy-related loss), "Acc+Eff" (using accuracy and efficiency losses) and "Acc+Eff+Uni" (using all the losses). As shown in Table 5, training with "Acc" will achieve the highest mAP, but the computation cost will be similar to "Uniform" method (GFLOPS/V = 65.76). Adding the efficiency loss term will decrease the computation cost drastically, whereas training with "Acc+Eff+Uni" will drop the GFLOPS even further. One reason is that the network tends to skip more frames in the inference stage. Finally, we use hyper-parameters $\alpha = 0.1$, $\beta = 0.3$ in our training.

Different Training Strategies. We explore several strategies for training the adaptive learning framework. As shown in Table 6, the best practice comes from "Warm-Up+Joint+Finetuning" so we adopt it in training our models.

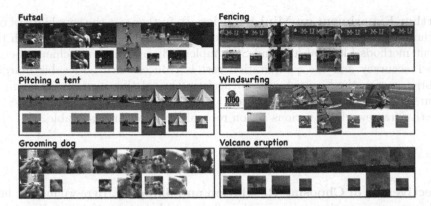

Fig. 4. Qualitative examples from ActivityNet and FCVID. We uniformly sample 8 frames per video and AR-Net chooses the proper resolutions or skipping. Relevant frames are kept in original resolution whereas non-informative frames are resized to lower resolution or skipped for computation efficiency.

4.4 Qualitative Analysis

An intuitive view of how AR-Net achieves efficiency is shown in Fig. 4. We conduct experiments on ActivityNet-v1.3 and FCVID testing sets. Videos are uniformly sampled in 8 frames. The upper row of each example shows original input frames, and the lower row shows the frames processed by our policy network for predictions. AR-Net keeps the most indicative frames (e.g. Futsal and Fencing) in original resolution and resizes or skips frames that are irrelevant or in low quality (blurriness). After being confident about the predictions, AR-Net will avoid using the original resolution even if informative contents appear again (e.g. Pitching a tent/Windsurfing). The last two examples show that AR-Net is able to capture both object-interaction (clipper-dog) and background changes.

5 Conclusion

We have demonstrated the power of adaptive resolution learning on a per frame basis for efficient video action recognition. Comprehensive experiments show that our method can work in a full range of accuracy-speed operating points, from a version that is both faster and more accurate than comparable visual-only models to a new, state-of-the-art accuracy-throughput version based on the EfficientNet [48] architecture. The proposed learning framework is model-agnostic, which allows applications to various sophisticated backbone networks and the idea can be generally adopted to explore other complex video understanding tasks.

Acknowledgement. This work is supported by IARPA via DOI/IBC contract number D17PC00341. The U.S. Government is authorized to reproduce and distribute reprints for Governmental purposes notwithstanding any copyright annotation thereon. This work is partly supported by the MIT-IBM Watson AI Lab.

References

1. Adelson, E.H., Anderson, C.H., Bergen, J.R., Burt, P.J., Ogden, J.M.: Pyramid methods in image processing. RCA Eng. **29**(6), 33–41 (1984)
2. Araujo, A., Negrevergne, B., Chevaleyre, Y., Atif, J.: Training compact deep learning models for video classification using circulant matrices. In: Leal-Taixé, L., Roth, S. (eds.) ECCV 2018. LNCS, vol. 11132, pp. 271–286. Springer, Cham (2019). https://doi.org/10.1007/978-3-030-11018-5_25
3. Bengio, E., Bacon, P.L., Pineau, J., Precup, D.: Conditional computation in neural networks for faster models. arXiv preprint arXiv:1511.06297 (2015)
4. Bengio, Y., Léonard, N., Courville, A.: Estimating or propagating gradients through stochastic neurons for conditional computation. arXiv preprint arXiv:1308.3432 (2013)
5. Caba Heilbron, F., Escorcia, V., Ghanem, B., Carlos Niebles, J.: ActivityNet: a large-scale video benchmark for human activity understanding. In: Proceedings of the IEEE Conference on Computer Vision and Pattern Recognition, pp. 961–970 (2015)
6. Cai, Z., Fan, Q., Feris, R.S., Vasconcelos, N.: A unified multi-scale deep convolutional neural network for fast object detection. In: Leibe, B., Matas, J., Sebe, N., Welling, M. (eds.) ECCV 2016. LNCS, vol. 9908, pp. 354–370. Springer, Cham (2016). https://doi.org/10.1007/978-3-319-46493-0_22
7. Carreira, J., Zisserman, A.: Quo Vadis, action recognition? A new model and the kinetics dataset. In: proceedings of the IEEE Conference on Computer Vision and Pattern Recognition, pp. 6299–6308 (2017)
8. Chen, C.F., Fan, Q., Mallinar, N., Sercu, T., Feris, R.: Big-little net: An efficient multi-scale feature representation for visual and speech recognition. arXiv preprint arXiv:1807.03848 (2018)
9. Chen, W., Wilson, J., Tyree, S., Weinberger, K., Chen, Y.: Compressing neural networks with the hashing trick. In: International Conference on Machine Learning, pp. 2285–2294 (2015)
10. Chéron, G., Laptev, I., Schmid, C.: P-CNN: pose-based CNN features for action recognition. In: Proceedings of the IEEE International Conference on Computer Vision, pp. 3218–3226 (2015)
11. Deng, J., Dong, W., Socher, R., Li, L.J., Li, K., Fei-Fei, L.: ImageNet: a large-scale hierarchical image database. In: 2009 IEEE Conference on Computer Vision and Pattern Recognition, pp. 248–255. IEEE (2009)
12. Donahue, J., et al.: Long-term recurrent convolutional networks for visual recognition and description. In: Proceedings of the IEEE Conference on Computer Vision and Pattern Recognition, pp. 2625–2634 (2015)
13. Dong, X., Huang, J., Yang, Y., Yan, S.: More is less: a more complicated network with less inference complexity. In: Proceedings of the IEEE Conference on Computer Vision and Pattern Recognition, pp. 5840–5848 (2017)
14. Fan, H., Xu, Z., Zhu, L., Yan, C., Ge, J., Yang, Y.: Watching a small portion could be as good as watching all: towards efficient video classification. In: IJCAI International Joint Conference on Artificial Intelligence (2018)
15. Fan, Q., Chen, C.F.R., Kuehne, H., Pistoia, M., Cox, D.: More is less: learning efficient video representations by big-little network and depthwise temporal aggregation. In: Advances in Neural Information Processing Systems, pp. 2261–2270 (2019)

16. Feichtenhofer, C., Fan, H., Malik, J., He, K.: Slowfast networks for video recognition. In: Proceedings of the IEEE International Conference on Computer Vision, pp. 6202–6211 (2019)
17. Feichtenhofer, C., Pinz, A., Wildes, R.P.: Spatiotemporal multiplier networks for video action recognition. In: Proceedings of the IEEE Conference on Computer Vision and Pattern Recognition, pp. 4768–4777 (2017)
18. Figurnov, M., et al.: Spatially adaptive computation time for residual networks. In: Proceedings of the IEEE Conference on Computer Vision and Pattern Recognition, pp. 1039–1048 (2017)
19. Gao, M., Yu, R., Li, A., Morariu, V.I., Davis, L.S.: Dynamic zoom-in network for fast object detection in large images. In: Proceedings of the IEEE Conference on Computer Vision and Pattern Recognition, pp. 6926–6935 (2018)
20. Gao, R., Oh, T.H., Grauman, K., Torresani, L.: Listen to look: Action recognition by previewing audio. arXiv preprint arXiv:1912.04487 (2019)
21. Gkioxari, G., Malik, J.: Finding action tubes. In: Proceedings of the IEEE Conference on Computer Vision and Pattern Recognition, pp. 759–768 (2015)
22. Glynn, P.W.: Likelihood ratio gradient estimation for stochastic systems. Commun. ACM **33**(10), 75–84 (1990)
23. Graves, A.: Adaptive computation time for recurrent neural networks. arXiv preprint arXiv:1603.08983 (2016)
24. Guo, Y., Shi, H., Kumar, A., Grauman, K., Rosing, T., Feris, R.: SpotTune: transfer learning through adaptive fine-tuning. In: Proceedings of the IEEE Conference on Computer Vision and Pattern Recognition, pp. 4805–4814 (2019)
25. Hara, K., Kataoka, H., Satoh, Y.: Can spatiotemporal 3D CNNs retrace the history of 2D CNNs and ImageNet? In: Proceedings of the IEEE conference on Computer Vision and Pattern Recognition, pp. 6546–6555 (2018)
26. He, K., Zhang, X., Ren, S., Sun, J.: Deep residual learning for image recognition. In: Proceedings of the IEEE Conference on Computer Vision and Pattern Recognition, pp. 770–778 (2016)
27. Howard, A.G., et al.: MobileNets: Efficient convolutional neural networks for mobile vision applications. arXiv preprint arXiv:1704.04861 (2017)
28. Iandola, F.N., Han, S., Moskewicz, M.W., Ashraf, K., Dally, W.J., Keutzer, K.: SqueezeNet: Alexnet-level accuracy with 50x fewer parameters and <0.5 mb model size. arXiv preprint arXiv:1602.07360 (2016)
29. Jang, E., Gu, S., Poole, B.: Categorical reparameterization with Gumbel-Softmax. arXiv preprint arXiv:1611.01144 (2016)
30. Jiang, Y.G., Wu, Z., Wang, J., Xue, X., Chang, S.F.: Exploiting feature and class relationships in video categorization with regularized deep neural networks. IEEE Trans. Pattern Anal. Mach. Intell. **40**(2), 352–364 (2017)
31. Karpathy, A., Toderici, G., Shetty, S., Leung, T., Sukthankar, R., Fei-Fei, L.: Large-scale video classification with convolutional neural networks. In: Proceedings of the IEEE Conference on Computer Vision and Pattern Recognition, pp. 1725–1732 (2014)
32. Kay, W., et al.: The kinetics human action video dataset. arXiv preprint arXiv:1705.06950 (2017)
33. Korbar, B., Tran, D., Torresani, L.: SCSampler: sampling salient clips from video for efficient action recognition. In: Proceedings of the IEEE International Conference on Computer Vision, pp. 6232–6242 (2019)
34. Laptev, I., Marszalek, M., Schmid, C., Rozenfeld, B.: Learning realistic human actions from movies. In: 2008 IEEE Conference on Computer Vision and Pattern Recognition, pp. 1–8. IEEE (2008)

35. Li, H., Kadav, A., Durdanovic, I., Samet, H., Graf, H.P.: Pruning filters for efficient ConvNets. arXiv preprint arXiv:1608.08710 (2016)
36. Lin, J., Gan, C., Han, S.: TSM: temporal shift module for efficient video understanding. In: Proceedings of the IEEE International Conference on Computer Vision, pp. 7083–7093 (2019)
37. Lin, T.Y., Dollár, P., Girshick, R., He, K., Hariharan, B., Belongie, S.: Feature pyramid networks for object detection. In: Proceedings of the IEEE Conference on Computer Vision and Pattern Recognition, pp. 2117–2125 (2017)
38. McGill, M., Perona, P.: Deciding how to decide: dynamic routing in artificial neural networks. In: Proceedings of the 34th International Conference on Machine Learning, vol. 70, pp. 2363–2372 (2017)
39. Monfort, M., et al.: Moments in time dataset: one million videos for event understanding. IEEE Trans. Pattern Anal. Mach. Intell. $42(2)$, 502–508 (2019)
40. Monfort, M., et al.: Multi-moments in time: Learning and interpreting models for multi-action video understanding. arXiv preprint arXiv:1911.00232 (2019)
41. Najibi, M., Singh, B., Davis, L.S.: AutoFocus: efficient multi-scale inference. In: Proceedings of the IEEE International Conference on Computer Vision, pp. 9745–9755 (2019)
42. Pedersoli, M., Vedaldi, A., Gonzalez, J., Roca, X.: A coarse-to-fine approach for fast deformable object detection. Pattern Recogn. $48(5)$, 1844–1853 (2015)
43. Perona, P., Malik, J.: Scale-space and edge detection using anisotropic diffusion. IEEE Trans. Pattern Anal. Mach. Intell. $12(7)$, 629–639 (1990)
44. Piergiovanni, A., Angelova, A., Ryoo, M.S.: Tiny video networks. arXiv preprint arXiv:1910.06961 (2019)
45. Sandler, M., Howard, A., Zhu, M., Zhmoginov, A., Chen, L.C.: MobileNetV2: inverted residuals and linear bottlenecks. In: Proceedings of the IEEE Conference on Computer Vision and Pattern Recognition, pp. 4510–4520 (2018)
46. Simonyan, K., Zisserman, A.: Two-stream convolutional networks for action recognition in videos. In: Advances in Neural Information Processing Systems, pp. 568–576 (2014)
47. Sutskever, I., Martens, J., Dahl, G., Hinton, G.: On the importance of initialization and momentum in deep learning. In: International Conference on Machine Learning, pp. 1139–1147 (2013)
48. Tan, M., Le, Q.V.: EfficientNet: Rethinking model scaling for convolutional neural networks. arXiv preprint arXiv:1905.11946 (2019)
49. Tran, D., Bourdev, L., Fergus, R., Torresani, L., Paluri, M.: Learning spatiotemporal features with 3D convolutional networks. In: Proceedings of the IEEE International Conference on Computer Vision, pp. 4489–4497 (2015)
50. Tran, D., Wang, H., Torresani, L., Feiszli, M.: Video classification with channel-separated convolutional networks. In: Proceedings of the IEEE International Conference on Computer Vision, pp. 5552–5561 (2019)
51. Tran, D., Wang, H., Torresani, L., Ray, J., LeCun, Y., Paluri, M.: A closer look at spatiotemporal convolutions for action recognition. In: Proceedings of the IEEE conference on Computer Vision and Pattern Recognition, pp. 6450–6459 (2018)
52. Veit, A., Belongie, S.: Convolutional networks with adaptive inference graphs. In: Ferrari, V., Hebert, M., Sminchisescu, C., Weiss, Y. (eds.) ECCV 2018. LNCS, vol. 11205, pp. 3–18. Springer, Cham (2018). https://doi.org/10.1007/978-3-030-01246-5_1
53. Wang, H., Kläser, A., Schmid, C., Liu, C.L.: Action recognition by dense trajectories. In: CVPR 2011, pp. 3169–3176. IEEE (2011)

54. Wang, L., et al.: Temporal segment networks: towards good practices for deep action recognition. In: Leibe, B., Matas, J., Sebe, N., Welling, M. (eds.) ECCV 2016. LNCS, vol. 9912, pp. 20–36. Springer, Cham (2016). https://doi.org/10.1007/978-3-319-46484-8_2

55. Wang, X., Girshick, R., Gupta, A., He, K.: Non-local neural networks. In: Proceedings of the IEEE Conference on Computer Vision and Pattern Recognition, pp. 7794–7803 (2018)

56. Wang, X., Yu, F., Dou, Z.-Y., Darrell, T., Gonzalez, J.E.: SkipNet: learning dynamic routing in convolutional networks. In: Ferrari, V., Hebert, M., Sminchisescu, C., Weiss, Y. (eds.) ECCV 2018. LNCS, vol. 11217, pp. 420–436. Springer, Cham (2018). https://doi.org/10.1007/978-3-030-01261-8_25

57. Wen, W., Xu, C., Wu, C., Wang, Y., Chen, Y., Li, H.: Coordinating filters for faster deep neural networks. In: Proceedings of the IEEE International Conference on Computer Vision, pp. 658–666 (2017)

58. Williams, R.J.: Simple statistical gradient-following algorithms for connectionist reinforcement learning. Mach. Learn. 8(3–4), 229–256 (1992)

59. Wu, W., He, D., Tan, X., Chen, S., Wen, S.: Multi-agent reinforcement learning based frame sampling for effective untrimmed video recognition. In: Proceedings of the IEEE International Conference on Computer Vision, pp. 6222–6231 (2019)

60. Wu, Z., et al.: BlockDrop: dynamic inference paths in residual networks. In: Proceedings of the IEEE Conference on Computer Vision and Pattern Recognition, pp. 8817–8826 (2018)

61. Wu, Z., Xiong, C., Jiang, Y.G., Davis, L.S.: LiteEval: a coarse-to-fine framework for resource efficient video recognition. In: Advances in Neural Information Processing Systems, pp. 7778–7787 (2019)

62. Wu, Z., Xiong, C., Ma, C.Y., Socher, R., Davis, L.S.: AdaFrame: adaptive frame selection for fast video recognition. In: Proceedings of the IEEE Conference on Computer Vision and Pattern Recognition, pp. 1278–1287 (2019)

63. Yeung, S., Russakovsky, O., Mori, G., Fei-Fei, L.: End-to-end learning of action detection from frame glimpses in videos. In: Proceedings of the IEEE Conference on Computer Vision and Pattern Recognition, pp. 2678–2687 (2016)

64. Zhang, X., Zhou, X., Lin, M., Sun, J.: ShuffleNet: an extremely efficient convolutional neural network for mobile devices. In: Proceedings of the IEEE Conference on Computer Vision and Pattern Recognition, pp. 6848–6856 (2018)

65. Zhou, B., Andonian, A., Oliva, A., Torralba, A.: Temporal relational reasoning in videos. In: Ferrari, V., Hebert, M., Sminchisescu, C., Weiss, Y. (eds.) ECCV 2018. LNCS, vol. 11205, pp. 831–846. Springer, Cham (2018). https://doi.org/10.1007/978-3-030-01246-5_49

Image-to-Voxel Model Translation for 3D Scene Reconstruction and Segmentation

Vladimir V. Kniaz[1,2], Vladimir A. Knyaz[1,2]([envelope]), Fabio Remondino[3],
Artem Bordodymov[1], and Petr Moshkantsev[1]

[1] State Research Institute of Aviation Systems (GosNIIAS), Moscow, Russia
{knyaz,vl.kniaz,bordodymov,moshkantsev}@gosniias.ru
[2] Moscow Institute of Physics and Technology (MIPT), Dolgoprudny, Russia
[3] Bruno Kessler Foundation (FBK), Trento, Italy
remondino@fbk.eu

Abstract. Objects class, depth, and shape are instantly reconstructed by a human looking at a 2D image. While modern deep models solve each of these challenging tasks separately, they struggle to perform simultaneous scene 3D reconstruction and segmentation. We propose a single shot image-to-semantic voxel model translation framework. We train a generator adversarially against a discriminator that verifies the object's poses. Furthermore, trapezium-shaped voxels, volumetric residual blocks, and 2D-to-3D skip connections facilitate our model learning explicit reasoning about 3D scene structure. We collected a SemanticVoxels dataset with 116k images, ground-truth semantic voxel models, depth maps, and 6D object poses. Experiments on ShapeNet and our SemanticVoxels datasets demonstrate that our framework achieves and surpasses state-of-the-art in the reconstruction of scenes with multiple non-rigid objects of different classes. We made our model and dataset publicly available (http://www.zefirus.org/SSZ).

Keywords: Single photo 3D reconstruction · 3D semantic segmentation

1 Introduction

While humans live and navigate in the 3D world, they reason about it semantically. Given only a class of an object, a human could easily imagine its 3D shape. Object's class, depth, and shape are closely related to each other, and a deep model should reason explicitly about them to truly understand a 3D scene.

There have been exciting recent progress in single image 3D object reconstruction [1–4]. While modern models can reconstruct the human body [5] or arbitrary object [3] from a single view, they are usually focused on the prediction of a single instance of a single object class. Recently proposed multilayer

Electronic supplementary material The online version of this chapter (https://doi.org/10.1007/978-3-030-58571-6_7) contains supplementary material, which is available to authorized users.

Fig. 1. Image-to-semantic voxel model translation using our SSZ model. Input color image (left), 2D-to-3D contour alignment (center), semantic voxel model output (right).

depth maps [6] make a step towards the 3D reconstruction of the whole scene. Still, they do not provide semantic labeling of the 3D scene. On the other hand, 3D scene semantic segmentation models [7] require a 3D model as input.

In this paper, we propose a Single Shot Z-space segmentation and 3D reconstruction model (SSZ) for single image-to-semantic voxel model translation. Different from modern baselines, our SSZ model performs joint 3D voxel model reconstruction and 3D scene semantic segmentation from a single image. Moreover, a modern architecture based on volumetric residual blocks allows our SSZ model to provide near-real-time performance at inference.

We hypothesize that semantic labeling of 3D object classes could aid a deep model learning explicit reasoning about 3D scene structure. To this end, we propose a multiclass semantic voxel model that represents the whole 3D scene visible by the camera. In our semantic voxel model, each voxel holds the ID of its class. Moreover, we leverage trapezium-shaped voxels to keep each voxel aligned with a corresponding pixel (see Fig. 1). Such 3D representation allows us to design direct 2D-to-3D skip connections, that leverage contour correspondences between an image and a 3D model. We use assumptions of Ronneberger et al. [8] and Sandler et al. [9] as a starting point to incorporate a U-net-like generator with inverted residuals blocks and skip connections into our framework.

Generative modeling [10] of 3D shapes has demonstrated promising progress recently [11]. Inspired by adversarial learning of 3D shapes, we incorporate a 3D pose discriminator into our framework. Specifically, we simultaneously train two models: an SSZ generator and an adversarial Pose6DoF discriminator (see Fig. 2). The aim of our Pose6DoF discriminator is twofold. Firstly, it estimates the poses of all object instances in the SSZ generator's output. Secondly, it qualifies each object instance as either being 'real' or 'fake.' The aim of our SSZ generator is fooling the discriminator Pose6DoF by producing a realistic and geometrically accurate semantic voxel model.

We collected a large SemanticVoxels dataset to train and evaluate our model and baselines. Our SemanticVoxels dataset includes 116k color images and pixel-level aligned semantic voxel models of nine object classes: person, car, truck, van, bus, building, tree, bicycle, ground.

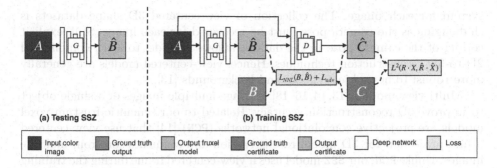

Fig. 2. SSZ framework.

Experiments on our SemanticVoxels dataset and various public benchmarks demonstrate that our SSZ model achieves the state-of-the-art in single-image 3D scene reconstruction. We show quantitative and qualitative results demonstrating our SSZ model ability to reconstruct a detailed voxel model of the whole scene from a single image. Moreover, our SSZ model produces both high-resolution 3D model and multiclass 3D semantic segmentation from a single image.

The developed model will be able to estimate shape, pose, and a class of all objects in the scene in such applications such as autonomous driving, robotics, and single photo 3D scene reconstruction.

We present four key technical contributions: (1) An SSZ generator architecture for single-shot 3D scene reconstruction and segmentation from a single image with 2D-to-3D skip connections and volumetric inverted residual blocks, (2) a generative-adversarial framework for training a volumetric generator against 6DoF pose reasoning discriminator, (3) a large SemanticVoxels dataset with 116k samples. Each sample includes color image, view-centered semantic voxel model, depth map, pose annotations of nine objects classes: person, car, truck, van, bus, building, tree, bicycle, ground, (4) an evaluation of our SSZ model and state-of-the-art baselines on ShapeNet, and our SemanticVoxels dataset.

2   Related Work

Single-Photo 3D Reconstruction. Deep networks for generation of 3D models from a single photo fall into two groups: object-centered models [12] and view-centered models [2, 3, 6, 13]. Object-centered models [12] reconstruct object 3D model in the same coordinate system for any camera pose with respect to the object. While the object-centered setting is generally easier in terms of data collection and model structure, most of the object-centered models fail to generalize to new object classes. The main reason for this is the absence of explicit reasoning about connections between object shape in the image and the reconstructed 3D shape.

View-centered models [1, 3, 13–15] overcome this problem using paired datasets. Such datasets include a separate 3D model in the camera coordinate system for each image. The collection of view-centered 3D shape datasets is challenging as the camera pose must be recovered for each image. Still, explicit coding of the camera pose in the dataset al.lows a model to learn complicated 2D-to-3D reconstruction techniques. Hence, view-centered models are generally more robust to new object classes and backgrounds [13].

Multi-view models [13,14,16–18] leverage multiple images of a single object to improve 3D reconstruction accuracy. Related to our semantic frustum voxel models are projective convolutional networks (PCN) [14] that use view-centered frame projection for 3D model reconstruction and segmentation from multiple images. Unlike PCN, our SSZ model uses a view-centered frame during the training time. Closely related to our Pose6DoF discriminator is geometric adversarial loss (GAL) [19] focused on the consistency of reconstructed 3D shapes. Unlike the GAL, our pose adversarial loss function is designed for multiple objects and focused on the scene structure.

3D Model Representations. While images are commonly represented as multichannel 2D tensors to train deep models, volumetric 3D shapes are more challenging to incorporate in deep learning pipeline. Therefore 3D reconstruction deep models could be divided into groups by the 3D model representation they use. **Voxel Models** divide object space into equal volume elements that encode probability p of space being either empty or occupied by an object. While voxel models are the most straightforward data representation for volumetric convolutional neural networks [12,20–31], they consume large amounts of GPU memory. Hence, the resolution of most modern methods is limited to $128 \times 128 \times 128$ voxels. Matryoshka networks [32] overcome this problem leveraging a memory-efficient shape encoding, which recursively decomposes a 3D shape into nested shape layers. Leveraging the semantic annotations for improving 3D reconstruction accuracy demonstrated promising results recently [33]. **Depth Maps** estimation methods [6,34–38] are closely connected to 3D model reconstruction. Still, only the visible surface of the object is being reconstructed in such methods. Closely related to our SSZ model is the property of depth maps to preserve contour correspondence between the input image and the reconstructed depth map. This correspondence allows using of skip connections between generator layers [8,39] to increase model resolution and robustness to new object classes. **Deformable Meshes** allow to use polygonal models for network training [40–48]. While this representation consumes less GPU memory than voxel models, it is best suited for symmetric, smooth objects such as hair [42] or human face [35,49–53]. The semantic description of the scene at the object level [54] is related to multiclass semantic voxel models in our SSZ model. Similar to our semantic voxel model is 3D-RCNN [55] for instance-level 3D object reconstruction. Unlike 3D-RCNN, our SSZ is a single-shot detector. **Frustum Voxel Models** [56–58] are similar to voxel models but utilize view-oriented projection similar to depth maps. Being designed specifically for single-photo 3D reconstruction, frustum voxel models (fruxel models) can significantly improve model performance for generator with skip connections. In this paper, we extend the fruxel model 3D representations for multiclass 3D scene reconstruction. We train our generator to produce tensors of $n \times w \times h \times d$ elements, where n is the number of classes, w, h, d number of elements for the width, height, and depth of a fruxel model.

3   Method

Our goal is training an SSZ generator $G : (A) \to B$ translating an input image A into a multiclass frustum voxel model of the scene F. Specifically, for an input image $A \in \mathbb{R}^{w \times h \times 3}$ our model predicts a probability tensor $B \in [0,1]^{n \times w \times h \times d}$, where n is the number of classes. Each element in B represents a probability $p(x, y, z)$ of point with coordinates (x, y, z) belonging to object class i. We found the resulting fruxel model $F \in \{0, 1, \ldots, n - 1\}^{w \times h \times d}$ as an $\arg\max$ of the probability map B.

$$F(x, y, z) = \arg\max_{i} B(i, x, y, z). \tag{1}$$

Inspired by generative models for 3D reconstruction, we train two models simultaneously: a generator network G and an adversarial discriminator D (see Fig. 2). The aim of our Pose6DoF discriminator $D : (A, F) \to C$ is predicting a certificate $C \in \{t, q, r\}^{u,v,w}$, where u, v, w is dimensions of the discriminator output, $t \in R^3$ is object translation in the view-centered coordinate frame, $q \in R^4$ is the object rotation quaternion, $r \in [0, 1]$ is the probability of object being 'real' or 'fake'. Certificate C describes the poses of object instances in the scene and qualifies them as either 'real' or 'fake.' The aim of our generator G is generating a realistic and geometrically accurate semantic voxel model F. To this end, the objective of our generator G is maximizing the probability of discriminator D making a mistake in certificate C qualifying a synthesized semantic voxel $\hat{F}$ as a real sample F from the training dataset. On the other hand, the generator is forced to minimize the error between ground truth object poses (t, q) and the predicted poses $(\hat{t}, \hat{q})$.

Two loss functions govern the training process of our framework: a negative log-likelihood loss $\mathcal{L}_{NLL}(B, \hat{B})$ and a pose adversarial loss $\mathcal{L}_{adv}(C, \hat{C})$. Inspired by the efficiency of negative log-likelihood loss for the task of 2D semantic segmentation [59], we leverage a similar loss function for our 3D semantic labeling. The aim of our $\mathcal{L}_{NLL}(B, \hat{B})$ loss is maximizing the probability $p(x, y, z)$ of voxel being labeled with the correct object class

$$\mathcal{L}_{NLL}(B, \hat{B}) = \frac{1}{q \cdot w \cdot h \cdot d} \sum_{x=0}^{w} \sum_{y=0}^{h} \sum_{z=0}^{d} \sum_{i=0}^{n} -k_i \cdot \log\left(\hat{B}(f, x, y, z)\right), \tag{2}$$

where k_i is a scalar weight of an object class i, $q = \sum_{i=0}^{n} k_i$ is the sum of weights for all classes, $f = F(x, y, z)$ is the index of the correct object class for point (x, y, z), $\sum_{f=1}^{n} \hat{B}(f, x, y, z) = 1$. The negative log-likelihood loss introduces a penalty only for voxels, where the predicted class does not equal to the target class. Hence, under such an objective, the voxels representing the empty space of the scene could be filled with any class without any penalty. To avoid such a scenario, we use an additional 'air' class that forces the loss function to include empty voxels in the training process.

We firstly present our semantic frustum voxel, in Sect. 3.1, and then discuss our SSZ generator in Sect. 3.2. After that, in Sect. 3.3, we introduce our Pose6DoF discriminator that provides the adversarial loss. Finally, we present our SemanticVoxels dataset in Sect. 3.4.

3.1   Semantic Frustum Voxel Model

Unlike the rectangular voxel model, the fruxel model leverages trapezium-shaped voxels. The trapezium of each fruxel lies on the ray that connects a pixel on the sensor matrix and a point on an object (see Fig. 3). Let $I = \{0, 1, \ldots, n-1\}$ be the set of n classes that the deep model has to predict in the image. Then the semantic voxel model $F \in \{0, 1, \ldots, n-1\}^{w \times h \times d}$ is a 3D tensor in which each element contains the index $i \in I$ of the class of an object located in the given fruxel.

To this end, the fruxel model can be regarded as a multilayer 3D semantic segmentation. Each slice is a boolean intersection of an object and a thin box orthogonal to the camera optical axis located at a given distance. A fruxel model can be described by the following set of parameters $\{z_n, z_f, d, \alpha\}$, where z_n is the distance from the camera to the nearest frustum clipping plane, z_f is the distance to the far clipping plane, d is the number of slices, and α is the camera's horizontal field of view (see Fig. 3).

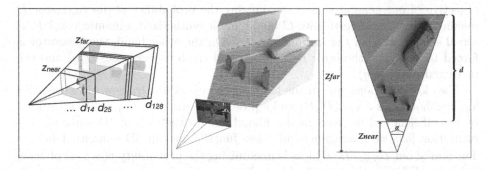

Fig. 3. Frustum voxel model: Slices generation by the boolean intersection of a cutting plane with 3D objects (left). A 3D model composed of trapezium-shaped elements (middle). Top view illustrating fruxel model parameters (right).

3.2   SSZ Generator

A defining feature of image-to-voxel translation problems is that they transform high-resolution 2D features to their 3D counterparts. While such translation can be achieved using hidden embedded representations [12], explicit feature translation using skip connections improves model generalization ability. We use assumptions made by Ronneberger et al. [8] and Sandler et al. [9] as a starting point for our SSZ generator. Namely, we connect the corresponding layers of an encoder and a decoder using skip connections that we term 'copy-inflate.'

While feature maps in the encoder are 3D tensors $M_e \in R^{w \times h \times c}$, their corresponding feature maps in the decoder are 4D tensors $M_d \in R^{w \times h \times d \times c}$, where c is the number of channels in a feature map. To match the dimensions, our 'copy-inflate' skip connections expand the new dimension by copying d times 2D slices of each channel in an encoder feature map M_e. While the 'copy-inflate' connection does not add new information to the expanded feature maps M_d, the pixel level contour correspondence between M_e and M_d allows the model to reason explicitly about relationships between 2D contours and the corresponding 3D shape.

We build the encoder and decoder of our model using inverted residual blocks [60,61]. This stimulates effective gradient propagation through our model. Moreover, modified inverted residual blocks allow near real-time inference time of the trained model. Each block of the encoder includes inverted residual blocks similar to [61] and an additional pointwise and depthwise convolutions that downscale the feature map.

We use volumetric inverted residual blocks to construct our decoder. Each volumetric inverted residual block includes a volumetric depth separable deconvolution layer followed by a Leaky ReLU activation and a pointwise volumetric convolution. We believe that depth separable convolution in our volumetric inverted residual blocks facilitates learning diverse filters for 2D and 3D features maps. The resulting generator architecture is presented in Fig. 4.

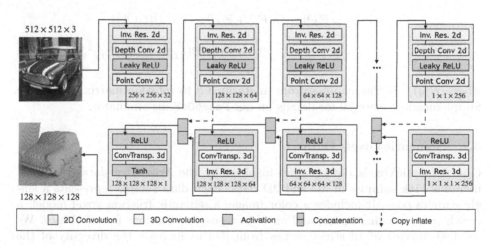

Fig. 4. SSZ generator.

3.3 Pose6DoF Discriminator

Our Pose6DoF discriminator aims to provide an adversarial loss function focused on the pose accuracy of the objects predicted by our SSZ generator. Different from modern volumetric discriminators [11], that qualify the input voxel model as being either 'real' or 'fake,' our Pose6DoF discriminator estimates 6DoF poses of objects in the scene and their perceptual realism. Hence, the architecture of our Pose6DoF discriminator fuses a pose estimation model and a discriminator.

We hypothesize that on additional pose term in an adversarial loss will facilitate the accuracy of our SSZ generator in terms of depth estimation. During training, our Pose6DoF discriminator receives either real fruxel model F from the dataset or a generator output $\hat{F}$. The objective of our Pose6DoF discriminator is twofold. Firstly, it must detect all instances of objects of all classes and predict their 6DoF poses. Secondly, for each instance it must predict if the instance is 'real' or 'fake.'

We use a PatchGAN discriminator [39] as a starting point for our Pose6DoF discriminator. Specifically, our architecture is similar to the encoder part of our SSZ generator with 2D convolutions replaced by volumetric convolutions. Our Pose6DoF is a conditional discriminator $D : (A, F) \rightarrow C$ that receives an image A and fruxel model F concatenated to a single tensor. Given the input (A, F) the model predicts a certificate $C \in \{t, q, r\}^{u,v,w}$. The discriminator output's structure is inspired by single-shot object detection models [62].

The aim of our adversarial loss $\mathcal{L}_{adv}(G, D)$ is twofold. Firstly, it introduces a penalty for incorrect object poses. Secondly, it penalizes unrealistic 3D object instances predicted by G

$$\mathcal{L}_{adv}(G, D) = \mathbb{E}_F[\log D(F)] + \mathbb{E}_A[\log(1 - D(G(A))] \\ + \sum_{j=0}^{m} \|R(\hat{q}_j)\hat{t}_j - R(q_j)t_j\|^2, \tag{3}$$

where $R(q)$ – is the mapping from quaternion q to rotation matrix. Please see Supplementary material for details on our Pose6DoF discriminator.

3.4 SemanticVoxels Dataset

Our SemanticVoxels dataset was inspired by the VoxelCity dataset [56]. It includes 116k samples of 3D and 2D data. Each data sample represents a single camera pose. It includes a color image, a semantic frustum voxel model, a depth map, a camera pose, and an object pose annotations for all classes. We used 8k images of 10 street scenes from [56] to increase the diversity of the dataset. SemanticVoxels dataset make the following contributions to the VoxelCity dataset: (1) 8k new real images of 20 street scenes, (2) 100k synthetic images of 200 scenes, (3) 116k new semantic voxel annotations for 9 object classes

We made our dataset consistent with the NuScenes dataset format [63]. Our dataset is divided into two splits: real and synthetic. The real split was generated using a Structure-from-Motion (SfM) technique similar to [64,65]. It contains

16k images. We present additional details on our SemanticVoxels dataset in the Supplementary material. Example scenes from the dataset are shown in Fig. 5.

Fig. 5. Examples of color images with 6D pose annotations and ground truth semantic voxel models from our SemanticVoxels dataset.

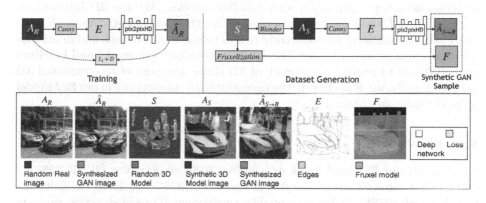

Fig. 6. Synthetic data generation using GAN. Training pix2pixHD to generate realistic color images from edges (left). Generating paired data samples by rendering a non-realistic 3D model A_S, calculating its edges E, and generating a realistic GAN image $\hat{A}_{S \to R}$ (right).

Synthetic Data Generation Using GANs. Generation of 3D datasets is challenging if it is required to obtain paired images and view-centered 3D models [66]. To overcome this problem, we developed a method based on generative modeling. Inspired by recent advances in generating realistic images from object contours [67–70], we hypothesize that object edges are very similar for real images and non-realistic images generated using the 3D model. Therefore, a ground truth color image for a voxel model could be generated from edges of a 3D model rendered in a non-realistic setup. Our pipeline is presented in Fig. 6.

Firstly, we generate a training dataset from random images of objects of given classes from the COCO dataset [71]. For each real image A, we generate contours E using a Canny operator [72]. We train the pix2pixHD [67] model on the task of edges-to-image translation.

We generate the dataset samples by creating virtual scenes S containing 3D models of various classes of objects. For each scene, we render a non-realistic image of the scene A_S and a corresponding frustum voxel model F. We extract the edges E from the image A_S and generate a realistic color image $\hat{A}_{S \rightarrow R}$ using the pix2pixHD [67] model.

4   Experiments

We evaluate our SSZ model and baselines on our SemanticVoxels dataset, the ShapeNet dataset [73], and the ScanNet dataset [74]. We train all models on the train split of ShapeNet and our SemanticVoxels datasets for the tasks of outdoor single photo 3D reconstruction. For the task of 3D Semantic Scene Completion, we use train and test splits of ScanNet dataset [74]. While our SSZ model simultaneously predicts voxel models for N classes of objects, all baselines predict only single class of object for a single photo. Therefore, we perform per-class accuracy compassion with baselines models. We use 3D Intersection over Union (IoU) metric. Our experiments are threefold. Firstly, we perform a qualitative evaluation to demonstrate rich 3D scene model details and multiclass reconstruction provided by our SSZ. Then, we evaluate our model and baselines quantitatively to prove the accuracy of 3D shape and pose of reconstructed 3D models. Finally, we demonstrate the necessity of all components in our SSZ model by performing an ablation study.

4.1   Baselines

We compare our SSZ model to four baselines DISN [4], Pix2Vox [3], 3D-R2N2 [2] and one 3D semantic scene completion baseline TS3DSC [75]. Deep Implicit Surface Network (DISN) [4] for high-quality single-view 3D reconstruction predicts a high-quality detail-rich 3D mesh from a single 2D image. The DISN model allows capturing the holes in a 3D shape using signed distance fields. Pix2Vox [3] exploits an encoder-decoder architecture to generate a coarse 3D volumes and refine them using a fusion block. 3D-R2N2 [2] utilizes a view-based generator that allows tackling single or multiview reconstruction problem. Two Stream 3D Semantic Scene Completion (TS3DSC) [75] leverages two stream model that uses the input depth and color modalities to perform semantic segmentation of indoor scenes. We train DISN, [3], 3D-R2N2 and our SSZ model on train splits of ShapeNet and our SemanticVoxels datasets. We train TS3DSC and our SSZ model on train split of ScanNet. We test all models on the test split of ShapeNet, Scan-Net and our SemanticVoxels datasets.

4.2   Training Details

Our SSZ framework was trained on the SemanticVoxels dataset using the PyTorch library [76]. For training on the ShapeNet dataset, we convert ground truth 3D models to fruxel models with parameters $\{z_n = 3, z_f = 10, d = 128, \alpha = 60°\}$. For training on the SemanticVoxels dataset, we use fruxel models with parameters $\{z_n = 2, z_f = 12, d = 128, \alpha = 40°\}$. The training was performed using the NVIDIA 2080 RTX GPU and took 82 h for the ShapeNet dataset and 173 h for our SemanticVoxels dataset. For network optimization, we use minibatch SGD with an Adam solver. We set the learning rate to 0.0002 with momentum parameters $\beta_1 = 0.5$, $\beta_2 = 0.999$ similar to [39].

4.3   Qualitative Evaluation

We evaluate our model and baselines qualitatively by reconstructing 3D scenes with multiple objects from single images. None of the compared baselines can to perform semantic segmentation of the resulting 3D model. Hence, to perform a fair evaluation, we extract a single class from our resulting fruxel model and compare it to the output of baselines. Qualitative results for ShapeNet [73] dataset are presented in Fig. 7. Pix2Vox and 3D-R2N2 models are the best competing baselines demonstrating the correct structure of the 3D shape. While the DISN model attempts to reconstruct the interior structure of the 3D model, its shape differs from the ground-truth model. The voxel model generated by our SSZ framework demonstrates more details and pose correspondence to the input image. The results for our SemanticVoxels dataset are presented in Fig. 8. Unlike the ShapeNet dataset our, SemanticVoxels dataset includes images with multiple objects. During the training stage, we use single-class ground truth 3D models for baselines. We select the 3D model of the object that occupies the largest area in the image. Only the Pix2Vox model can reconstruct the rough shape of the object. We believe that our 'copy-inflate' skip connections allow our model to reconstruct 3D scenes with multiple images. For more qualitative results on our SemanticVoxels dataset, see Supplementary material. Qualitative results for ScanNet [74] are given in Fig. 9. While the baseline TS3DSC [75] model receives both depth and color information as an input, our SSZ model still leverages only single color input image. Still our framework outperforms the TS3DSC both in fine details and number of reconstructed object classes.

4.4   Quantitative Results

We compare quantitative results in terms of 3D IoU. We present per-class 3D IoU for the ShapeNet dataset in Table 1. Pix2Vox and 3D-R2N2 are the next best performing models after our SSZ model. Pix2Vox model performs the best on plane models and boat models outperforming our model for these classes. Our SSZ model demonstrates the best mean IoU compared to baselines. Quantitative results on our SemanticVoxels dataset demonstrate that our SSZ model successfully reconstructs complex scenes with multiple non-rigid objects of different

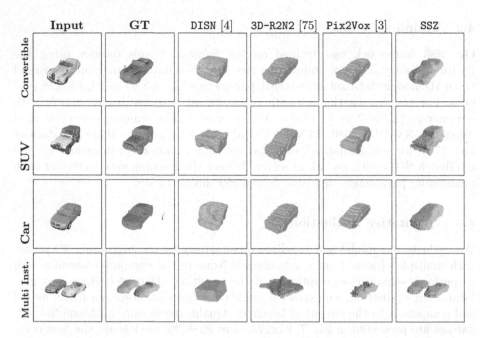

Fig. 7. Examples of 3D reconstruction using DISN [4], Pix2Vox [3], 3D-R2N2 [2], and our SSZ model on ShapeNet [77] dataset. Note that all baselines fail to reconstruct multi instance input images.

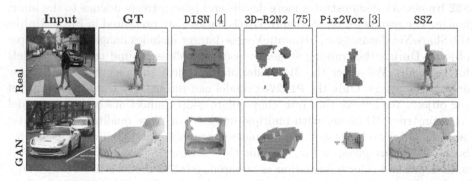

Fig. 8. Example of 3D reconstruction using DISN [4], Pix2Vox [3], 3D-R2N2 [2] and our SSZ on our SemanticVoxels dataset.

classes (see Table 2). 3D-R2N2 is the next best performing model for challenging non-rigid classes such as a human. Pix2Vox model demonstrates the next best results in mean IoU. Our SSZ model demonstrates best results in reconstructing non-rigid objects with complex structures such as humans.

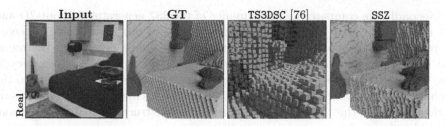

Fig. 9. Example of 3D reconstruction using **TS3DSC** [75] and our **SSZ** on ScanNet [74] dataset.

Table 1. Per-category IoU for different object classes for ShapeNet images.

Object class									
Method	Car	SUV	Conv.	Bike	Bus	Truck	Plane	Boat	Mean
DISN [4]	0.563	0.484	0.427	0.487	0.531	0.522	0.575	0.559	0.519
3D-R2N2 [13]	0.698	0.722	0.515	0.312	0.468	0.455	0.513	0.513	0.525
Pix2Vox [3]	0.732	0.714	0.577	0.356	0.471	0.465	**0.598**	**0.582**	0.562
SSZ	**0.804**	**0.745**	**0.653**	**0.531**	**0.562**	**0.518**	0.558	0.539	**0.614**
SSZ no 6D	0.597	0.586	0.463	0.393	0.412	0.386	0.408	0.395	0.455
SSZ no IR2D	0.682	0.598	0.544	0.433	0.474	0.428	0.457	0.431	0.506
SSZ no IR2D3D	0.594	0.604	0.474	0.429	0.418	0.401	0.441	0.390	0.469

Table 2. Per-category IoU for different object classes on our SemanticVoxels dataset.

Object Class									
Method	Person	Car	Van	Build.	Bicycle	Bus	Truck	Tree	Ground	Mean
DISN [4]	0.128	0.270	0.272	0.213	0.171	0.121	0.142	0.178	0.298	0.199
3D-R2N2 [3]	0.225	0.354	0.341	0.214	0.278	0.169	0.138	0.101	0.194	0.224
Pix2Vox [13]	0.140	0.286	0.247	0.306	0.246	0.267	0.256	0.282	0.253	0.254
SSZ	**0.618**	**0.822**	**0.745**	**0.585**	**0.531**	**0.662**	**0.518**	**0.558**	**0.539**	**0.620**
SSZ no 6D	0.452	0.611	0.538	0.440	0.407	0.495	0.400	0.418	0.380	0.461
SSZ no IR2D	0.502	0.702	0.604	0.458	0.000	0.558	0.432	0.469	0.436	0.462
SSZ no IR2D3D	0.499	0.611	0.607	0.433	0.000	0.505	0.388	0.430	0.438	0.435

4.5 Ablation Studies

We evaluate the necessity of all components of our model by performing 3D scene reconstructions using an ablated version of our model. We firstly remove our `Pose6DoF` discriminator to check the geometric accuracy of the reconstructed scene (see Fig. 10). The qualitative comparison demonstrates that the ablated version of our model introduces distortions of the scene geometry. Therefore, our pose loss forces the generator to learn to reconstruct invisible parts of an object and their dimensions along the camera's optical axis.

Secondly, we compare the performance of the SSZ generator without 2D and 3D inverted residual blocks. The ablated version of our model fails to reconstruct textureless objects such as ground and fine shape details. Furthermore, the ablated version could not reconstruct rare object classes such as bicycle (see Table 2). Therefore, all components of our SSZ framework contribute to the accuracy of the trained generator that allows it to achieve the state-of-the-art performance for the task of single-photo 3D reconstruction of multiclass nonrigid objects.

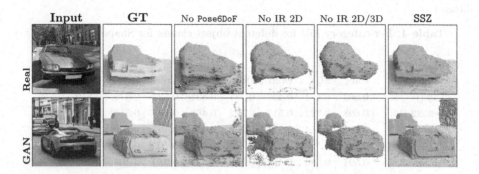

Fig. 10. Evaluation of ablated versions of our SSZ model.

5   Conclusions

We demonstrated that volumetric residual blocks could learn reconstruction and segmentation of 3D scenes from a single image. Furthermore, our frustum voxel model 3D scene representation allows using 2D-to-3D skip connections, facilitating the generalization ability of our SSZ model and robust reconstruction of previously unseen objects. Our main observation is that multiclass 3D scene reconstruction and semantic segmentation requires a similar number of model parameters compared to single class image-to-voxel model translation task. Moreover, rich semantic data in the training dataset al.lows our model to reason explicitly about geometric relationships between object classes.

Compared to state-of-the-art image-to-voxel model translation models, our SSZ framework surpasses leading results in both 3D IoU and pose accuracy for multiclass 3D scene reconstruction. Moreover, our SSZ model is end-to-end trainable. While modern GPUs pose hardware challenges for increasing voxel model resolution, graph convolution networks demonstrate promising results in voxel model super-resolution. The development of a mixed image-to-voxel model with graph convolution super-resolution is an exciting project that requires further work.

Acknowledgments. The reported study was funded by Russian Foundation for Basic Research (RFBR) according to the research project N° 17-29-04509.

References

1. Tatarchenko, M., Dosovitskiy, A., Brox, T.: Octree generating networks: efficient convolutional architectures for high-resolution 3D outputs. In: IEEE International Conference on Computer Vision, ICCV 2017, Venice, Italy, 22–29 October 2017, pp. 2107–2115 (2017)
2. Choy, C.B., Xu, D., Gwak, J.Y., Chen, K., Savarese, S.: 3D-R2N2: a unified approach for single and multi-view 3D object reconstruction. In: Leibe, B., Matas, J., Sebe, N., Welling, M. (eds.) ECCV 2016. LNCS, vol. 9912, pp. 628–644. Springer, Cham (2016). https://doi.org/10.1007/978-3-319-46484-8_38. As references [2] and [75] are same, we have deleted the duplicate reference and renumbered accordingly. Please check and confirm.
3. Xie, H., Yao, H., Sun, X., Zhou, S., Zhang, S.: Pix2Vox: context-aware 3D reconstruction from single and multi-view images. In: The IEEE International Conference on Computer Vision (ICCV) (October 2019)
4. Xu, Q., Wang, W., Ceylan, D., Mech, R., Neumann, U.: DISN: deep implicit surface network for high-quality single-view 3D reconstruction. In Wallach, H., Larochelle, H., Beygelzimer, A., dÁlché-Buc, F., Fox, E., Garnett, R. (eds.) Advances in Neural Information Processing Systems, vol. 32, pp. 492–502. Curran Associates, Inc. (2019)
5. Jackson, A.S., Manafas, C., Tzimiropoulos, G.: 3D human body reconstruction from a single image via volumetric regression. In: Leal-Taixé, L., Roth, S. (eds.) ECCV 2018. LNCS, vol. 11132, pp. 64–77. Springer, Cham (2019). https://doi.org/10.1007/978-3-030-11018-5_6
6. Shin, D., Ren, Z., Sudderth, E.B., Fowlkes, C.C.: 3D scene reconstruction with multi-layer depth and epipolar transformers. In: The IEEE International Conference on Computer Vision (ICCV) (October 2019)
7. Choy, C.B., Gwak, J., Savarese, S.: 4D spatio-temporal ConvNets: Minkowski convolutional neural networks. In: IEEE Conference on Computer Vision and Pattern Recognition, CVPR 2019, Long Beach, CA, USA, 16–20 June 2019, pp. 3075–3084 (2019)
8. Ronneberger, O., Fischer, P., Brox, T.: U-Net: convolutional networks for biomedical image segmentation. In: Navab, N., Hornegger, J., Wells, W.M., Frangi, A.F. (eds.) MICCAI 2015. LNCS, vol. 9351, pp. 234–241. Springer, Cham (2015). https://doi.org/10.1007/978-3-319-24574-4_28
9. Sandler, M., Howard, A., Zhu, M., Zhmoginov, A., Chen, L.C.: MobileNetV2: inverted residuals and linear bottlenecks, pp. 4510–4520 (2018)
10. Goodfellow, I., et al.: Generative adversarial nets. In: Advances in Neural Information Processing Systems, pp. 2672–2680 (2014)
11. Wu, J., Zhang, C., Xue, T., Freeman, W.T., Tenenbaum, J.B.: Learning a probabilistic latent space of object shapes via 3D generative-adversarial modeling. In: Advances in Neural Information Processing Systems, pp. 82–90 (2016)
12. Girdhar, R., Fouhey, D.F., Rodriguez, M., Gupta, A.: Learning a predictable and generative vector representation for objects. In: Leibe, B., Matas, J., Sebe, N., Welling, M. (eds.) ECCV 2016. LNCS, vol. 9910, pp. 484–499. Springer, Cham (2016). https://doi.org/10.1007/978-3-319-46466-4_29
13. Shin, D., Fowlkes, C., Hoiem, D.: Pixels, voxels, and views: a study of shape representations for single view 3D object shape prediction. In: IEEE Conference on Computer Vision and Pattern Recognition (CVPR) (2018)

14. Kalogerakis, E., Averkiou, M., Maji, S., Chaudhuri, S.: 3D shape segmentation with projective convolutional networks. In: The IEEE Conference on Computer Vision and Pattern Recognition (CVPR) (July 2017)
15. Zhu, R., Kiani Galoogahi, H., Wang, C., Lucey, S.: Rethinking reprojection: closing the loop for pose-aware shape reconstruction from a single image. In: The IEEE International Conference on Computer Vision (ICCV) (October 2017)
16. Leroy, V., Franco, J.-S., Boyer, E.: Shape reconstruction using volume sweeping and learned photoconsistency. In: Ferrari, V., Hebert, M., Sminchisescu, C., Weiss, Y. (eds.) ECCV 2018. LNCS, vol. 11213, pp. 796–811. Springer, Cham (2018). https://doi.org/10.1007/978-3-030-01240-3_48
17. Sridhar, S., Rempe, D., Valentin, J., Sofien, B., Guibas, L.J.: Multiview aggregation for learning category-specific shape reconstruction. In Wallach, H., Larochelle, H., Beygelzimer, A., dÁlché Buc, F., Fox, E., Garnett, R. (eds.) Advances in Neural Information Processing Systems, vol. 32, pp. 2351–2362. Curran Associates, Inc. (2019)
18. Insafutdinov, E., Dosovitskiy, A.: Unsupervised learning of shape and pose with differentiable point clouds. In: Bengio, S., Wallach, H., Larochelle, H., Grauman, K., Cesa-Bianchi, N., Garnett, R. (eds.) Advances in Neural Information Processing Systems, vol. 31, pp. 2802–2812. Curran Associates, Inc. (2018)
19. Jiang, L., Shi, S., Qi, X., Jia, J.: GAL: geometric adversarial loss for single-view 3D-object reconstruction. In: Ferrari, V., Hebert, M., Sminchisescu, C., Weiss, Y. (eds.) ECCV 2018. LNCS, vol. 11212, pp. 820–834. Springer, Cham (2018). https://doi.org/10.1007/978-3-030-01237-3_49
20. Wu, J., Wang, Y., Xue, T., Sun, X., Freeman, W.T., Tenenbaum, J.B.: MarrNet: 3D shape reconstruction via 2.5D sketches. In: Advances In Neural Information Processing Systems (2017)
21. Fan, H., Su, H., Guibas, L.J.: A point set generation network for 3D object reconstruction from a single image. In: The IEEE Conference on Computer Vision and Pattern Recognition (CVPR) (July 2017)
22. Li, K., Pham, T., Zhan, H., Reid, I.: Efficient dense point cloud object reconstruction using deformation vector fields. In: Ferrari, V., Hebert, M., Sminchisescu, C., Weiss, Y. (eds.) ECCV 2018. LNCS, vol. 11216, pp. 508–524. Springer, Cham (2018). https://doi.org/10.1007/978-3-030-01258-8_31
23. Zhang, X., Zhang, Z., Zhang, C., Tenenbaum, J., Freeman, B., Wu, J.: Learning to reconstruct shapes from unseen classes. In: Bengio, S., Wallach, H., Larochelle, H., Grauman, K., Cesa-Bianchi, N., Garnett, R. (eds.) Advances in Neural Information Processing Systems, vol. 31, pp. 2257–2268. Curran Associates, Inc. (2018)
24. Yang, G., Cui, Y., Belongie, S., Hariharan, B.: Learning single-view 3D reconstruction with limited pose supervision. In: Ferrari, V., Hebert, M., Sminchisescu, C., Weiss, Y. (eds.) ECCV 2018. LNCS, vol. 11219, pp. 90–105. Springer, Cham (2018). https://doi.org/10.1007/978-3-030-01267-0_6
25. Pavlakos, G., Zhou, X., Derpanis, K.G., Daniilidis, K.: Coarse-to-fine volumetric prediction for single-image 3D human pose. In: The IEEE Conference on Computer Vision and Pattern Recognition (CVPR) (July 2017)
26. Tulsiani, S., Zhou, T., Efros, A.A., Malik, J.: Multi-view supervision for single-view reconstruction via differentiable ray consistency. In: The IEEE Conference on Computer Vision and Pattern Recognition (CVPR) (July 2017)
27. Zhou, Y., Tuzel, O.: Voxelnet: end-to-end learning for point cloud based 3D object detection. In: The IEEE Conference on Computer Vision and Pattern Recognition (CVPR) (June 2018)

28. Moon, G., Yong Chang, J., Mu Lee, K.: V2V-PoseNet: voxel-to-voxel prediction network for accurate 3D hand and human pose estimation from a single depth map. In: The IEEE Conference on Computer Vision and Pattern Recognition (CVPR) (June 2018)

29. Sitzmann, V., Thies, J., Heide, F., Niessner, M., Wetzstein, G., Zollhofer, M.: DeepVoxels: Learning persistent 3D feature embeddings. In: The IEEE Conference on Computer Vision and Pattern Recognition (CVPR) (June 2019)

30. Gadelha, M., Wang, R., Maji, S.: Shape reconstruction using differentiable projections and deep priors. In: The IEEE International Conference on Computer Vision (ICCV) (October 2019)

31. Zheng, Z., Yu, T., Wei, Y., Dai, Q., Liu, Y.: DeepHuman: 3D human reconstruction from a single image. In: The IEEE International Conference on Computer Vision (ICCV) (October 2019)

32. Richter, S.R., Roth, S.: Matryoshka networks: predicting 3D geometry via nested shape layers. In: 2018 IEEE Conference on Computer Vision and Pattern Recognition, CVPR 2018, Salt Lake City, UT, USA, 18–22 June 2018, pp. 1936–1944 (2018)

33. Zhang, D., Han, J., Yang, Y., Huang, D.: Learning category-specific 3D shape models from weakly labeled 2D images. In: The IEEE Conference on Computer Vision and Pattern Recognition (CVPR) (July 2017)

34. Zheng, C., Cham, T.-J., Cai, J.: T^2Net: synthetic-to-realistic translation for solving single-image depth estimation tasks. In: Ferrari, V., Hebert, M., Sminchisescu, C., Weiss, Y. (eds.) ECCV 2018. LNCS, vol. 11211, pp. 798–814. Springer, Cham (2018). https://doi.org/10.1007/978-3-030-01234-2_47

35. Feng, M., Gilani, S.Z., Wang, Y., Mian, A.: 3D face reconstruction from light field images: a model-free approach. In: Ferrari, V., Hebert, M., Sminchisescu, C., Weiss, Y. (eds.) ECCV 2018. LNCS, vol. 11214, pp. 508–526. Springer, Cham (2018). https://doi.org/10.1007/978-3-030-01249-6_31

36. Kumar, S., Dai, Y., Li, H.: Monocular dense 3D reconstruction of a complex dynamic scene from two perspective frames. In: The IEEE International Conference on Computer Vision (ICCV) (October 2017)

37. Zhan, H., et al.: Unsupervised learning of monocular depth estimation and visual odometry with deep feature reconstruction. In: The IEEE Conference on Computer Vision and Pattern Recognition (CVPR) (June 2018)

38. Ma, X., Wang, Z., Li, H., Zhang, P., Ouyang, W., Fan, X.: Accurate monocular 3D object detection via color-embedded 3D reconstruction for autonomous driving. In: The IEEE International Conference on Computer Vision (ICCV) (October 2019)

39. Isola, P., Zhu, J.Y., Zhou, T., Efros, A.A.: Image-to-image translation with conditional adversarial networks. In: 2017 IEEE Conference on Computer Vision and Pattern Recognition (CVPR), pp. 5967–5976. IEEE (2017)

40. Kanazawa, A., Tulsiani, S., Efros, A.A., Malik, J.: Learning category-specific mesh reconstruction from image collections. In: Ferrari, V., Hebert, M., Sminchisescu, C., Weiss, Y. (eds.) ECCV 2018. LNCS, vol. 11219, pp. 386–402. Springer, Cham (2018). https://doi.org/10.1007/978-3-030-01267-0_23

41. Shimada, S., Golyanik, V., Theobalt, C., Stricker, D.: IsMo-GAN: adversarial learning for monocular non-rigid 3D reconstruction. In: The IEEE Conference on Computer Vision and Pattern Recognition (CVPR) Workshops (June 2019)

42. Zhou, Y., et al.: HairNet: single-view hair reconstruction using convolutional neural networks. In: Ferrari, V., Hebert, M., Sminchisescu, C., Weiss, Y. (eds.) ECCV 2018. LNCS, vol. 11215, pp. 249–265. Springer, Cham (2018). https://doi.org/10.1007/978-3-030-01252-6_15

43. Alp Guler, R., Trigeorgis, G., Antonakos, E., Snape, P., Zafeiriou, S., Kokkinos, I.: DenseReg: fully convolutional dense shape regression in-the-wild. In: The IEEE Conference on Computer Vision and Pattern Recognition (CVPR) (July 2017)
44. Shi, Y., Xu, K., Nießner, M., Rusinkiewicz, S., Funkhouser, T.: PlaneMatch: patch coplanarity prediction for robust RGB-D reconstruction. In: Ferrari, V., Hebert, M., Sminchisescu, C., Weiss, Y. (eds.) ECCV 2018. LNCS, vol. 11212, pp. 767–784. Springer, Cham (2018). https://doi.org/10.1007/978-3-030-01237-3_46
45. Wu, J., Zhang, C., Zhang, X., Zhang, Z., Freeman, W.T., Tenenbaum, J.B.: Learning shape priors for single-view 3D completion and reconstruction. In: Ferrari, V., Hebert, M., Sminchisescu, C., Weiss, Y. (eds.) ECCV 2018. LNCS, vol. 11215, pp. 673–691. Springer, Cham (2018). https://doi.org/10.1007/978-3-030-01252-6_40
46. Liu, C., Yang, J., Ceylan, D., Yumer, E., Furukawa, Y.: PlaneNet: piece-wise planar reconstruction from a single RGB image. In: The IEEE Conference on Computer Vision and Pattern Recognition (CVPR) (June 2018)
47. Agudo, A., Pijoan, M., Moreno-Noguer, F.: Image collection pop-up: 3D reconstruction and clustering of rigid and non-rigid categories. In: The IEEE Conference on Computer Vision and Pattern Recognition (CVPR) (June 2018)
48. Sinha, A., Unmesh, A., Huang, Q., Ramani, K.: SurfNet: generating 3D shape surfaces using deep residual networks. In: The IEEE Conference on Computer Vision and Pattern Recognition (CVPR) (July 2017)
49. Richardson, E., Sela, M., Or-El, R., Kimmel, R.: Learning detailed face reconstruction from a single image. In: The IEEE Conference on Computer Vision and Pattern Recognition (CVPR) (July 2017)
50. Dou, P., Shah, S.K., Kakadiaris, I.A.: End-to-end 3D face reconstruction with deep neural networks. In: The IEEE Conference on Computer Vision and Pattern Recognition (CVPR) (July 2017)
51. Tewari, A., et al.: MoFA: model-based deep convolutional face autoencoder for unsupervised monocular reconstruction. In: The IEEE International Conference on Computer Vision (ICCV) (October 2017)
52. Jackson, A.S., Bulat, A., Argyriou, V., Tzimiropoulos, G.: Large pose 3D face reconstruction from a single image via direct volumetric CNN regression. In: The IEEE International Conference on Computer Vision (ICCV) (October 2017)
53. Sela, M., Richardson, E., Kimmel, R.: Unrestricted facial geometry reconstruction using image-to-image translation. In: The IEEE International Conference on Computer Vision (ICCV) (October 2017)
54. Huang, S., Qi, S., Zhu, Y., Xiao, Y., Xu, Y., Zhu, S.-C.: Holistic 3D scene parsing and reconstruction from a single RGB image. In: Ferrari, V., Hebert, M., Sminchisescu, C., Weiss, Y. (eds.) ECCV 2018. LNCS, vol. 11211, pp. 194–211. Springer, Cham (2018). https://doi.org/10.1007/978-3-030-01234-2_12
55. Kundu, A., Li, Y., Rehg, J.M.: 3D-RCNN: instance-level 3D object reconstruction via render-and-compare. In: The IEEE Conference on Computer Vision and Pattern Recognition (CVPR) (June 2018)
56. Knyaz, V.A., Kniaz, V.V., Remondino, F.: Image-to-voxel model translation with conditional adversarial networks. In: Leal-Taixé, L., Roth, S. (eds.) ECCV 2018. LNCS, vol. 11129, pp. 601–618. Springer, Cham (2019). https://doi.org/10.1007/978-3-030-11009-3_37
57. Kniaz, V.V., Moshkantsev, P.V., Mizginov, V.A.: Deep learning a single photo voxel model prediction from real and synthetic images. In: Kryzhanovsky, B., Dunin-Barkowski, W., Redko, V., Tiumentsev, Y. (eds.) NEUROINFORMATICS 2019. SCI, vol. 856, pp. 3–16. Springer, Cham (2020). https://doi.org/10.1007/978-3-030-30425-6_1

58. Kniaz, V.V., Remondino, F., Knyaz, V.A.: Generative adversarial networks for single photo 3D reconstruction. In: ISPRS - International Archives of the Photogrammetry, Remote Sensing and Spatial Information Sciences, vol. XLII-2/W9, pp. 403–408 (2019)

59. Xiao, T., Liu, Y., Zhou, B., Jiang, Y., Sun, J.: Unified perceptual parsing for scene understanding. In: Ferrari, V., Hebert, M., Sminchisescu, C., Weiss, Y. (eds.) ECCV 2018. LNCS, vol. 11209, pp. 432–448. Springer, Cham (2018). https://doi.org/10.1007/978-3-030-01228-1_26

60. He, K., Zhang, X., Ren, S., Sun, J.: Deep residual learning for image recognition. CoRR abs/1512.03385 (2015)

61. Sandler, M., Howard, A.G., Zhu, M., Zhmoginov, A., Chen, L.: MobileNetV2: inverted residuals and linear bottlenecks. In: 2018 IEEE Conference on Computer Vision and Pattern Recognition, CVPR 2018, Salt Lake City, UT, USA, 18–22 June 2018, pp. 4510–4520 (2018)

62. Redmon, J., Farhadi, A.: YOLO9000: better, faster, stronger. In: 2017 IEEE Conference on Computer Vision and Pattern Recognition, CVPR 2017, Honolulu, HI, USA, 21–26 July 2017, pp. 6517–6525 (2017)

63. Caesar, H., et al.: nuScenes: A multimodal dataset for autonomous driving. arXiv preprint arXiv:1903.11027 (2019)

64. Locher, A., Havlena, M., Van Gool, L.: Progressive structure from motion. In: Ferrari, V., Hebert, M., Sminchisescu, C., Weiss, Y. (eds.) ECCV 2018. LNCS, vol. 11208, pp. 22–38. Springer, Cham (2018). https://doi.org/10.1007/978-3-030-01225-0_2

65. Mizginov, V.A., Kniaz, V.V.: Evaluating the accuracy of 3D object reconstruction from thermal images. In: ISPRS - International Archives of the Photogrammetry, Remote Sensing and Spatial Information Sciences, vol. XLII-2/W18, pp. 129–134 (2019)

66. Sun, X., et al.: Pix3D: dataset and methods for single-image 3D shape modeling. In: IEEE Conference on Computer Vision and Pattern Recognition (CVPR) (2018)

67. Wang, T., Liu, M., Zhu, J., Tao, A., Kautz, J., Catanzaro, B.: High-resolution image synthesis and semantic manipulation with conditional GANs. In: 2018 IEEE Conference on Computer Vision and Pattern Recognition, CVPR 2018, Salt Lake City, UT, USA, 18–22 June 2018, pp. 8798–8807 (2018)

68. Kniaz, V.V., Knyaz, V.A., Remondino, F.: The point where reality meets fantasy: mixed adversarial generators for image splice detection. In: Advances in Neural Information Processing Systems: Annual Conference on Neural Information Processing Systems 2019, NeurIPS 2019, 8–14 December 2019, Vancouver, BC, Canada, vol. 32, pp. 215–226 (2019)

69. Kniaz, V.V., Knyaz, V.A., Hladůvka, J., Kropatsch, W.G., Mizginov, V.: Thermal-GAN: multimodal color-to-thermal image translation for person re-identification in multispectral dataset. In: Leal-Taixé, L., Roth, S. (eds.) ECCV 2018. LNCS, vol. 11134, pp. 606–624. Springer, Cham (2019). https://doi.org/10.1007/978-3-030-11024-6_46

70. Kniaz, V.V., Bordodymov, A.N.: Long wave infrared image colorization for person re-identification. In: ISPRS - International Archives of the Photogrammetry, Remote Sensing and Spatial Information Sciences, vol. XLII-2/W12, pp. 111–116 (2019)

71. Lin, T.-Y., et al.: Microsoft COCO: common objects in context. In: Fleet, D., Pajdla, T., Schiele, B., Tuytelaars, T. (eds.) ECCV 2014. LNCS, vol. 8693, pp. 740–755. Springer, Cham (2014). https://doi.org/10.1007/978-3-319-10602-1_48

72. Canny, J.F.: A computational approach to edge detection. IEEE Trans. Pattern Anal. Mach. Intell. **8**(6), 679–698 (1986)
73. Chang, A.X., Funkhouser, T.A., et al.: ShapeNet: An information-rich 3D model repository. CoRR abs/1512.03012 (2015)
74. Dai, A., Chang, A.X., Savva, M., Halber, M., Funkhouser, T., Nießner, M.: Scan-Net: richly-annotated 3D reconstructions of indoor scenes. In: Proceedings of the Computer Vision and Pattern Recognition (CVPR). IEEE (2017)
75. Garbade, M., Chen, Y., Sawatzky, J., Gall, J.: Two stream 3D semantic scene completion. In: IEEE Conference on Computer Vision and Pattern Recognition Workshops, CVPR Workshops 2019, Long Beach, CA, USA, 16–20 June 2019, pp. 416–425 (2019)
76. Paszke, A., et al.: Automatic differentiation in PyTorch (2017)
77. Xiang, Y., Mottaghi, R., Savarese, S.: Beyond PASCAL: a benchmark for 3D object detection in the wild. In: IEEE Winter Conference on Applications of Computer Vision (WACV) (2014)

Consistency Guided Scene Flow Estimation

Yuhua Chen[1,2](✉), Luc Van Gool[2], Cordelia Schmid[1],
and Cristian Sminchisescu[1]

[1] Google Research, Mountain View, USA
yuhua.yc@gmail.com
[2] ETH Zurich, ZÜrich, Switzerland

Abstract. Consistency Guided Scene Flow Estimation ($CGSF$) is a self-supervised framework for the joint reconstruction of 3D scene structure and motion from stereo video. The model takes two temporal stereo pairs as input, and predicts disparity and scene flow. The model self-adapts at test time by iteratively refining its predictions. The refinement process is guided by a consistency loss, which combines stereo and temporal photo-consistency with a geometric term that couples disparity and 3D motion. To handle inherent modeling error in the consistency loss (e.g. Lambertian assumptions) and for better generalization, we further introduce a learned, output refinement network, which takes the initial predictions, the loss, and the gradient as input, and efficiently predicts a correlated output update. In multiple experiments, including ablation studies, we show that the proposed model can reliably predict disparity and scene flow in challenging imagery, achieves better generalization than the state-of-the-art, and adapts quickly and robustly to unseen domains.

Keywords: Scene flow · Disparity estimation · Stereo video · Geometric constraints · Self-supervised learning

1 Introduction

Scene flow is the task of jointly estimating the 3D structure and motion of a scene [34]. This is critical for a wide range of downstream applications, such as robotics, autonomous driving and augmented reality. Typically, scene flow is estimated from consecutive stereo pairs, and requires simultaneously solving two sub-problems: stereo matching and optical flow. Though closely related, the two tasks cover different aspects of scene flow: stereo matching seeks to estimate disparity from a static stereo pair, whereas the objective of optical flow is to find the correspondence between temporally adjacent frames.

Many end-to-end models powered by deep neural network have emerged for the scene flow estimation [1,15] and its components [5,13,29], and they showed

Electronic supplementary material The online version of this chapter (https://doi.org/10.1007/978-3-030-58571-6_8) contains supplementary material, which is available to authorized users.

promise in benchmarks. However, training such models relies on the availability of labeled data. Due to difficulty in acquiring real-world data, synthetic data [23] is widely used as the major supervision source for deep models, with 3D structure or motion generated automatically using computer graphics techniques. Unfortunately, synthetic data still exhibits noticeable appearance dissimilarity leading to domain shift, which often prevents models trained this way from generalizing to the real-world. This has been observed previously [27,31]. This issue can be partially addressed by finetuning on labeled real-world data. However, collecting ground-truth labels for scene flow can be extremely challenging, requiring the use of costly sensors and additional manual intervention [25,26]. This, however, may not always be feasible in many real-world scenarios, greatly limiting the applicability of deep models.

To address this issue, we present Consistency Guided Scene Flow (*CGSF*), a framework that additionally models output consistency. The framework begins with producing scene flow prediction using feedforward deep network. The predictions include disparity, optical flow and disparity change. These predictions are then coupled by a consistency loss which captures the photometric and geometric relations valid in scene flow, irrespective of domain shift. Therefore, the consistency loss can be a powerful cue in guiding predictions for better generalization in unseen domains. However, the consistency loss is inherently noisy due to the complexity of natural data, such as non-Lambertian surfaces or occlusion. As a result, the provided guidance is not always precise, and can exhibit undesired artifacts. To further correct such issues that are difficult to model explicitly, we further introduce a learned refinement module, which takes the initial predictions, the loss, and the gradient as input, and predicts an update to recursively refine the prediction. The refinement module is implemented as a neural network, and thus can be trained jointly with the original feedforward module.

Our *CGSF* model can be trained either using synthetic data, which can generalize well to real imagery, or trained self-supervised, using unlabeled data, based on the proposed consistency loss. In diverse experiments, we show our *CGSF* can reliably predict disparity and scene flow in challenging scenarios. Moreover, we observe that the proposed, learned refinement module, can significantly improve the results of the more classical feedforward network, by ensuring consistent predictions. In particular, we demonstrate that the proposed model significantly improves generalization to unseen domains, thus better supporting real-world applications of scene flow, where a degree of domain shift is inevitable.

2   Related Work

Scene Flow Estimation introduced by Vedula *et al.* [34], scene flow estimation aims to recover the 3D structure and motion of a scene. The task has been formulated as a variational inference problem by multiple authors [3,12,35,38]. Recently, several deep models have emerged for this task. Ilg *et al.* [14] combine networks for stereo and optical flow using an additional network to predict disparity change. Ma *et al.* [22] stack three networks to predicting disparity, flow and segmentation, then use a Gaussian-Newton solver to estimate per-object 3D motion. To leverage correlation between tasks, Jiang *et al.* [15] propose an encoder architecture shared among the tasks of disparity, optical flow, and segmentation. Similarly, Aleotti *et al.* [1] propose a lightweight architecture to share information between tasks. Complementary to previous work, our main objective is to improve generalization of the scene flow by means of additional constraints, self-supervised losses, and learnt refinement schemes.

Flow and Disparity Estimation. As scene flow requires simultaneously reasoning about two tasks: disparity and flow estimation, it has been largely influenced by the techniques used in end-to-end stereo matching and optical flow.

For optical flow estimation, FlowNet [8] represents the first attempt in building end-to-end deep models. FlowNet 2.0 [13] further improved performance by dataset scheduling and refinement. A spatial pyramid design is adopted in PWC-Net [29], which includes cost volume processing at multiple levels. PWC-Net achieved highly competitive performance on several benchmarks for optical flow estimation.

In stereo matching, Mayer *et al.* [23] introduce an architecture similar to FlowNet, for disparity estimation from rectified image pairs. Several techniques have been introduced to improve the matching accuracy, including 3D convolution in GC-Net [16], pyramid pooling in PSM-Net [5], *etc.* More recently, GA-Net [40] integrated two aggregation layers with good results.

Adaptation. Due to the practical difficulty of acquiring ground-truth labels, the aforementioned models are often trained on synthetic data, although a performance drop is observed when applied in the real-world [27,31].

To address this issue, several techniques [11,28,31–33,41] have been proposed to adapt the model to new domains where labels aren't available. For the purpose, either offline adaptation [31] or online adaptation [33] is performed to refine the model parameters in the new domain. One key difference in our work is that our refinement module operates on prediction (outputs) directly instead of network parameters, and it thus relies on the output consistency among outputs to overcome domain shift.

Self-supervision. On the other hand, self-supervised learning has been used with unlabelled data [4,9,10,18,36,39,42]. Some methods require collecting unlabelled data for offline training, which might not be always possible. Even so, trained model suffer from domain shift in new environments, which still requires online adaptation. Part of our modeling is based on similar ideas, in that we can also train with self-supervision in an offline stage. However, we additionally integrate output consistency terms in our refinement module, which makes our framework easier to self-adapt to new environments without collecting unlabeled data upfront.

Online Refinement. Online optimization under self-supervised consistency losses has shown to be effective for depth prediction in video [4,6]. In this work, we learn a refinement network to preserve the output consistency. Our refinement network shares ideas with learning-based optimization [2,19], where one aims to integrate iterative refinement into deep networks. Different metalearning ideas have also been explored in different applications, such as learning depth and pose estimation [7], 3D rigid motion estimation [21], or monocular reconstruction of static scenes [30]. Here we focus on problem-domain updates that integrate gradient information in order to ensure progress, for robustness, as well as computational efficiency. In contrast, our model consists of several novel geometric constraints for scene flow estimation, designed for self-supervision and overcoming domain shift.

3   Consistency Guided Scene Flow

3.1   Overview

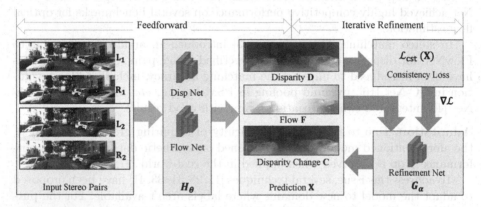

Fig. 1. Illustration of our proposed Consistency Guided Scene Flow ($CGSF$). The model can be obtained either using labeled data, or unlabeled images and self-supervision. At runtime, it self-adapts by producing a set of outputs using feedforward networks ($\mathbf{H}_\theta$, flow by blue arrows), then iteratively refining those estimates on two temporally adjacent stereo pairs, using a learned update (network $\mathbf{G}_\alpha$, flow by green arrows). The refinement process is guided by a consistency loss, which captures several intrinsic photometric and geometric constraints associated to scene flow. (Color figure online)

In this section we present our Consistency Guided Scene Flow framework ($CGSF$). An overview is given in Fig. 1. Given a couple of stereo images at subsequent timesteps ($\mathbf{L}_1, \mathbf{R}_1$) and ($\mathbf{L}_2, \mathbf{R}_2$), respectively, as input, the model predicts scene flow $\mathbf{X}$, $i.e.$, the 3D structure and motion of the environment. The 3D scene structure can be represented by the disparity in the first frame $\mathbf{D}_1$, as disparity is inversely proportional to depth. The 3D scene motion can be decomposed into the motion parallel to the image plane, represented by optical flow $\mathbf{F}_{1\to2}$, and the motion orthogonal to the image plane, represented as disparity change $\mathbf{C}_{1\to2}$.

At runtime, we formulate scene flow estimation as an iterative optimization problem. Our framework predicts scene flow in two stages: a more typical feedforward block and an iterative output refinement module (N.B. this is also feedforward, but has a recurrent structure). In the first stage, we rely on a feedforward module $\mathbf{H}_\theta$ to predict scene flow given input images. In the refinement stage, our geometric and photometric consistency losses are further optimized with respect to the outputs using a refinement network $\mathbf{G}_\alpha$. Both the feedforward module $\mathbf{H}_\theta$ and the refinement network $\mathbf{G}_\alpha$ are implemented as neural networks with learnt parameters θ and α. Therefore the two components can be trained jointly in an end-to-end process.

In the sequel, we introduce the feedforward module in Sect. 3.2. We formulate the geometric and photometric consistency terms for scene flow estimation in Sect. 3.3. We present the learned refinement network in Sect. 3.4 and describe the training and evaluation protocol in Sect. 3.5.

3.2 Feedforward Scene Flow Module

In the feedforward stage, the prediction of scene flow is obtained by passing the input images through disparity and flow networks. The disparity network predicts the 3D structure given stereo pairs. Specifically, the module predicts $\mathbf{D}_1$ from $(\mathbf{L}_1, \mathbf{R}_1)$, and $\mathbf{D}_2$ from $(\mathbf{L}_2, \mathbf{R}_2)$. Given $(\mathbf{L}_1, \mathbf{L}_2)$ as input, the flow network predicts optical flow $\mathbf{F}_{1\to2}$, and the disparity change $\mathbf{C}_{1\to2}$ which encodes the motion component orthogonal to the image plane.

In this work, we build the feedforward module upon GA-Net [40] and PWC-Net [29], mainly due to both competitive performance and implementation compatibility. Here we briefly introduce the architectures.

Disparity Network: We rely on GA-Net [40] to predict scene structure, i.e., $\mathbf{D}_1$ and $\mathbf{D}_2$. The network extracts features from a stereo pair with a shared encoder. Then features are used to build a cost volume, which is fed into a cost aggregation block for regularization, refinement and disparity prediction.

Flow Network: We modify PWC-Net [29] to predict the 3D motion, including optical flow $\mathbf{F}_{1\to2}$ and disparity change $\mathbf{C}_{1\to2}$. We follow the design in PWC-Net to construct a cost volume from the features of the first frame, and the warped features of the second frame. The cost volume is further processed to obtain the motion prediction. We increase the output channel from 2 to 3 to encode 3D motion.

In principle, our framework is agnostic to specific choices of model design—other options for the structure and motion networks are possible. This offers the flexibility of leveraging the latest advances in the field, and focus on our novel self-supervised geometric and photometric consistency losses, described next.

3.3 Scene Flow Consistency Loss

In this section we formulate the photometric and geometric constrains that are part of our proposed consistency loss.

Stereo Photometric Consistency. Photometric consistency between stereo pairs is widely used as a self-supervised loss in deep models [9,17]. The idea is to warp the source view via a differentiable bilinear map produced by the network prediction. The photometric difference between the warped source image and the target image can be used as a self-supervision signal.

Given a stereo pair $(\mathbf{L}, \mathbf{R})$, we use the left view $\mathbf{L}$ as the target image, and the right view $\mathbf{R}$ as the source image. Considering a pixel $\mathbf{p}$ in the left view, its correspondence in the right view can be obtained by subtracting its disparity value from its x coordinate. With a slight abuse of notation, we denote it as $\mathbf{p} - \mathbf{D}(\mathbf{p})$. If $\mathbf{p}$ corresponds to a 3D scene point visible in both views, its correspondence should be visually consistent. Following [9], we use a weighted sum of L1 loss and SSIM [37] loss as the photometric error, denoted as pe. Therefore the photometric stereo consistency model can be written as

$$\mathcal{L}_{pd}(\mathbf{p}) = pe(\mathbf{L}(\mathbf{p}), \mathbf{R}(\mathbf{p} - \mathbf{D}(\mathbf{p}))) \tag{1}$$

The stereo consistency applies to both $\mathbf{D}_1$ and $\mathbf{D}_2$.

Flow Photometric Consistency. We also rely on photometric consistency for temporal frames. Given a pixel $\mathbf{p}$ in the first frame $\mathbf{L}_1$, its correspondence in the second frame $\mathbf{L}_2$ can be obtained by displacing $\mathbf{p}$ using optical flow. We can write the flow photometric consistency as

$$\mathcal{L}_{pf}(\mathbf{p}) = \mathbf{O}_f(\mathbf{p}) \cdot pe(\mathbf{L}(\mathbf{p}), \mathbf{L}(\mathbf{p} + \mathbf{F}_{1\rightarrow2}(\mathbf{p}))) \tag{2}$$

$\mathbf{O}_f$ represents the occlusion map caused by optical flow. Similarly with previous work [20,24], we infer the occlusion map using a forward-backward flow consistency check. In more detail, an additional backward flow is computed and then warped by the the the forward flow $\mathbf{F}_{1\rightarrow2}$. We denote the computed warped backward flow map by $\hat{\mathbf{F}}_{2\rightarrow1}$. A forward-backward consistency check is performed to estimate the occlusion map

$$\mathbf{O}_f = [\![|\mathbf{F}_{1\rightarrow2} + \hat{\mathbf{F}}_{2\rightarrow1}|^2 < w_1(|\mathbf{F}_{1\rightarrow2}|^2 + |\hat{\mathbf{F}}_{2\rightarrow1}|^2) + w_2]\!] \tag{3}$$

where $[\![\cdot]\!]$ is the Iverson bracket, and we set $w_1 = 0.01, w_2 = 0.05$ in inferring the occlusion mask.

Disparity-Flow Consistency. We formulate a new consistency term to connect disparity and 3D motion. Given a pixel $\mathbf{p}$ in the left view of the first frame $\mathbf{L}_1$, its correspondence in $\mathbf{L}_2$ is associated by optical flow $\mathbf{F}_{1\rightarrow2}$ can be written as $\mathbf{p} + \mathbf{F}_{1\rightarrow2}(\mathbf{p})$. Thus its disparity value in the second frame should be $\mathbf{D}_2(\mathbf{p} + \mathbf{F}_{1\rightarrow2}(\mathbf{p}))$. On the other hand, $\mathbf{p}$'s disparity value in the second frame can also be obtained by adding the disparity change $\mathbf{C}_{1\rightarrow2}$ to the disparity of the first frame $\mathbf{D}_1$. Therefore the disparity flow consistency can be written as

$$\mathcal{L}_{df}(\mathbf{p}) = \mathbf{O}_f(\mathbf{p})\|\mathbf{D}_1(\mathbf{p}) + \mathbf{C}_{1\rightarrow2}(\mathbf{p}) - \mathbf{D}_2(\mathbf{p} + \mathbf{F}_{1\rightarrow2}(\mathbf{p}))\| \tag{4}$$

We use $\mathbf{O}_f$ to mask out occluded pixels as flow warping is used in the process.

Overall Consistency Loss. By integrating all previously derived terms, the consistency loss can be written as

$$\mathcal{L}_{cst} = \mathcal{L}_{pd} + \mathcal{L}_{pf} + \mathcal{L}_{df} \tag{5}$$

The consistency loss regularizes predictions resulting from the individual structure and flow networks $\mathbf{X}$, and captures several intrinsic geometric and photometric constraints that should always hold. To provide additional regularization of predictions, we use an edge-aware smoothness term as in [9]. This is applied to the disparity map $\mathbf{D}_1, \mathbf{D}_2$, optical flow $\mathbf{F}_{1\rightarrow 2}$, and disparity change $\mathbf{C}_{1\rightarrow 2}$.

3.4   Consistency Guided Refinement

In the refinement stage, the goal is to recursively improve scene flow prediction. We denote as $\mathbf{X}^t$ the scene flow prediction after t steps of refinement. The initial prediction from the classical feedforward module can be denoted as $\mathbf{X}^0$.

As the consistency loss $\mathcal{L}_{cst}$ reflects the intrinsic structure of scene flow, it can be used as an indicator of how good the prediction is. Therefore we aim to leverage the signal in consistency loss to guide online finetuning. To this end, we build a refinement network $\mathbf{G}_\alpha$ parameterized by α, which takes as input the previous prediction $\mathbf{X}^t$, the consistency loss over the previous prediction $\mathcal{L}_{cst}(\mathbf{X}^t)$, and the gradient on predictions $\nabla_{\mathbf{X}}\mathcal{L}_{cst}(\mathbf{X}^t)$. The reason for using the gradient is to provide an exact signal for the descent direction. The refinement network then predicts an update to refine the prediction to $\mathbf{X}^{t+1}$.

$$\mathbf{X}^{t+1} = \mathbf{X}^t + \mathbf{G}_\alpha(\mathbf{X}, \mathcal{L}_{cst}, \nabla_{\mathbf{X}}\mathcal{L}_{cst}) \tag{6}$$

For implementation, we first concatenate all predictions, including $\mathbf{D}_1, \mathbf{D}_2, \mathbf{C}_{1\rightarrow 2}$ each with size $W \times H \times 1$, and optical flow $\mathbf{F}_{1\rightarrow 2}$ with size $W \times H \times 2$. The concatenated prediction map is of dimension $W \times H \times 5$, with W and H being the width and height of the image, respectively. The gradient is of the same dimensionality as the prediction, and the loss map is of 1 channel. Therefore, all inputs can be concatenated as a $W \times H \times 11$ map. The benefit of using a concatenated map as input is that cross-channel correlations can be better captured. For instance, disparity information might be helpful to improve optical flow.

We implement the refinement module as a small fully convolutional network(FCN) operating on the input map, to provide dense (per pixel) output for the updates. The advantage is that the FCN architecture can learn to leverage the local inter-pixel context, which is helpful in reducing noise in the consistency loss, and in propagating information to and from neighbouring pixels. We use a lightweight design of 3 convolution layers, each with 512 hidden units and kernel size of 3×3. ReLU is used between convolution layers as the activation function. The light-weight design is motivated by the recurrent use of the module.

3.5   Training

To learn the parameters of the feedforward scene flow $\mathbf{H}_\theta$ and refinement network $\mathbf{G}_\alpha$, the framework can be initialized based on pre-training using synthetic data with ground-truth labels (whenever available), and then/or further trained using the self-supervised loss $\mathcal{L}_{cst}$, in order to better generalize to real imagery. When ground-truth labels are available, a standard supervised loss can be used

$$\mathcal{L}_{sup}(\mathbf{X}) = ||\mathbf{F}_{1\rightarrow 2} - \mathbf{F}^*_{1\rightarrow 2}|| + ||\mathbf{D}_1 - \mathbf{D}^*_1|| + ||\mathbf{C}_{1\rightarrow 2} - \mathbf{C}^*_{1\rightarrow 2}|| \qquad (7)$$

where $*$ indicates ground-truth. In either case, the network parameters θ, α can be learned jointly by minimizing the loss using stochastic gradient descent. The optimization objective writes

$$\arg\min_{\theta,\alpha} \sum_{t\in\{0,...,T\}} \mathcal{L}(\mathbf{X}^t) \qquad (8)$$

where the loss $\mathcal{L}$ can be either $\mathcal{L}_{sup}$(when the label is available) or $\mathcal{L}_{cst}$(in self-supervised training). The loss is applied to the initial prediction, as well as to the prediction after each refinement step (i.e. we supervise the augmented step update at each iteration). Essentially after each step we minimize the loss w.r.t. α so that the learnt descent direction produces as large of a loss decrease as possible, and aggregate in parallel over $T = 5$ refinement steps.

4   Experiments

In this section, we experimentally validate the proposed *CGSF*. First, we test our model on synthetic data on FlyingThings3D in Sect. 4.1. Then, in order to verify real-image generalization, we test the model on KITTI in Sect. 4.2. In Sect. 4.3 we provide ablation studies to provide further insight into our design choices. Finally, in Sect. 4.4 we show the performance of *CGSF* on different scenes captured by a stereo camera, in order to demonstrate the generalization to environments not seen in training.

4.1   Evaluation on Synthetic Data

First we evaluate the model on synthetic data. We use the FlyingThings3D [23] which is a synthetic dataset for scene flow estimation, containing $22,390$ stereo training pairs. Dense ground-truth labels are available in all images for disparity, optical flow and disparity change. We use the ground-truth to supervise our model, including the feedforward module and the refinement network.

In the refinement module, we use a set of trade-off weights to balance different consistency terms. We use $\omega_{pd}, \omega_{pf}, \omega_{df}$ to denote, respectively, the weight of stereo photometric consistency $\mathcal{L}_{pd}$, flow disparity consistency $\mathcal{L}_{pf}$, and disparity disparity-flow consistency $\mathcal{L}_{df}$. The weight of the smoothness term is denoted as ω_s. We set $\omega_{pd} = 1, \omega_{pf} = 1, \omega_{df} = 1, \omega_s = 0.1$. A stage-wise strategy is used in order to improve the stability of the training process. In more detail, we first train the disparity network and the flow network separately. For this part, we follow [29,40] in setting hyperparameters. These are then used as initialization for additional, joint fine-tuning. Specifically, we randomly initialize the weights of the refinement module, and jointly fine-tune the whole network including the pre-trained feedforward networks. To fine-tune the entire network, we use the Adam optimizer with $\beta_1 = 0.9$ and $\beta_2 = 0.999$. The learning rate is set to 10^{-4}. The network is trained on FlyingThings 3D for 10 epochs with a batch size of 4.

The models are evaluated on the test set of FlyingThings3D, which contains 4,370 images. As scene flow model requires 4 images as input, we drop the last frame of every sequence, resulting in a test set with 3,933 images. The performance is measured by end point error(EPE) for the three key outputs: optical flow, disparity, and disparity change. We use the results produced by the feedforward module without a refinement network as baseline. To facilitate the comparison with the state-of-the-art, we test against a recent model DWARF [1] in the same experimental setting. As shown in Table 1, the refinement model improves over the feedforward baseline in all three metrics, thus supporting the effectiveness of the consistency guided refinement process. Our model also outperforms DWARF [1] by a large margin. Again, this shows the benefit of geometrically modelling the consistency of scene flow outputs.

Table 1. Scene flow results on the FlyingThings3D test set. Results are evaluated as end point error (EPE). All models are trained on the training set of FlyingThings3D. Disparity change EPE represents the error of the motion orthogonal to the image plane.

	Disparity EPE	Flow EPE	Disparity change EPE *
DWARF [1]	2.00	6.52	2.23
Feedforward	0.83	7.02	2.02
CGSF (ours)	**0.79**	**5.98**	**1.33**

4.2 Generalization to Real Images

To verify the performance in real imagery where no labeled data is available, we evaluate on the KITTI scene flow dataset [25,26], which contains 200 training images with sparse ground-truth disparity and flow acquired by a lidar sensor. The ground-truth is only used in evaluation. To comply with the KITTI scene flow benchmark, the percentage of outliers in the following 4 categories is used as evaluation metrics, D1: outliers in the disparity of first frame (*i.e.*, $\mathbf{D}_1$), D2: outliers in second frame warped to the first frame (*i.e.*, $\mathbf{D}_1 + \mathbf{C}_{1 \to 2}$), F1: outliers in optical flow (*i.e.*, $\mathbf{F}_{1 \to 2}$), SF: outliers in either D1, D2 or F1. A pixel is considered correct if the prediction end-point error is smaller than 3 px or 5%.

Table 2. Evaluation on the KITTI 2015 scene flow dataset. The percentage of outliers is used as evaluation metric. A pixel is considered as correct if the prediction end-point error is smaller than 3 px or 5%. For training data, 'K(u)' stands for unsupervised training on KITTI, and 'F(s)' represents supervised training on FlyingThings3D.

Method	Training Data	D1	D2	F1	SF
Godard et al. [9]	K(u)	9.19	-	-	-
BridgeDepthFlow [18]	K(u)	8.62	-	26.72	-
UnOS [36]	K(u)	5.94	-	16.30	-
MADNet [33]	F(s)+ K(u)	8.41	-	-	-
DWARF [1]	F(s)	11.60	29.64	38.32	45.58
Feedforward	F(s)	11.53	27.83	33.09	43.55
CGSF (ours)	F(s)	7.10	19.68	27.35	35.40
CGSF (ours)	K(u)	6.65	17.69	23.05	31.52
CGSF (ours)	F(s)+ K(u)	5.75	15.53	20.45	28.14

As discussed in Sect. 3.3, our *CGSF* model can be trained with round-truth labels from synthetic data, or using self-supervision. We evaluate both strategies. For training using ground-truth on synthetic data, we already illustrated FlyingThings3D. For self-supervised training on KITTI, we use KITTI raw as a training set, with all test scenes excluded.

We compare with the supervised feedforward network without refinement as a baseline. Additionally, we compare with several recent competing methods, including self-supervised models based on stereo images [9] or stereo video [18,36], scene flow supervised on synthetic data [1], and an adaptation model for stereo estimation [33]. We initialize [33] with the pre-trained weights from synthetic data, and do unsupervised adaptation on KITTI raw (the same set used in our model's unsupervised training).

The results are summarized in Table 2. With the feedforward module only, the baseline achieves an error rate of 43.55%. The error can be significantly reduced to 35.40% by the proposed refinement network. Notably, the performance gain is much larger compared to the one in FlyingThings3D, which demonstrates that consistency plays a central and positive role in cross-domain scenarios. This indicates that consistency can be used as an effective model to overcome domain gaps and improve generalization.

Whenever collecting an unlabeled training set beforehand is possible, the model can also be trained under self-supervision. This results in an error rate of 31.52%, which demonstrates both the effectiveness of a self-supervised consistency loss, and good compatibility when supervision is available. Performance can be further improved by combining pre-training on synthetic data, and self-supervised finetuning. This combination results in the lowest scene flow error rate of 28.14%.

Compared to other component methods, our model outperforms the scene flow approach DWARF [1]. The performance of disparity estimation is also considerably better than the self-adaptive stereo model MADNet [33]. Compared to other self-supervised models relying on stereo data [9,18,36], our model achieves competitive results on disparity and flow estimation, while being additionally capable of predicting 3D motion.

Table 3. Ablation study for the consistency terms. Different consistency terms are used in the refinement module. All models are trained on FlyingThings3D and evaluated on KITTI.

Refinement	$\mathcal{L}_{pd}$	$\mathcal{L}_{pf}$	$\mathcal{L}_{df}$	D1	D2	F1	SF
				11.29	26.51	32.71	43.01
✓				10.40	25.15	32.05	42.43
✓	✓			7.95	22.48	31.38	39.80
✓		✓		9.84	23.92	29.06	39.64
✓			✓	9.11	21.14	30.95	39.59
✓	✓	✓		7.60	22.73	29.07	38.23
✓	✓	✓	✓	7.10	19.68	27.35	35.40

Fig. 2. Illustration of different consistency terms. From left to right we show results produced using $\mathcal{L}_{pd}, \mathcal{L}_{pf}, \mathcal{L}_{df}$. The first row presents the pixel-wise loss map of the feedforward prediction, where brighter is larger loss. The second row shows the error map for disparity estimation, when compared with the ground-truth label. Red indicates higher error, whereas blue indicates lower error.

4.3 Ablation Studies

We provide further experimental analysis on ablated versions of our model, for further insight into the design choices. To ensure a fair comparison, all models used in this section are trained on FlyingThings3D, and results are reported on KITTI2015 without self-supervised finetuning.

Consistency in Refinement Network. In the refinement network, the consistency loss is used as a guidance to refine the network outputs. The consistency loss mainly consists of three terms: a stereo photometric loss ($\mathcal{L}_{pd}$), a flow photometric loss ($\mathcal{L}_{pf}$) and a disparity flow consistency loss ($\mathcal{L}_{df}$). To understand the role of each loss, we conduct an ablation study where different combinations are used in the refinement network.

Table 4. Ablation study on the input to the refinement network. All models are trained on FlyingThings3D, and evaluated on KITTI.

$\mathbf{X}$	$\mathcal{L}$	$\nabla \mathcal{L}$	D1	D2	F1	SF
✓			10.40	25.15	32.05	42.43
✓	✓		9.77	22.80	30.95	40.47
✓		✓	7.44	20.01	28.20	36.31
✓	✓	✓	7.10	19.68	27.35	35.40

We summarize the results in Table 3. When no consistency is used, the refinement network only takes the prediction $\mathbf{X}$ as input. This baseline results in a scene flow error of of 42.43, slightly better than the feedforward result which is 43.01. This suggests that only $\mathbf{X}$ is insufficient in effectively guiding refinement. The error can be reduced by additionally including consistency terms, which supports the efficacy of our guided refinement strategy. The contributions of each loss term to the scene flow error are similar. However, each loss term exhibits different improvements over the three sub-measurements. Notably, $\mathcal{L}_{pd}$ improves $D1$ measure the most, $\mathcal{L}_{pf}$ improves $F1$ the most, whereas $\mathcal{L}_{df}$ reduces the $D2$ error, which is related to both disparity and optical flow. The results are understandable, as each loss intrinsically constraints different outputs. For example, the stereo photometric loss $\mathcal{L}_{pd}$ relates stronger to disparity, whereas the flow photometric loss $\mathcal{L}_{pf}$ better constrains flow.

To further understand the impact of different losses, in Fig. 2 we visualize refinement results by using only $\mathcal{L}_{pd}$, $\mathcal{L}_{pf}$ or $\mathcal{L}_{df}$. We observe that the photometric loss (the left and middle) is sparse and cannot provide sufficient signal in the textureless regions. As a result, the error in flat regions (such as road) remains large after refinement. On the other hand, the disparity flow consistency term $\mathcal{L}_{df}$ provides a denser signal, especially in textureless regions, and can reduce errors there. However, it still produces errors on the motion boundaries and in occluded areas, due to the output inconsistency in such regions.

Input to Refinement Network. In the refinement network, consistency is used to guide the change of scene flow predictions. In doing so, we use the current scene flow prediction $\mathbf{X}^t$, the consistency computed on the scene flow $\mathcal{L}_{cst}(\mathbf{X})$, and its gradient as input $\mathcal{L}_{cst}(\mathbf{X})$.

In this study, we study the influence of different inputs on the final performance. For this purpose, we train several versions of the refinement network, with various combinations of input features. As shown in Table 4, with only the variable as input, the refinement network achieved 42.43. By additionally including the loss and gradient as inputs, a further decrease of 0.96 and 6.12 are observed, respectively, which suggests that the gradient is a stronger signal for refinement, compared to the loss. Nevertheless, combining the two results in the best performance in scene flow, of 35.40 error rate. The results highlight the effectiveness of the gradient feature in the learned refinement network.

Online Refinement Strategies. In this experiment we compare our learned refinement module against alternative design choices. In this work we use a refinement network to predict an update from the loss signal, and to refine the scene flow prediction without updating the model parameters. Alternatively, one can perform online finetuning to update the model parameters, based on the same consistency loss. We refer to this approach as parameter finetuning. Another choice is to change the scene flow prediction directly, without passing through the network, which we refer to as output finetuning [6].

We test the two alternatives with the same consistency loss. The results are summarized in Table 5. As seen from the table, our learned refinement achieves similar performance with parameter finetuning. However, as multiple iterations of forward and backward passes are needed for finetuning network parameters, this approach results in a large run time of 120 s per image. Compared to parameter finetuning, our method is much faster.

Table 5. Ablation study of online refinement strategies. We use different online refinement strategies for scene flow estimation. All models are trained on FlyingThings3D and results are reported on KITTI.

Refinement method	D1	D2	F1	SF	Time
Outputs	8.53	22.82	30.61	39.95	0.5 s
Parameters	6.88	19.47	27.69	35.49	120 s
Learned (ours)	7.10	19.68	27.35	35.40	0.8 s

To further understand the difference among the three refinement strategies, we visualize the disparity outputs in Fig. 3. We can observe from the figure, that output finetuning is very noisy and sparse – this is due to properties of each pixel being refined independently. As shown previously, the loss signal is sparse and noisy, and is often invalid in occluded regions, which results in inaccurate updates. In contrast, our learned refinement can take advantage of this sparse signal and of contextual information. As a result, a much smoother refinement–similar to the one produced by parameter finetuning, but *two orders of magnitude faster*–is produced by the proposed learned refinement module.

Fig. 3. Qualitative results for different online refinement strategies. From left to right, we show the results refined with output finetuning, parameter finetuning and our proposed learning-based refinement. The first row illustrates disparity estimation, the second the accumulated updates, where brighter means larger change in disparity. The last row shows the error map evaluated against ground-truth. Red represents higher error, and blue lower error.

4.4   Performance for Unseen Real Visual Data

To test our method's generalization in other environments, we apply the model to real scenes captured by a ZED stereo camera and compare against results from the feedforward module. As shown in Fig. 4, our consistency guided refinement can notably improve the performance of disparity estimation in such cases. This again confirms that scene flow consistency can be a reliable model in overcoming domain shift, and support more robust performance in unseen scenarios.

Fig. 4. Disparity estimation results in real scenes different from training. Top: input left image, Middle: feedforward results, Bottom: results with consistency guided refinement. Note that refinement can significantly improve drastically incorrect predictions.

5   Conclusions

We have presented Consistency Guided Scene Flow (*CGSF*), a framework for the joint estimation of disparity and scene flow from stereo video. The consistency loss combines stereo and temporal photo-consistency with a novel geometric model which couples the depth and flow variables. Besides the usual online parameter and output finetuning strategies typical of self-supervised test-time domain adaptation, we introduce new, learned, output finetuning descent models with explicit gradient features, that produce good quality results, on par with parameter finetuning, but two orders of magnitude faster. Extensive experimental validation on benchmarks indicates that *CGSF* can reliably predict disparity and scene flow, with good generalization in cross-domain settings.

References

1. Aleotti, F., Poggi, M., Tosi, F., Mattoccia, S.: Learning end-to-end scene flow by distilling single tasks knowledge. In: AAAI (2020)
2. Andrychowicz, M., et al.: Learning to learn by gradient descent by gradient descent. In: Advances in Neural Information Processing Systems, pp. 3981–3989 (2016)
3. Basha, T., Moses, Y., Kiryati, N.: Multi-view scene flow estimation: a view centered variational approach. Int. J. Comput. Vis. **101**(1), 6–21 (2013)
4. Casser, V., Pirk, S., Mahjourian, R., Angelova, A.: Depth prediction without the sensors: leveraging structure for unsupervised learning from monocular videos. In: AAAI (2019)
5. Chang, J., Chen, Y.: Pyramid stereo matching network. In: CVPR (2018)
6. Chen, Y., Schmid, C., Sminchisescu, C.: Self-supervised learning with geometric constraints in monocular video: connecting flow, depth, and camera. In: ICCV (2019)
7. Clark, R., Bloesch, M., Czarnowski, J., Leutenegger, S., Davison, A.J.: LS-Net: Learning to solve nonlinear least squares for monocular stereo. arXiv preprint arXiv:1809.02966 (2018)
8. Dosovitskiy, A., et al.: FlowNet: learning optical flow with convolutional networks. In: ICCV (2015)
9. Godard, C., Mac Aodha, O., Brostow, G.J.: Unsupervised monocular depth estimation with left-right consistency. In: CVPR (2017)
10. Godard, C., Mac Aodha, O., Firman, M., Brostow, G.J.: Digging into self-supervised monocular depth estimation. In: ICCV (2019)
11. Guo, X., Li, H., Yi, S., Ren, J., Wang, X.: Learning monocular depth by distilling cross-domain stereo networks. In: Ferrari, V., Hebert, M., Sminchisescu, C., Weiss, Y. (eds.) ECCV 2018. LNCS, vol. 11215, pp. 506–523. Springer, Cham (2018). https://doi.org/10.1007/978-3-030-01252-6_30
12. Huguet, F., Devernay, F.: A variational method for scene flow estimation from stereo sequences. In: ICCV (2007)
13. Ilg, E., Mayer, N., Saikia, T., Keuper, M., Dosovitskiy, A., Brox, T.: FlowNet 2.0: evolution of optical flow estimation with deep networks. In: CVPR (2017)
14. Ilg, E., Saikia, T., Keuper, M., Brox, T.: Occlusions, motion and depth boundaries with a generic network for disparity, optical flow or scene flow estimation. In: Ferrari, V., Hebert, M., Sminchisescu, C., Weiss, Y. (eds.) ECCV 2018. LNCS, vol. 11216, pp. 626–643. Springer, Cham (2018). https://doi.org/10.1007/978-3-030-01258-8_38

15. Jiang, H., Sun, D., Jampani, V., Lv, Z., Learned-Miller, E., Kautz, J.: SENSE: a shared encoder network for scene-flow estimation. In: ICCV (2019)
16. Kendall, A., et al.: End-to-end learning of geometry and context for deep stereo regression. In: ICCV (2017)
17. Kuznietsov, Y., Stuckler, J., Leibe, B.: Semi-supervised deep learning for monocular depth map prediction. In: CVPR (2017)
18. Lai, H.Y., Tsai, Y.H., Chiu, W.C.: Bridging stereo matching and optical flow via spatiotemporal correspondence. In: CVPR (2019)
19. Li, K., Malik, J.: Learning to optimize. arXiv preprint arXiv:1606.01885 (2016)
20. Liu, P., Lyu, M., King, I., Xu, J.: SelFlow: self-supervised learning of optical flow. In: CVPR (2019)
21. Lv, Z., Dellaert, F., Rehg, J.M., Geiger, A.: Taking a deeper look at the inverse compositional algorithm. In: CVPR (2019)
22. Ma, W.C., Wang, S., Hu, R., Xiong, Y., Urtasun, R.: Deep rigid instance scene flow. In: CVPR (2019)
23. Mayer, N., et al.: A large dataset to train convolutional networks for disparity, optical flow, and scene flow estimation. In: CVPR (2016)
24. Meister, S., Hur, J., Roth, S.: UnFlow: unsupervised learning of optical flow with a bidirectional census loss. In: AAAI (2018)
25. Menze, M., Heipke, C., Geiger, A.: Joint 3D estimation of vehicles and scene flow. In: ISPRS Workshop on Image Sequence Analysis (ISA) (2015)
26. Menze, M., Heipke, C., Geiger, A.: Object scene flow. ISPRS J. Photogramm. Remote Sens. (JPRS) **140**, 60–76 (2018)
27. Pang, J., et al.: Zoom and learn: generalizing deep stereo matching to novel domains. In: CVPR (2018)
28. Poggi, M., Pallotti, D., Tosi, F., Mattoccia, S.: Guided stereo matching. In: CVPR (2019)
29. Sun, D., Yang, X., Liu, M.Y., Kautz, J.: PWC-Net: CNNs for optical flow using pyramid, warping, and cost volume. In: CVPR (2018)
30. Tang, C., Tan, P.: BA-Net: Dense bundle adjustment network. arXiv preprint arXiv:1806.04807 (2018)
31. Tonioni, A., Poggi, M., Mattoccia, S., Di Stefano, L.: Unsupervised adaptation for deep stereo. In: ICCV (2017)
32. Tonioni, A., Rahnama, O., Joy, T., Stefano, L.D., Ajanthan, T., Torr, P.H.: Learning to adapt for stereo. In: CVPR (2019)
33. Tonioni, A., Tosi, F., Poggi, M., Mattoccia, S., Stefano, L.D.: Real-time self-adaptive deep stereo. In: CVPR (2019)
34. Vedula, S., Baker, S., Rander, P., Collins, R., Kanade, T.: Three-dimensional scene flow. In: ICCV (1999)
35. Vogel, C., Schindler, K., Roth, S.: Piecewise rigid scene flow. In: ICCV (2013)
36. Wang, Y., Wang, P., Yang, Z., Luo, C., Yang, Y., Xu, W.: UnOS: unified unsupervised optical-flow and stereo-depth estimation by watching videos. In: CVPR (2019)
37. Wang, Z., Bovik, A.C., Sheikh, H.R., Simoncelli, E.P., et al.: Image quality assessment: from error visibility to structural similarity. IEEE Trans. Image Process. **13**(4), 600–612 (2004)
38. Wedel, A., Rabe, C., Vaudrey, T., Brox, T., Franke, U., Cremers, D.: Efficient dense scene flow from sparse or dense stereo data. In: Forsyth, D., Torr, P., Zisserman, A. (eds.) ECCV 2008. LNCS, vol. 5302, pp. 739–751. Springer, Heidelberg (2008). https://doi.org/10.1007/978-3-540-88682-2_56

39. Yin, Z., Shi, J.: GeoNet: unsupervised learning of dense depth, optical flow and camera pose. In: CVPR (2018)
40. Zhang, F., Prisacariu, V., Yang, R., Torr, P.H.: GA-Net: guided aggregation net for end-to-end stereo matching. In: CVPR (2019)
41. Zhong, Y., Li, H., Dai, Y.: Open-world stereo video matching with deep RNN. In: Ferrari, V., Hebert, M., Sminchisescu, C., Weiss, Y. (eds.) ECCV 2018. LNCS, vol. 11206, pp. 104–119. Springer, Cham (2018). https://doi.org/10.1007/978-3-030-01216-8_7
42. Zhou, T., Brown, M., Snavely, N., Lowe, D.G.: Unsupervised learning of depth and ego-motion from video. In: CVPR (2017)

Autoregressive Unsupervised Image Segmentation

Yassine Ouali$^{(\boxtimes)}$, Céline Hudelot, and Myriam Tami

Université Paris-Saclay, CentraleSupélec, MICS, 91190 Gif-sur-Yvette, France
{yassine.ouali,celine.hudelot,myriam.tami}@centralesupelec.fr

Abstract. In this work, we propose a new unsupervised image segmentation approach based on mutual information maximization between different constructed views of the inputs. Taking inspiration from autoregressive generative models that predict the current pixel from *past* pixels in a raster-scan ordering created with masked convolutions, we propose to use different *orderings* over the inputs using various forms of masked convolutions to construct different *views* of the data. For a given input, the model produces a pair of predictions with two valid orderings, and is then trained to maximize the mutual information between the two outputs. These outputs can either be low-dimensional features for representation learning or output clusters corresponding to semantic labels for clustering. While masked convolutions are used during training, in inference, no masking is applied and we fall back to the standard convolution where the model has access to the full input. The proposed method outperforms current state-of-the-art on unsupervised image segmentation. It is simple and easy to implement, and can be extended to other visual tasks and integrated seamlessly into existing unsupervised learning methods requiring different views of the data.

Keywords: Image segmentation · Autoregressive models ·
Unsupervised learning · Clustering · Representation learning

1 Introduction

Supervised deep learning has enabled great progress and achieved impressive results across a wide number of visual tasks, but it requires large annotated datasets for effective training. Designing such fully-annotated datasets involves a significant effort in terms of data cleansing and manual labeling. It is especially true for fine-grained annotations such as pixel-level annotations needed for segmentation tasks, where the annotation cost per image is considerably high [5,17]. This hurdle can be overcome with unsupervised learning, where unknown but useful patterns can be extracted from the easily accessible unlabeled data. Recent advances in unsupervised learning [7,22,27,36], that closed the performance gap with its supervised counterparts, make it a strong possible alternative.

Electronic supplementary material The online version of this chapter (https://doi.org/10.1007/978-3-030-58571-6_9) contains supplementary material, which is available to authorized users.

© Springer Nature Switzerland AG 2020
A. Vedaldi et al. (Eds.): ECCV 2020, LNCS 12352, pp. 142–158, 2020.
https://doi.org/10.1007/978-3-030-58571-6_9

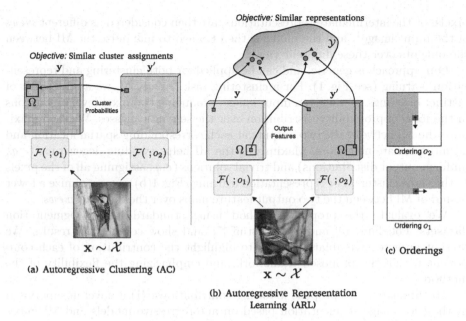

Fig. 1. Overview. Given an encoder-decoder type network $\mathcal{F}$ and two valid orderings (o_1, o_2) as illustrated in (c). The goal is to maximize the Mutual Information (MI) between the two outputs over the different *views*, *i.e.* different *orderings*. (a) For Autoregressive Clusterings (AC), we output the cluster assignments in the form of a probability distribution over pixels, and the goal is to have similar assignments regardless of the applied ordering. (b) For Autoregressive Representation Learning (ARL), the objective is to have similar representations at each corresponding spatial location and its neighbors over a window of small displacements Ω.

Recent works are mainly interested in two objectives, unsupervised representation learning and clustering. Representation learning aims to learn semantic features that are useful for down-stream tasks, be it classification, regression or visualization. In clustering, the unlabeled data points are directly grouped into semantic classes. In both cases, recent works showed the effectiveness of maximizing Mutual Information (MI) between different *views* of the inputs to learn useful and transferable features [13, 22, 36, 41] or discover clusters that accurately match semantic classes [21, 27].

Another line of study in unsupervised learning is generative modeling. In particular, for image modeling, generative autoregressive models [9, 34, 35, 40], such as PixelCNN, are powerful generative models with tractable likelihood computation. In this case, the high-dimensional data, *e.g.*, an image $\mathbf{x}$, is factorized as a product of conditionals over its pixels. The generative model is then trained to predict the current pixel x_i based on the past values $x_{\leq i-1}$ in a raster scan fashion using masked convolutions [34] (Fig. 3(a)).

In this work, instead of using a single left to right, top to bottom ordering, we propose to use several orderings obtained with different forms of masked convolutions and attention mechanism. The various *orderings* over the input pixels, or the intermediate representations, are then considered as different *views* of the input image[1], and the model is then trained to maximize the MI between the outputs over these different views.

Our approach is generic, and can be applied for both clustering and representation learning (see Fig. 1). For a clustering task (Fig. 1(a)), we apply a pair of distinct orderings over a given input image, producing two pixel-level predictions in the form of probability distribution over the semantic classes. We then maximize the MI between the two outputs at each corresponding spatial location and its intermediate neighbors. Maximizing the MI helps avoiding degeneracy (*e.g.*, uniform output distributions) and trivial solutions (*e.g.*, assigning all of the pixels to the same cluster). For representation learning (Fig. 1(b)), we maximize a lower bound of MI between the two output feature maps over the different *views*.

We evaluate the proposed method using standard image segmentation datasets: Potsdam [14] and COCO-stuff [5], and show competitive results. We present an extensive ablation study to highlight the contribution of each component within the proposed framework, and emphasizing the flexibility of the method.

To summarize, we propose following contributions: **(i)** a novel unsupervised method for image segmentation based on autoregressive models and MI maximization; **(ii)** various forms of masked convolutions to generate different orderings; **(iii)** an attention augmented version of masked convolutions for a larger receptive field, and a larger set of possible orderings; **(iv)** an improved performance above previous state-of-the-art on unsupervised image segmentation.

2   Related Works

Autoregressive Models. Many autoregressive models [9,10,15,31,34,37,40] for natural image modeling have been proposed. They model the joint probability distribution of high-dimensional images as a product of conditionals over the pixels. PixelCNN [34,35] specifies the conditional distribution of a sub-pixel (*i.e.*, a color channel of a pixel) as a full 256-way softmax, while PixelCNN++ [40] uses a mixture of logistics. In both cases, masked convolutions are used to process the initial image $\mathbf{x}$ in an autoregressive manner. In Image [37] and Sparse [10] transformers, self-attention [43] is used over the input pixels, while PixelSNAIL [9] combines both attention and masked convolutions.

Clustering and Unsupervised Representation Learning. Recent works in clustering aim at combining traditional clustering algorithms [19] with deep learning, such as using K-means style objectives when training deep nets training [6,12,18]. However, such objective can lead to trivial and degenerate solutions [6]. IIC [27] proposed to use a MI based objective which is intrinsically more robust to such trivial solutions. Unsupervised learning of representations [1,16, 22,36] rather aims to train a model, mapping the unlabeled inputs into some

---

[1] Throughout the paper, a *view* refers to the application of a given *ordering*. Both are used interchangeably.

lower-dimensional space, while preserving semantic information and discarding instance-specific details. The pre-trained model can then be fine-tuned on a down-stream task with fewer labels.

Unsupervised Learning and MI Maximization. Maximizing MI for unsupervised learning is not a new idea [2,19], and recent works demonstrated its effectiveness for unsupervised learning. For representation learning, the training objective is to maximize a lower bound of MI over continuous random variables between distinct views of the inputs. These views can be the input image and its representation [23], the global and local features [22], the features at different scales [1], a sequence of extracted patches from an image in some fixed order [36] or different modalities of the image [41]. For a clustering objective, with discrete random variables as outputs, the exact MI can be maximized over the different views, *e.g.*, IIC [27] maximizes the MI between the image and its augmented version.

Unsupervised Image Segmentation. Methods that learn the segmentation masks entirely from data with no supervision can be categorized as follows: (1) GAN based methods [4,8] that extract and redraw the main object in the image for object segmentation. Such methods are limited to only instances with two classes, a foreground and a background. The proposed method is more generalizable and is independent of the number of ground-truth classes; (2) Iterative methods [24] consisting of a two-step process. The features produced by a CNN are first grouped into clusters using spherical K-means. The CNN is then trained for better feature extraction to discriminate between the clusters. We propose an end-to-end method simplifying both training and inference; (3) MI maximization based methods [27] where the MI between two views of the same instance at the corresponding spatial locations is maximized. We propose an efficient and effective way to create different views of the input using masked convolutions. Another line of work consists of leveraging the learned representations of a deep network for unsupervised segmentation, *e.g.*, CRFs [29] and deep priors [29].

3   Method

Our goal is to learn a representation that maximizes the MI, denoted as I, between different views of the input. These views are generated using various orderings, capturing different aspects of the inputs. Formally, let $\mathbf{x} \sim \mathcal{X}$ be an unlabeled data point, and $\mathcal{F} : \mathcal{X} \rightarrow \mathcal{Y}$ be a deep representation to be learned as a mapping between the inputs and the outputs. For clustering, $\mathcal{Y}$ is the set of possible clusters corresponding to semantic classes, and for representation learning, $\mathcal{Y}$ corresponds to a lower-dimensional space of the output features. Let $(o_i, o_j) \in \mathcal{O}$ be two orderings o_i and o_j obtained from the set of possible and valid orderings $\mathcal{O}$ (Fig. 2). For two outputs $\mathbf{y} \sim \mathcal{F}(\mathbf{x}; o_i)$ and $\mathbf{y}' \sim \mathcal{F}(\mathbf{x}; o_j)$, the objective is to maximize the predictability of $\mathbf{y}$ from $\mathbf{y}'$ and vice-versa, where $\mathcal{F}(\mathbf{x}; o_i)$ corresponds to applying the learning function $\mathcal{F}$ with a given ordering o_i to process the image $\mathbf{x}$. This objective is equivalent to maximizing the MI between the two encoded variables:

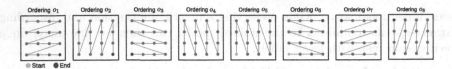

Fig. 2. Raster-scan type orderings.

$$\max_{\mathcal{F}} I(\mathbf{y}; \mathbf{y}') \tag{1}$$

We start by presenting different forms of masked convolutions to generate various raster-scan orderings, and propose an attention augmented variant (Sect. 3.1). We then formulate the training objective for maximizing Eq. (1) (Sect. 3.2). We finally conclude with a flexible design architecture for the function $\mathcal{F}$ (Sect. 3.3).

3.1 Orderings

Masked Convolutions. In neural autoregressive modeling [9,34,40], for an input image $\mathbf{x} \in \mathbb{R}^{H \times W \times 3}$ with 3 color channels, a raster-scan ordering is first imposed on the image (see Fig. 2, ordering o_1). Such an ordering, where the pixel x_i only depends on the pixels that come before it, is maintained using masked convolutions

Our proposition is to use all 8 possible raster-scan type orderings as the set of valid orderings $\mathcal{O}$ as illustrated in Fig. 2. A simple way to obtain them is to use a single ordering o_1 with the standard masked convolution (Fig. reffig3 (a)), along with geometric transformations g (*i.e.*, image rotations by multiples of 90 degrees and horizontal flips), resulting in 8 versions of the input image. We can then maximize the MI between the two outputs, *i.e.*, $I(\mathbf{y}; g^{-1}(\mathbf{y}'))$ with $\mathbf{y}' \sim \mathcal{F}(g(\mathbf{x}); o_j)$. In this case, since the masked weights are never trained, we cannot fall-back to the normal convolution where the function $\mathcal{F}$ has access to the full input during inference, greatly limiting the performance of such approach.

This point motivates our approach. Our objective is to learn all the weights of the masked convolution during training, and use an unmasked version during inference. This can be achieved by using a normal convolution, and for a given ordering o_i, we mask the corresponding weights during the forward pass to construct the desired view of the inputs. Then in the backward pass, we only update the unmasked weights and the masked weights remain unchanged. In this case, all of the weights will be learned and we will converge to a normal convolution given enough training iterations. During inference, no masking is applied, giving the function $\mathcal{F}$ full access to the inputs.

A straight forward way to implement this is to use 8 versions of the standard masked convolution to create the set $\mathcal{O}$ (Fig. 3(d)). However, for each forward pass, the majority of the weights are masked, resulting in a reduced receptive field and a fewer number of weights will be learned at each iteration, leading to some disparity between them.

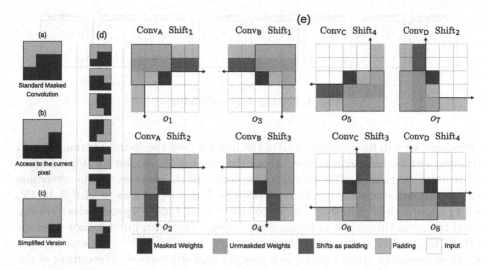

Fig. 3. Masked Convolutions. (a) Standard masked convolution used in autoregressive generative modeling, yielding an ordering o_1. (b) A relaxed version of standard masked convolution where we have access to the current pixel at each step. (c) A simplified version of masked convolution with a reduced number of masked weights. (d) The 8 versions of the standard masked convolution to construct all of the possible raster-scan type orderings. (e) The proposed types of masked convolutions with the corresponding shifts to obtain all of the 8 desired raster-scan types orderings. $F = 3$ in this case.

Given that we are interested in a discriminative task, rather than generative image modeling where the access to the current pixel is not allowed. We start by relaxing the conditional dependency, and allow the model to have access to the current pixel, reducing the number of masked locations by one (Fig. 3(b)). To further reduce the number of masked weights, for an $F \times F$ convolution, instead of masking the lower rows, we can simply shift the input by the same amount and only mask the weights of the last row. We thus reduce the number of masked weight from $\lfloor F^2/2 \rfloor$ (Fig. 3(b)) to $\lfloor F/2 \rfloor$ (Fig. 3(c)). With four possible masked convolutions: $\{\mathrm{Conv_A, Conv_B, Conv_C, Conv_D}\}$ and four possible shifts:[2] $\{\mathrm{Shift_1, Shift_3, Shift_2, Shift_4}\}$, we can create all of 8 raster-scan orderings as illustrated in Fig. 3(e). The proposed masked convolutions do not introduce any additional computational overhead, neither in training, nor inference, making them easy to implement and integrate into existing architectures with minor changes.

Attention Augmented Masked Convolutions. As pointed out by [34], the proposed masked convolutions are limited in terms of expressiveness since they create blind spots in the receptive field (Fig. 6). In our case, by applying different

---

[2] E.g., for $\mathrm{Shift_1}$ and a 3×3 convolution, an image of spatial dimensions $H \times W$ is first padded on the top resulting in $(H + 1) \times W$, the last row is then cropped, going back to $H \times W$.

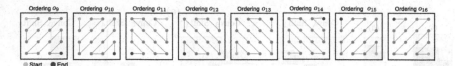

Fig. 4. Zigzag type orderings.

orderings, we will have access to all of the input **x** over the course of training, and this *bug* can be seen as a *feature* where the blind spots can be considered as an additional restriction. This restricted receptive filed, however, can be overcome using the self-attention mechanism [43]. Similar to previous works [3,44,45], we propose to add attention blocks to model long range dependencies that are hard to access through standalone convolutions. Given an input tensor of shape (H, W, C_{in}), after reshaping it into a matrix $X \in \mathbb{R}^{HW \times C_{in}}$, we can apply a masked version of attention [43] in a straight forward manner. The output of the attention operation is:

$$A = \text{Softmax}((QK^\top) \odot \mathbf{M}_{o_i})V \tag{2}$$

with $Q = XW_q$, $K = XW_k$ and $V = XW_v$, where $W_q, W_k \in \mathbb{R}^{C_{in} \times d}$ and $W_v \in \mathbb{R}^{C_{in} \times d}$ are learned linear transformations that map the input X to queries Q, keys K and values V, and $\mathbf{M}_{o_i} \in \mathbb{R}^{HW \times HW}$ corresponds to a masking operation to maintain the correct ordering o_i.

The output is then projected into the output space using a learned linear transformation $W^O \in \mathbb{R}^{d \times C_{in}}$ obtaining $X_{\text{att}} = AW^O$. The output of the attention operation X_{att} is concatenated channel wise with the input X, and then merged using a 1×1 convolution resulting in the output of the attention block.

Zigzag Orderings. Using attention gives us another benefit, we can extend the set of possible orderings to include zigzag type orderings introduced in [9] (Fig. 4). With zigzag orderings, the outputs at each spatial location will be mostly influenced by the values of the corresponding neighboring input pixels, which can give rise to more semantically meaningful representations compared to that of raster-scan orderings. This is done by simply using a mask $\mathbf{M}_{o_i}$ corresponding to the desired zigzag ordering o_i. Resulting in a set $\mathcal{O}$ of 16 possible and valid orderings o_i with $i \in \{1, \dots, 16\}$ in total. See Fig. 5 for an example.

3.2   Training Objective

In information theory, the MI $I(X; Y)$ between two random variables X and Y measures the *amount of information* learned from the knowledge of Y about X and vice-versa. The MI can be expressed as the difference of two entropy terms:

$$I(X; Y) = H(X) - H(X|Y) = H(Y) - H(Y|X) \tag{3}$$

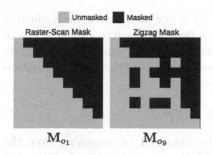

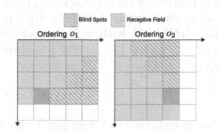

Fig. 5. Attention Masks. Examples of the different attention masks $\mathbf{M}_{o_i}$ of shape $HW \times HW$ applied for a given ordering o_i. With $HW = 9$.

Fig. 6. Blind Spots. Blind spots in the receptive field of pixel ■ as a result of using a masked convolution for a given ordering o_i.

Intuitively, $I(X;Y)$ can be seen as the reduction of uncertainty in one of the variables, when the other one is observed. If X and Y are independent, knowing one variable exposes nothing about the other, in this case, $I(X;Y) = 0$. Inversely, if the state of one variable is deterministic when the state of the other is revealed, the MI is maximized. Such an interpretation explains the goal behind maximizing Eq. (1). The neural network $\mathcal{F}$ must be able to preserve information and extract semantically similar representations regardless of the applied ordering o_i, and learn representations that encode the underlying shared information between the different views. The objective can also be interpreted as having a regularization effect, forcing the function $\mathcal{F}$ to focus on the different views and subparts of the input $\mathbf{x}$ to produce similar outputs, reducing the reliance on specific objects or parts of the image.

Let $p(\mathbf{y}, \mathbf{y}')$ be the joint distribution produced by sampling examples $\mathbf{x} \sim \mathcal{X}$ and then sampling two outputs $\mathbf{y} \sim \mathcal{F}(\mathbf{x}; o_i)$ and $\mathbf{y}' \sim \mathcal{F}(\mathbf{x}; o_j)$ with two possible orderings o_i and o_j. In this case, the MI in Eq. (1) can be defined as the Kullback–Leibler (KL) divergence between the joint and the product of the marginals:

$$I(\mathbf{y}, \mathbf{y}') = D_{\mathrm{KL}}(p(\mathbf{y}, \mathbf{y}') \| p(\mathbf{y})p(\mathbf{y}')) \tag{4}$$

To maximize Eq. (4), we can either maximize the exact MI for a clustering task over discrete predictions, or a lower bound for an unsupervised learning of representations over the continuous outputs. We will now formulate the loss functions $\mathcal{L}_{\mathrm{AC}}$ and $\mathcal{L}_{\mathrm{ARL}}$ of both objectives for a segmentation task.

Autoregressive Clustering (AC). In a clustering task, the goal is to train a neural network $\mathcal{F}$ to predict a cluster assignment corresponding to a given semantic class $k \in \{1, \ldots, K\}$ with K possible clusters at each spatial location. In this case, the encoder-decoder type network $\mathcal{F}$ is terminated with K-way softmax, outputting $\mathbf{y} \in [0,1]^{H \times W \times K}$ of the same spatial dimensions as the input. Concretely, for a given input image $\mathbf{x}$ and two valid orderings $(o_i, o_j) \in \mathcal{O}$, we forward pass the input through the network producing two output probability distributions $\mathcal{F}(\mathbf{x}; o_i) = p(\mathbf{y}|\mathbf{x}, o_i)$ and $\mathcal{F}(\mathbf{x}; o_j) = p(\mathbf{y}'|\mathbf{x}, o_j)$ over the K clusters and at each spatial location. After reshaping the outputs into two matrices of shape $HW \times K$, with each element corresponding to the probability of assigning pixel x_l with $l \in \{1, \ldots, HW\}$ to cluster k, we can compute the joint distribution $p(\mathbf{y}, \mathbf{y}')$ of shape $K \times K$ as follows:

$$p(\mathbf{y}, \mathbf{y}') = \mathcal{F}(\mathbf{x}; o_i)^\top \mathcal{F}(\mathbf{x}; o_j) \tag{5}$$

The marginals $p(\mathbf{y})$ and $p(\mathbf{y}')$ can then be obtained by summing over the rows and columns of $p(\mathbf{y}, \mathbf{y}')$. Similar to IIC [27], we symmetrize $p(\mathbf{y}, \mathbf{y}')$ using $[p(\mathbf{y}, \mathbf{y}') + p(\mathbf{y}, \mathbf{y}')^\top]/2$ to maximize the MI in both directions. The clustering loss $\mathcal{L}_{AC}$ in this case can be written as follows:

$$\mathcal{L}_{\mathrm{AC}} = \mathbb{E}_{\mathbf{x} \sim \mathcal{X}} \left[\mathbb{E}_{p(\mathbf{y}, \mathbf{y}')} \log \frac{p(\mathbf{y}, \mathbf{y}')}{p(\mathbf{y})p(\mathbf{y}')} \right] \tag{6}$$

In practice, instead of only maximizing the MI between two corresponding spatial locations, we maximize it between each spatial location and its intermediate neighbors over small displacements $\mathbf{u} \in \Omega$ (see Fig. 1). This can be efficiently implemented using a convolution operation as demonstrated in [27].

Autoregressive Representation Learning (ARL). Although the clustering objective in Eq. (6) can also be used as a pre-training objective for $\mathcal{F}$, Tschannen et al. [42] recently showed that maximizing the MI does not often results in transferable and semantically meaningful features, especially when the downstream task is a priori unknown. To this end, we follow recent representation learning works based on MI maximization [1,22,36,41], where a lower bound estimate of MI (e.g., InfoNCE [36], NWJ [33]) is maximized between different views of the inputs. These estimates are based on the simple intuitive idea, that if a critic f is able to differentiate between samples drawn from the joint distribution $p(\mathbf{y}, \mathbf{y}')$ and samples drawn from the marginals $p(\mathbf{y})p(\mathbf{y}')$, then the true MI is maximized. We refer the reader to [42] for a detailed discussion.

In our case, with image segmentation as the target down-stream task, we maximize the InfoNCE estimator [36] over the continuous outputs. Specifically, with two outputs $(\mathbf{y}, \mathbf{y}') \in \mathbb{R}^{H \times W \times C}$ as C-dimensional feature maps. The training objective is to maximize the infoNCE based loss $\mathcal{L}_{\mathrm{ARL}}$:

$$\mathcal{L}_{\mathrm{ARL}} = \mathbb{E}_{\mathbf{x} \sim \mathcal{X}} \left[\log \frac{e^{f(\mathbf{y}_l, \mathbf{y}_l')}}{\frac{1}{N} \sum_{m=1}^{N} e^{f(\mathbf{y}_l, \mathbf{y}_m')}} \right] \tag{7}$$

For an input image $\mathbf{x}$ and two outputs $\mathbf{y}$ and $\mathbf{y}'$. Let $\mathbf{y}_l$ and $\mathbf{y}_m'$ correspond to C-dimensional feature vectors at spatial positions l and m in the first and second outputs respectively. We start by creating N pairs of feature vectors $(\mathbf{y}_l, \mathbf{y}_m')$, with one positive pair drawn from the joint distribution and $N - 1$ negative pairs drawn from the marginals. A positive pair is a pair of feature vectors corresponding to the same spatial locations in the two outputs, i.e., a pair $(\mathbf{y}_l, \mathbf{y}'_m)$ with $m = l$. The negatives are pairs $(\mathbf{y}_l, \mathbf{y}'_m)$ corresponding to two distinct spatial positions $m \neq l$. In practice, we also consider small displacements Ω (Fig. 1) when constructing positives. Additionally, the negatives are generated from two distinct images, since two feature vectors might share similar characteristics even with different spatial positions. By maximizing Eq. (7), we push the model $\mathcal{F}$ to produce similar representations for the same spatial location regardless of the applied ordering, so that the critic function f is able to give high matching scores to the positive pairs and low matching to the negatives. We follow [22] and use separable critics $f(\mathbf{y}, \mathbf{y}') = \phi_1(\mathbf{y})^\top \phi_2(\mathbf{y}')$, where the functions ϕ_1/ϕ_2 non-linearly transform the outputs to a higher vector space, and $f(\mathbf{y}_l, \mathbf{y}'_m)$ produces a scalar corresponding to a matching score between the two representations at two spatial positions l and m of the two outputs.

Note that both losses $\mathcal{L}_{\mathrm{AC}}$ and $\mathcal{L}_{\mathrm{ARL}}$ can be applied interchangeably for both objectives, a case we investigate in our experiments (Sect. 4.1). For $\mathcal{L}_{\mathrm{AC}}$, we can consider the clustering objective as an intermediate task for learning useful representations. For $\mathcal{L}_{\mathrm{ARL}}$, during inference, K-means [28] algorithm can be applied over the outputs to obtain the cluster assignments.

3.3   Model

The representation $\mathcal{F}$ can be implemented in a general manner using three sub-parts, i.e., $\mathcal{F} = h \circ g_{ar} \circ d$, with a feature extractor h, an autoregressive encoder g_{ar} and a decoder d. With such a formulation, the function $\mathcal{F}$ is flexible and can take different forms. With h as an identity mapping, $\mathcal{F}$ becomes a fully autoregressive network, where we apply different orderings directly over the inputs. Inversely, if g_{ar} is an identity mapping, $\mathcal{F}$ becomes a generic encoder-decoder network, where h plays the role of an encoder. Additionally, h can be a simple convolutional stem that plays an important role in learning local features such as edges, or even multiple residual blocks [20] to extract higher representations. In this case, the orderings are applied over the hidden features using g_{ar}. g_{ar} is similar to h, containing a series of residual blocks, with two main differences, the proposed masked convolutions are used, and the batch normalization [25] layers are omitted to maintain the autoregressive dependency, with an optional attention block. The decoder d can be a simple conv1×1 to adapt the channels to the number of cluster K, followed by bilinear upsampling and a softmax operation for a clustering objective. For representation learning, d consists of two separable critics ϕ_1/ϕ_2, which are implemented as a series of conv$3 \times 3 - \mathrm{BN} - \mathrm{ReLU}$ and conv1×1 for projecting to a higher dimensional space. See sup. mat. for the architectural details.

4   Experiments

Datasets. The experiments are conducted on the newly established and challenging baselines by [27]. Potsdam [14] with 8550 RGBIR satellite images of size 200×200, of which 3150 are unlabeled. We experiment on both the 6-labels variant (roads and cars, vegetation and trees, buildings and clutter) and Potsdam-3,

Table 1. AC Ablations. Ablations studies conducted on Potsdam (POS) and Potsdam-3 (POS3) for Autoregressive Clusterings. We show the pixel classification accuracy (%).

Network $\mathcal{F} = h \circ g_{ar} \circ d$		POS	POS3
h	g_{ar}		
Random		28.5	38.2
$\mathcal{F}_1$ Id	5 Res. blocks	39.3	56.3
$\mathcal{F}_2$ Stem	5 Res. blocks	46.4	**66.4**
$\mathcal{F}_3$ Res. block	4 Res. blocks	**47.9**	64.5
$\mathcal{F}_4$ 5 Res. blocks	Id	35.1	63.4
$\mathcal{F}_5$ ResNet-18	Id	40.7	51.9

(a) **Variation of $\mathcal{F}$.**

$|\mathcal{O}|$	POS	POS3
2	43.2±2.19	59.5±5.12
4	45.6±3.22	63.55±3.52
8	**46.4**	**66.4**

(b) **Number of orderings.**

Orderings			POS	POS3
Raster-Scan	Zigzag	Attention		
✓	✗	✗	45.2	61.0
✓	✗	✓	47.9	66.3
✗	✓	✓	47.8	**66.5**
✓	✓	✓	**49.3**	65.4

(c) **Attention.**

Sampling o_i	POS	POS3
Random	46.4	**66.4**
No Rep.	48.6	64.8
Hard	**48.9**	65.2

(d) **Sampling of o_i.**

Type	Transf.	POS	POS3
None	-	46.4	66.4
Photometric	Col. Jittering	47.9	65.5
Geometric	Flip	46.7	68.0
Geometric	Rot.	**48.5**	68.3
Geo. & Pho.	All	**48.5**	**68.3**

(e) **Transformations.**

p	POS	POS3
0	46.4	**66.4**
0.1	**47.9**	64.7
0.2	46.9	65.1

(f) **Dropout.**

a 3-label variant formed by merging each of the pairs. We also use COCO-Stuff [5], a dataset containing *stuff* classes. Similarly, we use a reduced version of COCO-Stuff with 164k images and 15 coarse labels, reduced to 52k by taking only images with at least 75% stuff pixel. In addition to COCO-Stuff-3 with only 3 labels, sky, ground and plants.

Evaluation Metrics. We report the pixel classification Accuracy (Acc). For a clustering task, with a mismatch between the learned and ground truth clusters. We follow the standard procedure and find the best one-to-one permutation to match the output clusters to ground truth classes using the Hungarian algorithm [30]. The Acc is then computed over the labeled examples.

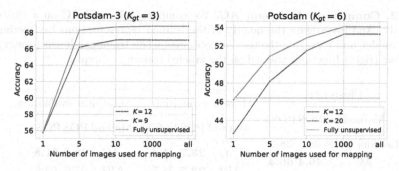

Fig. 7. Overclustering. The Acc obtained when using a number of output clusters greater than the number of ground truth classes $K > K_{gt}$. With variable number of images used to find the best many-to-one matching between the outputs and targets.

Implementation Details. The different variations of $\mathcal{F}$ are trained using ADAM with a learning rate of 10^{-5} to optimize both objectives in Eqs. (6) and (7). The training is conducted on NVidia V100 GPUs, and implemented using the PyTorch framework [38]. For more experimental details, see sup. mat.

4.1 Ablation Studies

We start by performing comprehensive ablation studies on the different components and variations of the proposed method. Table 1 and Fig. 7 show the ablation results for AC, and Table 2 shows a comparison between AC and ARL, analyzed as follows:

Variations of $\mathcal{F}$. Table 2a compares different variations of the network $\mathcal{F}$. With a fixed decoder d (*i.e.*, a 1×1Conv followed by bilinear upsampling and softmax function), we adjust h and g_{ar} going from a fully autoregressive model ($\mathcal{F}_1$) to a normal decoder-encoder network ($\mathcal{F}_4$ and $\mathcal{F}_5$). When using masked versions, we see an improvement over the normal case, with up to 8 points for Potsdam, and to a lesser extent for Potsdam-3 where the task is relatively easier with only three ground truth classes. When using a fully autoregressive model ($\mathcal{F}_1$), and applying the orderings directly over the inputs, maximizing the MI becomes much harder, and the model fails to learn meaningful representations. Inversely, when no masking is applied ($\mathcal{F}_4$ and $\mathcal{F}_5$), the task becomes comparatively simpler, and we see a drop in performance. The best results are obtained when applying the orderings over low-level features ($\mathcal{F}_2$ and $\mathcal{F}_3$). Interestingly, the unmasked versions yield results better than random, and perform competitively with 3 output classes for Potsdam-3, validating the effectiveness of maximizing the MI over small displacements $\mathbf{u} \in \Omega$. For the rest of the experiments we use $\mathcal{F}_2$ as our model.

Attention and Different Orderings. Table 2c shows the effectiveness of attention. With a single attention block added at a shallow level, we observe an improvement over the baseline, for both raster-scan and zigzag orderings, and

Table 2. Comparing ARL and AC. We compare ARL and AC on a clustering task (left). And investigate the quality of the learned representations by freezing the trained model, and reporting the test Acc obtained when training a linear (center) and non-linear (right) functions trained on the labeled training examples.

Clustering			Linear evaluation			Non-linear evaluation		
Method	POS	POS3	Method	POS	POS3	Method	POS	POS3
Random CNN	28.5	38.2	AC	**23.7**	**41.4**	AC	**68.0**	**81.8**
AC	**46.4**	**66.4**	ARL	**23.7**	38.5	ARL	47.6	63.5
ARL	45.1	57.1						

their combination, with up to 4 points for Potsdam. In this case, given the quadratic complexity of attention, we used an output stride of 4.

Data Augmentations. For a given training iteration, we pass the same image two times through the network, applying two different orderings at each forward pass. We can, however, pass a transformed version of the image as the second input. We investigate using photometric (*i.e.*, color jittering) and geometric (*i.e.*, rotations and H-flips) transformations. For geometric transformations, we bring the outputs back to the input coordinate space before computing the loss. Results are shown in Table 2e. As expected, we obtain relative improvements with data augmentations, highlighting the flexibility of the approach.

Dropout. To add some degree of stochasticity to the network, and as an additional regularization, we apply dropout to the intermediate activations within residual blocks. Table 2f shows a small increase in Acc for Potsdam.

Orderings. Until now, at each forward pass, we sample a pair of possible orderings with replacement from the set $\mathcal{O}$. With such a sampling procedure, we might end-up with the same pair of orderings for a given training iteration. As an alternative, we investigate two other sampling procedures. First, with no repetition (No Rep.), where we choose two distinct orderings for each training iteration. Second, using hard sampling, choosing two orderings with opposite receptive fields (*e.g.*, o_1 and o_6). Table 2d shows the obtained results. We see 2 points improvement when using hard sampling for Potsdam. For simplicity, we use random sampling for the rest of the experiments. Additionally, to investigate the effect of the number of orderings (*i.e.*, the cardinality of $\mathcal{O}$), we compute the Acc over different choices and sizes of $\mathcal{O}$. Table 2b shows best results are obtained when using all 8 raster-scan orderings. Interestingly, for some choices, we observe better results, which may be due to selecting orderings that do not share any receptive fields, as the ones used in hard sampling.

Overclustering. To compute the Acc for a clustering task using linear assignment, the output clusters are chosen to match the ground truth classes $K = K_{gt}$. Nonetheless, we can choose a higher number of clusters $K > K_{gt}$, and then find

Table 3. Unsupervised image segmentation. Comparison of AC with state-of-the-art methods on unsupervised segmentation.

	COCO-Stuff-3	COCO-Stuff	Potsdam-3	Potsdam
Random CNN	37.3	19.4	38.2	28.3
K-means [39]	52.2	14.1	45.7	35.3
SIFT [32]	38.1	20.2	38.2	28.5
Doersch 2015 [11]	47.5	23.1	49.6	37.2
Isola 2016 [26]	54.0	24.3	63.9	44.9
DeepCluster 2018 [6]	41.6	19.9	41.7	29.2
IIC 2019 [27]	72.3	27.7	65.1	45.4
AC	**72.9**	**30.8**	**66.5**	**49.3**

the best many-to-one matching between the output clusters and ground truths based a given number of labeled examples. In this case, however, we are not in a fully unsupervised case, given that we extract some information, although limited, from the labels. Figure 7 shows that, even with a very limited number of labeled examples used for mapping, we can obtain better results than the fully unsupervised case.

AC and ARL. To compare AC and ARL, we apply them interchangeably on both clustering and representation learning objectives. In clustering, for ARL, after PCA Whitening, we apply K-means over the output features to get the cluster assignments. In representation learning, we evaluate the quality of the learned representations using both linear and non-linear separability as a proxy for disentanglement, and as a measure of MI between representations and class labels. Table 2 shows the obtained results.

Clustering. As expected, AC outperforms ARL on a clustering task, given that the clusters are directly optimized by computing the exact MI during training.

Quality of the Learned Representations. Surprisingly, AC outperforms ARL on both linear and non-linear classifications. We hypothesize that unsupervised representation learning objectives that work well on image classification, fail in image segmentation due to the dense nature of the task. The model in this case needs to output distinct representations over pixels, rather than the whole image, which is a harder task to optimize. This might also be due to using only a small number of features (*i.e.*, N pairs) for each training iteration.

4.2 Comparison with the State-of-the-Art

Table 3 shows the results of the comparison. AC outperforms previous work, and by a good margin for harder segmentation tasks with a large number of output classes (*i.e.*, Potsdam and COCO-Stuff), highlighting the effectiveness of maximizing the MI between the different orderings as a training objective.

We note that no regularization or data augmentation were used, and we expect that better results can be obtained by combining AC with other procedures as demonstrated in the ablation studies.

5   Conclusion

We presented a novel method to create different *views* of the inputs using different *orderings*, and showed the effectiveness of maximizing the MI over these views for unsupervised image segmentation. We showed that for image segmentation, optimizing over the discrete outputs MI works better for both clustering and unsupervised representation learning, due to the dense nature of the task. Given the simplicity and ease of adoption of the method, we hope that the proposed approach can be adapted for other visual tasks and used in future works.

Acknowledgments. We gratefully acknowledge the support of Randstad corporate research chair, Saclay-IA platform of and Mésocentre computing center.

References

1. Bachman, P., Hjelm, R.D., Buchwalter, W.: Learning representations by maximizing mutual information across views. In: Advances in Neural Information Processing Systems, pp. 15509–15519 (2019)
2. Becker, S., Hinton, G.E.: Self-organizing neural network that discovers surfaces in random-dot stereograms. Nature **355**(6356), 161–163 (1992)
3. Bello, I., Zoph, B., Vaswani, A., Shlens, J., Le, Q.V.: Attention augmented convolutional networks. In: Proceedings of the IEEE International Conference on Computer Vision, pp. 3286–3295 (2019)
4. Bielski, A., Favaro, P.: Emergence of object segmentation in perturbed generative models. In: Advances in Neural Information Processing Systems, pp. 7256–7266 (2019)
5. Caesar, H., Uijlings, J., Ferrari, V.: Coco-stuff: thing and stuff classes in context. In: Proceedings of the IEEE Conference on Computer Vision and Pattern Recognition, pp. 1209–1218 (2018)
6. Caron, M., Bojanowski, P., Joulin, A., Douze, M.: Deep clustering for unsupervised learning of visual features. In: Ferrari, V., Hebert, M., Sminchisescu, C., Weiss, Y. (eds.) Computer Vision – ECCV 2018. LNCS, vol. 11218, pp. 139–156. Springer, Cham (2018). https://doi.org/10.1007/978-3-030-01264-9_9
7. Caron, M., Bojanowski, P., Mairal, J., Joulin, A.: Unsupervised pre-training of image features on non-curated data. In: Proceedings of the IEEE International Conference on Computer Vision, pp. 2959–2968 (2019)
8. Chen, M., Artières, T., Denoyer, L.: Unsupervised object segmentation by redrawing. In: Advances in Neural Information Processing Systems, pp. 12705–12716 (2019)
9. Chen, X., Mishra, N., Rohaninejad, M., Abbeel, P.: PixelSNAIL: an improved autoregressive generative model. In: International Conference on Machine Learning, pp. 864–872 (2018)
10. Child, R., Gray, S., Radford, A., Sutskever, I.: Generating long sequences with sparse transformers. arXiv preprint arXiv:1904.10509 (2019)

11. Doersch, C., Gupta, A., Efros, A.A.: Unsupervised visual representation learning by context prediction. In: Proceedings of the IEEE International Conference on Computer Vision, pp. 1422–1430 (2015)
12. Fard, M.M., Thonet, T., Gaussier, E.: Deep k-means: Jointly clustering with k-means and learning representations. arXiv preprint arXiv:1806.10069 (2018)
13. Federici, M., Dutta, A., Forré, P., Kushman, N., Akata, Z.: Learning robust representations via multi-view information bottleneck. arXiv preprint arXiv:2002.07017 (2020)
14. Gerke, M.: Use of the stair vision library within the ISPRS 2D semantic labeling benchmark (Vaihingen) (2014)
15. Germain, M., Gregor, K., Murray, I., Larochelle, H.: MADE: masked autoencoder for distribution estimation. In: International Conference on Machine Learning, pp. 881–889 (2015)
16. Gidaris, S., Singh, P., Komodakis, N.: Unsupervised representation learning by predicting image rotations. arXiv preprint arXiv:1803.07728 (2018)
17. Girshick, R., Donahue, J., Darrell, T., Malik, J.: Rich feature hierarchies for accurate object detection and semantic segmentation. In: Proceedings of the IEEE Conference on Computer Vision and Pattern Recognition, pp. 580–587 (2014)
18. Haeusser, P., Plapp, J., Golkov, V., Aljalbout, E., Cremers, D.: Associative deep clustering: training a classification network with no labels. In: Brox, T., Bruhn, A., Fritz, M. (eds.) GCPR 2018. LNCS, vol. 11269, pp. 18–32. Springer, Cham (2019). https://doi.org/10.1007/978-3-030-12939-2_2
19. Hartigan, J.A.: Direct clustering of a data matrix. J. Am. Stat. Assoc. **67**(337), 123–129 (1972)
20. He, K., Zhang, X., Ren, S., Sun, J.: Deep residual learning for image recognition. In: Proceedings of the IEEE Conference on Computer Vision and Pattern Recognition, pp. 770–778 (2016)
21. He, Z., Xu, X., Deng, S.: k-ANMI: a mutual information based clustering algorithm for categorical data. Inf. Fusion **9**(2), 223–233 (2008)
22. Hjelm, R.D., et al.: Learning deep representations by mutual information estimation and maximization. arXiv preprint arXiv:1808.06670 (2018)
23. Hu, W., Miyato, T., Tokui, S., Matsumoto, E., Sugiyama, M.: Learning discrete representations via information maximizing self-augmented training. In: Proceedings of the 34th International Conference on Machine Learning, vol. 70, pp. 1558–1567. JMLR.org (2017)
24. Hwang, J.J., et al.: SegSort: segmentation by discriminative sorting of segments. In: Proceedings of the IEEE International Conference on Computer Vision, pp. 7334–7344 (2019)
25. Ioffe, S., Szegedy, C.: Batch normalization: Accelerating deep network training by reducing internal covariate shift. arXiv preprint arXiv:1502.03167 (2015)
26. Isola, P., Zoran, D., Krishnan, D., Adelson, E.H.: Learning visual groups from co-occurrences in space and time. arXiv preprint arXiv:1511.06811 (2015)
27. Ji, X., Henriques, J.F., Vedaldi, A.: Invariant information clustering for unsupervised image classification and segmentation. In: Proceedings of the IEEE International Conference on Computer Vision, pp. 9865–9874 (2019)
28. Johnson, J., Douze, M., Jégou, H.: Billion-scale similarity search with GPUs. arXiv preprint arXiv:1702.08734 (2017)
29. Kanezaki, A.: Unsupervised image segmentation by backpropagation. In: 2018 IEEE International Conference on Acoustics, Speech and Signal Processing (ICASSP), pp. 1543–1547. IEEE (2018)

30. Kuhn, H.W.: The Hungarian method for the assignment problem. Naval Res. Logist. Q. **2**(1–2), 83–97 (1955)
31. Larochelle, H., Murray, I.: The neural autoregressive distribution estimator. In: Proceedings of the 14th International Conference on Artificial Intelligence and Statistics, pp. 29–37 (2011)
32. Lowe, D.G.: Distinctive image features from scale-invariant keypoints. Int. J. Comput. Vis. **60**(2), 91–110 (2004)
33. Nguyen, X., Wainwright, M.J., Jordan, M.I.: Estimating divergence functionals and the likelihood ratio by convex risk minimization. IEEE Trans. Inf. Theor. **56**(11), 5847–5861 (2010)
34. Van den Oord, A., Kalchbrenner, N., Espeholt, L., Vinyals, O., Graves, A., et al.: Conditional image generation with PixelCNN decoders. In: Advances in Neural Information Processing Systems, pp. 4790–4798 (2016)
35. van den Oord, A., Kalchbrenner, N., Kavukcuoglu, K.: Pixel recurrent neural networks. arXiv preprint arXiv:1601.06759 (2016)
36. van den Oord, A., Li, Y., Vinyals, O.: Representation learning with contrastive predictive coding. arXiv preprint arXiv:1807.03748 (2018)
37. Parmar, N., et al.: Image transformer. In: Dy, J., Krause, A. (eds.) Proceedings of the 35th International Conference on Machine Learning. Proceedings of Machine Learning Research, PMLR, Stockholmsmässan, Stockholm Sweden, 10–15 July 2018, vol. 80, pp. 4055–4064 (2018)
38. Paszke, A., et al.: Automatic differentiation in PyTorch (2017)
39. Pedregosa, F., et al.: Scikit-learn: machine learning in Python. J. Mach. Learn. Res. **12**, 2825–2830 (2011)
40. Salimans, T., Karpathy, A., Chen, X., Kingma, D.P.: PixelCNN++: Improving the PixelCNN with discretized logistic mixture likelihood and other modifications. arXiv preprint arXiv:1701.05517 (2017)
41. Tian, Y., Krishnan, D., Isola, P.: Contrastive multiview coding. arXiv preprint arXiv:1906.05849 (2019)
42. Tschannen, M., Djolonga, J., Rubenstein, P.K., Gelly, S., Lucic, M.: On mutual information maximization for representation learning. arXiv preprint arXiv:1907.13625 (2019)
43. Vaswani, A., et al.: Attention is all you need. In: Advances in Neural Information Processing Ssystems, pp. 5998–6008 (2017)
44. Wang, X., Girshick, R., Gupta, A., He, K.: Non-local neural networks. In: Proceedings of the IEEE Conference on Computer Vision and Pattern Recognition, pp. 7794–7803 (2018)
45. Zhang, H., Goodfellow, I., Metaxas, D., Odena, A.: Self-attention generative adversarial networks. arXiv preprint arXiv:1805.08318 (2018)

Controllable Image Synthesis via SegVAE

Yen-Chi Cheng[1,2]($\boxtimes$), Hsin-Ying Lee[1], Min Sun[2], and Ming-Hsuan Yang[1,3]

[1] University of California, Merced, Merced, USA
[2] National Tsing Hua University, Hsinchu City, Taiwan
charlescheng0117@gmail.com
[3] Google Research, Mountain View, USA

Abstract. Flexible user controls are desirable for content creation and image editing. A semantic map is commonly used intermediate representation for conditional image generation. Compared to the operation on raw RGB pixels, the semantic map enables simpler user modification. In this work, we specifically target at generating semantic maps given a label-set consisting of desired categories. The proposed framework, SegVAE, synthesizes semantic maps in an iterative manner using conditional variational autoencoder. Quantitative and qualitative experiments demonstrate that the proposed model can generate realistic and diverse semantic maps. We also apply an off-the-shelf image-to-image translation model to generate realistic RGB images to better understand the quality of the synthesized semantic maps. Finally, we showcase several real-world image-editing applications including object removal, insertion, and replacement.

1 Introduction

The recent success of deep generative models has made breakthroughs in a wide range of tasks such as image and video synthesis [2,9,11]. In addition to conventional generative models that aims to generate images from noise vectors sampled from prior distributions, conditional generative models have getting attention to handle various tasks including image-to-image translation (I2I) [6,15,43], text-to-image synthesis [5,41], and audio-to-video generation [18], to name a few. One major goal of these conditional generation tasks is to enable flexible user control, image editing, and content creation. Conditional generative models can greatly shorten the distance between professional creators and general users (Fig. 1).

Among all forms of conditional context, semantic maps are recently getting attention. Semantic maps can be used as an intermediate representation or directly as inputs. As an intermediate representation, semantic maps serve as mediums that facilitate the original tasks such as image generation from text and scene graph [5,7]. As inputs, semantic maps can be translated to realistic images via I2I models [27]. These I2I models enable editing on the semantic maps, which

Electronic supplementary material The online version of this chapter (https:// doi.org/10.1007/978-3-030-58571-6_10) contains supplementary material, which is available to authorized users.

A. Vedaldi et al. (Eds.): ECCV 2020, LNCS 12352, pp. 159–174, 2020.
https://doi.org/10.1007/978-3-030-58571-6_10

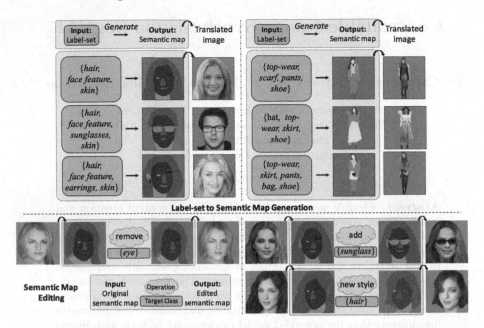

Fig. 1. Label-set to Semantic map generation. (*Top*) Given a label-set, SegVAE can generate diverse and realistic semantic maps. (*Bottom*) The proposed model enables several real-world flexible image editing.

is easier and more flexible than operating on the RGB space. However, in terms of image editing, users need to create semantic maps that are realistic in order to generate realistic RGB images. It is crucial to provide users greater flexibility and less overhead on image editing.

In this work, we focus on generating semantic maps given a label-set. The task is challenging for two reasons. First, the shape of components in the semantic maps not only need to be realistic, but also have to be mutually compatible. Second, the generation is inherently multimodal, that is, one label-set can correspond to multiple semantic maps. To handle these issues, we propose **SegVAE**, a VAE-based framework that can generate semantic maps in an iterative manner. For *compatibility*, the proposed model performs generation at each iteration conditioned on the label-set as well as previously generated components. For *diversity*, the proposed method learns a shape prior distribution that can be randomly sampled during the inference stage.

We evaluate the proposed methods through extensive qualitative and quantitative experiments. We conduct experiments on two diverse datasets, the Cele-bAMaskHQ [13] and HumanParsing [22] datasets, to demonstrate the general effectiveness of the proposed framework. We leverage Fréchet Inception Distance (FID) [3] and conduct a user study to evaluate realism. For diversity, we measure feature distances similar to the Learned Perceptual Image Patch Similarity (LPIPS) [42] metric. Furthermore, we demonstrate several real-world editing scenarios to showcase the superb controllability of the proposed method. We also apply an I2I model, SPADE [27], to synthesize realistic images based on the generated semantic maps to better visualize the quality of the proposed model.

We make the following contributions:

- We propose a new approach that can generate semantic maps from label-sets. Components in the generated semantic maps are mutually compatible and the overall semantic maps are realistic. SegVAE can also generate diverse results.
- We validate that our method performs favorably against existing methods and baselines in terms of realism and diversity on the CelebAMask-HQ and HumanParsing datasets.
- We demonstrate several real-world image editing applications using the proposed method. Our model enables flexible editing and manipulation. Our code and more results is available at https://github.com/yccyenchicheng/SegVAE.

2   Related Work

Generative Models. Generative models aim to model a data distribution given a set of samples from that distribution. The mainstream of generative models approximates the distribution through maximum likelihood. There are two branches of the maximum likelihood method. One stream of work explicitly models the data distribution. PixelRNN [25] and PixelCNN [24] are auto-regressive models that perform sequential generation where the next pixel value is predicted conditioned on all the previously generated pixel values. Variational autoencoder [11] model the real data distribution by maximizing the lower bound of the data log-likelihood. The other stream of work learns implicit data distribution. Generative adversarial networks [2] model the data distribution by a two-player game between a generator and a discriminator.

Based on conventional generative models, conditional generative models synthesize images based on various contexts. Conditional generative models can formulate a variety of topics in image editing and content creations, including super-resolution [12], image-to-image translation [16,43], text-to-image generation [37,41], video generation [20,39], and music-to-dance translation [18].

Generative Models with Semantic Maps. Semantic map is an important modality in generative modeling. There are two major ways of using semantic maps. First, semantic maps can be used as the conditional context for conditional image synthesis. Image-to-image translation models can learn the mapping from semantic maps to realistic RGB images [6,26,27,38]. Second, semantic maps can serve as an intermediate representation during the training of image synthesis conditioned on text or scene graph. [7,19,31,33,35]. Using semantic layouts provides rough guidance of the location and appearance of objects and further facilitate the training. In this work, we focus on generating semantic maps directly from a label-set. The proposed model enables flexible user editing and the generated results can be further used for photorealistic image generation.

Image Editing. Image editing is a process of altering images. Traditional image editing mostly focuses on low-level changing like image enhancement, image retouching, and image colorization. In this work, we target at generating and altering the content of images. For generation, previous work can synthesize desired output given instructions like a set of categories [8,17] or a sentence [34], or change the semantic information in a user-specified region of the target image [32]. Other stream of work can perform operations like object insertion [14,23], object removal [40], and object attribute editing [36]. The proposed method can achieve both generations: given specified label-sets, and editing including object insertion and removal (Fig. 2).

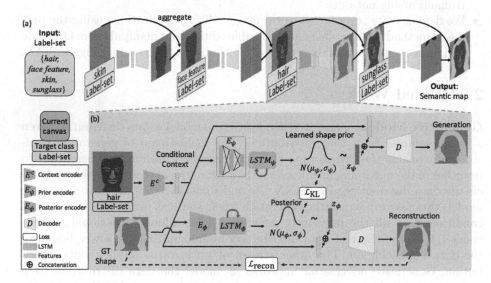

Fig. 2. Overview. (a) Given a label-set as input, we iteratively predict the semantic map of each category starting from a blank canvas. We initialize the initial canvas as a blank semantic map x_0. The generation conditions on the embedding of (*Current canvas, Target class, Label-set*). (b) In each iteration, the context encoder E^c encodes the input into the conditional context which is copied as the input to E_ϕ, E_ψ, and D. During training, the posterior encoder $\{E_\phi, LSTM_\phi\}$ takes the ground-truth semantic map of the target class as additional input to output $N(\mu_\phi, \sigma_\phi)$, which is then used to reconstruct the ground-truth semantic map. The prior encoder $\{E_\psi, LSTM_\psi\}$ encodes the conditional context to output $N(\mu_\psi, \sigma_\psi)$, which enables the stochastic sampling during test time.

3   Semantic Maps Generation

Our goal is to learn the mapping from label-sets $\mathcal{X}$ to semantic maps $\mathcal{Y} \subset \mathbb{R}^{H \times W \times C}$. A label-set $\mathbf{x} = [x_1, x_2, \ldots, x_c] \in \mathcal{X}$ is a binary vector with c classes, where $x_i \in \{0, 1\}$. A semantic map $y \in \mathcal{Y}$ denotes a c channels label map where

$Y_{i,j,k} \in \{0,1\}$ for class k, $k = 1, 2, \ldots, C$. The proposed **SegVAE** consist of a context encoder E_c, a posterior encoders $\{E_\phi, LSTM_\phi\}$, a learned prior encoders $\{E_\psi, LSTM_\psi\}$, and a decoder D. The context encoder E^c aims to encode information including label-set, current canvas, and target label into a context for the following conditional generation. The posterior network $\{E_\phi, LSTM_\phi\}$, consisting of a convolutional encoder and an LSTM, aims to conditionally encode input each iteration into an inference prior. The learned prior network $\{E_\psi, LSTM_\psi\}$, consisting of a fully-connected encoder and an LSTM, targets at learning a conditional prior distribution to be sampled from during inference time. The decoder D then learns the mapping from both posterior and learned prior distribution to semantic maps.

In this section, we first introduce the background knowledge of conditional variational auto-encoder in Sect. 3.1. Then we detail the proposed model in Sect. 3.2. Finally, we provide implementation details in Sect. 3.3.

3.1 Conditional VAE

Variational Autoencoder. A Variational Autoencoder (VAE) [11,29] attempts to explicitly model the real data distribution by maximizing the lower bound of the data log-likelihood. VAE leverages a simple prior $p_\theta(\mathbf{z})$ (e.g., Gaussian) and a complex likelihood $p_\theta(\mathbf{x}|\mathbf{z})$ on latent variable $\mathbf{z}$ to maximize the data likelihood $p_\theta(\mathbf{x})$. An inference network $q_\phi(\mathbf{z}|\mathbf{x})$ is introduced to approximate the intractable latent posterior $p_\theta(\mathbf{z}|\mathbf{x})$. Here θ and ϕ denote the parameters of the generation and inference networks. We then jointly optimize over θ and ϕ,

$$\log p_\theta(\mathbf{x}) = \log \int_{\mathbf{z}} p_\theta(\mathbf{x}|\mathbf{z})p(\mathbf{z}) \, dz$$
$$\geq \mathbb{E}_{q_\phi(\mathbf{z}|\mathbf{x})} \log p_\theta(\mathbf{x}|\mathbf{z}) - D_{\mathrm{KL}}(q_\phi(\mathbf{z}|\mathbf{x})||p(\mathbf{z})) \,. \tag{1}$$

With this inequality, the variational autoencoder aims to reconstruct data $\mathbf{x}$ with latent variable $\mathbf{z}$ sampled from the posterior $q_\phi(\mathbf{z}|\mathbf{x})$ while minimizing the KL-divergence between the prior $p(\mathbf{z})$ and posterior $q_\phi(\mathbf{z}|\mathbf{x})$.

Conditional Variational Autoencoder. A Conditional Variational Autoencoder (C-VAE) [30] is an extension of the VAE which condition on a prior information described by a variable or feature vector $\mathbf{c}$. The generation and inference network's output will base on the conditional variable $\mathbf{c}$, and the optimization over θ and ϕ becomes,

$$\log p_\theta(\mathbf{x}, \mathbf{c}) = \log \int_{\mathbf{z}} p_\theta(\mathbf{x}|\mathbf{z}, \mathbf{c})p(\mathbf{z}) \, dz$$
$$\geq \mathbb{E}_{q_\phi(\mathbf{z}|\mathbf{x})} \log p_\theta(\mathbf{x}|\mathbf{z}, \mathbf{c}) - D_{\mathrm{KL}}(q_\phi(\mathbf{z}|\mathbf{x}, \mathbf{c})||p(\mathbf{z}|\mathbf{c})) \,. \tag{2}$$

3.2 Iterative Generation with Learned Prior

A label-set consists of various amount of categories. To handle the dynamic amount of categories as well as capture dependency among categories, we leverage Long-Short Term Memory (LSTM) [4] as our recurrent backbone. However, how to perform stochastic generation and model data variations remain a challenge. The complexity is twofold. First, there are various possible combinations of categories to construct a label-set. For example, $y_1 = \{t\text{-}shirt, short, shoe\}$ and $y_2 = \{sunglasses, dress, bag\}$ represent two completely different outfit style. Second, in addition to label-set-level variations, category-level variations also need to be captured. For instance, each bag and $dress$ have diverse possible shapes. Moreover, the label-set-level variations and the category-level variations are not independent. For example, different choices of $t\text{-}shirt$ will affect the choices of $dress$ considering compatibility.

To handle these issues, we leverage C-VAE as our generative model. However, the usage of $\mathcal{N}(\mathbf{0}, \mathbf{I})$ which is conventionally used in VAE ignores dependencies between iterations since the priors are drawn independently at each iteration. Therefore, we adopt the similar idea from [1] to use a parameterized network ψ other than $\mathcal{N}(\mathbf{0}, \mathbf{I})$ for inferring the shape prior distribution. In order to learn the conditional prior, we first define our conditional context at iteration t as:

$$c_t = E^c(y_t, y, x_{1:t-1}),$$

(3)

where y_t is the current category to be generated, y represents the given label set, and x_k denote the semantic map at iteration k. The learned prior can thus be modeled with $\{E_\psi, LSTM_\psi\}$. At iteration t,

$$h_t = E_\psi(c_t)$$
$$\mu_\psi^t, \sigma_\psi^t = \text{LSTM}_\psi(h_t)$$
$$z_t \sim \mathcal{N}(\mu_\psi^t, \sigma_\psi^t).$$

(4)

The learned prior is trained with the help of the posterior network $\{E_\phi, LSTM_\phi\}$ and the decoder D. At iteration t, given x_t, the semantic map of current category, we perform reconstruction by

$$h_t = E_\phi(c_t, x_t)$$
$$\mu_\phi^t, \sigma_\phi^t = \text{LSTM}_\phi(h_t)$$
$$z_t \sim \mathcal{N}(\mu_\phi^t, \sigma_\phi^t)$$
$$\hat{x}_t = D(z_t, c_t).$$

(5)

Therefore, the model can be trained with a reconstruction loss and a KL loss at iteration t:

$$L_{\text{recon}}^t = \|\hat{x}_t - x_t\|_1$$
$$L_{\text{KL}}^t = -D_{\text{KL}}(\mathcal{N}(\mu_\phi^t, \sigma_\phi^t)\|\mathcal{N}(\mu_\psi^t, \sigma_\psi^t)).$$

(6)

We express the final objective as:

$$L = \mathbb{E}_{x,y}\Big[\sum_{i=1}^{|y|} \lambda_{\text{recon}} L_{\text{recon}}^i + \lambda_{\text{KL}} L_{\text{KL}}^i\Big],$$

(7)

where the hyper-parameters λs control the importance of both term.

In the inference time, given a label-set as input, we initialize an empty label map as x_0. We then generate x_k autoregressively by setting the inputs for p_ψ with the generated shapes $\hat{x}_{1:t-1}$.

Table 1. Realism and Diversity. We use the FID and a feature space distance metric to measure the realism and diversity ($\pm$ indicates the 95% C.I.).

Method	HumanParsing		CelebAMask-HQ	
	FID $\downarrow$	Diversity $\uparrow$	FID $\downarrow$	Diversity $\uparrow$
C-GAN	$171.1293^{\pm.3359}$	N/A	$76.0115^{\pm.1981}$	N/A
C-VAE$_{\text{sep}}$	$85.0505^{\pm.3052}$	$.1781^{\pm.040}$	$39.7445^{\pm.2254}$	$.1566^{\pm.033}$
C-VAE$_{\text{global}}$	$83.8214^{\pm.6747}$	$.1730^{\pm.034}$	$36.2903^{\pm.2084}$	$\mathbf{.1582}^{\pm.031}$
sg2im-orig [7]	$207.0786^{\pm.3324}$	N/A	$208.8142^{\pm.1876}$	N/A
sg2im [7]	$56.7421^{\pm.2206}$	$\underline{.2064}^{\pm.050}$	$34.7316^{\pm.3071}$	$.1476^{\pm.045}$
Ours w/o LSTM	$50.8830^{\pm.2374}$	$.2024^{\pm.045}$	$34.5073^{\pm.2156}$	$.1535^{\pm.034}$
Ours w/o Learned Prior	$\underline{44.6217}^{\pm.2881}$	$.1625^{\pm.054}$	$\underline{33.8060}^{\pm.3167}$	$.1492^{\pm.038}$
Ours	$\mathbf{39.6496}^{\pm.3543}$	$\mathbf{.2072}^{\pm.053}$	$\mathbf{28.8221}^{\pm.2732}$	$\underline{.1575}^{\pm.043}$
GT	$33.1562^{\pm.3801}$	$.2098^{\pm.050}$	$22.5981^{\pm.0870}$	$.1603^{\pm.045}$

3.3 Implementation Details

We implement our model in PyTorch [28]. For all experiments, we use the resolution of 128×128 for the input image and semantic map. For the context encoder E^c, we use two multilayer perceptrons to produce the embeddings of the label-set and target label, and fuse them with the current canvas. Then a six convolution layers will encode the embeddings and the current canvas into the conditional context. For the E_ψ, we apply a fully connected layers with LSTM followed by two multilayer perceptrons to output the mean and log variance. The E_ϕ is similar to E_ψ by replacing the fully connected layers with the convolution layers to encoder the ground truth semantic map. We use the latent code size of $z_\psi, z_\phi \in \mathbb{R}^{384}$ for all experiments. Finally, the D consists of five fractionally strided convolution layers. We apply the instance norm and spectral norm for all the architectures. For more details of the network architecture, please refer to the supplementary material.

For training, we use the Adam optimizer [10] with a learning rate of $5e^{-5}$, a batch size of 24, and $(\beta_1, \beta_2) = (0.5, 0.999)$. For the HumanParsing dataset, we use $\lambda_{\text{recon}} = 1$, $\lambda_{\text{KL}} = 1e^{-4}$ and $\lambda_{\text{recon}} = 1$, $\lambda_{\text{KL}} = 1e-7$ for the CelebAMask-HQ dataset. For the order of the iterative generation with learned prior, we use {*face, hair, left arm, right arm, left leg, right leg, upper clothes, dress, skirt, pants, left shoe, right shoe, hat, sunglasses, belt, scarf, bag*} for the HumanParsing dataset. In addition, {*skin, neck, hair, left eyebrow, right eyebrow, left ear, right ear, left eye, right eye, nose, lower lip, upper lip, mouth, hat, cloth, eyeglass, earrings, necklace*} for the CelebAMask-HQ dataset.

4   Experimental Results

Datasets. We perform the evaluation on two datasets:

- **HumanParsing.** The HumanParsing dataset [22], extended from [21], contains ~17,000 of street fashion images and 18 classes of semantic maps with pixel-annotations. It is composed of diverse appearances and multiple combinations of fashion items and human parts. We first clean the dataset by inspecting the aspect ratio of the ground truth semantic maps and remove those over ±1 standard deviation. For each example, we compute the bounding box of each class on the semantic map and crop them accordingly.
- **CelebAMask-HQ.** CelebAMask-HQ [13] is a large-scale face image dataset which includes 30,000 high-resolution paired face images and semantic maps. The semantic maps contain 19 classes of facial attributes and accessories. The various shapes of facial attributes and accessories make it suitable for testing.

We split the data into 80%, 10%, 10% for training, validation and testing.

Evaluated Method. We evaluate the following algorithms.

- **C-GAN.** We implement a conditional GAN which takes a label-set as input and generates the corresponding images. This method has to handle the class-dependency, compatibility between shapes, and the image quality at the same time, which imposes a great burden on a single model.
- **C-VAE$_{sep}$.** This baseline generates semantic maps for each category independently. The generated semantic maps are then aggregated to the final output.
- **C-VAE$_{global}$.** This baseline takes global context into consideration while generating semantic maps for each category. We encode the label-set into a global feature, which serves as the conditional context for the generation. With reference to the global feature, the generated shapes will be more compatible.
- **sg2im** [7]. Sg2im is a conditional generative model that takes a scene graph as input and output the corresponding image. To facilitate the learning, a semantic map is first predicted from the object embedding during the optimization process. We compare the predicted semantic maps from sg2im given a label-set as input, which can be seen as the simplest form of a scene graph. We use the official implementation provided by [7] for training. For a fair comparison, we provide ground truth bounding boxes for sg2im when generating the masks. We report both the metrics from the images translated from its predicted semantic maps using SPADE [27] and the images generated by sg2im (denoted by "sg2im" and "sg2im-orig" respectively in Table 1).

4.1   Quantitative Evaluation

Visual Quality. We evaluate the realism of the generated semantic maps using the Fréchet Inception Distance (FID) [3] metric. We first generate a semantic

Table 2. Compatibility and reconstructability. We train a shape predictor to measure the compatibility error (abbreviated as Compat. error) over the generated shapes. We adopt an auto-encoder to measure the quality of our generated results by computing the reconstruction error (denoted as Recon. error).

Method	HumanParsing		CelebAMask-HQ	
	Compat. error ↓	Recon. error ↓	Compat. error ↓	Recon. error ↓
C-VAE$_{sep}$	$.7823^{\pm.0161}$	$.6857^{\pm.010}$	$.1029^{\pm.0017}$	$.1165^{\pm.003}$
C-VAE$_{global}$	$.7345^{\pm.0141}$	$.6186^{\pm.018}$	$.1015^{\pm.0040}$	$.1142^{\pm.003}$
sg2im [7]	$.6983^{\pm.0176}$	$\mathbf{.5434^{\pm.012}}$	$.0844^{\pm.0020}$	$.1334^{\pm.003}$
Ours	$\mathbf{.6174^{\pm.0147}}$	$.5663^{\pm.011}$	$\mathbf{.0754^{\pm.0013}}$	$\mathbf{.0840^{\pm.001}}$

map given a label-set, then we use an off-the-shelf I2I model [27] to output the translated image. We compute FID with the official implementation from [3] on all compared methods to measure the realism of the generated semantic maps. Table 1 shows that the proposed model performs favorably against the baselines and the existing method.

Diversity. We measure the diversity by computing distance between the generated semantic maps using the distance metric similar to the LPIPS [42] metric. However, there are no general feature extractors for semantic maps. Therefore, we trained an auto-encoder on the ground truth semantic maps. We use the intermediate representation as the extracted features for semantic maps. We can then measure the feature distance between two semantic maps. We measure the diversity between 3000 pairs of generated semantic maps by sampling from the test-set. Table 1 shows that the proposed method generates diverse semantic maps without sacrificing visual quality.

Compatibility and Reconstruction Error. To evaluate the compatibility of a generated semantic maps, we design a metric measure the performance of all compared methods. A shape is compatible if it can be easily inferred from all the other class's semantic maps. We measure this quantitatively by training a shape predictor which takes a semantic map and a target label as input, and outputs the shape of the target class. The training pair of the data is created by excluding one of the class in the ground truth semantic map as the prediction target, and the remaining classes' semantic maps along with the class of the excluded target form the input. Then we use this shape predictor to compute the compatibility error for all the compared methods. Meanwhile, we also train an auto-encoder on the ground-truth semantic maps to measure if one generated result is close to the real data distribution. Given a generated semantic map as input, we calculate the reconstruction error between the input and the reconstructed result output by the auto-encoder. Table 2 shows that the proposed method generates compatible and reasonable semantic maps.

Prediction Order Analysis. We analyze how the prediction order will affect the performance of the proposed model at Tables 3. First, we organize the classes

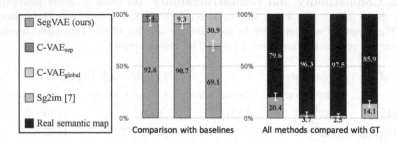

Fig. 3. User study. We conduct a user study to evaluate the realism of the generated semantic maps. We have two sets of comparison: the comparison with other algorithms, and all methods to real maps. Results showed that users favored SegVAE (gray bar) against all other compared methods in both settings.

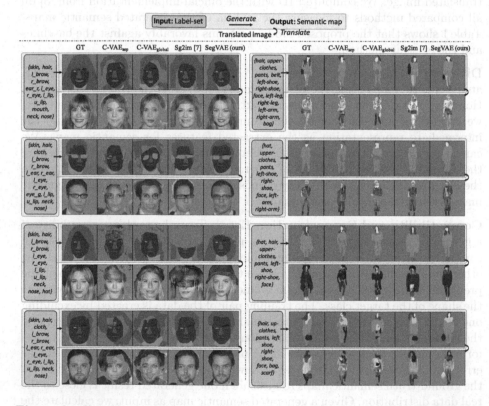

Fig. 4. Qualitative comparison. We present the generated semantic maps given label-sets on the CelebAMask-HQ (left) and the HumanParsing (right) datasets. The proposed model generates images with better visual quality compared to other methods. We also present the translated realistic images via SPADE. Please refer to Fig. 5 for the color mapping for each category.

Table 3. Prediction order analysis. (Upper) On the HumanParsing dataset, order–1 and order–2 perform similarly since both *Body, Clothes* provide great contexts for the model. In contrast, order–3 degrades the generation results and the diversity since *Accessories* offers limited contexts. (Lower) On the CelebAMask-HQ dataset, *Face* is crucial for serving as the initial canvas for the subsequent generation. Therefore order–1 outperforms order–2 and order–3. in FID. Similarly, order–3 largely constrains the possible generation for the remaining class and causes lower diversity.

Order (HumanParsing)	FID↓	Diversity↑
1 *Body → Clothes → Accessories* (Ours)	$\mathbf{39.6496}^{\pm.3543}$	$\mathbf{.2072}^{\pm.053}$
2 *Clothes → Body → Accessories*	$39.9008^{\pm.5263}$	$.2062^{\pm.0494}$
3 *Accessories → Body → Clothes*	$40.2909^{\pm.2195}$	$.2043^{\pm.0521}$
Order (CelebAMask-HQ)	FID↓	Diversity↑
1 *Face → Face features → Accessories* (Ours)	$\mathbf{28.8221}^{\pm.2732}$	$\mathbf{.1575}^{\pm.043}$
2 *Face features → Face → Accessories*	$30.6547^{\pm.1267}$	$.1517^{\pm.0376}$
3 *Accessories → Face → Face features*	$32.0325^{\pm.1294}$	$.1489^{\pm.0363}$

in each dataset into three major categories for two datasets where the class in each category has similar properties. Then, we train the proposed methods with different permutations of these orders.

HumanParsing. We organize the classes into *Body, Clothes, Accessories*. The classes in each category are

- *Body*: {*face, hair, left arm, right arm, left leg, right leg*}.
- *Clothes*: {*upper clothes, dress, skirt, pants, left shoe, right shoe*}.
- *Accessories*: {*hat, sunglasses, belt, scarf, bag*}.

Three orders are as follows. Order–1: *Body, Clothes, Accessories* (Ours), order–2: *Clothes, Body, Accessories*, and order–3: *Accessories, Body, Clothes*.

CelebAMask-HQ. We organize the classes into *Face, Face features, Accessories*. The classes in each category are

- *Face*: {*skin, neck, hair*}.
- *Face features*: {*left eyebrow, right eyebrow, left ear, right ear, left eye, right eye, nose, lower lip, upper lip, mouth*}.
- *Accessories*: {*hat, cloth, eyeglass, earrings, necklace*}.

We experiment on three prediction orders. Order–1: *Face, Face features, Accessories* (Ours), order–2: *Face features, Face, Accessories*, and order–3: *Accessories, Face, Face features*.

Table 3 shows how the prediction order affects the performance of realism and diversity. For the HumanParsing dataset, order–1 and order–2 perform similarly on FID and diversity since both *Body* and *Clothes* provide great contexts for the model. While in order–3, *Accessories* do not deliver good information as the other two categories and will constrain the possible shapes and locations when generating the semantic maps of *Body* and *Clothes*. This results in a degradation in FID and diversity. For the CelebAMask-HQ dataset, the *Face* category is essential. Acting as a canvas, it ensures the generation of the subsequent class is located in the semantically meaningful position, and gives the most degree of freedom when generating compatible shapes compared to other orders.

Ablation Studies. We analyze the contribution of each component of our method with ablation studies.

- **Ours w/o LSTM.** This model omits the LSTM when outputting the distribution of the learned prior and the posterior.
- **Ours w/o Learned Shape Prior.** This version adopts a fixed Gaussian distribution for the shape prior. The proposed method with fixed prior.

The results in Table 1 show the necessity of the proposed model's architecture design. LSTM serves as a crucial role to handle the dynamic among the classes as well as capture the dependency among them. On both datasets, the model yields significant improvements over FID in contrast to the model with fixed prior. Meanwhile, adopting the learned shape prior mainly contributes to the better diversity of the generated outputs and improves the realism.

User Study. To better explicitly evaluate the visual quality of the generated semantic maps without relying on the off-the-shelf image-to-image translation model, we conduct a user study. We perform two sets of comparisons. First, we compare the proposed method to baselines. Second, we compare all methods to ground-truth semantic maps. In each test, users are given two semantic maps generated from different methods and asked "which semantic map looks more realistic?". We ask each user to compare 20 pairs and collect results from a total of 60 subjects. Figure 3 presents the results of our user study.

4.2 Qualitative Evaluation

Visual Quality. We compare the visual quality of the generated semantic maps from the proposed method and the baseline methods. As shown in Fig. 4, the proposed model can generate semantic maps that are more realistic than others. The **C-VAE$_{sep}$** model generates each category independently. The generation of each semantic map is not only unaware of the shape of other categories, but even unknowing of what other categories are in this label-set. Although the individual semantic maps are reasonable, they are not mutually compatible after combination. The **C-VAE$_{global}$** model performs slightly better with taking the label-set information as an additional input. However, the generation process still disregards the appearance of each other. Finally, the proposed SegVAE outperforms sg2im from several perspectives. First, the iterative generation allows us to use teacher-forcing in training, which helps capture the dependency among components. Second, we can better capture the appearance distribution with the help of VAE. Finally, the learned latent space enables random sampling during inference time, which supports generating diverse outputs.

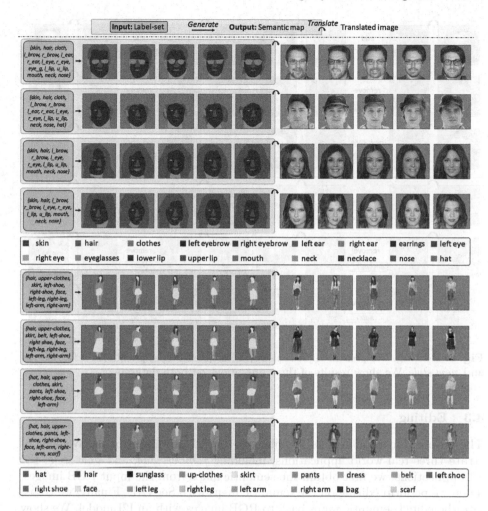

Fig. 5. Multi-modality. We demonstrate the ability of SegVAE to generate diverse results given a label-set on both datasets.

Multi-modality. We demonstrate the capability of the proposed method to generate diverse outputs in Fig. 5. SegVAE can generate diverse appearances of objects given the same label-set. For example, the eyeglasses (the first row of CelebAMask-HQ), the hat (the second row of CelebAMask-HQ), the skirt (the second row of HumanParsing), and the scarf (the fourth row of HumanParsing). The generated semantic maps are mutually compatible thanks to the iterative conditional generation process. In the fourth row of CelebAMask-HQ, the hair and face change jointly to different orientations. In the first row of HumanParsing, both left- and right-leg changes jointly to different poses.

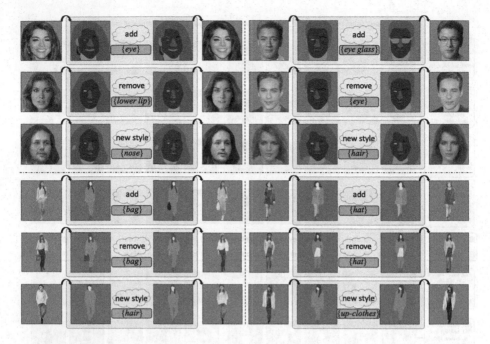

Fig. 6. Editing. We present three real-world image editing applications: *add*, *remove*, and *new style*. We show results of three operations on both datasets.

4.3 Editing

The proposed method enables flexible user-control for image editing. We demonstrate three real-world applications, including *remove*, *add*, and *new style*. For all applications, we first obtain the semantic maps from the input RGB images. Then we perform editing on the semantic maps with SegVAE. Finally, we translate the edited semantic maps back to RGB images with an I2I model. We show the results of image editing in Fig. 6. For *Remove*, we remove a category from the label-set. For *Add*, we add an additional category to the existing label-set to perform object insertion. For *New style*, we could alter the style of the targeted category due to the diverse outputs of the purposed method.

5   Conclusion

In this paper, we present a novel VAE-based framework with iterative generation process for label-set to semantic maps generation. To generate realistic appearance and mutually compatible shapes among the classes, we propose to generate the target shape in an autoregressive fashion by conditioning on the previously generated components. To handle the diverse output, we adopt a parameterized network for learning a shape prior distribution. Qualitative and quantitative results show that the generated semantic maps are realistic and diverse. We also apply an image-to-image translation model to generate RGB images to better understand the quality of the synthesized semantic maps. Finally, we showcase several real-world image-editing scenarios including removal, insertion, and replacement, which enables better user-control over the generated process.

Acknowledgement. This work is supported in part by the NSF CAREER Grant #1149783, MOST 108-2634-F-007-016-, and MOST 109-2634-F-007-016-.

References

1. Denton, E., Fergus, R.: Stochastic video generation with a learned prior. In: ICML (2018)
2. Goodfellow, I., et al.: Generative adversarial nets. In: NIPS (2014)
3. Heusel, M., Ramsauer, H., Unterthiner, T., Nessler, B., Hochreiter, S.: GANs trained by a two time-scale update rule converge to a local Nash equilibrium. In: NIPS (2017)
4. Hochreiter, S., Schmidhuber, J.: Long short-term memory. Neural Comput. **9**(8), 1735–1780 (1997)
5. Hong, S., Yang, D., Choi, J., Lee, H.: Inferring semantic layout for hierarchical text-to-image synthesis. In: CVPR (2018)
6. Isola, P., Zhu, J.Y., Zhou, T., Efros, A.A.: Image-to-image translation with conditional adversarial networks. In: CVPR (2017)
7. Johnson, J., Gupta, A., Fei-Fei, L.: Image generation from scene graphs. In: CVPR (2018)
8. Jyothi, A.A., Durand, T., He, J., Sigal, L., Mori, G.: LayoutVAE: stochastic scene layout generation from a label set. In: ICCV (2019)
9. Karras, T., Laine, S., Aila, T.: A style-based generator architecture for generative adversarial networks. In: CVPR (2019)
10. Kingma, D., Ba, J.: Adam: a method for stochastic optimization. In: ICLR (2015)
11. Kingma, D.P., Welling, M.: Auto-encoding variational Bayes. In: ICLR (2014)
12. Ledig, C., et al.: Photo-realistic single image super-resolution using a generative adversarial network. In: CVPR (2017)
13. Lee, C.H., Liu, Z., Wu, L., Luo, P.: MaskGAN: Towards diverse and interactive facial image manipulation. arXiv preprint arXiv:1907.11922 (2019)
14. Lee, D., Liu, S., Gu, J., Liu, M.Y., Yang, M.H., Kautz, J.: Context-aware synthesis and placement of object instances. In: NeurIPS (2018)
15. Lee, H.-Y., Tseng, H.-Y., Huang, J.-B., Singh, M., Yang, M.-H.: Diverse image-to-image translation via disentangled representations. In: Ferrari, V., Hebert, M., Sminchisescu, C., Weiss, Y. (eds.) ECCV 2018. LNCS, vol. 11205, pp. 36–52. Springer, Cham (2018). https://doi.org/10.1007/978-3-030-01246-5_3
16. Lee, H.-Y., et al.: DRIT++: diverse image-to-image translation via disentangled representations. Int. J. Comput. Vis. **128**(10), 2402–2417 (2020). https://doi.org/10.1007/s11263-019-01284-z
17. Lee, H.Y., et al.: Neural design network: graphic layout generation with constraints. In: ECCV (2020)
18. Lee, H.Y., et al.: Dancing to music. In: NeurIPS (2019)
19. Li, W., et al.: Object-driven text-to-image synthesis via adversarial training. In: CVPR (2019)

20. Li, Y., Min, M.R., Shen, D., Carlson, D., Carin, L.: Video generation from text. In: AAAI (2018)
21. Liang, X., et al.: Deep human parsing with active template regression. TPAMI **37**(12), 2402–2414 (2015)
22. Liang, X., et al.: Human parsing with contextualized convolutional neural network. In: ICCV (2015)
23. Lin, C.H., Yumer, E., Wang, O., Shechtman, E., Lucey, S.: ST-GAN: spatial transformer generative adversarial networks for image compositing. In: CVPR (2018)
24. Van den Oord, A., Kalchbrenner, N., Espeholt, L., Vinyals, O., Graves, A., et al.: Conditional image generation with PixelCNN decoders. In: NIPS (2016)
25. Van den Oord, A., Kalchbrenner, N., Kavukcuoglu, K.: Pixel recurrent neural networks. In: ICML (2016)
26. Pan, J., et al.: Video generation from single semantic label map. In: CVPR (2019)
27. Park, T., Liu, M.Y., Wang, T.C., Zhu, J.Y.: Semantic image synthesis with spatially-adaptive normalization. In: CVPR (2019)
28. Paszke, A., et al.: PyTorch: an imperative style, high-performance deep learning library. In: NeurIPS (2019)
29. Rezende, D.J., Mohamed, S., Wierstra, D.: Stochastic backpropagation and approximate inference in deep generative models. In: ICML (2014)
30. Sohn, K., Lee, H., Yan, X.: Learning structured output representation using deep conditional generative models. In: NIPS (2015)
31. Sun, W., Wu, T.: Image synthesis from reconfigurable layout and style. In: ICCV (2019)
32. Suzuki, R., Koyama, M., Miyato, T., Yonetsuji, T.: Spatially controllable image synthesis with internal representation collaging. arXiv preprint arXiv:1811.10153 (2018)
33. Talavera, A., Tan, D.S., Azcarraga, A., Hua, K.: Layout and context understanding for image synthesis with scene graphs. In: ICIP (2019)
34. Tan, F., Feng, S., Ordonez, V.: Text2Scene: generating compositional scenes from textual descriptions. In: CVPR (2019)
35. Tripathi, S., Bhiwandiwalla, A., Bastidas, A., Tang, H.: Heuristics for image generation from scene graphs. In: ICLR workshop (2019)
36. Tseng, H.Y., Fisher, M., Lu, J., Li, Y., Kim, V., Yang, M.H.: Modeling artistic workflows for image generation and editing. In: ECCV (2020)
37. Tseng, H.Y., Lee, H.Y., Jiang, L., Yang, W., Yang, M.H.: RetrieveGAN: image synthesis via differentiable patch retrieval. In: ECCV (2020)
38. Wang, T.C., Liu, M.Y., Zhu, J.Y., Tao, A., Kautz, J., Catanzaro, B.: High-resolution image synthesis and semantic manipulation with conditional GANs. In: CVPR (2018)
39. Wang, T.H., Cheng, Y.C., Lin, C.H., Chen, H.T., Sun, M.: Point-to-point video generation. In: ICCV (2019)
40. Yang, J., Hua, K., Wang, Y., Wang, W., Wang, H., Shen, J.: Automatic objects removal for scene completion. In: INFOCOM WKSHPS (2014)
41. Zhang, H., et al.: StackGAN: text to photo-realistic image synthesis with stacked generative adversarial networks. In: ICCV (2017)
42. Zhang, R., Isola, P., Efros, A.A., Shechtman, E., Wang, O.: The unreasonable effectiveness of deep features as a perceptual metric. In: CVPR (2018)
43. Zhu, J.Y., Park, T., Isola, P., Efros, A.A.: Unpaired image-to-image translation using cycle-consistent adversarial networks. In: ICCV (2017)

Off-Policy Reinforcement Learning for Efficient and Effective GAN Architecture Search

Yuan Tian[1(✉)], Qin Wang[1(✉)], Zhiwu Huang[1], Wen Li[2], Dengxin Dai[1],
Minghao Yang[3], Jun Wang[4], and Olga Fink[1]

[1] ETH Zürich, Zürich, Switzerland
{yutian,qwang,ofink}@ethz.ch, {zhiwu.huang,dai}@vision.ee.ethz.ch
[2] UESTC, Chengdu, China
liwenbnu@gmail.com
[3] Navinfo Europe, Eindhoven, The Netherlands
minghao.yang@navinfo.eu
[4] University College London, London, UK
junwang@cs.ucl.ac.uk

Abstract. In this paper, we introduce a new reinforcement learning
(RL) based neural architecture search (NAS) methodology for effective
and efficient generative adversarial network (GAN) architecture search.
The key idea is to formulate the GAN architecture search problem as
a Markov decision process (MDP) for smoother architecture sampling,
which enables a more effective RL-based search algorithm by target-
ing the potential global optimal architecture. To improve efficiency, we
exploit an off-policy GAN architecture search algorithm that makes efficient use of the samples generated by previous policies. Evaluation on two
standard benchmark datasets (i.e., CIFAR-10 and STL-10) demonstrates
that the proposed method is able to discover highly competitive architectures for generally better image generation results with a considerably
reduced computational burden: 7 GPU hours. Our code is available at
https://github.com/Yuantian013/E2GAN.

Keywords: Neural architecture search · Generative adversarial
networks · Reinforcement learning · Markov decision process ·
Off-policy

1 Introduction

Generative adversarial networks (GANs) have been successfully applied to a
wide range of generation tasks, including image generation [1,3,12,15,53], text

Y. Tian and Qin Wang—Equal contribution.

Electronic supplementary material The online version of this chapter (https://
doi.org/10.1007/978-3-030-58571-6_11) contains supplementary material, which is
available to authorized users.

© Springer Nature Switzerland AG 2020
A. Vedaldi et al. (Eds.): ECCV 2020, LNCS 12352, pp. 175–192, 2020.
https://doi.org/10.1007/978-3-030-58571-6_11

to image synthesis [40,44,62] and image translation [7,25], to name a few. To further improve the generation quality, several extensions and further developments have been proposed, ranging from regularization terms [4,14], progressive training strategy [26], utilizing attention mechanism [59,61], and to new architectures [3,27].

While designing favorable neural architectures of GANs has made great success, it typically requires a large amount of time, effort, and domain expertise. For instance, several state-of-the-art GANs [3,27] design appreciably complex generator or discriminator backbones for better generating high-resolution images. To alleviate the network engineering pain, an efficient automated architecture searching framework for GAN is highly needed. On the other hand, Neural architecture search (NAS) has been applied and proved effective in discriminative tasks such as image classification [30] and segmentation [33]. Encouraged by this, AGAN [52] and AutoGAN [11] have introduced neural architecture search methods for GAN based on reinforcement learning (RL), thereby enabling a significant speedup of architecture searching process.

Similar to the other architecture search tasks (image classification, image segmentation), recently proposed RL-based GAN architecture search method AGAN [52] optimized the entire architecture. Since the same policy might sample different architectures, it is likely to suffer from noisy gradients and a high variance, which potentially further harms the policy update stability. To circumvent this issue, multi-level architecture search (MLAS) has been used in Auto-GAN [52], and a progressive optimization formulation is used. However, because optimization is based on the best performance of the current architecture level, this progressive formulation potentially leads to a local minimum solution.

To overcome these drawbacks, we reformulate the GAN architecture search problem as a Markov decision process (MDP). The new formulation is partly inspired by the human-designed Progressive GAN [26], which has shown to improve generation quality progressively in intermediate outputs of each architecture cell. In our new formulation, a sequence of decisions will be made during the entire architecture design process, which allows state-based sampling and thus alleviates the variance. In addition, as we will show later in the paper, by using a carefully designed reward, this new formulation also allows us to target effective global optimization over the entire architecture.

More importantly, the MDP formulation can better facilitate off-policy RL training to improve data efficiency. The previously proposed RL-based GAN architecture search methods [11,52] are based on on-policy RL, leading to limited data efficiency that results in considerably long training time. Specifically, on-policy RL approach generally requires frequent sampling of a batch of architectures generated by current policy to update the policy. Moreover, new samples are required to be collected for each gradient step, while the previous batches are directly disposed. This quickly becomes very expensive as the number of gradient steps and samples increases with the complexity of the task, especially in the architecture search tasks. By comparison, off-policy reinforcement learning algorithms make use of past experience such that the RL agents are enabled to learn more efficiently. This has been proven to be effective in other RL tasks, including legged locomotion [32] and complex video games [38]. However, exploiting off-policy data for GAN architecture search poses new challenges. Training the policy network inevitably becomes unstable by using off-policy data, because these training samples are systematically different from the on-policy ones. This presents a great challenge to the stability and convergence of the algorithm [2]. Our proposed MDP formulation can make a difference here. By allowing state-based sampling, the new formulation alleviates this instability, and better supports the off-policy strategy.

The contributions of this paper are two-fold:

1. We reformulate the problem of neural architecture search for GAN as an MDP for smoother architecture sampling, which enables a more effective RL-based search algorithm and potentially more global optimization.
2. We propose an efficient and effective off-policy RL NAS framework for GAN architecture search (E^{2}GAN), which is 6 times faster than existing RL-based GAN search approaches with competitive performance.

We conduct a variety of experiments to validate the effectiveness of E^{2}GAN. Our discovered architectures yield better results compared to RL-based competitors. E^{2}GAN is efficient, as it is able to find a highly competitive model within **7 GPU hours**.

2 Related Work

Reinforcement Learning. Recent progress in model-free reinforcement learning (RL) [49] has fostered promising results in many interesting tasks ranging from gaming [37,48], to planning and control problems [6,18,19,23,31,58] and even up to the AutoML [34,41,65]. However, model-free deep RL methods are notoriously expensive in terms of their sample complexity. One reason of the poor sample efficiency is the use of on-policy reinforcement learning algorithms, such as trust region policy optimization (TRPO) [46], proximal policy optimization (PPO) [47] or REINFORCE [56]. On-policy learning algorithms **require new samples generated by the current policy for each gradient step**. On the contrary, off-policy algorithms aim to reuse past experience. Recent developments of the off-policy reinforcement learning algorithms, such as soft Actor-Critic (SAC) [17], have demonstrated substantial improvements in both performance and sample efficiency in previous on-policy methods.

Neural Architecture Search. Neural architecture search methods aim to automatically search for a good neural architecture for various tasks, such as image classification [30] and segmentation [33], in order to ease the burden of hand-crafted design of dedicated architectures for specific tasks. Several approaches have been proposed to tackle the NAS problem. Zoph and Le [65] proposed a reinforcement learning-based method that trains an RNN controller to design the neural network [65]. Guo et al. [16] exploited a novel graph convolutional neural networks for policy learning in reinforcement learning. Further successfully introduced approaches include evolutionary algorithm based methods [43], differentiable methods [35] and one-shot learning methods [5,35]. Early works of RL-based NAS algorithms [34,41,57,65] proposed to optimize the entire trajectory (i.e., the entire neural architecture). To the best of our knowledge, most of the previously proposed RL-based NAS algorithms used on-policy RL algorithms, such as REINFORCE or PPO, except [63] which uses Q-learning algorithm for NAS, which is a value-based method and only supports discrete state space problems. For on-policy algorithms, since each update requires new data collected by the current policy and the reward is based on the internal neural network architecture training, the on-policy training of RL-based NAS algorithms inevitably becomes computationally expensive.

GAN Architecture Search. Due to the specificities of GAN and their challenges, such as instability and mode collapse, the NAS approaches proposed for discriminative models cannot be directly transferred to the architecture search of GANs. Only recently, few approaches have been introduced tackling the specific challenges of the GAN architectures. Recently, AutoGAN has introduced a neural architecture search for GANs based on reinforcement learning (RL), thereby enabling a significant speedup of the process of architecture selection [11]. The AutoGAN algorithm is based on on-policy reinforcement learning. The proposed multi-level architecture search (MLAS) aims at progressively finding well-performing GAN architectures and completes the task in around 2 GPU days. Similarly, AGAN [52] uses reinforcement learning for generative architecture search in a larger search space. The computational cost for AGAN is comparably very expensive (1200 GPU days). In addition, AdversarialNAS [10] and DEGAS [9] adopted a different approach, i.e., differentiable searching strategy [35], for the GAN architecture search problem.

3   Preliminary

In this section, we briefly review the basic concepts and notations used in the following sections.

3.1   Generative Adversarial Networks

The training of GANs involves an adversarial competition between two players, a generator and a discriminator. The generator aims at generating realistic-looking images to 'fool' its opponent. Meanwhile, the discriminator aims to distinguish whether an image is real or fake. This can be formulated as a min-max optimization problem:

$$\min_{G} \max_{D} \mathbb{E}_{x \sim p_{real}}[\log D(x)] + \mathbb{E}_{z \sim p_z}[\log (1 - D(G(z)))], \tag{1}$$

where G and D are the generator and discriminator parametrized by neural networks. z is sampled from random noise. x are the real and $G(z)$ are the generated images.

3.2 Reinforcement Learning

A Markov decision process (MDP) is a discrete-time stochastic control process. At each time step, the process is in some state s, and its associated decision-maker chooses an available action a. Given the action, the process moves into a new state s' at the next step, and the agent receives a reward.

An MDP could be described as a tuple (S, A, r, P, ρ), where S is the set of states that is able to precisely describe the current situation, A is the set of actions, $r(s, a)$ is the reward function, $P(s'|s, a)$ is the transition probability function, and $\rho(s)$ is the initial state distribution.

MDPs can be particularly useful for solving optimization problems via reinforcement learning. In a general reinforcement learning setup, an agent is trained to interact with the environment and get a reward from its interaction. The goal is to find a policy π that maximizes the cumulative reward $J(\pi)$:

$$J(\pi) = \mathbb{E}_{\tau \sim \rho_\pi} \sum_{t=0}^{\infty} r(s_t, a_t) \tag{2}$$

While the standard RL merely maximizes the expected cumulative rewards, the maximum entropy RL framework considers a more general objective [64], which favors stochastic policies. This objective shows a strong connection to the exploration-exploitation trade-off, and could also prevent the policy from getting stuck in local optima. Formally, it is given by

$$J(\pi) = \mathbb{E}_{\tau \sim \rho_\pi} \sum_{t=0}^{\infty} [r(s_t, a_t) + \beta \mathcal{H}(\pi(\cdot|s_t))], \tag{3}$$

where β is the temperature parameter that controls the stochasticity of the optimal policy.

4 Problem Formulation

4.1 Motivation

Given a fixed search space, GAN architecture search agents aim to discover an optimal network architecture on a given generation task. Existing RL methods update the policy network by using batches of entire architectures sampled from the current policy. Even though these data samples are only used for the current update step, the sampled GAN architectures nevertheless require tedious training and evaluation processes. The sampling efficiency is therefore very low resulting in limited learning progress of the agents. Moreover, the entire architecture sampling leads to a high variance, which might influence the stability of the policy update.

The key motivation of the proposed methodology is to stabilize and accelerate the learning process by step-wise sampling instead of entire-trajectory-based sampling and making efficient use of past experiences from previous policies. To achieve this, we propose to formulate the GAN architecture search problem as an MDP and solve it by off-policy reinforcement learning.

4.2   GAN Architecture Search Formulated as MDP

We propose to formulate the GAN architecture search problem as a Markov decision process (MDP) which enables state-based sampling. It further boosts the learning process and overcomes the potential challenge of a large variance stemming from sampling entire architectures that makes it inherently difficult to train a policy using off-policy data.

Formulating GAN architecture search problem as an MDP provides a mathematical description of architecture search processes. An MDP can be described as a tuple (S, A, r, P, ρ), where S is the set of states that is able to precisely describe the current architecture (such as the current cell number, the structure or the performance of the architectures), A is the set of actions that defines the architecture design of the next cell, $r(s, a)$ is the reward function used to define how good the architecture is, $P(s'|s, a)$ is the transition probability function indicating the training process, and $\rho(s)$ is the initial architecture. We define a cell as an architecture block we are using to search in one step. The design details of states, actions, and rewards is discussed in Sect. 5.

It is important to highlight that the formulation proposed in this paper has two main differences compared to previous RL methods for neural architecture search. Firstly, it is essentially different to the classic RL approaches for NAS [65], which formulate the task as an optimization problem over the entire trajectory/architecture. Instead, the MDP formulation proposed here enables us to do the optimization based on the disentangled steps of cell design. Secondly, it is also different to the progressive formulation used by AutoGAN [11], where the optimization is based on the best performance of the current architecture level and can potentially lead to a local minimum solution. Instead, the proposed formulation enables us to potentially conduct a more global optimization using cumulative reward without the burden of calculating the reward over the full trajectory at once. It is important to point out that the multi-level optimization formulation used in AutoGAN [11] does not have this property.

5   Off-Policy RL for GAN Architecture Search

In this section, we integrate off-policy RL in the GAN architecture search by making use of the newly proposed MDP formulation. We introduce several innovations to address the challenges of an off-policy learning setup.

The MDP formulation of GAN architecture search enables us to use off-policy reinforcement learning for a step-wise optimization of the entire search process to maximize the cumulative reward.

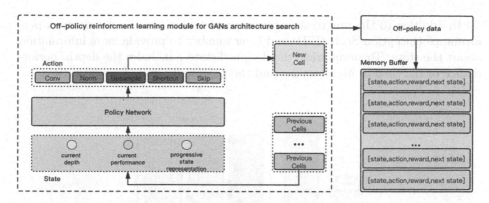

Fig. 1. Overview of the proposed E²GAN: the off-policy reinforcement learning module for GAN architecture search. The entire process comprises five steps: 1) The agent observes the current state s_t, which is designed as s = [Depth, Performance, Progressive state representation]. 2) The agent makes a decision a_t on how to design the cell added to previous cells according to the state information. a_t includes the skip options, upsampling operations, shortcut options, different types of convolution blocks and a normalization block 3) Progressively train the new architecture, obtain the reward r_t and the new state s_{t+1} information and then loop over it again. 4) Save the off-policy memory tuple $[s_t, a_t, r_t, s_{t+1}]$ into the memory buffer. 5) Sample a batch of data from the memory buffer to update the policy network.

5.1   RL for GAN Architecture Search

Before we move on to the off-policy solver, we need to design the state, reward, and action to meet the requirements of both the GAN architecture design, as well as of the MDP formulation.

State. MDP requires a state representation that can precisely represent the current network up to the current step. Most importantly, this state needs to be stable during training to avoid adding more variance to the training of the policy network. The stability requirement is particularly relevant since the policy network relies on it to design the next cell. The design of the state is one of the main challenges we face when adopting off-policy RL to GAN architecture search (Fig. 1).

Inspired by the progressive GAN [26], which has shown to improve generation quality in intermediate RGB outputs of each architecture cell, we propose a progressive state representation for GAN architecture search. Specifically, given a fixed batch of input noise, we adopt the average output of each cell as the progressive state representation. We down-sample this representation to impose a constant size across different cells. Note that there are alternative ways to encode the network information. For example, one could also deploy another network to encode the previous layers. However, we find the proposed design efficient and also effective.

In addition to the progressive state representation, we also use network performance (Inception Score/FID) and layer number to provide more information about the state. To summarize, the designed state s includes the depth, performance of the current architecture, and the progressive state representation.

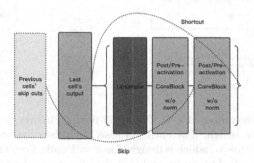

Fig. 2. The search space of a generator cell in one step. The search space is directly taken from AutoGAN [11].

Action. Given the current state, which encodes the information about previous layers, the policy network decides on the next action. The action describes the architecture of one cell. For example, if we follow the search space used by AutoGAN [11], action will contain skip options, upsampling operations, shortcut options, different types of convolution blocks, and the normalization option, as shown in Fig. 2.

This can then be defined as $a = [conv, norm, upsample, shortcut, skip]$. The action output by the agent will be carried out by a softmax classifier decoding into an operation. To demonstrate the effectiveness of our off-policy methods and enable a fair comparison, in all of our experiments, we use the same search space as AutoGAN [11], which means we search for generator cells, and the discriminator architecture is pre-designed and growing as the generator becomes deeper. More details on the search space are discussed in Sect. 6.

Reward. We propose to design the reward function as the **performance improvement** after adding the new cell. In this work, we use both Inception Score (IS) and Frchet Inception Distance (FID) as the indicators of the network performance. Since IS score is progressive (the higher the better) and FID score is degressive (the lower the better), the proposed reward function can be formulated as:

$$R_t(s, a) = IS(t) - IS(t-1) + \alpha(FID(t-1) - FID(t)), \qquad (4)$$

where α is a factor to balance the trade-off between the two indicators. We use $\alpha = 0.01$ in our main experiments. The motivation behind using a combined reward is based on an empirical finding indicating that IS and FID are not always consistent with each other and can lead to a biased choice of architectures. A detailed discussion about the choice of indicators is provided in Sect. 7.

By employing the performance improvement in each step instead of only using performance as proposed in [11], RL can maximize the expected sum of rewards over the entire trajectory. This enables us to target the potential global optimal structure with the highest reward:

$$J(\pi) = \sum_{t=0} \mathbb{E}_{(s_t,a_t) \sim p(\pi)} R(s_t, a_t) = \mathbb{E}_{architecture \sim p(\pi)} IS_{final} - \alpha FID_{final}, \quad (5)$$

where IS_{final} and FID_{final} are the final scores of the entire architecture.

5.2   Off-Policy RL Solver

The proposed designs of state, reward, and action fulfill the criteria of MDPs and makes it possible to stabilize the training using off-policy samples. We are now free to choose any off-policy RL solver to improve data efficiency.

In this paper, we apply the off-the-shelf soft actor-critic algorithm (SAC) [17], an off-policy actor-critic deep RL algorithm based on the maximum entropy reinforcement learning framework, as the learning algorithm. It has demonstrated to be 10 to 100 times more data-efficient compared to any other on-policy algorithms on traditional RL tasks. In SAC, the actor aims at maximizing expected reward while also maximizing entropy. This increases training stability significantly and improves the exploration during training.

For the learning of the critic, the objective function is defined as:

$$J(Q) = \mathbb{E}_{(s,a) \sim D} \left[\frac{1}{2} (Q(s, a) - Q_{target}(s, a))^2 \right] \quad (6)$$

where Q_{target} is the approximation target for Q :

$$Q_{target}(s, a) = Q(s, a) + \gamma Q_{target}(s', f(\epsilon, s')) \quad (7)$$

The objective function of the the policy network is given by:

$$J(\pi) = \mathbb{E}_D \left[\beta[\log(\pi_\theta(f_\theta(\epsilon, s)|s))] - Q(s, f_\theta(\epsilon, s)) \right] \quad (8)$$

where π_θ is parameterized by a neural network f_θ, ϵ is an input vector consisting of Gaussian noise, and the $\mathcal{D} = \{(s, a, s', r)\}$ is the replay buffer for storing the MDP tuples [38]. β is a positive Lagrange multiplier that controls the relative importance of the policy entropy versus the safety constraint.

5.3   Implementation of E^{2}GAN

In this section, we present the implementation details of the proposed off-policy RL framework E^{2}GAN. The training process is briefly outlined in Algorithm 1.

Algorithm 1. Pseudo code for E^{2}GAN search

Input hyperparameters, learning rates $\alpha_{\phi_Q}, \alpha_\theta$
Randomly initialize a Q network $Q(s, a)$ and policy network $\pi(a|s)$ with parameters
ϕ_Q, θ and the Lagrange multipliers β,
Initialize the parameters of target networks with $\overline{\phi}_Q \leftarrow \phi_Q$, $\overline{\theta} \leftarrow \theta$
for each iteration **do**
    Reset the weight and cells of E^{2}GAN
    for each time step **do**
        if Exploration **then**
            Sample a_t from $\pi(s)$, add the corresponding cell to E^{2}GAN
        else if Exploitation **then**
            Choose the best a_t from $\pi(s)$ and add the corresponding cell to E^{2}GAN
        end if
        Progressively train the E^{2}GAN
        Observe s_{t+1}, r_t and store (s_t, a_t, r_t, s_{t+1}) in $\mathcal{D}$
    end for
    for each update step **do**
        Sample mini-batches of transitions from $\mathcal{D}$ and update Q and π with gradients
        Update the target networks with soft replacement:

$$\overline{\phi}_Q \leftarrow \tau\phi_Q + (1 - \tau)\overline{\phi}_Q$$
$$\overline{\theta} \leftarrow \tau\theta + (1 - \tau)\overline{\theta}$$

    end for
end for

Agent Training. Since we reformulated the NAS as a multi-step MDP, our agent will make several decisions in any trajectory $\tau = [(s_1, a_1), ...(s_n, a_n)]$. In each step, the agent will collect this experience $[s_t, a_t, r_t, s_{t+1}]$ in the memory buffer $\mathcal{D}$. Once the threshold of the smallest memory length is reached, the agent is updated using the Adam [28] optimizer via the objective function presented in Eq. 8 by sampling a batch of data from the memory buffer $\mathcal{D}$ in an off-policy way.

The entire search comprises two periods: the exploration period and the exploitation period. During the exploration period, the agent will sample any possible architecture. While in the exploitation period, the agent will choose the best architecture, in order to quickly stabilize the policy.

The exploration period lasts for 70% of iterations, and the exploitation takes 30% iterations. Once the memory threshold is reached, for every exploration step, the policy will be updated once. For every exploitation step, the policy will be updated 10 times in order to converge quickly.

Proxy Task. We use a progressive proxy task in order to collect the rewards fast. When a new cell is added, we train the current full trajectory for one epoch and calculate the reward for the current cell. Within a trajectory, the previous cells' weights will be kept and trained together with the new cell. In order to accurately estimate the Q-value of each state-action pair, we reset the weight of the neural network after finishing the entire architecture trajectory design.

6 Experiments

6.1 Dataset

In this paper, we use the CIFAR-10 dataset [29] to evaluate the effectiveness and efficiency of the proposed E^{2}GAN framework. The CIFAR-10 dataset consists of 50,000 training images and 10,000 test images with a 32×32 resolution. We use its training set without any data augmentation technique to search for the architecture with the highest cumulative return for a GAN generator. Furthermore, to evaluate the transferability of the discovered architecture, we also adopt the STL-10 dataset [8] to train the network without any other data augmentation to make a fair comparison to previous works.

6.2 Search Space

To verify the effectiveness of the off-policy framework and to enable a fair comparison, we use the same search space as used in the AutoGAN experiments [11]. There are five control variables: 1) Skip operation, which is a binary value indicating whether the current cell takes a skip connection from any specific cell as its input. Note that each cell could take multiple skip connections from other preceding cells. 2) Pre-activation [21] and post-activation convolution block. 3) Three types of normalization operations, including batch normalization [24], instance normalization [51], and no normalization. 4) Upsampling operation which is standard in current image generation GAN, including bi-linear upsampling, nearest neighbor upsampling, and stride-2 deconvolution. 5) Shortcut operation.

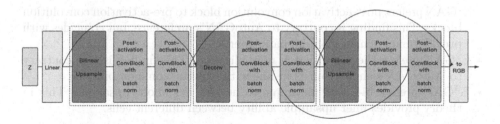

Fig. 3. The generator architecture discovered by E^{2}GAN on CIFAR-10.

6.3 Results

The generator architecture discovered by E^{2}GAN on the CIFAR-10 training set is displayed in Fig. 3. For the task of unconditional CIFAR-10 image generation (no class labels used), several notable observations could be summarized:

Table 1. Inception score and FID score of unconditional image generation task on CIFAR-10. We achieve **a highly competitive FID of 11.26** compared to published works. We mainly compare our approach with RL-based NAS approaches: AGAN [52] and AutoGAN [11]. Architectures marked by (*) are manually designed.

Methods	Inception score	FID	Search cost (GPU days)
DCGAN [42]	6.64 ± .14	–	*
Improved GAN [45]	6.86 ± .06	–	*
LRGAN [60]	7.17 ± .17	–	*
DFM [55]	7.72 ± .13	–	*
ProbGAN [20]	7.75	24.60	*
WGAN-GP, ResNet [14]	7.86 ± .07	–	*
Splitting GAN [13]	7.90 ± .09	–	*
SN-GAN [36]	8.22 ± .05	21.7 ± .01	*
MGAN [22]	8.33 ± .10	26.7	*
Dist-GAN [50]	–	17.61 ± .30	*
Progressive GAN [26]	**8.80 ± .05**	–	*
Improv MMD GAN [54]	8.29	16.21	*
Random search-1 [11]	8.09	17.34	–
Random search-2 [11]	7.97	21.39	–
AGAN [52]	8.29 ± .09	30.5	1200
AutoGAN-top1 [11]	8.55 ± .10	12.42	2
AutoGAN-top2 [11]	8.42 ± .07	13.67	2
AutoGAN-top3 [11]	8.41 ± .11	13.68	2
E^2GAN-top1	8.51 ± .13	**11.26**	0.3
E^2GAN-top2	8.50 ± .09	12.96	0.3
E^2GAN-top3	8.42 ± .11	12.48	0.3

* E^2GAN prefers post-activation convolution block to pre-activation convolution blocks. This finding is contrary to AutoGAN's preference, but coincides with previous experiences from human experts.
* E^2GAN prefers the use of batch normalization. This finding is also contrary to AutoGAN's choice, but is in line with experts' common practice.
* E^2GAN prefers bi-linear upsample to nearest neighbour upsample. This in theory provides finer upsample ability between different cells.

Our E^2GAN framework only takes about 0.3 GPU day for searching while the AGAN spends 1200 GPU days and AutoGAN spends 2 GPU days.

We train the discovered E^2GAN from scratch for 500 epochs and summarize the IS and FID scores in Table 1. On the CIFAR-10 dataset, our model achieves a **highly competitive FID 11.26** compared to published results by AutoGAN [11], and hand-crafted GAN [13,14,20,22,36,42,45,54,55,60]. In terms of IS score, E^2GAN is also highly competitive to AutoGAN [11]. We

Table 2. Inception score and FID score for the unconditional image generation task on STL-10. E²GAN uses the discovered architecture on CIFAR-10. Performance is significantly better than other RL-based competitors.

Methods	Inception score	FID	Search cost (GPU days)
D2GAN [39]	7.98	–	Manual
DFM [55]	8.51 ± .13	–	Manual
ProbGAN [20]	8.87 ± .095	46.74	Manual
SN-GAN [36]	9.10 ± .04	40.1 ± .50	Manual
Dist-GAN [50]	–	36.19	Manual
Improving MMD GAN [54]	9.34	37.63	Manual
AGAN [52]	9.23 ± .08	52.7	1200
AutoGAN-top1 [11]	9.16 ± .13	31.01	2
E²GAN-top1	**9.51 ± .09**	**25.35**	0.3

additionally report the performance of the top2 and top3 architectures discovered in one search. Both have higher performance than the respective AutoGAN counterparts.

We also test the transferability of E²GAN. We retrain the weights of the discovered E²GAN architecture using the STL-10 training and unlabeled set for the unconditional image generation task. **E²GAN achieves a highly-competitive performance on both IS (9.51) and FID (25.35)**, as shown in Table 2 (Fig. 4).

Fig. 4. The generated CIFAR-10 (left) and STL-10 (right) results of E²GAN which are randomly sampled without cherry-picking.

Because our main contribution is the new formulation and using off-policy RL for GAN architecture framework, we compare the proposed method directly with existing RL-based algorithms. We use the exact same searching space as AutoGAN, which does not include the search for a discriminator. As GAN training is an interactive procedure between generator and discriminator, one might expect better performance if the search is conducted on both networks. We report our scores using the exact same evaluation procedure provided by the authors of AutoGAN. The reported scores are based on the best models achieved during training on a 20 epoch evaluation interval. Mean and standard deviation of the IS score are calculated based on the 10-fold evaluation on 50,000 generated images. We additionally report the performance curve against training steps of E^2GAN and AutoGAN for three runs in the supplementary material.

Table 3. Performance on the unconditional image generation task for CIFAR-10 with different reward choices.

Methods	Inception score	FID	Search cost (GPU days)
AutoGAN-top1 [11]	8.55 ± .1	12.42	2
E^2GAN (IS and FID as reward)	8.51 ± .13	11.26	0.3
E^2GAN (IS only as reward)	**8.81 ± .11**	15.64	0.1

7 Discussion

7.1 Reward Choice: IS and FID

IS and FID scores are two main evaluation metrics for GAN. We conduct the ablation study of using different combinations. Specifically, IS only ($\alpha = 0$) and the combination of IS and FID ($\alpha = 0.01$) as the reward. Our agent successfully discovered two different architectures. When only IS is used as the reward, the agent discovered a different architecture using only 0.1 GPU day. The searched architecture achieved state-of-the-art IS score of 8.86, as shown in Table 3., but a relatively plain FID of 15.78. This demonstrates the effectiveness of the proposed method, as we are encouraging the agent to find the architecture with a higher IS score. Interestingly, this shows that, at least in certain edge cases, the IS and FID may not always have a strong positive correlation. This finding motivates us to include FID in the reward. When both IS and FID are used as the reward signal, the discovered architecture performs well in term of both metrics. This combined reward takes 0.3 GPU days (compared to 0.1 GPU days of IS only optimization) because of the relatively expensive cost of FID computation.

7.2 Reproducibility

We train our agent over 3 different seeds. As shown in Fig. 5, we observe that our agent steadily converged the policy in the exploitation period. E^2GAN can find similar architectures with relatively good performance on the proxy task.

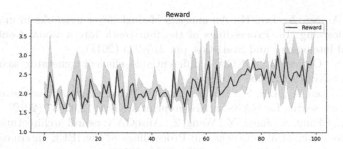

Fig. 5. Training curves on architecture searching. IS score on the proxy task against training time steps. E^{2}GAN shows relatively good stability and reproducibility.

8 Conclusion

We proposed a novel off-policy RL method, E^{2}GAN, to efficiently and effectively search for GAN architectures. We reformulated the problem as an MDP process, and overcame the challenges of using off-policy data. We first introduced a new progressive state representation. We additionally introduced a new reward, which allowed us to target the potential global optimization in our MDP formulation. The E^{2}GAN achieves state-of-the-art efficiency in GAN architecture searching, and the discovered architecture shows highly competitive performance.

Acknowledgement. The contributions of Yuan Tian, Qin Wang, and Olga Fink were funded by the Swiss National Science Foundation (SNSF) Grant no. PP00P2_176878.

References

1. Bao, J., Chen, D., Wen, F., Li, H., Hua, G.: CVAE-GAN: fine-grained image generation through asymmetric training. In: Proceedings of the IEEE International Conference on Computer Vision, pp. 2745–2754 (2017)
2. Bhatnagar, S., Precup, D., Silver, D., Sutton, R.S., Maei, H.R., Szepesvári, C.: Convergent temporal-difference learning with arbitrary smooth function approximation. In: Advances in Neural Information Processing Systems, pp. 1204–1212 (2009)
3. Brock, A., Donahue, J., Simonyan, K.: Large scale GAN training for high fidelity natural image synthesis. arXiv preprint arXiv:1809.11096 (2018)
4. Brock, A., Lim, T., Ritchie, J.M., Weston, N.: Neural photo editing with introspective adversarial networks. arXiv preprint arXiv:1609.07093 (2016)
5. Brock, A., Lim, T., Ritchie, J.M., Weston, N.: SMASH: one-shot model architecture search through hypernetworks. arXiv preprint arXiv:1708.05344 (2017)
6. Chao, M.A., Tian, Y., Kulkarni, C., Goebel, K., Fink, O.: Real-time model calibration with deep reinforcement learning. arXiv preprint arXiv:2006.04001 (2020)
7. Choi, Y., Choi, M., Kim, M., Ha, J.W., Kim, S., Choo, J.: StarGAN: unified generative adversarial networks for multi-domain image-to-image translation. In: Proceedings of the IEEE Conference on Computer Vision and Pattern Recognition, pp. 8789–8797 (2018)

8. Coates, A., Ng, A., Lee, H.: An analysis of single-layer networks in unsupervised feature learning. In: Proceedings of the fourteenth International Conference on Artificial Intelligence and Statistics, pp. 215–223 (2011)

9. Doveh, S., Giryes, R.: DEGAS: differentiable efficient generator search. arXiv preprint arXiv:1912.00606 (2019)

10. Gao, C., Chen, Y., Liu, S., Tan, Z., Yan, S.: AdversarialNAS: adversarial neural architecture search for GANs. arXiv preprint arXiv:1912.02037 (2019)

11. Gong, X., Chang, S., Jiang, Y., Wang, Z.: AutoGAN: neural architecture search for generative adversarial networks. In: Proceedings of the IEEE International Conference on Computer Vision, pp. 3224–3234 (2019)

12. Goodfellow, I., et al.: Generative adversarial nets. In: Advances in Neural Information Processing Systems, pp. 2672–2680 (2014)

13. Grinblat, G.L., Uzal, L.C., Granitto, P.M.: Class-splitting generative adversarial networks. arXiv preprint arXiv:1709.07359 (2017)

14. Gulrajani, I., Ahmed, F., Arjovsky, M., Dumoulin, V., Courville, A.C.: Improved training of wasserstein GANs. In: Advances in Neural Information Processing Systems, pp. 5767–5777 (2017)

15. Guo, Y., Chen, Q., Chen, J., Wu, Q., Shi, Q., Tan, M.: Auto-embedding generative adversarial networks for high resolution image synthesis. IEEE Trans. Multimed. **21**(11), 2726–2737 (2019)

16. Guo, Y., et al.: Nat: Neural architecture transformer for accurate and compact architectures. In: Advances in Neural Information Processing Systems, pp. 737–748 (2019)

17. Haarnoja, T., Zhou, A., Abbeel, P., Levine, S.: Soft actor-critic: off-policy maximum entropy deep reinforcement learning with a stochastic actor. arXiv preprint arXiv:1801.01290 (2018)

18. Han, M., Tian, Y., Zhang, L., Wang, J., Pan, W.: H infinity model-free reinforcement learning with robust stability guarantee. arXiv preprint arXiv:1911.02875 (2019)

19. Han, M., Zhang, L., Wang, J., Pan, W.: Actor-critic reinforcement learning for control with stability guarantee. arXiv preprint arXiv:2004.14288 (2020)

20. He, H., Wang, H., Lee, G.H., Tian, Y.: ProbGAN: towards probabilistic GAN with theoretical guarantees (2019)

21. He, K., Zhang, X., Ren, S., Sun, J.: Identity mappings in deep residual networks. In: Leibe, B., Matas, J., Sebe, N., Welling, M. (eds.) ECCV 2016. LNCS, vol. 9908, pp. 630–645. Springer, Cham (2016). https://doi.org/10.1007/978-3-319-46493-0_38

22. Hoang, Q., Nguyen, T.D., Le, T., Phung, D.: MGAN: training generative adversarial nets with multiple generators (2018)

23. Hwangbo, J., et al.: Learning agile and dynamic motor skills for legged robots. Sci. Robot. 4(26), eaau5872 (2019)

24. Ioffe, S., Szegedy, C.: Batch normalization: accelerating deep network training by reducing internal covariate shift. arXiv preprint arXiv:1502.03167 (2015)

25. Isola, P., Zhu, J.Y., Zhou, T., Efros, A.A.: Image-to-image translation with conditional adversarial networks. In: Proceedings of the IEEE Conference on Computer Vision and Pattern Recognition, pp. 1125–1134 (2017)

26. Karras, T., Aila, T., Laine, S., Lehtinen, J.: Progressive growing of GANs for improved quality, stability, and variation. arXiv preprint arXiv:1710.10196 (2017)

27. Karras, T., Laine, S., Aila, T.: A style-based generator architecture for generative adversarial networks. In: Proceedings of the IEEE Conference on Computer Vision and Pattern Recognition, pp. 4401–4410 (2019)

28. Kingma, D.P., Ba, J.: Adam: a method for stochastic optimization. arXiv preprint arXiv:1412.6980 (2014)
29. Krizhevsky, A., Hinton, G., et al.: Learning multiple layers of features from tiny images (2009)
30. Krizhevsky, A., Sutskever, I., Hinton, G.E.: ImageNet classification with deep convolutional neural networks. In: Advances in Neural Information Processing Systems, pp. 1097–1105 (2012)
31. Kumar, V., Gupta, A., Todorov, E., Levine, S.: Learning dexterous manipulation policies from experience and imitation. arXiv preprint arXiv:1611.05095 (2016)
32. Lillicrap, T.P., et al.: Continuous control with deep reinforcement learning. arXiv preprint arXiv:1509.02971 (2015)
33. Liu, C., et al.: Auto-deeplab: hierarchical neural architecture search for semantic image segmentation. In: Proceedings of the IEEE Conference on Computer Vision and Pattern Recognition, pp. 82–92 (2019)
34. Liu, C., et al.: Progressive neural architecture search. In: Proceedings of the European Conference on Computer Vision (ECCV), pp. 19–34 (2018)
35. Liu, H., Simonyan, K., Yang, Y.: DARTS: differentiable architecture search. In: International Conference on Learning Representations (2019). https://openreview.net/forum?id=S1eYHoC5FX
36. Miyato, T., Kataoka, T., Koyama, M., Yoshida, Y.: Spectral normalization for generative adversarial networks. arXiv preprint arXiv:1802.05957 (2018)
37. Mnih, V., et al.: Playing atari with deep reinforcement learning. arXiv preprint arXiv:1312.5602 (2013)
38. Mnih, V., et al.: Human-level control through deep reinforcement learning. Nature **518**(7540), 529–533 (2015)
39. Nguyen, T., Le, T., Vu, H., Phung, D.: Dual discriminator generative adversarial nets. In: Advances in Neural Information Processing Systems, pp. 2670–2680 (2017)
40. Park, T., Liu, M.Y., Wang, T.C., Zhu, J.Y.: Semantic image synthesis with spatially-adaptive normalization. In: Proceedings of the IEEE Conference on Computer Vision and Pattern Recognition, pp. 2337–2346 (2019)
41. Pham, H., Guan, M.Y., Zoph, B., Le, Q.V., Dean, J.: Efficient neural architecture search via parameter sharing. arXiv preprint arXiv:1802.03268 (2018)
42. Radford, A., Metz, L., Chintala, S.: Unsupervised representation learning with deep convolutional generative adversarial networks. arXiv preprint arXiv:1511.06434 (2015)
43. Real, E., et al.: Large-scale evolution of image classifiers. In: Proceedings of the 34th International Conference on Machine Learning, vol. 70, pp. 2902–2911. JMLR. org (2017)
44. Reed, S., Akata, Z., Yan, X., Logeswaran, L., Schiele, B., Lee, H.: Generative adversarial text to image synthesis. In: International Conference on Machine Learning, pp. 1060–1069 (2016)
45. Salimans, T., Goodfellow, I., Zaremba, W., Cheung, V., Radford, A., Chen, X.: Improved techniques for training GANs. In: Advances in Neural Information Processing Systems, pp. 2234–2242 (2016)
46. Schulman, J., Levine, S., Abbeel, P., Jordan, M., Moritz, P.: Trust region policy optimization. In: International Conference on Machine Learning, pp. 1889–1897 (2015)
47. Schulman, J., Wolski, F., Dhariwal, P., Radford, A., Klimov, O.: Proximal policy optimization algorithms. arXiv preprint arXiv:1707.06347 (2017)
48. Silver, D., Lever, G., Heess, N., Degris, T., Wierstra, D., Riedmiller, M.: Deterministic policy gradient algorithms (2014)

49. Sutton, R.S., Barto, A.G., Williams, R.J.: Reinforcement learning is direct adaptive optimal control. IEEE Control Syst. Mag. **12**(2), 19–22 (1992)
50. Tran, N.T., Bui, T.A., Cheung, N.M.: Dist-GAN: An improved GAN using distance constraints. In: Proceedings of the European Conference on Computer Vision (ECCV), pp. 370–385 (2018)
51. Ulyanov, D., Vedaldi, A., Lempitsky, V.: Instance normalization: the missing ingredient for fast stylization. arXiv preprint arXiv:1607.08022 (2016)
52. Wang, H., Huan, J.: AGAN: towards automated design of generative adversarial networks. arXiv preprint arXiv:1906.11080 (2019)
53. Wang, T.C., Liu, M.Y., Zhu, J.Y., Tao, A., Kautz, J., Catanzaro, B.: High-resolution image synthesis and semantic manipulation with conditional GANs. In: Proceedings of the IEEE Conference on Computer Vision and Pattern Recognition, pp. 8798–8807 (2018)
54. Wang, W., Sun, Y., Halgamuge, S.: Improving MMD-GAN training with repulsive loss function. In: International Conference on Learning Representations (2019). https://openreview.net/forum?id=HygjqjR9Km
55. Warde-Farley, D., Bengio, Y.: Improving generative adversarial networks with denoising feature matching (2016)
56. Williams, R.J.: Simple statistical gradient-following algorithms for connectionist reinforcement learning. Mach. Learn. **8**(3–4), 229–256 (1992)
57. Xie, S., Zheng, H., Liu, C., Lin, L.: SNAS: stochastic neural architecture search. arXiv preprint arXiv:1812.09926 (2018)
58. Xie, Z., Clary, P., Dao, J., Morais, P., Hurst, J., van de Panne, M.: Iterative reinforcement learning based design of dynamic locomotion skills for cassie. arXiv preprint arXiv:1903.09537 (2019)
59. Xu, T., et al.: AttnGAN: fine-grained text to image generation with attentional generative adversarial networks. In: Proceedings of the IEEE Conference on Computer Vision and Pattern Recognition, pp. 1316–1324 (2018)
60. Yang, J., Kannan, A., Batra, D., Parikh, D.: LR-GAN: layered recursive generative adversarial networks for image generation. arXiv preprint arXiv:1703.01560 (2017)
61. Zhang, H., Goodfellow, I., Metaxas, D., Odena, A.: Self-attention generative adversarial networks. In: International Conference on Machine Learning, pp. 7354–7363 (2019)
62. Zhang, H., et al.: StackGAN: text to photo-realistic image synthesis with stacked generative adversarial networks. In: Proceedings of the IEEE International Conference on Computer Vision, pp. 5907–5915 (2017)
63. Zhong, Z., Yan, J., Wu, W., Shao, J., Liu, C.L.: Practical block-wise neural network architecture generation. In: Proceedings of the IEEE Conference on Computer Vision and Pattern Recognition, pp. 2423–2432 (2018)
64. Ziebart, B.D.: Modeling purposeful adaptive behavior with the principle of maximum causal entropy (2010)
65. Zoph, B., Le, Q.V.: Neural architecture search with reinforcement learning. In: International Conference on Learning Representations (2017)

Efficient Non-Line-of-Sight Imaging
from Transient Sinograms

Mariko Isogawa[✉], Dorian Chan, Ye Yuan, Kris Kitani, and Matthew O'Toole

Carnegie Mellon University, Pittsburgh, PA 15213, USA
mariko.isogawa@ieee.org

Abstract. Non-line-of-sight (NLOS) imaging techniques use light that diffusely reflects off of visible surfaces (e.g., walls) to see around corners. One approach involves using pulsed lasers and ultrafast sensors to measure the travel time of multiply scattered light. Unlike existing NLOS techniques that generally require densely raster scanning points across the entirety of a relay wall, we explore a more efficient form of NLOS scanning that reduces both acquisition times and computational requirements. We propose a circular and confocal non-line-of-sight (C^2NLOS) scan that involves illuminating and imaging a common point, and scanning this point in a circular path along a wall. We observe that (1) these C^2NLOS measurements consist of a superposition of sinusoids, which we refer to as a transient sinogram, (2) there exists computationally efficient reconstruction procedures that transform these sinusoidal measurements into 3D positions of hidden scatterers or NLOS images of hidden objects, and (3) despite operating on an order of magnitude fewer measurements than previous approaches, these C^2NLOS scans provide sufficient information about the hidden scene to solve these different NLOS imaging tasks. We show results from both simulated and real C^2NLOS scans (Project page: https://marikoisogawa.github.io/project/c2nlos).

Keywords: Computational imaging · Non-line-of-sight imaging

1 Introduction

The ability to image objects hidden outside of a camera's field of view has many potential applications [23], including autonomous driving, search and rescue, and remote imaging. Over the last decade, many different technologies have been used for non-line-of-sight (NLOS) imaging, including transient imaging [2,6,7,10–13, 16,19,22,25,27–29,32,33,35], conventional cameras [4,8,17,18,30,31], WiFi or radio frequency measurements [1,20], thermal imaging [24], and even audio-based techniques [21]. Transient imaging refers to measuring a scene's temporal response to a pulse of light, and is one of the more successful approaches to reconstructing high-quality 3D shape of hidden scenes.

Electronic supplementary material The online version of this chapter (https://doi.org/10.1007/978-3-030-58571-6_12) contains supplementary material, which is available to authorized users.

© Springer Nature Switzerland AG 2020
A. Vedaldi et al. (Eds.): ECCV 2020, LNCS 12352, pp. 193–208, 2020.
https://doi.org/10.1007/978-3-030-58571-6_12

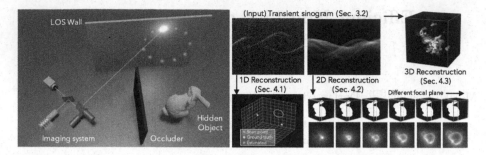

Fig. 1. A circular and confocal non-line-of-sight (C^2NLOS) system scans points along a circular path on a relay wall. Exploiting the sinusoidal properties of C^2NLOS measurements, a circular scan of a wall is sufficient to reconstruct images. C^2NLOS operates on far fewer measurements than existing NLOS techniques.

NLOS imaging techniques are fundamentally dependent on the spatial scanning patterns they utilize. Initially, methods used exhaustive measurements of 5D transients [2,10,16,33], requiring explicit scanning of both virtual sources and sensors on a line-of-sight (LOS) wall. To mitigate these issues, alternative approaches proposed co-locating the source and sensor points [27], reducing the dimensionality of the required scanning to just two spatial dimensions which significantly expedites computation. However, even these techniques still require a full raster scan of a wall, which is limited to 2 Hz to 4 Hz for state-of-the-art NLOS systems [22]—too slow for real-time capture.

All of these previous NLOS techniques motivate the following two-fold question. First, what is the dimensionality of the smallest set of measurements that is sufficient for reconstructing a NLOS image? And second, among all measurement sets of this size, which ones lend themselves to efficient reconstruction algorithms? Answering these questions involves many complicated considerations, including the need to define the exact reconstruction problem we are solving.

While we do not provide definitive answers to these questions in this paper, we take first steps towards addressing them. In particular, we identify the subset of measurements produced by a circular and confocal non-line-of-sight (C^2NLOS) scan, which yields powerful properties that facilitate fast reconstructions. As shown in Fig. 1, C^2NLOS scanning involves sampling points that form a circle on a visible surface, reducing the dimensionality of transient measurements under this regime to just 2 dimensions. Our key observation is that NLOS images can be obtained with far fewer measurements than previously expected or demonstrated by existing NLOS systems and reconstruction techniques. With off-the-shelf large beam scanning galvo systems (e.g., Thorlabs GVS012), circular scanning is also fast and potentially supports real-time NLOS tasks at 130 Hz.

In addition to having smaller dimensionality and being efficient to acquire, C^2NLOS measurements satisfy the requirements set out above, sufficiency and computational efficiency, for two important NLOS reconstruction problems.

The first problem is localizing a discrete number of small objects ("scatterers"). We show that C^2NLOS measurements are sufficient for this task, and enable recovery of the unknown locations through a straightforward Hough voting procedure [3]. The second problem is reconstructing a single planar object. For small planar objects, we show that this problem can be reduced to one equivalent to computed tomography, and therefore can be solved using techniques developed for that task such as the inverse Radon transform [15]. Both results rely on a theoretical analysis that shows that the transient measurements from C^2NLOS scanning are a superposition of sinusoids (referred to as a *transient sinogram*) with different amplitudes, phases, and offsets. A one-to-one mapping directly relates the parameters of these sinusoids to the 3D position of the hidden scatterers.

Motivated by the above results, we also empirically investigate two related problems. We show that accurate 2D images of large planar scenes can be obtained by solving a simple linear least squares problem based on C^2NLOS measurements. Furthermore, we demonstrate that approximate 3D reconstructions of the NLOS scene can be efficiently recovered from C^2NLOS measurements.

To summarize, our contributions are the following: (i) we provide a theoretical analysis of our proposed C^2NLOS scanning procedure which shows that the measurements consist of a superposition of sinusoids, producing a transient sinogram; (ii) we propose efficient reconstruction procedures that build on these sinusoidal properties to localize hidden objects and reconstruct NLOS images; and (iii) we show that the C^2NLOS measurements are sufficient for reconstructing 1D, 2D, and 3D NLOS images from both simulated and real transients, while using far fewer measurements than existing methods.

It should be stated up front that our reconstruction quality is strictly worse than conventional methods that make use of a larger set of transient measurements and longer capture times. In contrast to past NLOS works where the objective is to improve reconstruction quality, our key objective is to show that **a circular scan of transients is sufficient to reconstruct a NLOS image.**

2   Overview of Transient NLOS Imaging

NLOS imaging has received significant attention, with solutions that operate on a wide variety of different principles. However, a common approach to NLOS imaging involves using transient sources and sensors that operate on visible or near-IR light; we refer to these as transient NLOS imaging systems.

C^2NLOS imaging is a transient-based technique which shares many similarities to previous work in confocal NLOS imaging [27]. We therefore review the general NLOS image formation model, followed by confocal NLOS imaging.

General NLOS Imaging [33]. In Fig. 2(a), a laser sends a pulse of light towards a 3D point $\mathbf{x}''$ on a visible wall, and the light diffusely scatters from that point at time $t = 0$. The scattered light illuminates the objects hidden around a corner, and a fraction of that light reflects back towards the wall in response. A transient sensor (e.g., a SPAD) then measures the temporal response at a point $\mathbf{x}'$ on the

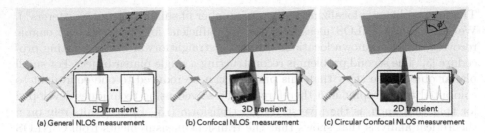

(a) General NLOS measurement   (b) Confocal NLOS measurement   (c) Circular Confocal NLOS measurement

Fig. 2. Illustration of transient NLOS scans. A pulsed laser illuminates a point $\mathbf{x}''$, while a transient sensor images a point $\mathbf{x}'$ on a LOS wall. By changing $\mathbf{x}''$ and $\mathbf{x}'$, we obtain a diverse set of transients that can help identify the position, shape, and appearance of objects hidden from sight. **(a)** Conventional NLOS imaging scans several combinations of light source positions $\mathbf{x}''$ and detector positions $\mathbf{x}'$ on the wall to obtain a 5D transient measurement. **(b)** Confocal NLOS imaging illuminates and images the same point, i.e., $\mathbf{x}'' = \mathbf{x}'$, producing a 3D transient measurement. **(c)** C^{2}NLOS imaging proposes confocally scanning only those points that lie on a circle, yielding a 2D transient measurement. We propose a transformation that reduces this transient image into a sum of sinusoids, called a *transient sinogram*, where the amplitude, phase, and offset of each sinusoid corresponds to the position of a hidden scatterer.

wall, also known as a transient measurement [26]. The transient measurement, $\tau(\mathbf{x}', \mathbf{x}'', t)$, represents the amount of light detected at point $\mathbf{x}'$ at time t, given illumination from point $\mathbf{x}''$ at time $t = 0$. For simplicity, we ignore the travel time between the system to the wall itself, which can be accounted for given the wall's geometry relative to the position of the laser and sensor.

The standard image formation model for NLOS imaging is

$$\tau(\mathbf{x}', \mathbf{x}'', t) = \iiint_\Omega \rho(\mathbf{x}) \frac{\delta \left(\|\mathbf{x} - \mathbf{x}'\| + \|\mathbf{x} - \mathbf{x}''\| - tc \right)}{\|\mathbf{x} - \mathbf{x}'\|^2 \|\mathbf{x} - \mathbf{x}''\|^2} \, d\mathbf{x}, \qquad (1)$$

where the function $\rho(\mathbf{x})$ represents the albedo of objects at every point $\mathbf{x}$, and $c = 3 \times 10^8$ m/s is the speed of light. The expression inside the Dirac delta $\delta(\cdot)$ relates the distance light travels through the hidden volume to its time of flight. The denominator accounts for the decrease in the intensity of light as a function of distance traveled, as given by the inverse square law.

This image formation model makes three underlying assumptions: (i) it only models three-bounce light paths, (ii) the model ignores the effect of a material's reflectance function and surface orientation, and (iii) the model assumes no occlusions within the hidden volume.

Equation (1) can be discretized into a linear system of equations

$$\boldsymbol{\tau} = \mathbf{A}\boldsymbol{\rho}, \qquad (2)$$

where $\boldsymbol{\tau}$ and $\boldsymbol{\rho}$ are discretized and vectorized representations of the measurements and volume, respectively. Recovering the hidden scene's geometry involves solving the linear system in Eq. (2). Unfortunately, the matrix $\mathbf{A}$ can be extremely large in practice. In general, the matrix maps a 3D volume ρ to a 5D transient measurement τ (4D spatial + 1D temporal). In this case, the matrix is far too large to construct, store, and invert directly.

As a result, many works have explored different sampling patterns that reduce the size of the measurements and simplify the reconstruction procedure. Certain approaches simply fix the light source and scan the sensor (or vice versa), producing 2D spatial measurements [6,11]. SNLOS [28] temporally focuses the light reflecting off of a single voxel, by simultaneously illuminating and imaging the wall over an ellipse. To scan a 2D or 3D set of voxels, ellipses of different shapes and sizes are used. Keyhole NLOS imaging [25] illuminates and detects light at a single point on the LOS wall, and relies on the motion of the hidden object to produce measurements for NLOS imaging. Confocal NLOS imaging [22,27] scans the source and sensor together, and is described next in more detail.

Confocal NLOS Imaging [27]. Confocal NLOS imaging (Fig. 2(b)) co-locates the source and sensor by setting $\mathbf{x}' = \mathbf{x}''$, and samples a regular 2D grid of points on the wall. This sampling strategy has a number of practical advantages. First, it simplifies the NLOS calibration process, since the shape of the wall is given by direct reflections. Second, confocal scans capture light from retroreflective objects, which helps to enable NLOS imaging at interactive rates [22]. Finally, there exist computationally and memory efficient algorithms for recovering hidden volumes from confocal scans without explicit construction of matrix $\mathbf{A}$.

When co-locating the source and detector, Eq. (1) reduces to

$$\tau(\mathbf{x}', t) = \iiint_\Omega \rho(\mathbf{x}) \, \frac{\delta\left(2\|\mathbf{x}' - \mathbf{x}\| - tc\right)}{\|\mathbf{x}' - \mathbf{x}\|^4} \, d\mathbf{x}. \tag{3}$$

As discussed by O'Toole et al. [27], a change of variables $v = (tc/2)^2$ produces

$$\tilde{\tau}(\mathbf{x}', v) \equiv v^{\frac{3}{2}} \, \tau(\mathbf{x}', \tfrac{2}{c}\sqrt{v}) = \iiint_\Omega \rho(\mathbf{x}) \, \delta\left(\|\mathbf{x}' - \mathbf{x}\|^2 - v\right) \, d\mathbf{x}. \tag{4}$$

When the relay wall is planar (i.e., $z' = 0$), the 3D spatio-temporal response $\tilde{\tau}(\mathbf{x}', v)$ of a scatterer becomes shift-invariant with respect to its 3D position $\mathbf{x}$. Equation (4) can then be expressed as a simple 3D convolution, which can be efficiently evaluated using a fast Fourier transform. The inverse problem involves a simple 3D deconvolution procedure called the light cone transform (LCT).

3   The Geometry of Circular and Confocal Scanning

While previous approaches have successfully reduced both capture and reconstruction times, the scanning paths required by these techniques inherently restrict scanning speeds on current hardware. Typical NLOS imaging systems, such as the one developed by Lindell et al. [22], use a pair of large galvo mirrors to raster scan the wall. The mirrors can only be driven up to a maximum of

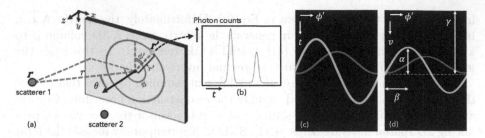

Fig. 3. Geometry of a C^2NLOS scan for individual scatterers. **(a)** The system con-focally scans the red circle of radius r' one point at a time to image hidden objects. **(b)** Each point produces a transient, i.e., the temporal response to a pulse of light. This signal represents the travel time from a point on the wall, to the scatterers, and back again. **(c)** Scanning different points on the circle produces a collection of tran-sients. Note that the signals represented here are only approximately sinusoidal. **(d)** By resampling the transients through a change of variables $v = (tc/2)^2$ (as explained in Eq. (4)), we obtain a transient sinogram. Every scatterer produces a unique sinusoid with a specific amplitude α, phase β, and offset γ. The parameters of these sinusoids are directly related to the spherical coordinates of the scatterers; see Eq. (10). (Color figure online)

65 Hz for a square wave pattern, capping scanning to just 130 lines per second. As a result, even the 2D grids utilized by confocal approaches [22,27] are limited to just a few hertz (e.g., 32×32 at 4 Hz, or 64×64 at 2 Hz), impractical for dynamic scenes. Higher dimensional non-confocal measurements are even slower. Although smaller mirrors enable higher-frequency modulation (e.g., MEMS mir-rors operate at kHz rates), this would greatly reduce the light efficiency of the system, lowering the quality of the output measurement.

This fundamental mechanical limitation motivates the following question: *can we further reduce the scanning path to just a single dimension, while still capturing useful information about the hidden scene?* We analyze the case of a circular and confocal scan (see Fig. 2(c)). Such a sinusoidal pattern could eas-ily be captured at 130 Hz under current galvo-mirror systems—a typical NLOS setup can capture an entire 1D circular scan in the time it takes to capture a single row of a 2D grid scan. At the same time, these C^2NLOS scans encode significant information about the hidden scene. We investigate their properties in further detail in the rest of this section.

3.1 Equation (4) in Spherical Coordinates

We start by analyzing the form of Eq. (4) when expressed in spherical coor-dinates. As shown in Fig. 3(a), we express the position of voxels in the hidden scene and scanning positions on the wall as $\mathbf{r} = (r, \theta, \phi)$ and $\mathbf{r}' = (r', \theta', \phi')$ respectively, where

$$x = r\sin(\theta)\cos(\phi), \quad y = r\sin(\theta)\sin(\phi), \quad z = r\cos(\theta), \qquad (5)$$

for an azimuth angle $0 \le \phi \le 2\pi$, a zenith angle $0 \le \theta \le \pi$, and a radius $r \ge 0$.

Through a change of variables, we can rewrite the confocal NLOS image formation model of Eq. (4) as

$$\tilde{\tau}(\mathbf{r}', v) \equiv v^{\frac{3}{2}} \, \tau(\mathbf{r}', \tfrac{2}{c}\sqrt{v}) = \iiint_{\Omega} \rho(\mathbf{r}) \, \delta \left(d(\mathbf{r}', \mathbf{r})^2 - v \right) \, r^2 \sin(\theta) \, dr \, d\theta \, d\phi, \quad (6)$$

where the distance function $d(\cdot, \cdot)$ expressed in spherical coordinates is

$$v(\mathbf{r}') \equiv d(\mathbf{r}', \mathbf{r})^2 = r^2 + r'^2 - 2rr' \left(\sin(\theta) \sin(\theta') \cos(\phi - \phi') + \cos(\theta) \cos(\theta') \right). \quad (7)$$

We restrict scatterers to be on one side of the wall, by setting $\theta \le \pi/2$.

3.2   Transient Sinograms

We assume that our C^2NLOS scans points along a wall where $\theta' = \pi/2$, the points on the wall are on a circle of fixed radius r', and the center of the circle is the origin $\mathbf{0}$. By applying these assumptions to Eq. (7), we get

$$v(\phi') = r^2 + r'^2 - 2rr' \sin(\theta) \cos(\phi - \phi') = \gamma - \alpha \cos(\beta - \phi'), \quad (8)$$

where

$$\alpha = 2rr' \sin(\theta), \quad \beta = \phi, \quad \gamma = r^2 + r'^2. \quad (9)$$

Here, α, β, and γ represent the amplitude, phase, and offset of a sinusoid. Therefore, after resampling the transient measurements (Fig. 3(c)) with the substitution $v = (tc/2)^2$, the transient measurement resulting from a C^2NLOS scan becomes a 2D image representing a superposition of different sinusoids, where each sinusoid represents a different point in the hidden space (see Fig. 3(d)). We therefore refer to the corresponding measurement as a *transient sinogram* τ_{circ}.

Consider scatterers of the form $\mathbf{r} = (r, 0, 0)$ for all $r \ge 0$. These scatterers produce a sinusoid with zero amplitude, because all points on the circle are equidistant to the scatterer. As we change the zenith angle $\mathbf{r} = (r, \theta, 0)$ for $0 \le \theta \le \pi/2$, the amplitude of the sinusoid also increases up to a maximum of $2rr'$ when scatterers are adjacent to the wall. Finally, introducing an azimuth angle $\mathbf{r} = (r, \theta, \phi)$ for $0 \le \phi \le 2\pi$ produces a phase shift of the sinusoid.

After identifying the amplitude, phase, and offset of each scatterer's sinusoid, inverting the expression in Eq. (9) recovers the scatterer's position:

$$r = \sqrt{\gamma - r'^2}, \quad \theta = \arcsin \left(\frac{\alpha}{2rr'} \right), \quad \phi = \beta. \quad (10)$$

This expression becomes useful when estimating the positions of one or a handful of scatterers around a corner, as discussed in Sect. 4.1.

In addition to computing the position of scatterers, another NLOS objective is to reconstruct images of the hidden scene. Consider an object that lies on the surface of a sphere of known radius r and centered about point $\mathbf{0}$ on the wall. This scenario occurs when sufficiently-small planar objects are oriented towards the origin **0**. (For planar objects tilted away from the origin, one can scan a different circle centered about another point on the wall.) According to Eq. (9), the measurement consists of a combination of sinusoids, all of which have identical offsets. This simplifies the measurement into a conventional sinogram image, the same type of measurement used in computed tomography (CT) [15]. We exploit this property in Sect. 4.2 to recover 2D images of the hidden scene.

4   Reconstructing Images from Transient Sinograms

4.1   1D Reconstruction: Estimating 3D Positions

Given a transient sinogram τ_{circ}, our first goal is to recover the 3D position of an object located at $\mathbf{x} = (x, y, z)$ by estimating its corresponding sinusoid parameters α, β, and γ, as described in Eq. (10). The challenge is to perform this operation both accurately and robustly, e.g., in the presence of sensor noise.

We propose a convolutional approach to the Hough transform for fixed-period sinusoids, based loosely on [36]. First, we generate a 2D Hough kernel representing a sinusoid of a given amplitude. Through a FFT-based convolution between this kernel and the transient sinogram, we obtain a parameter-space image that produces large responses in areas where the kernel aligns well with the sinusoid in the transient sinogram. Second, we repeat this procedure multiple times for kernels representing sinusoids with different amplitudes, producing a three dimensional parameter-space volume. The location of the voxels with the highest values in the volume represent the parameters of the sinusoids in the transient sinogram. Using these sinusoids, we can then recover the scatterers in the hidden scene by applying Eq. (10). We illustrate this process in Fig. 6(left).

4.2   2D Reconstructions

Consider the scenario where the hidden scene can be approximately modelled as a single planar object. We propose two ways to reconstruct a 2D image of this object. First, the inverse Radon transform is an integral transform used to solve the CT reconstruction problem; it is therefore possible to directly apply the inverse Radon transform technique on transient sinograms to recover a 2D image. This assumes that the planar patch is small, and tangent to the surface of a sphere of radius r, with the same center as the C^2NLOS scan. Second, since it is shown transient sinograms preserve information about the hidden scene and the measurements are much smaller when compared to conventional NLOS scans, it becomes computationally feasible to explicitly construct a matrix $\mathbf{A}$ that directly maps points from a hidden 2D plane to the C^2NLOS measurements, and solve a discrete linear system (i.e., Eq. (2)) directly.

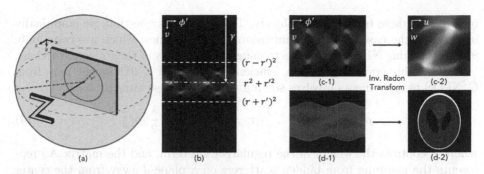

Fig. 4. Inverse Radon reconstruction based 2D imaging. **(a)** Suppose the hidden Z is a planar object that approximately lies on the surface of a sphere of radius r, and the C^2NLOS scan radius is r'. **(b)** Each scatterer on the surface of this sphere produces a sinusoidal response with a temporal offset $\gamma = r^2 + r'^2$ within a range $[(r - r')^2, (r + r')^2]$. **(c-1)** The transient sinogram is cropped with this range to recover a 2D image **(c-2)** via the inverse Radon transform. This is inspired by 2D image recovery with X-ray computed tomography (CT), shown in **(d-1)** and **(d-2)**.

Inverse Radon Reconstruction. When the hidden object lies on the surface of a sphere of radius r with the same center as the scanning circle (see Fig. 4(a)), each point on the hidden object produces a sinusoid with the same temporal offset γ, as shown in Fig. 4(b). We then recover a 2D image of the object from these measurements by using a standard inverse Radon transform procedure.

We choose a value for the radius r, either manually or automatically by computing the mean transient response. All sinusoids from points on this sphere have a corresponding offset $\gamma = r^2 + r'^2$. Because the maximum amplitude of sinusoids is $2rr'$, the transient response is contained within a temporal range $[\gamma - 2rr', \gamma + 2rr'] = [(r - r')^2, (r + r')^2]$. We therefore crop the transient sinogram accordingly, and apply the inverse Radon transform (see Fig. 4(d-1, d-2)) directly to the results to recover a 2D image (see Fig. 4(c-1, c-2)). The pixel coordinate of the recovered image associated for each sinusoid is given by

$$[u, w] = [\alpha \cos(\beta), \alpha \sin(\beta)] \qquad \text{(from Radon transform)} \quad (11)$$
$$= [2rr' \sin(\theta) \cos(\phi), 2rr' \sin(\theta) \sin(\phi)] \quad \text{(from Eq. (9))} \quad (12)$$
$$= 2r'[x, y] \qquad \text{(from Eq. (5))} \quad (13)$$

In other words, the recovered image simply represents a scaled orthographic projection of the hidden object onto the relay wall.

Linear Inversion. Our analysis with the Radon Transform demonstrates that significant information about the hidden scene is encoded in a transient sinogram. However, in practice, most common objects are not fully contained within the surface of a sphere, instead consisting of multiple depths and distances from the center of the scanning circle. With that in mind, an important question that arises is whether a C^2NLOS measurement contains enough information to reconstruct these more general objects. To explore this question, we empirically investigate the case of large 2-dimensional planar scenes, which are commonly used by existing NLOS techniques to gauge the accuracy of their reconstructions.

Under this constrained case, efficient recovery of a 2D image ρ_{2D} from C^2NLOS measurements involves solving a linear-least squares problem:

$$\rho_{2D} = \arg\min_{\rho} \quad \frac{1}{2}\|\tau_{\text{circ}} - \mathbf{A}_d\rho\|_2^2 + \frac{\lambda}{2}\|\rho\|_2^2, \tag{14}$$

where λ controls the weight of the regularization term, and the matrix $\mathbf{A}_d$ represents the mapping from hidden scatterers on a plane d away from the center of the scanning circle, to C^2NLOS measurements.

Both our Radon reconstruction and planar inversion algorithms require knowledge of the sphere or plane containing the hidden object. If the object is not contained within the surface of the sphere/plane, the recovered images are blurred; we show an analysis in the supplement. Changing the value for r or d is analogous to a manual refocusing operation that can help produce a clearer image.

4.3   3D Reconstruction: 3D Imaging via a Modified LCT

A natural follow-up question that arises is whether a transient sinogram is sufficient for performing a full 3D reconstruction. Empirically, we show that it is feasible to recover full 3D volumes of the hidden scene from C^2NLOS measurements. Although this involves solving an underconstrained system due to the limited number of measurements, approximate reconstructions can be achieved by applying non-negativity, sparsity, and total variation priors on the hidden volume, commonly utilized by previous approaches [2,11,12,27].

We propose a modified version of the iterative light cone transform (LCT) procedure used in confocal NLOS imaging [27]. Because a C^2NLOS measurement is a subset of a full confocal NLOS measurement, we simply add a sampling term to the iterative LCT procedure, solving the following optimization problem:

$$\rho_{3D} = \arg\min_{\rho} \quad \frac{1}{2}\|\tau_{\text{circ}} - \mathbf{M}\mathbf{A}\rho\|_2^2 + \Gamma(\rho), \tag{15}$$

where the matrix $\mathbf{A}$ maps a 3D volume to a confocal NLOS measurement, the matrix $\mathbf{M}$ subsamples the confocal NLOS measurement to produce a C^2NLOS measurement, and $\Gamma(\cdot)$ represents our non-negativity, sparsity, and total variation priors. Because the matrix $\mathbf{A}$ can be modelled as a convolution operation, the above expression can be optimized efficiently without having to construct $\mathbf{A}$ explicitly. We describe our procedure in detail in the supplement.

There are some drawbacks to this formulation. In its current form, it makes no explicit usage of the sinusoidal properties of C^2NLOS measurements that we utilized for object detection and 2D imaging, that could simplify the reconstruction. At the same time, the matrix $\mathbf{M}$ complicates a frequency analysis of the LCT, making it much more unclear which parts of the hidden scene can and cannot be reconstructed. We plan to investigate these phenomena in the future.

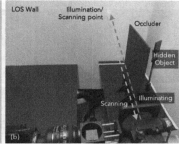

Fig. 5. (a) Our hardware prototype. (b) A hidden scene with a single NLOS object (a retroreflector) used for our object localization experiments.

5 Experiments

Baseline Algorithms. No existing algorithms operate on C^2NLOS scans, or even just 1D scans. Thus, we compare our method with two volume reconstruction approaches that rely on full 2D confocal scans: LCT [27] and FK [22]. We identify the peak and compute a maximum intensity projection from each of the output volumes to generate 1D and 2D reconstructions, respectively. To estimate scatterer positions, we also test a trilateration-based approach ("3 Points") that uses only three scanning points [27], which we describe in the supplement.

Hardware. Our prototype C^2NLOS system (Fig. 5) is based on the system proposed in O'Toole et al. [27]. Please refer to the supplemental material for more details. To estimate the computational efficiency of each algorithm, we ran each reconstruction algorithm on a 2017 Macbook Pro (2.5 GHz Intel Core i7).

Transient Measurement Data. For object localization, we use real captured data from our C^2NLOS acquisition system (see Fig. 6(a)), as well as simulated data. In our hardware acquisition system, we captured transients of size $1024(\phi') \times 4096(t)$ from a circular scanning pattern of diameter 1.0 m. To qualitatively evaluate our single-object localization, we synthesized transients of size $64 \times 64 \times 2048$ from 100 randomly generated NLOS scenes, where we placed a single scatterer at a random location in a $1.0\,m \times 1.0\,m \times 1.0\,m$ volume 2.0 m away from the LOS wall. We used 200 scenes in the two-object case. For 2D imaging, we used simulated transient data from the Z-NLOS Dataset [9,14], which we resized to $64 \times 64 \times 2048$. For 3D imaging, we test our algorithm on real captured data provided by O'Toole et al. [27], as well as simulated data from the Z-NLOS Dataset, all rescaled to $64 \times 64 \times 512$. In all cases, to synthesize C^2NLOS data, we sampled 360 angles along the inscribed circle of the confocal grid.

On a typical NLOS hardware setup, the 64×64 grid data used by FK/LCT would only be captured at roughly 2 Hz. In contrast, C^2NLOS measurements can be captured at 130 Hz, corresponding to just 1.6% of the capture time.

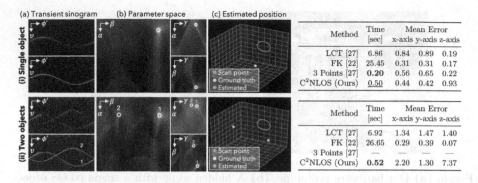

Fig. 6. Estimating the position of (i) one and (ii) two scatterers. **Left:** Given a transient measurement in (a) top, we generate a sinusoid parameter space (b). The sinusoid parameters that best fit the transient sinogram (see (a) bottom) are obtained by finding its peak (see annotations on (b)). The 3D position of the object is reconstructed with the estimated parameters. **Right:** Quantitative evaluation with mean estimation error and computational time. Despite only requiring roughly 1.6% of the capture time of LCT or FK, C^2NLOS estimated the position within almost the same order of accuracy as the other methods. Our approach was also faster than LCT and FK.

5.1   1D Reconstruction: Object Localization

Figure 6(left) demonstrates our methodology for estimating a scatterer's position with real captured transient data, using the approach described in Sect. 4.1. Please note that the proposed method is applicable for more than two objects without loss of generality. Due to the robustness of Hough voting, our method detects the position of the hidden object(s) even though the transient measurements are quite noisy. See supplemental materials for more results.

For quantitative validation, Fig. 6(right) compares our method to the baseline approaches using the experimental setup outlined in the previous section. Despite the much smaller number of spatial samples, C^2NLOS was able to achieve similar accuracy to LCT or FK, both of which require an order-of-magnitude more measurements. Computationally, our method was also faster than LCT and FK, but slower than the 3-Points method in the single object case. However, note that the 3-Points method does not generalize beyond a single object.

5.2   2D Reconstruction: 2D Plane Imaging

Figure 7 shows the qualitative and quantitative 2D imaging results on large planar scenes. Despite requiring just 1.6% of the capture time, the linear inversion method was able to visualize the hidden image plane. At the same time, even though our inverse Radon reconstruction approach was not designed for large planar objects, it still recovers an approximate reconstruction of the 2D scene.

As we mentioned in Sect. 4.2, changing the value for the radius r of the sphere or distance d is analogous to a manual refocusing operation. Figure 8 shows the results with the proposed Radon reconstruction-based method, in which the

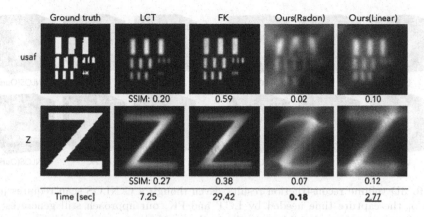

	Ground truth	LCT	FK	Ours(Radon)	Ours(Linear)
usaf		SSIM: 0.20	0.59	0.02	0.10
z		SSIM: 0.27	0.38	0.07	0.12
Time [sec]		7.25	29.42	**0.18**	2.77

Fig. 7. Quantitative and qualitative results on 2D imaging on large planar scenes. Despite sampling far fewer measurements than LCT and FK, both of our inverse Radon reconstruction/linear inversion-based methods reconstructed images that were similar in quality. The SSIM scores for the proposed methods were slightly worse than LCT or FK. However, our methods were much more computationally efficient (e.g., inverse Radon reconstruction yielded a 50× speedup over LCT).

Different focal plane (r) ⟶

Fig. 8. Our inverse Radon reconstruction-based 2D imaging with different focus planes (right focuses towards larger depth). Even for non-planar objects like a bunny, C^2NLOS measurements contain sufficient information about the hidden object for an inverse Radon transform to approximately reconstruct its visual appearance.

results with larger r (farther from the wall) are shown to the right. Our method was able to visualize not only flat objects, but also objects with a wider range of depths, as shown by the *bunny* scene.

For quantitative validation, we used SSIM [34] as a metric. As shown in Fig. 7, both of our 2D imaging methods yield slightly worse results compared to LCT and FK. However, both our Radon-reconstruction and linear-inversion procedures are significantly faster than LCT and FK.

5.3   3D Reconstruction: 3D Volume Imaging

We use the Alternating Direction Method of Multipliers (ADMM) [5] to minimize the optimization problem from Eq. (15). We show a full derivation in the supplement. Because of the iterative optimization process required by our strong priors, our reconstruction operator is inherently slower than both FK and LCT. However, our method yields similar runtimes to the iterative versions of LCT and the Gram operator [2], both of which use a similar optimization formulation.

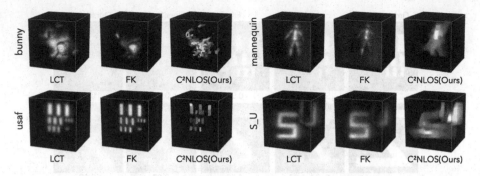

Fig. 9. 3D volume reconstruction results. Even though a C^2NLOS scan requires just 1.6% of the capture time needed by LCT and FK, our approach still generates an approximate reconstruction. More results in the supplement.

In order to evaluate our 3D reconstructions, we test LCT, FK, and our modified LCT procedure on a variety of different scenes in Fig. 9. In general, while FK and LCT demonstrate much higher reconstruction quality, our approach still captures important features of the hidden scene, like the presence and depth of multiple planar objects in the S_U scene and the overall pose in the *mannequin* scene. Empirically, this shows that significant volumetric information of the hidden scene can be recovered from a single transient sinogram.

6   Conclusion

We show that a transient sinogram acquired through C^2NLOS scanning is sufficient for solving a number of imaging tasks, even though the dimensionality of the measurement is smaller than those captured by existing NLOS methods. Through an analysis of the image formation model, we explain how the measurements are fundamentally sinusoidal and lend themselves to efficient reconstruction algorithms, including a Hough voting procedure for estimating the 3D position of scatterers and an inverse Radon technique for recovering 2D images of hidden objects. We empirically demonstrate that the measurements can also be applied to recover full 3D volumes. We believe these contributions mark a significant step in our understanding of *efficient* imaging techniques for revealing objects hidden just around a corner.

Acknowledgements. We thank Ioannis Gkioulekas for helpful discussions and feedback on this work. M. Isogawa is supported by NTT Corporation. M. O'Toole is supported by the DARPA REVEAL program.

References

1. Adib, F., Hsu, C.Y., Mao, H., Katabi, D., Durand, F.: Capturing the human figure through a wall. ACM Trans. Graph. (TOG) **34**(6), 1–13 (2015)

2. Ahn, B., Dave, A., Veeraraghavan, A., Gkioulekas, I., Sankaranarayanan, A.C.: Convolutional approximations to the general non-line-of-sight imaging operator. In: IEEE International Conference on Computer Vision (ICCV), pp. 7888–7898 (2019)
3. Ballard, D.H.: Generalizing the Hough transform to fetect arbitrary shapes. In: Readings in Computer Vision, pp. 714–725 (1987)
4. Bouman, K.L., et al.: Turning corners into cameras: principles and methods. In: IEEE International Conference on Computer Vision (ICCV), pp. 2289–2297 (2017)
5. Boyd, S., Parikh, N., Chu, E., Peleato, B., Eckstein, J.: Distributed optimization and statistical learning via the alternating direction method of multipliers. Found. Trends Mach. Learn. **3**(1), 1–122 (2011)
6. Buttafava, M., Zeman, J., Tosi, A., Eliceiri, K., Velten, A.: Non-line-of-sight imaging using a time-gated single photon avalanche diode. Opt. Express **23**(16), 20997–21011 (2015)
7. Chan, S., Warburton, R.E., Gariepy, G., Leach, J., Faccio, D.: Non-line-of-sight tracking of people at long range. Opt. Express **25**(9), 10109–10117 (2017)
8. Chandran, S., Jayasuriya, S.: Adaptive lighting for data-driven non-line-of-sight 3D localization and object identification. In: The British Machine Vision Conference (BMVC) (2019)
9. Galindo, M., Marco, J., O'Toole, M., Wetzstein, G., Gutierrez, D., Jarabo, A.: A dataset for benchmarking time-resolved non-line-of-sight imaging. In: ACM SIGGRAPH 2019 Posters, pp. 1–2 (2019)
10. Gupta, O., Willwacher, T., Velten, A., Veeraraghavan, A., Raskar, R.: Reconstruction of hidden 3D shapes using diffuse reflections. Opt. Express **20**(17), 19096–19108 (2012)
11. Heide, F., Heidrich, W., Hullin, M.B.: Diffuse mirrors: 3D reconstruction from diffuse indirect illumination using inexpensive time-of-flight sens. In: IEEE Conference on Computer Vision and Pattern Recognition (CVPR), pp. 3222–3229 (2014)
12. Heide, F., O'Toole, M., Zang, K., Lindell, D.B., Diamond, S., Wetzstein, G.: Non-line-of-sight imaging with partial occluders and surface normals. ACM Trans. Graph. **38**(3), 1–10 (2019)
13. Isogawa, M., Yuan, Y., O'Toole, M., Kitani, K.M.: Optical non-line-of-sight physics-based 3D human pose estimation. In: IEEE Conference on Computer Vision and Pattern Recognition (CVPR), pp. 7013–7022 (2020)
14. Jarabo, A., Marco, J., Muñoz, A., Buisan, R., Jarosz, W., Gutierrez, D.: A framework for transient rendering. ACM Trans. Graph. (ToG) **33**(6), 1–10 (2014)
15. Kak, A.C., Slaney, M., Wang, G.: Principles of computerized tomographic imaging. Med. Phys. **29**(1), 107–107 (2002)
16. Kirmani, A., Hutchison, T., Davis, J., Raskar, R.: Looking around the corner using transient imaging. In: IEEE International Conference on Computer Vision (ICCV), pp. 159–166 (2009)
17. Klein, J., Peters, C., Laurenzis, M., Hullin, M.: Tracking objects outside the line of sight using 2D intensity images. Sci. Rep. **6**(32491), 1–9 (2016)
18. Klein, J., Peters, C., Laurenzis, M., Hullin, M.: Non-line-of-sight MoCap. In: ACM SIGGRAPH Emerging Technologies, pp. 18:1–18:2 (2017)
19. La Manna, M., Kine, F., Breitbach, E., Jackson, J., Sultan, T., Velten, A.: Error backprojection algorithms for non-line-of-sight imaging. IEEE Trans. Pattern Anal. Mach. Intell. **41**(7), 1615–1626 (2019)
20. Li, T., Fan, L., Zhao, M., Liu, Y., Katabi, D.: Making the invisible visible: action recognition through walls and occlusions. In: Proceedings of the IEEE International Conference on Computer Vision, pp. 872–881 (2019)

21. Lindell, D.B., Wetzstein, G., Koltun, V.: Acoustic non-line-of-sight imaging. In: IEEE Conference on Computer Vision and Pattern Recognition (CVPR), pp. 6780–6789 (2019)
22. Lindell, D.B., Wetzstein, G., O'Toole, M.: Wave-based non-line-of-sight imaging using fast F-K migration. ACM Trans. Graph. (TOG) **38**(4), 116 (2019)
23. Maeda, T., Satat, G., Swedish, T., Sinha, L., Raskar, R.: Recent advances in imaging around corners. In: arXiv (2019)
24. Maeda, T., Wang, Y., Raskar, R., Kadambi, A.: Thermal non-line-of-sight imaging. In: IEEE International Conference on Computational Photography (ICCP), pp. 1–11 (2019)
25. Metzler, C.A., Lindell, D.B., Wetzstein, G.: Keyhole imaging: non-line-of-sight imaging and tracking of moving objects along a single optical path at long standoff distances. In: arXiv (2019)
26. O'Toole, M., Heide, F., Lindell, D.B., Zang, K., Diamond, S., Wetzstein, G.: Reconstructing transient images from single-photon sensors. In: IEEE Conference on Computer Vision and Pattern Recognition (CVPR), pp. 2289–2297 (2017)
27. O'Toole, M., Lindell, D.B., Wetzstein, G.: Confocal non-line-of-sight imaging based on the light-cone transform. Nature **555**(7696), 338 (2018)
28. Pediredla, A., Dave, A., Veeraraghavan, A.: SNLOS: Non-line-of-sight scanning through temporal focusing. In: IEEE International Conference on Computational Photography (ICCP), pp. 1–13 (2019)
29. Redo-Sanchez, A., et al.: Terahertz time-gated spectral imaging for content extraction through layered structures. Nat. Commun. **7**, 12665 (2016)
30. Saunders, C., Murray-Bruce, J., Goyal, V.K.: Computational periscopy with an ordinary digital camera. Nature **565**(7740), 472–475 (2019)
31. Tancik, M., Satat, G., Raskar, R.: Flash photography for data-driven hidden scene recovery. In: arXiv (2018)
32. Tsai, C.Y., Sankaranarayanan, A.C., Gkioulekas, I.: Beyond volumetric albedo - a surface optimization framework for non-line-of-sight imaging. In: IEEE Conference on Computer Vision and Pattern Recognition (CVPR) (2019)
33. Velten, A., Willwacher, T., Gupta, O., Veeraraghavan, A., Bawendi, M.G., Raskar, R.: Recovering three-dimensional shape around a corner using ultrafast time-of-flight imaging. Nat. Commun. **3**, 745 (2012)
34. Wang, Z., Bovik, A.C., Sheikh, H.R., Simoncelli, E.P.: Image quality assessment: from error visibility to structural similarity. IEEE Trans. Image Process. **13**(4), 600–612 (2004)
35. Xin, S., Nousias, S., Kutulakos, K.N., Sankaranarayanan, A.C., Narasimhan, S.G., Gkioulekas, I.: A theory of Fermat paths for non-line-of-sight shape reconstruction. In: IEEE Conference on Computer Vision and Pattern Recognition (CVPR) (2019)
36. Zou, C.C., Ge, S.: A Hough transform-based method for fast detection of fixed period sinusoidal curves in images. In: International Conference on Signal Processing (ICSP), vol. 1, pp. 909–912 (2002)

Texture Hallucination for Large-Factor Painting Super-Resolution

Yulun Zhang[1]([⊠]), Zhifei Zhang[2], Stephen DiVerdi[2], Zhaowen Wang[2], Jose Echevarria[2], and Yun Fu[1]

[1] Northeastern University, Boston, USA
yulun100@gmail.com
[2] Adobe Research, San Jose, USA

Abstract. We aim to super-resolve digital paintings, synthesizing realistic details from high-resolution reference painting materials for very large scaling factors (e.g., 8×, 16×). However, previous single image super-resolution (SISR) methods would either lose textural details or introduce unpleasing artifacts. On the other hand, reference-based SR (Ref-SR) methods can transfer textures to some extent, but is still impractical to handle very large factors and keep fidelity with original input. To solve these problems, we propose an efficient high-resolution hallucination network for very large scaling factors with efficient network structure and feature transferring. To transfer more detailed textures, we design a wavelet texture loss, which helps to enhance more high-frequency components. At the same time, to reduce the smoothing effect brought by the image reconstruction loss, we further relax the reconstruction constraint with a degradation loss which ensures the consistency between downscaled super-resolution results and low-resolution inputs. We also collected a high-resolution (e.g., 4K resolution) painting dataset PaintHD by considering both physical size and image resolution. We demonstrate the effectiveness of our method with extensive experiments on PaintHD by comparing with SISR and Ref-SR state-of-the-art methods.

Keywords: Texture hallucination · Large-factor · Painting super-resolution · Wavelet texture loss · Degradation loss

1 Introduction

Image super-resolution (SR) aims to reconstruct high-resolution (HR) output with details from its low-resolution (LR) counterpart. Super-resolution for digital painting images has important values in both culture and research aspects. Many historical masterpieces were damaged and their digital replications are in low-resolution (LR), low-quality due to technological limitation in old days. Recovery

Electronic supplementary material The online version of this chapter (https://doi.org/10.1007/978-3-030-58571-6_13) contains supplementary material, which is available to authorized users.

© Springer Nature Switzerland AG 2020
A. Vedaldi et al. (Eds.): ECCV 2020, LNCS 12352, pp. 209–225, 2020.
https://doi.org/10.1007/978-3-030-58571-6_13

of their fine details is crucial for maintaining and protecting human heritage. It is also a valuable research problem for computer scientists to restore high-resolution (HR) painting due to the rich content and texture of paintings in varying scales. A straightforward way to solve this problem is to borrow some knowledge from natural image SR [5,35,37], which however is not enough.

Super-resolving painting images is particularly challenging as vary large upscaling factors (8×, 16×, or even larger) are required to recover the brush and canvas details of artworks, so that a viewer can fully appreciate the aesthetics as from the original painting. One state-of-the-art (SOTA) single image super-resolution (SISR) method RCAN [35] can upscale input with large scaling factors with high PSNR values. But, it would suffer from over-smoothing artifacts, because most high-frequency components (e.g., textures) have been lost in the input. It's hard to recover high-frequency information from LR input directly. Some reference-based SR (Ref-SR) methods try to transfer high-quality textures from another reference image. One SOTA Ref-SR method SRNTT [37] matches features between input and reference. Then, feature swapping is conducted in a multi-level way. SRNTT performs well in the texture transfer. However, the results of SRNTT could be affected by the reference obviously. Also, it's hard for SRNTT to transfer high-quality textures when scaling factor becomes larger.

Based on the analyses above, we try to transfer detailed textures from reference images and also tackle with large scaling factors. Fortunately, there is a big abundance of existing artworks scanned in high-resolution, which provide the references for the common texture details shared among most paintings.

To this end, we collect a large-scale high-quality dataset PaintHD for oil painting images with diverse contents and styles. We explore new deep network architectures with efficient texture transfer (i.e., match feature in smaller scale and swap feature in fine scale) for large upscaling factors. We also design wavelet-based texture loss and degradation loss to achieve high perceptual quality and fidelity at the same time. The network architecture helps tackle large scaling factors better. The wavelet-based texture loss and degradation loss contribute to achieve better visual results. Our proposed method can hallucinate realistic details based on the given reference images, which is especially desired for large factor image upscaling. Compared to the previous SOTA SISR and Ref-SR methods, our proposed method achieves significantly improved quantitative (perceptual index (PI) [1]) and visual results, which are further verified in our human subjective evaluation (i.e., user study). In Fig. 1, we compare with other state-of-the-art methods for large scaling factor (e.g., 16×). We can see our method can transfer more vivid and faithful textures.

In summary, the main contributions of this work are:

- We proposed a reference-based image super-resolution framework for large upscaling factors (e.g., 8× and 16×) with novel training objectives. Specifically, we proposed wavelet texture loss and degradation loss, which allow to transfer more detailed and vivid textures.

- We collected a new digital painting dataset PaintHD with high-quality images and detailed meta information, by considering both physical and resolution sizes. Such a high-resolution dataset is suitable for painting SR.
- We achieved significantly improved quantitative and visual results over previous single image super-resolution (SISR) and reference based SR (Ref-SR) state-of-the-arts. A new technical direction is opened for Ref-SR with large upscaling factor on painting images.

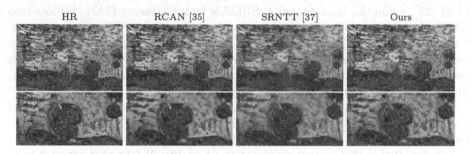

Fig. 1. Visual comparisons for the scaling factor of 16× (the first row) and zoom-in patches (the second row). We compare with state-of-the-art SISR and Ref-SR methods.

2 Related Work

Recent work on deep-learning-based methods for image SR [20,22,25,35–37] is clearly outperforming more traditional methods [3,9,28] in terms of either PSNR/SSIM or visual quality. Here, we focus on the former for conciseness.

2.1 Single Image Super-Resolution

Single image super-resolution (SISR) recovers a high-resolution image directly from its low-resolution (LR) counterpart. The pioneering SRCNN proposed by Dong et al. [5], made the breakthrough of introducing deep learning to SISR, achieving superior performance than traditional methods. Inspired by this seminal work, many representative works [6,16,17,22,26,29,35] were proposed to further explore the potential of deep learning and have continuously raised the baseline performance of SISR. In SRCNN and follow-ups VDSR [16] and DRCN [17], the input LR image is upscaled to the target size through interpolation before fed into the network for recovery of details. Later works demonstrated that extracting features from LR directly and learning the upscaling process would improve both quality and efficiency. For example, Dong et al. [6] provide the LR image directly to the network and use a deconvolution for upscaling. Shi et al. [26] further speed up the upscaling process using sub-pixel convolutions, which became widely adopted in recent works. Current state-of-the-art performance is achieved by EDSR [22] and RCAN [35]. EDSR takes inspiration from ResNet [13], using long-skip and sub-pix convolutions to achieve stronger edge and finer texture. RCAN introduced channel attention to learn high-frequency information.

Once larger upscaling factors were achievable, e.g., 4×, 8×, many empirical studies [20,25,37] demonstrated that the commonly used quality measurements PSNR and SSIM proved to be not representative of visual quality, i.e., higher visual quality may result in lower PSNR; a fact first investigated by Johnson et al. [15] and Ledig et al. [20]. The former investigated perceptual loss using VGG [27], while the later proposed SRGAN by introducing GAN [11] loss into SISR, which boosted significantly the visual quality compared to previous works. Based on SRGAN [20], Sajjadi et al. [25] further adopted texture loss to enhance textural reality. Along with higher visual quality, those GAN-based SR methods also introduce artifacts or new textures synthesized depending on the content, which would contribute to increased perceived fidelity.

Although SISR has been studied for decades, it is still limited by its ill-posed nature, making it difficult to recover fine texture detail for upscaling factors of 8× or 16×. So, most existing SISR methods are limited to a maximum of 4×. Otherwise, they suffer serious degradation of quality. Works that attempted to achieve 8× upscaling, e.g., LapSRN [19] and RCAN [35], found visual quality would degrade quadratically with the increase of upscaling factor.

2.2   Reference-Based Super-Resolution

Different from SISR, reference-based SR (Ref-SR) methods attempt to utilize self or external information to enhance the texture. Freeman et al. [8] proposed the first work on Ref-SR, which replaced LR patches with fitting HR ones from a database/dictionary. [7,14] considered the input LR image itself as the database, from which references were extracted to enhance textures. These methods benefit the most from repeated patterns with perspective transformation. Light field imaging is an area of interest for Ref-SR, where HR references can be captured along the LR light field, just with a small offset. Thus, making easier to align the reference to the LR input, facilitating the transfer of high-frequency information in [2,38]. CrossNet [39] took advantage of deep learning to align the input and reference by estimating the flow between them and achieved SOTA performance.

A more generic scenario for Ref-SR is to relax the constraints on references, i.e., the references could present large spacial/color shift from the input. More extremely, references and inputs could contain unrelated content. Sun et al. [28] used global scene descriptors and internet-scale image databases to find similar scenes that provide ideal example textures. Yue et al. [33] proposed a similar idea, retrieving similar images from the web and performing global registration and local matching. Recent works [31,37] leveraged deep models and significantly improved Ref-SR performance, e.g., visual quality and generalization capacity.

Our proposed method further extends the feasible scaling factor of previous Ref-SR methods from 4× to 16×. More importantly, as oppose to the previous approach [37], which transfers the high-frequency information from reference as a style transfer task, we conduct texture transfer only in high-frequency band, which reduces the transfer effect on the low-frequency content.

3 Approach

We aim to hallucinate the SR image I_{SR} for large scaling factor s from its low-resolution (LR) input I_{LR} and transfer highly detailed textures from high-resolution (HR) reference I_{Ref}. However, most previous Ref-SR methods [37,39] could mainly handle relatively small scaling factors (e.g., ×4). To achieve visually pleasing I_{SR} with larger scaling factors, we firstly build a more compact network (see Fig. 2) and then apply novel loss functions to the output.

3.1 Pipeline

We first define L levels according to scaling factor s, where $s = 2^L$. Inspired by SRNTT [37], we conduct texture swapping in the feature space to transfer highly detailed textures to the output (Fig. 2). The feature upscaler acts as the mainstream of upscaling the input LR image. Meanwhile, the reference feature that carries richer texture is extracted by the deep feature extractor. At the finest layer (largest scale) the reference feature is transferred to the output.

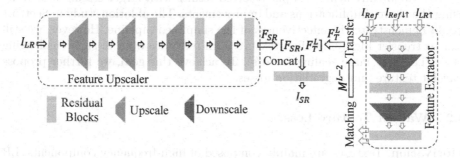

Fig. 2. The pipeline of our proposed method.

As demonstrated in recent works [21,35], the batch normalization (BN) layers commonly used in deep models for stabilizing the training process turns to degrade the SR performance. Therefore, we avoid BN layer in our feature upscaling model. More importantly, the GPU memory usage is largely reduced, as the BN layer consumes similar amount of GPU memory as convolutional layer [22].

To efficiently transfer high-frequency information from the reference, we swap features at the finest level L, where the reference features are swapped according to the local feature matching between the input and reference. Since patch matching is time-consuming, it is conducted at lower level (small spatial size), i.e., we obtain feature matching information M^{L-2} in level $L-2$ via

$$M^{L-2} = H_M^{L-2}\left(\phi^{L-2}\left(I_{LR\uparrow}\right), \phi^{L-2}\left(I_{Ref\downarrow\uparrow}\right)\right), \tag{1}$$

where $H_M^{L-2}(\cdot)$ denotes feature matching operation in level $L-2$. $\phi^{L-2}(\cdot)$ is a neural feature extractor (e.g., VGG19 [27]) matching the same level. $I_{LR\uparrow}$ is upscaled by Bicubic interpolation with scaling factor s. To match the frequency band of $I_{LR\uparrow}$, we first downscale and then upscale it with scaling factor s. For each patch from $\phi^{L-2}(I_{LR\uparrow})$, we could find its best matched patch from $\phi^{L-2}(I_{Ref\downarrow\uparrow})$ with highest similarity.

Then, using the matching information M^{L-2}, we transfer features at level L and obtain the new feature F_T^L via

$$F_T^L = H_T^L\left(\phi^L\left(I_{Ref}\right), M^{L-2}\right), \tag{2}$$

where $H_T^L(\cdot)$ denotes feature transfer operation. $\phi^L\left(I_{Ref}\right)$ extracts neural feature from the high-resolution reference I_{Ref} at level L.

On the other hand, we also extract deep feature from the LR input I_{LR} and upscale it with scaling factor s. Let's denote the upscaled input feature as F_{SR} and the operation as $H_{FSR}(\cdot)$, namely $F_{SR} = H_{FSR}(I_{LR})$. To introduce the transferred feature F_T^L into the image hallucination, we fuse F_T^L and F_{SR} by using residual learning, and finally reconstruct the output I_{SR}. Such a process can be expressed as follows

$$I_{SR} = H_{Rec}\left(H_{Res}\left(\left[F_{SR}, F_T^L\right]\right) + F_{SR}\right), \tag{3}$$

where $[F_{SR}, F_T^L]$ refers to channel-wise concatenation, $H_{Res}(\cdot)$ denotes several residual blocks, and $H_{Rec}(\cdot)$ denotes a reconstruction layer.

We can already achieve super-resolved results with larger scaling factors by using the above simplifications and improvements. The ablation study in Sect. 5.1 would demonstrate the effectiveness of the simplified pipeline. However, we still aim to transfer highly-detailed texture from reference even in such challenging cases (i.e., very large scaling factors). To achieve this goal, we further propose wavelet texture and degradation losses.

3.2   Wavelet Texture Loss

Motivation. Textures are mainly composed of high-frequency components. LR images contain less high-frequency components, when the scaling factor goes larger. If we apply the loss functions (including texture loss) on the color image space, it's still hard to recover or transfer more high-frequency ones. However, if we pay more attention to the high-frequency components and relax the reconstruction of color image space, such an issue could be alleviated better. Specifically, we aim to transfer as many textures as possible from reference by applying texture loss on the high-frequency components. Wavelet is a proper way to decompose the signal into different bands with different frequency levels.

Haar Wavelet. Inspired by the excellent WCT^2 [32], where a wavelet-corrected transfer was proposed, we firstly apply Haar wavelet to obtain different components. The Haar wavelet transformation has four kernels, $\left\{LL^T, LH^T, HL^T, HH^T\right\}$, where L^T and H^T denote the low and high pass filters,

$$L^T = \frac{1}{\sqrt{2}} \begin{bmatrix} 1 & 1 \end{bmatrix}, \ H^T = \frac{1}{\sqrt{2}} \begin{bmatrix} -1 & 1 \end{bmatrix}. \tag{4}$$

As a result, such a wavelet operation would split the signal into four channels, capturing low-frequency and high-frequency components. We denote the extraction operations for these four channels as $H_W^{LL}(\cdot)$, $H_W^{LH}(\cdot)$, $H_W^{HL}(\cdot)$, and $H_W^{HH}(\cdot)$ respectively. Then, we aim to pay more attention to the recovery of high-frequency components with the usage of wavelet texture loss.

Wavelet Texture Loss. As investigated in WCT^2 [32], in Haar wavelet, the low-pass filter can extract smooth surface and parts of texture and high-pass filters capture higher frequency components (e.g., horizontal, vertical, and diagonal edge like textures).

Ideally, it's a wise choice to apply texture loss on each channel split by Haar wavelet. However, as we calculate texture loss in different scales, such a choice would suffer from very heavy GPU memory usage and running time. Moreover, as it's very difficult for the network to transfer highly detailed texture with very large scaling factors, focusing on the reconstruction of more desired parts would be a better choice. Consequently, we propose a wavelet texture loss with HH kernel and formulate it as follows

$$\mathcal{L}_{tex} = \sum_l \lambda_l \left\| Gr \left(\phi^l \left(H_W^{HH} \left(I_{SR} \right) \right) \right) - Gr \left(F_T^l \right) \right\|_F, \tag{5}$$

where $H_W^{HH}(\cdot)$ extracts high-frequency component from the upscaled output I_{SR} with HH kernel. F_T^l is the transferred feature in feature map space of ϕ^l. $Gr(\cdot)$ calculates the Gram matrix for each level l, where λ_l is the corresponding normalization weight. $\|\cdot\|_F$ denotes Frobenius norm.

As shown in Eq. (5), we mainly focus on the texture reconstruction of higher frequency components, which would transfer more textures with somehow creative ability. Then, we further relax the reconstruction constraint by proposing a degradation loss.

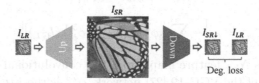

Fig. 3. The illustration of our proposed degradation loss. We try to minimize the degradation loss $\mathcal{L}_{deg}$ between the downscaled output $I_{SR\downarrow}$ and the original input I_{LR}.

3.3 Degradation Loss

Motivation. Most previous single image SR methods (e.g., RCAN [35]) mainly concentrate on minimizing the loss between the upscaled image I_{SR} and ground truth I_{GT}. For small scaling factors (e.g., ×2), those methods would achieve excellent results with very high PSNR values. However, when the scaling factor goes very large (e.g., 16×), the results of those methods would suffer from heavy smoothing artifacts and lack favorable textures (see Fig. 1). On the other hand, as we try to transfer textures to the results as many as possible, emphasizing on the overall reconstruction in the upscaled image may also smooth some transferred textures. To alleviate such texture oversmoothing artifacts, we turn to additionally introduce the LR input I_{LR} into network optimization.

Degradation Loss. Different from image SR, which is more challenging to obtain favorable results, image downscaling could be relatively easier. It's possible to learn a degradation network H_D, that maps the HR image to an LR one. We train such a network by using HR ground truth I_{GT} as input and try to minimize the loss between its output $H_D(I_{GT})$ and the LR counterpart I_{LR}.

With the degradation network H_D, we are able to mimic the degradation process from I_{GT} to I_{LR}, which can be a many-to-one case. Namely, there exists many upscaled images corresponding to the original LR image I_{LR}, which helps to relax the constraints on the reconstruction. To make use of this property, we try to narrow the gap between the downscaled output $I_{SR\downarrow}$ and the original LR input I_{LR}. As shown in Fig. 3, we formulate it as a degradation loss

$$\mathcal{L}_{deg} = \|I_{SR\downarrow} - I_{LR}\|_1 = \|H_D(I_{SR}) - I_{LR}\|_1, \tag{6}$$

where $I_{SR\downarrow}$ denotes the downscaled image from I_{SR} with scaling factor s and $\|\cdot\|_1$ denotes ℓ_1-norm. With the proposed loss functions, we further give details about the implementation.

3.4   Implementation Details

Loss Functions. We also adopt another three common loss functions [15,20,25,37]: reconstruction ($\mathcal{L}_{rec}$), perceptual ($\mathcal{L}_{per}$), and adversarial ($\mathcal{L}_{adv}$) losses. We briefly introduce them as follows.

$$\mathcal{L}_{rec} = \|I_{SR} - I_{GT}\|_1, \tag{7}$$

$$\mathcal{L}_{per} = \frac{1}{N_{5,1}} \sum_{i=1}^{N_{5,1}} \left\| \phi_i^{5,1}(I_{SR}) - \phi_i^{5,1}(I_{GT}) \right\|_F, \tag{8}$$

where $\phi^{5,1}$ extracts $N_{5,1}$ feature maps from 1-st convolutional layer before 5-th max-pooling layer of the VGG-19 [27] network. $\phi_i^{5,1}$ is the i-th feature map.

We also adopt WGAN-GP [12] for adversarial training [11], which can be expressed as follows

$$\min_G \max_D \mathbb{E}_{I_{GT} \sim \mathbb{P}_r} [D(I_{GT})] - \mathbb{E}_{I_{SR} \sim \mathbb{P}_g} [D(I_{SR})], \tag{9}$$

where G and D denote generator and discriminator respectively, and $I_{SR} = G(I_{LR})$. $\mathbb{P}_r$ and $\mathbb{P}_g$ represent data and model distributions. For simplicity, here, we mainly focus on the adversarial loss for generator and show it as follows

$$\mathcal{L}_{adv} = -\mathbb{E}_{I_{SR} \sim \mathbb{P}_g} [D(I_{SR})]. \tag{10}$$

Training. The weights for $\mathcal{L}_{rec}$, $\mathcal{L}_{tex}$, $\mathcal{L}_{deg}$, $\mathcal{L}_{per}$, and $\mathcal{L}_{adv}$ are 1, 10^{-4}, 1, 10^{-4}, and 10^{-6} respectively. To stabilize the training process, we pre-train the network for 2 epochs with $\mathcal{L}_{rec}$ and $\mathcal{L}_{tex}$. Then, all the losses are applied to train another 20 epochs. We implement our model with TensorFlow and apply Adam optimizer [18] with learning rate 10^{-4}.

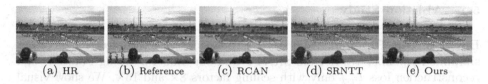

| (a) HR | (b) Reference | (c) RCAN | (d) SRNTT | (e) Ours |

Fig. 4. Visual results (8×) of RCAN [35], SRNTT [37], and our method on CUFED5. Our result is visually more pleasing than others, and generates plausible texture details.

Fig. 5. Examples from our collected PaintHD dataset.

4 Dataset

For large upscaling factors, e.g., 8× and 16×, input images with small size, e.g., 30×30, but with rich texture in its originally HR counterpart will significantly increase the arbitrariness/smoothness for texture recovery because fewer pixels result in looser content constraints on the texture recovery. Existing datasets for Ref-SR are unsuitable for such large upscaling factors (see Fig. 4). Therefore, we collect a new dataset of high-resolution painting images that carry rich and diverse stroke and canvas texture.

The new dataset, named PaintHD, is sourced from the Google Art Project [4], which is a collection of very large zoom-able images. In total, we collected over 13,600 images, some of which achieve gigapixel. Intuitively, an image with more pixels does not necessarily present finer texture since the physical size of the corresponding painting may be large as well. To measure the richness of texture, the physical size of paintings is considered to calculate pixel per inch (PPI) for each image. Finally, we construct the training set consisting of 2,000 images and the testing set of 100 images with relatively higher PPI. Figure 5 shows some examples of PaintHD, which contains abundant textures.

To further evaluate the generalization capacity of the proposed method, we also test on the CUFED5 [37] dataset, which is designed specifically for Ref-SR validation. There are 126 groups of samples. Each group consists of one HR image and four references with different levels of similarity to the HR image.

For simplicity, we adopt the most similar reference for each HR image to construct the testing pairs. The images in CUFED5 are of much lower resolution, e.g., 500×300, as compared to the proposed PaintHD dataset.

5   Experimental Results

5.1   Ablation Study

Effect of Our Pipeline. We firstly try to demonstrate the effectiveness of our simplified pipeline. We re-train SRNTT and our model by using PaintHD and reconstruction loss $\mathcal{L}_{rec}$ only with scaling factors $8\times$ and $16\times$. We show visual comparisons about $8\times$ in Fig. 6(a). We can see the color of the background by our method is more faithful to the ground truth. Furthermore, our method achieves sharper result than that of SRNTT. Such a observation can be much clearer, when the scaling factor becomes $16\times$ (e.g., see Fig. 6(b)). As a result, our method transfers more textures and achieve shaper results. We also provide quantitative results about 'SRNTT-$\mathcal{L}_{rec}$' and 'Ours–$\mathcal{L}_{rec}$' in Table 1, where we'll give more details and analyses. In summary, these comparisons demonstrate the effectiveness of our simplified pipeline.

Effect of Wavelet Texture Loss. The wavelet texture loss is imposed on the high-frequency band of the feature maps, rather than directly applying on raw features like SRNTT [37] and traditional style transfer [10]. Comparison between the wavelet texture loss and tradition texture loss is illustrated in Fig. 7. To highlight the difference, weights on texture losses during training are increased by 100 times as compared to the default setting in Sect. 3.4. Let's compare Figs. 7(c) and 7(d), the result without wavelet is significantly affected by the texture/color from the reference (Fig. 7(b)), lost identity to the input content. By contrast, the result with wavelet still preserves similar texture and color to the ground truth (Fig. 7(a)).

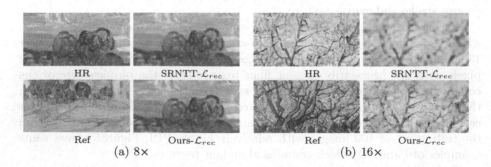

Fig. 6. Visual comparisons between SRNTT and ours by using $\mathcal{L}_{rec}$ only

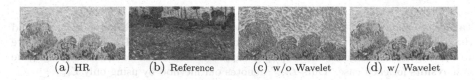

(a) HR   (b) Reference   (c) w/o Wavelet   (d) w/ Wavelet

Fig. 7. Comparison of super-resolved results with and without wavelet

Effect of Degradation Loss. To demonstrate the effectiveness of our proposed degradation loss $\mathcal{L}_{deg}$, we train one of our models with $\mathcal{L}_{rec}$ only and another same model with $\mathcal{L}_{rec}$ and $\mathcal{L}_{deg}$ with scaling factor 8×. We show the visual comparison in Fig. 8, where we can see result with $\mathcal{L}_{rec}$ only would suffer from some blurring artifacts (see Fig. 8(c)). While, in Fig. 8(d), $\mathcal{L}_{deg}$ helps suppress such artifacts to some degree. This is mainly because the degradation loss $\mathcal{L}_{deg}$ alleviates the training difficulty in the ill-posed image SR problem. Such observations not only demonstrate the effectiveness of $\mathcal{L}_{deg}$, but also are consistent with our analyses in Sect. 3.3.

5.2   Quantitative Results

We compare our method with state-of-the-art SISR and Ref-SR methods. The SISR methods are EDSR [22], RCAN [35], and SRGAN [20], where RCAN [35] achieved state-of-the-art performance in terms of PSNR (dB). Due to limited space, we only introduce the state-of-the-art Ref-SR method SRNTT [37] for comparison. However, most of those methods are not originally designed for very large scaling factors. Here, to make them suitable for 8× and 16× SR, we adopt them with some modifications. In 8× case, we use RCAN [35] to first upscale the input I_{LR} by 2×. The upscaled intermediate result would be the input for EDSR and SRGAN, which then upscale the result by 4×. Analogically, in 16× case, we use RCAN to first upscale I_{LR} by 4×. The intermediate result would be def into RCAN, EDSR, and SRGAN, which further upscale it by 4×. For SRNTT and our method, we would directly upscale the input by 8× or 16×. SRNTT is re-trained with our PaintHD training data by its authors.

We not only compute the pixel-wise difference with PSNR and SSIM [30], but also evaluate perceptual quality with perceptual index (PI) [1] by considering Ma's score [23] and NIQE [24]. Specifically, PI = 0.5((10 − Ma) + NIQE). Lower PI value reflects better perceptual quality. We show quantitative results in Table 1, where we have some interesting and thought-provoking observations.

First, SISR methods would obtain higher PSNR and SSIM values than those of Ref-SR methods. This is reasonable because SISR methods mainly target to minimize MSE, which helps to pursue higher PSNR values. But, when the scaling factor goes to larger (e.g., 16×), the gap among SISR methods also becomes very smaller. It means that it would be difficult to distinguish the performance between different SISR methods by considering PSNR/SSIM.

Based on the observations and analyses above, we conclude that we should turn to other more visually-perceptual ways to evaluate the performance of SR

Table 1. Quantitative results (PSNR/SSIM/PI) of different SR methods for 8× and 16× on two datasets: CUFED5 [37] and our collected PaintHD. The methods are grouped into two categories: SISR (top group) and Ref-SR (bottom). We highlight the best results for each case. 'Ours-$\mathcal{L}_{rec}$' denotes our method by using only $\mathcal{L}_{rec}$

Data	CUFED5		PaintHD	
Scale	8×	16×	8×	16×
Bicubic	21.63/0.572/9.445	19.75/0.509/10.855	23.73/0.432/9.235	22.33/0.384/11.017
EDSR	23.02/0.653/7.098	20.70/0.548/8.249	24.42/0.477/7.648	22.90/0.405/8.943
RCAN	23.37/0.666/6.722	20.71/0.548/8.188	24.43/0.478/7.448	22.91/0.406/8.918
SRGAN	22.93/0.642/5.714	20.54/0.537/7.367	24.21/0.466/7.154	22.75/0.396/7.955
SRNTT-$\mathcal{L}_{rec}$	22.34/0.612/7.234	20.17/0.528/8.373	23.96/0.449/7.992	22.47/0.391/8.464
SRNTT	21.08/0.548/2.502	19.09/0.418/2.956	22.90/0.377/3.856	21.48/0.307/4.314
Ours-$\mathcal{L}_{rec}$	22.40/0.635/4.520	19.71/0.526/5.298	24.02/0.461/5.253	22.13/0.375/5.815
Ours	20.36/0.541/2.339	18.51/0.442/2.499	22.49/0.361/3.670	20.69/0.259/4.131

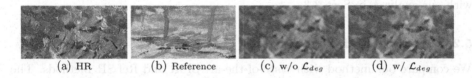

(a) HR   (b) Reference   (c) w/o $\mathcal{L}_{deg}$ (d) w/ $\mathcal{L}_{deg}$

Fig. 8. Comparison of super-resolved results (8×) with and without degradation loss

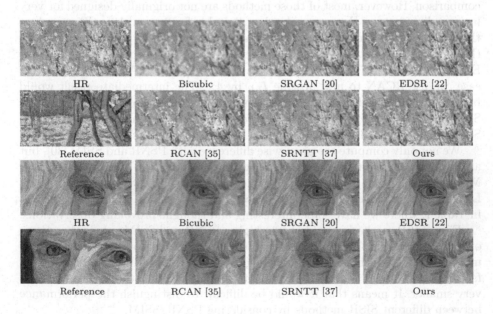

HR   Bicubic   SRGAN [20]   EDSR [22]

Reference   RCAN [35]   SRNTT [37]   Ours

HR   Bicubic   SRGAN [20]   EDSR [22]

Reference   RCAN [35]   SRNTT [37]   Ours

Fig. 9. Visual results (8×) of different SR methods on PaintHD

methods, instead of only depending on PSNR/SSIM values. So, we further evaluate the PI values of each SR method. We can see 'Ours-$\mathcal{L}_{rec}$' achieves lower PI values than those of 'SRNTT-$\mathcal{L}_{rec}$', which is consistent with the analyses in Sect. 5.1. SRNTT [37] would achieve lower PI values than other SISR methods. It's predictable, as SRNTT transfers textures from high-quality reference. However, our method would achieve the lowest PI values among all the compared methods. Such quantitative results indicate that our method obtains outputs with better visual quality. To further support our analyses, we further conduct visual results comparisons and user study.

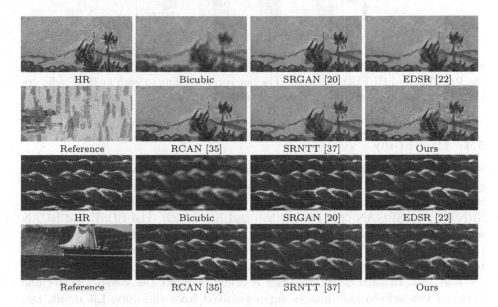

Fig. 10. Visual results (16×) of different SR methods on PaintHD

5.3 Visual Comparisons

As our PaintHD contains very high-resolution images with abundant textures, it's a practical way for us to show the zoom-in image patches for comparison. To better view the details of high-resolution image patches, it's hard for us to show image patches from too many methods. As a result, we only show visual comparison with state-of-the-art SISR and Ref-SR methods: SRGAN [20], EDSR [22], RCAN [35], and SRNTT [37].

We show visual comparisons in Figs. 9 and 10 for 8× and 16× cases respectively. Take 8× case as an example, SISR methods could handle it to some degree, because the LR input has abundant details for reconstruction. But, SISR methods still suffer from some blurring artifacts due to use PSNR-oriented loss function (e.g., ℓ_1-norm loss). By transferring textures from reference and using other loss functions (e.g., texture, perceptual, and adversarial losses), SRNTT [37] performs visually better than RCAN. But SRNTT still can hardly transfer more detailed textures. In contrast, our method would obviously address the blurring artifacts and can transfer more vivid textures.

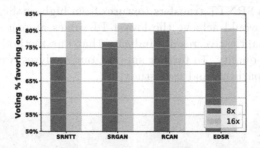

Fig. 11. User study on the results of SRNTT, SRGAN, RCAN, EDSR, and ours on the PaintHD and CUFED5 datasets. The bar corresponding to each method indicates the percentage favoring ours as compared to the method

5.4 User Study

Since the traditional metric PSNR and SSIM do not consistent to visual quality [15,20,25,37], we conducted user study by following the setting of SRNTT [37] to compare our results with those from other methods, i.e., SRNTT [34], SRGAN [20], RCAN [35], and EDSR [22]. The EDSR and RCAN achieve state-of-the-art performance in terms of PSNR/SSIM, while SRGAN (SISR) and SRNTT (Ref-SR) focus more on visual quality. All methods are tested on a random subset of CUFED5 and PaintHD at the upscaling factor of 8× and 16×. In each query, the user is asked to select the visually better one between two side-by-side images super-resolved from the same LR input, i.e., one from ours and the other from another method. In total, we collected 3,480 votes, and the results are shown in Fig. 11. The height of a bar indicates the percentage of users who favor our results as compared to those from a corresponding method. In general, our results achieve better visual quality at both upscaling scales, and the relative quality at 16× further outperforms the others.

5.5 Effect of Different References

For Ref-SR methods, investigation on the effect from references is an interesting and opening problem, e.g., how the references affect SR results, how to control (i.e., utilize or suppress) such effect, etc. This section intends to explore the effect of references in the proposed Ref-SR method. As shown in Fig. 12, the same LR input is super-resolved using different reference images, respectively. We can see that the results keep similar content structures as the input. If we give a further look at the details, we find each result has specific textures from the corresponding reference. It indicates that our method keeps the main structures to the LR input, but also adaptively transfers texture details from reference.

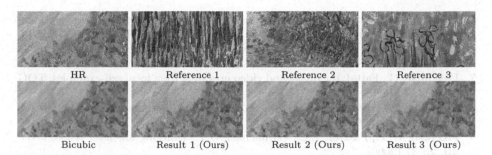

Fig. 12. Visual results with scaling factor 8× using different reference images

6 Conclusions

We aim to hallucinate painting images with very large upscaling factors and transfer high-resolution (HR) detailed textures from HR reference images. Such a task could be very challenging. The popular single image super-resolution (SISR) could hardly transfer textures from reference images. On the other hand, reference-based SR (Ref-SR) could transfer textures to some degree, but could hardly handle very large scaling factors. We address this problem by first construct an efficient Ref-SR network, being suitable for very large scaling factor. To transfer more detailed textures, we propose a wavelet texture loss to focus on more high-frequency components. To alleviate the potential over-smoothing artifacts caused by reconstruction constraint, we further relax it by proposed a degradation loss. We collect high-quality painting dataset PaintHD, where we conduct extensive experiments and compare with other state-of-the-art methods. We achieved significantly improvements over both SISR and Ref-SR methods.

Acknowledgments. This work was supported by the Adobe gift fund.

References

1. Blau, Y., Mechrez, R., Timofte, R., Michaeli, T., Zelnik-Manor, L.: The 2018 pirm challenge on perceptual image super-resolution. In: ECCV (2018)
2. Boominathan, V., Mitra, K., Veeraraghavan, A.: Improving resolution and depth-of-field of light field cameras using a hybrid imaging system. In: ICCP (2014)
3. Chang, H., Yeung, D.Y., Xiong, Y.: Super-resolution through neighbor embedding. In: CVPR (2004)
4. Commons, W.: Google art project (2018). https://commons.wikimedia.org/wiki/Category:Google_Art_Project
5. Dong, C., Loy, C.C., He, K., Tang, X.: Learning a deep convolutional network for image super-resolution. In: Fleet, D., Pajdla, T., Schiele, B., Tuytelaars, T. (eds.) ECCV 2014. LNCS, vol. 8692, pp. 184–199. Springer, Cham (2014). https://doi.org/10.1007/978-3-319-10593-2_13

6. Dong, C., Loy, C.C., Tang, X.: Accelerating the super-resolution convolutional neural network. In: Leibe, B., Matas, J., Sebe, N., Welling, M. (eds.) ECCV 2016. LNCS, vol. 9906, pp. 391–407. Springer, Cham (2016). https://doi.org/10.1007/978-3-319-46475-6_25

7. Freedman, G., Fattal, R.: Image and video upscaling from local self-examples. TOG **30**, 1–11 (2011)

8. Freeman, W.T., Jones, T.R., Pasztor, E.C.: Example-based super-resolution. IEEE Comput. Graph. Appl. **2**, 56–65 (2002)

9. Freeman, W.T., Pasztor, E.C., Carmichael, O.T.: Learning low-level vision. IJCV **40**, 25–47 (2000)

10. Gatys, L.A., Ecker, A.S., Bethge, M.: Image style transfer using convolutional neural networks. In: CVPR (2016)

11. Goodfellow, I., et al.: Generative adversarial nets. In: NeurIPS (2014)

12. Gulrajani, I., Ahmed, F., Arjovsky, M., Dumoulin, V., Courville, A.C.: Improved training of wasserstein gans. In: NeurIPS (2017)

13. He, K., Zhang, X., Ren, S., Sun, J.: Deep residual learning for image recognition. In: CVPR (2016)

14. Huang, J.B., Singh, A., Ahuja, N.: Single image super-resolution from transformed self-exemplars. In: CVPR (2015)

15. Johnson, J., Alahi, A., Fei-Fei, L.: Perceptual losses for real-time style transfer and super-resolution. In: Leibe, B., Matas, J., Sebe, N., Welling, M. (eds.) ECCV 2016. LNCS, vol. 9906, pp. 694–711. Springer, Cham (2016). https://doi.org/10.1007/978-3-319-46475-6_43

16. Kim, J., Kwon Lee, J., Mu Lee, K.: Accurate image super-resolution using very deep convolutional networks. In: CVPR (2016)

17. Kim, J., Kwon Lee, J., Mu Lee, K.: Deeply-recursive convolutional network for image super-resolution. In: CVPR (2016)

18. Kingma, D., Ba, J.: Adam: a method for stochastic optimization. In: ICLR (2014)

19. Lai, W.S., Huang, J.B., Ahuja, N., Yang, M.H.: Deep laplacian pyramid networks for fast and accurate super-resolution. In: CVPR (2017)

20. Ledig, C., et al.: Photo-realistic single image super-resolution using a generative adversarial network. In: CVPR (2017)

21. Lee, C.Y., Xie, S., Gallagher, P., Zhang, Z., Tu, Z.: Deeply-supervised nets. In: AISTATS (2015)

22. Lim, B., Son, S., Kim, H., Nah, S., Lee, K.M.: Enhanced deep residual networks for single image super-resolution. In: CVPRW (2017)

23. Ma, C., Yang, C.Y., Yang, X., Yang, M.H.: Learning a no-reference quality metric for single-image super-resolution. CVIU **158**, 1–16 (2017)

24. Mittal, A., Soundararajan, R., Bovik, A.C.: Making a "completely blind" image quality analyzer. SPL **20**, 209–212 (2012)

25. Sajjadi, M.S., Schölkopf, B., Hirsch, M.: EnhanceNet: single image super-resolution through automated texture synthesis. In: ICCV (2017)

26. Shi, W., et al.: Real-time single image and video super-resolution using an efficient sub-pixel convolutional neural network. In: CVPR (2016)

27. Simonyan, K., Zisserman, A.: Very deep convolutional networks for large-scale image recognition. arXiv preprint arXiv:1409.1556 (2014)

28. Sun, L., Hays, J.: Super-resolution from internet-scale scene matching. In: ICCP (2012)

29. Wang, Z., Liu, D., Yang, J., Han, W., Huang, T.: Deep networks for image super-resolution with sparse prior. In: ICCV (2015)

30. Wang, Z., Bovik, A.C., Sheikh, H.R., Simoncelli, E.P.: Image quality assessment: from error visibility to structural similarity. TIP **13**, 600–612 (2004)
31. Yang, W., Xia, S., Liu, J., Guo, Z.: Reference-guided deep super-resolution via manifold localized external compensation. TCSVT **29**, 1270–1283 (2018)
32. Yoo, J., Uh, Y., Chun, S., Kang, B., Ha, J.W.: Photorealistic style transfer via wavelet transforms. In: ICCV (2019)
33. Yue, H., Sun, X., Yang, J., Wu, F.: Landmark image super-resolution by retrieving web images. TIP **22**, 4865–4878 (2013)
34. Zhang, H., Patel, V.M.: Densely connected pyramid dehazing network. In: CVPR (2018)
35. Zhang, Y., Li, K., Li, K., Wang, L., Zhong, B., Fu, Y.: Image super-resolution using very deep residual channel attention networks. In: Ferrari, V., Hebert, M., Sminchisescu, C., Weiss, Y. (eds.) ECCV 2018. LNCS, vol. 11211, pp. 294–310. Springer, Cham (2018). https://doi.org/10.1007/978-3-030-01234-2_18
36. Zhang, Y., Tian, Y., Kong, Y., Zhong, B., Fu, Y.: Residual dense network for image super-resolution. In: CVPR (2018)
37. Zhang, Z., Wang, Z., Lin, Z., Qi, H.: Image super-resolution by neural texture transfer. In: CVPR (2019)
38. Zheng, H., Guo, M., Wang, H., Liu, Y., Fang, L.: Combining exemplar-based approach and learning-based approach for light field super-resolution using a hybrid imaging system. In: ICCV (2017)
39. Zheng, H., Ji, M., Wang, H., Liu, Y., Fang, L.: CrossNet: an end-to-end reference-based super resolution network using cross-scale warping. In: ECCV (2018)

Learning Progressive Joint Propagation for Human Motion Prediction

Yujun Cai[1(✉)], Lin Huang[3], Yiwei Wang[5], Tat-Jen Cham[1], Jianfei Cai[1,2], Junsong Yuan[3], Jun Liu[6], Xu Yang[1], Yiheng Zhu[4], Xiaohui Shen[4], Ding Liu[4], Jing Liu[4], and Nadia Magnenat Thalmann[1]

[1] Nanyang Technological University, Singapore, Singapore
{yujun001,s170018}@e.ntu.edu.sg, {astjcham,nadiathalmann}@ntu.edu.sg
[2] Monash University, Melbourne, Australia
jianfei.cai@monash.edu
[3] State University of New York at Buffalo University, Buffalo, USA
{lhuang27,jsyuan}@buffalo.edu
[4] ByteDance Research, New York, USA
{shenxiaohui,yiheng.zhu,liuding,jing.liu}@bytedance.com
[5] National University of Singapore, Singapore, USA
wangyw_seu@foxmail.com
[6] SUTD, Singapore, Singapore
jun_liu@sutd.edu.sg

Abstract. Despite the great progress in human motion prediction, it remains a challenging task due to the complicated structural dynamics of human behaviors. In this paper, we address this problem in three aspects. First, to capture the long-range spatial correlations and temporal dependencies, we apply a transformer-based architecture with the global attention mechanism. Specifically, we feed the network with the sequential joints encoded with the temporal information for spatial and temporal explorations. Second, to further exploit the inherent kinematic chains for better 3D structures, we apply a progressive-decoding strategy, which performs in a central-to-peripheral extension according to the structural connectivity. Last, in order to incorporate a general motion space for high-quality prediction, we build a memory-based dictionary, which aims to preserve the global motion patterns in training data to guide the predictions. We evaluate the proposed method on two challenging benchmark datasets (Human3.6M and CMU-Mocap). Experimental results show our superior performance compared with the state-of-the-art approaches.

Keywords: 3D motion prediction · Transformer network · Progressive decoding · Dictionary module

Electronic supplementary material The online version of this chapter (https://doi.org/10.1007/978-3-030-58571-6_14) contains supplementary material, which is available to authorized users.

A. Vedaldi et al. (Eds.): ECCV 2020, LNCS 12352, pp. 226–242, 2020.
https://doi.org/10.1007/978-3-030-58571-6_14

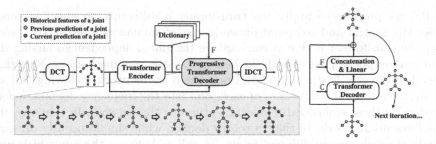

Fig. 1. Left: **Overview of our proposed network architecture for 3D motion prediction.** Given a sequence of 3D human poses, we apply Discrete Cosine Transform (DCT) to encode the temporal information of each joint into frequency coefficients. The DCT coefficients of sequential joints are then fed into the transformer-based architecture for progressive predictions. Additionally, we use memory-based dictionary to incorporate the global motion knowledge into the model. We apply inverse DCT (IDCT) to convert the predicted DCT coefficients back to the temporal domain. Right: **Progressive decoding strategy.** We predict the DCT coefficients of the target joints progressively, which performs in a central-to-peripheral manner in accordance with the kinematic chains (bottom left), with the encoded context feature **C** and the dictionary information **F**.

1   Introduction

Human motion prediction aims to forecast a sequence of future dynamics based on an observed series of human poses. It has extensive applications in robotics, computer graphics, healthcare and public safety [20,24,26,40,41], such as human robot interaction [25], autonomous driving [35] and human tracking [18].

Due to the inherent temporal nature of this task, many existing methods [14,33,43] resort to recurrent neural networks (RNN) and their variants for temporal modeling. However, simply relying on the temporal coherence is not enough, since the bio-mechanical dynamics of human behavior are extremely complicated, which not only correspond to temporal smoothness, but also highly relate to spatial joint dependencies. To address this issue, previous work attempted to embed the spatial configurations into the modeling space, so as to enhance the validity of the 3D structures. For instance, Li *et al.* [28] relied on a convolutional filter to capture the dependencies across the spatial and temporal domains. The range of such dependencies, however, is strongly limited by the size of the convolutional kernel. Mao *et al.* [32] applied Discrete Cosine Transform (DCT) to encode temporal information and designed a Graph Neural Network (GNN) to model spatial correlations. Although achieving good results, it forgoes the prevailing sequential decoding architecture and thus cannot explicitly leverage context features that may lead to further improvement.

Based on these observations, we aim to efficiently capture long-range spatial-temporal dependencies while also incorporating the advantage of sequential modeling. In particular, motivated by substantial performance gains achieved by transformer-based networks [11,12,37,42] in Natural Language Processing

(NLP), we propose to apply the transformer architecture to simultaneously model the spatial and temporal dependencies of human motion. A key benefit of the transformer is that it can capture the global dependencies among the input and output sequences with the help of the attention mechanism. Note that instead of directly feeding sequential poses into the network, following [32] we encode the temporal trajectories of each joint into the frequency domain, before transferring these embedded temporal features to the network. In this way, the model essentially works in the trajectory domain while simultaneously drawing global attention among different joints, as well as between the input historical trajectories and the output predictions.

Moreover, we would like to point out that simply using the transformer for motion prediction does not fully exploit the kinematic chains of body skeletons, yet these are important since they underlie the motions in human behavior. For instance, absolute displacement of a wrist is often mediated by initial movement of the shoulder, followed by the elbow. Inspired by spatial explorations in 3D human pose estimation [8,27], we propose to exploit the structural configurations by predicting the joint trajectories progressively in a central-to-peripheral manner. More precisely, as depicted in Fig. 1 (bottom left), we first estimate the future dynamics of the central body as seed points, and then sequentially propagate the joint predictions based on the kinematic connections.

In addition, the typical approach for most encoder-decoder frameworks, when decoding the motion predictions, is to mainly focus on the single source video that is being processed. This may not be the optimal, since partial motions of many actions follow certain types of general patterns (*e.g.* walking feet, waving hands and bending knees), which may appear in multiple videos with similar but not identical context. Thus, we further propose to incorporate a general motion space into the predictions. Specially, inspired by the memory scheme that is widely utilized in Question Answering (QA) [39,46], we design a memory-based dictionary to store the common actions across different videos in training data. From the dictionary, we can query the historical motions $\mathbf{C}$ and construct the future dynamics $\mathbf{F}$ to guide the predictions, as shown in Fig. 1 (left).

In summary, our contributions of this work are threefold:

- We propose to leverage the transformer-based architecture to simultaneously exploit the spatial correlations and the temporal smoothness of human motion, by treating the sequential joints with the encoded temporal features as the input of the network.
- To further exploit the structural connectivity of human skeletons, we deploy a progressive decoding strategy to predict the future joint dynamics in a central-to-peripheral manner in accordance with the kinematic chains of a human body.
- To incorporate the general motion space for high quality results, we build a memory-based dictionary to guide the predictions, which preserves the correspondences between the historical motion features and the representative future dynamics.

We conducted comprehensive experiments on two widely-used benchmarks for human motion prediction: the Human3.6M dataset and the CMU-Mocap dataset, and our proposed method improves state-of-the-art performance in both datasets.

2   Related Work

Human Motion Prediction. Human motion predictions have been extensively studied in the past few years. Early approaches tackled this problem with Hidden Markov Model [4], linear dynamics system [36], and Gaussian Process latent variable models [44], etc., which commonly suffer from the computational resources and can be easily stuck in non-periodical actions. Recently, due to the success of the sequence-to-sequence inference, RNN-based architectures have been widely used in state-of-the-art approaches [2,5,14,17,45]. For instance, Fragkiadaki et al. [14] proposed a Encoder- Recurrent-Decoder (ERD) framework, which maps pose data into a latent space and propagates it across the temporal domain through LSTM cells. To facilitate more realistic human motions, Gui et al. [19] introduced an adversarial training and Wang et al. [43] employed imitation learning into the sequential modeling. While pushing the boundaries of the motion predictions, many of these RNN-based models directly use a fully-connected layer to learn the representation of human pose, which to some extent overlook the inherent spatial configurations of human body.

Structural-Aware Prediction. Several recent works [1,22,27,29–32] tried to embed the spatial articulations of human body to enhance the validity of the 3D structures. For example, Jain et al. [22] proposed to encode the spatial and temporal structure of the pose via a manually designed spatio-temporal graph. Although taking structural configurations into account, these graphs, however, have limited flexibility for discovering long-range interactions between different joints. To address this issue, Mao et al. [32] leveraged GNN-based architectures, where all joints are linked together for full explorations. While achieving good results, this method does not explicitly utilize the kinematic chains of body structure. In contrast, to leverage the long-range connections while also exploiting the structural connectivity of body skeletons, we apply a transformer-based architecture to capture the long-range spatial and temporal dependencies of human motion. Additionally, we propose to progressively propagate the joint predictions in a central-to-peripheral manner to further exploit the spatial configurations.

Transformer Network. The transformer has become the state-of-the-art approach in Natural Language Processing (NLP), with extensive architectures such as Bert [12], GPT [37], XLNet [11]. Recently, it is also investigated in Computer Vision, such as Image GPT [10] and Object Detection [9]. Compared with the traditional recurrent neural network (RNN) that explicitly models the compatibility of adjacent tokens, the transformer takes an entirely different global attention mechanism, which allows to capture the long-term dependencies between the input and the output sequences. Inspired from this, we propose to leverage transformer-based architecture to capture the spatio-temporal correlations

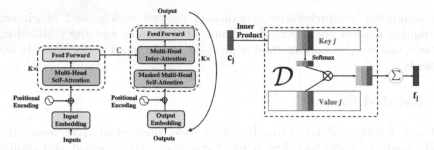

Fig. 2. Left: **The architecture of the conventional transformer** [42], where the far left side is the transformer-encoder that encodes the input into context features **C**, while the relatively right side is the decoder that recursively generates the output sequence with the encoded context features. Right: **Query and reconstruction procedure in memory-based dictionary for joint** j. The input is the observed context features encoded from the historical trajectories, and the output is the constructed features for predicting future dynamics.

of human motion. Particularly, instead of directly taking the sequential poses as the input, we follow [32] to apply DCT to encode the trajectory of each joint. The sequential joints with encoded temporal patterns are then fed into the network for global explorations.

3   Methodology

3.1   Overview

Figure 1 gives an overview of our proposed network architecture. Given a series of human motion poses $\mathbf{X}_{1:T} = [\mathbf{x}_1, \mathbf{x}_2, ..., \mathbf{x}_T]$, where $\mathbf{x}_t$ denotes the pose at frame t, our target is to generate a corresponding prediction $\mathbf{X}_{T+1:T+T_f}$ for the future T_f frames. To achieve this goal, different from most existing work that employ RNN-based architectures to model the temporal information of human motions, we leverage the transformer network to capture the long-range spatial and temporal correlations of human motions with the help of the attention mechanism. Specifically, we apply Discrete Cosine Transform (DCT) to encode the temporal information of each joint into frequency space and feed the network with the sequential joints with encoded temporal patterns. Additionally, motivated by the inherent structural connectivity of body skeletons, we explicitly stagger the decoding into predefined progressive steps. This is performed in a central-to-peripheral manner according to the kinematic chains, with a total update at the final stage (see Fig. 1 bottom-left). To create a generalized and full-spectrum human motion space across the different videos in training data, we further introduce a dictionary as an auxiliary decoder to enhance the prediction quality. The whole model is trained in an end-to-end manner with backpropagation. Next, we describe the individual components in detail.

3.2   Revisiting Transformer

The transformer architecture is a core pillar underpinning of many state-of-the-art methods in Natural Language Processing (NLP) since [12], showing superior performance compared to conventional RNN-based structures. This is mainly because RNNs have difficulties in modelling long-term dependencies, while the transformer overcomes this limitation by leveraging the global attention mechanism to draw the dependencies between the entire input and output sequences, without regard to their distances. In particular, as shown in Fig. 2 (left), the transformer employs an attention-based encoder-decoder framework, where the encoder applies self-attention to extract the useful context from the input sequence, and the decoder consecutively produces the prediction based on the global dependencies between the context features and the previous output sequences. To make use of the sequential order, the transformer additionally inserts a "positional encoding" module to the embeddings at the bottom of the encoder and decoder stacks, assigning each dimension of each token with a unique encoded value.

3.3   Transformer for Pose Prediction

Motivated by the substantial performance gain induced by the transform architecture in NLP, we propose to solve the pose prediction problem with the help of a transformer-based network. A straightforward way is to take the human pose at each time step as corresponding to a "word" in the machine translation task, and then predict the pose at the next time step as akin to predicting the next word. However, doing so blindly ignores the spatial dependencies between joints, which have proven to be highly effective in state-of-the-art methods for pose estimation [8,13,15,16,27,29] and pose prediction [28,32].

To tackle this issue and leverage both the spatial and temporal dependencies of human poses, following [32] we encode the temporal information of each joint into frequency space. Specifically, we first replicate the last pose x_T for T_f times to generate a temporal sequence of length $T + T_f$, and then compute the DCT coefficients of each joint. In this way, the task becomes that of generating an output sequence $\hat{X}_{1:T+T_f}$ from an input sequence $X_{1:T+T_f}$, with our true objective to predict $X_{T+1:T+T_f}$.

We then feed the obtained DCT coefficients into the transformer-based network, so as to capture the spatial dependencies with the help of the attention mechanism. A key benefit of this design is that the network essentially works in the trajectory space while simultaneously modeling the spatial dependencies among the input and the output joint sequences. Moreover, thanks to the positional encoding, the joint index can be explicitly injected into motion features, allowing the network to not only learn the trajectory of each joint, but also incorporates the joint identities into this process. To encourage smoothness between the input and output trajectories, we also apply the residual scheme at the end of the decoding (see Fig. 1 right).

3.4   Progressive Joint Propagation

The conventional transformer decoder works auto-regressively during inference, that is, conditioning each output word on previously generated outputs. In terms of pose prediction, we observe that human motion is naturally propagated sequentially based on the kinematic chains of body skeletons. For instance, a person may initiate movement of the left shoulder, which then drives the movement of the left elbow and eventually that of the left wrist.

Motivated by this, we propose to progressively express the 3D pose predictions in a similar manner. In particular, as shown in Fig. 1 bottom-left, we treat the central eight joints as the seed joints, and estimate their future motions first, based on their historical motions. Next we sequentially propagate the joint predictions from center to periphery, according to the structural connectivity of the body skeleton. Figure 1 (right) depicts the details of the progressive decoding process: we iteratively predict the residual DCT coefficients of the joints, given the encoded context feature $\mathbf{C} = [\mathbf{c}_1, \mathbf{c}_2, ..., \mathbf{c}_J]$ and the auxiliary information $\mathbf{F} = [\mathbf{f}_1, \mathbf{f}_2, ..., \mathbf{f}_J]$ from the dictionary, where J is the number of joints. Mathematically, for the sth progressive decoding, we formulate the computational process as:

$$\mathbf{X}_{in}^{(s)} = [\hat{\mathbf{X}}_p; \mathbf{X}_h^{(s)}], \tag{1}$$

$$\hat{\mathbf{X}}_{out}^{(s)} = \mathbf{X}_h^{(s)} + \text{Decoder}(\mathbf{X}_{in}^{(s)}, \mathbf{C}, \mathbf{F}^{(s)}), \tag{2}$$

$$\hat{\mathbf{X}}_p = [\hat{\mathbf{X}}_p; \hat{\mathbf{X}}_{out}^{(s)}], \tag{3}$$

where $\mathbf{X}_{in}^{(s)}$ denotes the input of the progressive decoder at stage s, which is a combination of the previously predicted joint sequence $\hat{\mathbf{X}}_p$ and the historical motion of the target joints $\mathbf{X}_h^{(s)}$. $\hat{\mathbf{X}}_{out}^{(s)}$ is the output of the sth decoder, which summarizes the historical motions $\mathbf{X}_h^{(s)}$ and the generated residual DCT coefficients. $\mathbf{F}^{(s)}$ refers to the auxiliary information used for stage s, containing the guided future dynamics of the target joints at stage s. Note that each time we generate the estimation of certain joints $\hat{\mathbf{X}}_{out}$, we merge them into the previously predicted joint sequence $\hat{\mathbf{X}}_p$ for the next iteration. In this way, we ensure that the estimation is propagated along the structural connectivity and the entire body prediction is constructed in the order of the kinematic chains via the progressive joint propagation. To further refine the full-body prediction, we add a total updating stage at the end of the progressive decoder.

3.5   Dictionary

One potential limitation of the encoder-decoder framework (e.g. the transformer, the RNN-based modeling) is that the decoder mainly focuses on one input sequence that is currently being processed while decoding. However, partial motions of many actions follow certain common patterns (e.g. walking feet, bending knees), which may appear in multiple videos with similar but not identical context features. To incorporate this generalized motion prior knowledge for better prediction quality, we design a memory-based dictionary to guide the motion prediction, inspired by the memory scheme [39,46,47] leveraged to preserve a knowledge base for comprehensive understanding. The dictionary is built to store the full spectrum of correspondences between the observed motion features and the representative future dynamics of each joint across different videos in training data. Note that although the correspondences are mainly constructed for each joint, the global motion of the full body is also taken into account, due to the self-attention mechanism of the transformer encoder.

We propose to learn this dictionary via query and construction processes. This dictionary $\mathcal{D}$ is defined as:

$$\mathcal{D} = \left\{ \left(\mathbf{D}_j^{key}, \mathbf{D}_j^{value} \right) \mid j = 1, 2, \ldots, J \right\}, \tag{4}$$

where $\mathbf{D}_j^{key}, \mathbf{D}_j^{value} \in \mathbb{R}^{N \times M}$ are the key and the value matrices respectively for joint j, N is the number of memory cells/clusters for each joint, and M is the dimension of a feature stored in a memory cell. As shown in Fig. 2 (right), the key matrix is used to score an observed motion query of each memory cell so as to better combine the value elements. Mathematically, given an encoded context motion feature $\mathbf{c}_j \in \mathbb{R}^M$ of joint j, the query process can be written as:

$$\mathbf{q}_j = \text{softmax} \left(\mathbf{D}_j^{key} \mathbf{c}_j \right), \tag{5}$$

where $\mathbf{q}_j$ is the query result in the memory network for joint j. Then we define the construction process as

$$\mathbf{f}_j = \left(\mathbf{D}_j^{value} \right)^T \mathbf{q}_j, \tag{6}$$

where $\mathbf{f}_j$ is the feature vector constructed by the memory network for joint j, representing the future dynamics summarized from the learned generalized motion space. In our implementation, we set N as 100 and M as 512.

3.6 Training Strategy

Since the construction of the dictionary relies on the context features from the transformer encoder, we first train the whole network without the dictionary module. Then we learn the dictionary and finetune the whole model subsequently. For the first stage, we employ the following loss function, which aims to minimize the differences between the predicted sequential poses converted from the DCT coefficients and the corresponding ground truth:

$$L = \sum_{s=1}^{S} \lambda_s \sum_{j \in \mathcal{J}_s} \sum_{t=1}^{T+T_f} \mathcal{P}(\hat{x}_{j,t}, x_{j,t}^{GT}) \tag{7}$$

Here $\hat{x}_{j,t}$ refers to the prediction of the jth joint in frame t and $x_{j,t}^{GT}$ is the corresponding ground truth. S is the number of the progressive decoding stages,

$\mathcal{J}_s$ is the set of joints to be predicted at stage s, λ_s is the weight for each stage, T and T_f represent the length of observed frames and predicted frames respectively. $\mathcal{P}$ is a distance function that uses L_1 loss for joint angle representation and L_2 loss for 3D joint coordinates, both of which are typical representations in motion prediction literature. Following [32], we sum the errors over both future and observed time steps, to provide more signals for the learning process.

Having trained the transformer encoder and decoder, we next learn the dictionary module. Specifically, given the observed motion features $\mathbf{C}$, we seek to query for similar historical motion patterns and produce the auxiliary information $\mathbf{F}$ containing future dynamics for each joint. The auxiliary information is typically concatenated with the features generated from the decoder and sent into the final linear layer of the progressive decoder (see Fig. 1 right), so as to produce the prediction of each joint. Formally, we train the dictionary by penalizing the difference between the produced joint predictions and the corresponding ground truth:

$$L_d = \sum_{j=1}^{J} \sum_{t=1}^{T+T_f} \mathcal{P}(\hat{x}_{j,t}, x_{j,t}^{GT}) \tag{8}$$

where J is the number of joints.

Finally, we finetune the whole model in an end-to-end manner, with the same loss function (Eq. (7)) as proposed in the first training stage.

4   Experiments

4.1   Implementation Details

In our experiments, we chose the conventional transformer proposed in [42], with 8 headers and 512 hidden units for each module. Both the encoder and the progressive decoder contain a stack of $K = 4$ identical layers. To accelerate the convergence, we applied the scheduled sampling scheme [3] during training, which randomly replaces part of the previous joint predictions with the ground truth in the input to the progressive decoder. The whole model was implemented within the PyTorch framework. For the first training stage described in Sect. 3.6, we set $\lambda_s = 1$, and trained for 40 epochs with the Adam optimizer [23]. The learning rate started from 5e−4, with a shrink factor of 0.96 applied every two epochs. For the second stage, we learned the dictionary for 20 epochs with the learning rate of 5e−4. Finally, the whole network was finetuned in an end-to-end manner, using a relatively small learning rate of 5e−5. All experiments were conducted on a single NVIDIA Titan V GPU, with a batch size of 128 for both training and evaluation.

Table 1. Short-term prediction results in Mean Angle Error (MAE) on Human3.6M for the main actions due to limited space. The best result is marked in bold. The full table can be found in supplementary.

Milliseconds	Walking				Eating				Smoking				Directions				Greeting				Average			
	80	160	320	400	80	160	320	400	80	160	320	400	80	160	320	400	80	160	320	400	80	160	320	400
Zero-velocity [33]	0.39	0.68	0.99	1.15	0.27	0.48	0.73	0.86	0.26	0.48	0.97	0.95	0.39	0.59	0.79	0.89	0.54	0.89	1.30	1.49	0.40	0.78	1.07	1.21
Residual sup. [33]	0.28	0.49	0.72	0.81	0.23	0.39	0.62	0.76	0.33	0.61	1.05	1.15	0.26	0.47	0.72	0.84	0.75	1.17	1.74	1.83	0.36	0.67	1.02	1.15
convSeq2Seq [28]	0.33	0.54	0.68	0.73	0.22	0.36	0.58	0.71	0.26	0.49	0.96	0.92	0.39	0.60	0.80	0.91	0.51	0.82	1.21	1.38	0.38	0.68	1.01	1.13
AGED w/o adv [19]	0.28	0.42	0.66	0.73	0.22	0.35	0.61	0.74	0.30	0.55	0.98	0.99	0.26	0.46	0.71	0.81	0.61	0.95	1.44	1.61	0.32	0.62	0.96	1.07
AGED w/ adv [19]	0.22	0.36	0.55	0.67	0.17	**0.28**	0.51	0.64	0.27	0.43	**0.82**	0.84	0.23	0.39	0.63	0.69	0.56	0.81	1.30	1.46	0.31	0.54	0.85	0.97
Imitation [43]	0.21	0.34	0.53	0.59	0.17	0.30	0.52	0.65	0.23	0.44	0.87	0.85	0.27	0.46	0.81	0.89	0.43	0.75	1.17	1.33	0.31	0.57	0.90	1.02
GNN [32]	0.18	0.31	**0.49**	0.56	0.16	0.29	0.50	0.62	0.22	0.41	0.86	0.80	0.26	0.45	0.71	0.79	0.36	0.60	0.95	1.13	0.27	0.51	0.83	0.95
Ours	**0.17**	**0.30**	0.51	**0.55**	**0.16**	0.29	**0.50**	**0.61**	**0.21**	**0.40**	0.85	**0.78**	**0.22**	**0.39**	**0.62**	**0.69**	**0.34**	**0.58**	**0.94**	1.12	**0.25**	**0.49**	**0.83**	**0.94**

Table 2. Short-term prediction results in Mean Per Joint Position Error (MPJPE) on Human3.6M for the main actions due to limited space. The best result is marked in bold. A 3D suffix to a method indicates that the method was directly trained on 3D joint positions. Otherwise, the results were obtained by converting the joint angle to 3D positions. The best result is marked in bold and the full table can be found in supplementary.

Milliseconds	Walking				Eating				Smoking				Directions				Greeting				Average			
	80	160	320	400	80	160	320	400	80	160	320	400	80	160	320	400	80	160	320	400	80	160	320	400
Residual sup. [33]	21.7	38.1	58.9	68.8	15.1	28.6	54.8	67.4	20.8	39.0	66.1	76.1	27.9	44.8	63.5	78.2	29.3	56.0	110.2	125.6	27.9	51.6	88.9	103.4
Residual sup. 3D [33]	23.8	40.4	62.9	70.9	17.6	34.7	71.9	87.7	19.7	36.6	61.8	73.9	36.5	56.4	81.5	97.3	37.9	74.1	139.0	158.8	30.8	57.0	99.8	115.5
convSeq2Seq [28]	21.8	37.5	55.9	63.0	13.3	24.5	48.6	60.0	15.4	25.5	39.3	44.5	26.7	43.3	59.0	72.4	30.4	58.6	110.0	122.8	24.9	44.9	75.9	88.1
convSeq2Seq 3D [28]	17.1	31.2	53.8	61.5	13.7	25.9	52.5	63.3	11.1	21.0	33.4	38.3	22.0	37.2	59.6	73.4	24.5	46.2	90.0	103.1	19.6	37.8	68.1	80.2
GNN [32]	11.1	19.0	32.0	39.1	9.2	19.5	40.3	48.9	9.2	16.6	26.1	29.0	11.2	23.2	52.7	64.1	14.2	27.7	67.1	82.9	13.5	27.0	54.2	65.0
GNN 3D [32]	8.9	15.7	29.2	**33.4**	8.8	18.9	39.4	47.2	7.8	14.9	25.3	28.7	12.6	24.4	48.2	58.4	14.5	30.5	74.2	89.0	12.1	25.0	51.0	61.3
Ours	9.6	18.0	33.1	39.1	9.1	19.5	40.2	48.8	7.2	14.2	24.7	29.7	**9.3**	**22.0**	51.6	63.2	15.4	30.7	71.8	82.8	11.9	26.1	53.2	64.5
Ours 3D	**7.9**	**14.5**	**29.1**	34.5	**8.4**	**18.1**	**37.4**	**45.3**	**6.8**	**13.2**	**24.1**	**27.5**	11.1	22.7	**48.0**	**58.4**	**13.2**	**28.0**	**64.5**	**77.9**	**10.7**	**23.8**	**50.0**	**60.2**

Table 3. Short and long-term prediction of 3D joint positions in MPJPE on CMU-Mocap dataset.

Milliseconds	Basketball					Basketball signal					Directing traffic					Jumping					Running				
	80	160	320	400	1000	80	160	320	400	1000	80	160	320	400	1000	80	160	320	400	1000	80	160	320	400	1000
Residual sup. 3D [33]	18.4	33.8	59.5	70.5	106.7	12.7	23.8	40.3	46.7	77.5	15.2	29.6	55.1	66.1	127.1	36.0	68.7	125.0	145.5	195.5	**15.6**	**19.4**	**31.2**	36.2	43.3
GNN 3D [32]	14.0	25.4	49.6	61.4	106.1	3.5	6.1	**11.7**	15.2	**53.9**	7.4	15.1	31.7	42.2	152.4	16.9	34.4	76.3	96.8	**164.6**	25.5	36.7	39.3	39.9	58.2
Ours 3D	**11.6**	**21.7**	**44.4**	**57.3**	**90.9**	**2.6**	**4.9**	12.7	18.7	75.8	**6.2**	**12.7**	**29.1**	**39.6**	149.1	**12.9**	**27.6**	**73.5**	**92.2**	176.6	23.5	34.2	35.2	**36.1**	**43.1**
Milliseconds	Soccer					Walking					Washwindow					Average									
	80	160	320	400	1000	80	160	320	400	1000	80	160	320	400	1000	80	160	320	400	1000					
Residual sup. 3D [33]	20.3	39.5	71.3	84	129.6	8.2	13.7	21.9	24.5	52.2	8.4	15.8	29.3	35.4	61.1	16.8	30.5	54.2	63.6	99.0					
GNN 3D [32]	11.3	21.5	44.2	55.8	117.5	7.7	11.8	19.4	23.1	40.2	5.9	11.9	30.3	40.0	79.3	11.5	20.4	37.8	46.8	96.5					
Ours 3D	**9.2**	**18.4**	**39.2**	**49.5**	**93.9**	**6.7**	**10.7**	21.7	27.5	**37.4**	**5.4**	**11.3**	**29.2**	39.6	79.1	**9.8**	**17.6**	**35.7**	**45.1**	**93.2**					

4.2 Datasets and Evaluation Metrics

We evaluated our method on two publicly available datasets: the Human3.6M dataset [21] and the CMU-Mocap dataset[1] for 3D human motion prediction.

Human3.6M: The Human3.6M dataset [21] is a large-scale and commonly used dataset for human motion prediction, which consists of 7 subjects performing 15 actions, such as "Walking", "Sitting" and "Smoking". Following the standard setup in [19,28,32,33,43], the global rotations, translations and constant joints

---

[1] Available at http://mocap.cs.cmu.edu/.

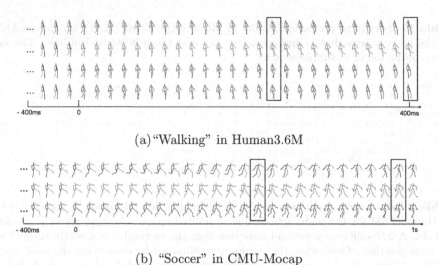

(a) "Walking" in Human3.6M

(b) "Soccer" in CMU-Mocap

Fig. 3. (a) **Qualitative comparison of long-term prediction on Human 3.6M dataset.** From top to bottom, we show the ground truth, the results of Residual sup. [33], GCN [32] and our method. The results show that our approach generates more realistic and accurate results. (b) **Qualitative analysis for the impact of the dictionary.** From top to bottom, we show the ground truth, the results without and with the dictionary module. We see that adding the dictionary facilitates more descriptive future dynamics.

were excluded from our experiments. We down-sampled each sequence to 25 frames per second and applied the evaluation on subject 5 (S5), as proposed in [28,32,33].

CMU-Mocap: To show the generalization ability of our proposed method, we also evaluated our performance on the CMU mocap dataset (CMU-Mocap). Following [28,32], we selected eight actions for evaluation, including "basketball", "baseball", "soccer", etc. The data processing is the same as for Human3.6M.

Evaluation Metric: The evaluation was performed under two metrics. Following [19,28,32,33,43], we first report the Euclidean distance between the predicted and the ground-truth joint angles in Euler angle representation, which can be referred to as Mean Angle Error (MAE). In [32], an alternative metric of Mean Per Joint Position Error (MPJPE) in millimeters is adopted, which is also widely used in 3D pose estimation field [6–8,13,15,27,34,38,48]. Compared with MAE, MPJPE has been noted to be more effective in measuring the predicted human poses due to the inherent ambiguity in angle space, where two different sets of angles can yield the same 3D pose. To show this, we measured the MPJPE in two ways: directly using 3D coordinates to train the network (via DCT/IDCT), and converting Euler angles into 3D joint locations.

Table 4. Long-term prediction of 3D joint positions in MPJPE on Human 3.6M dataset. Our method using 3D coordinates yields the best performance.

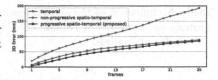

Fig. 4. Average 3D position error of each predicted frame for all actions on Human 3.6M dataset. The error accumulates much faster with the temporal model and our proposed progressive spatio-temporal method achieves the best results.

Milliseconds	Walking		Eating		Smoking		Discussion		Average	
	560	1000	560	1000	560	1000	560	1000	560	1000
Residual sup. [33]	79.4	91.6	82.6	110.8	89.5	122.6	121.9	154.3	93.3	119.8
Residual sup. 3D [33]	73.8	86.7	101.3	119.7	85.0	118.5	120.7	147.6	95.2	118.1
convSeq2Seq [28]	69.2	81.5	71.8	91.4	50.3	85.2	101.0	143.0	73.1	100.3
convSeq2Seq 3D [28]	59.2	71.3	66.5	85.4	42.0	67.9	84.1	116.9	62.9	85.4
GNN [32]	55.0	60.8	68.1	79.5	42.2	70.6	93.8	119.7	64.8	82.6
GNN 3D [32]	42.3	51.3	**56.5**	68.6	32.3	60.5	**70.5**	103.5	50.4	71.0
Ours	51.8	58.7	59.3	76.5	40.3	76.8	82.6	107.7	58.5	79.9
Ours 3D	**36.8**	**41.2**	58.4	**67.9**	**29.2**	**58.3**	74.0	**103.1**	**49.6**	**67.6**

4.3 Comparison with the State-of-the-art Methods

For fair comparison, we report both short-term (10 frames in 400 ms) and long-term predictions (25 frames in 1 s) for the two datasets, given the input of consecutive 10-frame human poses.

Results on Human3.6M: For short term predictions, we evaluated our results under both MAE (Table 1) and MPJPE (Table 2) protocols, in comparison to state-of-the-art baselines [19,28,32,33,43]. As previously mentioned, for MPJPE we can either directly use 3D coordinates or convert angles to 3D joint locations. As can be seen, our proposed method consistently outperformed all the state-of-the-art methods on most actions for both MAE and MPJPE protocols. The improvement is more obvious when measuring with the MPJPE metric, for which the best performance was achieved when directly using 3D joint locations during training. Moreover, we would like to point out that a high error in angle space (*e.g.* Phoning Action under MAE protocol) does not necessarily generate worse results in 3D (Phoning under MPJPE protocol). This can be explained by the inherent ambiguity of the angle representation, since two different sets of angles can generate the same 3D human pose. Based on this observation, for the following experiments, we mainly report our results under the MPJPE metric, using the 3D coordinates for training.

Besides the short term predictions, we also compared our results with the state-of-the-art methods [28,32,33] in long-term scenarios. For fair comparison, we report our results for 4 main classes used in the previous work, including the "Walking", "Eating", "Smoking" and "Discussion" actions under MPJPE evaluation. As shown in Table 4, similar to the short-term results, our results surpassed all other state-of-the-art methods, reducing the average errors to 49.6 mm in 560 ms and 67.6 mm in 1000 ms predictions when directly training and evaluating with the 3D joint locations.

For qualitative analysis, we provided visual comparisons with the state-of-the-art approaches [32,33] for long-term (Fig. 3(a)) scenario, which further underscored how our method generates more realistic results, matching the ground truth better.

Table 5. Influence of the spatial temporal explorations and the progressive-decoding strategy on 4 actions of Human3.6M. For fair comparison, we exclude the dictionary module for all models.

Milliseconds	Walking				Eating				Smoking				Discussion				Average			
	80	160	320	400	80	160	320	400	80	160	320	400	80	160	320	400	80	160	320	400
Temporal	28.9	47.2	69.7	77.8	17.2	31.6	58.3	69.0	18.8	35.7	65.4	76.1	27.9	53.1	82.0	87.9	23.2	41.9	68.9	77.7
Non-progressive spatial-temporal	10.5	17.1	31.9	35.7	10.1	21.2	40.7	47.5	8.6	15.9	26.5	30.4	10.6	24.1	47.5	51.3	9.9	19.5	36.6	41.2
Progressive spatial-temporal (proposed)	8.3	15.1	30.3	35.2	8.8	19.3	39.0	46.1	7.1	14.0	24.9	28.1	8.9	22.1	44.3	49.1	8.3	17.6	34.6	39.6

Table 6. Impact of the propagating directions on Human3.6 M dataset under the MPJPE protocol. The outward direction performs in the proposed central-to-peripheral extension while the inward direction contrastly propagate the predictions from the outside to inside body.

Milliseconds	Walking				Eating				Smoking				Discussion				Average			
	80	160	320	400	80	160	320	400	80	160	320	400	80	160	320	400	80	160	320	400
Inward Propagation	8.9	15.8	30.5	34.9	8.9	19.5	38.9	46.7	7.6	15.0	25.0	29.2	9.4	23.0	45.3	49.9	8.7	18.3	34.9	40.2
Outward Propagation(proposed)	7.9	14.5	29.1	33.5	8.4	18.1	37.4	45.3	6.8	13.2	24.1	27.5	8.3	21.7	43.9	48.0	7.8	16.8	33.6	38.5

Table 7. The impact of the dictionary module on Human3.6M dataset under the MJMPE metric.

Milliseconds	Walking				Eating				Smoking				Discussion				Average			
	80	160	320	400	80	160	320	400	80	160	320	400	80	160	320	400	80	160	320	400
w/o dictionary	8.3	15.1	30.3	35.2	8.8	19.3	39.0	46.1	7.1	14.0	24.9	28.1	8.9	22.1	44.3	49.1	8.3	17.6	34.6	39.6
w/ dictionary(proposed)	7.9	14.5	29.1	33.5	8.4	18.1	37.4	45.3	6.8	13.2	24.1	27.5	8.3	21.7	43.9	48.0	7.8	16.8	33.6	38.5

Results on CMU-Mocap: Table 3 compared the performance of our approach with the previously reported results [32,33] on the CMU-Mocap dataset. For fair comparison, all methods were directly trained with 3D joint coordinates and evaluated under the MPJPE protocol. It can be seen that compared with the state-of-the-art methods, our approach achieved the best results on average and over most of the action classes.

4.4 Ablation Study

Advantages of Spatio-Temporal Correlation and Joint Propagation. We first quantify the importance of leveraging both spatial and temporal correlations and assess the effectiveness of the progressive-decoding strategy. For fair comparisons, we excluded the dictionary from the model and ablated our proposed method (progressive spatio-temporal) with the following baselines: **1) temporal:** We used the straightforward way of applying the transformer network, which treats a pose at each time step as a "word" in machine translation task and sequentially generates the pose prediction of each frame; **2) non-progressive spatio-temporal:** We used DCT to encode the temporal information of each joint and fed the sequential joints into the transformer network, so as to capture the spatial and temporal dependencies. However, the decoder generates the whole body predictions at one step, without progressively producing the results.

As shown in Table 5, compared with the temporal baseline, exploiting both the spatial and temporal correlations (non-progressive spatio-temporal) considerably improved the performance by a large margin, reducing the average MPJPE error from 77.7 mm to 41.2 mm in 400 ms prediction. This result can be further enhanced by applying our proposed progressive-decoding strategy, dropping the MPJPE error to 39.6 mm in 400 ms prediction. Moreover, as illustrated in Fig. 4, the 3D errors accumulated much faster with the temporal model than the spatio-temporal approaches, and the proposed progressive joint propagation consistently outperformed the non-progressive counterpart across all time steps.

Impact of the Propagating Direction. Despite the overall effectiveness of progressive joint propagation, we wanted to investigate how the propagation direction impacts the results. To address this, we employed the progressive-decoding in two directions: the outward (proposed) direction that propagates from the body center to the periphery, and the inward (opposite) direction that propagates from outside to the center. As shown in Table 6, the outward propagation yielded superior performance, indicating the benefit of guiding joint extension with the more stable motion cues from the center body.

Impact of Using the Dictionary. We examined the impact of the dictionary quantitatively and qualitatively. As presented in Table 7, adding the dictionary consistently reduced the 3D errors among the four main action classes on the Human 3.6M dataset, which quantitatively shows the effectiveness of dictionary module. To gain more insight into what the dictionary has learned and how the dictionary enhances the prediction quality, in Fig. 3(b), we qualitatively compared our method with or without the dictionary. As can be seen, when adding the dictionary for general motion guidance, we produce more plausible and descriptive future dynamics, such as "smooth running" after kicking a ball when playing soccer.

Acknowledgement. This research/project is supported by the National Research Foundation, Singapore under its International Research Centres in Singapore Funding Initiative. Any opinions, findings and conclusions or recommendations expressed in this material are those of the author(s) and do not reflect the views of National Research Foundation, Singapore This research is partially supported by the Monash FIT Start-up Grant, start-up funds from University at Buffalo and SUTD project PIE-SGP-Al-2020-02.

References

1. Aksan, E., Kaufmann, M., Hilliges, O.: Structured prediction helps 3D human motion modelling. In: Proceedings of the IEEE International Conference on Computer Vision, pp. 7144–7153 (2019)

2. Barsoum, E., Kender, J., Liu, Z.: HP-GAN: Probabilistic 3D human motion prediction via GAN. In: Proceedings of the IEEE Conference on Computer Vision and Pattern Recognition Workshops, pp. 1418–1427 (2018)
3. Bengio, S., Vinyals, O., Jaitly, N., Shazeer, N.: Scheduled sampling for sequence prediction with recurrent neural networks. In: Advances in Neural Information Processing Systems, pp. 1171–1179 (2015)
4. Brand, M., Hertzmann, A.: Style machines. In: Proceedings of the 27th Annual Conference on Computer Graphics and Interactive Techniques, pp. 183–192 (2000)
5. Butepage, J., Black, M.J., Kragic, D., Kjellstrom, H.: Deep representation learning for human motion prediction and classification. In: Proceedings of the IEEE Conference on Computer Vision and Pattern Recognition, pp. 6158–6166 (2017)
6. Cai, Y., Ge, L., Cai, J., Magnenat-Thalmann, N., Yuan, J.: 3D hand pose estimation using synthetic data and weakly labeled RGB images. IEEE Trans. Pattern Anal. Mach. Intell. (2020)
7. Cai, Y., Ge, L., Cai, J., Yuan, J.: Weakly-supervised 3D hand pose estimation from monocular RGB images. In: Ferrari, V., Hebert, M., Sminchisescu, C., Weiss, Y. (eds.) ECCV 2018. LNCS, vol. 11210, pp. 678–694. Springer, Cham (2018). https://doi.org/10.1007/978-3-030-01231-1_41
8. Cai, Y., et al.: Exploiting spatial-temporal relationships for 3D pose estimation via graph convolutional networks. In: Proceedings of the IEEE International Conference on Computer Vision, pp. 2272–2281 (2019)
9. Carion, N., Massa, F., Synnaeve, G., Usunier, N., Kirillov, A., Zagoruyko, S.: End-to-end object detection with transformers. arXiv preprint arXiv:2005.12872 (2020)
10. Chen, M., et al.: Generative pretraining from pixels (2020)
11. Dai, Z., Yang, Z., Yang, Y., Carbonell, J., Le, Q.V., Salakhutdinov, R.: Transformer-XL: attentive language models beyond a fixed-length context. arXiv preprint arXiv:1901.02860 (2019)
12. Devlin, J., Chang, M.W., Lee, K., Toutanova, K.: BERT: pre-training of deep bidirectional transformers for language understanding. arXiv preprint arXiv:1810.04805 (2018)
13. Fang, H.S., Xu, Y., Wang, W., Liu, X., Zhu, S.C.: Learning pose grammar to encode human body configuration for 3D pose estimation. In: Thirty-Second AAAI Conference on Artificial Intelligence (2018)
14. Fragkiadaki, K., Levine, S., Felsen, P., Malik, J.: Recurrent network models for human dynamics. In: Proceedings of the IEEE International Conference on Computer Vision, pp. 4346–4354 (2015)
15. Ge, L., Cai, Y., Weng, J., Yuan, J.: Hand pointnet: 3D hand pose estimation using point sets. In: Proceedings of the IEEE Conference on Computer Vision and Pattern Recognition, pp. 8417–8426 (2018)
16. Ge, L., et al.: 3D hand shape and pose estimation from a single RGB image. In: Proceedings of the IEEE Conference on Computer Vision and Pattern Recognition, pp. 10833–10842 (2019)
17. Ghosh, P., Song, J., Aksan, E., Hilliges, O.: Learning human motion models for long-term predictions. In: 2017 International Conference on 3D Vision (3DV), pp. 458–466. IEEE (2017)
18. Gong, H., Sim, J., Likhachev, M., Shi, J.: Multi-hypothesis motion planning for visual object tracking. In: 2011 International Conference on Computer Vision, pp. 619–626. IEEE (2011)
19. Gui, L.Y., Wang, Y.X., Liang, X., Moura, J.M.: Adversarial geometry-aware human motion prediction. In: Proceedings of the European Conference on Computer Vision (ECCV), pp. 786–803 (2018)

20. Gupta, A., Martinez, J., Little, J.J., Woodham, R.J.: 3D pose from motion for cross-view action recognition via non-linear circulant temporal encoding. In: Proceedings of the IEEE Conference on Computer Vision and Pattern Recognition, pp. 2601–2608 (2014)
21. Ionescu, C., Papava, D., Olaru, V., Sminchisescu, C.: Human3. 6M: large scale datasets and predictive methods for 3D human sensing in natural environments. IEEE Trans. Pattern Anal. Mach. Intell. **36**(7), 1325–1339 (2013)
22. Jain, A., Zamir, A.R., Savarese, S., Saxena, A.: Structural-RNN: deep learning on spatio-temporal graphs. In: Proceedings of the IEEE Conference on Computer Vision and Pattern Recognition, pp. 5308–5317 (2016)
23. Kingma, D.P., Ba, J.: Adam: a method for stochastic optimization. arXiv preprint arXiv:1412.6980 (2014)
24. Koppula, H., Saxena, A.: Learning spatio-temporal structure from RGB-D videos for human activity detection and anticipation. In: International Conference on Machine Learning, pp. 792–800 (2013)
25. Koppula, H.S., Saxena, A.: Anticipating human activities for reactive robotic response. In: IROS, Tokyo, p. 2071 (2013)
26. Kovar, L., Gleicher, M., Pighin, F.: Motion graphs. In: ACM SIGGRAPH 2008 classes, pp. 1–10 (2008)
27. Lee, K., Lee, I., Lee, S.: Propagating LSTM: 3D pose estimation based on joint interdependency. In: Ferrari, V., Hebert, M., Sminchisescu, C., Weiss, Y. (eds.) ECCV 2018. LNCS, vol. 11211, pp. 123–141. Springer, Cham (2018). https://doi.org/10.1007/978-3-030-01234-2_8
28. Li, C., Zhang, Z., Sun Lee, W., Hee Lee, G.: Convolutional sequence to sequence model for human dynamics. In: Proceedings of the IEEE Conference on Computer Vision and Pattern Recognition, pp. 5226–5234 (2018)
29. Liu, J., et al.: Feature boosting network for 3D pose estimation. IEEE Trans. Pattern Anal. Mach. Intell. **42**, 494–501 (2019)
30. Liu, J., Shahroudy, A., Wang, G., Duan, L.Y., Kot, A.C.: Skeleton-based online action prediction using scale selection network. IEEE Trans. Pattern Anal. Mach. Intell. **42**(6), 1453–1467 (2019)
31. Liu, J., Shahroudy, A., Xu, D., Kot, A.C., Wang, G.: Skeleton-based action recognition using spatio-temporal LSTM network with trust gates. IEEE Trans. Pattern Anal. Mach. Intell. **40**(12), 3007–3021 (2017)
32. Mao, W., Liu, M., Salzmann, M., Li, H.: Learning trajectory dependencies for human motion prediction. In: Proceedings of the IEEE International Conference on Computer Vision, pp. 9489–9497 (2019)
33. Martinez, J., Black, M.J., Romero, J.: On human motion prediction using recurrent neural networks. In: Proceedings of the IEEE Conference on Computer Vision and Pattern Recognition, pp. 2891–2900 (2017)
34. Martinez, J., Hossain, R., Romero, J., Little, J.J.: A simple yet effective baseline for 3D human pose estimation. In: Proceedings of the IEEE International Conference on Computer Vision, pp. 2640–2649 (2017)
35. Paden, B., Čáp, M., Yong, S.Z., Yershov, D., Frazzoli, E.: A survey of motion planning and control techniques for self-driving urban vehicles. IEEE Trans. Intell. Veh **1**(1), 33–55 (2016)
36. Pavlovic, V., Rehg, J.M., MacCormick, J.: Learning switching linear models of human motion. In: Advances in Neural Information Processing Systems, pp. 981–987 (2001)

37. Radford, A., Narasimhan, K., Salimans, T., Sutskever, I.: Improving language understanding by generative pre-training (2018). https://s3-us-west-2.amazonaws.com/openai-assets/researchcovers/languageunsupervised/languageunderstanding paper.pdf

38. Yang, S., Liu, J., Lu, S., Er, M.H., Kot, A.C.: Collaborative learning of gesture recognition and 3D hand pose estimation with multi-order feature analysis. In: Proceedings of the European Conference on Computer Vision (ECCV) (2020)

39. Sukhbaatar, S., Weston, J., Fergus, R., et al.: End-to-end memory networks. In: Advances in Neural Information Processing Systems, pp. 2440–2448 (2015)

40. Li, T., Liu, J., Zhang, W., Duan, L.: Hard-net: hardness-aware discrimination network for 3D early activity prediction. In: Proceedings of the European Conference on Computer Vision (ECCV) (2020)

41. Troje, N.F.: Decomposing biological motion: a framework for analysis and synthesis of human gait patterns. J. Vis. **2**(5), 2–2 (2002)

42. Vaswani, A., et al.: Attention is all you need. In: Advances in Neural Information Processing Systems, pp. 5998–6008 (2017)

43. Wang, B., Adeli, E., Chiu, H.K., Huang, D.A., Niebles, J.C.: Imitation learning for human pose prediction. In: Proceedings of the IEEE International Conference on Computer Vision, pp. 7124–7133 (2019)

44. Wang, J.M., Fleet, D.J., Hertzmann, A.: Gaussian process dynamical models for human motion. IEEE Trans. Pattern Anal. Mach. Intell. **30**(2), 283–298 (2007)

45. Wang, Z., et al.: Learning diverse stochastic human-action generators by learning smooth latent transitions. arXiv preprint arXiv:1912.10150 (2019)

46. Xiong, C., Merity, S., Socher, R.: Dynamic memory networks for visual and textual question answering. In: International Conference on Machine Learning, pp. 2397–2406 (2016)

47. Yang, X., Tang, K., Zhang, H., Cai, J.: Auto-encoding scene graphs for image captioning. In: Proceedings of the IEEE Conference on Computer Vision and Pattern Recognition, pp. 10685–10694 (2019)

48. Fan, Z., Jun Liu, Y.W.: Adaptive computationally efficient network for monocular 3D hand pose estimation. In: Proceedings of the European Conference on Computer Vision (ECCV) (2020)

Image Stitching and Rectification
for Hand-Held Cameras

Bingbing Zhuang$^{(\boxtimes)}$ and Quoc-Huy Tran

NEC Labs America, Princeton, USA
bzhuang@nec-labs.com

Abstract. In this paper, we derive a new differential homography that can account for the scanline-varying camera poses in Rolling Shutter (RS) cameras, and demonstrate its application to carry out RS-aware image stitching and rectification at one stroke. Despite the high complexity of RS geometry, we focus in this paper on a special yet common input—two consecutive frames from a video stream, wherein the inter-frame motion is restricted from being arbitrarily large. This allows us to adopt simpler differential motion model, leading to a straightforward and practical minimal solver. To deal with non-planar scene and camera parallax in stitching, we further propose an RS-aware spatially-varying homogarphy field in the principle of As-Projective-As-Possible (APAP). We show superior performance over state-of-the-art methods both in RS image stitching and rectification, especially for images captured by hand-held shaking cameras.

Keywords: Rolling Shutter · Image rectification · Image stitching · Differential homography · Homography field · Hand-held cameras

1 Introduction

Rolling Shutter (RS) cameras adopt CMOS sensors due to their low cost and simplicity in manufacturing. This stands in contrast to Global Shutter (GS) CCD cameras that require specialized and highly dedicated fabrication. Such discrepancy endows RS cameras great advantage for ubiquitous employment in consumer products, e.g., smartphone cameras [44] or dashboard cameras [12]. However, the expediency in fabrication also causes a serious defect in image capture—instead of capturing different scanlines all at once as in GS cameras, RS cameras expose each scanline one by one sequentially from top to bottom. While static RS camera capturing a static scene is fine, the RS effect comes to haunt us as soon as images are taken during motion, i.e., images could be severely distorted due to scanline-varying camera poses (see Fig. 1).

Electronic supplementary material The online version of this chapter (https://doi.org/10.1007/978-3-030-58571-6_15) contains supplementary material, which is available to authorized users.

© Springer Nature Switzerland AG 2020
A. Vedaldi et al. (Eds.): ECCV 2020, LNCS 12352, pp. 243–260, 2020.
https://doi.org/10.1007/978-3-030-58571-6_15

RS distortion has been rearing its ugly head in various computer vision tasks. There is constant pressure to either remove the RS distortion in the front-end image capture [25,48,50,61], or design task-dependent RS-aware algorithms in the back end [2,10,15,42,46,51,54]. While various algorithms have been developed for each of them in isolation, algorithms achieving both in a holistic way are few [24,52,62,66]. In this paper, we make contributions towards further advancement in this line. Specifically, we propose a novel differential homography and demonstrate its application to carry out RS image stitching and rectification at one stroke.

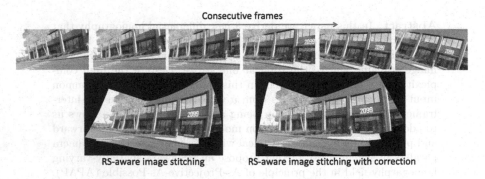

Fig. 1. Example results of RS-aware image stitching and rectification.

RS effect complicates the two-view geometry significantly compared to its GS counterpart, primarily because 12 additional unknown parameters are required to model the intra-frame velocity of the two cameras. Thus, despite the recent effort of Lao et al. [24] in solving a generic RS homography for discrete motion, the complexity of RS geometry significantly increases the number of required correspondences (36 points for full model and 13.5 points after a series of approximations). Inspired by prior work [66] that demonstrates dramatic simplification in differential RS relative pose estimation compared to its discrete counterpart [10], we focus in this paper on the special yet common case where the inputs are two consecutive frames from a video. In this case, the inter-frame motion is restricted from being arbitrarily large, allowing us to adopt the simpler differential homography model [39]. Furthermore, the intra-frame motion could be directly parameterized by the inter-frame motion via interpolation, thereby reducing the total number of unknown parameters to solve. In particular, we derive an RS-aware differential homography under constant acceleration motion assumption, together with a straightforward solver requiring only 5 pairs of correspondences, and demonstrate its application to simultaneous RS image stitching and rectification. Since a single homography warping is only exact under pure rotational camera motion or for 3D planar scene, it often causes misalignment when such condition is not strictly met in practice. To address such model inadequacy, we extend the single RS homography model to a spatially-varying RS homography field following the As-Projective-As-Possible (APAP) principle [63], thereby lending itself to handling complex scenes. We demonstrate example results in Fig. 1, where multiple images are stitched and rectified by concatenating pairwise warping from our method.

We would also like to emphasize our advantage over the differential Structure-from-Motion (SfM)-based rectification method [66]. Note that [66] computes the rectification for each pixel separately via pixel-wise depth estimation from optical flow and camera pose. As such, potential gross errors in optical flow estimates could lead to severe artifacts in the texture-less or non-overlapping regions. In contrast, the more parsimonious homography model offers a natural defense against wrong correspondences. Despite its lack of full 3D reconstruction, we observe good empirical performance in terms of visual appearance.

In summary, our contributions include:

- We derive a novel differential homography model together with a minimal solver to account for the scanline-varying camera poses of RS cameras.
- We propose an RS-aware spatially-varying homography field for improving RS image stitching.
- Our proposed framework outperforms state-of-the-art methods both in RS image rectification and stitching.

2   Related Work

RS Geometry. Since the pioneering work of Meingast et al. [41], considerable efforts have been invested in studying the geometry of RS cameras. These include relative pose estimation [10,47,66], absolute pose estimation [2,3,23,26,40,56], bundle adjustment [15,22], SfM/Reconstruction [20,54,55,58], degeneracies [4,21,68], discrete homography [24], and others [5,45]. In this work, we introduce RS-aware differential homography, which is of only slighly higher complexity than its GS counterpart.

RS Image Rectification. Removing RS artifacts using a *single* input image is inherently an ill-posed problem. Works in this line [25,48,50] often assume simplified camera motions and scene structures, and require line/curve detection in the image, if available at all. Recent methods [49,68] have started exploring deep learning for this task. However, their generalization ability to different scenes remains an open problem. In contrast, *multi-view* approaches, be it geometric-based or learning-based [35], are more geometrically grounded. In particular, Ringaby and Forssen [52] estimate and smooth a sequence of camera rotations for eliminating RS distortions, while Grundmann et al. [11] and Vasu et al. [61] use a mixture of homographies to model and remove RS effects. Such methods often rely on nontrivial iterative optimization leveraging a large set of correspondences. Recently, Zhuang et al. [66] present the first attempt to derive minimal solver for RS rectification. It takes a minimal set of points as input and lends itself well to RANSAC, leading to a more principled way for robust estimation. In the same spirit, we derive RS-aware differential homography and show important advantages. Note that our minimal solver is orthogonal to the optimization-based methods, e.g. [52,61], and can serve as their initialization. Very recently, Albl et al. [1] present an interesting way for RS undistortion from two cameras, yet require specific camera mounting.

GS Image Stitching. Image stitching [59] has achieved significant progress over the past few decades. Theoretically, a single homography is sufficient to align two input images of a common scene if the images are captured with no parallax or the scene is planar [13]. In practice, this condition is often violated, causing misalignments or ghosting artifacts in the stitched images. To overcome this issue, several approaches have been proposed such as spatially-varying warps [27,29,33,34,63], shape-preserving warps [7,8,30], and seam-driven methods [17,18,31,65]. All of the above approaches assume a GS camera model and hence they cannot handle RS images, i.e., the stitched images may contain RS distortion-induced misalignment. While Lao et al. [24] demonstrate the possibility of stitching in spite of RS distortion, we present a more concise and straightforward method that works robustly with hand-held cameras.

3   Homography Preliminary

GS Discrete Homography. Let us assume that two calibrated cameras are observing a 3D plane parameterized as (n, d), with n denoting the plane normal and d the camera-to-plane distance. Denoting the relative camera rotation and translation as $R \in SO(3)$ and $t \in \mathbb{R}^3$, a pair of 2D correspondences x_1 and x_2 (in normalized plane) can be related by $\hat{x}_2 \propto H\hat{x}_1$, where $H = R + tn^\top/d$ is defined as the *discrete* homography [13] and $\hat{x} = [x^\top, 1]^\top$. $\propto$ indicates equality up to a scale. Note that H in the above format subsumes the pure rotation-induced homography as a special case by letting $d \to \infty$. Each pair of correspondence $\{x_1^i, x_2^i\}$ gives two constraints $a_i h = 0$, where $h \in \mathbb{R}^9$ is the vectorized form of H and the coefficients $a_i \in \mathbb{R}^{2 \times 9}$ can be computed from $\{x_1^i, x_2^i\}$. In *GS discrete 4-point solver*, with the minimal of 4 points, one can solve h via:

$$Ah = 0, \quad s.t. \ \|h\| = 1, \tag{1}$$

which has a closed-form solution by Singular Value Decomposition (SVD). A is obtained by stacking all a_i.

GS Spatially-Varying Discrete Homography Field. In image stitching application, it is often safe to make zero-parallax assumption as long as the (non-planar) scene is far enough. However, it is also not uncommon that such assumption is violated to the extent that warping with just one global homography causes unpleasant misalignments. To address this issue, APAP [63] proposes to compute a spatially-varying homograpy field for each pixel x:

$$h^*(x) = \arg\min_h \sum_{i \in \mathcal{I}} \|w_i(x)a_i h\|^2, \quad s.t. \ \|h\| = 1, \tag{2}$$

where $w_i(x) = \max(\exp(-\frac{\|x-x_i\|^2}{\sigma^2}), \tau)$ is a weight. σ and τ are the pre-defined scale and regularization parameters respectively. $\mathcal{I}$ indicates the inlier set returned from GS discrete 4-point solver with RANSAC (motivated by [60]). The optimization has a closed-form solution by SVD. On the one hand, Eq. 2 encourages the warping to be globally As-Projective-As-Possible (APAP) by making use of all the inlier correspondences, while, on the other hand, it allows local deformations guided by nearby correspondences to compensate for model deficiency. Despite being a simple tweak, it yet leads to considerable improvement in image stitching.

GS Differential Homography. Suppose the camera is undergoing an instantaneous motion [19], consisting of rotational and translational velocity (ω, v). It would induce a motion flow $u \in \mathbb{R}^2$ in each image point x. Denoting $\tilde{u} = [u^\top, 0]^\top$, we have[1]

$$\tilde{u} = (I - \hat{x}e_3^\top)H\hat{x}, \tag{3}$$

where $H = -(\lfloor \omega \rfloor_\times + vn^\top/d)$ is defined as the *differential* homography [39]. I represents identity matrix and $e_3 = [0, 0, 1]^\top$. $\lfloor . \rfloor_\times$ returns the corresponding skew-symmetric matrix from the vector. Each flow estimate $\{u_i, x_i\}$ gives two effective constraints out of the three equations included in Eq. 3, denoted as $b_i h = u_i$, where $b_i \in \mathbb{R}^{2 \times 9}$ can be computed from x_i. In GS *differential 4-point solver*, with a minimal of 4 flow estimates, H can be computed by solving:

$$Bh = U, \tag{4}$$

which admits closed-form solution by pseudo inverse. B and U are obtained by stacking all b_i and u_i, respectively. Note that, we can only recover $H_L = H + \varepsilon I$ with an unknown scale ε, because B has a one-dimensional null space. One can easily see this by replacing H in Eq. 3 with εI and observing that the right hand side vanishes, regardless of the value of x. ε can be determined subsequently by utilizing the special structure of calibrated H. However, this is not relevant in our paper since we focus on image stitching on general uncalibrated images.

4   Methods

4.1   RS Motion Parameterization

Under the discrete motion model, in addition to the 6-Degree of Freedom (DoF) inter-frame relative motion (R, t), 12 additional unknown parameters (ω_1, v_1) and (ω_2, v_2) are needed to model the intra-frame camera velocity, as illustrated in Fig. 2(a). This quickly increases the minimal number of points and the algorithm complexity to compute an RS-aware homography. Instead, we aim to solve for the case of continuous motion, i.e., a relatively small motion between two consecutive frames. In this case, we only need to parameterize the relative motion (ω, v) between the two first scanlines (one can choose other reference scanlines

---

[1] See our supplementary material for derivations.

without loss of generality) of the image pair, and the poses corresponding to all the other scanlines can be obtained by interpolation, as illustrated in Fig. 2(b). In particular, it is shown in [66] that a *quadratic* interpolation can be derived under constant *acceleration* motion. Formally, the absolute camera rotation and translation $(r_1^{y_1}, p_1^{y_1})$ (resp. $(r_2^{y_2}, p_2^{y_2})$)) of scanline y_1 (resp. y_2) in frame 1 (resp. 2) can be written as:

$$r_1^{y_1} = \beta_1(k, y_1)\boldsymbol{\omega}, \quad p_1^{y_1} = \beta_1(k, y_1)\boldsymbol{v}, \tag{5}$$
$$r_2^{y_2} = \beta_2(k, y_2)\boldsymbol{\omega}, \quad p_2^{y_2} = \beta_2(k, y_2)\boldsymbol{v}, \tag{6}$$

where

$$\beta_1(k, y_1) = (\frac{\gamma y_1}{h} + \frac{1}{2}k(\frac{\gamma y_1}{h})^2)(\frac{2}{2+k}), \tag{7}$$

$$\beta_2(k, y_2) = (1 + \frac{\gamma y_2}{h} + \frac{1}{2}k(1 + \frac{\gamma y_2}{h})^2)(\frac{2}{2+k}). \tag{8}$$

Here, k is an extra unknown motion parameter describing the acceleration, which is assumed to be in the same direction as velocity. γ denotes the the readout time ratio [66], i.e. the ratio between the time for scanline readout and the total time between two frames (including inter-frame delay). h denotes the total number of scanlines in a image. Note that the absolute poses $(r_1^{y_1}, p_1^{y_1})$ and $(r_2^{y_2}, p_2^{y_2})$ are all defined w.r.t the first scanline of frame 1. It follows that the relative pose between scanlines y_1 and y_2 reads:

$$\boldsymbol{\omega}_{y_1 y_2} = r_2^{y_2} - r_1^{y_1} = (\beta_2(k, y_2) - \beta_1(k, y_1))\boldsymbol{\omega}, \tag{9}$$
$$\boldsymbol{v}_{y_1 y_2} = p_2^{y_2} - p_1^{y_1} = (\beta_2(k, y_2) - \beta_1(k, y_1))\boldsymbol{v}. \tag{10}$$

We refer the readers to [66] for the detailed derivation of the above equations.

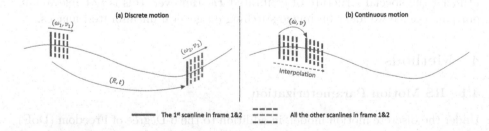

Fig. 2. Illustration of discrete/continuous camera motion and their motion parameters.

4.2   RS-Aware Differential Homography

We are now in a position to derive the RS-aware differential homography. First, it is easy to verify that Eq. 3 also applies uncalibrated cameras, under which case $H = -K(\lfloor\boldsymbol{\omega}\rfloor_\times + \boldsymbol{v}\boldsymbol{n}^\top/d)K^{-1}$, with $\boldsymbol{u}$ and $\boldsymbol{x}$ being raw measurements in pixels.

K denotes the unknown camera intrinsic matrix. Given a pair of correspondence by $\{u, x\}$, we can plug $(\omega_{y_1 y_2}, v_{y_1 y_2})$ into Eq. 3, yielding

$$\tilde{u} = (\beta_2(k, y_2) - \beta_1(k, y_1))(I - \hat{x} e_3^{\top})H\hat{x} = \beta(k, y_1, y_2)(I - \hat{x} e_3^{\top})H\hat{x}. \qquad (11)$$

Here, we can define $H_{RS} = \beta(k, y_1, y_2)H$ as the RS-aware differential homography, which is now scanline dependent.

5-Point Solver. In addition to H, we now have one more unknown parameter k to solve. Below, we show that 5 pairs of correspondences are enough to solve for k and H, using the so-called hidden variable technique [9]. To get started, let us first rewrite Eq. 11 as:

$$\beta(k, y_1, y_2)bh = u. \qquad (12)$$

Next, we move u to the left hand side and stack the constraints from 5 points, leading to:

$$C\hat{h} = 0, \qquad (13)$$

where

$$C = \begin{bmatrix} \beta_1(k, y_1^1, y_2^1)b_1, & -u_1 \\ \beta_2(k, y_1^2, y_2^2)b_2, & -u_2 \\ \beta_3(k, y_1^3, y_2^3)b_3, & -u_3 \\ \beta_4(k, y_1^4, y_2^4)b_4, & -u_4 \\ \beta_5(k, y_1^5, y_2^5)b_5, & -u_5 \end{bmatrix}, \qquad \hat{h} = [h^T, 1]^T. \qquad (14)$$

It is now clear that, for h to have a solution, C must be rank-deficient. Further observing that $C \in \mathbb{R}^{10 \times 10}$ is a square matrix, rank deficiency indicates vanishing determinate, i.e.,

$$det(C) = 0. \qquad (15)$$

This gives a univariable polynomial equation, whereby we can solve for k efficiently. h can subsequently be extracted from the null space of C.

DoF Analysis. In fact, only 4.5 points are required in the minimal case, since we have one extra unknown k while each point gives two constraints. Utilizing 5 points nevertheless leads to a straightforward solution as shown. *Yet, does this lead to an over-constrained system?* No. Recall that we can only recover $H + \varepsilon I$ up to an arbitrary ε. Here, due to the one extra constraint, a specific value is chosen for ε since the last element of $\hat{h}$ is set to 1. Note that a true ε, thus H, is not required in our context since it does not affect the warping. This is in analogy to uncalibrated SfM [13] where a projective reconstruction up to an arbitrary projective transformation is not inferior to the Euclidean reconstruction in terms of reprojection error.

Plane Parameters. Strictly speaking, the plane parameters slightly vary as well due to the intra-frame motion. This is however not explicitly modeled in Eq. 11, due to two reasons. First, although the intra-frame motion is in a similar range as the inter-frame motion (Fig. 2(b)) and hence has a large impact in terms of motion, it induces merely a small perturbation to the absolute value of the scene parameters, which can be safely ignored (see supplementary for a more formal characterization). Second, we would like to keep the solver as simple as possible as along as good empirical results are obtained (see Sect. 5).

Motion Infidelity vs. Shutter Fidelity. Note that the differential motion model is always an approximation specially designed for small motion. This means that, unlike its discrete counterpart, its fidelity decreases with increasing motion. Yet, we are only interested in relatively large motion such that the RS distortion reaches the level of being visually unpleasant. Therefore, a natural and scientifically interesting question to ask is, whether the benefits from modeling RS distortion (Shutter Fidelity) are more than enough to compensate for the sacrifices due to the approximation in motion model (Motion Infidelity). Although a theoretical characterization on such comparison is out of the scope of this paper, via extensive experiments in Sect. 5, we fortunately observe that the differential RS model achieves overwhelming dominance in this competition.

Degeneracy. *Are there different pairs of* k *and* H *that lead to the same flow field* u? Although such degeneracy does not affect stitching, it does make a difference to rectification (Sect. 4.4). We leave the detailed discussion to the supplementary, but would like the readers to be assured that such cases are very rare, in accordance with Horn [19] that motion flow is hardly ambiguous.

More Details. Firstly, note that although $\{u, x\}$ is typically collected from optical flow in classical works [16,38] prior to the advent of keypoint descriptors (e.g., [37,53]), we choose the latter for image stitching for higher efficiency. Secondly, if we fix $k = 0$, i.e., constant velocity model, (ω, v) could be solved using a linear 4-point minimal solver similar to the GS case. However, we empirically find its performance to be inferior to the constant acceleration model in shaking cameras, and shall not be further discussed here.

4.3 RS-Aware Spatially-Varying Differential Homography Field

Can GS APAP [63] Handle RS Distortion by Itself? As aforementioned, the adaptive weight in APAP (Eq. 2) permits local deformations to account for the local discrepancy from the global model. However, we argue that APAP alone is still not capable of handling RS distortion. The root cause lies in the GS homography being used—although the warping of pixels near correspondences are less affected, due to the anchor points role of correspondences, the warping of other pixels still relies on the transformation propagated from the correspondences and thus the model being used does matter here.

RS-Aware APAP. Obtaining a set of inlier correspondences $\mathcal{I}$ from our RS differential 5-point solver with RANSAC, we formulate the spatially-varying RS-aware homography field as:

$$h^*(x) = \arg\min_h \sum_{i \in \mathcal{I}} \|w_i(x)(\beta(k, y_1, y_2)b_i h - u_i)\|^2, \tag{16}$$

where $w_i(x)$ is defined in Sect. 3. Since k is a pure motion parameter independent of the scene, we keep it fixed in this stage for simplicity. Normalization strategy [14] is applied to (u, x) for numerical stability. We highlight that the optimization has a simple closed-form solution, yet is geometrically meaningful in the sense that it minimizes the error between the estimated and the observed flow u. This stands in contrast with the discrete homography for which minimizing reprojection error requires nonlinear iterative optimization. In addition, we also observe higher stability from the differential model in cases of keypoints concentrating in a small region (see supplementary for discussions).

4.4   RS Image Stitching and Rectification

Once we have the homography H (either a global one or a spatially-varying field) mapping from frame 1 to frame 2, we can warp between two images for stitching. Referring to Fig. 2(b) and Eq. 11, for each pixel $x_1 = [x_1, y_1]^\top$ in frame 1, we find its mapping $x_2 = [x_2, y_2]^\top$ in frame 2 by first solving for y_2 as:

$$y_2 = y_1 + \lfloor (\beta_2(k, y_2) - \beta_1(k, y_1))(I - \hat{x}_1 e_3^\top) H \hat{x}_1 \rfloor_y, \qquad (17)$$

which admits a closed-form solution. $\lfloor . \rfloor_y$ indicates taking the y coordinate. x_2 can be then obtained easily with known y_2. Similarly, x_1 could also be projected to the GS canvas defined by the pose corresponding to the first scanline of frame 1, yielding its rectified point x_{g1}. x_{g1} can be solved according to

$$x_1 = x_{g1} + \lfloor \beta_1(k, y_1)(I - \hat{x}_{g1} e_3^\top) H \hat{x}_{g1} \rfloor_{xy}, \qquad (18)$$

where $\lfloor . \rfloor_{xy}$ indicates taking x and y coordinate.

5   Experiments

5.1   Synthetic Data

Data Generation. First, we generate motion parameters (ω, v) and k with desired constraints. For each scanline y_1 (resp. y_2) in frame 1 (resp. 2), we obtain its absolute pose as $(R(\beta_1(k, y_1)\omega), \beta_1(k, y_1)v)$ (resp. $(R(\beta_2(k, y_2)\omega), \beta_2(k, y_2)v))$. Here, $R(\theta) = \exp(\lfloor \theta \rfloor_\times)$ with exp: so(3) $\rightarrow$ SO(3). Due to the inherent depth-translation scale ambiguity, the magnitude of v is defined as the ratio between the translation magnitude and the average scene depth. The synthesized image plane is of size 720×1280 with a $60°$ horizontal Field Of View (FOV). Next, we randomly generate a 3D plane, on which we sample 100 3D points within FOV. Finally, we project each 3D point X to the RS image. Since we do not know which scanline observes X, we first solve for y_1 from the quadratic equation:

$$y_1 = \lfloor \pi(R(\beta_1(k, y_1)\omega)(X - \beta_1(k, y_1)v)) \rfloor_y, \qquad (19)$$

where $\pi([a, b, c]^{\top})=[a/c, b/c]^{\top}$. x_1 can then be obtained easily with known y_1. Likewise, we obtain the projection in frame 2.

Comparison Under Various Configurations. First, we study the performance under the noise-free case to understand the intrinsic and noise-independent behavior of different solvers, including discrete GS 4-point solver ('GS-disc'), differential GS 4-point solver ('GS-diff') and our RS 5-point solver ('RS-ConstAcc'). Specifically, we test the performance with varying RS readout time ratio γ, rotation magnitude $\|\omega\|$, and translation magnitude $\|v\|$. To get started, we first fix $(\|\omega\|, \|v\|)$ to $(3°, 0.03)$, and increase γ from 0 to 1, indicating zero to strongest RS effect. Then, we fix $\gamma = 1$, $\|v\| = 0.03$ while increasing $\|\omega\|$ from $0°$ to $9°$. Finally, we fix $\gamma = 1$, $\|\omega\| = 3°$ while increasing $\|v\|$ from 0 to 0.1. We report averaged reprojection errors over all point pairs in Fig. 3(a)–(c). The curves are averaged over 100 configurations with random plane and directions of ω and v.

First, we observe that 'GS-diff' generally underperforms 'GS-disc' as expected due to its approximate nature (cf. 'Motion Infidelity' in Sect. 4.2). In (a), although 'RS-ConstAcc' performs slightly worse than 'GS-disc' under small RS effect ($\gamma <= 0.1$), it quickly surpasses 'GS-disc' significantly with increasing γ (cf. 'Shutter Fidelity' in Sect. 4.2). Moreover, this is constantly true in (b) and (c) with the gap becoming bigger with increasing motion magnitude. Such observations suggest that the gain due to handling RS effect overwhelms the degradation brought about by the less faithful differential motion model. Further, we conduct investigation with noisy data by adding Gaussian noise (with standard deviations $\sigma_g = 1$ and $\sigma_g = 2$ pixels) to the projected 2D points. The updated results in the above three settings are shown in Fig. 3(d)–(f) and Fig. 3(g)–(i) for $\sigma_g = 1$ and $\sigma_g = 2$ respectively. Again, we observe considerable superiority of the RS-aware model, demonstrating its robustness against noise. We also conduct evaluation under different values of k, with $(\|\omega\|, \|v\|) = (3°, 0.03)$, $\gamma = 1$, $\sigma_g = 1$. We plot $\beta_1(k, y_1)$ against $\frac{\gamma y_1}{h}$ with different values of k in Fig. 4(a) to have a better understanding of scanline pose interpolation. The reprojection error curves are plotted in Fig. 4(b). We observe that the performance of 'GS-disc' drops considerably with k deviating from 0, while 'RS-ConstAcc' maintains almost constant accuracy. Also notice the curves are not symmetric as $k > 0$ indicates acceleration (increasing velocity) while $k < 0$ indicates deceleration (decreasing velocity).

5.2   Real Data

We find that the RS videos used in prior works, e.g. [11,15,52], often contain small jitters without large viewpoint change across consecutive frames. To demonstrate the power of our method, we collect 5 videos (around 2k frames in total) with hand-held RS cameras while running, leading to large camera shaking and RS distortion. Following [35], we simply set $\gamma = 1$ to avoid its nontrival calibration [41] and find it works well for our camera.

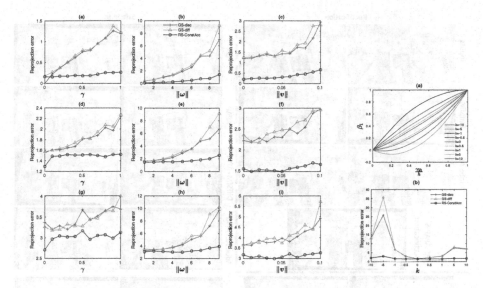

Fig. 3. Quantitative comparison under different configurations.   **Fig. 4.** Quantitative comparison under different values of k.

Two-View Experiments. Below we discuss the two-view experiment results.

Qualitative Evaluation. We first present a few qualitative examples to intuitively demonstrate the performance gap, in terms of RS image rectification and stitching. For RS image rectification, we compare our method with the differential SfM based approach [66] ('DiffSfM') and the RS repair feature in Adobe After Effect ('Adobe AE'). For RS image stitching, we compare with the single GS discrete homography stitching ('GS') and its spatially-varying extension [63]('APAP'). In addition, we also evaluate the sequential approaches which feed 'DiffSfM' (resp. 'Adobe AE') into 'APAP', denoted as 'DiffSfM+APAP' (resp. 'Adobe AE+APAP'). We denote our single RS homography stitching without rectification as 'RS', our spatially-varying RS homography stitching without rectification as 'RS-APAP', and our spatially-varying RS homography stitching with rectification as 'RS-APAP & Rectification'.

In general, we observe that although 'DiffSfM' performs very well for pixels with accurate optical flow estimates, it may cause artifacts elsewhere. Similarly, we find 'Adobe AE' to be quite robust on videos with small jitters, but often introduces severe distortion with the presence of strong shaking. Due to space limit, we show two example results here and leave more to the supplementary.

In the example of Fig. 5, despite that 'DiffSfM' successfully rectifies the door and tube to be straight, the boundary parts (red circles) are highly skewed— these regions have no correspondences in frame 2 to compute flow. 'Adobe AE' manages to correct the images to some extent, yet bring evident distortion in the boundary too, as highlighted. 'RS-APAP & Rectification' nicely corrects

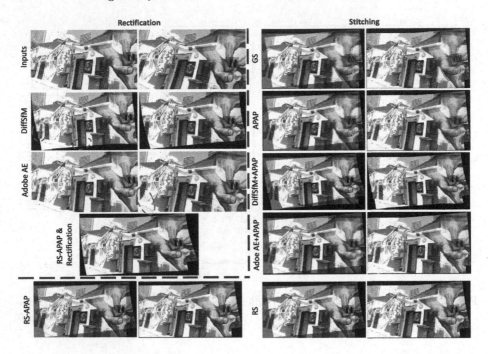

Fig. 5. Comparison of rectification/stitching on real RS images. Best viewed in screen.

the distortion with the two images readily stitched together. Regarding image stitching, we overlay two images after warping with the discrepancy visualized by green/red colors, beside which we show the linearly blended images. As can be seen, 'GS' causes significant misalignments. 'APAP' reduces them to some extent but not completely. The artifacts due to 'DiffSfM' and 'Adobe AE' persist in the stitching stage. Even for those non-boundary pixels, there are still misalignments as the rectification is done per frame in isolation, independent of the subsequent stitching. In contrast, we observe that even one single RS homography ('RS') suffices to warp the images accurately here, yielding similar result as 'RS-APAP'.

We show one more example in Fig. 6 with partial results (the rest are in the supplementary). 'DiffSfM' removes most of the distortion to the extent that 'APAP' warps majority of the scene accurately ('DiffSfM+APAP'), yet, misalignments are still visible as highlighted, again, due to its sequential nature. We would like to highlight that APAP plays a role here to remove the misalignment left by the 'RS' and leads to the best stitching result.

Quantitative Evaluation. Here, we conduct quantitative evaluation to characterize the benefits brought about by our RS model. For every pair of consecutive frames, we run both 'GS-disc' and 'RS-ConstAcc', each with 1000 RANSAC trials. We compute for each pair the median reprojection error among all the correspondences, and plot its cumulative distribution function (CDF) across all

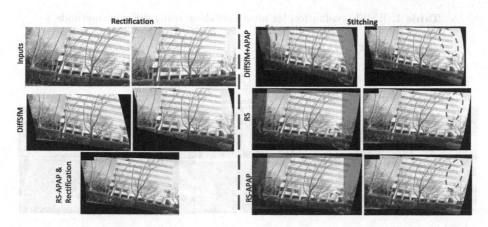

Fig. 6. Comparison of rectification/stitching on real RS images. Best viewed in screen.

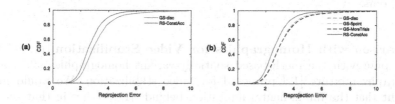

Fig. 7. Quantitative evaluation under standard setting & further study.

the frame pairs, as shown in Fig. 7(a). Clearly, 'RS-ConstAcc' has higher-quality warping with reduced reprojection errors.

Although the above comparison demonstrates promising results in favor of the RS model, we would like to carry out further studies for more evidence, due to two reasons. First, note that the more complicated RS model has higher DoF and it might be the case that the smaller reprojection errors are simply due to over-fitting to the observed data, rather than due to truly higher fidelity of the underlying model. Second, different numbers (4 vs. 5) of correspondences are sampled in each RANSAC trial, leading to different amount of total samples used by the two algorithms. To address these concerns, we conduct two further investigations accordingly. First, for each image pair, we reserve 500 pairs of correspondences as test set and preclude them from being sampled during RANSAC. We then compare how well the estimated models perform on this set. Second, we test two different strategies to make the total number of samples equivalent—'GS-MoreTrials': increases the number of RANSAC trials for 'GS-disc' to $1000 \times 5/4 = 1250$; 'GS-5point': samples non-minimal 5 points and get a solution in least squares sense in each trial. As shown in Fig. 7(b), although 'GS-5point' does improve the warping slightly, all the GS-based methods still lag behind the RS model, further validating the utility of our RS model.

Table 1. RMSE evaluation for image stitching using different methods.

Method	GS	Mesh-based [36]	Mixture [11]	APAP [63]	RS-APAP
RMSE [0–255]	5.72	5.15	3.65	3.27	**3.05**

Fig. 8. Qualitative comparison to DiffSfM [66], the method of Lao and Ait-Aider [24], and the method of Vasu et al. [61]. Stitched images with rectification are shown for [24] and ours.

Comparison with Homographies for Video Stabilization [11,36]. Here, we compare with the mesh-based spatially-variant homographies [36] and the homography mixture [11] proposed for video stabilization. We would like to highlight that the fundamental limitation behind [11,36] lies in that the individual homography is still GS-based, whereas ours explicitly models RS effect. We follow [28,32] to evaluate image alignment by the RMSE of one minus normalized cross correlation (NCC) over a neighborhood of 3×3 window for the overlapping pixel x_i and x_j, i.e. $RMSE = \sqrt{\frac{1}{N}\sum_\pi (1 - NCC(x_i, x_j))^2}$, with N being the total number of pixels in the overlapping region π. As shown in Table 1, RS-APAP achieves lower averaged RMSE than [11,36]. Surprisingly, [36] is not significantly better than GS, probably as its shape-preserving constraint becomes too strict for our strongly shaky videos. We also note that, in parallel with MDLT, our RS model could be integrated into [11,36] as well; this is however left as future works.

Test on Data from [66]. We also compare with [24,61] on the 6 image pairs used in [66], with 2 shown in Fig. 8 and 4 in the supplementary. We show the results from our single RS model without APAP for a fair comparison to [24,66]. First, we observe that our result is not worse than the full 3D reconstuction method [66]. In addition, it can be seen that our method performs on par with [24,61], while being far more concise and simpler.

Multiple-View Experiments. We demonstrate an extension to multiple images by concatenating the pairwise warping (note that the undertermined ε's do not affect this step). We show an example in Fig. 9 and compare with the multi-image APAP [64], AutoStitch [6] and Photoshop. AutoStitch result exhibits severe ghosting effects. APAP repairs them but not completely.

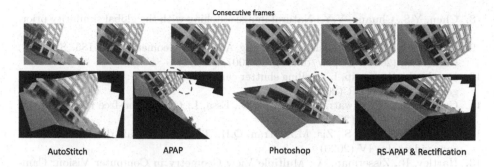

Fig. 9. Qualitative comparison on multiple image stitching.

Photoshop applies advanced seam cutting for blending, yet can not obscure the misalignments. Despite its naive nature, our simple concatenation shows superior stitching results.

6   Conclusion

We propose a new RS-aware differential homography together with its spatially-varying extension to allow local deformation. At its core is a novel minimal solver strongly governed by the underlying RS geometry. We demonstrate its application to RS image stitching and rectification at one stroke, achieving good performance. We hope this work could shed light on handling RS effect in other vision tasks such as large-scale SfM/SLAM [4,43,57,67,69].

Acknowledgement. We would like to thank Buyu Liu, Gaurav Sharma, Samuel Schulter, and Manmohan Chandraker for proofreading and support of this work. We are also grateful to all the reviewers for their constructive suggestions.

References

1. Albl, C., Kukelova, Z., Larsson, V., Polic, M., Pajdla, T., Schindler, K.: From two rolling shutters to one global shutter. In: CVPR (2020)
2. Albl, C., Kukelova, Z., Pajdla, T.: R6p-rolling shutter absolute camera pose. In: CVPR (2015)
3. Albl, C., Kukelova, Z., Pajdla, T.: Rolling shutter absolute pose problem with known vertical direction. In: CVPR (2016)
4. Albl, C., Sugimoto, A., Pajdla, T.: Degeneracies in rolling shutter SfM. In: Leibe, B., Matas, J., Sebe, N., Welling, M. (eds.) ECCV 2016. LNCS, vol. 9909, pp. 36–51. Springer, Cham (2016). https://doi.org/10.1007/978-3-319-46454-1_3
5. Bapat, A., Price, T., Frahm, J.M.: Rolling shutter and radial distortion are features for high frame rate multi-camera tracking. In: CVPR (2018)
6. Brown, M., Lowe, D.G.: Automatic panoramic image stitching using invariant features. Int. J. Comput. Vis. **74**(1), 59–73 (2007)
7. Chang, C.H., Sato, Y., Chuang, Y.Y.: Shape-preserving half-projective warps for image stitching. In: CVPR (2014)

8. Chen, Y.S., Chuang, Y.Y.: Natural image stitching with the global similarity prior. In: ECCV (2016)
9. Cox, D.A., Little, J., O'shea, D.: Using Algebraic Geometry, vol. 185. Springer, Heidelberg (2006). https://doi.org/10.1007/b138611
10. Dai, Y., Li, H., Kneip, L.: Rolling shutter camera relative pose: generalized epipolar geometry. In: CVPR (2016)
11. Grundmann, M., Kwatra, V., Castro, D., Essa, I.: Calibration-free rolling shutter removal. In: ICCP (2012)
12. Haresh, S., Kumar, S., Zia, M.Z., Tran, Q.H.: Towards anomaly detection in dashcam videos. In: IV (2020)
13. Hartley, R., Zisserman, A.: Multiple View Geometry in Computer Vision. Cambridge University Press, Cambridge (2003)
14. Hartley, R.I.: In defense of the eight-point algorithm. IEEE Trans. Pattern Anal. Mach. Intell. **19**(6), 580–593 (1997)
15. Hedborg, J., Forssén, P.E., Felsberg, M., Ringaby, E.: Rolling shutter bundle adjustment. In: CVPR (2012)
16. Heeger, D.J., Jepson, A.D.: Subspace methods for recovering rigid motion I: algorithm and implementation. Int. J. Comput. Vis. **7**(2), 95–117 (1992)
17. Herrmann, C., et al.: Robust image stitching with multiple registrations. In: Ferrari, V., Hebert, M., Sminchisescu, C., Weiss, Y. (eds.) ECCV 2018. LNCS, vol. 11206, pp. 53–69. Springer, Cham (2018). https://doi.org/10.1007/978-3-030-01216-8_4
18. Herrmann, C., Wang, C., Bowen, R.S., Keyder, E., Zabih, R.: Object-centered image stitching. In: Ferrari, V., Hebert, M., Sminchisescu, C., Weiss, Y. (eds.) ECCV 2018. LNCS, vol. 11207, pp. 846–861. Springer, Cham (2018). https://doi.org/10.1007/978-3-030-01219-9_50
19. Horn, B.K.: Motion fields are hardly ever ambiguous. Int. J. Comput. Vis. **1**(3), 259–274 (1988)
20. Im, S., Ha, H., Choe, G., Jeon, H.G., Joo, K., So Kweon, I.: High quality structure from small motion for rolling shutter cameras. In: ICCV (2015)
21. Ito, E., Okatani, T.: Self-calibration-based approach to critical motion sequences of rolling-shutter structure from motion. In: CVPR (2017)
22. Klingner, B., Martin, D., Roseborough, J.: Street view motion-from-structure-from-motion. In: ICCV (2013)
23. Kukelova, Z., Albl, C., Sugimoto, A., Pajdla, T.: Linear solution to the minimal absolute pose rolling shutter problem. In: Jawahar, C.V., Li, H., Mori, G., Schindler, K. (eds.) ACCV 2018. LNCS, vol. 11363, pp. 265–280. Springer, Cham (2019). https://doi.org/10.1007/978-3-030-20893-6_17
24. Lao, Y., Aider, O.A.: Rolling shutter homography and its applications. In: IEEE Trans. Pattern Anal. Mach. Intell. (2020)
25. Lao, Y., Ait-Aider, O.: A robust method for strong rolling shutter effects correction using lines with automatic feature selection. In: CVPR (2018)
26. Lao, Y., Ait-Aider, O., Bartoli, A.: Rolling shutter pose and ego-motion estimation using shape-from-template. In: Ferrari, V., Hebert, M., Sminchisescu, C., Weiss, Y. (eds.) ECCV 2018. LNCS, vol. 11206, pp. 477–492. Springer, Cham (2018). https://doi.org/10.1007/978-3-030-01216-8_29
27. Lee, K.Y., Sim, J.Y.: Warping residual based image stitching for large parallax. In: CVPR (2020)
28. Li, S., Yuan, L., Sun, J., Quan, L.: Dual-feature warping-based motion model estimation. In: ICCV (2015)
29. Liao, T., Li, N.: Single-perspective warps in natural image stitching. IEEE Trans. Image Process. **29**, 724–735 (2019)

30. Lin, C.C., Pankanti, S.U., Natesan Ramamurthy, K., Aravkin, A.Y.: Adaptive as-natural-as-possible image stitching. In: CVPR (2015)
31. Lin, K., Jiang, N., Cheong, L.-F., Do, M., Lu, J.: SEAGULL: seam-guided local alignment for parallax-tolerant image stitching. In: Leibe, B., Matas, J., Sebe, N., Welling, M. (eds.) ECCV 2016. LNCS, vol. 9907, pp. 370–385. Springer, Cham (2016). https://doi.org/10.1007/978-3-319-46487-9_23
32. Lin, K., Jiang, N., Liu, S., Cheong, L.F., Do, M., Lu, J.: Direct photometric alignment by mesh deformation. In: CVPR (2017)
33. Lin, W.Y., Liu, S., Matsushita, Y., Ng, T.T., Cheong, L.F.: Smoothly varying affine stitching. In: CVPR (2011)
34. Liu, F., Gleicher, M., Jin, H., Agarwala, A.: Content-preserving warps for 3D video stabilization. ACM Trans. Graph. (TOG) 28(3), 1–9 (2009)
35. Liu, P., Cui, Z., Larsson, V., Pollefeys, M.: Deep shutter unrolling network. In: CVPR (2020)
36. Liu, S., Yuan, L., Tan, P., Sun, J.: Bundled camera paths for video stabilization. ACM Trans. Graph. (TOG) 32(4), 1–10 (2013)
37. Lowe, D.G.: Distinctive image features from scale-invariant keypoints. Int. J. Comput. Vis. 60(2), 91–110 (2004)
38. Ma, Y., Košecká, J., Sastry, S.: Linear differential algorithm for motion recovery: a geometric approach. Int. J. Comput. Vis. 36(1), 71–89 (2000)
39. Ma, Y., Soatto, S., Kosecka, J., Sastry, S.S.: An Invitation to 3-D Vision: From Images to Geometric Models, vol. 26. Springer, Heidelberg (2012)
40. Magerand, L., Bartoli, A., Ait-Aider, O., Pizarro, D.: Global optimization of object pose and motion from a single rolling shutter image with automatic 2D-3D matching. In: Fitzgibbon, A., Lazebnik, S., Perona, P., Sato, Y., Schmid, C. (eds.) ECCV 2012. LNCS, vol. 7572, pp. 456–469. Springer, Heidelberg (2012). https://doi.org/10.1007/978-3-642-33718-5_33
41. Meingast, M., Geyer, C., Sastry, S.: Geometric models of rolling-shutter cameras. In: Workshop on Omnidirectional Vision, Camera Networks and Non-Classical Cameras (2005)
42. Mohan, M.M., Rajagopalan, A., Seetharaman, G.: Going unconstrained with rolling shutter deblurring. In: ICCV (2017)
43. Mur-Artal, R., Montiel, J.M.M., Tardos, J.D.: ORB-SLAM: a versatile and accurate monocular slam system. IEEE Trans. Rob. 31(5), 1147–1163 (2015)
44. Muratov, O., Slynko, Y., Chernov, V., Lyubimtseva, M., Shamsuarov, A., Bucha, V.: 3DCapture: 3D reconstruction for a smartphone. In: CVPRW (2016)
45. Oth, L., Furgale, P., Kneip, L., Siegwart, R.: Rolling shutter camera calibration. In: CVPR (2013)
46. Punnappurath, A., Rengarajan, V., Rajagopalan, A.: Rolling shutter super-resolution. In: ICCV (2015)
47. Purkait, P., Zach, C.: Minimal solvers for monocular rolling shutter compensation under ackermann motion. In: WACV (2018)
48. Purkait, P., Zach, C., Leonardis, A.: Rolling shutter correction in Manhattan world. In: ICCV (2017)
49. Rengarajan, V., Balaji, Y., Rajagopalan, A.: Unrolling the shutter: CNN to correct motion distortions. In: CVPR (2017)
50. Rengarajan, V., Rajagopalan, A.N., Aravind, R.: From bows to arrows: rolling shutter rectification of urban scenes. In: CVPR (2016)
51. Rengarajan, V., Rajagopalan, A.N., Aravind, R., Seetharaman, G.: Image registration and change detection under rolling shutter motion blur. IEEE Trans. Pattern Anal. Mach. Intell. 39(10), 1959–1972 (2016)

52. Ringaby, E., Forssén, P.E.: Efficient video rectification and stabilisation for cell-phones. Int. J. Comput. Vis. **96**(3), 335–352 (2012)
53. Rublee, E., Rabaud, V., Konolige, K., Bradski, G.: ORB: an efficient alternative to SIFT or SURF. In: ICCV (2011)
54. Saurer, O., Koser, K., Bouguet, J.Y., Pollefeys, M.: Rolling shutter stereo. In: ICCV (2013)
55. Saurer, O., Pollefeys, M., Hee Lee, G.: Sparse to dense 3D reconstruction from rolling shutter images. In: CVPR (2016)
56. Saurer, O., Pollefeys, M., Lee, G.H.: A minimal solution to the rolling shutter pose estimation problem. In: IROS (2015)
57. Schonberger, J.L., Frahm, J.M.: Structure-from-motion revisited. In: CVPR (2016)
58. Schubert, D., Demmel, N., Usenko, V., Stuckler, J., Cremers, D.: Direct sparse odometry with rolling shutter. In: ECCV (2018)
59. Szeliski, R., et al.: Image alignment and stitching: a tutorial. Found. Trends® Comput. Graph. Vis. **2**(1), 1–104 (2007)
60. Tran, Q.-H., Chin, T.-J., Carneiro, G., Brown, M.S., Suter, D.: In defence of RANSAC for outlier rejection in deformable registration. In: Fitzgibbon, A., Lazebnik, S., Perona, P., Sato, Y., Schmid, C. (eds.) ECCV 2012. LNCS, vol. 7575, pp. 274–287. Springer, Heidelberg (2012). https://doi.org/10.1007/978-3-642-33765-9_20
61. Vasu, S., Mohan, M.M., Rajagopalan, A.: Occlusion-aware rolling shutter rectification of 3D scenes. In: CVPR (2018)
62. Vasu, S., Rajagopalan, A.N., Seetharaman, G.: Camera shutter-independent registration and rectification. IEEE Trans. Image Process. **27**(4), 1901–1913 (2017)
63. Zaragoza, J., Chin, T.J., Brown, M.S., Suter, D.: As-projective-as-possible image stitching with moving DLT. In: CVPR (2013)
64. Zaragoza, J., Chin, T.J., Tran, Q.H., Brown, M.S., Suter, D.: As-projective-as-possible image stitching with moving DLT. IEEE Trans. Pattern Anal. Mach. Intell. **36**(7), 1285–1298 (2014)
65. Zhang, F., Liu, F.: Parallax-tolerant image stitching. In: CVPR (2014)
66. Zhuang, B., Cheong, L.F., Hee Lee, G.: Rolling-shutter-aware differential SFM and image rectification. In: ICCV (2017)
67. Zhuang, B., Cheong, L.F., Hee Lee, G.: Baseline desensitizing in translation averaging. In: CVPR (2018)
68. Zhuang, B., Tran, Q.H., Ji, P., Cheong, L.F., Chandraker, M.: Learning structure-and-motion-aware rolling shutter correction. In: CVPR (2019)
69. Zhuang, B., Tran, Q.H., Lee, G.H., Cheong, L.F., Chandraker, M.: Degeneracy in self-calibration revisited and a deep learning solution for uncalibrated SLAM. In: IROS (2019)

PARSENET: A Parametric Surface Fitting Network for 3D Point Clouds

Gopal Sharma[1]($\boxtimes$) iD, Difan Liu[1] iD, Subhransu Maji[1] iD,
Evangelos Kalogerakis[1] iD, Siddhartha Chaudhuri[2,3], and Radomír Měch[2]

[1] University of Massachusetts Amherst, Amherst, USA
{gopalsharma,dliu,smaji,kalo}@cs.umass.edu
[2] Adobe Research, San Jose, USA
{sidch,rmech}@adobe.com
[3] IIT, Bombay, Bombay, India

Abstract. We propose a novel, end-to-end trainable, deep network called PARSENET that decomposes a 3D point cloud into parametric surface patches, including B-spline patches as well as basic geometric primitives. PARSENET is trained on a large-scale dataset of man-made 3D shapes and captures high-level semantic priors for shape decomposition. It handles a much richer class of primitives than prior work, and allows us to represent surfaces with higher fidelity. It also produces repeatable and robust parametrizations of a surface compared to purely geometric approaches. We present extensive experiments to validate our approach against analytical and learning-based alternatives. Our source code is publicly available at: https://hippogriff.github.io/parsenet.

1 Introduction

3D point clouds can be rapidly acquired using 3D sensors or photogrammetric techniques. However, they are rarely used in this form in design and graphics applications. Observations from the computer-aided design and modeling literature [3,4,14,16] suggest that designers often model shapes by constructing several non-overlapping patches placed seamlessly. The advantage of using several patches over a single continuous patch is that a much more diverse variety of geometric features and surface topologies can be created. The decomposition also allows easier interaction and editing. The goal of this work is to automate the time-consuming process of converting a 3D point cloud into a piecewise parametric surface representation as seen in Fig. 1.

An important question is how surface patches should be represented. Patch representations in CAD and graphics are based on well-accepted geometric properties: (a) *continuity* in their tangents, normals, and curvature, making patches

Electronic supplementary material The online version of this chapter (https://doi.org/10.1007/978-3-030-58571-6_16) contains supplementary material, which is available to authorized users.

Fig. 1. PARSENET decomposes point clouds (top row) into collections of assembled parametric surface patches including B-spline patches (bottom row). On the right, a shape is edited using the inferred parametrization.

appear smooth, (b) *editability*, such that they can easily be modified based on a few intuitive degrees of freedom (DoFs), *e.g.*, control points or axes, and (c) *flexibility*, so that a wide variety of surface geometries can be captured. Towards this goal, we propose PARSENET, a **parametric surface fitting network** architecture which produces a compact, editable representation of a point cloud as an assembly of geometric primitives, including open or closed B-spline patches.

PARSENET models a richer class of surfaces than prior work which *only* handles basic geometric primitives such as planes, cuboids and cylinders [11, 12,17,24]. While such primitives are continuous and editable representations, they lack the richness and flexibility of spline patches which are widely used in shape design. PARSENET includes a novel neural network (SPLINENET) to estimate an open or closed B-spline model of a point cloud patch. It is part of a *fitting module* (Sect. 3.2) which can also fit other geometric primitive types. The fitting module receives input from a *decomposition module*, which partitions a point cloud into segments, after which the fitting module estimates shape parameters of a predicted primitive type for each segment (Sect. 3.1). The entire pipeline, shown in Fig. 2, is fully differentiable and trained end-to-end (Sect. 4). An optional geometric postprocessing step further refines the output.

Compared to purely analytical approaches, PARSENET produces decompositions that are more consistent with high-level semantic priors, and are more robust to point density and noise. To train and test PARSENET, we leverage a recent dataset of man-made parts [8]. Extensive evaluations show that PARSENET outperforms baselines (RANSAC and SPFN [11]) by 14.93% and 13.13% respectively for segmenting a point cloud into patches, and by 50%, and 47.64% relative error respectively for parametrizing each patch for surface reconstruction (Sect. 5).

To summarize, our contributions are:

- The first proposed end-to-end differentiable approach for representing a raw 3D point cloud as an assembly of parametric primitives *including* spline patches.
- Novel decomposition and primitive fitting modules, including SPLINENET, a fully-differentiable network to fit a cubic B-spline patch to a set of points.
- Evaluation of our framework vs prior analytical and learning-based methods.

2   Related Work

Our work builds upon related research on parametric surface representations and methods for primitive fitting. We briefly review relevant work in these areas. Of course, we also leverage extensive prior work on neural networks for general shape processing: see recent surveys on the subject [1].

Parametric Surfaces. A parametric surface is a (typically diffeomorphic) mapping from a (typically compact) subset of $\mathbb{R}^2$ to $\mathbb{R}^3$. While most of the geometric primitives used in computer graphics (spheres, cuboids, meshes etc.) can be represented parametrically, the term most commonly refers to curved surfaces used in engineering CAD modelers, represented as spline patches [3]. There are a variety of formulations – *e.g.* Bézier patches, B-spline patches, NURBS patches – with slightly different characteristics, but they all construct surfaces as weighted combinations of control parameters, typically the positions of a sparse grid of points which serve as editing handles. More specifically, a B-spline patch is a smoothly curved, bounded, parametric surface, whose shape is defined by a sparse grid of control points $\mathbf{C} = \{\mathbf{c}_{p,q}\}$. The surface point with parameters $(u, v) \in [u_{\min}, u_{\max}] \times [v_{\min}, v_{\max}]$ and *basis functions* [3] $b_p(u)$, $b_q(v)$ is given by:

$$\mathbf{s}(u, v) = \sum_{p=1}^{P} \sum_{q=1}^{Q} b_p(u) b_q(v) \mathbf{c}_{p,q} \tag{1}$$

Please refer to supplementary material for more details on B-spline patches.

Fitting Geometric Primitives. A variety of analytical (*i.e.* not learning-based) algorithms have been devised to approximate raw 3D data as a collection of geometric primitives: dominant themes include Hough transforms, RANSAC and clustering. The literature is too vast to cover here, we recommend the comprehensive survey of Kaiser *et al.* [7]. In the particular case of NURBS patch fitting, early approaches were based on user interaction or hand-tuned heuristics to extract patches from meshes or point clouds [2,6,10]. In the rest of this section, we briefly review recent methods that *learn* how to fit primitives to 3D data.

Several recent papers [20,22,24,27] also try to approximate 3D shapes as unions of cuboids or ellipsoids. Paschalidou *et al.* [12,13] extended this to superquadrics. Sharma *et al.* [17,18] developed a neural parser that represents a test shape as a collection of basic primitives (spheres, cubes, cylinders) combined with boolean operations. Tian *et al.* [23] handled more expressive construction rules (*e.g.* loops) and a wider set of primitives. Because of the choice of simple primitives, such models are naturally limited in how well they align to complex input objects, and offer less flexible and intuitive parametrization for user edits.

More relevantly to our goal of modeling arbitrary curved surfaces, Gao *et al.* [5] parametrize 3D point clouds as extrusions or surfaces of revolution, generated by B-spline cross-sections detected by a 2D network. This method requires translational/rotational symmetry, and does not apply to general curved patches. Li *et al.* [11] proposed a supervised method to fit primitives to 3D point clouds,

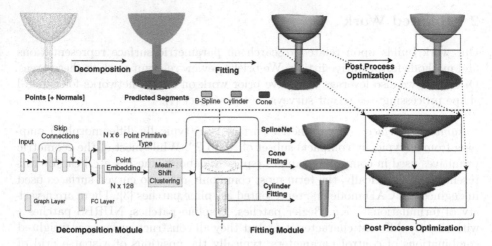

Fig. 2. Overview of PARSENET **pipeline.** (1) The *decomposition module* (Sect. 3.1) takes a 3D point cloud (with optional normals) and decomposes it into segments labeled by primitive type. (2) The *fitting module* (Sect. 3.2) predicts parameters of a primitive that best approximates each segment. It includes a novel SPLINENET to fit B-spline patches. The two modules are jointly trained end-to-end. An optional postprocess module (Sect. 3.3) refines the output.

first predicting per-point segment labels, primitive types and normals, and then using a differential module to estimate primitive parameters. While we also chain segmentation with fitting in an end-to-end way, we differ from Li *et al.* in two important ways. First, our differentiable metric-learning segmentation produces improved results (Table 1). Second, a major goal (and technical challenge) for us is to significantly improve expressivity and generality by incorporating B-spline patches: we achieve this with a novel differentiable spline-fitting network. In a complementary direction, Yumer *et al.* [26] developed a neural network for fitting a single NURBS patch to an unstructured point cloud. While the goal is similar to our spline-fitting network, it is not combined with a decomposition module that jointly learns how to express a shape with *multiple* patches covering different regions. Further, their fitting module has several non-trainable steps which are not obviously differentiable, and hence cannot be used in our pipeline.

3   Method

The goal of our method is to reconstruct an input point cloud by predicting a set of parametric patches closely approximating its underlying surface. The first stage of our architecture is a *neural decomposition module* (Fig. 2) whose goal is to segment the input point cloud into regions, each labeled with a parametric patch type. Next, we incorporate a *fitting module* (Fig. 2) that predicts each patch's shape parameters. Finally, an optional post-processing *geometric opti-*

mization step refines the patches to better align their boundaries for a seamless surface.

The input to our pipeline is a set of points $\mathbf{P} = \{\mathbf{p}_i\}_{i=1}^N$, represented either as 3D positions $\mathbf{p}_i = (x, y, z)$, or as 6D position + normal vectors $\mathbf{p}_i = (x, y, z, n_x, n_y, n_z)$. The output is a set of surface patches $\{\mathbf{s}_k\}$, reconstructing the input point cloud. The number of patches is automatically determined. Each patch is labeled with a type t_k, one of: sphere, plane, cone, cylinder, open/closed B-spline patch. The architecture also outputs a real-valued vector for each patch defining its geometric parameters, *e.g.* center and radius for spheres, or B-spline control points and knots.

3.1 Decomposition Module

The first module (Fig. 2) decomposes the point cloud $\mathbf{P}$ into a set of segments such that each segment can be reliably approximated by one of the above mentioned surface patch types. To this end, the module first embeds the input points into a representation space used to reveal such segments. As discussed in Sect. 4, the representations are learned using metric learning, such that points belonging to the same patch are embedded close to each other, forming a distinct cluster.

Embedding Network. To learn these point-wise representations, we incorporate edge convolution layers (EdgeConv) from DGCNN [25]. Each EdgeConv layer performs a graph convolution to extract a representation of each point with an MLP on the input features of its neighborhood. The neighborhoods are dynamically defined via nearest neighbors in the input feature space. We stack 3 Edge-Conv layers, each extracting a 256-D representation per point. A max-pooling layer is also used to extract a global 1024-D representation for the whole point cloud. The global representation is tiled and concatenated with the representations from all three EdgeConv layers to form intermediate point-wise (1024 + 256)-D representations $\mathbf{Q} = \{\mathbf{q}_i\}$ encoding both local and global shape information. We found that a global representation is useful for our task, since it captures the overall geometric shape structure, which is often correlated with the number and type of expected patches. This representation is then transformed through fully connected layers and ReLUs, and finally normalized to unit length to form the point-wise embedding $\mathbf{Y} = \{\mathbf{y}_i\}_{i=1}^N$ (128-D) lying on the unit hypersphere.

Clustering. A mean-shift clustering procedure is applied on the point-wise embedding to discover segments. The advantage of mean-shift clustering over other alternatives (*e.g.*, k-means or mixture models) is that it does not require the target number of clusters as input. Since different shapes may comprise different numbers of patches, we let mean-shift produce a cluster count tailored for each input. Like the pixel grouping of [9], we implement mean-shift iterations as differentiable recurrent functions, allowing back-propagation. Specifically, we initialize mean-shift by setting all points as seeds $\mathbf{z}_i^{(0)} = \mathbf{y}_i, \forall y_i \in R^{128}$. Then, each mean-shift iteration t updates each point's embedding on the unit hypersphere:

$$\mathbf{z}_i^{(t+1)} = \sum_{j=1}^{N} \mathbf{y}_j g(\mathbf{z}_i^{(t)}, \mathbf{y}_j) / (\sum_{j=1}^{N} g(\mathbf{z}_i^{(t)}, \mathbf{y}_j)) \tag{2}$$

where the pairwise similarities $g(\mathbf{z}_i^{(t)}, \mathbf{y}_j)$ are based on a von Mises-Fisher kernel with bandwidth β: $g(\mathbf{z}_i, \mathbf{y}_j) = \exp(\mathbf{z}_i^T \mathbf{y}_j / \beta^2)$ (iteration index dropped for clarity). The embeddings are normalized to unit vectors after each iteration. The bandwidth for each input point cloud is set as the average distance of each point to its 150th neighboring point in the embedding space [19]. The mean-shift iterations are repeated until convergence (this occurs around 50 iterations in our datasets). We extract the cluster centers using non-maximum suppression: starting with the point with highest density, we remove all points within a distance β, then repeat. Points are assigned to segments based on their nearest cluster center. The point memberships are stored in a matrix $\mathbf{W}$, where $\mathbf{W}[i, k] = 1$ means point i belongs to segment k, and 0 means otherwise. The memberships are passed to the fitting module to determine a parametric patch per segment. During training, we use soft memberships for differentiating this step (more details in Sect. 4.3).

Segment Classification. To classify each segment, we pass the per-point representation $\mathbf{q}_i$, encoding local and global geometry, through fully connected layers and ReLUs, followed by a softmax for a per-point probability $P(t_i = l)$, where l is a patch type (*i.e.*, sphere, plane, cone, cylinder, open/closed B-spline patch). The segment's patch type is determined through majority voting over all its points.

3.2   Fitting Module

The second module (Fig. 2) aims to fit a parametric patch to each predicted segment of the point cloud. To this end, depending on the segment type, the module estimates the shape parameters of the surface patch.

Basic Primitives. Following Li *et al.* [11], we estimate the shape of basic primitives with least-squares fitting. This includes center and radius for spheres; normal and offset for planes; center, direction and radius for cylinders; and apex, direction and angle for cones. We also follow their approach to define primitive boundaries.

B-Splines. Analytically parametrizing a set of points as a spline patch in the presence of noise, sparsity and non-uniform sampling, can be error-prone. Instead, predicting control points directly with a neural network can provide robust results. We propose a neural network SPLINENET, that inputs points of a segment, and outputs a fixed size control-point grid. A stack of three EdgeConv layers produce point-wise representations concatenated with a global representation extracted from a max-pooling layer (as for decomposition, but weights are not shared). This equips each point i in a segment with a 1024-D representation ϕ_i. A segment's representation is produced by max-pooling over its points, as identified through the membership matrix $\mathbf{W}$ extracted previously:

$$\phi_k = \max_{i=1\dots N}(\mathbf{W}[i,k] \cdot \phi_i). \tag{3}$$

Finally, two fully-connected layers with ReLUs transform ϕ_k to an initial set of 20×20 control points $\mathbf{C}$ unrolled into a 1200-D output vector. For a segment with a small number of points, we upsample the input segment (with nearest neighbor interpolation) to 1600 points. This significantly improved performance for such segments (Table 2). For closed B-spline patches, we wrap the first row/column of control points. Note that the network parameters to produce open and closed B-splines are not shared. Figure 5 visualizes some predicted B-spline surfaces.

3.3   Post-processing Module

SPLINENET produces an initial patch surface that approximates the points belonging to a segment. However, patches might not entirely cover the input point cloud, and boundaries between patches are not necessarily well-aligned. Further, the resolution of the initial control point grid (20×20) can be further adjusted to match the desired surface resolution. As a post-processing step, we perform an optimization to produce B-spline surfaces that better cover the input point cloud, and refine the control points to achieve a prescribed fitting tolerance.

Optimization. We first create a grid of 40×40 points on the initial B-spline patch by uniformly sampling its UV parameter space. We tessellate them into quads. Then we perform a maximal matching between the quad vertices and the input points of the segment, using the Hungarian algorithm with L2 distance costs. We then perform an as-rigid-as-possible (ARAP) [21] deformation of the tessellated surface towards the matched input points. ARAP is an iterative, detail-preserving method to deform a mesh so that selected vertices (pivots) achieve targets position, while promoting locally rigid transformations in one-ring neighborhoods (instead of arbitrary ones causing shearing/stretching). We use the boundary vertices of the patch as pivots so that they move close to their matched input points. Thus, we promote coverage of input points by the B-spline patches. After the deformation, the control points are re-estimated with least-squares [14].

Refinement of B-spline Control Points. After the above optimization, we again perform a maximal matching between the quad vertices and the input points of the segment. As a result, the input segment points acquire 2D parameter values in the patch's UV parameter space, which can be used to re-fit any other grid of control points [14]. In our case, we iteratively upsample the control point grid by a factor of 2 until a fitting tolerance, measured via Chamfer distance, is achieved. If the tolerance is satisfied by the initial control point grid, we can similarly

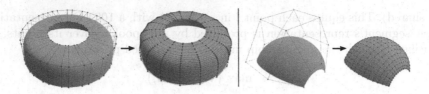

Fig. 3. Standardization: Examples of B-spline patches with a variable number of control points (shown in red), each standardized with 20×20 control points. Left: closed B-spline and Right: open B-spline. (Please zoom in.) (Color figure online)

downsample it iteratively. In our experiments, we set the fitting tolerance to 5×10^{-4}. In Fig. 5 we show the improvements from the post-processing step.

4   Training

To train the neural decomposition and fitting modules of our architecture, we use supervisory signals from a dataset of 3D shapes modeled through a combination of basic geometric primitives and B-splines. Below we describe the dataset, then we discuss the loss functions and the steps of our training procedure.

4.1   Dataset

The ABC dataset [8] provides a large source of 3D CAD models of mechanical objects whose file format stores surface patches and modeling operations that designers used to create them. Since our method is focused on predicting surface patches, and in particular B-spline patches, we selected models from this dataset that contain at least one B-spline surface patch. As a result, we ended up with a dataset of 32K models (24K, 4K, 4K train, test, validation sets respectively). We call this ABCPARTSDATASET. All shapes are centered in the origin and scaled so they lie inside unit cube. To train SPLINENET, we also extract 32K closed and open B-spline surface patches each from ABC dataset and split them into 24K, 4K, 4K train, test, validation sets respectively. We call this SPLINEDATASET. We report the average number of different patch types in supplementary material.

Preprocessing. Based on the provided metadata in ABCPARTSDATASET, each shape can be rendered based on the collection of surface patches and primitives it contains (Fig. 4). Since we assume that the inputs to our architecture are point clouds, we first sample each shape with 10K points randomly distributed on the shape surface. We also add noise in a uniform range $[-0.01, 0.01]$ along the normal direction. Normals are also perturbed with random noise in a uniform range of $[-3, 3]$ degrees from their original direction.

4.2   Loss Functions

We now describe the different loss functions used to train our neural modules. The training procedure involving their combination is discussed in Sect. 4.3.

Embedding Loss. To discover clusters of points that correspond well to surface patches, we use a metric learning approach. The point-wise representations **Z** produced by our decomposition module after mean-shift clustering are learned such that point pairs originating from the same surface patch are embedded close to each other to favor a cluster formation. In contrast, point pairs originating from different surface patches are pushed away from each other. Given a triplet of points (a, b, c), we use the triplet loss to learn the embeddings:

$$\ell_{emb}(a, b, c) = \max\left(0, \ \|\mathbf{z}_a - \mathbf{z}_b\|^2 - \|\mathbf{z}_a - \mathbf{z}_c\|^2 + \tau\right), \tag{4}$$

where τ the margin is set to 0.9. Given a triplet set $\mathcal{T}_S$ sampled from each point set S from our dataset $\mathcal{D}$, the embedding objective sums the loss over triplets:

$$L_{emb} = \sum_{S \in \mathcal{D}} \frac{1}{|\mathcal{T}_S|} \sum_{(a,b,c) \in \mathcal{T}_S} \ell_{emb}(a, b, c). \tag{5}$$

Segment Classification Loss. To promote correct segment classifications according to our supported types, we use the cross entropy loss: $L_{class} = -\sum_{i \in S} \log(p_i^t)$ where p_t^i is the probability of the ith point of shape S belonging to its ground truth type t, computed from our segment classification network.

Control Point Regression Loss. This loss function is used to train SPLINENET. As discussed in Sect. 3.2, SPLINENET produces 20×20 control points per B-spline patch. We include a supervisory signal for this control point grid prediction. One issue is that B-spline patches have a variable number of control points in our dataset. Hence we reparametrize each patch by first sampling $M = 3600$ points and estimating a new 20×20 reparametrization using least-squares fitting [10, 14], as seen in the Fig. 3. In our experiments, we found that this standardization produces no practical loss in surface reconstructions in our dataset. Finally, our reconstruction loss should be invariant to flips or swaps of control points grid in u and v directions. Hence we define a loss that is invariant to such permutations:

$$L_{cp} = \sum_{S \in \mathcal{D}} \frac{1}{|\mathcal{S}^{(b)}|} \sum_{s_k \in \mathcal{S}^{(b)}} \frac{1}{|\mathbf{C}_k|} \min_{\pi \in \Pi} \|\mathbf{C}_k - \pi(\hat{\mathbf{C}}_k)\|^2 \tag{6}$$

where $\mathcal{S}^{(b)}$ is the set of B-spline patches from shape $\mathcal{S}$, $\mathbf{C}_k$ is the predicted control point grid for patch s_k ($|\mathbf{C}_k| = 400$ control points), $\pi(\hat{\mathbf{C}}_k)$ is permutations of the ground-truth control points from the set Π of 8 permutations for open and 160 permutations for closed B-spline.

Laplacian Loss. This loss is also specific to B-Splines using SPLINENET. For each ground-truth B-spline patch, we uniformly sample ground truth surface, and measure the surface Laplacian capturing its second-order derivatives. We also uniformly sample the predicted patches and measure their Laplacians. We then establish Hungarian matching between sampled points in the ground-truth and predicted patches, and compare the Laplacians of the ground-truth points

$\hat{\mathbf{r}}_m$ and corresponding predicted ones $\mathbf{r}_n$ to improve the agreement between their derivatives as follows:

$$L_{lap} = \sum_{S \in \mathcal{D}} \frac{1}{|\mathcal{S}^{(b)}| \cdot M} \sum_{s_k \in \mathcal{S}^{(b)}} \sum_{\mathbf{r}_n \in s_k} ||\mathcal{L}(\mathbf{r}_n) - \mathcal{L}(\hat{\mathbf{r}}_m)||^2 \qquad (7)$$

where $\mathcal{L}(\cdot)$ is the Laplace operator on patch points, and $M = 1600$ point samples.

Patch Distance Loss. This loss is applied to both basic primitive and B-splines patches. Inspired by [11], the loss measures average distances between predicted primitive patch s_k and uniformly sampled points from the ground truth patch as:

$$L_{dist} = \sum_{S \in \mathcal{D}} \frac{1}{K_S} \sum_{k=1}^{K_S} \frac{1}{M_{\hat{s}_k}} \sum_{n \in \hat{s}_k} D^2(\mathbf{r}_n, \mathbf{s}_k), \qquad (8)$$

where K_S is the number of predicted patches for shape S, $M_{\hat{s}_k}$ is number of sampled points $\mathbf{r}_n$ from ground patch $\hat{s}_k$, $D^2(\mathbf{r}_n, \mathbf{s}_k)$ is the squared distance from $\mathbf{r}_n$ to the predicted primitive patch surface $\mathbf{s}_k$. These distances can be computed analytically for basic primitives [11]. For B-splines, we use an approximation based on Chamfer distance between sample points.

4.3   Training Procedure

One possibility for training is to start it from scratch using a combination of all losses. Based on our experiments, we found that breaking the training procedure into the following steps leads to faster convergence and to better minima:

- We first pre-train the networks of the decomposition module using ABC-PARTSDATASET with the sum of embedding and classification losses: $L_{emb} + L_{class}$. Both losses are necessary for point cloud decomposition and classification.
- We then pre-train the SPLINENET using SPLINEDATASET for control point prediction exclusively on B-spline patches using $L_{cp} + L_{lap} + L_{dist}$. We note that we experimented training the B-spline patch prediction only with the patch distance loss L_{dist} but had worse performance. Using both the L_{cp} and L_{lap} loss yielded better predictions as shown in Table 2.
- We then jointly train the decomposition and fitting module end-to-end with all the losses. To allow backpropagation from the primitives and B-splines fitting to the embedding network, the mean shift clustering is implemented as a recurrent module (Eq. 2). For efficiency, we use 5 mean-shift iterations during training. It is also important to note that during training, Eq. 3 uses *soft* point-to-segment memberships, which enables backpropagation from the fitting module to the decomposition module and improves reconstructions. The soft memberships are computed based on the point embeddings $\{\mathbf{z}_i\}$ (after the mean-shift iterations) and cluster center embedding $\{\mathbf{z}_k\}$ as follows:

$$\mathbf{W}[i, k] = \frac{\exp(\mathbf{z}_k^T \mathbf{z}_i / \beta^2)}{\sum_{k'} \exp(\mathbf{z}_{k'}^T \mathbf{z}_i / \beta^2)} \qquad (9)$$

Please see supplementary material for more implementation details.

5   Experiments

Table 1. Primitive fitting on ABCPARTSDATASET. We compare PARSENET with nearest neighbor (NN), RANSAC [15], and SPFN [11]. We show results with points (p) and points and normals (p+n) as input. The last two rows shows our method with end-to-end training and post-process optimization. We report 'seg iou' and 'label iou' metric for segmentation task. We report the residual error (res) on all, geometric and spline primitives, and the coverage metric for fitting.

Method	Input	seg iou	label iou	res (all)	res (geom)	res (spline)	P cover
NN	p	54.10	61.10	–	–	–	–
RANSAC	p+n	67.21	–	0.0220	0.0220	-	83.40
SPFN	p	47.38	68.92	0.0238	0.0270	0.0100	86.66
SPFN	p+n	69.01	79.94	0.0212	0.0240	0.0136	88.40
PARSENET	p	71.32	79.61	0.0150	0.0160	0.0090	87.00
PARSENET	p+n	81.20	87.50	0.0120	0.0123	0.0077	92.00
PARSENET + e2e	p+n	82.14	88.60	0.0118	0.0120	0.0076	92.30
PARSENET + e2e + opt	p+n	**82.14**	**88.60**	**0.0111**	**0.0120**	**0.0068**	**92.97**

Our experiments compare our approach to alternatives in three parts: (a) evaluation of the quality of segmentation and segment classification (Sect. 5.1), (b) evaluation of B-spline patch fitting, since it is a major contribution of our work (Sect. 5.2), and (c) evaluation of overall reconstruction quality (Sect. 5.3). We include evaluation metrics and results for each of the three parts next.

5.1   Segmentation and Labeling Evaluation

Evaluation Metrics. We use the following metrics for evaluating the point cloud segmentation and segment labeling based on the test set of ABCPARTSDATASET:

- **Segmentation mean IOU** ("seg mIOU"): this metric measures the similarity of the predicted segments with ground truth segments. Given the ground-truth point-to-segment memberships $\hat{\mathbf{W}}$ for an input point cloud, and the predicted ones $\mathbf{W}$, we measure: $\frac{1}{K} \sum_{k=1}^{K} IOU(\hat{\mathbf{W}}[:, k], h(\mathbf{W}[:, k]))$ where h represents a membership conversion into a one-hot vector, and K is the number of ground-truth segments.
- **Segment labeling IOU** ("label mIOU"): this metric measures the classification accuracy of primitive type prediction averaged over segments: $\frac{1}{K} \sum_{k=1}^{K} \mathcal{I} [t_k = \hat{t}_k]$ where t_k and $\hat{t}_k$ is the predicted and ground truth primitive type respectively for k^{th} segment and $\mathcal{I}$ is an indicator function.

We use Hungarian matching to find correspondences between predicted segments and ground-truth segments.

Comparisons. We first compare our method with a nearest neighbor (NN) baseline: for each test shape, we find its most similar shape from the training set using Chamfer distance. Then for each point on the test shape, we transfer the labels and primitive type from its closest point in $\mathcal{R}^3$ on the retrieved shape.

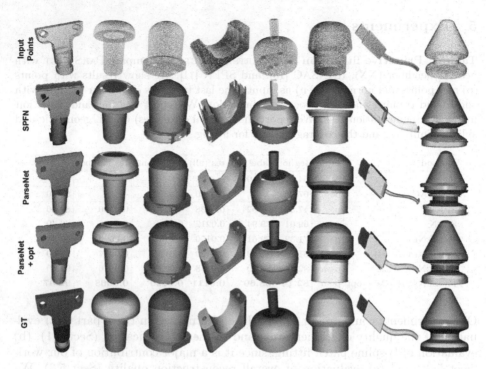

Fig. 4. Given the input point clouds with normals of the first row, we show surfaces produced by SPFN [11] (second row), PARSENET without post-processing optimization (third row), and full PARSENET including optimization (fourth row). The last row shows the ground-truth surfaces from our ABCPARTSDATASET.

We also compare against efficient RANSAC algorithm [15]. The algorithm only handles basic primitives (cylinder, cone, plane, sphere, and torus), and offers poor reconstruction of B-splines patches in our dataset. Efficient RANSAC requires per point normals, which we provide as the ground-truth normals. We run RANSAC 3 times and report the performance with best coverage.

We then compare against the supervised primitive fitting (SPFN) approach [11]. Their approach produces per point segment membership, and their network is trained to maximize relaxed IOU between predicted membership and ground truth membership, whereas our approach uses learned point embeddings and clustering with mean-shift clustering to extract segments. We train SPFN network using their provided code on our training set using their proposed losses. We note that we include B-splines patches in their supported types. We train their network in two input settings: (a) the network takes only point positions as input, (b) it takes point and normals as input. We train our PARSENET on our training set in the same two settings using our loss functions.

The performance of the above methods are shown in Table 1. The lack of B-spline fitting hampers the performance of RANSAC. The SPFN method with points and normals as input performs better compared to using only points

Table 2. Ablation study for B-spline fitting. The error is measured using Chamfer Distance (CD is scaled by 100). The acronyms "cp": control-points regression loss, "dist" means patch distance loss, and "lap" means Laplacian loss. We also include the effect of post-processing optimization "opt". We report performance with and without upsampling ("ups") for open and closed B-splines.

Loss				Open splines		Closed splines	
cp	dist	lap	opt	w/ ups	w/o ups	w/ ups	w/o ups
✓				2.04	2.00	5.04	3.93
✓	✓			1.96	2.00	4.9	3.60
✓	✓	✓		1.68	1.59	3.74	3.29
✓	✓	✓	✓	**0.92**	**0.87**	**0.63**	**0.81**

as input. Finally, ParSeNet with only points as input performs better than all other alternatives. We observe further gains when including point normals in the input. Training ParSeNet end-to-end gives 13.13% and 8.66% improvement in segmentation mIOU and label mIOU respectively over SPFN with points and normals as input. The better performance is also reflected in Fig. 4, where our method reconstructs patches that correspond to more reasonable segmentations compared to other methods. In the supplementary material we evaluate methods on the TraceParts dataset [11], which contains only basic primitives (cylinder, cone, plane, sphere, torus). We outperform prior work also in this dataset.

5.2 B-Spline Fitting Evaluation

Evaluation Metrics. We evaluate the quality of our predicted B-spline patches by computing the Chamfer distance between densely sampled points on the ground-truth B-spline patches and densely sampled points on predicted patches. Points are uniformly sampled based on the 2D parameter space of the patches. We use 2K samples. We use the test set of our SplineDataset for evaluation.

Ablation Study. We evaluate the training of SplineNet using various loss functions while giving 700 points per patch as input, in Table 2. All losses contribute to improvements in performance. Table 2 shows that upsampling is effective for closed splines. Figure 5 shows the effect of optimization to improve the alignment of patches and the adjustment of resolution in the control point grid. See supplementary material for more experiments on SplineNet's robustness.

5.3 Reconstruction Evaluation

Evaluation Metrics. Given a point cloud $\mathbf{P} = \{\mathbf{p}_i\}_{i=1}^{N}$, ground-truth patches $\{\cup_{k=1}^{K}\hat{\mathbf{s}}_k\}$ and predicted patches $\{\cup_{k=1}^{K}\mathbf{s}_k\}$ for a test shape in ABCParts-Dataset, we evaluate the patch-based surface reconstruction using the following:

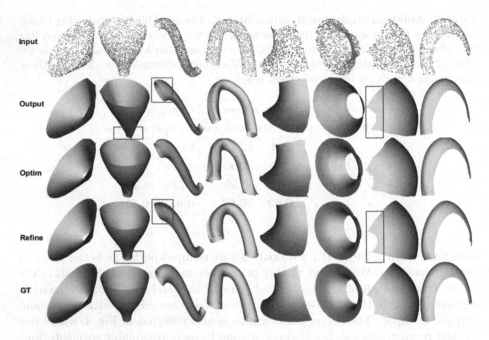

Fig. 5. Qualitative evaluation of B-spline fitting. From top to bottom: input point cloud, reconstructed surface by SPLINENET, reconstructed surface by SPLINENET with post-processing optimization, reconstruction by SPLINENET with control point grid adjustment and finally ground truth surface. Effect of post process optimization is highlighted in red boxes. (Color figure online)

- **Residual error** ("res") measures the average distance of input points from the predicted primitives following [11]: $L_{dist} = \sum_{k=1}^{K} \frac{1}{M_k} \sum_{n \in \hat{s}_k} D(\mathbf{r}_n, \mathbf{s}_k)$ where K is the number of segments, M_k is number of sampled points $\mathbf{r}_n$ from ground patch $\hat{s}_k$, $D(\mathbf{r}_n, \mathbf{s}_k)$ is the distance of $\mathbf{r}_n$ from predicted primitive patch $\mathbf{s}_k$.
- **P-coverage** ("P-cover") measures the coverage of predicted surface by the input surface also following [11]: $\frac{1}{N} \sum_{i=1}^{N} \mathbf{I} \left[\min_{k=1}^{K} D(\mathbf{p}_i, \mathbf{s}_k) < \epsilon \right]$ ($\epsilon = 0.01$).

We note that we use the matched segments after applying Hungarian matching algorithm, as in Sect. 5.1, to compute these metrics.

Comparisons. We report the performance of RANSAC for geometric primitive fitting tasks. Note that RANSAC produces a set of geometric primitives, along with their primitive type and parameters, which we use to compute the above metrics. Here we compare with the SPFN network [11] trained on our dataset using their proposed loss functions. We augment their per point primitive type prediction to also include open/closed B-spline type. Then for classified segments as B-splines, we use our SPLINENET to fit B-splines. For segments classified as geometric primitives, we use their geometric primitive fitting algorithm.

Results. Table 1 reports the performance of our method, SPFN and RANSAC. The residual error and P-coverage follows the trend of segmentation metrics. Interestingly, our method outperforms SPFN even for geometric primitive predictions (even without considering B-splines and our adaptation). Using points and normals, along with joint end-to-end training, and post-processing optimization offers the best performance for our method by giving 47.64% and 50% reduction in relative error in comparison to SPFN and RANSAC respectively.

6   Conclusion

We presented a method to reconstruct point clouds by predicting geometric primitives and surface patches common in CAD design. Our method effectively marries 3D deep learning with CAD modeling practices. Our architecture predictions are editable and interpretable. Modelers can refine our results based on standard CAD modeling operations. In terms of limitations, our method often makes mistakes for small parts, mainly because clustering merges them with bigger patches. In high-curvature areas, due to sparse sampling, PARSENET may produce more segments than ground-truth. Producing seamless boundaries is still a challenge due to noise and sparsity in our point sets. Generating training point clouds simulating realistic scan noise is another important future direction.

Acknowledgements. This research is funded in part by NSF (#1617333, #1749833) and Adobe. Our experiments were performed in the UMass GPU cluster funded by the MassTech Collaborative. We thank Matheus Gadelha for helpful discussions.

References

1. Ahmed, E.: Deep learning advances on different 3D data representations: a survey. Computing Research Repository (CoRR) abs/1808.01462 (2019)
2. Eck, M., Hoppe, H.: Automatic reconstruction of B-spline surfaces of arbitrary topological type. In: SIGGRAPH (1996)
3. Farin, G.: Curves and Surfaces for CAGD, 5th edn. Morgan Kaufmann, San Francisco (2002)
4. Foley, J.D., van Dam, A., Feiner, S.K., Hughes, J.F.: Computer Graphics: Principles and Practice, 2nd edn. Addison-Wesley Longman Publishing Co. Inc., Boston (1990)
5. Gao, J., Tang, C., Ganapathi-Subramanian, V., Huang, J., Su, H., Guibas, L.J.: DeepSpline: data-driven reconstruction of parametric curves and surfaces. Computing Research Repository (CoRR) abs/1901.03781 (2019)
6. Hoppe, H., et al.: Piecewise smooth surface reconstruction. In: Proceedings of SIGGRAPH (1994)
7. Kaiser, A., Ybanez Zepeda, J.A., Boubekeur, T.: A survey of simple geometric primitives detection methods for captured 3D data. Comput. Graph. Forum **38**(1), 167–196 (2019)
8. Koch, S., et al.: ABC: a big cad model dataset for geometric deep learning. In: Proceedings of the IEEE/CVF Conference on Computer Vision and Pattern Recognition (CVPR), June 2019

9. Kong, S., Fowlkes, C.: Recurrent pixel embedding for instance grouping. In: 2018 Conference on Computer Vision and Pattern Recognition (CVPR) (2018)
10. Krishnamurthy, V., Levoy, M.: Fitting smooth surfaces to dense polygon meshes. In: SIGGRAPH (1996)
11. Li, L., Sung, M., Dubrovina, A., Yi, L., Guibas, L.J.: Supervised fitting of geometric primitives to 3D point clouds. In: Proceedings of the IEEE/CVF Conference on Computer Vision and Pattern Recognition (CVPR), June 2019
12. Paschalidou, D., Ulusoy, A.O., Geiger, A.: Superquadrics revisited: Learning 3D shape parsing beyond cuboids. In: 2019 IEEE/CVF Conference on Computer Vision and Pattern Recognition (CVPR), pp. 10336–10345 (2019)
13. Paschalidou, D., Gool, L.V., Geiger, A.: Learning unsupervised hierarchical part decomposition of 3d objects from a single RGB image. In: Proceedings of the IEEE/CVF Conference on Computer Vision and Pattern Recognition (CVPR), June 2020
14. Piegl, L., Tiller, W.: The NURBS Book. Monographs in Visual Communication, 2nd edn. Springer, Heidelberg (1997). https://doi.org/10.1007/978-3-642-59223-2
15. Schnabel, R., Wahl, R., Klein, R.: Efficient RANSAC for point-cloud shape detection. Comput. Graph. Forum **26**, 214–226 (2007)
16. Schneider, P.J., Eberly, D.: Geometric Tools for Computer Graphics. Elsevier Science Inc., Amsterdam (2002)
17. Sharma, G., Goyal, R., Liu, D., Kalogerakis, E., Maji, S.: CSGNet: neural shape parser for constructive solid geometry. In: 2018 IEEE/CVF Conference on Computer Vision and Pattern Recognition (CVPR), pp. 5515–5523 (2018)
18. Sharma, G., Goyal, R., Liu, D., Kalogerakis, E., Maji, S.: Neural shape parsers for constructive solid geometry. Computing Research Repository (CoRR) abs/1912.11393 (2019). http://arxiv.org/abs/1912.11393
19. Silverman, B.W.: Density Estimation for Statistics and Data Analysis. Chapman & Hall, London (1986)
20. Smirnov, D., Fisher, M., Kim, V.G., Zhang, R., Solomon, J.: Deep parametric shape predictions using distance fields. In: Proceedings of the IEEE/CVF Conference on Computer Vision and Pattern Recognition (CVPR), June 2020
21. Sorkine, O., Alexa, M.: As-rigid-as-possible surface modeling. In: Symposium on Geometry Processing, pp. 109–116 (2007)
22. Sun, C., Zou, Q., Tong, X., Liu, Y.: Learning adaptive hierarchical cuboid abstractions of 3D shape collections. ACM Trans. Graph. (SIGGRAPH Asia) **38**(6), 1–3 (2019)
23. Tian, Y., et al.: Learning to infer and execute 3D shape programs. In: International Conference on Learning Representations (2019)
24. Tulsiani, S., Su, H., Guibas, L.J., Efros, A.A., Malik, J.: Learning shape abstractions by assembling volumetric primitives. In: Proceedings of the IEEE Conference on Computer Vision and Pattern Recognition (CVPR), July 2017
25. Wang, Y., Sun, Y., Liu, Z., Sarma, S.E., Bronstein, M.M., Solomon, J.M.: Dynamic graph CNN for learning on point clouds. ACM Trans. Graph. **38**(5), 1–12 (2019)
26. Yumer, M.E., Kara, L.B.: Surface creation on unstructured point sets using neural networks. Comput. Aided Des. **44**(7), 644–656 (2012)
27. Zou, C., Yumer, E., Yang, J., Ceylan, D., Hoiem, D.: 3D-PRNN: generating shape primitives with recurrent neural networks. In: The IEEE International Conference on Computer Vision (ICCV) (2017)

The Group Loss for Deep Metric Learning

Ismail Elezi[1]([✉]), Sebastiano Vascon[1], Alessandro Torcinovich[1],
Marcello Pelillo[1], and Laura Leal-Taixé[2]

[1] Ca' Foscari University of Venice, Venice, Italy
ismail.elezi@gmail.com
[2] Technical University of Munich, Munich, Germany

Abstract. Deep metric learning has yielded impressive results in tasks
such as clustering and image retrieval by leveraging neural networks to
obtain highly discriminative feature embeddings, which can be used to
group samples into different classes. Much research has been devoted to
the design of smart loss functions or data mining strategies for training
such networks. Most methods consider only pairs or triplets of samples
within a mini-batch to compute the loss function, which is commonly
based on the distance between embeddings. We propose *Group Loss*,
a loss function based on a differentiable label-propagation method that
enforces embedding similarity across *all* samples of a group while promoting, at the same time, low-density regions amongst data points belonging
to different groups. Guided by the smoothness assumption that "similar
objects should belong to the same group", the proposed loss trains the
neural network for a classification task, enforcing a consistent labelling
amongst samples within a class. We show state-of-the-art results on clustering and image retrieval on several datasets, and show the potential of
our method when combined with other techniques such as ensembles. To
facilitate further research, we make available the code and the models at
https://github.com/dvl-tum/group_loss.

Keywords: Deep metric learning · Image retrieval · Image clustering

1 Introduction

Measuring object similarity is at the core of many important machine learning
problems like clustering and object retrieval. For visual tasks, this means learning
a distance function over images. With the rise of deep neural networks, the focus
has rather shifted towards learning a feature embedding that is easily separable
using a simple distance function, such as the Euclidean distance. In essence,
objects of the same class (similar) should be close by in the learned manifold,
while objects of a different class (dissimilar) should be far away.

Electronic supplementary material The online version of this chapter (https://
doi.org/10.1007/978-3-030-58571-6_17) contains supplementary material, which is
available to authorized users.

A. Vedaldi et al. (Eds.): ECCV 2020, LNCS 12352, pp. 277–294, 2020.
https://doi.org/10.1007/978-3-030-58571-6_17

Historically, the best performing approaches get deep feature embeddings from the so-called siamese networks [3], which are typically trained using the contrastive loss [3] or the triplet loss [36,47]. A clear drawback of these losses is that they only consider pairs or triplets of data points, missing key information about the relationships between all members of the mini-batch. On a mini-batch of size n, despite that the number of pairwise relations between samples is $\mathcal{O}(n^2)$, contrastive loss uses only $\mathcal{O}(n/2)$ pairwise relations, while triplet loss uses $\mathcal{O}(2n/3)$ relations. Additionally, these methods consider only the relations between objects of the same class (positives) and objects of other classes (negatives), without making any distinction that negatives belong to different classes. This leads to not taking into consideration the global structure of the embedding space, and consequently results in lower clustering and retrieval performance. To compensate for that, researchers rely on other tricks to train neural networks for deep metric learning: intelligent sampling [21], multi-task learning [53] or hard-negative mining [35]. Recently, researchers have been increasingly working towards exploiting in a principled way the global structure of the embedding space [4,10,31,44], typically by designing ranking loss functions instead of following the classic triplet formulations.

In a similar spirit, we propose *Group Loss*, a novel loss function for deep metric learning that considers the similarity between all samples in a mini-batch. To create the mini-batch, we sample from a fixed number of classes, with samples coming from a class forming a *group*. Thus, each mini-batch consists of several randomly chosen groups, and each group has a fixed number of samples. An iterative, fully-differentiable label propagation algorithm is then used to build feature embeddings which are similar for samples belonging to the same group, and dissimilar otherwise.

At the core of our method lies an iterative process called replicator dynamics [8,46], that refines the local information, given by the softmax layer of a neural network, with the global information of the mini-batch given by the similarity between embeddings. The driving rationale is that the more similar two samples are, the more they affect each other in choosing their final label and tend to be grouped together in the same group, while dissimilar samples do not affect each other on their choices. Neural networks optimized with the Group Loss learn to provide similar features for samples belonging to the same class, making clustering and image retrieval easier.

Our **contribution** in this work is four-fold:

- We propose a novel loss function to train neural networks for deep metric embedding that takes into account the local information of the samples, as well as their similarity.
- We propose a differentiable label-propagation iterative model to embed the similarity computation within backpropagation, allowing end-to-end training with our new loss function.
- We perform a comprehensive robustness analysis showing the stability of our module with respect to the choice of hyperparameters.

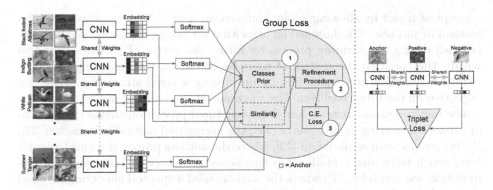

Fig. 1. A comparison between a neural model trained with the Group Loss (left) and the triplet loss (right). Given a mini-batch of images belonging to different classes, their embeddings are computed through a convolutional neural network. Such embeddings are then used to generate a similarity matrix that is fed to the Group Loss along with prior distributions of the images on the possible classes. The green contours around some mini-batch images refer to *anchors*. It is worth noting that, differently from the triplet loss, the Group Loss considers multiple classes and the pairwise relations between all the samples. Numbers from ① to ③ refer to the Group Loss steps, see Sect. 3.1 for the details.

- We show state-of-the-art qualitative and quantitative results in several standard clustering and retrieval datasets.

2   Related Work

Classical Metric Learning Losses. The first attempt at using a neural network for feature embedding was done in the seminal work of Siamese Networks [3]. A cost function called *contrastive loss* was designed in such a way as to minimize the distance between pairs of images belonging to the same cluster, and maximize the distance between pairs of images coming from different clusters. In [5], researchers used the principle to successfully address the problem of face verification. Another line of research on convex approaches for metric learning led to the triplet loss [36,47], which was later combined with the expressive power of neural networks [35]. The main difference from the original Siamese network is that the loss is computed using triplets (an anchor, a positive and a negative data point). The loss is defined to make the distance between features of the anchor and the positive sample smaller than the distance between the anchor and the negative sample. The approach was so successful in the field of face recognition and clustering, that soon many works followed. The majority of works on the Siamese architecture consist of finding better cost functions, resulting in better performances on clustering and retrieval. In [37], the authors generalized the concept of triplet by allowing a joint comparison among $N-1$ negative examples instead of just one. [39] designed an algorithm for taking advantage of the minibatches during the training process by lifting the vector of pairwise distances within the batch to the matrix of pairwise distances, thus enabling the algorithm to learn feature embedding by optimizing a novel structured prediction objective on the lifted problem. The work was later extended in [38], proposing a new metric learning scheme based on structured prediction that is designed to optimize a clustering quality metric, i.e., the normalized mutual information [22]. Better results were achieved on [43], where the authors proposed a novel angular loss, which takes angle relationship into account. A very different problem formulation was given by [17], where the authors used a spectral clustering-inspired approach to achieve deep embedding. A recent work presents several extensions of the triplet loss that reduce the bias in triplet selection by adaptively correcting the distribution shift on the selected triplets [50].

Sampling and Ensemble Methods. Knowing that the number of possible triplets is extremely large even for moderately-sized datasets, and having found that the majority of triplets are not informative [35], researchers also investigated sampling. In the original triplet loss paper [35], it was found that using semi-hard negative mining, the network can be trained to a good performance, but the training is computationally inefficient. The work of [21] found out that while the majority of research is focused on designing new loss functions, selecting training examples plays an equally important role. The authors proposed a distance-weighted sampling procedure, which selects more informative and stable examples than traditional approaches, achieving excellent results in the process. A similar work was that of [9] where the authors proposed a hierarchical version of triplet loss that learns the sampling all-together with the feature embedding. The majority of recent works has been focused on complementary research directions such as intelligent sampling [6,9,21,45,48] or ensemble methods [15,24,34,49,51]. As we will show in the experimental section, these can be combined with our novel loss.

Other Related Problems. In order to have a focused and concise paper, we mostly discuss methods which tackle image ranking/clustering in standard datasets. Nevertheless, we acknowledge related research on specific applications such as person re-identification or landmark recognition, where researchers are also gravitating towards considering the global structure of the mini-batch. In [10] the authors propose a new hashing method for learning binary embeddings of data by optimizing Average Precision metric. In [11,31] authors study novel metric learning functions for local descriptor matching on landmark datasets. [4] designs a novel ranking loss function for the purpose of few-shot learning. Similar works that focus on the global structure have shown impressive results in the field of person re-identification [1,54].

Classification-Based Losses. The authors of [23] proposed to optimize the triplet loss on a different space of triplets than the original samples, consisting of an anchor data point and similar and dissimilar learned proxy data points.

These proxies approximate the original data points so that a triplet loss over the proxies is a tight upper bound of the original loss. The final formulation of the loss is shown to be similar to that of softmax cross-entropy loss, challenging the long-hold belief that classification losses are not suitable for the task of metric learning. Recently, the work of [52] showed that a carefully tuned normalized softmax cross-entropy loss function combined with a balanced sampling strategy can achieve competitive results. A similar line of research is that of [55], where the authors use a combination of normalized-scale layers and Gram-Schmidt optimization to achieve efficient usage of the softmax cross-entropy loss for metric learning. The work of [30] goes a step further by taking into consideration the similarity between classes. Furthermore, the authors use multiple centers for class, allowing them to reach state-of-the-art results, at a cost of significantly increasing the number of parameters of the model. In contrast, we propose a novel loss that achieves state-of-the-art results without increasing the number of parameters of the model.

3   Group Loss

Most loss functions used for deep metric learning [9, 17, 21, 35, 37–39, 43–45] do not use a classification loss function, e.g., cross-entropy, but rather a loss function based on embedding distances. The rationale behind it, is that what matters for a classification network is that the output is correct, which does not necessarily mean that the embeddings of samples belonging to the same class are similar. Since each sample is classified independently, it is entirely possible that two images of the same class have two distant embeddings that both allow for a correct classification. We argue that a classification loss can still be used for deep metric learning if the decisions do not happen independently for each sample, but rather jointly for a whole *group*, i.e., the set of images of the same class in a mini-batch. In this way, the method pushes for images belonging to the same class to have similar embeddings.

Towards this end, we propose *Group Loss*, an iterative procedure that uses the global information of the mini-batch to refine the local information provided by the softmax layer of a neural network. This iterative procedure categorizes samples into different *groups*, and enforces consistent labelling among the samples of a group. While softmax cross-entropy loss judges each sample in isolation, the Group Loss allows us to judge the overall class separation for *all* samples. In Sect. 3.3, we show the differences between the softmax cross-entropy loss and Group Loss, and highlight the mathematical properties of our new loss.

3.1   Overview of Group Loss

Given a mini-batch $\mathcal{B}$ consisting of n images, consider the problem of assigning a class label $\lambda \in \Lambda = \{1, \ldots, m\}$ to each image in $\mathcal{B}$. In the remainder of the manuscript, $X = (x_{i\lambda})$ represents a $n \times m$ (non-negative) matrix of image-label soft assignments. In other words, each row of X represents a probability distribution over the label set Λ ($\sum_\lambda x_{i\lambda} = 1$ for all $i = 1 \ldots n$).

Our model consists of the following steps (see also Fig. 1 and Algorithm 1):

① **Initialization**: Initialize X, the image-label assignment using the softmax outputs of the neural network. Compute the $n \times n$ pairwise similarity matrix W using the neural network embedding.

② **Refinement**: Iteratively, refine X considering the similarities between all the mini-batch images, as encoded in W, as well as their labeling preferences.

③ **Loss computation**: Compute the cross-entropy loss of the refined probabilities and update the weights of the neural network using backpropagation.

We now provide a more detailed description of the three steps of our method.

3.2   Initialization

Image-Label Assignment Matrix. The initial assignment matrix denoted $X(0)$, comes from the softmax output of the neural network. We can replace some of the initial assignments in matrix X with one-hot labelings of those samples. We call these randomly chosen samples *anchors*, as their assignments do not change during the iterative refine process and consequently do not directly affect the loss function. However, by using their correct label instead of the predicted label (coming from the softmax output of the NN), they guide the remaining samples towards their correct label.

Similarity Matrix. A measure of similarity is computed among all pairs of embeddings (computed via a CNN) in $\mathcal{B}$ to generate a similarity matrix $W \in \mathbb{R}^{n \times n}$. In this work, we compute the similarity measure using the Pearson's correlation coefficient [28]:

$$\omega(i,j) = \frac{\mathrm{Cov}[\phi(I_i), \phi(I_j)]}{\sqrt{\mathrm{Var}[\phi(I_i)]\mathrm{Var}[\phi(I_j)]}} \tag{1}$$

for $i \neq j$, and set $\omega(i,i)$ to 0. The choice of this measure over other options such as cosine layer, Gaussian kernels, or learned similarities, is motivated by the observation that the correlation coefficient uses data standardization, thus providing invariance to scaling and translation – unlike the cosine similarity, which is invariant to scaling only – and it does not require additional hyperparameters, unlike Gaussian kernels [7]. The fact that a measure of the linear relationship among features provides a good similarity measure can be explained by the fact that the computed features are actually a highly non-linear function of the inputs. Thus, the linear correlation among the embeddings actually captures a non-linear relationship among the original images.

3.3   Refinement

In this core step of the proposed algorithm, the initial assignment matrix $X(0)$ is refined in an iterative manner, taking into account the similarity information provided by matrix W. X is updated in accordance with the *smoothness assumption*, which prescribes that similar objects should share the same label.

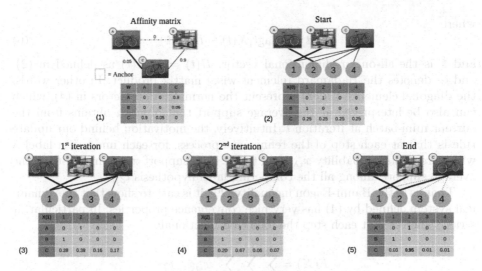

Fig. 2. A toy example of the refinement procedure, where the goal is to classify sample C based on the similarity with samples A and B. (1) The Affinity matrix used to update the soft assignments. (2) The initial labeling of the matrix. (3-4) The process iteratively refines the soft assignment of the unlabeled sample C. (5) At the end of the process, sample C gets the same label of A, (A, C) being more similar than (B, C).

To this end, let us define the *support* matrix $\Pi = (\pi_{i\lambda}) \in R^{n \times m}$ as

$$\Pi = WX \tag{2}$$

whose (i, λ)-component

$$\pi_{i\lambda} = \sum_{j=1}^{n} w_{ij} x_{j\lambda} \tag{3}$$

represents the *support* that the current mini-batch gives to the hypothesis that the i-th image in $\mathcal{B}$ belongs to class λ. Intuitively, in obedience to the smoothness principle, $\pi_{i\lambda}$ is expected to be high if images similar to i are likely to belong to class λ (Fig. 2).

Given the initial assignment matrix $X(0)$, our algorithm refines it using the following update rule:

$$x_{i\lambda}(t+1) = \frac{x_{i\lambda}(t)\pi_{i\lambda}(t)}{\sum_{\mu=1}^{m} x_{i\mu}(t)\pi_{i\mu}(t)} \tag{4}$$

where the denominator represents a normalization factor which guarantees that the rows of the updated matrix sum up to one. This is known as multi-population replicator dynamics in evolutionary game theory [46] and is equivalent to non-linear relaxation labeling processes [29, 32].

In matrix notation, the update rule (4) can be written as:

$$X(t+1) = Q^{-1}(t) \left[X(t) \odot \Pi(t) \right] \tag{5}$$

where

$$Q(t) = \mathrm{diag}([X(t) \odot \Pi(t)]\, \mathbb{1}) \tag{6}$$

and $\mathbb{1}$ is the all-one m-dimensional vector. $\Pi(t) = WX(t)$ as defined in (2), and $\odot$ denotes the Hadamard (element-wise) matrix product. In other words, the diagonal elements of $Q(t)$ represent the normalization factors in (4), which can also be interpreted as the average support that object i obtains from the current mini-batch at iteration t. Intuitively, the motivation behind our update rule is that at each step of the refinement process, for each image i, a label λ will increase its probability $x_{i\lambda}$ if and only if its support $\pi_{i\lambda}$ is higher than the average support among all the competing label hypothesis Q_{ii}.

Thanks to the Baum-Eagon inequality [29], it is easy to show that the dynamical system defined by (4) has very nice convergence properties. In particular, it strictly increases at each step the following functional:

$$F(X) = \sum_{i=1}^{n} \sum_{j=1}^{n} \sum_{\lambda=1}^{m} w_{ij} x_{i\lambda} x_{j\lambda} \tag{7}$$

which represents a measure of "consistency" of the assignment matrix X, in accordance to the smoothness assumption (F rewards assignments where highly similar objects are likely to be assigned the same label). In other words:

$$F(X(t+1)) \geq F(X(t)) \tag{8}$$

with equality if and only if $X(t)$ is a stationary point. Hence, our update rule (4) is, in fact, an algorithm for maximizing the functional F over the space of row-stochastic matrices. Note, that this contrasts with classical gradient methods, for which an increase in the objective function is guaranteed only when infinitesimal steps are taken, and determining the optimal step size entails computing higher-order derivatives. Here, instead, the step size is implicit and yet, at each step, the value of the functional increases.

3.4   Loss Computation

Once the labeling assignments converge (or in practice, a maximum number of iterations is reached), we apply the cross-entropy loss to quantify the classification error and backpropagate the gradients. Recall, the refinement procedure is optimized via *replicator dynamics*, as shown in the previous section. By studying Eq. (5), it is straightforward to see that it is composed of fully differentiable operations (matrix-vector and scalar products), and so it can be easily integrated within backpropagation. Although the refining procedure has no parameters to be learned, its gradients can be backpropagated to the previous layers of the neural network, producing, in turn, better embeddings for similarity computation.

Algorithm 1: The Group Loss

Input: input : Set of pre-processed images in the mini-batch $\mathcal{B}$, set of labels y,
neural network ϕ with learnable parameters θ, similarity function ω,
number of iterations T

1 Compute feature embeddings $\phi(\mathcal{B}, \theta)$ via the forward pass
2 Compute the similarity matrix $W = [\omega(i,j)]_{ij}$
3 Initialize the matrix of priors $X(0)$ from the softmax layer
4 **for** $t = 0, \ldots, T\text{-}1$ **do**
5 $\quad$ $Q(t) = \text{diag}([X(t) \odot \Pi(t)]\,\mathbb{1})$
6 $\quad$ $X(t+1) = Q^{-1}(t)\,[X(t) \odot \Pi(t)]$
7 Compute the cross-entropy $J(X(T), y)$
8 Compute the derivatives $\partial J/\partial \theta$ via backpropagation, and update the weights θ

3.5 Summary of the Group Loss

In this section, we proposed the Group Loss function for deep metric learning. During training, the Group Loss works by grouping together similar samples based on both the similarity between the samples in the mini-batch and the local information of the samples. The similarity between samples is computed by the correlation between the embeddings obtained from a CNN, while the local information is computed with a softmax layer on the same CNN embeddings. Using an iterative procedure, we combine both sources of information and effectively bring together embeddings of samples that belong to the same class.

During inference, we simply forward pass the images through the neural network to compute their embeddings, which are directly used for image retrieval within a nearest neighbor search scheme. The iterative procedure is not used during inference, thus making the feature extraction as fast as that of any other competing method.

4 Experiments

In this section, we compare the Group Loss with state-of-the-art deep metric learning models on both image retrieval and clustering tasks. Our method achieves state-of-the-art results in three public benchmark datasets.

4.1 Implementation Details

We use the PyTorch [27] library for the implementation of the Group Loss. We choose GoogleNet [40] with batch-normalization [12] as the backbone feature extraction network. We pretrain the network on *ILSVRC 2012-CLS* dataset [33]. For pre-processing, in order to get a fair comparison, we follow the implementation details of [38]. The inputs are resized to 256×256 pixels, and then randomly cropped to 227×227. Like other methods except for [37], we use only a center crop during testing time. We train all networks in the classification task for 10 epochs. We then train the network in the Group Loss task for 60 epochs using RAdam optimizer [18]. After 30 epochs, we lower the learning rate by multiplying it by 0.1. We find the hyperparameters using random search [2]. We use small mini-batches of size 30–100. As sampling strategy, on each mini-batch, we first randomly sample a fixed number of classes, and then for each of the chosen classes, we sample a fixed number of samples.

4.2   Benchmark Datasets

We perform experiments on 3 publicly available datasets, evaluating our algorithm on both clustering and retrieval metrics. For training and testing, we follow the conventional splitting procedure [39].

CUB-200-2011 [42] is a dataset containing 200 species of birds with 11,788 images, where the first 100 species (5,864 images) are used for training and the remaining 100 species (5,924 images) are used for testing.

Cars 196 [16] dataset is composed of 16,185 images belonging to 196 classes. We use the first 98 classes (8,054 images) for training and the other 98 classes (8,131 images) for testing.

Stanford Online Products dataset [39], contains 22,634 classes with 120,053 product images in total, where 11,318 classes (59,551 images) are used for training and the remaining 11,316 classes (60,502 images) are used for testing.

4.3   Evaluation Metrics

Based on the experimental protocol detailed above, we evaluate retrieval performance and clustering quality on data from unseen classes of the 3 aforementioned datasets. For the retrieval task, we calculate the percentage of the testing examples whose K nearest neighbors contain at least one example of the same class. This quantity is also known as Recall@K [13] and is the most used metric for image retrieval evaluation.

Similar to all other approaches, we perform clustering using K-means algorithm [20] on the embedded features. Like in other works, we evaluate the clustering quality using the Normalized Mutual Information measure (NMI) [22]. The choice of NMI measure is motivated by the fact that it is invariant to label permutation, a desirable property for cluster evaluation.

4.4   Results

We now show the results of our model and comparison to state-of-the-art methods. Our main comparison is with other loss functions, e.g., triplet loss. To compare with perpendicular research on intelligent sampling strategies or ensembles, and show the power of the Group Loss, we propose a simple ensemble version of our method. Our ensemble network is built by training l independent neural networks with the same hyperparameter configuration. During inference, their

Fig. 3. Retrieval results on a set of images from the *CUB-200-2011* (left), *Cars 196* (middle), and *Stanford Online Products* (right) datasets using our Group Loss model. The left column contains query images. The results are ranked by distance. The green square indicates that the retrieved image is from the same class as the query image, while the red box indicates that the retrieved image is from a different class. (Color figure online)

embeddings are concatenated. Note, that this type of ensemble is much simpler than the works of [15, 25, 34, 49, 51], and is given only to show that, when optimized for performance, our method can be extended to ensembles giving higher clustering and retrieval performance than other methods in the literature. Finally, in the interest of space, we only present results for Inception network [40], as this is the most popular backbone for the metric learning task, which enables fair comparison among methods. In supplementary material, we present results for other backbones, and include a discussion about the methods that work by increasing the number of parameters (capacity of the network) [30], or use more expressive network architectures.

Quantitative Results

Loss Comparison. In Table 1 we present the results of our method and compare them with the results of other approaches. On the *CUB-200-2011* dataset, we outperform the other approaches by a large margin, with the second-best model (Classification [52]) having circa 6 percentage points (*pp*) lower absolute accuracy in Recall@1 metric. On the NMI metric, our method achieves a score of 69.0 which is 2.8*pp* higher than the second-best method. Similarly, on *Cars 196*, our method achieves best results on Recall@1, with Classification [52] coming second with a 4*pp* lower score. On *Stanford Online Products*, our method reaches the best results on the Recall@1 metric, around 2*pp* higher than Classification [52] and Proxy-NCA [23]. On the same dataset, when evaluated on the NMI score, our loss outperforms any other method, be those methods that exploit advanced sampling, or ensemble methods.

Loss with Ensembles. In Table 2 we present the results of our ensemble, and compare them with the results of other ensemble and sampling approaches. Our ensemble method (using 5 neural networks) is the highest performing model in *CUB-200-2011*, outperforming the second-best method (Divide and Conquer [34]) by 1*pp* in Recall@1 and by 0.4*pp* in NMI. In *Cars 196* our method

Table 1. Retrieval and Clustering performance on *CUB-200-2011*, *CARS 196* and *Stanford Online Products* datasets. Bold indicates best results.

Loss	CUB-200-2011					CARS 196					Stanford Online Products			
	R@1	R@2	R@4	R@8	NMI	R@1	R@2	R@4	R@8	NMI	R@1	R@10	R@100	NMI
Triplet [35]	42.5	55	66.4	77.2	55.3	51.5	63.8	73.5	82.4	53.4	66.7	82.4	91.9	89.5
Lifted Structure [39]	43.5	56.5	68.5	79.6	56.5	53.0	65.7	76.0	84.3	56.9	62.5	80.8	91.9	88.7
Npairs [37]	51.9	64.3	74.9	83.2	60.2	68.9	78.9	85.8	90.9	62.7	66.4	82.9	92.1	87.9
Facility Location [38]	48.1	61.4	71.8	81.9	59.2	58.1	70.6	80.3	87.8	59.0	67.0	83.7	93.2	89.5
Angular Loss [43]	54.7	66.3	76	83.9	61.1	71.4	81.4	87.5	92.1	63.2	70.9	85.0	93.5	88.6
Proxy-NCA [23]	49.2	61.9	67.9	72.4	59.5	73.2	82.4	86.4	88.7	64.9	73.7	–	–	90.6
Deep Spectral [17]	53.2	66.1	76.7	85.2	59.2	73.1	82.2	89.0	93.0	64.3	67.6	83.7	93.3	89.4
Classification [52]	59.6	72	81.2	88.4	66.2	81.7	88.9	93.4	96	70.5	73.8	88.1	**95**	89.8
Bias Triplet [50]	46.6	58.6	70.0	–	–	79.2	86.7	91.4	–	–	63.0	79.8	90.7	–
Ours	**65.5**	**77.0**	**85.0**	**91.3**	**69.0**	**85.6**	**91.2**	**94.9**	**97.0**	**72.7**	**75.7**	**88.2**	94.8	**91.1**

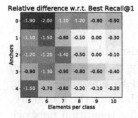

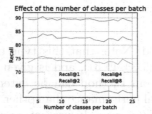

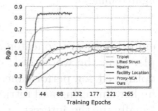

Fig. 4. The effect of the number of anchors and the number of samples per class.

Fig. 5. The effect of the number of classes per mini-batch.

Fig. 6. Recall@1 as a function of training epochs on Cars196 dataset. Figure adapted from [23].

outperforms the second best method (ABE 8 [15]) by 2.8*pp* in Recall@1. The second best method in NMI metric is the ensemble version of RLL [44] which gets outperformed by 2.4*pp* from the Group Loss. In *Stanford Online Products*, our ensemble reaches the third-highest result on the Recall@1 metric (after RLL [44] and GPW [45]) while increasing the gap with the other methods in NMI metric.

Qualitative Results

In Fig. 3 we present qualitative results on the retrieval task in all three datasets. In all cases, the query image is given on the left, with the four nearest neighbors given on the right. Green boxes indicate the cases where the retrieved image is of the same class as the query image, and red boxes indicate a different class. As we can see, our model is able to perform well even in cases where the images suffer from occlusion and rotation. On the *Cars 196* dataset, we see a successful retrieval even when the query image is taken indoors and the retrieved image outdoors, and vice-versa. The first example of *Cars 196* dataset is of particular interest. Despite that the query image contains 2 cars, its four nearest neighbors have the same class as the query image, showing the robustness of the algorithm to uncommon input image configurations. We provide the results of t-SNE [19] projection in the supplementary material.

Table 2. Retrieval and Clustering performance of our ensemble compared with other ensemble and sampling methods. Bold indicates best results.

Loss+Sampling	CUB-200-2011					CARS 196					Stanford Online Products			
	R@1	R@2	R@4	R@8	NMI	R@1	R@2	R@4	R@8	NMI	R@1	R@10	R@100	NMI
Samp. Matt. [21]	63.6	74.4	83.1	90.0	69.0	79.6	86.5	91.9	95.1	69.1	72.7	86.2	93.8	90.7
Hier. triplet [9]	57.1	68.8	78.7	86.5	–	81.4	88.0	92.7	95.7	–	74.8	88.3	94.8	–
DAMLRRM [48]	55.1	66.5	76.8	85.3	61.7	73.5	82.6	89.1	93.5	64.2	69.7	85.2	93.2	88.2
DE-DSP [6]	53.6	65.5	76.9	61.7	–	72.9	81.6	88.8	–	64.4	68.9	84.0	92.6	89.2
RLL 1 [44]	57.4	69.7	79.2	86.9	63.6	74	83.6	90.1	94.1	65.4	76.1	89.1	95.4	89.7
GPW [45]	65.7	77.0	86.3	91.2	–	84.1	90.4	94.0	96.5	–	78.2	90.5	96.0	–
Teacher-Student														
RKD [26]	61.4	73.0	81.9	89.0	–	82.3	89.8	94.2	96.6	-	75.1	88.3	95.2	–
Loss+Ensembles														
BIER 6 [24]	55.3	67.2	76.9	85.1	–	75.0	83.9	90.3	94.3	-	72.7	86.5	94.0	–
HDC 3 [51]	54.6	66.8	77.6	85.9	–	78.0	85.8	91.1	95.1	-	70.1	84.9	93.2	–
ABE 2 [15]	55.7	67.9	78.3	85.5	–	76.8	84.9	90.2	94.0	–	75.4	88.0	94.7	–
ABE 8 [15]	60.6	71.5	79.8	87.4	–	85.2	90.5	94.0	96.1	–	76.3	88.4	94.8	–
A-BIER 6 [25]	57.5	68.7	78.3	86.2	–	82.0	89.0	93.2	96.1	–	74.2	86.9	94.0	
D and C 8 [34]	65.9	76.6	84.4	90.6	69.6	84.6	90.7	94.1	96.5	70.3	75.9	88.4	94.9	90.2
RLL 3 [44]	61.3	72.7	82.7	89.4	66.1	82.1	89.3	93.7	96.7	71.8	**79.8**	**91.3**	**96.3**	90.4
Ours 2-ensemble	65.8	76.7	85.2	91.2	68.5	86.2	91.6	95.0	97.1	72.6	75.9	88.0	94.5	**91.1**
Ours 5-ensemble	**66.9**	**77.1**	**85.4**	**91.5**	**70.0**	**88.0**	**92.5**	**95.7**	**97.5**	**74.2**	76.3	88.3	94.6	**91.1**

4.5 Robustness Analysis

Number of Anchors. In Fig. 4, we show the effect of the number of anchors with respect to the number of samples per class. We do the analysis on *CUB-200-2011* dataset and give a similar analysis for *CARS* dataset in the supplementary material. The results reported are the percentage point differences in terms of Recall@1 with respect to the best performing set of parameters (see Recall@1 = 64.3 in Table 1). The number of anchors ranges from 0 to 4, while the number of samples per class varies from 5 to 10. It is worth noting that our best setting considers 1 or 2 anchors over 9 samples. Moreover, even when we do not use any anchor, the difference in Recall@1 is no more than 2*pp*.

Number of Classes per Mini-Batch. In Fig. 5, we present the change in Recall@1 on the *CUB-200-2011* dataset if we increase the number of classes we sample at each iteration. The best results are reached when the number of classes is not too large. This is a welcome property, as we are able to train on small mini-batches, known to achieve better generalization performance [14].

Convergence Rate. In Fig. 6, we present the convergence rate of the model on the *Cars 196* dataset. Within the first 30 epochs, our model achieves state-of-the-art results, making our model significantly faster than other approaches. The other models except Proxy-NCA [23], need hundreds of epochs to converge.

Implicit Regularization and Less Overfitting. In Figs. 7 and 8, we compare the results of training vs. testing on *Cars 196* [16] and *Stanford Online Products* [39] datasets. We see that the difference between Recall@1 at train and test time

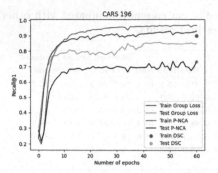
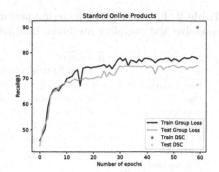

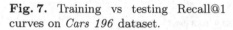

Fig. 7. Training vs testing Recall@1 curves on *Cars 196* dataset.

Fig. 8. Training vs testing Recall@1 curves on *Stanford Online Products* dataset.

is small, especially on *Stanford Online Products* dataset. On *Cars 196* the best results we get for the training set are circa 93% in the Recall@1 measure, only 7.5 percentage points (*pp*) better than what we reach in the testing set. From the works we compared the results with, the only one which reports the results on the training set is [17]. They reported results of over 90% in all three datasets (for the training sets), much above the test set accuracy which lies at 73.1% on *Cars 196* and 67.6% on *Stanford Online Products* dataset. [41] also provides results, but it uses a different network.

We further implement the P-NCA [23] loss function and perform a similar experiment, in order to be able to compare training and test accuracies directly with our method. In Fig. 7, we show the training and testing curves of P-NCA on the *Cars 196* [16] dataset. We see that while in the training set, P-NCA reaches results of 3*pp* higher than our method, in the testing set, our method outperforms P-NCA by around 10*pp*. Unfortunately, we were unable to reproduce the results of the paper [23] on *Stanford Online Products* dataset. Furthermore, even when we turn off *L2*-regularization, the generalization performance of our method does not drop at all. Our intuition is that by taking into account the structure of the entire manifold of the dataset, our method introduces a form of regularization. We can clearly see a smaller gap between training and test results when compared to competing methods, indicating less overfitting.

5   Conclusions and Future Work

In this work, we propose the Group Loss, a novel loss function for metric learning. By considering the content of a mini-batch, it promotes embedding similarity across all samples of the same class, while enforcing dissimilarity for elements of different classes. This is achieved with a differentiable layer that is used to train a convolutional network in an end-to-end fashion. Our model outperforms state-of-the-art methods on several datasets, and shows fast convergence. In our work, we did not consider any advanced sampling strategy. Instead, we randomly sample objects from a few classes at each iteration. Sampling has shown to have a very important role in feature embedding [21]. As future work, we will explore sampling techniques which can be suitable for our module.

Acknowledgements. This research was partially funded by the Humboldt Foundation through the Sofja Kovalevskaja Award. We thank Michele Fenzi, Maxim Maximov and Guillem Braso Andilla for useful discussions.

References

1. Alemu, L.T., Shah, M., Pelillo, M.: Deep constrained dominant sets for person re-identification. In: IEEE/CVF International Conference on Computer Vision, ICCV, pp. 9854–9863 (2019)
2. Bergstra, J., Bengio, Y.: Random search for hyper-parameter optimization. J. Mach. Learn. Res. **13**, 281–305 (2012)
3. Bromley, J., Guyon, I., LeCun, Y., Säckinger, E., Shah, R.: Signature verification using a "siamese" time delay neural network. In: Advances in Neural Information Processing Systems, NIPS, pp. 737–744 (1994)
4. Çakir, F., He, K., Xia, X., Kulis, B., Sclaroff, S.: Deep metric learning to rank. In: IEEE Conference on Computer Vision and Pattern Recognition, CVPR, pp. 1861–1870 (2019)
5. Chopra, S., Hadsell, R., LeCun, Y.: Learning a similarity metric discriminatively, with application to face verification. In: IEEE Computer Vision and Pattern Recognition, CVPR, pp. 539–546 (2005)
6. Duan, Y., Chen, L., Lu, J., Zhou, J.: Deep embedding learning with discriminative sampling policy. In: IEEE Computer Vision and Pattern Recognition, CVPR (2019)
7. Elezi, I., Torcinovich, A., Vascon, S., Pelillo, M.: Transductive label augmentation for improved deep network learning. In: International Conference on Pattern Recognition, ICPR, pp. 1432–1437 (2018)
8. Erdem, A., Pelillo, M.: Graph transduction as a noncooperative game. Neural Comput. **24**(3), 700–723 (2012)
9. Ge, W., Huang, W., Dong, D., Scott, M.R.: Deep metric learning with hierarchical triplet loss. In: Ferrari, V., Hebert, M., Sminchisescu, C., Weiss, Y. (eds.) ECCV 2018. LNCS, vol. 11210, pp. 272–288. Springer, Cham (2018). https://doi.org/10.1007/978-3-030-01231-1_17
10. He, K., Çakir, F., Bargal, S.A., Sclaroff, S.: Hashing as tie-aware learning to rank. In: IEEE Conference on Computer Vision and Pattern Recognition, CVPR, pp. 4023–4032 (2018)
11. He, K., Lu, Y., Sclaroff, S.: Local descriptors optimized for average precision. In: IEEE Conference on Computer Vision and Pattern Recognition, CVPR, pp. 596–605 (2018)
12. Ioffe, S., Szegedy, C.: Batch normalization: accelerating deep network training by reducing internal covariate shift. In: International Conference on Machine Learning, ICML, pp. 448–456 (2015)
13. Jégou, H., Douze, M., Schmid, C.: Product quantization for nearest neighbor search. IEEE Trans. Pattern Anal. Mach. Intell. **33**(1), 117–128 (2011)
14. Keskar, N.S., Mudigere, D., Nocedal, J., Smelyanskiy, M., Tang, P.T.P.: On large-batch training for deep learning: Generalization gap and sharp minima. In: International Conference on Learning Representations, ICLR (2017)

15. Kim, W., Goyal, B., Chawla, K., Lee, J., Kwon, K.: Attention-based ensemble for deep metric learning. In: Ferrari, V., Hebert, M., Sminchisescu, C., Weiss, Y. (eds.) ECCV 2018. LNCS, vol. 11205, pp. 760–777. Springer, Cham (2018). https://doi.org/10.1007/978-3-030-01246-5_45

16. Krause, J., Stark, M., Deng, J., Fei-Fei, L.: 3D object representations for fine-grained categorization. In: International IEEE Workshop on 3D Representation and Recognition (3dRR 2013), Sydney, Australia (2013)

17. Law, M.T., Urtasun, R., Zemel, R.S.: Deep spectral clustering learning. In: Proceedings of the 34th International Conference on Machine Learning, ICML, pp. 1985–1994 (2017)

18. Liu, L., Jiang, H., He, P., Chen, W., Liu, X., Gao, J., Han, J.: On the variance of the adaptive learning rate and beyond. In: International Conference on Learning Representations, ICLR (2020)

19. van der Maaten, L., Hinton, G.E.: Visualizing non-metric similarities in multiple maps. Mach. Learn. **87**(1), 33–55 (2012)

20. MacQueen, J.: Some methods for classification and analysis of multivariate observations. In: Proceedings of the Fifth Berkeley Symposium on Mathematical Statistics and Probability, vol. 1. pp. 281–297 (1967)

21. Manmatha, R., Wu, C., Smola, A.J., Krähenbühl, P.: Sampling matters in deep embedding learning. In: IEEE International Conference on Computer Vision, ICCV, pp. 2859–2867 (2017)

22. McDaid, A.F., Greene, D., Hurley, N.J.: Normalized mutual information to evaluate overlapping community finding algorithms. CoRR abs/1110.2515 (2011)

23. Movshovitz-Attias, Y., Toshev, A., Leung, T.K., Ioffe, S., Singh, S.: No fuss distance metric learning using proxies. In: IEEE International Conference on Computer Vision, ICCV, pp. 360–368 (2017)

24. Opitz, M., Waltner, G., Possegger, H., Bischof, H.: BIER - boosting independent embeddings robustly. In: IEEE International Conference on Computer Vision, ICCV, pp. 5199–5208 (2017)

25. Opitz, M., Waltner, G., Possegger, H., Bischof, H.: Deep metric learning with BIER: boosting independent embeddings robustly. IEEE Trans. Pattern Anal. Mach. Intell. **42**(2), 276–290 (2020)

26. Park, W., Kim, D., Lu, Y., Cho, M.: Relational knowledge distillation. In: IEEE Computer Vision and Pattern Recognition, CVPR (2019)

27. Paszke, A., et al.: Automatic differentiation in pytorch. In: NIPS Workshops (2017)

28. Pearson, K.: Notes on regression and inheritance in the case of two parents. Proc. R. Soc. London **58**, 240–242 (1895)

29. Pelillo, M.: The dynamics of nonlinear relaxation labeling processes. J. Math. Imaging Vis. **7**(4), 309–323 (1997)

30. Qian, Q., et al.: SoftTriple loss: Deep metric learning without triplet sampling. In: IEEE/CVF International Conference on Computer Vision, ICCV, pp. 6449–6457 (2019)

31. Revaud, J., Almazán, J., Rezende, R.S., de Souza, C.R.: Learning with average precision: Training image retrieval with a listwise loss. In: IEEE/CVF International Conference on Computer Vision, ICCV, pp. 5106–5115 (2019)

32. Rosenfeld, A., Hummel, R.A., Zucker, S.W.: Scene labeling by relaxation operations. IEEE Trans. Syst. Man Cybern. **6**, 420–433 (1976)

33. Russakovsky, O., et al.: ImageNet large scale visual recognition challenge. Int. J. Comput. Vis. **115**(3), 211–252 (2015)

34. Sanakoyeu, A., Tschernezki, V., Büchler, U., Ommer, B.: Divide and conquer the embedding space for metric learning. In: IEEE Computer Vision and Pattern Recognition, CVPR (2019)
35. Schroff, F., Kalenichenko, D., Philbin, J.: FaceNet: a unified embedding for face recognition and clustering. In: IEEE Conference on Computer Vision and Pattern Recognition, CVPR, pp. 815–823 (2015)
36. Schultz, M., Joachims, T.: Learning a distance metric from relative comparisons. In: Advances in Neural Information Processing Systems, NIPS, pp. 41–48 (2003)
37. Sohn, K.: Improved deep metric learning with multi-class n-pair loss objective. In: Advances in Neural Information Processing Systems, NIPS, pp. 1849–1857 (2016)
38. Song, H.O., Jegelka, S., Rathod, V., Murphy, K.: Deep metric learning via facility location. In: IEEE Conference on Computer Vision and Pattern Recognition, CVPR, pp. 2206–2214 (2017)
39. Song, H.O., Xiang, Y., Jegelka, S., Savarese, S.: Deep metric learning via lifted structured feature embedding. In: IEEE Conference on Computer Vision and Pattern Recognition, CVPR, pp. 4004–4012 (2016)
40. Szegedy, C., Liu, W., Jia, Y., Sermanet, P., Reed, S.E., Anguelov, D., Erhan, D., Vanhoucke, V., Rabinovich, A.: Going deeper with convolutions. In: IEEE Conference on Computer Vision and Pattern Recognition, CVPR. pp. 1–9 (2015)
41. Vo, N., Hays, J.: Generalization in metric learning: should the embedding layer be embedding layer? In: IEEE Winter Conference on Applications of Computer Vision, WACV, pp. 589–598 (2019)
42. Wah, C., Branson, S., Welinder, P., Perona, P., Belongie, S.: The Caltech-UCSD Birds-200-2011 Dataset. Technical report CNS-TR-2011-001, California Institute of Technology (2011)
43. Wang, J., Zhou, F., Wen, S., Liu, X., Lin, Y.: Deep metric learning with angular loss. In: IEEE International Conference on Computer Vision, ICCV, pp. 2612–2620 (2017)
44. Wang, X., Hua, Y., Kodirov, E., Hu, G., Garnier, R., Robertson, N.M.: Ranked list loss for deep metric learning. In: IEEE Conference on Computer Vision and Pattern Recognition, CVPR, pp. 5207–5216 (2019)
45. Wang, X., Han, X., Huang, W., Dong, D., Scott, M.R.: Multi-similarity loss with general pair weighting for deep metric learning. In: IEEE Computer Vision and Pattern Recognition, CVPR (2019)
46. Weibull, J.: Evolutionary Game Theory. MIT Press, Cambridge (1997)
47. Weinberger, K.Q., Saul, L.K.: Distance metric learning for large margin nearest neighbor classification. J. Mach. Learn. Res. 10, 207–244 (2009)
48. Xu, X., Yang, Y., Deng, C., Zheng, F.: Deep asymmetric metric learning via rich relationship mining. In: IEEE Computer Vision and Pattern Recognition, CVPR
49. Xuan, H., Souvenir, R., Pless, R.: Deep randomized ensembles for metric learning. In: Ferrari, V., Hebert, M., Sminchisescu, C., Weiss, Y. (eds.) ECCV 2018. LNCS, vol. 11220, pp. 751–762. Springer, Cham (2018). https://doi.org/10.1007/978-3-030-01270-0_44
50. Yu, B., Liu, T., Gong, M., Ding, C., Tao, D.: Correcting the triplet selection bias for triplet loss. In: Ferrari, V., Hebert, M., Sminchisescu, C., Weiss, Y. (eds.) ECCV 2018. LNCS, vol. 11210, pp. 71–86. Springer, Cham (2018). https://doi.org/10.1007/978-3-030-01231-1_5
51. Yuan, Y., Yang, K., Zhang, C.: Hard-aware deeply cascaded embedding. In: IEEE International Conference on Computer Vision, CVPR, pp. 814–823 (2017)
52. Zhai, A., Wu, H.: Classification is a strong baseline for deep metric learning. In: British Machine Vision Conference BMVC, p. 91 (2019)

53. Zhang, X., Zhou, F., Lin, Y., Zhang, S.: Embedding label structures for fine-grained feature representation. In: IEEE Conference on Computer Vision and Pattern Recognition, CVPR, pp. 1114–1123 (2016)
54. Zhao, K., Xu, J., Cheng, M.: RegularFace: deep face recognition via exclusive regularization. In: IEEE Conference on Computer Vision and Pattern Recognition, CVPR, pp. 1136–1144 (2019)
55. Zheng, X., Ji, R., Sun, X., Zhang, B., Wu, Y., Huang, F.: Towards optimal fine grained retrieval via decorrelated centralized loss with normalize-scale layer. In: Conference on Artificial Intelligence, AAAI, pp. 9291–9298 (2019)

Learning Object Depth from Camera Motion and Video Object Segmentation

Brent A. Griffin[(✉)] and Jason J. Corso

University of Michigan, Ann Arbor, USA
{griffb,jjcorso}@umich.edu

Abstract. Video object segmentation, i.e., the separation of a target object from background in video, has made significant progress on real and challenging videos in recent years. To leverage this progress in 3D applications, this paper addresses the problem of learning to estimate the depth of segmented objects given some measurement of camera motion (e.g., from robot kinematics or vehicle odometry). We achieve this by, first, introducing a diverse, extensible dataset and, second, designing a novel deep network that estimates the depth of objects using only segmentation masks and uncalibrated camera movement. Our data-generation framework creates artificial object segmentations that are scaled for changes in distance between the camera and object, and our network learns to estimate object depth even with segmentation errors. We demonstrate our approach across domains using a robot camera to locate objects from the YCB dataset and a vehicle camera to locate obstacles while driving.

Keywords: Depth estimation · Video object segmentation · Robotics

1 Introduction

Perceiving environments in three dimensions (3D) is important for locating objects, identifying free space, and motion planning in robotics and autonomous vehicles. Although these domains typically rely on 3D sensors to measure depth and identify free space (e.g., LiDAR [12] or RGBD cameras [10]), classifying and understanding raw 3D data is a challenging and ongoing area of research [21,23,30,40]. Alternatively, RGB cameras are less expensive and more ubiquitous than 3D sensors, and there are many more datasets and methods based on RGB images [8,17,27]. Thus, even when 3D sensors are available, RGB images remain a critical modality for understanding data and identifying objects [11,52].

To identify objects in a sequence of images, video object segmentation (VOS) addresses the problem of densely labeling target objects in video. VOS is a hotly studied area of video understanding, with frequent developments and improving

Electronic supplementary material The online version of this chapter (https://doi.org/10.1007/978-3-030-58571-6_18) contains supplementary material, which is available to authorized users.

© Springer Nature Switzerland AG 2020
A. Vedaldi et al. (Eds.): ECCV 2020, LNCS 12352, pp. 295–312, 2020.
https://doi.org/10.1007/978-3-030-58571-6_18

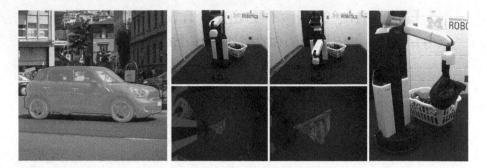

Fig. 1. Depth from Video Object Segmentation. Video object segmentation algorithms can densely segment target objects in a variety of settings (DAVIS [38], *left*). Given object segmentations and a measure of camera movement (e.g., from vehicle odometry or robot kinematics, *right*), our network can estimate an object's depth

performance on challenging VOS benchmark datasets [25,38,39,49,55]. These algorithmic advances in VOS support learning object class models [36,47], scene parsing [28,48], action recognition [31,43,44], and video editing applications [5].

Given that many VOS methods perform well in unstructured environments, in this work, we show that VOS can similarly support 3D perception for robots and autonomous vehicles. We take inspiration from work in psychology that establishes how people perceive depth motion from the optical expansion or contraction of objects [19,46], and we develop a deep network that learns object depth estimation from uncalibrated camera motion and video object segmentation (see Fig. 1). We depict our optical expansion model in Fig. 2, which uses a moving pinhole camera and binary segmentation masks for an object in view. To estimate an object's depth, we only need segmentations at two distances with an estimate of relative camera movement. Notably, most autonomous hardware platforms already measure movement, and even hand-held devices can track movement using an inertial measurement unit or GPS. Furthermore, although we do not study it here, if hardware-based measurements are not available, structure from motion is also plausible to recover camera motion [20,34,42].

In recent work [14], we use a similar model for VOS-based visual servo control, depth estimation, and mobile robot grasping. However, our previous analytic depth estimation method does not adequately account for segmentation errors. For real-world objects in complicated scenes, segmentation quality can change among frames, with typical errors including: incomplete object segmentation, partial background inclusion, or segmenting the wrong object. Thus, we develop and train a deep network that learns to accommodate segmentation errors and reduces object depth estimation error from [14] by as much as 59%.

The first contribution of our paper is developing a learning-based approach to object depth estimation using motion and segmentation, which we experimentally evaluate in multiple domains. To the best of our knowledge, this work is the first to use a learned, segmentation-based approach to depth estimation, which

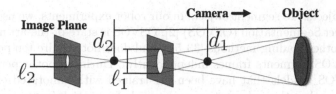

Fig. 2. Optical Expansion and Depth. An object's projection onto the image plane scales inversely with the depth between the camera and object. We determine an object's depth (d) using video object segmentation, relative camera movement, and corresponding changes in scale (ℓ). In this example, $d_1 = \frac{d_2}{2}$, $\ell_1 = 2\ell_2$, and $d_1\ell_1 = d_2\ell_2$

has many advantages. First, we use segmentation masks as input, so our network does not rely on application-specific visual characteristics and is useful in multiple domains. Second, we process a series of observations simultaneously, thereby mitigating errors associated with any individual camera movement or segmentation mask. Third, our VOS implementation operates on streaming video and our method, using a single forward pass, runs in real-time. Fourth, our approach only requires a single RGB camera and relative motion (no 3D sensors). Finally, our depth estimation accuracy will improve with future innovations in VOS.

A second contribution of our paper is the Object Depth via Motion and Segmentation (ODMS) dataset.[1] This is the first dataset for VOS-based depth estimation and enables learning-based algorithms to be leveraged in this problem space. ODMS data consist of a series of object segmentation masks, camera movement distances, and ground truth object depth. Due to the high cost of data collection and user annotation [3,50], manually collecting training data would either be cost prohibitive or severely limit network complexity to avoid overfitting. Instead, we configure our dataset to continuously generate synthetic training data with random distances, object profiles, and even perturbations, so we can train networks of arbitrary complexity. Furthermore, because our network input consists simply of binary segmentation masks and distances, we show that domain transfer from synthetic training data to real-world applications is viable. Finally, as a benchmark evaluation, we create four ODMS validation and test sets with over 15,650 examples in multiple domains, including robotics and driving.

2 Related Work

We use video object segmentation (VOS) to process raw input video and output the binary segmentation masks we use to estimate object depth in this work. Unsupervised VOS usually relies on generic object motion and appearance cues [9,16,24,37,53,54], while semi-supervised VOS segments objects that are specified in user-annotated examples [1,6,15,32,35,58]. Thus, semi-supervised VOS can learn a specific object's visual characteristics and reliably segment dynamic

---

[1] Dataset and source code website: https://github.com/griffbr/ODMS.

or static objects. To segment objects in our robot experiments, we use One-Shot Video Object Segmentation (OSVOS) [2]. OSVOS is state-of-the-art in VOS, has influenced other leading methods [33,51], and does not require temporal consistency (OSVOS segments frames independently). During robot experiments, we apply OSVOS models that have been pre-trained with annotated examples of each object rather than annotating an example frame at inference time.

We take inspiration from many existing datasets in this work. VOS research has benefited from benchmark datasets like SegTrackv2 [25,49], DAVIS [38,39], and YouTube-VOS [55], which have provided increasing amounts of annotated training data. The recently developed MannequinChallenge dataset [26] trained a network to predict dense depth maps from videos with people, with improved performance when given an additional human-mask input. Among automotive datasets, Cityscapes [7] focuses on *semantic segmentation* (i.e., assigning class labels to all pixels), KITTI [13] includes benchmarks separate from segmentation for single-image depth completion and prediction, and SYNTHIA [41] has driving sequences with simultaneous ground truth for semantic segmentation and depth images. In this work, our ODMS dataset focuses on **O**bject **D**epth via **M**otion and **S**egmentation, establishing a new benchmark for segmentation-based 3D perception in robotics and driving. In addition, ODMS is arbitrarily extensible, which makes learning-based methods feasible in this problem space.

3   Optical Expansion Model

Our optical expansion model (Fig. 2) forms the theoretical underpinning for our learning-based approach in Sect. 4 and ODMS dataset in Sect. 5. In this section, we derive the complete model and analytic solution for segmentation-based depth estimation. We start by defining the inputs we use to estimate depth. Assume we are given a set of $n \geq 2$ observations that consist of masks

$$M := \{M_1, M_2, \cdots, M_n\} \tag{1}$$

segmenting an object and corresponding camera positions on the optical axis

$$z := \{z_1, z_2, \cdots, z_n\}. \tag{2}$$

Each binary mask image M_i consists of pixel-level labels where 1 indicates a pixel belongs to a specific segmented object and 0 is background. For the solutions in this work, the optical axis's origin and absolute position of z is inconsequential.

3.1   Relating Depth and Scale

We use changes in scale of an object's segmentation mask to estimate depth. As depicted in Fig. 2, we relate depth and scale across observations using

$$d_i \ell_i = d_j \ell_j \implies \frac{\ell_j}{\ell_i} = \frac{d_i}{d_j}, \tag{3}$$

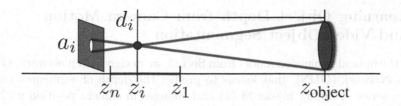

Fig. 3. Calculating Object Depth. First, we define d_i in terms of its component parts z_{object} and z_i (6). Second, we relate measured changes in camera pose z_i and segmentation area a_i across observations (7). Finally, we solve for z_{object} using (8)

where ℓ_i is the object's projected scale in $\mathbf{M}_i$, d_i is the distance on the optical axis from z_i to the visible perimeter of the segmented object, and $\frac{\ell_j}{\ell_i}$ is the object's change in scale between $\mathbf{M}_i$ and $\mathbf{M}_j$. Notably, it is more straightforward to track changes in scale using area (i.e., the sum of mask pixels) than length measurements. Thus, we use Galileo Galilei's Square-cube law to modify (3) as

$$a_j = a_i \left(\frac{\ell_j}{\ell_i} \right)^2 \implies \frac{\ell_j}{\ell_i} = \frac{\sqrt{a_j}}{\sqrt{a_i}} = \frac{d_i}{d_j}, \tag{4}$$

where a_i is an object's projected area at d_i and $\frac{\sqrt{a_j}}{\sqrt{a_i}}$ is equal to the change in scale between $\mathbf{M}_i$ and $\mathbf{M}_j$. Combining (3) and (4), we relate observations as

$$d_i \sqrt{a_i} = d_j \sqrt{a_j} = c, \tag{5}$$

where c is a constant corresponding to an object's orthogonal surface area.

3.2 Object Depth Solution

To find object depth d_i in (5), we first redefine d_i in terms of its components as

$$d_i := z_i - z_{\text{object}}, \tag{6}$$

where z_{object} is the object's static position on the optical axis and $\dot{z}_{\text{object}} = 0$ (see Fig. 3). Substituting (6) in (5), we can now relate observations as

$$(z_i - z_{\text{object}})\sqrt{a_i} = (z_j - z_{\text{object}})\sqrt{a_j} = c. \tag{7}$$

From (7), we can solve z_{object} from any two unique observations ($z_i \neq z_j$) as

$$z_{\text{object}} = \frac{z_i \sqrt{a_i} - z_j \sqrt{a_j}}{\sqrt{a_i} - \sqrt{a_j}} = \frac{z_i - z_j \frac{\sqrt{a_j}}{\sqrt{a_i}}}{1 - \frac{\sqrt{a_j}}{\sqrt{a_i}}}. \tag{8}$$

Substituting z_{object} in (6), we can now find object depth d_i at any observation.

4   Learning Object Depth from Camera Motion and Video Object Segmentation

Using the optical expansion model from Sect. 3, we design a deep network, **O**bject **D**epth **N**etwork (ODN), that learns to predict the depth of segmented objects given a series of binary masks M (1) and changes in camera position z (2). To keep ODN broadly applicable, we formulate a normalized relative distance input in Sect. 4.1. In Sects. 4.2 and 4.3, we derive three unique losses for learning depth estimation. After some remarks on using intermediate observations in Sect. 4.4, we detail our ODN architecture in Sect. 4.5.

4.1   Normalized Relative Distance Input

To learn to estimate a segmented object's depth, we first derive a normalized relative distance input that increases generalization. As in Sect. 3, assume we are given a set of n segmentation masks M with corresponding camera positions z. We can use M and z as inputs to predict object depth, however, a direct z input enables a learned prior based on absolute camera position, which limits applicability at inference. To avoid this, we define a relative distance input

$$\Delta \mathbf{z} := \{z_2 - z_1, z_3 - z_1, \cdots, z_n - z_1\}, \tag{9}$$

where $z_1, z_2, \cdots, z_n$ are the sorted z positions with the minimum z_1 closest to the object (see Fig. 3) and $\Delta \mathbf{z} \in \mathbb{R}^{n-1}$. Although $\Delta \mathbf{z}$ consists only of relative changes in position, it still requires learning a specific SI unit of distance and enables a prior based on camera movement range. Thus, we normalize (9) as

$$\bar{\mathbf{z}} := \left\{ \frac{z_i - z_1}{z_n - z_1} | z \in \mathbf{z}, 1 < i < n \right\}, \tag{10}$$

where $z_n - z_1$ is the camera move range, $\frac{z_i - z_1}{z_n - z_1} \in (0, 1)$, and $\bar{\mathbf{z}} \in \mathbb{R}^{n-2}$.

Using $\bar{\mathbf{z}}$ as our camera motion input increases the general applicability of ODN. First, $\bar{\mathbf{z}}$ uses the relative difference formulation, so ODN does not learn to associate depth with an absolute camera position. Second, $\bar{\mathbf{z}}$ is dimensionless, so our trained ODN can use camera movements on the scale of millimeters or kilometers (it makes no difference). Finally, $\bar{\mathbf{z}}$ is made a more compact motion input by removing the unnecessary constants $\frac{z_1 - z_1}{z_n - z_1} = 0$ and $\frac{z_n - z_1}{z_n - z_1} = 1$ in (10).

4.2   Normalized Relative Depth Loss

Our basic depth loss, given input masks M (1) and relative distances $\Delta \mathbf{z}$ (9), is

$$\mathcal{L}_d(\mathbf{W}) := |d_1 - f_d(\mathsf{M}, \Delta \mathbf{z}, \mathbf{W})|, \tag{11}$$

where **W** are the trainable network parameters, d_1 is the ground truth object depth at z_1 (6), and $f_d \in \mathbb{R}$ is the predicted depth. To use the normalized distance input $\bar{\mathbf{z}}$ (10), we modify (11) and define a normalized depth loss as

$$\mathcal{L}_{\bar{d}}(\mathbf{W}) := \left| \frac{d_1}{z_n - z_1} - f_{\bar{d}}(\mathsf{M}, \bar{\mathbf{z}}, \mathbf{W}) \right|, \tag{12}$$

where $\frac{d_1}{z_n - z_1}$ is the normalized object depth and $f_{\bar{d}}$ is a dimensionless depth prediction that is in terms of the input camera movement range. To use $f_{\bar{d}}$ at inference, we multiply the normalized output $f_{\bar{d}}$ by $(z_n - z_1)$ to find d_1.

4.3   Relative Scale Loss

We increase depth accuracy and simplify ODN's prediction by learning to estimate relative changes in segmentation scale. In Sect. 4.2, we define loss functions that use a similar input-output paradigm to the analytic solution in Sect. 3. However, training ODN to directly predict depth requires learning many operations. Alternatively, if ODN only predicts the relative change in segmentation scale, we can finish calculating depth using (8). Thus, we define a loss for predicting the relative scale as

$$\mathcal{L}_\ell(\mathbf{W}) := \left| \frac{\ell_n}{\ell_1} - f_\ell(\mathsf{M}, \bar{\mathbf{z}}, \mathbf{W}) \right|, \tag{13}$$

where $\frac{\ell_n}{\ell_1} = \frac{d_1}{d_n} \in (0,1)$ (3) is the ground truth distance-based change in scale between $\mathbf{M}_n$ and $\mathbf{M}_1$ and f_ℓ is the predicted scale change. To use f_ℓ at inference, we output $f_\ell \approx \frac{\ell_n}{\ell_1}$ and, using (4) to substitute $\frac{\ell_j}{\ell_i}$ for $\frac{\sqrt{a_j}}{\sqrt{a_i}}$ in (8), find z_{object} as

$$z_{\text{object}} = \frac{z_1 - z_n f_\ell}{1 - f_\ell} \approx \frac{z_1 - z_n \left(\frac{\ell_n}{\ell_1} \right)}{1 - \left(\frac{\ell_n}{\ell_1} \right)}. \tag{14}$$

After finding z_{object} in (14), we use (6) to find object depth as $d_1 = z_1 - z_{\text{object}}$.

4.4   Remarks on Using Intermediate Observations

Although the ground truth label d_1 in (11)–(12) is determined only by camera position z_1 and label $\frac{\ell_n}{\ell_1}$ in (13) is determined only by endpoint masks $\mathbf{M}_n$, $\mathbf{M}_1$, we emphasize that intermediate mask and distance inputs are still useful. Consider that, first, the ground truth mask scale monotonically decreases across all observations (i.e., $\forall i, \ell_{i+1} < \ell_i$). Second, the distance inputs make it possible to extrapolate d_1 and $\frac{\ell_n}{\ell_1}$ from intermediate changes in scale. Third, if z_1, z_n, $\mathbf{M}_1$, or $\mathbf{M}_n$ have significant errors, intermediate observations provide the best prediction for d_1 or $\frac{\ell_n}{\ell_1}$. Finally, experiments in Sect. 6.1 show that intermediate observations improve performance for networks trained on (11), (12), or (13).

4.5   Object Depth Estimation Network Architecture

Our ODN architecture is shown in Fig. 4. The input to the first convolution layer consists of n 112×112 binary segmentation masks and, for three configurations in Sect. 6.1, a radial image. The first convolution layer uses 14×14 kernels, and the remaining convolution layers use 3×3 kernels in four residual blocks [18]. After average pooling the last residual block, the relative camera position

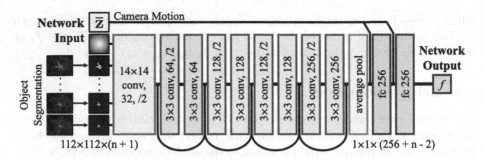

Fig. 4. Object depth network architecture

(e.g., $\bar{\mathbf{z}}$) is included with the input to the first two fully-connected layers, which use ReLU activation and 20% dropout for all inputs during training [45]. After the first two fully-connected layers, our ODN architecture ends with one last fully-connected neuron that, depending on chosen loss, is the output object depth $f_d(\mathsf{M}, \Delta\mathbf{z}, \mathbf{W}) \in \mathbb{R}$ using (11), normalized object depth $f_{\bar{d}}(\mathsf{M}, \bar{\mathbf{z}}, \mathbf{W})$ using (12), or relative scale $f_\ell(\mathsf{M}, \bar{\mathbf{z}}, \mathbf{W})$ using (13).

5 ODMS Dataset

To train our object depth networks from Sect. 4, we introduce the **O**bject **D**epth via **M**otion and **S**egmentation dataset (ODMS). In Sect. 5.1, we explain how ODMS continuously generates new labeled training data, making learning-based techniques feasible in this problem space. In Sect. 5.2, we describe the robotics-, driving-, and simulation-based test and validation sets we develop for evaluation. Finally, in Sect. 5.3, we detail our ODMS training implementation.

5.1 Generating Random Object Masks at Scale

Camera Distance and Depth. We generate new training data by, first, determining n random camera distances (i.e., $\mathbf{z}$ (2)) for each training example. To make ODMS configurable, assume we are given a minimum camera movement range ($\Delta z_{\min}$) and minimum and maximum object depths ($d_{\min}, d_{\max}$). Using these parameters, we define distributions for uniform random variables to find the endpoints

$$z_1 \sim \mathcal{U}[d_{\min}, d_{\max} - \Delta z_{\min}], \tag{15}$$

$$z_n \sim \mathcal{U}[z_1 + \Delta z_{\min}, d_{\max}], \tag{16}$$

and, for $1 < i < n$, the remaining intermediate camera positions

$$z_i \sim \mathcal{U}(z_1, z_n). \tag{17}$$

Using (15)–(17) to select $\mathbf{z} = \{z_1, \cdots, z_n\}$ ensures that the random camera movement range is independent of the number of observations n. For the object depth label d_1, we choose an optical axis such that $z_{\text{object}} = 0$ and $d_1 = z_1$ (6). We generate data in this work using $\Delta z_{\min} = d_{\min} = 0.1$ m and $d_{\max} = 0.7$ m.

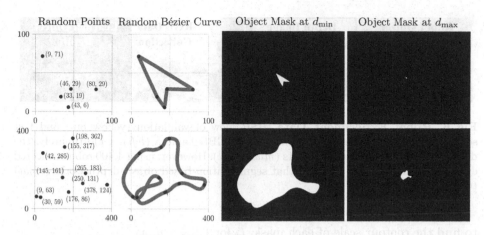

Fig. 5. Generating Random Object Masks at Scale. Initializing from a random number of points within a variable boundary (*left*), random curves complete the contour of each simulated object (*middle left*). These contours are then scaled for each simulated distance and output as a filled binary mask (*right*). Each generated object is unique

Random Object Contour and Binary Masks. After determining $\mathbf{z}$, we generate a random object with n binary masks (i.e., M (1)) scaled for each distance in $\mathbf{z}$ (see Fig. 5). To make each object unique, we randomly select parameters that change the object's size ($s_\mathbf{p}$), number of contour points ($n_\mathbf{p}$), and contour smoothness (r_B, ρ_B). In this work, we randomly select $s_\mathbf{p}$ from $\{100, 200, 300, 400\}$ and $n_\mathbf{p}$ from $\{3, 4, \cdots, 10\}$. Using $s_\mathbf{p}$ and $n_\mathbf{p}$, we select each of the random initial contour points, $\mathbf{p}_i \in \mathbb{R}^2$ for $1 \le i \le n_\mathbf{p}$, as

$$\mathbf{p}_i = [x_i, y_i]', \ x_i \sim \mathcal{U}[0, s_\mathbf{p}], \ y_i \sim \mathcal{U}[0, s_\mathbf{p}]. \tag{18}$$

To complete the object's contour, we use cubic Bézier curves with random smoothness to connect each set of adjacent coordinates $\mathbf{p}_i$, $\mathbf{p}_j$ from (18). Essentially, r_B and ρ_B determine polar coordinates for the two intermediate Bézier control points of each curve. $\arctan(\rho_B)$ is the rotation of a control point away from the line connecting $\mathbf{p}_i$ and $\mathbf{p}_j$, while r_B is the relative radius of a control point away from $\mathbf{p}_i$ (e.g., $r_B = 1$ has a radius of $\|\mathbf{p}_i - \mathbf{p}_j\|$). In this work, we randomly select r_B from $\{0.01, 0.05, 0.2, 0.5\}$ and ρ_B from $\{0.01, 0.05, 0.2\}$ for each object. In general, lower r_B and ρ_B values result in a more straight-edged contour, while higher values result in a more curved and widespread contour. As two illustrative examples in Fig. 5, the top "straight-edged" object uses $r_B = \rho_B = 0.01$ and the bottom "curved" object uses $r_B = 0.5$ and $\rho_B = 0.2$.

To simulate object segmentation over multiple distances, we scale the generated contour to match each distance $z_i \in \mathbf{z}$ from (15)–(17) and output a set of binary masks $\mathbf{M}_i \in \mathsf{M}$ (1). We let the initial contour represent the object's image projection at $d_{\min}$, and designate this initial scale as $\ell_{\min} = 1$. Having chosen an optical axis such that $z_{\text{object}} = 0$ in (6) (i.e., $d_i = z_i$), we modify (3)

Fig. 6. Robot Experiment Data. HSR view of validation (yellow bin) and test set objects (blue bin) using head-mounted RGBD camera (*left*). Unfortunately, the depth image is missing many objects (*middle left*). However, using 4,400 robot-collected examples (*middle right*), we find that segmentation-based object depth works (*right*) (Color figure online)

to find the contour scale of each mask, ℓ_i for $1 \leq i \leq n$, as

$$\ell_i = \frac{d_{\min}\ell_{\min}}{d_i} = \frac{d_{\min}}{z_i}. \tag{19}$$

After finding ℓ_i, we scale, fill, and add the object contour to each mask $\mathbf{M}_i$. In this work, we position the contour by centering the scaled boundary $(\ell_i s_{\mathbf{p}})$ in a 480×640 mask. Our complete object-generating process is shown in Fig. 5.

5.2   Robotics, Driving, and Simulation Validation and Test Sets

We test object depth estimation in a variety of settings using four ODMS validation and test sets. These are based on robot experiments, driving, and simulated data with and without perturbations and provide a repeatable benchmark for ablation studies and future methods. All examples include $n \geq 10$ observations.

Robot Validation and Test Set. Our robot experiment data provide an evaluation for object depth estimation from a physical platform using video object segmentation on real-world objects in a practical use case. We collect data using a Toyota Human Support Robot (HSR), which has a 4-DOF manipulator arm with an end effector-mounted wide-angle grasp camera [56,57]. Using HSR's prismatic torso, we collect 480×640 grasp-camera images as the end effector approaches an object of interest, with the intent that HSR can estimate the object's depth using motion and segmentation. We use 16 custom household objects for our validation set and 24 YCB objects [4] for our test set (Fig. 6, left). For each object, we collect 30 images distanced 2 cm apart of the object in isolation and, as an added challenge, 30 more images in a cluttered setting (see Fig. 6, middle right). The ground truth object depth (d_1) is manually measured at the closest camera position and propagated to the remaining images using HSR's kinematics and encoder values, which also measure camera positions ($\mathbf{z}$). To generate binary masks (M), we segment objects using OSVOS [2], which we fine-tune on each object using three annotated images from outside of the

Fig. 7. Driving Test Set Examples and Results. The ODN_ℓ object depth error is -6 and -23 cm for the pedestrians, -10 cm for the bicycle, and -4 cm for the car

validation and test sets. We vary the input camera movement range between 18–58 cm and object depth (d_1) between 11–60 cm to generate 4,400 robot object depth estimation examples (1,760 validation and 2,640 test).

Driving Validation and Test Set. Our driving data provide an evaluation for object depth estimation in a faster moving automotive domain with greater camera movement and depth distances. Our goal is to track driving obstacles using an RGB camera, segmentation, and vehicle odometry. Challenges include changing object perspectives, camera rotation from vehicle turning, and moving objects. We collect data using the SYNTHIA Dataset [41], which includes ground truth semantic segmentation, depth images, and vehicle odometry in a variety of urban scenes and weather conditions. To generate binary masks (M), we use SYNTHIA's semantic segmentation over a series of 760×1280 frames for unique instances of pedestrians, bicycles, and cars (see Fig. 7). For each instance, the ground truth object depth (d_1) is the mean depth image values contained within corresponding mask $\mathbf{M}_1$. As the vehicle moves, we track changes in camera position ($\mathbf{z}$) along the optical axis of position z_1. With an input camera movement range between 4.2–68 m and object depth (d_1) between 1.5–62 m, we generate 1,250 driving object depth estimation examples (500 validation and 750 test).

Simulation Validation and Test Sets. Finally, we generate a set of normal and perturbation-based data for simulated objects. The normal set and the continuously-generated training data we use in Sect. 5.3 both use the same mask-generating procedure from Sect. 5.1, so the normal set provides a consistent evaluation for the type of simulated objects we use during training.

To test robustness for segmentation errors, we also generate a set of simulated objects with random perturbations added to each mask, $\mathbf{M}_i$ for $1 \leq i \leq n$, as

$$p_i \sim \mathcal{N}(0,1), \ \mathbf{M}_{i,p} = \begin{cases} \text{dilate}(\mathbf{M}_i, \lfloor p_i + 0.5 \rfloor) & \text{if } p_i \geq 0 \\ \text{erode}(\mathbf{M}_i, \lfloor p_i + 0.5 \rfloor) & \text{if } p_i < 0 \end{cases}, \quad (20)$$

where $\mathcal{N}(0,1)$ is a Gaussian distribution with $\mu = 0$, $\sigma^2 = 1$, p_i randomly determines the perturbation type and magnitude, and $\mathbf{M}_{i,p}$ is the perturbed version of initial mask $\mathbf{M}_i$. Notably, the sign of p_i determines a dilation or

Table 1. ODMS test set tesults

Config. ID	Object Depth Method	n Input Masks	Mean Percent Error (21)				
			Robot Objects	Driving Objects	Simulated Objects		All Sets
					Normal	Perturb	
ODN_ℓ	$\mathcal{L}_\ell$ (13)	10	19.3	**30.1**	8.3	18.2	**19.0**
$ODN_{\bar{d}}$	$\mathcal{L}_{\bar{d}}$ (12)	10	18.5	30.9	8.2	18.5	19.0
ODN_d	$\mathcal{L}_d$ (11)	10	**18.1**	47.5	**5.1**	**11.2**	20.5
VOS-DE	[14]	10	32.6	36.0	7.9	33.6	27.5

erosion perturbation, and the rounded magnitude of p_i determines the number of iterations using a square connectivity equal to one. When generating perturbed masks $\mathbf{M}_{i,p}$, we make no other changes to input data or ground truth labels.

We generate 5,000 object depth estimation examples (2,000 validation and 3,000 test) for both the normal and perturbation-based simulation sets.

5.3 Training Object Depth Networks Using ODMS

Using the architecture in Sect. 4.5, we train networks for depth loss $\mathcal{L}_d$ (11), normalized relative depth loss $\mathcal{L}_{\bar{d}}$ (12), and relative scale loss $\mathcal{L}_\ell$ (13). We call these networks ODN_d, $ODN_{\bar{d}}$, and ODN_ℓ respectively. We train each network with a batch size of 512 randomly-generated training examples using the framework in Sect. 5.1 with $n = 10$ observations per prediction. We train each network for 5,000 iterations using the Adam Optimizer [22] with a 1×10^{-3} learning rate, which takes 2.6 days using a single GPU (GTX 1080 Ti). Notably, the primary time constraint for training is generating new masks, and we can train a similar configuration with $n = 2$ for 5,000 iterations in 15 h.

6   Experimental Results

Our primary experiments and analysis use the four ODMS test sets. For each test set, the number of network training iterations is determined by the best validation performance, which we check at every ten training iterations. We determine the effectiveness of each depth estimation method using the mean percent error for each test set, which is calculated for each example as

$$\text{Percent Error} = \left| \frac{d_1 - \hat{d}_1}{d_1} \right| \times 100\%, \tag{21}$$

where d_1 and $\hat{d}_1$ are ground truth and predicted object depth at final pose z_1.

6.1   ODMS Test Results

Object depth estimation results for all four ODMS test sets are provided in Table 1 for our three ODN configurations and VOS-DE [14]. We use $n = 10$

Table 2. ODMS test set results vs. Number of observations

Config.	Depth	Overall Mean Percent Error				Average Training Iterations			
ID	Method	$n = 2$	$n = 3$	$n = 5$	$n = 10$	$n = 2$	$n = 3$	$n = 5$	$n = 10$
ODN_ℓ	$\mathcal{L}_\ell$ (13)	**20.4**	**19.9**	20.0	**19.0**	**2,590**	**3,460**	**3,060**	**3,138**
$ODN_{\bar{d}}$	$\mathcal{L}_{\bar{d}}$ (12)	22.7	20.9	**19.9**	19.0	3,993	4,330	3,265	3,588
ODN_d	$\mathcal{L}_d$ (11)	21.6	21.2	20.5	20.5	4,138	4,378	4,725	3,300
VOS-DE	[14]	50.3	29.7	27.6	27.5	N/A	N/A	N/A	N/A

Table 3. Test results with perturb training data and radial input image

Config.	Object Depth	Radial Input	Type of Training	Mean Percent Error (21)				
						Simulated		All
ID	Method	Image	Data	Robot	Driving	Normal	Perturb	Sets
Perturb Training Data								
$ODN_{\ell p}$	$\mathcal{L}_\ell$ (13)	No	Perturb	22.2	**29.0**	11.1	13.0	18.8
$ODN_{\bar{d}p}$	$\mathcal{L}_{\bar{d}}$ (12)	No	Perturb	25.8	31.4	11.1	13.2	20.4
ODN_{dp}	$\mathcal{L}_d$ (11)	No	Perturb	20.1	60.9	7.3	**8.2**	24.1
Radial Input Image								
$ODN_{\ell r}$	$\mathcal{L}_\ell$ (13)	Yes	Normal	**13.1**	31.7	8.6	17.9	**17.8**
$ODN_{\bar{d}r}$	$\mathcal{L}_{\bar{d}}$ (12)	Yes	Normal	15.2	30.9	8.4	18.5	18.3
ODN_{dr}	$\mathcal{L}_d$ (11)	Yes	Normal	13.4	48.6	**5.6**	11.2	19.7

observations, and "All Sets" is an aggregate score across all test sets. Notably, VOS-DE uses only the largest connected region of each mask to reduce noise.

The relative scale-based ODN_ℓ performs best on the Driving set and overall. We show a few quantitative depth estimation examples for ODN_ℓ in Fig. 6 and Fig. 7. Normalized depth-based $ODN_{\bar{d}}$ comes in second overall, and depth-based ODN_d performs best in three categories but worst in driving. Basically, ODN_d gets a performance boost from a camera movement range- and depth-based prior (i.e., $\Delta\mathbf{z}$ and f_d in (11)) at the cost of applicability to other domains where the scale of camera input and depth will vary. On the other hand, the generalization of $ODN_{\bar{d}}$ and ODN_ℓ from small distances in training to large distances in Driving is highly encouraging. VOS-DE performs the worst overall, particularly on test sets with segmentation errors or moving objects. However, VOS-DE does perform well on normal simulated objects, which only have mask discretization errors.

Results on Changing the Number of Observations. Object depth estimation results for varied number of observations are provided in Table 2. We repeat training and validation for each new configuration to learn depth estimation with less observations. As n changes, each test set example uses the same endpoint observations (i.e., $\mathbf{M}_1, \mathbf{M}_n, z_1, z_n$). However, the $n - 2$ intermediate observations are evenly distributed and do change (e.g., $n = 2$ has none). Notably, at $n = 2$, VOS-DE is equivalent to (8) and $\bar{\mathbf{z}} \in \mathbb{R}^{n-2}$ (10) gives no input to $ODN_{\bar{d}}$, ODN_ℓ.

ODN_ℓ has the most consistent and best performance for all n settings, aside from a second place to $ODN_{\bar{d}}$ at $n = 5$. ODN_ℓ also requires the fewest training iterations for all n. In general, $ODN_{\bar{d}}$ and ODN_d performance starts to decrease for $n \leq 3$. VOS-DE performance decreases most significantly at $n = 2$, having 2.5 times the error of ODN_ℓ at $n = 2$. Amazingly, all $n = 2$ ODN configurations outperform $n = 10$ VOS-DE. Thus, even with significantly less input data, our learning-based approach outperforms prior work.

Results with Perturbation Training Data. We train each $n = 10$ ODN on continuously-generated perturbation data (20) from Sect. 5.2. As shown in Table 3, this improves performance for each ODN on the Perturb test set, and demonstrates that we can learn robust depth estimation for specific errors. The perturbed ODN_ℓ configuration, $ODN_{\ell p}$, improves performance overall and has the best Driving result of any method.

Results with Radial Input Image. For our final ODMS results in Table 3, we train each $n = 10$ ODN with an added input radial image for convolution. Pixel values $\in [0, 1]$ are scaled radially from 1 at the center to 0 at each corner (see Fig. 4). This serves a similar purpose to coordinate convolution [29] but simply focuses on how centered segmentation mask regions are. This improves overall performance for each ODN, particularly on the Robot test, where objects are generally centered for grasping and peripheral segmentation errors can be ignored. Notably, $ODN_{\ell r}$ has the best Robot and overall result of any method.

6.2 Robot Object Depth Estimation and Grasping Experiments

As a live robotics demonstration, we use $ODN_{\ell r}$ to locate objects for grasping. Experiments start with HSR's grasp camera approaching an object while generating segmentation masks at 1 cm increments using pre-trained OSVOS. Once ten masks are available, $ODN_{\ell r}$ starts predicting depth as HSR continues approaching and generating masks. Because $ODN_{\ell r}$'s prediction speed is negligible compared to HSR's data-collection speed, we use the median depth estimate of multiple permutations of collected data to improve robustness against segmentation errors. Once $ODN_{\ell r}$ estimates the object to be within 20 cm of grasping, HSR stops collecting data and grasps the object at that depth. Using this active depth estimation process, we are able to successfully locate and grasp consecutive objects at varied heights in a variety of settings, including placing laundry in a basket and clearing garbage off a table (see Fig. 1). We show these robot experiments in our Supplementary Video at: https://youtu.be/c90Fg_whjpI.

7   Conclusions

We introduce the **O**bject **D**epth via **M**otion and **S**egmentation (ODMS) dataset, which continuously generates synthetic training data with random camera motion, objects, and even perturbations. Using the ODMS dataset, we train the first deep network to estimate object depth from motion and segmentation, leading to as much as a 59% reduction in error over previous work. By using ODMS's simple binary mask- and distance-based input, our network's performance transfers across sim-to-real and diverse application domains, as demonstrated by our results on the robotics-, driving-, and simulation-based ODMS test sets. Finally, we use our network to perform object depth estimation in real-time robot grasping experiments, demonstrating how our segmentation-based approach to depth estimation is a viable tool for real-world applications requiring 3D perception from a single RGB camera.

Acknowledgements. We thank Madan Ravi Ganesh, Parker Koch, and Luowei Zhou for various discussions throughout this work. Toyota Research Institute ("TRI") provided funds to assist the authors with their research but this article solely reflects the opinions and conclusions of its authors and not TRI or any other Toyota entity.

References

1. Bao, L., Wu, B., Liu, W.: CNN in MRF: video object segmentation via inference in A CNN-based higher-order spatio-temporal MRF. In: IEEE Conference on Computer Vision and Pattern Recognition (CVPR) (2018)
2. Caelles, S., Maninis, K.K., Pont-Tuset, J., Leal-Taixé, L., Cremers, D., Van Gool, L.: One-shot video object segmentation. In: IEEE Conference on Computer Vision and Pattern Recognition (CVPR) (2017)
3. Caelles, S., et al.: The 2018 DAVIS challenge on video object segmentation. CoRR abs/1803.00557 (2018)
4. Calli, B., Walsman, A., Singh, A., Srinivasa, S., Abbeel, P., Dollar, A.M.: Benchmarking in manipulation research: using the Yale-CMU-Berkeley object and model set. IEEE Robot. Autom. Mag. **22**(3), 36–52 (2015)
5. Chen, D.J., Chen, H.T., Chang, L.W.: Video object co-segmentation. In: ACM International Conference on Multimedia (2012)
6. Chen, Y., Pont-Tuset, J., Montes, A., Van Gool, L.: Blazingly fast video object segmentation with pixel-wise metric learning. In: Computer Vision and Pattern Recognition (CVPR) (2018)
7. Cordts, M., et al.: The cityscapes dataset for semantic urban scene understanding. In: Proceedings of the IEEE Conference on Computer Vision and Pattern Recognition (CVPR) (2016)
8. Deng, J., Dong, W., Socher, R., Li, L.J., Li, K., Fei-Fei, L.: ImageNet: a large-scale hierarchical image database. In: IEEE Conference on Computer Vision and Pattern Recognition (CVPR) (2009)
9. Faktor, A., Irani, M.: Video segmentation by non-local consensus voting. In: British Machine Vision Conference (BMVC) (2014)
10. Ferguson, M., Law, K.: A 2D–3D object detection system for updating building information models with mobile robots. In: 2019 IEEE Winter Conference on Applications of Computer Vision (WACV) (2019)
11. Florence, V., Corso, J.J., Griffin, B.: Robot-supervised learning for object segmentation. In: The IEEE International Conference on Robotics and Automation (ICRA) (2020)

12. Gan, L., Zhang, R., Grizzle, J.W., Eustice, R.M., Ghaffari, M.: Bayesian spatial kernel smoothing for scalable dense semantic mapping. IEEE Robot. Autom. Lett. (RA-L) 5(2), 790–797 (2020)
13. Geiger, A., Lenz, P., Urtasun, R.: Are we ready for autonomous driving? The Kitti vision benchmark suite. In: 2012 IEEE Conference on Computer Vision and Pattern Recognition (CVPR) (2012)
14. Griffin, B., Florence, V., Corso, J.J.: Video object segmentation-based visual servo control and object depth estimation on a mobile robot. In: IEEE Winter Conference on Applications of Computer Vision (WACV) (2020)
15. Griffin, B.A., Corso, J.J.: BubbleNets: learning to select the guidance frame in video object segmentation by deep sorting frames. In: The IEEE Conference on Computer Vision and Pattern Recognition (CVPR) (2019)
16. Griffin, B.A., Corso, J.J.: Tukey-inspired video object segmentation. In: IEEE Winter Conference on Applications of Computer Vision (WACV) (2019)
17. He, K., Gkioxari, G., Dollar, P., Girshick, R.: Mask R-CNN. In: The IEEE International Conference on Computer Vision (ICCV) (2017)
18. He, K., Zhang, X., Ren, S., Sun, J.: Deep residual learning for image recognition. In: The IEEE Conference on Computer Vision and Pattern Recognition (CVPR) (2016)
19. Ittelson, W.H.: Size as a cue to distance: radial motion. Am. J. Psychol. 64(2), 188–202 (1951)
20. Kasten, Y., Galun, M., Basri, R.: Resultant based incremental recovery of camera pose from pairwise matches. In: IEEE Winter Conference on Applications of Computer Vision (WACV) (2019)
21. Khan, S.H., Guo, Y., Hayat, M., Barnes, N.: Unsupervised primitive discovery for improved 3d generative modeling. In: The IEEE Conference on Computer Vision and Pattern Recognition (CVPR) (2019)
22. Kingma, D.P., Ba, J.: Adam: A method for stochastic optimization. In: International Conference on Learning Representations (ICLR) (2014)
23. Kumawat, S., Raman, S.: LP-3DCNN: unveiling local phase in 3D convolutional neural networks. In: The IEEE Conference on Computer Vision and Pattern Recognition (CVPR) (2019)
24. Lee, Y.J., Kim, J., Grauman, K.: Key-segments for video object segmentation. In: IEEE International Conference on Computer Vision (ICCV) (2011)
25. Li, F., Kim, T., Humayun, A., Tsai, D., Rehg, J.M.: Video segmentation by tracking many figure-ground segments. In: The IEEE International Conference on Computer Vision (ICCV) (2013)
26. Li, Z., et al.: Learning the depths of moving people by watching frozen people. In: The IEEE Conference on Computer Vision and Pattern Recognition (CVPR) (2019)
27. Lin, T.Y., et al.: Microsoft COCO: common objects in context. In: Fleet, D., Pajdla, T., Schiele, B., Tuytelaars, T. (eds.) ECCV 2014. LNCS, vol. 8693, pp. 740–755. Springer, Cham (2014). https://doi.org/10.1007/978-3-319-10602-1_48
28. Liu, B., He, X.: Multiclass semantic video segmentation with object-level active inference. In: IEEE Conference on Computer Vision and Pattern Recognition (CVPR) (2015)
29. Liu, R., et al.: An intriguing failing of convolutional neural networks and the coord-Conv solution. In: Advances in Neural Information Processing Systems, vol. 31 (NIPS)

30. Liu, Y., Fan, B., Xiang, S., Pan, C.: Relation-shape convolutional neural network for point cloud analysis. In: The IEEE Conference on Computer Vision and Pattern Recognition (CVPR) (2019)
31. Lu, J., Xu, R., Corso, J.J.: Human action segmentation with hierarchical supervoxel consistency. In: IEEE Conference on Computer Vision and Pattern Recognition (CVPR) (2015)
32. Luiten, J., Voigtlaender, P., Leibe, B.: Premvos: Proposal-generation, refinement and merging for video object segmentation. In: Asian Conference on Computer Vision (ACCV) (2018)
33. Maninis, K., et al.: Video object segmentation without temporal information. IEEE Trans. Pattern Anal. Mach. Intell. **41**, 1515–1530 (2018)
34. Mur-Artal, R., Tards, J.D.: ORB-SLAM2: an open-source slam system for monocular, stereo, and RGB-D cameras. IEEE Trans. Robot. (T-RO) **33**, 1255-1262 (2017)
35. Oh, S.W., Lee, J.Y., Sunkavalli, K., Kim, S.J.: Fast video object segmentation by reference-guided mask propagation. In: IEEE Conference on Computer Vision and Pattern Recognition (CVPR) (2018)
36. Oneata, D., Revaud, J., Verbeek, J., Schmid, C.: Spatio-temporal object detection proposals. In: Fleet, D., Pajdla, T., Schiele, B., Tuytelaars, T. (eds.) ECCV 2014. LNCS, vol. 8691, pp. 737–752. Springer, Cham (2014). https://doi.org/10.1007/978-3-319-10578-9_48
37. Papazoglou, A., Ferrari, V.: Fast object segmentation in unconstrained video. In: Proceedings of the IEEE International Conference on Computer Vision (ICCV) (2013)
38. Perazzi, F., Pont-Tuset, J., McWilliams, B., Van Gool, L., Gross, M., Sorkine-Hornung, A.: A benchmark dataset and evaluation methodology for video object segmentation. In: IEEE Conference on Computer Vision and Pattern Recognition (CVPR) (2016)
39. Pont-Tuset, J., Perazzi, F., Caelles, S., Arbelaez, P., Sorkine-Hornung, A., Gool, L.V.: The 2017 DAVIS challenge on video object segmentation. CoRR abs/1704.00675 (2017)
40. Qi, C.R., Su, H., Mo, K., Guibas, L.J.: PointNet: deep learning on point sets for 3D classification and segmentation. In: The IEEE Conference on Computer Vision and Pattern Recognition (CVPR) (2017)
41. Ros, G., Sellart, L., Materzynska, J., Vazquez, D., Lopez, A.M.: The SYNTHIA dataset: a large collection of synthetic images for semantic segmentation of urban scenes. In: The IEEE Conference on Computer Vision and Pattern Recognition (CVPR) (2016)
42. Schonberger, J.L., Frahm, J.M.: Structure-from-motion revisited. In: The IEEE Conference on Computer Vision and Pattern Recognition (CVPR) (2016)
43. Soomro, K., Idrees, H., Shah, M.: Action localization in videos through context walk. In: IEEE International Conference on Computer Vision (ICCV) (2015)
44. Soomro, K., Idrees, H., Shah, M.: Predicting the where and what of actors and actions through online action localization. In: IEEE Conference on Computer Vision and Pattern Recognition (CVPR) (2016)
45. Srivastava, N., Hinton, G., Krizhevsky, A., Sutskever, I., Salakhutdinov, R.: DropOut: a simple way to prevent neural networks from overfitting. J. Mach. Learn. Res. **15**, 1929–1958 (2014)
46. Swanston, M.T., Gogel, W.C.: Perceived size and motion in depth from optical expansion. Percept. Psychophys. **39**, 309–326 (1986)

47. Tang, K., Sukthankar, R., Yagnik, J., Fei-Fei, L.: Discriminative segment annotation in weakly labeled video. In: IEEE Conference on Computer Vision and Pattern Recognition (CVPR) (2013)
48. Tighe, J., Lazebnik, S.: SuperParsing: scalable nonparametric image parsing with superpixels. Int. J. Comput. Vis. **101**(2), 352–365 (2012)
49. Tsai, D., Flagg, M., Nakazawa, A., Rehg, J.M.: Motion coherent tracking using multi-label MRF optimization. Int. J. Comput. Vis. **100**(2), 190–202 (2012)
50. Vijayanarasimhan, S., Grauman, K.: What's it going to cost you?: Predicting effort vs. informativeness for multi-label image annotations. In: IEEE Conference on Computer Vision and Pattern Recognition (CVPR) (2009)
51. Voigtlaender, P., Leibe, B.: Online adaptation of convolutional neural networks for video object segmentation. In: British Machine Vision Conference (BMVC) (2017)
52. Wang, C., et al.: DenseFusion: 6D object pose estimation by iterative dense fusion. In: The IEEE Conference on Computer Vision and Pattern Recognition (CVPR) (2019)
53. Wehrwein, S., Szeliski, R.: Video segmentation with background motion models. In: British Machine Vision Conference (BMVC) (2017)
54. Xu, C., Corso, J.J.: LIBSVX: a supervoxel library and benchmark for early video processing. Int. J. Comput. Vis. **119**(3), 272–290 (2016)
55. Xu, N., Yang, L., Fan, Y., Yue, D., Liang, Y., Yang, J., Huang, T.S.: Youtube-VOS: a large-scale video object segmentation benchmark. CoRR abs/1809.03327 (2018)
56. Yamaguchi, U., Saito, F., Ikeda, K., Yamamoto, T.: HSR, human support robot as research and development platform. The Abstracts of the international conference on advanced mechatronics : toward evolutionary fusion of IT and mechatronics : ICAM 2015, vol. 6, pp. 39–40 (2015)
57. Yamamoto, T., Terada, K., Ochiai, A., Saito, F., Asahara, Y., Murase, K.: Development of human support robot as the research platform of a domestic mobile manipulator. ROBOMECH J. **6**(1), 4 (2019)
58. Yang, L., Wang, Y., Xiong, X., Yang, J., Katsaggelos, A.K.: Efficient video object segmentation via network modulation. In: IEEE Conference on Computer Vision and Pattern Recognition (CVPR) (2018)

OnlineAugment: Online Data Augmentation with Less Domain Knowledge

Zhiqiang Tang[1][(✉)], Yunhe Gao[1], Leonid Karlinsky[2], Prasanna Sattigeri[2], Rogerio Feris[2], and Dimitris Metaxas[1]

[1] Rutgers University, New Brunswick, USA
{zhiqiang.tang,yunhe.gao,dnm}@rutgers.edu
[2] IBM Research AI, Long Beach, USA
LEONIDKA@il.ibm.com, {psattig,rsferis}@us.ibm.com

Abstract. Data augmentation is one of the most important tools in training modern deep neural networks. Recently, great advances have been made in searching for optimal augmentation policies in the image classification domain. However, two key points related to data augmentation remain uncovered by the current methods. First is that most if not all modern augmentation search methods are *offline* and learning policies are isolated from their usage. The learned policies are mostly constant throughout the training process and are *not adapted* to the current training model state. Second, the policies rely on class-preserving image processing functions. Hence applying current offline methods to new tasks may require domain knowledge to specify such kind of operations. In this work, we offer an orthogonal *online* data augmentation scheme together with three new augmentation networks, co-trained with the target learning task. It is both more efficient, in the sense that it does not require expensive offline training when entering a new domain, and more adaptive as it adapts to the learner state. Our augmentation networks require less domain knowledge and are easily applicable to new tasks. Extensive experiments demonstrate that the proposed scheme alone performs on par with the state-of-the-art offline data augmentation methods, as well as improving upon the state-of-the-art in combination with those methods.

1 Introduction

Data augmentation is widely used in training deep neural networks. It is an essential ingredient of many state-of-the-art deep learning systems on image classification [9,21,33,42], object detection [8,14], segmentation [12,32,39], as well as text classification [40]. Current deep neural networks may have billions

---

Electronic supplementary material The online version of this chapter (https://doi.org/10.1007/978-3-030-58571-6_19) contains supplementary material, which is available to authorized users.

© Springer Nature Switzerland AG 2020
A. Vedaldi et al. (Eds.): ECCV 2020, LNCS 12352, pp. 313–329, 2020.
https://doi.org/10.1007/978-3-030-58571-6_19

of parameters, tending to overfit the limited training data. Data augmentation aims to increase both the quantity and diversity of training data, thus alleviates overfitting and improves generalization.

Traditionally, data augmentation relies on hand-crafted policies. Designing the polices is usually inspired by domain knowledge and further verified by testing performance [17,34]. For example, the typical routine in training CIFAR classifiers uses random cropping and horizontal flip to conduct data augmentation. Intuitively, these operations do not change the image labels, and they can also improve testing performance in practice.

Recently, AutoML techniques [2,45] are used to automate the process of discovering augmentation polices. The resulted approaches, such as AutoAugment [6] and its variants [18,21,24,44] are quite successful and achieve state-of-the-art results. We name them *offline data augmentation* since the policy learning and usage are isolated. Moreover, these approaches use pre-specified image processing functions as augmentation operations. Defining the basic operations requires domain knowledge, which may impede their applications to more tasks.

In this paper, we propose *OnlineAugment*, which jointly optimizes data augmentation and target network training in an online manner. The merits of OnlineAugment lie in three-fold. First, it is orthogonal to the offline methods. Their complementary nature makes it possible to apply them together. Second, through the online learning, the augmentation network can adapt to the target network through training from the start to the end, saving it from the inconveniences of pre-training [23] or early stopping [29]. Third, it is easy to implement and train OnlineAugment. In contrast, learning offline policies usually rely on distributed training, as there are many parallel optimization processes.

Furthermore, we propose more general data augmentation operations with less domain knowledge. Instead of using pre-defined image processing functions, such as rotation and color, we design neural networks to perform data augmentation. Specifically, we devise three learnable models: augmentation STN (A-STN), deformation VAE (D-VAE), and Perturbation VAE (P-VAE). It is nontrivial to craft STN [19] and VAE [20] to conduct data augmentation. We also propose new losses to regularize them in training. Besides, OnlineAugment integrates both adversarial training and meta-learning in updating the augmentation networks. Adversarial training is to prevent overfitting, whereas meta-learning encourages generalization.

In summary, our key contributions are:

– We propose a new online data augmentation scheme based on meta-learned augmentation networks co-trained with the target task. Our framework is complementary to the state-of-the-art offline methods such as AutoAugment. Experiments on CIFAR, SVHN, and ImageNet show that on its own, OnlineAugment achieves comparable performances to AutoAugment. More excitingly, OnlineAugment can further boost state-of-the-art performances if used jointly with AutoAgument policies.

- We propose three complementary augmentation models responsible for different types of augmentations. They replace the image processing functions commonly used in contemporary approaches and make our method both more adaptive and less dependent on domain knowledge.
- We show that the proposed OnlineAugment can generalize to tasks different from object classification by applying it to a liver&tumor segmentation task, demonstrating improved performance compared with the state-of-the-art RandAugment on this task.

2 Related Work

Data augmentation has been shown to improve the generalization of machine learning models and is especially effective in training deep neural networks. It is essential in the situation where only limited data is available for the target task, but is also crucial for generalization performance in case the data is abundant.

Known class-preserving transformation has been routinely used to expand labeled datasets for training image classifiers. These include operations such as cropping, horizontal and vertical flips, and rotation [5,21,33]. Recently, reinforcement learning has been used to learn the optimal sequence of such transformations for a given dataset that leads to improved generalization [29]. AutoAugment [6] falls under this category of methods and actively explores policies and validates their effectiveness by repeatedly training models from scratch. Due to the large search space, the searching process, based on reinforcement learning, severely suffers from high computational demand. Subsequent works [7,18] in this direction have been aimed at reducing the computational complexity of the search strategies. However, they all follow the formulation of AutoAugment that first searches policies using a sampled small dataset, and then applies them to the final large dataset. Thus the policy learning and usage are isolated. Adversarial AutoAugment [43] jointly optimizes the polices and target learner. However, the learned policies are still based on domain-specific image processing functions.

More general transformations, such as Gaussian noise and dropout, are also effective in expanding the training set [10,35,36]. Spatial Transformer Network (STN) can perform more adaptive transformations than image processing functions such as rotation. However, it was designed for localization, not for data augmentation. In this paper, we craft it to conduct data augmentation. Generative models are also helpful for data augmentation. DAGAN [1] employs a Generative Adversarial Network (GAN) [15] to learn data augmentation for few-shot classification. In this work, we devise two augmentation models based on Variational Auto-encoder (VAE) [20], as another popular generative model.

Adversarial training [16,22,27] can serve as a general data augmentation framework. It aims to generate adversarial perturbations on input data. The adversarial examples are further used in training models to improve their robustness. It has been shown that adversarial training can hurt model generalization although it can boost robustness [27,38]. Concurrent work AdvProp [37] successfully adapts adversarial training to advance model generalization. It uses

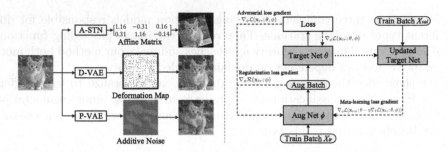

Fig. 1. Augmentation illustrations (**Left**) and OnlineAugment scheme (**Right**). We propose three models to conduct spatial transformation, deformation, and noise perturbation. OnlineAugment can jointly optimize each plug-in augmentation network with the target network. Updating the augmentation network incorporates adversarial training, meta-learning, and some novel regularizations.

the common adversarial attack methods, such as PGD and I-FGSM, to generate additive noises. In contrast, our models can learn to generate more diverse augmentations: spatial transformation, deformation, and additive noises. We also use adversarial training together with meta-learning.

Learning data augmentation is to train the target learner better, i.e., learning to learn better. Validation data have been used in meta-learning literatures for few-shot learning [26,30,31], where very limited training data are available. Here we follow the MAML [11] algorithm to set a meta-objective for the augmentation network. That is, augmentations conducted on a training mini-batch is evaluated on another validation one.

3   The Online Data Augmentation Formulation

In this section, we introduce our online data augmentation paradigm: updating target model θ and augmentation model ϕ alternately. In this way, data augmentation and target model are learned jointly. Benefiting from the joint learning, the augmentation model ϕ can adapt to the target model θ in training.

For simplicity, let $\mathbf{x}$ be the annotated data, including both input and target. Note that $\mathbf{x}$ can come from any supervised task such as image classification or semantic segmentation. Let θ and ϕ denote the target and augmentation models. During training, the target model θ learns from the augmented data $\phi(\mathbf{x})$ instead of the original x. Note that ϕ will also transform the ground truth annotation if necessary. For example, in semantic segmentation, ϕ applies the same spatial transformations to both an image and its segmentation mask. Without loss of generality, we assume θ and ϕ are parameterized by deep neural networks, which are mostly optimized by SGD and its variants. Given a training mini-batch $\mathbf{x}_{tr}$ sampled from training set $\mathcal{D}_{tr}$, θ is updated by stochastic gradient:

$$\nabla_\theta \mathcal{L}(\mathbf{x}_{tr}; \theta, \phi), \tag{1}$$

Algorithm 1: OnlineAugment: Online Data Augmentation

Input: Initial target model θ, initial augmentation model ϕ, training set $\mathcal{D}_{tr}$, and validation set $\mathcal{D}_{val}$

1 **while** *not converged* **do**
2   Sample mini-batches $\mathbf{x}_{tr}$ and $\mathbf{x}_{val}$ from $\mathcal{D}_{tr}$ and $\mathcal{D}_{val}$ respectively
3   Update augmentation model ϕ by stochastic gradient:
      $\nabla_\phi \mathcal{L}(\mathbf{x}_{val}; \theta - \eta \nabla_\theta \mathcal{L}(\mathbf{x}_{tr}; \theta, \phi)) + \lambda \nabla_\phi \mathcal{R}(\mathbf{x}_{tr}; \phi) - \beta \nabla_\phi \mathcal{L}(\mathbf{x}_{tr}; \theta, \phi)$
4   Update target model θ by stochastic gradient: $\nabla_\theta \mathcal{L}(\mathbf{x}_{tr}; \theta, \phi)$
5 **end**

Output: Optimized target model θ^*

---

where the choice of $\mathcal{L}$ depends on the task. In the case of object classification, $\mathcal{L}$ is a cross entropy function.

The goal of data augmentation is to improve the generalization of the target model. To this end, we draw on inspirations from adversarial training and meta-learning. Adversarial training aims to increase the training loss of the target model by generating hard augmentations. It can effectively address the overfitting issue of the target model. Meta-learning, on the other hand, can measure the impact of augmented data on the performance of validation data. If a validation set $\mathcal{D}_{val}$ is possible, we can sample from it a validation mini-batch $\mathbf{x}_{val}$. Otherwise, we can simulate the meta-tasks by sampling two separate mini-batches from train set $\mathcal{D}_{tr}$ as $\mathbf{x}_{tr}$ and $\mathbf{x}_{val}$. Mathematically, the stochastic gradient of augmentation model ϕ is computed as:

$$\nabla_\phi \mathcal{L}(\mathbf{x}_{val}; \theta - \eta \nabla_\theta \mathcal{L}(\mathbf{x}_{tr}; \theta, \phi)) + \lambda \nabla_\phi \mathcal{R}(\mathbf{x}_{tr}; \phi) - \beta \nabla_\phi \mathcal{L}(\mathbf{x}_{tr}; \theta, \phi), \quad (2)$$

where $\mathcal{L}(\mathbf{x}_{val}; \theta - \eta \nabla_\theta \mathcal{L}(\mathbf{x}_{tr}; \theta, \phi))$, $\mathcal{R}(\mathbf{x}_{tr}; \phi)$, and $-\mathcal{L}(\mathbf{x}_{tr}; \theta, \phi)$ are the generalization, regularization, and adversarial losses. λ and β are the balancing weights. $\theta - \eta \nabla_\theta \mathcal{L}(\mathbf{x}_{tr}; \theta, \phi)$ represents the updated target network by augmented data $\phi(\mathbf{x}_{tr})$. For simplicity, here we use a vanilla gradient descent with learning rate η. Other more complex optimizers are also applicable. For efficient training, we use the second-order approximation [25] to compute the meta-gradient.

$\mathcal{R}(\mathbf{x}; \phi)$ measures the distance between the original and augmented data. Adding this regularization term is to constrain the augmented data within reasonable distributions. Otherwise, adversarial training may cause meaningless augmentations that hurt training. Theoretically, the generalization term can also help regularize the augmentations implicitly. In practice, we find that the explicit regularization term is critical for practical adversarial training. Besides, adversarial training is performed by minimizing the negative training loss $-\mathcal{L}(\mathbf{x}_{tr}; \theta, \phi)$. In this way, the augmentation model ϕ learn to generate hard augmentations. The training scheme is presented in Algorithm 1 and the right figure in Fig. 1.

Relation to Offline Augmentation Methods. The formulation of our online augmentation differs from the previous offline ones [6,7,18] mainly in three aspects. First, OnlineAugment alternates updating the target model θ and augmentation model ϕ. The offline methods usually perform a full optimization

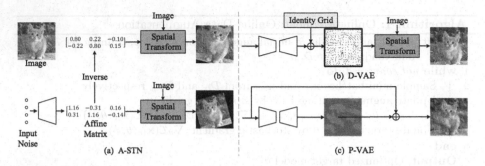

Fig. 2. Augmentation models: A-STN **(a)**, D-VAE **(b)**, and P-VAE **(c)**. A-STN, conditioned on Gaussian noise, generate a transformation matrix. Both the matrix and its inverse are applied to an image for diversity. D-VAE or P-VAE takes an image as input, generating deformation grid maps or additive noise maps. The three models are trainable if plugged in the training scheme in Fig. 1.

for θ in each step of updating ϕ. Second, to get the optimized target model, the offline methods usually require a two-stage training: learning policies and applying them. However, OnlineAugment can optimize the target model in one training process. Third, we use adversarial training in learning the augmentation model. The offline methods only have one generalization objective, maximizing performance on validation data.

Relation to Adversarial Training Methods. Adversarial training [16,22, 27] is mainly used to improve the robustness of the target model. Some works [27,38] have shown that robust models usually come at the cost of degraded generalization to clean data. The goal of OnlineAugment is generalization rather than robustness. To pilot adversarial training for generalization, we design new regularization terms and add meta-learning in OnlineAugment.

4   Data Augmentation Models

After introducing the OnlineAugment scheme, we present three different data augmentation models in this section. The three models are motivated by our analysis of possible data transformations. Specifically, we summarize them into three types: global spatial transformation, local deformation, and intensity perturbation. Each transformation corresponds to a model below. They either change pixel locations or values. Note that the pixel in this work refers to an element in a generic feature map, not necessarily an image. Technically, we design the augmentation models based on the spatial transformer network (STN) [19] and variational auto-encoder (VAE) [20].

4.1   Global Spatial Transformation Model

There are several commonly used spatial transformation functions such as rotation, scale, and translation, which can be unified into more general ones, such as affine transformation. It is well-known that STN [19] can perform general spatial transformations. Briefly, STN contains three parts: a localization network, a grid generator, and a sampler. The last two modules are deterministic and differentiable functions, denoted as τ. Therefore, our focus is to design a new localization network ϕ that outputs the transformation matrix.

Augmentation STN (A-STN). Suppose we use affine transformation, the output should be a 6-dimension vector, further re-shaped into a 2×3 transformation matrix. Traditionally, the STN localization network uses images or feature maps as its input. Here we also provide an alternative input of Gaussian noises. Our design is motivated by the observation that the global spatial transformations are transferable in data augmentation. That is, the same spatial transformation is applicable to different images or feature maps in augmenting training data. Therefore, conditioning on the images or feature maps may not be necessary for generating the augmentation transformation.

The architecture of the localization network ϕ depends on the choices of its input. It can be a convolutional neural network (CNN) or a multi-layer perceptron (MLP) if conditioned on the generic feature map or 1-D Gaussian noise. We will give its detailed architectures in the experiment. Moreover, the MLP localization network itself is also transferable as it is unrelated to the target task. However, we may need to craft new CNN localization networks for different tasks. Therefore, it is preferable to implement the localization network ϕ as an MLP in practice.

Double Cycle-consistency Regularization. To apply the spatial transformation model to Algorithm 1, we need to design a proper regularization term $\mathcal{R}$. Empirically, increasing the spatial variance of training data can enhance the generalization power of the model. However, excessive spatial transformations probably bring negative impacts. To constrain the spatial transformations within reasonable scopes, we propose a novel double cycle-consistency regularization, see in Fig. 2 (a). The key idea is to measure the lost information during the spatial transformation process. Mathematically, we compute the double cycle-consistency loss:

$$\mathcal{R}_c^s(\mathbf{x}; \phi) = \|\tau_\phi^{-1}(\tau_\phi(\mathbf{x})) - \mathbf{x}\|_2^2 + \|\tau_\phi(\tau_\phi^{-1}(\mathbf{x})) - \mathbf{x}\|_2^2, \tag{3}$$

where $\tau_\phi(\mathbf{x}) = \tau(\mathbf{x}, \phi(\mathbf{z}))$. The deterministic function τ transforms the image or feature map $\mathbf{x}$ using the generated affine matrix $\phi(\mathbf{z})$, where $\mathbf{z}$ is the Gaussian noise. τ_ϕ^{-1} denotes the inverse transformation of τ_ϕ. Ideally, applying a transformation followed by its inverse will recover the original input, and vice versa. In reality, whichever applied first may cause some irreversible information loss. For example, the zoom-in transformation discards the region falling out of scope. Applying the zoom-out transformation afterwards will produce zero or boundary padding, which is different from the original image region. We find a single cycle-consistency loss will lead to biased transformations. The localization network ϕ tends to output zoom-out transformations whose inverse can easily recover the original input. Fortunately, imposing the double cycle-consistency constraint can avoid the biases effectively, thereby producing more diverse transformations.

4.2 Local Deformation Model

Apart from the global spatial transformation model, we propose another complementary deformation model. The global transformation applies the same transformation matrix to all the pixels of an image or feature map. In the local deformation, each pixel, however, has an independent transformation.

Input and Output. It is cumbersome and also unnecessary to produce all the transformation matrices. Recall that STN performs transformations by the grid sampling. A better choice is to predict a grid map directly. For 2D transformations, the grid map has the shape $h \times w \times 2$, where h and w are the height and width of the input feature map. Each location in the grid map indicates the 2D coordinates to sample a pixel. A grid map is personalized to an image or feature map as each pixel has its own transformation. Different from a low-dimension affine matrix, a deformation grid map may be unlikely to transfer. Therefore, our deformation model is conditioned on the image or feature map, generating the grid map.

Deformation VAE (D-VAE). The deformation model ϕ, see in Fig. 2 (b), builds on the Variational Autoencoders (VAE) [20], a popular generative model. A VAE model consists of an encoder and a decoder. Similar to the original VAE, our deformation VAE also uses images or feature maps as the encoder input. However, in our setting, the decoder outputs the deformation grid maps instead of the reconstructed input. We refer to the deformation grid maps as deformation deltas Δ_ϕ^d. They are added on the grid maps of identity mapping id to perform grid sampling τ. The transformed input $\tau(\mathbf{x}, \Delta_\phi^d + id)$ serves as the reconstructed input. Following the original VAE, our deformation VAE is also trained to minimize both the reconstruction loss and the KL-divergence between the encoded distribution and the standard normal distribution:

$$\mathcal{R}_v^d(\mathbf{x}; \phi) = \|\mathbf{x} - \tau(\mathbf{x}, \Delta_\phi^d + id)\|_2^2 + \mathcal{KL}(\mathcal{N}(\mu_\phi(\mathbf{x}), \Sigma_\phi(\mathbf{x})), \mathcal{N}(0, I)), \quad (4)$$

where $\mu_\phi(\mathbf{x})$ and $\Sigma_\phi(\mathbf{x})$ are the encoded mean and variance, parameterizing the Gaussian distribution.

Smoothness Regularization. Smooth deformations are essential to preserving the quality of deformed data. Otherwise, the deformed data may become noisy as each pixel is sampled from an independent location in the original image or feature map. This is especially important for location-sensitive tasks such as semantic segmentation. Given an arbitrary pixel i and its neighbours $j \in \mathcal{N}(i)$, we enforce the local smoothness constraint on the deformation deltas:

$$\mathcal{R}_s^d(\mathbf{x}; \phi) = \sum_i \sum_{j \in \mathcal{N}(i)} \|\Delta_\phi^d(i) - \Delta_\phi^d(j)\|_2^2. \quad (5)$$

The smoothness regularization can make the deformations consistent for nearby pixels. In the experiment, we use the combination $\lambda_v^d \mathcal{R}_v^d(\mathbf{x}; \phi) + \lambda_s^d \mathcal{R}_s^d(\mathbf{x}; \phi)$ to regularize our deformation augmentation model.

4.3 Intensity Perturbation Model

The above two models perform data augmentation by changing the pixel locations. Here we propose another model to manipulate the pixel values instead. As an analogy, the offline data augmentation methods [6,7,18] use some built-in image texture processing functions such as colour and brightness. These functions are designed based on the domain knowledge for natural images. In contrast, our intensity perturbation is more general without domain knowledge.

Perturbation VAE (P-VAE). Specifically, the intensity perturbation model ϕ, see in Fig. 2 (c), conditioned on the image or feature map, generates additive noises Δ_ϕ^p. As the deformation, we use the VAE model to learn the intensity perturbation. The reconstructed input is the sum of the input and generated noises $\mathbf{x} + \Delta_\phi^p$. Therefore, we can compute the VAE loss as:

$$\mathcal{R}_v^p(\mathbf{x}; \phi) = \|\Delta_\phi^p\|_2^2 + \mathcal{KL}(\mathcal{N}(\mu_\phi(\mathbf{x}), \Sigma_\phi(\mathbf{x})), \mathcal{N}(0, I)), \qquad (6)$$

where $\mu_\phi(\mathbf{x})$ and $\Sigma_\phi(\mathbf{x})$ are the mean and variance of the encoded Gaussian distribution. Note that P-VAE produces deltas Δ_ϕ^p in the image or feature map domain while the deltas Δ_ϕ^d, predicted by D-VAE, lie in the grid map domain. It results in the different reconstruction losses in Eqs. 6 and 4.

Relation to Adversarial Attacks. Additive noise is a common tool in generating adversarial examples [27,37]. Here we explore its potential in data augmentation. Although the adversarial examples serve as augmented data in adversarial training, they are mainly to improve the model's robustness. Some evidence [28] have shown that adversarial training usually sacrifices the model generalization to clean data. However, our intensity perturbation model can improve the generalization through the OnlineAugment. Recently, concurrent work AdvProp [37] successfully adapts the PGD attack [27] to data augmentation. In contrast, we design the perturbation VAE model to generate additive noises.

5 Experiments

In this section, we empirically evaluate OnlineAugment with the three models.

5.1 Experimental Settings

Applying OnlineAugment is simple in practice. The augmentation models A-STN, D-VAE, and P-VAE requires neither pre-training [23] nor early stopping [29]. Because they can adapt to the target network during online training. Inspired by AdvProp [37], we use multiple batch normalization layers to merge different types of augmentations. A-STN, D-VAE, and P-VAE are trained by Adam optimizer with the same learning rate of $1e-3$, weight decay $1e-4$, and $\beta_1 = 0.5$. Other Adam hyper-parameters are set by default in Pytorch.

A-STN. We design the noise conditioned A-STN as a 6-layer MLP. Specifically, it takes only 1-dimensional Gaussian noises as input and outputs 6-dimensional affine parameters. Each hidden layer generates 8-dimension features. Batch normalization, ReLU, and dropout (0.5) are applied after each linear layer. The loss weights are set as $\lambda_c^s = 0.1$ and $\beta^s = 0.1$.

D-VAE. D-VAE consists of an encoder and a decoder. The encoder maps an image to the 32-dimensional latent space. It includes 5 3×3 convolutional layers and three linear layers. The first convolutional layer increases the channel number from 3 to 32. After that, the feature channels double if the convolution stride is 2. There are two convolutional layers on each resolution. The first linear layer takes the reshaped convolutional features and outputs 512-dimensional latent features. Another two linear layers generate the mean and variance vectors of encoded Gaussian distributions. The decoder is simply the reverse of the encoder with transposed convolutions. The last layer is a 1×1 convolution producing 2-channel grid maps. We use the weights $\lambda_v^d = 1$, $\lambda_s^d = 10$, and $\beta^d = 1e - 2$.

P-VAE. It shares almost the same architecture as D-VAE. The only difference is the last layer in the decoder, because P-VAE needs to generate additive noises on the images. The latent space dimension is set to 8 for P-VAE. We also set the hyper-parameters $\lambda_v^p = 1e - 3$ and $\beta^p = 10$.

Image Classification. We use datasets CIFAR-10, CIFAR-100, SVHN, and ImageNet with their standard training/test splits. To tune hyper-parameters efficiently, we also sample reduced datasets: R-CIFAR-10, R-CIFAR-100, and R-CIFAR-SVHN. Each of them consists of 4000 examples. The sampling is reproducible using the public sklearn StratifiedShuffleSplit function with random state 0. We report top-1 classification accuracy in most tables except for Table 6 with top-1 errors. The target networks are Wide-ResNet-28-10 [41] (W-ResNet), Shake-Shake network [13], and ResNet-50 [17]. We use Cutout [10] as the baselines in Tables 1, 2, 3, and 4.

Medical Image Segmentation. To test the generalization ability of our approach, we further conduct experiments on the medical image segmentation dataset LiTS [3]. LiTS published 131 liver CT images as a training set with liver and tumor annotations. Since these experiments are to prove the effectiveness of our augmentation algorithm, pursuing the highest performance is not our goal, we use the 2D UNet as the segmentation network to segment CT images on the axial plane slice by slice. We randomly split the 131 CT images into 81 training cases, 25 validation cases, and 25 test cases. We first resample all images to $2 \times 2 \times 2$ mm, then center crop each slice to 256 in size, and finally normalize the image window $[-200, 250]$ to $[0, 1]$ as the input of the network. Only A-STN and D-VAE are presented in this task, since P-VAE has no obvious performance improvement. Compared with classification tasks, segmentation tasks are sensitive to location. Therefore, for A-STN and D-VAE, we not only perform a bilinear grid sample on the images, but also perform a nearest neighbor grid sample for the label masks using the same grid.

We also compared our proposed OnlineAugment with RandAugment [7]. We slightly modify RandAugment to fit our setting. As the number of transformations involved is relatively small, all transformations are used during training.

Table 1. Evaluation of the Gaussian noise input and double cycle-consistency regularization in A-STN. We compare them to the image condition and single cycle-consistency. Double cycle-consistency outperforms the single one. With the double one, the noise and image inputs get comparable accuracy.

Dataset	Model	Cutout	Image input +1 cycle	Image input +2 cycles	Noise input +1 cycle	Noise input +2 cycles
R-CIFAR-10	W-ResNet	80.95	83.24	84.76	82.62	**84.94**

Table 2. Evaluation of the smoothness regularization (SR) in D-VAE. We report the results on both image classification and segmentation. The smoothness regularization is more useful for the location-sensitive image segmentation task.

Dataset	Model	Baseline	D-VAE only	D-VAE + SR
R-CIFAR-10	W-ResNet	80.95 (Cutout)	82.72	**82.86**
Liver segmentation	U-Net	66.0 (No Aug.)	68.51	**70.49**

Therefore, for global spatial transformation, the search space is the magnitude of 4 transforms, including rotate, translate-x, translate-y, and scale. For the deformation model, the search space is the magnitude of local deformations. At each iteration, the magnitude of each transformation is uniformly and randomly sampled between 0 and the upper bound for both global spatial transformation and local deformation.

5.2   Experimental Results

The experiments consist of ablation studies for the three models, comparisons with AutoAugment [6], and their orthogonality. The comparisons with state-of-the-art methods are reported on image classification and medical segmentation.

A-STN. The A-STN may be conditioned on image or Gaussian noise. We compare these two choices in this ablation study. Besides, we also compare its regularization with single or double cycle-consistency losses. Table 1 gives the comparisons. The double cycle-consistency obtains higher accuracy than the single cycle one. Because it can make A-STN produce more diverse transformations. With the double-cycle consistency regularization, the noise and image conditions achieve comparable accuracy. We use the noise condition A-STN in other experiments since its architecture is transferable between tasks.

D-VAE. The smoothness regularization comes as an additional component in the D-VAE. We evaluate its effectiveness in both CIFAR-10 classification and liver segmentation tasks. Table 2 presents the results. Interestingly, the smoothness regularization has little effect on classification accuracy. However, it makes a difference (%2) for the liver segmentation. Because the liver segmentation is

Table 3. Comparisons of P-VAE to AdvProp [37] with iterative gradient methods PGD [27], GD, and I-FGSM [4]. Adversarial training plus only the noise regularization can make P-VAE comparable to AdvProp with GD or I-FGSM.

Dataset	Model	Cutout	AP+PGD	AP+GD	AP+I-FGSM	P-VAE
R-CIFAR-10	W-ResNet	80.95	83.00	83.90	83.92	**84.08**

Table 4. Ours *v.s.* AutoAugment (AA). The three models helps separately, and they together may perform on a par with AA. The stochastic shake-shake operations may interfere with the online learning, reducing the improvements.

Dataset	Model	Cutout	AA	A-STN	D-VAE	P-VAE	Comb
R-CIFAR-10	Wide-ResNet-28-10	80.95	85.43	84.94	82.72	84.18	**85.65**
	Shake-Shake (26 2 × 32d)	85.42	**87.71**	86.62	86.51	86.34	87.12
R-CIFAR-100	Wide-ResNet-28-10	41.64	47.87	46.55	45.42	47.45	**48.31**
	Shake-Shake (26 2 × 32d)	44.41	**48.18**	46.81	46.53	46.30	47.27
R-SVHN	Wide-ResNet-28-10	90.16	93.27	92.73	91.32	91.61	**93.29**
	Shake-Shake (26 2 × 32d)	94.03	**94.63**	94.15	94.06	94.12	94.21

a location-sensitive task. The smoothness regularization can remove the noises along the boundaries of segmentation masks.

P-VAE. The P-VAE generates additive noises to perform data augmentation. AdvProp [28] has a similar goal, but utilizes the iterative gradient methods for the generation. For a fair comparison with AdvProp, we use only adversarial training and the noise regularization in training P-VAE. Table 3 shows the comparisons. P-VAE compares favorably to AdvProp with GD and I-FGSM. On the one hand, P-VAE learns some noise distributions while the iterative methods rely on the gradient ascent rules. On the other hand, P-VAE generates structured noises, while the iterative approaches produce more complex ones.

OnlineAugment *v.s.* AutoAugment. AutoAugment is a representative offline augmentation method. Here we evaluate OnlineAugment by comparing with it. Table 4 provides the separate results of three data augmentation models, as well as their combined. Each model, independently, can boost the generalization of two target networks on three datasets. Combining them can bring further improvements, achieving comparable performance as AutoAugment. We can also observe that the improvements for the Shake-Shake network [13] are lower than those of the Wide ResNet [41]. One possible explanation is that the stochastic shake-shake operations may affect the online learning of data augmentation.

OnlineAugment + AutoAugment. Apart from comparing OnlineAugment with AutoAugment, it is more interesting to investigate their orthogonality. Table 5 summarizes the results. We can find that OnlineAugment can bring consistent improvements on top of AutoAugment for different target networks and datasets. Their orthogonality comes from the differences in training schemes and

Table 5. Ours+AutoAugment (AA). We use A-STN, D-VAE, and P-VAE on top of the AutoAugment polices. Surprisingly, each model can further improve AutoAugment performance. It demonstrates that OnlineAugment is orthogonal to AutoAugment. The three models use more general augmentation operations.

Dataset	Model	AA	+A-STN	+D-VAE	+P-VAE	+Comb.
R-CIFAR-10	Wide-ResNet-28-10	85.43	89.39	87.40	87.63	**89.40**
	Shake-Shake (26 2 × 32d)	87.71	89.25	88.43	88.52	**89.50**
R-CIFAR-100	Wide-ResNet-28-10	47.87	52.94	50.01	51.02	**53.72**
	Shake-Shake (26 2 × 32d)	48.18	**50.58**	50.42	50.87	50.11
R-SVHN	Wide-ResNet-28-10	93.27	94.32	93.72	94.17	**94.69**
	Shake-Shake (26 2 × 32d)	94.63	95.21	94.87	**95.28**	95.06

Table 6. Comparisons with state-of-the-art methods. We compare our OnlineAugment with AutoAugment (AA), PBA [18], and Fast AutoAugment (FAA) [24] on three datasets. OnlineAugment alone obtains comparable test errors. Combining it with AutoAugment produces the lowest errors on three datasets.

Dataset	Model	Baseline	Cutout	AA	PBA	FAA	Ours	Ours+AA
CIFAR-10	Wide-ResNet-28-10	3.9	3.1	2.6	2.6	2.7	2.4	**2.0**
CIFAR-100	Wide-ResNet-28-10	18.8	18.4	17.1	16.7	17.3	16.6	**16.3**
ImageNet	ResNet-50	23.7	–	22.4	–	22.4	22.5	**22.0**

augmentation models. Different from OnlineAugment, AutoAugment learns data augmentation policies in an offline manner. Moreover, the three models (A-STN, D-VAE, and P-VAE) generate different augmentations from the image processing functions in AutoAugment. Note that OnlineAugment is also orthogonal to other offline methods [6,7,18] since they have similar policies as AutoAugment.

Comparisons with State-of-the-Art Methods. Besides AutoAugment, we also compare OnlineAugment with other state-of-the-art methods such as Fast AutoAugment (FAA) and Population-based Augmentation (PBA). They all belong to offline data augmentation. OnlineAugment alone gets the lowest test errors on CIFAR-10 and CIFAR-100 and comparable errors on ImageNet. Further, OnlineAugment, together with AutoAugment, achieves new state-of-the-art results on all the three image classification datasets.

Comparisons with RandAugment on LiTS Dataset. OnlineAugment can also apply to medical image segmentation easily. Table 7 gives the comparisons with state-of-the-art RandAugment. A-STN has comparable scores as RandAugment STN. However, both D-VAE and its joint application with A-STN outperform the corresponding RandAugment parts, especially on the tumor segmentation. Figure 3 illustrates the augmented images of A-STN, and D-VAE along with the training process. The augmentation is relatively large at the beginning and gradually becomes small as the training converges.

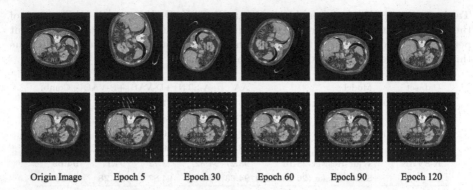

Fig. 3. Visualization of two augmentation modules: A-STN (**top**) and D-VAE (**bottom**). Red line is the contour of liver while green line is the contour of tumor. Our OnlineAugment can generate diverse augmented images. Moreover, it can also adapt to the target network. As the target network converges during training, the magnitude of the augmentation will also decrease.

Table 7. OnlineAugment *v.s.* RandAugment on LiTS measured by Dice score coefficient. Although A-STN is comparable to RandAug STN, D-VAE alone and its combination with A-STN obtain higher scores than the RandAug variants.

Method	Liver	Tumor	Average
No augmentation	89.04	44.73	66.88
RandAug STN	**93.86**	50.54	72.20
RandAug deformation	90.49	46.93	68.71
RandAug combine	91.91	51.11	71.51
Ours A-STN	92.01	52.26	72.13
Ours D-VAE	90.18	50.81	70.49
Ours combine	93.12	**53.58**	**73.35**

6   Conclusion

In this paper, we have presented OnlineAugment - a new and powerful data augmentation technique. Our method adapts online to the learner state throughout the entire training. We have designed three new augmentation networks that are capable of learning a wide variety of local and global geometric and photometric transformations, requiring less domain knowledge of the target task. Our OnlineAugment integrates both adversarial training and meta-learning for efficient training. We also design essential regularization techniques to guide adaptive online augmentation learning. Extensive experiments demonstrate the utility of the approach to a wide variety of tasks, matching (without requiring expensive offline augmentation policy search) the performance of the powerful AutoAugment policy, as well as improving upon the state-of-the-art in augmentation techniques when used jointly with AutoAugment.

Acknowledgment. This work has been partially supported by NSF 1763523, 1747778, 1733843 and 1703883 Awards to Dimitris Metaxas and the Defense Advanced Research Projects Agency (DARPA) under Contract No. FA8750-19-C-1001 to Leonid Karlinsky and Rogerio Feris.

References

1. Antoniou, A., Storkey, A., Edwards, H.: Data augmentation generative adversarial networks. arXiv preprint arXiv:1711.04340 (2017)
2. Baker, B., Gupta, O., Naik, N., Raskar, R.: Designing neural network architectures using reinforcement learning. arXiv preprint arXiv:1611.02167 (2016)
3. Bilic, P., et al.: The liver tumor segmentation benchmark (LiTS). arXiv preprint arXiv:1901.04056 (2019)
4. Chang, T.J., He, Y., Li, P.: Efficient two-step adversarial defense for deep neural networks. arXiv preprint arXiv:1810.03739 (2018)
5. Ciregan, D., Meier, U., Schmidhuber, J.: Multi-column deep neural networks for image classification. In: CVPR (2012)
6. Cubuk, E.D., Zoph, B., Mane, D., Vasudevan, V., Le, Q.V.: AutoAugment: learning augmentation strategies from data. In: CVPR, pp. 113–123 (2019)
7. Cubuk, E.D., Zoph, B., Shlens, J., Le, Q.V.: RandAugment: practical automated data augmentation with a reduced search space. arXiv preprint arXiv:1909.13719 (2019)
8. Dai, J., Li, Y., He, K., Sun, J.: R-FCN: object detection via region-based fully convolutional networks. In: NeurIPS (2016)
9. DeVries, T., Taylor, G.W.: Dataset augmentation in feature space. arXiv preprint arXiv:1702.05538 (2017)
10. DeVries, T., Taylor, G.W.: Improved regularization of convolutional neural networks with cutout. arXiv preprint arXiv:1708.04552 (2017)
11. Finn, C., Abbeel, P., Levine, S.: Model-agnostic meta-learning for fast adaptation of deep networks. In: ICML, pp. 1126–1135. JMLR.org (2017)
12. Fu, J., et al.: Dual attention network for scene segmentation. In: CVPR, pp. 3146–3154 (2019)
13. Gastaldi, X.: Shake-shake regularization. arXiv preprint arXiv:1705.07485 (2017)
14. Girshick, R., Radosavovic, I., Gkioxari, G., Dollár, P., He, K.: Detectron (2018)
15. Goodfellow, I., et al.: Generative adversarial nets. In: NeurIPS, pp. 2672–2680 (2014)
16. Goodfellow, I.J., Shlens, J., Szegedy, C.: Explaining and harnessing adversarial examples. arXiv preprint arXiv:1412.6572 (2014)
17. He, K., Zhang, X., Ren, S., Sun, J.: Deep residual learning for image recognition. In: CVPR (2016)
18. Ho, D., Liang, E., Stoica, I., Abbeel, P., Chen, X.: Population based augmentation: Efficient learning of augmentation policy schedules. arXiv preprint arXiv:1905.05393 (2019)
19. Jaderberg, M., Simonyan, K., Zisserman, A., et al.: Spatial transformer networks. In: NeurIPS, pp. 2017–2025 (2015)
20. Kingma, D.P., Welling, M.: Auto-encoding variational bayes. arXiv preprint arXiv:1312.6114 (2013)
21. Krizhevsky, A., Sutskever, I., Hinton, G.E.: ImageNet classification with deep convolutional neural networks. In: NeurIPS, pp. 1097–1105 (2012)

22. Kurakin, A., Goodfellow, I., Bengio, S.: Adversarial machine learning at scale. arXiv preprint arXiv:1611.01236 (2016)
23. Lee, D., Park, H., Pham, T., Yoo, C.D.: Learning augmentation network via influence functions. In: CVPR (2020)
24. Lim, S., Kim, I., Kim, T., Kim, C., Kim, S.: Fast autoaugment. In: NeurIPS, pp. 6662–6672 (2019)
25. Liu, H., Simonyan, K., Yang, Y.: Darts: Differentiable architecture search. arXiv preprint arXiv:1806.09055 (2018)
26. Lorraine, J., Duvenaud, D.: Stochastic hyperparameter optimization through hypernetworks. arXiv preprint arXiv:1802.09419 (2018)
27. Madry, A., Makelov, A., Schmidt, L., Tsipras, D., Vladu, A.: Towards deep learning models resistant to adversarial attacks. arXiv preprint arXiv:1706.06083 (2017)
28. Raghunathan, A., Xie, S.M., Yang, F., Duchi, J.C., Liang, P.: Adversarial training can hurt generalization. arXiv preprint arXiv:1906.06032 (2019)
29. Ratner, A.J., Ehrenberg, H., Hussain, Z., Dunnmon, J., Ré, C.: Learning to compose domain-specific transformations for data augmentation. In: NeurIPS, pp. 3236–3246 (2017)
30. Ravi, S., Larochelle, H.: Optimization as a model for few-shot learning (2016)
31. Ren, M., et al.: Meta-learning for semi-supervised few-shot classification. arXiv preprint arXiv:1803.00676 (2018)
32. Ronneberger, O., Fischer, P., Brox, T.: U-Net: convolutional networks for biomedical image segmentation. In: Navab, N., Hornegger, J., Wells, W.M., Frangi, A.F. (eds.) MICCAI 2015. LNCS, vol. 9351, pp. 234–241. Springer, Cham (2015). https://doi.org/10.1007/978-3-319-24574-4_28
33. Simard, P.Y., Steinkraus, D., Platt, J.C., et al.: Best practices for convolutional neural networks applied to visual document analysis. In: ICDAR, vol. 3 (2003)
34. Simonyan, K., Zisserman, A.: Very deep convolutional networks for large-scale image recognition. arXiv preprint arXiv:1409.1556 (2014)
35. Srivastava, N., Hinton, G., Krizhevsky, A., Sutskever, I., Salakhutdinov, R.: Dropout: a simple way to prevent neural networks from overfitting. JMLR 15(1), 1929–1958 (2014)
36. Taylor, L., Nitschke, G.: Improving deep learning using generic data augmentation. arXiv preprint arXiv:1708.06020 (2017)
37. Xie, C., Tan, M., Gong, B., Wang, J., Yuille, A., Le, Q.V.: Adversarial examples improve image recognition. arXiv preprint arXiv:1911.09665 (2019)
38. Xie, C., Wu, Y., Maaten, L.v.d., Yuille, A.L., He, K.: Feature denoising for improving adversarial robustness. In: CVPR, pp. 501–509 (2019)
39. Yang, M., Yu, K., Zhang, C., Li, Z., Yang, K.: Denseaspp for semantic segmentation in street scenes. In: CVPR (2018)
40. Yang, Z., Dai, Z., Yang, Y., Carbonell, J., Salakhutdinov, R.R., Le, Q.V.: XLNET: generalized autoregressive pretraining for language understanding. In: NeurIPS, pp. 5754–5764 (2019)
41. Zagoruyko, S., Komodakis, N.: Wide residual networks. arXiv preprint arXiv:1605.07146 (2016)
42. Zhang, H., Cisse, M., Dauphin, Y.N., Lopez-Paz, D.: mixup: beyond empirical risk minimization. arXiv preprint arXiv:1710.09412 (2017)
43. Zhang, X., Wang, Q., Zhang, J., Zhong, Z.: Adversarial autoaugment. In: ICLR (2019)

44. Zoph, B., Cubuk, E.D., Ghiasi, G., Lin, T.Y., Shlens, J., Le, Q.V.: Learning data augmentation strategies for object detection. arXiv preprint arXiv:1906.11172 (2019)
45. Zoph, B., Le, Q.V.: Neural architecture search with reinforcement learning. arXiv preprint arXiv:1611.01578 (2016)

Learning Pairwise Inter-plane Relations for Piecewise Planar Reconstruction

Yiming Qian[⊠] and Yasutaka Furukawa

Simon Fraser University, Burnaby, Canada
{yimingq,furukawa}@sfu.ca

Abstract. This paper proposes a novel single-image piecewise planar reconstruction technique that infers and enforces inter-plane relationships. Our approach takes a planar reconstruction result from an existing system, then utilizes convolutional neural network (CNN) to (1) classify if two planes are orthogonal or parallel; and 2) infer if two planes are touching and, if so, where in the image. We formulate an optimization problem to refine plane parameters and employ a message passing neural network to refine plane segmentation masks by enforcing the inter-plane relations. Our qualitative and quantitative evaluations demonstrate the effectiveness of the proposed approach in terms of plane parameters and segmentation accuracy.

Keywords: Piecewise planar · Reconstruction · Deep learning · Single-view

1 Introduction

Inter-plane relationships convey rich geometric information for underlying scene structure. Man-made environments are full of parallelism and orthogonality, whose information would constrain surface orientations. Planes meet along a line, where knowing the presence and location of such contact lines would further refine plane parameters and produce precise plane segmentation.

With the emergence of deep learning, state-of-the-art piecewise planar reconstruction methods are capable of finding plane instances and estimating their parameters even from a single image [10,12,24]. However, these approaches reconstruct plane instances independently, and reconstructions suffer from inter-plane inconsistencies. For example, depth values are inconsistent at plane boundaries, leading to clear visual artifacts in the 3D models. Plane segmentation is also erroneous at its boundaries with many holes in-between, yielding gaps and cracks in the 3D models, which could cause unpleasant user experiences in AR applications (*e.g.*, a virtual ball gets stuck or goes through cracks into walls) (Fig. 1).

Electronic supplementary material The online version of this chapter (https://doi.org/10.1007/978-3-030-58571-6_20) contains supplementary material, which is available to authorized users.

© Springer Nature Switzerland AG 2020
A. Vedaldi et al. (Eds.): ECCV 2020, LNCS 12352, pp. 330–345, 2020.
https://doi.org/10.1007/978-3-030-58571-6_20

This paper proposes a novel single-image piecewise planar reconstruction technique that takes and improves existing piecewise planar reconstruction by detecting and enforcing inter-plane relationships. More concretely, given a piecewise planar reconstruction (*i.e.*, a set of plane parameters and segmentation masks), convolutional neural networks (CNNs) first infer two types of inter-plane relationships: 1) If two planes are orthogonal, parallel, or neither; and 2) If two planes are in contact and, if so, where in the image.

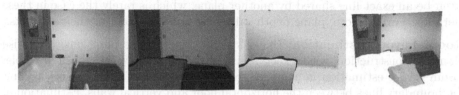

Fig. 1. This paper takes a piecewise planar reconstruction and improves its plane parameters and segmentation masks by inferring and utilizing inter-plane relationships. From left to right, input image, segmented plane instances, recovered depthmap, reconstructed 3D planar model

With the relationships, we formulate an optimization problem to refine plane parameters so that 1) plane normals agree with the inferred orthogonality or parallelism; and 2) plane intersections project onto the estimated contact lines. Lastly, we employ message passing neural networks to refine plane segmentation while ensuring that the plane segmentation and parameters become consistent.

We have utilized ScanNet [3] to generate ground-truth inter-plane relationships and introduced three new inter-plane consistency metrics. We have built the proposed algorithm in combination with two state-of-the-art piecewise planar reconstruction methods (PlaneRCNN [10] and the work by Yu *et al.* [24]). Our qualitative and quantitative evaluations demonstrate that the proposed approach consistently improves the accuracy of the plane parameters and segmentation. Code and data are available at https://github.com/yi-ming-qian/interplane.

2   Related Work

We first review piecewise planar reconstruction literature, and then study other techniques relevant to our paper.

Piecewise Planar Reconstruction: Traditional approaches for piecewise planar reconstruction require multiple views or depth information [5,6,14,19,20,25]. They generate plane proposals from 3D points by heuristics (*e.g.*, RANSAC based plane fitting), then assign a proposal to each pixel via a global inference (*e.g.*, Markov Random Field). Deng *et al.* [4] proposed a learning-based approach to recover planar regions, while still requiring depth information as input. Recently, Chen *et al.* [12] revisited the piecewise planar depthmap reconstruction problem from a single image with an end-to-end learning framework

(PlaneNet). PlaneRecover [23] later proposed an unsupervised learning approach. Both PlaneNet and PlaneRecover require the maximum number of planes in an image as a prior (*i.e.*, 10 in PlaneNet and 5 in PlaneRecover). To handle arbitrary number of planes, PlaneRCNN employs a detection architecture from the recognition community to handle arbitrary number of planes [10]. Yu *et al.* employs an associative embedding technique instead [24]. These methods produce impressive reconstructions, but plane segmentation masks are almost always imprecise at their boundaries. For example, a plane boundary should often be an exact line shared by another plane, which is rarely the case in these methods. Furthermore, plane depth values are not consistent at their contacts.

Room Layout Estimation: Under special structural assumptions, piecewise planar reconstruction with exact segmentation boundary has been possible. Room layout estimation is one such example, where the methods seek to find the boundary lines between the horizontal floor and vertical walls. Estimation of plane geometry/parameters is automatic from the segmentation thanks to the structural assumption [7,13,21,27].

Segmentation with Piecewise Linear Boundary: While not necessarily a reconstruction task, segmentation with compact linear boundary is a closely related work. KIPPI is a polygonal image segmentation technique, which detects and extends line segments to form polygonal shapes [1]. Planar graph reconstruction is a similar task, effective for floorplan reconstruction [2], floorplan vectorization [11], or outdoor architectural parsing [26]. The key difference in our problem is that we solve reconstruction and segmentation, where plane parameters and segmentation boundaries are tightly coupled. In fact, the earlier work by Kushal and Seitz [9] exploits this relationship to reconstruct a piecewise smooth 3D model. Their method extracts boundary first, which is often challenging and requires manual work, then performs piecewise smooth surface reconstruction. Our work solves reconstruction and segmentation simultaneously.

3D Primitive-Based Reconstruction: 3D primitive based reconstruction produces piecewise planar/smooth models with clean boundary lines. Constructive solid geometry with 3D solid primitives was used for large-scale building reconstruction with an assumption of a block world [22]. More recently, a data-driven approach was proposed for CSG model reconstruction [17]. They produce high-quality 3D models but were demonstrated mostly on synthetic objects. This work tackles complex cluttered indoor scenes.

Plane Identification: Given a pair of images, a CNN was trained to identify the same plane in the image pair, which was used for the loop-closing in the SLAM application [18]. This work exploits much richer class of pairwise plane relationships for a single image planar reconstruction.

3   Algorithm

Our system takes a piecewise planar reconstruction as input, and refines its plane parameters and segmentation masks by exploiting inter-plane relationships.

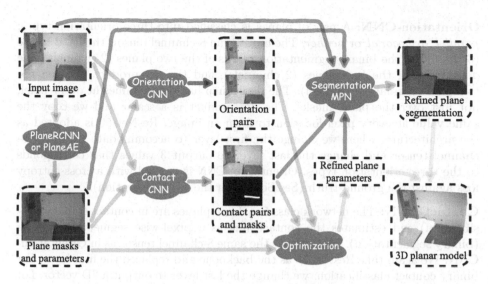

Fig. 2. System overview. Given a single RGB input, we use PlaneRCNN or PlaneAE to produce initial plane segmentation masks and parameters. We then use Orientation-CNN and Contact-CNN for pairwise relationship reasoning. Next, we solve an optimization problem to refine the plane parameters, followed by a message passing neural network (Segmentation-MPN) to refine plane segmentation

In practice, we have used two state-of-the-art methods for generating our inputs: PlaneRCNN by Liu *et al.* [10] and the work by Yu *et al.*, which we refer to as PlaneAE for convenience [24].

Our process consists of three steps (See Fig. 2). First, we use CNNs to infer two inter-plane relationships for every pair of plane instances. Second, we formulate an optimization problem to refine plane parameters by enforcing the inter-plane relationships. Third, we jointly refine the plane segmentation masks by a message passing neural network to be consistent with the refined plane parameters and the inter-plane relationships. We now explain the details.

3.1 Inter-plane Relationships Learning

We consider two types of pairwise inter-plane relationships.

- **Orientation**: Are two planes parallel or orthogonal?
- **Contact**: Are two planes in contact? Where is the contact line in an image?

Manhattan structure is prevalent for man-made environments and the orientation relationship would effectively constrain surface normals for many pairs of planes. Plane-contacts are straight lines, whose information would constrain surface normal/offset parameters and provide precise segmentation boundaries. We employ standard CNNs to infer both relationships.

Orientation-CNN: A pair of planes is classified into three orientation types: *parallel, orthogonal,* or *neither.* The input is an 8-channel tensor: the RGB image (3 channels), the binary segmentation masks of the two planes (2 channels), the depthmaps of the two planes (2 channels), and the dot-product between the two plane normals (1 channel). The depthmap has depth values at every pixel, not just over the plane masks. The dot-product is a scalar and we copy the same value at every pixel location to form an image. ResNet-50 is adopted as the architecture, where we change the first layer to accommodate the input 8-channel tensor and change the last layer to output 3 values that corresponds to the three orientation types. Orientation-CNN is trained with a cross-entropy loss against the ground-truth (See Sect. 4 for the GT preparation).

Contact-CNN: The network classifies if two planes are in contact (binary classification) and estimates the contact line as a pixel-wise segmentation mask (binary segmentation). The input is the same 8-channel tensor as in Orientation-CNN. We again take ResNet-50 as the backbone and replaced the first layer. For binary contact classification, we change the last layer to output a 2D vector. For binary contact segmentation, we attach a branch of bilinear upsampling and convolution layers to the last residual block of ResNet-50, which is adopted from the binary segmentation branch of [24]. The output size of the segmentation mask is the same as the input image. The network is trained with a cross-entropy loss against the ground-truth, where the loss for the segmentation mask is averaged over all the pixels. The classification and segmentation losses are enforced with equal weights. For a non-contact plane pair, an empty mask is the supervision.

3.2 Plane Parameter Refinement

We solve the following optimization problem to refine the plane parameters. Our variables are the plane normal N_i and the offset d_i for each plane: $N_i \cdot X = d_i$. X is a 3D point coordinate.

$$\min_{\{N_i, d_i\}} E_{unit} + E_{input} + E_{parallel} + E_{ortho} + E_{contact}, \tag{1}$$

$$E_{unit} = 10 \sum_{i \in P} (N_i \cdot N_i - 1)^2, \tag{2}$$

$$E_{input} = 10 \sum_{i \in P} w_i (N_i \cdot \overline{N}_i)^2 + \sum_{i \in P} \sum_{p \in M_i} w_i (N_i \cdot \overline{X}_i^p - d_i)^2 / |M_i|, \tag{3}$$

$$E_{parallel} = \sum_{(i,j) \in P_{pa}} w_i w_j (N_i \cdot N_j - 1)^2, \tag{4}$$

$$E_{ortho} = \sum_{(i,j) \in P_{or}} w_i w_j (N_i \cdot N_j)^2, \tag{5}$$

$$E_{contact} = \sum_{(i,j) \in P_{co}} \sum_{p \in M_{i,j}} w_i w_j (D_i^p - D_j^p)^2 / |M_{i,j}|. \tag{6}$$

- E_{unit} enforces N_i to have a unit norm. P denotes the set of planes.

- E_{input} keeps the solution close to the original and breaks the scale/rotational ambiguities inherent in the other terms. The first term is on the plane normal. $\overline{\mathbf{N}}_i$ denotes the initial plane normal. w_i is a rescaled segmentation area: $\sum_{i \in P} w_i = 1$. The second term measures the deviation from the initial depthmap. $\overline{\mathbf{X}}_i^p$ denotes the 3D coordinate of a pixel p based on the initial plane parameters. The plane equation residual is summed over the mask M_i of the i_{th} plane.
- $E_{parallel}$ and E_{ortho} enforces the parallel and orthogonal relationships, respectively. P_{pa} and P_{or} denotes the pairs of planes with the inferred parallel and orthogonal relationships, respectively.
- $E_{contact}$ measures the consistency of depth values along the plane contacts between pairs of planes P_{co} with the inferred contact relationships. For every pixel p in the plane contact area $M_{i,j}$ estimated by the Contact-CNN, we compute the depth values $(\mathbf{D}_i^p, \mathbf{D}_j^p)$ based on their plane parameters. The term evaluates the average depth value discrepancy.

The energy terms are well normalized by the rescaled segmentation areas (w_i). We rescale E_{unit} and the first term of E_{input} by a factor of 10 and keep the balancing weights fixed throughout the experiments. E_{unit} has a large weight because its role is close to a hard constraint (ensuring that the plane normal is a unit vector). E_{input} has a large weight because the normal estimation is usually more accurate than the offset estimation in the initial input from PlaneRCNN and PlaneAE. We use an off-the-shelf BFGS optimization library in SciPy to solve the problem [15].

3.3   Plane Segmentation Refinement (Segmentation-MPN)

PlaneRCNN [10] jointly refines plane segmentation by "ConvAccu Module", which is a special case of more general convolutional message passing neural architecture (Conv-MPN) [26]. PlaneAE [24] estimates segmentation masks jointly by associative embedding. However, there are two major issues in their segmentation results. First, they ignore inter-plane contact relationships: Plane parameters would not be consistent with the boundaries, and the 3D model would look broken (gaps and discontinuities). Second, they tend to under-segment (especially PlaneRCNN) because the ground-truth is often under-segmented, too.[1]

We follow PlaneRCNN and utilize Conv-MPN for joint segmentation refinement. We add the binary split mask as the 5_{th} channel to the input so that the network knows when the segmentation boundary becomes consistent with the plane parameters. A plane may have multiple contacts, and the union of all the split-masks is formed for each plane. We make the following modifications to address the above two issues (See Fig. 3).

---

[1] Ground-truth segmentation comes from plane-fitting to 3D points [10]. For being conservative, they focus on high confidence areas with high point densities only, dropping the plane boundaries.

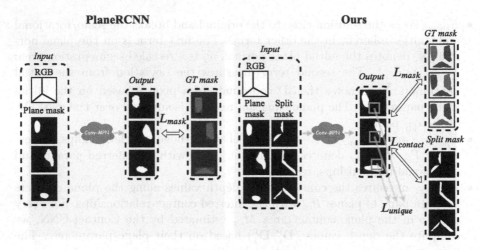

Fig. 3. Contact-aware joint segmentation refinement. We follow PlaneRCNN [10] and utilize Conv-MPN [26] architecture. (Left) In the original formulation in PlaneRCNN, the mask loss (L_{mask}) tries to make the output equal to the under-segmented "ground-truth". (Right) In the new formulation, we change the definition of negative samples (blue pixels) in the mask loss (L_{mask}) to prevent under-segmentation. Furthermore, we add a contact loss $L_{contact}$ with the split mask so that the plane segmentation boundary becomes consistent with the plane parameters. The same split mask is also added to the input of the network. Lastly, we add L_{unique} to prevent over-segmentation and ensure that a pixel (green boxes) belongs to at most one plane (Color figure online)

Resolving Parameter Inconsistencies: Our idea is simple. For each pair of planes with the inferred contact mask, we compute the exact plane boundary inside the mask as a line from the refined plane parameters. We split the mask into two regions along the line and send them as images to Conv-MPN. The split mask serves as the input as well as the loss so that Conv-MPN will learn to satisfy the contact consistency. More precisely, we compute the 3D intersection line from the refined plane parameters and project the line into the image, where the intrinsic parameters are given for each image in the database. After splitting the mask into two regions along the line at the pixel-level, we can determine easily which split mask should belong to which plane by comparing the current plane segmentation and the line. We simply add a cross entropy loss $L_{contact}$ for pixels inside the split contact mask.

Resolving Under-Segmentation: In the original PlaneRCNN formulation [10], the cross entropy loss was defined with the under-segmented "ground-truth" plane mask. The red and blue pixels in Fig. 3 illustrate the positive and negative pixels for the loss (L_{mask}). We modify the definition of negative samples in this mask loss (L_{mask}) to be the union of the other under-segmented "ground-truth" regions instead, allowing Conv-MPN to grow beyond the under-segmented "ground-truth". In order to prevent over-segmentation this time, we introduce a new loss (L_{unique}) which prevents a pixel from belonging to multiple

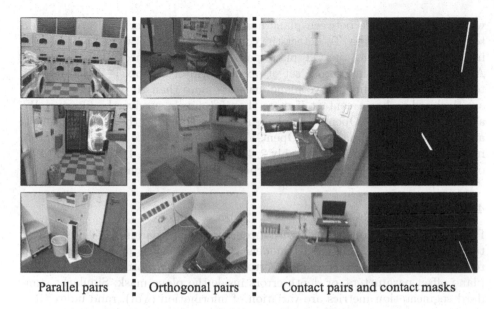

Parallel pairs   Orthogonal pairs   Contact pairs and contact masks

Fig. 4. Inter-plane relationships dataset. Here we show three example pairs for each relationship type, where the PlaneRCNN plane masks are colored by red and blue. For contact pairs, we also show the contact lines as overlays (green) in the third column and as the binary masks in the last column. Note that our relationship annotations are automatically generated from the ScanNet database [3] (Color figure online)

planes. To be precise, the loss is defined at each pixel as

$$L_{unique} = -\log(2 - \max(1, \alpha)). \tag{7}$$

α is the sum of the top 2 mask probabilities at a pixel. The sum of the three terms L_{mask}, $L_{contact}$, and L_{unique} becomes the loss without rescaling.

4   Dataset and Metrics

Inter-plane relationship learning is a new task, where this paper generates the ground-truth and introduces new evaluation metrics (See Fig. 4).

4.1   Dataset

We borrow the piecewise planar reconstruction dataset by Liu *et al.* [10,12], which was originally constructed from ScanNet [3]. We follow the same process in splitting the dataset into training and testing sets. Note that the camera intrinsic parameters are associated with each image. We generate inter-plane relationship labels (parallel, orthogonal, and contact) as follows.

First, we associate each PlaneRCNN plane segment to a corresponding GT segment with the largest overlap. To detect parallel and orthogonal plane pairs, we check if the angle between plane normals are either 0 or 90 degrees with a tolerance of 10 degrees. To detect the contact relationship, we compute the 3D intersection line using the GT plane parameters, and project onto the image. After rastering the line into a set of pixels, we filter out pixels if the distance to the closest pixel in the two plane masks is more than 20 pixels. Two planes are declared to be in contact if more than 5% pixels survive the filtering. We apply 5×5 dilation (OpenCV implementation, 5 times) to the remaining pixels and apply 5×5 Gaussian blur (OpenCV implementation) to obtain the contact mask. The process produced roughly $2,472,000$ plane pairs. 16%, 47%, and 12% of the pairs are labeled as parallel, perpendicular, and in contact, respectively.

4.2 Metrics

Piecewise planar reconstruction with inconsistent plane parameters and segmentation information leads to 3D models with large visual artifacts. Standard reconstruction metrics are angular errors in the plane normals, errors in the plane offset parameters, or depth errors inside the plane mask. Similarly, standard segmentation metrics are variation of information (VoI), rand index (RI), segmentation covering (SC), and intersection over union (IoU) [10,24]. However, these metrics are evaluated per-plane and do not reflect the visual quality of 3D models well, where inter-plane inconsistencies become more noticeable. This paper introduces three new metrics.

Relative Orientation Error (ROE): For each plane pair, we compute the angle between their normals using the GT plane parameters and the reconstructed parameters. The discrepancy of the two angles averaged over all the plane pairs is the metric.

Contact consistency error (CCE): Depth values of the two planes must be the same along the contact line. CCE measures the average depth value discrepancy along the ground-truth contact line. Note a difference from the contact energy term $E_{contact}$ Eq. (6) from the optimization, which measures the discrepancy along the contact line predicted by Contact-CNN. This metric measures the discrepancy along the ground-truth line.

Segmentation Metric Over Contact Mask: This is a simple modification to the standard segmentation metrics. We simply compute the standard metrics (VoI, RI, SC, and IoU) inside the contact line mask instead of an entire image. Segmentation masks must be accurate at its boundaries to achieve high scores.

5   Experiments

We have implemented our approach in Python using the PyTorch library. We train our networks with the Adam optimizer [8] and set the learning rate to 10^{-4}. The batch size of 24 is used for Orientation-CNN and Contact-CNN, and the batch size of 1 is used for segmentation-MPN. The training of each network takes about 10 to 15 h on an NVIDIA GTX 1080 Ti GPU with 11 GB of RAM.

The average run-times of our algorithm (pairwise relationship prediction, BFGS optimization, and segmentation refinement) are shown in Table 1 when testing on an image with the resolution of 224×224.

Table 1. Average running time in seconds of our method

Input method	Relationship prediction	BFGS optimization	Segmentation-MPN	Total
PlaneRCNN	0.35	1.36	1.24	2.95
PlaneAE	0.15	0.84	0.95	1.94

Table 2. Quantitative evaluation of reconstruction accuracy. The unit of the offset error, the depth error and CCE is in centimeters. The unit of normal error and ROE is in degrees. The color cyan denotes the best result in each triplet

	Normal error	Offset error	Depth error	ROE	CCE
PlaneRCNN	12.37	20.12	21.97	12.12	12.92
+Ours (w/o contact)	11.38	19.81	21.98	10.09	14.82
+Ours (all)	11.11	20.09	21.93	10.06	9.25
PlaneAE	9.77	15.53	17.60	11.28	13.05
+Ours (w/o contact)	9.38	15.55	17.40	10.71	13.24
+Ours (all)	9.68	15.85	17.36	10.69	11.59

5.1   Planar Reconstruction

Table 2 provides the quantitative evaluation of the geometrical reconstruction accuracy. The table reports the three standard reconstruction metrics (mean angular error of plane normals, mean absolute error of plane offset parameters, and mean depth error inside the ground-truth segmentation mask) and the new ROE and CCE metrics. We tested the proposed system with PlaneRCNN or PlaneAE while running their released official code. As an ablation study, we also run our optimization process while removing the contact term ($E_{contact}$).

As shown in Table 2, our approach consistently improves normal-error, depth-error, ROE, and CCE metrics, in particular, the last two inter-plane consistency metrics. The offset error rather increased, because it conflicts with the depth error which our optimization minimizes. The offset-error does not take into account the surface region on the plane, and we believe that the depth-error is more informative. The use of the plane-contact constraints have dramatic effects on the CCE metric as expected. ROE and CCE reflect the visual quality of the reconstructed 3D models more accurately as shown in Fig. 5. The models are rendered from viewpoints close to the original in the top half, where the proposed method consistently improves segmentation at plane boundaries,

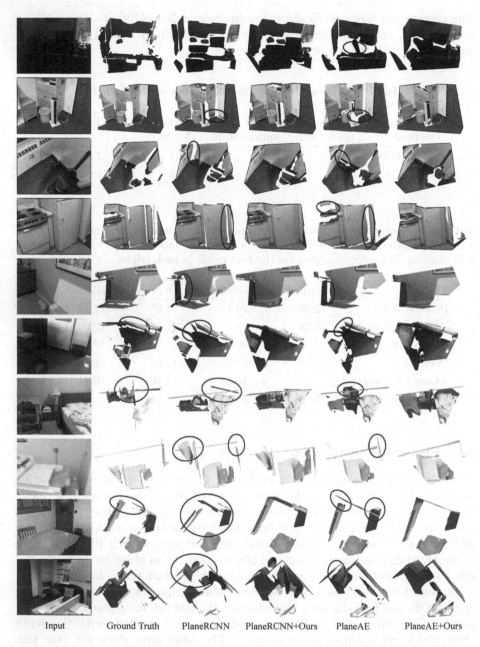

Input   Ground Truth   PlaneRCNN   PlaneRCNN+Ours   PlaneAE   PlaneAE+Ours

Fig. 5. Visual comparison of 3D planar reconstruction results. From left to right, it shows the input RGB image, the ground truth, the PlaneRCNN results [10], our results with PlaneRCNN, the PlaneAE results [24], our results with PlaneAE. The proposed approach fixes incomplete and inconsistent reconstructions at various places, highlighted in red ovals. Also refer to the supplementary video for the best assessment (Color figure online)

often completely closing the gaps in-between. Models are rendered from lateral viewpoints in the bottom half. It is clear that planes meet exactly at their contacts with our approach, while 3D models by PlaneRCNN or PlaneAE often suffer from severe artifacts due to plane gaps and intersections. Also refer to the supplementary video for the best assessment of the visual quality.

5.2   Plane Instance Segmentation

"Ground-truth" plane segmentation in the PlaneRCNN dataset have large errors. We have randomly chosen 50 testing images and manually annotated ground-truth plane segmentation by the LabelMe tool [16] (See the second column of Fig. 6). Following [10,24], we employ four segmentation metrics mentioned in Sect. 4.2 (VoI, RI, SC, and IoU). To further evaluate the segmentation accuracy along the contact plane boundary, we have annotated the plane contact lines with LabelMe and computed the same metrics only inside the contact lines (See Sect. 4.2). Table 3 shows that our approach consistently improves segmentation accuracy over both PlaneRCNN and PlaneAE, especially along the contact lines. Figure 6 qualitatively demonstrates that our approach produces more complete segmentation, especially at plane boundaries. Furthermore, our plane segmentation boundaries are exact straight lines that are consistent with the plane parameters, while the boundaries are usually curved in the raw PlaneRCNN and PlaneAE results. It is also noteworthy that we faithfully recover the T-junctions in an indoor scene as shown in both Fig. 5 and Fig. 6.

Table 3. Quantitative evaluation of plane segmentation. The smaller the better for VoI, while the larger the better for the other metrics. The color cyan denotes the best result in each pair

Method	Evaluation on the entire image				Evaluation on contact line only			
	VoI↓	RI	SC	IoU%	VoI↓	RI	SC	IoU%
PlaneRCNN	0.967	0.910	0.788	78.98	2.301	0.744	0.456	39.90
PlaneRCNN+Ours	0.822	0.936	0.830	80.90	2.146	0.778	0.508	48.96
PlaneAE	1.183	0.881	0.735	69.86	2.253	0.735	0.466	38.90
PlaneAE+Ours	1.002	0.882	0.753	69.26	2.101	0.733	0.486	41.72

5.3   Pairwise Relationship Inference

Table 4 evaluates the inter-plane relationship classification (parallel, orthogonal, and contact) and the contact mask estimation by our two CNN modules (Orientation-CNN and Contact-CNN). We compare against three baseline methods that use PlaneRCNN for reconstruction and simple heuristics to infer the relationships between planes.

Input   Ground Truth   PlaneRCNN   PlaneRCNN+Ours   PlaneAE   PlaneAE+Ours

Fig. 6. Visual comparison of planar segmentation results. From left to right, it shows the input RGB image, our ground-truth manual annotation by LabelMe [16], the PlaneRCNN results [10], our results with PlaneRCNN, the PlaneAE results [24], and our results with PlaneAE. Improvements by the proposed approach are noticeable at various places, as highlighted in the red ovals (Color figure online)

- *PlaneRCNN-Angle* is a baseline for the orientation classification utilizing PlaneRCNN reconstruction. It simply takes the plane surface normals from PlaneRCNN, calculates the angle differences for pairs of planes, then classifies the relationship (parallel, orthogonal, or neither) based on the angular difference with a tolerance of 10 degrees.
- *PlaneRCNN-Contact1* is a baseline for the contact inference utilizing PlaneRCNN plane masks. We perform the dilation operation 5 times (by OpenCV implementation) to expand each PlaneRCNN plane mask. A pair of planes is deemed to be in contact if the intersection of their expanded masks have more than 10 pixels. The intersection region is reported as the contact mask.
- *PlaneRCNN-Contact2* is a baseline for the contact inference utilizing PlaneRCNN plane masks as well as parameters. We follow the steps of generating ground-truth contact information in Sect. 4, while replacing the GT plane parameters by the PlaneRCNN parameters. This baseline takes into account both 2D segmentation masks and 3D plane depths in judging the contact relationship.

Table 4. Inter-plane relationship evaluation on the two CNN modules (Orientation-CNN and Contact-CNN). F1-scores are used for the parallel, orthogonal, and contact relationship classifier. IoU metric is used for the contact mask prediction. We compare against a few baseline methods (PlaneRCNN-Angle, PlaneRCNN-Contact1, and PlaneRCNN-Contact2). We also conduct an ablation study where we control the amount of input information. The color cyan and orange denote the best and the second best results

Method	F1-score (parallel)	F1-score (orthogonal)	F1-score (contact)	IoU% (contact mask)
PlaneRCNN-Angle	0.51	0.68	–	–
PlaneRCNN-Contact1	–	–	0.64	35.75
PlaneRCNN-Contact2			0.69	21.60
Ours (mask)	0.37	0.51	0.69	42.84
Ours (mask+RGB)	0.45	0.58	0.69	41.40
Ours (mask+RGB+depth)	0.59	0.74	0.72	42.64
Ours (all)	0.60	0.76	0.75	45.43

Table 4 demonstrates that the proposed approach performs the best in all the metrics. While all the baselines perform reasonably well by utilizing the PlaneRCNN reconstruction results, our simple CNN solutions (Orientation-CNN and Contact-CNN) infer inter-plane relationships the best. The ablation study (the last 4 rows) shows that the CNN modules consistently improves numbers as more input information is given.

6   Conclusion

This paper proposed a novel single-image piecewise planar reconstruction technique that infers and enforces inter-plane relationships. Our approach utilizes CNNs to infer the relationships, refines the plane parameters by optimization, and employs a message passing neural network for jointly refining the plane segmentation, while enforcing the inter-plane consistency constraints. We have generated ground-truth inter-plane relationship labels and introduced three new metrics in assessing reconstruction and segmentation. Qualitative and quantitative evaluations demonstrate the effectiveness of the proposed method.

Acknowledgments. This research is partially supported by NSERC Discovery Grants, NSERC Discovery Grants Accelerator Supplements, and DND/NSERC Discovery Grant Supplement.

References

1. Bauchet, J.P., Lafarge, F.: KIPPI: kinetic polygonal partitioning of images. In: Proceedings of the IEEE Conference on Computer Vision and Pattern Recognition, pp. 3146–3154 (2018)
2. Chen, J., Liu, C., Wu, J., Furukawa, Y.: Floor-SP: inverse cad for floorplans by sequential room-wise shortest path. In: Proceedings of the IEEE International Conference on Computer Vision, pp. 2661–2670 (2019)
3. Dai, A., Chang, A.X., Savva, M., Halber, M., Funkhouser, T., Nießner, M.: ScanNet: richly-annotated 3d reconstructions of indoor scenes. In: Proceedings of the IEEE Conference on Computer Vision and Pattern Recognition, pp. 5828–5839 (2017)
4. Deng, Z., Todorovic, S., Latecki, L.J.: Unsupervised object region proposals for RGB-D indoor scenes. Comput. Vis. Image Underst. **154**, 127–136 (2017)
5. Furukawa, Y., Curless, B., Seitz, S.M., Szeliski, R.: Manhattan-world stereo. In: 2009 IEEE Conference on Computer Vision and Pattern Recognition, pp. 1422–1429. IEEE (2009)
6. Gallup, D., Frahm, J.M., Pollefeys, M.: Piecewise planar and non-planar stereo for urban scene reconstruction. In: 2010 IEEE Computer Society Conference on Computer Vision and Pattern Recognition, pp. 1418–1425. IEEE (2010)
7. Hedau, V., Hoiem, D., Forsyth, D.: Recovering the spatial layout of cluttered rooms. In: 2009 IEEE 12th International Conference on Computer Vision, pp. 1849–1856. IEEE (2009)
8. Kingma, D.P., Ba, J.: Adam: a method for stochastic optimization. arXiv preprint arXiv:1412.6980 (2014)
9. Kushal, A., Seitz, S.M.: Single view reconstruction of piecewise swept surfaces. In: 2013 International Conference on 3D Vision-3DV 2013, pp. 239–246. IEEE (2013)
10. Liu, C., Kim, K., Gu, J., Furukawa, Y., Kautz, J.: PlanerCNN: 3D plane detection and reconstruction from a single image. In: Proceedings of the IEEE Conference on Computer Vision and Pattern Recognition, pp. 4450–4459 (2019)
11. Liu, C., Wu, J., Kohli, P., Furukawa, Y.: Raster-to-vector: revisiting floorplan transformation. In: Proceedings of the IEEE International Conference on Computer Vision, pp. 2195–2203 (2017)

12. Liu, C., Yang, J., Ceylan, D., Yumer, E., Furukawa, Y.: PlaneNet: piece-wise planar reconstruction from a single RGB image. In: Proceedings of the IEEE Conference on Computer Vision and Pattern Recognition, pp. 2579–2588 (2018)
13. Liu, C., Schwing, A.G., Kundu, K., Urtasun, R., Fidler, S.: Rent3D: floor-plan priors for monocular layout estimation. In: Proceedings of the IEEE Conference on Computer Vision and Pattern Recognition, pp. 3413–3421 (2015)
14. Monszpart, A., Mellado, N., Brostow, G.J., Mitra, N.J.: RAPTER: rebuilding man-made scenes with regular arrangements of planes. ACM Trans. Graph. **34**(4), 103–111 (2015)
15. Nocedal, J., Wright, S.: Numerical Optimization. Springer, New York (2006). https://doi.org/10.1007/978-0-387-40065-5
16. Russell, B.C., Torralba, A., Murphy, K.P., Freeman, W.T.: LabelMe: a database and web-based tool for image annotation. Int. J. Comput. Vis. **77**(1–3), 157–173 (2008)
17. Sharma, G., Goyal, R., Liu, D., Kalogerakis, E., Maji, S.: CSGNET: neural shape parser for constructive solid geometry. In: Proceedings of the IEEE Conference on Computer Vision and Pattern Recognition, pp. 5515–5523 (2018)
18. Shi, Y., Xu, K., Nießner, M., Rusinkiewicz, S., Funkhouser, T.: PlaneMatch: patch coplanarity prediction for robust RGB-D reconstruction. In: Ferrari, V., Hebert, M., Sminchisescu, C., Weiss, Y. (eds.) ECCV 2018. LNCS, vol. 11212, pp. 767–784. Springer, Cham (2018). https://doi.org/10.1007/978-3-030-01237-3_46
19. Silberman, N., Hoiem, D., Kohli, P., Fergus, R.: Indoor segmentation and support inference from RGBD images. In: Fitzgibbon, A., Lazebnik, S., Perona, P., Sato, Y., Schmid, C. (eds.) ECCV 2012. LNCS, vol. 7576, pp. 746–760. Springer, Heidelberg (2012). https://doi.org/10.1007/978-3-642-33715-4_54
20. Sinha, S., Steedly, D., Szeliski, R.: Piecewise planar stereo for image-based rendering (2009)
21. Sun, C., Hsiao, C.W., Sun, M., Chen, H.T.: HorizonNet: learning room layout with 1D representation and pano stretch data augmentation. In: Proceedings of the IEEE Conference on Computer Vision and Pattern Recognition, pp. 1047–1056 (2019)
22. Xiao, J., Furukawa, Y.: Reconstructing the world's museums. Int. J. Comput. Vis. **110**(3), 243–258 (2014)
23. Yang, F., Zhou, Z.: Recovering 3D planes from a single image via convolutional neural networks. In: Ferrari, V., Hebert, M., Sminchisescu, C., Weiss, Y. (eds.) ECCV 2018. LNCS, vol. 11214, pp. 87–103. Springer, Cham (2018). https://doi.org/10.1007/978-3-030-01249-6_6
24. Yu, Z., Zheng, J., Lian, D., Zhou, Z., Gao, S.: Single-image piece-wise planar 3D reconstruction via associative embedding. In: Proceedings of the IEEE Conference on Computer Vision and Pattern Recognition, pp. 1029–1037 (2019)
25. Zebedin, L., Bauer, J., Karner, K., Bischof, H.: Fusion of Feature- and Area-Based Information for Urban Buildings Modeling from Aerial Imagery. In: Forsyth, D., Torr, P., Zisserman, A. (eds.) ECCV 2008. LNCS, vol. 5305, pp. 873–886. Springer, Heidelberg (2008). https://doi.org/10.1007/978-3-540-88693-8_64
26. Zhang, F., Nauata, N., Furukawa, Y.: Conv-mpn: Convolutional message passing neural network for structured outdoor architecture reconstruction. In: Proceedings of the IEEE Conference on Computer Vision and Pattern Recognition (2020)
27. Zheng, J., Zhang, J., Li, J., Tang, R., Gao, S., Zhou, Z.: Structured3D: a large photo-realistic dataset for structured 3d modeling. arXiv preprint arXiv:1908.00222 (2019)

Intra-class Feature Variation Distillation for Semantic Segmentation

Yukang Wang[2], Wei Zhou[2], Tao Jiang[2], Xiang Bai[2], and Yongchao Xu[1(✉)]

[1] School of Computer Science, Wuhan University, Wuhan, China
yongchao.xu@whu.edu.cn
[2] School of EiC, Huazhong University of Science and Technology, Wuhan, China
{wangyk,weizhou,taojiang,xbai,yongchao.xu}@hust.edu.cn

Abstract. Current state-of-the-art semantic segmentation methods usually require high computational resources for accurate segmentation. One promising way to achieve a good trade-off between segmentation accuracy and efficiency is knowledge distillation. In this paper, different from previous methods performing knowledge distillation for densely pairwise relations, we propose a novel intra-class feature variation distillation (IFVD) to transfer the intra-class feature variation (IFV) of the cumbersome model (teacher) to the compact model (student). Concretely, we compute the feature center (regarded as the prototype) of each class and characterize the IFV with the set of similarity between the feature on each pixel and its corresponding class-wise prototype. The teacher model usually learns more robust intra-class feature representation than the student model, making them have different IFV. Transferring such IFV from teacher to student could make the student mimic the teacher better in terms of feature distribution, and thus improve the segmentation accuracy. We evaluate the proposed approach on three widely adopted benchmarks: Cityscapes, CamVid and Pascal VOC 2012, consistently improving state-of-the-art methods. The code is available at https://github.com/YukangWang/IFVD.

Keywords: Semantic segmentation · Knowledge distillation · Intra-class feature variation

1 Introduction

Semantic segmentation is a fundamental topic in computer vision, which aims to assign each pixel in the input image with a unique category label. The recent surge of work based on fully convolutional networks [25] (FCNs) has lead to vast performance improvements for semantic segmentation algorithms. However, seeking for high segmentation accuracy often comes at a cost of more runtime. Most state-of-the-art semantic segmentation frameworks [10,13,41,43,46] usually require high computational resources, which limits their use in many real-world applications such as autonomous driving, virtual reality, and robots.

© Springer Nature Switzerland AG 2020
A. Vedaldi et al. (Eds.): ECCV 2020, LNCS 12352, pp. 346–362, 2020.
https://doi.org/10.1007/978-3-030-58571-6_21

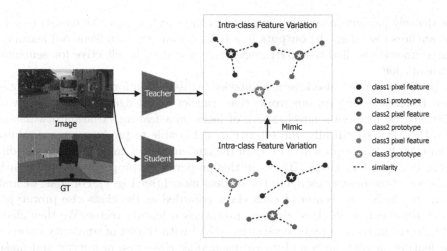

Fig. 1. The teacher model and the student model are endowed with different intra-class feature variation, which can be characterized as the set of similarity (dashed lines) between the feature on each pixel and its corresponding class-wise prototype. Higher similarity means lower variation. Our motivation is to transfer such variation of the teacher model to the student model, which makes the student model mimic the teacher model better, and thus improves the accuracy of the student model.

To tackle this problem, some real-time architectures for semantic segmentation have been proposed, *e.g.*, ENet [28], ESPNet [26], ICNet [45] and BiSeNet [40].

Model compression is a popular way to achieve high efficiency. In general, existing methods can be roughly divided into three categories: quantization [31,37], pruning [2,14,15,36] and knowledge distillation [19,33,44]. The quantization-based methods represent the parameters of filter kernels and weighting matrices using fewer bits. The pruning-based approaches aim to trim the network by removing redundant connections between neurons of adjacent layers. The notion of knowledge distillation is first proposed in [7] and then popularized by Hinton *et al.* [19]. The key idea is to utilize the soft probabilities of a cumbersome model (teacher) to supervise the training of a compact model (student). Later, in [21,44], the authors suggest transferring attention maps of the teacher model to the student model. In [27,30,35], the authors also attempt to transfer pairwise or triple-wise relations. Prior works using knowledge distillation are mostly devoted to classification tasks and achieve impressive results.

Some recent works [18,24] adopt knowledge distillation for semantic segmentation. Similar to the classification task, a straightforward scheme is to align individual pixel-wise outputs. This forces the student model to mimic the teacher model in terms of output probability maps. Different from the classification task, semantic segmentation has a structured output. The long-range dependencies are crucial for semantic segmentation, and the teacher model and student model usually capture different long-range contextual information due to their differences in receptive fields. Motivated by this, in [18,24], the authors propose to transfer the densely pairwise relations computed in the feature space. Moreover, in [24], the authors also align the outputs in a holistic manner via adversarial learning. These knowledge distillation strategies are proved to be effective for semantic segmentation.

In this paper, we also leverage knowledge distillation for semantic segmentation. Different from previous works that transfer knowledge on densely pairwise relations, we propose a novel notion of intra-class feature variation distillation (IFVD). More specifically, the teacher model is able to produce a more robust intra-class feature representation than the student model, making them have different degrees of variation. Based on this property, we propose to transfer such variation of the teacher model to the student model (see Fig. 1). For that, we first compute the feature center of each class, regarded as the class-wise prototype, which represents each class with one prototypical feature vector. We then characterize the intra-class feature variation (IFV) with the set of similarity between the feature on each pixel and its corresponding class-wise prototype and make the student model mimic such IFV of the teacher model, improving the segmentation accuracy of the student model. Extensive experiments demonstrate that the proposed IFVD consistently achieves noticeable improvements on the student model.

The main contributions of this paper are two-fold: 1) We propose a novel notion of intra-class feature variation distillation for semantic segmentation. More specifically, we force the student model to mimic the set of similarity between the feature on each pixel and its corresponding class-wise prototype, alleviating the difference of feature distributions between the student model and the teacher model. This helps to improve the segmentation accuracy of the student model. To the best of our knowledge, this is the first application of the intra-class feature variation concept to knowledge distillation for semantic segmentation. 2) The proposed intra-class feature variation distillation consistently improves upon existing methods using knowledge distillation for semantic segmentation, further boosting the state-of-the-art results of the compact model on three popular benchmark datasets.

The reminder of this paper is organized as follows. We shortly review some related works in Sect. 2 and clarify the differences with our approach. We then detail the proposed method, aptly named IFVD in Sect. 3, followed by extensive experiments in Sect. 4. Lastly, we conclude and give some perspectives on the future work in Sect. 5.

2   Related Work

We shortly review some related works on semantic segmentation and vision tasks leveraging knowledge distillation for boosting the accuracy while maintaining the efficiency of the compact model.

2.1   Semantic Segmentation

Semantic segmentation is one of the most fundamental topics in computer vision. The recent rapid development of deep neural networks has had a tremendous impact on semantic segmentation. Following the pioneer work [25] that adopts fully convolution network for semantic segmentation, many efforts have been made to boost the segmentation performance by exploiting the multi-scale context. For instance, Chen et al. [8] and Yu et al. [42] utilize dilated convolution to enlarge the receptive field and preserve the spatial size of the feature map. Chen et al. further develop DeeplabV3+ [10] with an encoder-decoder structure to recover the spatial information. PSPNet [46] apply the pyramid pooling to aggregate contextual information. Recently, some methods resort to the attention mechanism to guide the network learning and alleviate inconsistency in segmentation. For example, Yu et al. [41] adopt channel attention to select the features. OCNet [43] focuses on the context aggregation by spatial attention. In [13], the authors consider the combination of spatial and channel attention. These state-of-the-art methods aim to boost the segmentation performance at the cost of high computational resources.

Highly efficient semantic segmentation has been recently studied to address the above issue. ENet [28] explores spatial decomposition of convolutional kernels and achieves similar accuracy to SegNet [4] with 79x less parameters. ESPNet [26] designs an efficient spatial pyramid module that decomposes the standard convolution into point-wise convolution followed by spatial pyramid to reduce computational cost. In [45], the authors propose ICNet, an image cascade network based on the compressed PSPNet for real-time semantic segmentation. Yu et al. [40] introduce BiSeNet contains a spatial path and a context path to raise efficiency.

2.2   Vision Tasks Using Knowledge Distillation

Knowledge distillation has been widely studied in recent years. The concept is popularized by Hinton et al. in [19], which represents the process of training a student model with the objective of matching the soft probabilities of a teacher model. Similar ideas can also be found in [3,5,7]. With knowledge distillation, the student model performs well in terms of accuracy while maintaining efficiency. Various knowledge distillation schemes have been proposed recently. Romero et al. [33] utilize additional linear projection layers to minimize the discrepancy of high-level features. Zagoruyko et al. [44] and Huang et al. [21] transfer the attention map of the teacher model to the student model. Yim et al. [39] consider the flow knowledge between layers. Peng et al. [30] introduce correlation congruence for knowledge distillation to transfer not only the instance-level information but also the correlation between instances. Xu et al. [38] apply knowledge distillation based on conditional adversarial networks.

Prior works are mostly devoted to image classification. With growing interests in this topic, knowledge distillation approaches are proposed in other vision

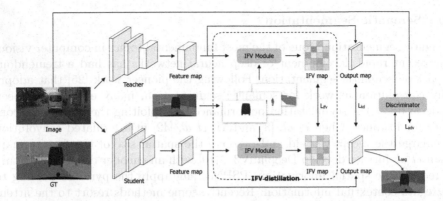

Fig. 2. Pipeline of the proposed intra-class feature variation distillation (IFVD). We introduce an IFV module to obtain the intra-class feature variation (IFV) maps. Knowledge transfer is then applied to the IFV maps of the teacher model and the student model. The original knowledge distillation loss (the KL divergence on outputs of teacher and student models) and adversarial learning are also included in our pipeline to further align the student model to the teacher model in the output space.

tasks, including semantic segmentation. He *et al.* [18] adapt the knowledge distillation with an additional auto-encoder and also transfer the densely pairwise affinity maps to the student model. Liu *et al.* [24] propose structured knowledge distillation (SKD), which also transfers pairwise relations and forces the outputs of the student model to mimic the teacher model from a holistic view via adversarial learning. The self-attention distillation (SAD) is introduced in [20] to explore attention maps derived from high-level features as the distillation target for shallow layers.

Most of the existing knowledge distillation approaches for semantic segmentation rely on transferring pairwise relations. However, our proposed IFVD solves the problem from a different aspect, which focuses on the intra-class feature variation (IFV). We propose to characterize the IFV with the set of similarity between the feature on each pixel and its corresponding class-wise prototype. The class-wise prototype is a prototypical representation for each class. This kind of similarity indicates how compact the intra-class feature distribution is. On the other hand, the stronger teacher model usually provides a more robust intra-class feature representation than the student model. Different feature distributions make the difference in semantic segmentation. The proposed IFVD forces the student model to explicitly mimic the intra-class feature variation, alleviating the difference in feature distribution between the student model and the teacher model. This is beneficial for improving the segmentation accuracy of the student model.

3 Method

3.1 Overview

Semantic segmentation densely classifies each pixel into a class category. Though many efforts have been made to maintain the intra-class consistency, intra-class variation in feature space still exists. Indeed, it is almost impossible for current CNN models to learn exactly the same feature for those pixels within the same category. Equipped with different feature extractors, the cumbersome model (teacher) and the compact model (student) have different degrees of intra-class feature variation. On the other hand, feature representation learning plays an important role in semantic segmentation. Different feature distributions lead to different segmentation results. The intra-class feature variation (IFV) is closely related to the feature distribution. Transferring such knowledge from teacher to student could make the student mimic the teacher better in terms of feature distribution, and thus improve the performance of the student model. Therefore, we propose to perform the knowledge distillation on the intra-class feature variation. The overall pipeline of the proposed method, dubbed intra-class feature variation distillation (IFVD), is depicted in Fig. 2. In Sect. 3.2, we introduce the intra-class feature variation map to characterize the IFV of a model. We then detail the intra-class feature variation distillation in Sect. 3.3.

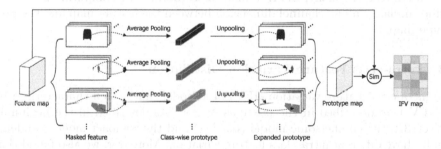

Fig. 3. Illustration of the proposed IFV module for computing the IFV map of a model. The masked feature for each class is generated from the feature map and the down-sampled label map (of the same size as the underlying feature map). Then the prototype of each class is obtained by masked average pooling and expanded to form the prototype map. Finally, we characterize the intra-class feature variation by computing the pixel-wise cosine similarity along channel dimension between the feature map and the prototype map.

3.2 Intra-class Feature Variation Map

We characterize the intra-class feature variation of a model using the map of feature similarity between each pixel and its corresponding class-wise prototype. Such intra-class feature variation (IFV) maps can be easily obtained in two steps.

First, we compute the prototype for each class c by averaging the features on all pixels having the same class label c. Then we perform the cosine similarity function between the feature of each pixel and its corresponding class-wise prototype. Formally, the IFV map M is computed as follows:

$$M(p) = sim(f(p), \frac{1}{|\mathcal{S}_p|} \sum_{q \in \mathcal{S}_p} f(q)), \tag{1}$$

where $f(p)$ denotes the feature on pixel p, $\mathcal{S}_p$ is the set of pixels having the same label as pixel p, $|\mathcal{S}_p|$ stands for the size of the set $\mathcal{S}_p$, and sim is a similarity function. Specifically, we adopt the *Cosine* similarity for all experiments in this paper.

As shown in Fig. 3, to embed the proposed IFVD in existing deep neural networks, we propose an IFV module including the above steps. Concretely, we first down-sample the label map with the nearest interpolation to match the spatial size of the feature map. Then we select the region of the same label for each class and apply the average pooling on the masked feature along the spatial dimension. In this way, the prototype of each class is obtained. We then expand each class-wise prototype by unpooling operation on the masked region. In consequence, a prototype map with the same size as the input feature map is produced, in which each position stores the corresponding class-wise prototypical feature vector. Finally, the IFV map M is obtained by computing pixel-wise cosine similarity along channel dimension between the feature map and the prototype map.

3.3 Intra-class Feature Variation Distillation

The intra-class feature variation (IFV) of a model can be well characterized by the IFV map described in the previous section. As described in the beginning of Sect. 3.1, the cumbersome model (teacher) and the compact model (student) usually have different intra-class feature variation. Moreover, we also found that there is still a bias of IFV after using existing knowledge distillation strategies. Therefore, we propose the intra-class feature variation distillation (IFVD), which aims to make the student model mimic better the teacher model.

A straightforward idea to achieve this goal is to minimize the distance between intra-class feature variation maps of the teacher model and the student model. Specifically, we employ the conventional Mean Squared (L2) loss as below:

$$L_{ifv} = \frac{1}{N} \sum_{p \in \Omega} (M_s(p) - M_t(p))^2, \tag{2}$$

where N is the number of pixels, Ω denotes the image domain, M_t and M_s represent the corresponding intra-class feature variation map (computed by Eq. (1)) of the teacher model and the student model, respectively.

The loss function in Eq. (2) makes the student model to mimic the intra-class feature variation of the teacher model. The original knowledge distillation loss and adversarial learning are also included in our pipeline to make the student model not only mimic the feature distribution but also the output score map of the teacher model.

The original KD loss is a conventional and widely adopted objective for many vision tasks. It adds a strong congruent constraint on predictions. Formally, we minimize the Kullback-Leibler (KL) divergence between the output score maps S of the teacher model and the student model as follows:

$$L_{kd} = \frac{1}{N} \sum_{p \in \Omega} \sum_{i=1}^{C} S_s^i(p) \, log \, \frac{S_s^i(p)}{S_t^i(p)}, \tag{3}$$

where C denotes the total number of classes, $S_s^i(p)$ and $S_t^i(p)$ denote the probability of i-th class on pixel p produced by the student model and the teacher model, respectively.

Adversarial learning for knowledge distillation can be first found in [38]. Liu et al. [24] shares the similar idea for semantic segmentation, named holistic distillation. We also leverage the adversarial learning performed in the output space. More specifically, we first train a discriminator to distinguish whether an input is from the teacher model or the student model, by assessing how well the raw image and the segmentation map match. Then the segmentation network is trained to fool the discriminator. Formally, the loss for training discriminator L_d and adversarial item L_{adv} can be formulated as follows:

$$L_d = \mathbb{E}_{z_s \sim p_s(z_s)}[D(z_s|I)] - \mathbb{E}_{z_t \sim p_t(z_t)}[D(z_t|I)], \tag{4}$$

$$L_{adv} = \mathbb{E}_{z_s \sim p_s(z_s)}[D(z_s|I)], \tag{5}$$

where $\mathbb{E}[\cdot]$ represents the expectation operator. $D(\cdot)$ is an embedding network as the discriminator. I and z are the input image and the corresponding segmentation map.

For the proposed intra-class feature variation distillation (IFVD), the whole training objective is composed of a conventional cross-entropy loss L_{seg} for semantic segmentation and three loss items for knowledge distillation:

$$L = L_{seg} + \lambda_1 L_{kd} - \lambda_2 L_{adv} + \lambda_3 L_{ifv}, \tag{6}$$

where λ_1, λ_2, λ_3 are set to 10, 0.1 and 50, respectively.

During training, we alternatively optimize the discriminator D with L_d in Eq. (4) and the segmentation network with L in Eq. (6).

4   Experiments

To validate the effectiveness of the proposed IFVD, we conduct experiments on three common segmentation benchmark datasets: Cityscapes [11], CamVid [6] and Pascal VOC 2012 [12].

4.1   Datasets and Evaluation Metrics

Cityscapes [11] is a challenging benchmark collected for urban scene parsing. The dataset contains 5000 finely annotated images divided into 2975, 500 and 1525 images for training, validation and testing, respectively. It provides 30 common classes and 19 of them are used for evaluation. Similar to [24], we do not use the coarsely labeled data.

CamVid [6] is an automotive dataset extracted from high resolution video frames. It is split into 367 images for training and 233 images for testing. 11 classes are utilized for evaluation. The 12th class represents the unlabeled data that we ignore during training.

Pascal VOC 2012 [12] is a segmentation benchmark containing 20 foreground object categories and one background class. Following prior works [8,46], we use the augmented data with extra annotations provided by [16] resulting in 10582, 1449 and 1456 images for training, validation and testing, respectively. We use the *train* split for training and report performance on the *val* split.

Evaluation Metrics. In all experiments, we adopt the commonly used mean Intersection-over-Union (mIoU) to measure segmentation accuracy. All models are tested under a single-scale setting. For a more robust and fair comparison, we report the average results of multiple models from the final epoch. The number of parameters is obtained by summing the number of elements for every parameter group in PyTorch [29] and "FLOPs" are calculated with the PyTorch version implementation [1] on a fixed input size (512×1024).

4.2   Implementation Details

Network Architectures. For a fair comparison, we experiment on the same cumbersome and compact networks as [24]. More specifically, we adopt the segmentation architecture PSPNet [46] with ResNet101 [17] backbone as the teacher model for all experiments. The student model also utilizes PSPNet [46] as the segmentation architecture but with different backbone networks. For the backbone of student model, we conduct experiments on ResNet18 [17] and ResNet18 (0.5), the width-halved version of ResNet18, respectively. We further replace the student backbone with EfficientNet-B0 [34] and EfficientNet-B1 [34] to validate the effectiveness of the proposed IFVD when the teacher model and the student model are of different architectural types.

Training Details. For all our experiments, we first pretrain the teacher model following the training process of [46] and then keep the parameters frozen during the distillation progress. For the training process of the student, we use SGD as the optimizer with the "poly" learning rate policy where the learning rate equals to the base one multiplying $base\_lr * (1 - \frac{iter}{total\_iter})^{power}$. The base learning rate $base\_lr$ is initialized to 0.01 and the power is set to 0.9. We employ a batch size of 8 and 40000 iterations without specification. For the data augmentation, we only apply random flipping and random scaling in the range of $[0.5, 2]$. We choose image crop size as 512×512 for the limited GPU memory. The implementation is based on the PyTorch [29] platform. All our distillation experiments are carried out on a workstation with an Intel Xeon 16-core CPU (3.5 GHz), 64 GB RAM, and a single NIVIDIA Titan Xp GPU card of 12 GB memory.

Table 1. Ablation study on Cityscapes.

Method			val mIoU (%)
T: ResNet101			78.56
S: ResNet18			69.10
$Loss_{kd}$	$Loss_{adv}$	$Loss_{ifv}$	val mIoU (%)
✓			70.51 (+1.41)
✓	✓		72.47 (+3.37)
✓	✓	✓	74.54 (+5.44)

4.3 Ablation Study

As introduced in Sect. 3.3, the proposed IFVD contains three loss items for knowledge distillation, $Loss_{kd}$, $Loss_{adv}$ and $Loss_{ifv}$. Therefore, we study their contributions, respectively, on Cityscapes. Specifically, we first train the teacher model with ResNet101 backbone and then perform the knowledge distillation on the student model with ResNet18 backbone. As shown in Table 1, the original KD loss improves the student model without distillation by 1.41%. The gain increases to 3.37% when adversarial learning is also adopted. Further aligning the intra-class feature variation (IFV) boosts the improvement to 5.44%. The gap between student and teacher is reduced from 9.46% to 4.02%. These results demonstrate the effectiveness of the proposed IFVD, which is also complementary to other existing methods.

4.4 Results

Cityscapes. We first evaluate the proposed IFVD on the Cityscapes dataset [11]. Since the method in [24] does not provide experimental results with EfficientNet, we have implemented [24] with EfficientNet using the code released by [24]. The quantitative results are listed in Table 2. IFVD improves the student model built on ResNet18 without distillation by 5.44% on *val* set and 5.14% on *test* set. We also apply the proposed distillation scheme on ResNet18 (0.5), which is a width-halved version of the original ResNet18 and not pretrained on ImageNet. The proposed IFVD leads to an improvement of 7.95% on *val* set and 9.58% on *test* set. When the teacher model and the student model are of different architectural types, similar consistent improvements can also be obtained. Specifically, with the student model built on EfficientNet-B0, IFVD achieves a

6.36% and 4.46% mIoU boosting over the baseline model, on *val* set and *test* set, respectively. The gains shift to 6.10% and 4.51% when EfficientNet-B1 is adopted as the student model. Compared with SKD [24] relying on transferring pairwise relations, the proposed IFVD achieves consistent improvements, ranging from 0.72% to 3.37% on all involved student networks. These results demonstrate the effectiveness of the proposed IFVD. Some qualitative comparisons, *e.g.*, with ResNet18 as the student backbone, are illustrated in Fig. 4.

Table 2. Quantitative results on Cityscapes. * means the results we reproduced using the released code of [24], which does not provide experimental results with EfficientNet.

Method	*val* mIoU(%)	*test* mIoU(%)	Params (M)	FLOPs (G)
Some related semantic segmentation methods				
ENet [28]	-	58.3	0.3580	3.612
ESPNet [26]	-	60.3	0.3635	4.422
ERFNet [32]	-	68.0	2.067	25.60
ICNet [45]	-	69.5	26.5	28.3
FCN [25]	-	65.3	134.5	333.9
RefineNet [23]	-	73.6	118.1	525.7
OCNet [43]	-	80.1	62.58	548.5
PSPNet [46]	-	78.4	70.43	574.9
Comparison with different distillation schemes				
T: ResNet101	78.56	76.78	70.43	574.9
S: ResNet18	69.10	67.60	13.07	125.8
+ SKD [24]	72.70	71.40		
+ IFVD (ours)	74.54	72.74		
S: ResNet18 (0.5)	55.40	54.10	3.27	31.53
+ SKD [24]	61.60	60.50		
+ IFVD (ours)	63.35	63.68		
S: EfficientNet-B0	58.37	58.06	4.19	7.967
+ SKD* [24]	62.90	61.80		
+ IFVD (ours)	64.73	62.52		
S: EfficientNet-B1	60.40	59.91	6.70	9.896
+ SKD* [24]	63.13	62.59		
+ IFVD (ours)	66.50	64.42		

CamVid. We then evaluate the proposed IFVD on CamVid dataset [6]. The quantitative results are listed in Table 3. The proposed IFVD improves the model without distillation by 1.5% while slightly improving SKD [24] by 0.8%. Moreover, the gains shift to 2.5% and 0.5% when employing the student model

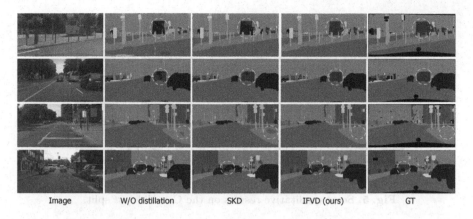

Image   W/O distillation   SKD   IFVD (ours)   GT

Fig. 4. Some qualitative comparisons on the Cityscapes *val* split.

Table 3. The segmentation performance on CamVid *test* set. * means the results we reproduced using the released code of [24], which does not provide experimental results with EfficientNet.

Method	*test* mIoU (%)	Params (M)
Some related semantic segmentation methods		
FCN [25]	57.0	134.5
ENet [28]	51.3	0.3580
ESPNet [26]	57.8	0.3635
FC-DenseNet56 [22]	58.9	1.550
SegNet [4]	55.6	29.46
ICNet [45]	67.1	26.5
BiSeNet-ResNet18 [40]	68.7	49.0
Comparison with different distillation schemes		
T: ResNet101	77.52	70.43
S: ResNet18	70.3	13.07
+ SKD [24]	71.0	
+ IFVD (ours)	71.8	
S: EfficientNet-B0	61.9	4.19
+ SKD* [24]	63.9	
+ IFVD (ours)	64.4	

built on EfficientNet-B0. Some qualitative comparisons based on ResNet18 are depicted in Fig. 5.

Pascal VOC. We also conduct experiments on PASCAL VOC dataset [12] to further verify the distillation ability of the proposed IFVD on visual object segmentation. As depicted in Table 4, IFVD improves the baseline model by 3.27%

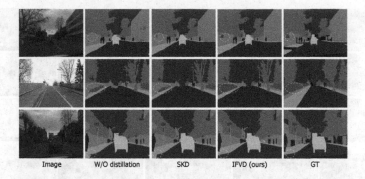

Fig. 5. Some qualitative results on the CamVid *test* split.

Table 4. The performance on Pascal VOC 2012 *val* set. * means the results we reproduced using the released implementation of [24], which does not conduct experiments
on this dataset.

Method	*val* mIoU (%)
Some related semantic segmentation methods	
CRF-RNN [47]	72.90
DeepLab-LargeFOV [8]	75.54
DeepLabV3 [9]	78.51
Comparison with different distillation schemes	
T: ResNet101	77.82
S: ResNet18	70.78
+ SKD* [24]	73.05
+ IFVD (ours)	74.05
S: EfficientNet-B0	69.28
+ SKD* [24]	70.24
+ IFVD (ours)	71.07

while outperforming SKD [24] by 1.00%. We then evaluate our method with
the student model built on EfficientNet-B0. The proposed IFVD surpasses the
baseline model by 1.79% while improving SKD by 0.83%. Visualization results
when employing ResNet18 as the student backbone are given in Fig. 6.

4.5 Discussion

Experimental results prove that the proposed IFVD can consistently boost the
accuracy of the student model. Besides, we also analyze the discrepancy between
the IFV of teacher and student models before and after distillation on Cityscapes.
As depicted in Fig. 7, we observe that both the student models without distillation and with the state-of-the-art SKD [24] have a relatively high average bias to

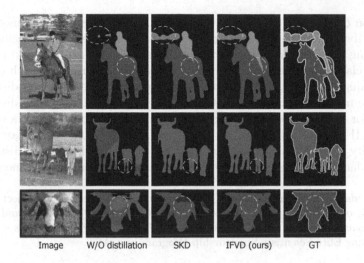

Image   W/O distillation   SKD   IFVD (ours)   GT

Fig. 6. Visual improvements on the Pascal VOC 2012 *val* split.

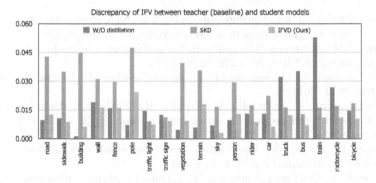

Fig. 7. Discrepancy between the intra-class feature variation of teacher and student models. We first obtain the IFV maps of teacher and student models, and then compute the average discrepancy between them with L1 distance for each class on Cityscapes.

the teacher model. After applying the proposed IFVD, the average discrepancy is significantly decreased, implying that IFVD can make the student better mimic the teacher in terms of feature distribution and thus improve the performance. Finally, one may wonder what would happen if we use the global prototype computed on the whole training dataset. We have conducted such an experiment and the mIoU slightly reduced to 73.86% (−0.68%) on Cityscapes. This is probably due to the high intra-class variability in training data.

5   Conclusion

We propose a novel intra-class feature variation distillation (IFVD) for semantic segmentation. Different from existing methods that perform knowledge distillation on pairwise relations, we attempt to alleviate the difference in feature distribution of the teacher model and student model. This is achieved by transferring the set of similarity between the feature on each pixel and its corresponding class-wise prototype. We conduct extensive experiments on three popular benchmark datasets, and consistently improve the model without distillation by a large margin. Comparison with the state-of-the-art knowledge distillation method for semantic segmentation also demonstrates the effectiveness of the proposed IFVD. In the future, we would like to explore the inter-class feature separability in addition to intra-class feature variation for knowledge distillation. We also plan to explore such spirit in other tasks than semantic segmentation.

Acknowledgement. This work was supported in part by the Major Project for New Generation of AI under Grant no. 2018AAA0100400, NSFC 61703171, and NSF of Hubei Province of China under Grant 2018CFB199. Dr. Yongchao Xu was supported by the Young Elite Scientists Sponsorship Program by CAST.

References

1. https://github.com/warmspringwinds/pytorch-segmentation-detection/blob/master/pytorch_segmentation_detection/utils/flops_benchmark.py
2. Alvarez, J.M., Salzmann, M.: Learning the number of neurons in deep networks. In: Proceedings of NIPS, pp. 2270–2278 (2016)
3. Ba, J., Caruana, R.: Do deep nets really need to be deep? In: Proceedings of NIPS, pp. 2654–2662 (2014)
4. Badrinarayanan, V., Kendall, A., Cipolla, R.: SegNet: a deep convolutional encoder-decoder architecture for image segmentation. IEEE Trans. Pattern Anal. Mach. Intell. **39**(12), 2481–2495 (2017)
5. Breiman, L., Shang, N.: Born again trees. University of California, Berkeley, Berkeley, CA, Technical report **1**, 2 (1996)
6. Brostow, G.J., Shotton, J., Fauqueur, J., Cipolla, R.: Segmentation and recognition using structure from motion point clouds. In: Forsyth, D., Torr, P., Zisserman, A. (eds.) ECCV 2008. LNCS, vol. 5302, pp. 44–57. Springer, Heidelberg (2008). https://doi.org/10.1007/978-3-540-88682-2_5
7. Buciluă, C., Caruana, R., Niculescu-Mizil, A.: Model compression. In: Proceedings of SIGKDD, pp. 535–541 (2006)
8. Chen, L.C., Papandreou, G., Kokkinos, I., Murphy, K., Yuille, A.L.: Deeplab: semantic image segmentation with deep convolutional nets, atrous convolution, and fully connected CRFs. IEEE Trans. Pattern Anal. Mach. Intell. **40**(4), 834–848 (2018)
9. Chen, L.C., Papandreou, G., Schroff, F., Adam, H.: Rethinking atrous convolution for semantic image segmentation. arXiv preprint arXiv:1706.05587 (2017)
10. Chen, L.-C., Zhu, Y., Papandreou, G., Schroff, F., Adam, H.: Encoder-decoder with atrous separable convolution for semantic image segmentation. In: Ferrari, V., Hebert, M., Sminchisescu, C., Weiss, Y. (eds.) ECCV 2018. LNCS, vol. 11211, pp. 833–851. Springer, Cham (2018). https://doi.org/10.1007/978-3-030-01234-2_49
11. Cordts, M., et al.: The cityscapes dataset for semantic urban scene understanding. In: Proceedings of CVPR, pp. 3213–3223 (2016)
12. Everingham, M., Van Gool, L., Williams, C.K., Winn, J., Zisserman, A.: The pascal visual object classes (VOC) challenge. Int. J. Comput. Vis. **88**(2), 303–338 (2010)

13. Fu, J., et al.: Dual attention network for scene segmentation. In: Proceedings of CVPR, pp. 3146–3154 (2019)
14. Han, S., Mao, H., Dally, W.J.: Deep compression: compressing deep neural networks with pruning, trained quantization and Huffman coding. In: Proceedings of ICLR (2016)
15. Han, S., Pool, J., Tran, J., Dally, W.: Learning both weights and connections for efficient neural network. In: Proceedings of NIPS, pp. 1135–1143 (2015)
16. Hariharan, B., Arbeláez, P., Bourdev, L., Maji, S., Malik, J.: Semantic contours from inverse detectors. In: Proceedings of ICCV, pp. 991–998 (2011)
17. He, K., Zhang, X., Ren, S., Sun, J.: Deep residual learning for image recognition. In: Proceedings of CVPR, pp. 770–778 (2016)
18. He, T., Shen, C., Tian, Z., Gong, D., Sun, C., Yan, Y.: Knowledge adaptation for efficient semantic segmentation. In: Proceedings of CVPR, pp. 578–587 (2019)
19. Hinton, G., Vinyals, O., Dean, J.: Distilling the knowledge in a neural network. In: Proceedings of NIPS Workshop (2014)
20. Hou, Y., Ma, Z., Liu, C., Loy, C.C.: Learning lightweight lane detection CNNs by self attention distillation. In: Proceedings of ICCV, pp. 1013–1021 (2019)
21. Huang, Z., Wang, N.: Like what you like: knowledge distill via neuron selectivity transfer. arXiv preprint arXiv:1707.01219 (2017)
22. Jégou, S., Drozdzal, M., Vazquez, D., Romero, A., Bengio, Y.: The one hundred layers tiramisu: fully convolutional densenets for semantic segmentation. In: Proceedings of CVPR, pp. 11–19 (2017)
23. Lin, G., Milan, A., Shen, C., Reid, I.: Refinenet: multi-path refinement networks for high-resolution semantic segmentation. In: Proceedings of CVPR, pp. 1925–1934 (2017)
24. Liu, Y., Chen, K., Liu, C., Qin, Z., Luo, Z., Wang, J.: Structured knowledge distillation for semantic segmentation. In: Proceedings of CVPR, pp. 2604–2613 (2019)
25. Long, J., Shelhamer, E., Darrell, T.: Fully convolutional networks for semantic segmentation. In: Proceedings of CVPR, pp. 3431–3440 (2015)
26. Mehta, S., Rastegari, M., Caspi, A., Shapiro, L., Hajishirzi, H.: ESPNet: efficient spatial pyramid of dilated convolutions for semantic segmentation. In: Ferrari, V., Hebert, M., Sminchisescu, C., Weiss, Y. (eds.) ECCV 2018. LNCS, vol. 11214, pp. 561–580. Springer, Cham (2018). https://doi.org/10.1007/978-3-030-01249-6_34
27. Park, W., Kim, D., Lu, Y., Cho, M.: Relational knowledge distillation. In: Proceedings of CVPR, pp. 3967–3976 (2019)
28. Paszke, A., Chaurasia, A., Kim, S., Culurciello, E.: Enet: a deep neural network architecture for real-time semantic segmentation. arXiv preprint arXiv:1606.02147 (2016)
29. Paszke, A., et al.: Automatic differentiation in pytorch. In: Proceedings of NIPS Workshop (2017)
30. Peng, B., et al.: Correlation congruence for knowledge distillation. In: Proceedings of ICCV, pp. 5007–5016 (2019)
31. Rastegari, M., Ordonez, V., Redmon, J., Farhadi, A.: XNOR-Net: ImageNet classification using binary convolutional neural networks. In: Leibe, B., Matas, J., Sebe, N., Welling, M. (eds.) ECCV 2016. LNCS, vol. 9908, pp. 525–542. Springer, Cham (2016). https://doi.org/10.1007/978-3-319-46493-0_32
32. Romera, E., Alvarez, J.M., Bergasa, L.M., Arroyo, R.: Erfnet: efficient residual factorized convnet for real-time semantic segmentation. IEEE Trans. Intell. Transp. Syst. 19(1), 263–272 (2017)
33. Romero, A., Ballas, N., Kahou, S.E., Chassang, A., Gatta, C., Bengio, Y.: Fitnets: hints for thin deep nets. In: Proceedings of ICLR (2015)

34. Tan, M., Le, Q.: Efficientnet: rethinking model scaling for convolutional neural networks. In: Proceedings of ICML, pp. 6105–6114 (2019)
35. Tung, F., Mori, G.: Similarity-preserving knowledge distillation. In: Proceedings of ICCV, pp. 1365–1374 (2019)
36. Wen, W., Wu, C., Wang, Y., Chen, Y., Li, H.: Learning structured sparsity in deep neural networks. In: Proceedings of NIPS, pp. 2074–2082 (2016)
37. Wu, J., Leng, C., Wang, Y., Hu, Q., Cheng, J.: Quantized convolutional neural networks for mobile devices. In: Proceedings of CVPR, pp. 4820–4828 (2016)
38. Xu, Z., Hsu, Y.C., Huang, J.: Training shallow and thin networks for acceleration via knowledge distillation with conditional adversarial networks. In: Proceedings of ICLR Workshop (2018)
39. Yim, J., Joo, D., Bae, J., Kim, J.: A gift from knowledge distillation: fast optimization, network minimization and transfer learning. In: Proceedings of CVPR, pp. 4133–4141 (2017)
40. Yu, C., Wang, J., Peng, C., Gao, C., Yu, G., Sang, N.: BiSeNet: bilateral segmentation network for real-time semantic segmentation. In: Ferrari, V., Hebert, M., Sminchisescu, C., Weiss, Y. (eds.) ECCV 2018. LNCS, vol. 11217, pp. 334–349. Springer, Cham (2018). https://doi.org/10.1007/978-3-030-01261-8_20
41. Yu, C., Wang, J., Peng, C., Gao, C., Yu, G., Sang, N.: Learning a discriminative feature network for semantic segmentation. In: Proceedings of CVPR, pp. 1857–1866 (2018)
42. Yu, F., Koltun, V.: Multi-scale context aggregation by dilated convolutions. In: Proceedings of ICLR (2016)
43. Yuan, Y., Wang, J.: Ocnet: object context network for scene parsing. arXiv preprint arXiv:1809.00916 (2018)
44. Zagoruyko, S., Komodakis, N.: Paying more attention to attention: improving the performance of convolutional neural networks via attention transfer. In: Proceedings of ICLR (2017)
45. Zhao, H., Qi, X., Shen, X., Shi, J., Jia, J.: ICNet for real-time semantic segmentation on high-resolution images. In: Ferrari, V., Hebert, M., Sminchisescu, C., Weiss, Y. (eds.) ECCV 2018. LNCS, vol. 11207, pp. 418–434. Springer, Cham (2018). https://doi.org/10.1007/978-3-030-01219-9_25
46. Zhao, H., Shi, J., Qi, X., Wang, X., Jia, J.: Pyramid scene parsing network. In: Proceedings of CVPR, pp. 2881–2890 (2017)
47. Zheng, S., et al.: Conditional random fields as recurrent neural networks. In: Proceedings of CVPR, pp. 1529–1537 (2015)

Temporal Distinct Representation Learning for Action Recognition

Junwu Weng[1,3], Donghao Luo[2(✉)], Yabiao Wang[2], Ying Tai[2], Chengjie Wang[2], Jilin Li[2], Feiyue Huang[2], Xudong Jiang[3], and Junsong Yuan[4]

[1] Tencent AI Lab, Shenzhen, China
calweng@tencent.com
[2] Tencent Youtu Lab, Shanghai, China
{michaelluo,caseywang,yingtai,jasoncjwang,
jerolinli,garyhuang}@tencent.com
[3] School of EEE, Nanyang Technological University, Singapore, Singapore
exdjiang@ntu.edu.sg
[4] Department of CSE, The State University of New York, Buffalo, USA
jsyuan@buffalo.edu

Abstract. Motivated by the previous success of Two-Dimensional Convolutional Neural Network (2D CNN) on image recognition, researchers endeavor to leverage it to characterize videos. However, one limitation of applying 2D CNN to analyze videos is that different frames of a video share the same 2D CNN kernels, which may result in repeated and redundant information utilization, especially in the spatial semantics extraction process, hence neglecting the critical variations among frames. In this paper, we attempt to tackle this issue through two ways. 1) Design a sequential channel filtering mechanism, i.e., Progressive Enhancement Module (PEM), to excite the discriminative channels of features from different frames step by step, and thus avoid repeated information extraction. 2) Create a Temporal Diversity Loss (TD Loss) to force the kernels to concentrate on and capture the variations among frames rather than the image regions with similar appearance. Our method is evaluated on benchmark temporal reasoning datasets Something-Something V1 and V2, and it achieves visible improvements over the best competitor by 2.4% and 1.3%, respectively. Besides, performance improvements over the 2D-CNN-based state-of-the-arts on the large-scale dataset Kinetics are also witnessed.

Keywords: Video representation learning · Action recognition · Progressive Enhancement Module · Temporal Diversity Loss

1 Introduction

Owing to the computer vision applications in many areas like intelligent surveillance and behavior analysis, how to characterize and understand videos becomes

---

J. Weng and D. Luo—Equal contribution. This work is done when Junwu Weng is an intern at Youtu Lab.

A. Vedaldi et al. (Eds.): ECCV 2020, LNCS 12352, pp. 363–378, 2020.
https://doi.org/10.1007/978-3-030-58571-6_22

an intriguing topic in the computer vision community. To date, a large number of deep learning models [10,12–14,20,23,25,29,33] have been proposed to analyze videos. The RNN-based models [29,30] are common tools for sequence modeling for its sequential nature of visual representation processing, by which the order of a sequence can be realized. However, in these models the spatial appearance and temporal information are learned separately. Motivated by the success in image recognition, Convolutional Neural Network (CNN) becomes popular for video analysis. 3D CNNs [4,20,25,26] are widely used in video analysis as they can jointly learn spatial and temporal features from videos. However, their large computational complexities impede them from being applied in real scenarios. In contrast, 2D CNNs are light-weight, but do not bear the ability for temporal modeling. To bridge the gap between image recognition and video recognition, considerable 2D-CNN-based researches [9,10,23,33,34] recently attempt to equip the conventional 2D CNNs with a temporal modeling ability, and some improvements are witnessed.

However, another direction seems to be less explored for 2D-CNN-based video analysis, namely diversifying visual representations among video frames. Although the 2D CNN takes multiple frames of a video at once as input, the frames captured from the same scene share the same convolution kernels. A fact about CNN is that each feature channel generated by the kernel convolution from the high-level layers highly reacts to a specific semantic pattern. Hence, with 2D CNN, the yielded features from different frames may share multiple similar channels, which thereafter results in repeated and redundant information extraction for video analysis. If the majority part of frames is background, these repeated redundant channels tend to describe the background scene rather than the regions of interest. This tendency may lead to the ignorance of the motion information which can be more critical than the scene information for action understanding [2,8,24,27]. Besides, the customary strategy that features from different frames of a video are learned under the same label of supervision will make this issue even more severe. We observe that for one temporal reasoning dataset like Something-Something [5], video samples under the same category are from various scenes and the actions therein are performed with various objects. The scene and object information may not be directly useful for the recognition task. Thus, a 2D-CNN-based method like TSN [23] is easy to overfit as the model learns many scene features and meanwhile neglects the variations among frames, e.g. the motion information. We state that due to this redundant information extraction, the previously proposed temporal modeling method cannot fully play its role. In this paper, we propose two ways to tackle the issue.

We first introduce an information filtering module, i.e., Progressive Enhancement Module (PEM), to adaptively and sequentially enhance the discriminative channels and meanwhile suppress the repeated ones of each frame's feature with the help of motion historical information. Specifically, the PEM progressively determines the enhancements for the current frame's feature maps based on the motion observation in previous time steps. This sequential way of enhancement learning explicitly takes the temporal order of frames into consideration, which enables the network itself to effectively avoid gathering similar channels and fully utilize the information from different temporal frames. After PEM, we set a temporal modeling module that temporally fuses the enhanced features to help the discriminative information from different frames interact with each other.

Furthermore, the convolution kernels are calibrated by the Temporal Diversity Loss (TD Loss) so that they are forced to concentrate on and capture the variations among frames. We locate a loss right after the temporal modeling module. By minimizing the pair-wise cosine similarity of the same channels between different frames, the kernels can be well adjusted to diversify the representations across frames. As the TD Loss acts as a regularization enforced to the network training, it does not add an extra complexity to the model and keeps a decent accuracy-speed tradeoff.

We evaluate our method on three benchmark datasets. The proposed model outperforms the best state-of-the-arts by 2.4%, 1.3% and 0.8% under the $8f$ setting on the Something-SomethingV1, V2 and the Kinctics400 datasets, respectively, as shown in Table 1 and Table 2. The proposed PEM and TD Loss outperform the baseline by 2.6% and 2.3% on Something-Something V1, respectively. The experimental results demonstrate the effectiveness of our proposed 2D-CNN-based model on video analysis.

Our contributions can be summarized as follows:

- We propose a Progressive Enhancement Module for channel-level information filtering, which effectively excites the discriminative channels of different frames and meanwhile avoids repeated information extraction.
- We propose a Temporal Diversity Loss to train the network. The loss calibrates the convolution kernels so that the network can concentrate on and capture the variations among frames. The loss also improves the recognition accuracy without adding an extra network complexity.

2   Related Work

2D-CNNs for Video Analysis. Due to the previous great success in classifying images of objects, scenes, and complex events [3,6,18,19], convolutional neural networks have been introduced to solve the problem of video understanding. Using two-dimensional convolutional network is a straightforward way to characterize videos. In Temporal Segment Network [23], 2D CNN is utilized to individually extract a visual representation for each sampled frame of a video, and an average pooling aggregation scheme is applied for temporal modeling. To further tackle the temporal reasoning of 2D CNNs, Zhou et al. proposed a Temporal Relational Network [33] to hierarchically construct the temporal relationship among video frames. Ji et al. introduced a simple but effective shift operation between frames into 2D CNN, and proposed the Temporal Shift Module [10]. Following the same direction, the Temporal Enhancement Interaction Network (TEINet) [11] introduces a depth-wise temporal convolution for light-weight temporal modeling. Similar methods include Temporal Bilinear Network [9] and Approximate Bilinear Module [34], which re-design the bilinear pooling for temporal modeling. These methods attempt to equip the 2D CNN with an ability of temporal modeling. However, one neglected limitation of the 2D CNN is the redundant feature extraction among frames or the lack of temporal representation diversity. This is the battle field to which our proposed method is engaged. We first propose a Progressive Enhancement Module before temporal modeling to enhance the discriminative channels and meanwhile suppress the redundant channels of different frames sequentially. Furthermore, after the temporal modeling module, we create a Temporal Diversity loss to force the convolution kernels to capture the variations among frames.

Channel Enhancement. The idea of enhancing the discriminative channels for recognition first appears in image recognition. In Squeeze-and-Excitation Network (SENet) [7], an attention sub-branch in the convolutional layer is involved to excite the discriminative channels of frame's features. Inheriting from the SENet, to emphasize the motion cues in videos, TEINet uses the difference between feature maps of two consecutive frames for channel-level enhancement learning. In our method, we expand the receptive field of this channel enhancement module. At each time step, the enhancement module is able to be aware of the motion conducted in previous frames, therefore avoiding activating the channels emphasized previously.

Diversity Regularization. In fine-grained image recognition, to adaptively localize discriminative parts, attention models are widely used. However, the previously proposed attention models perform poorly in classifying fine-grained objects as the learned attentions tend to be similar to each other. In [31,32], attention maps are regularized to be diverse in the spatial domain to capture the discriminative parts. In this paper, we take the temporal diversity of the feature maps into consideration and propose the Temporal Diversity Loss. The TD Loss directly sets the regularization on the visual representation of each frame to obtain the discriminative and dynamic features for video analysis.

3 Proposed Method

In this section, we elaborate on the two contributions of this work. We first give the framework of the proposed method in Sect. 3.1. The Progressive Enhancement Module is introduced in Sect. 3.2. In Sect. 3.3, the Temporal Diversity Loss for diverse representation modeling is described. The illustration of the whole framework is shown in Fig. 1.

3.1 Framework

In our model, each video frame is represented by a tensor $\boldsymbol{X}_t^b \in \mathbb{R}^{C_b \times W_b \times H_b}$, which bears C_b stacked feature maps with width W_b and height H_b, and b indicates the block index. In the following, we use C, W and H instead to simplify the

Progressive Enhancement Module   **Temporal Diversity Regularization**

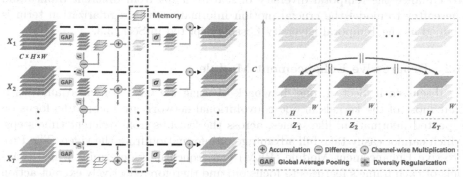

Fig. 1. An illustration of the proposed framework. In PEM, 1) features of each frame are GAP-ed and down-sampled to get a vector. 2) The differencing operation is performed on the vectors of each two consecutive frames. 3) The *memory* vector (in the red box) accumulates historical difference information. 4) With the Sigmoid function, the channel-level enhancement is obtained to excite discriminative channels of each frame. To compress the model complexity, the 1×1 convolution operation in $f(\cdot)$ reduces the vector dimensionality and the one before $\sigma(\cdot)$ recovers it back to C. In TD regularization, the same channels of each frame pair are regularized to be distinguished from each other.

notations. Given a video sequence/clip with T sampled frames $V = \{X_t\}_{t=1}^T$, the goal of our established deep network is to extract a discriminative visual representation of V and predict its class label $k \in \{1, 2, ..., K\}$, where K is the number of categories. Each block of the network takes the T frames as input and outputs the feature maps for the next block, which is formulated as follows:

$$(X_1^b, \cdots, X_T^b) = \mathcal{F}(X_1^{b-1}, \cdots, X_T^{b-1}; \theta^b), \tag{1}$$

where $\mathcal{F}$ is the feature mapping function, which involves the Progressive Attention for information filtering (Sect. 3.2) and temporal information interaction. θ is the block parameters to be optimized. The input and output of the network are denoted as X^0 and X^B, and B is the total number of blocks.

The output feature maps $\{X_t^B\}_{t=1}^T$ are gathered by average pooling, and are further fed into the Softmax function for category prediction. This mapping is defined as $\hat{y} = \mathcal{G}(X_1^B, \cdots, X_T^B)$, where $\hat{y} \in [0, 1]^K$ contains the prediction scores of K categories. Therefore, the loss function is defined as

$$\mathcal{L} = \mathcal{L}_c + \lambda \mathcal{L}_r = - \sum_{i=1}^K y_i \cdot log\, \hat{y}_i + \lambda \mathcal{L}_r, \tag{2}$$

where $\mathcal{L}_c$ is the Cross Entropy Loss for category supervision. y_i is the groundtruth label concerning class i, and it is an element of the one-hot vector $y \in \{0, 1\}^K$. $\mathcal{L}_r$ is the regularization term for network training, and λ balances the importance between category supervision and network regularization.

To enhance the temporal diversity of feature maps from different frames and thereafter to model the crucial motion information, the regularization term is defined as the Temporal Diversity Loss as depicted in Sect. 3.3.

3.2 Progressive Enhancement Module

As discussed in Sect. 1, one drawback of using 2D CNN for video analysis is that most of the kernels in one convolutional network are inclined to focus on repeated information, like scenes, across the features from different time steps, which cannot easily take full advantage of information from the video. The Progressive Enhancement Module (PEM) can sequentially determine which channels of each frame's features to focus on, and therefore effectively extract action related information. In each block, the feature maps $\{X_t^{b-1}\}_{t=1}^T$ from the preceding block are first fed into the Progressive Enhancement Module for information filtering, as illustrated in Fig. 1. Let $a_t^b \in \mathbb{R}^C$ denote the enhancement vector to excite the discriminative channels of each frame. This operation is defined as

$$U_t^b = X_t^{b-1} \odot a_t^b, \tag{3}$$

where U_t^b is the t-th frame output of PEM in the b-th block, and $\odot$ is a channel-wise multiplication. For notational simplicity, we remove the block-index notation b in the following description.

The input feature maps $\{X_t^{b-1}\}_{t=1}^T$ are first aggregated across the spatial dimensions by using Global Average Pooling (GAP), and the channel-wise statistics $\{x_t\}_{t=1}^T$, $x \in \mathbb{R}^C$ are then obtained. Each pair of neighboring frames in $\{x_t\}_{t=1}^T$ is then fed into two individual 1×1 convolution operations f_1 and f_2 with ReLU activation, respectively, for feature selection. As discussed in [11], taking the difference of channel statistics between two consecutive frames as input for channel-level enhancement learning is more effective for video analysis than the original channel-wise statistics $\{x_t\}_{t=1}^T$ proposed in Squeeze-and-Excitation Network [7], which is especially designed for image recognition. We choose to use the difference of channel statistics between two consecutive frames as the input of PEM. With the differencing operation, we obtain the difference of channel-wise statistics $\{d_t\}_{t=1}^T$. The differencing operation is defined as

$$d_t = f_2(x_{t+1}) - f_1(x_t), \tag{4}$$

and the difference of the last frame, d_T, is set as a vector with ones to maintain the magnitude of the memory vector.

To extend the receptive field of enhancement learning, we here introduce an accumulation operation into the learning of channel-level enhancement for each frame. By the accumulation, the enhancement module of each current frame can be aware of the vital motion information in the previous timings, and not be trapped into the local temporal window as in [11]. The accumulated vector m, named as *memory*, accumulates d at each time step, and the accumulation operation is controlled by $\gamma \in [0, 1]$, as defined in Eq. (5):

$$m_t = (1 - \gamma) \cdot m_{t-1} + \gamma \cdot d_t, \qquad \gamma = \sigma(W_g(m_{t-1} \| d_t)). \tag{5}$$

The factor γ is determined by the accumulated vector m_{t-1} and the difference information d_t, where $\|$ denotes a concatenation operation, W_g is a projection matrix for linear transformation, and $\sigma(\cdot)$ is a Sigmoid activation function. The final enhancement vector a is then generated by

$$a_t = \sigma(W_a m_t), \tag{6}$$

where W_a is a matrix linearly projecting m into a new vector space. With PEM, the network is able to progressively select the motion-related channels in each frame, and adaptively filter the discriminative information for video analysis. The enhanced feature maps $\{U_t\}_{t=1}^{T}$ are then fed into a temporal modeling module for temporal information fusion, and we write the output as $\{Z_t\}_{t=1}^{T}$, $Z \in \mathbb{R}^{C \times W \times H}$.

3.3   Temporal Diversity Loss

It is well-known that feature maps from high-level layers tend to have responses to specific semantic patterns. Convolution kernels that focus on the background of a video may generate similar semantic patterns for the same channels of features from different frames, which may lead to redundant visual feature extraction for video analysis. To calibrate the kernels in 2D CNN and force the network to focus on and capture the variations among frames of a video sequence, we propose the Temporal Diversity Loss to regularize the network toward learning distinguished visual features for different frames. For the feature map Z_t from each frame, its C vectorized channel features are denoted as $\{z_t^c\}_{c=1}^{C}$, $z \in \mathbb{R}^{WH}$. We use the Cosine Similarity to measure the similarities of a specific channel between two frames of each video frame pair, and then define the loss as:

$$\mathcal{L}_\mu = \sum_c \frac{1}{|\mathbb{I}|} \sum_{(i,j) \in \mathbb{I}} \eta(z_i^c, z_j^c), \tag{7}$$

where $\mathbb{I} = \{(i,j) \,|\, i \neq j, 1 \leqslant i,j \leqslant T\}$, $|\cdot|$ indicates the total number of elements in a set, and $\eta(\cdot)$ defines the Cosine Similarity measure, namely $\eta(x,y) = \frac{x^\top y}{\|x\|_2 \cdot \|y\|_2}$. Considering that the static information among frames is also beneficial to recognition, we only use C_μ ($C_\mu < C$) channels for temporal diversity regularization. A further analysis will be discussed in Sect. 4.5. With the proposed Temporal Diversity $\mathcal{L}_\mu$, the regularization term $\mathcal{L}_r$ is then defined as $\mathcal{L}_r = \sum_{b=1}^{B_\mu} \mathcal{L}_\mu^b$, where B_μ is the number of blocks with temporal diversity regularization.

4   Experiments

In this section, the proposed method is evaluated on three benchmark datasets, the Something-Something V1 dataset [5], Something-Something V2 dataset [16], and the Kinetics400 dataset [1]. We first briefly introduce these three datasets and the experiment settings in Sect. 4.1 and Sect. 4.2, respectively. Then, our method is compared with the state-of-the-arts in Sect. 4.3. The ablation study is conducted in Sect. 4.4 to evaluate the performance of each individual module of our proposed method. In Sect. 4.5, we evaluate the proposed method in detail, including parameter, position sensitivity analysis and visualization.

4.1   Datasets

Something-Something V1&V2 are crowd-sourced datasets focusing on temporal modeling. In these two datasets, the scenes and objects in each single action category are various, which strongly requires the considered model to focus on the temporal variations among video frames. The V1 & V2 datasets include 108,499/220,847 videos, respectively, containing 174 action categories in both versions.

Kinetics400 is a large-scale YouTube-like dataset, which contains 400 human action classes, with at least 400 video clips for each category. The average duration of video clips in this dataset is around 10s. Unlike Something-Something datasets, Kinetics is less sensitive to temporal relationships, so the scene information is of importance in its recognition.

4.2   Experimental Setup

In all the conducted experiments, we use the ResNet-50 [6] as our backbone considering the tradeoff between performance and efficiency, and our model is pre-trained by ImageNet [3]. We set the Progressive Enhancement Module (PEM) in front of all the blocks of the ResNet backbone. Given that the early stages of the Convolutional Network focus more on spatial appearance modeling and the later ones focus on temporal modeling [15,

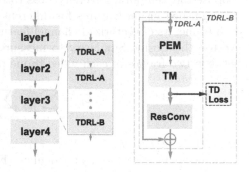

Fig. 2. Block Illustration

21] and for better convergence, we regularize the temporal diversity of feature maps in the last blocks of each of the last three layers. The Temporal Diversity Loss (TD Loss) is located right after the temporal modeling module. What follows the temporal modeling module is the convolution operation (ResConv) taken from the ResNet block, which includes one 1×1, one 3×3, and one 1×1 2D convolutions. The position of the PEM and the temporal diversity regularization are illustrated in Fig. 2. We define the TDRL-A as the block without the TD Loss, and TDRL-B as the one with the TD Loss, where TDRL stands for Temporal Distinct Representation Learning. The ratio of channels regularized by Temporal Diversity Loss in each feature is 50%. Without loss of generality, we use the Temporal Interaction Module proposed in [11] as our temporal modeling module (TM). λ for loss balancing is set as 2×10^{-4}.

Table 1. Comparison with the state-of-the-arts on Something-Something V1&V2 (Top1 Accuracy %). The notation 'I' or 'K' in the backbone column indicates that the model is pre-trained with ImageNet or Kinetics400 dataset. The subscripts of 'Val' and 'Test' indicate the version of the Something-Something dataset. '2S' indicates two streams.

Method	Backbone	Frames	FLOPs	Val$_1$	Test$_1$	Val$_2$	Test$_2$
I3D [26]	Res3D-50 (IK)	$32f \times 2$	306G	41.6	–	–	–
NL I3D [26]			334G	44.4	–	–	–
NL I3D+GCN [26]			606G	46.1	45.0	–	–
TSM [10]	Res2D-50 (IK)	$8f$	33G	45.6	–	–	–
		$8f \times 2$	65G	47.3	–	61.7	–
		$16f$	65G	47.2	46.0	–	–
TSM$_{En}$ [10]		$16f + 8f$	98G	49.7	–	–	–
TSM-2S [10]		$16f + 16f$	–	52.6	50.7	64.0	64.3
TEINet [11]	Res2D-50(I)	$8f$	33G	47.4	–	61.3	60.6
		$8f \times 10$	990G	48.8	–	64.0	62.7
		$16f$	66G	49.9	–	62.1	60.8
		$16f \times 10$	1980G	51.0	44.7	64.7	63.0
TEINet$_{En}$ [11]		$8f + 16f$	99G	52.5	46.1	66.5	64.6
GST [15]	Res2D-50(I)	$8f$	29.5G	47.0	–	61.6	60.0
		$16f$	59G	48.6	–	62.6	61.2
Ours	Res2D-50(I)	$8f$	33G	**49.8**	**42.7**	**62.6**	**61.4**
		$8f \times 2$	198G	**50.4**	–	**63.5**	–
		$16f$	66G	**50.9**	**44.7**	**63.8**	**62.5**
		$16f \times 2$	396G	**52.0**	–	**65.0**	–
		$8f + 16f$	99G	**54.3**	**48.3**	**67.0**	**65.1**

Pre-processing. We follow a similar pre-processing strategy to that described in [25]. To be specific, we first resize the shorter side of RGB images to 256, and center crop a patch followed by scale-jittering. The image patches are then resized to 224 × 224 before being fed into the network. Owing to the various lengths of video sequences, we adopt different temporal sampling strategies for different datasets. The network takes a clip of a video as input. Each clip consists of 8 or 16 frames. For the Kinetics dataset, we uniformly sample 8 or 16 frames from the consecutive 64 frames randomly sampled in each video. For the Something-Something dataset, due to the limited duration of video samples, we uniformly sample 8 or 16 frames from the whole video.

Training. For the Kinetics dataset, we train our model for 100 epochs. The initial learning rate is set as 0.01, and is scaled with 0.1 at 50, 75, and 90 epochs. For the Something-Something dataset, the model is trained with 50

Table 2. Comparison with the state-of-the-arts on Kinetics400 (%). The notations 'I', 'Z', 'S' in the backbone column indicate that the model is pre-trained with ImageNet, trained from scratch, or pre-trained with the Sport1M dataset, respectively.

Method	Backbone	GFLOPs×views	Top-1	Top-5
I3D$_{64f}$ [26]	Inception V1(I)	108×N/A	72.1	90.3
I3D$_{64f}$ [26]	Inception V1(Z)	108×N/A	67.5	87.2
NL+I3D$_{32f}$ [25]	Res3D-50(I)	70.5×30	74.9	91.6
NL+I3D$_{128f}$ [25]	Res3D-50(I)	282×30	76.5	92.6
NL+I3D$_{128f}$ [25]	Res3D-101(I)	359×30	77.7	93.3
Slowfast [4]	Res3D-50(Z)	36.1×30	75.6	92.1
Slowfast [4]	Res3D-101(Z)	106×30	77.9	93.2
NL+Slowfast [4]	Res3D-101(Z)	234×30	**79.8**	**93.9**
LGD-3D$_{128f}$ [17]	Res3D-101(I)	N/A×N/A	79.4	94.4
R(2+1)D$_{32f}$ [21]	Res2D-34(Z)	152×10	72.0	90.0
R(2+1)D$_{32f}$ [21]	Res2D-34(S)	152×10	74.3	91.4
ARTNet$_{16f}$+TSN [22]	Res2D-18(Z)	23.5×250	70.7	89.3
S3D-G$_{64f}$ [28]	Inception V1(I)	71.4×30	74.7	93.4
TSM$_{16f}$ [10]	Res2D-50(I)	65×30	74.7	91.4
TEINet$_{8f}$ [11]	Res2D-50(I)	33×30	74.9	91.8
TEINet$_{16f}$ [11]	Res2D-50(I)	66×30	76.2	92.5
Ours$_{8f}$	Res2D-50(I)	33 × 30	**75.7**	**92.2**
Ours$_{16f}$		66 × 30	**76.9**	**93.0**

epochs in total. The initial learning rate is set as 0.01 and reduced by a factor of 10 at 30, 40, and 45 epochs. In the training, Stochastic Gradient Decent (SGD) is utilized with momentum 0.9 and weight decay of 1×10^{-4}. The experiments are conducted on *Tesla M40* GPUs, and the batch size is set as 64. The memory vector can be initialized by zeros, or the difference vector d_t from the first or last frame, and we experimentally find that the last frame difference d_{T-1} can achieve slightly better performance. We therefore use d_{T-1} as the memory initialization in the experiments.

Inference. For fair comparison with the state-of-the-arts, we follow two different data processing settings to evaluate our model. In single-clip (8 or 16 frames) comparison, namely model trained with 8 frames only ($8f$), or with 16 frames only ($16f$), we use center cropping for input image processing. The analysis experiments are under the $8f$ setting. In multi-clip comparison, we follow the widely applied settings in [10,25] to resize the shorter side of images to 256 and take 3 crops (left, middle, right) in each frame. Then we uniformly sample N clips ($8f \times N$ or $16f \times N$) in each video and obtain the classification scores for each clip individually, and the final prediction is based on the average classification score of the N clips.

4.3   Comparison with State-of-the-Arts

We compare the proposed method with the state-of-the-arts on the Something-SomethingV1&V2 and the Kinetics400 datasets under different settings for fair comparison. The results are shown in Table 1 and Table 2, respectively. Table 1 shows that on the Something-Something V1 dataset, our proposed method outperforms the so far best model, TEINet [11], by 2.4%, 1.3%, and 1.8% under the $8f$, $16f$, and $8f + 16f$ settings on the validation set, respectively. Our performance under the two-clips setting is even better than TEINet's performance under the ten-clips setting. On the Something-Something V2 dataset, the performance of our model under the $8f$ setting is even better or the same as the TEINet and GST under the $16f$ setting, which indicates that we can use only half of the inputs of these two models to achieve the same or better accuracy. These results verify the effectiveness of the temporal representation diversity learning. On the Kinetics dataset, the results are reported under the ten-clips-three-crops setting. As can be seen from Table 2, our proposed model outperforms all the 2D-CNN-based models under different settings, and it even performs better than the 3D-CNN-based nonlocal [25] and slowfast [4] networks with less frames input. We can also witness consistent improvement on the test set of V2, and our model beats TEI by 1.2% under the $8f + 16f$ setting.

Table 3. Ablation study - TSM [10] (%)   **Table 4.** Ablation study - TIM [11] (%)

Method	Top-1	Top-5
Baseline [10]	45.6	74.2
+PEM	48.1	77.4
+TDLoss	47.5	76.8
+PEM+TDLoss	48.4	77.4

Method	Top-1	Top-5
Baseline [11]	46.1	74.7
+MEM [11]	47.4	76.6
+PEM	48.7	77.8
+TDLoss	48.4	77.3
+PEM+TDLoss	49.8	78.1

4.4   Ablation Study

In this section, we evaluate the performances of different modules in our model. We use the single-clip $8f$ setting for the experiment conducted in this section. We use a temporal shift module (TSM) [10] and a temporal interaction module (TIM) [11], respectively, as the baseline in our experiment to show the generality of our model cooperating with different temporal modeling modules. As can be seen from Table 3, with the PEM and the TD Loss, there are 2.5% and 1.9% Top-1 accuracy improvements over the TSM, respectively. With both the PEM and TD Loss, the improvement reaches 2.8%. Similarly, as shown in Table 4, PEM gives 2.6% Top-1 accuracy improvement over the baseline, and it outperforms MEM [11] by 1.3%, which also involves a channel enhancement module. With the TD Loss, there is 2.3% improvement over the baseline. We can see from Table 4 that there is 3.7% improvement over the baseline when both the PEM and TD

Loss are applied. One more thing we need to point out is that, after 50 epochs training, the TIM baseline's training accuracy reaches 79.03%, while with the PEM and the TD Loss, the training accuracies are down to 77.98% and 74.45%, respectively. This training accuracy decline shows that our proposed method can avoid overfitting, and force the model to learn the essential motion cues.

Table 5. TDLoss Ratio (%)   **Table 6.** Block Position (%)   **Table 7.** Impact of λ (%)

Method	Top-1	Order	Top-1	λ	Top-1
baseline	46.1	TM	46.1	0×10^{-4}	46.1
+25% TDLoss	47.7	PEM B. TM	48.7	1×10^{-4}	47.9
+50% TDLoss	48.4	PEM A. TM	49.0	2×10^{-4}	48.4
+75% TDLoss	47.8	TDLoss B. TM	46.9	3×10^{-4}	47.8
+100% TDLoss	47.3	TDLoss A. TM	48.4	4×10^{-4}	48.0

4.5   Detailed Analysis

Ratio of Channel Regularization. The ratio of channel regularization indicates that how many channels are involved for diversity regularization. We set the ratio from 0% (baseline) to 100% to evaluate the impact of the TD loss in this section. The results are shown in Table 5. From this table we can see that when half of the channels are regularized, the model achieves the best performance, 48.4%. If all the channels are set under the regularization, the model reaches the lowest accuracy 47.3%. This comparison shows that not all the channels require the regularization, and channels without regularization are still useful for the recognition task. However, no matter how many channels are involved in the loss, good improvement is still witnessed over the baseline, TIM.

Position of Blocks. In this part, we discuss where to insert the PEM and TD Loss in each block. The two modules are located before (B.) or after (A.) the temporal module (TM) individually to see the impact of position on accuracy. We follow the position of MEM in TEINet [11] for fair comparison. The results are shown in Table 6. As can be seen, for PEM, there is no much difference between the two locations. It can fairly provide stable improvement on two different positions. For the TD loss, we discover that when it is located before the TM, the improvement over the baseline is limited. Because TM is inclined to make the representation similar to each other, the following ResConv cannot well extract the video representation. While when the TD regularization is after TM, there is 2.3% improvement over the baseline. The TD loss effectively diversifies the representations among different frames after TM.

Fig. 3. Visualization of the features excited and suppressed by PEM. The features are organized in the temporal order, and they are from the first block of the first layer. **R1**: the images in this row are the input images of the network. **R2**: the features in this row are those before PEM. The channels of each of these features are divided by three groups, and the channels in each group are gathered by average pooling to generate a 3-channels feature, presented as an RGB image. **R3-4**: Each of the feature map in the these two rows is the average of channels picked from the features before PEM. Each feature map in the third row is gathering of ten channels with the highest enhancement, and each one in the fourth row is gathered with the lowest enhancement.

Loss Balancing Factor λ. We analyze the impact of the loss balancing factor λ on the accuracy in this section. We set λ from 1×10^{-4} to 4×10^{-4}. The result comparisons are shown in Table 7. As can be seen, the fluctuation is in the range of 0.6%, which shows that the proposed TD Loss is not very sensitive to λ when this factor is in an appropriate range. No matter which λ we set, the involvement of the TD Loss can still help improve the accuracy over the baseline, which shows the effectiveness of the proposed temporal diversity loss.

Visualization. We visualize feature maps from different blocks to show the effect of the PEM and TD Loss. The experiment is conducted under the Kinetics dataset. We show the feature maps filtered by the PEM in Fig. 3. There are two video samples shown in the figure. The input images are uniformly sampled from a video. From Fig. 3 we can see that the top ten enhanced channels mainly focus on the motion, while the top ten suppressed channels highly respond to the static background. This visualization shows that the proposed PEM can well discover which are the motion-related channels and which are the repeated static background channels. By enhancing the motion-related ones and suppress the repeated ones, the redundant information can be filtered out and the discriminative one can be well kept. As can be seen from Fig. 4, with the TD Loss, the feature maps after TM can well encode the information from the current frame and its neighboring frames, while the motion encoded in the features after

TM without the TD regularization is very limited. The figures indicate that the TD loss can calibrate the temporal convolution kernels and also enhance the temporal interactions among them.

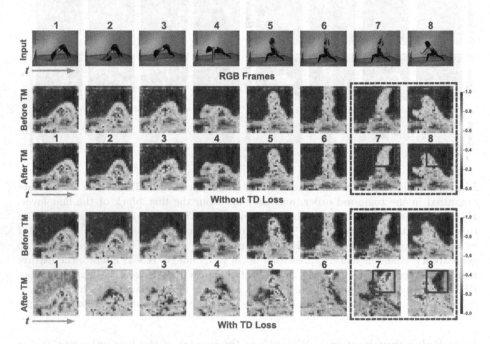

Fig. 4. Visualization of feature maps before and after TM w/ or w/o the TD loss. These feature maps are uniformly sampled from one video and are organized following the temporal order. They are from the last block of the second layer. **R1**: The images are the input to the network. The purple dashed rectangles mark and illustrate the difference between feature maps with and without TD Loss. **w/ TD Loss**, the feature maps can well encode action from neighboring frames, and emphasize the variations among them, as marked by red rectangles in the last row. **w/o TD loss**, the features cannot enhance those variations, as marked by red rectangles in the third row.

5   Conclusions

In this work, we proposed two ways to tackle the issue that the 2D CNN cannot well capture large variations among frames of videos. We first introduced the Progressive Enhancement Module to sequentially excite the discriminative channels of frames. The learned enhancement can be aware of the frame variations in the past time and effectively avoid the redundant feature extraction process. Furthermore, the Temporal Diversity Loss was proposed to diversify the representations after temporal modeling. With this loss, the convolutional kernels are effectively calibrated to capture the variations among frames. The experiments were conducted on three datasets to validate our contributions, showing the effectiveness of the proposed PEM and TD loss.

Acknowledgement. We thank Dr. Wei Liu from Tencent AI Lab for his valuable advice.

References

1. Carreira, J., Zisserman, A.: Quo vadis, action recognition? a new model and the kinetics dataset. In: CVPR, pp. 6299–6308 (2017)
2. Choi, J., Gao, C., Messou, J.C., Huang, J.B.: Why can't i dance in the mall, learning to mitigate scene bias in action recognition. In: NeurIPS, pp. 853–865 (2019)
3. Deng, J., Dong, W., Socher, R., Li, L.J., Li, K., Fei-Fei, L.: Imagenet: a large-scale hierarchical image database. In: CVPR, pp. 248–255. IEEE (2009)
4. Feichtenhofer, C., Fan, H., Malik, J., He, K.: Slowfast networks for video recognition. In: ICCV, pp. 6202–6211 (2019)
5. Goyal, R., et al.: The "something something" video database for learning and evaluating visual common sense. In: ICCV, vol. 1, p. 5 (2017)
6. He, K., Zhang, X., Ren, S., Sun, J.: Deep residual learning for image recognition. In: CVPR, pp. 770–778 (2016)
7. Hu, J., Shen, L., Sun, G.: Squeeze-and-excitation networks. In: CVPR, pp. 7132–7141 (2018)
8. Jiang, Y.-G., Dai, Q., Xue, X., Liu, W., Ngo, C.-W.: Trajectory-based modeling of human actions with motion reference points. In: Fitzgibbon, A., Lazebnik, S., Perona, P., Sato, Y., Schmid, C. (eds.) ECCV 2012. LNCS, vol. 7576, pp. 425–438. Springer, Heidelberg (2012). https://doi.org/10.1007/978-3-642-33715-4_31
9. Li, Y., Song, S., Li, Y., Liu, J.: Temporal bilinear networks for video action recognition. In: AAAI, vol. 33, pp. 8674–8681 (2019)
10. Lin, J., Gan, C., Han, S.: Tsm: Temporal shift module for efficient video understanding. In: ICCV, pp. 7083–7093 (2019)
11. Liu, Z., et al.: Teinet: towards an efficient architecture for video recognition. In: AAAI, vol. 2, p. 8 (2020)
12. Lu, X., Ma, C., Ni, B., Yang, X., Reid, I., Yang, M.-H.: Deep regression tracking with shrinkage loss. In: Ferrari, V., Hebert, M., Sminchisescu, C., Weiss, Y. (eds.) Computer Vision – ECCV 2018. LNCS, vol. 11218, pp. 369–386. Springer, Cham (2018). https://doi.org/10.1007/978-3-030-01264-9_22
13. Lu, X., Wang, W., Ma, C., Shen, J., Shao, L., Porikli, F.: See more, know more: Unsupervised video object segmentation with co-attention siamese networks. In: CVPR, pp. 3623–3632 (2019)
14. Lu, X., Wang, W., Shen, J., Tai, Y.W., Crandall, D.J., Hoi, S.C.: Learning video object segmentation from unlabeled videos. In: CVPR, pp. 8960–8970 (2020)
15. Luo, C., Yuille, A.L.: Grouped spatial-temporal aggregation for efficient action recognition. In: ICCV, pp. 5512–5521 (2019)
16. Mahdisoltani, F., Berger, G., Gharbieh, W., Fleet, D., Memisevic, R.: On the effectiveness of task granularity for transfer learning. arXiv:1804.09235 (2018)
17. Qiu, Z., Yao, T., Ngo, C.W., Tian, X., Mei, T.: Learning spatio-temporal representation with local and global diffusion. In: CVPR, pp. 12056–12065 (2019)
18. Simonyan, K., Zisserman, A.: Very deep convolutional networks for large-scale image recognition. In: ICLR (2014)
19. Szegedy, C., et al.: Going deeper with convolutions. In: CVPR, pp. 1–9 (2015)
20. Tran, D., Bourdev, L., Fergus, R., Torresani, L., Paluri, M.: Learning spatiotemporal features with 3D convolutional networks. In: ICCV, pp. 4489–4497 (2015)

21. Tran, D., Wang, H., Torresani, L., Ray, J., LeCun, Y., Paluri, M.: A closer look at spatiotemporal convolutions for action recognition. In: CVPR, pp. 6450–6459 (2018)
22. Wang, L., Li, W., Li, W., Van Gool, L.: Appearance-and-relation networks for video classification. In: CVPR, pp. 1430–1439 (2018)
23. Wang, L., Xiong, Y., Wang, Z., Qiao, Yu., Lin, D., Tang, X., Van Gool, L.: Temporal segment networks: towards good practices for deep action recognition. In: Leibe, B., Matas, J., Sebe, N., Welling, M. (eds.) ECCV 2016. LNCS, vol. 9912, pp. 20–36. Springer, Cham (2016). https://doi.org/10.1007/978-3-319-46484-8_2
24. Wang, X., Farhadi, A., Gupta, A.: Actions transformations. In: CVPR, pp. 2658–2667 (2016)
25. Wang, X., Girshick, R., Gupta, A., He, K.: Non-local neural networks. In: CVPR, pp. 7794–7803 (2018)
26. Wang, X., Gupta, A.: Videos as space-time region graphs. In: Ferrari, V., Hebert, M., Sminchisescu, C., Weiss, Y. (eds.) ECCV 2018. LNCS, vol. 11209, pp. 413–431. Springer, Cham (2018). https://doi.org/10.1007/978-3-030-01228-1_25
27. Wang, Y., Hoai, M.: Pulling actions out of context, explicit separation for effective combination. In: CVPR, pp. 7044–7053 (2018)
28. Xie, S., Sun, C., Huang, J., Tu, Z., Murphy, K.: Rethinking spatiotemporal feature learning: speed-accuracy trade-offs in video classification. In: Ferrari, V., Hebert, M., Sminchisescu, C., Weiss, Y. (eds.) ECCV 2018. LNCS, vol. 11219, pp. 318–335. Springer, Cham (2018). https://doi.org/10.1007/978-3-030-01267-0_19
29. Xingjian, S., Chen, Z., Wang, H., Yeung, D.Y., Wong, W.K., Woo, W.c.: Convolutional LSTM network: a machine learning approach for precipitation nowcasting. In: NeurIPS, pp. 802–810 (2015)
30. Zhang, P., Lan, C., Xing, J., Zeng, W., Xue, J., Zheng, N.: View adaptive recurrent neural networks for high performance human action recognition from skeleton data. In: ICCV, pp. 2117–2126 (2017)
31. Zhao, B., Wu, X., Feng, J., Peng, Q., Yan, S.: Diversified visual attention networks for fine-grained object classification. T-MM **19**(6), 1245–1256 (2017)
32. Zheng, H., Fu, J., Mei, T., Luo, J.: Learning multi-attention convolutional neural network for fine-grained image recognition. In: CVPR, pp. 5209–5217 (2017)
33. Zhou, B., Andonian, A., Oliva, A., Torralba, A.: Temporal relational reasoning in videos. In: Ferrari, V., Hebert, M., Sminchisescu, C., Weiss, Y. (eds.) ECCV 2018. LNCS, vol. 11205, pp. 831–846. Springer, Cham (2018). https://doi.org/10.1007/978-3-030-01246-5_49
34. Zhu, X., Xu, C., Hui, L., Lu, C., Tao, D.: Approximated bilinear modules for temporal modeling. In: ICCV, pp. 3494–3503 (2019)

Representative Graph Neural Network

Changqian Yu[1,2] , Yifan Liu[2] , Changxin Gao[1] , Chunhua Shen[2] ,
and Nong Sang[1(✉)]

[1] Key Laboratory of Image Processing and Intelligent Control,
School of Artificial Intelligence and Automation,
Huazhong University of Science and Technology, Wuhan, China
{changqian_yu,cgao,nsang}@hust.edu.cn
[2] The University of Adelaide, Adelaide, Australia

Abstract. Non-local operation is widely explored to model the long-range dependencies. However, the redundant computation in this operation leads to a prohibitive complexity. In this paper, we present a Representative Graph (RepGraph) layer to dynamically sample a few representative features, which dramatically reduces redundancy. Instead of propagating the messages from all positions, our RepGraph layer computes the response of one node merely with a few representative nodes. The locations of representative nodes come from a learned spatial offset matrix. The RepGraph layer is flexible to integrate into many visual architectures and combine with other operations. With the application of semantic segmentation, without any bells and whistles, our RepGraph network can compete or perform favourably against the state-of-the-art methods on three challenging benchmarks: ADE20K, Cityscapes, and PASCAL-Context datasets. In the task of object detection, our RepGraph layer can also improve the performance on the COCO dataset compared to the non-local operation. Code is available at https://git.io/RepGraph.

Keywords: Representative graph · Dynamic sampling · Semantic segmentation · Deep learning

1 Introduction

Modelling long-range dependencies is of vital importance for visual understanding, e.g., semantic segmentation [11,18,44] and object detection/segmentation [2, 16,37]. The previous dominant paradigm is dependent on the deep stacks of local operators, e.g., convolution operators, which are yet limited by inefficient computation, hard optimization and insufficient effective receptive field [29].

Part of the work was done when C. Yu was visiting The University of Adelaide.

Electronic supplementary material The online version of this chapter (https://doi.org/10.1007/978-3-030-58571-6_23) contains supplementary material, which is available to authorized users.

© Springer Nature Switzerland AG 2020
A. Vedaldi et al. (Eds.): ECCV 2020, LNCS 12352, pp. 379–396, 2020.
https://doi.org/10.1007/978-3-030-58571-6_23

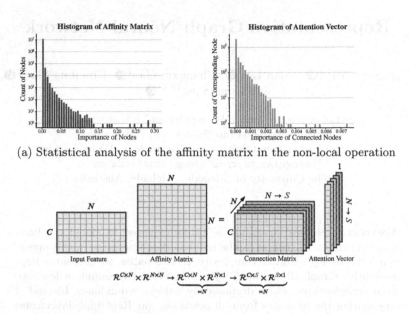

(a) Statistical analysis of the affinity matrix in the non-local operation

(b) Computation diagram of the non-local operation

Fig. 1. Illustration of the affinity matrix. (a) The statistical analysis of the affinity matrix. In Non-local, the affinity matrix models the importance of all other positions to each position. The histogram of the weights of all the positions is on the left, while that of one position is on the right. These statistical results indicate some *representative* positions exhibit principal importance. (b) The computation diagram of Non-local. The computation in the left can be decoupled into N groups of connection matrix and attention vector. The connection matrix determines which positions require connecting to the current position, while the attention vector assigns the weight to the connection edge. Here, the N above the connection matrix represents N nodes are connected to the current position. Therefore, for each position, we can select S representative nodes to connect and compute a corresponding attention vector to reduce the complexity

To solve this issue, a family of non-local methods [6,16,37,41,44,47] is proposed to capture the long-range relations in feature representation. The non-local operation computes the response at a position as a weighted sum of the features at all positions, whose weights are assigned by a dense affinity matrix. This affinity matrix models the importance of all other positions to each position. Intuitively, there is some redundancy in this affinity matrix, leading to a prohibitive computation complexity. For each position, some other positions may contribute little to its response. This assumption drives us to study further the distributions of importance in the affinity matrix. We perform the statistical analysis on this affinity matrix to help to understand in Fig. 1(a). It is surprising to see that the distribution is extremely imbalanced, which implies that *some representative positions contribute principal impact, while the majority of positions have little contribution.* Therefore, if the affinity matrix can only compute the response with only a few representative positions, the computation redundancy can be dramatically reduced.

Based on previous observations, we rethink Non-local methods from the graphical model perspective and propose an efficient, flexible, and generic operation to capture the long-range dependencies, termed **Representative Graph** (RepGraph). Considering each feature position as a node, Non-local constructs a complete graph (fully-connected graph) and assigns a weight to each connection edge via the affinity map. Thus, for each feature node, the computation of non-local graph can be decoupled into two parts: (i) a connection matrix; (ii) a corresponding attention vector, as illustrated in Fig. 1(b). The connection matrix determines which nodes make contributions to each node, while the attention vector assigns the weight for each connection edge.

To reduce the redundant computation, for each node, the *RepGraph* layer dynamically selects a few representative nodes as the neighbourhoods instead of all nodes. The corresponding weight is assigned to the edge to propagate the long-range dependencies. Specifically, the *RepGraph* layer first regresses an offset matrix conditioned on the current node. With the offset matrix, this layer samples the representative nodes on the graph, and then compute an affinity map as the weight to aggregate these representative features.

Meanwhile, the *RepGraph* layer is easy to combine with other mechanisms. Motivated by the pyramid methods [3,51], we can spatially group some feature elements as a graph node instead of only considering one element, named *Grid Representative Graph (Grid RepGraph)*. Besides, inspired by the channel group mechanism [15,33,39,45,50], we can also divide the features into several groups, and conduct computation in each corresponding group, termed *Group RepGraph*.

There are several merits of our *RepGraph* layer: (i) The *RepGraph* layer can dramatically reduce the redundant computation of Non-local. Specifically, the RepGraph layer is around 17 times smaller in computation complexity and over 5 times faster than Non-local with a 256×128 input. (ii) The *RepGraph* layer learns a compact and representative feature representation, which is more efficient and effective than non-local operation; (iii) Our *RepGraph* layer can be flexibly integrated into other neural networks or operations.

We showcase the effectiveness of *RepGraph* operations in the application of semantic segmentation. Extensive evaluations demonstrate that the *RepGraph* operations can compete or perform favorably against the *state-of-the-art* semantic segmentation approaches. To demonstrate the generality of *RepGraph* operations, we further conduct the experiments of object detection/segmentation tasks on the COCO dataset [28]. In the comparison of non-local blocks, our *RepGraph* operations can increase the accuracy further.

2   Related Work

Non-local Methods and Compact Representation. Motivated by the non-local means [1], [37] proposes the non-local neural network to model the long-range dependences in the application of video classification [5,37], object detection and segmentation [16,37,47]. The relation network [16] embeds the geometry feature with the self-attention manner [34] to model the relationship between object proposals. OCNet [44] extends the non-local block with pyramid methods [4,51]. CFNet [47] explores the co-occurrent context to help the scene understanding, while DANet [11] applies the self-attention on both the spatial and channel dimension. Meanwhile, CPNet [41] explores the supervised self-attention matrix to capture the intra-context and inter-context.

The redundant computation in these nonlocal methods leads to a prohibitive computational complexity, which hinders its application, especially in some dense prediction tasks. Therefore, there are mainly two ways to explore the compact representation of non-local operations: (i) Matrix factorization. A^2-Net [5] computes the affinity matrix between channels. LatentGNN [49] embeds the features into a latent space to get a low-complexity matrix. CGNL [45] groups the channels and utilizes the Taylor expansion reduce computation. CCNet [18] introduces a recurrent criss-cross attention. (ii) Input restricting. Non-local has a quadratic complexity with the size of the input feature. Therefore, restricting the input size is a straightforward approach to reduce complexity. [55] utilizes a pyramid pooling manner to compress the input of the key and value branch. ISA [17] adopts the interlacing mechanism to spatially group the input.

In this paper, we explore a compact and general representation to model the dependencies. Non-local can be a special case of our work, as illustrated in Fig. 1 (b). In contrast to previous compact methods, our work dynamically sample the representative nodes to efficiently reduces the spatial redundancy.

Graph Neural Network. Our work is also related to the graphical neural network [22,23,53]. Non-local [34,37] can be viewed as a densely-connected graph, which models the relationships between any two nodes. Meanwhile, GAT [35] introduces a graph attentional layer, which performs self-attention on each node. In contrast to both dense graphical models, our work constructs a sparse graph, on which each node is simply connected to a few representative nodes.

Deformable Convolution. Our work needs to learn an offset matrix to locate some representative nodes, which is related to the deformable convolution [8]. The learned offset matrix in DCN is applied on the regular grid positions of convolution kernels, and the number of the sampled positions requires matching with the kernel size. However, our work applies the learned offset to each node position directly. The number of sampled nodes can be unlimited theoretically.

3   Representative Graph Neural Networks

In this section, we first revisit Non-local from the graphical model perspective in Sect. 3.1. Next, we introduce the motivation, formulation, and several instantiations of the representative graph layer in Sect. 3.2. Finally, the extended instantiations of the representative graph layer are illustrated in Sect. 3.3.

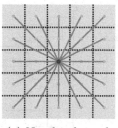 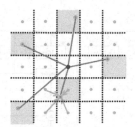

(a) Non-local graph   (b) Representative graph

Fig. 2. Comparison of non-local graph and representative graph. (a) The non-local graph is a fully-connected graph, leading to prohibitive complexity. (b) The representative graph only computes the relationships with some representative nodes, e.g., five in the figure, for each output node. The sampled nodes with fractional positions are interpolated with the nodes at four integral neighbourhood positions

3.1 Revisiting Non-local Graph Neural Network

Following the formulation of the non-local operator in [37], we describe a fully-connected graphical neural network.

For a 2D input feature with the size of $C \times H \times W$, where C, H, and W denote the channel dimension, height, and width respectively, it can be interpreted as a set of features, $\mathbf{X} = [\mathbf{x}_1, \mathbf{x}_2, \cdots, \mathbf{x}_N]^\mathsf{T}$, $\mathbf{x}_i \in \mathbb{R}^C$, where N is the number of nodes (e.g., $N = H \times W$), and C is the node feature dimension.

With the input features, we can construct a fully-connected graph $\mathcal{G} = (\mathcal{V}, \mathcal{E})$ with $\mathcal{V}$ as the nodes, and $\mathcal{E}$ as the edges, as illustrated in Fig. 2(a). The graphical model assigns each feature element $\mathbf{x}_i$ as a node $v_i \in \mathcal{V}$, while the edge $(v_i, v_j) \in \mathcal{E}$ encodes the relationship between node v_i and node v_j. Three linear transformation, parameterized by three weight matrices $W_\phi \in \mathbb{R}^{C' \times C}$, $W_\theta \in \mathbb{R}^{C' \times C}$, and $W_g \in \mathbb{R}^{C' \times C}$ respectively, are applied on each node. Therefore, the formulation of the non-local graph network can be interpreted as:

$$\tilde{\mathbf{x}}_i = \frac{1}{\mathcal{C}(\mathbf{x})} \sum_{\forall j} f(\mathbf{x}_i, \mathbf{x}_j) g(\mathbf{x}_j) = \frac{1}{\mathcal{C}(\mathbf{x})} \sum_{\forall j} \delta(\theta(\mathbf{x}_i)\phi(\mathbf{x}_j)^\mathsf{T}) g(\mathbf{x}_j), \quad (1)$$

where j enumerates all possible positions, δ is the softmax function, and $\mathcal{C}(\mathbf{x})$ is a normalization factor.

We can rewrite the formulation in Eq. 1 in a matrix form:

$$\tilde{\mathbf{X}} = \delta(\mathbf{X}_\theta \mathbf{X}_\phi^\mathsf{T}) \mathbf{X}_\mathbf{g} = \mathbf{A}(\mathbf{X}) \mathbf{X}_\mathbf{g}, \quad (2)$$

where $\mathbf{A}(\mathbf{X}) \in \mathbb{R}^{N \times N}$ indicates the affinity matrix, $X_\theta \in \mathbb{R}^{N \times C'}$, $X_\phi \in \mathbb{R}^{N \times C'}$, and $X_g \in \mathbb{R}^{N \times C'}$. The matrix multiplication results in a prohibitive computation complexity: $\mathcal{O}(C' \times N^2)$. In some visual understanding tasks, e.g., semantic segmentation and object detection, the input usually has a large resolution, which is unfeasible to compute the dense affinity matrix. It is thus desirable to explore a more compact and efficient operation to model the long-range dependencies.

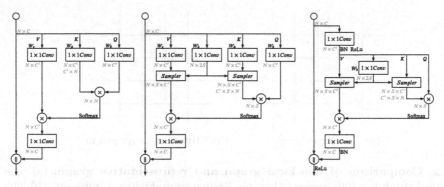

(a) Non-local block   (b) Simple Representative Graph layer   (c) Bottleneck Representative Graph layer

Fig. 3. Instantiations of representative graph layer. (a) is the structure of the non-local block; (b) is the structure of our Simple RepGraph layer, which utilizes learned offset matrix to sample the representative features of the value and key branches; (c) is the structure of our Bottleneck RepGraph layer, following the bottleneck design. Here, ‖ means the aggregation operation, e.g., *summation* or *concatenation*

3.2 Representative Graph Layer

Motivation. As showed in Fig. 1(b), we can reconstruct the matrix multiplication as a new form:

$$\mathcal{R}^{N\times N} \times \mathcal{R}^{N\times C'} \to \underbrace{\mathcal{R}^{1\times N} \times \mathcal{R}^{N\times C'}}_{=N}, \tag{3}$$

where $\mathcal{R}^{N\times C'}$, as the connection matrix, determines which nodes are connected to current node, while $\mathcal{R}^{1\times N}$ as the attention vector assigns the weight to corresponding edge.

Based on our observation discussed in Sect. 1, we can select a few representative nodes (e.g., S) for each node instead of propagating the messages from all nodes. Therefore, the number of connected nodes for each node can be reduced from N to S (usually $S \ll N$), which dramatically reduces the prohibitive computation complexity. The new pipeline can be transformed as:

$$\underbrace{\mathcal{R}^{1\times N} \times \mathcal{R}^{N\times C'}}_{=N} \to \underbrace{\mathcal{R}^{1\times S} \times \mathcal{R}^{S\times C'}}_{=N}, \tag{4}$$

where S is the number of the representative nodes. This reconstruction reduces the computation cost from $\mathcal{O}(C'\times N^2)$ to $\mathcal{O}(C'\times N\times S)$, usually $S \ll N$ (e.g., for a 65×65 input feature, $N = 65 \times 65 = 4225$, while $S = 9$ in our experiments).

Formulation. Based on the observations, we can dynamically sample some nodes to construct the Representative Graph, as illustrated Fig. 2(b).

For each position i of the node feature, we sample a set of representative node features:

$$\mathcal{F}(\mathbf{x}(i)) = \{\mathbf{s}(n)|n = 1, 2, \cdots, S\}, \tag{5}$$

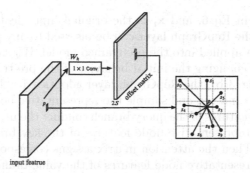

Fig. 4. Illustration of representative nodes sampler. For each position p, the layer adopts one 1×1 convolution operation to regress an offset matrix to sample S representative nodes. The offset matrix has $2S$ channels, the values of which are typically fractional

where $s(n) \in \mathcal{R}^{C'}$ is the sampled representative node feature.

Given the sampling function $\mathcal{F}(\mathbf{x}_i)$, Eq. 1 can be reformulated as:

$$\tilde{\mathbf{x}}(i) = \frac{1}{\mathcal{C}(\mathbf{x})} \sum_{\forall n} \delta(\mathbf{x}_\theta(i)\mathbf{s}_\phi(n)^\mathsf{T})\mathbf{s}_g(n), \tag{6}$$

where n only enumerates the sampled positions, δ is the softmax function, $\mathbf{x}_\theta(i) = W_\theta\mathbf{x}(i), \mathbf{s}_\phi(i) = W_\phi\mathbf{s}(i), \mathbf{s}_g(i) = W_g\mathbf{s}(i)$.

Representative Nodes Sampler. Motivated by [8], we can instantiate Eq. 5 via offset regression. Conditioned on the node features, we can learn an offset matrix to dynamically select nodes. Therefore, for each position p, Eq. 5 can be reformulated as:

$$\mathcal{F}(\mathbf{x}(p)) = \{\mathbf{x}(p + \Delta p_n)|n = 1, 2, \cdots, S\}, \tag{7}$$

where Δp_n is the regressed offset.

Due to the regression manner, the offset Δp_n is commonly fractional. Thus, we utilize bilinear interpolation [20] to compute the correct values of the fractional position with the node feature at four integral neighbourhood positions:

$$\mathbf{x}(p_s) = \sum_{\forall t} G(t, p_s)\mathbf{x}(t), \tag{8}$$

where $p_s = p + \Delta p_n$, t is four neighbourhood integral positions, and G is bilinear interpolation kernel.

As illustrated in Fig. 5, we adopt a 1×1 convolutional layer to regress the offset matrix for each node feature, which has $2S$ channel dimensions. After bilinear interpolation, the RepGraph layer can sample S representative nodes.

Instantiations. We can instantiate Eq. 6 with a residual structure [14], as illustrated in Fig. 3(b). We define the RepGraph layer as:

$$\mathbf{y}_i = W_y\tilde{\mathbf{x}}_i + \mathbf{x}_i, \tag{9}$$

where $\tilde{\mathbf{x}}_i$ is given in Eq. 6, and $\mathbf{x}_i$ is the original input feature. This residual structure enables the RepGraph layer can be inserted to any pre-trained model. We note that when applied into the pre-trained model, W_y should be initialized to zero in avoid of changing the initial behavior of the pre-trained model.

As shown in Fig. 3(b), the RepGraph layer adopts a 1×1 convolution layer to regress the offset matrix, and sample the representative nodes of the key and value branch. The features of the query branch conduct the matrix multiplication with the sampled representative node features of the key branch to obtain the attention matrix. Then the attention matrix assigns corresponding weights and aggregates the representative node features of the value branch.

Meanwhile, motivated by the bottleneck design [14,39], we re-design the Rep-Graph layer as a bottleneck structure, as illustrated in Fig. 3(c). We note that when applied to the pre-trained architectures, the weights and biases of last convolution and batch normalization should be initialized to zero, and the ReLU function should be removed.

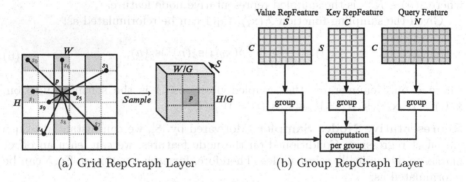

(a) Grid RepGraph Layer   (b) Group RepGraph Layer

Fig. 5. Illustration of extended instantiations of the repGraph layer. (a) is Grid RepGraph layer, which spatially grids the input features into several groups, e.g., the features in the red box. Each group has an anchor coordinate, showed in blue cube. The learned offset matrix is applied on the anchor coordinate to sample S representative node features. G indicates how many elements to group along a dimension, e.g., $G = 2$ in the top figure. (b) is Group RepGraph layer, which divides the feature of query branch, sampled representative feature of value branch and key branch into several channel groups respectively. Then, the same computation shown in Eq. 6 is conducted in each corresponding group (Color figure online)

3.3   Extended Instantiations

Motivated by pyramid methods [3,51], and channel group mechanism [15,39,45], it is easy to instantiate the RepGraph layer with diverse structures.

Grid RepGraph Layer. Instead of considering one input feature element as a node, we can spatially group varying quantity of elements as a node. First, we spatially grid input feature into several groups. The left-top element in each group is the anchor position. Then, we utilize the average pooling to group the input features to regress the offset matrix spatially. The learned offset coordinates are applied to the anchor positions to sample some representative nodes for each group. Finally, we conduct the matrix multiplication on the grid features.

Group RepGraph Layer. Channel group mechanism is widely used in lightweight recognition architectures, which can reduce the computation and increase the capacity of the model [15,33,39,45,50]. It is easy to be applied on the RepGraph layer. With the input features $\mathbf{x}_\theta(i), \mathcal{F}(\mathbf{x}_\phi(j)), \mathcal{F}(\mathbf{x}_g(j))$, we can divide all C' channels into G groups, each of which has $\tilde{C} = C'/G$ channels. Then, the RepGraph computation of Eq. 6 can be performed in each group independently. Finally, we concatenate the output features of all the groups along the dimension of channels as the final output features.

4   Experiments on Semantic Segmentation

We perform comprehensive ablative evaluation on challenging ADE20K [54] dataset. We also report performance on Cityscapes [7] and PASCAL-Context [30] to investigate the effectiveness of our work.

Datasets. The ADE20K dataset contains 20 K training images and 2 K validation images. It is a challenging scene understanding benchmark due to the complex scene and up to 150 category labels.

Cityscapes is a large urban street scene parsing benchmark, which contains 2,975, 500, 1,525 fine-annotation images for training, validation, and testing, respectively. Besides, there are additional 20,000 coarse-annotation images for training. In our experiments, we only use the fine-annotation set. The images of this benchmark are all in 2048 × 1024 resolution with 19 semantic categories.

PASCAL-Context [30] augments 10,103 images from PASCAL VOC 2010 dataset [10] for scene understanding, which considers both the stuff and thing categories. This dataset can be divided into 4,998 images for training and 5,105 images for testing. The most common 59 categories are used for evaluation.

Training. We utilize the SGD algorithm with 0.9 momentum to fine-tune the RepGraph network. For the ADE20K and PASCAL-Context datasets, we train our model starting with the initial learning rate of 0.02, the weight decay of 0.0001, and the batch size of 16. For the Cityscapes dataset, the initial rate is 0.01 with the weight decay of 0.0005, while the batch size is 8. We note that we adopt the "poly" learning rate strategy [3], in which the initial learning rate is multiplied by $(1 - \frac{iter}{iter_{max}})^{0.9}$. Besides, the synchronized batch normalization [19, 31,46] is applied to train our models. We train our models for 100K, 40K, 80K iterations on ADE20K, Cityscapes, PASCAL-Context datasets, respectively.

For the data augmentation, we randomly horizontally flip, randomly scale and crop the input images to a fixed size for training, which scales include $\{0.75, 1, 1.25, 1.5, 1.75, 2.0\}$. Meanwhile, the cropped resolutions are 520 × 520 for ADE20K and PASCAL-Context, and 769 × 769 for Cityscapes dataset.

Inference. In the inference phase, we adopt the sliding-window evaluation strategy [43,51,52]. Moreover, multi-scale and flipped inputs are employed to improve the performance, which scales contain {0.5, 0.75, 1.0, 1.25} for the ADE20K and PASCAL-Context datasets, and {0.5, 0.75, 1, 1.5} for the Cityscapes dataset.

Table 1. Ablations on ADE20K. We show mean IoU (%) and pixel accuracy (%) as the segmentation performance

model, R50	mIoU	pixAcc
R50 baseline	36.48	77.57
NL baseline	40.97	79.96
$S=1$	42.53	80.08
9	**43.12**	80.27
12	42.60	80.43
15	42.99	80.45
18	42.85	80.44
27	43.06	**80.64**

model, R50		mIoU	pixAcc
baseline		36.48	77.57
+NL	sum	40.3	79.96
	concate	40.97	80.01
+Simple	sum	42.61	80.191
	concate	42.98	80.41
+Bottleneck	sum	42.67	**80.46**
	concate	**43.12**	80.27

model, R50	mIoU	pixAcc
baseline	36.48	77.57
res$_2$	41.52	79.67
res$_3$	**41.59**	**79.97**
res$_4$	41.25	79.69
res$_5$	41.34	79.89

model, R50	mIoU	pixAcc
baseline	36.48	77.57
1-layer	41.59	**79.97**
3-layer	**41.86**	79.85
5-layer	41.76	79.89

(a) **Representative nodes:** 1 RepGraph layer of diverse nodes is inserted after the last stage of R50 baseline

(b) **Instantiations:** 1 RepGraph layer of different structure is inserted after the last stage of ResNet-50 baseline

(c) **Stages:** 1 Bottleneck RepGraph layer is inserted into different stages of ResNet-50 baseline

(d) **Deeper non-local models:** we insert 1, 3, and 5 Bottleneck RepGraph layer into the ResNet-50 baseline

4.1 Ablative Evaluation on ADE20K

This section provides an ablative evaluation on ADE20K comparing segmentation accuracy and computation complexity. We train all models on the training set and evaluate on the validation set. We adopt the pixel accuracy (pixAcc) and mean intersection of union (mIoU) as the evaluation metric.

Baselines. Similar to [3,4,46,51,52], we adopt dilated ResNet (ResNet-50) [14] with pre-trained weights as our *backbone baseline*. An auxiliary loss function with the weight of 0.4 is integrated into the fourth stage of the backbone network [41, 51,52]. We utilize one 3×3 convolution layer followed by batch normalization [19] and ReLU activation function on the output of the last backbone stage to reduce the channel dimension to 512. Based on this output, we apply one non-local block (NL) as the *NL baseline*. Table 1(a) shows the segmentation performance of backbone baseline and NL baseline.

Instantiations. Table 1(b) shows the different structures of RepGraph layer, as illustrated in Fig. 3. The simple RepGraph layer (SRG) has a similar structure with the non-local operation, while the bottleneck RepGraph layer (BRG) combines the residual bottleneck [14,39] with the simple RepGraph layer. The number of sampled representative nodes is 9. Meanwhile, we also compare the different fusion methods (*summation* and *concatenation*) of diverse structures. The bottleneck RepGraph layer has stronger representation ability, which achieves better performance than the simple RepGraph layer. Therefore, in the rest of this paper, we use the bottleneck RepGraph layer version by default.

How Many Representative Nodes to Sample? Table 1(a) compares the performance of choosing different number of representative nodes. It shows *all*

Table 2. Practical GFLOPs of different blocks with the input feature of 256 × 128 resolution (1/8 of the 1024 × 2048 image). The batch size of the input feature is 1, while the input channel $C = 2048$ and middle channel $C' = 256$. The inference time is measured on one NVIDIA RTX 2080Ti card. The decrease of our methods in term of computation and inference time is compared with NL

Input size	Model	GFLOPs	Inference time (ms)
256 × 128	NL [44]	601.4	146.65
	DANet [11]	785.01	279.56
	SRG [ours]	45.31 (↓ 556.09)	60.89 (↓ 85.76)
	BRG [ours]	34.96 (↓ 566.44)	25.96 (↓ 120.69)

Table 3. Extended instantiations of RepGraph layer. We can spatially group the spatial nodes, termed *Grid RepGraph*, or divide the channel into several groups, termed *Group RepGraph*. We show mean IoU (%) and pixel accuracy (%) as the segmentation performance

model, R50	mIoU	pixAcc
baseline	36.48	77.57
Grid RG($g_s = 1$)	43.12	80.27
$g_s = 5$	42.40	80.17
13	41.82	80.01
65	41.23	79.73

model, R50	mIoU	pixAcc
baseline	36.48	77.57
Group RG($g_c = 1$)	43.12	80.27
$g_c = 4$	42.78	80.20
8	43.01	80.32
16	42.96	80.19
32	42.38	80.18

(a) **Spatial group**: g_s is the number of spatially grouped elements in one dimension, (e.g., for a 2D input, $g_s = 5$ indicates groups 5 × 5 elements as a graph node)

(b) **Channel group**: g_c indicates how many channels require dividing into on group

the models can improve the performance over the ResNet-50 baseline and are better than the NL baseline, which validates the effectiveness and robustness of our RepGraph layer. We employ $S = 9$ as our default. Interestingly, even only choosing one representative node ($s = 1$) for each position can also lead to a 1.56% performance improvement. This validates reducing redundancy in non-local helps to more effective representation. For better understanding, we show some visualization of learned sampling positions in the supplementary material.

Next, we investigate the combination with the pre-trained model (e.g., ResNet). Due to insertion into the pre-trained model, we can not change the initial behaviour of the pre-trained model. Therefore, we have to choose the summation version of bottleneck RepGraph layer and remove the last ReLU function of this layer. Meanwhile, the parameters of the last convolution layer and batch normalization require to initialize as zero.

Which Stage to Insert RepGraph Layer? We insert the bottleneck Rep-Graph layer before the last block of different backbone stages, as shown in Table 1 (c). The improvements over the backbone baseline validate the RepGraph layer can be a generic component to extract features.

Going Deeper with RepGraph Layer. Table 1(d) shows the performance with more RepGraph layers. We add 1 (to res$_3$), 3 (to res$_3$, res$_4$, res$_5$ respectively), and 5 (1 to res$_3$, 2 to res$_4$, 2 to res$_5$). With more layers, the performance can be improved further. This improvement validates the RepGraph layer can model some complementary information not encoded in the pre-trained model.

Computation Complexity. The theoretical computational complexity of non-local operation and RepGraph layer is $\mathcal{O}(C \times N^2)$ and $\mathcal{O}(C \times S \times N)$ respectively. Meanwhile, Table 2 shows the practical GFLOPs and inference time of non-local operation [37], DANet [11] and RepGraph layer with the input size of 256×128 (1/8 of the 1024×2048 image). Here, we use the concatenation fusion method in each block. The RepGraph layer can dramatically reduce the computation complexity and have fewer inference time compared to the non-local operation.

Then, we show some extended instantiations of RepGraph layer.

Table 4. Quantitative evaluations on the ADE20K validation set. The proposed RGNet performs favorably against the *state-of-the-art* segmentation algorithms

Model	Reference	Backbone	*mIoU*	*picAcc*
RefineNet [26]	CVPR2017	ResNet-152	40.7	–
UperNet [38]	ECCV2018	ResNet-101	42.66	81.01
PSPNet [51]	CVPR2017	ResNet-269	44.94	81.69
DSSPN [25]	CVPR2018	ResNet-101	43.68	81.13
PSANet [52]	ECCV2018	ResNet-101	43.77	81.51
SAC [48]	ICCV2017	ResNet-101	44.30	**81.86**
EncNet [46]	CVPR2018	ResNet-101	44.65	81.69
CFNet [47]	CVPR2019	ResNet-101	44.89	–
CCNet [18]	ICCV2019	ResNet-101	45.22	–
ANL [55]	ICCV2019	ResNet-101	45.24	–
DMNet [12]	ICCV2019	ResNet-101	<u>45.50</u>	
RGNet	–	ResNet-50	44.02	81.12
RGNet	–	ResNet-101	**45.8**	<u>81.76</u>

Extension. Table 3 shows some extended instantiations of the RepGraph layer. Instead of considering one feature element as a graph node, we can spatially group a few pixels as a graph node to construct the RepGraph layer, termed *Grid RepGraph*. We argue that the Grid RepGraph layer computes the relationships between representative nodes and local nodes in one group. The sampling

Table 5. Quantitative evaluations on Cityscapes test set. The proposed RGNet performs favorably against the *state-of-the-art* segmentation methods. We train our model with *trainval-fine* set, and evaluate on the *test* set

Model	Reference	Backbone	$mIoU$
GCN [32]	CVPR2017	ResNet-101	76.9
DUC [36]	WACV2018	ResNet-101	77.6
DSSPN [25]	CVPR2018	ResNet-101	77.8
SAC [48]	ICCV2017	ResNet-101	78.1
PSPNet [51]	CVPR2017	ResNet-101	78.4
BiSeNet [42]	ECCV2018	ResNet-101	78.9
AAF [21]	ECCV2018	ResNet-101	79.1
DFN [43]	CVPR2018	ResNet-101	79.3
PSANet [52]	ECCV2018	ResNet-101	80.1
DenseASPP [40]	CVPR2018	DenseNet-161	80.6
ANL [55]	ICCV2019	ResNet-101	81.3
CPNet [41]	CVPR2020	ResNet-101	81.3
CCNet [18]	ICCV2019	ResNet-101	81.4
DANet [11]	CVPR2019	ResNet-101	**81.5**
RGNet	–	ResNet-101	**81.5**

of representative nodes can capture long-range information, while the spatial grouping enables the short-range contextual modelling.

Inspired by [39, 45], the channel of RepGraph layer can be divided into a few groups, called *Group RepGraph* layer. This structure can increase the cardinality and capture the correlation in diverse channel groups. Although there is a little performance decrease, the extended instantiations are more efficient.

4.2   Performance Evaluation

In this section, we compare the RepGraph network (RGNet) with other *state-of-the-art* methods on three datasets: ADE20K, Cityscapes, and PASCAL-Context.

ADE20K. Table 4 shows the comparison results with other *state-of-the-art* algorithms on ADE20K dataset. *Without any bells and whistles*, our RGNet with ResNet-101 as backbone achieves mean IoU of 45.8% and pixel accuracy of 81.76%, which outperforms previous *state-of-the-art* methods. Our RGNet with ResNet-50 obtains mean IoU of 44.04% and pixel accuracy of 81.12%, even better than the PSANet [52], PSPNet [51], UperNet [38], and RefineNet [26] with deeper backbone networks.

Cityscapes. Table 5 shows the comparison with previous results on Cityscapes [7] dataset. We train our model with *trainval* set of merely the fine annotation images, and evaluate on the *test* set. The compared methods only

Table 6. Quantitative evaluations on the PASCAL-Context validation set. The proposed RGNet performs favorably against the *state-of-the-art* segmentation methods.

Model	Reference	Backbone	$mIoU$
CRF-RNN [53]	ICCV2015	VGG-16	39.3
RefineNet [26]	CVPR2017	ResNet-152	47.3
PSPNet [51]	CVPR2017	ResNet-101	47.8
CCL [9]	CVPR2018	ResNet-101	51.6
EncNet [46]	CVPR2018	ResNet-101	51.7
DANet [11]	CVPR2019	ResNet-101	52.6
ANL [55]	ICCV2019	ResNet-101	52.8
EMANet [24]	ICCV2019	ResNet-101	<u>53.1</u>
CPNet [41]	CVPR2020	ResNet-101	**53.9**
RGNet	–	ResNet-101	**53.9**

Table 7. Adding 1 RepGraph layer to Mask R-CNN for COCO **object detection** and **instance segmentation**. The backbone is ResNet-50 with FPN [27]

	Method	AP^{box}	AP^{box}_{50}	AP^{box}_{75}	AP^{mask}	AP^{mask}_{50}	AP^{mask}_{75}
R50	Baseline	38.0	59.6	41.0	34.6	56.4	36.5
	+1 NL	39.0	61.1	41.9	35.5	**58.0**	37.4
	+1 RGL	**39.6**	**61.4**	**42.1**	**36.0**	57.9	**37.9**

use the fine-annotation images as well. The RGNet achieves mean IoU of 81.5%, which competes with previous *state-of-the-art* methods. However, as shown in Table 5, the RGNet is more efficient than the DANet, which applies the self-attention mechanism on the spatial and channel dimension respectively.

PASCAL-Context. Table 6 shows the results on the PASCAL-Context dataset compared with other methods. The RGNet achieves mean IoU of 53.9% on the *val* set, which sets *state-of-the-art* result.

5   Experiments on Detection

To investigate the generalization ability of our work, we conduct experiments on object detection. Following [37], we set the Mask R-CNN [13] as our baseline. All experiments are trained on COCO [28] *train*2017 and tested on *test*2017.

We add one RepGraph layer before the last block of res$_4$ of ResNet backbone network in the Mack R-CNN. Table 7 shows the box AP and mask AP on COCO dataset. As we can see, using just one RepGraph layer can improve the performance over the baseline. Meanwhile, adding one RepGraph layer achieves *better* performance than adding one non-local operation.

6   Concluding Remarks

We present a Representative Graph (RepGraph) layer to model long-range dependencies via dynamically sample a few representative nodes. The RepGraph layer is compact and general component for visual understanding. Meanwhile, the RepGraph layer is easy to integrate into any pre-trained model or combined with other designs. On the semantic segmentation and object detection task, the RepGraph layer can achieve promising improvement over baseline and non-local operation. We believe the *RepGraph* layer can be an efficient and general block to the visual understanding community.

Acknowledgment. This work is supported by the National Natural Science Foundation of China (No. 61433007 and 61876210).

References

1. Buades, A., Coll, B., Morel, J.M.: A non-local algorithm for image denoising. In: Proceedings of the IEEE Conference on Computer Vision and Pattern Recognition (CVPR), vol. 2, pp. 60–65. IEEE (2005)
2. Cao, Y., Xu, J., Lin, S., Wei, F., Hu, H.: GCNet: non-local networks meet squeeze-excitation networks and beyond. arXiv (2019)
3. Chen, L.C., Papandreou, G., Kokkinos, I., Murphy, K., Yuille, A.L.: DeepLab: semantic image segmentation with deep convolutional nets, atrous convolution, and fully connected CRFs. arXiv (2016)
4. Chen, L.C., Papandreou, G., Schroff, F., Adam, H.: Rethinking atrous convolution for semantic image segmentation. arXiv (2017)
5. Chen, Y., Kalantidis, Y., Li, J., Yan, S., Feng, J.: A^ 2-nets: double attention networks. In: Advances in Neural Information Processing Systems (NeurIPS), pp. 352–361 (2018)
6. Chen, Y., Rohrbach, M., Yan, Z., Shuicheng, Y., Feng, J., Kalantidis, Y.: Graph-based global reasoning networks. In: Proceedings of the IEEE Conference on Computer Vision and Pattern Recognition (CVPR), pp. 433–442 (2019)
7. Cordts, M., et al.: The cityscapes dataset for semantic urban scene understanding. In: Proceedings of the IEEE Conference on Computer Vision and Pattern Recognition (CVPR) (2016)
8. Dai, J., et al.: Deformable convolutional networks. In: Proceedings of the IEEE International Conference on Computer Vision (ICCV), pp. 764–773 (2017)
9. Ding, H., Jiang, X., Shuai, B., Qun Liu, A., Wang, G.: Context contrasted feature and gated multi-scale aggregation for scene segmentation. In: Proceedings of the IEEE Conference on Computer Vision and Pattern Recognition (CVPR), pp. 2393–2402 (2018)
10. Everingham, M., Van Gool, L., Williams, C.K.I., Winn, J., Zisserman, A.: The PASCAL visual object classes challenge 2012 (VOC2012) results (2012). http://www.pascal-network.org/challenges/VOC/voc2012/workshop/index.html
11. Fu, J., Liu, J., Tian, H., Fang, Z., Lu, H.: Dual attention network for scene segmentation. In: Proceedings of the IEEE Conference on Computer Vision and Pattern Recognition (CVPR) (2019)

12. He, J., Deng, Z., Qiao, Y.: Dynamic multi-scale filters for semantic segmentation. In: Proceedings of the IEEE International Conference on Computer Vision (ICCV), October 2019
13. He, K., Gkioxari, G., Dollár, P., Girshick, R.: Mask R-CNN. In: Proceedings of the IEEE International Conference on Computer Vision (ICCV), pp. 2961–2969 (2017)
14. He, K., Zhang, X., Ren, S., Sun, J.: Deep residual learning for image recognition. In: Proceedings of the IEEE Conference on Computer Vision and Pattern Recognition (CVPR) (2016)
15. Howard, A.G., et al.: MobileNets: efficient convolutional neural networks for mobile vision applications. arXiv (2017)
16. Hu, H., Gu, J., Zhang, Z., Dai, J., Wei, Y.: Relation networks for object detection. In: Proceedings of the IEEE Conference on Computer Vision and Pattern Recognition (CVPR) (2018)
17. Huang, L., Yuan, Y., Guo, J., Zhang, C., Chen, X., Wang, J.: Interlaced sparse self-attention for semantic segmentation. arXiv (2019)
18. Huang, Z., Wang, X., Huang, C., Wei, Y., Liu, W.: CCNet: criss-cross attention for semantic segmentation (2019)
19. Ioffe, S., Szegedy, C.: Batch normalization: accelerating deep network training by reducing internal covariate shift. In: Proceedings of the International Conference on Machine Learning (ICML), pp. 448–456 (2015)
20. Jaderberg, M., Simonyan, K., Zisserman, A., et al.: Spatial transformer networks. In: Advances in Neural Information Processing Systems (NeurIPS), pp. 2017–2025 (2015)
21. Ke, T.W., Hwang, J.J., Liu, Z., Yu, S.X.: Adaptive affinity fields for semantic segmentation. In: Proceedings of the European Conference on Computer Vision (ECCV), pp. 587–602 (2018)
22. Krähenbühl, P., Koltun, V.: Efficient inference in fully connected CRFs with Gaussian edge potentials. In: Advances in Neural Information Processing Systems (NeurIPS) (2011)
23. Lafferty, J., McCallum, A., Pereira, F.C.: Conditional random fields: probabilistic models for segmenting and labeling sequence data. In: Proceedings of the International Conference on Machine Learning (ICML) (2001)
24. Li, X., Zhong, Z., Wu, J., Yang, Y., Lin, Z., Liu, H.: Expectation-maximization attention networks for semantic segmentation. In: Proceedings of the IEEE International Conference on Computer Vision (ICCV), October 2019
25. Liang, X., Zhou, H., Xing, E.P.: Dynamic-structured semantic propagation network. In: Proceedings of the IEEE Conference on Computer Vision and Pattern Recognition (CVPR), pp. 752–761 (2018)
26. Lin, G., Milan, A., Shen, C., Reid, I.: RefineNet: multi-path refinement networks with identity mappings for high-resolution semantic segmentation. In: Proceedings of the IEEE Conference on Computer Vision and Pattern Recognition (CVPR) (2017)
27. Lin, T.Y., Dollár, P., Girshick, R., He, K., Hariharan, B., Belongie, S.: Feature pyramid networks for object detection. In: Proceedings of the IEEE Conference on Computer Vision and Pattern Recognition (CVPR), pp. 2117–2125 (2017)
28. Lin, T.-Y., et al.: Microsoft COCO: common objects in context. In: Fleet, D., Pajdla, T., Schiele, B., Tuytelaars, T. (eds.) ECCV 2014. LNCS, vol. 8693, pp. 740–755. Springer, Cham (2014). https://doi.org/10.1007/978-3-319-10602-1_48

29. Luo, W., Li, Y., Urtasun, R., Zemel, R.: Understanding the effective receptive field in deep convolutional neural networks. In: Advances in Neural Information Processing Systems (NeurIPS), pp. 4898–4906 (2016)

30. Mottaghi, R., et al.: The role of context for object detection and semantic segmentation in the wild. In: Proceedings of the IEEE Conference on Computer Vision and Pattern Recognition (CVPR) (2014)

31. Peng, C., et al.: MegDet: a large mini-batch object detector. In: Proceedings of the IEEE Conference on Computer Vision and Pattern Recognition (CVPR), pp. 6181–6189 (2018)

32. Peng, C., Zhang, X., Yu, G., Luo, G., Sun, J.: Large kernel matters-improve semantic segmentation by global convolutional network. In: Proceedings of the IEEE Conference on Computer Vision and Pattern Recognition (CVPR) (2017)

33. Sandler, M., Howard, A., Zhu, M., Zhmoginov, A., Chen, L.C.: Inverted residuals and linear bottlenecks: mobile networks for classification. arXiv 1801 (2018)

34. Vaswani, A., et al.: Attention is all you need. In: Advances in Neural Information Processing Systems (NeurIPS) (2017)

35. Veličković, P., Cucurull, G., Casanova, A., Romero, A., Lio, P., Bengio, Y.: Graph attention networks (2018)

36. Wang, P., et al.: Understanding convolution for semantic segmentation. In: Proceedings of the IEEE Winter Conference on Applications of Computer Vision (WACV) (2018)

37. Wang, X., Girshick, R., Gupta, A., He, K.: Non-local neural networks. In: Proceedings of the IEEE Conference on Computer Vision and Pattern Recognition (CVPR) (2018)

38. Xiao, T., Liu, Y., Zhou, B., Jiang, Y., Sun, J.: Unified perceptual parsing for scene understanding. In: Proceedings of the European Conference on Computer Vision (ECCV). pp. 418–434 (2018)

39. Xie, S., Girshick, R., Dollár, P., Tu, Z., He, K.: Aggregated residual transformations for deep neural networks. In: Proceedings of the IEEE Conference on Computer Vision and Pattern Recognition (CVPR), pp. 1492–1500 (2017)

40. Yang, M., Yu, K., Zhang, C., Li, Z., Yang, K.: DenseASPP for semantic segmentation in street scenes. In: Proceedings of the IEEE Conference on Computer Vision and Pattern Recognition (CVPR), pp. 3684–3692 (2018)

41. Yu, C., Wang, J., Gao, C., Yu, G., Shen, C., Sang, N.: Context prior for scene segmentation. In: Proceedings of the IEEE/CVF Conference on Computer Vision and Pattern Recognition, pp. 12416–12425 (2020)

42. Yu, C., Wang, J., Peng, C., Gao, C., Yu, G., Sang, N.: BiSeNet: bilateral segmentation network for real-time semantic segmentation. In: Proceedings of the European Conference on Computer Vision (ECCV), pp. 325–341 (2018)

43. Yu, C., Wang, J., Peng, C., Gao, C., Yu, G., Sang, N.: Learning a discriminative feature network for semantic segmentation. In: Proceedings of the IEEE Conference on Computer Vision and Pattern Recognition (CVPR) (2018)

44. Yuan, Y., Wang, J.: OCNet: object context network for scene parsing. arXiv (2018)

45. Yue, K., Sun, M., Yuan, Y., Zhou, F., Ding, E., Xu, F.: Compact generalized non-local network. In: Advances in Neural Information Processing Systems (NeurIPS), pp. 6510–6519 (2018)

46. Zhang, H., et al.: Context encoding for semantic segmentation. In: Proceedings of the IEEE Conference on Computer Vision and Pattern Recognition (CVPR), pp. 7151–7160 (2018)

47. Zhang, H., Zhang, H., Wang, C., Xie, J.: Co-occurrent features in semantic segmentation. In: Proceedings of the IEEE Conference on Computer Vision and Pattern Recognition (CVPR), pp. 548–557 (2019)
48. Zhang, R., Tang, S., Zhang, Y., Li, J., Yan, S.: Scale-adaptive convolutions for scene parsing. In: Proceedings of the IEEE International Conference on Computer Vision (ICCV), pp. 2031–2039 (2017)
49. Zhang, S., Yan, S., He, X.: LatentGNN: learning efficient non-local relations for visual recognition. In: Proceedings of the International Conference on Machine Learning (ICML) (2019)
50. Zhang, X., Zhou, X., Lin, M., Sun, J.: ShuffleNet: an extremely efficient convolutional neural network for mobile devices. In: Proceedings of the IEEE Conference on Computer Vision and Pattern Recognition (CVPR), pp. 6848–6856 (2018)
51. Zhao, H., Shi, J., Qi, X., Wang, X., Jia, J.: Pyramid scene parsing network. In: Proceedings of the IEEE Conference on Computer Vision and Pattern Recognition (CVPR) (2017)
52. Zhao, H., Zhang, Y., Liu, S., Shi, J., Loy, C.C., Lin, D., Jia, J.: PSANet: pointwise spatial attention network for scene parsing. In: Proceedings of the European Conference on Computer Vision (ECCV) (2018)
53. Zheng, S., et al.: Conditional random fields as recurrent neural networks. In: Proceedings of the IEEE International Conference on Computer Vision (ICCV) (2015)
54. Zhou, B., Zhao, H., Puig, X., Fidler, S., Barriuso, A., Torralba, A.: Semantic understanding of scenes through the ADE20K dataset. CoRR abs/1608.05442 (2016)
55. Zhu, Z., Xu, M., Bai, S., Huang, T., Bai, X.: Asymmetric non-local neural networks for semantic segmentation. In: Proceedings of the IEEE International Conference on Computer Vision (ICCV), pp. 593–602 (2019)

Deformation-Aware 3D Model Embedding and Retrieval

Mikaela Angelina Uy[1]([✉]), Jingwei Huang[1], Minhyuk Sung[2], Tolga Birdal[1], and Leonidas Guibas[1]

[1] Stanford University, Stanford, USA
mikacuy@stanford.edu
[2] Adobe Research, San Jose, USA

Abstract. We introduce a new problem of *retrieving* 3D models that are *deformable* to a given query shape and present a novel deep *deformation-aware* embedding to solve this retrieval task. 3D model retrieval is a fundamental operation for recovering a clean and complete 3D model from a noisy and partial 3D scan. However, given a finite collection of 3D shapes, even the closest model to a query may not be satisfactory. This motivates us to apply 3D model deformation techniques to adapt the retrieved model so as to better fit the query. Yet, certain restrictions are enforced in most 3D deformation techniques to preserve important features of the original model that prevent a perfect fitting of the deformed model to the query. This gap between the deformed model and the query induces *asymmetric* relationships among the models, which cannot be handled by typical metric learning techniques. Thus, to retrieve the best models for fitting, we propose a novel deep embedding approach that learns the asymmetric relationships by leveraging location-dependent egocentric distance fields. We also propose two strategies for training the embedding network. We demonstrate that both of these approaches outperform other baselines in our experiments with both synthetic and real data. Our project page can be found at deformscan2cad.github.io.

Keywords: 3D model retrieval · Deformation-aware embedding · Non-metric embedding

1 Introduction

A fundamental task in 3D perception is the 3D reconstruction, where the shape and appearance of a real object are captured into digital form through a scanning process. The result of 3D scanning is usually imperfect, due to sensor noise, outliers, motion blur, and scanning pattern artifacts. Despite the advances in robust techniques for fusing scans [9,16,17,30,47,65], the quality of the produced 3D shapes can be far from what is desired. Recently, we are witnessing

Electronic supplementary material The online version of this chapter (https://doi.org/10.1007/978-3-030-58571-6_24) contains supplementary material, which is available to authorized users.

© Springer Nature Switzerland AG 2020
A. Vedaldi et al. (Eds.): ECCV 2020, LNCS 12352, pp. 397–413, 2020.
https://doi.org/10.1007/978-3-030-58571-6_24

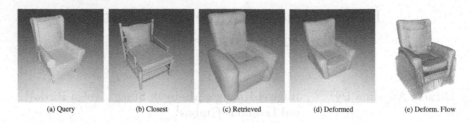

(a) Query   (b) Closest   (c) Retrieved   (d) Deformed   (e) Deform. Flow

Fig. 1. Example of deformation-aware 3D model retrieval. Given a query (a), the closest 3D model in terms of Chamfer distance has distinct geometric and semantic differences. The model retrieved with our framework (c) better fits the query *after* deformation (d). The deformation flow is visualized in (e).

growing efforts to replace the observed noisy, cluttered and partial scans with clean geometry, such as artist-created CAD models [5,6,15,39]. In this way, eventually, an entire scene can be virtualized into a set of 3D models that are free of noise, partiality, and scanning artifacts – while maintaining the semantically valid structure and realistic appearance. One straightforward way to achieve this goal is to replace the sensor data by a known CAD model *retrieved* from an existing repository.

Unfortunately, such retrieval is only viable when there is an almost exact match between the scan and the model. Given the tremendous variety of real 3D shapes, it is implausible to expect that a CAD model in the repository can exactly match the input or the user's desire – even with the recent advent of large-scale 3D repositories [10,58,61,62]. The closest shape in the database from the query might still have subtle but semantically important geometric or structural differences, leading to an undesirable gap in various settings (e.g., the difference in global structure in Fig. 1 (b)). To reduce such differences, we propose to retrieve a CAD model (Fig. 1 (c)) with similar structure to the query, so that we can apply a deformation operation to fit the query (Fig. 1 (d)) better than the closest shape (Fig. 1 (b)). One challenge is to efficiently retrieve such a CAD model especially given that the deformation requires significant time to compute. In light of this, we propose an efficient *deformation-aware* 3D model retrieval framework that finds a 3D model best matching the input *after* a deformation. Such an approach of joint retrieval and fitting can help more closely reconstruct the target with the same initial pool of 3D models (Fig. 1 (d)) while maintaining retrieval efficiency.

A key issue in this deformation-aware retrieval is in dealing with the *scope* of the deformation of each 3D model. Since the goal of 3D model retrieval is to take advantage of the high fidelity and fine structure of shape representation of manmade models, it is desired to maintain such beneficial properties in the deformation. The long literature of 3D shape deformation has also stemmed from this preservation intent and has investigated diverse ways of constraining or regularizing the deformation; for example, making a smooth function of the deformation with a coarse set of control points [34–36,41,51,64] or having per-edge or per-face regularization functions preserving local geometric details, given a mesh representation of a model [32,40,42,56,57]. Such constraints/regularizations aim to ensure production of *plausible* variations without losing the original 3D model's features – although they simultaneously confine the scope of deformation and prevent it from exactly matching the target. Thus, given a function deforming a *source* model to match the *target* under appropriate regularizations, we consider the notion of the *fitting gap*, defined as the difference between the *deformed* source model and the target.

We introduce a novel deep embedding technique that maps a collection of 3D models into a latent space based on the fitting gap as characterized by a given deformation function. Our embedding technique is agnostic to the exact nature of the deformation function and only requires values of the fitting gap for sampled pairs of the source and target models in training. Due to the *asymmetric* nature of the fitting gap and the lack of a *triangle inequality*, the embedding cannot be accomplished with typical metric learning techniques [11,26,50]. Hence, we propose a novel approach, learning a location-dependent *egocentric* anisotropic distance field from the fitting gaps and suggest two network training strategies: one based on margin loss and the other based on regression loss. In test time, given a query shape, the retrieval can be performed by computing the egocentric distance from all 3D models in the database and finding the one that gives the smallest distance.

In our experiments with ShapeNet [10] dataset, we demonstrate that our framework outperforms all the other baseline methods and also that the second regression-based training strategy provides consistently better performance across different categories of the shapes. We also test our framework with queries of 3D scans and images. In the case of real 3D scans, our outputs show even a smaller average fitting gap when compared with human selected 3D models.

In summary, our contributions are:

- defining a new task, that of retrieving a 3D CAD model in a *deformation-aware* fashion;
- introducing a novel *asymmetric* distance notion called *fitting gap*, measuring shape difference after deforming one model toward the other;
- formulating an *egocentric anisotropic distance field* on a latent embedding space so as to respect the asymmetry of the fitting gap;
- proposing two deep network training strategies to learn the said embedding;
- demonstrating that our framework outperforms baselines in the experiments with ShapeNet and presenting results for 3D object reconstruction in a real scan-to-CAD application as well as an image-to-CAD scenario.

2   Related Work

3D Model Deformation. 3D model deformation has been a decades-long problem in geometry. Given a shape represented with a mesh, the problem is defined as finding the best positions of vertices in a way that the new shape fits a target while preserving local geometric details.

Previous work has introduced various ways of formulating the regularization conserving the local geometric details, which are mainly classified into three categories. The first is so-called *free-form* [36,51] approaches. These methods use the voxel grids of the volume enclosing the surface as control points and define a smooth deformation function interpolating weights from the control points to the mesh vertices. The second are *cage-based* approaches [34,35,41,64], which take the control points not from voxel grids but from a coarse scaffold mesh surrounding the input. The last is *vertex-based* approaches [32,40,42,56,57]. In these methods, the objective function for the optimization is directly defined with the mesh vertex positions, which describe geometric properties that should be preserved, such as mesh Laplacian [40,57] or local rigidity [32,42,56].

Recently, neural networks also have been applied to these three (free-form [28,33,38,69], cage-based [68], and vertex-based [24,63]) approaches of the 3D shape deformation. The purposes of leveraging neural networks in the deformation vary, including: better handling partiality in the target [28], finding per-point correspondences in an unsupervised way [24], enabling taking data in other modalities (e.g., color images or depth scans) as input [33,38,63], correlating shape variations with semantic meanings [69], and deformation transfer [68].

In this work, we propose a deformation-aware retrieval technique that can employ any of the deformation methods introduced above as a *given* function for generating plausible deformations. We assume that, based on the regularization of preserving geometric properties, the given deformation function *guarantees* the plausibility of the deformed 3D model while minimizing the fitting distance.

Retrieval via Deep Embedding. With deep embedding, retrieval problems have been formulated in diverse ways depending on their characteristics.

A significant progress has been made on learning *similarity metrics*, after Chopra *et al.* [13] and Hadsell *et al.* [26] introduced pioneering work for Siamese network architecture and contrastive loss. Given positive and negative samples of the query, the contrastive loss is defined as pulling and pushing the positive and negative samples in the embedding, respectively. While the contrastive loss is often defined with two separate losses for each of them [52,60], in the retrieval, considering *relative* distances can engage more flexibility in the embedding function. Thus, later work has more exploited margin losses [21,27], coupling positive and negative samples and pushing the distance between them to be greater than a threshold. Researchers have also verified that the performance can be improved with a better strategy of triplet sampling, such as hard negative mining [50,52] that takes the farthest positive and the closest negative samples at each time. In Sect. 3.2, we introduce an embedding approach incorporating techniques above, although our problem is fundamentally different from the metric learning due to *asymmetry*. Thus, we focus on dealing with the asymmetry.

Another direction is *graph embedding*, which is more general in terms of handling asymmetric relationships (when considering *directed* graphs). The basic goal of the graph embedding is to represent adjacencies among nodes in the graph with similarity in the embedding space. Thus, it can be formulated as regressing the existence or weight of edges [2,66]. However, recent work focuses more on learning high-order proximity, with the assumption that *neighbors of neighbors are neighbors*, and leverages ideas of random walk in the embedding [19,25,48]. This *transitivity* assumption, however, is *not* guaranteed to hold in our problem. In Sect. 3.3, we introduce our second embedding approach following the idea of similarity regression but without exploiting the random walk procedure.

Although metric learning has been previously adapted for 3D point sets [18], it is shown that non-metric learning is able to generate a more complex, accurate and perceptually meaningful similarity model [22,59]. While similarity search on non-metric spaces is widespread in the classical retrieval systems [12,46,53–55], simultaneous learning and non-metric embedding of deep features is still an open problem. In this paper, we address this gap for the particular problem of deformation-aware 3D shape retrieval.

3   Deformation-Aware Embedding

We propose an efficient deformation-aware retrieval framework which retrieves a 3D model from the database that can best match the query shape through deformation— in the context of the deformation, we will also use the terms *source* and *target* for the *database* and *query* shapes, respectively. For the framework, we develop a deep embedding technique that maps a given collection of 3D models $\mathbf{X}$ into a latent space based on a given notion of *distance after deformation*. While in principle any shape can be deformed to any other shape under the same topology, such notion of *fitting gap* emerges from the consideration of constraints or regularizations in the deformation. A 3D model, which can be easily converted into a

$$\mathcal{D}(\text{🪑}; \text{🪑}) = \text{🪑}$$
$$\mathcal{D}(\text{🪑}; \text{🪑}) = \text{🪑}$$
$$\neq$$
$$d(\text{🪑}, \text{🪑}) \neq d(\text{🪑}, \text{🪑})$$

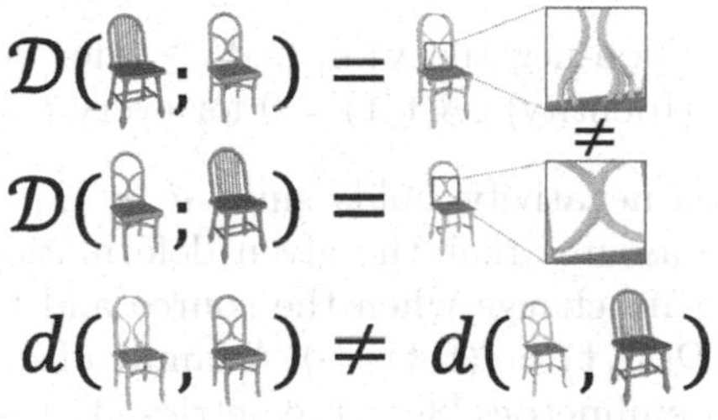

Fig. 2. *Fitting gap is asymmetric.* The four bars of the red chair can deform close to the two bars of the green chair, achieving a small fitting gap. However, it is harder to deform the green chair into the red chair as we cannot split two bars into four, hence resulting in a larger fitting gap. (Color figure online)

mesh, typically has delicate geometric structure that faithfully describes sharp edges and smooth surfaces. Thus, in the deformation of meshes, previous research has paid attention to preserve the fine geometric structure and proposed a variety of techniques regularizing the deformation – in ways to maintain mesh Laplacian [40,57], local rigidity [32,42,56], and surface smoothness [36,51]. Such regularizations, however, obviously may limit the scope of deformation of each 3D model, meaning that a model may not exactly reach the other target shape via deformation. Thus, given a pair of the source and target models $\mathbf{s}, \mathbf{t} \in \mathbf{X}$ and a deformation function $\mathcal{D} : (\mathbf{X} \times \mathbf{X}) \to \mathbf{X}$ warping the source shape $\mathbf{s}$ to best match the target shape $\mathbf{t}$ under the regularizations, we define the fitting gap

$e_{\mathcal{D}}(\mathbf{s}, \mathbf{t})$ from $\mathbf{s}$ to $\mathbf{t}$ as how much the deformed source shape $\mathcal{D}(\mathbf{s}; \mathbf{t})$ *deviates* from the target shape $\mathbf{t}$:

$$e_{\mathcal{D}}(\mathbf{s}, \mathbf{t}) = d(\mathcal{D}(\mathbf{s}; \mathbf{t}), \mathbf{t}), \tag{1}$$

where $d : (\mathbf{X} \times \mathbf{X}) \rightarrow [0, \infty)$ is a function measuring the difference between two 3D models. In other words, the fitting gap is *shape difference after the source deformation* (0 means perfect fitting). Considering the given deformation function $\mathcal{D}$ as a black-box, our goal of the embedding is to build a latent space reflecting the fitting gap characterized by the deformation function so that given a query (target) $\mathbf{t}$, the 3D model $\hat{\mathbf{s}} \in \mathbf{X} \setminus \{\mathbf{t}\}$ that gives the smallest fitting gap $e_{\mathcal{D}}(\hat{\mathbf{s}}, \mathbf{t})$ can be retrieved for downstream applications.

Note that such definition of the fitting gap does not guarantee *symmetry* given arbitrary deformation function $\mathcal{D}$: $\exists \mathbf{s}, \mathbf{t} \in \mathbf{X}$ s.t. $e_{\mathcal{D}}(\mathbf{s}, \mathbf{t}) \neq e_{\mathcal{D}}(\mathbf{t}, \mathbf{s})$; a counterexample can be found as shown in Fig. 2. Moreover, any notion of transitivity such as directional triangular inequality ($e_{\mathcal{D}}(\mathbf{s}, \mathbf{t}) + e_{\mathcal{D}}(\mathbf{t}, \mathbf{u}) \leq e_{\mathcal{D}}(\mathbf{s}, \mathbf{u})$) is not guaranteed. For both reasons, the fitting gap is not a *metric*. The only properties of metrics that are satisfied with the fitting gap are the following two:

1. (Non-negativity) $e_{\mathcal{D}}(\mathbf{s}, \mathbf{t}) \geq 0$ for every $\mathbf{s}, \mathbf{t} \in \mathbf{X}$.
2. (Identity) $e_{\mathcal{D}}(\mathbf{t}, \mathbf{t}) = 0$ for every $\mathbf{t} \in \mathbf{X}$. [1]

Non-negativity holds since d in Eq. (1) is a distance function. For identity, we assume that the given deformation function $\mathcal{D}$ satisfies $\mathcal{D}(\mathbf{t}, \mathbf{t}) = \mathbf{t}$ (making no change when the source and target are the same), and thus $e_{\mathcal{D}}(\mathbf{t}, \mathbf{t}) = d(\mathcal{D}(\mathbf{t}), \mathbf{t}) = d(\mathbf{t}, \mathbf{t}) = 0$. A family of such bivariate functions is often called pseudosemimetrics [8] or premetrics [3]. Embedding based on such a notion has been underexplored.

Next, we illustrate how we encode the fitting gap among 3D models on a latent embedding space (Sect. 3.1) and then propose two strategies of training our embedding network (Sect. 3.2 and 3.3).

3.1   Embedding with Egocentric Distances

Consider an embedding network $\mathcal{F} : \mathbf{X} \rightarrow \mathbb{R}^k$ that maps each 3D model in $\mathbf{X}$ to a point in a k-dimensional latent space. The key in our embedding is to allow the network to properly encode *asymmetric* relationships among 3D models described with the fitting gap while satisfying the properties including non-negativity and identity. Given this, in addition to mapping a 3D model $\mathbf{s} \in \mathbf{X}$ to a point in the embedding space, we propose another network $\mathcal{G} : \mathbf{X} \rightarrow \mathbb{S}_+^k$ that predicts an *egocentric* anisotropic distance field for each 3D model, represented with a $k \times k$ positive-semidefinite (PSD) matrix. Analogous to Mahalanobis

---

[1] This is *not* exactly the same with the property of metrics, *identity of indiscernibles*, meaning the two-way identity ($e_{\mathcal{D}}(\mathbf{s}, \mathbf{t}) = 0 \Leftrightarrow \mathbf{s} = \mathbf{t}$). We cannot guarantee that $e_{\mathcal{D}}(\mathbf{s}, \mathbf{t}) = 0 \Rightarrow \mathbf{s} = \mathbf{t}$ from our definition of $e_{\mathcal{D}}$. Nevertheless, this is not necessary in the retrieval problem.

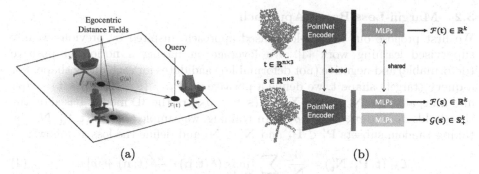

Fig. 3. (a) Visual illustration of our embedding space and egocentric distance. **(b)** Our Siamese network architecture. The PointNet [49] encoder branches to two MLPs: the embedding network $\mathcal{F}$ and the egocentric distance field network $\mathcal{G}$. Both the embedding vector $\mathcal{F}(\mathbf{s})$ and the distance field $\mathcal{G}(\mathbf{s})$ are predicted for the source $\mathbf{s}$, while only the embedding vector $\mathcal{F}(\mathbf{t})$ is predicted for the target $\mathbf{t}$. These are used to calculate for their asymmetric fitting gap.

distance [45], we define the egocentric distance function $\delta : \mathbf{X} \times \mathbf{X} \to [0, \infty)$ given the target and *observer* 3D models $\mathbf{t}, \mathbf{s} \in \mathbf{X}$ as follows:

$$\delta(\mathbf{t}; \mathbf{s}) = \sqrt{(\mathcal{F}(\mathbf{t}) - \mathcal{F}(\mathbf{s}))^T \, \mathcal{G}(\mathbf{s}) \, (\mathcal{F}(\mathbf{t}) - \mathcal{F}(\mathbf{s}))}. \qquad (2)$$

Although it is a common practice to employ Mahalanobis distance in metric learning [7,37,43], we do *not* learn a metric. Hence, we propose to vary the PSD matrix (the inverse covariance matrix in the Mahalanobis distance) depending on the *observer* shape so that it can characterize the fitting gap of the observer shape over the latent space. We remark that, in retrieval, each model in the database that can be *retrieved* becomes an *observer* when computing the distance from the query to the model since we deform the retrieved 3D model to fit the query (see Fig. 3(a)). Also, note that the function δ satisfies non-negativity (since $\mathcal{G}(\mathbf{s}) \succeq 0$) and identity ($\forall \mathbf{s}, \; \delta(\mathbf{s}; \mathbf{s}) = 0$).

When considering the goal of retrieval (Sect. 3), our desire is to learn a egocentric distance function δ that satisfies for every t that

$$\operatorname*{argmin}_{\mathbf{s} \in \mathbf{X} \setminus \{\mathbf{t}\}} e_{\mathcal{D}}(\mathbf{s}, \mathbf{t}) = \operatorname*{argmin}_{\mathbf{s} \in \mathbf{X} \setminus \{\mathbf{t}\}} \delta(\mathbf{t}; \mathbf{s}). \qquad (3)$$

Since it is practically impossible to compute the deformation function $\mathcal{D}$ for all ordered pairs of 3D models in $\mathbf{X}$ due to the intensive computation time, we leverage the inductive bias of neural networks generalizing the prediction to unseen data points. Thus, in network training, we select a fixed size subset of models $\mathbf{X}_\mathbf{t} \setminus \{\mathbf{t}\} \subset \mathbf{X}$ for every model $\mathbf{t} \in \mathbf{X}$ and only use the set of source-target pairs $\{(\mathbf{s}, \mathbf{t}) \mid \mathbf{s} \in \mathbf{X}_\mathbf{t}, \forall \mathbf{t} \in \mathbf{X}\}$ in the training while precomputing the fitting gap. In the following subsections, we introduce two training strategies with different loss functions. The difference between these two strategies is also analyzed with experiments in Sect. 5.

3.2 Margin-Loss-Based Approach

We first propose our margin-loss-based approach, inspired by previous weakly supervised learning work [4]. We leverage on having a notion of positive (deformable) and negative (not deformable) candidates for each query shape. For a query (target) shape $\mathbf{t}$, we define a positive set $\mathbf{P_t} = \{\mathbf{s} \in \mathbf{X_t} \,|\, e_{\mathcal{D}}(\mathbf{s}, \mathbf{t}) \leq \sigma_P\}$ and a negative set $\mathbf{N_t} = \{\mathbf{s} \in \mathbf{X_t} \,|\, e_{\mathcal{D}}(\mathbf{s}, \mathbf{t}) > \sigma_N\}$ of the 3D models based on the thresholds σ_P and σ_N ($\sigma_P < \sigma_N$). In training, we sample triplets $(\mathbf{t}, \mathbf{P'_t}, \mathbf{N'_t})$ by taking random subsets $\mathbf{P'_t} \subset \mathbf{P_t}$ and $\mathbf{N'_t} \subset \mathbf{N_t}$ and define the loss as follows:

$$\mathcal{L}_M\left(\mathbf{t}, \mathbf{P'_t}, \mathbf{N'_t}\right) = \frac{1}{N'_t} \sum_{n \in N'_t} [\max_{p \in P'_t} \left(\delta\left(\mathbf{t}; \mathbf{p}\right)\right) - \delta\left(\mathbf{t}; \mathbf{n}\right) + m]_+, \qquad (4)$$

where $[\ldots]_+$ denotes the hinge loss [14] and m is a margin parameter. This is in contrast to the loss of Arandjelovi et al. [4] where the best/closest positive is taken to handle false positives. The intuition for our loss is that the distance from the query to the furthest positive candidate should always be pulled closer than any of the negative candidates.

3.3 Regression-Based Approach

We also propose another training strategy that uses a regression loss instead of defining the positive and negative sets. Since we only need to learn *relative* scales of the fitting gap $e_{\mathcal{D}}(\mathbf{s}, \mathbf{t})$ for each query $\mathbf{t}$ in retrieval, inspired by Stochastic Neighbor Embedding (SNE) [29], we first convert the fitting gap into a form of *probability* as follows:

$$p(\mathbf{s}; \mathbf{t}) = \frac{\exp\left(-e_{\mathcal{D}}^2(\mathbf{s}, \mathbf{t})/2\sigma_t^2\right)}{\sum_{\mathbf{s} \in \mathbf{X'_t}} \exp\left(-e_{\mathcal{D}}^2(\mathbf{s}, \mathbf{t})/2\sigma_t^2\right)}, \qquad (5)$$

where $\mathbf{X'_t} \subset \mathbf{X_t}$ is a randomly sampled fixed size subset and σ_t is a pre-computed constant for each shape $\mathbf{t}$, which is determined in a way to satisfy the following condition (which is based on Shannon entropy) [44]:

$$\log_2 \tau = - \sum_{\mathbf{s} \in \mathbf{X'_t}} p(\mathbf{s}; \mathbf{t}) \log_2(p(\mathbf{s}; \mathbf{t})), \qquad (6)$$

where τ is a perplexity parameter determining the extent of the neighborhood. Note that we regress the probabilities $p(\mathbf{s}; \mathbf{t})$ since we do not have access to the entire distribution of $p(\cdot; \mathbf{t})$ but only to the models in the subset $\mathbf{X'_t}$ for each $\mathbf{t}$. This is contrast to SNE which seeks to fully match the given and predicted distributions. We similarly convert the learned asymmetric distance $\delta(\mathbf{t}; \mathbf{s})$ into a form of probability:

$$\hat{p}(\mathbf{s}; \mathbf{t}) = \frac{\delta^2(\mathbf{t}; \mathbf{s})}{\sum_{\mathbf{s} \in \mathbf{X'_t}} \delta^2(\mathbf{t}; \mathbf{s})}. \qquad (7)$$

The following $l1$-distance is finally defined as regression loss:

$$\mathcal{L}_R(\mathbf{t}, \mathbf{X'_t}) = \frac{1}{\mathbf{X'_t}} \sum_{\mathbf{s} \in \mathbf{X'_t}} |\hat{p}(\mathbf{s}; \mathbf{t}) - p(\mathbf{s}; \mathbf{t})|. \qquad (8)$$

4   Implementation Details

In our implementation, we first convert 3D CAD models into meshes to compute deformation. In order to cope with the multiple connected components of the CAD models in the deformation, we particularly convert the CAD models into *watertight* meshes using the method of Huang *et al.* [31]. We further simplify them with a mesh decimation technique [23] for efficient computation. For the deformation function $\mathcal{D}$, we use a simplified version of ARAP deformation [56]— refer to the supplementary for the details. For computing the distance between shapes and feeding the 3D shape information to the network, we also generate point clouds from the meshes by uniformly sampling 2,048 points. The distance function $d(\mathbf{x}, \mathbf{y})$ (see Eq. (1)) measuring the shape difference between two 3D models $\mathbf{x}, \mathbf{y} \in \mathbf{X}$ is defined as average two-way Chamfer distance (CD) between the point sets resampled on the meshes $\mathbf{x}, \mathbf{y}$ following previous work [1,20,63,68]. We remark that our embedding framework does *not* require any specific type of the deformation function, and in the embedding, the given deformation function is only used to precompute the fitting gap between two shapes in the sampled pairs. See Sect. 2 for more options of the deformation function.

Network Architecture for $\mathcal{F}$ and $\mathcal{G}$ and training details. Figure 3(b) illustrates our network design. We build a Siamese architecture taking a pair of source $\mathbf{s}$ and target $\mathbf{t}$ point clouds with PointNet [49] encoder (the earlier part until the *maxpool* layer) as our shared encoder. The outputs after the *maxpool* then pass through two separate branches of *MLP*; one is $\mathcal{F}$ that predicts the location in the k-dimensional latent embedding space, and the other is $\mathcal{G}$ that predicts the egocentric distance field (the PSD matrix, see Sect. 3.1). In $\mathcal{G}$, we predict a *positive diagonal* matrix as our PSD matrix using a sigmoid activation and adding $\epsilon = 1e^{-6}$. We use $k = 256$ for most of our experiments but also demonstrate the effect of varying the dimension of the latent space in the supplementary material.

In training, we further randomly downsample the point clouds with 2,048 points to 1,024 points for memory efficiency (but the entire 2,048 points are used in baseline methods). We set the minibatch size as 8 for the query $\mathbf{t}$, and $|\mathbf{P}'_{\mathbf{t}}| = 2$ and $|\mathbf{N}'_{\mathbf{t}}| = 13$ for the margin-loss-based and $|\mathbf{X}'_{\mathbf{t}}| = 15$ for the regression-based approaches. We use Adam optimizer with a learning rate of 0.001 and train for 350 epochs for all cases.

Remark that the resolution of the 3D model in retrieval is not affected by the resolution of input point clouds fed into our network. A 3D model in any resolution can be retrieved in their original format.

5   Results

We present our experimental evaluation to demonstrate the advantage of our embedding framework for deformation-aware 3D model retrieval. We also

Table 1. Quantitative results of retrievals. See Sect. 5 for baselines and evaluation metrics. The numbers multiplied by $1e^{-2}$ are reported. Bold is the smallest, and underscore is the second smallest. Our retrieval results give smaller *after*-deformation distances $e_D^m(s,t)$ while the *before*-deformation distances $d^m(s,t)$ are large.

Method		Table		Chair		Sofa		Car		Plane	
		Top-1	Top-3	Top-1	Top-3	Top-1	Top-3	Top-1	Top-3	Top-1	Top-3
Mean $d^m(s,t)$	Ranked CD	**4.467**	**3.287**	**4.412**	**3.333**	**3.916**	**2.985**	**2.346**	**1.860**	**2.530**	**1.540**
	AE	<u>4.867</u>	3.491	<u>4.710</u>	<u>3.473</u>	4.223	<u>3.178</u>	2.579	1.942	3.045	1.789
	CD-Margin	4.875	<u>3.449</u>	4.750	3.518	<u>3.087</u>	4.151	<u>2.525</u>	<u>1.905</u>	<u>2.801</u>	<u>1.655</u>
	Ours-Margin	6.227	4.026	5.664	3.889	4.825	3.400	2.962	2.142	3.442	1.885
	Ours-Reg	5.955	3.979	5.751	3.981	5.091	3.628	3.119	2.263	3.436	1.976
Mean $e_D^m(s,t)$	Ranked CD	<u>2.095</u>	1.284	1.937	1.186	1.450	0.886	<u>1.138</u>	<u>0.716</u>	1.199	<u>0.569</u>
	AE	2.180	1.292	1.991	1.196	1.521	0.887	1.214	0.753	1.392	0.634
	CD-Margin	2.362	1.373	2.134	1.242	1.587	0.909	1.249	0.773	1.315	0.620
	Ours-Margin	2.127	<u>1.251</u>	<u>1.915</u>	<u>1.144</u>	<u>1.420</u>	<u>0.835</u>	1.226	0.747	<u>1.300</u>	0.586
	Ours-Reg	**1.969**	**1.129**	**1.752**	**1.054**	**1.338**	**0.788**	**1.112**	**0.681**	**1.199**	**0.529**

showcase applications of our approach in two real scenarios: Scan-to-CAD (Sect. 5.2) and Image-to-CAD[2].

Baselines. We compare the proposed margin-loss-based (*Ours-Margin*, Sect. 3.2) and regression-based (*Ours-Reg*, Sect. 3.3) approaches with three retrieval baselines (we also compare with more baselines in the supplementary):

1. Ranked by Chamfer Distance (*Ranked CD*): This retrieves the closest 3D models by Chamfer Distance (CD), which is our distance function d in Sect. 4.
2. Autoencoder (*AE*): This learns an embedding space by training a point cloud autoencoder as defined in [1]. The dimension of the latent space is 1024, which is larger than that of our space.
3. Chamfer Distance Triplet (*CD-Margin*): This baseline is the same with *Ours-Margin* (Sect. 3.2) except for that the distance for the hinge loss is defined as the Euclidean distance over the latent space instead of our egocentric asymmetric distance. The positive and negative candidates are sampled by taking 20 closest models ordered by CD and random 50 models, respectively.

The Chamfer Distance Triplet (*CD-Margin*) is trained in the same way with our margin-loss-based approach (*Ours-Margin*) described in Sect. 3.2; the minibatches are generated with 8 queries and 2 positive and 13 negative random candidates for each of them. We use a margin value $m = 0.5$ for *CD-Margin* and also normalize the latent codes to have a unit $l2$-norm as done in FaceNet [50].

Note that neither of the three baselines above leverage the information about *deformability*, meaning how a 3D model can be deformed to fit the query.

Evaluation Metrics. To avoid sampling bias of the point clouds, in the evaluations, we measure the distance between two shapes as a two-way *point-to-mesh* Chamfer distance; we also use a denser point cloud including 50k

---

[2] Due to space restrictions we present results of Image-to-CAD in our supplementary material.

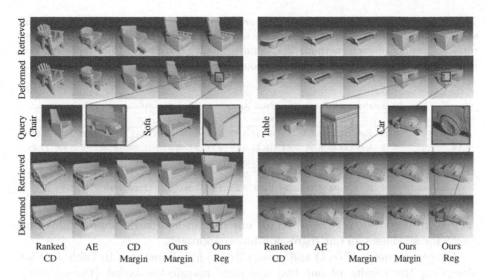

Fig. 4. Visualization of retrieval followed by deformation on ShapeNet. Our network is able to retrieve models that better fit after deformation despite having large geometric distances initially. Notice the big back part of the retrieved chair and the thick seat of the retrieved sofa, attributes that are not identical to the query. Yet, these parts properly fit the target after deformation. Our network is also able to retrieve a sofa with legs and a car with a trunk that are present in the desired targets. Moreover, our deformation-aware *retrieval & deformation* approach also allows us to preserve fine-details of the source model post-deformation as shown in the zoomed in regions. See supplementary for more results.

uniformly sampled points in this case. We denote this new distance function as $d^m : (\mathbf{X} \times \mathbf{X}) \rightarrow [0, \infty)$ and the accompanying fitting gap function as $c_{\mathcal{D}}^m(\mathbf{s}, \mathbf{t}) - d^m(\mathcal{D}(\mathbf{s}; \mathbf{t}), \mathbf{t})$. Also, for simplicity, we will use the notations $d^m(\mathbf{s}, \mathbf{t})$ and $e_{\mathcal{D}}^m(\mathbf{s}, \mathbf{t})$ as the source-target distances *before* and *after* the source deformation in the rest of the paper. We report the mean of these numbers for the best among top-N retrieved models; $N = 1, 3$ are reported. For a partial scan input, we use a *one-way* point-to-mesh distance; see Sect. 5.2 for the details.

5.1   Experiments on ShapeNet [10]

We experiment with four classes in ShapeNet [10] dataset: *Table, Chair, Sofa* and *Car*. We train/evaluate the networks per class with the training/test splits of Yang *et al.* [67]. In the evaluations, we take all models in the test set as queries and retrieve 3D models from the same test set but except for the query. For our training data, we precompute the fitting gap $e_{\mathcal{D}}$ (Sect. 3). To obtain source-target pairs, we sample 100 source models for every target $\mathbf{t} \in \mathbf{X}$, i.e. $|\mathbf{X_t}| = 100$, which consist of the 50 closest models by the distance d in Sect. 3.1 (not including $\mathbf{t}$ itself) and another 50 random models. We use $\sigma_P = 3.5e^{-4}, 3e^{-4}, 2e^{-4}$, and $1.2e^{-4}$ and $\sigma_N = 7.5e^{-4}, 6e^{-4}, 4e^{-4}$, and $2e^{-4}$ for the table, chair, sofa, and car

Table 2. Ranking evaluations with 150 models per query. The models are randomly selected and sorted by $e^m_{\mathcal{D}}(\mathbf{s}, \mathbf{t})$ (the query is not included). All results are for the top-1 retrieval results of each method. The numbers multiplied by $1e^{-2}$ are reported. Bold is the smallest, and underscore is the second smallest.

Method	Table			Chair			Sofa			Car			Plane		
	Mean d^m	Mean $e^m_{\mathcal{D}}$	Mean Rank	Mean d^m	Mean $e^m_{\mathcal{D}}$	Mean Rank	Mean d^m	Mean $e^m_{\mathcal{D}}$	Mean Rank	Mean d^m	Mean $e^m_{\mathcal{D}}$	Mean Rank	Mean d^m	Mean $e^m_{\mathcal{D}}$	Mean Rank
Ranked-CD	**6.24**	3.20	12.53	**5.65**	2.61	11.37	**4.73**	1.87	14.07	**2.75**	<u>1.31</u>	<u>12.0</u>	**1.83**	**1.26**	**5.53**
AE	6.95	3.11	11.69	6.08	2.61	10.21	5.19	1.91	14.43	3.09	1.39	14.55	2.60	1.68	17.91
CD-Margin	<u>6.77</u>	3.19	12.55	<u>6.02</u>	2.72	13.24	<u>5.07</u>	1.93	15.76	<u>3.02</u>	1.48	18.94	<u>2.36</u>	1.56	12.27
Ours-Margin	8.89	<u>2.88</u>	<u>8.86</u>	7.15	<u>2.37</u>	<u>8.15</u>	5.83	<u>1.67</u>	<u>9.09</u>	3.61	1.34	12.95	2.65	1.48	10.67
Ours-Reg	8.59	**2.71**	**7.05**	7.39	**2.24**	**6.32**	6.23	**1.62**	**7.91**	3.80	**1.24**	**7.80**	2.64	<u>1.42</u>	<u>8.96</u>

classes, respectively, and $m = 10$ for our margin-loss-based approach. We use $\tau = 5$ for all classes in our regression-based approach.

We report mean $d^m(\mathbf{s}, \mathbf{t})$ and mean $e^m_{\mathcal{D}}(\mathbf{s}, \mathbf{t})$ for all methods in Table 1. When observing the results of our two methods, margin-loss-based (*Ours-Margin*) and regression-based (*Ours-Reg*) approaches, the distance *before* deformation ($d^m(\mathbf{s}, \mathbf{t})$) is farther than the baselines, but the distance *after* deformation ($e^m_{\mathcal{D}}(\mathbf{s}, \mathbf{t})$) is smaller. Such a result is shown consistently in all classes, particularly for *Ours-Reg* results. This indicates that our methods can discover 3D models that can better align with the query shape through the given deformation operation.

Also, *Ours-Reg* achieves better results than *Ours-Margin* consistently for all classes. The advantage of *Ours-Reg* is that it can discriminate among all models in $\mathbf{X_t}$, while *Ours-Margin* can only consider *inter*-relationships across the positive set $\mathbf{P_t}$ and the negative set $\mathbf{N_t}$ but not *intra*-relationships in each set. Hence, *Ours-Reg* can achieve a better understanding of the overall distribution of the data. *Ours-Margin* also has a trade-off for the thresholds of $\sigma_{\mathbf{P}}$ and $\sigma_{\mathbf{N}}$; too tight thresholds may result in overfitting, and too loose thresholds can make the two sets less distinguishable. We empirically found good thresholds for each class, but finding the optimum thresholds is a very time-consuming task requiring an extensive binary search (Table 2).

In Fig. 4, we visualize some examples of retrieved models and their deformations given query models. The models retrieved by our methods have large distance before deformation but better fit after deformation compared with the results of other methods. For example, the chair and sofa retrieved by our methods as shown in Fig. 4 have bigger back parts than the queries, but they become smaller properly after operating the deformation. Our network is able to be agnostic to the details that are easy to recover via deformations such as chair body size, and table leg thickness. It rather retrieves based on the overall shape of the model that can be deformed to fit the desired target. On the other hand, the small geometric details can be inherited from the retrieved model and be preserved during deformation. It is also noticeable that our retrieval is more structurally faithful as we observe the presence of legs in the retrieved sofa or the trunk of the car that are essential for valid deformation.

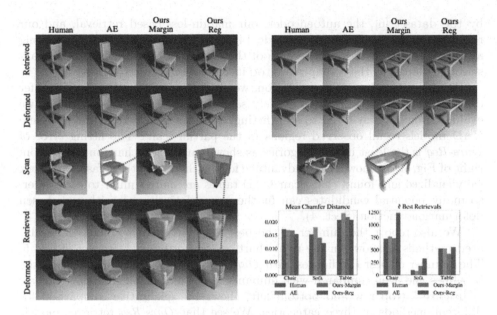

Fig. 5. (Top row and bottom left) Qualitative results of Scan-to-CAD. **(Bottom right)** Quantitative Results: We compare different retrieval methods on the Scan2CAD [6] dataset. The left chart shows the mean fitting errors and the right chart shows the number of best candidates retrieved by different methods. *Ours-Reg* achieves the minimum overall fitting errors and the maximum number of best retrievals among all categories compared with other methods. See supplementary for more results.

We also report the *rank* of retrieved models when we sort the test models based on $e_D^m(\mathbf{s}, \mathbf{t})$. Since it is computationally extremely expensive to compute the deformation for all pairs in our dataset, for each 3D model, we randomly sample 150 other models and use them for the ranking; $e_D^m(\mathbf{s}, \mathbf{t})$ and $d^m(\mathbf{s}, \mathbf{t})$ are precomputed for them. The results in Sect. 5.1 show the mean rank of the top-1 retrieval results out of the selected 150 models. *Our-Reg* and *Our-Margin* achieve the best and the second best mean ranks compared with the baseline methods in all classes except for cars; most of the car models are structurally similar to each other. *Our-Reg* still provides the best mean rank for cars.

5.2 Scan-to-CAD

We also evaluate our method for the real scan-to-CAD conversion problem [6]. We use our models trained on ShapeNet [10] and directly evaluate our performance on the Scan2CAD [6] dataset. Scan2CAD provides partial 3D scans of indoor scenes, which are segmented to each object instance. We normalize and align the object scans to the ShapeNet canonical space using the 9DoF alignment provided in [6]. We use our embedding for retrieval and then apply the deformation function (Sect. 4) to the retrieved CAD to fit the scan. Similar to previous works [63,68], we reflect the scan about the vertical symmetric plane before fitting. Our evaluation is performed on three common categories: chairs, sofas, and tables. We compare different methods including human annotations defined by the dataset [6], the autoencoder, our margin-loss-based retrieval, and our regression-based retrieval. We exclude 149 extremely partial scans (2% among all scans) which cover less than 10% of the regions (after reflection) of human-selected shapes, as these shapes are too incomplete to be recognizable.

Similar to the ShapeNet evaluation, we also measure *point-to-mesh* Chamfer distance that is uniformly and densely sampled with $50k$ points. However, we evaluated on one-way CAD to scan fitting, since our goal is to fit the complete CAD models to all observed regions in the partial scans. The fitting error of *Ours-Reg* is the least in all categories as shown on the left chart on the bottom right of Fig. 5. We show a clear advantage for the chairs and the sofas. For tables, we visualized and found that Scan2CAD tables are quite similar to each other, so many potential candidates can fit the scan relatively well with our chosen deformation function (Sect. 4).

We also report the number of the best-retrieved models among the evaluated methods as shown in the right chart on the bottom-right corner of Fig. 5. The number of best candidates with *Ours-Reg* is significantly higher than the baselines and even compared with human-selected models on chairs and sofas.

Figure 5 (top row and bottom left) shows the qualitative comparison for different methods in three categories. We see that *Ours-Reg* retrieves models that are more similar to that of the target scan. For example, ours is the only method that retrieves the model with the same connectivity of parts compared to the target as shown by the legs of the chair and the top-less table scan. For the sofa example, we retrieve a model with a large distance but which is similar in shape to the observed regions of the scan, hence the deformed model fits the scan better than other methods. By deforming the CAD model, we additionally preserve important CAD features including sharp edges and corners.

6   Conclusion

We proposed a *deformation-aware* 3D model retrieval framework that enables finding a 3D model best matching a query after the deformation. Due to the feature-preserving regularizations in most deformation techniques, 3D models generally cannot exactly match the query through deformation but induce a *fitting gap*. This gap, describing the *deformability* one to the other, is *asymmetric* by definition and thus not a metric. Hence, we introduced a novel embedding technique that can encode such relationships with *egocentric* distance fields given any arbitrary deformation function and proposed two strategies for network training. We demonstrated that our approach outperforms other baselines in the experiments with ShapeNet and also presented results in scan-to-CAD and image-to-CAD applications. We plan to further investigate the relationships among 3D models defined by the deformation in the future.

Acknowledgements. This work is supported by a Google AR/VR University Research Award, a Vannevar Bush Faculty Fellowship, a grant from the Stanford SAIL Toyota Research Center, and gifts from the Adobe Corporation and the Dassault Foundation.

References

1. Achlioptas, P., Diamanti, O., Mitliagkas, I., Guibas, L.J.: Learning representations and generative models for 3D point clouds. In: ICML (2018)
2. Ahmed, A., Shervashidze, N., Narayanamurthy, S., Josifovski, V., Smola, A.J.: Distributed large-scale natural graph factorization. In: WWW (2013)
3. Aldrovandi, R., Pereira, J.: An Introduction to Geometrical Physics. World Scientific (1995)
4. Arandjelović, R., Gronat, P., Torii, A., Pajdla, T., Sivic, J.: NetVLAD: CNN architecture for weakly supervised place recognition. In: CVPR (2016)
5. Avetisyan, A., Dahnert, M., Dai, A., Savva, M., Chang, A.X., Nießner, M.: Scan2CAD: learning cad model alignment in RGB-D scans. In: CVPR (2019)
6. Avetisyan, A., Dai, A., Nießner, M.: End-to-end cad model retrieval and 9DoF alignment in 3D scans. In: ICCV (2019)
7. Bellet, A., Habrard, A., Sebban, M.: A survey on metric learning for feature vectors and structured data (2013)
8. Buldygin, V., et al.: Metric Characterization of Random Variables and Random Processes. American Mathematical Society (2000)
9. Bylow, E., Sturm, J., Kerl, C., Kahl, F., Cremers, D.: Real-time camera tracking and 3D reconstruction using signed distance functions. In: RSS (2013)
10. Chang, A.X., et al.: Shapenet: an information-rich 3D model repository (2015)
11. Chechik, G., Sharma, V., Shalit, U., Bengio, S.: Large scale online learning of image similarity through ranking. J. Mach. Learn. Res. **11**, 1109–1135 (2010)
12. Chen, L., Lian, X.: Efficient similarity search in nonmetric spaces with local constant embedding. IEEE Trans. Knowl. Data Eng. **20**(3), 321–336 (2008)
13. Chopra, S., Hadsell, R., LeCun, Y.: Learning a similarity metric discriminatively, with application to face verification. In: CVPR (2005)
14. Cortes, C., Vapnik, V.: Support-vector networks. Mach. Learn. **20**(3), 273–297 (1995)
15. Dahnert, M., Dai, A., Guibas, L., Nießner, M.: Joint embedding of 3D scan and cad objects. In: ICCV (2019)
16. Dai, A., Nießner, M., Zollhöfer, M., Izadi, S., Theobalt, C.: BundleFusion: real-time globally consistent 3D reconstruction using on-the-fly surface reintegration. In: ACM SIGGRAPH (2017)
17. Dai, A., Ruizhongtai Qi, C., Nießner, M.: Shape completion using 3D-encoder-predictor CNNs and shape synthesis. In: CVPR (2017)
18. Deng, H., Birdal, T., Ilic, S.: PPFNet: global context aware local features for robust 3D point matching. In: Proceedings of the IEEE Conference on Computer Vision and Pattern Recognition, pp. 195–205 (2018)
19. Dong, Y., Chawla, N.V., Swami, A.: metapath2vec: scalable representation learning for heterogeneous networks. In: KDD (2017)
20. Fan, H., Su, H., Guibas, L.J.: A point set generation network for 3D object reconstruction from a single image. In: CVPR (2016)
21. G, V.K.B., Carneiro, G., Reid, I.: Learning local image descriptors with deep siamese and triplet convolutional networks by minimizing global loss functions. In: CVPR (2016)
22. Garcia, N., Vogiatzis, G.: Learning non-metric visual similarity for image retrieval. Image Vis. Comput. **82**, 18–25 (2019)
23. Garland, M., Heckbert, P.S.: Simplifying surfaces with color and texture using quadric error metrics. In: Visualization (1998)

24. Groueix, T., Fisher, M., Kim, V.G., Russell, B.C., Aubry, M.: Deep self-supervised cycle-consistent deformation for few-shot shape segmentation. In: Eurographics Symposium on Geometry Processing (2019)
25. Grover, A., Leskovec, J.: node2vec: scalable feature learning for networks. In: KDD (2016)
26. Hadsell, R., Chopra, S., LeCun, Y.: Dimensionality reduction by learning an invariant mapping. In: CVPR (2006)
27. Han, X., Leung, T., Jia, Y., Sukthankar, R., Berg, A.C.: MatchNet: unifying feature and metric learning for patch-based matching. In: CVPR (2015)
28. Hanocka, R., Fish, N., Wang, Z., Giryes, R., Fleishman, S., Cohen-Or, D.: ALIGNet: partial-shape agnostic alignment via unsupervised learning. ACM Trans. Graph. **38**(1), 1–14 (2018)
29. Hinton, G.E., Roweis, S.T.: Stochastic neighbor embedding. In: NIPS (2003)
30. Huang, J., Dai, A., Guibas, L.J., Nießner, M.: 3Dlite: towards commodity 3D scanning for content creation. In: ACM SIGGRAPH Asia (2017)
31. Huang, J., Su, H., Guibas, L.: Robust watertight manifold surface generation method for shapenet models (2018)
32. Igarashi, T., Moscovich, T., Hughes, J.F.: As-rigid-as-possible shape manipulation. In: ACM SIGGRAPH (2005)
33. Jack, D., et al.: Learning free-Form deformations for 3D object reconstruction. In: ICCV (2018)
34. Joshi, P., Meyer, M., DeRose, T., Green, B., Sanocki, T.: Harmonic coordinates for character articulation. In: ACM SIGGRAPH (2007)
35. Ju, T., Schaefer, S., Warren, J.: Mean value coordinates for closed triangular meshes. In: ACM SIGGRAPH (2005)
36. Kraevoy, V., Sheffer, A., Shamir, A., Cohen-Or, D.: Non-homogeneous resizing of complex models. In: ACM SIGGRAPH Asia (2006)
37. Kulis, B., et al.: Metric learning: a survey. Found. Trends® Mach. Learn. **5**(4), 287–364 (2013)
38. Kurenkov, A., et al.: DeformNet: free-form deformation network for 3D shape reconstruction from a single image. In: WACV (2018)
39. Li, Y., Dai, A., Guibas, L., Nießner, M.: Database-assisted object retrieval for real-time 3D reconstruction. In: Eurographics (2015)
40. Lipman, Y., Sorkine, O., Cohen-Or, D., Levin, D., Rossi, C., Seidel, H.P.: Differential coordinates for interactive mesh editing. In: Shape Modeling Applications (2004)
41. Lipman, Y., Levin, D., Cohen-Or, D.: Green coordinates. In: ACM SIGGRAPH (2008)
42. Lipman, Y., Sorkine, O., Levin, D., Cohen-Or, D.: Linear rotation-invariant coordinates for meshes. In: ACM SIGGRAPH (2005)
43. Liu, E.Y., Guo, Z., Zhang, X., Jojic, V., Wang, W.: Metric learning from relative comparisons by minimizing squared residual. In: ICDM (2012)
44. van der Maaten, L., Hinton, G.: Visualizing data using t-SNE. J. Mach. Learn. Res. **9**, 2579–2605 (2008)
45. Mahalanobis, P.C.: On the generalized distance in statistics. In: Proceedings of the National Institute of Science. National Institute of Science of India (1936)
46. Morozov, S., Babenko, A.: Non-metric similarity graphs for maximum inner product search. In: Advances in Neural Information Processing Systems (2018)
47. Newcombe, R.A., et al.: KinectFusion: real-time dense surface mapping and tracking. In: ISMAR (2011)

48. Perozzi, B., Al-Rfou, R., Skiena, S.: Deepwalk: online learning of social representations. In: KDD (2013)
49. Qi, C.R., Su, H., Mo, K., Guibas, L.J.: PointNet: deep learning on point sets for 3D classification and segmentation. In: CVPR (2017)
50. Schroff, F., Kalenichenko, D., Philbin, J.: FaceNet: a unified embedding for face recognition and clustering. In: CVPR (2015)
51. Sederberg, T.W., Parry, S.R.: Free-form deformation of solid geometric models. In: ACM SIGGRAPH (1986)
52. Simo-Serra, E., Trulls, E., Ferraz, L., Kokkinos, I., Fua, P., Moreno-Noguer, F.: Discriminative learning of deep convolutional feature point descriptors. In: ICCV (2015)
53. Skopal, T.: On fast non-metric similarity search by metric access methods. In: Ioannidis, Y., et al. (eds.) EDBT 2006. LNCS, vol. 3896, pp. 718–736. Springer, Heidelberg (2006). https://doi.org/10.1007/11687238_43
54. Skopal, T., Bustos, B.: On nonmetric similarity search problems in complex domains. ACM Comput. Surv. (CSUR) 43(4), 1–50 (2011)
55. Skopal, T., Lokoč, J.: NM-tree: flexible approximate similarity search in metric and non-metric spaces. In: Bhowmick, S.S., Küng, J., Wagner, R. (eds.) DEXA 2008. LNCS, vol. 5181, pp. 312–325. Springer, Heidelberg (2008). https://doi.org/10.1007/978-3-540-85654-2_30
56. Sorkine, O., Alexa, M.: As-rigid-as-possible surface modeling. In: Eurographics Symposium on Geometry Processing (2007)
57. Sorkine, O., Cohen-Or, D., Lipman, Y., Alexa, M., Rössl, C., Seidel, H.P.: Laplacian surface editing. In: Eurographics Symposium on Geometry Processing (2004)
58. Stratasys: GrabCAD community. https://grabcad.com/library
59. Tan, X., Chen, S., Li, J., Zhou, Z.H.: Learning non-metric partial similarity based on maximal margin criterion. In: 2006 IEEE Computer Society Conference on Computer Vision and Pattern Recognition (CVPR 2006), vol. 1. IEEE (2006)
60. Tian, Y., Fan, B., Wu, F.: L2-Net: deep learning of discriminative patch descriptor in euclidean space. In: CVPR (2017)
61. Trimble: 3D warehouse. https://3dwarehouse.sketchup.com/
62. TurboSquid: TurboSquid. https://www.turbosquid.com/
63. Wang, W., Ceylan, D., Mech, R., Neumann, U.: 3DN: 3D deformation network. In: CVPR (2019)
64. Weber, O., Ben-Chen, M., Gotsman, C.: Complex barycentric coordinates with applications to planar shape deformation. In: Eurographics (2009)
65. Whelan, T., Leutenegger, S., Salas-Moreno, R.F., Glocker, B., Davison, A.J.: ElasticFusion: dense slam without a pose graph. Robot.: Sci. Syst. (2011)
66. Hamilton, W.L., Ying, R., Leskovec, J.: Representation learning on graphs: methods and applications. IEEE Data Eng. Bull. (2017)
67. Yang, G., Huang, X., Hao, Z., Liu, M.Y., Belongie, S., Hariharan, B.: Pointflow: 3D point cloud generation with continuous normalizing flows. In: ICCV (2019)
68. Yifan, W., Aigerman, N., Kim, V., Chaudhuri, S., Sorkine-Hornung, O.: Neural cages for detail-preserving 3D deformations (2019)
69. Yumer, E., Mitra, N.J.: Learning semantic deformation flows with 3D convolutional networks. In: ECCV (2016)

Atlas: End-to-End 3D Scene Reconstruction from Posed Images

Zak Murez[1(✉)], Tarrence van As[2], James Bartolozzi[1], Ayan Sinha[1],
Vijay Badrinarayanan[3], and Andrew Rabinovich[2]

[1] Magic Leap Inc., Sunnyvale, CA, USA
zak@murez.com, bartolozzij@gmail.com, asinha@magicleap.com
[2] InsideIQ Inc., San Francisco, CA, USA
{tarrence,andrew}@insideiq.team
[3] Wayve.ai, London, UK
vijay@wayve.ai

Abstract. We present an end-to-end 3D reconstruction method for a
scene by directly regressing a truncated signed distance function (TSDF)
from a set of posed RGB images. Traditional approaches to 3D reconstruction rely on an intermediate representation of depth maps prior
to estimating a full 3D model of a scene. We hypothesize that a direct
regression to 3D is more effective. A 2D CNN extracts features from
each image independently which are then back-projected and accumulated into a voxel volume using the camera intrinsics and extrinsics. After
accumulation, a 3D CNN refines the accumulated features and predicts
the TSDF values. Additionally, semantic segmentation of the 3D model
is obtained without significant computation. This approach is evaluated
on the Scannet dataset where we significantly outperform state-of-the-
art baselines (deep multiview stereo followed by traditional TSDF fusion)
both quantitatively and qualitatively. We compare our 3D semantic segmentation to prior methods that use a depth sensor since no previous
work attempts the problem with only RGB input.

Keywords: Multiview stereo · TSDF · 3D reconstruction

1 Introduction

Reconstructing the world around us is a long standing goal of computer vision.
Recently many applications have emerged, such as autonomous driving and augmented reality, which rely heavily upon accurate 3D reconstructions of the surrounding environment. These reconstructions are often estimated by fusing depth

T. van As, J. Bartolozzi and V. Badrinarayanan—Work done at Magic Leap.

Electronic supplementary material The online version of this chapter (https://
doi.org/10.1007/978-3-030-58571-6_25) contains supplementary material, which is
available to authorized users.

measurements from special sensors, such as structured light, time of flight, or LIDAR, into 3D models. While these sensors can be extremely effective, they require special hardware making them more cumbersome and expensive than systems that rely solely on RGB cameras. Furthermore, they often suffer from noise and missing measurements due to low albedo and glossy surfaces as well as occlusion.

Another approach to 3D reconstruction is to use monocular [18,31,32], binocular [3,5] or multivew [23,27,28,51] stereo methods which take RGB images (one, two, or multiple respectively) and predict depth maps for the images. Despite the plethora of recent research, these methods are still much less accurate than depth sensors, and do not produce satisfactory results when fused into a 3D model.

Fig. 1. Overview of our method. Features from each image are backprojected along rays and accumulated into a feature volume. Then a 3D CNN refines the features and regresses a TSDF volume. Finally a mesh is extracted from the TSDF. Semantic Labels can also be output.

In this work, we observe that depth maps are often just intermediate representations that are then fused with other depth maps into a full 3D model. As such, we propose a method that takes a sequence of RGB images and directly predicts a full 3D model in an end-to-end trainable manner. This allows the network to fuse more information and learn better geometric priors about the world, producing much better reconstructions. Furthermore, it reduces the complexity of the system by eliminating steps like frame selection, as well as reducing the required compute by amortizing the cost over the entire sequence.

Our method is inspired by two main lines of work: cost volume based multi view stereo [28,57] and Truncated Signed Distance Function (TSDF) refinement [12,15]. Cost volume based multi view stereo methods construct a cost volume using a plane sweep. Here, a reference image is warped onto the target image for each of a fixed set of depth planes and stacked into a 3D cost volume. For the correct depth plane, the reference and target images will match while for other depth planes they will not. As such, the depth is computed by taking the argmin over the planes. This is made more robust by warping image features extracted by a CNN instead of the raw pixel measurements, and by filtering the cost volume with another CNN prior to taking the argmin.

TSDF refinement starts by fusing depth maps from a depth sensor into an initial voxel volume using TSDF fusion [10], in which each voxel stores the truncated signed distance to the nearest surface. Note that a triangulated mesh can then be extracted from this implicit representation by finding the zero crossing surface using marching cubes [34]. TSDF refinement methods [12,15] take this noisy, incomplete TSDF as input and refine it by passing it through a 3D convolutional encoder-decoder network.

Similar to cost volume multi view stereo approaches, we start by using a 2D CNN to extract features from a sequence of RGB images. These features are then back projected into a 3D volume using the known camera intrinsics and extrinsics. However, unlike cost volume approaches which back project the features into a target view frustum using image warping, we back project into a canonical voxel volume, where each pixel gets mapped to a ray in the volume (similar to [46]). This avoids the need to choose a target image and allows us to fuse an entire sequence of frames into a single volume. We fuse all the frames into the volume using a simple running average. Next, as in both cost volume and TSDF refinement, we pass our voxel volume through a 3D convolutional encoder-decoder to refine the features. Finally, as in TSDF refinement, our feature volume is used to regress the TSDF values at each voxel (see Fig. 1).

We train and evaluate our network on real scans of indoor rooms from the Scannet [11] dataset. Our method significantly outperforms state-of-the-art multi view stereo baselines [28,51] producing accurate and complete meshes.

As an additional bonus, for minimal extra compute, we can add an additional head to our 3D CNN and perform 3D semantic segmentation. While the problems of 3D semantic and instance segmentation have received a lot of attention recently [21,25], all previous methods assume the depth was acquired using a depth sensor. Although our 3D segmentations are not competitive with the top performers on the Scannet benchmark leader board, we establish a strong baseline for the new task of 3D semantic segmentation from multi view RGB.

2   Related Work

2.1   3D Reconstruction

Reconstructing a 3D model of a scene usually involves acquiring depth for a sequence of images and fusing the depth maps using a 3D data structure. The most common 3D structure for depth accumulation is the voxel volume used by TSDF fusion [10]. However, surfels (oriented point clouds) are starting to gain popularity [44,55]. These methods are usually used with a depth sensor, but can also be applied to depth maps predicted from monocular or stereo images.

With the rise of deep learning, monocular depth estimation has seen huge improvements [18,31,32], however their accuracy is still far below state-of-the-art stereo methods. A popular classical approach to stereo [23] uses mutual information and semi global matching to compute the disparity between two images. Similar approaches have been incorporated into SLAM systems such as COLMAP [42,43] and CNN-SLAM [50]. More recently, several end-to-end plane sweep algorithms have been proposed. DeepMVS [27] uses a patch matching network. MVDepthNet [51] constructs the cost volume from raw pixel measurements and performs 2D convolutions, treating the planes as feature channels. GPMVS [26] builds upon this and aggregates information into the cost volume over long sequences using a Gaussian process. MVSNet [57] and DPSNet [28] construct the cost volume from features extracted from the images using a 2D CNN. They then filter the cost volume using 3D convolutions on the 4D tensor. R-MVSNet [58] reduces the memory requirements of MVSNet by replacing the 3D CNN with a recurrent CNN, while P-MVSNet [6] starts with a low resolution MVSNet and then iteratively refines the estimate using their point flow module. All of these methods require choosing a target image to predict depth for and then finding suitable neighboring reference images. Recent binocular stereo methods [3,5] use a similar cost volume approach, but avoid frame selection by using a fixed baseline stereo pair. Depth maps over a sequence are computed independently (or weakly coupled in the case of [26]). In contrast to these approaches, our method constructs a single coherent 3D model from a sequence of input images directly.

While TSDF fusion is simple and effective, it cannot reconstruct partially occluded geometry and requires averaging many measurements to reduce noise. As such, learned methods have been proposed to improve the fusion. OctNet-Fusion [40] uses a 3D encoder-decoder to aggregate multiple depth maps into a TSDF and shows results on single objects and portions of scans. ScanComplete [15] builds upon this and shows results for entire rooms. SG-NN [12] improves upon ScanComplete by increasing the resolution using sparse convolutions [21] and training using a novel self-supervised training scheme. 3D-SIC [24] focuses on 3D instance segmentation using region proposals and adds a per instance completion head. Routed fusion [54] uses 2D filtering and 3D convolutions in view frustums to improve aggregation of depth maps.

More similar in spirit to ours are networks that take one or more images and directly predict a 3D representation. 3D-R2N2 [9] encodes images to a latent space and then decodes a voxel occupancy volume. Octtree-Gen [49] increases the resolution by using an octtree data structure to improve the efficiency of 3D voxel volumes. Deep SDF [38] chooses to learn a generative model that can output an SDF value for any input position instead of discretizing the volume. These methods encode the input to a small latent code and report results on single objects, mostly from shapenet [4]. This small latent code is unlikely to contain enough information to be able to reconstruct an entire scene (follow up work [2], concurrent with ours, addresses this problem, but they do not apply it to RGB only reconstruction). Pix2Vox [56] encodes each image to a latent code and then decodes a voxel representation for each and then fuses them. This is similar to ours, but we explicitly model the 3D geometry of camera rays allowing us to learn better representations and scale to full scenes. SurfNet [45] learns a 3D offset from a template UV map of a surface. Point set generating networks [17] learns to generate point clouds with a fixed number of points. Pixel2Mesh++ [52] uses a graph convolutional network to directly predict a triangulated mesh. Mesh-RCNN [20] builds upon 2D object detection [22] and adds an additional head to predict a voxel occupancy grid for each instance and then refines them using a graph convolutional network on a mesh.

Back projecting image features into a voxel volume and then refining them using a 3D CNN has also been used for human pose estimation [29,59]. These works regress 3D heat maps that are used to localize joint locations.

Deep Voxels [46] and the follow up work of scene representation networks [47] accumulate features into a 3D volume forming an unsupervised representation of the world which can then be used to render novel views without the need to form explicit geometric intermediate representations.

2.2 3D Semantic Segmentation

In addition to reconstructing geometry, many applications require semantic labeling of the reconstruction to provide a richer representation. Broadly speaking, there are two approaches to solving this problem: 1) Predict semantics on 2D input images using a 2D segmentation network [1,7,22] and back project the labels to 3D [35–37] 2) Directly predict the semantic labels in the 3D space. All of these methods assume depth is provided by a depth sensor. A notable exception is Kimera [41], which uses multiview stereo [23] to predict depth, however, they only show results on synthetic data and ground truth 2D segmentations.

SGPN [53] formulates instance segmentation as a 3D point cloud clustering problem. Predicting a similarity matrix and clustering the 3D point cloud to derive semantic and instance labels. 3D-SIS [25] improves upon these approaches by fusing 2D features in a 3D representation. RGB images are encoded using a 2D CNN and back projected onto the 3D geometry reconstructed from depth maps. A 3D CNN is then used to predict 3D object bounding boxes and semantic labels. SSCN [21] predicts semantics on a high resolution voxel volume enabled by sparse convolutions.

In contrast to these approaches, we propose a strong baseline to the relatively untouched problem of 3D semantic segmentation without a depth sensor.

3 Method

Our method takes as input an arbitrary length sequence of RGB images, each with known intrinsics and pose. These images are passed through a 2D CNN backbone to extract features. The features are then back projected into a 3D voxel volume and accumulated using a running average. Once the image features have been fused into 3D, we regress a TSDF directly using a 3D CNN (See Fig. 2). We also experiment with adding an additional head to predict semantic segmentation.

3.1 Feature Volume Construction

Let $I_t \in \mathbb{R}^{3 \times h \times w}$ be an image in a sequence of T RGB images. We extract features $F_t = F(I_t) \in \mathbb{R}^{c \times h \times w}$ using a standard 2D CNN where c is the feature dimension. These 2D features are then back projected into a 3D voxel volume

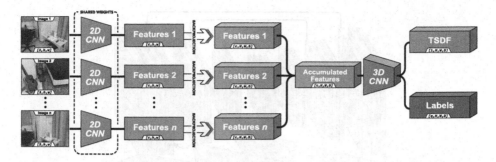

Fig. 2. Schematic of our method. Features are extracted from a sequence of images using a 2D CNN and then back projected into a 3D volume. These volumes are accumulated and then passed through a 3D CNN to directly regress a TSDF reconstruction of the scene. We can also jointly predict the 3D semantic segmentation of the scene.

using the known camera intrinsics and extrinsics, assuming a pinhole camera model. Consider a voxel volume $V \in \mathbb{R}^{c \times H \times W \times D}$

$$V_t(:, i, j, k) = F_t(:, \hat{i}, \hat{j}), \quad \text{with} \tag{1}$$

$$\begin{bmatrix} \hat{i} \\ \hat{j} \end{bmatrix} = \Pi K_t P_t \begin{bmatrix} i \\ j \\ k \\ 1 \end{bmatrix}, \tag{2}$$

where P_t and K_t are the extrinsics and intrinsics matrices for image t respectively, Π is the perspective mapping and : is the slice operator. Here (i, j, k) are the voxel coordinates in world space and $(\hat{i}, \hat{j})$ are the pixel coordinates in image space. Note that this means that all voxels along a camera ray are filled with the same features corresponding to that pixel.

These feature volumes are accumulated over the entire sequence using a weighted running average similar to TSDF fusion as follows:

$$\bar{V}_t = \frac{\bar{V}_{t-1} \bar{W}_{t-1} + V_t}{\bar{W}_{t-1} + W_t}, \tag{3}$$

$$\bar{W}_t = \bar{W}_{t-1} + W_t. \tag{4}$$

For the weights we use a binary mask $W_t(i, j, k) \in \{0, 1\}$ which stores if voxel (i, j, k) is inside or outside the view frustum of the camera.

3.2   3D Encoder-Decoder

Once the features are accumulated into the voxel volume, we use a 3D convolutional encoder-decoder network to refine the features and regress the output TSDF (Fig. 3). Each layer of the encoder and decoder uses a set of $3 \times 3 \times 3$

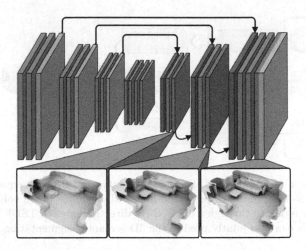

Fig. 3. Our 3D encoder-decoder architecture. Blue boxes denote residual blocks, green boxes are stride 2 convolutions and red boxes are trilinear upsampling. The arrows from the encoder to the decoder indicate skip connections. Our network predicts TSDFs in a coarse to fine manner with the previous resolution being used to sparsify the next resolution (shown as small arrows in the decoder). (Color figure online)

residual blocks. Downsampling is implemented with $3 \times 3 \times 3$ stride 2 convolution, while upsampling uses trilinear interpolation followed by a $1 \times 1 \times 1$ convolution to change the feature dimension. The feature dimension is doubled with each downsampling and halved with each upsampling. All convolution layers are followed by batchnorm and relu. We also include additive skip connections from the encoder to the decoder.

At the topmost layer of the encoder-decoder, we use a $1 \times 1 \times 1$ convolution followed by a tanh activation to regress the final TSDF values. For our semantic segmentation models we also include an additional $1 \times 1 \times 1$ convolution to predict the segmentation logits.

We also include intermediate output heads at each decoded resolution prior to upsampling. These additional predictions are used both for intermediate supervision to help the network train faster, as well as to guide the later resolutions to focus on refining predictions near surfaces. At each resolution, any voxel that is predicted beyond a fraction (.99) of the truncation distance is clamped to one at the following resolutions. Furthermore, loss is only backpropageted for non-clamped voxels. Without this, the loss at the higher resolutions is dominated by the large number of empty space voxels and the network has a harder time learning fine details.

Note that since our features are back projected along entire rays, the voxel volume is filled densely and thus we cannot take advantage of sparse convolutions [21] in the encoder. However, the multiscale outputs can be used to sparsify the feature volumes in the decoder allowing for the use of sparse convolutions similar to [12]. In practice, we found that we were able to train our models at $4\,\text{cm}^3$ voxel resolution without the need for sparse convolutions.

4   Implementation Details

We use a Resnet50-FPN [33] followed by the merging method of [30] with 32 output feature channels as our 2D backbone. Our 3D CNN consists of a four scale resolution pyramid where we double the number of channels each time we half the resolution. The encoder consists of (1, 2, 3, 4) residual blocks at each scale respectively, and the decoder consists of (3, 2, 1) residual blocks.

We supervise the multiscale TSDF reconstructions using ℓ_1 loss to the ground truth TSDF values. Following [14], we log-transform the predicted and target values before applying the ℓ_1 loss, and only backpropagate loss for voxels that were observed in the ground truth (i.e. have TSDF values strictly less than 1.) However, to prevent the network from hallucinating artifacts behind walls, outside the room, we also mark all the voxels where their entire vertical column is equal to 1 and penalize in these areas too. The intuition for this is that if the entire vertical column was not observed it was probably not within the room. To construct the ground truth TSDFs we run TSDF fusion at each resolution on the full sequences, prior to training.

We train the network end-to-end using 50 images selected randomly throughout the full sequence. We use a voxel size of $4\,\text{cm}^3$ with a grid of $(160 \times 160 \times 64)$ voxels, corresponding to a volume of $(6.4 \times 6.4 \times 2.56)\,\text{m}$. At test time, we accumulate the feature volumes in place (since we do not need to store the intermediate activations for backpropagation), allowing us to operate on arbitrary length sequences (often thousands of frames for ScanNet) and we use a $400 \times 400 \times 104$ sized voxel grid corresponding to a volume of $(16 \times 16 \times 4.16)\,\text{m}$. We use the ADAM optimizer with a learning rate of $5e-4$ and 16bit mixed precision operations. Training the network takes around $24\,\text{h}$ on 8 Titan RTX GPUs with a batch size of 8 (1 sequence per GPU) and synchronized batchnorm. Our model is implemented with PyTorch and PyTorch Lightning [16].

5   Results

We evaluate our method on ScanNet [11], which consists of 2.5M images across 707 distinct spaces. Standard train/validation/test splits are adopted. The 3D reconstructions are benchmarked using standard 2D depth metrics (Table 2) and 3D metrics (Table 3), which are defined in Table 1. We also show qualitative comparisons in Fig. 6 where our method really stands out.

We compare our method to 4 state-of-the-art baselines: COLMAP [42, 43], MVDepthNet [51], GPMVS [26], and DPSNet [28]. For COLMAP we use the default dense reconstruction parameters but use the ground truth poses provided by Scannet. For each of the learned methods we fine tuned the models provided by the authors on Scannet. At inference time, 6 reference frames were selected temporally with stride 10 centered around the target view. We also mask the boundary pixels since the networks have visible edge effects that cause poor depth predictions here (leading to 92.8% completeness).

To evaluate these in 3D we fuse the predicted depth maps using two techniques: TSDF Fusion [10] and point cloud fusion. For COLMAP we use their default point cloud fusion, while for the other methods we use the implementation of [19]. We found point cloud fusion was more robust to the outliers present in the depth predictions than our implementation of TSDF Fusion. As such, we only report the point cloud fusion results in Table 3 which are strictly better than the TSDF Fusion results (Note that the L_1 metric is computed using the TSDF Fusion approach as it is not computed in the point cloud fusion approach).

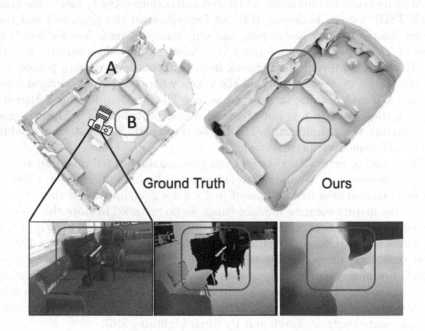

Fig. 4. Our method learns to fill holes that are missing from the ground truth. These holes arise from two causes: A) limitations of depth sensors on low albedo and specular surfaces, and B) unobserved regions caused by occlusion and incomplete scans. While other multiview stereo method often learn to predict depth for these troublesome surfaces, they are not able to complete unobserved geometry.

As seen in Fig. 4 our method is able to fill holes that are missing from the ground truth. These holes arise from two causes: A) limitations of depth sensors on low albedo and specular surfaces, and B) unobserved regions caused by occlusion and incomplete scans. While other multiview stereo method often learn to predict depth for these troublesome surfaces, they are not able to complete unobserved geometry. On the other hand, since our method directly regresses the full TSDF for a scene, it is able to reason about and complete unobserved regions. However, this means that we must take extra care when evaluating the point cloud metrics, otherwise we will be falsely penalized in these regions. We remove geometry that was not observed in the ground truth by taking the rendered depth maps from our predicted mesh and re-fuse them using TSDF Fusion into a trimmed mesh. This guarantees that there is no mesh in areas that were not observed in the ground truth.

Our method achieves state-of-the-art on about half of the metrics and is competitive on all metrics. However, as seen in Fig. 6, qualitatively our results our significantly better than previous methods. While the L_1 metric on the TSDF seems to reflect this performance gap better, the inability of the other metrics to capture this indicates a need for additional more perceptual metrics.

As mentioned previously, we augment the existing 3D-CNN with a semantic segmentation head, requiring only a single $1 \times 1 \times 1$ convolution, to be able to not only reconstruct the 3D structure of the scene but also provide semantic labels to the surfaces. Since no prior work attempts to do 3D semantic segmentation from only RGB images, and there are no established benchmarks, we propose a new evaluation procedure. The semantic labels from the predicted mesh are transferred onto the ground truth mesh using nearest neighbor lookup on the vertices, and then the standard IOU metric can be used. The results are reported in Table 4 and Fig. 7 (note that this is an unfair comparison since all prior methods include depth as input).

Table 1. Definitions of metrics: n is the number of pixels with both valid ground truth and predictions, d and d^* are the predicted and ground truth depths (the predicted depth from our method is computed by rendering the predicted mesh). t and t^* are the predicted and ground truth TSDFs while p and p^* are the predicted and ground truth point clouds.

2D		3D	
Abs Rel	$\frac{1}{n}\sum |d - d^*|/d^*$	L1	$\mathrm{mean}_{t^* < 1}|t \ \ t^*|$
Abs Diff	$\frac{1}{n}\sum |d - d^*|$	Acc	$\mathrm{mean}_{p \in P}(\min_{p^* \in P^*} ||p - p^*||)$
Sq Rel	$\frac{1}{n}\sum |d - d^*|^2/d^*$	Comp	$\mathrm{mean}_{p^* \in P^*}(\min_{p \in P} ||p - p^*||)$
RMSE	$\sqrt{\frac{1}{n}\sum |d - d^*|^2}$	Prec	$\mathrm{mean}_{p \in P}(\min_{p^* \in P^*} ||p - p^*|| < .05)$
$\delta < 1.25^i$	$\frac{1}{n}\sum (\max(\frac{d}{d^*}, \frac{d^*}{d}) < 1.25^i)$	Recal	$\mathrm{mean}_{p^* \in P^*}(\min_{p \in P} ||p - p^*|| < .05)$
Comp	% valid predictions	F-score	$\frac{2 \times \mathrm{Perc} \times \mathrm{Recal}}{\mathrm{Perc} + \mathrm{Recal}}$

From the results in Table 4 we see that our approach is surprisingly competitive with (and even beats some) prior methods that include depth as input. Having depth as an input makes the problem significantly easier because the only source of error is from the semantic predictions. In our case, in order to correctly label a vertex we must both predict the geometry correct as well as the semantic label. From Fig. 7 we can see that mistakes in geometry compounds with mistakes in semantics which leads to lower IOUs.

Table 2. 2D depth metrics

Method	AbsRel	AbsDiff	SqRel	RMSE	$\delta < 1.25$	$\delta < 1.25^2$	$\delta < 1.25^3$	Comp
COLMAP [43]	.137	.264	.138	.502	.834	.908	.938	.871
MVDepthNet [51]	.098	.191	.061	.293	.896	.977	.994	.928
GPMVS [26]	.130	.239	.339	.472	.906	.967	.980	.928
DPSNet [28]	.087	.158	**.035**	**.232**	.925	**.984**	**.995**	.928
Ours (plain)	**.061**	**.120**	.042	.248	**.940**	.972	.985	**.999**
Ours (semseg)	.065	.124	.043	.251	.936	.971	.986	**.999**

Table 3. 3D geometry metrics

Method	L_1	Acc	Comp	Prec	Recal	F-score
COLMAP [43]	.599	.069	.135	.634	**.505**	**.558**
MVDepthNet [51]	.518	.040	.240	.831	.208	.329
GPMVS [26]	.475	**.031**	.879	**.871**	.188	.304
DPSNet [28]	.421	.045	.284	.793	.223	.344
Ours (plain)	**.162**	.065	.130	.725	.383	.499
Ours (semseg)	.172	.074	**.124**	.711	.413	.520

Table 4. 3D semantic label benchmark

Method	mIOU
ScanNet [11]	30.6
PointNet++ [39]	33.9
SPLATNet [48]	39.3
3DMV [13]	48.4
3DMV-FTSDF	50.1
PointNet++SW	52.3
SparseConvNet [21]	72.5
MinkowskiNet [8]	**73.4**
Ours	34.0

ScanNet 3D Semantic Segmentation metrics. We transfer our labels from the predicted mesh to the ground truth mesh using nearest neighbors.

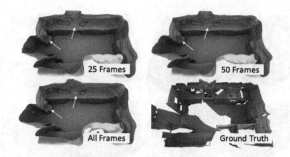

Fig. 5. Quality as a function of number of input frames at inference time. There is almost no degradation with as few as 25 frames (out of 784 total).

Table 5. Inference time

Method	Per frame time (sec)	Per sequence time (sec)
COLMAP [43]	2.076	0
MVDepthNet [51]	0.048	0
GPMVS [26]	0.051	0
DPSNet [28]	0.322	0
Ours	.071	.840

In Fig. 5 we show an example of how our method degrades as the number of frames is reduced at inference time. We see that there is almost no degradation with as few as 25 frames. See accompanying video for more examples.

5.1   Inference Time

Since our method only requires running a small 2D CNN on each frame, the cost of running the large 3D CNN is amortized over a sequence of images. On the other hand, MVS methods must run all their compute on every frame. Note that they must also run depth map fusion to accumulate the depth maps into a mesh, but we do not include this additional time here. We report inference times using 2 neighbors. All models are run on a single NVidia TiTan RTX GPU. From Table 5 we can see that after approximately 4 frames, ours becomes faster than DPSNet (note that most Scannet scenes are a few thousands of frames).

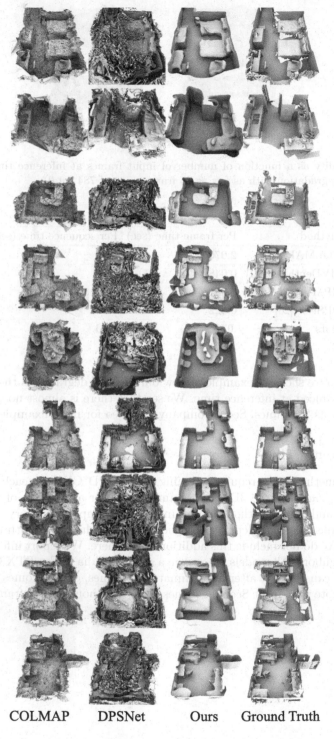

COLMAP   DPSNet   Ours   Ground Truth

Fig. 6. Qualitative 3D reconstruction results.

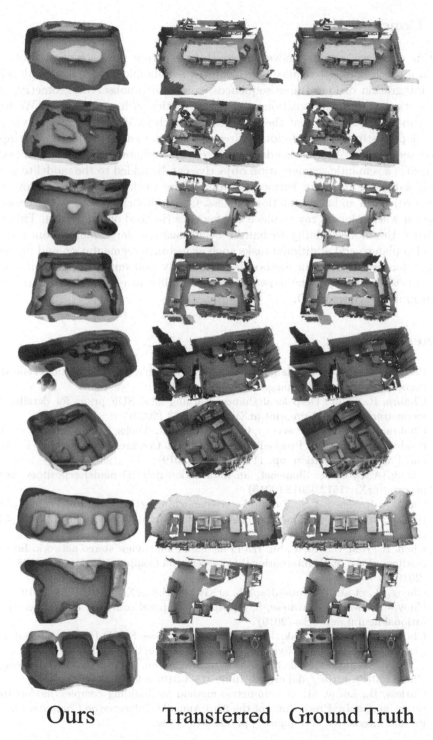

Ours   Transferred   Ground Truth

Fig. 7. Qualitative 3D semantic segmentations. Left to right: Ours, our labels transferred to the ground truth mesh, ground truth labels. We are able to accurately segment the 3D scene despite not using a depth sensor.

6 Conclusions

In this work, we present a novel approach to 3D scene reconstruction. Notably, our approach does not require depth inputs; is unbounded temporally, allowing the integration of long frame sequences; completes unobserved geometry; and supports the efficient prediction of other quantities such as semantics. We have experimentally verified that the classical approach to 3D reconstruction via per view depth estimation is inferior to direct regression to a 3D model from an input RGB sequence. We have also demonstrated that without significant additional compute, a semantic segmentation objective can be added to the model to accurately label the resultant surfaces. In our future work, we aim to improve the back projection and accumulation process. One approach is to allow the network to learn where along a ray to place the features (instead of uniformly). This will improve the models ability to handle occlusions and large multi room scenes. We also plan to add additional tasks such as instance segmentation and intrinsic image decomposition. Our method is particularly well suited for intrinsic image decomposition because the network has the ability to reason with information from multiple views in 3D.

References

1. Badrinarayanan, V., Kendall, A., Cipolla, R.: Segnet: a deep convolutional encoder-decoder architecture for image segmentation (2015)
2. Chabra, R., et al.: Deep local shapes: learning local SDF priors for detailed 3D reconstruction. arXiv preprint arXiv:2003.10983 (2020)
3. Chabra, R., Straub, J., Sweeney, C., Newcombe, R., Fuchs, H.: Stereodrnet: dilated residual stereonet. In: Proceedings of the IEEE Conference on Computer Vision and Pattern Recognition, pp. 11786–11795 (2019)
4. Chang, A.X., et al.: Shapenet: an information-rich 3D model repository. arXiv preprint arXiv:1512.03012 (2015)
5. Chang, J.R., Chen, Y.S.: Pyramid stereo matching network. In: Proceedings of the IEEE Conference on Computer Vision and Pattern Recognition, pp. 5410–5418 (2018)
6. Chen, R., Han, S., Xu, J., Su, H.: Point-based multi-view stereo network. In: Proceedings of the IEEE International Conference on Computer Vision, pp. 1538–1547 (2019)
7. Cheng, B., et al.: Panoptic-deeplab. arXiv preprint arXiv:1910.04751 (2019)
8. Choy, C., Gwak, J., Savarese, S.: 4D spatio-temporal convnets: minkowski convolutional neural networks (2019)
9. Choy, C.B., Xu, D., Gwak, J.Y., Chen, K., Savarese, S.: 3D-R2N2: a unified approach for single and multi-view 3D object reconstruction. In: Leibe, B., Matas, J., Sebe, N., Welling, M. (eds.) ECCV 2016. LNCS, vol. 9912, pp. 628–644. Springer, Cham (2016). https://doi.org/10.1007/978-3-319-46484-8_38
10. Curless, B., Levoy, M.: A volumetric method for building complex models from range images. In: Proceedings of the 23rd Annual Conference on Computer Graphics and Interactive Techniques, pp. 303–312 (1996)

11. Dai, A., Chang, A.X., Savva, M., Halber, M., Funkhouser, T., Nießner, M.: Scannet: richly-annotated 3D reconstructions of indoor scenes. In: Proceedings of Computer Vision and Pattern Recognition (CVPR). IEEE (2017)

12. Dai, A., Diller, C., Nießner, M.: SG-NN: sparse generative neural networks for self-supervised scene completion of RGB-D scans. arXiv preprint arXiv:1912.00036 (2019)

13. Dai, A., Nießner, M.: 3DMV: joint 3D-multi-view prediction for 3D semantic scene segmentation (2018)

14. Dai, A., Qi, C.R., Nießner, M.: Shape completion using 3D-encoder-predictor CNNs and shape synthesis (2016)

15. Dai, A., Ritchie, D., Bokeloh, M., Reed, S., Sturm, J., Nießner, M.: Scancomplete: large-scale scene completion and semantic segmentation for 3D scans. In: Proceedings of the IEEE Conference on Computer Vision and Pattern Recognition, pp. 4578–4587 (2018)

16. Falcon, W.: Pytorch lightning. GitHub. https://github.com/PyTorchLightning/pytorch-lightning Cited by 3 (2019)

17. Fan, H., Su, H., Guibas, L.J.: A point set generation network for 3D object reconstruction from a single image. In: Proceedings of the IEEE Conference on Computer Vision and Pattern Recognition, pp. 605–613 (2017)

18. Fu, H., Gong, M., Wang, C., Batmanghelich, K., Tao, D.: Deep ordinal regression network for monocular depth estimation. In: Proceedings of the IEEE Conference on Computer Vision and Pattern Recognition, pp. 2002–2011 (2018)

19. Galliani, S., Lasinger, K., Schindler, K.: Massively parallel multiview stereopsis by surface normal diffusion. In: Proceedings of the IEEE International Conference on Computer Vision, pp. 873–881 (2015)

20. Gkioxari, G., Malik, J., Johnson, J.: Mesh R-CNN. In: Proceedings of the IEEE International Conference on Computer Vision, pp. 9785–9795 (2019)

21. Graham, B., Engelcke, M., van der Maaten, L.: 3D semantic segmentation with submanifold sparse convolutional networks. In: Proceedings of the IEEE Conference on Computer Vision and Pattern Recognition, pp. 9224–9232 (2018)

22. He, K., Gkioxari, G., Dollár, P., Girshick, R.: Mask R-CNN. In: Proceedings of the IEEE International Conference on Computer Vision, pp. 2961–2969 (2017)

23. Hirschmuller, H.: Stereo processing by semiglobal matching and mutual information. IEEE Trans. Pattern Anal. Mach. Intell. **30**(2), 328–341 (2007)

24. Hou, J., Dai, A., Nießner, M.: 3D-SIC: 3D semantic instance completion for RGB-D scans. arXiv preprint arXiv:1904.12012 (2019)

25. Hou, J., Dai, A., Nießner, M.: 3D-SIS: 3D semantic instance segmentation of RGB-D scans (2018)

26. Hou, Y., Kannala, J., Solin, A.: Multi-view stereo by temporal nonparametric fusion. In: Proceedings of the IEEE International Conference on Computer Vision, pp. 2651–2660 (2019)

27. Huang, P.H., Matzen, K., Kopf, J., Ahuja, N., Huang, J.B.: Deepmvs: learning multi-view stereopsis. In: Proceedings of the IEEE Conference on Computer Vision and Pattern Recognition, pp. 2821–2830 (2018)

28. Im, S., Jeon, H.G., Lin, S., Kweon, I.S.: Dpsnet: end-to-end deep plane sweep stereo. In: 7th International Conference on Learning Representations, ICLR 2019. International Conference on Learning Representations, ICLR (2019)

29. Iskakov, K., Burkov, E., Lempitsky, V., Malkov, Y.: Learnable triangulation of human pose. In: Proceedings of the IEEE International Conference on Computer Vision, pp. 7718–7727 (2019)

30. Kirillov, A., Girshick, R., He, K., Dollár, P.: Panoptic feature pyramid networks. In: Proceedings of the IEEE Conference on Computer Vision and Pattern Recognition, pp. 6399–6408 (2019)
31. Lasinger, K., Ranftl, R., Schindler, K., Koltun, V.: Towards robust monocular depth estimation: mixing datasets for zero-shot cross-dataset transfer. arXiv preprint arXiv:1907.01341 (2019)
32. Lee, J.H., Han, M.K., Ko, D.W., Suh, I.H.: From big to small: multi-scale local planar guidance for monocular depth estimation. arXiv preprint arXiv:1907.10326 (2019)
33. Lin, T.Y., Dollár, P., Girshick, R., He, K., Hariharan, B., Belongie, S.: Feature pyramid networks for object detection. In: Proceedings of the IEEE Conference on Computer Vision and Pattern Recognition, pp. 2117–2125 (2017)
34. Lorensen, W.E., Cline, H.E.: Marching cubes: a high resolution 3D surface construction algorithm. ACM Siggraph Comput. Graph. **21**(4), 163–169 (1987)
35. McCormac, J., Clark, R., Bloesch, M., Davison, A., Leutenegger, S.: Fusion++: volumetric object-level slam. In: 2018 International Conference on 3D Vision (3DV), pp. 32–41. IEEE (2018)
36. McCormac, J., Handa, A., Davison, A., Leutenegger, S.: Semanticfusion: dense 3D semantic mapping with convolutional neural networks. In: 2017 IEEE International Conference on Robotics and Automation (ICRA), pp. 4628–4635. IEEE (2017)
37. Narita, G., Seno, T., Ishikawa, T., Kaji, Y.: Panopticfusion: online volumetric semantic mapping at the level of stuff and things. arXiv preprint arXiv:1903.01177 (2019)
38. Park, J.J., Florence, P., Straub, J., Newcombe, R., Lovegrove, S.: Deepsdf: learning continuous signed distance functions for shape representation. In: Proceedings of the IEEE Conference on Computer Vision and Pattern Recognition, pp. 165–174 (2019)
39. Qi, C.R., Yi, L., Su, H., Guibas, L.J.: Pointnet++: deep hierarchical feature learning on point sets in a metric space (2017)
40. Riegler, G., Osman Ulusoy, A., Geiger, A.: Octnet: learning deep 3D representations at high resolutions. In: Proceedings of the IEEE Conference on Computer Vision and Pattern Recognition, pp. 3577–3586 (2017)
41. Rosinol, A., Abate, M., Chang, Y., Carlone, L.: Kimera: an open-source library for real-time metric-semantic localization and mapping. In: IEEE International Conference on Robotics and Automation (ICRA) (2020)
42. Schönberger, J.L., Frahm, J.M.: Structure-from-motion revisited. In: Conference on Computer Vision and Pattern Recognition (CVPR) (2016)
43. Schönberger, J.L., Zheng, E., Pollefeys, M., Frahm, J.M.: Pixelwise view selection for unstructured multi-view stereo. In: European Conference on Computer Vision (ECCV) (2016)
44. Schöps, T., Sattler, T., Pollefeys, M.: Surfelmeshing: online surfel-based mesh reconstruction. IEEE Trans. Pattern Anal. Mach. Intell. (2019)
45. Sinha, A., Unmesh, A., Huang, Q., Ramani, K.: Surfnet: generating 3D shape surfaces using deep residual networks. In: Proceedings of the IEEE Conference on Computer Vision and Pattern Recognition, pp. 6040–6049 (2017)
46. Sitzmann, V., Thies, J., Heide, F., Nießner, M., Wetzstein, G., Zollhofer, M.: Deepvoxels: learning persistent 3D feature embeddings. In: Proceedings of the IEEE Conference on Computer Vision and Pattern Recognition, pp. 2437–2446 (2019)
47. Sitzmann, V., Zollhöfer, M., Wetzstein, G.: Scene representation networks: continuous 3D-structure-aware neural scene representations. In: Advances in Neural Information Processing Systems (2019)

48. Su, H., et al.: Splatnet: sparse lattice networks for point cloud processing (2018)
49. Tatarchenko, M., Dosovitskiy, A., Brox, T.: Octree generating networks: efficient convolutional architectures for high-resolution 3D outputs. In: Proceedings of the IEEE International Conference on Computer Vision, pp. 2088–2096 (2017)
50. Tateno, K., Tombari, F., Laina, I., Navab, N.: CNN-slam: real-time dense monocular slam with learned depth prediction. In: Proceedings of the IEEE Conference on Computer Vision and Pattern Recognition, pp. 6243–6252 (2017)
51. Wang, K., Shen, S.: Mvdepthnet: real-time multiview depth estimation neural network. In: 2018 International Conference on 3D Vision (3DV), pp. 248–257. IEEE (2018)
52. Wang, N., Zhang, Y., Li, Z., Fu, Y., Liu, W., Jiang, Y.G.: Pixel2Mesh: generating 3D mesh models from single RGB images. In: Proceedings of the European Conference on Computer Vision (ECCV), pp. 52–67 (2018)
53. Wang, W., Yu, R., Huang, Q., Neumann, U.: SGPN: similarity group proposal network for 3D point cloud instance segmentation. In: In Proceedings of the IEEE Conference on Computer Vision and Pattern Recognition, pp. 2569–2578 (2018)
54. Weder, S., Schönberger, J., Pollefeys, M., Oswald, M.R.: Routedfusion: learning real-time depth map fusion. arXiv preprint arXiv:2001.04388 (2020)
55. Whelan, T., Leutenegger, S., Salas-Moreno, R., Glocker, B., Davison, A.: Elasticfusion: Dense slam without a pose graph. Robotics: Science and Systems (2015)
56. Xie, H., Yao, H., Sun, X., Zhou, S., Zhang, S.: Pix2Vox: context-aware 3D reconstruction from single and multi-view images. In: Proceedings of the IEEE International Conference on Computer Vision, pp. 2690–2698 (2019)
57. Yao, Y., Luo, Z., Li, S., Fang, T., Quan, L.: Mvsnet: depth inference for unstructured multi-view stereo. In: Proceedings of the European Conference on Computer Vision (ECCV), pp. 767–783 (2018)
58. Yao, Y., Luo, Z., Li, S., Shen, T., Fang, T., Quan, L.: Recurrent MVSNet for high-resolution multi-view stereo depth inference. In: Proceedings of the IEEE Conference on Computer Vision and Pattern Recognition, pp. 5525–5534 (2019)
59. Zimmermann, C., Ceylan, D., Yang, J., Russell, B., Argus, M., Brox, T.: FreiHAND: a dataset for markerless capture of hand pose and shape from single RGB images. In: Proceedings of the IEEE International Conference on Computer Vision, pp. 813–822 (2019)

Multiple Class Novelty Detection Under Data Distribution Shift

Poojan Oza[1]([✉]), Hien V. Nguyen[2], and Vishal M. Patel[1]

[1] Johns Hopkins University, 3400 N. Charles St, Baltimore, MD 21218, USA
{poza,vp36}@jhu.edu
[2] University of Houston, Houston, TX 77004, USA
hienvnguyen@uh.edu

Abstract. The novelty detection models learn a decision boundary around multiple categories of a given dataset. This helps such models in detecting any novel classes encountered during testing. However, in many cases, the test data distribution can be different from that of the training data. For such cases, the novelty detection models risk detecting a known class as novel due to the dataset distribution shift. This scenario is often ignored while working with novelty detection. To this end, we consider the problem of multiple class novelty detection under dataset distribution shift to improve the novelty detection performance. Firstly, we discuss the problem setting in detail and show how it affects the performance of current novelty detection methods. Secondly, we show that one could improve those novelty detection methods with a simple integration of domain adversarial loss. Finally, we propose a method which brings together the techniques from novelty detection and domain adaptation to improve generalization of multiple class novelty detection on different domains. We evaluate the proposed method on digits and object recognition datasets and show that it provides improvements over the baseline methods.

Keywords: Dataset distribution shift · Multiple class novelty detection

1 Introduction

In recent years, improving robustness of convolutional neural networks (CNNs) has received an increasing amount of attention [2,6]. Many problems such as countering adversarial/trojan/poison attacks [8,25,26,47], detecting novel categories [7,35,37,39,40,42] and out-of-distribution samples [10,13,24,54] etc. tackle different aspects of robustness of CNNs. One of the practical aspect related to model robustness is detection of samples belonging to novel categories during testing. Specifically, when the CNN models are tested in the real world environment, it is highly likely that the models will observe samples from categories that were not present during training. To tackle such cases, it would be better

Electronic supplementary material The online version of this chapter (https://doi.org/10.1007/978-3-030-58571-6_26) contains supplementary material, which is available to authorized users.

A. Vedaldi et al. (Eds.): ECCV 2020, LNCS 12352, pp. 432–449, 2020.
https://doi.org/10.1007/978-3-030-58571-6_26

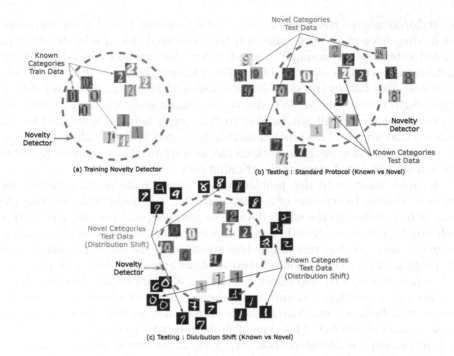

Fig. 1. An overview of the proposed problem setting. (a) We have a training data with samples from multiple known categories. Here, we have used the SVHN dataset with digits 0, 1 and 2 as known categories. These data samples are used to learn a novelty detector to enclose the known categories. (b) In a standard novelty detection testing protocol, the test data follows the same distribution as the training data. As shown in the figure, typically the novelty detector is able to distinguish between known categories and novel categories. Here, digits 7, 8 and 9 sampled from the SVHN dataset are used as novel categories. As illustrated in the figure, the learned novelty detector is able to differentiate between known and novel digits from the SVHN dataset correctly. (c) This figure illustrates the scenario where the test data does not follow the distribution of the training dataset. When tested with known (0, 1, 2) and novel (7, 8, 9) digits from the MNIST dataset, due to the distribution shift, the learned novelty detector performs poorly. This problem arises due to the fact that while training any novelty detector to enclose the known categories of a particular dataset, it also encloses the style/domain of that dataset. This creates a problem as shown in this figure, where the data from known categories, which follow a different distribution will have high risk of being detected as novel category.

to first identify whether the given sample is from a novel category or not and only then should be passed through CNN for classification if it is identified as known. This problem is commonly referred to as novelty detection.

There has been a lot of work done in the literature for the novelty detection task [3,4,7,34,40,42]. Typically, the novelty detection methods try to learn a decision boundary that encloses the known categories given in the dataset. However, while trying to enclose the known categories, these methods also enclose the style/domain of the dataset. As a result, samples from known categories but having different style/domain, will have increased risk of false detection as a novel category. For example, a novelty detection method trained on SVHN digits dataset will be correctly able to detect known categories from novel, only if the test data follows the same distribution as SVHN. But, if the test data is from a digits dataset like MNIST, due to the domain shift, it is highly likely that the novelty detector will not be able to distinguish between novel and known categories accurately. This problem is also illustrated in Fig. 1. Most of the earlier novelty detection methods work on the assumption that the test data would follow a similar distribution as the training data.

A simple solution to this problem would be to create another dataset for the new domain. In the case of novelty detection, one could avoid labeling the dataset by considering the whole dataset as one class, and training any off-the-shelf novelty detection algorithm on it. However, most datasets contain multiple categories and ignoring this multi-class structure of the dataset could restrict the performance of the novelty detection algorithm. If we wish to exploit the multi-class structure to help novelty detection, it would require labeling efforts that are costly and time consuming. This problem can be solved to an extent by transferring the knowledge from a labeled dataset that has different style/domain to the dataset of interest. This type of problem setting has been widely studied as unsupervised domain adaptation [11,14,49], in the literature, and specifically deals with the dataset distribution shift issue. However, most of the work on this topic has been done for the task of classification [11,14,49,52], segmentation [15,50,55], detection [9,16,19] etc. and to the best of our knowledge no work is available in the literature that addresses the distribution shift problem for novelty detection.

To this end, we consider the problem of multiple-class novelty detection under dataset distribution shift. Since no prior work has been done for this specific problem, we first describe the problem statement in detail and provide trivial baselines for this task based on novelty detection and domain adaptation approaches. Furthermore, we propose a novelty detection method that can address the data distribution shift problem and help improve over the trivial baselines. Moreover, we discuss the differences between the closely related problem setting such as open-set domain adaptation [36] and also provide experimental analysis to show that their performance is sub-optimal in the problem setting considered in this paper.

To summarize, this paper makes the following contributions:

- We consider novelty detection under dataset distribution shift. To the best of our knowledge this is the first work to consider data distribution shift in the context of novelty detection.
- We show the effects of distribution shift on current novelty detection methods and provide a few baselines that combine novelty detection and domain adaptation techniques.
- We propose an algorithm to mitigate data distribution shift for novelty detection, and show that it can improve the detection performance over the trivial novelty detection baselines.

2   Related Work

Novelty Detection. Earlier works in novelty detection were based on Principle Component Analysis (PCA) [51], Mixture Models [30], Support Vector Machines [46] etc. Typically, these methods work on features extracted from the image and learn a decision boundary to enclose the extracted features from the dataset. However, most of the methods for novelty detection have shifted to CNNs in recent years due to their outstanding representation learning capability. Especially, unsupervised learning strategies such as auto-encoders [1] and generative adversarial networks [12] are among the most popular algorithms for novelty detection. Some approaches use auto-encoders [1] for novelty detection. However, such approaches are not optimal since auto-encoder often suffer from blurry reconstructions. Sabokrou *et al.* [42] proposed a novelty detection algorithm using a de-noising auto-encoder based generative adversarial network. Specifically, during training, input is injected with gaussian noise and auto-encoders are tasked to provide clean reconstructions. The reconstructions are supervised with a combination of adversarial loss and reconstruction loss. Finally, discriminator prediction probability of the reconstructed image is used as the novelty detection score. Pidhorskyi *et al.* [40] proposed another method based on adversarial auto-encoders [29]. Specifically, the encoder is trained to learn a feature embedding that are Gaussian distributed and the overall network is designed to reconstruct the original image. Both of these approaches are shown to work reasonably well when there are multiple categories present in the dataset and both show a marginal drop in the performance with increased number of categories. Recent works such as OC-GAN [38] and non-adversarial generative method [7] consider a specific case where it is assumed that there is only one category available in the dataset. With that assumption, they learn a one-class novelty detector to enclose a particular given category. The authors of these approaches have not evaluated the performance of their methods in the case when there are multiple categories present in the dataset. Moreover, when the dataset contains only one category, it is better to just train the novelty detector on the data from the new domain. The problem of distribution shift is much more relevant when datasets contain multiple categories, which is a more realistic scenario. However, all of these approaches do not consider the scenario of distribution shift in the dataset.

Domain Adaptation. Unsupervised domain adaptation problem has been well-studied in the literature for image classification task. It is defined as aligning domains having distinct distributions, namely source and target containing same categories. In unsupervised domain adaptation, it is assumed that images in the source dataset are available with category labels, while no label information is provided for the target images. The most popular approaches for this task are based on CNNs. Some of these approaches include feature distribution alignment [11,44,48,52], similarity learning [41], residual transfer [27,28], and generative adversarial network-based methods [14,17,31,45]. These methods mostly consider a setting where both source and target datasets have equal number of categories. Recently, some works have started to consider different settings where the number of categories in source and target are not the same. These extensions include partial domain adaptation [5], universal domain adaptation [53] and open-set domain adaptation [36]. Partial domain adaptation assumes that target domain categories are a subset of the source domain categories and hence only a part of the source dataset is useful during adaptation. Whereas open-set domain adaptation assumes that the source domain categories are a subset of the target domain categories and hence only a part of the target data is useful for the adaptation. Universal domain adaptation brings both open-set and partial settings together into a single framework. All of these modifications to the original domain adaptation problem setting are designed to improve the domain adaptation performance on more practical scenarios.

The most related problem to the proposed scenario available in the literature is open-set domain adaptation proposed by Busto and Gall et al. [36]. However, we would like to point out that there are some key differences between open-set domain adaptation and the proposed approach. Specifically, in open-set domain adaptation, the target categories are a superset of the source categories, i.e., there are some unknown categories available in the target dataset. Since, no labels are provided for the target domain, the challenge for open-set domain adaption method is to separate out the samples belonging to known and unknown categories in the available target dataset. This extends the domain adaptation capability to a real-world scenario where the target category set will be a superset of the source. In the proposed problem, we do not modify the domain adaptation setting like the open-set domain adaptation, but on the contrary, utilize the domain adaptation techniques to improve generalization of novelty detection methods on different data domains. Specifically, in the proposed problem we have labeled data from the source domain and unlabeled data from the target domain and both of these domains share the same category set. Also, unlike open-set domain adaptation, where unknown category data samples are accessible during training, in the proposed problem setting, unknown category data samples are only observed during testing. The end goal for the proposed problem is to utilize the source domain information to create a better novelty detection model for the target domain data. Since both methods follow different problem settings, either of the methods would not be optimal for the other problem setting. We provide an experiment and discuss this point in more detail in the supplementary material.

3   Novelty Detection Vs Distribution Shift

We provide a preliminary experimental analysis to show the effect of dataset distribution shift on the performance of novelty detection. For this experiment, we consider a novelty detector [42], referred to as Adversarially learned One-Class Classifier (ALOCC). The ALOCC method is trained on the MNIST dataset. For training, we consider digits 0 to 4 as known categories and the remaining digits as novel categories. Figure 2(a) shows the ROC curve illustrating the performance of the novelty detector when evaluated on the MNIST data (Blue curve).

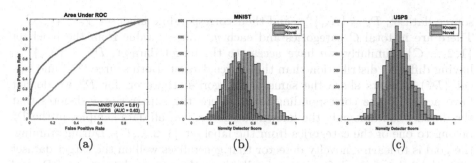

(a)   (b)   (c)

Fig. 2. (a) Area under the ROC plot when a novelty detector is evaluated on the MNIST and USPS datasets. (b) Histogram of scores corresponding to the MNIST dataset. (c) Histogram of scores corresponding to the USPS dataset. (Color figure online)

The novelty detector achieves area under the curve of 0.81. In order to simulate the data distribution shift, we evaluate the novelty detector on the USPS dataset, again considering 0 to 4 digits as known categories and the remaining digits as novel categories. As we can see from Fig. 2(a), the performance on the USPS dataset (red curve) drops by ∼20% compared to the MNIST dataset. Also, by looking at the histogram of score predictions in Fig. 2(b) and Fig. 2(c), it is clear that compared to MNIST, USPS scores for both known and novel categories on average are shifted towards the left. This shows that the novelty detector trained on MNIST has high risk of detecting USPS known categories as novel. This is due to the shift in the distribution between MNIST and USPS datasets.

4   Robust Novelty Detection Under Distribution Shift

In this section, we first formulate the problem and then discuss some baseline methods. Finally, we present the proposed method in detail.

4.1   Problem Setting

Typically, a novelty detection model is developed using a training dataset having multiple categories which we refer to as the source dataset. This trained model is then tested in the real-world where the goal is to detect any test input samples belonging to novel categories. However, as discussed in Sect. 1, these models have high risk of detecting any test samples belonging to known categories as unknown, when the test samples are from a different distribution than that of the training dataset. The goal of the proposed problem setting is to generalize the novelty detection models on a dataset having different distribution, which we refer to as the target dataset. The terminology of referring labeled dataset as source and unlabeled dataset as target is borrowed from the domain adaptation literature. Formally, in the proposed problem setting, we have access to the source dataset, $\mathcal{D}_s = \{X_{si}\}_{i=1}^{N_s}$ and their corresponding label set $\mathcal{Y}_s = \{y_{si}\}_{i=1}^{N_s}$. There are in total C categories and each y_{si} takes a value from the label set $\{1, 2, ..., C\}$. Similarly, we have access to the target dataset, $\mathcal{D}_t^k = \{X_{ti}\}_{i=1}^{N_t}$, having different distribution than the source dataset. Both source $(\mathcal{D}_s)$ and target $(\mathcal{D}_t^k)$ datasets share the same C categories. However, for $\mathcal{D}_t^k$ we do not have access to the corresponding labels. Here, the superscript k denotes that the dataset contains only the known categories, i.e., all data samples in the $\mathcal{D}_t^k$ belong to one of the categories from the label set $\{1, 2, ..., C\}$. During training, the goal is to learn a novelty detector that generalizes well on the target dataset with the help of the information available in the source dataset, i.e., $\mathcal{D}_s$ and $\mathcal{Y}_s$. The learned novelty detector is evaluated using a test set from the target dataset $(\mathcal{D}_t^{k:test})$ having known categories and a target set containing data from unknown categories $(\mathcal{D}_t^u)$. Here, superscript u denotes that the dataset contains only novel categories. Note that data from $\mathcal{D}_t^u$ is not utilized during training but only used while evaluating the novelty detection performance on the target set.

4.2 Simple Approaches

As discussed in Sect. 1 and shown by preliminary experiment in Sect. 3 the dataset distribution shift is one of the unexplored problems in novelty detection. Following the problem setting and notations described in previous section, in this section, we explore some potential solutions for tackling this problem. Since there are no prior works available in the literature on this problem, we develop a few baselines by considering similar works from the literature. The block diagrams of these methods are illustrated in Fig. 3(a)–(d). In what follows, we describe these baseline approaches in detail.

Softmax. The most simple baseline would be to utilize the labeled source data to train a feature extractor and classifier network to perform multi-class classification. However, classification networks are prone to novel classes even in the source domain, hence would not translate well for the target domain novelty detection.

ALOCC. Another approach would be to disregard the source domain information and only use the target domain unlabeled data to train any off-the-shelf novelty detector algorithm. For this baseline, we utilize ALOCC method for novelty detection proposed in [42]. Specifically, ALOCC trains an auto-encoder which aims to reconstruct a clean image from the input image using Gaussian noise. This auto-encoder network is trained in generative adversarial framework and the score from the discriminator of the reconstructed image is used for novelty detection. The dataset will have multiple categories, however ALOCC remains agnostic to that by considering multiple categories as one.

GRL. Gradient reversal layer [11] has been widely used to reduce the domain gap between two datasets having different distributions for the classification task. GRL baseline can be considered as an extension to the Softmax baseline such that the domain gap issue between source and target is addressed by the gradient reversal layer.

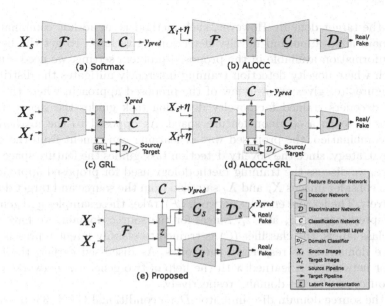

Fig. 3. Illustration of multiple potential solutions to address the distribution shift problem for novelty detection. (a) Softmax: Simplest approach which utilizes the labeled source data to train a classification network. The maximum softmax probability can be used as the novelty score. (b) ALOCC: Another approach which directly utilizes the unlabeled target data to train an off-the-shelf novelty detector. We utilize, a novelty detection algorithm proposed in [42]. Here, η denotes the Gaussian noise added to the input image. (c) GRL: Uses labeled source and unlabeled target data to learn a domain invariant feature space using a gradient reversal layer [11]. The maximum softmax prediction probability can be used as the novelty score. (d) ALOCC+GRL: A combination of both novelty detector [42] and domain invariant feature learning [11] in an ad-hoc manner. (e) Proposed method: A shared feature space is learned through cross-domain mappings. The corss-domain mappings helps to learn a better feature space which is especially useful for novelty detection.

ALOCC+GRL. This is the final baseline which combines the gradient reversal training to reduce the domain gap between source and target, together with the novelty detection training specified in the ALOCC. This ad-hoc combination provides a strong baseline for the proposed setting, since GRL is able to take care of the domain gap and with the help of domain invariant feature space, the ALOCC is able to learn a more general novelty detector which is likely to perform better on the target domain.

4.3   Proposed Method

ALOCC+GRL is the most related method out of all the methods described above. Also, it is able to exploit both novelty detection training and domain adversarial loss to learn a domain invariant feature space. This should help the novelty detector mitigate the effects of distribution shift and perform reasonably well on the target domain. However, such method is an ad-hoc combination of the domain adaptation and novelty detection algorithms. To get the best out of the information available in the proposed problem setting, we need a unified approach where novelty detection training inherently mitigates the distribution shift. Figure 3(e) gives an overview of the proposed approach, where the cross-domain decoders trained for novelty detection task guides the shared feature extractor to learn a common feature space. As opposed to the method with ad-hoc combination, the proposed way of learning can benefit from the unified training strategy, since the novelty detection task guides the feature space learning. Here, we discuss the training methodology used for proposed approach.

Let's consider images X_s and X_t sampled from the source and target domain, respectively. The feature encoder network ($\mathcal{F}$), takes these samples and generates latent representations z_s and z_t. Since, for the source domain, we have access to the class labels, the classifier ($\mathcal{C}$) is trained to classify latent representations of source domain in to respective categories. As discussed earlier, the feature extractor network $\mathcal{F}$ is learned with the help of two generator networks $\mathcal{G}_s$ and $\mathcal{G}_t$ for source and target domain, respectively.

For the source domain discriminator D_s, a conditional GAN [33] based approach is used. This specifically helps the generator networks when datasets contain multiple categories. Following the conditional GAN formulation proposed by [33], the discriminator network D_s has two parts. The first part referred to as, D_s^b, identifies whether the samples generated by $\mathcal{G}_s$ are real or fake by a binary classification. On the other hand, the second part referred to as, D_s^a, classifies the generated images into one of the known categories. $\mathcal{G}_s$ takes in the latent representations z_s and z_t to generate images $\hat{X}_{s2s}$ and $\hat{X}_{t2s}$, respectively. This process can be described as follows,

$$z_s = \mathcal{F}(X_s), \quad z_t = \mathcal{F}(X_s)$$
$$\hat{X}_{t2s} = \mathcal{G}_s(z_t), \quad \hat{X}_{s2s} = \mathcal{G}_s(z_s). \tag{1}$$

For the target domain discriminator D_t, a binary classifier based on the cross entropy loss is used. The generator network $\mathcal{G}_t$ generates the image samples from the source and the target domain, using latent representations z_s and z_t, respectively. This process can be described as follows,

$$\hat{X}_{s2t} = \mathcal{G}_t(z_s), \quad \hat{X}_{t2t} = \mathcal{G}_t(z_t). \tag{2}$$

The classifier loss function can be defined as follows

$$\mathcal{L}_{ce} = \mathbb{E}_{\{X,y\} \sim \{\mathcal{D}_s, \mathcal{Y}_s\}}[\ell_{ce}(\mathcal{C}(\mathcal{F}(X)), y)], \tag{3}$$

where, $\mathcal{L}_{ce}$ is the overall classification loss computed on the labeled source data and ℓ_{ce} is the categorical cross entropy loss. Considering $\hat{y} = \mathcal{C}(z_s)$ as the predicted probability vector, ℓ_{ce} can be expressed as follows

$$\ell_{ce}(\hat{y}, y) = -\sum_{j=1}^{C} y_j \log[\hat{y}_j]. \tag{4}$$

To train the source discriminator in the conditional GAN framework, we need to perform real/fake classification and categorical classification, which can be expressed as

$$\mathcal{L}_{cGAN}^{D_s} = \mathbb{E}_{X \sim \mathcal{D}_s}[\log(1 - D_s^b(X))] + \mathbb{E}_{X \sim \mathcal{D}_s}[\log(D_s^b(\hat{X}_{t2s}))]$$

$$+ \mathbb{E}_{X \sim \mathcal{D}_t^k}[\log(D_s^b(\hat{X}_{s2s}))] + \mathbb{E}_{X \sim \mathcal{D}_s, y \sim \mathcal{Y}_s}[\ell_{ce}(D_s^a(\hat{X}_{s2s}), y)], \quad (5)$$

where, the first term in the equation trains the discriminator D_s^b to identify data sampled from the source dataset $\mathcal{D}_s$ as real images. The second and third term train the discriminator to identify images generated by $\mathcal{G}_s$, i.e., $\hat{X}_{t2s}$ and $\hat{X}_{s2s}$, as fake. The fourth term is a classification loss similar to Eq. 3, where the generated images $\hat{X}_{s2s}$ are classified in to the category corresponding to the source input images using D_s^a.

After the discriminator update, the source generator is trained to generate images such that the discriminator network is fooled into identifying the generated images, $\hat{X}_{s2s}$ and $\hat{X}_{t2s}$ as real source images. To further improve the image generation quality, we add L1 reconstruction loss, denoted as ℓ_r, on the generated source images, $\hat{X}_{s2s}$. The loss functions described above can be mathematically formulated as

$$\mathcal{L}_{cGAN}^{\mathcal{G}_s} = \mathbb{E}_{X \sim \mathcal{D}_s}[\log(1 - D_s^b(\mathcal{G}_s(X)))] + \mathbb{E}_{X \sim \mathcal{D}_t^k}[\log(1 - D_s^b(\mathcal{G}_s(X)))], \quad (6)$$

$$\mathcal{L}_{rs}^{\mathcal{G}_s} = \mathbb{E}_{X \sim \mathcal{D}_s}[\ell_r(\hat{X}_{s2s}, X)], \quad (7)$$

where

$$\ell_r(\hat{X}, X) = \|X - \hat{X}\|_1. \quad (8)$$

Similar to the source domain discriminator and generator, we apply the same GAN losses for the target domain discriminator D_t, and generator $\mathcal{G}_t$. Since, the target domain labels are not available, a traditional GAN formulation is used [12], instead of the conditional GAN formulation [33] used for source domain. Additionally, similar to the source domain, we add L1 reconstruction loss on the generated target images, $\hat{X}_{t2t}$, to further improve the image generation quality in the target domain. These losses can be written as follows

$$\mathcal{L}_{GAN}^{D_t} = \mathbb{E}_{X \sim \mathcal{D}_t}[\log(1 - D_t(X))] + \mathbb{E}_{X \sim \mathcal{D}_s}[\log(D_t(\hat{X}_{s2t}))]$$

$$+ \mathbb{E}_{X \sim \mathcal{D}_t^k}[\log(D_t(\hat{X}_{t2t}))], \quad (9)$$

$$\mathcal{L}_{GAN}^{\mathcal{G}_t} = \mathbb{E}_{X \sim \mathcal{D}_t^k}[\log(1 - D_t(\mathcal{G}_t(X)))] + \mathbb{E}_{X \sim \mathcal{D}_s}[\log(1 - D_t(\mathcal{G}_t(X)))], \quad (10)$$

$$\mathcal{L}_{rt}^{\mathcal{G}_t} = \mathbb{E}_{X \sim \mathcal{D}_t^k}[\ell_r(\hat{X}_{t2t}, X)]. \quad (11)$$

Finally, the loss function for the feature encoder network consists of both the classification loss on the source and the adaptation loss from the conditional GAN module. The final loss for the network $\mathcal{F}$ can be expressed as

$$\mathcal{L}_{total}^{\mathcal{F}} = \mathcal{L}_{ce} + \lambda_1 \mathcal{L}_{cGAN}^{\mathcal{G}_s} + \lambda_2 \mathcal{L}_{GAN}^{\mathcal{G}_t}, \quad (12)$$

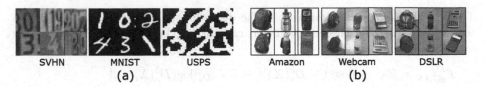

SVHN   MNIST   USPS   Amazon   Webcam   DSLR

(a)   (b)

Fig. 4. Sample images from the datasets used for conducting experiments. (a) Digits (b) Office-31.

where λ_1 and λ_2 are parameters. The loss functions defined above, $\mathcal{L}_{cGAN}^{\mathcal{G}_s}$, $\mathcal{L}_{cGAN}^{D_s}$, $\mathcal{L}_{GAN}^{\mathcal{G}_t}$, $\mathcal{L}_{GAN}^{D_t}$, $\mathcal{L}_{ce}^{\mathcal{C}}$, $\mathcal{L}_{total}^{\mathcal{F}}$, $\mathcal{L}_{rt}^{\mathcal{G}_t}$ and $\mathcal{L}_{rs}^{\mathcal{G}_s}$, are minimized iteratively to update the parameters of their respective networks. The overall training procedure for the proposed method is summarized in Algorithm 1.

5   Experiments and Results

For experiments, we consider all the baseline methods discussed in Sect. 4.2 and the proposed method described in Sect. 4.3. We use SVHN [32], MNIST [23] and USPS [18] digit recognition datasets, as well as the Office-31 [43] object recognition datasets to conduct experiments (see Fig. 4). We evaluate the performance of different methods using the Area Under the ROC (AUROC) Curve metric, which is the most commonly used evaluation metric for novelty detection.

Algorithm 1. Pseudocode for Training Proposed Method

Require: Network models $\mathcal{F}, \mathcal{C}, \mathcal{G}_s, \mathcal{D}_s, \mathcal{G}_t, \mathcal{D}_s$
Require: Initial parameters $\Theta_f, \Theta_c, \Theta_{g_s}, \Theta_{d_s}, \Theta_{g_t}, \Theta_{d_t}$
Require: Source data, $\mathcal{D}_s, \mathcal{Y}_s$ Target data , $\mathcal{D}_t^k$
Require: Hyper-parameters : $N, lr, \lambda_1, \lambda_2$
1: **while** not done **do**
2:     **for** each batch with size N **do**
3:         **for** i = 1 to N **do**
4:             Feed-forward using Eq. (1) – Eq. (2)
5:         **end for**
6:         Calculate Losses based on Eq. (3) – Eq.(12)
7:         Update Θ_{d_s}, $\Theta_{d_s} \leftarrow \Theta_{d_s} - lr * \nabla_{\Theta_{d_s}} \mathcal{L}_{cGAN}^{D_s}$
8:         Update Θ_{d_t}, $\Theta_{d_t} \leftarrow \Theta_{d_t} - lr * \nabla_{\Theta_{d_t}} \mathcal{L}_{GAN}^{D_t}$
9:         Update Θ_{g_s}, $\Theta_{g_s} \leftarrow \Theta_{g_s} - lr * \nabla_{\Theta_{g_s}} \mathcal{L}_{cGAN}^{G_s}$
10:        Update Θ_f, $\Theta_f \leftarrow \Theta_f - lr * \nabla_{\Theta_f} \mathcal{L}_{total}^{\mathcal{F}}$
11:        Update Θ_c, $\Theta_c \leftarrow \Theta_c - lr * \nabla_{\Theta_c} \mathcal{L}_{ce}$
12:        Update Θ_{g_t}, $\Theta_{g_t} \leftarrow \Theta_{g_t} - lr * \nabla_{\Theta_{g_t}} \mathcal{L}_{rt}^{G_t}$
13:        Update Θ_{g_s}, $\Theta_{g_s} \leftarrow \Theta_{g_s} - lr * \nabla_{\Theta_{g_s}} \mathcal{L}_{rs}^{G_s}$
14:    **end for**
15: **end while**
16: **Output:** Learned parameters $\hat{\Theta}_f, \hat{\Theta}_s, \hat{\Theta}_{g_s}, \hat{\Theta}_{d_s}, \hat{\Theta}_{d_t}, \hat{\Theta}_{g_t}$

Each datasets are divided into known and novel categories for novelty detection. Details regarding the splits are described in the following sections. The novel categories are not utilized during training and only used during inference. The following methods are comapred.

- **Softmax baseline:** In this baseline, only the feature extractor network $\mathcal{F}$ and the classification network $\mathcal{C}$ are trained on the labeled source dataset using the cross entropy loss. This is the simplest baseline and follows the traditional CNN training for recognition. Maximum softmax probability score is used for novelty detection.
- **ALOCC:** ALOCC is a method proposed in [42], which utilizes a feature extractor network $\mathcal{F}$ and a decoder network $\mathcal{G}$ supervised in a generative adversarial framework with the help of a discriminator network D_i. The training is done directly on the unlabeled target data. The input is injected with a Gaussian noise η and networks $\mathcal{F}$ and $\mathcal{G}$ are forced to reconstruct a clean image. The network parameters are learned by optimizing a combination of GAN and reconstruction losses. The discriminator score of the reconstructed input $D(\mathcal{G}(\mathcal{F}(X + \eta)))$ is used for novelty detection.
- **GRL:** Gradient reversal baseline extends the softmax baseline by improving the feature space to be domain invariant. This makes the maximum softmax probability much more reliable for the novelty detection task on the target domain. For GRL, feature extractor $\mathcal{F}$ and classifier network $\mathcal{C}$ are trained using the cross entropy loss and domain classifier D_f is employed with a gradient reversal layer [11] to enforce the feature space to be domain invariant. Here, the method utilizes both labeled source data and unlabeled target data for training the network parameters.
- **ALOCC+GRL:** ALOCC+GRL combines the two method described above in an ad-hoc fashion. The ALOCC training is done as described above, which involves reconstructing a clean image when the input to the network is injected with Gaussian noise. For this baseline we add noise to both source and target data. The feature extractor network $\mathcal{F}$ is also trained to perform classification of labeled source data through classification network $\mathcal{C}$. Additionally, the feature space of network $\mathcal{F}$ is enforced to be domain invariant through domain classifier D_f and gradient reversal layer. Combination of scores from ALOCC and maximum softmax probability is used to perform novelty detection. The training utilizes both labeled source and unlabeled target data.
- **Proposed method:** The proposed method is used as described in Sect. 4.3. We use addition of maximum softmax probability scores and loss from target generator (i.e. discriminator score of generated image and reconstruction loss) for novelty detection.

In all experiments, we use Adam optimizer [20] with the learning rate (η) of 0.0001 and batch size (N) of 64. The hyper-parameter λ_1 and λ_2 are both set equal to 0.03. The parameters are chosen using validation performance from the source domain data. Details regarding the network architectures used for $\mathcal{F}$, $\mathcal{C}$, $\mathcal{G}_s$, $\mathcal{G}_t$, D_s and D_t are provided in supplementary material.

Table 1. Performance on the digits datasets - SVHN, MNIST and USPS evaluated using area under the roc metric. (S), (T) and (ST) respectively denote only labeled source data, only unlabeled target data and both labeled source-unlabeled target data used for training.

Method	SVHN→MNIST	MNIST→USPS	USPS→MNIST	SVHN→USPS	Average performance
Softmax (S)	0.642	0.602	0.651	0.587	0.620
ALOCC (T)	0.702	0.633	0.702	0.633	0.667
GRL (ST)	0.718	0.863	0.859	0.667	0.776
ALOCC+GRL (ST)	0.851	0.903	0.895	0.845	0.873
Proposed (ST)	**0.919**	**0.945**	**0.928**	**0.895**	**0.921**

Digits: SVHN, USPS, MNIST. In the first set of experiments, SVHN, USPS and MNIST digit datasets are used to create four different scenarios, SVHN→MNIST, SVHN→USPS, USPS→MNIST and MNIST→USPS. First five digits, digits 0 to 4, are used as known categories and the remaining digits, digit 5 to 9, are considered as novel categories. Only the known categories are used during training and novel categories are used only for evaluating the methods. For the problem setting proposed in this paper, we utilize training split provided by the respective datasets to train the models and test split are used for evaluating the performance. All images in SVHN, MNIST and USPS are resized to 32 × 32. The feature extractor used in this paper is inspired from the LeNet architecture [22] (details are provided in supplementary material).

The performance of each method is reported in the Table 1. The softmax baseline performs worst out of all the methods. This is expected as softmax baseline is trained on only labeled source dataset. Also, it is not specifically trained for the novelty detection task. ALOCC performs better than softmax as it is trained on the target dataset and is specifically designed for the task of novelty detection. GRL baseline learns a domain invariant feature encoder, and hence is able to produce reasonable softmax probabilities on the target dataset. ALOCC+GRL combines the ideas from domain adversarial training and novelty detection training. Specifically, ALOCC learns a good model for novelty detection task and GRL helps the feature extractor of the ALOCC model to learn domain invariant feature. Additional training with classification loss on the labeled source data helps the ALOCC+GRL to better utilize multi-class structure of the dataset, making it the best performing method among the baselines. All of the above methods are simple extensions or ad-hoc combinations of the work available in the literature. Whereas, the proposed approach tackles the

Table 2. AUC performance of different methods on the Office31 [43] datasset.

Methods	A→D	A→W	W→A	W→D	D→A	D→W	Average
Softmax	0.719	0.835	0.655	0.862	0.606	0.842	0.737
ALOCC	0.776	0.725	0.608	0.983	0.570	0.884	0.758
GRL	0.766	0.730	0.624	**0.988**	0.572	0.890	0.762
ALOCC+GRL	0.783	0.759	0.640	0.987	0.576	0.898	0.774
Proposed	**0.877**	**0.863**	**0.824**	0.938	**0.807**	**0.940**	**0.877**

distribution shift issue along with novelty detection training in a single model. This helps the proposed approach perform better than the ad-hoc solutions, performing ~5% better than ALOCC+GRL.

Office31 : Amazon, Webcam, DSLR. Finally, we evaluate the proposed method on the Office31 benchmark [43]. The Office31 benchmark has a total 31 object categories and three different domains. Image samples for the dataset are acquired in three different domains, i.e. Amazon (A), Webcam (W) and DSLR (D). First 10 categories from all three domains are considered as known. Categories from $11, 12, ..., 30$ are considered as novel categories for all domains. For all the methods compared, AlexNet [21] is used as the base feature extractor. During training we freeze all the convolutional layers of AlexNet and only fine tune the fully-connected layers. For training the generator networks $\mathcal{G}_s$ and $\mathcal{G}_t$ we resize the images to 32×32 and the discriminator architectures are used accordingly (more details in supplementary material). Three domains of the dataset form in total 6 pairs of source→target combinations. For each source→target combination, we report AUROC performance.

The peformance of each method is reported in Table 2. Overall the trend of performance improvements are similar to the digits experiment. Among all the methods, softmax baseline achieves the lowest performance. ALOCC improves by ~2% over the softmax baseline, while GRL is able to improve ~1% over ALOCC. Utilizing gradient reversal along with ALOCC training further improves the performance by ~1%. The proposed approach on average performs better than the other approaches. Specifically, the proposed approach on average provides ~9% improvement over the next best baseline of ALOCC+GRL.

6   Conclusion

We considered the problem of novelty detection under dataset distribution shift and showed the challenges it poses with experiments. To the best of our knowledge, this is the first work to address such problem for novelty detection. We also discussed the differences between the proposed problem setting and some of the related problems like open-set domain adaptation. We also developed a few trivial baseline methods based on the related works available in the literature by combining the techniques from novelty detection and domain adaptation. Finally, we proposed an approach to tackle the distribution shift by learning a shared feature space that can generalize better in comparison with the baseline methods.

Acknowledgement. This work was supported by the NSF grant 1910141.

References

1. Amarbayasgalan, T., Jargalsaikhan, B., Ryu, K.H.: Unsupervised novelty detection using deep autoencoders with density based clustering. Appl. Sci. **8**(9), 1468 (2018)
2. Amodei, D., Olah, C., Steinhardt, J., Christiano, P., Schulman, J., Mané, D.: Concrete problems in ai safety. arXiv preprint arXiv:1606.06565 (2016)
3. Baweja, Y., Oza, P., Perera, P., Patel, V.M.: Anomaly detection-based unknown face presentation attack detection. In: International Joint Conference on Biometrics (IJCB), Houston, TX (2020)
4. Bhattacharjee, S., Mandal, D., Biswas, S.: Multi-class novelty detection using mixup technique. In: The IEEE Winter Conference on Applications of Computer Vision. pp. 1400–1409 (2020)
5. Cao, Z., Ma, L., Long, M., Wang, J.: Partial adversarial domain adaptation. In: Proceedings of the European Conference on Computer Vision (ECCV). pp. 135–150 (2018)
6. Carlini, N., Wagner, D.: Towards evaluating the robustness of neural networks. In: 2017 IEEE Symposium on Security and Privacy (SP). pp. 39–57. IEEE (2017)
7. Chen, C., et al.: Novelty detection via non-adversarial generative network. arXiv preprint arXiv:2002.00522 (2020)
8. Chen, X., Liu, C., Li, B., Lu, K., Song, D.: Targeted backdoor attacks on deep learning systems using data poisoning. arXiv preprint arXiv:1712.05526 (2017)
9. Chen, Y., Li, W., Sakaridis, C., Dai, D., Van Gool, L.: Domain adaptive faster r-cnn for object detection in the wild. In: Proceedings of the IEEE conference on computer vision and pattern recognition. pp. 3339–3348 (2018)
10. DeVries, T., Taylor, G.W.: Learning confidence for out-of-distribution detection in neural networks. arXiv preprint arXiv:1802.04865 (2018)
11. Ganin, Y., Lempitsky, V.: Unsupervised domain adaptation by backpropagation. arXiv preprint arXiv:1409.7495 (2014)
12. Goodfellow, I., et al.: Generative adversarial nets. In: Advances in Neural Information Processing Systems. pp. 2672–2680 (2014)
13. Hendrycks, D., Gimpel, K.: A baseline for detecting misclassified and out-of-distribution examples in neural networks. arXiv preprint arXiv:1610.02136 (2016)
14. Hoffman, J., et al.: Cycada: Cycle-consistent adversarial domain adaptation. arXiv preprint arXiv:1711.03213 (2017)
15. Hoffman, J., Wang, D., Yu, F., Darrell, T.: Fcns in the wild: Pixel-level adversarial and constraint-based adaptation. arXiv preprint arXiv:1612.02649 (2016)
16. Hsu, H.K., et al.: Progressive domain adaptation for object detection. In: Proceedings of the IEEE Conference on Computer Vision and Pattern Recognition Workshops. pp. 1–5 (2019)

17. Hu, L., Kan, M., Shan, S., Chen, X.: Duplex generative adversarial network for unsupervised domain adaptation. In: Proceedings of the IEEE Conference on Computer Vision and Pattern Recognition. pp. 1498–1507 (2018)
18. Hull, J.J.: A database for handwritten text recognition research. IEEE Trans. Pattern Anal. Mach. Intell. 16(5), 550–554 (1994)
19. Kim, T., Jeong, M., Kim, S., Choi, S., Kim, C.: Diversify and match: a domain adaptive representation learning paradigm for object detection. In: Proceedings of the IEEE Conference on Computer Vision and Pattern Recognition. pp. 12456–12465 (2019)
20. Kingma, D.P., Ba, J.: Adam: A method for stochastic optimization. arXiv preprint arXiv:1412.6980 (2015)
21. Krizhevsky, A., Sutskever, I., Hinton, G.E.: Imagenet classification with deep convolutional neural networks. In: Advances in Neural Information Processing Systems. pp. 1097–1105 (2012)
22. LeCun, Y., Bottou, L., Bengio, Y., Haffner, P., et al.: Gradient-based learning applied to document recognition. Proc. IEEE 86(11), 2278–2324 (1998)
23. LeCun, Y., Cortes, C., Burges, C.: MNIST handwritten digit database (2010)
24. Liang, S., Li, Y., Srikant, R.: Enhancing the reliability of out-of-distribution image detection in neural networks. arXiv preprint arXiv:1706.02690 (2017)
25. Liu, K., Dolan-Gavitt, B., Garg, S.: Fine-pruning: defending against backdooring attacks on deep neural networks. In: Bailey, M., Holz, T., Stamatogiannakis, M., Ioannidis, S. (eds.) RAID 2018. LNCS, vol. 11050, pp. 273–294. Springer, Cham (2018). https://doi.org/10.1007/978-3-030-00470-5_13
26. Liu, Y., Xie, Y., Srivastava, A.: Neural trojans. In: 2017 IEEE International Conference on Computer Design (ICCD). pp. 45–48. IEEE (2017)
27. Long, M., Zhu, H., Wang, J., Jordan, M.I.: Unsupervised domain adaptation with residual transfer networks. In: Advances in Neural Information Processing Systems. pp. 136–144 (2016)
28. Long, M., Zhu, H., Wang, J., Jordan, M.I.: Deep transfer learning with joint adaptation networks. In: Proceedings of the 34th International Conference on Machine Learning-Volume 70. pp. 2208–2217. JMLR. org (2017)
29. Makhzani, A., Shlens, J., Jaitly, N., Goodfellow, I., Frey, B.: Adversarial autoencoders. arXiv preprint arXiv:1511.05644 (2015)
30. Markou, M., Singh, S.: Novelty detection: a review–part 1: statistical approaches. Signal Process. 83(12), 2481–2497 (2003). 4
31. Murez, Z., Kolouri, S., Kriegman, D., Ramamoorthi, R., Kim, K.: Image to image translation for domain adaptation. In: Proceedings of the IEEE Conference on Computer Vision and Pattern Recognition. pp. 4500–4509 (2018)
32. Netzer, Y., Wang, T., Coates, A., Bissacco, A., Wu, B., Ng, A.Y.: Reading digits in natural images with unsupervised feature learning (2011)
33. Odena, A., Olah, C., Shlens, J.: Conditional image synthesis with auxiliary classifier gans. In: Proceedings of the 34th International Conference on Machine Learning. vol. 70. pp. 2642–2651. JMLR. org (2017)
34. Oza, P., Patel, V.M.: One-class convolutional neural network. IEEE Signal Process. Lett. 26(2), 277–281 (2018)
35. Oza, P., Patel, V.M.: Utilizing patch-level category activation patterns for multiple class novelty detection. In: European Conference on Computer Vision. Springer (2020)
36. Panareda Busto, P., Gall, J.: Open set domain adaptation. In: Proceedings of the IEEE International Conference on Computer Vision. pp. 754–763 (2017)

37. Perera, P., et al.: Generative-discriminative feature representations for open-set recognition. In: Proceedings of the IEEE/CVF Conference on Computer Vision and Pattern Recognition. pp. 11814–11823 (2020)
38. Perera, P., Nallapati, R., Xiang, B.: Ocgan: One-class novelty detection using gans with constrained latent representations. In: Proceedings of the IEEE Conference on Computer Vision and Pattern Recognition. pp. 2898–2906 (2019)
39. Perera, P., Patel, V.M.: Learning deep features for one-class classification. IEEE Trans. Image Process. **28**(11), 5450–5463 (2019)
40. Pidhorskyi, S., Almohsen, R., Doretto, G.: Generative probabilistic novelty detection with adversarial autoencoders. In: Advances in Neural Information Processing Systems. pp. 6822–6833 (2018)
41. Pinheiro, P.O.: Unsupervised domain adaptation with similarity learning. In: Proceedings of the IEEE Conference on Computer Vision and Pattern Recognition. pp. 8004–8013 (2018)
42. Sabokrou, M., Khalooei, M., Fathy, M., Adeli, E.: Adversarially learned one-class classifier for novelty detection. In: Proceedings of the IEEE Conference on Computer Vision and Pattern Recognition. pp. 3379–3388 (2018)
43. Saenko, K., Kulis, B., Fritz, M., Darrell, T.: Adapting visual category models to new domains. In: Daniilidis, K., Maragos, P., Paragios, N. (eds.) ECCV 2010. LNCS, vol. 6314, pp. 213–226. Springer, Heidelberg (2010). https://doi.org/10.1007/978-3-642-15561-1_16
44. Saito, K., Watanabe, K., Ushiku, Y., Harada, T.: Maximum classifier discrepancy for unsupervised domain adaptation. In: Proceedings of the IEEE Conference on Computer Vision and Pattern Recognition. pp. 3723–3732 (2018)
45. Sankaranarayanan, S., Balaji, Y., Castillo, C.D., Chellappa, R.: Generate to adapt: aligning domains using generative adversarial networks. In: Proceedings of the IEEE Conference on Computer Vision and Pattern Recognition. pp. 8503–8512 (2018)
46. Schölkopf, B., Smola, A.J., Bach, F., et al.: Learning with kernels: support vector machines, regularization, optimization, and beyond. MIT press, Cambridge (2002)
47. Shao, R., Perera, P., Yuen, P.C., Patel, V.M.: Open-set adversarial defense. In: European Conference on Computer Vision. (2020)
48. Shu, R., Bui, H.H., Narui, H., Ermon, S.: A dirt-t approach to unsupervised domain adaptation. arXiv preprint arXiv:1802.08735 (2018)
49. Sun, B., Saenko, K.: Deep CORAL: correlation alignment for deep domain adaptation. In: Hua, G., Jégou, H. (eds.) ECCV 2016. LNCS, vol. 9915, pp. 443–450. Springer, Cham (2016). https://doi.org/10.1007/978-3-319-49409-8_35
50. Tsai, Y.H., Hung, W.C., Schulter, S., Sohn, K., Yang, M.H., Chandraker, M.: Learning to adapt structured output space for semantic segmentation. In: Proceedings of the IEEE Conference on Computer Vision and Pattern Recognition. pp. 7472–7481 (2018)
51. Turk, M., Pentland, A.: Face recognition using eigenfaces. In: Proceedings 1991 IEEE Computer Society Conference on Computer Vision and Pattern Recognition. pp. 586–587 (1991)
52. Tzeng, E., Hoffman, J., Saenko, K., Darrell, T.: Adversarial discriminative domain adaptation. In: Proceedings of the IEEE Conference on Computer Vision and Pattern Recognition. pp. 7167–7176 (2017)
53. You, K., Long, M., Cao, Z., Wang, J., Jordan, M.I.: Universal domain adaptation. In: Proceedings of the IEEE Conference on Computer Vision and Pattern Recognition. pp. 2720–2729 (2019)

54. Zhang, H., Patel, V.M.: Sparse representation-based open set recognition. IEEE Trans. Pattern Anal. Mach. Intell. **39**(8), 1690–1696 (2016)
55. Zhang, Y., David, P., Foroosh, H., Gong, B.: A curriculum domain adaptation approach to the semantic segmentation of urban scenes. IEEE Trans. Pattern Anal. Mach. Intell. (2019)

Colorization of Depth Map via Disentanglement

Chung-Sheng Lai[1]([✉]), Zunzhi You[2], Ching-Chun Huang[1], Yi-Hsuan Tsai[3], and Wei-Chen Chiu[1]

[1] National Chiao Tung University, Taiwan, China
[2] Sun Yat-sen University, Guangzhou, China
[3] NEC Labs America, New Jersey, USA

Abstract. Vision perception is one of the most important components for a computer or robot to understand the surrounding scene and achieve autonomous applications. However, most of the vision models are based on the RGB sensors, which in general are vulnerable to the insufficient lighting condition. In contrast, the depth camera, another widely-used visual sensor, is capable of perceiving 3D information and being more robust to the lack of illumination, but unable to obtain appearance details of the surrounding environment compared to RGB cameras. To make RGB-based vision models workable for the low-lighting scenario, prior methods focus on learning the colorization on depth maps captured by depth cameras, such that the vision models can still achieve reasonable performance on colorized depth maps. However, the colorization produced in this manner is usually unrealistic and constrained to the specific vision model, thus being hard to generalize for other tasks to use. In this paper, we propose a depth map colorization method via disentangling appearance and structure factors, so that our model could 1) learn depth-invariant appearance features from an appearance reference and 2) generate colorized images by combining a given depth map and the appearance feature obtained from any reference. We conduct extensive experiments to show that our colorization results are more realistic and diverse in comparison to several image translation baselines.

Keywords: Depth colorization · Disentanglement · Image translation

1 Introduction

Recognizing the surrounding objects or the environment based on the visual sensory is one of the fundamental topics in computer vision. Most of the existing computer vision algorithms, including object recognition, simultaneous localization and mapping (SLAM) for robot navigation and position, or the ones used

Electronic supplementary material The online version of this chapter (https://doi.org/10.1007/978-3-030-58571-6_27) contains supplementary material, which is available to authorized users.

© Springer Nature Switzerland AG 2020
A. Vedaldi et al. (Eds.): ECCV 2020, LNCS 12352, pp. 450–466, 2020.
https://doi.org/10.1007/978-3-030-58571-6_27

Fig. 1. RGB and Depth cameras are two most popular visual sensors nowadays, while most of the typical computer vision models (e.g., object detection) are trained upon the data acquired by RGB cameras. However, if there is no sufficient illumination in the environment, the RGB camera usually cannot well capture image details, thus leading to inaccurate recognition. In comparison, the active sensing of depth cameras is able to function well under such low-lighting situation to produce depth maps. In this paper we aim to utilize this advantage of depth cameras and colorize the depth map, such that the vision models would still be able to perform their tasks.

in autonomous driving, are applied on the images or videos taken by RGB cameras. Under the condition of having sufficient lighting environment, appearance details of objects can be well captured in RGB images, in which the vision models are trained to perform recognition on such images. As the RGB image is formed by recording the scattered light coming from the illuminated surface of the surrounding environment into the camera, appearance details shown in the image would gradually diminish when the environmental illumination becomes lower, which leads to undesirable performance of recognition for vision models. The case of having insufficient lighting is actually quite common in our daily life, e.g., indoor navigation or surveillance in a dark room, autonomous driving in the evening, or cave exploration by a robot. How to maintain the ability of visual perception in such cases is an important topic for the research community.

Depth camera is another popular visual sensor for perceiving the depth information and it is nowadays equipped to various robots and autonomous vehicles, where the rough structure/shape of the surrounding objects is well preserved in the resultant depth maps. Depth camera can still function smoothly in the low-lighting environment via its active sensing, e.g., based on the (infrared) laser design. However, although depth camera is able to provide more robust sensory ability against different illumination conditions, it is incapable of capturing appearance details (e.g., color and texture) of the objects as the RGB cameras do. Thus, the complementary property of RGB and depth cameras has attracted wide research interests [14,21,23] to have them integrated together for achieving better performance in visual perception and recognition.

Nevertheless, the combination between RGB and depth cameras does not guarantee to fully resolve the challenge for recognizing objects in the low-lighting environment. Therefore, several works [1–3,5,19] propose to tackle this problem from another perspective via performing the colorization on depth maps, where the colorized images are used as input for computer vision models to perform their recognition tasks. We observe that these works are either based on the hand-crafted colorization approaches or aiming to find the specific colorization manner in order to boost the performance of a certain computer vision model, and thus the colorized results are usually unrealistic and hard to be used for different tasks. In this paper, we instead propose to focus on the problem of learning depth map colorization without being constrained on any specific applications and target for generating realistic colorization results. In particular, the resultant colorization produced by our model is expected to paint the given depth map with (photo-)realistic textures and still maintain the overall structure/shape of the objects, such that the RGB-based vision models can be easily adapted to the colorized depth maps with less efforts.

We tackle the depth map colorization problem based on a hypothesis: an RGB image is composed of the structure factor and the appearance factor, where the former can be well captured by the corresponding depth map. This hypothesis of the disentanglement for RGB images is realized by our proposed model, which has three main components: structure sub-network, appearance sub-network, and a mixing sub-network (see Fig. 2). Given a depth map that we would like to colorize and a reference RGB-Depth image-pair as the source of appearance, the mixing sub-network takes 1) the structure factor extracted by the structure sub-network from the given depth map and 2) the appearance factor extracted by the appearance sub-network from the reference image-pair, as the input and then outputs the colorized depth map.

Based on our proposed model, a depth map can be colorized into different appearances by utilizing various reference RGB-Depth image-pairs. Each of our designed model is learned to obtain its function, i.e, extraction of structure/appearance factors for structure/appearance sub-networks and image generation for mixing sub-network. In addition, we apply several designs to improve our training procedure, such as the random flipping of reference image-pair and the time-invariant property of a video sequence. Experiments are conducted on the NYU-Depth v2 [20] and the SceneNet RGB-D [17] datasets. We provide the quantitative and qualitative evaluation on both the quality and diversity of the colorized depth maps, and demonstrate the efficacy of our method on maintaining performance for RGB-based computer vision models, in comparison to several baselines.

2   Related Work

Depth Colorization. Previous works [1–3,5,19] on depth colorization mainly focus on how to transfer the depth maps into the format compatible with RGB images, such that the computer vision models which are primitively learned or designed for other data domains (e.g., RGB images) can still be adopted. For instance, Eitel *et al.* [3] propose a hand-crafted way to map the normalized depth values into RGB color channels (i.e., from highest depth values to lowest ones, they are gradually mapped into red, green, and blue colors). In [1], since a depth map contains rich 3D information, they instead propose to convert a depth image into a map of 3D surface normal, where the magnitude along each axis of a normal vector is encoded into RGB color channels respectively. Although the colorization obtained by these two methods do have the RGB colors, they are dissimilar to the typical images taken by regular RGB cameras, which may not be utilizable by typical RGB-based computer vision models. More recently, the work of [2] tackles the depth map colorization problem from the perspective of transfer learning, where a deep network is learned to find the optimal transformation from depth into RGB images, with respect to a given pre-trained Conv-Net. Since the given Conv-Net is pre-trained for a specific task, the learned transform and the resultant colorized depth maps are actually not realistic and thus less generalizable for direct usage by other models. Our goal in this paper is distinct from aforementioned approaches since we aim to generate the (photo-)realistic colorization on depth maps and our model is not designed specifically for any particular pre-trained models. There are also other approaches in performing colorization on the gray-scale images [7,11]. However, their input gray-scale images are the monochrome photos which already have quite some appearance details. Hence these gray-scale photos are fundamentally different from our target depth maps in this paper, which only represent the rough structure/shape of objects in the surrounding environment.

Image-to-Image Translation. Another way to tackle the depth map colorization problem is to treat it as a special case of image-to-image translation task, where we take RGB images and depth maps as two data domains, and learn the translation between them. Image-to-image translation methods have been developed widely. For instance, Isola *et al.* [8] leverage the conditional generative adversarial network (GAN) [4] for learning the translation from one domain to another (with taking one domain as condition), where their method needs the paired data across domains for training. Zhu *et al.* [24] utilize the cycle consistency for learning the translation networks between two image domains, without requiring paired data. However, those methods are only able to produce one-to-one translation, i.e., the mapping between domains is deterministic, and thus the translated outputs lack diversity. Instead, the work of [25] extends the image-to-image translation from one-to-one mapping into one-to-many. With taking the data from one domain as condition, their method learns to model a distribution of plausible translated outputs for another domain based on the conditional generative modeling. However, as which will be shown later in our experiments, applying such models in the task of depth map colorization could suffer from the issue of mode collapse. Moreover, the resultant images may not be sufficiently realistic nor maintain the structure as in the input depth map. In comparison, our method is based on learning the disentanglement of RGB images and can generate realistic colorization with high image quality and diversity.

3   Proposed Method for Depth Map Colorization

As motivated in the introduction, the objective of our proposed method is to colorize a given depth map D by taking the appearance information from

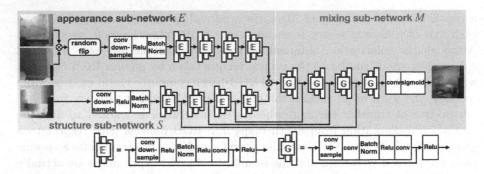

Fig. 2. Overview of the proposed model, which is composed of three main components: structure sub-network, appearance sub-network, and a mixing sub-network (shaded in green, blue, and red background respectively). (Color figure online)

a reference of RGB-Depth image-pair $\{I^R, D^R\}$. The architecture of the proposed model is illustrated in Fig. 2, consisting of three sub-networks: structure sub-network S, appearance sub-network E, and mixing sub-network M. In the following, we will describe how we achieve the depth map colorization in details.

3.1 Disentanglement via Self-supervised Learning

The main assumption behind our model design is that: an RGB image I can be disentangled into the structure and appearance components, where they should be independent from each other. In particular, we hypothesize that the structure information has been fully maintained in the corresponding depth map D. Thus, the structure sub-network S is designed to extract the structure factor $v_S = S(D)$ from the input depth map D. In addition, while following the assumption above, the appearance information of an RGB image should be obtainable by subtracting the structure information from it. Hence, the appearance sub-network E takes an RGB-Depth image-pair $\{I^R, D^R\}$ as input, and then learns to extract the structure-invariant appearance factor $v_E = E(I^R, D^R)$ from I^R. Upon having both v_S and v_E, the mixing sub-network M combines them and produces the colorization result, which ideally should be a (photo-)realistic RGB image with its structure and appearance similar/related to D and I^R respectively.

Self-Supervised Learning. Our task is to colorize a given depth map D by using the appearance reference from any arbitrary RGB-Depth image-pair $\{I^R, D^R\}$. Since D and $\{I^R, D^R\}$ are unnecessary a pair that belongs to the same scene, there is no dataset under such setting that we can directly use to supervise our models. Moreover, it is impossible to collect a dataset with proper ground truths, i.e., finding multiple real-world images related to the same depth map having different appearance and the corresponding appearance references.

To address the problem of having no proper dataset, we propose a *self-supervised learning* scheme. Basically, we use the RGB-Depth image-pair

$\{I^R, D^R\}$ and its depth map D^R as the input for the appearance sub-network E and structure sub-network S respectively. Then the resultant colorization produced by the mixing sub-network M should be able to well reconstruct an RGB image $\hat{I}^R = M(E(I^R, D^R), S(D^R))$. Nevertheless, directly using the objective defined on such reconstruction for training our model could be problematic.

The main reason is as follows. The primary motivation behind our model design is to make the appearance sub-network extract only the structure-invariant appearance information from the reference RGB-Depth image-pair, i.e., to achieve the disentanglement between the structure factor v_S and the appearance factor v_E, such that we are able to flexibly colorize a depth map D with any arbitrary appearance reference for producing diverse colorization results with the well-maintained structure of D. However, regarding our self-supervised learning scheme, since the input D^R for the structure sub-network S is used again in the input pair $\{I^R, D^R\}$ for the appearance sub-network E, the mixing sub-network M could have a trivial solution via learning to ignore $S(D^R)$, as M already receives all the information from E to reconstruct $\hat{I}^R$ to be similar to I^R. In other words, there is no guarantee to achieve the disentanglement between $v_S = S(D^R)$ and $v_E = E(I^R, D^R)$ solely via using the aforementioned reconstruction.

Random Flipping. In order to resolve such issue and still keep the benefit of self-supervised learning, we introduce a *random flipping* step to randomly flip the reference RGB-Depth pair $\{I^R, D^R\}$ before passing it to the appearance sub-network. Such random flipping operation F helps to alleviate the dependency between the inputs for both appearance and structure sub-networks, i.e., $\{F(I^R), F(D^R)\}$ and D^R respectively (note that I^R and D^R are under the same flipping). Therefore, the mixing sub-network is encouraged to jointly consider $v_S = S(D^R)$ and $v'_E = E(F(I^R), F(D^R))$ for achieving the reconstruction of I^R. In particular, the appearance factor v'_E extracted by E is enhanced to be structure invariant, and our colorization model is encouraged to acquire the structural information mainly from the structure sub-network S, as the input D^R for S and the colorization output $\hat{I}^R = M(v'_E, v_S)$ should be consistent in structure even when the reference RGB-Depth pair $\{I^R, D^R\}$ is flipped. We define an objective to calculate the L1, L2, and the perceptual errors [9]:

$$\mathcal{L}_r = \left\| I, \hat{I} \right\|_1 + \left\| I, \hat{I} \right\|_2 + \sum_l \left\| \phi_l(I), \phi_l(\hat{I}) \right\|_2, \tag{1}$$

where I and $\hat{I}$ are input and reconstructed images respectively, and ϕ_l denotes the feature representation obtained from the l-th layer of an ImageNet-pretrained VGG network using `relu1_1`, `relu2_1`, `relu3_1`, and `relu4_1` layers. The objective based on our self-supervised scheme and the random flipping step considers (1) in reconstruction:

$$\mathcal{L}_{rec} = \mathcal{L}_r(I^R, M(v'_E, v_S)). \tag{2}$$

As shown in Fig. 2, both appearance sub-network E and structure sub-network S share the similar network architecture. The only difference is that

S has the skip-connections to the mixing sub-network M over multiple convolution layers, serving a purpose to help the mixing sub-network preserve the structure details of the input depth map D^R.

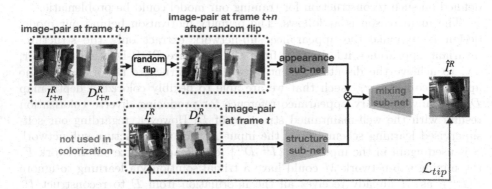

Fig. 3. Illustration of using Time Invariant Property (TIP) to provide additional supervised signals for our model training.

Time Invariant Property (TIP). To further improve the self-supervised signal to deal with the lack of ground truths to train our colorization network, we propose another design to facilitate the model training, named as *Time Invariant Property (TIP)*. The basic idea is to leverage the characteristics of the RGB-D video: We assume that the consecutive frames in an RGB-D video sequence share similar or even the identical appearances, but only have difference in the structure which is related to their depth maps. For instance, the RGB-D video sequences used for our experiments are taken in indoor scene by a moving camera, where the textures/appearances between consecutive frames are similar to each other.

This assumption then provides additional supervision to train the colorization model. One training scheme is illustrated in Fig. 3. Given an RGB-D video sequence, we use the depth map at time stamp t as the input to the structure sub-network S, and its neighboring RGB-Depth image-pair at time stamp $t + n$ as the appearance reference, to perform the colorization. Since the appearance features among neighboring frames are similar, we treat the RGB image at time stamp t as the ground truth of colorization for network training. However, there could exist a potential concern where the depth map structure of the appearance reference could be similar to the target depth map, which may break the disentanglement assumption. Fortunately, the proposed random flipping operation can well decorrelate these two depth maps and ensure our time invariant property. The reconstruction loss with TIP is similar to (2):

$$\mathcal{L}_{tip} = \mathcal{L}_r(I_t^R, M(v'_{E,t+n}, v_{S,t})), \tag{3}$$

where $v'_{E,t+n}$ denotes the extracted appearance factor from the reference pair I^R_{t+n}, D^R_{t+n} at time stamp t+n, $v_{S,t}$ denotes the extracted structure factor for the input depth map D^R_t at time stamp t, and I^R_t denotes the image at time stamp t.

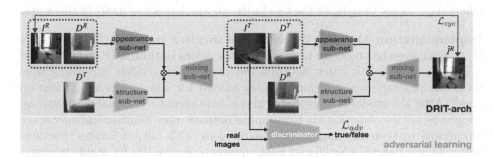

Fig. 4. Illustration of the DRIT-arch and adversarial learning used for improving our model training (cf. Sect. 3.2).

3.2 Adversarial Learning and Cycle Consistency

To further improve the robustness of our proposed model (denoted as "Full Model" in the following sections), we introduce two additional training techniques, as shown in Fig. 4. First, we utilize the adversarial learning approach [4] via utilizing a discriminator on the colorization output to make the results more realistic. Second, as inspired by a recent work (i.e., DRIT [12,13]) on learning disentanglement for improving image-to-image translation, we apply a similar idea (denoted as *DRIT-arch*) to enforce cycle consistency and stabilize our network training. To better explain the overall procedure of DRIT-arch as illustrated in Fig. 4, we denote the reference RGB-Depth image-pair as $\{I^R, D^R\}$, and name the input depth map for colorization as D^T. Note that D^T is unrelated to the reference $\{I^R, D^R\}$. Then our network first produces the colorized output $I^T = M(E(I^R, D^R), S(D^T))$, which should have the appearance factor from $\{I^R, D^R\}$ and a similar structure to D^T. Then, we pair I^T and D^T as a new source of appearance reference and use it to colorize D^R, where the resultant colorization should well reconstruct I^R:

$$\mathcal{L}_{cyc} = \mathcal{L}_r(I^R, M(E(I^T, D^T), S(D^R))). \tag{4}$$

This cycle consistency provides us another supervision to train the network. It is worth mentioning that the cycle consistency can be applied without relying on the TIP assumption. Since there is no ground truth for I^T, we adopt an adversarial loss $\mathcal{L}_{adv}$ [16] to make the colorized output similar to real images.

Overall Objective. The overall objective for our model training involves the above-mentioned self-supervised loss via random flipping and time invariant property in (3), the cycle-consistency loss in (4), and the adversarial loss $\mathcal{L}_{adv}$:

$$\mathcal{L}_{all} = \mathcal{L}_{tip} + \mathcal{L}_{cyc} + \lambda_{adv}\mathcal{L}_{adv}, \tag{5}$$

where λ_{adv} serves to balance the loss function, which is set as 0.001 in this work.

Implementation Details. We follow the standard training scheme of GAN [4] to optimize the objective in (5), using the Adam optimizer [10] with a fixed learning rate of 0.001. First, we train our model from scratch only using time invariant property with random flipping via (3) for 100 epochs as a warm-up stage. After the model is more stable and able to produce reasonable results, we adopt the full loss function via (5) to make outputs more realistic and encourage our model to keep the appearance factor along with output images. Furthermore, we use PatchGANs [8] and least-squares objective [16] for stable training. More details are provided in the supplementary material about the network architecture and training procedure. Our project page is at https://github.com/alanlai199/ColorizeDepthNet.

4 Experimental Results

Dataset. We adopt two datasets in our experiments: NYU Depth v2 [20] and SceneNet RGB-D [17]. The NYU Depth v2 dataset is composed of a collection of RGB-D video sequences and is originally proposed for learning indoor scene segmentation task. Here we use all the 284 raw video clips in the training set as we would like to leverage the time invariant property within the video sequences, while all the 654 RGB-D images in its test set (originally for evaluating segmentation) are used for testing. The SceneNet RGB-D dataset has a large scale collection of synthetic RGB-D videos, which are with photo-realistic quality in rendering. Here we randomly select 50,728 short video clips and 493 RGB-D images of different room-layouts from its training and test sets for our model learning and testing respectively.

4.1 Evaluation Metrics and Baselines for Comparison

There are two different quantitative evaluation schemes for the colorization results in our experiments. For the first evaluation scheme, we aim to quantify the performance of reconstruction, i.e., colorization on a depth map by using its corresponding ground truth RGB image. Here we adopt the well-know PSNR (peak signal-to-noise ratio, higher the better) metric for the assessment on the reconstructed image with respect to the ground truth RGB image.

For the second scheme, we target to evaluate the image quality and the diversity of the colorized depth maps. Here we adopt Fréchet Inception distance (FID [6], lower the better), which is commonly used in GAN-related works, as our metric. FID basically compares the similarity between two sets of data based on the distance between their distributions in the space of Inception feature representation [22]. Regarding both NYU Depth v2 and SceneNet RGB-D datasets, we choose 5 distinct RGB-Depth image-pairs from each of their test sets as our appearance references, and perform colorization on all the testing depth maps of each dataset. The colorization outputs are then compared with the real RGB images in the testing set, by using FID scores.

Three models of image-to-image translation are used as our baselines for comparison, including CycleGAN [24], Pix2Pix [8], and BicycleGAN [25]. We take RGB images and depth maps as two different data domains for training the baselines. Both CycleGAN and Pix2Pix can only produce one-to-one mapping, which means they can only generate one RGB output image for each input depth map. BicycleGAN acts more similar to our model; ideally it is able to colorize a given depth map into various appearances, where the appearance feature could be extracted from a reference RGB image, which is then combined with a given depth map as the input to achieve colorization. Note that, the generators in all baseline models have similar architecture as the one for BicycleGAN, in which the capacity of the generator is larger than our proposed model, i.e., 4×10^7 v.s. 1.5×10^7 (ours) in terms of the number of parameters.

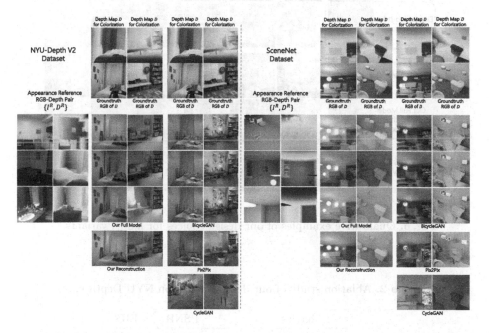

Fig. 5. Qualitative results of our framework and image-to-image translation baselines.

Table 1. Quantitative evaluation on the NYU Depth v2 and SceneNet RGB-D datasets, in terms of PSNR for reconstruction and FID [6] for both quality/diversity of the colorization results, with comparison to the image-to-image translation baselines.

Dataset	NYU Depth v2		SceneNet RGB-D	
Metrics	PSNR	FID	PSNR	FID
Cycle GAN	8.9948	245.2066	9.7859	187.3561
Pix2Pix	10.9974	142.2589	11.8593	152.3537
BicycleGAN	10.7301	145.3382	15.5830	192.1874
Our Full Model	**12.1115**	**45.1402**	**22.3333**	**92.7267**

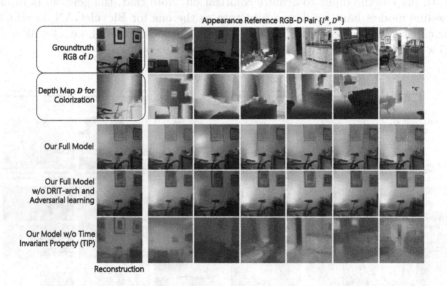

Fig. 6. Qualitative examples of our design choices for model variants.

Table 2. Ablation study of our design choices on NYU Depth v2.

Metrics	PSNR	FID
Our Full Model	12.1115	**45.1402**
w/o Random Flipping	13.8649	58.9894
w/o Time Invariant Property	**16.1137**	138.9675
w/o DRIT-arch & Discriminator	12.7394	55.9795

4.2   Quantitative and Qualitative Results

In Fig. 5 and Table 1, we show the quantitative and qualitative evaluations respectively for our proposed model and the image-to-image translation baselines. For both evaluation schemes described previously, we observe that our full model performs favorably on colorization in comparison to baselines, where the resultant images have clearer edges, realistic appearance, and larger variety/diversity. In particular, our colorization results demonstrate the flexibility of our proposed method for adding different appearances into the same depth map via learning disentanglement, while the BicycleGAN baseline suffers from the mode collapse problem (i.e., produces the same colorization result no matter which appearance reference is given). As both the Pix2Pix and CycleGAN can only produce one-to-one mapping, it is not surprising to see lower diversity. In addition, we often observe noisy patterns in the baseline results, in which it verifies the difficulty of such depth colorization task for image-to-image translation models. Based on our reconstruction results, it is also worth noting that the appearance features extracted from the appearance reference are actually high-level and invariant to the structure, e.g., the objects on the same position in both ground truth RGB image and our reconstruction may not have the identical appearance.

4.3   Ablation Study

We perform an ablation study to investigate the contributions of our design choices in the proposed model on NYU Depth v2. The quantitative and qualitative evaluations of different variants are provided in the Fig. 6 and Table 2. Having all the designs in the full model achieves the best performance in terms of FID, showing that the results are the most realistic and diverse ones compared to other model variants. Also, both the random flipping operation and time invariant property (TIP) contribute to model learning, thus helping to produce more realistic colorization. Especially, the TIP plays an important role to largely improve the diversity as indicated by the FID scores. Regarding the DRIT-arch and adversarial learning with discriminator, they together benefit the training of disentanglement and improve the image quality of colorization. It is also worth noting that, although the model variant without TIP can achieve the best performance in PSNR, it can only perform well in the case of reconstruction (i.e., colorization on a depth map by having its corresponding ground truth RGB image as the appearance reference) but fail to nicely paint the depth map with other appearance sources, which leads to much worse FID scores and colorization results with artifacts as clearly shown in Fig. 6 (some structure information from the appearance reference stains the colorization in the bottom row).

4.4   Recognition and Temporal Consistency

As motivated in this paper, we would like to colorize the depth maps such that the vision models originally trained on RGB images can still function reasonably

Table 3. Comparisons between different methods in terms of consistency in average precision for object detection on NYU Depth v2 (top) and SceneNet (bottom) test sets. Here, we randomly select 5 appearance reference image-pairs and exclude them from the testing set for the "Reconstruction" setting, while using depth maps and corresponding reference image-pairs for the "Our Full Model" setting.

	chair	sofa	bed	tv	table	person	sink	fridge	toilet	oven
Ill-Lighted	3.5	9.5	19.4	15.3	12.6	26.8	28.4	31.3	33.2	12.6
CycleGAN	8.4	1.7	0.2	0.1	4.9	0.6	0.0	0.0	0.0	0.0
Pix2Pix	38.0	46.6	52.0	10.9	37.8	35.9	39.7	55.7	76.0	5.5
BicycleGAN	46.2	31.4	45.4	7.3	35.9	31.7	20.3	38.1	20.9	2.5
Reconstruction	**71.0**	**76.3**	82.5	**39.7**	**77.7**	**69.0**	59.7	**77.9**	88.1	**46.2**
Our Full Model	69.9	71.4	**85.0**	36.1	75.1	59.6	**61.7**	66.4	**90.0**	35.7

	chair	toilet	bench	bowl	pottedplant
Ill-Lighted	18.7	25.0	25.0	0.0	0.0
CycleGAN	33.0	15.9	8.3	3.6	0.0
Pix2Pix	0.0	0.0	4.9	12.8	6.1
BicycleGAN	23.4	21.5	25.0	6.3	0.0
Reconstruction	**70.3**	**75.4**	32.1	**68.8**	**66.7**
Our Full Model	65.1	67.0	**68.8**	62.5	44.4

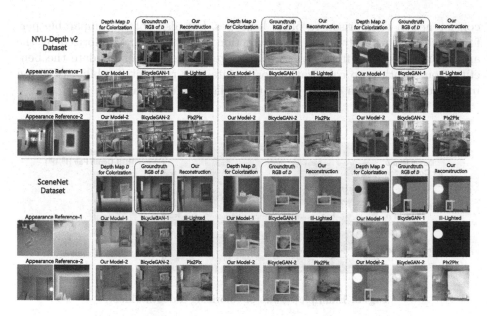

Fig. 7. Examples for recognition consistency. Our reconstruction and colorization show higher detection consistency with respect to the original image than the other methods.

on the colorization results even when the illumination is insufficient. Therefore, given a depth map D and its corresponding RGB image I taken under sufficient lighting, we expect that the vision model would have similar/consistent recognition outputs across I and the colorization of D produced by our proposed method. In order to verify if such consistency exists, we adopt an off-the-shelf object detector, YOLOv3 [18] pre-trained on the COCO dataset [15], to perform the object detection on both ground truth RGB images and the colorization results, and then evaluate the consistency between their detection results.

The metric of consistency is defined upon the average precision of object detection on colorization results by considering the detection results on the original RGB images as the ground truths bounding boxes (IoU $\geq$ 0.5). Note that we do not perform any fine-tuning on the detector towards colorization. As COCO dataset has 80 object categories where most of them do not appear in NYU-Depth-v2, we manually select 10 object classes which frequently appear in NYU-Depth-v2 as our targets for verification. Similarly, for SceneNet, 5 object classes are chosen. In addition to having the comparison with the aforementioned image-translation methods in terms of consistency, we introduce another baseline which applies gamma-correction on the original RGB images for simulating the photos taken under ill-lighting situation (gamma equals to 10 in our experiments).

The quantitative and qualitative results are shown in Fig. 7 and Table 3, respectively. The colorization results produced by our full model (using the appearance reference distinct from the original image) not only have higher consistency in comparison to other baselines, but also obtain comparable performance with respect to the reconstruction (i.e., depth map colorized by the appearance reference from its original image). These results validate the benefit of our depth map colorization for maintaining recognition ability of vision models up to a certain degree under the ill-lighting environment.

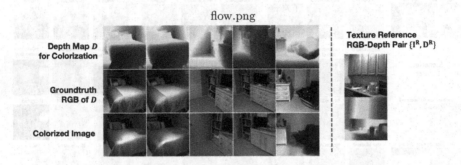

Fig. 8. Example results of colorizing a depth video.

Moreover, we experiment on colorizing a video sequence of depth maps, based on a fixed RGB-Depth image-pair as the appearance reference, in order to testify the temporal consistency of our colorization results, i.e., the same object should be colorized similarly across video frames. As shown in the qualitative results of Fig. 8, our model is able to produce temporally smooth colorization, and we are able to well recognize the objects despite their different appearances compared to original RGB images.

5   Conclusions

We present a method for colorizing the depth map via disentanglement of image appearance and structure. A practical application is to provide an alternative, clear, and colorful view of the ill-lighting scene. Unlike previous works which usually produce unrealistic images, our model focuses on generating realistic colorization with the flexibility of using any reference image as the source of appearance information. Several self-supervised designs are adopted to realize our model training, such as random flipping, time invariant property (TIP), adversarial learning, and cycle consistency. The ablation study demonstrates the contributions of each design to encourage the image disentanglement that benefits colorization. Results on both the recognition and temporal consistencies further verifies the applicability of our proposed colorization model.

Acknowledgment. This project is supported by MOST109-2636-E-009-018, MOST-109-2634-F-009-020, and MOST-109-2634-F-009-015. Thanks to the National Center for High Performance Computing for computation facilities.

References

1. Bo, L., Ren, X., Fox, D.: Unsupervised feature learning for rgb-d based object recognition. In: Desai, J., Dudek G., Khatib, O., Kumar, V. (eds). Experimental Robotics. Springer Tracts in Advanced Robotics, vol 88. Springer, Heidelberg (2013) https://doi.org/10.1007/978-3-319-00065-7_27

2. Carlucci, F.M., Russo, P., Caputo, B.: $(DE)^2CO$: Deep depth colorization. IEEE Robot. Autom. Lett. **3**(3), 2386–2393 (2018)

3. Eitel, A., Springenberg, J.T., Spinello, L., Riedmiller, M., Burgard, W.: Multimodal deep learning for robust rgb-d object recognition. In: 2015 IEEE/RSJ International Conference on Intelligent Robots and Systems (IROS). pp. 681–687. IEEE (2015)

4. Goodfellow, I., et al.: Generative adversarial nets. In: Advances in Neural Information Processing Systems. pp. 2672–2680 (2014)

5. Gupta, S., Girshick, R., Arbeláez, P., Malik, J.: Learning rich features from rgb-d images for object detection and segmentation. In: Fleet, D., Pajdla, T., Schiele, B., Tuytelaars, T. (eds.) ECCV 2014. LNCS, vol. 8695, pp. 345–360. Springer, Cham (2014). https://doi.org/10.1007/978-3-319-10584-0_23

6. Heusel, M., Ramsauer, H., Unterthiner, T., Nessler, B., Hochreiter, S.: Gans trained by a two time-scale update rule converge to a local nash equilibrium. In: Advances in Neural Information Processing Systems. pp. 6626–6637 (2017)

7. Iizuka, S., Simo-Serra, E., Ishikawa, H.: Let there be color! joint end-to-end learning of global and local image priors for automatic image colorization with simultaneous classification. ACM Trans. Graph. (ToG) **35**(4), 1–11 (2016)

8. Isola, P., Zhu, J.Y., Zhou, T., Efros, A.A.: Image-to-image translation with conditional adversarial networks. In: Proceedings of the IEEE Conference on Computer Vision and Pattern Recognition. pp. 1125–1134 (2017)

9. Johnson, J., Alahi, A., Fei-Fei, L.: Perceptual losses for real-time style transfer and super-resolution. In: Leibe, B., Matas, J., Sebe, N., Welling, M. (eds.) ECCV 2016. LNCS, vol. 9906, pp. 694–711. Springer, Cham (2016). https://doi.org/10.1007/978-3-319-46475-6_43

10. Kingma, D.P., Ba, J.: Adam: A method for stochastic optimization. arXiv preprint arXiv:1412.6980 (2014)

11. Larsson, G., Maire, M., Shakhnarovich, G.: Learning representations for automatic colorization. In: Leibe, B., Matas, J., Sebe, N., Welling, M. (eds.) ECCV 2016. LNCS, vol. 9908, pp. 577–593. Springer, Cham (2016). https://doi.org/10.1007/978-3-319-46493-0_35

12. Lee, H.Y., Tseng, H.Y., Huang, J.B., Singh, M., Yang, M.H.: Diverse image-to-image translation via disentangled representations. In: Proceedings of the European Conference on Computer Vision (ECCV). pp. 35–51 (2018)

13. Lee, H.Y., et al.: DRIT++: Diverse image-to-image translation via disentangled representations. Int. J. Comput. Vis. **128**(10), 2402–2417 (2020). https://doi.org/10.1007/s11263-019-01284-z

14. Li, Y., Zhang, J., Cheng, Y., Huang, K., Tan, T.: Df^{2}net: Discriminative feature learning and fusion network for rgb-d indoor scene classification. In: Thirty-Second AAAI Conference on Artificial Intelligence (2018)

15. Lin, T.Y., et al.: Microsoft COCO: common objects in context. In: Fleet, D., Pajdla, T., Schiele, B., Tuytelaars, T. (eds.) ECCV 2014. LNCS, vol. 8693, pp. 740–755. Springer, Cham (2014). https://doi.org/10.1007/978-3-319-10602-1_48

16. Mao, X., Li, Q., Xie, H., Lau, R.Y., Wang, Z., Paul Smolley, S.: Least squares generative adversarial networks. In: Proceedings of the IEEE International Conference on Computer Vision. pp. 2794–2802 (2017)

17. McCormac, J., Handa, A., Leutenegger, S., Davison, A.J.: Scenenet rgb-d: Can 5m synthetic images beat generic imagenet pre-training on indoor segmentation? In: Proceedings of the IEEE International Conference on Computer Vision. pp. 2678–2687 (2017)
18. Redmon, J., Farhadi, A.: Yolov3: An incremental improvement. arXiv preprint arXiv:1804.02767 (2018)
19. Schwarz, M., Schulz, H., Behnke, S.: Rgb-d object recognition and pose estimation based on pre-trained convolutional neural network features. In: 2015 IEEE International Conference on Robotics and Automation (ICRA). pp. 1329–1335. IEEE (2015)
20. Silberman, N., Hoiem, D., Kohli, P., Fergus, R.: Indoor segmentation and support inference from rgbd images. In: Fitzgibbon, A., Lazebnik, S., Perona, P., Sato, Y., Schmid, C. (eds.) ECCV 2012. LNCS, vol. 7576, pp. 746–760. Springer, Heidelberg (2012). https://doi.org/10.1007/978-3-642-33715-4_54
21. Song, S., Lichtenberg, S.P., Xiao, J.: Sun rgb-d: A rgb-d scene understanding benchmark suite. In: Proceedings of the IEEE Conference on Computer Vision and Pattern Recognition. pp. 567–576 (2015)
22. Szegedy, C., et al.: Going deeper with convolutions. In: Proceedings of the IEEE Conference on Computer Vision and Pattern Recognition. pp. 1–9 (2015)
23. Yuan, Y., Xiong, Z., Wang, Q.: Acm: Adaptive cross-modal graph convolutional neural networks for rgb-d scene recognition. Proc. AAAI Conf. Artifi. Intell. **33**, 9176–9184 (2019)
24. Zhu, J.Y., Park, T., Isola, P., Efros, A.A.: Unpaired image-to-image translation using cycle-consistent adversarial networks. In: Proceedings of the IEEE International Conference on Computer Vision. pp. 2223–2232 (2017)
25. Zhu, J.Y., et al.: Toward multimodal image-to-image translation. In: Advances in Neural Information Processing Systems. pp. 465–476 (2017)

Beyond Controlled Environments: 3D Camera Re-localization in Changing Indoor Scenes

Johanna Wald[1](✉), Torsten Sattler[2,3], Stuart Golodetz[4], Tommaso Cavallari[4], and Federico Tombari[1,5]

[1] Technical University of Munich, Munich, Germany
johanna.wald@tum.de
[2] Chalmers University of Technology, Gothenburg, Sweden
[3] CIIRC, Czech Technical University in Prague, Prague, Czechia
[4] Five AI Ltd., Cambridge, England
[5] Google Inc., Mountain View, USA

Abstract. Long-term camera re-localization is an important task with numerous computer vision and robotics applications. Whilst various outdoor benchmarks exist that target lighting, weather and seasonal changes, far less attention has been paid to appearance changes that occur indoors. This has led to a mismatch between popular indoor benchmarks, which focus on static scenes, and indoor environments that are of interest for many real-world applications. In this paper, we adapt *3RScan* – a recently introduced indoor RGB-D dataset designed for object instance re-localization – to create *RIO10*, a new long-term camera re-localization benchmark focused on indoor scenes. We propose new metrics for evaluating camera re-localization and explore how state-of-the-art camera re-localizers perform according to these metrics. We also examine in detail how different types of scene change affect the performance of different methods, based on novel ways of detecting such changes in a given RGB-D frame. Our results clearly show that long-term indoor re-localization is an unsolved problem. Our benchmark and tools are publicly available at https://www.waldjohannau.github.io/RIO10.

1 Introduction

Visual re-localization is the problem of estimating the precise position and orientation from which a given image was taken with respect to a known scene. It is a key component of advanced computer vision applications such as AR/VR [8,22,41,61,69,72,95], and robotics systems such as self-driving cars [19] and drones [59]. Real-world scenes are highly dynamic, exhibiting changes in illumination, appearance and/or geometry. These changes are caused by a variety of factors, including the time of day, the presence of artificial light sources

Electronic supplementary material The online version of this chapter (https://doi.org/10.1007/978-3-030-58571-6_28) contains supplementary material, which is available to authorized users.

© Springer Nature Switzerland AG 2020
A. Vedaldi et al. (Eds.): ECCV 2020, LNCS 12352, pp. 467–487, 2020.
https://doi.org/10.1007/978-3-030-58571-6_28

Train Setup: RGB-D scan at time T_0 Test Setup: RGB-D scans at different points in time

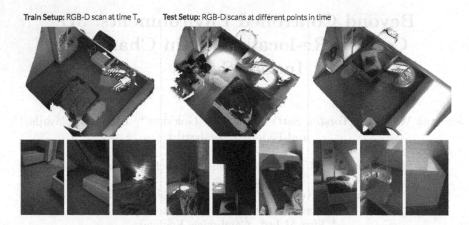

Fig. 1. Visual re-localization in changing indoor scenes: we introduce a new benchmark based on *3RScan* [97], together with a new evaluation methodology, for measuring 6DoF re-localization performance given a reference RGB(-D) sequence of an indoor scene at time T_0 (left), and query sequences taken at different points in time (center and right).

and, most prominently, humans interacting with their environments, *e.g.* by redecorating a room, or using furniture and objects in day-to-day life. Like human perception, visual re-localization algorithms should be as robust as possible to such changes to enable long-term operation in the real world. However, the datasets traditionally used for evaluating visual re-localization performance [27,45,49,57,58,80,83,93] either do not contain such changes [49,83,93] or do not provide a means of quantifying their impact [27,45,57,58,80,86]. Only recently released datasets such as Aachen Day-Nigh [79,80], (extended) CMU Seasons [7,79], RobotCar Seasons [62,79], and SILDa [9] explicitly model such changes. By providing a reference representation and test images taken under different conditions, the corresponding works point out failure cases of existing re-localization algorithms, in turn motivating the community to devise more robust methods [2,11,34,37,50,70,75,88,89]. However, these datasets mostly focus on outdoor scenes, where most changes are cyclic (*e.g.* day-night, seasonal and weather changes) and can thus easily be predicted by neural networks [2,70].

As shown in Fig. 1, indoor scenes are arguably more diverse, and exhibit changes – including complex illumination changes, as well as geometric and appearance variations caused by human interaction – that are harder to predict. The only indoor datasets exhibiting these types of changes [21,86] were captured in public spaces, where there is limited human interaction with the environment. Just as importantly, these datasets do not quantify changes, and do not provide the means to measure their impact on re-localization performance. They therefore cannot be used to measure to what degree existing re-localization algorithms are able to handle realistic changes occurring in everyday indoor scenes.

This paper makes the following **contributions**: (1) We construct an **indoor re-localization benchmark** based on a recently released dataset, *3RScan* [97]. *3RScan* captures everyday scenes over a long period of time (*c.f.* Fig. 1) and thus depicts a wide range of changes not captured by other datasets from the literature. (2) We propose a **novel framework to quantify changes in (indoor) scenes**, covering appearance, geometric, and semantic changes. This enables us, for what to the best of our knowledge is the first time, to quantifiably measure the impact of different types of change on the accuracy of the camera poses predicted by visual re-localization algorithms. (3) We evaluate state-of-the-art methods for re-localization in static indoor and changing outdoor scenes, and show through detailed experiments that indoor re-localization in real-world scenes is far from being solved. (4) Based on our experiments, we propose a set of **open challenges** for the community to work on. We make our benchmark, framework, and evaluation protocols **publicly available**. We think this benchmark closes a gap in the literature by going beyond controlled indoor environments, similar to recent high-impact benchmarks modelling outdoor scene changes [7,62,79,80].

2   Related Work

Benchmarks. A variety of datasets exist to target different aspects of the camera re-localization problem (*c.f.* Table 1)[1]. For the task of re-localizing in *outdoor* scenes that change over time, a multitude of benchmarks exists that look at day vs. night changes, season and weather changes, and long-term geometric changes based on e.g. changing vegetation or construction projects. *Aachen Day-Night* [79] extends the Aachen dataset [80] to support evaluation of a re-localizer's ability to estimate the poses of night-time, outdoor, RGB-only images against a day-time 3D model. *RobotCar Seasons* [79] is based on a subset of the outdoor Oxford RobotCar dataset [62]. It focuses on re-localization across different seasons and weather conditions, but also contains a challenge related to localizing low-quality night-time images. While RobotCar Seasons covers an urban region, the (extended) *CMU-Seasons* dataset [7,79] also covers more vegetated outdoor scenes. *SILDa* [9] depicts a small block of buildings in London and provides test images under changing conditions such as weather and illumination changes.

For many years, the most popular *indoor* datasets have been *7-Scenes* [83] and *12-Scenes* [93], which only contain static scenes and exhibit no changes between train and test time. There do exist indoor datasets containing changes, e.g. *InLoc* [86] consists of non-sequential RGB-D training images that are registered to floor plans of university buildings [99], and RGB-only query images taken at a later date by hand-held devices. Moreover, *InLoc* and *NCLT* [21] both contain scene changes such as moved objects. However, neither provide any means

---

[1] We exclude other semantic indoor [5,26,30,44,84,85] and submap merging [40] datasets that are neither designed for camera re-localization, nor include scene changes. We also exclude outdoor datasets unsuited to measure re-localization performance in changing scenes [28,45,49,57,58], and purely synthetic datasets [54,73].

of quantifying the impact that different changes have on re-localization performance. In this paper, we address this problem by introducing a novel framework to properly quantify the effects of changes in indoor scenes.

Table 1. Overview of camera re-localization benchmarks

Dataset	Train images	Test/Val images	Setup	Sequential	Time span
7-Scenes [38]	26000	17000	Indoor	Yes	No
12-Scenes [93]	16926	5702	Indoor	Yes	No
InLoc [86]	9972	329	Indoor	No	Few days
Aachen Day-Night [79]	4328	922	Outdoor	No	Few years
Extended CMU-Seasons [79]	60937	56613	Outdoor	Yes	2 years
RobotCar Seasons [79]	26121	11934	Outdoor	Yes	1 year
SILDa [9]	8334	6064	Outdoor	Yes	1 year
NCLT [21]	N/A	N/A	Both	Yes	15 months
RIO10 (Ours)	52562	200159	Indoor	Yes	1 year

Camera Re-localization Methods can be broadly divided into four types: *Image retrieval* methods typically match the query image against images with known poses in a database [35,39], but can struggle to generalise to novel poses. Strategies to mitigate this include the use of synthesized views [36,90], interpolation between database poses [10,51,91,102], and triangulation based on relative poses [103,104]. To achieve scalability in terms of memory and run-time, place recognition methods [3,90] typically use compact image-level descriptors. Such methods perform well under appearance and limited viewpoint changes [79].

Direct pose regression methods, which aim to directly regress a pose from the query image, are often based on pose regression networks [1,47–49,64,100], although decision forest [46], GAN [20] and LSTM [29,96] variants also exist. On the whole, they have not yet matched the precision of state-of-the-art structure-based and RGB-D methods indoors. Recent work by Sattler *et al.* [81] has suggested that they are conceptually similar to image retrieval, and may thus face ongoing challenges in generalising to novel poses and achieving highly accurate pose predictions. Some direct pose regression methods [18,53,71,92] now exploit the relative poses between images to improve accuracy, and in some cases [71,92] have achieved accuracies that are competitive with state-of-the-art RGB-D methods. However, thus far they have had to rely on estimated poses from previous frames, making them effectively camera tracking approaches that are incomparable with methods that are able to re-localize from only a single image.

Structure-based methods typically match 2D features in the image with 3D points in the scene, and then pass the correspondences to a RANSAC-based backend for camera pose estimation. A classic example is Active Search [78], which performs efficient bidirectional matching using SIFT-based visual vocabularies. Hierarchical localization methods [45,75,77,86,87] use an initial image retrieval step to make matching more efficient, *i.e.*they first determine a set of potentially visible locations and restrict 2D-3D matching to these. For long-term localization under changing conditions, state-of-the-art methods typically rely on learned features [34,37,75,98], *e.g.* HF-Net [75] uses sparse SuperPoint [32] and DOAP [43] features, whilst [34] uses sparse higher-level features extracted from deeper layers of a CNN. Both achieve state-of-the-art results on outdoor benchmarks from [79] and outperform approaches based on dense feature matching [37,86,98]. Another popular approach to outdoor long-term localization is to use semantic information [50,82,88,89]. However, [87] argues that most of these approaches are not directly applicable to indoor scenes. Similarly, object-based localization methods [4,6,52,74] do not seem applicable in the context of re-localization in changing indoor scenes, as many objects are likely to change their position.

Scene coordinate regression (SCoRe) methods densely regress the scene coordinates of query image pixels using a regression forest [13,23–25,40,42,65–67,83,94], a neural network [12,14–17,33,55,56,101], or both [63]. The correspondences are used to generate pose hypotheses using PnP/Kabsch that are then refined using RANSAC. These methods can be categorised based on whether they expect RGB [12–16,33,55,56,65,66,101] or RGB-D [23–25,42,67,83,94] input at test time, and whether they require offline training (most methods) or can be used online [23–25]. Better performance has typically been achieved using RGB-D [24] rather than RGB-only [14,15] input, although RGB-only methods are gradually closing the gap. The state-of-the-art SCoRe relocaliser for indoor RGB-D scenes is currently Grove v2 [24], an online regression forest method, although a network-based variant of this [23] performs better outdoors.

A few approaches defy such a categorisation. Valentin *et al.* [93] use continuous pose optimisation to refine the results of an initial matching process based on a retrieval forest and multiscale navigation graph. Nakashima *et al.* [68] replace the feature matching step in hierarchical localization with dense regression. Other methods perform retrieval using a point cloud [31] or 3D model [60] constructed from multiple query images, or hallucinate a subvolume and match that against a database [82]. Since our main contribution here is to propose a new benchmark and metrics for evaluating camera re-localization in changing indoor scenes, we focus our attentions on those re-localizers that are known to currently have state-of-the-art performance on static indoor scenes or dynamic outdoor scenes, and explore how their performance is affected when the scenes change.

3   Benchmark Dataset

The original *3RScan* [97], which was the first large-scale, real-world dataset of changing indoor environments, consists of 1482 3D scans of around 450 natural indoor environments. Each scene has m globally aligned 3D models, each reconstructed from an RGB-D sequence s recorded at time T_s, using a hand-held

Table 2. Scene statistics and images of the reference/train scan of *RIO10*.

Scene	S01	S02	S03	S04	S05	S06	S07	S08	S09	S10
Rescans	6	8	7	10	5	12	8	5	5	8
Max Day-Span Between Captures	176	165	369	176	163	173	104	229	1	168
# Object Instances	39	33	20	28	44	49	39	61	67	63
# Changed Object Instances	5–9	5–6	2–3	1–5	1–2	1–6	6–10	1–5	5–6	7–9

Google Tango phone with camera intrinsics $K_s \in \mathbb{R}^{3\times3}$. Reasonably accurate camera poses $\{P_{s,1}, ..., P_{s,k_s}\}$ for each sequence s (of length k_s) are determined via an offline bundle adjustment framework, based on fisheye images. A pose

$$P_{s,i} \in \mathbb{R}^{4\times4} = \begin{bmatrix} R_{s,i} & t_{s,i} \\ \mathbf{0}^\top & 1 \end{bmatrix} \tag{1}$$

is defined by a rotation matrix $R_{s,i} \in \mathbb{R}^{3\times3}$ and a translation vector $t_{s,i} \in \mathbb{R}^3$. Note that $P_{s,i}$ transforms from the local camera coordinate system to the 3D model coordinate system. Whilst originally designed for object re-localization, *3RScan* can also – when slightly adapted – enable benchmarking of related tasks such as long-term camera re-localization. Due to the large size of the original dataset, we have chosen to focus on a 10-scene subset of it, which we call *RIO10*, for our experiments and evaluation protocol (*c.f.* Table 2). We split the sequences and 3D models into training, validation (one sequence per scene) and testing sets, leaving us with 10 train, 10 validation and 54 test sequences overall. The provided 3D models have both color and semantics (see Fig. 2), and are defined as $\{\mathcal{M}_s : 0 \leq s < m\}$, where $\mathcal{M}_0$ is our reference/training scan, and each other scan $\mathcal{M}_s$ is a test or validation scan. The 10 scenes chosen for *RIO10* were selected due partly to their scanning frequency, and partly to their scene and change diversity. Indeed, they are among the scenes in *3RScan* with the highest time span and scanning frequency (5–12 scans each). *RIO10* features many different indoor scenarios (messy laundry basements, offices or bathrooms) and different types of change (*e.g.* diversity in lighting, both subtle and significant movements of large/small and rigid/non-rigid objects, and ambiguous changes where objects of the same appearance move). Whilst we decided to evaluate on only a small subset of *3RScan*, the remaining scans are still useful for training future models. To simplify evaluation, each test 3D model and camera pose is provided in the training sequence's reference frame. Due to the low resolution and frame-rate of the raw Tango depth maps, we generated depth renderings of the 3D models for each RGB frame, together with ground-truth 2D instance segmentations. For reproducibility, all data, along with the evaluation tools and per-frame statistics, will be made publicly available.

4   Evaluating Re-localization in Changing Indoor Scenes

Having described our benchmark dataset, we now propose an evaluation methodology for the well-studied camera re-localization problem, as well as novel ways to quantify scene changes. Compared to common evaluation measures from previous camera re-localization benchmarks, we show the advantages of alternative metrics such as the normalised absolute correspondence re-projection error (Sect. 4.2) when measuring camera re-localization performance. To analyse how re-localization methods are able to generalise to changes in the scene, we propose various measures to quantify the change in each image. This is important, since it gives us an understanding of whether and how different methods are affected by different types of scene change.

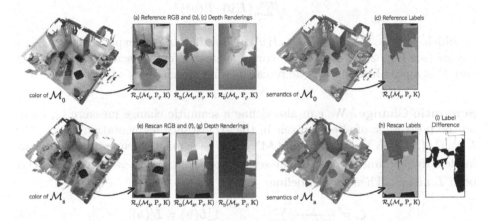

Fig. 2. We render synthetic RGB, depth and semantic images from our 3D reference and test models $\mathcal{M}_0$ and $\mathcal{M}_s$, and use them to compute the scene change measures described in Sect. 4.1. See the main text for details.

4.1   Quantifying Change in (Indoor) Scenes

In the following, we introduce different measures to quantify the extent to which an RGB-D frame in one of the test sequences has changed with respect to the same view of the reference scan. To compute the measures, we make use of synthetic views of the globally aligned semantic and textured 3D models in *3RScan* (see Sect. 3). To produce these synthetic views, we define three different rendering functions: $\mathcal{R}_C$ for color, $\mathcal{R}_D$ for depth, and $\mathcal{R}_S$ for semantics. Each of these takes a 3D model $\mathcal{M}$, a pose matrix $P \in \mathbb{R}^{4\times4}$, and a camera intrinsics matrix $K \in \mathbb{R}^{3\times3}$, and produces a $w \times h$ synthetic view of $\mathcal{M}$ as seen from P using a camera with intrinsics K (see Fig. 2 for examples).

Visual Appearance Change. Given these rendering functions, we can define measures for the visual appearance change between two different models $\mathcal{M}$ and $\mathcal{M}'$ as seen from a given pose P by a camera with intrinsics K. Let $I = \mathcal{R}_C(\mathcal{M}, P, K)$ and $I' = \mathcal{R}_C(\mathcal{M}', P, K)$ be color renderings of the two models from P. Given these, we consider two different measures of the visual appearance change – the normalized correlation coefficient ρ_v, defined as

$$\rho_v = \frac{\sum_u (I(u) - I'(u))^2}{\sqrt{(\sum_u I(u)^2) \cdot (\sum_u I'(u)^2)}}, \tag{2}$$

and the normalized sum of squared differences ζ_v, defined as

$$\zeta_v = \frac{\sum_u (\bar{I}(u) \cdot \bar{I}'(u))^2}{\sqrt{\sum_u (\bar{I}(u) \cdot \bar{I}'(u))^2}}, \tag{3}$$

in which $\bar{I}(u) = I(u) - \frac{1}{w \cdot h} \sum_{u'} I(u')$. Note that in our experiments, $\mathcal{M}$ is a rescan (see Fig. 2(e)), $\mathcal{M}'$ is the corresponding reference scan (see Fig. 2(a)), and P is a pose from one of the rescan/testing sequences.

Semantic Change. We can also define a semantic change measure ζ_s, based on the percentage of altered pixels in the 2D instance segmentation images. Let $L = \mathcal{R}_S(\mathcal{M}, P, K)$ and $L' = \mathcal{R}_S(\mathcal{M}', P, K)$ be semantic renderings of the two models from P, and $V_{\{L,L'\}}^{(s)}$ be the set of pixels that have a valid instance ID in both L and L'. Then we can define

$$\zeta_s = \frac{1}{\left|V_{\{L,L'\}}^{(s)}\right|} \sum_{u \in V_{\{L,L'\}}^{(s)}} \mathbb{1}\left[L(u) \neq L'(u)\right]. \tag{4}$$

Geometric Change. We can define a geometric change measure ζ_g based on the average per-pixel difference between a depth rendering of each model. Let $D = \mathcal{R}_D(\mathcal{M}, P, K)$ and $D' = \mathcal{R}_D(\mathcal{M}', P, K)$ be depth renderings of the two models from P, and $V_\Delta^{(d)}$ be the set of pixels that have a valid depth value for all $D'' \in \Delta$, with $V_D^{(d)} \equiv V_{\{D\}}^{(d)}$. Then we can define

$$\zeta_g = \frac{1}{\left|V_{\{D,D'\}}^{(d)}\right|} \sum_{u \in V_{\{D,D'\}}^{(d)}} \|D(u) - D'(u)\|_2. \tag{5}$$

We report ζ_g as a value in millimeters. Note that this measure would be particularly high for the depth renderings from pose P_j in Fig. 2, since in one of the models, a door has been moved so as to block the view.

Change Statistics. Please note that change statistics for each scene can be found in the supplementary material.

4.2 Measuring Re-localization Performance

Given a sequence of ground truth poses as 3D orientations $\{R_1, ..., R_p\}$ (where $R_i \in \mathbb{R}^{3\times3}$) and absolute 3D locations $\{t_1, ..., t_p\}$ (with $t_i \in \mathbb{R}^3$), as well as corresponding pose estimates $\{\hat{R}_1, ..., \hat{R}_p\}$ and $\{\hat{t}_1, ..., \hat{t}_p\}$, common evaluation protocols are based on absolute pose errors. More specifically, it is common to compute the absolute translation error as a Euclidean distance in meters, namely $\Delta t_i = ||\hat{t}_i - t_i||$, and the absolute orientation error as an angle in degrees, namely $\Delta\theta_i = ||\frac{180}{\pi} \cdot 2 \cdot \arccos[q(R_i)^{-1} \cdot q(\hat{R}_i)]||$, in which $q(R)$ denotes the quaternion corresponding to the rotation matrix R. Methods can then be ranked by comparing their values for $\mathcal{E}_a$ or $\bar{\mathcal{E}}_a$, the fraction of images localized within (Eq. 6) or outside of (Eq. 7) the given error thresholds ($\epsilon_t, \epsilon_\theta$):

$$\mathcal{E}_a(\epsilon_t, \epsilon_\theta) = \frac{1}{p}\sum_{i=1}^p \mathbb{1}\left[\Delta t_i < \epsilon_t \text{ and } \Delta\theta_i < \epsilon_\theta\right] \qquad (6)$$

$$\bar{\mathcal{E}}_a(\epsilon_t, \epsilon_\theta) = \frac{1}{p}\sum_{i=1}^p \mathbb{1}\left[\Delta t_i \geq \epsilon_t \text{ or } \Delta\theta_i \geq \epsilon_\theta\right] \qquad (7)$$

Commonly chosen thresholds for $\mathcal{E}_a$ in indoor setups are $(0.05\,\mathrm{m}, 5°)$ or $(0.1\,\mathrm{m}, 10°)$. However, these values are manually selected, and do not correlate with the visual appearance of a scene: a one-pixel shift could potentially lead to a pose error of only a few millimeters when objects are close, but a few meters if objects are far from the camera. Instead of using hard thresholds, [49] independently reports the medians $\widetilde{\Delta t}$ and $\widetilde{\Delta\theta}$ of the absolute translation and angular errors. However, these median errors can correspond to completely different frames, and there is in fact no guarantee with this measure that any single frame has both a low translation error and a low angular error, even if both the medians are low. In this paper, we eschew both of these approaches and instead propose a new measure that, rather than being based on the absolute translation and angular errors, is directly based on the difference in appearance between an image from the ground truth pose and an image from the predicted pose.

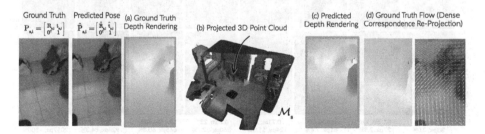

Fig. 3. Given ground truth and predicted camera poses $P_{s,i}$ and $\hat{P}_{s,i}$, we compute the flow errors $\delta_f^{(i)}(u)$ for DCRE by back-projecting the rendered depth image $D = \mathcal{R}_D(\mathcal{M}_s, P_{s,i}, K_s)$ in (a) using $\Pi_{K_s}^{-1}$ to get a 3D point cloud (b) that is then transformed by $\hat{P}_{s,i}^{-1} P_{s,i}$. The flow errors are the displacements between the projections of the points in this transformed point cloud and the pixels in the original image. See Eq. 8.

Dense Correspondence Re-projection Error (DCRE). Our new measure, which we call the *Dense Correspondence Re-Projection Error*, is defined as a ground truth re-projection error of the 2D flow of dense 3D points rendered from an underlying 3D model (see Fig. 3). The flow is computed according to our ground truth and predicted camera poses. Specifically, the 3D model for the sequence of interest s is first rendered from the ground truth pose $P_{s,i}$. This gives us a high-resolution dense depth map $D_i = \mathcal{R}_D(\mathcal{M}_s, P_{s,i}, K_s)$ that can be back-projected into a 3D point cloud using the back-projection function $\Pi_{K_s}^{-1}$. The points in the cloud are then transformed by $\hat{P}_{s,i}^{-1} P_{s,i}$ before being projected back down onto the image plane using Π_{K_s} to get a new depth map. The flow error $\delta_f^{(i)}$ at a pixel u in frame i can then be defined as

$$\delta_f^{(i)}(u) = \Pi_{K_s}(\hat{P}_{s,i}^{-1} P_{s,i} \Pi_{K_s}^{-1}(u, D_i)) - u. \tag{8}$$

Intuitively, the overall frame error $\mathcal{E}_{DCRE}^{(i)}$ is then the average magnitude of the 2D correspondence displacement, normalised by the image diagonal, *i.e.*

$$\mathcal{E}_{DCRE}^{(i)} = \frac{1}{\left|V_{D_i}^{(d)}\right|} \sum_{u \in V_{D_i}^{(d)}} \min\left(\frac{\|\delta_f^{(i)}(u)\|}{\sqrt{w^2 + h^2}}, 1\right). \tag{9}$$

This can then be extended to a DCRE-based error $\mathcal{E}_f(\epsilon_f)$ for the whole sequence:

$$\mathcal{E}_f(\epsilon_f) = \frac{1}{p} \sum_{i=1}^{p} \mathbb{1}\left[\mathcal{E}_{DCRE}^{(i)} < \epsilon_f\right]. \tag{10}$$

Fig. 4. Some example poses predicted by the methods evaluated in Sect. 4.2, their absolute pose errors in m/°, and the DCRE in pixels and the percentage of the image diagonal this represents in each case. See also Figs. 6, 7 and 9.

One major advantage of such a measure is that it gives us an error that correlates with visual perception (see examples in Fig. 4). Another desirable property of

DCRE is the fact that it is represented by a single number, which is in contrast to absolute pose errors, which struggle to combine the translation error Δt_i with the angular error $\Delta\theta_i$. Furthermore, a (cumulative) DCRE histogram can provide us with a good way of characterising the performance of a method (see Sect. 5.2), since it represents the poses within a wide error range.

5 Experiments

To evaluate the impact of appearance changes on indoor camera re-localization, we analyse the performance of state-of-the-art re-localizers on *RIO10* using both common evaluation metrics and our newly proposed DCRE measure (Sect. 4.2). We also conduct experiments to evaluate how robust different re-localizers are with respect to various types of change, as suggested in Sect. 4.1.

5.1 Classifying Frame Difficulty

Scene changes are one factor that can make single-image re-localization challenging, but other factors (*e.g.* scene context and texture, or the pose novelty with respect to the training trajectory) can also play a significant role. We thus propose to rank the difficulty of each query image based on the following three properties. More details can be found in the supplementary material.

Variance of Laplacian. Many feature-based methods struggle when confronted with motion blur and a lack of texture. To be able to detect such images, we compute the variance of the Laplacian of the image, which we refer to as σ.

Field of View Context. Besides a lack of texture, a lack of scene context can present another major challenge for camera re-localizers. To estimate the field of view of a particular frame, we first back-project the depth map. The volume of the convex hull of the resulting 3D points, combined with the camera center, gives an estimate of the context observed in a particular view (see Fig. 5).

Fig. 5. (a) High $13.1\,\mathrm{m}^3$, (b) medium $1.0\,\mathrm{m}^3$ and (c) low $0.1\,\mathrm{m}^3$ frame coverage.

Pose Novelty. Another major challenge for camera re-localizers is the novelty of query poses with respect to the training trajectory. Given a sequence of poses

$\{P'_0, ..., P'_p\}$ from the train set, and a ground truth query pose P, we can define the pose novelty η as the minimum of some dissimilarity function ϵ_η between all pose combinations, such that $\eta = \min_{\forall P'_i \in \{P'_0,...,P'_p\}} \epsilon_\eta(P, P'_i)$.

5.2   Re-localization Performance

In the following, we evaluate a selection of state-of-the-art algorithms that cover the most common types of re-localization approach: hand-crafted structure-based methods [76], learned methods[2] that expect either RGB [34,75] or RGB-D [24,25] input, and image retrieval methods [3,90]. In our first experiment, we evaluate on all 165 744 query test images, without any filtering. We list the overall performance of each method in Table 3 by reporting $\mathcal{E}_f(0.05)$ and $\mathcal{E}_f(0.15)$, based on our newly introduced DCRE metric. For comparison, we also report the recall based on the absolute pose error $\mathcal{E}_a$, with the often-used thresholds $(\epsilon_t, \epsilon_\theta) = (0.05m, 5°)$. Further, we also quantify the number of re-localization outliers[3], by reporting both the percentage of frames with a high $\mathcal{E}_a$ error, with $(\epsilon_t, \epsilon_\theta) = (0.5m, 25°)$, high DCRE error, with $\mathcal{E}_f(0.5)$, and failed re-localizations (no predicted pose or NaN). Single numbers are still not really descriptive of the dynamics of each algorithm. We thus visualize cumulative plots in Fig. 6 using DCRE, as well as Δt_i and $\Delta \theta_i$ for comparison. These graphs shed some light on the behavior of the methods that we analyze. For example, it is interesting that the best-performing methods according to the threshold-based metrics $\mathcal{E}_a$ and $\mathcal{E}_f$, such as Grove v2 and D2-Net, output increasingly inaccurate poses, as evidenced by the steady increase in their DCRE values towards the right of the plot. By contrast, Active Search tends to provide poses for a smaller number of query frames but, crucially, does not output overly incorrect poses, as evidenced by the plateauing of its DCRE plot. While some of this information can also be gained by analysing the numbers in Table 3, we find that the cumulative plot provides a deeper, more intuitive characterisation of each method. An ideal method should yield a cumulative DCRE that is as similar to a step function as possible: first rising quickly to correctly re-localize a good fraction of the frames, and then plateauing (signalling failed re-localizations instead of producing highly incorrect poses).

Scene Changes. To see how scene changes affect a method's performance, we plot the overall error/performance of the best methods with images of increasing visual (ζ_v and ρ_v), geometric ζ_g and semantic change ζ_s. A clear correlation between scene changes and overall performance is observable in Fig. 7.

Object Re-Localization vs. Camera Re-Localization. Rigidly moving objects cause new types of absolute camera pose estimation ambiguities. Poses become ambiguous when a changed object occupies most of the view. An example is given in Fig. 8, where localizing the test image (c) from the rescan (b) is practically impossible given only the reference scan (a). The correct reference

---

[2] Training details for HF-Net can be found in the supplementary material. .

[3] We define $\bar{\mathcal{E}}_f(\epsilon_f) = \frac{1}{p}\sum_{i=1}^{p} \mathbb{1}\left[\mathcal{E}_{DCRE}^{(i)} \geq \epsilon_f\right]$. .

Table 3. Comparison of all methods w.r.t. their inlier/outlier ratios, median pose errors and DCRE errors. *Obj.* is the fraction of failure cases where the methods re-localized against a moved object. *N/A* denotes invalid/missing predictions.

Method	Inlier				Outlier			
	$\mathcal{E}_a(0.05\,\text{m}, 5°)$	$(\widetilde{\Delta t}, \widetilde{\Delta\theta})$	$\mathcal{E}_f(0.05)$	$\mathcal{E}_f(0.15)$	N/A	$\bar{\mathcal{E}}_a(0.5\,\text{m}, 25°)$	$\bar{\mathcal{E}}_f(0.5)^3$	Obj.
Active Search [78]	0.0696	(0.16, 4.68)	0.171	0.243	0.684	0.0891	0.028	0.149
Grove [25]	0.2300	(0.06, 1.74)	0.334	0.391	0.452	0.144	0.106	0.065
Grove v2 [24]	0.2742	(0.11, 2.60)	0.406	0.485	0.162	0.332	0.262	0.051
HFNet [75]	0.0182	(1.56, 72.33)	0.057	0.098	0	0.900	0.714	0.005
HF-Net Trained[2] [75]	0.0725	(0.84, 24.17)	0.180	0.288	0	0.685	0.427	0.065
D2Net [34]	0.1553	(0.55, 14.90)	0.365	0.506	0.014	0.513	0.194	0.033
NetVLAD [3]	0.0002	(0.93, 31.44)	0.006	0.125	0	0.798	0.452	0.016
DenseVLAD [90]	0.0003	(0.98, 32.26)	0.008	0.124	0.006	0.772	0.520	0.014

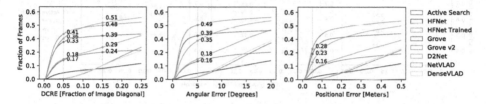

Fig. 6. Cumulative plots of the absolute pose recall and DCRE for all camera re-localization methods.

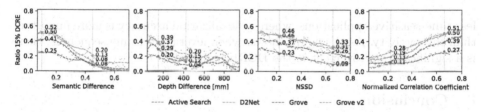

Fig. 7. The charts show the performance of the best methods with respect to semantic ζ_s, geometric ζ_g and visual change (ζ_v and ρ_v). Each dot represents the performance $\mathcal{E}_f(0.15)$ of a particular method on frames with increasing change measured by ζ_s, ζ_g, ζ_v and ρ_v respectively. Note that the dashed lines denote running averages.

view of the GT pose would produce the reference view pictured in (d). Instead, when an object instance dominates the view, the camera might incorrectly localize with respect to the visible object. We report the fraction of these cases (out of all failure cases) in the last column of Table 3.

Sequences. We experimented with sequence lengths s_Δ of (a) 10, (b) 30, and (c) 100 consecutive frames. The corresponding DCRE plots can be found in Fig. 9. We chose the values 10 and 30 to model interactive applications, where using a small number of consecutive frames can help tackle motion blur and object instance ambiguities; whereas longer sequences of up to 100 frames can be used in

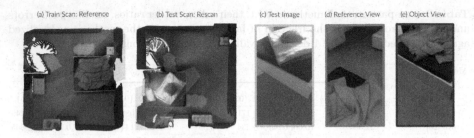

Fig. 8. Given the reference scan (a) for training, localizing the image (c) from a rescan (b) is practically impossible. A camera re-localization method might localize an object (e) instead of the global scene (d).

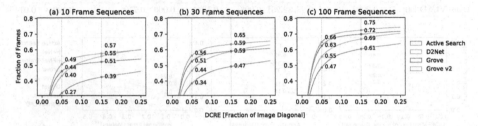

Fig. 9. Cumulative plots of the DCRE for the best-performing camera re-localization methods using (a) short, (b) medium, and (c) long sequences of frames.

less time-sensitive applications, where re-localization accuracy is more important than interactivity. As the figure shows, when leveraging frame sequences, there is a significant improvement in the DCRE numbers.

6 Conclusion

In this paper, we have both curated a suitable dataset for long-term indoor camera re-localization, and defined a set of metrics for quantifying changes in indoor scenes. For the first time, this enables an evaluation of the impact of changes in indoor scenes on re-localization performance, thus closing a significant gap in the literature. We have also introduced DCRE, a new metric to measure re-localization performance, and shown that many methods experience a loss of performance when exposed to scene regions that have undergone changes of visual, geometric and semantic nature, *e.g.* as caused by rigid/non-rigid object movements. We have further analysed the behaviour of camera re-localizers on frames that capture rigidly moving objects. Large semantic changes, *e.g.* caused by large objects in a scene changing their position, are a particular problem. In such situations, the methods potentially re-localize with respect to the object dominating the camera's field of view, rather than with respect to the scene. Results for state-of-the-art re-localizers on our new benchmark show that none of them is fully capable of handling everyday changes observed in indoor scenes: indeed, there is significant room for improvement. Using short image sequences, rather than individual images, for re-localization naturally improves performance, but is not sufficient to solve our benchmark. We believe that long-term camera re-localization in indoor scenes requires the learning of higher-level concepts of a scene – such as its semantics, and/or object-level understanding of poses, dynamics and appearance variations – so as to subsequently be able to reason about scene changes. In this way, we would expect the camera pose estimation task to gradually become more tightly coupled to general scene understanding going forwards.

Acknowledgements. This work was supported by the Centre Digitisation Bavaria (ZD.B), the Swedish Foundation for Strategic Research (Semantic Mapping and Visual Navigation for Smart Robots), the Chalmers AI Research Centre (CHAIR) (VisLo-cLearn), Five AI Ltd. and Google Inc.

References

1. Acharya, D., Khoshelham, K., Winter, S.: BIM-PoseNet: indoor camera localisation using a 3D indoor model and deep learning from synthetic images. J. Photogramm. Remote Sens. **150**, 245–258 (2019)
2. Anoosheh, A., Sattler, T., Timofte, R., Pollefeys, M., Gool, L.V.: Night-to-day image translation for retrieval-based localization. In: International Conference on Robotics and Automation. IEEE (2019)
3. Arandjelović, R., Gronat, P., Torii, A., Pajdla, T., Sivic, J.: NetVLAD: CNN architecture for weakly supervised place recognition. In: Conference on Computer Vision and Pattern Recognition. IEEE (2016)
4. Ardeshir, S., Zamir, A.R., Torroella, A., Shah, M.: GIS-assisted object detection and geospatial localization. In: Fleet, D., Pajdla, T., Schiele, B., Tuytelaars, T. (eds.) ECCV 2014. LNCS, vol. 8694, pp. 602–617. Springer, Cham (2014). https://doi.org/10.1007/978-3-319-10599-4_39
5. Armeni*, I., Sax*, A., Zamir, A.R., Savarese, S.: Joint 2D-3D-Semantic Data for Indoor Scene Understanding. arXiv:1702.01105 (2017)
6. Atanasov, N., Zhu, M., Daniilidis, K., Pappas, G.J.: Localization from semantic observations via the matrix permanent. Int. J. Robot. Res. **35**(1–3), 73–99 (2016)
7. Badino, H., Huber, D., Kanade, T.: Visual topometric localization. In: Intelligent Vehicles Symposium (IV) (2011)
8. Bae, H., Walker, M., White, J., Pan, Y., Sun, Y., Golparvar-Fard, M.: Fast and scalable structure-from-motion based localization for high-precision mobile augmented reality systems. J. Mobile User Exp. **5**(1), 1–21 (2016)
9. Balntas, V., et al.: (SILDa): Scape imperial localisation dataset. https://image-matching-workshop.github.io/challenge/ (2019)
10. Balntas, V., Li, S., Prisacariu, V.: RelocNet: continuous metric learning relocalisation using neural nets. In: Ferrari, V., Hebert, M., Sminchisescu, C., Weiss, Y. (eds.) European Conference on Computer Vision(2018)
11. Benbihi, A., Geist, M., Pradalier, C.: ELF: embedded localisation of features in pre-trained CNN. In: International Conference on Computer Vision. IEEE (2019)
12. Brachmann, E., et al.: DSAC - Differentiable RANSAC for camera localization. In: Conference on Computer Vision and Pattern Recognition. IEEE (2017)

13. Brachmann, E., Michel, F., Krull, A., Yang, M.Y., Gumhold, S., Rother, C.: Uncertainty-driven 6D pose estimation of objects and scenes from a single rgb image. In: Conference on Computer Vision and Pattern Recognition. IEEE (2016)
14. Brachmann, E., Rother, C.: Learning less is more - 6D camera localization via 3d surface regression. In: Conference on Computer Vision and Pattern Recognition. IEEE (2018)
15. Brachmann, E., Rother, C.: Expert sample consensus applied to camera re-localization. In: International Conference on Computer Vision. IEEE (2019)
16. Brachmann, E., Rother, C.: Neural-guided ransac: learning where to sample model hypotheses. In: International Conference on Computer Vision. IEEE (2019)
17. Brachmann, E., Rother, C.: Visual Camera Re-Localization from RGB and RGB-D Images Using DSAC. arXiv:2002.12324 (2020)
18. Brahmbhatt, S., Gu, J., Kim, K., Hays, J., Kautz, J.: Geometry-aware learning of maps for camera localization. In: Conference on Computer Vision and Pattern Recognition. IEEE (2018)
19. Bresson, G., Alsayed, Z., Yu, L., Glaser, S.: Simultaneous localization and mapping: a survey of current trends in autonomous driving. Trans. Intell. Veh. **2**(3), 194–220 (2017)
20. Bui, M., Baur, C., Navab, N., Ilic, S., Albarqouni, S.: Adversarial Networks for Camera Pose Regression and Refinement. (2019)
21. Carlevaris-Bianco, N., Ushani, A.K., Eustice, R.M.: University of Michigan North Campus long-term vision and lidar dataset. Int. J. Robot. Res. **35**(9), 1023–1035 (2016)
22. Castle, R., Klein, G., Murray, D.W.: Video-rate localization in multiple maps for wearable augmented reality. In: International Symposium on Wearable Computers. pp. 15–22. IEEE (2008)
23. Cavallari*, T., Bertinetto, L., Mukhoti, J., Torr, P., Golodetz*, S.: Let's take this online: adapting scene coordinate regression network predictions for online rgb-d camera relocalisation. In: International Conference on 3D Vision. IEEE, Québec, Canada (2019)
24. Cavallari*, T., et al.: Real-time rgb-d camera pose estimation in novel scenes using a relocalisation cascade. IEEE Trans. Pattern Anal. Mach. Intell. (2019)
25. Cavallari, T., et al.: On-the-fly adaptation of regression forests for online camera relocalisation. In: Conference on Computer Vision and Pattern Recognition (2017)
26. Chang, A., et al.: Matterport3D: learning from rgb-d data in indoor environments. In: International Conference on 3D Vision. IEEE (2017)
27. Chen, D.M., et al.: City-scale landmark identification on mobile devices. In: Conference on Computer Vision and Pattern Recognition. IEEE (2011)
28. Chen, D.M., et al.: City-scale landmark identification on mobile devices. In: Conference on Computer Vision and Pattern Recognition. pp. 737–744. IEEE (2011)
29. Clark, R., Wang, S., Markham, A., Trigoni, N., Wen, H.: VidLoc: a deep spatio-temporal model for 6-dof video-clip relocalization. In: Conference on Computer Vision and Pattern Recognition. pp. 6856–6864. IEEE (2017)
30. Dai, A., Chang, A.X., Savva, M., Halber, M., Funkhouser, T., Nießner, M.: Scan-Net: richly-annotated 3d reconstructions of indoor scenes. In: Conference on Computer Vision and Pattern Recognition. IEEE (2017)
31. Deng, L., Chen, Z., Chen, B., Duan, Y., Zhou, J.: Incremental image set querying based localization. Neurocomputing **208**, 315–324 (2016)
32. DeTone, D., Malisiewicz, T., Rabinovich, A.: SuperPoint: self-supervised interest point detection and description. In: Conference on Computer Vision and Pattern Recognition Workshops. IEEE (2018)

33. Duong, N.D., Kacete, A., Sodalie, C., Richard, P.Y., Royan, J.: xyzNet: towards machine learning camera relocalization by using a scene coordinate prediction network. In: International Symposium on Mixed and Augmented Reality. IEEE (2018)

34. Dusmanu, M., et al.: D2-Net: a trainable CNN for joint detection and description of local features. In: Conference on Computer Vision and Pattern Recognition. IEEE (2019)

35. Gálvez-López, D., Tardós, J.D.: Real-time loop detection with bags of binary words. In: International Conference on Intelligent Robots and Systems. pp. 51–58. IEEE (2011)

36. Gee, A.P., Mayol-Cuevas, W.: 6D Relocalisation for RGBD cameras using synthetic view regression. In: British Machine Vision Conference. pp. 1–11. BMVA (2012)

37. Germain, H., Bourmaud, G., Lepetit, V.: Sparse-to-dense hypercolumn matching for long-term visual localization. In: International Conference on 3D Vision. IEEE (2019)

38. Glocker, B., Izadi, S., Shotton, J., Criminisi, A.: Real-time RGB-D camera relocalization. In: International Symposium on Mixed and Augmented Reality. IEEE (2013)

39. Glocker, B., Shotton, J., Criminisi, A., Izadi, S.: Real-time RGB-D camera relocalization via randomized ferns for keyframe encoding. IEEE Trans. Vis. Comput. Graph. 21(5), 571–583 (2015)

40. Golodetz*, S., et al.: Collaborative large-scale dense 3d reconstruction with online inter-agent pose optimisation. IEEE Trans. Vis. Comput. Graph. 24(11), 2895–2905 (2018)

41. Golodetz*, S., et al.: SemanticPaint: interactive segmentation and learning of 3d worlds. In: ACM SIGGRAPH Emerging Technologies. p. 22 (2015)

42. Guzman-Rivera, A., et al.: Multi-output learning for camera relocalization. In: Conference on Computer Vision and Pattern Recognition. pp. 1114–1121. IEEE (2014)

43. He, K., Lu, Y., Sclaroff, S.: Local descriptors optimized for average precision. In: Conference on Computer Vision and Pattern Recognition. pp. 596–605. IEEE (2018)

44. Hua, B.S., Pham, Q.H., Nguyen, D.T., Tran, M.K., Yu, L.F., Yeung, S.K.: SceneNN: a scene meshes dataset with aNNotations. In: International Conference on 3D Vision. IEEE (2016)

45. Irschara, A., Zach, C., Frahm, J.M., Bischof, H.: From structure-from-motion point clouds to fast location recognition. In: Conference on Computer Vision and Pattern Recognition. IEEE (2009)

46. Kacete, A., Wentz, T., Royan, J.: Decision forest for efficient and robust camera relocalization. In: International Symposium on Mixed and Augmented Reality. pp. 20–24. IEEE (2017)

47. Kendall, A., Cipolla, R.: Modelling uncertainty in deep learning for camera relocalization. In: International Conference on Robotics and Automation. IEEE (2016)

48. Kendall, A., Cipolla, R.: Geometric loss functions for camera pose regression with deep learning. In: Conference on Computer Vision and Pattern Recognition. IEEE (2017)

49. Kendall, A., Grimes, M., Cipolla, R.: PoseNet: a convolutional network for real-time 6-dof camera relocalization. In: International Conference on Computer Vision. pp. 2938–2946. IEEE (2015)

50. Larsson, M., Stenborg, E., Toft, C., Hammarstrand, L., Sattler, T., Kahl, F.: fine-grained segmentation networks: self-supervised segmentation for improved long-term visual localization. In: International Conference on Computer Vision. IEEE (2019)
51. Laskar*, Z., Melekhov*, I., Kalia, S., Kannala, J.: Camera relocalization by computing pairwise relative poses using convolutional neural network. In: International Conference on Computer Vision Workshops. pp. 929–938. IEEE (2017)
52. Li, J., Meger, D., Dudek, G.: Semantic mapping for view-invariant relocalization. In: International Conference on Robotics and Automation. IEEE (2019)
53. Li, Q., et al.: Relative Geometry-Aware Siamese Neural Network for 6DOF Camera Relocalization. arXiv:1901.01049v2 (2019)
54. Li, W., et al.: InteriorNet: Mega-scale multi-sensor photo-realistic indoor scenes dataset. In: British Machine Vision Conference. BMVA (2018)
55. Li, X., Ylioinas, J., Kannala, J.: Full-frame scene coordinate regression for image-based localization. In: Robotics: Science and Systems (2018)
56. Li, X., Ylioinas, J., Verbeek, J., Kannala, J.: scene coordinate regression with angle-based reprojection loss for camera relocalization. In: Leal-Taixé, L., Roth, S. (eds.) European Conference on Computer Vision (2018)
57. Li, X., Wu, C., Zach, C., Lazebnik, S., Frahm, J.-M.: Modeling and recognition of landmark image collections using iconic scene graphs. In: Forsyth, D., Torr, P., Zisserman, A. (eds.) ECCV 2008. LNCS, vol. 5302, pp. 427–440. Springer, Heidelberg (2008). https://doi.org/10.1007/978-3-540-88682-2_33
58. Li, Y., Snavely, N., Huttenlocher, D., Fua, P.: Worldwide pose estimation using 3d point clouds. In: Fitzgibbon, A., Lazebnik, S., Perona, P., Sato, Y., Schmid, C. (eds.) ECCV 2012. LNCS, vol. 7572, pp. 15–29. Springer, Heidelberg (2012). https://doi.org/10.1007/978-3-642-33718-5_2
59. Lim, H., Sinha, S.N., Cohen, M.F., Uyttendaele, M.: Real-time image-based 6-dof localization in large-scale environments. In: Conference on Computer Vision and Pattern Recognition. IEEE (2012)
60. Lu, G., Yan, Y., Kolagunda, A., Kambhamettu, C.: A fast 3d indoor-localization approach based on video queries. In: MultiMedia Modeling. pp. 218–230 (2016)
61. Lynen, S., Sattler, T., Bosse, M., Hesch, J., Pollefeys, M., Siegwart, R.: Get out of my lab: large-scale, real-time visual-inertial localization. In: Robotics: Science and Systems (2015)
62. Maddern, W., Pascoe, G., Linegar, C., Newman, P.: 1 year, 1000km: the oxford robotcar dataset. Int. J. Robot. Res. **36**(1), 3–15 (2017)
63. Massiceti, D., Krull, A., Brachmann, E., Rother, C., Torr, P.H.S.: Random forests versus neural networks - what's best for camera localization? In: International Conference on Robotics and Automation. IEEE (2017)
64. Melekhov, I., Ylioinas, J., Kannala, J., Rahtu, E.: Image-based Localization using hourglass networks. In: International Conference on Computer Vision Workshops. pp. 879–886. IEEE (2017)
65. Meng, L., Chen, J., Tung, F., Little, J.J., de Silva, C.W.: exploiting random rgb and sparse features for camera pose estimation. In: British Machine Vision Conference. BMVA (2016)
66. Meng, L., Chen, J., Tung, F., Little, J.J., Valentin, J., de Silva, C.W.: Backtracking regression forests for accurate camera relocalization. In: International Conference on Intelligent Robots and Systems. IEEE (2017)
67. Meng, L., Tung, F., Little, J.J., Valentin, J., de Silva, C.W.: exploiting points and lines in regression forests for rgb-d camera relocalization. In: International Conference on Intelligent Robots and Systems. IEEE (2018)

68. Nakashima, R., Seki, A.: SIR-Net: scene-independent end-to-end trainable visual relocalizer. In: International Conference on 3D Vision. IEEE (2019)
69. Paucher, R., Turk, M.: Location-based augmented reality on mobile phones. In: Conference on Computer Vision and Pattern Recognition Workshops. pp. 9–16. IEEE (2010)
70. Porav, H., Maddern, W., Newman, P.: Adversarial training for adverse conditions: robust metric localisation using appearance transfer. In: International Conference on Robotics and Automation. IEEE (2018)
71. Radwan, N., Valada, A., Burgard, W.: VLocNet++: deep multitask learning for semantic visual localization and odometry. Robot. Autom. Lett. **3**(4), 4407–4414 (2018)
72. Rodas, N.L., Barrera, F., Padoy, N.: Marker-less ar in the hybrid room using equipment detection for camera relocalization. In: Navab, N., Hornegger, J., Wells, W.M., Frangi, A.F. (eds.) MICCAI 2015. LNCS, vol. 9349, pp. 463–470. Springer, Cham (2015). https://doi.org/10.1007/978-3-319-24553-9_57
73. Saeedi, S., et al.: Characterizing visual localization and mapping datasets. In: International Conference on Robotics and Automation. IEEE (2019)
74. Salas-Moreno, R.F., Newcombe, R.A., Strasdat, H., Kelly, P.H.J., Davison, A.J.: SLAM++: simultaneous localisation and mapping at the level of objects. In: Conference on Computer Vision and Pattern Recognition. IEEE (2013)
75. Sarlin, P.E., Cadena, C., Siegwart, R., Dymczyk, M.: From coarse to fine: robust hierarchical localization at large scale. In: Conference on Computer Vision and Pattern Recognition. IEEE (2019)
76. Sattler, T., Leibe, B., Kobbelt, L.: Fast image-based localization using direct 2d-to-3d matching. In: International Conference on Computer Vision. pp. 667–674. IEEE (2011)
77. Sattler, T., Leibe, B., Kobbelt, L.: Improving image-based localization by active correspondence search. In: Fitzgibbon, A., Lazebnik, S., Perona, P., Sato, Y., Schmid, C. (eds.) ECCV 2012. LNCS, vol. 7572, pp. 752–765. Springer, Heidelberg (2012). https://doi.org/10.1007/978-3-642-33718-5_54
78. Sattler, T., Leibe, B., Kobbelt, L.: Efficient & effective prioritized matching for large-scale image-based localization. IEEE Trans. Pattern Anal. Mach. Intell. **39**(9), 1744–1756 (2016)
79. Sattler, T., et al.: Benchmarking 6dof outdoor visual localization in changing conditions. In: Conference on Computer Vision and Pattern Recognition. IEEE, Piscataway, NJ (2018)
80. Sattler, T., Weyand, T., Leibe, B., Kobbelt, L.: image retrieval for image-based localization revisited. In: British Machine Vision Conference. BMVA (2012)
81. Sattler, T., Zhou, Q., Pollefeys, M., Leal-Taixé, L.: Understanding the limitations of cnn-based absolute camera pose regression. In: Conference on Computer Vision and Pattern Recognition. IEEE (2019)
82. Schönberger, J.L., Pollefeys, M., Geiger, A., Sattler, T.: Semantic visual localization. In: Conference on Computer Vision and Pattern Recognition. IEEE (2018)
83. Shotton, J., Glocker, B., Zach, C., Izadi, S., Criminisi, A., Fitzgibbon, A.: Scene coordinate regression forests for camera relocalization in rgb-d images. In: Conference on Computer Vision and Pattern Recognition. pp. 2930–2937. IEEE (2013)
84. Silberman, N., Hoiem, D., Kohli, P., Fergus, R.: Indoor segmentation and support inference from rgbd images. In: Fitzgibbon, A., Lazebnik, S., Perona, P., Sato, Y., Schmid, C. (eds.) ECCV 2012. LNCS, vol. 7576, pp. 746–760. Springer, Heidelberg (2012). https://doi.org/10.1007/978-3-642-33715-4_54

85. Song, S., Lichtenberg, S.P., Xiao, J.: SUN RGB-D: A RGB-D scene understanding benchmark suite. In: Conference on Computer Vision and Pattern Recognition. pp. 567–576. IEEE (2015)
86. Taira, H., et al.: InLoc: Indoor visual localization with dense matching and view synthesis. In: Conference on Computer Vision and Pattern Recognition. IEEE (2018)
87. Taira, H., et al.: Is This the right place? geometric-semantic pose verification for indoor visual localization. In: International Conference on Computer Vision. IEEE (October 2019)
88. Toft, C., Olsson, C., Kahl, F.: Long-term 3d localization and pose from semantic labellings. In: International Conference on Computer Vision. IEEE (2017)
89. Toft, C., et al.: Semantic match consistency for long-term visual localization. In: Ferrari, V., Hebert, M., Sminchisescu, C., Weiss, Y. (eds.) European Conference on Computer Vision (2018)
90. Torii, A., Arandjelović, R., Sivic, J., Okutomi, M., Pajdla, T.: 24/7 place recognition by view synthesis. In: Conference on Computer Vision and Pattern Recognition. IEEE (2015)
91. Torii, A., Sivic, J., Pajdla, T.: Visual localization by linear combination of image descriptors. In: International Conference on Computer Vision Workshops. IEEE (2011)
92. Valada*, A., Radwan*, N., Burgard, W.: Deep auxiliary learning for visual localization and odometry. In: International Conference on Robotics and Automation. IEEE (2018)
93. Valentin, J., et al.: Learning to navigate the energy landscape. In: International Conference on 3D Vision. pp. 323–332. IEEE (2016)
94. Valentin, J., Nießner, M., Shotton, J., Fitzgibbon, A., Izadi, S., Torr, P.: Exploiting uncertainty in regression forests for accurate camera relocalization. In: Conference on Computer Vision and Pattern Recognition. IEEE (2015)
95. Valentin, J., et al.: SemanticPaint: interactive 3d labeling and learning at your fingertips. IEEE Trans. Graph. **34**(5), 154 (2015)
96. Walch, F., et al.: Image-based localization using LSTMs for structured feature correlation. In: International Conference on Computer Vision. IEEE (2017)
97. Wald, J., Avetisyan, A., Navab, N., Tombari, F., Niessner, M.: RIO: 3D object instance re-localization in changing indoor environments. In: International Conference on Computer Vision. IEEE (2019)
98. Widya, A.R., Torii, A., Okutomi, M.: Structure from motion using dense cnn features with keypoint relocalization. IEEE Trans. Comput. Vis. Appl. **10**(1), 6 (2018)
99. Wijmans, E., Furukawa, Y.: Exploiting 2D floorplan for building-scale panorama RGBD alignment. In: Conference on Computer Vision and Pattern Recognition. IEEE (2017)
100. Wu, J., Ma, L., Hu, X.: Delving deeper into convolutional neural networks for camera relocalization. In: International Conference on Robotics and Automation. IEEE (2017)
101. Yang*, L., Bai*, Z., Tang, C., Li, H., Furukawa, Y., Tan, P.: SANet: scene agnostic network for camera localization. In: International Conference on Computer Vision. IEEE (2019)
102. Zamir, A.R., Shah, M.: Accurate image localization based on google maps street view. In: Daniilidis, K., Maragos, P., Paragios, N. (eds.) European Conference on Computer Vision (2010)

103. Zhang, W., Kosecka, J.: Image based localization in urban environments. In: 3DIM-PVT. IEEE (2006)
104. Zhou, Q., Sattler, T., Pollefeys, M., Leal-Taixe, L.: To learn or not to learn: visual localization from essential matrices. In: International Conference on Robotics and Automation. IEEE (2020)

GeoGraph: Graph-Based Multi-view Object Detection with Geometric Cues End-to-End

Ahmed Samy Nassar[1]([✉]), Stefano D'Aronco[2], Sébastien Lefèvre[1], and Jan D. Wegner[2]

[1] IRISA, Université Bretagne Sud, Vannes, France
{ahmed-samy-mohamed.nassar,sebastien.lefevre}@irisa.fr
[2] EcoVision Lab, Photogrammetry and Remote Sensing Group, ETH Zurich, Zurich, Switzerland
{stefano.daronco,jan.wegner}@geod.baug.ethz.ch

Abstract. In this paper we propose an end-to-end learnable approach that detects static urban objects from multiple views, re-identifies instances, and finally assigns a geographic position per object. Our method relies on a Graph Neural Network (GNN) to, detect all objects and output their geographic positions given images and approximate camera poses as input. Our GNN simultaneously models relative pose and image evidence, and is further able to deal with an arbitrary number of input views. Our method is robust to occlusion, with similar appearance of neighboring objects, and severe changes in viewpoints by jointly reasoning about visual image appearance and relative pose. Experimental evaluation on two challenging, large-scale datasets and comparison with state-of-the-art methods show significant and systematic improvements both in accuracy and efficiency, with 2–6% gain in detection and re-ID average precision as well as 8x reduction of training time.

Keywords: Object detection · Re-identification · Graph Neural Networks · Urban objects · Multi-view

1 Introduction

We present an end-to-end trainable multi-view object detection and re-identification approach centered on Graph Neural Networks (GNN). Unlike images, much data is not structured on a grid but naturally follows a graph structure. GNNs apply directly to graphs and thus their applications vary over many disciplines like predicting molecular properties for chemical compounds [15,29] and proteins [12], social influence prediction [43], object tracking [3,13], or detection of fake news [35]. Here, we propose to solve the problem of multi-view detection and re-identification of static objects in urban scenes using Graph Neural Networks. Given a set of ground-level images with coarse relative pose

© Springer Nature Switzerland AG 2020
A. Vedaldi et al. (Eds.): ECCV 2020, LNCS 12352, pp. 488–504, 2020.
https://doi.org/10.1007/978-3-030-58571-6_29

information, we detect, re-identify and finally assign geographic coordinates to thousands of urban objects with an end-to-end learnable approach.

Maintaining complete and accurate maps of urban objects is essential for a wide range of applications like autonomous driving, or maintenance of infrastructure by local municipalities. Despite much research in this field [23,38,49,54], updating maps is often still carried out via field surveys, which is a time-consuming and costly process. Here, we propose to accomplish this task by leveraging publicly available imagery that comes with coarse camera pose information.

What makes this task challenging is the relatively poor image quality of street-level panoramas (e.g., image stitching artefacts, motion blur) or dash cam image sequences (e.g., motion blur, narrow field of view) compared to data acquired through dedicated mobile mapping campaigns. Basically, wide baselines between consecutive acquisitions, and inaccurate camera poses information hinder establishing dense pixel-level correspondences between images. We thus propose to integrate image evidence and pose information into a single, end-to-end trainable neural network that uses images and coarse poses as input and outputs the geo-location of each distinct object in the scene. In contrast to a rigorous structure-from-motion approach, our method learns the joint distribution over different warping functions of the same object instance across multiple views together with the relative pose information. Unlike recent research in this domain, e.g., [2,23,26,49], our method employs an end-to-end approach that helps to jointly learn features to carry out the detection, re-identification, and geo-localization tasks. And differently to other end-to-end works such as [38], our approach for re-identification is based on a GNN that enables the use of multiple views (2+) and is much more computationally efficient in comparison to a siamese approach.

As illustrated in Fig. 1, our method works as follows: using a set of street-level images that come with coarse camera pose information as input, an object detector predicts several object bounding boxes for each of the views. We then construct a fully connected graph connecting all the object instances across the images. Next, the graph is fed through a GNN whose goal is to separate it into multiple disconnected sub-graphs, each representing a distinct object in the scene. The GNN has access to both image evidence and coarse pose information, so that it can learn to merge geometric view information with the corresponding object features from different viewpoints and to ensure high quality object re-identification. Finally, once that the distinct objects are re-identified, the proposed end-to-end architecture estimates their geo-location.

Our contributions are: i) an efficient end-to-end, multi-view detector for static objects *ii*) that implements a novel method for incorporating graphs inside any anchor-based object detector. We further *iii*) formulate a GNN approach that jointly uses coarse relative camera pose information and image evidence to detect distinct objects in the scene. We validate our method experimentally on two different datasets of street-level panoramas and dash cam image sequences. Our

Fig. 1. Illustration of our multi-view scenario. Red circle: Camera acquisition location. Green circle: target object to be detected. Orange line: distance between camera and object. (Color figure online)

GNN formulation for multi-view object detection and instance re-identification outperforms existing methods while being much more computationally efficient.

2   Related Work

Our proposed method is related to many different research topics in computer vision like pose estimation, urban object detection, and instance re-identification. A full review is beyond the scope of this paper and we rather provide here some representative works for each different topic and highlight the differences with our proposal.

Urban object detection from ground-level images is an application closely related to our paper. In [2,49], the authors propose a method to detect and geo-locate street-trees from Google street-view panorama and aerial images with a hierarchical workflow. Trees are first detected in all images, detections are then projected to geographic coordinates. The detection scores are back-projected into images and re-evaluated, finally a conditional random field integrates all image evidence with other learned priors. In [55] a method is proposed to detect and geo-locate poles in Google street-view panoramas using object detectors along with a modified brute-force line-of-bearing approach to estimate pole locations. Authors in [23] perform a semantic segmentation of images and estimate monocular depth before feeding both sources of evidence into a Markov random field to geo-locate traffic signs. [54] detects road objects from ground level imagery and places them into the right location using semantic segmentation and a topological binary tree. All previously mentioned methods have in common that they propose hierarchical, multi-step workflows where pose and image evidence are treated separately unlike ours, which models them jointly. The most similar work to ours is [38], which proposes to jointly leverage relative camera pose information and image evidence as an end-to-end trainable siamese CNN. [19] detects trees as blobs from satellite imagery and a Digital Surface Model using semantic segmentation. Here, we propose to formulate the problem as a graph neural network, which, intuitively, better represents the underlying data structure of multi-view object detection. Our GNN provides greater flexibility to add an arbitrary number of views (as opposed to a siamese CNN), is computationally drastically less costly, and achieves significantly better quantitative results. A large body of literature addresses urban object detection from an autonomous driving perspective with various existing public benchmark datasets like famous KITTI [14], CityScapes [6], or Mapillary [33,39]. As opposed to our case, in this scenario dense image sequences are acquired with minor viewpoint changes in driving direction with forward facing cameras and often relative pose information of good accuracy, enabling object detection and re-identification across views [5,24,56]. In our setup, relative pose information is coarse and the viewpoints among the images might be remarkably different, i.e., large baseline between the cameras, making the correspondences matching a much harder task.

Learning to predict camera poses using deep learning was made popular by PoseNet [20] and still motivates various studies [9,37,51]. Estimating a human hand's appearance from any viewpoint can be achieved by coupling pose with image content [42]. Full human pose estimation is another task that benefits from combined reasoning across pose and scene content, for instance in [32], authors employ a multi-task CNN to estimate pose and recognize action. We rely here on public imagery without fine-grained camera pose information, which requires a different approach.

Multiple object tracking (MOT) and person re-identification is related to our setting, but significantly differs in that objects are moving while cameras are usually fixed. Again, many deep learning-based solutions have been reported, usually employing a siamese CNN [28], as it is an effective technique to measure similarity between image patches. In [25], for instance, authors propose to learn features using a siamese CNN for multi-modal inputs (images and optical flow maps). In [48], a siamese CNN and temporally constrained metrics are jointly learned to create a tracklet affinity model. [44] uses a combination of CNNs and recurrent neural networks (RNN) in order to match pairs of detections. Authors in [52], instead, solve the re-identification problem with a so-called center loss that tries to minimize the distance between candidate boxes in the feature space. A work that is closely related to ours is [3]. Authors formulate their MOT for person re-identification into a graph setup. The graph is composed of nodes that hold CNN features of the image crops of the persons over time, with edges created between all these instances. A message passing network is then used to propagate the node features throughout the graph. Similar to our work, the edges between these nodes are then classified to re-identify the person. This paper however focuses on a single camera setup, whereas in our case we need to re-identify objects from different views.

Graph neural networks (GNN) naturally adapt to non-grid structured data like molecules, social networks, point clouds, or road networks. Graph convolutional networks (GCNs), as introduced by [4], originally proposed a convolutional approach on spectral graphs, which was further extended in [7,22,27]. Another line of research investigated GCNs in the spatial domain [1,11,15,34,40], where spatial neighborhoods of nodes inside graphs are convolved. In order to make processing on large graphs more efficient, recent methods pool nodes in order to perform subgraph-level classification [17,47]. These methods are described as fixed-pooling methods because they are based on the graph topology. Another idea is pooling nodes into a coarser representation based on weighted aggregations that are learned from the graph directly [8,13,53]. In our approach, a GNN network is used to capitalize on the data structure by classifying edges between nodes to find the correspondence. We use the spatial convolution operator GraphConv [36] since spatial-based convolutions have proven to be more efficient, and to generalize better on other data [17,50].

3   Method

We now describe in detail the proposed method. It is convenient to think of our architecture as composed of three stages: object detector, a GNN object re-identification and a geo-localization predictor, see Fig. 2. Note that, though we can see the model as made of three stages, the training is still conducted in an end-to-end manner, as the all the different parts support back-propagation.

3.1   Object Detection

In general, any state-of-the-art object detector could be used here. We choose EfficientDet [46] as it can provide state-of-the-art accuracy performance with a moderate amount of parameters and computations. The benefit of using an anchor based detector, is that our method can be adapted to other state-of-the-art methods [18,31] that also use an anchor based solution. The whole pipeline could, however, easily be adapted to work with anchor-free object detectors if desired.

The input to the object detector is a set of multiple images, which represent a scene, alongside with their metadata $M = \{C^*_{lat}, C^*_{lng}, h^\circ\}$ where $C^*_{lat}, C^*_{lng}, h^\circ$ represent the cameras's latitude, longitude and heading angle respectively, which corresponds to the location in the 3D world of the cameras. Similar to most object detectors, we feed the images through the *backbone*, which is in our case an ImageNet-pretrained CNN, to extract features. The features maps are then fed to both a classifier network and a regression network in order to predict the class of the objects and regress the coordinates of its bounding box, respectively. During the training phase we obviously have access to the bounding box ground truth with objects IDs of the annotated instances.

We use the Focal Loss introduced in [30] to train the object detection classifier. This loss was selected as it helps to handle the class imbalance between

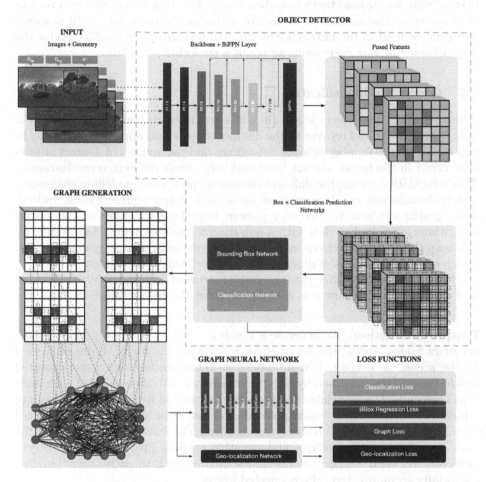

Fig. 2. Architecture of GeoGraph. A batch of images from multiple views and camera metadata information M pertaining to them are passed through the backbone network (EfficientNet) and the multi-scale feature aggregator (BiFPN) of the object detector that provides different levels of features. Anchors are then generated across the feature layers, and passed through two sub-networks to provide classification and box predictions. Based on the IoU of the ground truth with the anchors we select the positive and negative anchors. The features of these anchors are used to generate a dense fully connected graph. The graph is then fed to a GNN to predict if the nodes are corresponding by classifying their respective edge. In Parallel, the regressed bounding boxes of the positive anchors are passed to the Geo-Localization Network to regress the geo-coordinate.

positive and negative samples. In order to calculate the detection losses, we measure Intersection Over Union (IoU) and select the anchors that have the best overlap with our ground truth bounding boxes. This task is achieved by a threshold that splits the anchors into positive and negative proposals; both proposal will then be used in the next stage of our architecture (see Sect. 3.2). As for the object bounding box regression, we adopt a smooth-L_1 loss [16].

3.2   Object Re-identification

After detecting the objects across the different views, we need a method that is able to re-identify and recover all the distinct objects that appear of the scene. In this case both the number of input detections, and the number of distinct objects that occur in the scene, are not fixed and vary across different scene instances. This irregularity among the different instances poses some modelling challenges, which, fortunately, can be overcome by using a graph representation. Indeed, since graphs are usually used to represent irregular data, most of the graphs algorithms are suited to deal with a non-fixed number of nodes. As a result, we can map the object detections as nodes of a graph, and then use graph methods, which can handle graphs of different sizes, to perform object re-identification. In the following, we first define how the graph is created from the object detections, and then we describe how it is used to carry out the re-identification task.

Graph Generation. We generate a graph $\mathcal{G} = (V, E)$ where V represents the set of N nodes, and E the set of edges connecting the nodes. From each view in the scene, we extract as many nodes as there are features vectors located inside the anchors proposed by the object detector. We then think of each node v as containing the associated feature vector extracted from the feature map to which we concatenate the coarse pose information of the image and the predicted bounding box values. The features selected from the feature map include all the ones contained in the positive and negative anchors predicted by the object detector. We then connect all the nodes in the graph to each other, building essentially an undirected fully connected graph.

During the training phase we build a second undirected graph, $\mathcal{G}_{gt}$, which contains the same nodes as $\mathcal{G}$ but with edges encoding the identification information. Using the groundtruth annotations, we set $e_{ij} = 1$ if nodes i and j belong to the same object, regardless of which images the nodes i and j are associated to. Otherwise, we set $e_{ij} = 0$, meaning that the nodes are disconnected. We basically connect each pair of nodes only if they come from the same object. Intuitively, it is convenient to think of $\mathcal{G}_{gt}$ as made of a set of disconnected sub-graph components, each representing a single individual object in the scene.

Graph Neural Network. At this stage we are provided with an input graph $\mathcal{G}$, which is a fully connected graph among all the feature cells of all the objects detected in the different views. The goal here is to train a GNN that receives as input $\mathcal{G}$, and disentangles the nodes of the graph that belong to different objects, i.e., the GNN should recover $\mathcal{G}_{gt}$.

We compose our GNN out of 3 GraphConv [36] layers with a ReLU activation after each convolution. The GraphConv uses message passing to aggregate information from the neighborhood of i, denoted as $\mathcal{N}_i$, to update the feature representation H by:

$$H^{(k+1)}(v) = f_1^{W_1^{(k)}}\left(H^{(k)}(v), f_2^{W_2^{(k)}}\left(\left\{H^{(k)}(w) | w \in \mathcal{N}(v)\right\}\right)\right), \qquad (1)$$

where k represents the layer of the GNN, W^k are the trainable/learned weights, $f_2^{W_2^{(k)}}$ is the aggregation function of $\mathcal{N}(v)$, and $f_1^{W_1^{(k)}}$ merges the neighborhood features. At this point in our network, we insert a dropout [45] layer for regularization. The output feature representations of the nodes are then passed to a modified or stripped down EdgePooling layer [8] for the edge classification. This operation consists in concatenating the features of all the neighboring nodes in the graph, and passing them through a linear transformation followed by a sigmoid non-linearity:

$$s_{ij} = \sigma\left(W \cdot (H_i \| H_j) + b\right), \qquad (2)$$

where $\sigma()$ denotes the sigmoid function and $\|$ operator denotes a concatenation operation. s_{ij} represents the probability for the nodes i and j to belong to the same object in the scene. In this case the groundtruth value for each edge comes from $\mathcal{G}_{gt}$ and, as for the object detection, we train this classifier using focal loss to accommodate for dataset imbalance.

Note that by relying on a graph formulation we are able to effortlessly deal with a varying number of distinct objects in the scenes, focusing on "link prediction" instead of "graph classification". In fact, as we simply aim at disentangling the graph to separate the objects, the method is oblivious of the number of distinct objects in the scene (i.e., the object number is not hard-coded), and it is able to separate the graph into any number of disconnected components.

3.3   Geo-localization

We estimate the geo-coordinates of the identified objects similarly to [38,49]. The regressed bounding boxes values are projected to real world geographic coordinates by taking advantage of the camera information that is coupled with the image. In order to perform this operation we further assume that the terrain is locally flat. By using the projection equations Eq. (3) and (4) we are able to map the object bounding box pixel locations x and y in East, North, Up (ENU) coordinates e_x, e_y, e_z and secondly recover the position of the object in the real world O_{lat}, O_{lng}.

$$(e_x, e_y, e_z) = \left(R\cos[C_{lat}]\sin[O_{lng} - C_{lat}], R\sin[O_{lat} - C_{lat}], -\mathrm{h}^\circ\right) \qquad (3)$$

$$\begin{aligned} x &= \left(\pi + \arctan(e_x, e_y) - \mathrm{h}^\circ\right) W/2\pi \\ y &= \left(\pi/2 - \arctan(C_h, z)\right) H/\pi \end{aligned} \qquad (4)$$

where R denotes the Earth's radius, W and H are the image's width and height, C_h denotes camera's height and $z = \sqrt{e_x^2 + e_y^2}$ is an estimate of the object's distance from the camera. In order to improve the geo-localization accuracy we refine the predictions by feeding the geo-coordinates computed using Eq. (3) and (4) through a neural network. The geo-localization network is trained using the groundtruth through regression to obtain the object's geo-coordinate using a Mean Square Error (MSE) loss.

3.4 Inference Operations

At inference time, the operations carried out in the whole pipeline are slightly different. First, the object detector generates the proposals for the anchors with classification confidences and bounding boxes. A threshold is then applied to the classification score to select only the detection proposals with a high classification confidence. Afterwards, Non Maximum Suppression (NMS) is used to filter further proposals and reduce redundancy.

With the remaining proposals, we create a fully connected graph as described before, with each node representing a feature vector contained inside the proposals, at which we concatenate the image's camera metadata information. The generated graph is then fed to the GNN network for edge classification. Finally, we classify the edges scores by applying a threshold on them with a decision boundary of 0.5. At this point, the obtained graph is supposed to be made of several disconnected components, one for each of the distinct objects in the scene. We remove sequentially each set of connected components until no nodes are left.

We finally compute the geo-location of the identified objects by utilizing the camera metadata information and the location of the bounding box in the image for all the views where the identified object appears. All the objects geo-coordinates computed from each different view are then separately refined with the geo-localization network and, finally, averaged to obtain the final prediction.

4   Experiments

4.1   Datasets

Pasadena Multi-View ReID. Instance labeled trees are ignored in most urban object datasets where they are rather labeled as vegetation. We consider the Pasadena Multi-View ReID [38] dataset that provides labeled instances of different trees acquired in Pasadena, California. The dataset offers approximately 4 Google Street View panoramic views for each tree instance. A scene of 4 views could contain multiple labeled instances, averaging 2 instances per scene, and other trees that are not instance labeled. There is a total of 6,020 individual tree instances.

The dataset consists of 6,141 panorama images of size 2048×1024 px. In total, there are around 25,061 annotated objects in the dataset. Each annotation includes the object's bounding box values, image geo-coordinates, camera heading, estimate of object distance from camera, ID and geo-coordinate of object. In our experiments, we follow the same data split introduced in [38], and allocate 4,298 images for training, 921 for validation, and 922 for testing.

Mapillary. The second dataset we consider is a crowdsourced one provided by Mapillary[1], that is different from the image segmentation dataset, Mapillary Vistas [39]. Normally, the dataset contains different types of objects, but this subset contains traffic signs only in an area of $2\,km^2$ London, England. In comparison to the Pasadena Multi-View ReID, the images acquired in this dataset are dominantly captured consecutively by forward-faced cameras mounted on vehicles with the object mostly facing change in scale with the same viewpoint, with the other instances being from pedestrians' smartphone cameras.

Given its crowdsourced nature, this dataset presents interesting challenges such as images being acquired at different times of the day, various camera sensors as well as image sizes. There are 31,442 different instances of traffic signs labeled in 74,320 images. An object instance appears on average in 4 images, and there are approximately 2 object instances in each image. Almost entirely, all instances of signs in the image are annotated. Each object instance in the dataset comes with its bounding box values, object ID, image geo-coordinates, instance geo-coordinates, heading of camera, in which images the object appears, and its height. It is important to note that the object geo-coordinate is attained through 3D Structure From Motion techniques (SFM). In contrast to the Pasadena Multi-View ReID, the objects are much smaller in comparison to trees, and much difficult to capture sideways due to the physical property of signs being thin. On the other hand, the dataset is much larger, thus easing the training process.

4.2   Implementation Details

We implemented GeoGraph using PyTorch [41]. For the object detector, a PyTorch implementation of EfficientDet was used. The backbone chosen for the EfficientDet was "EfficientNet-B5". As for the GNN component, we relied on the PyTorch Geometric package [10]. The Dropout [45] layers are used with a drop probability of 0.2. The learning rate is set to 0.001 initially with ADAM [21] as the optimizer. Each epoch takes approximately 45 min during training time on a NVIDIA 1080 Ti GPU ([38] needs 270 min). Our network uses 34.75M parameters while [38] uses 50M. We significantly reduce inference time per image from 0.78 ms [38] to 0.32 ms.

4.3   Object Detection and Re-identification

In Table 1 we report the results achieved by our method in the different datasets as well as state-of-the-art performance. The effectiveness of our approach is evaluated by correctly identifying an instance of an object across multiple views, as

---

[1] www.mapillary.com.

also visually illustrated in Fig. 3 and Fig. 4. Typically, the object detection method influences the re-identification process as a better mean Average Precision (mAP) ensures that the object is fed to the next stage of the pipeline for the re-identification. Moreover, note that the object detection scores for the proposed method does not change between the 2 and 2+ views, this is because the object detection is always carried out on a single image at the time. Our method outperforms SSD-ReID-Geo [38] for detection mAP by 2.2% with the Pasadena dataset, and 1.7% with the Mapillary dataset. GeoGraph improvement can be attributed to the superiority of EfficientDet over SSD.

Our experiments for re-identification aim at validating whether using graphs with coarse pose information would assist in identifying the same object instance across views. The performance of the GNN component is based on whether the detections of the same object across different views have connecting edges. Therefore to calculate our mAP, we consider as true positives correctly predicted edges between a pair of detections with no other edge connections to different objects in the scene. Otherwise we consider them as false positives. In order to ensure a fair comparison with other methods, we perform experiments with a similar number of views. As shown in Table 1, increasing the views leads to higher re-identification mAP, with an improvement of 3.2% for Pasadena and 4.2% for Mapillary.

4.4   Geolocalization

The geo-localization component is evaluated in terms of a Mean Absolute Error (MAE) of the distance, measured in meters, between the predicted geo-coordinate averaged over the different views and the ground truth as shown in Fig. 5. The metric chosen to measure the distance is the Haversine distance which is defined as:

$$d = 2R \arcsin\left(\left(\sin^2\left(\frac{O_{lat} - G_{lat}}{2}\right)\right.\right.$$
$$\left.\left. + \cos(G_{lat})\cos(O_{lat})\sin^2\left(\frac{O_{lng} - G_{lng}}{2}\right)\right)^{0.5}\right), \quad (5)$$

where O_{lat}, O_{lng} represent the detection's predicted geo-coordinates, and G_{lat}, G_{lng} represent the object's ground truth. As reported in Table 1, for the Pasadena dataset, the geo-localization error decreases as the number of views increases (12% improvement). As for Mapillary, we report again lower error with our GeoGraph and 6 views w.r.t. SSD-ReID-Geo [38] (3.4% improvement). However, we surprisingly did not outperform GeoGraph results achieved with only 2 views. This is probably be due to the way the ground truth of the Mapillary dataset is acquired (see Sect. 4.1), and adding more views brings a lot of noise in the representation of a scene and of the objects it contains.

Table 1. Quantitative assessment of our GeoGraph framework and related work on object detection, re-identification, and geo-localization tasks.

Method	# Views	Dataset	Detection mAP	Re-ID mAP	Geo-localization error (m)
MRF [23]	4	Pasadena	0.742	-	3.83
SSD-ReID-Geo [38]	2	Pasadena	0.682	0.731	3.13
Our GeoGraph	2	Pasadena 2*}	0.742	**0.754**	**2.94**
Our GeoGraph	4	Pasadena		**0.763**	**2.75**
MRF [23]	4	Mapillary	0.919	-	4.62
SSD-ReID-Geo [38]	2	Mapillary	0.902	0.882	4.36
Our GeoGraph	2	Mapillary 2*}	0.919	**0.902**	**3.88**
Our GeoGraph	6	Mapillary		**0.924**	4.21

4.5   Ablation Studies

Since the graphs are generated during training are created online, we assess this component separately to be able to evaluate its effect. In these experiments, we build the graph from our ground-truth by generating CNN features from the image crops of multi-view images, which served as our node features. Using the labeled instances, edges were associated between the different instances of image crops across the different views. Throughout this experiment, the same settings of the GNN were used as mentioned in Sect. 3.2. We compare our method to a siamese CNN with a ResNet50 backbone trained with a contrastive loss that classified whether the two crops of the object are similar or not.

Table 2. Results for our graph matching method component evaluated with bypassing the object detector, and using image crops. We show a comparison between a Siamese CNN, a GNN based on CNN features and a GNN based on CNN features and camera metadata information to classify if pairs of objects are the same or not.

Method	Dataset	F1-score
Siamese CNN	Pasadena	0.509
GNN	Pasadena	0.601
GNN-Geo	Pasadena	**0.640**
Siamese CNN	Mapillary	0.721
GNN	Mapillary	0.823
GNN-Geo	Mapillary	**0.873**

We can observe from results reported in Table 2 that adding geometric cues consistently helped to improve re-identification. Through different examination with different forms of the graph construction, we have found out that creating edges between nodes across multiple views but also within the same image in a fully connected dense manner led to better results than in the case where edges between nodes of the same image (i.e. detections within same image) are ignored. This can be explained by the fact that node aggregation performs better with fully connected graphs.

5   Conclusion

In this paper we have tackled the problems of object detection, re-identification across multiple views and geo-localization with a unified, end-to-end learnable framework. We propose a method that integrates both image and pose information and use a GNN to perform object re-identification. The advantage of the our GNN over standard Siamese CNN is the ability to deal with any number of views and be computational efficient. Experiments conducted on two public datasets have shown the relevance of our GeoGraph framework, which achieves high detection accuracy together with low geo-localization error. Furthermore, our approach is robust to occlusion, neighboring objects of similar appearance, and severe changes in viewpoints.

Fig. 3. Sample results obtained on the Pasadena dataset for multi-view object detection and re-identification. Trees were correctly detected (green) and further accurately re-identified across different views (cyan) when possible. (Color figure online)

The proposed framework could be improved if based on a better geo-localization component. Furthermore, using the proposals generated from each view could improve the quality of the object detection step. Finally, while only street view images were used in our paper, our GeoGraph framework is compatible with other types of images. We thus would like to combine these ground-level

Fig. 4. Sample results obtained on the Mapillary dataset for multi-view object detection and re-identification. Here all detected objects (signs) were both detected and further re-identified (cyan) due to the higher similarity between views. (Color figure online)

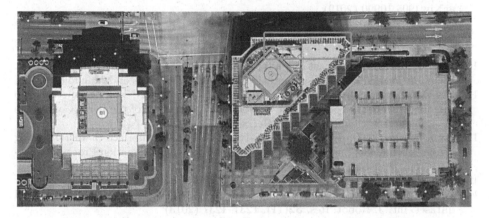

Fig. 5. Sample of geo-localization results for Pasadena comparing different methods. Green, blue, yellow and red circles represent the ground-truth, GeoGraph, SSD-ReID-Geo and MRF respectively. The orange bounding box exhibits how ground level imagery can be helpful to detect object obscured by buildings from aerial view. (Color figure online)

views with aerial views in order to improve the overall performance and to make the best of multiple viewpoints following [26].

Acknowledgment. This project was supported by funding provided by the Hasler Foundation. We thank Mapillary for providing the dataset.

References

1. Atwood, J., Towsley, D.: Diffusion-convolutional neural networks. In: Advances in Neural Information Processing Systems, pp. 1993–2001 (2016)

2. Branson, S., Wegner, J.D., Hall, D., Lang, N., Schindler, K., Perona, P.: From Google Maps to a fine-grained catalog of street trees. ISPRS J. Photogrammetry Remote Sensing **135**, 13–30 (2018)
3. Brasó, G., Leal-Taixé, L.: Learning a neural solver for multiple object tracking. arXiv preprint arXiv:1912.07515 (2019)
4. Bruna, J., Zaremba, W., Szlam, A., LeCun, Y.: Spectral networks and locally connected networks on graphs. arXiv preprint arXiv:1312.6203 (2013)
5. Chen, X., Ma, H., Wan, J., Li, B., Xia, T.: Multi-view 3D object detection network for autonomous driving. In: Proceedings of the IEEE Conference on Computer Vision and Pattern Recognition, pp. 1907–1915 (2017)
6. Cordts, M., et al.: The cityscapes dataset for semantic urban scene understanding. In: Proceedings of the IEEE Conference on Computer Vision and Pattern Recognition, pp. 3213–3223 (2016)
7. Defferrard, M., Bresson, X., Vandergheynst, P.: Convolutional neural networks on graphs with fast localized spectral filtering. In: Advances in Neural Information Processing Systems, pp. 3844–3852 (2016)
8. Diehl, F.: Edge contraction pooling for graph neural networks. arXiv preprint arXiv:1905.10990 (2019)
9. En, S., Lechervy, A., Jurie, F.: RPNet: an end-to-end network for relative camera pose estimation. In: Proceedings of the European Conference on Computer Vision, pp. 738–745 (2018)
10. Fey, M., Lenssen, J.E.: Fast graph representation learning with PyTorch geometric. In: ICLR Workshop on Representation Learning on Graphs and Manifolds (2019)
11. Fey, M., Lenssen, J.E., Weichert, F., Müller, H.: SplineCNN: fast geometric deep learning with continuous b-spline kernels. In: Proceedings of the IEEE Conference on Computer Vision and Pattern Recognition, pp. 869–877 (2018)
12. Fout, A., Byrd, J., Shariat, B., Ben-Hur, A.: Protein interface prediction using graph convolutional networks. In: Advances in Neural Information Processing Systems, pp. 6530–6539 (2017)
13. Gao, H., Ji, S.: Graph U-Nets. arXiv preprint arXiv:1905.05178 (2019)
14. Geiger, A., Lenz, P., Stiller, C., Urtasun, R.: Vision meets robotics: the KITTI dataset. Int. J. Robot. Res. **32**(11), 1231–1237 (2013)
15. Gilmer, J., Schoenholz, S.S., Riley, P.F., Vinyals, O., Dahl, G.E.: Neural message passing for quantum chemistry. In: Proceedings of the International Conference on Machine Learning, vol. 70, pp. 1263–1272 (2017)
16. Girshick, R.: Fast R-CNN. In: Proceedings of the IEEE International Conference on Computer Vision, pp. 1440–1448 (2015)
17. Hamilton, W., Ying, Z., Leskovec, J.: Inductive representation learning on large graphs. In: Advances in Neural Information Processing Systems, pp. 1024–1034 (2017)
18. He, K., Gkioxari, G., Dollár, P., Girshick, R.: Mask R-CNN. In: Proceedings of the IEEE International Conference on Computer Vision, pp. 2961–2969 (2017)
19. Kampffmeyer, M., Salberg, A.B., Jenssen, R.: Semantic segmentation of small objects and modeling of uncertainty in urban remote sensing images using deep convolutional neural networks. In: Proceedings of the IEEE Conference on Computer Vision and Pattern Recognition Workshops, pp. 1–9 (2016)
20. Kendall, A., Grimes, M., Cipolla, R.: Posenet: a convolutional network for real-time 6-DOF camera relocalization. In: Proceedings of the IEEE International Conference on Computer Vision, pp. 2938–2946 (2015)
21. Kingma, D.P., Ba, J.: Adam: a method for stochastic optimization. arXiv preprint arXiv:1412.6980 (2014)

22. Kipf, T.N., Welling, M.: Semi-supervised classification with graph convolutional networks. arXiv preprint arXiv:1609.02907 (2016)
23. Krylov, V.A., Kenny, E., Dahyot, R.: Automatic discovery and geotagging of objects from street view imagery. Remote Sensing 10(5), 661 (2018)
24. Ku, J., Mozifian, M., Lee, J., Harakeh, A., Waslander, S.L.: Joint 3D proposal generation and object detection from view aggregation. In: Proceedings of the IEEE/RSJ International Conference on Intelligent Robots and Systems, pp. 1–8 (2018)
25. Leal-Taixé, L., Canton-Ferrer, C., Schindler, K.: Learning by tracking: siamese CNN for robust target association. In: Proceedings of the IEEE Conference on Computer Vision and Pattern Recognition Workshops, pp. 33–40 (2016)
26. Lefèvre, S., Tuia, D., Wegner, J.D., Produit, T., Nassar, A.S.: Toward seamless multiview scene analysis from satellite to street level. Proc. IEEE 105(10), 1884–1899 (2017)
27. Levie, R., Monti, F., Bresson, X., Bronstein, M.M.: CayleyNets: graph convolutional neural networks with complex rational spectral filters. IEEE Trans. Signal Process. 67(1), 97–109 (2019)
28. Li, W., Zhao, R., Xiao, T., Wang, X.: Deepreid: deep filter pairing neural network for person re-identification. In: Proceedings of the IEEE Conference on Computer Vision and Pattern Recognition, pp. 152–159 (2014)
29. Li, Y., Vinyals, O., Dyer, C., Pascanu, R., Battaglia, P.: Learning deep generative models of graphs. arXiv preprint arXiv:1803.03324 (2018)
30. Lin, T.Y., Goyal, P., Girshick, R., He, K., Dollár, P.: Focal loss for dense object detection. In: Proceedings of the IEEE International Conference on Computer Vision, pp. 2980–2988 (2017)
31. Liu, Y., et al.: CBNet: a novel composite backbone network architecture for object detection. arXiv preprint arXiv:1909.03625 (2019)
32. Luvizon, D.C., Picard, D., Tabia, H.: 2D/3D pose estimation and action recognition using multitask deep learning. In: Proceedings of the IEEE Conference on Computer Vision and Pattern Recognition, pp. 5137–5146 (2018)
33. Ma, D., Fan, H., Li, W., Ding, X.: The state of mapillary: an exploratory analysis. ISPRS Int. J. Geo Inf. 9(1), 10 (2020)
34. Monti, F., Boscaini, D., Masci, J., Rodola, E., Svoboda, J., Bronstein, M.M.: Geometric deep learning on graphs and manifolds using mixture model CNNs. In: Proceedings of the IEEE Conference on Computer Vision and Pattern Recognition, pp. 5115–5124 (2017)
35. Monti, F., Frasca, F., Eynard, D., Mannion, D., Bronstein, M.M.: Fake news detection on social media using geometric deep learning. arXiv preprint arXiv:1902.06673 (2019)
36. Morris, C., et al.: Weisfeiler and leman go neural: higher-order graph neural networks. In: Proceedings of the AAAI Conference on Artificial Intelligence, vol. 33, pp. 4602–4609 (2019)
37. Nakajima, Y., Saito, H.: Robust camera pose estimation by viewpoint classification using deep learning. Comput. Vis. Media 3(2), 189–198 (2017). https://doi.org/10.1007/s41095-016-0067-z
38. Nassar, A.S., Lefèvre, S., Wegner, J.D.: Simultaneous multi-view instance detection with learned geometric soft-constraints. In: Proceedings of the IEEE International Conference on Computer Vision, pp. 6559–6568 (2019)
39. Neuhold, G., Ollmann, T., Bulò, S.R., Kontschieder, P.: The mapillary vistas dataset for semantic understanding of street scenes. In: Proceedings of the IEEE International Conference on Computer Vision, pp. 5000–5009 (2017)

40. Niepert, M., Ahmed, M., Kutzkov, K.: Learning convolutional neural networks for graphs. In: Proceedings of the International Conference on Machine Learning, pp. 2014–2023 (2016)
41. Paszke, A., et al.: Automatic differentiation in PyTorch. In: NIPS Autodiff Workshop (2017)
42. Poier, G., Schinagl, D., Bischof, H.: Learning pose specific representations by predicting different views. In: Proceedings of the IEEE Conference on Computer Vision and Pattern Recognition, pp. 60–69 (2018)
43. Qiu, J., Tang, J., Ma, H., Dong, Y., Wang, K., Tang, J.: Deepinf: social influence prediction with deep learning. In: Proceedings of the ACM SIGKDD International Conference on Knowledge Discovery & Data Mining, pp. 2110–2119 (2018)
44. Sadeghian, A., Alahi, A., Savarese, S.: Tracking the untrackable: Learning to track multiple cues with long-term dependencies. In: Proceedings of the IEEE International Conference on Computer Vision, pp. 300–311 (2017)
45. Srivastava, N., Hinton, G., Krizhevsky, A., Sutskever, I., Salakhutdinov, R.: Dropout: a simple way to prevent neural networks from overfitting. J. Mach Learn. Res. **15**(1), 1929–1958 (2014)
46. Tan, M., Pang, R., Le, Q.V.: Efficientdet: scalable and efficient object detection. arXiv preprint arXiv:1911.09070 (2019)
47. Veličković, P., Cucurull, G., Casanova, A., Romero, A., Lio, P., Bengio, Y.: Graph attention networks. arXiv preprint arXiv:1710.10903 (2017)
48. Wang, B., et al.: Joint learning of convolutional neural networks and temporally constrained metrics for tracklet association. In: Proceedings of the IEEE Conference on Computer Vision and Pattern Recognition Workshops, pp. 1–8 (2016)
49. Wegner, J.D., Branson, S., Hall, D., Schindler, K., Perona, P.: Cataloging public objects using aerial and street-level images-urban trees. In: IEEE Conference on Computer Vision and Pattern Recognition, pp. 6014–6023 (2016)
50. Wu, Z., Pan, S., Chen, F., Long, G., Zhang, C., Yu, P.S.: A comprehensive survey on graph neural networks. arXiv preprint arXiv:1901.00596 (2019)
51. Xiang, Y., Schmidt, T., Narayanan, V., Fox, D.: PoseCNN: a convolutional neural network for 6D object pose estimation in cluttered scenes. In: Robotics: Science and Systems (2018)
52. Xiao, J., Xie, Y., Tillo, T., Huang, K., Wei, Y., Feng, J.: IAN: the individual aggregation network for person search. Pattern Recogn. **87**, 332–340 (2019)
53. Ying, Z., You, J., Morris, C., Ren, X., Hamilton, W., Leskovec, J.: Hierarchical graph representation learning with differentiable pooling. In: Advances in Neural Information Processing Systems, pp. 4800–4810 (2018)
54. Zhang, C., Fan, H., Li, W., Mao, B., Ding, X.: Automated detecting and placing road objects from street-level images. arXiv preprint arXiv:1909.05621 (2019)
55. Zhang, W., Witharana, C., Li, W., Zhang, C., Li, X., Parent, J.: Using deep learning to identify utility poles with crossarms and estimate their locations from Google street view images. Sensors **18**(8), 2484 (2018)
56. Zhao, J., Zhang, X.N., Gao, H., Yin, J., Zhou, M., Tan, C.: Object detection based on hierarchical multi-view proposal network for autonomous driving. In: Proceedings of the International Joint Conference on Neural Networks, pp. 1–6 (2018)

Localizing the Common Action Among a Few Videos

Pengwan Yang[1,2(✉)], Vincent Tao Hu[2], Pascal Mettes[2], and Cees G. M. Snoek[2]

[1] Peking University, Beijing, China
yangpengwan2016@gmail.com
[2] University of Amsterdam, Amsterdam, The Netherlands
taohu620@gmail.com

Abstract. This paper strives to localize the temporal extent of an action in a long untrimmed video. Where existing work leverages many examples with their start, their ending, and/or the class of the action during training time, we propose few-shot common action localization. The start and end of an action in a long untrimmed video is determined based on just a hand-full of trimmed video examples containing the same action, without knowing their common class label. To address this task, we introduce a new 3D convolutional network architecture able to align representations from the support videos with the relevant query video segments. The network contains: (*i*) a mutual enhancement module to simultaneously complement the representation of the few trimmed support videos and the untrimmed query video; (*ii*) a progressive alignment module that iteratively fuses the support videos into the query branch; and (*iii*) a pairwise matching module to weigh the importance of different support videos. Evaluation of few-shot common action localization in untrimmed videos containing a single or multiple action instances demonstrates the effectiveness and general applicability of our proposal.
Code: https://github.com/PengWan-Yang/commonLocalization

Keywords: Common action localization · Few-shot learning

1 Introduction

The goal of this paper is to localize the temporal extent of an action in a long untrimmed video. This challenging problem [8,32] has witnessed considerable progress thanks to deep learning solutions, *e.g.* [12,26,37], fueled by the availability of large-scale video datasets containing the start, the end, and the class of the action [3,6,17]. Recently, weakly-supervised alternatives have appeared, *e.g.* [1,18,24,25,31,34,43,47]. They avoid the need for hard to obtain start and

---

P. Yang and V. T. Hu—Equal contribution.

Electronic supplementary material The online version of this chapter (https://doi.org/10.1007/978-3-030-58571-6_30) contains supplementary material, which is available to authorized users.

© Springer Nature Switzerland AG 2020
A. Vedaldi et al. (Eds.): ECCV 2020, LNCS 12352, pp. 505–521, 2020.
https://doi.org/10.1007/978-3-030-58571-6_30

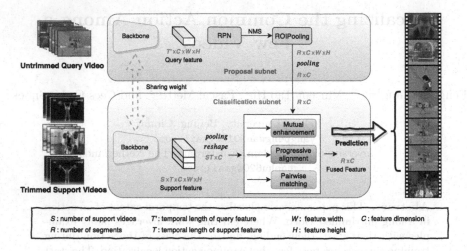

Fig. 1. Common action localization in an untrimmed query video from three trimmed support videos during inference. The action is localized in the query video based on the common action in the support videos.

end time annotations, but still require hundreds of videos labeled with their action class. In this paper, we also aim for a weakly-supervised setup, but we avoid the need for any action class labels. We propose few-shot *common* action localization, which determines the start and end of an action in a long untrimmed video based on just a hand-full of trimmed videos containing the same action, without knowing their common class label.

We are inspired by recent works on few-shot object detection [7,16,35,36]. Dong *et al.* [7] start from a few labeled boxes per object and a large pool of unlabeled images. Pseudo-labels for the unlabeled images are utilized to iteratively refine the object detection result. Both Shaban *et al.* [36] and Hu *et al.* [16] further relax the labeling constraint by only requiring a few examples to contain a common object, without the strict need to know their class name. Hu *et al.* [16] introduce two modules to reweigh the influence of each example and to leverage spatial similarity between support and query images. We also require that our few examples contain a common class and we adopt a reweighting module. Different from Hu *et al.*, we have no module to focus on masking objects spatially in images. Instead, we introduce three alternative modules optimized for localizing actions temporally in long untrimmed videos, as illustrated in Fig. 1.

We make three contributions in this work. First, we consider common action localization from the few-shot perspective. All we require is that the few trimmed video examples share a common action, which may be obtained from social tags, hash tags or off-the-shelve action classifiers. Second, we propose a network architecture for few-shot common action localization, along with three modules able to align representations from the support videos with the relevant query video segments. The mutual enhancement module strengthens the representations of the query and support representations simultaneously by building upon non-local blocks [44]. The progressive alignment module iteratively integrates the support branch into the query branch. Lastly, the pairwise matching module learns to weigh the importance of different support videos. As a third contribution, we reorganize the videos in ActivityNet1.3 [3] and Thumos14 [17] to allow for experimental evaluation of few-shot common action localization in long untrimmed videos containing a single or multiple action instances.

2 Related Work

Action Localization from Many Examples. Standard action localization is concerned with finding the start and end times of actions in videos from many training videos with labeled temporal boundaries [2,9,37]. A common approach is to employ sliding windows to generate segments and subsequently classify them with action classifiers [5,11,37,42,46]. Due to the computational cost of sliding windows, several approaches model the temporal evolution of actions and predict an action label at each time step [9,27,38,48]. The R-C3D action localization pipeline [45] encodes the frames with fully-convolutional 3D filters, generates action proposals, then classifies and refines them. In this paper, we adopt the proposal subnet of R-C3D to obtain class-agnostic action proposals. In weakly-supervised localization, the models are learned from training videos without temporal annotations. They only rely on the global action class labels [30,31,43]. Different from both standard and weakly-supervised action localization, our *common* action localization focuses on finding the common action in a long untrimmed query video given a few (or just one) trimmed support videos without knowing the common action class label, making our task class-agnostic. Furthermore, the videos used to train our approach contain actions that are not seen during testing.

Action Localization from Few Examples. Yang *et al.* [46] pioneered few-shot *labeled* action localization, where a few (or at least one) positive labeled and several negative labeled videos steer the localization via an end-to-end meta-learning strategy. It relies on sliding windows to swipe over the untrimmed query video to generate fixed boundary proposals. Rather then relying on a few positive and many negative action class labels, our approach does not require any predefined positive nor negative action labels, all we require is that the few support videos have the same action in *common*. Moreover, we propose a network architecture with three modules that predicts proposals of arbitrary length from commonality only.

Action Localization from One Example. Closest to our work is video re-localization by Feng *et al.* [10], which introduces localization in an untrimmed query video from a *single* unlabeled support video. They propose a bilinear matching module with gating functions for the localization. Compared to video relocalization, we consider a more general and realistic setting, where more than one support video can be used. Furthermore, we consider untrimmed videos of longer temporal extent and we consider action localization from a single frame.

To enable action localization under these challenging settings, we introduce modules that learn to enhance and align the query video with one or more support videos, while furthermore learning to weigh individual support videos. We find that our proposed common action localization formulation obtains better results, both in existing and in our new settings.

Action Localization from No Examples. Localization has also been investigated from a zero-shot perspective by linking actions to relevant objects [19, 20,29]. Soomro *et al.* [39] tackle action localization in an unsupervised setting, where no annotations are provided overall. While zero-shot and unsupervised action localization show promise, current approaches are not competitive with (weakly-)supervised alternatives, hence we focus on the few-shot setting.

3   Method

3.1   Problem Description

For the task of few-shot common action localization, we are given a set of trimmed support videos S_c^N, where N is small, and an untrimmed query video Q_c. Both the support and query videos contain activity class c, although its label is not provided. The goal is to learn a function $f(S_c^N, Q_c)$ that outputs the temporal segments for activity class c in the query video. The function $f(\cdot, \cdot)$ is parametrized by a deep network consisting of a support and query branch. During training, we have access to a set of support-query tuples $T = \{(S_l^N, Q_l)\}_{l \in \mathcal{L}_{\text{train}}}$. During both validation and testing, we are only given a few trimmed support videos with corresponding long untrimmed query video. The data is divided such that $\mathcal{L}_{\text{train}} \cup \mathcal{L}_{\text{val}} \cup \mathcal{L}_{\text{test}} = \emptyset$.

3.2   Architecture

We propose an end-to-end network to solve the few-shot common action localization problem. A single query video and a few support videos are fed into the backbone, a C3D network [40], to obtain video representations. The weights of the backbone network are shared between the support and query videos. For the query video, a proposal subnet predicts temporal segments of variable length containing potential activities [45]. Let $\mathcal{F}_Q \in \mathbb{R}^{R \times C}$ denote the feature representation of the query video for R temporal proposal segments, each of dimensionality C. Let $\mathcal{F}_S \in \mathbb{R}^{ST \times C}$ denote the representations of the S support videos, where we split each support video into T fixed temporal parts. The main goal of the network is to align the support representations with the relevant query segment representation:

$$\mathcal{F} = \phi(\mathcal{F}_Q, \mathcal{F}_S). \tag{1}$$

In Eq. 1, $\mathcal{F} \in \mathbb{R}^{R \times C}$ denotes the temporal segment representations after alignment with the support representations through ϕ. In our common localization network, representations $\mathcal{F}$ are fed to fully-connected layers that perform a

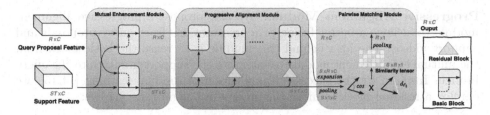

Fig. 2. **Modules for aligning representations** from the support videos with the relevant query video segments. The mutual enhancement module augments the support and query representations simultaneously through message passing. Then, the progressive alignment module fuses the support into the query branch through recursive use of the basic block. Finally, the pairwise matching module reweighs the fused features according to the similarity between the enhanced query segments and the enhanced support videos.

binary classification to obtain the likelihood that each proposal segment matches with the support actions, which is followed by a temporal regression to refine the activity start- and end-times for all segments.

In our network, we consider the following: *i*) the representations of the support videos need to be aligned with the representations of the activity in the query video, *ii*) not all support videos are equally informative, and *iii*) common action localization is a support-conditioned localization task, where the activityness of different query segments should be guided by the support videos. We propose three modules, namely mutual enhancement module, progressive alignment module, and pairwise matching module to deal with these considerations.

Mutual Enhancement Module. Building on the recent success of the transformer structure [41] and the non-local block [44], which are forms of self-attention, we propose a module which can simultaneously enhance the representations of the support and query videos from each other. The basic block for this module is given as:

$$m(I_1, I_2) = c_1(soft(c_2(I_1) \times c_3(I_2^T)) \times c_4(I_2)) + I_1, \qquad (2)$$

where c_1, c_2, c_3, c_4 are fully-connected layers, *soft* denotes the softmax activation, and $\times$ denotes matrix multiplication. I_1 and I_2 denote the two inputs. A detailed overview and illustration of the basic block is provided in the supplementary materials. Based on the basic block, we design a mutual enhancement module to learn mutually-enforced representations, both for query proposals and support videos, as shown in Fig. 2. The mutual enhancement module has two streams $m_{s \to q}$, $m_{q \to s}$ that are responsible for enhancing query proposals and support videos respectively. The inputs to the mutual enhancement module, $\mathcal{F}_Q$ and $\mathcal{F}_S$, will be enhanced by each other:

$$m_{s \to q} = m(\mathcal{F}_Q, \mathcal{F}_S), \qquad (3)$$

$$m_{q \to s} = m(\mathcal{F}_S, \mathcal{F}_Q). \qquad (4)$$

Progressive Alignment Module. We also propose a progressive alignment module to achieve a better fusion of representations from query proposals and support videos. The idea behind this module is to reuse the basic block from the mutual enhancement module to integrate the support branch into the query branch. Inspired by the successful application of residual learning [14,15], we employ a residual block to make the progressive alignment effective:

$$r(I) = c_1(relu(c_2(I))) + I, \tag{5}$$

where c_1, c_2 are fully-connected layers, *relu* denotes the ReLU activation. A detailed overview and illustration of the residual block is provided in the supplementary materials. We first take query proposal representations from the first module $m_{s \to q}$ as 0-depth outcome $\mathcal{P}_0$. On top, we adopt our basic block m to integrate this outcome with $m_{q \to s}$ which has been recalibrated by our residual block r. We perform this operation multiple times in a recursive manner, *i.e.*:

$$\mathcal{P}_0 = m_{s \to q}, \tag{6}$$

$$\mathcal{P}_k = m(\mathcal{P}_{k-1}, r(m_{q \to s})), \quad k = 1, 2, \dots, n. \tag{7}$$

where we set $n = 3$ in practice. The advantage of a progressive design is that it strengthens the integration of the support branch into the query branch as we increase the number of basic block iterations. By using the same efficient basic blocks as our first module, the computational overhead is small. An illustration of the progressive alignment module is shown in Fig. 2.

Pairwise Matching Module. In common action localization, a small number of support videos is used. Intuitively, not every support video is equally informative for the query segments. In addition, different query segments should not be treated equally either. To address these intuitions, we add a means to weigh the influence between each support video and each query segment, by introducing a pairwise matching module.

The input for the matching module are all segments of the query video and all support videos. The pair-wise matching is a mapping PMM : $(\mathbb{R}^{R \times C}, \mathbb{R}^{S \times T \times C}) \mapsto \mathbb{R}^{S \times R \times 1}$. To align the two components, we first perform an expansion operation e on the query segments, denoted as $e(\mathcal{P}_n) \in \mathbb{R}^{S \times R \times C}$. Then a pooling p is applied over the support videos along the temporal dimension, denoted as $p(m_{q \to s}) \in \mathbb{R}^{S \times 1 \times C}$. Afterwards, we perform an auto broadcasting operation b on $p(m_{q \to s})$, which can broadcast the dimension of $p(m_{q \to s})$ from $\mathbb{R}^{S \times 1 \times C}$ to $\mathbb{R}^{S \times R \times C}$ to align with the dimension of $e(\mathcal{P}_n)$. For query segments $\mathcal{P}_n$ and for support videos $m_{q \to s}$, their match is given by the cosine similarity (*cos*) and ℓ_2 Euclidean distance (d_{ℓ_2}) along the segment axis:

$$M = cos(\mathcal{P}_n, m_{q \to s}) = \frac{<e(\mathcal{P}_n), b(p(m_{q \to s}))>}{\|e(\mathcal{P}_n)\| \cdot \|b(p(m_{q \to s}))\|}, \tag{8}$$

$$N = d_{\ell_2}(\mathcal{P}_n, m_{q \to s}) = \|e(\mathcal{P}_n) - b(p(m_{q \to s}))\|. \tag{9}$$

We combine both distance measures:

$$W = \text{PMM}(\mathcal{P}_n, m_{q \to s}) = M \odot \sigma(-N), \tag{10}$$

where σ denotes the Sigmoid operation. Tensor $W \in \mathbb{R}^{S \times R \times 1}$ can be interpreted as a weight tensor to achieve attention over the R and S dimensions. $W[i, j]$ is a scalar depicting the similarity between the j-th query segment representation and the i-th support representation. For the j-th query segment representation, $W[:, j] \in \mathbb{R}^{S \times 1}$ corresponds to the weight for different support videos, while for the i-th support representation, $W[i, :] \in \mathbb{R}^{R \times 1}$ resembles the weight for different query segments. In the end, we enforce the pairwise matching weight W:

$$\phi(\mathcal{F}_Q, \mathcal{F}_S) = \mathcal{P}_n \odot \text{AP}(W), \tag{11}$$

where AP denotes an average pooling operation along the support dimension, in other words, $\text{AP} : \mathbb{R}^{S \times R \times 1} \mapsto \mathbb{R}^{R \times 1}$.

3.3   Optimization

To optimize our network on the training set, we employ both a classification loss and a temporal regression loss. Different than *e.g.*, R-C3D [45], our classification task is specifically dependent on the few support videos. Accordingly, the loss function is given as:

$$L = \frac{1}{N_{cls}} \sum_i L_{cls}(a_i, a_i^*) + \frac{1}{N_{reg}} \sum_i a_i^* L_{reg}(t_i, t_i^*), \tag{12}$$

where N_{cls} and N_{reg} stand for batch size and the number of proposal segments, while i denotes the proposal segment index in a batch, a_i is the predicted probability of the proposal segment, a_i^* is the ground truth label, and t_i represents predicted relative offset to proposals. In the context of this work, the ground truth label is class-agnostic and hence binary (foreground/background), indicating the presence of an action or not. Lastly, t_i^* represents the coordinate transformation of ground truth segments to proposals.

The above loss function is applied on two parts: the support-agnostic part and the support-conditioned part. All losses for the two parts are optimized jointly. In the support-agnostic part, the foreground/background classification loss L_{cls} predicts whether the proposal contains an activity, or not, and the regression loss L_{reg} optimizes the relative displacement between proposals and ground truths. For the support-conditioned part, the loss L_{cls} predicts whether the proposal has the same common action as the one among the few support videos. The regression loss L_{reg} optimizes the relative displacement between activities and ground truths. We note explicitly that this is done for the training set only.

During inference, the proposal subnet generates proposals for the query video. The proposals are refined by Non-Maximum Suppression (NMS) with a threshold of 0.7. Then the selected proposals are fused with the support videos through the mutual enhancement, progressive alignment, and pairwise matching modules.

Table 1. Overview of the common (multi-)instance datasets. The common instance datasets contain a single target action per video, while the common multi-instance datasets contain more frames and more actions per video, adding to the challenge of few-shot common action localization.

	Common instance		Common multi-instance	
	ActivityNet	Thumos	ActivityNet	Thumos
Video statistics				
number of instances	1	1	1.6	14.3
number of frames	266.9	284.6	444.5	5764.2
length (sec)	89.0	11.4	148.2	230.6
number of train videos	10035	3580	6747	1665
number of val+test videos	2483	775	1545	323
Class statistics				
number of train actions	160	16	160	16
number of val+test actions	40	4	40	4

The obtained representation is fed to the classification subnet to again perform binary classification and the boundaries of the predicted proposals are further refined by the regression layer. Finally, we conduct NMS based on the confidence scores of the refined proposals to remove redundant ones, and the threshold in NMS is set a little bit smaller than the overlap threshold θ in evaluation ($\theta = 0.1$ in this paper).

Optimizing for Long Videos. The longer the untrimmed query video, the larger the need for common localization, as manual searching for the activity becomes problematic. In our setup, the length of the input video is set to 768 frames to fit the GPU memory. When the query video is longer than 768 frames, we employ multi-scale segment generation [37]. We apply temporal sliding windows of 256, 512, and 768 frames with 75% overlap. Consequently, we generate a set of candidates $\Phi = \{(s_h, \psi_h, \psi'_h)\}_{h=1}^{H}$ as input for the proposal subnet, where H is the total number of sliding windows, and ψ_h and ψ'_h are the starting time and ending time of the h-th segment s_h. All refined proposals of all candidate segments together go through the NMS to remove redundant proposals.

4   Experimental Setup

4.1   Datasets

Existing video datasets are usually created for classification [17,22], temporal localization [3], captioning [4], or summarization [13]. To evaluate few-shot common action localization, we have revised two existing datasets, namely ActivityNet1.3 [3] and Thumos14 [17]. Both datasets come with temporal annotations suitable for our evaluation. We consider both common instance and common

Table 2. Module evaluation on ActivityNet and Thumos in the common instance setting. All three modules have a positive mAP effect on the localization performance with only a slight increase in parameters.

MEM	PAM	PMM	ActivityNet		Thumos	
			one-shot	five-shot	one-shot	five-shot
			42.4	42.5	37.5	38.4
	✓		49.7	52.0	42.3	44.5
	✓	✓	51.3	53.6	44.8	46.0
✓	✓		52.5	55.3	47.6	49.6
✓	✓	✓	**53.1**	**56.5**	**48.7**	**51.9**

multi-instance, where the latter deals with query videos containing multiple instances of the same action.

Common Instance. For the revision of ActivityNet1.3, we follow the organization of Feng *et al.* [10]. We divide videos that contain multiple actions into independent videos, with every newly generated video consisting of just one action and background. Next we discard videos longer than 768 frames. We split the remaining videos into three subsets, divided by action classes. We randomly select 80% of the classes for training, 10% of the classes for validation, and the remaining 10% of the classes for testing. Besides ActivityNet, we also revise the Thumos dataset using the same protocol.

Common Multi-instance. Query videos in real applications are usually unconstrained and contain multiple action segments. Therefore, we also split the original videos of ActivityNet1.3 and Thumos14 into three subsets according to their action classes without any other video preprocessing. As a result, we obtain long query videos with multiple action instances. The support videos are still trimmed action videos.

During training, the support videos and query video are randomly paired, while the pairs are fixed for validation and testing. The differences between the common instance and common multi-instance video datasets are highlighted in Table 1.

4.2 Experimental Details

We use PyTorch [33] for implementation. Our network is trained with Adam [23] with a learning rate of 1e−5 on one Nvidia GTX 1080TI. We use 40k training iterations and learning rate is decayed to 1e−6 after 25k iterations. To be consistent with the training process of our baselines [10,49], we use the same C3D backbone [40]. The backbone is pre-trained on Sports-1M [21] and is fine-tuned with a class-agnostic proposal loss on the training videos for each dataset. The batch size is set to 1. The proposal score threshold is set as 0.7. The proposal number after NMS is 128 in training and 300 in validation and testing.

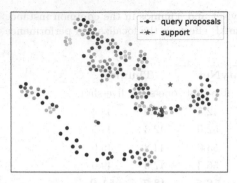

Without our modules.   With our modules.

Fig. 3. Module evaluation by t-SNE visualization of support and query representations. Colors of query proposals indicate their overlap with the ground truth action, the darker the better. Without our modules (left), both relevant and irrelevant query proposals are near the support videos. Afterwards (right), only relevant proposals remain close to the support videos, highlighting the effectiveness of our modules for localizing common actions among a few videos.

4.3   Evaluation

Following [10,37], we measure the localization performance using (mean) Average Precision. A prediction is correct when it has the correct foreground/background prediction and has a ground truth overlap larger than the overlap threshold. The overlap is set to 0.5 unless specified otherwise.

5   Experimental Results

5.1   Ablation Study

Module Evaluation. We evaluate the effect of the mutual enhancement module (MEM), the progressive alignment module (PAM), and the pairwise matching module (PMM) for our task on the common instance datasets. We report results using one and five support videos in Table 2. To validate the effectiveness of our modules, we compare to our baseline system without any modules. Here the support representations are averaged and added to the query representations. We observe that the progressive alignment module increases over the baseline considerably, showing its efficacy. Adding the pairwise matching on top of the progressive alignment or using the mutual enhancement before the progressive alignment further benefits few-shot common action localization. Combining all three modules works best.

To get insight into the workings of our modules for common action localization, we have analysed the feature distribution before and after the use of our modules. In Fig. 3, we show the t-SNE embedding [28] before and after we align the five support videos with the 300 proposals in one query video. We observe

Table 3. Influence of noisy support videos on common-instance ActivityNet for the five-shot setting. The result shows that our approach is robust to the inclusion of noisy support videos, whether they come from the same or different classes.

No noise	56.5
1 noisy support video	53.5
2 noisy support videos of different class	51.9
2 noisy support videos of same class	50.6

that after the use of our modules, the proposals with high overlap are closer to the support videos, indicating our ability to properly distill the correct action locations using only a few support videos. Irrelevant proposals are pushed away from the support videos, which results in a more relevant selection of action locations.

Few-Shot Evaluation. Our common action localization is optimized to work with multiple examples as support. To show this capability, we have measured the effect of gradually increasing the number of support videos, we found that the mAP gradually increases as we enlarge the number of support videos from one to six on common-instance ActivityNet. We obtain an mAP of 53.1 (one shot), 53.8 (two shots), 54.9 (three shots), 55.4 (four shots), 56.5 (five shots), 56.8 (six shots). The results show that our approach obtains high accuracy with only a few support videos. Using more than one support video is beneficial for common action localization in our approach, showing that we indeed learn from using more than one support video. Results stagnate when using more than six examples.

Effect of Support Video Length. We ablate the effect of the length of the support videos on the localization performance in Fig. 4a. We sample 16, 32, 48 and 64 frames for each support video respectively. We find that the result gradually increases with longer support videos, which indicates that temporal information in the support videos is beneficial to our modules for common action localization.

Influence of Action Proportion in Query Video. Figure 4b shows that for query videos with a dominant action, we can obtain high scores. An open challenge remains localizing very short actions in very long videos.

Influence of Noisy Support Videos. To test the robustness of our approach, we have investigated the effect of including noisy support videos in the five-shot setting. The results are shown in Table 3. When one out of five support videos contains the wrong action, the performance drops only 3% from 56.5 to 53.5. The performance drop remains marginal when replacing two of the five support videos with noisy videos. When two noisy support videos are from the same class, the drop is larger, which is to be expected, as this creates a stronger bias towards a distractor class. Overall, we find that our approach is robust to noise for common action localization.

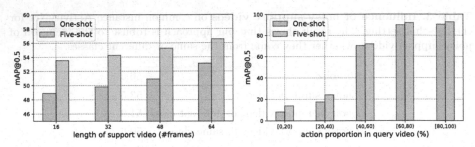

Effect of support video length.   Effect of action ratio in query video.

Fig. 4. Ablation studies on the length of the support videos and the action proportion in the query video. Both studies are on common-instance ActivityNet. Left: The longer the support videos, the better we perform, as we can distill more knowledge from the limited provided supervision. Right: High scores can be obtained when the common action is dominant, localization of short actions in long videos remains challenging.

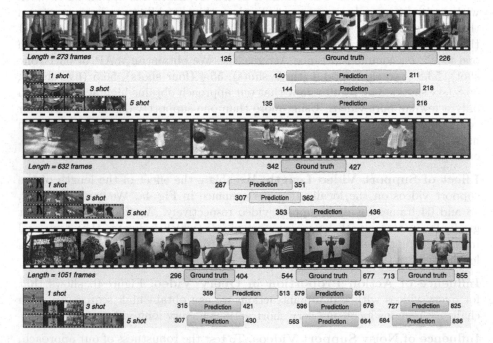

Fig. 5. Qualitative result of predictions by our approach under 1-shot, 3-shot and 5-shot settings. Correct predictions with an overlap larger than 0.5 are marked in green, and incorrect predictions are marked in red. The length and start-end boundary of segment are indicated in frame numbers. (Color figure online)

Table 4. One-shot comparison on common instance ActivityNet. Results marked with * obtained with author provided code. In both settings, our approach is preferred across all overlaps, highlighting its effectiveness.

	Overlap threshold					
	0.5	0.6	0.7	0.8	0.9	0.5:0.9
Common instance						
Hu et al. [16] *	41.0	33.0	27.1	15.9	6.8	24.8
Feng et al. [10]	43.5	35.1	27.3	16.2	6.5	25.7
This paper	**53.1**	**40.9**	**29.8**	**18.2**	**8.4**	**29.5**
Common multi-instance						
Hu et al. [16] *	29.6	23.2	12.7	7.4	3.1	15.2
Feng et al. [10] *	31.4	25.5	16.1	8.9	3.2	17.0
This paper	**42.1**	**36.0**	**18.5**	**11.1**	**7.0**	**22.9**

Qualitative Results. To visualize the result of our method, we show three cases in Fig. 5. For the first example, we can find the common action location from one support video. Adding more support videos provides further context, resulting in a better fit. For the second one, our method can recover the correct prediction only when five support videos are used. As shown in the third case, our method can also handle the multi-instance scenario. We show a query video with three instances. With only one support video, we miss one instance and have low overlap with another. When more support videos are added, we can recover both misses.

5.2   Comparisons with Others

To evaluate the effectiveness of our proposed approach for common action localization, we perform three comparative evaluations.

One-Shot Comparison. For the one-shot evaluation, we compare to the one-shot video re-localization of Feng et al. [10] and to Hu et al. [16], which focuses on few-shot common object detection. We evaluate on the same setting as Feng et al. [10], namely the revised ActivityNet dataset using the one-shot setting (common instance). Note that we both use the C3D base network. To evaluate the image-based approach of Hu et al. [16], we use their proposed similarity module on the temporal video proposals, rather than spatial proposals based on author provided code [16]. The results in Table 4 show that across all overlap thresholds, our approach is preferred. At an overlap threshold of 0.5, we obtain an mAP of 53.1 compared to 41.0 for [16] and 43.5 for [10]. It is of interest to note that without our three modules, we obtain only 42.4 (Table 2). This demonstrates that a different training setup or a different model architecture by itself does not benefit common action localization. We attribute our improvement to the better alignment between the support and query representations as a result of our three

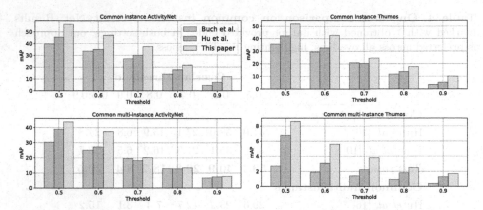

Fig. 6. Five-shot comparison. We evaluate our method as well as modified versions of Hu *et al.* [16] and Buch *et al.* [2] on all common instance and multi-instance datasets, we obtain favourable results. Detailed numerical results are provided in supplementary file to facilitate the comparison for the follow-up works. Best viewed in color. (Color figure online)

Table 5. Localization from images on the common instance datasets. Our method generalizes beyond videos as support input and outperforms Zhang *et al.* [49]

	ActivityNet		Thumos	
	one-shot	five-shot	one-shot	five-shot
Zhang *et al.*	45.2	48.5	36.9	38.9
This paper	**49.2**	**52.8**	**43.0**	**45.6**

modules. Next to a comparison on the common instance dataset, we also perform the same experiment on the longer multi-instance ActivityNet variant. In this more challenging setting, our approach again outperforms the baselines. We note that we are not restricted to the one-shot setting, where the baseline by Feng *et al.* [10] is.

Five-Shot Comparison. Second, we evaluate the performance of our approach on all datasets in the five-shot setting. We compare to a modified version of SST by Buch *et al.* [2]. We add a fusion layer on top of the original GRU networks in SST to incorporate the support feature, and then choose the proposal with the largest confidence score. SST is used as baseline, because the approach of Feng *et al.* [10] cannot handle more than one support video. We also include another comparison to Hu *et al.* [16]. This time also using their feature reweighting module. The results are shown in Fig. 6. We observe that our method performs favorably compared to the two baselines on all datasets, reaffirming the effectiveness of our method. Also note that even when our support videos are noisy (Table 3), we are still better than the baselines without any noise based on Buch *et al.* [2] and Hu *et al.* [16] (39.7 and 45.4 for a threshold of 0.5 on common instance ActivityNet). The large amount of distractor actions in the long videos of common multi-instance Thumos results in lower overall scores, indicating that common action localization is far from a solved problem.

Localization from Images. Next to using videos, we can also perform common action localization using images as support. This provides a challenging setting, since any temporal information is lost. We perform localization from support images by inflating the images to create static support videos. We perform a common action localization on common instance ActivityNet and Thumos. We compare to the recent approach of Zhang *et al.* [49], which focuses on video retrieval from images. Results in Table 5 show we obtain favourable results on both datasets, even though our approach is not designed for this setting.

6   Conclusion

In this paper we consider action localization in a query video given a few trimmed support videos that contain a common action, without specifying the label of the action. To tackle this challenging problem, we introduce a new network architecture along with three modules optimized for temporal alignment. The first module focuses on enhancing the representations of the query and support representation simultaneously. The second module progressively integrates the representations of the support branch into the query branch, to distill the common action in the query video. The third module weighs the different support videos to deal with non-informative support examples. Experiments on reorganizations of ActivityNet and Thumos dataset, both with settings containing a single and multiple action instances per video, show that our approach can robustly localize the action which is common amongst support videos in both standard and long untrimmed query videos.

References

1. Bojanowski, P., et al.: Weakly supervised action labeling in videos under ordering constraints. In: Fleet, D., Pajdla, T., Schiele, B., Tuytelaars, Tinne (eds.) ECCV 2014. LNCS, vol. 8693, pp. 628–643. Springer, Cham (2014). https://doi.org/10.1007/978-3-319-10602-1_41
2. Buch, S., Escorcia, V., Shen, C., Ghanem, B., Carlos Niebles, J.: Sst: single-stream temporal action proposals. In: CVPR (2017)
3. Caba Heilbron, F., Escorcia, V., Ghanem, B., Car-los Niebles, J.: Activitynet: a large-scale video benchmark for human activity understanding. In: CVPR (2015)
4. Chen, D.L., Dolan, W.B.: Collecting highly parallel data for paraphrase evaluation. In: ACL (2011)
5. Dai, X., Singh, B., Zhang, G., Davis, L.S., Chen, Y.Q: Temporal context network for activity localization in videos. In: ICCV (2017)
6. Damen, D.: Scaling egocentric vision: the epic-kitchens dataset. In: ECCV (2018)
7. Dong, X., Zheng, L., Ma, F., Yang, Y., Meng, D.: Few-example object detection with model communication. PAMI **41**(7), 1641–1654 (2018)

8. Duchenne, O., Laptev, I., Sivic, J., Bach, F., Ponce, J.: Automatic annotation of human actions in video. In ICCV (2009)
9. Escorcia, V., Caba Heilbron, F., Niebles, J.C., Ghanem, B.: DAPs: deep action proposals for action understanding. In: Leibe, B., Matas, J., Sebe, N., Welling, M. (eds.) ECCV 2016. LNCS, vol. 9907, pp. 768–784. Springer, Cham (2016). https://doi.org/10.1007/978-3-319-46487-9_47
10. Feng, Y., Ma, L., Liu, W., Zhang, T., Luo, J.: Video re-localization. In: ECCV (2018)
11. Gao, J., Chen, K., Nevatia, R.: Ctap: Complementary temporal action proposal generation. In: ECCV (2018)
12. Gao, J., Yang, Z., Sun, C., Chen, K., Nevatia, R.: Turn tap: temporal unit regression network for temporal action proposals. In: ICCV (2017)
13. Gygli, M., Grabner, H., Riemenschneider, H., Van Gool, L.: Creating summaries from user videos. In: Fleet, D., Pajdla, T., Schiele, B., Tuytelaars, Tinne (eds.) ECCV 2014. LNCS, vol. 8695, pp. 505–520. Springer, Cham (2014). https://doi.org/10.1007/978-3-319-10584-0_33
14. He, K., Zhang, X., Ren, S., Sun, J.: Deep residual learning for image recognition. In: CVPR (2016)
15. Hu, J., Shen, L., Sun, G.: Squeeze-and-excitation networks. In: CVPR (2018)
16. Hu, T., Mettes, P., Huang, J.-H., Snoek, C.G.M.: SILCO: show a few images, localize the common object. In: ICCV(2019)
17. Idrees, H., et al.: The THUMOS challenge on action recognition for videos "in the wild". In: CVIU (2017)
18. Jain, M., Ghodrati, A., Snoek, C.G.M.: ActionBytes: learning from trimmed videos to localize actions. In: CVPR (2020)
19. Jain, M., van Gemert, J.C., Mensink, T., Snoek, C.G.M.: Objects2action: classifying and localizing actions without any video example. In: ICCV (2015)
20. Kalogeiton, V., Weinzaepfel, P., Ferrari, V., Schmid, C.: Joint learning of object and action detectors. In: ICCV (2017)
21. Karpathy, A., Toderici, G., Shetty, S., Leung, T., Sukthankar, R., Fei-Fei, L.: Large-scale video classification with convolutional neural networks. In: CVPR (2014)
22. Kay, W., et al.: The kinetics human action video dataset. arXiv (2017)
23. Kingma, D.P., Ba, J.: Adam: a method for stochastic optimization. arXiv (2014)
24. Kuehne, H., Richard, A., Gall, J.: A hybrid RNN-HMM approach for weakly supervised temporal action segmentation. arXiv (2019)
25. Singh, K.K., Lee, Y.J.: Hide-and-seek: forcing a network to be meticulous for weakly-supervised object and action localization. In: ICCV (2017)
26. Lin, T., Zhao, X., Su, H., Wang, C., Yang, M.: BSN: boundary sensitive network for temporal action proposal generation. In: ECCV (2018)
27. Ma, S., Sigal, L., Sclaroff, S.: Learning activity progression in LSTMS for activity detection and early detection. In: CVPR (2016)
28. van der Maaten, L., Hinton, G.: Visualizing data using t-SNE. JMLR 9, 2579–2605 (2008)
29. Mettes, P., Snoek, C.G.M.: Spatial-aware object embeddings for zero-shot localization and classification of actions. In: ICCV (2017)
30. Nguyen, P., Liu, T., Prasad, G., Han, G.: Weakly supervised action localization by sparse temporal pooling network. In: CVPR (2018)
31. Nguyen, P.X., Ramanan, D., Charless C.F.: Weakly-supervised action localization with background modeling. In: ICCV (2019)
32. Oneata, D., Verbeek, J., Cordelia, S.: Action and event recognition with fisher vectors on a compact feature set. In: ICCV (2013)

33. Pasze, A., et al.: Automatic differentiation in pytorch. In: NeurIPS (2017)
34. Paul, S., Roy, S., Roy-Chowdhury, A.K.: W-talc: Weakly-supervised temporal activity localization and classification. In: ECCV (2018)
35. Sawatzky, J., Garbade, M., Gall, J.: Ex paucis plura: learning affordance segmentation from very few examples. In: Brox, T., Bruhn, A., Fritz, M. (eds.) GCPR 2018. LNCS, vol. 11269, pp. 169–184. Springer, Cham (2019). https://doi.org/10.1007/978-3-030-12939-2_13
36. Shaban, A., Rahimi, A., Gould, S., Boots, B., Hartley, R.: Learning to find common objects across image collections. In: ICCV (2019)
37. Shou, Z., Wang, D., Chang, S.-F.: Temporal action localization in untrimmed videos via multi-stage CNNS. In: CVPR (2016)
38. Singh, B., Marks, T.K., Jones, M., Tuzel, O., Shao, M.: A multi-stream bi-directional recurrent neural network for fine-grained action detection. In: CVPR (2016)
39. Soomro, K., Shah, M.: Unsupervised action discovery and localization in videos. In: ICCV (2017)
40. Tran, D., Bourdev, L., Fergus, R., Torresani, L., Paluri, M.: Learning spatiotemporal features with 3D convolutional networks. In: ICCV (2015)
41. Vaswani, A., et al.: Attention is all you need. In: NeurIPS (2017)
42. Wang, L., Qiao, Y., Tang, X.: Action recognition and detection by combining motion and appearance features. THUMOS14 Action Recogn. Challenge, 1(2), 2 (2014)
43. Wang, L., Xiong, Y., Lin, D., Van Gool, L.: Untrimmednets for weakly supervised action recognition and detection. In: CVPR (2017)
44. Wang, X., Girshick, R., Gupta, A., He, K.: Non-local neural networks. In: CVPR (2018)
45. Xu, H., Das, A., Saenko, K.: R-C3D: Region convolutional 3D network for temporal activity detection. In: ICCV (2017)
46. Yang, H., He, X., Porikli, F.: One-shot action localization by learning sequence matching network. In: CVPR (2018)
47. Yang, J., Yuan, J.: Common action discovery and localization in unconstrained videos. In: ICCV (2017)
48. Yeung, S., Russakovsky, O., Mori, G., Fei-Fei, L.: End-to-end learning of action detection from frame glimpses in videos. In: CVPR (2016)
49. Zhang, Z., Zhao, Z., Lin, Z., Song, J., Cai, D.: Localizing unseen activities in video via image query. In: IJCAI (2019)

TAFSSL: Task-Adaptive Feature Sub-Space Learning for Few-Shot Classification

Moshe Lichtenstein[1], Prasanna Sattigeri[1], Rogerio Feris[1], Raja Giryes[2], and Leonid Karlinsky[1(✉)]

[1] IBM Research AI, Cambridge, USA
leonidka@il.ibm.com
[2] Tel Aviv University, Tel Aviv, Israel

Abstract. Recently, Few-Shot Learning (FSL), or learning from very few (typically 1 or 5) examples per novel class (unseen during training), has received a lot of attention and significant performance advances. While number of techniques have been proposed for FSL, several factors have emerged as most important for FSL performance, awarding SOTA even to the simplest of techniques. These are: the backbone architecture (bigger is better), type of pre-training (meta-training vs multi-class), quantity and diversity of the base classes (the more the merrier), and using auxiliary self-supervised tasks (a proxy for increasing the diversity). In this paper we propose TAFSSL, a simple technique for improving the few shot performance in cases when some additional unlabeled data accompanies the few-shot task. TAFSSL is built upon the intuition of reducing the feature and sampling noise inherent to few-shot tasks comprised of novel classes unseen during pre-training. Specifically, we show that on the challenging *mini*ImageNet and *tiered*ImageNet benchmarks, TAFSSL can improve the current state-of-the-art in both transductive and semi-supervised FSL settings by more than 5%, while increasing the benefit of using unlabeled data in FSL to above 10% performance gain.

Keywords: Transductive · Semi-supervised · Few-Shot Learning

1 Introduction

The great success of Deep Learning (DL) methods to solve complex computer vision problems can be attributed in part to the emergence of large labeled datasets [27,40] and strong parallel hardware. Yet in many practical situations, the amount of data and/or labels available for training or adapting the DL model to a new target task is prohibitively small. In extreme cases, we might be interested in learning from as little as one example per novel class. This is the

Electronic supplementary material The online version of this chapter (https://doi.org/10.1007/978-3-030-58571-6_31) contains supplementary material, which is available to authorized users.

© Springer Nature Switzerland AG 2020
A. Vedaldi et al. (Eds.): ECCV 2020, LNCS 12352, pp. 522–539, 2020.
https://doi.org/10.1007/978-3-030-58571-6_31

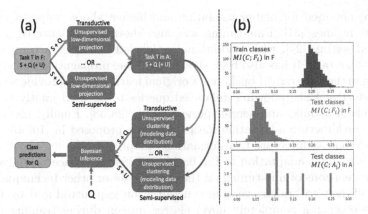

Fig. 1. (a) TAFSSL overview: red and blue pathways are for semi-supervised and transductive FSL respectively. T - few-shot task; S - support set; Q - query set; U - optional set of additional unlabeled examples (semi-supervised FSL); F - original feature space; A - task adapted feature sub-space. **(b) Improved SNR in A:** the normalized (by min entropy) Mutual Information (MI) between either train or test classes and the features in F (of dimension 1024) or in A (7-dim) provides the motivation to use A over F. Computed on *mini*ImageNet

typical scenario of Few-Shot Learning (FSL), a very active and exciting research topic of many concurrent works [22,47,51,52]. While many great techniques have been proposed to improve FSL performance, recent studies [3,15,52] have shown that there exist a number of important factors that can improve the FSL performance, largely regardless of the model and the learning algorithm used. These include: (i) significant performance gains observed while increasing the size and the number of parameters of the backbone generating the feature representations of the images [3,52]; (ii) gains while pre-training the FSL model on the base classes dataset as a regular multi-class classifier (to all base classes at once) [52], as opposed to the popular meta-training by generating a lot of synthetic few-shot tasks from random small groups of base classes [22,51]; (iii) gains when pre-training on more (diverse) base classes (e.g. higher empirical FSL performance on seemingly more difficult *tiered*ImageNet benchmark than on supposedly simpler *mini*ImageNet benchmark [22,52]; (iv) gains when artificially increasing the diversity and complexity of the base classes dataset by introducing additional self-supervised tasks during pre-training [15]. Correctly using these factors allows the simple Nearest Neighbor classifier to attain state-of-the-art FSL performance [52] improving upon more sophisticated FSL techniques.

All the aforementioned factors and gains concern the base classes pre-training stage of the FSL methods backbones. Much less attention has been given to adapting the feature spaces resulting from these backbones to the novel classes few-shot tasks during test time. It has been shown that some moderate gains can be obtained from using the few training examples (support set) of the novel tasks to fine-tune the backbones (changing the feature spaces slightly), with best gains obtained for higher resolution and higher 'shots' (support examples per class) regimes [31]. Fine-tuning was also shown to be effective for semi-supervised setting [24], where additional unlabeled examples accompany each novel few-shot task. It has also been shown that label propagation and clustering operating in the pre-trained backbone's original feature space provide some gains for transductive FSL (allowing unlabeled queries to be used jointly to predict their labels in a bulk) and semi-supervised FSL [28,38]. Finally, meta-learned backbone architecture adaptation mechanics were proposed in [10] allowing for slight backbone architecture transformations adaptive to the few-shot test task.

However, slight adaptation of the backbone's feature space to a given task, using few iterations of fine-tuning on the support set or other techniques, might not be sufficient to bridge over the generalization gap introduced by the FSL backbone observing completely novel classes unseen during training (as confirmed by the relatively moderate performance gains obtained from these techniques). Intuitively, we could attribute this in part to many of the feature space dimensions (feature vector entries) becoming 'useless' for a given set of novel classes in the test few-shot task. Indeed, every feature vector entry can be seen as a certain 'pattern detector' which fires strongly when a certain visual pattern is observed on the input image. The SGD (or other) backbone training is making sure all of these patterns are discriminative for the classes used for pre-training. But, due to likely over-fitting, many of these patterns are base classes specific, and do not fire for the novel test classes. Hence, their corresponding feature vector entries will mainly produce 'noise values' corresponding to 'pattern not observed'. In other words, the ratio of feature vector entries that can be used for recognition of novel classes to ones which mainly output 'noise' significantly decreases for test few-shot task (Fig. 1b). And it is unlikely that small modifications to the feature space recovers a significant portion of the 'noise producing' feature entries. The high level of noise in the feature vectors intuitively has significant adverse implications on the performance of the FSL classifier operating on this vector, especially the popular distance based classifiers like nearest-neighbor [52] and Prototypical Networks (PN) [47] are affected. In light of this intuition, we conjecture that for a significant performance boost, we need to concentrate our efforts on the so-called *Task-Adaptive Feature Sub-Space Learning (TAFSSL)* - seeking sub-spaces of the backbone's feature space that are discriminative for the novel classes of the test few-shot task and which are 'as noise free as possible', that is most of the sub-space dimensions indeed 'find' the patterns they represent in the images of the novel categories belonging to the task.

In this paper we set to explore TAFSSL under the transductive and the semi-supervised few-shot settings. In many practical applications of FSL, alongside the few labeled training examples (the support set) of the few shot task, additional unlabeled examples containing instances of the target novel classes are available. Such is the situation in transductive FSL which assumes that the query samples arrive in a 'bulk' and not one-by-one, and hence we can answer all the queries 'at once' while using the query set as unlabeled data. Similar situation exists in semi-supervised FSL, where unlabeled set of images simply accompanies the few-shot task. As can be observed from our experiments, TAFSSL, and especially TAFSSL accompanied by specific (proposed) forms of clustering based approaches, provides very significant boost to FSL performance under the transductive and semi-supervised setting. Specifically, we obtain over 7% and over 10% absolute improvement of the popular 1-shot *mini*ImageNet [51] and *tiered*ImageNet [38] few-shot benchmarks in the transductive FSL setting, and 13% and over 10% absolute improvement in semi-supervised FSL setting (over corresponding state-of-the-art while using their respective evaluation protocols). Figure 1a illustrates an overview of the proposed approach.

To summarize, we offer the following contributions: (i) we highlight the Task-Adaptive Feature Sub-Space Learning (TAFSSL) as an important factor for Few-Shot Learning (FSL), we explore several TAFSSL methods and demonstrate significant performance gains obtained using TAFSSL for transductive and semi-supervised FSL; (ii) we propose two variants of clustering that can be used in conjunction with TAFSSL to obtain even greater performance improvements; (iii) we obtain new state-of-the-art transductive and semi-supervised FSL results on two popular benchmarks: *mini*ImageNet and *tiered*ImageNet; (iv) we offer an extensive ablation study of the various aspects of our approach, including sub-space dimension, unlabeled data quantity, effects of out-of-distribution noise in unlabeled data, backbone architectures, and finally - effect of class imbalance (skew) in unlabeled data (so-far unexplored in all previous works).

2   Related Work

Here we briefly review the modern Few-Shot Learning (FSL) approaches, focusing in more detail on the transductive and semi-supervised FSL methods that leverage unlabeled data. The *meta-learning* methods [23,47,50,51,57] learn from few-shot tasks (or episodes) rather then from individual labeled samples. Each such task is a small dataset, with few labeled training examples (a.k.a. support), and a few test examples (a.k.a. query). The goal is to learn a model that can adapt to new tasks with novel categories unseen during training. The *gradient-based meta learners* [3,12,22,25,30,32,36,41,58] search for models can transfer well to novel few-shot tasks. Typically, in these methods higher order derivatives are used to optimize the loss the model would have after applying few gradient steps. At test time, simple fine-tuning is used. In [11] ensemble methods for few-shot learning are proposed. The *metric learning* based methods [7,14,20,32,39,43,47,49,54,55] a non linear metric is optimized on base classes and applied to unseen few-shot test tasks. In [7,46] distance to class prototype is replaced by distance to a class sub-space. As opposed to [7] and [46] that try to optimize a sub-space for each class, in TAFSSL we seek a single sub-space optimally adapted to the entire data of the few-shot task - labeled and unlabeled. Notably, in [52] non-meta-learning pre-training was used in combination with 'large' backbones (e.g. DenseNet [19]) and a nearest-neighbor classifier to achieve state-of-the-art results. The *generative and augmentation-based* methods [1,2,4,6,9,16,17,26,33,37,44,45,48,53,56] are methods that (learn to) generate more samples from the one or a few training examples in a given few-shot learning task.

Transductive and semi-supervised FSL: In many practical applications, in addition to the labeled support set, additional unlabeled data accompanies the few-shot task. Transductive FSL [8,21,28,35] assumes that the set of task queries arrives in a bulk and can be used as a source of unlabeled data, allowing query samples to 'learn' from each other. In [8] the queries are used in fine-tuning in conjunction with entropy minimization loss in order to maximize the certainty of their predictions. In semi-supervised FSL [24,28,38,46] the unlabeled data comes in addition to the support set and is assumed to have a similar distribution to the target classes (although some unrelated samples noise is also allowed). In the LST [24] self-labeling and soft attention are used on the unlabeled samples intermittently with fine-tuning on the labeled and self-labeled data. Similarly to LST, [38] updates the class prototypes using k-means like iterations initialized from the PN prototypes. Their method also includes down-weighting the potential distractor samples (likely not to belong to the target classes) in the unlabeled data. In [46] unlabeled examples are used through soft-label propagation. In [42] semi-supervised few-shot domain adaptation is considered. In [14,21,28] graph neural networks are used for sharing information between labeled and unlabeled examples in semi-supervised [14,28] and transductive [21] FSL setting. Notably, in [28] a Graph Construction network is used to predict the task specific graph for propagating labels between samples of semi-supervised FSL task.

3   Method

Here we derive the formal definition of TAFSSL and examine several approaches for it. In addition, we propose several ways to combine TAFSSL with clustering, which is shown to be very beneficial to the performance in Sect. 4.

3.1   FSSL and TAFSSL

Let a CNN backbone $\mathcal{B}$ (e.g. ResNet [18] or DenseNet [19]) pre-trained for FSL on a (large) dataset $\mathcal{D}_b$ with a set of base (training) classes $\mathcal{C}_b$. Here for simplicity, we equally refer to all different forms of pre-training proposed for FSL in the literature, be it meta-training [51] or 'regular' training of a multi-class classifier for all the classes $\mathcal{C}_b$ [52]. Denote by $\mathcal{B}(x) \in \mathcal{F} \subset \mathbf{R}^m$ to be a feature vector corresponding to an input image x represented in the feature space $\mathcal{F}$ by the backbone $\mathcal{B}$. Under this notation, we define the goal of linear Feature Sub-Space Learning (FSSL) to find an 'optimal' (for a certain task) linear sub-space $\mathcal{A}$ of $\mathcal{F}$ and a linear mapping W of size $r \times m$ (typically with $r \ll m$) such that:

$$\mathbf{R}^r \supset \mathcal{A} \ni A = W \cdot \mathcal{B}(x) \tag{1}$$

is the new representation of an input image x as a vector A in the feature subspace $\mathcal{A}$ (spanned by rows of W).

Now, consider an n-way + k-shot few-shot test task $\mathcal{T}$ with a query set Q, and a support set: $S = \{s_i^j | 1 \le i \le n, 1 \le j \le k, \mathcal{L}(s_i^j) = i\}$, where $\mathcal{L}(x)$ is the class label of image x, so in S we have k training samples (shots) for each of the n classes in the task $\mathcal{T}$. Using the PN [47] paradigm we assume $k = 1$ (otherwise support examples of the same class are averaged to a single class prototype) and that each $q \in Q$ is classified using Nearest Neighbor (NN) in $\mathcal{F}$:

$$CLS(q) = \operatorname*{argmin}_i \|\mathcal{B}(s_i^1) - \mathcal{B}(q)\|^2 \qquad (2)$$

Then, in the context of this given task $\mathcal{T}$, we can define linear Task-Adaptive FSSL (TAFSSL) as a search for a linear sub-space $\mathcal{A}_{\mathcal{T}}$ of the feature space $\mathcal{F}$ defined by a $\mathcal{T}$-specific projection matrix $W_{\mathcal{T}}$, such that the probability:

$$\frac{exp(-\tau \cdot \|W_{\mathcal{T}} \cdot (\mathcal{B}(s^1_{\mathcal{L}(q)}) - \mathcal{B}(q))\|^2)}{\sum_i exp(-\tau \cdot \|W_{\mathcal{T}} \cdot (\mathcal{B}(s_i^1) - \mathcal{B}(q))\|^2)} \qquad (3)$$

of predicting q to belong to the same class as the 'correct' support $s^1_{\mathcal{L}(q)}$ is maximized, while of course the true label $\mathcal{L}(q)$ is unknown at test time (here τ in Eq. 3 is a temperature parameter, we used $\tau = 1$).

Discussion. Using the 'pattern detectors' intuition from Sect. 1, lets consider the activations of each dimension F_d of $F \in \mathcal{F}$ as a random variable with a Mixture of (two) Gaussians (MoG) distribution:

$$F_d \sim P_d = \rho_n \cdot N(\mu_n, \sigma_n) + \rho_s \cdot N(\mu_s, \sigma_s) \qquad (4)$$

where (μ_n, σ_n) and (μ_s, σ_s) are the expectation and variance of the F_d's distribution of activations when F_d does not detect (noise) or detects (signal) the pattern respectively. The ρ_n and ρ_s are the noise and the signal prior probabilities respectively ($\rho_n + \rho_s = 1$). For brevity, we drop the index d from the distribution parameters. Naturally, for the training classes C_b, for most dimensions F_d the $\rho_s \gg 0$ implying that the dimension is 'useful' and does not produce only noise (Fig. 1b, top). However, for the new (unseen during training) classes of a test task $\mathcal{T}$ this is no longer the case, and it is likely that for the majority of dimensions $\rho_s^{\mathcal{T}} \approx 0$ (Fig. 1b, middle). Assuming (for the time being) that F_d are conditionally independent, the square Euclidean distance could be seen as an aggregation of votes for the 'still useful' (for the classes of $\mathcal{T}$) patterns, and a sum of squares of i.i.d (zero mean) Gaussian samples for the patterns that are 'noise only' on the classes of $\mathcal{T}$. The latter 'noise dimensions' randomly increase the distance on the expected order of $N^{\mathcal{T},\mathcal{F}} \cdot \sigma_n^2$, where $N^{\mathcal{T},\mathcal{F}}$ is the number of *noise features* of the feature space $\mathcal{F}$ for the classes of task $\mathcal{T}$. Using this intuition, if we could find such a TAFSSL sub-space $\mathcal{A}_{\mathcal{T}}$ adapted to the task $\mathcal{T}$ so that $N^{\mathcal{T},\mathcal{S}_{\mathcal{T}}}$ is reduced (Fig. 1b, bottom), we would improve the performance of the NN classifier on $\mathcal{T}$. With only few labeled samples in the support set S, we cannot expect to effectively learn the $W_{\mathcal{T}}$ projection to the sub-space $\mathcal{A}_{\mathcal{T}}$

using SGD on S. Yet, when unlabeled data accompanies the task $\mathcal{T}$ (Q in transductive FSL, or an additional set of unlabeled samples U in semi-supervised FSL), we can use this data to find such $W_{\mathcal{T}}$ that: (a) the dimensions of $\mathcal{A}_{\mathcal{T}}$ are 'disentangled', meaning their pairwise independence is maximized; (b) after the 'disentanglement' we choose the dimensions that are expected to 'exhibit the least noise' or in our previous MoG notation have the largest ρ_s values.

Luckily, simple classical methods can be used for TAFSSL approximating the requirements (a) and (b). Both Principle Component Analysis (PCA) [34] and Independent Component Analysis (ICA) [5] applied in $\mathcal{F}$ on the set of samples: $S \cup Q$ (transductive FSL) or $S \cup U$ (semi-supervised FSL) can approximate (a). PCA under the approximate joint Gaussianity assumption of $\mathcal{F}$, and ICA under approximate non-Gaussianity assumption. In addition, if after the PCA rotation we subtract the mean, the variance of the (zero-mean) MoG mixtures for the transformed (independent) dimensions would be:

$$\rho_n \cdot (\mu_n^2 + \sigma_n^2) + \rho_s \cdot (\mu_s^2 + \sigma_s^2) \tag{5}$$

Then assuming μ_n and σ_n are roughly the same for all dimensions (which is reasonable due to heavy use of Batch Normalization (BN) in the modern backbones), choosing the dimensions with higher variance in PCA would lead to larger ρ_s, μ_s, and σ_s - all of which are likely to increase the signal-to-noise ratio of the NN classifier. Larger μ_s leads to patterns with stronger 'votes', larger σ_s means wider range of values that may better discriminate multiple classes, and larger ρ_s means patterns that are more frequent for classes of $\mathcal{T}$. Similarly, the dimensions with bigger ρ_s exhibit stronger departure from Gaussianity and hence would be chosen by ICA.

TAFSSL Summary. To summarize, following the discussion above, both PCA and ICA are good simple approximations for TAFSSL using unlabeled data and therefore we simply use them to perform the 'unsupervised low-dimensional projection' in the first step of our proposed approach (Fig. 1a). As we show in the Results Sect. 4, even on their own (when directly followed by an NN classifier) they lead to significant FSL performance boosts (Tables 1 and 2).

3.2 Clustering

It was shown that clustering is a useful tool for transductive and semi-supervised FSL [38]. There, it was assumed that modes of the task $\mathcal{T}$ data distribution (including both labeled and unlabeled image samples) correspond classes. However, in the presence of feature 'noise' in $\mathcal{F}$, as discussed is Sect. 3.1, the 'class' modes may become mixed with the noise distribution modes, that may blur the class modes boundaries or swallow the class modes altogether. Indeed, the performance gains in [38] were not very high.

In contrast, after applying PCA or ICA based TAFSSL, the feature noise levels are usually significantly reduced (Fig. 1b) making the task-adapted feature sub-space $\mathcal{A}_{\mathcal{T}}$ of the original feature space $\mathcal{F}$ to be much more effective for clustering. We propose two clustering-based algorithms, the Bayesian K-Means (BKM) and Mean-Shift Propagation (MSP). In the Results Sect. 4 we show that following PCA or ICA based TAFSSL, these clustering techniques add about 5% to the performance. They are used to perform the 'unsupervised clustering' + 'bayesian inference' steps of our approach (Fig. 1a).

The **BKM** is a soft k-means [29] variant accompanied with Bayesian inference for computing class probabilities for the queries. In BKM, each k-means cluster, obtained for the entire set of (labeled + unlabeled) task $\mathcal{T}$ data, is treated as a Gaussian mixture distribution with a mode for each class. The BKM directly computes the class probability for each query $q \in Q$ by averaging the posterior of q in each of the mixtures using weights being the probability of q to belong to each cluster. BKM details are provided in Algorithm 1.

Algorithm 1. Bayesian K-Means (BKM)

Cluster the samples of task $\mathcal{T}$ ($Q \cup S$ or $U \cup S$ in transductive or semi-supervised FSL respectively) into k clusters, associating each to c_k - the centroid of cluster k.

for each $s \in S$, $q \in Q$, and k **do**

$$P(cluster(q) = k) = \frac{\exp(-||q - c_k||^2)}{\sum_j \exp(-||q - c_j||^2)}$$

$$P(cluster(s) = k) = \frac{\exp(-||s - c_k||^2)}{\sum_j \exp(-||s - c_j||^2)}$$

$$P(\mathcal{L}(q) = i | cluster(q) = k) = \sum_{\mathcal{L}(s)=i} \frac{\exp(-||q - s||^2) \cdot P(cluster(s) = k)}{\sum_{t \in S} \exp(-||q - t||^2) \cdot P(cluster(t) = k)}$$

$$P(\mathcal{L}(q) = i) = \sum_k P(\mathcal{L}(q) = i | cluster(q) = k) \cdot P(cluster(q) = k)$$

The **MSP** is a mean-shift [13] based approach, that is used to update the prototype of each class. In MSP we perform a number of mean-shift like iterations on the prototypes [47] of the classes taken within the distribution of all the (labeled and unlabeled) samples of $\mathcal{T}$. In each iteration, for each prototype p_i (of class i), we compute a set of K most confident samples within a certain confidence radius and use the mean of this set as the next prototype (of class i). The K itself is balanced among the classes. The details of MSP are summarized in Algorithm 2 box. Following MSP, the updated prototypes are used in standard NN classifier fashion to obtain the class probabilities.

3.3 Implementation Details

All the proposed TAFSSL approaches were implemented in PyTorch. We have used the PyTorch native version of SVD for PCA, and FastICA from sklearn for ICA. The k-means from sklearn was used for BKM. The sub-space dimensions were 4 for PCA based TAFSSL, and 10 for ICA based TAFSSL. These were set using validation (Sect. 4.4). The $T = 0.3$ and $N = 4$ were used for MSP, and $k = 5$ for BKM, all set using validation. We used the backbones implementations from [52]. Unless otherwise specified, DenseNet backbone was used (for backbones ablation, please see Sect. 4.4). The most time consuming of the proposed TAFSSL

Algorithm 2. Mean-Shift Propagation (MSP)

Initialize:
Compute prototypes: $\{p_i = \frac{1}{k} \cdot \sum_{s \in S, \mathcal{L}(s)=i} s\}$, where k is # of shots in task $\mathcal{T}$
for N times **do**
    Compute $P(\mathcal{L}(x) = i) = \frac{\exp(-||x-p_i||^2)}{\sum_j \exp(-||x-p_j||^2)}$, $\forall x \in Q \cup S$ (or $x \in U \cup S$)
    Compute predictions $c(x) = \operatorname*{argmax}_i P(\mathcal{L}(x) = i)$
    $K_i = \sum_x \mathbb{1}_{(c(x)=i) \wedge (P(\mathcal{L}(x)=i)>T)}$, where T is a threshold parameter
    $K = min_i\{K_i\}$
    Compute the new prototypes: $\{p_i = \frac{1}{K} \cdot \sum_{x \in \hat{S}_i} x\}$, where $\hat{S}_i$ are the top K
samples that have $c(x) = i$ sorted in decreasing order of $P(\mathcal{L}(x) = i)$
return labels $c(q), \forall q \in Q$

---

approaches (ICA + BKM) runs in below 0.05 seconds (CPU) for a typical 1-shot and 5-way episode with 15 queries per class.

4   Results

We have evaluated our approach on the popular few-shot classification benchmarks, namely *mini*ImageNet [51] and *tiered*ImageNet [38], used in all transductive and semi-supervised FSL works [8,21,24,28,28,35,38,46]. On these benchmarks, we used the standard evaluation protocols, exactly as in corresponding (compared) works. The results of the transductive and semi-supervised FSL evaluation, together with comparison to previous methods, are summarized in Tables 1 and 2 respectively and are detailed and discussed in the following sections. All the performance numbers are given in accuracy % and the 0.95 confidence intervals are reported. The tests are performed on 10,000 random 5-way episodes, with 1 or 5 shots (number of support examples per class), and with 15 queries per episode (unless otherwise specified). For each dataset, the standard train/validation/test splits were used. For each dataset, training subset was used to pre-train the backbone (from scratch) as a regular multi-class classifier to all the train classes, same as in [52]; the validation data was used to select the best model along the training epochs and to choose the hyper-parameters; and episodes generated from the test data (with test categories unseen during training and validation) were used for meta-testing to obtain the final performance. In all experiments not involving BKM, the class probabilities were computed using the NN classifier to the class prototypes.

4.1   FSL Benchmarks Used in Our Experiments

The *mini*ImageNet benchmark (Mini) [51] is a standard benchmark for few-shot image classification, that has 100 randomly chosen classes from ILSVRC-2012 [40]. They are randomly split into disjoint subsets of 64 meta-training, 16 meta-validation, and 20 meta-testing classes. Each class has 600 images of size 84×84. We use the same splits as [22] and prior works.

The *tiered*ImageNet benchmark (Tiered) [38] is a larger subset of ILSVRC-2012 [40], consisted of 608 classes grouped into 34 high-level classes. These are divided into disjoint 20 meta-training high-level classes, 6 meta-validation classes, and 8 meta-testing classes. This corresponds to 351, 97, and 160 classes for meta-training, meta-validation, and meta-testing respectively. Splitting using higher level classes effectively minimizes the semantic similarity between classes belonging to the different splits. All images are of size 84 × 84.

4.2 Transductive FSL Setting

Table 1. Transductive setting

	Mini 1-shot	Mini 5-shot	Tiered 1-shot	Tiered 5-shot
Simple shot [52]	64.30 ± 0.20	81.48 ± 0.14	71.26 ± 0.21	86.59 ± 0.15
TPN [28]	55.51 ± 0.86	69.86 ± 0.65	59.91 ± 0.94	73.30 ± 0.75
TEAM [35]	60.07 ± N.A	75.90 ± N.A	-	-
EGNN + trans. [21]	-	76.37 ± N.A	-	80.15 ± N.A
Trans. Fine-Tuning [8]	65.73 ± 0.68	78.40 ± 0.52	73.34 ± 0.71	85.50 ± 0.50
Trans-mean-sub	65.58 ± 0.20	81.45 ± 0.14	73.49 ± 0.21	86.56 ± 0.15
Trans-mean-sub(*)	65.88 ± 0.20	82.20 ± 0.14	73.75 ± 0.21	87.16 ± 0.15
PCA	70.53 ± 0.25	80.71 ± 0.16	80.07 ± 0.25	86.42 ± 0.17
ICA	72.10 ± 0.25	81.85 ± 0.16	80.82 ± 0.25	86.97 ± 0.17
BKM	72.05 ± 0.24	80.34 ± 0.17	79.82 ± 0.25	85.67 ± 0.18
PCA + BKM	75.11 ± 0.26	82.24 ± 0.17	83.19 ± 0.25	87.83 ± 0.17
ICA + BKM	75.79 ± 0.26	82.83 ± 0.16	83.39 ± 0.25	88.00 ± 0.17
MSP	71.39 ± 0.27	82.67 ± 0.15	76.01 ± 0.27	87.13 ± 0.15
PCA + MSP	76.31 ± 0.26	84.54 ± 0.14	84.06 ± 0.25	89.13 ± 0.15
ICA + MSP	**77.06 ± 0.26**	**84.99 ± 0.14**	**84.29 ± 0.25**	**89.31 ± 0.15**

In these experiments we consider the transductive FSL setting, where the set of queries is used as the source of the unlabeled data. This setting is typical for cases when an FSL classifier is submitted a bulk of query data for offline evaluation. In Table 1 we report the performance of our proposed TAFSSL (PCA, ICA), clustering (BKM, MSP), and TAFSSL+clustering (PCA/ICA + BKM/MSP) approaches and compare them to a set of baselines and state-of-the-art (SOTA) transductive FSL methods from the literature: TPN [28] and Transductive Fine-Tuning [8]. We also compare to SOTA regular FSL result of [52] in order to highlight the effect of using the unlabeled queries for prediction. As baselines, we try to maximally adapt the method of [52] to the transductive FSL setting. These are the so-called "trans-mean-sub" that on each test episode subtracts the mean of all the samples ($S \cup Q$) from all the samples followed by L2 normalization (in order reduce the episode bias); and the "trans-mean-sub(*)" where we do the same but computing and subtracting the means of the S and Q sample sets separately (in order to better align their distributions). As can be seen from

Table 1, on both the Mini and the Tiered transductive FSL benchmarks, the top performing of our proposed TAFSSL based approaches (ICA+MSP) consistently outperforms all the previous (transductive and non-transductive) SOTA and the baselines by more then 10% in the more challenging 1-shot setting and by more then 2% in the 5-shot setting, underlining the benefits of using the transductive setting, and the importance of TAFSSL to this setting. In the following section, we only evaluate the ICA based TAFSSL variants as it was found to consistently outperform the PCA based variant under all settings.

4.3   Semi-supervised FSL Setting

In this section we evaluate our proposed approaches in the semi-supervised FSL setting. In this setting, we have an additional set of unlabeled samples U that accompanies the test task T. In U we usually expect to have additional samples from the T's target classes distribution, possibly mixed with addi-

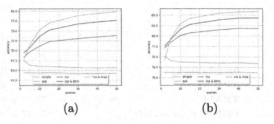

(a)   (b)

Fig. 2. Num. queries (transductive). (a) *mini*ImageNet; (b) *tiered*ImageNet

tional unrelated samples from some number of distracting classes (please see Sect. 4.4 for an ablation on this). In Table 2 we summarize the performance of our proposed TAFSSL based approaches, and compare them to the SOTA semi-supervised FSL methods of [24, 28, 38, 46]. In addition, we also present results for varying number of additional unlabeled samples in U (semi-supervised). As can be seen from Table 2 the TAFSSL-based approaches outperform all competing methods by a large margins of over 8% and 4% accuracy gain in both the Mini and the Tiered benchmarks in 1-shot and 5-shot settings respectively. Interestingly, same as for the transductive FSL, for the semi-supervised FSL the ICA+MSP approach is the best performing.

4.4   Ablation Study

Number of Queries in Transductive FSL. Since the unlabelled data in transductive FSL is comprised entirely from the query samples, the size of the query set Q in the meta-testing episodes affects the performance. To test this we have evaluated the proposed TAFSSL ICA-based methods, as well as two baselines, namely SimpleShot [52], and its adaptation to transductive setting "trans-mean-sub*" (sub). All methods were tested varying the number of queries from 2 to 50. The results of this ablation on both the Tiered and Mini benchmarks are shown on Fig. 2. As can be seen from the figure, already for as little as 5 queries a substantial gap can be observed (for both the benchmarks) between the proposed best performing ICA+MSP technique and the best of the baselines.

Table 2. Semi supervised settingSemi supervised setting

	# Unlabeled	Mini 1-shot	Mini 5-shot	Tiered 1-shot	Tiered 5-shot
TPN [28]	360	52.78 ± 0.27	66.42 ± 0.21	-	-
PSN [46]	100	-	68.12 ± 0.67	-	71.15 ± 0.67
TPN [28]	1170	-	-	55.74 ± 0.29	71.01 ± 0.23
SKM [38]	100	62.10 ± N.A	73.60 ± N.A	68.60 ± N.A	81.00 ± N.A
TPN [28]	100	62.70 ± N.A	74.20 ± N.A	72.10 ± N.A	83.30 ± N.A
LST [24]	30	65.00 ± 1.90	-	75.40 ± 1.60	-
LST [24]	50	-	77.80 ± 0.80	-	83.40 ± 0.80
LST [24]	100	70.10 ± 1.90	78.70 ± 0.80	77.70 ± 1.60	85.20 ± 0.80
ICA	30	72.00 ± 0.24	81.31 ± 0.16	80.24 ± 0.24	86.57 ± 0.17
ICA	50	72.66 ± 0.24	81.96 ± 0.16	80.86 ± 0.24	87.03 ± 0.17
ICA	100	72.80 ± 0.24	82.27 ± 0.16	80.91 ± 0.25	87.14 ± 0.17
ICA + BKM	30	75.70 ± 0.22	83.59 ± 0.14	82.97 ± 0.23	88.34 ± 0.15
ICA + BKM	50	76.46 ± 0.22	84.36 ± 0.14	83.51 ± 0.22	88.81 ± 0.15
ICA + BKM	100	76.83 ± 0.22	84.83 ± 0.14	83.73 ± 0.22	88.95 ± 0.15
ICA + MSP	30	78.55 ± 0.25	84.84 ± 0.14	85.04 ± 0.24	88.94 ± 0.15
ICA + MSP	50	79.58 ± 0.25	85.41 ± 0.13	85.75 ± 0.24	89.32 ± 0.15
ICA + MSP	100	80.11 ± 0.25	85.78 ± 0.13	86.00 ± 0.23	89.39 ± 0.15

Out of Distribution Noise (distraction Classes) in Unlabeled Data. In many applications, the unlabeled data may become contaminated with samples "unrelated" to the few-shot task $\mathcal{T}$ target classes. This situation is most likely to arise in the semi supervised FSL setting, as in transductive FSL the unlabeled samples are the queries and unless we are inter-

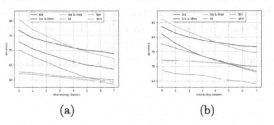

(a)   (b)

Fig. 3. The affect of the unlabeled data noise. Plots for LST [24], TPN [28], and SKM [38] are from original papers. (a) *mini*ImageNet; (b) *tiered*ImageNet

ested in open-set FSL mode (to the best of our knowledge not explored yet), these are commonly expected to belong only to the target classes distribution. In the semi-supervised FSL literature [24,28,38], this type of noise is evaluated using additional random samples from random "distracting" classes added to the unlabeled set. In Fig. 3 we compare our proposed ICA-based TAFSSL approaches to SOTA semi-supervised FSL methods [24,28,38]. By varying the number of distracting classes from 0 to 7, we see that about 8% accuracy gap is maintained between top TAFSSL method and the top baseline across all the tested noise levels.

The Number of TAFSSL Sub-space Dimensions. An important parameter for TAFSSL is the number of the dimensions of the sub-space selected by the TAFSSL approach. In Fig. 4 we explore the effect of the number of chosen dimensions in ICA-based TAFFSL on both the Mini and the Tiered benchmarks. As can be seen from the figure, the optimal number of dimensions for ICA-based TAFSSL approaches is 10, which is consistent between both test and validation sets. Interestingly, the same number 10 is consistent between the two benchmarks. Similarly, using validation, the optimal dimension for PCA-based TAFSSL was found to be 4 (also consistently on the two benchmarks).

Backbone Architectures. The choice of backbone turned out to be an important factor for FSL methods performance [3, 52]. In Table 3 we evaluate the performance of one of the proposed TAFSSL approaches, namely PCA+MSP while using different backbones pre-trained on the training set to compute

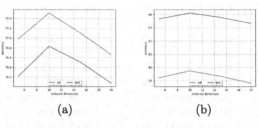

(a)   (b)

Fig. 4.   ICA   dim.   vs   accuracy.   (a) *mini*ImageNet (b) *tiered*ImageNet

the base feature space $\mathcal{F}$. We used the 1-shot transductive FSL setting on both Mini and Tiered benchmarks for this evaluation. As can be seen from the table, larger backbones produce better performance for the TAFSSL approach. In addition, we list the reported performance of the competing SOTA transductive FSL methods in the same table for direct comparison using the same backbones. As can be seen, above 8% accuracy advantage is maintained by our proposed approach above the top previous method using the corresponding WRN architecture.

Table 3. Backbones comparison. The 1-shot transductive FSL setting for *mini*ImageNet (Mini) and *tiered*ImageNet (Tiered) was used for this comparison

	Backbone	Mini 1-shot	Tiered 1-shot
TPN [28]	Conv-4	55.51 ± 0.86	59.91 ± 0.94
TPN [28]	ResNet-12	59.46 ± N.A	-
Transductive Fine-Tuning [8]	WRN	65.73 ± 0.68	73.34 ± 0.71
PCA + MSP	Conv-4	56.63 ± 0.27	60.27 ± 0.29
PCA + MSP	ResNet-10	70.93 ± 0.28	76.27 ± 0.28
PCA + MSP	ResNet-18	73.73 ± 0.27	80.60 ± 0.27
PCA + MSP	WRN	73.72 ± 0.27	81.61 ± 0.26
PCA + MSP	DenseNet	76.31 ± 0.26	84.06 ± 0.25

Unbalanced (long-Tail) Test Classes Distribution in Unlabeled Data.
In all previous transductive FSL works, balanced test tasks (in terms of the
number of queries for each class) were used. While this is fine for experimental
evaluation, in practical applications there is no guarantee that the bulk of queries
sent for offline evaluation will be class-balanced. In fact, class-skew (lack of
balance) is much more likely. To test the effect of query set skew, we have
evaluated the proposed ICA-based TAFSSL approaches, as well as the Simple-
Shot [52] and its transductive adaptation "trans-mean-sub*" (sub) baselines,
under varying levels of this skew. The level of skew was controlled through the
so-called "unbalanced factor" parameter R: in each test episode, for each class
$15 + uni([0, R])$ query samples were randomly chosen (here uni refers to a uniform
distribution). Figure 5 shows the effect of varying R from 10 to 50, while at
the extreme setting (50) above factor 4 skew is possible between the classes in
terms of the number of associated queries. Nevertheless, as can be seen from the
figure, the effect of lack of balance on the performance of the TAFSSL based
approaches is minimal, leading to at most 1% performance loss at $R = 50$. Since
no prior work offered a similar evaluation design, we believe that the proposed
protocol may become an additional important tool for evaluating transductive
FSL methods under lack of query set balance in the future.

5   Summary and Conclusions

In this paper we have shown
that the Feature Sub-Space
Learning (FSSL), and specifically it's Task Adaptive variant (TAFSSL), has a significant
positive effect on FSL performance. We have explored different methods for benefiting
from TAFSSL in FSL and have
shown great promise for this

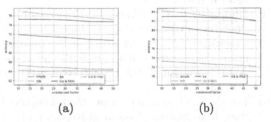

(a)   (b)

Fig. 5. Unbalanced. (a) *mini*ImageNet (b)
*tiered*ImageNet

kind of techniques by achieving large margin improvements over transductive
and semi-supervised FSL state-of-the-art, as well as over methods that do not
use additional unlabeled data, thus highlighting the benefit of the latter. Potential future work directions include using TAFSSL with meta-training, e.g. by
propagating training episodes gradients through pyTorch PCA/ICA implementations, and the proposed clustering techniques BKM/MSP; exploring non-linear
TAFSSL variants (e.g. kernel or DNN TAFSSL); further exploring the effect of
TAFSSL in *any-shot* learning and the significance of the *way* parameter of the
task; exploring the benefits of TAFSSL in cross-domain few-shot learning where
the FSL backbone pre-training occurs in different visual domain from the one
test classes are sampled from.

Acknowledgment. This material is based upon work supported by the Defense Advanced Research Projects Agency (DARPA) under Contract No. FA8750-19-C-1001. Any opinions, ndings and conclusions or recommendations expressed in this material are those of the author(s) and do not necessarily reect the views of DARPA. Raja Giryes is supported by ERC-StG grant no. 757497 (SPADE).

References

1. Alfassy, A., et al.: LaSO: Label-Set Operations networks for multi-label few-shot learning. In: CVPR (2019)
2. Antoniou, A., Storkey, A., Edwards, H.: Data Augmentation Generative Adversarial Networks. arXiv:1711.04340 (2017). https://arxiv.org/pdf/1711.04340.pdf
3. Chen, W.Y., Liu, Y.C., Kira, Z., Wang, Y.C., Huang, J.B.: A closer look at few-shot classification. In: ICLR (2019)
4. Chen, Z., Fu, Y., Zhang, Y., Jiang, Y.G., Xue, X., Sigal, L.: Multi-level semantic feature augmentation for one-shot learning. IEEE Trans. Image Process. **28**(9), 4594–4605 (2019). https://doi.org/10.1109/tip.2019.2910052
5. Comon, P.: Independent component analysis, A new concept? Technical Report (1994)
6. Cubuk, E.D., Zoph, B., Mané, D., Vasudevan, V., Le, Q.V.: AutoAugment: Learning Augmentation Policies from Data. https://arxiv.org/pdf/1805.09501v1.pdf
7. Devos, A., Grossglauser, M.: Subspace Networks for Few-shot Classification. Technical Report (2019)
8. Dhillon, G.S., Chaudhari, P., Ravichandran, A., Soatto, S.: A Baseline For Few-Shot Image Classification. Technical Report (2019)
9. Dosovitskiy, A., Springenberg, J.T., Tatarchenko, M., Brox, T.: Learning to generate chairs, tables and cars with convolutional networks. IEEE Trans. Pattern Anal. Mach. Intell. **39**(4), 692–705 (2017). https://doi.org/10.1109/TPAMI.2016.2567384
10. Doveh, S., et al.: MetAdapt: Meta-Learned Task-Adaptive Architecture for Few-Shot Classification. Technical Report (2019)
11. Dvornik, N., Schmid, C., Mairal, J.: Diversity with cooperation: ensemble methods for few-shot classification. In: The IEEE International Conference on Computer Vision (ICCV) (2019). http://arxiv.org/abs/1903.11341
12. Finn, C., Abbeel, P., Levine, S.: Model-Agnostic Meta-Learning for Fast Adaptation of Deep Networks. arXiv:1703.03400 (2017). http://arxiv.org/abs/1703.03400
13. Fukunaga, K., Hostetler, L.D.: The estimation of the gradient of a density function, with applications in pattern recognition. IEEE Trans. Inf. Theory **21**(1), 32–40 (1975). https://doi.org/10.1109/TIT.1975.1055330
14. Garcia, V., Bruna, J.: Few-Shot Learning with Graph Neural Networks, pp. 1–13. arXiv:1711.04043 (2017). http://arxiv.org/abs/1711.04043
15. Gidaris, S., Bursuc, A., Komodakis, N., Pérez, P., Cord, M.: Boosting Few-Shot Visual Learning with Self-Supervision, 6 2019. http://arxiv.org/abs/1906.05186
16. Guu, K., Hashimoto, T.B., Oren, Y., Liang, P.: Generating Sentences by Editing Prototypes. Arxiv:1709.08878 (2017). https://arxiv.org/pdf/1709.08878.pdf

17. Hariharan, B., Girshick, R.: Low-shot visual recognition by shrinking and hallucinating features. In: IEEE International Conference on Computer Vision (ICCV) (2017). https://arxiv.org/pdf/1606.02819.pdf
18. He, K., Zhang, X., Ren, S., Sun, J.: Deep Residual Learning for Image Recognition. arXiv:1512.03385 (2015). https://arxiv.org/pdf/1512.03385.pdf
19. Huang, G., Liu, Z., Maaten, V.D.L., Weinberger, K.Q.: Densely connected convolutional networks. In: 2017 IEEE Conference on Computer Vision and Pattern Recognition (CVPR) pp. 2261–2269 (2017). https://doi.org/10.1109/CVPR.2017. 243, https://arxiv.org/pdf/1608.06993.pdf
20. Jiang, X., Havaei, M., Varno, F., Chartrand, G.: Learning To Learn With Conditional Class Dependencies, pp. 1–11 (2019)
21. Kim, J., Kim, T., Kim, S., Yoo, C.D.: Edge-Labeling Graph Neural Network for Few-shot Learning. Technical Report
22. Lee, K., Maji, S., Ravichandran, A., Soatto, S.: Meta-Learning with Differentiable Convex Optimization. In: CVPR (2019). https://github.com/kjunelee/ MetaOptNet
23. Li, H., Eigen, D., Dodge, S., Zeiler, M., Wang, X.: Finding Task-Relevant Features for Few-Shot Learning by Category Traversal, vol. 1 (2019). http://arxiv.org/abs/ 1905.11116
24. Li, X., et al.: Learning to Self-Train for Semi-Supervised Few-Shot Classification, 6 2019. http://arxiv.org/abs/1906.00562
25. Li, Z., Zhou, F., Chen, F., Li, H.: Meta-SGD: Learning to Learn Quickly for Few-Shot Learning. arXiv:1707.09835 (2017). http://arxiv.org/abs/1707.09835
26. Lim, S., Kim, I., Kim, T., Kim, C., Brain, K., Kim, S.: Fast AutoAugment. Technical Report (2019)
27. Lin, T.-Y., et al.: Microsoft COCO: common objects in context. In: Fleet, D., Pajdla, T., Schiele, B., Tuytelaars, T. (eds.) ECCV 2014. LNCS, vol. 8693, pp. 740–755. Springer, Cham (2014). https://doi.org/10.1007/978-3-319-10602-1_48
28. Liu, Y., et al.: Learning To Propagate Labels: Transductive Propagation Networfor For Few-Shot Learning (2019)
29. Lloyd, S.P., Lloyd, S.P.: Least squares quantization in PCM. IEEE Trans. Inf. Theory, 28, 129–137 (1982). https://citeseerx.ist.psu.edu/viewdoc/summary?doi=10. 1.1.131.1338
30. Munkhdalai, T., Yu, H.: Meta Networks. arXiv:1703.00837 (2017). https://doi.org/ 10.1093/mnrasl/slx008, http://arxiv.org/abs/1703.00837
31. Nakamura, A., Harada, T.: Revisiting Fine-Tuning for Few-Shot Learning. Technical Report
32. Oreshkin, B.N., Rodriguez, P., Lacoste, A.: TADAM: task dependent adaptive metric for improved few-shot learning. NeurIPS, 5 2018. http://arxiv.org/abs/ 1805.10123
33. Park, D., Ramanan, D.: Articulated pose estimation with tiny synthetic videos. In: IEEE Conference on Computer Vision and Pattern Recognition (CVPR), pp. 58–66, October 2015. https://doi.org/10.1109/CVPRW.2015.7301337
34. Pearson, K.: On lines and planes of closest fit to systems of points in space. Lond. Edinb. Dublin Philos. Mag. J. Sci. 2(11), 559–572 (1901). https://doi.org/10.1080/ 14786440109462720
35. Qiao, L., Shi, Y., Li, J., Wang, Y., Huang, T., Tian, Y.: Transductive Episodic-Wise Adaptive Metric for Few-Shot Learning (2019). http://arxiv.org/abs/1910. 02224
36. Ravi, S., Larochelle, H.: Optimization as a model for few-shot learning. In: ICLR, pp. 1–11 (2017). https://openreview.net/pdf?id=rJY0-Kcll

37. Reed, S., et al.: Few-shot autoregressive density estimation: towards learning to learn distributions, pp. 1–11 (2018). arXiv:1710.10304 (2016)
38. Ren, M., et al.: Meta-learning for semi-supervised few-shot classification. In: ICLR, 3 2018. http://arxiv.org/abs/1803.00676, http://bair.berkeley.edu/blog/2017/07/18/
39. Rippel, O., Paluri, M., Dollar, P., Bourdev, L.: Metric Learning with Adaptive Density Discrimination, pp. 1–15. arXiv:1511.05939 (2015). http://arxiv.org/abs/1511.05939
40. Russakovsky, O., et al.: ImageNet large scale visual recognition challenge. In: IJCV, 9 2015. http://arxiv.org/abs/1409.0575
41. Rusu, A.A., et al.: Meta-learning with latent embedding optimization. In: ICLR, 7 2018. http://arxiv.org/abs/1807.05960
42. Saito, K., Kim, D., Sclaroff, S., Darrell, T., Saenko, K.: Semi-supervised domain adaptation via minimax entropy. In: ICCV, 4 2019. http://arxiv.org/abs/1904.06487
43. Santoro, A., Bartunov, S., Botvinick, M., Wierstra, D., Lillicrap, T.: Meta-learning with memory-augmented neural networks. J. Mach. Learn. Res. (Proceedings of The 33rd International Conference on Machine Learning), vol. 48, pp. 1842–1850 (2016). https://doi.org/10.1002/2014GB005021
44. Schwartz, E., Karlinsky, L., Feris, R., Giryes, R., Bronstein, A.M.: Baby steps towards few-shot learning with multiple semantics, pp. 1–11 (2019). http://arxiv.org/abs/1906.01905
45. Schwartz, E., et al.: Delta-Encoder: an effective sample synthesis method for few-shot object recognition. NeurIPS (2018). https://arxiv.org/pdf/1806.04734.pdf
46. Simon, C., Koniusz, P., Harandi, M.: Projective sub-space networks for few-shot learning. In: ICLR 2019 OpenReview. https://openreview.net/pdf?id=rkzfuiA9F7
47. Snell, J., Swersky, K., Zemel, R.: Prototypical networks for few-shot learning. In: NIPS (2017). http://arxiv.org/abs/1703.05175
48. Su, H., Qi, C.R., Li, Y., Guibas, L.J.: Render for CNN viewpoint estimation in images using CNNs trained with rendered 3D model views.pdf. In: IEEE International Conference on Computer Vision (ICCV), pp. 2686–2694 (2015)
49. Sung, F., Yang, Y., Zhang, L., Xiang, T., Torr, P.H.S., Hospedales, T.M.: Learning to Compare: Relation Network for Few-Shot Learning. https://arxiv.org/pdf/1711.06025.pdf
50. Sung, F., Yang, Y., Zhang, L., Xiang, T., Torr, P.H.S., Hospedales, T.M.: Learning to Compare: Relation Network for Few-Shot Learning. arXiv:1711.06025 (2017), http://arxiv.org/abs/1711.06025
51. Vinyals, O., Blundell, C., Lillicrap, T., Kavukcuoglu, K., Wierstra, D.:Matching networks for one shot learning. In: NIPS (2016).https://doi.org/10.1109/CVPR.2016.95, http://arxiv.org/abs/1606.04080
52. Wang, Y., Chao, W.L., Weinberger, K.Q., van der Maaten, L.: SimpleShot: Revisiting Nearest-Neighbor Classification for Few-Shot Learning, 11 2019. http://arxiv.org/abs/1911.04623
53. Wang, Y.X., Girshick, R., Hebert, M., Hariharan, B.: Low-Shot Learning from Imaginary Data. arXiv:1801.05401 (2018). http://arxiv.org/abs/1801.05401
54. Weinberger, K.Q., Saul, L.K.: Distance metric learning for large margin nearest neighbor classification. J. Mach. Learn. Res. 10, 207–244 (2009). https://doi.org/10.1126/science.277.5323.215
55. Xing, C., Rostamzadeh, N., Oreshkin, B.N., Pinheiro, P.O.: Adaptive Cross-Modal Few-Shot Learning (2019). https://arxiv.org/pdf/1902.07104.pdf, http://arxiv.org/abs/1902.07104

56. Yu, A., Grauman, K.: Semantic jitter: dense supervision for visual comparisons via synthetic images. In: Proceedings of the IEEE International Conference on Computer Vision, pp. 5571–5580, October 2017. https://doi.org/10.1109/ICCV.2017.594
57. Zhang, J., Zhao, C., Ni, B., Xu, M., Yang, X.: Variational few-shot learning. In: IEEE International Conference on Computer Vision (ICCV) (2019)
58. Zhou, F., Wu, B., Li, Z.: Deep Meta-Learning: Learning to Learn in the Concept Space. Technical Report, 2 2018. http://arxiv.org/abs/1802.03596

Traffic Accident Benchmark for Causality Recognition

Tackgeun You[1,2] and Bohyung Han[2(✉)]

[1] Department of CSE, POSTECH, Pohang, Korea
`tackgeun.you@postech.ac.kr`
[2] Department of ECE and ASRI, Seoul National University, Seoul, Korea
`bhhan@snu.ac.kr`

Abstract. We propose a brand new benchmark for analyzing causality in traffic accident videos by decomposing an accident into a pair of events, cause and effect. We collect videos containing traffic accident scenes and annotate cause and effect events for each accident with their temporal intervals and semantic labels; such annotations are not available in existing datasets for accident anticipation task. Our dataset has the following two advantages over the existing ones, which would facilitate practical research for causality analysis. First, the decomposition of an accident into cause and effect events provides atomic cues for reasoning on a complex environment and planning future actions. Second, the prediction of cause and effect in an accident makes a system more interpretable to humans, which mitigates the ambiguity of legal liabilities among agents engaged in the accident. Using the proposed dataset, we analyze accidents by localizing the temporal intervals of their causes and effects and classifying the semantic labels of the accidents. The dataset as well as the implementations of baseline models are available in the code repository (https://github.com/tackgeun/CausalityInTrafficAccident).

1 Introduction

Developing an autonomous driving system is one of the major problems in artificial intelligence. This problem has long been viewed as an extremely challenging task since it requires high-level scene understanding in addition to various low-level recognitions. Despite such challenges, autonomous driving has drawn wide attention, and significant improvement has been achieved over the past few years by virtue of advances in computer vision technologies.

Autonomous driving provides convenience to drivers, however, it also raises concerns about traffic accidents, creating the following needs. First, autonomous driving systems should be able to anticipate accidents, take a series of actions to mitigate fatalities, and help drivers escape from the accident. Second, they need to provide an interpretable reasoning process for an accident and deal with liability issues between self-driving vehicles, their manufacturers, passengers, and insurance companies.

A. Vedaldi et al. (Eds.): ECCV 2020, LNCS 12352, pp. 540–556, 2020.
https://doi.org/10.1007/978-3-030-58571-6_32

Despite various issues in autonomous driving systems, the research related to traffic accident analysis is rarely explored due to the following two reasons. First, it is challenging to construct a comprehensive video dataset with traffic accidents due to huge variations in the characteristics of accidents and the environment of traffic scenes. Second, the categories of traffic accidents are ill-defined while the diversity of dataset is crucial to learn robust models for accident recognition.

With the challenges, a few methods [5,11,20,26] mainly focus on the accident anticipation task that aims at forecasting accidents a few seconds earlier. However, the methods simply predict accidents without sophisticated analysis and potential to be extended to accident avoidance systems. On the other hand, Najm *et al.* [17] analyze a traffic accident as a composition of a *cause* and an *effect* event, based on the real-world traffic accident statistics reported by the police. According to [17], an effect event corresponds to the time interval that a vehicle is engaged to an accident, while a cause event means a precrash behavior of the vehicle that potentially leads to an accident. For example, at a road junction, a cause of *'a car driving at red light'* may result in an effect of *'a collision between two vehicles'* as illustrated in Fig. 1. Decomposing a traffic accident scene into a cause and an effect has advantages beyond simple accident anticipation in autonomous driving. First, identifying semantic labels for cause or effect in an accident provides atomic cues for accident analysis and future action planning. Second, the interpretability given by predicting cause and effect events can deal with liability issues between multiple agents.

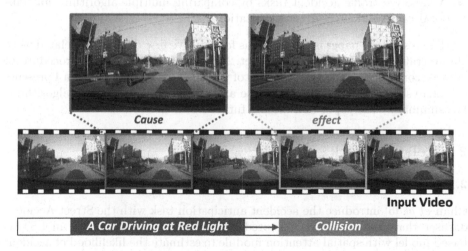

Fig. 1. An example of traffic accident video in our dataset, which is associated with a cause (in red) and an effect (in green) events. Both the cause and the effects have their semantic labels: *a car driving at red light* in the cause and *a collision between two vehicles* in the effect. (Color figure online)

Motivated by such advantages, we constructed a novel video dataset for causality analysis in traffic accident scenes, which is referred to as CTA (Causality in Traffic Accident). We collected 1,935 videos of traffic accidents, which are captured by dashcams or monitoring cameras, from video repositories on the web. We annotate the semantic labels of cause and effect and their temporal intervals in each accident video. The detailed information of the semantic labels, including their kinds and distributions, is presented in Fig. 2.

Based on the traffic accident analysis dataset, we propose a novel task, temporal cause and effect event localization. As illustrated in Fig. 1, given a video including a traffic accident, the task aims to localize temporal intervals of cause and effect events as well as to identify their semantic labels, simultaneously. To deal with the problem, we adopt several action recognition algorithms—action detection and segmentation—as baseline methods. Experimental results show that modeling long-range contextual information is critical to achieve competitive performance for the localization of cause and effect events.

The main contributions of this paper are summarized below.

- We introduce a traffic accident analysis benchmark, denoted by CTA, which contains temporal intervals of a cause and an effect in each accident and their semantic labels provided by [17].
- We construct the dataset based on the semantic taxonomy in crash avoidance research [17], which makes the distribution of the benchmark coherent to the semantic taxonomy and the real-world statistics.
- We analyze traffic accident tasks by comparing multiple algorithms for temporal cause and effect event localization.

The rest of the paper is organized as follows. We first discuss the related work about traffic accident analysis in Sect. 2. Section 3 describes the procedure of dataset construction and the statistics of the collected dataset. Section 4 presents the analysis of our dataset using cause and effect event localization algorithms. We summarize the paper and discuss future works in Sect. 5.

2   Related Work

2.1   Traffic Accident Anticipation

Chan et al. [5] introduce the accident anticipation task with the Street Accident dataset that contain videos captured by dashcams. They propose an LSTM-based model with spatial attention module to estimate the likelihood of accident occurrence in the near future for each frame. Zeng et al. [26] propose a multi-task learning approach to improve accident anticipation accuracy, which also localizes risky regions associated with accidents. Herzig et al. [11] present the Collision dataset, which includes near-miss incident scenes in addition to accident videos. They propose spatio-temporal action graphs that effectively model the relationship between objects associated with an accident. Kataoka et al. [12,20] introduce a large-scale dataset for accident anticipation, referred to as near-miss

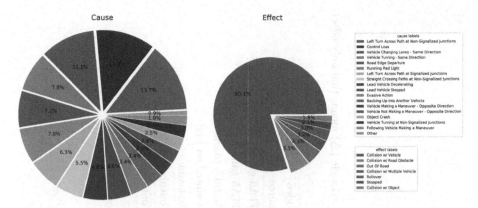

Fig. 2. The distributions of semantic labels for cause (left) and effect (right) events. According to the figure, 80.1% of accidents in this dataset are related with the collision of two vehicles.

incident database (NIDB), and propose an adaptive loss function to facilitate the earliest anticipation of an accident.

On the other hand, Yao *et al.* [25] propose a traffic accident detection method based on self-supervision about the future location of vehicles in a scene. By exploiting an additional dataset, their approach manages to outperform [5] without the temporal location supervision of accidents.

There exist a few datasets based on synthetic videos obtained from the GTA5 game to reduce accident video collection cost. Aliakbarian *et al.* [2] collect synthetic driving videos with several scenarios including traffic accidents at scale by constructing a simulator. Kim *et al.* [13] introduce a domain adaptation benchmark for accident anticipation by collecting real and synthetic traffic accident videos. Our traffic accident analysis could take advantage of synthetic datasets by generating videos at a lower cost. However, it is not straightforward to simulate the real distribution of accident cause and effect and generate diverse videos relevant to our objective without sophisticated duration during the dataset construction process.

The accident anticipation task is limited to predicting the occurrence of an accident without its semantic understanding. In contrast, we focus on more challenging tasks—localizing cause and effect events of an accident and estimating semantic labels of an accident—and expect our research to facilitate in-depth analysis of traffic accident scenes.

2.2 Causality in Visual Domain

Causality indicates influence by which an event contributes to the generation of another one, where the former event is referred to as the cause and the latter one is referred to as the effect. The simplest mathematical expression for causality is a bivariate model, which consists of a single cause variable, a single effect

Table 1. Comparison of traffic accident datasets. The asterisk (*) indicates averaged duration. The triangle (△) means that only effect type is provided.

Dataset	# of accidents	Causality	Semantic labels	Duration (sec)	Accident type	Video source
VIENA² [2]	~1,200	-	△	5	synthetic	GTA5 game
GTACrash [13]	7,720	-	-	2	synthetic	GTA5 game
Street Accident [5]	678	-	△	5	real	Youtube (dashcam)
NIDB [12,20]	4,595	-	-	10–15	near-miss	Mounted on taxi
Collision [11]	803	-	△	*40	real+near-miss	Dashcam
YouTubeCrash [13]	122	-	-	2	real	Youtube (dashcam)
CTA (ours)	1,935	✓	✓	*17.7	real	Youtube

variable, and a directed edge from the cause to the effect. Research on causality often addresses properties of the directed edge, which describe the causal relation between cause and effect variables.

Lopez-Paz *et al.* [16] propose a binary classifier that identifies whether given two variables X and Y have a causal $(X \rightarrow Y)$ or an anti-causal $(Y \rightarrow X)$ relation. Based on the binary classifier, they reveal causal relationships between object presence and visual features. Causality in videos is explored in [18,23], where they both aim to classify whether a video is played in a forward or a backward direction. Lebeda *et al.* [15] propose a statistical tool to analyze causality by separating camera motion from the observed one in a scene.

In contrast to the prior works exploring causal relationships, our novelty lies in addressing causality to represent and analyze traffic accident videos—how videos are decomposed, what types of accidents happen, and which prior events trigger the accidents.

2.3   Action Understanding

Action understanding algorithm is a core component for video understanding, visual surveillance and autonomous driving. We review action classification and localization tasks in this subsection.

Action Classification. This task, also referred to as action recognition, categorizes an input video into one or more semantic action classes. There have been a lot of works for this problem, which are often related to video representation learning. Primitive video representation learning methods for action classification include two-stream networks [9,19], C3D [21], 3D-ResNet [10], and I3D [4] while TSN [22] learns augmented representations on top of the standard methods by sparse and uniform sampling of video segments.

Action Localization. The objective of action localization is to identify action class labels and their temporal intervals in a video. There are three kinds of mainstream algorithms—proposal-based action detection, single-stage action detection, and temporal action segmentation; they commonly follow the successful design practices in the image domain.

Proposal-based action detection [6,24,27,28] first extracts proposals for the temporal regions that are likely to have action instances, and then classifies the individual proposals. Single-stage action detection [3] estimates action intervals from the predefined temporal anchors by regression. Contrary to the two detection-based methods predicting an action label per temporal interval, action segmentation methods [8,14] perform frame-level prediction and obtain temporal information of actions. Note that we tested all three types of action localization methods on our traffic accident analysis benchmark; action segmentation methods are often designed to capture long-range temporal dependency effectively, and results in superior performance in our dataset.

3   Traffic Accident Dataset for Causality Understanding

This section describes how we collected the traffic accident dataset for causality understanding, and presents its statistics.

3.1   Semantic Taxonomy of Traffic Accident

We constructed a unique dataset, CTA, based on the semantic taxonomy from the report of precrash typology [17], which specifies causes and effect events of accidents observed in the real-world[1]. The prior works related to traffic accident [2,5,11,13,20,25] have little consideration about semantic taxonomy of accidents, and often suffer from intrinsic biases in datasets.

We decompose a traffic accident into a matching pair of events—a cause and an effect. Following the concept of causality, the cause event of an accident corresponds to risky behavior of an agent, such as a vehicle and a pedestrian, that may lead to the accident. On the other hand, the effect event of an accident is related to physical damage of the agents involved in the accident. In principle, a single accident may have multiple causes because many agents can contribute to the accident, but all videos in our dataset contain only a single pair of cause and event.

For each cause and effect event, we assign semantic labels, which correspond to the specific activities of agents that eventually result in accidents. The semantic labels are obtained from the real-world statistics [17].

Our dataset is constructed based on the semantic taxonomy described above; each video has annotation for a cause and an effect, which are associated with semantic labels. Figure 1 illustrates the relationship between a video, a pair of cause and effect events, and semantic labels. The list of semantic labels of cause and effect events of our benchmark is shown in Fig. 4 and Table 4.

3.2   Construction of Dataset

Collecting Accident Videos. To acquire diverse types of traffic accident scenes, we collect traffic accident videos downloaded from several Youtube channels. Because a single Youtube video may contain multiple traffic accidents, we split the video into distinct sub-clips without shot changes and make each sub-clip associated with only a single accident. The sub-clip split process consists of the following two steps; 1) initial shot boundaries are obtained using a built-in shot boundary detector in FFmpeg[2], and 2) wrong shot boundaries are eliminated and re-annotated manually. Given the sub-clips, we perform an additional filtering step to exclude 1) videos in low resolutions, 2) videos zoomed in or out near the moment of the accident, 3) videos that have ambiguity in determining semantic labels, and 4) too complex videos having multiple cause and effect

---

[1] 2004 General Estimates System (GES) crash database [1] contains a nationally representative sample of police reports dealing with all types of a vehicle crash.

[2] https://ffmpeg.org/.

Fig. 3. An example view of our annotation tool that supports spatio-temporal annotations. We maintain two kinds of annotations: one for cause and effect events (upper right) and the other for object instances (lower right). The bounding box for the 34th instance denotes the spatio-temporal start position of the cause of the 18th accident, which has a cause semantic label *'vehicle turning'* and an effect label *'Collision with Vehicle'*.

events. By applying the procedures described above, 59.8% of accident videos are survived. Eventually, 1,935 videos (corresponding to 9.53 hours) with only a single traffic accident remain in our dataset. They are split into 1,355 (70%), 290 (15%) and 290 (15%) videos for train, validation and testing, respectively. Most of the videos in our dataset are captured by dashcam while there exists a small fraction (~12%) of videos from monitoring cameras.

Annotating Videos. Figure 3 illustrates our annotation tool. We annotate temporal intervals and semantic labels of cause and effect in traffic accidents via the following two steps; 1) we determine the semantic labels of cause and effect in each candidate video, and 2) we annotate the temporal intervals for cause and effect events. After that, the temporal intervals are adjusted for their consistency with the semantic labels. Note that the semantic label estimation solely depends on visual information because no other information is accessible.

We annotate an effect event first and the label of a cause event is conditioned on the one corresponding to the matching effect. The start time of an effect is the moment that a vehicle begins to suffer any physical damage while its end time corresponds to the frame at which there is no more event happening to all the involved objects. On the other hand, the duration a cause is from the frame that a vehicle starts any abnormal movements or wrongdoings to the moment that such atypical activities end. In practice, the end time of a cause is often ambiguous and annotated as the same time with the start time of an effect.

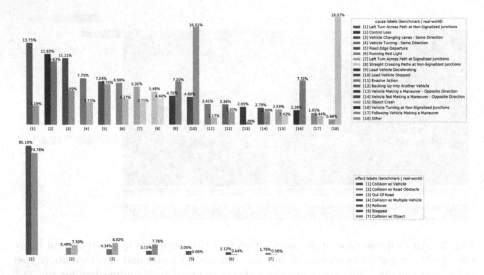

Fig. 4. The distribution of semantic labels for cause (top) and effect (bottom) observed in the proposed dataset and the real-world statistics. For each semantic label, the darker bar denotes our benchmark dataset while the lighter one indicates the real-world.

3.3   Statistics of Our Dataset

Figure 4 demonstrates the distribution of semantic labels of cause in both our benchmark dataset and the real-world statistics. Our dataset covers 18 semantic labels in cause and 7 semantic labels in effect while the distributions of semantic labels in the benchmark and the real-world are roughly consistent. However, the distributions are particularly different for *other* class. This is partly because we use a subset of semantic classes in the real-world data for the construction of our benchmark dataset and all the semantic classes missing in our dataset now belong to *other* class. The missing classes are mostly related to violent accidents such as collisions with pedestrians or animals; they are removed from YouTube. Although they may induce unwanted bias in the dataset, our dataset is constructed based on the semantic taxonomy with the real-world statistics.

4   Traffic Accident Benchmark

We demonstrate the task—temporal cause and effect events classification and localization—for traffic accident benchmark and introduce the evaluation method with simulating real-world which exploits real-world distribution for performance evaluation.

4.1   Temporal Cause and Effect Events Recognition

The main target task of our dataset is temporal cause and effect event recognition, which consists of two subtasks, classification and localization. The classification task aims to identify semantic labels for each cause and effect event while the objective of the localization task to estimate the temporal interval for each cause and effect event. Compared to the standard action recognition task, where each action or its instance is predicted independently, our problem need to consider temporal constraints of cause and effect—the cause event always precedes the effect event—and understand causal relation of the two events—the dynamics of vehicles is consistent with the causality of the accident.

4.2 Baselines

We adopt temporal segment networks (TSN) [22] as the baseline algorithm for action classification, where two consensus functions, average and linear function, are utilized for evaluation. For action localization, three baselines with unique characteristics are tested. The first baseline is Single-Stream Temporal Action Proposals (SST) [3], which employs a Gated Recurrent Units (GRU) [7] to classify a label for each proposal corresponding to a video segment. For this baseline, we train two additional variant models by replacing the forward GRU with a backward GRU (Backward SST) and bi-directional GRU (Bi-SST). The second option is R-C3D [24], which is a simple extension of R-CNN for object detection; it detects actions by proposal generation followed by classification. The third one is Multi-Stage Temporal Convolutional Network (MS-TCN) [8], which consists of repeated building blocks of Single Stage Temporal Convolutional Network (SS-TCN). SS-TCN consists of 1D dilated convolutions to model long-range dependencies and perform frame-level dense predictions.

We use I3D [4] RGB stream for our video representation of all baselines. The detailed architectures of all baselines and their training details (*e.g.*, learning rate, hyper-parameters, etc.) are described in the code repository.

4.3 Evaluation Metrics

Classification Accuracy. We use the standard metric for the evaluation of classification methods. Note that we perform classification over semantic labels and the accuracies of individual classes are averaged to report the final score.

Accuracy with Temporal IoU. We adopt the "accuracy" at a temporal Intersection over Union (tIoU) threshold, which measures the percentage of the predictions that have tIoUs larger than the threshold. Given the tIoU threshold τ, the accuracy is defined by

$$\text{accuracy}^\tau = \frac{1}{N} \sum_{n=1}^{N} \mathbb{1} \left[\frac{(\text{prediction}_n \cap \text{gt}_n)}{(\text{prediction}_n \cup \text{gt}_n)} > \tau \right], \tag{1}$$

where gt denotes ground-truth interval and N is the number of examples, and $\mathbb{1}[\cdot]$ is an indicator function.

We use top-1 accuracy for evaluation, which takes the temporal interval with the highest score as the prediction.

Evaluation with Prior Distribution. We also evaluate the algorithms based on the weighted accuracy, which leverages the real-world distribution of semantic classes as prior information. This is possible because our benchmark dataset is constructed based on the real-world accident distribution. The weighted mean accuracy is computed by

$$\text{weighted mean accuracy}^\tau = \sum_{c \in \mathcal{C}} w_c \cdot \text{accuracy}_c^\tau, \tag{2}$$

where w_c indicates the frequency of a semantic class c in the real-world. If w_c is identical to all c's, the metric is equivalent to (unweighted) mean accuracy. Note that the weighted mean accuracy penalizes predictions for labels that rarely happen in the real-world and this weighting scheme is crucial for planning actions to mitigate the fatalities.

Table 2. Performance comparisons of action classification methods.

Method	Top-1 mean accuracy (%)			Top-2 mean accuracy (%)		
	Cause	Effect	Mean	Cause	Effect	Mean
Trivial Prediction	13.7	80.1	46.9	25.5	85.6	55.6
TSN [22] (average)	18.8	43.8	31.3	31.3	87.5	59.4
TSN (linear)	31.3	87.5	59.4	37.5	93.8	65.7

4.4   Analysis of Action Classification Performance

Action Classification. We compared between TSN with two consensus functions and the trivial prediction, which outputs the most frequent semantic labels of cause and effect event. According to Table 2, TSN with average consensus function is worse than the trivial prediction. In contrast, TSN with linear consensus function outperforms the trivial prediction. This is because the average consensus function ignores the temporal order of video frames while the linear function preserves the temporal order of frame features in a video.

4.5   Analysis of Action Localization Performance

Trivial Prediction via Averaging Temporal Intervals. To evaluate the performance of the baseline algorithms, we computed the accuracy of the trivial prediction, which is given by the average interval of all ground-truths for cause and effect in the training dataset. We compute the average intervals for both un-normalized and normalized videos, where the normalization means the equalization of video lengths. Table 3 presents that the trivial methods are not successful in most cases compared to the baselines.

Table 3. Performances of the baseline algorithms for temporal cause and effect event localization on the test set of our dataset (CTA).

Algorithm type	Method	Accuracy (%) at a tIoU threshold								
		tIoU > 0.3			tIoU > 0.5			tIoU > 0.7		
		cause	effect	mean	cause	effect	mean	cause	effect	mean
Trivial prediction	Un-normalized	13.45	26.55	20.00	9.31	15.52	12.42	2.41	4.48	3.45
	Normalized	21.72	37.24	29.48	11.38	19.66	15.52	2.41	6.90	4.66
Single-stage detection	SST [3]	23.45	31.72	27.59	17.24	17.24	17.24	6.90	6.55	6.72
	Backward SST	30.00	44.83	37.41	17.93	24.83	21.38	5.17	6.21	5.69
	Bi-SST	29.66	54.48	42.07	17.24	27.24	22.24	5.17	10.00	7.59
	SS-TCN + SST	32.41	48.97	40.69	20.00	30.00	25.00	9.31	12.76	11.03
Single-stage detection	R-C3D [24]	36.21	58.62	47.41	22.07	38.28	30.17	8.62	13.10	10.86
Segmentation	SS-TCN [8]	38.28	54.97	46.62	23.86	36.48	30.17	10.55	17.10	13.83
	MS-TCN [8]	41.45	57.45	49.45	28.07	37.86	32.97	11.10	17.72	14.41

Table 4. Localization performance of MS-TCN for individual semantic classes. The semantic labels of cause and effect are sorted in a descending order of frequency.

	Semantic label	Accuracy (%)		
		tIoU > 0.3	tIoU > 0.5	tIoU > 0.7
Cause	[1] Left turn across path at non-signalized junctions	38.71	25.81	12.90
	[2] Control Loss	74.19	35.48	12.90
	[3] Vehicle changing lanes: same direction	17.24	13.79	6.90
	[4] Vehicle turning: same direction	44.00	36.00	16.00
	[5] Road edge departure	45.83	33.33	25.00
	[6] Running red light	31.58	26.32	21.05
	[7] Left turn across path at signalized junctions	56.25	50.00	25.00
	[8] Straight crossing paths at non-signalized junctions	50.00	31.82	4.55
	[9] Lead vehicle decelerating	35.29	35.29	29.41
	[10] Lead vehicle stopped	33.33	26.67	13.33
	[11] Evasive action	50.00	30.00	20.00
	[12] Backing up into another vehicle	50.00	25.00	12.50
	[13] Vehicle making a maneuver: opposite direction	37.50	25.00	25.00
	[14] Vehicle not making a maneuver: opposite direction	66.67	66.67	33.33
	[15] Object crash	33.33	8.33	8.33
	[16] Vehicle turning at non-signalized junctions	37.50	37.50	12.50
	[17] Following vehicle making a maneuver	40.00	20.00	20.00
	[18] Other	50.00	25.00	0.00
	Mean accuracy	43.97	30.67	16.59
	Weighted mean accuracy (benchmark)	43.45	30.00	15.86
	Weighted mean accuracy (real-world)	44.51	30.31	13.39
Effect	[1] Collision with vehicle	56.83	36.56	18.06
	[2] Collision with road obstacle	43.75	12.50	6.25
	[3] Out of road	80.00	66.67	20.00
	[4] Collision with multiple vehicle	44.44	22.22	11.11
	[5] Rollover	44.44	33.33	22.22
	[6] Stopped	66.67	50.00	33.33
	[7] Collision with object	75.00	37.50	25.00
	Mean accuracy	58.73	36.96	19.42
	Weighted mean accuracy (benchmark)	57.24	36.55	17.93
	Weighted mean accuracy (real-world)	57.14	36.47	16.97

Variants of Single-Stage Detection Methods. Table 3 also presents that effect localization performance is sensitive to the choice of GRUs in SST while cause localization is relatively stable in the direction of GRU placement. We observe that the contextual information from future frames, which can be acquired by backward SST better, is crucial for recognizing effect events. Exploiting both contextual information from past and future frames as in Bi-SST delivers the best performance.

Detection vs. Segmentation. The methods for temporal segmentation such as SS-TCN and MS-TCN tend to achieve better performance than detection-based techniques, especially at high tIoU thresholds, although the proposal-based detection method, R-C3D is comparable to segmentation-based approaches. This is partly because action localization methods based on detection are designed to

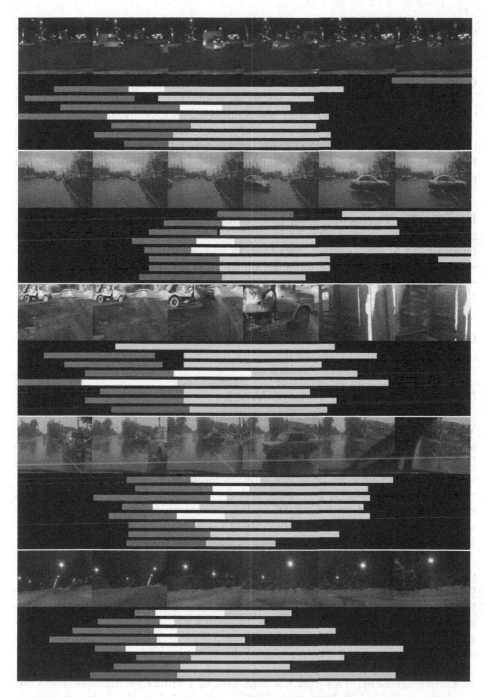

Fig. 5. The qualitative localization results of the 7 baselines algorithms placed with same order in Table 3 and the ground-truths. A bar indicates the duration of a cause or an effect while it has the following color codes: temporal interval of predicted cause, predicted effect, predicted cause and effect (overlapped) ground-truth cause and ground-truth effect. (Color figure online)

identify multiple events in a video while the videos in our dataset contain only a single instance of cause and effect.

GRU vs. Stack of Dilated Convolutions. To verify the effectiveness of SS-TCN without the advantage of action segmentation over action detection, we tested the accuracy of SST after replacing GRU in SST by SS-TCN, which is denoted by SS-TCN+SST. SS-TCN+SST outperforms all variants of SST with large margins at all tIoU thresholds as presented in Table 3. Note that while Bi-directional GRU is capable of modeling long-range dependencies, it turns out that stacking of 1D dilated convolutions is more effective.

Localization Performance of Individual Semantic Classes. Table 4 shows the localization performance of individual semantic classes, where the results from MS-TCN are reported. Note that, in addition to the naïve mean accuracy, we present two versions of weighted mean accuracy; they are differentiated by whether the weights are from the real-word distribution or the sampled distribution in our benchmark.

Qualitative Results. Figure 5 illustrates the qualitative results of predictions given by the compared algorithms.

5   Discussion and Future Works

We introduced a traffic accident benchmark and demonstrated temporal cause and effect event classification and localization performance of several baseline approaches. Our benchmark annotates cause and effect events separately to facilitate research for causality understanding and takes advantage of real-world grounded semantic taxonomy and the associated distribution for building dataset. Our dataset contains 1,935 traffic accident videos, each of which is annotated with a pair of temporal intervals of cause and effect with their semantic labels.

Spatio-temporal cause and effect localization would be a straightforward extension of our work towards capturing object-level cause and effect information, but it requires additional annotations for individual objects in videos. In the current version of the dataset, we discard the traffic accident videos with the ambiguous semantic labels for cause and effect events. Also, there exists only a single semantic label for each cause and effect event, and additional efforts should be made for the construction of the more comprehensive dataset.

Acknowledgement. This work was supported by Institute for Information & Communications Technology Promotion (IITP) grant funded by the Korea government (MSIT) [2017-0-01780, 2017-0-01779] and Microsoft Research Asia. We also appreciate Jonghwan Mun and Ilchae Jung for valuable discussion.

References

1. National automotive sampling system (NASS) general estimates system (GES) analytical user's manual, pp. 1988–2004 (2005). https://one.nhtsa.gov/Data/National-Automotive-Sampling-System-(NASS)
2. Aliakbarian, M.S., Saleh, F.S., Salzmann, M., Fernando, B., Petersson, L., Andersson, L.: VIENA^2: a driving anticipation dataset. In: Jawahar, C.V., Li, H., Mori, G., Schindler, K. (eds.) ACCV 2018. LNCS, vol. 11361, pp. 449–466. Springer, Cham (2019). https://doi.org/10.1007/978-3-030-20887-5_28
3. Buch, S., Escorcia, V., Shen, C., Ghanem, B., Niebles, J.C.: SST: Single-stream temporal action proposals. In: CVPR (2017)
4. Carreira, J., Zisserman, A.: Quo vadis, action recognition? a new model and the kinetics dataset. In: CVPR (2017)
5. Chan, F.-H., Chen, Y.-T., Xiang, Y., Sun, M.: Anticipating accidents in dashcam videos. In: Lai, S.-H., Lepetit, V., Nishino, K., Sato, Y. (eds.) ACCV 2016. LNCS, vol. 10114, pp. 136–153. Springer, Cham (2017). https://doi.org/10.1007/978-3-319-54190-7_9
6. Chao, Y.W., Vijayanarasimhan, S., Seybold, B., Ross, D.A., Deng, J., Sukthankar, R.: Rethinking the faster R-CNN architecture for temporal action localization. In: CVPR (2018)
7. Cho, K., van Merrienboer, B., Gulcchre, C., Bougares, F., Schwenk, H., Bengio, Y.: Learning phrase representations using RNN encoder-decoder for statistical machine translation. In: EMNLP (2014)
8. Farha, Y.A., Gall, J.: Ms-tcn: Multi-stage temporal convolutional network for action segmentation. In: CVPR (2019)
9. Feichtenhofer, C., Pinz, A., Zisserman, A.: Convolutional two-stream network fusion for video action recognition. In: CVPR (2016)
10. Hara, K., Kataoka, H., Satoh, Y.: Can spatiotemporal 3D CNNs retrace the history of 2D CNNs and imagenet? In: CVPR, pp. 6546–6555 (2018)
11. Herzig, R., et al.: Spatio-temporal action graph networks. In: ICCVW (2019)
12. Kataoka, H., Suzuki, T., Oikawa, S., Matsui, Y., Satoh, Y.: Drive video analysis for the detection of traffic near-miss incidents. In: ICRA (2018)
13. Kim, H., Lee, K., Hwang, G., Suh, C.: Crash to not Crash: learn to identify dangerous vehicles using a simulator. In: AAAI (2019)
14. Lea, C., Flynn, M.D., Vidal, R., Reiter, A., Hager, G.D.: Temporal convolutional networks for action segmentation and detection. In: CVPR (2017)
15. Lebeda, K., Hadfield, S., Bowden, R.: Exploring causal relationships in visual object tracking. In: ICCV (2015)
16. Lopez-Paz, D., Nishihara, R., Chintala, S., Schölkopf, B., Bottou, L.: Discovering causal signals in images. In: CVPR (2017)
17. Najm, W.G., Smith, J.D., Yanagisawa, M.: Pre-crash scenario typology for crash avoidance research (2007). https://rosap.ntl.bts.gov/view/dot/6281
18. Pickup, L.C., et al.: Seeing the arrow of time. In: CVPR (2014)
19. Simonyan, K., Zisserman, A.: Two-stream convolutional networks for action recognition in videos. In: NIPS (2014)
20. Suzuki, T., Kataoka, H., Aoki, Y., Satoh, Y.: Anticipating traffic accidents with adaptive loss and large-scale incident db. In: CVPR (2018)
21. Tran, D., Bourdev, L., Fergus, R., Torresani, L., Paluri, M.: Learning spatiotemporal features with 3d convolutional networks. In: ICCV (2015)

22. Wang, L., et al.: Temporal segment networks: towards good practices for deep action recognition. In: Leibe, B., Matas, J., Sebe, N., Welling, M. (eds.) ECCV 2016. LNCS, vol. 9912, pp. 20–36. Springer, Cham (2016). https://doi.org/10.1007/978-3-319-46484-8_2
23. Wei, D., Lim, J., Zisserman, A., Freeman, W.T.: Learning and using the arrow of time. In: CVPR (2018)
24. Xu, H., Das, A., Saenko, K.: R-c3d: region convolutional 3D network for temporal activity detection. In: ICCV (2017)
25. Yao, Y., Xu, M., Wang, Y., Crandall, D.J., Atkins, E.M.: Unsupervised traffic accident detection in first-person videos. In: IROS (2019)
26. Zeng, K.H., Chou, S.H., Chan, F.H., Niebles, J.C., Sun, M.: Agent-centric risk assessment: accident anticipation and risky region localization. In: CVPR (2017)
27. Zeng, R., et al.: Graph convolutional networks for temporal action localization. In: ICCV (2019)
28. Zhao, Y., Xiong, Y., Wang, L., Wu, Z., Tang, X., Lin, D.: Temporal action detection with structured segment networks. In: ICCV (2017)

Face Anti-Spoofing with Human Material Perception

Zitong Yu[1], Xiaobai Li[1], Xuesong Niu[2,3], Jingang Shi[1,4],
and Guoying Zhao[1(✉)]

[1] Center for Machine Vision and Signal Analysis, University of Oulu, Oulu, Finland
{zitong.yu,xiaobai.li,guoying.zhao}@oulu.fi
[2] Key Laboratory of Intelligent Information Processing of Chinese Academy
of Sciences (CAS), Institute of Computing Technology, CAS, Beijing, China
xuesong.niu@vipl.ict.ac.cn
[3] University of Chinese Academy of Sciences, Beijing, China
[4] School of Software Engineering, Xi'an Jiaotong University, Xi'an, China

Abstract. Face anti-spoofing (FAS) plays a vital role in securing the
face recognition systems from presentation attacks. Most existing FAS
methods capture various cues (e.g., texture, depth and reflection) to distinguish the live faces from the spoofing faces. All these cues are based
on the discrepancy among physical materials (e.g., skin, glass, paper and
silicone). In this paper we rephrase face anti-spoofing as a material recognition problem and combine it with classical human material perception,
intending to extract discriminative and robust features for FAS. To this
end, we propose the Bilateral Convolutional Networks (BCN), which is
able to capture intrinsic material-based patterns via aggregating multi-
level bilateral macro- and micro- information. Furthermore, Multi-level
Feature Refinement Module (MFRM) and multi-head supervision are
utilized to learn more robust features. Comprehensive experiments are
performed on six benchmark datasets, and the proposed method achieves
superior performance on both intra- and cross-dataset testings. One highlight is that we achieve overall $11.3 \pm 9.5\%$ EER for cross-type testing
in SiW-M dataset, which significantly outperforms previous results. We
hope this work will facilitate future cooperation between FAS and material communities.

Keywords: Face anti-spoofing · Material perception · Bilateral
filtering

1 Introduction

In recent years, face recognition [1–3] has been widely used in various interactive
and payment scene due to its high accuracy and convenience. However, such

Electronic supplementary material The online version of this chapter (https://
doi.org/10.1007/978-3-030-58571-6_33) contains supplementary material, which is
available to authorized users.

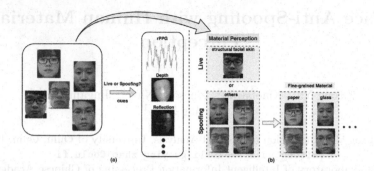

Fig. 1. (a) Face anti-spoofing can be regarded as a binary classification (live or spoofing) problem, which relies on the intrinsic cues such as rPPG, depth, reflection and so on. (b) Face anti-spoofing can be also treated as a material perception problem.

biometric system is vulnerable to presentation attacks (PAs). Typical examples of physical PAs include print, video replay, 3D masks and makeup. In order to detect such PAs and secure the face recognition system, face anti-spoofing (FAS) has attracted more attention from both academia and industry.

In the past decade, several hand-crafted feature based [4–9] and deep learning based [10–13] methods have been proposed for presentation attack detection (PAD). On one hand, the classical hand-crafted descriptors leverage local relationship among the neighbours as the discriminative features, which is robust for describing the detailed invariant information (e.g., color texture, moiré pattern and noise artifacts) between the live and spoofing faces. On the other hand, due to the stacked convolution operations with nonlinear activation, the convolutional neural networks (CNN) hold strong representation abilities to distinguish the bona fide from PA. However, most existing CNN and hand-crafted features are designed for universal image recognition tasks, which might not represent fine-grained spoofing patterns in FAS task.

According to the known intrinsic cues in face anti-spoofing task, many state-of-the-art methods introduced task-oriented priori knowledge for feature representation. As shown in Fig. 1(a), there are three famous human-defined cues (i.e., rPPG, depth and reflection) for FAS task. Firstly, frequency distribution dissimilarity of rPPG signals [14–17] recovered from live skin surface and spoofing face can be utilized as there are no or weaker blood volume changes in spoofing faces. Secondly, structural facial depth difference between live and spoofing faces [16,18,19] can be adopted as significant cue as most spoofing faces are broadcasted in plane presentation attack instruments (PAIs). Thirdly, reflectance difference [20,21] is also one kind of reliable cues as human facial skin and spoofing surfaces react differently to changes in illumination. Despite the human-defined cues are helpful to enhance the modeling capability respectively, it is still difficult to describe intrinsic and robust features for FAS task.

An interesting and essential question for FAS task is how human beings differentiate live or spoofing faces, and what can be learned by

machine intelligent systems? In real-world cases, spoofing faces are always broadcasted by physical spoofing carriers (e.g., paper, glass screen and resin mask), which have obvious material properties difference with human facial skin. Such difference can be explicitly described as human-defined cues (e.g., rPPG, depth and reflection) or implicitly learned according to the material property uniqueness of structural live facial skin. Therefore, as illustrated in Fig. 1(b), we assume that discrepancy of the structural materials between human facial skin and physical spoofing carriers are the essence of distinguishing live faces from spoofing ones.

Motivated by the discussions above, we rephrase face anti-spoofing task as structural material recognition problem and our goal is to learn intrinsic and robust features for distinguishing structural facial skin material from the others (i.e., materials for physical spoofing carriers). According to the study inspired by classical human material perception [22], bilateral filtering plays a vital role in representing macro- and micro- cues for various materials. In this paper, we integrate traditional bilateral filtering operator into the state-of-the-art FAS deep learning framework, intending to help networks to learn more intrinsic material-based patterns. Our contributions include:

- We design novel Bilateral Convolutional Networks (BCN), which is able to capture intrinsic material-based patterns via aggregating multi-level bilateral macro- and micro- information.
- We propose to use Multi-level Feature Refinement Module (MFRM) and material based multi-head supervision to further boost the performance of BCN. The former one refines the multi-scale features via reassembling weights of local neighborhood while the latter forces the network to learn robust shared features for multi-head auxiliary tasks.
- Our proposed method achieves outstanding performance on six benchmark datasets with both intra- and cross-dataset testing protocols. We also conduct fine-grained material recognition experiments on SiW-M dataset to validate the effectiveness of our proposed method.

2 Related Work

2.1 Face Anti-Spoofing

Traditional face anti-spoofing methods usually extract hand-crafted features from the facial images to capture the spoofing patterns. Several classical local descriptors such as LBP [4,6], SIFT [9], SURF [23] and HOG [7] are utilized to extract frame level features while video level methods usually capture dynamic cues like dynamic texture [24], micro–motion [25] and eye blinking [26]. More recently, a few deep learning based methods are proposed for FAS task. Some frame-level CNN methods [13,27–31] are supervised by binary scalars or pixel-wise binary maps. In contrast, auxiliary depth [12,16,18,19] and reflection [32] supervisions are introduced to learn detailed cues effectively. In order to learn generalized features for unseen attacks and environment, few-shot learning [10], zero-shot learning [10,33] and domain generalization [34–36] are introduced for FAS task. Meanwhile, several video-level CNN methods are presented to exploit the dynamic spatio-temporal [11,37–39] or rPPG [14–16,40–42] features for PAD. Despite introducing task-oriented priori knowledge (e.g., auxiliary depth, reflection and rPPG), deep learning based methods are still difficult to extract rich intrinsic features among live faces and various kinds of PAs.

2.2 Human and Machine Material Perception

Our world consists of not only objects and scenes but also of materials of various kinds. The perception of materials by humans usually focuses on optical and mechanical properties. Maloney and Brainard [43] demonstrates the research concerns about perception of material surface properties other than color and lightness, such as gloss or roughness. Fleming [44] proposes statistical appearance models to describe visual perception of materials. Nishida [45] presents that material perception is visual estimation of optical modulation of image statistics. Inspired by human material perception, several machine intelligent methods are designed for material classification. Techniques derived from the domain of texture analysis can be adopted for material recognition by machines [46]. Varma and Zisserman [47] utilizes joint distribution of intensity values over image patch exemplars for material classification under unknown viewpoint and illumination. Sharan et al. [22] uses bilateral based low and mid-level image features for material recognition. Aiming to keep the details of features, deep dilated convolutional network is used for material perception [48].

In terms of vision applications, concepts of human material perception have been developed into image quality assessment [49] and video quality assessment [50]. For face anti-spoofing task, few works [20,21,51] consider discrepant surface reflectance properties of live or spoofing faces. However, only considering surface reflectance properties is not always reliable for material perception [22]. In order to learn more generalized material-based features for FAS, we combine the state-of-the-art FAS methods with classical human material perception [22].

3   Methodology

In this section, we first introduce the Bilateral Convolutional Networks (BCN) in Sect. 3.1, then present Multi-level Feature Refinement Module (MFRM) in Sect. 3.2, and at last introduce the material based multi-head supervision for face anti-spoofing in Sect. 3.3. The overall framework is shown in Fig. 2.

3.1   Bilateral Convolutional Networks

Inspired by classical material perception [22] that utilizes bilateral filtering [52] for exacting subsequent macro- and micro- features, we try to adopt bilateral filtering technique for FAS task. The main issue is that in [22], several hand-crafted features are designed after bilateral filtering, which limits the feature

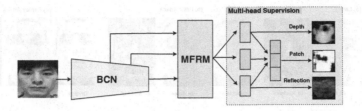

Fig. 2. The overall framework consists of Bilateral Convolutional Networks (BCN), Multi-level Feature Refinement Module (MFRM) and multi-head supervision.

representation capacity. In this subsection, we propose two solutions to integrate bilateral filtering with the state-of-the-art deep networks for FAS task.

Bilateral Filtering. The first solution is straightforward: The bilateral filtered frames are taken as network inputs instead of the original RGB frames. The bilateral filter is utilized to smooth the original frame while preserving its main edges. Each pixel is a weighted mean of its neighbors where the weights decrease with the distance in space and with the intensity difference. With Gaussian function $g_\sigma(x)) = exp(-x^2/\sigma^2)$, the bilateral filter of image I at pixel p is defined by:

$$Bi\_Base(I)_p = \frac{1}{k} \sum_{q \in I} g_{\sigma_s}(\|p - q\|) g_{\sigma_r}(|I_p - I_q|) I_q,$$

$$with: \qquad k = \sum_{q \in I} g_{\sigma_s}(\|p - q\|) g_{\sigma_r}(|I_p - I_q|), \tag{1}$$

where σ_s and σ_r control the influence of spatial neighborhood distance and intensity difference respectively, and k normalizes the weights. Give the input image I, bilateral filter is able to create a two-scale decomposition [53] where the output of the filter produces a large-scale base image $Bi\_Base(I)$ and the residual detail image $Bi\_Residual(I)$ can be obtained by $Bi\_Residual(I) = I - Bi\_Base(I)$. We use the fast approximation version[1] of the bilateral filter [54] with default parameters for implementation.

Typical samples before and after bilateral filtering are visualized in Fig. 3. There are obvious differences in bilateral base and residual images between live and spoofing faces despite their similarities in the original RGB images. As shown in Fig. 3(b) 'Bi_Base', the print attack face made of paper material is rougher and less glossy. Moreover, it can be seen from Fig. 3(b)(c) 'Bi_Residual' that the high-frequency activation in eyes and eyebrow region is stronger, which might be caused by discrepant surface reflectance properties among materials (e.g., skin, paper and glass). These visual evidences are consistent with classical human material perception [22] that macro- cues from bilateral base and micro-cues from bilateral residual are helpful for material perception.

---

[1] http://people.csail.mit.edu/jiawen/software/bilateralFilter-1.0.m.

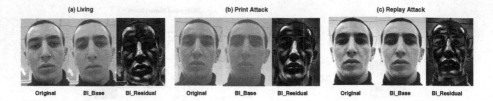

Fig. 3. Samples visualization for (a) live faces, (b) print attack, and (c) replay attack. 'Bi_Base' denotes frames after bilateral filtering while 'Bi_Residual' denotes residual result between original and bilateral filtered frames respectively. The intensity values of bilateral residual images are enlarged by four times for better visual effects.

In this paper, Auxiliary(Depth) [16] is chosen as our baseline deep model. The bilateral filtered (i.e., bilateral base and residual) images can forward the baseline model directly and predict the corresponding results. The ablation study of different kinds of inputs will be discussed in Sect. 4.3.

Deep Bilateral Networks. The drawbacks of the above-mentioned solution are mainly of two folds: 1) directly replacing original inputs with bilateral images might lead to information loss, which limits the feature representation capability for neural networks, and 2) it is an inefficient way to learn multi-level bilateral features as the bilateral filter is only adopted in the input space. Aiming to overcome these drawbacks, we propose a novel method called Bilateral Convolutional Networks (BCN) to integrate traditional bilateral filtering with deep networks properly.

In order to filter the deep features instead of original images, the deep bilateral operator (DBO) is introduced. Mimicking the process of gray-scale or color image filtering, given the deep feature maps $\mathcal{F} \in \mathbb{R}^{H \times W \times C}$ with height H, width W and C channels, channel-wise deep bilateral filtering is operated. Considering the small spatial distance for the widely used convolution with 3×3 kernel, the distance decay term in Eq. (1) can be removed (see *Appendix A* for corresponding ablation study), which is more efficient and lightweight when operating in deep hidden space. Hence deep bilateral operator for each channel of $\mathcal{F}$ can be formulated as

$$DBO(\mathcal{F})_p = \frac{1}{k} \sum_{q \in \mathcal{F}} g_{\sigma_r}(|\mathcal{F}_p - \mathcal{F}_q|)\mathcal{F}_q,$$

$$with: \quad k = \sum_{q \in \mathcal{F}} g_{\sigma_r}(|\mathcal{F}_p - \mathcal{F}_q|). \tag{2}$$

Now performing DBO for features in different levels, it is easy to obtain multi-level bilateral base features. Nevertheless, how to get multi-level bilateral residual features is still unknown. As our goal is to represent aggregated bilateral base and residual features $\mathcal{F}_{Bi}$, inspired by residual learning in ResNet [55], bilateral residual features $\mathcal{F}_{Residual}$ can be learned dynamically via shortcut connecting with bilateral base features $\mathcal{F}_{Base}$, i.e., $\mathcal{F}_{Residual} = \mathcal{F}_{Bi} - \mathcal{F}_{Base}$. The architecture of the proposed Bilateral Convolutional Networks is illustrated

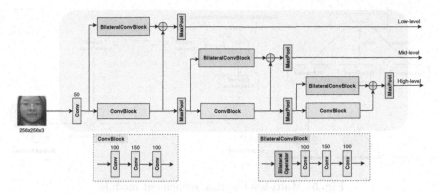

Fig. 4. The proposed BCN architecture. The number of filters are shown on top of each convolutional layer, the size of all filters is 3×3 with stride 1 for convolutional and 2 for pooling layers. Each output from 'ConvBlock' and 'BilateralConvBlock' in the same level will be operated with element-wise addition.

in Fig. 4. As 'BilateralConvBlock' and 'ConvBlock' have same convolutional structure but unshared parameters, it is possible to learn $\mathcal{F}_{Base}$ and $\mathcal{F}_{Residual}$ from 'BilateralConvBlock' and 'ConvBlock' respectively. Compared with baseline model Auxiliary(Depth) [16] without 'BilateralConvBlock', BCN is able to learn more intrinsic features via aggregating multi-level bilateral macro- and micro- information.

3.2 Multi-level Feature Refinement Module

In the baseline model Auxiliary(Depth) [16], multi-level features are concatenated directly for subsequent head supervision. We argue that such coarse features are not optimal for fine-grained material-based FAS task. Hence Multi-level Feature Refinement Module (MFRM) is introduced after BCN (see Fig. 2), which aims to refine and fuse the coarse low-mid-high level features from BCN via context-aware feature reassembling.

As illustrated in Fig. 5, features $\mathcal{F}$ from low-mid-high levels are refined via reassembling features with local context-aware weights. Unlike [56] which aims for feature upsampling, here we focus on the general multi-level feature refinement. The refined features $\mathcal{F}'$ can be formulated as

$$\mathcal{F}'_{level} = \mathcal{F}_{level} \otimes \mathcal{N}(\psi(\phi(\mathcal{F}_{level}))), \ level \in \{low, mid, high\}, \qquad (3)$$

where ϕ, ψ, $\mathcal{N}$ and $\otimes$ represent channel compressor, content encoder, kernel normalizer and refinement operator, respectively. The channel compressor adopts a 1×1 convolution layer to compress the input feature channel from C to C', making the refinement module more efficient. The content encoder utilizes a convolution layer of kernel size 5×5 to generate refinement kernels based on the content of input features $\mathcal{F}$, and then each $K \times K$ refinement kernel is normalized with a softmax function spatially in kernel normalizer. Given the

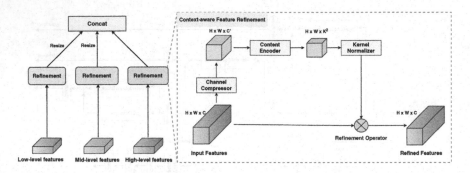

Fig. 5. Multi-level feature refinement module.

location $l = (i, j)$, channel c and corresponding normalized refinement kernel $\mathcal{W}_l$, the output refined features $\mathcal{F}'$ are expressed as

$$\mathcal{F}'_{(i,j,c)} = \sum_{n=-r}^{r} \sum_{m=-r}^{r} \mathcal{W}_{l(n,m)} \cdot \mathcal{F}_{(i+n,j+m,c)}, \; with \; r = \lfloor K/2 \rfloor. \tag{4}$$

In essence, MFRM exploits the semantic and contextual information to reallocate the contributions of the local neighbors, which is possible to obtain more intrinsic features. For instance, our module is able to refine the discriminative cues (e.g. moiré pattern) from salient regions according to their local context. We also compare the refinement method with other classical feature attention based methods such as spatial attention [57], channel attention [58] and non-local attention [59] in Sect. 4.3.

3.3   Material Based Multi-head Supervision

As material categorization is complex and depends on various fine-grained cues (e.g., surface shape, reflectance and texture), it is impossible to learn robust and intrinsic material-based patterns via only one simple supervision (e.g., softmax binary loss and depth regression loss). For the sake of learning intrinsic material-based features, material based multi-head supervision is proposed. As shown in Fig. 2, three-head supervision is utilized to guide the multi-level fused features from MFRM: 1) depth-head supervision, intending to force the model to learn structural surface shape information; 2) reflection-head supervision, helping networks to learn surface reflectance property; and 3) patch-head supervision, guiding to learn fine-grained surface texture cues.

Loss Function. Appropriate loss functions should be designed to supervise the network training. Given an input face image I, the network predicts the depth map D_{pre}, reflection map R_{pre} and patch map P_{pre}. Then the loss functions can be formulated as:

$$\mathcal{L}_{depth} = \frac{1}{H \times W} \sum_{i \in H, j \in W} \left\| D_{pre(i,j)} - D_{gt(i,j)} \right\|_2^2, \tag{5}$$

$$\mathcal{L}_{reflection} = \frac{1}{H \times W \times C} \sum_{i \in H, j \in W, c \in C} \left\| R_{pre(i,j,c)} - R_{gt(i,j,c)} \right\|_2^2, \qquad (6)$$

$$\mathcal{L}_{patch} = \frac{1}{H \times W} \sum_{i \in H, j \in W} -(P_{gt(i,j)} log(P_{pre(i,j)}) + (1 - P_{gt(i,j)}) log(1 - P_{pre(i,j)})),$$
$$(7)$$

where D_{gt}, R_{gt} and P_{gt} denote ground truth depth map, reflection map and patch map respectively. Finally, the overall loss function is $\mathcal{L}_{overall} = \mathcal{L}_{depth} + \mathcal{L}_{reflection} + \mathcal{L}_{patch}$.

Ground Truth Generation. Dense face alignment [60,61] is adopted to estimate facial 3D shapes and generate the facial depth maps with size 32×32. The reflection maps are estimated by the state-of-the-art reflection estimation network [62] and then face regions are cropped from reflection maps to avoid being overfitted to backgrounds. We normalize live depth maps and spoofing reflection maps in a range of $[0,1]$, while setting spoofing depth maps and live reflection maps to 0, which is similar to [16,32]. The patch maps are generated simply by downsampling original images and filling each patch position with corresponding binary label (i.e., live 1 and spoofing 0).

4 Experiments

4.1 Datasets and Metrics

Six databases including OULU-NPU [63], SiW [16], CASIA-MFSD [64], Replay-Attack [65], MSU-MFSD [66] and SiW-M [33] are used in our experiments. OULU-NPU and SiW are large-scale high-resolution databases, containing four and three protocols to validate the generalization (e.g., unseen illumination and attack medium) of models respectively, which are utilized for intra testing. CASIA-MFSD, Replay-Attack and MSU-MFSD are databases which contain low-resolution videos, and are used for cross testing. SiW-M is designed for fine-grained material recognition and cross-type testing for unseen attacks as there are rich attacks types (totally 13 types) inside.

Performance Metrics. In OULU-NPU and SiW dataset, we follow the original protocols and metrics, i.e., Attack Presentation Classification Error Rate (APCER), Bona Fide Presentation Classification Error Rate (BPCER), and ACER [67] for a fair comparison. Half Total Error Rate (HTER) is adopted in the cross testing between CASIA-MFSD and Replay-Attack. Area Under Curve (AUC) is utilized for intra-database cross-type test on CASIA-MFSD, Replay-Attack and MSU-MFSD. For the cross-type test on SiW-M, APCER, BPCER, ACER and Equal Error Rate (EER) are employed.

4.2 Implementation Details

Our proposed method is implemented with Pytorch. The default settings $\sigma_r = 1.0$ and $C' = 20, K = 5$ are adopted for BCN and MFRM, respectively. In the

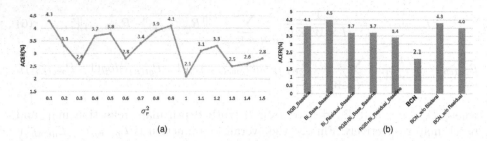

Fig. 6. (a) Impact of σ_r in BCN. (b) Comparison among various kinds of inputs for baseline model Auxilary(Depth) [16] and BCN. Lower ACER, better performance.

Table 1. Results of network composition and supervision.

Model	ACER (%)
D (Baseline)	4.1
D+R	2.8
D+P	2.3
D+R+P	1.8
D+R+P+MFRM	1.2
D+R+P+MFRM+BCN	0.8

Table 2. Ablation study of refinement methods in MFRM.

Model	ACER (%)
D+R+P	1.8
D+R+P+Spatial Attention [57]	1.5
D+R+P+Channel Attention [58]	9.5
D+R+P+Non-local Attention [59]	12.7
D+R+P+Context-aware Reassembling	1.2

training stage, models are trained with Adam optimizer and the initial learning rate (lr) and weight decay (wd) are 1e–4 and 5e–5, respectively. We train models with maximum 1300 epochs while lr halves every 500 epochs. The batch size is 7 on a Nvidia P100 GPU. In the testing stage, we calculate the mean value of the predicted depth map $\mathcal{D}_{test}$, reflection map $\mathcal{R}_{test}$ and patch map $\mathcal{P}_{test}$ as the final score $\mathcal{S}_{test}$:

$$\mathcal{S}_{test} = mean(\mathcal{D}_{test}) + mean(1 - \mathcal{R}_{test}) + mean(\mathcal{P}_{test}). \tag{8}$$

4.3 Ablation Study

In this subsection, all ablation studies are conducted on Protocol-1 (different illumination condition and location between train and test sets) of OULU-NPU [63] to explore the details of our proposed BCN, MFRM and multi-head supervision.

Impact of σ_r and Bilateral Operator in BCN. According to Eq. (2) and Gaussian function $g_{\sigma_r}(x)) = exp(-x^2/\sigma_r^2)$, σ_r controls the strength of neighbor feature differences, i.e., the higher σ_r, the more contributions are given to the neighbor with large differences. As illustrated in Fig. 6(a), the best performance (ACER = 2.1%) is obtained when $\sigma_r^2 = 1.0$ in BCN. We use this setting for the following experiments. According to the quantitative index shown in Fig. 6(b), BCN (ACER = 2.1%) could decrease the ACER by half when campared with the results of 'RGB_Baseline' (ACER = 4.1%). In order to validate whether the improvement from BCN is due to the extra parameters from 'BilateralConvBlock' in Fig. 4, we remove the bilateral operator in these blocks. However, as shown in Fig. 6(b) 'BCN_w/o Bilateral', it even works worse than the baseline (4.3% versus 4.1% ACER), indicating that the network easily overfits by introducing extra parameters without bilateral operators. We are also curious about the efficacy of bilateral residual term. After removing bilateral residual structure from BCN, the ACER index sharply changes from 2.1% (see 'BCN') to 4.0% (see 'BCN_w/o Residual'). It implies that the micro- patterns from bilateral residual branch are also important for FAS task.

Influence of Various Input Types. As discussed in Sect. 3.1, the first solution is to adopt bilateral filtered images as network inputs. The results in Fig. 6(b) show that 'Bi_Residual_Baseline' with bilateral residual inputs performs better (0.4% ACER lower) than that of original RGB baseline. While combing the multi-level features from both original RGB and bilateral filtered images (i.e., 'RGB+Bi_Base_Baseline' and 'RGB+Bi_Residual_Baseline' in Fig. 6(b)), the performance further boosts. In contrast, BCN with only original RGB input outperforms the first solution methods for a large margin, implying that deep bilateral base and residual features in BCN are more robust.

Advantage of MFRM and Multi-head Supervision. Table 1 shows the ablation study about the network composition and supervision. 'D', 'R', 'P' are short for depth, reflection and patch heads, respectively. It is clear that multi-head supervision facilitates the network to learn more intrinsic features thus boost the performance. Furthermore, with both MFRM and multi-head supervision, our model is able to reduce ACER from baseline 4.1% to 1.2%. Ultimately, the full version of our method 'D+R+P+MFRM+BCN' achieves excellent performance with 0.8% ACER.

Impact of Refinement Methods in MFRM. We investigate four feature refinement methods in MFRM and the results are shown in Table 2. It is surprised that only spatial attention [57] (the second row) boosts the performance while SE block based channel attention [58] (the third row) and non-local block based self-attention [59] (the fourth row) perform poorly when domain shifts (e.g., illumination changes). We adopt context-aware reassembling as defaulted setting in MFRM as it can obtain more generalized features and improve baseline 'D+R+P' by 0.6% ACER. In summary, we use 'D+R+P+MFRM+BCN (with $\sigma_r^2 = 1.0$)' for all the following tests.

Table 3. The results of intra testing on four protocols of OULU-NPU.

Prot.	Method	APCER (%)↓	BPCER (%)↓	ACER (%)↓
1	GRADIANT [68]	1.3	12.5	6.9
	BASN [32]	1.5	5.8	3.6
	STASN [38]	1.2	2.5	1.9
	Auxiliary [16]	1.6	1.6	1.6
	FaceDs [13]	1.2	1.7	1.5
	FAS-TD [37]	2.5	0.0	1.3
	DeepPixBiS [30]	0.8	0.0	**0.4**
	Ours	0.0	1.6	0.8
2	DeepPixBiS [30]	11.4	0.6	6.0
	FaceDs [13]	4.2	4.4	4.3
	Auxiliary [16]	2.7	2.7	2.7
	BASN [32]	2.4	3.1	2.7
	GRADIANT [68]	3.1	1.9	2.5
	STASN [38]	4.2	0.3	2.2
	FAS-TD [37]	1.7	2.0	1.9
	Ours	2.6	0.8	**1.7**
3	DeepPixBiS [30]	11.7 ± 19.6	10.6 ± 14.1	11.1 ± 9.4
	FAS-TD [37]	5.9 ± 1.9	5.9 ± 3.0	5.9 ± 1.0
	GRADIANT [68]	2.6 ± 3.9	5.0 ± 5.3	3.8 ± 2.4
	BASN [32]	1.8 ± 1.1	3.6 ± 3.5	2.7 ± 1.6
	FaceDs [13]	4.0 ± 1.8	3.8 ± 1.2	3.6 ± 1.6
	Auxiliary [16]	2.7 ± 1.3	3.1 ± 1.7	2.9 ± 1.5
	STASN [38]	4.7 ± 3.9	0.9 ± 1.2	2.8 ± 1.6
	Ours	2.8 ± 2.4	2.3 ± 2.8	**2.5 ± 1.1**
4	DeepPixBiS [30]	36.7 ± 29.7	13.3 ± 14.1	25.0 ± 12.7
	GRADIANT [68]	5.0 ± 4.5	15.0 ± 7.1	10.0 ± 5.0
	Auxiliary [16]	9.3 ± 5.6	10.4 ± 6.0	9.5 ± 6.0
	FAS-TD [37]	14.2 ± 8.7	4.2 ± 3.8	9.2 ± 3.4
	STASN [38]	6.7 ± 10.6	8.3 ± 8.4	7.5 ± 4.7
	FaceDs [13]	1.2 ± 6.3	6.1 ± 5.1	5.6 ± 5.7
	BASN [32]	6.4 ± 8.6	3.2 ± 5.3	**4.8 ± 6.4**
	Ours	2.9 ± 4.0	7.5 ± 6.9	5.2 ± 3.7

4.4 Intra Testing

The intra testing is carried out on both the OULU-NPU and the SiW datasets. We strictly follow the four protocols on OULU-NPU and three protocols on SiW for the evaluation. All compared methods including STASN [38] are trained without extra datasets for a fair comparison.

Results on OULU-NPU. As shown in Table 3, our proposed method ranks first or second on all the four protocols (0.4%, 1.7%, 2.5% and 5.2% ACER, respectively), which indicates the proposed method performs well at the generalization of the external environment, attack mediums and input camera variation. Note that DeepPixBis [30] utilizes patch map for supervision but performing poorly in unseen attack mediums and camera types while BASN [30] exploits depth and reflection map as guidance but ineffective in unseen external environment. Our method works well for all 4 protocols as the extracted material-based features are intrinsic and generalized.

Results on SiW. We also compare our method with four state-of-the-art methods [16,32,37,38] on SiW dataset. Our method performs the best for all three protocols (0.36%, 0.11%, 2.45% ACER, respectively), revealing the excellent generalization capacity for 1) variations of face pose and expression, 2) variations of different spoof mediums, and 3) unknown presentation attack. More detailed results of each protocol are shown in *Appendix C*.

4.5 Inter Testing

To further validate whether our model is able to learn intrinsic features, we conduct cross-type and cross-dataset testing to verify the generalization capacity to unknown presentation attacks and unseen environment, respectively.

Cross-type Testing. Here we use CASIA-MFSD [64], Replay-Attack [65] and MSU-MFSD [66] to perform intra-dataset cross-type testing between replay and print attacks. Our proposed method achieves the best overall performance (96.77% AUC) among state-of-the-art methods [10,33,69,70], indicating the learned features generalized well among unknown attacks. More details can be found in *Appendix D*. Moreover, we also conduct cross-type testing on the latest SiW-M [33] dataset. As illustrated in Table 4, the proposed method achieves the best average ACER (11.2%) and EER (11.3%) among 13 attacks, which indicates our method actually learns material-based intrinsic patterns from rich kinds of material hence generalized well in unseen material type.

Cross-dataset Testing. In this experiment, we first train on the CASIA-MFSD and test on Replay-Attack, which is named as protocol CR. And then exchanging the training dataset and the testing dataset reciprocally, named protocol RC. Our proposed method has 16.6% HTER on protocol CR, outperforming all prior state-of-the-arts. For protocol RC, we also achieve comparable performance with 36.4% HTER. As our method is frame-level based, the performance might be further improved via introducing the temporal dynamic features in FAS-TD [37].

Table 4. The evaluation and comparison of the cross-type testing on SiW-M [33].

Method	Metrics(%)	Replay	Print	Mask Attacks					Makeup Attacks			Partial Attacks			Average
				Half	Silicone	Trans.	Paper	Manne.	Obfusc.	Imperson.	Cosmetic	Funny Eye	Paper Glasses	Partial Paper	
SVM+LBP [63]	APCER	19.1	15.4	40.8	20.3	70.3	0.0	4.6	96.9	35.3	11.3	53.3	58.5	0.6	32.8±29.8
	BPCER	22.1	21.5	21.9	21.4	20.7	23.1	22.9	21.7	12.5	22.2	18.4	20.0	22.9	21.0±2.9
	ACER	20.6	18.4	31.3	21.4	45.5	11.6	13.8	59.3	23.9	16.7	35.9	39.2	11.7	26.9±14.5
	EER	20.8	18.6	36.3	21.4	37.2	7.5	14.1	51.2	19.8	16.1	34.4	33.0	7.9	24.5±12.9
Auxiliary [16]	APCER	23.7	7.3	27.7	18.2	97.8	8.3	16.2	100.0	18.0	16.3	91.8	72.2	0.4	38.3±37.4
	BPCER	10.1	6.5	10.9	11.6	6.2	7.8	9.3	11.6	9.3	7.1	6.2	8.8	10.3	8.9± 2.0
	ACER	16.8	6.9	19.3	14.9	52.1	8.0	12.8	55.8	13.7	11.7	49.0	40.5	5.3	23.6±18.5
	EER	14.0	4.3	11.6	12.4	24.6	7.8	10.0	72.3	10.1	9.4	21.4	18.6	4.0	17.0±17.7
DTN [33]	APCER	1.0	0.0	0.7	24.5	58.6	0.5	3.8	73.2	13.2	12.4	17.0	17.0	0.2	17.1±23.3
	BPCER	18.6	11.9	29.3	12.8	13.4	8.5	23.0	11.5	9.6	16.0	21.5	22.6	16.8	16.6 ±6.2
	ACER	9.8	6.0	15.0	18.7	36.0	4.5	7.7	48.1	11.4	14.2	19.3	19.8	8.5	16.8 ±11.1
	EER	10.0	2.1	14.4	18.6	26.5	5.7	9.6	50.2	10.1	13.2	19.8	20.5	8.8	16.1± 12.2
Ours	APCER	12.4	5.2	8.3	9.7	13.6	0.0	2.5	30.4	0.0	12.0	22.6	15.9	1.2	10.3±9.1
	BPCER	13.2	6.2	13.1	10.8	16.3	3.9	2.3	34.1	1.6	13.9	23.2	17.1	2.3	12.2±9.4
	ACER	12.8	5.7	10.7	10.3	14.9	1.9	2.4	32.3	0.8	12.9	22.9	16.5	1.7	11.2±9.2
	EER	13.4	5.2	8.3	9.7	13.6	5.8	2.5	33.8	0.0	14.0	23.3	16.6	1.2	11.3±9.5

Table 5. Fine-grained material recognition in SiW-M dataset. The evaluation metric is accuracy (%).

Method	Live	Replay	Print	Mask	Makeup	Overall
ResNet50 (pre-trained) [55]	88.4	93.9	84.2	92.6	**98.6**	91.3
Patch (Ours)	91.5	98.0	87.7	95.9	73.9	90.1
Patch+BCN (Ours)	83.7	**100.0**	**93.0**	96.0	94.2	92.0
Patch+BCN+MFRM (Ours)	**96.1**	**100.0**	**93.0**	95.1	82.6	**93.7**

4.6   Analysis and Visualization

Fine-grained Material Recognition. Face anti-spoofing is usually regarded as a binary classification problem despite we treat it as a binary material perception problem (i.e., structural facial skin versus others) in this paper. It is curious whether the model learns material-based intrinsic features despite it achieves state-of-the-art performance in most FAS datasets. As there are rich spoofing material types in SiW-M dataset, we separate it into five material categories, i.e., live, replay, print, mask and makeup, which are made of structural facial skin, plain glass, wrapped paper, structural fiber and foundation, respectively. Half samples of the each category are used for training and the remaining parts are utilized for testing. Only patch map supervision with five categories is utilized as the baseline because depth and reflection maps are not suitable for multi-category classification. As shown in Table 5, with the BCN and MFRM, the overall accuracy boosts by 1.9% and extra 1.7% respectively, outperforming ResNet50 [55] pre-trained in ImageNet. It implies intrinsic patterns among materials might be captured by BCN and MFRM.

Features Visualization. The low-level features of BCN and the predicted maps are visualized in Fig. 7. It is clear that the bilateral base and residual features between live and spoofing faces are quite different. For the bilateral base features of print attacks (see the 2nd and 3rd column in Fig. 7), the random noises in the hair region are obvious which is caused by the rough surface of the paper

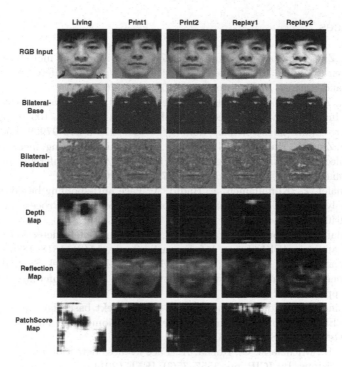

Fig. 7. Features visualization on live face (the first column) and spoofing faces (four columns to the right). The six rows represent the RGB images, low-level bilateral base features, low-level bilateral residual features in BCN, predicted depth maps, reflection maps and patch maps, respectively. Best view when zoom in.

material. Moreover, the micro- patterns in bilateral residual features reveal more details of facial outline in spoofing attacks but blurriness in live faces.

5 Conclusions

In this paper, we rephrase face anti-spoofing (FAS) task as a material recognition problem and combine FAS with classical human material perception [22]. To this end, Bilateral Convolutional Networks are proposed for capturing material-based bilateral macro- and micro- features. Extensive experiments are performed to verify the effectiveness of the proposed method. Our future works include: 1) to learn intrinsic material features via disentangling them with material-unrelated features (e.g., face id and face attribute features); and 2) to establish a more suitable cross-material based FAS benchmark.

Acknowledgment. This work was supported by the Academy of Finland for project MiGA (grant 316765), ICT 2023 project (grant 328115), and Infotech Oulu. We also acknowledge CSC-IT Center for Science, Finland, for computational resources.

References

1. Guo, J., Zhu, X., Zhao, C., Cao, D., Lei, Z., Li, S.Z.: Learning meta face recognition in unseen domains. In: Proceedings of the IEEE/CVF Conference on Computer Vision and Pattern Recognition, pp. 6163–6172 (2020)
2. Guo, J., Zhu, X., Lei, Z., Li, S.Z.: Face synthesis for eyeglass-robust face recognition. In: Zhou, J., et al. (eds.) CCBR 2018. LNCS, vol. 10996, pp. 275–284. Springer, Cham (2018). https://doi.org/10.1007/978-3-319-97909-0_30
3. Cao, D., Zhu, X., Huang, X., Guo, J., Lei, Z.: Domain balancing: face recognition on long-tailed domains. In: Proceedings of the IEEE/CVF Conference on Computer Vision and Pattern Recognition, pp. 5671–5679 (2020)
4. Boulkenafet, Z., Komulainen, J., Hadid, A.: Face anti-spoofing based on color texture analysis. In: IEEE International Conference on Image Processing (ICIP), pp. 2636–2640 (2015)
5. Boulkenafet, Z., Komulainen, J., Hadid, A.: Face spoofing detection using colour texture analysis. IEEE Trans. Inf. Forensics Secur. 11(8), 1818–1830 (2016)
6. de Freitas Pereira, T., Anjos, A., De Martino, J.M., Marcel, S.: LBP-top based countermeasure against face spoofing attacks. In: Asian Conference on Computer Vision, pp. 121–132 (2012)
7. Komulainen, J., Hadid, A., Pietikainen, M.: Context based face anti-spoofing. In: 2013 IEEE Sixth International Conference on Biometrics: Theory, Applications and Systems (BTAS), pp. 1–8 (2013)
8. Peixoto, B., Michelassi, C., Rocha, A.: Face liveness detection under bad illumination conditions. In: ICIP, pp. 3557–3560. IEEE (2011)
9. Patel, K., Han, H., Jain, A.K.: Secure face unlock: spoof detection on smartphones. IEEE Trans. Inf. Forensics Secur. 11(10), 2268–2283 (2016)
10. Qin, Y., et al.: Learning meta model for zero-and few-shot face anti-spoofing. In: The Thirty-Fourth AAAI Conference on Artificial Intelligence (AAAI) (2020)
11. Wang, Z., et al.: Deep spatial gradient and temporal depth learning for face anti-spoofing. In: Proceedings of the IEEE/CVF Conference on Computer Vision and Pattern Recognition, pp. 5042–5051 (2020)
12. Yu, Z., et al.: Searching central difference convolutional networks for face anti-spoofing. In: Proceedings of the IEEE/CVF Conference on Computer Vision and Pattern Recognition, pp. 5295–5305 (2020)
13. Jourabloo, A., Liu, Y., Liu, X.: Face de-spoofing: anti-spoofing via noise modeling. In: Proceedings of the European Conference on Computer Vision (ECCV), pp. 290–306 (2018)
14. Lin, B., Li, X., Yu, Z., Zhao, G.: Face liveness detection by RPPG features and contextual patch-based CNN. In: Proceedings of the 2019 3rd International Conference on Biometric Engineering and Applications, pp. 61–68. ACM (2019)
15. Li, X., Komulainen, J., Zhao, G., Yuen, P.C., Pietikäinen, M.: Generalized face anti-spoofing by detecting pulse from face videos. In: 2016 23rd International Conference on Pattern Recognition (ICPR), pp. 4244–4249. IEEE (2016)
16. Liu, Y., Jourabloo, A., Liu, X.: Learning deep models for face anti-spoofing: binary or auxiliary supervision. In: Proceedings of the IEEE Conference on Computer Vision and Pattern Recognition, pp. 389–398 (2018)
17. Liu, S.Q., Lan, X., Yuen, P.C.: Remote photoplethysmography correspondence feature for 3D mask face presentation attack detection. In: Proceedings of the European Conference on Computer Vision (ECCV), pp. 558–573 (2018)

18. Atoum, Y., Liu, Y., Jourabloo, A., Liu, X.: Face anti-spoofing using patch and depth-based CNNs. In: 2017 IEEE International Joint Conference on Biometrics (IJCB), pp. 319–328 (2017)
19. Guo, J., Zhu, X., Xiao, J., Lei, Z., Wan, G., Li, S.Z.: Improving face anti-spoofing by 3D virtual synthesis. In: 2019 International Conference on Biometrics (ICB), pp. 1–8. IEEE (2019)
20. Tan, X., Li, Y., Liu, J., Jiang, L.: Face liveness detection from a single image with sparse low rank bilinear discriminative model. In: Daniilidis, K., Maragos, P., Paragios, N. (eds.) ECCV 2010. LNCS, vol. 6316, pp. 504–517. Springer, Heidelberg (2010). https://doi.org/10.1007/978-3-642-15567-3_37
21. Li, L., Xia, Z., Jiang, X., Ma, Y., Roli, F., Feng, X.: 3D face mask presentation attack detection based on intrinsic image analysis. arXiv preprint arXiv:1903.11303 (2019)
22. Sharan, L., Liu, C., Rosenholtz, R., Adelson, E.H.: Recognizing materials using perceptually inspired features. Int. J. Comput. Vision 103(3), 348–371 (2013)
23. Boulkenafet, Z., Komulainen, J., Hadid, A.: Face antispoofing using speeded-up robust features and fisher vector encoding. IEEE Signal Process. Lett. 24(2), 141–145 (2017)
24. Komulainen, J., Hadid, A., Pietikäinen, M.: Face spoofing detection using dynamic texture. In: Park, J.-I., Kim, J. (eds.) ACCV 2012. LNCS, vol. 7728, pp. 146–157. Springer, Heidelberg (2013). https://doi.org/10.1007/978-3-642-37410-4_13
25. Siddiqui, T.A., et al.: Face anti-spoofing with multifeature videolet aggregation. In: 2016 23rd International Conference on Pattern Recognition (ICPR), pp. 1035–1040. IEEE (2016)
26. Pan, G., Sun, L., Wu, Z., Lao, S.: Eyeblink-based anti-spoofing in face recognition from a generic webcamera. In: IEEE International Conference on Computer Vision, pp. 1–8 (2007)
27. Yu, Z., et al.: Auto-fas: searching lightweight networks for face anti-spoofing. In: ICASSP 2020-2020 IEEE International Conference on Acoustics, Speech and Signal Processing (ICASSP), pp. 996–1000. IEEE (2020)
28. Li, L., Feng, X., Boulkenafet, Z., Xia, Z., Li, M., Hadid, A.: An original face anti-spoofing approach using partial convolutional neural network. In: IPTA, pp. 1–6 (2016)
29. Patel, K., Han, H., Jain, A.K.: Cross-database face antispoofing with robust feature representation. In: Chinese Conference on Biometric Recognition, pp. 611–619 (2016)
30. George, A., Marcel, S.: Deep pixel-wise binary supervision for face presentation attack detection. In: International Conference on Biometrics. Number CONF (2019)
31. Yu, Z., et al.: Multi-modal face anti-spoofing based on central difference networks. In: Proceedings of the IEEE/CVF Conference on Computer Vision and Pattern Recognition Workshops, pp. 650–651 (2020)
32. Kim, T., Kim, Y., Kim, I., Kim, D.: BASN: enriching feature representation using bipartite auxiliary supervisions for face anti-spoofing. In: Proceedings of the IEEE International Conference on Computer Vision Workshops (2019)
33. Liu, Y., Stehouwer, J., Jourabloo, A., Liu, X.: Deep tree learning for zero-shot face anti-spoofing. In: Proceedings of the IEEE Conference on Computer Vision and Pattern Recognition, pp. 4680–4689 (2019)
34. Jia, Y., Zhang, J., Shan, S., Chen, X.: Single-side domain generalization for face anti-spoofing. In: Proceedings of the IEEE/CVF Conference on Computer Vision and Pattern Recognition, pp. 8484–8493 (2020)

35. Wang, G., Han, H., Shan, S., Chen, X.: Cross-domain face presentation attack detection via multi-domain disentangled representation learning. In: Proceedings of the IEEE/CVF Conference on Computer Vision and Pattern Recognition, pp. 6678–6687 (2020)

36. Shao, R., Lan, X., Li, J., Yuen, P.C.: Multi-adversarial discriminative deep domain generalization for face presentation attack detection. In: Proceedings of the IEEE Conference on Computer Vision and Pattern Recognition, pp. 10023–10031 (2019)

37. Wang, Z., Zhao, C., Qin, Y., Zhou, Q., Lei, Z.: Exploiting temporal and depth information for multi-frame face anti-spoofing. arXiv preprint arXiv:1811.05118 (2018)

38. Yang, X., et al.: Face anti-spoofing: Model matters, so does data. In: Proceedings of the IEEE Conference on Computer Vision and Pattern Recognition (2019)

39. Lin, C., Liao, Z., Zhou, P., Hu, J., Ni, B.: Live face verification with multiple instantialized local homographic parameterization. In: IJCAI, pp. 814–820 (2018)

40. Yu, Z., Li, X., Zhao, G.: Remote photoplethysmograph signal measurement from facial videos using spatio-temporal networks. arXiv preprint arXiv:1905.02419 (2019)

41. Yu, Z., Li, X., Niu, X., Shi, J., Zhao, G.: Autohr: a strong end-to-end baseline for remote heart rate measurement with neural searching. arXiv preprint arXiv:2004.12292 (2020)

42. Yu, Z., Peng, W., Li, X., Hong, X., Zhao, G.: Remote heart rate measurement from highly compressed facial videos: an end-to-end deep learning solution with video enhancement. In: Proceedings of the IEEE International Conference on Computer Vision, pp. 151–160 (2019)

43. Maloney, L.T., Brainard, D.H.: Color and material perception: achievements and challenges. J. Vis. **10**(9), 19 (2010)

44. Fleming, R.W.: Visual perception of materials and their properties. Vis. Res. **94**, 62–75 (2014)

45. Nishida, S.: Image statistics for material perception. Curr. Opinion Behav. Sci. **30**, 94–99 (2019)

46. Adelson, E.H.: On seeing stuff: the perception of materials by humans and machines. In: Human vision and electronic imaging VI, vol. 4299, pp. 1–12. International Society for Optics and Photonics (2001)

47. Varma, M., Zisserman, A.: A statistical approach to material classification using image patch exemplars. IEEE Trans. Pattern Anal. Mach. Intell. **31**(11), 2032–2047 (2008)

48. Jiang, X., Du, J., Sun, B., Feng, X.: Deep dilated convolutional network for material recognition. In: 2018 Eighth International Conference on Image Processing Theory, Tools and Applications (IPTA), pp. 1–6. IEEE (2018)

49. Ling, S., Callet, P.L., Yu, Z.: The role of structure and textural information in image utility and quality assessment tasks. Electron. Imaging **2018**(14), 1–13 (2018)

50. Deng, B.W., Yu, Z.T., Ling, B.W., Yang, Z.: Video quality assessment based on features for semantic task and human material perception. In: 2016 IEEE International Conference on Consumer Electronics-China (ICCE-China), pp. 1–4. IEEE (2016)

51. Li, L., Xia, Z., Jiang, X., Ma, Y., Roli, F., Feng, X.: 3D face mask presentation attack detection based on intrinsic image analysis. IET Biometrics **9**(3), 100–108 (2020)

52. Tomasi, C., Manduchi, R.: Bilateral filtering for gray and color images. In: ICCV, vol. 98, p. 2 (1998)

53. Durand, F., Dorsey, J.: Fast bilateral filtering for the display of high-dynamic-range images. In: ACM Transactions on Graphics (TOG), vol. 21, pp. 257–266. ACM (2002)
54. Paris, S., Durand, F.: A fast approximation of the bilateral filter using a signal processing approach. In: Leonardis, A., Bischof, H., Pinz, A. (eds.) ECCV 2006. LNCS, vol. 3954, pp. 568–580. Springer, Heidelberg (2006). https://doi.org/10.1007/11744085_44
55. He, K., Zhang, X., Ren, S., Sun, J.: Deep residual learning for image recognition. In: Proceedings of the IEEE Conference on Computer Vision and Pattern Recognition, pp. 770–778 (2016)
56. Wang, J., Chen, K., Xu, R., Liu, Z., Loy, C.C., Lin, D.: Carafe: content-aware reassembly of features. arXiv preprint arXiv:1905.02188 (2019)
57. Woo, S., Park, J., Lee, J.Y., So Kweon, I.: Cbam: convolutional block attention module. In: Proceedings of the European Conference on Computer Vision (ECCV), pp. 3–19 (2018)
58. Hu, J., Shen, L., Sun, G.: Squeeze-and-excitation networks. In: Proceedings of the IEEE Conference on Computer Vision and Pattern Recognition, pp. 7132–7141 (2018)
59. Wang, X., Girshick, R., Gupta, A., He, K.: Non-local neural networks. In: Proceedings of the IEEE Conference on Computer Vision and Pattern Recognition, pp. 7794–7803 (2018)
60. Guo, J., Zhu, X., Yang, Y., Yang, F., Lei, Z., Li, S.Z.: Towards fast, accurate and stable 3D dense face alignment. In: Proceedings of the European Conference on Computer Vision (ECCV) (2020)
61. Feng, Y., Wu, F., Shao, X., Wang, Y., Zhou, X.: Joint 3D face reconstruction and dense alignment with position map regression network. In: Proceedings of the European Conference on Computer Vision (ECCV) (2017)
62. Zhang, X., Ng, R., Chen, Q.: Single image reflection separation with perceptual losses. In: Proceedings of the IEEE Conference on Computer Vision and Pattern Recognition, pp. 4786–4794 (2018)
63. Boulkenafet, Z., Komulainen, J., Li, L., Feng, X., Hadid, A.: OULU-NPU: a mobile face presentation attack database with real-world variations. In: FGR, pp. 612–618 (2017)
64. Zhang, Z., Yan, J., Liu, S., Lei, Z., Yi, D., Li, S.Z.: A face antispoofing database with diverse attacks. In: ICB, pp. 26–31 (2012)
65. Chingovska, I., Anjos, A., Marcel, S.: On the effectiveness of local binary patterns in face anti-spoofing. In: Biometrics Special Interest Group, pp. 1–7 (2012)
66. Wen, D., Han, H., Jain, A.K.: Face spoof detection with image distortion analysis. IEEE Trans. Inf. Forensics Secur. 10(4), 746–761 (2015)
67. International Organization for Standardization: ISO/IEC JTC 1/SC 37 biometrics: information technology biometric presentation attack detection part 1: Framework (2016). https://www.iso.org/obp/ui/iso
68. Boulkenafet, Z., et al.: A competition on generalized software-based face presentation attack detection in mobile scenarios. In: 2017 IEEE International Joint Conference on Biometrics (IJCB), pp. 688–696. IEEE (2017)
69. Arashloo, S.R., Kittler, J., Christmas, W.: An anomaly detection approach to face spoofing detection: a new formulation and evaluation protocol. IEEE Access 5, 13868–13882 (2017)
70. Xiong, F., AbdAlmageed, W.: Unknown presentation attack detection with face RGB images. In: 2018 IEEE 9th International Conference on Biometrics Theory, Applications and Systems (BTAS), pp. 1–9. IEEE (2018)

How Can I See My Future? FvTraj: Using First-Person View for Pedestrian Trajectory Prediction

Huikun Bi[1,2]([✉]), Ruisi Zhang[3], Tianlu Mao[1,2], Zhigang Deng[4], and Zhaoqi Wang[1,2]

[1] Beijing Key Laboratory of Mobile Computing and Pervasive Device, Institute of Computing Technology, Chinese Academy of Sciences, Beijing, China
{bihuikun,ltm,zqwang}@ict.ac.cn
[2] University of Chinese Academy of Sciences, Beijing, China
[3] University of Utah, Salt Lake City, USA
ruisi.zhang@utah.edu
[4] University of Houston, Houston, USA
zdeng4@uh.edu

Abstract. This work presents a novel **First-person View** based **Traj**ectory predicting model (FvTraj) to estimate the future trajectories of pedestrians in a scene given their observed trajectories and the corresponding first-person view images. First, we render first-person view images using our in-house built **First-person View Sim**ulator (FvSim), given the ground-level 2D trajectories. Then, based on multi-head attention mechanisms, we design a social-aware attention module to model social interactions between pedestrians, and a view-aware attention module to capture the relations between historical motion states and visual features from the first-person view images. Our results show the dynamic scene contexts with ego-motions captured by first-person view images via FvSim are valuable and effective for trajectory prediction. Using this simulated first-person view images, our well structured FvTraj model achieves state-of-the-art performance.

Keywords: Deep learning · Human behavior · Trajectory prediction · Crowd simulation · Multi-head attention

1 Introduction

Pedestrian trajectory prediction has attracted increasing attention of researchers in computer vision community due to its various potential applications including robotic navigation, autonomous driving, and anomaly detection [5,21]. It is often necessary to consider all three major inherent properties of pedestrian trajectory prediction: social interactions, multimodality, and scene contexts. The first two properties have been well considered in the state-of-the-art frameworks [1,13,17,18]. Scene contexts are particularly essential yet challenging for modern studies, since they contain both the stationary obstacles

© Springer Nature Switzerland AG 2020
A. Vedaldi et al. (Eds.): ECCV 2020, LNCS 12352, pp. 576–593, 2020.
https://doi.org/10.1007/978-3-030-58571-6_34

Fig. 1. (a) A top-down view image [26] contains large-scale scene contexts. (b) A first-person view image from the First-Person Locomotion (FPL) dataset [47] contains dynamic scene contexts (i.e., moving pedestrians). (c) A simulated scenario using FvSim. (d), (e), and (f) are the first-person view images of the pedestrian p_3 in (c) at step t_1, t_2, and t_3, respectively. Note, the first-person view images are individual-specific and are not shared among pedestrians in a scene.

(e.g., buildings, trees) and dynamic objects (e.g., moving pedestrians). Recently, researchers have started to exploit scene contexts for pedestrian trajectory prediction [9,22,37,47], using either top-down view images (Fig. 1(a)) or first-person view images (Fig. 1(b)). However, both methods suffer from the following limitations.

Top-down view images are easy to access and applicable to anomaly detection, but provide limited dynamic scene contexts. Prior works [9,22,37] introduced the top-down view images (Fig. 1(a)), which are shared between pedestrians, to mainly capture the stationary obstacles. But it is difficult to capture each individual pedestrian's detailed dynamic information (e.g., poses, ego-motions, visual occlusion information) due to the pixel-precise in a top-down view image.

First-person view images provide detailed dynamic scene contexts with ego-motions, but is difficult to access for each pedestrian in a scene. They are applicable to various applications like blind navigation [19,27], robotic navigation [36], and autonomous driving [8,33,39]. They (Fig. 1(b)) can well capture moving pedestrians by observing the ego-motion of each pedestrian (i.e., camera wearer), the pedestrian's visual perspective effect on the neighbors, and pedestrians' detailed poses [47]. Obtaining comprehensive and accurate scene contexts requires the first-person view images from each pedestrian in a scene, since the images from a single pedestrian can only provide partial scene contexts and the relative position of each pedestrian. In reality, to do so we need to mount at least one camera per pedestrian in a scene, which is expensive, time-consuming, and sometimes infeasible.

To overcome these limitations, we first build an in-house simulator *FvSim* using Unity to generate a dynamic virtual environment and render the corresponding first-person view images for each pedestrian based on the observed trajectories. This environment is proportional to the real-world environment using SI units, which can be generalized to any dataset collected in real world using unit conversions and some linear transformations between coordinate systems. Unlike physically collecting images required a large number of camera-wearing robots moving in a given scene, our FvSim requires zero physical cameras (i.e., low-cost) to provide desired information of given pedestrians, which is ideal for capturing dynamic scene contexts. We also use FvSim to evaluate the effectiveness and importance of first-person view information for some trajectory-prediction tasks.

We then propose *FvTraj*, a model to predict future trajectories of pedestrians, by considering two given inputs: the observed trajectory of each pedestrian in a scene, and the pedestrians' corresponding first-person view images simulated by FvSim. Without any preconceived scene contexts (e.g., top-down view information), FvTraj considers trajectory prediction holistically by taking into account historical motion patterns, social interactions, and self dynamic scene contexts with ego-motions. Through experimental comparisons with various state-of-the-art models, we show that FvTraj can achieve better performance.

The main contributions of this work can be summarized as: (1) To address the problem of hardware limitation commonly faced in the pedestrian trajectory prediction task, we develop FvSim, a trajectory simulator that is capable of providing multi-view information in the scene. We show the first-person view images via FvSim could be valuable and effective for trajectory prediction. (2) We develop FvTraj, a novel architecture to predict future trajectories of pedestrians based on historical trajectories and the corresponding first-person view images of each pedestrian in a scene. Our FvTraj uses social-aware attention and view-aware attention based on a multi-attention mechanism, which captures both social behaviors and visual features including ego-motions.

2   Related Work

In this section, we will mainly focus on the reviewing of recent related efforts on pedestrian trajectory prediction [1,7,9,13,18,29,37].

Social Interaction Schemes. Prior works had successfully presented that hand-crafted features of pedestrians are essential for modeling social interactions [3,16,24,31,32,44,45]. Recently, some works [1,13,14] modeled complex human-human interactions using DNN-based methods, which adopt social pooling schemes to describe the social behaviors and assign equal importance of neighboring pedestrians. Attention-based models [2,37,43,49] intentionally select useful information from neighboring pedestrians based on the relative locations and motion correlations. Furthermore, by adopting a graph to describe the pedestrians in a scene, a graph attention model (GAT) was proposed to model social interactions in order to generate realistic pedestrian trajectories [17,22].

Semantic Scene Contexts. The physical scene around pedestrians is important for trajectory prediction, because visually stationary or dynamic obstacles (e.g., buildings, trees, and moving pedestrians) generally influence pedestrians' trajectories. Lee et al. [25] built a scene context fusion unit to encode semantic context information in dynamic scenes. Sadeghian et al. [38] proposed the Carnet that uses single-source and multi-source attention mechanisms to visualize fine-grained semantic elements of navigation scenes. Sadeghian et al. [37] proposed Sophie that could produce plausible social trajectories using pre-trained

CNN to extract the visual features. Choi et al. [9] visually extract spatiotemporal features of static road structures, road topology, and road appearance. Liang et al. [28] proposed a person interaction module to encode both the nearby scene of a person, as well as the explicit geometric relations and the surrounding object types in the scene. Kosaraju et al. [22] proposed Social-BiGAT that applies soft attention to capture physical features in the scene context.

First-Person View. In some applications like autonomous driving and robotic navigation, the most naturally accessible visual input for trajectory prediction is the first-person view [6,29,40,47]. Yagi et al. [47] proposed a method to predict the future location of a person seen in a first-person video based on the ego-motions of the video, poses, scales, and locations of the person. Yao et at. [48] proposed an unsupervised approach for traffic accident detection in first-person videos. Lai et at. [23] proposed a new collision avoidance system for the first-person viewpoint, to show the trajectory of people and to predict the future location. Ma et al. [29] proposed Trafficpredict to predict the trajectories of heterogeneous agents based on a proposed first-person view driving dataset. Of the particular interest in the field of autonomous driving, there is a variety of driving datasets recorded in the first-person view (i.e., collected by the cameras rigidly attached to vehicles), which could be potentially used to train a model to predict the trajectories of heterogeneous road users [12,30,35].

3 Methodology

As aforementioned, our proposed *FvTraj* model can output the future trajectories of pedestrians in a scene, given their previous motion states and the corresponding first-person view images simulated by the *FvSim* simulator.

3.1 Problem Formulation

Trajectory prediction for pedestrians can be formally defined as the problem of predicting the future trajectory of any focus pedestrian in a scene, given the pedestrian's previous states and the scene information. We consider the previous states of a pedestrian $p^i (i \in [1, N])$ in a N-pedestrians scene as a two-dimensional (2D) position $X_t^i = (x_t^i, y_t^i)$ within an observation period from time step $t = 1$ to $t = T_{obs}$. We denote the trajectory of p^i in a period from $t = T_{start}$ to $t = T_{end}$ as $X_{t \in [T_{start}, T_{end}]}^i$. In our case, the scene information is described as the first-person view image I_t^i of the pedestrian p^i within the same observation period, which is denoted as $I_{t \in [1, T_{obs}]}^i$. Each focus pedestrian in the scene does not share their first-person view images with others. Given the above two input variables, $X_{t \in [1, T_{obs}]}^i$ and $I_{t \in [1, T_{obs}]}^i$ ($i \in [1, N]$), the goal of our model is to output the 2D position of each pedestrian in the scene within the prediction period from $t = T_{obs} + 1$ to $t = T_{pred}$, which is denoted as $X_{t \in [T_{obs}+1, T_{pred}]}^i$.

Although the first-person view images are accessible in some applications, it is difficult to access the first-person view images for all pedestrians in the scene

Fig. 2. (a) A frame in HOTEL dataset [34]. The orange dots represent the labeled pedestrians. (b) The corresponding simulated scenario for (a) using a top-down view. (c) The focus pedestrian's first-person view image (i.e., red dot in (a)). (d) The camera settings for pedestrians in FvSim. (Color figure online)

due to practical cost and technical difficulty. This could be formally defined as the problem of simulating the first-person view images for each pedestrian in a scene, given their observed states.

3.2 Model Overview

FvSim–using Unity–extends given 2D pedestrian trajectories into a 3D simulated scene, from which we can obtain multi-view information, especially first-person views for each pedestrian (Fig. 2(c)). FvSim is proportional to the real-world environment using SI units. The input of FvSim is ground-level 2D trajectory data from a given dataset, which is either presented in or converted to our coordinate system defined in our simulated environment. We prepare 27 3D human models with walking behavior embedded. It enables FvSim to randomly assign a prepared human model to each pedestrian from a given dataset. Since the body, head, and gaze orientations are necessary required information for FvSim but not accessible from the original datasets (e.g. ETH [34] and UCY [26]), we assume they are aligned with the focus pedestrian's forward direction (i.e., the direction of the computed velocity using 2D trajectories). FvSim assumes the height of each pedestrian is 1.75 m, and the first-person view is provided via a camera with a 144° wide-angle [14] and an optical axis parallel to the ground plane, which is rigidly mounted on each pedestrian's head 1.63 m above the ground (Fig. 2(d)).

As illustrated in Fig. 3, FvTraj is composed of five modules: (1) a Traj-Encoder (Sect. 3.3), a trajectory encoder that captures historical motion patterns of each pedestrian; (2) a View-Encoder (Sect. 3.4), an encoder module that extracts visual features from the simulated first-person view image sequence; (3) a Social-aware attention module (Sect. 3.5) that builds relations with other socially interacted pedestrians in the scene; (4) a View-aware attention module (Sect. 3.6) that captures the latent relations between motions and visual features (i.e., extracted from the first-person view images with ego-motion information) using an attention mechanism; (5) a Traj-Decoder (Sect. 3.7) that generates multimodal pedestrian trajectories given all observed information including pedestrians' historical trajectories, social interactions with other pedestrians in the scene, and the dynamic scene contexts from the first-person view images.

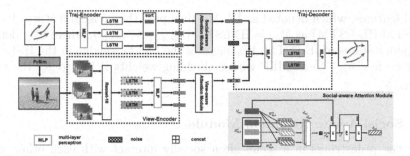

Fig. 3. Pipeline overview of the FvTraj. Given the pedestrian trajectories in the observation period, we use FvSim to simulate the corresponding crowd scenario and render the first-person view images for each pedestrian. The Traj-Encoder and the View-Encoder are used to extract latent representations for observed pedestrian trajectories, and the first-person view images, respectively. Their outputs are fed into the follow-up social-aware attention and view-aware attention modules to capture social behaviors and visual view-aware features based on multi-head attention mechanisms. The final multimodal trajectories are produced by the Traj-Decoder. Social-aware attention module (with yellow background). It captures the latent social interactions between the focus pedestrian p^i and the other pedestrians. In this module, we use a multi-head attention to calculate the scaled dot product attentions over all other pedestrians except p^i for each of the four heads (i.e., $n = 4$). Followed by an MLP, the social-aware attention module finally returns the social interaction representations e^i_{soci}. (Color figure online)

3.3 Trajectory Encoder

We build Traj-Encoder, an encoder for any given pedestrian $p^i (i \in [1, N])$ in a scene to capture the historical motion patterns. Given the observed trajectory $X^i_{t \subset [1, T_{obs}]}$, we calculate its relative displacements $\Delta X^i_t = X^i_t - X^i_{t-1}$. Then, ΔX^i_t is embedded into a high dimensional space using a multi-layer perceptron (MLP) and then fed into an LSTM (TE-LSTM) as follows:

$$h^i_{te,t} = \text{TE-LSTM}\left(h^i_{te,t-1}, \text{MLP}(\Delta X^i_t, W^{emb}_{rel}); W_{te}\right), \qquad (1)$$

where $h^i_{te,t}$ is the hidden states of TE-LSTM, which carries latent representations of historical motion states of p^i, W^{emb}_{rel} denotes the embedding weights of MLP, and W_{te} denotes the LSTM weights in the trajectory encoder TE-LSTM. In our model, all the pedestrians in the scene share the same parameter values in TE-LSTM.

3.4 View Image Encoder

We build View-Encoder, an encoder for any given first-person view image I^i_t of the corresponding pedestrian p^i. The simulated first-person view images with the original size of 768×1024 are resized to 36×48 for FvTraj. We use a ResNet-18 model [15] pre-trained on ImageNet [10] and fine tune the model to extract visual features, which denoted as V^i. We then pass these visual features V^i into an LSTM (IE-LSTM) as $h^i_{ie,t} = \text{IE-LSTM}\left(h^i_{ie,t-1}, V^i_t; W_{ie}\right)$, where $h^i_{ie,t}$ denotes the hidden states of IE-LSTM, W_{ie} denotes the LSTM weights in the IE-LSTM. Then we feed $h^i_{ie,t}$ to an MLP with embedding weights W^{emb}_{ie} to get the visual feature $\hat{h}^i_{ie,t}$.

3.5   Social-Aware Attention Module

Since the pedestrians in a scene often socially interact with each other, modeling social interactions among the pedestrians is important to the realism of real-world crowds, besides the purpose of collision avoidance. We build a social-aware attention module (Fig. 3) based on a multi-head attention mechanism [42] to learn latent social interactions between a focus pedestrian and all other pedestrians in the scene. Inspired by the REFER module [20], which can learn latent relationships between a given question and a dialog history in the visual dialog task and reach the state-of-the-art performance, we design a similar structure for this module.

Similar to the prior works [2,11,37], we sort the order of the pedestrians other than the focus pedestrian based on their relative distances between the focus pedestrian and themselves. We denote the concatenated hidden states (i.e., which are calculated in the trajectory encoder) of these sorted pedestrians as $H^i_{te,t}$, which carry the latent representations of historical motion patterns.

To capture how the sorted pedestrians influence the future trajectories of the focus pedestrian, we use the scaled dot product attention [42] to obtain the interactions between the focus pedestrian p^i and the others as follows:

$$\alpha^i_{te,n} = Attn((h^i_{te,t}W^h_{te,n}), (H^i_{te,t}W^H_{te,n})), \quad Attn(a,b) = \text{softmax}(\frac{ab^T}{\sqrt{d_{te}}})b, \quad (2)$$

where $W^h_{te,n}$ and $W^H_{te,n}$ are the linear weights to transform the hidden states into d_{te} dimensions, respectively.

To stabilize the learning process, we operate a multi-head attention mechanism [42] by calculating the attention n times with distinct $W^h_{te,n}$ and $W^H_{te,n}$ using Eq. 2, yielding $\alpha^i_{te,1}, ..., \alpha^i_{te,n}$. The multi-head representations are concatenated as α^i_M, followed by a linear function as $\alpha^i_M = \alpha^i_{te,1} \oplus ... \oplus \alpha^i_{te,n}$, where $\oplus$ is a concatenation operation. Note that α^i_M is then passed into another linear function with weights W^M_{te}. To add their hidden states $h^i_{te,t}$, we apply a residual connection [15] and employ layer normalization (LN) [4] as $\lambda^i = \text{LN}(\alpha^i_M W^M_{te} + h^i_{te,t})$.

To obtain the social interaction representations e^i_{soci} for the pedestrian p^i in the scene, we again adopt an MLP with weights W_{soci}, followed by the other residual connection and LN as $e^i_{soci} = \text{LN}(\text{MLP}(\lambda^i, W_{soci}) + \lambda^i)$.

3.6   View-Aware Attention Module

We also build a view-aware attention module to extract visual features from the first-person view images in the observation period, which adopts the module structure from the previous social-aware attention module (Sect. 3.5). Similarly, we exploit the multi-head attention mechanism to concatenate information, followed by residual connection and LN to obtain the relationships between a given latent motion pattern representation and the historical latent visual features extracted from the first-person view images, denoted as e^i_{view}. Note that only the structure of the social-aware attention module and that of the view-aware attention module are the same, the parameter values in the two modules are not shared and could be different.

The input of first-person view information is not shared between pedestrians in opposition to the historical trajectory information. Considering the visually dynamic and continuous scene context of pedestrians, we denote $\hat{h}^i_{ie,t}$ with the latent representations of visual features of p^i from view image encoder at $t \in [1, T_{obs}]$ as H^i_{ie}. The shape of H^i_{ie} is $T_{obs} \times d_{ie}$, where d_{ie} is the dimension of $\hat{h}^i_{ie,t}$. Based on the hidden states $h^i_{te,t}$ of p^i in the trajectory encoder, we can obtain the scaled dot product attention as $\alpha^i_{ie,n} = Attn((h^i_{te,t}\hat{W}^h_{ie,n}), (H^i_{ie}W^H_{ie,n}))$, where $\hat{W}^h_{ie,n}$ and $W^H_{ie,n}$ are linear weights to transform the hidden states into d_{ie} dimensions, respectively.

3.7 Trajectory Decoder

We build the Traj-Decoder, a trajectory decoder that generates future trajectories for each pedestrian in a scene. To mimic the actual motions of pedestrians, we consider their major inherent properties: multimodality, self historical motion patterns, social interactions with other pedestrians, and scene contexts.

Traj-Decoder utilizes an LSTM decoder (TD-LSTM), inspired by the previous works [13,17,37] that exploit a noise vector z sampled from a multivariate normal distribution to produce multimodal future trajectories. We use the concatenation of four components: (1) the latent representation of the motion patterns in the observation period from the last step of LSTM trajectory encoder $h^i_{te,T_{obs}}$, (2) the embedding of social interactions between the focus pedestrian and the other pedestrians e^i_{soci}, (3) the captured view-aware representation e^i_{view} from the first-person view images with scene contexts, and (4) the sampled noise vector z. The output of this concatenation is then passed through an MLP with weights W^{emb}_{td} to initialize the hidden states of the LSTM decoder. Based on the Seq2seq framework [41], the latter process can be represented as:

$$h^i_{td,T_{obs}+1} = \text{MLP}(h^i_{te,T_{obs}} \oplus e^i_{soci} \oplus e^i_{view} \oplus z, W^{emb}_{td}), \tag{3}$$

where $h^i_{td,T_{obs}+1}$ denotes the initialized hidden states of TD-LSTM.

The recursion equation of the Traj-Decoder for p^i in the prediction period is:

$$h^i_{td,t} = \text{TD-LSTM}(h^i_{td,t-1}, \text{MLP}(\Delta\hat{X}^i_t, W^{emb}_{rel}); W_{td}), \tag{4}$$

where $\Delta\hat{X}^i_t$ is the relative positions based on the predicted results at the last step. Note that $\Delta\hat{X}^i_t$ at the first step $T_{obs} + 1$ of the prediction period is the same as the last input of TE-LSTM at step T_{obs}. The MLP with weights W^{emb}_{rel} shares the parameters with MLP in Eq. 1. W_{td} and $h^i_{td,t}$ are the LSTM weights and hidden states in TD-LSTM, respectively.

Lastly, we pass the hidden states $h^i_{td,t}$ in TE-LSTM into another MLP with weights W_d one at a time to calculate the relative positions $\Delta \hat{X}^i_t$ in the prediction period, and we obtain the predicted positions based on $\Delta \hat{X}^i_t$ and the last 2D positions, represented as $\Delta \hat{X}^i_t = \text{MLP}(h^i_{td,t}, W_d)$, and $\hat{X}^i_t = \Delta \hat{X}^i_t + \hat{X}^i_{t-1}$.

3.8   Training and Implementation Details

Losses. The entire network is trained end-to-end by minimizing the L2 loss ($L = ||\Delta X^i_t - \Delta \hat{X}^i_t||_2$), which is the difference between the predicted trajectories in the prediction period and the ground-truth trajectories [2,13,17,37]. Based on a noise vector z, FvTraj can produce multimodal trajectories. We adopt a similar training process, following the variety loss in the previous works [2,13,17,37]. For each training step, we generate k possible trajectories according to the randomly sampled z, and then choose the best result as the prediction.

Implementation Details. In the Traj-Encoder, the 2D position of each pedestrian is embedded into a vector of 32 dimensions, and followed by LSTMs with 64 hidden states. In the View-Encoder, the first-person view images at each step in the observation period are processed into 1000 dimensions using ResNet-18, and followed by LSTMs with 128 hidden states. The output of the LSTMs in View-Encoder is further processed by a two-layer MLP ($128 \times 64 \times 64$) with ReLU activation functions. In the social-aware attention module, the number of multi-head attention is $n = 4$. $h^i_{te,t}$ and $H^i_{te,t}$ are projected into 16 dimensions. The MLP for λ^i comprises 2-layer 1D convolution operations with ReLU activation functions. In the view-aware attention module, the parameters have the same dimensions as those in the social-aware attention module. In the Traj-Decoder, we add a 32 dimension noise vector. The concatenation of $h^i_{te,T_{obs}} \oplus e^i_{soci} \oplus e^i_{view} \oplus z$ is fed into a 3-layer MLP ($224 \times 192 \times 128 \times 64$), with ReLU functions and batch normalizations. The hidden states of the LSTM in the Traj-Decoder is fixed to 64 dimensions. The $h^i_{td,t}$ with 64 dimensions will finally transformed into 2D relative positions. The initial learning rate is set to 0.001 and decayed into 0.0001 after 20 epochs. The learning process adopts Adam optimizer to iteratively update the network with a batch size 8 for 500 epochs.

4   Experiment Results

We compared FvTraj with state-of-the-art pedestrian trajectory prediction models, and presented quantitative and qualitative evaluation in this section. We used two relevant and publicly accessible datasets: ETH [34] and UCY [26]. The ETH dataset comprises two distinct scenes: ETH and HOTEL, and the UCY dataset comprises three distinct scenes: ZARA1, ZARA2, and UCY. We used the data preprocessing method proposed in S-GAN [13], and the corrected ETH-Univ

Table 1. Quantitative results for the predicted positions. We use ADE and FDE in meters to evaluate the task of predicting the trajectories within a period of 12 steps (4.8 s), given the previous observed 8 steps (3.2 s). The lower evaluation is the better.

Dataset	Without scene contexts		With scene contexts		Ours			
	S-GAN [13]	STGAT [17]	Sophie [37]	Bi-GAT [22]	FvTraj	FvTraj-noSocial	FvTraj-noView	FvTraj
	20-20	20-20	20-20	20-20	1-1	5-20	5-20	5-20
ETH	0.87/1.62	0.65/1.12	0.70/1.43	0.69/1.29	0.62/1.23	0.60/1.22	0.58/1.21	**0.56/1.14**
HOTEL	0.67/1.37	0.35/0.66	0.76/1.67	0.49/1.01	0.53/1.10	0.34/0.70	0.42/0.89	**0.28/0.55**
UNIV	0.76/1.52	**0.52/1.10**	0.54/1.24	0.55/1.32	0.57/1.19	0.55/1.16	0.56/1.16	0.52/1.12
ZARA1	0.35/0.68	0.34/0.69	**0.30/0.63**	0.30/0.62	0.42/0.89	0.39/0.80	0.37/0.78	0.37/0.78
ZARA2	0.42/0.84	**0.29/0.60**	0.38/0.78	0.36/0.75	0.38/0.79	0.35/0.69	0.33/0.67	0.32/0.68
Average	0.61/1.21	0.43/0.83	0.54/1.15	0.48/1.00	0.50/1.04	0.45/0.91	0.45/0.94	**0.41/0.85**

frame rate presented in the work [49]. Following a similar approach as in the prior works [13,22,37], we used a leave-one-out method to use four scenes as the training data and the remaining one scene as the test data. In our experiments, the pedestrian trajectories for the initial eight steps (i.e., the observation period on a timescale of 3.2 s) are given, and we aim to predict trajectories for the next 12 steps (i.e., the prediction period on a timescale of 4.8 s).

Baselines. We compared FvTraj to four state-of-the-art pedestrian trajectory prediction models, including two models without scene contexts: Social-GAN (**S-GAN**) [13] and a spatial-temporal graph attention network (**STGAT**) [17], and the other two with scene contexts: the social GAN with attention networks (**Sophie**) [37] and the Bicycle-GAN with graph attention networks (**Social-BiGAT**) [22]. The results of STGAT are obtained by our implementations of the ADE and FDE metrics and evaluation of the trained models that are released by the authors. The results of S-GAN, Sophie, and Social-BiGAT are obtained from the original papers [13,22,37].

Evaluation Metrics. Inspired by prior works [13,22,37], we chose Average Displacement Error (**ADE**) and Final Displacement Error (**FDE**) as the evaluation metrics. ADE is the average Euclidean distance error between the predicted result and the ground truth over the whole sequence. FDE is the Euclidean distance error at the last step between the predicted result and the ground truth.

Ablation Study. We performed an ablation study using various control settings to evaluate the contribution of each major component of our model. FvTraj is our final model with all the components; FvTraj-noSocial is a version of our model without the social-aware attention module; FvTraj-noView is a version of our model without both the view image encoder and the view-aware attention module. The model with N-K variety loss represents that the model with the lowest ADE and FDE selected from K randomly sampled trajectories after N times training, which is similar to the prior works [13,22,37].

4.1   Quantitative Evaluation

The quantitative comparison results between our model to the baseline models are reported in Table 1, which include ADE and FDE for the predicted trajectories within the prediction period of 12 steps given the observed eight steps.

For ETH, HOTEL, and UNIV, the baseline models with scene contexts (i.e., Sophie and Bi-GAT) outperformed S-GAN but not STGAT. FvTraj outperformed both S-GAN and STGAT, except the performance of FvTraj and STGAT on UNIV are similar. These results suggest that the contribution of the top-down view images used in the baselines is not as obvious as that of the first-person view images used in FvTraj. ETH, HOTEL, and UNIV can be characterized as a spacious environment with few stationary obstacles such that the main obstacles in the scene are the moving pedestrians. It is our conjecture that the success of FvTraj in these scenes is due to that the first-person view images can better capture the detailed motion of each pedestrian, especially the ego-motions.

For ZARA1, the baseline models with scene contexts (i.e., Sophie and Bi-GAT) outperformed both S-GAN and STGAT, but FvTraj outperformed neither S-GAN nor STGAT. For ZARA2, both Sophie and Bi-GAT outperformed S-GAN but not STGAT, so does the FvTraj model. The results seem to suggest that the contribution of the top-down view images might be more than that of the first-person view images used in the FvTraj model. ZARA1 and ZARA2 can be characterized as the environment with some large-scale stationary obstacles such that the pedestrians' motions would be limited. It is possible that the performance of the FvTraj model is no better than the baseline models in these cases, due to the lacking of stationary scene contexts in our simulated first-person view images. By considering the performance of baseline models, it is reasonable to believe the performance of FvTraj can be further improved by introducing the simulated stationary obstacles in our FvSim.

In terms of our proposed module-based architecture, we found that incorporating both the social-aware attention module and the view-aware attention module can significantly improve the performances on ETH, HOTEL, and UNIV. However, we cannot find noticeable differences between FvTraj-noView and FvTraj for ZARA1 and ZARA2. This might be caused by the same reason described above, which is the lacking of stationary scene contexts in our simulated images.

The baseline models were evaluated using 20-20 variety loss, and FvTraj was evaluated using 5–20 variety loss. We choose K for FvTraj to be consistent with the four baseline models. We chose the reduced $N = 5$ due to the computational complexity of FvTraj, which contains the computationally intensive architecture of networks and the pre-processing procedure of first-person view images sequence for each pedestrian in the scene. It is reasonable to believe the performance of FvTraj can be further improved if we increase $N = 5$ to $N = 20$.

Figure 4 shows the effect of varying K from $K = 20$ to $K = 1$ when evaluating the generalization of each model. Although we found that the increase of K generally leads to better accuracy in terms of ADE and FDE for all the five models, the effect of varying K on the performance of FvTraj is not significant

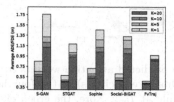

Fig. 4. Quantitative results for the predicted positions demonstrate the effect of the variety loss. Reducing K results in a higher average ADE/FDE across all five scenes, and less change means better generalization. Note, we use $N = 5$ for FvTraj, and $N = 20$ for S-GAN, STGAT, Sophie, and Social-BiGAT.

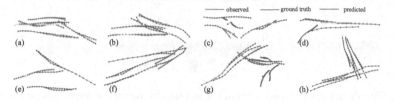

Fig. 5. Visual comparisons between the ground truth and the predicted trajectories by FvTraj across eight scenes. Each scene shows at least one of the scenarios among pedestrians: individual following, group following, meeting, and collision avoiding.

Fig. 6. Visualization of the predicted trajectory distributions ($K = 20$) and the final trajectories. The trajectories in the observation period and the prediction period are illustrated as solid and dash lines, respectively.

compared to the four baseline models. The average ADE and FDE of our model with 5-1 various loss are 0.47 and 0.96, respectively. When K is increased to 20, the average ADE and FDE of our model decrease to 0.41 and 0.85, respectively, which leads to a performance increase of 13.7% and 12.9%, respectively. This result indicates across all five scenes, on average, drawing more samples from our model does not cause a significant increase in accuracy. Therefore, our FvTraj is more robust and better generalized than all the baseline models.

4.2 Qualitative Evaluation

To better evaluate the performance of FvTraj, we visualize the predicted trajectories (Fig. 5) across eight scenes given the observed trajectories, compared to the ground truth. We are aware that the multimodality of pedestrians might be caused by scene contexts, self intentions, destinations, etc. Although the predicted trajectories in Fig. 5(c), (d), (g), and (h) seems do not to agree to the ground truth, they might still be reasonable and safe for the pedestrians.

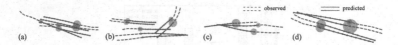

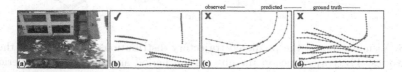

Fig. 7. Visualization of the predicted attention weights by FvTraj. Here, we visualize the average attention weights (green circles) of the four head attentions used in the social-aware attention module at T_{obs}. Note, the green circles' radii are proportional to the attention weights, the red circles represent the position of the focus pedestrian at T_{obs}, the red trajectories represent the focus pedestrian whose attention weights are predicted, and the blue trajectories represent the other pedestrians in the scene. (Color figure online)

Fig. 8. Visualization of learned attention weights by our view-aware attention module of 8 steps in observation period and simulated first-person view images by FvSim for 3 corresponding steps. Each scene shows at least one of the scenarios among pedestrians: meeting, following, and collision avoiding. The colored circles' radii are proportional to the attention weights, the red trajectories represent the focus pedestrian whose attention weights are predicted, and the blue trajectories show the other pedestrians.

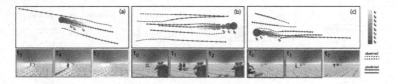

Fig. 9. Visualization of the predicted pedestrian trajectories using FvTraj for ZARA1. FvTraj is not optimized for the scene packed with large-scaled stationary obstacles, such as (a) ZARA1, shown in the top-down view. Here, (b) FvTraj can successfully predict the trajectories, (c) and (d) but sometimes may fail, especially for the cases that the pedestrians' intention changed dramatically to avoid the obstacles.

These predicted trajectories are more conservative in terms of safety, especially in meeting scenes to avoid potential and future collisions. This is of particular interest for some specific applications such as robotic navigation and blind navigation.

Figure 6 shows the predicted trajectory distribution in various scenes. Figures 6 (a) and (b) describe two meeting scenes with three pedestrians; Figs. 6(c) and (d) describe two meeting scenes with two pedestrians. We observe that: (1) the directions of the potential trajectories of a single pedestrian could be far apart (i.e., the pedestrian colored in green in Fig. 6(c), (2) the trajectories of neighboring pedestrians have been well considered, (3) pedestrian collision is unlikely to occur due to the inexistence of overlapping among the predicted trajectory distributions at any step, and (4) the variance of the predicted trajectory distribution is reduced with the increased probability of collisions occurring between pedestrians. Since these observed scenarios are likely to happen in real world, which suggests that FvTraj can well capture the fundamental factors including multimodality, social interactions, and scene contexts.

We visualize the learned attention weights (Fig. 7) using the social-aware attention module. We observe that social module assigns higher attention weights to the pedestrians: (1) who have relative small Euclidean distances from the focus pedestrians, (2) who move toward the focus pedestrians, and (3) whose observed trajectories are close to the focus pedestrians' observed trajectory. These observations implicitly address our safety concerns, which implies the social-aware attention module can well capture the social interactions within a scene.

The Contribution of First-Person View Information. Table 1 shows the comparison between our full-model FvTraj and FvTraj-noView, which is a model without first-person view information. Adding first-person view information to FvTraj leads to performance increases of 9.8% and 10.6% for average ADE and FDE, respectively. Figure 8 shows simulated first-person view images can well capture ego-motions for the focus pedestrians using learned attention weights by view-aware attention module. Ego-motions (i.e, the focus pedestrian's visual perspective effect on the neighbors and moving intentions) are important in trajectory prediction, which is difficult to capture using third-person view images or social-aware module (focusing on capturing historical motion and social patterns learned from numerical inputs). Combining the view-aware and the social-aware modules, FvTraj can well capture all these important features.

Failure Cases. Figure 9 shows the visual comparisons between the ground truth and the predicted trajectory using FvTraj for ZARA1. Although the differences between our predicted trajectories and the ground truth are not significantly noticeable for most of the cases (Fig. 9(b)), the differences in some specific cases (Fig. 9(c) and (d)) are noticeable. We observe that the effect of the stationary obstacles (e.g., buildings, parked vehicles) on pedestrians' trajectories in ZARA1 cannot be neglected. It seems that pedestrians intentionally maintain a relatively large distance from the stationary obstacles, which are not well captured in FvTraj. These qualitative results for ZARA1 are consistent with the qualitative results described in Sect. 4.1. These results suggest more work is required to understand the relationship between the stationary obstacles and the dynamic scene contexts, which motivates us to develop an advanced FvSim in our future work. Although current FvSim without any scene context may cause failure cases, simulation without scene contexts are universal and can be applicable to any scenes without any scene-related constraint.

5   Conclusion

This work presents a novel first-person view based trajectory prediction model, FvTraj. To obtain the first-person view information in an efficient way, we develop a simulator, FvSim, to generate a 3D simulated scenario with multi-view information including the first-person view, given the observed 2D trajectories. FvTraj takes into account historical motion patterns of pedestrians, social interactions, and the first-person view scene contexts, based on multi-head attention mechanisms to predict realistic and plausible trajectories. Our experimental results suggested that: (1) the first-person view information successfully introduces detailed dynamic scene contexts with ego-motions, (2) FvTraj is well structured for the pedestrian trajectory prediction task, and (3) FvTraj achieves state-of-the-art performance via comparisons with baseline models.

Acknowledgement. This work was supported in part by the National Key Research and Development Program of China under Grant 2018AAA0103000, 2017YFC0804900, and 2018YFB1700905, in part by the National Natural Science Foundation of China under Grant 61532002, 61972379, and 61702482. Zhigang Deng was in part supported by US NSF grant IIS-1524782.

References

1. Alahi, A., Goel, K., Ramanathan, V., Robicquet, A., Fei-Fei, L., Savarese, S.: Social LSTM: human trajectory prediction in crowded spaces. In: Proceedings of IEEE Conference on Computer Vision and Pattern Recognition (CVPR) (2016)
2. Amirian, J., Hayet, J.B., Pettré, J.: Social ways: learning multi-modal distributions of pedestrian trajectories with GANs. In: Proceedings of IEEE Conference on Computer Vision Pattern Recognition Workshops (CVPRW) (2019)
3. Antonini, G., Bierlaire, M., Weber, M.: Discrete choice models of pedestrian walking behavior. Transp. Res. Part B: Methodol. **40**(8), 667–687 (2006)
4. Ba, J.L., Kiros, J.R., Hinton, G.E.: Layer normalization. arXiv preprint arXiv:1607.06450 (2016)
5. Bagautdinov, T., Alahi, A., Fleuret, F., Fua, P., Savarese, S.: Social scene understanding: end-to-end multi-person action localization and collective activity recognition. In: Proceedings of IEEE Conference on Computer Vision and Pattern Recognition (CVPR), pp. 4315–4324 (2017)
6. Bertasius, G., Chan, A., Shi, J.: Egocentric basketball motion planning from a single first-person image. In: The IEEE Conference on Computer Vision and Pattern Recognition (CVPR), June 2018
7. Bi, H., Fang, Z., Mao, T., Wang, Z., Deng, Z.: Joint prediction for kinematic trajectories in vehicle-pedestrian-mixed scenes. In: Proceedings of IEEE International Conference on Computer Vision (ICCV) (2019)
8. Caesar, H., et al.: nuScenes: a multimodal dataset for autonomous driving. arXiv preprint arXiv:1903.11027 (2019)
9. Choi, C., Dariush, B.: Looking to relations for future trajectory forecast. In: Proceedings of IEEE International Conference on Computer Vision (ICCV) (2019)
10. Deng, J., Dong, W., Socher, R., Li, L.J., Li, F.F.: Imagenet: a large-scale hierarchical image database. In: 2009 IEEE Computer Society Conference on Computer Vision and Pattern Recognition (CVPR 2009), Miami, Florida, USA, 20–25 June 2009 (2009)
11. Felsen, P., Lucey, P., Ganguly, S.: Where will they go? Predicting fine-grained adversarial multi-agent motion using conditional variational autoencoders. In: The European Conference on Computer Vision (ECCV), September 2018

12. Geiger, A., Lenz, P., Stiller, C., Urtasun, R.: Vision meets robotics: the kitti dataset. Int. J. Robot. Res. **32**(11), 1231–1237 (2013)
13. Gupta, A., Johnson, J., Fei-Fei, L., Savarese, S., Alahi, A.: Social GAN: socially acceptable trajectories with generative adversarial networks. In: Proceedings of IEEE Conference on Computer Vision and Pattern Recognition (CVPR) (2018)
14. Hasan, I., Setti, F., Tsesmelis, T., Del Bue, A., Galasso, F., Cristani, M.: Mx-LSTM: mixing tracklets and vislets to jointly forecast trajectories and head poses. In: Proceedings of IEEE Conference on Computer Vision and Pattern Recognition (CVPR) (2018)
15. He, K., Zhang, X., Ren, S., Sun, J.: Deep residual learning for image recognition. CoRR abs/1512.03385 (2015). http://arxiv.org/abs/1512.03385
16. Helbing, D., Molnar, P.: Social force model for pedestrian dynamics. Phys. Rev. E **51**(5), 4282 (1995)
17. Huang, Y., Bi, H., Li, Z., Mao, T., Wang, Z.: STGAT: modeling spatial-temporal interactions for human trajectory prediction. In: Proceedings of IEEE International Conference on Computer Vision (ICCV) (2019)
18. Ivanovic, B., Pavone, M.: The trajectron: probabilistic multi-agent trajectory modeling with dynamic spatiotemporal graphs. In: Proceedings of IEEE International Conference on Computer Vision (ICCV) (2019)
19. Johnson, L.A., Higgins, C.M.: A navigation aid for the blind using tactile-visual sensory substitution. In: Proceedings of International Conference on IEEE Engineering in Medicine and Biology Society, pp. 6289–6292 (2006)
20. Kang, G., Lim, J., Zhang, B.: Dual attention networks for visual reference resolution in visual dialog. CoRR abs/1902.09368 (2019). http://arxiv.org/abs/1902.09368
21. Kantorovitch, J., Väre, J., Pehkonen, V., Laikari, A., Seppälä, H.: An assistive household robot-doing more than just cleaning. J. Assistive Technol. **8**(2), 64–76 (2014)
22. Kosaraju, V., Sadeghian, A., Martín-Martín, R., Reid, I., Rezatofighi, S.H., Savarese, S.: Social-bigat: multimodal trajectory forecasting using bicycle-GAN and graph attention networks. arXiv preprint arXiv:1907.03395 (2019)
23. Lai, G.Y., Chen, K.H., Liang, B.J.: People trajectory forecasting and collision avoidance in first-person viewpoint. In: 2018 IEEE International Conference on Consumer Electronics-Taiwan (ICCE-TW), pp. 1–2. IEEE (2018)
24. Lee, J.G., Han, J., Whang, K.Y.: Trajectory clustering: a partition-and-group framework. In: Proceedings of ACM SIGMOD International Conference on Management of Data, pp. 593–604 (2007)
25. Lee, N., Choi, W., Vernaza, P., Choy, C.B., Torr, P.H.S., Chandraker, M.: Desire: distant future prediction in dynamic scenes with interacting agents. In: Proceedings of IEEE Conference on Computer Vision and Pattern Recognition (CVPR) (2017)
26. Lerner, A., Chrysanthou, Y., Lischinski, D.: Crowds by example. In: Proceedings of Computer Graphics Forum, vol. 26, pp. 655–664 (2007)
27. Leung, T.S., Medioni, G.: Visual navigation aid for the blind in dynamic environments. In: Proceedings of IEEE Conference on Computer Vision and Pattern Recognition Workshops, pp. 565–572 (2014)
28. Liang, J., Jiang, L., Carlos Niebles, J., Hauptmann, A.G., Fei-Fei, L.: Peeking into the future: predicting future person activities and locations in videos. In: Proceedings of IEEE Conference on Computer Vision and Pattern Recognition (CVPR) (2019)

29. Ma, Y., Zhu, X., Zhang, S., Yang, R., Wang, W., Manocha, D.: Trafficpredict: trajectory prediction for heterogeneous traffic-agents. In: Proceedings of AAAI Conference on Artificial Intelligence, pp. 6120–6127 (2019)
30. Maddern, W., Pascoe, G., Linegar, C., Newman, P.: 1 year, 1000 km: the oxford robotcar dataset. Int. J. Robot. Res. **36**(1), 3–15 (2017)
31. Mehran, R., Oyama, A., Shah, M.: Abnormal crowd behavior detection using social force model. In: Proceedings of IEEE Conference on Computer Vision and Pattern Recognition (CVPR), pp. 935–942 (2009)
32. Morris, B., Trivedi, M.: Learning trajectory patterns by clustering: experimental studies and comparative evaluation. In: Proceedings of IEEE Conference on Computer Vision and Pattern Recognition (CVPR), pp. 312–319 (2009)
33. Patil, A., Malla, S., Gang, H., Chen, Y.: The H3D dataset for full-surround 3D multi-object detection and tracking in crowded urban scenes. CoRR abs/1903.01568 (2019). http://arxiv.org/abs/1903.01568
34. Pellegrini, S., Ess, A., Schindler, K., Van Gool, L.: You'll never walk alone: modeling social behavior for multi-target tracking. In: Proceedings of IEEE Conference on Computer Vision (ICCV), pp. 261–268 (2009)
35. Ramanishka, V., Chen, Y.T., Misu, T., Saenko, K.: Toward driving scene understanding: a dataset for learning driver behavior and causal reasoning. In: IEEE Conference on Computer Vision and Pattern Recognition, pp. 7699–7707 (2018)
36. Rios-Martinez, J., Spalanzani, A., Laugier, C.: From proxemics theory to socially-aware navigation: a survey. Int. J. Soc. Robot. **7**(2), 137–153 (2015)
37. Sadeghian, A., Kosaraju, V., Sadeghian, A., Hirose, N., Rezatofighi, H., Savarese, S.: Sophie: an attentive GAN for predicting paths compliant to social and physical constraints. In: Proceedings of IEEE Conference on Computer Vision and Pattern Recognition (CVPR) (2019)
38. Sadeghian, A., Legros, F., Voisin, M., Vesel, R., Alahi, A., Savarese, S.: Car-net: clairvoyant attentive recurrent network. In: Proceedings of European Conference on Computer Vision (ECCV), pp. 151–167 (2018)
39. Song, X., et al.: Apollocar3d: a large 3D car instance understanding benchmark for autonomous driving. CoRR abs/1811.12222 (2018). http://arxiv.org/abs/1811.12222
40. Soo Park, H., Hwang, J.J., Niu, Y., Shi, J.: Egocentric future localization. In: The IEEE Conference on Computer Vision and Pattern Recognition (CVPR), June 2016
41. Sutskever, I., Vinyals, O., Le, Q.V.: Sequence to sequence learning with neural networks. CoRR abs/1409.3215 (2014). http://arxiv.org/abs/1409.3215
42. Vaswani, A., et al.: Attention is all you need. CoRR abs/1706.03762 (2017). http://arxiv.org/abs/1706.03762
43. Vemula, A., Muelling, K., Oh, J.: Social attention: modeling attention in human crowds. In: Proceedings of IEEE International Conference on Robotics and Automation (ICRA), pp. 1–7 (2018)
44. Wang, X., Ma, K.T., Ng, G.W., Grimson, W.E.L.: Trajectory analysis and semantic region modeling using nonparametric hierarchical Bayesian models. Int. J. Computer Vision **95**(3), 287–312 (2011)
45. Wang, X., Ma, X., Grimson, W.E.L.: Unsupervised activity perception in crowded and complicated scenes using hierarchical Bayesian models. IEEE Trans. Pattern Anal. Mach. Intell. **31**(3), 539–555 (2009)
46. Xu, Y., Piao, Z., Gao, S.: Encoding crowd interaction with deep neural network for pedestrian trajectory prediction. In: Proceedings of IEEE Conference on Computer Vision and Pattern Recognition (CVPR) (2018)

47. Yagi, T., Mangalam, K., Yonetani, R., Sato, Y.: Future person localization in first-person videos. In: Proceedings of IEEE Conference on Computer Vision and Pattern Recognition (CVPR) (2018)
48. Yao, Y., Xu, M., Wang, Y., Crandall, D.J., Atkins, E.M.: Unsupervised traffic accident detection in first-person videos. CoRR abs/1903.00618 (2019). http://arxiv.org/abs/1903.00618
49. Zhang, P., Ouyang, W., Zhang, P., Xue, J., Zheng, N.: SR-LSTM: state refinement for LSTM towards pedestrian trajectory prediction. In: Proceedings of IEEE Conference on Computer Vision and Pattern Recognition (CVPR) (2019)

Multiple Expert Brainstorming for Domain Adaptive Person Re-Identification

Yunpeng Zhai[1,2], Qixiang Ye[3], Shijian Lu[4], Mengxi Jia[1], Rongrong Ji[5],
and Yonghong Tian[2(✉)]

[1] School of Electronic and Computer Engineering, Peking University, Beijing, China
{ypzhai,mxjia}@pku.edu.cn
[2] Department of Computer Science and Technology, Peking University,
Beijing, China
yhtian@pku.edu.cn
[3] University of Chinese Academy of Sciences, Beijing, China
qxye@ucas.ac.cn
[4] Nanyang Technological University, Singapore, Singapore
shijian.lu@ntu.edu.sg
[5] Xiamen University, Xiamen, China
rrji@xmu.edu.cn

Abstract. Often the best performing deep neural models are ensembles of multiple base-level networks, nevertheless, ensemble learning with respect to domain adaptive person re-ID remains unexplored. In this paper, we propose a multiple expert brainstorming network (MEB-Net) for domain adaptive person re-ID, opening up a promising direction about model ensemble problem under unsupervised conditions. MEB-Net adopts a mutual learning strategy, where multiple networks with different architectures are pre-trained within a source domain as expert models equipped with specific features and knowledge, while the adaptation is then accomplished through brainstorming (mutual learning) among expert models. MEB-Net accommodates the heterogeneity of experts learned with different architectures and enhances discrimination capability of the adapted re-ID model, by introducing a regularization scheme about authority of experts. Extensive experiments on large-scale datasets (Market-1501 and DukeMTMC-reID) demonstrate the superior performance of MEB-Net over the state-of-the-arts. Code is available at https://github.com/YunpengZhai/MEB-Net.

Keywords: Domain adaptation · Person re-ID · Ensemble learning

1 Introduction

Person re-identification (re-ID) aims to match persons in an image gallery collected from non-overlapping camera networks [14,16,40]. It has attracted increasing interest from the computer vision community thanks to its wide applications

© Springer Nature Switzerland AG 2020
A. Vedaldi et al. (Eds.): ECCV 2020, LNCS 12352, pp. 594–611, 2020.
https://doi.org/10.1007/978-3-030-58571-6_35

in security and surveillance. Though supervised re-ID methods have achieved very decent results, they often experience catastrophic performance drops while applied to new domains. Domain adaptive person re-ID that can well generalize across domains remains an open research challenge.

Unsupervised domain adaptation (UDA) in re-ID has been studied extensively in recent years. Most existing works can be broadly grouped into three categories. The first category attempts to align feature distributions between source and target domains [35,39], aiming to minimize the inter-domain gap for optimal adaptation. The second category addresses the domain gap by employing generative adversarial networks (GAN) for converting sample images from a source domain to a target domain while preserving the person identity as much as possible [5,22,24,36]. To leverage the target sample distribution, the third category adopts self-supervised learning and clustering to predict pseudo-labels of target-domain samples iteratively to fine-tune re-ID models [7,8,15,30,37,43]. Nevertheless, the optimal performance is often achieved by ensemble that integrates multiple sub-networks and their discrimination capability. However, ensemble learning in domain adaptive re-ID remains unexplored. How to leverage specific features and knowledge of multiple networks and optimally adapt them to an unlabelled target domain remains to be elaborated.

In this paper, we present an multiple expert brainstorming network (MEB-Net), which learns and adapts multiple networks with different architectures for optimal re-ID in an unlabelled target domain. MEB-Net conducts iterative training where clustering for pseudo-labels and models feature learning are alternately executed. For feature learning, MEB-Net adopts a mutual learning strategy where networks with different architectures are pre-trained in a source domain as expert models equipped with specific features and knowledge. The adaptation is accomplished through brainstorming-based mutual learning among multiple expert models. To accommodate the heterogeneity of experts learned with different architectures, a regularization scheme is introduced to modulate the experts' authority according to their feature distributions in the target domain, and further enhances the discrimination capability of the re-ID model.

The contributions of this paper are summarized as follows.

- We propose a novel multiple expert brainstorming network (MEB-Net) based on mutual learning among expert models, each of which is equipped with knowledge of an architecture.
- We design an authority regularization to accommodate the heterogeneity of experts learned with different architectures, modulating the authority of experts and enhance the discrimination capability of re-ID models.
- Our MEB-Net approach achieves significant performance gain over the state-of-the-art on commonly used datasets: Market-1501 and DukeMTMC-reID.

2   Related Works

2.1   Unsupervised Domain Adaptive Re-ID

Unsupervised domain adaptation (UDA) for person re-ID defines a learning problem for target domains where source domains are fully labeled while sample labels in target domains are totally unknown. Methods have been extensively explored in recent years, which take three typical approaches as follows.

Feature Distribution Alignment. In [21], Lin *et al.* proposed minimizing the distribution variation of the source's and the target's mid-level features based on Maximum Mean Discrepancy (MMD) distance. Wang *et al.* [35] utilized additional attribute annotations to align feature distributions of source and target domains in a common space.

Image-Style Transformation. GAN-based methods have been extensively explored for domain adaptive person re-ID [5,22,24,36,49]. HHL [49] simultaneously enforced cameras invariance and domain connectedness to improve the generalization ability of models on the target set. PTGAN [36], SPGAN [5], ATNet [22] and PDA-Net [18] transferred images with identity labels from source into target domains to learn discriminative models.

Self-supervised Learning. Recently, the problem about how to leverage the large number of unlabeled samples in target domains have attracted increasing attention [7,23,37,38,41,44,50]. Clustering [7,43,46] and graph matching [41] methods have been explored to predict pseudo-labels in target domains for discriminative model learning. Reciprocal search [23] and exemplar-invariance approaches [38] were proposed to refine pseudo labels, taking camera-invariance into account concurrently. SSG [8] utilized both global and local feature of persons to build multiple clusters, which are then assigned pseudo-labels to supervise the model training.

However, existing works barely explored the domain adaptive person re-ID task using methods of model ensemble, which have achieved impressive performance on many other tasks.

2.2   Knowledge Transfer

Distilling knowledge from well trained neural networks and transferring it to another model/network has been widely studied in recent years [1–3,11,19,42]. The typical approach of knowledge transfer is the teacher-student model learning, which uses the soft output distribution of a teacher network to supervise a student network, so as to make student models learn discrimination ability from teacher models.

The mean-teacher model [33] averaged model weights at different training iterations to create supervisions for unlabeled samples. Deep mutual learning [45] adopted a pool of student models by training them with supervision from each other. Mutual mean teaching [9] designed a symmetrical framework with hard

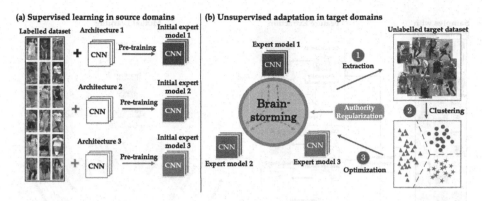

Fig. 1. Overview of proposed multiple expert brainstorming network (MEB-Net). Multiple expert networks with different architectures are first pre-trained in the source domain and then adapted to the target domain through brainstorming.

pseudo-labels as well as refined soft labels for unsupervised domain adaptive re-ID. However, existing methods with teacher-student mechanisms mostly adopted a symmetrical framework which largely neglected the different confidence of teacher networks when they are heterogeneous.

2.3 Model Ensemble

There is a considerable number of previous works on ensembles with neural networks. A typical approach [13,29,31,34] generally create a series of networks with shared weights during training and then implicitly ensemble them at test time. Another approach [28] focus on label refinery by well trained networks for training a new model with higher discrimination capability. However, these methods cannot be directly used on unsupervised domain adaptive re-ID tasks, where the training set and the testing set share non-overlapping label space.

3 The Proposed Approach

We study the problem of unsupervised domain adaptive re-ID using model ensemble methods from a source-domain to a target-domain. The labelled source-domain dataset are denoted as $S = \{X_s, Y_s\}$, which has N_s sample images with M_s unique identities. X_s and Y_s denote the sample images and the person identities, where each sample x_s in X_s is associated with a person identity y_s in Y_s. The N_t sample images in the target-domain $T = \{X_t\}$ have no identity available. We aim to leverage the labelled sample images in S and the unlabelled sample images in T to learn a transferred re-ID model for the target-domain T.

3.1 Overview

MEB-Net adopts a two-stage training scheme including supervised learning in source domains (Fig. 1a) and unsupervised adaptation to target domains

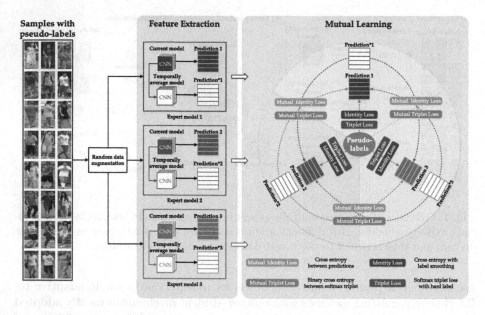

Fig. 2. Flowchart of proposed expert brainstorming in MEB-Net, which consists of two components, feature extraction and mutual learning. In mutual learning, multiple expert networks are organized to collaboratively learn from each other by their predictions and the pseudo-labels, and improve themselves for the target domain in an unsupervised mutual learning manner. More details are described in Sect. 3.4.

(Fig. 1b). In the initialization phase, multiple expert models with different network architectures are pre-trained by the source dataset in a supervised manner. Afterwards the trained experts are adapted to the target domain by iteratively brainstorming with each other using the unlabelled target-domain samples. In each iterative epoch, pseudo-labels are predicted for target samples via clustering which are then utilized to fine-tune the expert networks by mutual learning. In addition, the authority regularization is employed to modulate the authority of expert networks according to their discrimination capability during training. In this way, the knowledge from multiple networks is fused, enhanced, and transferred to the target domain, as described in Algorithm 1.

3.2   Learning in Source Domains

The proposed MEB-Net aims to transfer the knowledge of multiple networks from a labelled source domain to an unlabelled target domain. For each architecture, a deep neural network (DNN) model $\mathcal{M}^k$ parameterized with θ^k (a pre-trained expert) is first trained in a supervised manner. $\mathcal{M}^k$ transforms each sample image $x_{s,i}$ into a feature representation $f(x_{s,i}|\theta^k)$, and outputs a predicted probability $p_j(x_{s,i}|\theta^k)$ of image $x_{s,i}$ belonging to the identity j. The cross

---

Algorithm 1. Multiple Expert Brainstorming Network

Input: Source domain dataset $\mathcal{S} = \{X_s, Y_s\}$, target domain dataset $\mathcal{T} = \{X_t\}$.
Input: K network architectures $\{\mathcal{A}^k\}$.
Output: Expert model parameters $\{\theta^k\}$.
 1: Initialize pre-trained weights θ^k of model $\mathcal{M}^k$ with each architecture $\mathcal{A}^k$.
 2: **for** each epoch **do**
 3:    Extract average features on $\mathcal{T}$: $f(X_t) = \frac{1}{K} \sum_{k=1}^{K} f(X_t|\Theta^k)$.
 4:    Generate pseudo-labels $\widetilde{Y}_t$ of X_t by clustering samples using $f(X_t)$.
 5:    Evaluate authority w of each expert model by inter-/intra-cluster scatter.
 6:    **for** each iteration T, mini-batch $\mathcal{B} \subset \mathcal{T}$ **do**
 7:       Calculate soft-labels from each temporally average model with $\{\Theta_T^k\}$:
          $p(x_{t,i \in \mathcal{B}}|\Theta_T^k)$, $\mathcal{P}_{i \in \mathcal{B}}(\Theta_T^k)$.
 8:       Calculate output of each current model with $\{\theta^k\}$: $p(x_{t,i \in \mathcal{B}}|\theta^k)$, $\mathcal{P}_{i \subset \mathcal{B}}(\theta^k)$.
 9:       Update parameters $\{\theta^k\}$ by optimizing Eq. 14 with authority $\{w^e\}$.
10:       Update temporally average model weights $\{\Theta_T^k\}$ following Eq. 4.
11:    **end for**
12: **end for**
13: **Return** Expert model parameters $\{\theta^k\}$

---

entropy loss with label smoothing is defined as

$$\mathcal{L}_{s,id}^k = \frac{1}{N_s} \sum_{i=1}^{N_s} \sum_{j=1}^{M_s} q_j \log p_j(x_{s,i}|\theta^k) \tag{1}$$

where $q_j = 1 - \varepsilon + \frac{\varepsilon}{M_s}$ if $j = y_{s,i}$, otherwise $q_j = \frac{\varepsilon}{M_s}$. ε is a small constant, which is set as 0.1. The softmax triplet loss is also defined as

$$\mathcal{L}_{s,tri}^k = -\frac{1}{N_s} \sum_{i=1}^{N_s} \log \frac{e^{\|f(x_{s,i}|\theta^k) - f(x_{s,i-}|\theta^k)\|}}{e^{\|f(x_{s,i}|\theta^k) - f(x_{s,i+}|\theta^k)\|} + e^{\|f(x_{s,i}|\theta^k) - f(x_{s,i-}|\theta^k)\|}} \tag{2}$$

where $x_{s,i+}$ denotes the hardest positive sample of the anchor $x_{s,i}$, and $x_{s,i-}$ denotes the hardest negative sample. $\| \cdot \|$ denotes the L_2 distance. The overall loss is therefore calculated as

$$\mathcal{L}_s^k = \mathcal{L}_{s,id}^k + \mathcal{L}_{s,tri}^k. \tag{3}$$

With K network architectures, the supervised learning thus produces K pre-trained re-ID models each of which acts as an expert for brainstorming.

3.3 Clustering in the Target Domain

In the target domain, MEB-Net consists of a clustering-based pseudo-label generation procedure and a feature learning procedure, which are mutually enforced. Each epoch consists of three steps: (1) For sample images in the target domain, each expert model extracts convolutional features $f(X_t|\theta^k)$ and determines the ensemble features by averaging features extracted by multiple expert models $f(X_t) = \frac{1}{K}\sum_{k=1}^{K} f(X_t|\theta^k)$; (2) A mini-batch k-means clustering is performed on $f(X_t)$ to classify all target-domain samples into M_t different clusters; (3) The produced cluster IDs are used as pseudo-labels $\widetilde{Y}_t$ for the training samples X_t. The steps 3 and 4 in Algorithm 1 summarize this clustering process.

3.4   Expert Brainstorming

With multiple expert models $\{\mathcal{M}^k\}$ with different architectures which absorb rich knowledge from the source domain, MEB-Net aims to organize them to collaboratively learn from each other and improve themselves for the target domain in an unsupervised mutual learning manner, Fig. 2.

In each training iteration, the same batch of images in the target domain are first fed to all the expert models $\{\mathcal{M}^k\}$ parameterized by $\{\theta^k\}$, to predict the classification confidence predictions $\{p(x_{t,i}|\theta^k)\}$ and feature representations $\{f(x_{t,i}|\theta^k)\}$. To transfer knowledge from one expert to others, the class predictions of each expert can serve as soft class labels for training other experts. However, directly using the current predictions as soft labels to train each model decreases the independence of expert models' outputs, which might result in an error amplification. To avoid this error, MEB-Net leverages the temporally average model of each expert model, which preserves more original knowledge, to generate reliable soft pseudo labels for supervising other experts. The parameters of the temporally average model of expert $\mathcal{M}^k$ at current iteration T are denoted as Θ_T^k, which is updated as

$$\Theta_T^k = \alpha\Theta_{T-1}^k + (1-\alpha)\theta^k, \tag{4}$$

where $\alpha \in [0,1]$ is the scale factor, and the initial temporal average parameters are $\Theta_0^k = \theta^k$. Utilizing this temporal average model of expert $\mathcal{M}^e$, the probability for each identity j is predicted as $p_j(x_{t,i}|\Theta_T^e)$, and the feature representation is calculated as $f(x_{t,i}|\Theta_T^e)$.

Mutual Identity Loss. For each expert model $\mathcal{M}^k$, the mutual identity loss of models learned by a certain expert $\mathcal{M}^e$ is defined as the cross entropy between the class prediction of the expert $\mathcal{M}^k$ and the temporal average model of the expert $\mathcal{M}^e$, as

$$\mathcal{L}_{mid}^{k\leftarrow e} = -\frac{1}{N_t}\sum_{i=1}^{N_t}\sum_{j=1}^{M_t} p_j(x_{t,i}|\Theta_T^e)\log p_j(x_{t,i}|\theta^k). \tag{5}$$

The mutual identity loss for expert $\mathcal{M}^k$ is set as the average of above losses of models learned by all other experts, as

$$\mathcal{L}_{mid}^k = \frac{1}{K-1}\sum_{e\neq k}^{K}\mathcal{L}_{mid}^{k\leftarrow e} \tag{6}$$

Mutual Triplet Loss. For each expert model $\mathcal{M}^k$, the mutual triplet loss of models learned by a certain expert $\mathcal{M}^e$ is also defined as binary cross entropy, as

$$\mathcal{L}_{mtri}^{k \leftarrow e} = -\frac{1}{N_t} \sum_{i=1}^{N_t} \left[\mathcal{P}_i(\Theta_T^e) \log \mathcal{P}_i(\theta^k) + (1 - \mathcal{P}_i(\Theta_T^e)) \log(1 - \mathcal{P}_i(\theta^k)) \right], \quad (7)$$

where $\mathcal{P}_i(\theta^k)$ denotes the softmax of the feature distance between negative sample pairs:

$$\mathcal{P}_i(\theta^k) = \frac{e^{\|f(x_{t,i}|\theta^k)-f(x_{t,i-}|\theta^k)\|}}{e^{\|f(x_{t,i}|\theta^k)-f(x_{t,i+}|\theta^k)\|} + e^{\|f(x_{t,i}|\theta^k)-f(x_{t,i-}|\theta^k)\|}}, \quad (8)$$

where $x_{t,i+}$ denotes the hardest positive sample of the anchor $x_{t,i}$ according to the pseudo-labels $\widetilde{Y}_t$, and $x_{t,i-}$ denotes the hardest negative sample. $\|\cdot\|$ denotes L_2 distance. The mutual triplet loss for expert $\mathcal{M}^k$ is calculated as the average of above triplet losses of models learned by all other experts, as

$$\mathcal{L}_{mtri}^k = \frac{1}{K-1} \sum_{e \neq k}^K \mathcal{L}_{mtri}^{k \leftarrow e}, \quad (9)$$

Voting Loss. In order to learn stable and discriminative knowledge from the pseudo-labels obtained by clustering as described in Sect. 3.3, we introduce voting loss which consists of the identity loss and the triplet loss. For each expert model $\mathcal{M}^k$, the identity loss is defined as cross entropy with label smoothing, as

$$\mathcal{L}_{id}^k = \frac{1}{N_t} \sum_{i=1}^{N_t} \sum_{j=1}^{M_t} q_j \log p_j(x_{t,i}|\theta^k), \quad (10)$$

where $q_j = 1 - \varepsilon + \frac{\varepsilon}{M_t}$ if $j = \widetilde{y}_{t,i}$, otherwise $q_j = \frac{\varepsilon}{M_t}$. ε is small constant. The softmax triplet loss is defined as:

$$\mathcal{L}_{tri}^k = -\frac{1}{N_t} \sum_{i=1}^{N_t} \log \frac{e^{\|f(x_{t,i}|\theta^k)-f(x_{t,i-}|\theta^k)\|}}{e^{\|f(x_{t,i}|\theta^k)-f(x_{t,i+}|\theta^k)\|} + e^{\|f(x_{t,i}|\theta^k)-f(x_{t,i-}|\theta^k)\|}}, \quad (11)$$

where $x_{t,i+}$ denotes the hardest positive sample of the anchor $x_{t,i}$, and $x_{t,i-}$ denotes the hardest negative sample. $\|\cdot\|$ denotes L_2 distance. The voting loss is defined by summarizing the identity loss and the triplet loss:

$$\mathcal{L}_{vot}^k = \mathcal{L}_{id}^k + \mathcal{L}_{tri}^k, \quad (12)$$

Overall Loss. For each expert model $\mathcal{M}^k$, the individual brainstorming loss is defined by

$$\mathcal{L}_{bs}^k = \mathcal{L}_{mid}^k + \mathcal{L}_{mtri}^k + \mathcal{L}_{vot}^k, \quad (13)$$

The overall loss is defined by the sum loss of the individual brainstorming for each expert model.

$$\mathcal{L}_{meb} = \sum_{k=1}^K \mathcal{L}_{bs}^k. \quad (14)$$

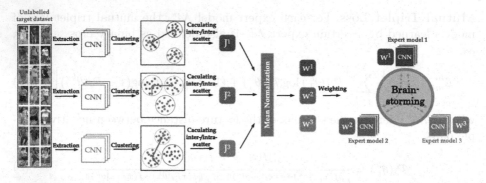

Fig. 3. Illustration of our proposed authority regularization. It modulates the authority of different experts according to the inter-/intra-cluster scatter of each single expert. A larger scatter means better discrimination capability.

3.5   Authority Regularization

Expert networks with different architectures are equipped with various knowledge, and thus have different degrees of discrimination capability in the target domain. To accommodate the heterogeneity of experts, we propose an authority regularization (AR) scheme, which modulates the authority of different experts according to the inter-/intra-cluster scatter of each single expert, Fig. 3. Specifically, for each expert $\mathcal{M}$ we extract sample features $f(x|\Theta_T)$ and cluster all the training samples in the target domain into M_t groups as $\mathbb{C}$. The intra-cluster scatter of the cluster $\mathbb{C}_i$ is defined as

$$S_{intra}^i = \sum_{x \in \mathbb{C}_i} \|f(x|\Theta_T) - \mu_i\|^2, \tag{15}$$

where $\mu_i = \sum_{x \in \mathbb{C}_i} f(x|\Theta_T)/n_t^i$ is the average feature of the cluster $\mathbb{C}_i$ (with n_t^i samples). The inter-cluster scatter is defined as

$$S_{inter} = \sum_{i=1}^{M_t} n_i^t \|\mu_i - \mu\|^2, \tag{16}$$

where $\mu = \sum_{i=1}^{N_t} f(x_{t,i}|\Theta_T)/N_t$ is the average feature of all training samples in the target domain. To evaluate the discrimination of each expert model in the unlabeled target domain, the inter-/intra-cluster scatter J is defined as

$$J = \frac{S_{inter}}{\sum_{i=1}^{M_t} S_{intra}^i}. \tag{17}$$

J gets larger when the inter-cluster scatter is larger or the intra-cluster scatter is smaller. And a larger J means better discrimination capability. Before feature learning in each epoch, we calculate J scatter for each expert $\mathcal{M}^e$ as J^e, and defined expert authority w^e as the mean normalization of J^e, as

$$w^e = \frac{J^e}{\sum_{k=1}^{K} J^k / K} = \frac{K J^e}{\sum_{k=1}^{K} J^k}. \tag{18}$$

We re-define the mutual identity loss in Eq. 6 and the mutual triplet loss in Eq. 9 as the weighted sum of $\mathcal{L}_{mid}^{k \leftarrow e}$ and $\mathcal{L}_{mtri}^{k \leftarrow e}$ for other experts, as

$$\mathcal{L}_{mid}^{k} = \frac{1}{K-1} \sum_{e \neq k}^{K} w^e \mathcal{L}_{mid}^{k \leftarrow e}, \tag{19}$$

and

$$\mathcal{L}_{mtri}^{k} = \frac{1}{K-1} \sum_{e \neq k}^{K} w^e \mathcal{L}_{mtri}^{k \leftarrow e}. \tag{20}$$

With the regularization scheme, MEB-Net modulates the authority of experts to facilitate discrimination in the target domain.

4   Experiments

4.1   Datasets and Evaluation Metrics

We evaluate the proposed method on Market-1501 [47] and DukeMTMC-reID [27,48].

Market-1501: This dataset contains 32,668 images of 1,501 identities from 6 disjoint cameras, among which 12,936 images from 751 identities form a training set, 19,732 images from 750 identities (plus a number of distractors) form a gallery set, and 3,368 images from 750 identities form a query set.

DukeMTMC-reID: This dataset is a subset of the DukeMTMC. It consists of 16,522 training images, 2,228 query images, and 17,661 gallery images of 1,812 identities captured using 8 cameras. Of the 1812 identities, 1,404 appear in at least two cameras and the rest (distractors) appear in a single camera.

Evaluation Metrics: In evaluations, we use one dataset as the target domain and the other as the source domain. The used metrics are Cumulative Matching Characteristic (CMC) curve and mean average precision (mAP).

4.2   Implementation Details

MEB-Net is trained by two stages: *pre-training in source domains* and the *adaptation in target domains*.

Stage 1: Pre-training in Source Domains: We first pre-train three supervised expert models on the source dataset as described in Sect. 3.2. We adopt three architectures: DenseNet-121 [12], ResNet-50 [10] and Inception-v3 [32] as backbone networks for the three experts, and initialize them by using parameters pre-trained on the ImageNet [4]. Zero padding is employed on the final features to obtain representations of the same 2048 dimensions for all networks. During training, the input image is resized to 256×128 and traditional image augmentation was performed via random flipping and random erasing. For each identity from the training set, a mini-batch of 64 is sampled with $P = 16$ randomly selected identities and $K = 4$ randomly sampled images for computing the hard batch triplet loss. We use the Adam [17] with weight decay 0.0005 to optimize parameters. The initial learning rate is set to 0.00035 and is decreased to $1/10$ of its previous value on the 40th and 70th epoch in the total 80 epochs.

Stage 2: Adaptation in Target Domains. For unsupervised adaptation on target datasets, we follow the same data augmentation strategy and triplet loss setting. The temporal ensemble momentum α in Eq. 4 is set to 0.999. The learning rate is fixed to 0.00035 for overall 40 epochs. In each epoch, we conduct mini-batch k-means clustering and the number of groups M_t is set as 500 for all target datasets. Each epoch consists of 800 training iterations. During testing, we only use one expert network for feature representations.

4.3   Comparison with State-of-the-Arts

We compare MEB-Net with state-of-the-art methods including: hand-crafted feature approaches (LOMO[20], BOW[47], UMDL[25]), feature alignment based methods (MMFA[21], TJ-AIDL[35], UCDA-CCE[26]), GAN-based methods (SPGAN [5], ATNet[22], CamStyle[51], HHL[49], ECN[50] and PDA-Net[18]), pseudo-label prediction based methods (PUL[6], UDAP[30], PCB-PAST[44], SSG[8] MMT[9]). Table 1 shows the person Re-ID performance while adapting from Market1501 to DukeMTMC-reID and vice versa.

Hand-Crafted Feature Approaches. As Table 1 shows, MEB-Net outperforms hand-crafted feature approaches including LOMO, BOW and UMDL by large margins, as deep network can learn more discriminative representations than hand-crafted features.

Feature Alignment Approaches. MEB-Net significantly exceeds the feature alignment unsupervised Re-ID models. The reason lies in that it explores and utilizes the similarity between unlabelled sample in target domains in an more effective manner of brainstorming.

GAN-Based Approaches. The performance of these approaches is diverse. In particular, ECN performs better than most methods using GANs because it enforces cameras in-variance as well as latent sample relations. However, MEB-Net can achieve higher performance than GAN-based methods without generating new images, which indicates its more efficient use of the unlabelled samples.

Pseudo-labels Based Approaches. The line of approaches perform clearly better than other approaches in most cases, as they fully make use of the unlabelled target samples by assigning pseudo-labels to them according to

Table 1. Comparison with state-of-the-art methods: For the adaptation on Market-1501 and that on DukeMTMC-reID. The top-three results are highlighted with bold, italic, and underline fonts, respectively.

Methods	Market-1501				DukeMTMC-reID			
	mAP	R-1	R-5	R-10	mAP	R-1	R-5	R-10
LOMO [20]	8.0	27.2	41.6	49.1	4.8	12.3	21.3	26.6
Bow [47]	14.8	35.8	52.4	60.3	8.3	17.1	28.8	34.9
UMDL [25]	12.4	34.5	52.6	59.6	7.3	18.5	31.4	37.6
MMFA [21]	27.4	56.7	75.0	81.8	24.7	45.3	59.8	66.3
TJ-AIDL [35]	26.5	58.2	74.8	81.1	23.0	44.3	59.6	65.0
UCDA-CCE [26]	30.9	60.4	–	–	31.0	47.7	–	–
ATNet [22]	25.6	55.7	73.2	79.4	24.9	45.1	59.5	64.2
SPGAN+LMP [5]	26.7	57.7	75.8	82.4	26.2	46.4	62.3	68.0
CamStyle [51]	27.4	58.8	78.2	84.3	25.1	48.4	62.5	68.9
HHL [49]	31.4	62.2	78.8	84.0	27.2	46.9	61.0	66.7
ECN [50]	43.0	75.1	87.6	91.6	40.4	63.3	75.8	80.4
PDA-Net [18]	47.6	75.2	86.3	90.2	45.1	63.2	77.0	82.5
PUL [6]	20.5	45.5	60.7	66.7	16.4	30.0	43.4	48.5
UDAP [30]	53.7	75.8	89.5	93.2	49.0	68.4	80.1	83.5
PCB-PAST [44]	54.6	78.4	–	–	54.3	72.4	–	–
SSG [8]	<u>58.3</u>	<u>80.0</u>	<u>90.0</u>	<u>92.4</u>	<u>53.4</u>	<u>73.0</u>	<u>80.6</u>	<u>83.2</u>
MMT-500[9]	*71.2*	*87.7*	*94.9*	*96.9*	*63.1*	*76.8*	*88.0*	*92.2*
MEB-Net(Ours)	**76.0**	**89.9**	**96.0**	**97.5**	**66.1**	**79.6**	**88.3**	**92.2**

sample feature similarities. For a fair comparison, we report MMT-500 with the cluster number of 500, which is the same as the proposed MEB-Net. As Table 1 shows, MEB-Net achieves an mAP of 76.0% and a rank-1 accuracy of 89.9% for the DukeMTMC-reID→Market1501 transfer, which outperforms the state-of-the-art (by MMT-500) by 4.8% and 2.2%, respectively. And for Market1501→DukeMTMC-reID transfer, MEB-Net obtains an mAP of 66.1% and a rank-1 accuracy of 79.6% which outperforms the state-of-the-art by 3.0% and 2.8%, respectively.

4.4 Ablation Studies

Detailed ablation studies are performed to evaluate the components of MEB-Net as shown in Table 2.

Supervised Models vs. Direct Transfer. We first derive the upper and lower performance bounds by the supervised models (trained using labelled target-domain images) and the direct transfer models (trained using labelled source-domain images) for the ablation studies as shown in Table 2. We evaluate all

Table 2. Ablation studies: *Supervised Models:* - Re-ID models trained using the labelled target-domain training images. *Direct Transfer:* - Re-ID models trained by labelled source-domain training images. $\mathcal{L}_{vot}$ (Eq. 12), Θ_T (Eq. 4), $\mathcal{L}_{mid}$ (Eq. 6) and $\mathcal{L}_{mtri}$ (Eq. 9) are described in Sect. 3.4. *AR:* Authority Regularization as described in Sect. 3.5.

Methods	Market-1501				DukeMTMC-reID			
	mAP	R-1	R-5	R-10	mAP	R-1	R-5	R-10
Supervised models	82.5	93.7	98.1	98.5	67.1	82.1	90.0	92.1
Direct Transfer	31.5	60.6	75.7	80.8	29.7	46.5	61.8	67.7
Baseline(Only $\mathcal{L}_{vot}$)	69.5	86.8	94.9	96.6	60.6	75.0	85.5	89.4
MEB-Net w/o Θ_T	70.7	87.1	94.8	96.7	58.3	72.6	83.6	88.5
MEB-Net w/o $\mathcal{L}_{mid}$	70.2	87.9	94.8	96.6	60.4	75.0	86.1	89.3
MEB-Net w/o $\mathcal{L}_{mtri}$	74.9	88.4	95.8	97.7	63.0	76.6	87.3	90.8
MEB-Net w/o AR	75.5	89.3	95.9	97.4	65.4	77.9	88.9	91.9
MEB-Net	76.0	89.9	96.0	97.5	66.1	79.6	88.3	92.2

three architectures and report the best results in Table 2. It can be observed that the huge performance gaps between the Direct Transfer models and the Supervised Models due to the domain shift.

Voting Loss: We create baseline ensemble models that only use voting loss. Specifically, pseudo-labels are predicted by averaging the features outputted from all expert networks, and then used to supervise the training of each expert network individually by optimizing the voting loss. As Table 1 shows, the Baseline model outperforms the Direct Transfer model by a large margin. This shows that the voting loss effectively make use of the ensemble models to predict more accurate pseudo-labels and fine-tune each network.

Temporally Average Networks: The model removing the temporally average models is denoted as "MEB-Net w/o Θ_T". For this experiment, we directly use the prediction of the current networks parameterized by θ_T instead of the temporally average networks with parameters Θ_T as soft labels. As Table 2 shows, distinct drops of 5.3% mAP and 2.8% rank-1 accuracy are observed for Market1501→DukeMTMC-reID transfer. Without using temporally average models, networks tend to degenerate to be homogeneous, which substantially decreases the learning capability.

Effectiveness of Mutual Learning: We evaluate the mutual learning component in Sect. 3.4 from two aspects: the mutual identity loss and the mutual triplet loss. The former is denoted as "MEB-Net w/o $\mathcal{L}_{mid}$". Results show that mAP drops from 76.0% to 70.2% on Market-1501 dataset and from 66.1% to 60.4% on DukeMTMC-reID dataset. Similar drops can also be observed when studying the mutual triplet loss, which are denoted as "MEB-Net w/o $\mathcal{L}_{mtri}$". For example, the mAP drops to 74.9% and 63.0% for DukeMTMC-reID→Market-1501 and vice versa, respectively. The effectiveness of the mutual learning, including both two mutual loss, can be largely attributed to that it enhances the discrimination capability of all expert networks.

Authority Regularization: We verify the effectiveness of the proposed authority regularization (Sect. 3.5) of MEB-Net. Specifically, we remove the authority regularization, and set authority $w = 1$ (in Eq. 19 and Eq. 20) equally for all expert models. The model is denoted as "MEB-Net w/o AR", of which the results are shown in Table 1. Experiments without authority regularization shows distinct drops on both Market-1501 and DukeMTMC-reID datasets, which indicates that equivalent brainstorming among experts hinders feature discrimination because an unprofessional expert may provide erroneous supervision.

Table 3. mAP (%) of networks of different architectures for DukeMTMC-reID → Market-1501 transfer: *Supervised* - supervised models; *Dire. tran.* - direct transfer; *Sing. tran.* - single model transfer; *Base. ens.* - baseline ensemble.

Architectures	Supervised	Dire. tran	Sing. tran	Base. ens	MEB-Net
DenseNet-121	**80.0**	30.8	57.8	69.5	<u>76.0</u>
ResNet-50	**82.5**	31.5	62.4	65.6	<u>72.2</u>
Inception-v3	**68.3**	28.5	51.5	62.3	<u>71.3</u>

4.5 Discussion

Comparison with Baseline Ensemble

Considering that ensemble models usually achieve more superior performance than a single model, we compare mAPs of our approach with other baseline methods, including single model transfer and baseline model ensemble. Results are shown in Table. 3. The baseline model ensemble uses all networks to extract average features of unlabelled samples for pseudo-label prediction, but without mutual learning among them while adaptation in the target domain. The improvement of baseline ensemble than single model transfer is because of more accurate pseudo-labels. However, MEB-Net performs significantly better than all compared methods. It validates that MEB-Net provides a more effective ensemble method with respect to domain adaptive person re-ID.

Number of Epochs. We evaluate the mAP of MEB-Net after each epoch, respectively. As shown in Fig. 4, the models become stronger when the iterative clustering proceeds. The performance is improved in early epochs, and finally converges after 20 epochs for both datasets.

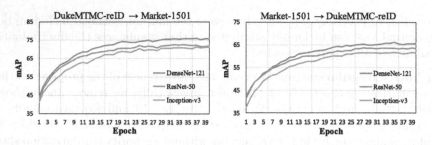

Fig. 4. Evaluation with different *epoch*. The performance of all networks ascend to a stable value after 20 epochs.

5 Conclusion

The paper proposed a multiple expert brainstorming network (MEB-Net) for domain adaptive person re-ID. MEB-Net adopts a mutual learning strategy, where networks of each architecture are pre-trained to initialize several expert models while the adaptation is accomplished through brainstorming (mutual learning) among expert models. Furthermore, an authority regularization scheme was introduced to tackle the heterogeneity of experts. Experiments demonstrated the effectiveness of MEB-Net for improving the discrimination ability of re-ID models. Our approach efficiently assembled discrimination capability of multiple networks while requiring solely a single model during inference time throughout.

Acknowledgement. This work is partially supported by grants from the National Key R&D Program of China under grant 2017YFB1002400, the National Natural Science Foundation of China (NSFC) under contract No. 61825101, U1611461 and 61836012.

References

1. Anil, R., Pereyra, G., Passos, A., Ormandi, R., Dahl, G.E., Hinton, G.E.: Large scale distributed neural network training through online distillation. arXiv preprint arXiv:1804.03235 (2018)
2. Bagherinezhad, H., Horton, M., Rastegari, M., Farhadi, A.: Label refinery: improving ImageNet classification through label progression. arXiv preprint arXiv:1805.02641 (2018)
3. Chen, T., Goodfellow, I., Shlens, J.: Net2Net: accelerating learning via knowledge transfer. arXiv preprint arXiv:1511.05641 (2015)
4. Deng, J., Dong, W., Socher, R., Li, L., Li, K., Li, F.: ImageNet: a large-scale hierarchical image database. In: IEEE CVPR (2009)
5. Deng, W., Zheng, L., Ye, Q., Kang, G., Yang, Y., Jiao, J.: Image-image domain adaptation with preserved self-similarity and domain-dissimilarity for person re-identification. In: IEEE CVPR (2018)
6. Fan, H., Zheng, L., Yan, C., Yang, Y.: Unsupervised person re-identification: clustering and fine-tuning. TOMCCAP **14**(4), 83:1–83:18 (2018)

7. Fan, H., Zheng, L., Yang, Y.: Unsupervised person re-identification: clustering and fine-tuning. CoRR abs/1705.10444 (2017)
8. Fu, Y., Wei, Y., Wang, G., Zhou, Y., Shi, H., Huang, T.S.: Self-similarity grouping: a simple unsupervised cross domain adaptation approach for person re-identification. In: Proceedings of the IEEE International Conference on Computer Vision (ICCV), pp. 6112–6121 (2019)
9. Ge, Y., Chen, D., Li, H.: Mutual mean-teaching: pseudo label refinery for unsupervised domain adaptation on person re-identification. arXiv preprint arXiv:2001.01526 (2020)
10. He, K., Zhang, X., Ren, S., Sun, J.: Deep residual learning for image recognition. In: The IEEE Conference on Computer Vision and Pattern Recognition (CVPR), June 2016
11. Hinton, G., Vinyals, O., Dean, J.: Distilling the knowledge in a neural network. arXiv preprint arXiv:1503.02531 (2015)
12. Huang, G., Liu, Z., Van Der Maaten, L., Weinberger, K.Q.: Densely connected convolutional networks. In: Proceedings of the IEEE Conference on Computer Vision and Pattern Recognition (CVPR), pp. 4700–4708 (2017)
13. Huang, G., Sun, Yu., Liu, Z., Sedra, D., Weinberger, K.Q.: Deep networks with stochastic depth. In: Leibe, B., Matas, J., Sebe, N., Welling, M. (eds.) ECCV 2016. LNCS, vol. 9908, pp. 646–661. Springer, Cham (2016). https://doi.org/10.1007/978-3-319-46493-0_39
14. Jia, M., Zhai, Y., Lu, S., Ma, S., Zhang, J.: A similarity inference metric for RGB-infrared cross-modality person re-identification. In: IJCAI 2020, June 2020
15. Jin, X., Lan, C., Zeng, W., Chen, Z.: Global distance-distributions separation for unsupervised person re-identification. arXiv preprint arXiv:2006.00752 (2020)
16. Jin, X., Lan, C., Zeng, W., Chen, Z., Zhang, L.: Style normalization and restitution for generalizable person re-identification. In: Proceedings of the IEEE/CVF Conference on Computer Vision and Pattern Recognition, pp. 3143–3152 (2020)
17. Kingma, D.P., Ba, J.: Adam: a method for stochastic optimization. arXiv preprint arXiv:1412.6980 (2014)
18. Li, Y.J., Lin, C.S., Lin, Y.B., Wang, Y.C.F.: Cross-dataset person re-identification via unsupervised pose disentanglement and adaptation. In: Proceedings of the IEEE International Conference on Computer Vision (ICCV), pp. 7919–7929 (2019)
19. Li, Y., Yang, J., Song, Y., Cao, L., Luo, J., Li, L.J.: Learning from noisy labels with distillation. In: Proceedings of the IEEE International Conference on Computer Vision (ICCV), pp. 1910–1918 (2017)
20. Liao, S., Hu, Y., Zhu, X., Li, S.Z.: Person re-identification by local maximal occurrence representation and metric learning. In: The IEEE Conference on Computer Vision and Pattern Recognition (CVPR), June 2015
21. Lin, S., Li, H., Li, C., Kot, A.C.: Multi-task mid-level feature alignment network for unsupervised cross-dataset person re-identification. In: BMVC (2018)
22. Liu, J., Zha, Z.J., Chen, D., Hong, R., Wang, M.: Adaptive transfer network for cross-domain person re-identification. In: IEEE CVPR (2019)
23. Liu, Z., Wang, D., Lu, H.: Stepwise metric promotion for unsupervised video person re-identification. In: IEEE ICCV, pp. 2448–2457 (2017)
24. Lv, J., Wang, X.: Cross-dataset person re-identification using similarity preserved generative adversarial networks. In: Liu, W., Giunchiglia, F., Yang, B. (eds.) KSEM, pp. 171–183 (2018)
25. Peng, P., et al.: Unsupervised cross-dataset transfer learning for person re-identification. In: The IEEE Conference on Computer Vision and Pattern Recognition (CVPR), June 2016

26. Qi, L., Wang, L., Huo, J., Zhou, L., Shi, Y., Gao, Y.: A novel unsupervised camera-aware domain adaptation framework for person re-identification. In: Proceedings of the IEEE International Conference on Computer Vision (ICCV), pp. 8080–8089 (2019)

27. Ristani, E., Solera, F., Zou, R.S., Cucchiara, R., Tomasi, C.: Performance measures and a data set for multi-target, multi-camera tracking. In: IEEE ECCV Workshops (2016)

28. Shen, Z., He, Z., Xue, X.: Meal: Multi-model ensemble via adversarial learning. In: Proceedings of the AAAI Conference on Artificial Intelligence, vol. 33, pp. 4886–4893 (2019)

29. Singh, S., Hoiem, D., Forsyth, D.: Swapout: Learning an ensemble of deep architectures. In: Advances in Neural Information Processing Systems, pp. 28–36 (2016)

30. Song, L., et al.: Unsupervised domain adaptive re-identification: Theory and practice. CoRR abs/1807.11334 (2018)

31. Srivastava, N., Hinton, G., Krizhevsky, A., Sutskever, I., Salakhutdinov, R.: Dropout: a simple way to prevent neural networks from overfitting. J. Mach. Learn. Res. **15**(1), 1929–1958 (2014)

32. Szegedy, C., Vanhoucke, V., Ioffe, S., Shlens, J., Wojna, Z.: Rethinking the inception architecture for computer vision. In: Proceedings of the IEEE Conference on Computer Vision and Pattern Recognition (CVPR), pp. 2818–2826 (2016)

33. Tarvainen, A., Valpola, H.: Mean teachers are better role models: weight-averaged consistency targets improve semi-supervised deep learning results. In: Advances in Neural Information Processing Systems, pp. 1195–1204 (2017)

34. Wan, L., Zeiler, M., Zhang, S., Le Cun, Y., Fergus, R.: Regularization of neural networks using dropconnect. In: International Conference on Machine Learning, pp. 1058–1066 (2013)

35. Wang, J., Zhu, X., Gong, S., Li, W.: Transferable joint attribute-identity deep learning for unsupervised person re-identification. In: IEEE CVPR (2018)

36. Wei, L., Zhang, S., Gao, W., Tian, Q.: Person transfer GAN to bridge domain gap for person re-identification. In: IEEE CVPR (2018)

37. Wu, J., Liao, S., Lei, Z., Wang, X., Yang, Y., Li, S.Z.: Clustering and dynamic sampling based unsupervised domain adaptation for person re-identification. In: IEEE ICME, pp. 886–891 (2019)

38. Wu, Y., Lin, Y., Dong, X., Yan, Y., Ouyang, W., Yang, Y.: Exploit the unknown gradually: one-shot video-based person re-identification by stepwise learning. In: IEEE CVPR (2018)

39. Yang, F., et al.: Part-aware progressive unsupervised domain adaptation for person re-identification. IEEE Trans. Multimed. (2020)

40. Yang, F., Yan, K., Lu, S., Jia, H., Xie, X., Gao, W.: Attention driven person re-identification. Pattern Recogn. **86**, 143–155 (2019)

41. Ye, M., Ma, A.J., Zheng, L., Li, J., Yuen, P.C.: Dynamic label graph matching for unsupervised video re-identification. In: IEEE ICCV, pp. 5152–5160 (2017)

42. Yim, J., Joo, D., Bae, J., Kim, J.: A gift from knowledge distillation: fast optimization, network minimization and transfer learning. In: Proceedings of the IEEE Conference on Computer Vision and Pattern Recognition (CVPR), pp. 4133–4141 (2017)

43. Zhai, Y., Lu, S., Ye, Q., Shan, X., Chen, J., Ji, R., Tian, Y.: Ad-cluster: augmented discriminative clustering for domain adaptive person re-identification. In: IEEE/CVF Conference on Computer Vision and Pattern Recognition (CVPR), June 2020

44. Zhang, X., Cao, J., Shen, C., You, M.: Self-training with progressive augmentation for unsupervised cross-domain person re-identification. In: Proceedings of the IEEE International Conference on Computer Vision (ICCV), pp. 8222–8231 (2019)
45. Zhang, Y., Xiang, T., Hospedales, T.M., Lu, H.: Deep mutual learning. In: Proceedings of the IEEE Conference on Computer Vision and Pattern Recognition (CVPR), pp. 4320–4328 (2018)
46. Zheng, L., et al.: MARS: a video benchmark for large-scale person re-identification. In: Leibe, B., Matas, J., Sebe, N., Welling, M. (eds.) ECCV 2016. LNCS, vol. 9910, pp. 868–884. Springer, Cham (2016). https://doi.org/10.1007/978-3-319-46466-4_52
47. Zheng, L., Shen, L., Tian, L., Wang, S., Wang, J., Tian, Q.: Scalable person re-identification: a benchmark. In: The IEEE International Conference on Computer Vision (ICCV), December 2015
48. Zheng, Z., Zheng, L., Yang, Y.: Unlabeled samples generated by GAN improve the person re-identification baseline in vitro. In: IEEE ICCV (2017)
49. Zhong, Z., Zheng, L., Li, S., Yang, Y.: Generalizing a person retrieval model hetero- and homogeneously. In: Ferrari, V., Hebert, M., Sminchisescu, C., Weiss, Y. (eds.) ECCV 2018. LNCS, vol. 11217, pp. 176–192. Springer, Cham (2018). https://doi.org/10.1007/978-3-030-01261-8_11
50. Zhong, Z., Zheng, L., Luo, Z., Li, S., Yang, Y.: Invariance matters: exemplar memory for domain adaptive person re-identification. In: IEEE CVPR (2019)
51. Zhong, Z., Zheng, L., Zheng, Z., Li, S., Yang, Y.: CamStyle: a novel data augmentation method for person re-identification. IEEE TIP **28**(3), 1176–1190 (2019)

NASA
Neural Articulated Shape Approximation

Boyang Deng[1]([✉]), J. P. Lewis[1], Timothy Jeruzalski[1], Gerard Pons-Moll[2], Geoffrey Hinton[1], Mohammad Norouzi[1], and Andrea Tagliasacchi[1,3]

[1] Google Research, Mountain View, USA
bydeng@google.com
[2] MPI for Informatics, Saarland Informatics Campus, Saarbrücken, Germany
[3] University of Toronto, Toronto, Canada

Abstract. Efficient representation of articulated objects such as human bodies is an important problem in computer vision and graphics. To efficiently simulate deformation, existing approaches represent 3D objects using polygonal meshes and deform them using skinning techniques. This paper introduces neural articulated shape approximation (NASA), an alternative framework that enables representation of articulated deformable objects using neural indicator functions that are conditioned on pose. Occupancy testing using NASA is straightforward, circumventing the complexity of meshes and the issue of water-tightness. We demonstrate the effectiveness of NASA for 3D tracking applications, and discuss other potential extensions.

Keywords: 3D deep learning · Neural object representation · Articulated objects · Deformation · Skinning · Occupancy · Neural implicit functions

1 Introduction

There has been a surge of recent interest in representing 3D geometry using implicit functions parameterized by neural networks [10,20,37,39]. Such representations are flexible, continuous, and differentiable. Neural implicit functions are useful for "inverse graphics" pipelines for scene understanding [54], as back propagation through differentiable representations of 3D geometry is often required. That said, neural models of *articulated* objects have received little attention. Articulated objects are particularly important to represent animals and humans, which are central in many applications such as computer games and animated movies, as well as augmented and virtual reality.

Although parametric models of human body such as SMPL [33] have been integrated into neural network frameworks for self-supervision [27,38,40,53],

Electronic supplementary material The online version of this chapter (https://doi.org/10.1007/978-3-030-58571-6_36) contains supplementary material, which is available to authorized users.

© Springer Nature Switzerland AG 2020
A. Vedaldi et al. (Eds.): ECCV 2020, LNCS 12352, pp. 612–628, 2020.
https://doi.org/10.1007/978-3-030-58571-6_36

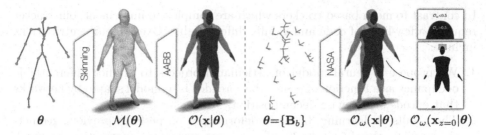

Fig. 1. Teaser – (left) Traditional articulated models map pose parameters θ to a polygonal mesh $\mathcal{M}(\theta)$ via linear blend skinning; if one desires to *query* the occupancy of this representation, acceleration data structures need to be computed (e.g. axis align bounding box tree). (right) Conversely, NASA learns an *implicit* neural occupancy $\mathcal{O}_\omega$, which can be queried directly.

these approaches depend heavily on polygonal mesh representations. Mesh representations require expert supervision to construct, and are not flexible for capturing topology variations. Furthermore, geometric representations often should fulfill several purposes simultaneously such as modeling the surface for rendering, or representing the volume to test intersections with the environment, which are not trivial when polygonal meshes are used [24]. Although neural models have been used in the context of articulated deformation [3], they *relegate* query execution to classical acceleration data structures, thus sacrificing full differentiability (Fig. 1).

Our method represents articulated objects with a neural model, which outputs a differentiable occupancy of the articulated body in a specific pose. Like previous geometric learning efforts [9,12,37,39], we represent geometry by *indicator functions* – also referred to as *occupancy* functions – that evaluate to 1 inside the object and 0 otherwise. Unlike previous approaches, which focused on collections of static objects described by (unknown) shape parameters, we look at learning indicator functions as we vary *pose parameters*, which will be discovered by training on animation sequences. We show that existing methods [9,37,39] cannot encode pose variation reliably, because it is hard to learn the occupancy of every point in space as a function of a latent pose vector.

Instead, we introduce NASA, a neural decoder that exploits the structure of the underlying deformation driving the articulated object. Exploiting the fact that 3D geometry in *local* body part coordinates does not significantly change with pose, we classify the occupancy of 3D points as seen from the coordinate frame of each part. Our main architecture combines a collection of per-part learnable indicator functions with a per-part pose encoder to model localized non-rigid deformations. This leads to a significant boost in generalization to unseen poses, while retaining the useful properties of existing methods: differentiability, ease of spatial queries such as intersection testing, and continuous surface outputs. To demonstrate the flexibility of NASA, we use it to track point clouds by finding the maximum likelihood estimate of the pose under NASA's occupancy model.

In contrast to mesh based trackers which are complex to implement, our tracker requires a few lines of code and is fully differentiable. Overall, our contributions include:

1. We propose a neural model of articulated objects to predict differentiable occupancy as a function of pose – the core idea is to model shapes by networks that encode a piecewise decomposition;
2. The results on learning 3D body deformation outperform previous geometric learning algorithms [9,39,39], and our surface reconstruction accuracy approaches that of mesh-based statistical body models [33];
3. The differentiable occupancy supports constant-time queries (.06 ms/query on an NVIDIA GTX 1080), avoiding the need to convert to separate representations, or the dynamic update of spatial acceleration data structures;
4. We derive a technique that employs occupancy functions for tracking 3D geometry via an implicit occupancy template, without the need to ever compute distance functions.

2   Related Work

Neural articulated shape approximation provides a single framework that addresses problems that have previously been approached separately. The related literature thus includes a number of works across several different research topics.

Skinning Algorithms. Efficient articulated deformation is traditionally accomplished with a skinning algorithm that deforms vertices of a mesh surface as the joints of an underlying abstract skeleton change. The classic linear blend skinning (LBS) algorithm expresses the deformed vertex as a weighted sum of that vertex rigidly transformed by several adjacent bones; see [23] for details. LBS is widely used in computer games, and is a core ingredient of some popular vision models [33]. Mesh sequences of general (not necessarily articulated) deforming objects have also been represented with skinning for the purposes of compression and manipulation, using a collection of non-hierarchical "bones" (i.e. transformations) discovered with clustering [25,30]. LBS has well-known disadvantages: the deformation has a simple algorithmic form that cannot produce pose-dependent detail, it results in characteristic volume-loss effects such as the "collapsing elbow" and "candy wrapper" artifacts [31, Figs. 2, 3], and for best results the weights must be *manually* painted by artists. It is possible to add pose-dependent detail with a shallow or deep net regression [3,31], but this process operates as a correction to classical LBS deformation.

Object Intersection Queries. Registration, template matching, 3D tracking, collision detection, and other tasks require efficient inside/outside tests. A disadvantage of polygonal meshes is that they do not efficiently support these queries, as meshes often contain thousands of individual triangles that must be tested for each query. This has led to the development of a variety of spatial data structures to accelerate point-object queries [32,43], including voxel grids, octrees, kdtrees, and others. In the case of deforming objects, the spatial data structure must

Fig. 2. Notation – (left) The ground truth occupancy $\mathcal{O}(\mathbf{x}|\bar{\boldsymbol{\theta}})$ in the rest frame and the pose parameters $\bar{\boldsymbol{\theta}} \equiv \{\bar{\mathbf{B}}_b\}_{b=1}^{B}$ representing the transformations of B bones. (right) T frames of an animation associated with pose parameters $\{\boldsymbol{\theta}_t\}_{t=1}^{T}$ with corresponding occupancy $\{\mathcal{O}(\mathbf{x}|\boldsymbol{\theta}_t)\}_{t=1}^{T}$; each $\boldsymbol{\theta}_t$ encodes the transformations of B bones. Note we shorthand $\{*_y\}$ to indicate an ordered set $\{*_y\}_{y=1}^{Y}$.

be repeatedly rebuilt as the object deforms. A further problem is that typically meshes may be constructed (or deformed) without regard to being "watertight" and thus do not have a clearly defined interior [24].

Part-Based Representations. For object intersection queries on articulated objects, it can be more efficient to approximate the overall shape in terms of a moving collection of rigid parts, such as spheres or ellipsoids, that support efficient querying [41]; see **supplementary material** for further discussion. Unfortunately this has the drawback of introducing a second approximate representation that does not exactly match the originally desired deformation. A further core challenge, and subject of continuing research, is the automatic creation of such *part-based* representations [1,19,21]. Unsupervised part discovery has been recently tackled by a number of deep learning approaches [8,12,13,17,34]. In general these methods address analysis and correspondence across shape collections, but do not target accurate representations of articulated objects, and do not account for pose-dependent deformations.

Neural Implicit Object Representation. Finally, several recent works represent objects with neural implicit functions [9,37,39]. These works focus on the neural representation of *static* shapes in an *aligned* canonical frame and do not target the modeling of transformations. Our core contributions are to show that these architectures have difficulties in representing complex and detailed *articulated* objects (e.g. human bodies), and that a simple architectural change can address these shortcomings. Comparisons to these closely related works will be revisited in more depth in Sect. 6.

3   Neural Articulated Shape Approximation

This paper investigates the use of neural networks and implicit functions for modeling articulated shapes in $\mathbb{R}^d$. Let $\boldsymbol{\theta}$ denotes a vector representing the pose of an articulated shape, and let $\mathcal{O}: \mathbb{R}^d \rightarrow \{0,1\}$ denotes an occupancy function defining the exterior and interior of an articulated body. We are interested in modeling the joint distribution of pose and occupancy, which can be decomposed using the chain rule into a conditional occupancy term, and a pose prior term:

$$p(\boldsymbol{\theta}, \mathcal{O}) = p(\mathcal{O}|\boldsymbol{\theta})\,p(\boldsymbol{\theta}) \tag{1}$$

This paper focuses on building an expressive model of $p(\mathcal{O}|\boldsymbol{\theta})$, that is, occupancy conditioned on pose. Figure 2 illustrates this problem for $d = 2$, and clarifies the notation. There is extensive existing research on pose priors $p(\boldsymbol{\theta})$ for human bodies and other articulated objects [4,27,48]. Our work is orthogonal to such prior models, and any parametric or non-parametric $p(\boldsymbol{\theta})$ can be combined with our $p(\mathcal{O}|\boldsymbol{\theta})$ to obtain the joint distribution $p(\boldsymbol{\theta}, \mathcal{O})$. We delay the discussion of pose priors until Sect. 5.2, where we define a particularly simple prior that nevertheless supports sophisticated tracking of moving humans.

In what follows we describe different ways of building a pose conditioned occupancy function, denoted $\mathcal{O}_\omega(\mathbf{x}|\boldsymbol{\theta})$, which maps a 3D point $\mathbf{x}$ and a pose $\boldsymbol{\theta}$ onto a real valued occupancy value. Our goal is to learn a parametric occupancy $\mathcal{O}_\omega(\mathbf{x}|\boldsymbol{\theta})$ that mimics a ground truth occupancy $\mathcal{O}(\mathbf{x}|\boldsymbol{\theta})$ as closely as possible, based on the following probabilistic interpretation:

$$p(\mathcal{O}|\boldsymbol{\theta}) \propto \prod_{\mathbf{x}\in\mathbb{R}^d} \exp\{-(\mathcal{O}_\omega(\mathbf{x}|\boldsymbol{\theta}) - \mathcal{O}(\mathbf{x}|\boldsymbol{\theta}))^2\}\,, \tag{2}$$

where we assume a standard normal distribution around the predicted real valued occupancy $\mathcal{O}_\omega(\mathbf{x}|\boldsymbol{\theta})$ to score an occupancy $\mathcal{O}(\mathbf{x}|\boldsymbol{\theta})$.

We are provided with a collection of T ground-truth occupancies $\{\mathcal{O}(\mathbf{x}|\boldsymbol{\theta}_t)\}_{t=1}^T$ associated with T poses. With a slight abuse of notation, we will henceforth use $\mathbf{x}$ to represent both a vector in $\mathbb{R}^d$, and its $\mathbb{R}^{d+1}$ homogeneous representation $[\mathbf{x}; 1]$. In our formulation, each pose parameter $\boldsymbol{\theta}$ represents a set of B *posed* bones/transformations, i.e., $\boldsymbol{\theta} \equiv \{\mathbf{B}_b\}_{b=1}^B$. To help disambiguate the part-whole relationship, we also assume that for each mesh vertex $v \in \mathbf{V}$, the body part associations $\mathbf{w}(v)$ are available, where $\mathbf{w}(v) \in [0, 1]^B$ with $\|\mathbf{w}(v)\|_1 = 1$.

Given pose parameters $\boldsymbol{\theta}$, we desire to query the corresponding indicator function $\mathcal{O}(\mathbf{x}|\boldsymbol{\theta})$ at a point $\mathbf{x}$. This task is more complicated than might seem, as in the general setting this operation requires the computation of generalized winding numbers to resolve ambiguous configurations caused by self-intersections and non-necessarily watertight geometry [24]. However, when given a database of poses $\boldsymbol{\Theta} = \{\boldsymbol{\theta}_t\}_{t=1}^T$ and corresponding *ground truth* indicator $\{\mathcal{O}(\mathbf{x}|\boldsymbol{\theta}_t)\}_{t=1}^T$, we can formulate our problem as the minimization of the objective:

$$\mathcal{L}_{\text{occupancy}}(\omega) = \sum_{\boldsymbol{\theta}\in\boldsymbol{\Theta}} \mathbb{E}_{\mathbf{x}\sim p(\mathbf{x})}\left[(\mathcal{O}(\mathbf{x}|\boldsymbol{\theta}) - \mathcal{O}_\omega(\mathbf{x}|\boldsymbol{\theta}))^2\right] \tag{3}$$

where $p(\mathbf{x})$ is a density representing the sampling distribution of points in $\mathbb{R}^d$ (Sect. 4.4) and $\mathcal{O}_\omega$ is a neural network with parameters ω that represents our *neural articulated shape approximator*. We adopt a sampling distribution $p(\mathbf{x})$ that randomly samples in the volume surrounding a posed character, along with additional samples in the vicinity of the deformed surface.

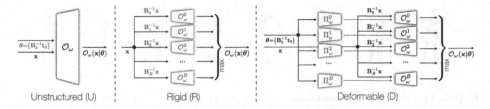

Fig. 3. The three architectures for $p(\mathcal{O}|\theta)$. The unstructured model employs a global MLP conditioned on pose, the rigid model expresses geometry as a composition of B *rigid* elements, while the deformable model via a composition of B *deformable* elements; we highlight the differences between models in red. (Color figure online)

4   Pose Conditioned Occupancy $\mathcal{O}(\mathbf{x}|\theta)$

We investigate several neural architectures for the problem of articulated shape approximation; see Fig. 3. We start by introducing an unstructured architecture (U) in Sect. 4.1. This baseline variant does not explicitly encode the knowledge of articulated deformation. However, typical articulated deformation models [33] express deformed mesh vertices $\mathbf{V}$ reusing the information stored in rest vertices $\bar{\mathbf{V}}$. Hence, we can assume that computing the function $\mathcal{O}(\mathbf{x}|\theta)$ in the deformed pose can be done by reasoning about the information stored at rest pose $\mathcal{O}(\mathbf{x}|\bar{\theta})$. Taking inspiration from this observation, we investigate two different architecture variants, one that models geometry via a *piecewise-rigid* assumption (Sect. 4.2), and one that relaxes this assumption and employs a *quasi-rigid* decomposition, where the shape of each element can deform according to the pose (Sect. 4.3); see Fig. 4.

4.1   Unstructured Model – "U"

Recently, a series of papers [9,37,39] tackled the problem of modeling occupancy across shape datasets as $\mathcal{O}_\omega(\mathbf{x}|\beta)$, where β is a latent code learned to encode the shape. These techniques employ deep and fully connected networks, which one can adapt to our setting by replacing the shape β with pose parameters θ, and using a neural network that takes as input $[\mathbf{x}, \theta]$. Leaky ReLU activations are used for inner layers of the neural net and a sigmoid activation is used for the final output so that the occupancy prediction lies in the $[0, 1]$ range.

To provide pose information to the network, one can simply concatenate the set of affine bone transformations to the query point to obtain $[\mathbf{x}, \{\mathbf{B}_b\}]$ as the input. This results in an input tensor of size $3 + 16 \times B$. Instead, we propose to represent pose as $\{\mathbf{B}_b^{-1}\mathbf{t}_0\}$, where $\mathbf{t}_0$ is the translation vector of the *root* bone in homogeneous coordinates, resulting in a smaller input of size $3 + 3 \times B$; we ablate this choice against other alternatives in the **supplementary material**. Our unstructured baseline takes the form:

$$\mathcal{O}_\omega(\mathbf{x}|\theta) = \text{MLP}_\omega(\mathbf{x}, \underbrace{\{\mathbf{B}_b^{-1}\mathbf{t}_0\}}_{\text{pose}}) \qquad (4)$$

Fig. 4. Our NASA representation models an articulated object as a collection of *deformable* components. The shape of each component is controlled by the pose of the subject, in a way that take inspiration from pose-space correctives [31].

4.2   Piecewise Rigid Model – "R"

The simplest structured deformation model for articulated objects assumes objects can be represented via a *piecewise rigid* composition of elements; e.g. [36, 41]:

$$\mathcal{O}(\mathbf{x}|\boldsymbol{\theta}) = \max_b \{\mathcal{O}^b(\mathbf{x}|\boldsymbol{\theta})\} \tag{5}$$

We observe that if these elements are related to corresponding rest-pose elements through the rigid transformations $\{\mathbf{B}_b\}$, then it is possible to *query* the corresponding rest-pose indicator as:

$$\mathcal{O}_\omega(\mathbf{x}|\boldsymbol{\theta}) = \max_b \{\bar{\mathcal{O}}_\omega^b(\mathbf{B}_b^{-1}\mathbf{x})\} \tag{6}$$

where, similar to (4), we can represent each of components via a *learnable* indicator $\bar{\mathcal{O}}_\omega^b(.) = \mathrm{MLP}_\omega^b(.)$. This formulation assumes that the local shape of each learned bone component stays *constant* across the range of poses when viewed from the corresponding coordinate frame, which is only a crude approximation of the deformation in realistic characters, and other deformable shapes.

4.3   Piecewise Deformable Model – "D"

We can generalize our models by combining the model of (4) to the one in (6), hence allowing the shape of each element to be *adjusted* according to pose:

$$\mathcal{O}_\omega(\mathbf{x}|\boldsymbol{\theta}) = \max_b \{\bar{\mathcal{O}}_\omega^b(\underbrace{\mathbf{B}_b^{-1}\mathbf{x}}_{\text{query}}|\boldsymbol{\theta})\} \tag{7}$$

Similar to (6) we use a *collection* of learnable indicator functions in rest pose $\{\mathcal{O}_\omega^b\}$, and to encode pose conditionals we take inspiration from (4). More specifically, we express our model as:

$$\mathcal{O}_\omega(\mathbf{x}|\boldsymbol{\theta}) = \max_b \{\bar{\mathcal{O}}_\omega^b(\mathbf{B}_b^{-1}\mathbf{x}, \underbrace{\Pi_\omega^b\left[\{\mathbf{B}_b^{-1}\mathbf{t}_0\}\right]}_{\text{part-specific pose}})\} \tag{8}$$

Similarly to (6), we model $\bar{\mathcal{O}}_\omega^b(.)$ via dense layers $\mathrm{MLP}_\omega^b : \mathbb{R}^{3+D} \to \mathbb{R}$. The operator $\Pi_\omega^b : \mathbb{R}^{B \times 3} \to \mathbb{R}^D$ is a learnable *linear* subspace projection – one per each bone b.

This choice is driven by the intuition that in typical skinned deformation models only *small subset* of the coordinate frames affect the deformation of a part. We employ $D = 4$ throughout, see ablations in the supplementary material. Our experiments reveal that this bottleneck greatly improves generalization.

4.4   Technical Details

The overall training loss for our model is:

$$\mathcal{L}(\omega) = \mathcal{L}_{\text{occupancy}}(\omega) + \lambda\mathcal{L}_{\text{weights}}(\omega) \tag{9}$$

where $\lambda = 5e^{-1}$ was found through hyper-parameter tuning. We now detail the weights auxiliary loss, the architecture backbones, and the training procedure.

Auxiliary Loss – Skinning Weights. As most deformable models are equipped with skinning weights, we exploit this additional source of information to facilitate learning of the part-based models (i.e. "R" and "D"). We label each mesh vertex $\mathbf{v}$ with the index of the corresponding highest skinning weight value $b^*(v) = \arg\max_b w(v)[b]$, and use the loss:

$$\mathcal{L}_{\text{weights}}(\omega) = \tfrac{1}{V}\tfrac{1}{B}\sum_{\theta\in\Theta}\sum_{\mathbf{v}}\sum_{b}\left(\bar{\mathcal{O}}_\omega^b(\mathbf{v}|\boldsymbol{\theta}) - \mathcal{I}_b(\mathbf{v})\right)^2 \tag{10}$$

where $\mathcal{I}_b(\mathbf{v}) = 0.5$ when $b = b^*$, and $\mathcal{I}_b(\mathbf{v}) = 0$ otherwise – recall that by convention the 0.5 level set is the surface represented by the occupancy function. Without such a loss, we could end up in the situation where a single (deformable) part could end up being used to describe the entire deformable model, and the trivial solution (zero) would be returned for all other parts.

Network Architectures. To keep our experiments comparable across baselines, we use the same network architecture for all the models while varying the *width* of the layers. The network backbone is similar to DeepSDF [39], but simplified to 4 layers. Each layer has a residual connection, and uses the Leaky ReLU activation function with the leaky factor 0.1. All layers have the *same* number of neurons, which we set to 960 for the unstructured model and 40 for the structured ones. For the piecewise (6) and deformable (8) models the neurons are distributed across $B = 24$ different channels (note $B \times 40 = 960$). Similar to the use of grouped filters/convolutions [22,29], such a structure allows for significant performance boosts compared to unstructured models (4), as the different branches can be executed in *parallel* on separate compute devices.

Training. All models are trained with the Adam optimizer, with batch size 12 and learning rate $1e - 4$. For better gradient propagation, we use *softmax* whenever a max was employed in our expressions. For each optimization step, we use 1024 points sampled uniformly within the bounding box and 1024 points sampled near the ground truth surface. We also sample 2048 vertices out of 6890 mesh vertices at each step for $\mathcal{L}_{weights}$. The models are trained for 200K iterations for approximately 6 h on a single NVIDIA Tesla V100.

5   Dense Articulated Tracking

Following the probabilistic interpretation of Sect. 3, we introduce an application
of NASA to dense articulated 3D *tracking*; see [47]. Note that this section does
not claim to beat the state-of-the-art in tracking of deformable objects [44,51,
52], but rather it seeks to show *how* neural occupancy functions can be used
effectively in the development of dense tracking techniques. Taking the negative
log of the joint probability in (1), the tracking problems can be expressed as the
minimization of a pair of energies [47]:

$$\arg \min_{\boldsymbol{\theta}^{(t)}} E_{\text{fit}}(\mathbf{D}^{(t)}, \boldsymbol{\theta}^{(t)}) + E_{\text{prior}}(\boldsymbol{\theta}^{(t)}) \qquad (11)$$

where $\mathbf{D} = \{\mathbf{x}_n\}_{n=1}^N$ is a point cloud in $\mathbb{R}^d$, and the superscript (t) indicates the
point cloud and the pose associated with the tth frame. The optimization for $\boldsymbol{\theta}^{(t)}$
is initialized with the minimizer computed at frame $(t-1)$. We also assume $\boldsymbol{\theta}^{(0)}$
is provided as ground truth, but discriminative models could also be employed to
obtain an initialization [27,45]. In what follows, we often drop the (t) superscript
for clarity of notation. We now discuss different aspects of this problem when
an implicit representation of the model is used, including the implementation
of fitting (Sect. 5.1) and prior (Sect. 5.2) energies, as well as details about the
iterative optimization scheme (Sect. 5.3).

5.1   Fitting Energy

If we could compute the Signed Distance Function (SDF) Φ of an occupancy $\mathcal{O}$
at a query point $\mathbf{x}$, then the fitness of $\mathcal{O}$ to input data could be measured as:

$$E_{\text{fit}}(\mathbf{D}, \boldsymbol{\theta}) = \sum_{\mathbf{x} \in \mathbf{D}} \|\Phi(\mathbf{x}|\mathcal{O}, \boldsymbol{\theta})\|^2 \qquad (12)$$

The time complexity of computing SDF from an occupancy $\mathcal{O}$ that is discretized
on a grid is *linear* in the number of voxels [16]. However, the number voxels grows
as $O(n^d)$, making naive SDF computation impractical for high resolutions (large
n) or high dimensions (in practice, $d{\geq}3$ is already problematic). Spatial acceleration data structures (kdtrees and octrees) are commonly employed, but these
data structures still require an overall $O(n \log(n))$ pre-processing (where n is the
number of polygons), and they need to be re-built at every frame (as $\boldsymbol{\theta}$ changes),
and do not support implicit representations.

Recently, Dou et al. [14] proposed to smooth an occupancy function with a
Gaussian blur kernel to *approximate* Φ in the near field of the surface. Following
this idea, our fitting energy can be re-expressed as:

$$E_{\text{fit}}(\mathbf{D}, \boldsymbol{\theta}) = \sum_{\mathbf{x} \in \mathbf{D}} \|\mathcal{N}_{0,\sigma^2} \circledast \mathcal{O}(\mathbf{x}|\boldsymbol{\theta}) - 0.5\|^2 \qquad (13)$$

where $\mathcal{N}_{0,\sigma^2}$ is a Gaussian kernel with a zero mean and a variance σ^2, and $\circledast$ is the
convolution operator. This approximation is suitable for tracking, as large values

of distance should be associated with *outliers* in a registration optimization [6], and therefore ignored. Further, this approximation can be explained via the algebraic relationship between heat kernels and distance functions [11]. Note that we *intentionally* use $\mathcal{O}$ instead of $\mathcal{O}_\omega$, as what follows is applicable to *any* implicit representation, not just our neural occupancy $\mathcal{O}_\omega$.

Dou et al. [14] used (13) being given a voxelized representation of $\mathcal{O}$, and relying on GPU implementations to efficiently compute 3D convolutions $\circledast$. To circumvent these issues, we re-express the convolution via stochastic sampling:

$$\mathcal{O}(\mathbf{x}|\boldsymbol{\theta}) \circledast \mathcal{N}_{0,\sigma^2} = \int \mathcal{O}(\mathbf{s}|\boldsymbol{\theta}) g(\mathbf{x} - \mathbf{s}|0, \sigma^2)\, ds \quad \text{(definition of convolution) (14)}$$

$$= \int \mathcal{O}(\mathbf{s}|\boldsymbol{\theta}) g(\mathbf{s} - \mathbf{x}|0, \sigma^2)\, ds \quad \text{(symmetry of Gaussian)} \quad (15)$$

$$= \int \mathcal{O}(\mathbf{s}|\boldsymbol{\theta}) g(\mathbf{s}|\mathbf{x}, \sigma^2)\, ds \quad \text{(definition of Gaussian)} \quad (16)$$

$$= \mathbb{E}_{\mathbf{s} \sim \mathcal{N}_{\mathbf{x},\sigma^2}} [\mathcal{O}(\mathbf{s}|\boldsymbol{\theta})] \quad \text{(definition of expectation)} \quad (17)$$

Overall, Eq. 17 allows us to design a tracking solution that directly operates on occupancy functions, *without* the need to compute signed distance functions [48], closest points [47], or 3D convolutions [14]. It further provides a direct cost/accuracy control in terms of the number of samples used to approximate the expectation in (17). However, the gradients ∇_θ of (17) also need to be available – we achieve this by applying the *re-parameterization* trick [28] to (17):

$$\nabla_\theta \left[\mathbb{E}_{\mathbf{s} \sim \mathcal{N}_{\mathbf{x},\sigma^2}} [\mathcal{O}(\mathbf{s}|\boldsymbol{\theta})] \right] = \mathbb{E}_{\mathbf{s} \sim \mathcal{N}_{0,1}} [\nabla_\theta \mathcal{O}(\mathbf{x} + \sigma\mathbf{s}|\boldsymbol{\theta})] \quad (18)$$

5.2 Pose Prior Energy

An issue of generative tracking is that once the model is too far from the target (e.g. fast motion) there will be no proper gradient to correct it. If we directly optimize for transformation without any constraints, there is a high chance that the model will degenerate into such a case. To address this, we impose a prior:

$$E_{\text{prior}}(\boldsymbol{\theta} = \{\mathbf{B}_b\}) = \sum_{(b_1,b_2)\in\mathcal{E}} \left\| (\bar{\mathbf{t}}_{b_2} - \bar{\mathbf{t}}_{b_1}) - \mathbf{B}_{b_1}^{-1}\mathbf{t}_{b_2} \right\|_2^2 \quad (19)$$

where $\mathcal{E}$ is the set of directed edges (b_1, b_2) on the pre-defined directed rig with b_1 as the parent, and recall $\mathbf{t}_b$ is the translation vector of matrix $\mathbf{B}_b$. One can view this loss as aligning the vector pointing to t_{b_2} at run-time with the vector at rest pose, i.e. $(\bar{\mathbf{t}}_{b_2} - \bar{\mathbf{t}}_{b_1})$. We emphasize that more sophisticated priors exist, and could be applied, including employing a hierarchical skeleton [48], or modeling the density of joint angles [4]. The simple prior used here is chosen to highlight the effectiveness of our neural occupancy model *independent* of such priors.

5.3   Iterative Optimization

One would be tempted to use the gradients of (13) to track a point cloud via *iterative* optimization. However, it is known that when optimizing rotations *centering* the optimization about the current state is heavily advisable [47]. Indexing time by (t) and given the update rule $\boldsymbol{\theta}^{(t)} = \boldsymbol{\theta}^{(t-1)} + \Delta\boldsymbol{\theta}^{(t)}$, the iterative optimization of (13) can be expressed as:

$$\arg\min_{\Delta\boldsymbol{\theta}^{(t)}} \sum_{\mathbf{x} \in \mathbf{D}^{(t)}} \left\| \mathbb{E}_{\mathbf{s} \sim \mathcal{N}_{\mathbf{x},\sigma^2}} \left[\mathcal{O}_\omega(\mathbf{s}|\boldsymbol{\theta}^{(t-1)} + \Delta\boldsymbol{\theta}^{(t)}) \right] - 0.5 \right\|^2 \tag{20}$$

where in what follows we omit the index (t) for brevity of notation. As the pose $\boldsymbol{\theta}$ is represented by matrices, we represent the transformation differential as:

$$\mathcal{O}_\omega(\mathbf{x}|\boldsymbol{\theta} + \Delta\boldsymbol{\theta}) = \mathcal{O}_\omega(\mathbf{x}|\{(\mathbf{B}_b \Delta\mathbf{B}_b)^{-1}\}) = \mathcal{O}_\omega(\mathbf{x}|\{\Delta\mathbf{B}_b^{-1}\mathbf{B}_b^{-1}\}), \tag{21}$$

resulting in the optimization:

$$\arg\min_{\{\Delta\mathbf{B}_b^{-1}\}} \sum_{\mathbf{x} \in \mathbf{D}} \left\| \mathbb{E}_{\mathbf{s} \sim \mathcal{N}_{\mathbf{x},\sigma^2}} \left[\mathcal{O}_\omega(\mathbf{s}|\{\Delta\mathbf{B}_b^{-1}\mathbf{B}_b^{-1}\}) \right] - 0.5 \right\|^2 \tag{22}$$

where we parameterize the rotational portion of elements in the collection $\{\Delta\mathbf{B}_b^{-1}\}$ by two (initially orthogonal) vectors [57], and re-orthogonalize them *before* inversion within each optimization update $\mathbf{B}_b^{(i+1)} = \mathbf{B}_b^{(i)}(\Delta\mathbf{C}_b^{(i)})^{-1}$, where $\Delta\mathbf{C}_b = \Delta\mathbf{B}_b^{-1}$ are the quantities the solver optimizes for. In other words, we optimize for the *inverse* of the coordinate frames in order to avoid back-propagation through matrix inversion.

6   Results and Discussion

We describe the training data (Sect. 6.1), quantitatively evaluate the performance of our neural 3D representation on several datasets (Sect. 6.2), as well as demonstrate its usability for tracking applications (Sect. 6.3). We conclude by contrasting our technique to recent methods for implicit-learning of geometry (Sect. 6.4). Ablation studies validating *each* of our technical choices can be found in the **supplementary material**.

6.1   Training Data

Our training data consists of sampled indicator function values, transformation frames ("bones") per pose, and skinning weights. The samples used for training (3) come from two sources (each comprising a total of $100,000$ samples): ① we randomly sample points uniformly within a bounding box scaled to 110% of its original diagonal dimension; ② we perform Poisson disk sampling on the surface, and randomly displace these points with isotropic normal noise with $\sigma = .03$. The ground truth indicator function at these samples are computed

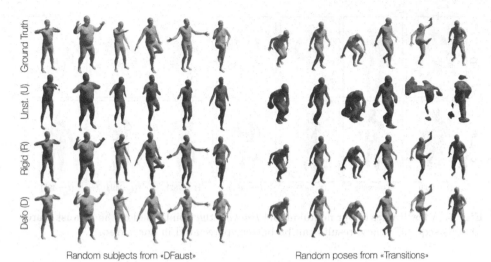

Random subjects from «DFaust»   Random poses from «Transitions»

Fig. 5. The qualitative performance of our three models in reconstructing the occupancy function on the (left) DFaust and (right) Transitions dataset.

by casting randomized rays and checking the *parity* (i.e. counting the number of intersections) – generalized winding numbers [24] or sign-agnostic losses [2] could also be used for this purpose. The test reconstruction performance is evaluated by comparing the predicted indicator values against the ground truth samples on the full set of 100, 000 samples. We evaluate using mean Intersection over Union (IoU), Chamfer-L1 [15] and F-score (F%) [50] with a threshold set to 0.0001. The meshes are obtained from the "DFaust" [5] and "Transitions" sub-datasets of AMASS [35], as detailed in Sect. 6.2.

Table 1. AMASS/DFaust

Model	mIoU↑	Chamfer L1↓	F%↑
U	.702	.00631	46.15
R	.932	.00032	93.94
D	.959	.00004	98.54

Table 2. AMASS/Transitions

Model	mIoU↑	Chamfer L1↓	F%↑
U	.520	.01057	26.83
R	.936	.00006	96.71
D	.965	.00002	99.42

6.2   Reconstruction

We employ the "DFaust" portion of the AMASS dataset to verify that our model can be used effectively *across* different subjects. This dataset contains 10 subjects, 10 sequences/subject, and ≈300 frames/sequence on average. We train 100 different models by optimizing (9): for each subject we use 9 sequences for

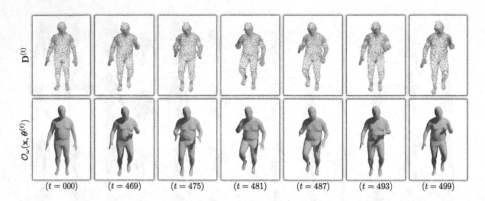

$D^{(t)}$

$\mathcal{O}_\omega(x, \theta^{(t)})$

| $(t = 000)$ | $(t = 469)$ | $(t = 475)$ | $(t = 481)$ | $(t = 487)$ | $(t = 493)$ | $(t = 499)$ |

Fig. 6. A few frames of our neural model *tracking* the point cloud of the DFaust "hard" (02-09) sequence; these results can be better appreciated in our **video**.

training, leaving one out for testing to compute our metrics. We average these metrics across the 100 runs, and report these in Table 1. Note how learning a deformable model via decomposition provides *striking* advantages, as quantified by the fact that the rigid (R) baseline is consistently better than the unstructured (U) baseline under *any* metric – a +49% in F-score. Similar improvements can be noticed by comparing the rigid (R) to the deformable (D) model, where the latter achieves an additional +5% in F-score. Figure 5 (second row) gives a qualitative visualization of how the unstructured models struggles in generalizing to poses that are sufficiently different from the ones in the training set.

We employ the "Transitions" portion of the AMASS dataset to further study the performance of the model when more training data and a larger diversity of motions) is available for a *single* subject. This dataset contains 110 sequences of one individual, with ≈1000+ frames/sequence. We randomly sample ≈250 frames from each sequence, randomly select 80 sequences for training, and keep the remaining 30 sequences for testing; see our **supplementary material**. Results are shown in Table 2. The conclusions are analogous to the ones we made from DFaust. Further, note that in this more difficult dataset containing a larger variety of more complex motions, the unstructured model struggles even more significantly ($U{\rightarrow}R$: +70% in F-score). As the model is exposed to more poses compared to DFaust, the reconstruction performance is also improved. Moving from DFaust to Transitions results in a +1% in F-score for the deformable model.

Table 3. DFaust "easy" (00-01)

$p(\mathcal{O}|\theta)$	$p(\theta)$	⊛	mIoU↑	Chamfer L1↓	F%↑
U	✓	✓	.845	.00383	61.63
D	✓	✓	**.968**	**.00004**	**99.08**
oracle	–	–	.976	.00004	99.01

Table 4. DFaust "hard" (02-09)

$p(\mathcal{O}|\theta)$	$p(\theta)$	⊛	mIoU↑	Chamfer L1↓	F%↑
U	✓	✓	.686	.00700	50.63
D	✓	✓	**.948**	**.00006**	**96.48**
oracle	–	–	.959	.00006	96.80

6.3 Tracking

We validate our tracking technique on two sequences from the DFaust dataset; see Fig. 6. Note these are test sequences, and were *not* used to train our model. The prior $p(\boldsymbol{\theta})$ (Sect. 5.2) and the stochastic optimization ⊛ (Sect. 5.1) can be applied to both unstructured (U) and structured (D) representations, with the latter leading to significantly better tracking performance. The quantitative results reported for the "easy" (Table 3) and "hard" (Table 4) tracking sequences are best understood by watching our **supplementary video**. It is essential to re-state that we are not trying to beat traditional baselines, but rather seek to *illustrate* how NASA, once trained, can be readily used as a 3D representation for classical vision tasks. For the purpose of this illustration, we use only noisy panoptic point clouds (i.e. complete [14] rather than incomplete [48] data), and do not use any discriminative per-frame re-initializer as would typically be employed in a contemporary tracking system.

6.4 Discussion

The recent success of neural implicit representations of geometry, introduced by [9,37,39], has heavily relied on the fact that the geometry in ShapeNet datasets [7] is *canonicalized*: scaled to unit ranges and consistently oriented. Research has highlighted the importance of expressing information in a canonical frame [55], and one could interpret our method as a way to achieve this within the realm of articulated motion. To understand the shortcomings of unstructured models, one should remember that as an object moves, much of the local geometric details remain *invariant* to articulation. However, unstructured pose conditioned models are forced to *memorize* these details in any pose they seek to reconstruct. Hence, as one evaluates unstructured models *outside* of their training manifold, their performance *collapses* – as quantified by the +49% performance change as we move from unstructured to rigid models; see Table 1. One could also argue that given sufficient capacity, a neural network *should* be able to learn the *concept* of coordinate frames and transformations. However, multiplicative relationships between inputs (e.g. dot products) are difficult to learn for neural networks [26, Sec. 2.3]. As changes of coordinate frames are nothing but collections of dot products, one could use this reasoning to justify the limited performance of unstructured models. We conclude by clearly contrasting our method, targeting the modeling of $\mathcal{O}(\mathbf{x}|\boldsymbol{\theta})$ to those that address shape completion $\mathcal{O}(\mathbf{x}|\mathbf{D})$ [2,18,42,56]. In contrast to these, our solution, to the best of our knowledge, represents the first attempt to create a "neural implicit rig" – from a computer graphics perspective – for articulated deformation modeling.

 One limitation of our work is the reliance on $\{\tilde{\mathbf{B}}_b\}$, which could be difficult to obtain in in-the-wild settings, as well as skinning weights to guide the part-decomposition; how to automatically regress these quantities from raw observations is an open problem. Our model is also currently limited to *individual* subjects, and to be competitive to mesh-based models one would also have to learn identity parameters (i.e. the β parameters of SMPL [33]). Finally, our representation currently fails to capture high frequency features (e.g. see the geometric details of the face region in Fig. 5); however, recent research on implicit representations [46,49] can likely mitigate this issue.

7 Conclusions

We introduce a novel neural representation of a particularly important class of 3D objects: *articulated* bodies. We use a structured neural occupancy approach, enabling both direct occupancy queries and deformable surface representations that are competitive with classic hand-crafted mesh representations. The representation is fully differentiable, and enables tracking of realistic articulated bodies – traditionally a complex task – to be almost *trivially* implemented. Crucially, our work demonstrates the value of incorporating a task-appropriate inductive bias into the neural architecture. By acknowledging and encoding the quasi-rigid part structure of articulated bodies, we represent this class of objects with higher quality, and significantly better generalization.

References

1. Anguelov, D., Koller, D., Pang, H.C., Srinivasan, P., Thrun, S.: Recovering articulated object models from 3D range data. In: Uncertainty in Artificial Intelligence (2004)
2. Atzmon, M., Lipman, Y.: SAL: sign agnostic learning of shapes from raw data. arXiv preprint arXiv:1911.10414 (2019)
3. Bailey, S.W., Otte, D., Dilorenzo, P., O'Brien, J.F.: Fast and deep deformation approximations. In: SIGGRAPH (2018)
4. Bogo, F., Kanazawa, A., Lassner, C., Gehler, P., Romero, J., Black, M.J.: Keep It SMPL: automatic estimation of 3D human pose and shape from a single image. In: Leibe, B., Matas, J., Sebe, N., Welling, M. (eds.) ECCV 2016. LNCS, vol. 9909, pp. 561–578. Springer, Cham (2016). https://doi.org/10.1007/978-3-319-46454-1_34
5. Bogo, F., Romero, J., Pons-Moll, G., Black, M.J.: Dynamic FAUST: registering human bodies in motion. In: IEEE Conference on Computer Vision and Pattern Recognition (CVPR) (2017)
6. Bouaziz, S., Tagliasacchi, A., Pauly, M.: Sparse iterative closest point. In: SGP (2013)
7. Chang, A.X., et al.: Shapenet: an information-rich 3D model repository. arXiv:1512.03012 (2015)
8. Chen, Z., Yin, K., Fisher, M., Chaudhuri, S., Zhang, H.: Bae-net: branched autoencoder for shape co-segmentation. In: ICCV (2019)
9. Chen, Z., Zhang, H.: Learning implicit fields for generative shape modeling. In: CVPR (2019)
10. Chibane, J., Alldieck, T., Pons-Moll, G.: Implicit functions in feature space for 3D shape reconstruction and completion. In: CVPR (2020)
11. Crane, K., Weischedel, C., Wardetzky, M.: Geodesics in heat: a new approach to computing distance based on heat flow. ACM TOG **32**(5), 1–11 (2013)

12. Deng, B., Genova, K., Yazdani, S., Bouaziz, S., Hinton, G., Tagliasacchi, A.: Cvxnet: learnable convex decomposition. In: CVPR (2020)
13. Deng, B., Kornblith, S., Hinton, G.: Cerberus: a multi-headed derenderer. arXiv:1905.11940 (2019)
14. Dou, M., et al.: Fusion4d: real-time performance capture of challenging scenes. ACM TOG **35**(4), 1–13 (2016)
15. Fan, H., Su, H., Guibas, L.J.: A point set generation network for 3D object reconstruction from a single image. In: CVPR (2017)
16. Felzenszwalb, P.F., Huttenlocher, D.P.: Distance transforms of sampled functions. Theory Comput. **8**(1), 415–428 (2012)
17. Gao, L., et al.: SDM-NET: deep generative network for structured deformable mesh. ACM TOG **38**(6), 1–15 (2019)
18. Genova, K., Cole, F., Sud, A., Sarna, A., Funkhouser, T.: Deep structured implicit functions. In: CVPR (2019)
19. de Goes, F., Goldenstein, S., Velho, L.: A hierarchical segmentation of articulated bodies. In: SGP (2008)
20. Groueix, T., Fisher, M., Kim, V.G., Russell, B.C., Aubry, M.: Atlasnet: a papier-mâché approach to learning 3D surface generation. arXiv preprint arXiv:1802.05384 (2018)
21. Huang, Q., Koltun, V., Guibas, L.: Joint shape segmentation with linear programming. ACM TOG (2011)
22. Ioannou, Y., Robertson, D., Cipolla, R., Criminisi, A.: Deep roots: improving CNN efficiency with hierarchical filter groups. In: CVPR (2017)
23. Jacobson, A., Deng, Z., Kavan, L., Lewis, J.: Skinning: real-time shape deformation. In: ACM SIGGRAPH Courses (2014)
24. Jacobson, A., Kavan, L., Sorkine-Hornung, O.: Robust inside-outside segmentation using generalized winding numbers. ACM TOG **32**(4), 1–12 (2013)
25. James, D.L.: Twigg, C.D.: Skinning mesh animations. In: SIGGRAPH (2005)
26. Joseph-Rivlin, M., Zvirin, A., Kimmel, R.: Momen(e)t: flavor the moments in learning to classify shapes. In: CVPR Workshops (2019)
27. Kanazawa, A., Black, M.J., Jacobs, D.W., Malik, J.: End-to-end recovery of human shape and pose. In: CVPR (2018)
28. Kingma, D.P., Welling, M.: Auto-encoding variational bayes. arXiv preprint arXiv:1312.6114 (2013)
29. Krizhevsky, A., Sutskever, I., Hinton, G.: Imagenet classification with deep convolutional neural networks. In: NIPS (2012)
30. Le, B.H., Deng, Z.: Smooth skinning decomposition with rigid bones. ACM TOG **31**(6), 1–10 (2012)
31. Lewis, J.P., Cordner, M., Fong, N.: Pose space deformation: a unified approach to shape interpolation and skeleton-driven deformation. In: SIGGRAPH (2000)
32. Lin, M.C., Manocha, U.D., Cohen, J.: Collision detection: algorithms and applications (1996)
33. Loper, M., Mahmood, N., Romero, J., Pons-Moll, G., Black, M.J.: SMPL: a skinned multi-person linear model. In: SIGGRAPH Asia (2015)
34. Lorenz, D., Bereska, L., Milbich, T., Ommer, B.: Unsupervised part-based disentangling of object shape and appearance. arXiv:1903.06946 (2019)
35. Mahmood, N., Ghorbani, N., Troje, N.F., Pons-Moll, G., Black, M.J.: AMASS: archive of motion capture as surface shapes. In: ICCV (2019)
36. Melax, S., Keselman, L., Orsten, S.: Dynamics based 3D skeletal hand tracking. In: Graphics Interface (2013)

37. Mescheder, L., Oechsle, M., Niemeyer, M., Nowozin, S., Geiger, A.: Occupancy networks: learning 3D reconstruction in function space. arXiv:1812.03828 (2018)
38. Omran, M., Lassner, C., Pons-Moll, G., Gehler, P., Schiele, B.: Neural body fitting: unifying deep learning and model based human pose and shape estimation. In: International Conference on 3D Vision (3DV) (2018)
39. Park, J.J., Florence, P., Straub, J., Newcombe, R., Lovegrove, S.: DeepSDF: learning continuous signed distance functions for shape representation. In: CVPR (2019)
40. Pavlakos, G., Zhu, L., Zhou, X., Daniilidis, K.: Learning to estimate 3D human pose and shape from a single color image. In: CVPR (2018)
41. Remelli, E., Tkach, A., Tagliasacchi, A., Pauly, M.: Low-dimensionality calibration through local anisotropic scaling for robust hand model personalization. In: ICCV (2017)
42. Saito, S., Huang, Z., Natsume, R., Morishima, S., Kanazawa, A., Li, H.: PIFu: pixel-aligned implicit function for high-resolution clothed human digitization. In: CVPR (2019)
43. Samet, H.: Applications of Spatial Data Structures: Computer Graphics, Image Processing, and GIS. Addison-Wesley Longman Publishing Co., Inc., Boston (1990)
44. Shen, J., et al.: The phong surface: efficient 3D model fitting using lifted optimization (2020)
45. Shotton, J., et al.: Real-time human pose recognition in parts from single depth images. In: CVPR (2011)
46. Sitzmann, V., Martel, J.N.P., Bergman, A.W., Lindell, D.B., Wetzstein, G.: Implicit neural representations with periodic activation functions (2020)
47. Tagliasacchi, A., Bouaziz, S.: Dynamic 2D/3D registration. In: Proceedings of Symposium on Geometry Processing (Technical Course Notes) (2018)
48. Tagliasacchi, A., Schröder, M., Tkach, A., Bouaziz, S., Botsch, M., Pauly, M.: Robust articulated-ICP for real-time hand tracking. In: SGP (2015)
49. Tancik, M., et al.: Fourier features let networks learn high frequency functions in low dimensional domains. arXiv preprint arXiv:2006.10739 (2020)
50. Tatarchenko, M., Richter, S.R., Ranftl, R., Li, Z., Koltun, V., Brox, T.: What do single-view 3D reconstruction networks learn? In: CVPR (2019)
51. Taylor, J., et al.: Articulated distance fields for ultra-fast tracking of hands interacting. ACM Trans. Graph. (TOG) 36(6), 1–12 (2017)
52. Tkach, A., Tagliasacchi, A., Remelli, E., Pauly, M., Fitzgibbon, A.: Online generative model personalization for hand tracking. ACM Trans. Graph. (Proc. SIGGRAPH Asia) 36(6), 1–11 (2017)
53. Tung, H.Y., Tung, H.W., Yumer, E., Fragkiadaki, K.: Self-supervised learning of motion capture. In: Advances in Neural Information Processing Systems, pp. 5236–5246 (2017)
54. Valentin, J., Keskin, C., Pidlypenskyi, P., Makadia, A., Sud, A., Bouaziz, S.: Tensorflow graphics: computer graphics meets deep learning (2019)
55. Wang, H., Sridhar, S., Huang, J., Valentin, J., Song, S., Guibas, L.J.: Normalized object coordinate space for category-level 6D object pose and size estimation. In: CVPR (2019)
56. Xu, Q., Wang, W., Ceylan, D., Mech, R., Neumann, U.: DISN: deep implicit surface network for high-quality single-view 3D reconstruction. In: NeurIPS (2019)
57. Zhou, Y., Barnes, C., Lu, J., Yang, J., Li, H.: On the continuity of rotation representations in neural networks. In: CVPR (2019)

Towards Unique and Informative Captioning of Images

Zeyu Wang[1](✉) (iD), Berthy Feng[1,2] (iD), Karthik Narasimhan[1] (iD),
and Olga Russakovsky[1] (iD)

[1] Princeton University, Princeton, USA
{zeyuwang,karthikn,olgarus}@cs.princeton.edu, bfeng@caltech.edu
[2] California Institute of Technology, Pasadena, USA

Abstract. Despite considerable progress, state of the art image captioning models produce generic captions, leaving out important image details. Furthermore, these systems may even misrepresent the image in order to produce a simpler caption consisting of common concepts. In this paper, we first analyze both modern captioning systems and evaluation metrics through empirical experiments to quantify these phenomena. We find that modern captioning systems return higher likelihoods for incorrect distractor sentences compared to ground truth captions, and that evaluation metrics like SPICE can be 'topped' using simple captioning systems relying on object detectors. Inspired by these observations, we design a new metric (SPICE-U) by introducing a notion of *uniqueness* over the concepts generated in a caption. We show that SPICE-U is better correlated with human judgements compared to SPICE, and effectively captures notions of diversity and descriptiveness. Finally, we also demonstrate a general technique to improve any existing captioning model – by using mutual information as a re-ranking objective during decoding. Empirically, this results in more unique and informative captions, and improves three different state-of-the-art models on SPICE-U as well as average score over existing metrics (Code is available at https://github. com/princetonvisualai/SPICE-U).

1 Introduction

Over the last few years, there has been considerable progress in image captioning, with current methods producing fluent captions for a variety of images [2,8,26,41,42,45,48]. However, all these systems tend to produce generic captions, re-using a small set of common concepts to describe vastly different images. Consider the example caption in Fig. 1, produced by a state of the art model [8]. Despite obvious differences between the sixteen images, the model produces the same caption, missing several other details specific to certain images and generating incorrect facts about others. A human, on the other hand, would identify unique aspects of each image, such as whether the person is serving, is it a match or a practice, the type of tennis court, the color of the person's shirt, etc. While the inadequacies of the captioning models can be partially attributed

© Springer Nature Switzerland AG 2020
A. Vedaldi et al. (Eds.): ECCV 2020, LNCS 12352, pp. 629–644, 2020.
https://doi.org/10.1007/978-3-030-58571-6_37

Fig. 1. Diverse images from the COCO validation set for which a trained captioning system [8] generates the same caption: "A man holding a tennis racket on a tennis court". The caption misses important details, such as the action of the person, the type of tennis court, whether there is audience, etc.

to the "mode collapse" problem of current techniques and loss functions like cross-entropy, the issue is more fundamental—defining and benchmarking image captioning adequately remains a challenging task.

To this end, we investigate modern captioning systems in terms of their ability to produce *unique and complete* captions. Specifically, we find that the problem of producing common concepts is deeply ingrained in modern captioning systems. As we demonstrate empirically, one reason for this could be that end-to-end training results in strong language model priors that lead to models preferring more commonly occurring sentences, irrespective of whether they are relevant to the image or not. For instance, we find that state-of-the-art captioning systems [2,8,27] incorrectly assign higher likelihoods to irrelevant common captions compared to even ground truth captions paired with a particular image. Furthermore, we also show that this is not just a problem with the captioning models – existing evaluation metrics frequently fail to reward diversity and uniqueness in captions, in fact *preferring* simple automatically generated captions to more descriptive captions produced by human annotators.

In this paper, we take a step towards quantitatively characterizing these deficiencies by proposing a new measure which captures the ability of a caption to uniquely identify an image. We convert a caption into a set of objects, attributes, and relations. For each such concept, we compute its uniqueness as a function of the global number of images containing the concept. This is then aggregated over concepts to compute the uniqueness of the overall caption. This uniqueness metric is orthogonal to standard measures like precision and recall, and allows us to combine them using a harmonic mean to define a new metric, SPICE-U. We empirically demonstrate that this metric correlates better with human judgements than the commonly-used SPICE [1] metric.

Next, we propose techniques to improve current captioning systems at producing unique, more meaningful captions. We employ the strategy of re-ranking captions during the decoding process by maximizing mutual information between the image and the caption (inspired by a similar line of work in machine translation [18]). Our method achieves an absolute improvement of up to 1.6% in SPICE-U and a relative improvement of up to 2.4% on the average across different metrics. The captions produced are more informative and relevant to the image while not losing out on fluency.

To summarize, the contributions of this paper are:

- quantitatively demonstrating limitations of current captioning systems and metrics.
- proposing a new metric (SPICE-U) that measures the ability of captions to be unique and descriptive.
- investigating new decoding objectives to generate more informative captions.

2 Related Work

Discriminative Captioning. A number of recent approaches address the task of producing discriminative captions [22,24,27,28,37]. One such method considers the task of distinguishing a target image from a distractor image using generated captions [37]. The proposed method balances the objectives of maximizing the probability of seeing the predicted caption conditioned on the target image and minimizing the probability of seeing the predicted caption conditioned on the distractor image. Other methods [24,27] incorporate image retrieval into the training process, encouraging the generation of captions that are more likely to be uniquely aligned to the original image than to other images. While these approaches help generate more discriminative captions, they are approximate versions of maximizing mutual information between the image and caption, which we aim to do explicitly.

Descriptive Captioning. Prior work has also focused on improving the amount of information present in a single generated caption. Dense captioning [9] aims to identify all the salient regions in an image and describe each with a caption. Diverse image annotation [44] focuses on describing as much of the image as possible with a limited number of tags. Entity-aware captioning [25] employs hashtags as additional input. Image paragraph captioning [13,29] aims to produce more than a single sentence for an image. While these papers do capture some notion of expressiveness, they do not explicitly quantify it or examine trade-offs such as the caption length or uniqueness of generated concepts.

Diversity and Mutual Information in Captioning. Another related line of research to this paper is the area of diversity-promoting objectives for captioning [21,34,39,40,43]. While the similarity lies in aiming to prevent generic, dull captions, these approaches do not explicitly try to make sure that the information content of the caption matches well with the image. In terms of measuring diversity, some papers propose metrics that use corpus-level statistics to provide coarse judgements [21,34,43]. For instance, one can measure how distinct a set of different captions are for a single image, or how many different captions a model generates across the entire test set. In contrast, our metric provides measurements for *each image-caption pair* using aggregated corpus-level information.

Using mutual information to re-rank scores has been explored in speech recognition [3,31], machine translation [12,17,18,36], conversational agents [50], and multimodal search and retrieval [5,7,47]. Maximizing the mutual information as an objective (during either training or inference) has provided reasonable performance gains on all the above tasks. However, to the best of our knowledge, ours is the first work to explore re-ranking via maximizing mutual information specifically to improve the uniqueness of machine-generated captions.

Image Captioning Metrics. The most commonly used metrics for image captioning evaluation are BLEU [30], METEOR [16], CIDEr [38], and SPICE [1]. BLEU, METEOR, and CIDEr all rely on n-gram matching between the candidate caption and reference captions. BLEU and METEOR are traditionally used in machine translation and thus concerned with syntactical soundness. CIDEr measures the similarity between the candidate caption and "consensus" of the set of reference captions, essentially calculating how often n-grams in the candidate appear in the reference set. SPICE (Semantic Propositional Image Caption Evaluation) is more concerned with the semantics of a caption. It scores a caption based on how closely it matches the scene graph of the target image, where a scene graph consists of a set of object classes, set of relation types, and set of attribute types. While other metrics capture "naturalness" of captions, SPICE correlates better with human judgement by focusing on semantic correctness. Attempts at combining metrics have also been made (e.g. SPIDER [23]). More recent work [33] points out existing models often hallucinate objects when generating captions and proposes the CHAIR score to explicitly evaluate this problem. In contrast to the above rule-base metrics, recent work has also proposed learning statistical models to evaluate captioning systems [4,6]. While these metrics provide a good measure for the accuracy of a caption, they do not explicitly evaluate how descriptive or informative a caption is. Our metric (SPICE-U) incorporates a new 'uniqueness' measure, while also capturing notions of caption fluency and accuracy through traditional precision and recall components.

3   Analysis: Prevalence and Causes of Common Concepts in Captions

Current image captioning systems produce captions that are surprisingly fluent and frequently accurate, but generic and uninformative. We begin by demonstrating that the problem of generating common concept is deeply ingrained in both the current captioning systems and in the evaluation metrics. These two factors are closely related as captioning systems are trained to optimize performance on existing metrics. To analyze the captioning systems in the absence of any pre-defined metrics, we take a look directly at the underlying probability distributions learned by the models; to further demonstrate the brittleness of the metrics we design a simple competing baseline that outperforms state-of-the-art captioning systems on standard metrics (this section). Equipped with this analysis, we then go on to propose a new metric (Sect. 4) along with a potential technical solution (Sect. 5) to address the problem.

3.1 Captioning Systems Prefer Common Concepts

Modern captioning systems are trained to maximize the likelihood of generating the correct caption sentence s conditioned on the image I, or $P(s|I)$. Even though the model is learned jointly and does not neatly decompose, intuitively the probability distribution is influenced by two factors: (1) whether a particular concept appears in the image, and (2) the likelihood that the particular concept would appear in a caption. We run a simple experiment to showcase that the latter language prior plays a surprisingly strong role in modern captioning models, helping to partially explain why the systems frequently resort to returning generic image captions corresponding to common concepts.

Table 1. Five most common captions in the COCO [20] training set with appearance numbers (based on exact matches over the entire sentence). In Sect. 3 we demonstrate that captioning models frequently prefer such distractors to ground truth human captions of the images.

a man riding a wave on top of a surfboard (160)
a man flying through the air while riding a skateboard (137)
a man riding skis down a snow covered slope (124)
a man holding a tennis racquet on a tennis court (122)
a large long train on a steel track (116)

To do so, we examine the learned probability distribution of the bottom-up top-down attention model [2] trained on the popular Karpathy split [11] of the COCO dataset [20]. On every validation image, we compare the model's likelihood of the human generated ground truth captions for this image with the model's likelihood corresponding to generic distractor sentences applied to this image. For distractor sentences, we use the five captions that appear most frequently in training set (Table 1). During evaluation, to ensure that these distractor sentences are not correct description of the corresponding image, we use the code from [33] to only keep the sentences that contain at least one hallucinated object not present in the image. We observe that in an amazing 73% of the images the model returns a higher likelihood $P(d|I)$ for one of these *wrong* distractor sentences d than its likelihood $P(g|I)$ of one of the ground truth caption, i.e., $\exists d, g : P(d|I) > P(g|I)$. Figure 2 qualitatively illustrates why this is the case: an incorrect caption associated with common concepts may end up with a higher overall $P(s|I)$ than a correct caption albeit with rare words, which would receive lower language model scores.

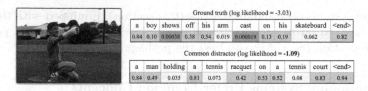

Fig. 2. The ground truth caption "a boy shows off his arm cast on his skateboard" has much lower mean log likelihood (-3.03) according to the captioning model of [2] than a common (on this dataset) but incorrect caption "a man holding a tennis racquet on a tennis court." Numbers under each word w_k correspond to $P(w_k|I, w_{<k})$ of the captioning model, color-coded according to their magnitude. This preference for common captions even at the expense of accuracy is a problem in modern captioning models.

3.2 Captioning Metrics Prefer Common Concepts

We now demonstrate that the problem is not just in the captioning models but also in the metrics used to evaluate those models, such as SPICE [1].

Background: SPICE. While older metrics such as BLEU [30], METEOR [16] and CIDEr [38] aim to evaluate both the correctness and the fluency of a caption through n-gram matching, SPICE takes a departure from fluency to focus primarily on caption correctness, i.e., whether the caption reflects visual concepts that are indeed in the image. Here, a *visual concept* is a concrete thing or abstract notion that can be both localized in an image and described using natural language. For the purposes of evaluation, visual concepts are restricted to objects, their attributes, and their relations [1,10,14].

Consider an image with a set of visual concepts $\mathbf{G}$ and a set of predicted visual concepts $\mathbf{P}$. The accuracy of this description $\mathbf{P}$ is commonly measured using *precision* and *recall* with regard to the ground truth concepts $\mathbf{G}$ [1], where:

$$\text{Rec}(\mathbf{P};\mathbf{G}) = \frac{|\mathbf{P} \cap \mathbf{G}|}{|\mathbf{G}|}, \qquad \text{Pr}(\mathbf{P};\mathbf{G}) = \frac{|\mathbf{P} \cap \mathbf{G}|}{|\mathbf{P}|}$$

The SPICE metric trades off between them using the harmonic mean:

$$\text{SPICE}(\mathbf{P};\mathbf{G}) = \frac{2}{1/\text{Rec}(\mathbf{P};\mathbf{G}) + 1/\text{Pr}(\mathbf{P};\mathbf{G})} \tag{1}$$

We can observe that this metric ignores entirely the uniqueness of concepts and implicitly rewards models which predict common concepts (which are easier to recognize) over rare yet more distinctive concepts.

Findings. We run a simple experiment to show that the SPICE metric can be fooled by very simple baseline models that only recognize the **10** *most common object classes* in images, and nothing else![1] To do so, we design an object-based

---

[1] The objects classes are: man, person, tree, ground, shirt, wall, sky, window, building, and head.

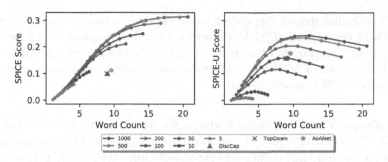

Fig. 3. Comparison of state of the art TopDown model [2], DiscCap model [27], AoANet model [8], and our object detection-based models (best viewed in color). The x-axis is the average caption length in words. The y-axis is the SPICE score [1] (left) and proposed SPICE-U score (right) on 1,076 images (the intersection of the COCO [20] and the Visual Genome dataset [14] which not appear in the training set of both object detection and captioning models). The different curves of the object-based model correspond to running different numbers of object detectors (e.g., detecting only the 1000, 500, etc. most common object classes in the image) and producing simplistic captions of the form "There is a tennis ball, court and person". For each curve, performance is shown across varying detection thresholds from 0.1 to 0.9. A simple object-based model that only outputs the 10 most common object classes seen in images (brown) outperforms a state of the art discriminative captioning model (green triangle) on SPICE, but not on SPICE-U. (Color figure online)

captioning model consisting of a set of object detectors. The object detectors are trained jointly as a Faster R-CNN model [32], on the Visual Genome training dataset [14].[2] Given a set of detected objects such as "tennis ball," "court" and "person," the final caption is generated following a template as: "There is a tennis ball, court and person".[3] We evaluate the accuracy of this system using the SPICE (Eq. 1). The evaluation is done on 1,076 images (the intersection of the COCO [20] and the Visual Genome dataset [14] which not appear in the training set of both object detection and captioning models) using their ground truth concept annotations from Visual Genome.

To help interpret the results, we compare this baseline model with three modern captioning systems: the bottom-up and top-down attention model [2], which combines the bottom-up region features generated from object detector with top-down attention mechanism, the model of Luo et al. [27], which includes a "discriminability" loss to encourage unique captions, and the model of Huang et al. [8], which extends conventional models with a stronger attention mechanism. The models are trained on the COCO dataset [20] with the split of [11]. Figure 3 (left) details the results of the experiment. Surprisingly, according to this metric an object detector that only knows **10** object classes rivals a state of

---

[2] The trained object detectors are taken from the bottom-up part of the captioning model [2].

[3] The resulting model is similar to *Baby Talk* [15], which uses object, attribute, and relationship classifiers to generate image descriptions.

the art captioning model: our object-based captioning model achieves a SPICE score of 0.11 versus 0.10 of [27]! This occurs even despite producing fewer words on average per caption: 6.4 versus 9.1. Further, we observe that given access to a (still limited) set of 500 object detectors, our simple baseline produces significantly higher SPICE scores ($\geq$0.3).

Conclusions. These surprising findings are likely due to two reasons. First, the SPICE score gives equal weight to different concepts. This means that, for example, a caption that names generic objects like "tree" and "person" scores the same as a caption that identifies the two unique objects in the image, such as "volleyball" or "gazebo", giving a perhaps unfair advantage to our simple baseline. We will address this by proposing a new uniqueness-based metric in Sect. 4. Second, modern captioning systems are optimized to rely too heavily on the common concepts, failing to fully leverage their image understanding capabilities, and we propose some strategies to mitigate that in Sect. 5.

4   SPICE-U: A Uniqueness-Aware Metric

Inspired by the observations in Sect. 3, we introduce the SPICE-U metric ("Semantic Propositional Image Caption Evaluation with Uniqueness") to encourage captions to capture the diversity and uniqueness of real-world images.

Uniqueness. We define the uniqueness of a single visual concept p as:

$$\text{Un}(p) = \frac{\#\text{ images not containing p}}{\#\text{ images total}} \tag{2}$$

This is similar to the notion of *inverse document frequency* (IDF) in text retrieval [35], which allows for weighting down common words in text. While this concept is also used in CIDEr [38], they compute IDF over n-grams, not visual concepts. Note that our definition of uniqueness is complementary to saliency – while saliency measures how prominent a concept is in the image, uniqueness aims to identify parts of the image that make it *interesting*. Future work could involve investigating combinations of these.

For computational tractability, we approximate the denominator using a large set of images (e.g. the training set). For example, if p is *tree*, contained in 28,186 of 113,287 images in the COCO training set [20], Un[*tree*] = 0.75. We realize that this approximation introduces some dependence on the corpus, but this is similar to calculating IDF using a large text corpus in metrics like CIDEr. Further, even measures like recall implicitly make corpus-specific assumptions, e.g. by considering the set of ground truth concepts to be those concepts seen in the dataset.

To define the uniqueness of a set of predictions $\mathbf{P}$, we want to consider the uniqueness of its constituent concepts. One natural definition would be:

$$\mathrm{Un}(\mathbf{P}) = \sum_{p \in \mathbf{P}} \mathrm{Un}(p) \tag{3}$$

However, this definition is undesirable for several reasons. First, it's not between 0 and 1, making it difficult to reason about in comparison with precision and recall. Second, and more problematically, it increases with every additional concept (unless the concept is present in 100% of the training images), encouraging long captions. Finally, it encourages the models to make incorrect predictions and detect unusual concepts not present in the image just to increase the uniqueness score.

Instead, we use a definition that measures the uniqueness of a set of predictions compared to the best (most unique) set of predictions which could have been made. To do so, consider alternative predictions $\mathbf{A}$ of the same length as $\mathbf{P}$. As to not encourage a reduction in accuracy through uniqueness, we further assume $\mathbf{A}$ consists only of the concepts that appear either within $\mathbf{P}$ or within the ground truth set $\mathbf{G}$. Concretely:

$$\mathcal{A}(\mathbf{P}; \mathbf{G}) = \{\mathbf{A} : \mathbf{A} \in \mathbf{G} \cup \mathbf{P}, |\mathcal{A}| = |\mathbf{P}|\} \tag{4}$$

For example, if the image contains a *cat* and a *dog*, and the prediction was *cat* and *fish*:

$$\mathcal{A}(\{(cat, fish)\}, \{(cat, dog)\}) = \{(cat, dog), (cat, fish), (dog, fish)\} \tag{5}$$

Given this definition, we then define the *uniqueness* of a prediction as:

$$\mathrm{Uniq}(\mathbf{P}; \mathbf{G}) = \frac{\mathrm{Un}(\mathbf{P}) - \min_{\mathbf{A} \in \mathcal{A}(\mathbf{G};\mathbf{P})} \mathrm{Un}(\mathbf{A})}{\max_{\mathbf{A} \in \mathcal{A}(\mathbf{G};\mathbf{P})} \mathrm{Un}(\mathbf{A}) - \min_{\mathbf{A} \in \mathcal{A}(\mathbf{G};\mathbf{P})} \mathrm{Un}(\mathbf{A})} \tag{6}$$

Intuitively, this measures how unique the caption is compared to others of the same length that could have been conceivably generated. For example, consider an image that contains a *person* (uniqueness score of 0.75), *table* (score of 0.87), and *elephant* (score of 0.98). If the model captions only one of these objects and nothing else, it will be rewarded with a uniqueness score of 1 if the object it chooses is *elephant*, 0 if it outputs *person*, and 0.52 if it outputs *table*. Note that predicting a more unique, yet incorrect, object would not give the model an additional reward. Similarly, if the image did not contain an *elephant*, then the model would receive the full uniqueness score of 1 for predicting the most unique object *table*. This ensures that models are rewarded for noticing unique things in the image but not unfairly penalized on images with only common concepts.

Combined Metric. The uniqueness-aware measure of the quality of a caption is then a combination through harmonic mean of SPICE (Eq. 1), and uniqueness (Eq. 6):

$$\mathrm{SPICE\text{-}U}(\mathbf{P}; \mathbf{G}) = \frac{2}{1/\mathrm{SPICE}(\mathbf{P}; \mathbf{G}) + 1/\mathrm{Uniq}(\mathbf{P}; \mathbf{G})} \tag{7}$$

Table 2. Evaluation of various metrics against human judgements. First five columns show pairwise judgment accuracy with fifty reference captions on the PASCAL-50 dataset (HC: both sentences written by humans for the corresponding image, HI: both sentences written by humans – one for the corresponding image and one for a random image, HM: one caption written by human and another generated by a model, MM: captions generated by two different models.) The last column is Pearson's correlation between human preferences and each metric on images from PASCAL-50.

	HC	HI	HM	MM	ALL	Pearson's
BLEU-4	55.00	97.30	92.60	61.80	76.68	0.581
ROUGE	54.60	98.70	96.00	62.00	77.83	0.732
METEOR	57.50	**99.30**	**96.90**	62.30	79.00	0.710
CIDEr	53.00	**99.30**	92.10	67.10	77.88	0.641
SPICE	**66.80**	98.50	93.80	**71.10**	82.55	0.749
SPICE-U	66.50	98.60	94.40	70.80	**82.58**	**0.767**

Consider the example above of an image that contains a *person*, *table* and *elephant*, and two captions: "There is a table" and "There is an elephant." The original SPICE score of Eq. 1 would be 0.5 for both captions (recall 1/3, precision 1), failing to recognize that one is a much more useful caption than the other. However, SPICE-U score would be 0.67 for "There is an elephant" and 0.51 for "There is a table," correctly selecting the most informative description.[4]

Advantage of SPICE-U. We follow the setup of [1] to analyze correlation of SPICE-U with human judgements when determining the similarity of sentences. We use the PASCAL-50S dataset [38], which contains 50 ground truth captions for each image. Human annotators were provided with a pair of candidate sentences (b, c) and asked which was more similar to sentence a, which is one of the ground truth captions for an image. Consider an image with a set of ground truth captions $A = \{a_k\}$ and a reference pair of sentences (b, c) as above, where without loss of generality we assume that humans favored b over c for this image (i.e., on average over all a_k, humans found a_k to be more similar to b than c). We say that a metric agrees with humans if $\text{metric}(b, A) \geq \text{metric}(c, A)$. From Table 2, we observe that SPICE-U achieves better judgement accuracy than other metrics and comparable accuracy with SPICE, especially outperforming SPICE on HM pairs. This shows that SPICE-U can indeed capture the diverse nature of human written captions and can help separate two captions that are both correct but differ in quality. Despite being a standard test on PASCAL-50S, measuring the accuracy abstracts away detailed human preferences, and causes issue when two candidate captions get similar human votes. To mitigate this, we

---

[4] For "There is a person" uniqueness is 0, since it's the most common of the objects, and SPICE-U score is 0 by definition.

Algorithm 1. Generating caption with beam decoding and re-ranking

---

Input: Caption model with parameter θ_c, language model with parameter θ_l, image I, weighting factor λ

Output: Generated caption s

1: Beam decode top-k captions $\{s^{(1)}, ..., s^{(k)}\}$ along with probabilities $\{P(s^{(1)}|I;\theta_c), ..., P(s^{(k)}|I;\theta_c)\}$ with caption model

2: Generate probabilities for entire captions $\{P(s^{(1)};\theta_l), ..., P(s^{(k)};\theta_l)\}$ with language model

3: $s \leftarrow \arg\max_{s^{(i)}} \log P(s^{(i)}|I;\theta_c) - \lambda \log P(s^{(i)};\theta_l)$

---

also evaluate Pearson's correlation between human preferences and each metric[5]. SPICE-U achieves the best correlation score among all metrics.

5 Generating Unique and Informative Captions

SPICE-U aims to capture the uniqueness of a particular caption given an image. Intuitively, any captioning model that maximizes SPICE-U must forge a strong connection between the semantic concepts in the image and the linguistic concepts in the caption it generates. However, in the predominant (current) regime of end-to-end training with loss functions such as cross entropy, there is no explicit objective which enables this connection.

Formally, current captioning models decode using the following objective:

$$\hat{s} = \arg\max_s \log P(s|I;\theta) \tag{8}$$

where s is the caption, I is the image and θ are the learned parameters of the model. However, this ignores the dependency from the caption to the image $P(I|s)$, which is critical for ensuring that the caption adequately (and uniquely) describes the image. A similar observation was made in machine translation [17, 18] where the input and output are sentences in two different languages.

One solution to this problem is to maximize mutual information (MMI) instead of cross-entropy:

$$\hat{s} = \arg\max_s \log \frac{P(I,s)}{P(I)P(s)^\lambda}$$

$$= \arg\max_s \log P(s|I) - \lambda \log P(s) \tag{9}$$

$$= \arg\max_s (1-\lambda) \log P(s|I) + \lambda \log P(I|s)$$

However, since training a model to predict $P(I|s)$ is not trivial [19,46,49], we propose to use second line in the MMI objective above to *re-rank captions* produced by a standard beam decoding mechanism. To this end, we train language

---

[5] We calculate the correlation between the mean value of human votes (+1 if they prefer caption b over caption c, −1 otherwise) and the score $R_m(b) - R_m(c)$, where $R_m(s)$ is the score of sentence s given by metric m.

models to obtain likelihood estimates for captions, $\log P(s) = \sum_i \log P(s_i|s_{<i})$. In particular, we investigate three variants of language models:

1. **Unigram LM:** A simple unigram language model estimated from the train set, $P(s) = \prod_i P(s_i)$
2. **LSTM LM:** An LSTM language model trained on captions in the train set.
3. **Interpolated LM:** A log-linear interpolation[6] between the variants above:

$$P_{int}(s_i|s_{<i}) = P_{uni}(s_i)^\alpha P_{LSTM}(s_i|s_{<i})^{1-\alpha} \tag{10}$$

We generate the top-k captions using the baseline model and then re-rank them using their newly computed scores, described in Algorithm 1.

6   Experiments

Data. We conduct experiments on the COCO [20] dataset which contains images of everyday scenes with common objects in their natural context. For captioning task, every image is annotated with five human captions, mostly short sentences summarizing the important parts of the scene. We adopt the popular split of this dataset from Karpathy et al. [11], which contains 113,287 images for training and 5,000 images for validation and test respectively.

Model. We use three recent captioning models as our baselines. The bottom-up and top-down attention model (TopDown) from Anderson et al. [2] utilizes object detector to propose salient image regions as bottom-up features and then uses top-down attention to decide weight for each region. The discriminative captioning model (DiscCap) from Luo et al. [27] is trained explicitly with proposed 'discriminability' loss besides standard cross-entropy loss to encourage unique captions that can distinguish between different images. The attention on attention model (AoANet) from Huang et al. [8] extends conventional attention mechanism with another attention to determine the relevance between attention results and queries. We use off-the-shelf implementations for these models[7]. For language model, we train a one-layer LSTM with hidden size of 512 and embedding size of 300.

Re-Ranking. We use the captioning model with beam decoding to generate top 10 candidates along with probabilities $P(s|I)$ for re-ranking. The language model is then used to generate the $P(s)$ for each candidate caption and finally the caption with the maximum mutual information is selected according to Eq. 9 as the predicted caption.

---

[6] We also tried linear interpolation and it works not as good as the log-linear interpolation.

[7] The TopDown model from https://github.com/poojahira/image-captioning-bottom-up-top-down, the DiscCap from https://github.com/ruotianluo/DiscCaptioning and AoANet from https://github.com/husthuaan/AoANet.

The hyperparameters λ (language model weight in Eq. 9) and α (coefficient in interpolation model, Eq. 10) are selected for each model on the validation set using a grid search (0 to 1, step size of 0.1).

We cross-validate with the objective of optimizing the geometric mean[8] across several evaluation metrics (BLEU-4, METEOR, CIDEr, CHAIRs, SPICE and SPICE-U). The resulting hyperparameters are: $\lambda = 0.3$ on TopDown+Unigram, $\lambda = 0.2$ on TopDown+LSTM, $\lambda = 0.4, \alpha = 0.8$ on TopDown+Interpolated, $\lambda = 1.0$ on DiscCap+Unigram, $\lambda = 0.1$ on DiscCap+LSTM, $\lambda = 0.8, \alpha = 0.9$ on DiscCap+Interpolated, and $\lambda = 0.4$ on AoANet+Unigram, $\lambda = 0.1$ on AoANet+LSTM, $\lambda = 0.5, \alpha = 0.9$ on AoANet+Interpolated.

Table 3. Comparison of three different state-of-the-art captioning systems [2,8,27], along with our proposed re-ranking schemes, evaluated using different metrics on the COCO test split from [11].

	BLEU	METEOR	CIDEr	CHAIRs ($\downarrow$)	SPICE	SPICE-U	GeoMean
TopDown [2]	**23.03**	28.98	**108.13**	8.68	20.62	23.70	12.63
TopDown+Unigram	22.88	**29.06**	107.04	8.10	**20.82**	25.05	12.89
TopDown+LSTM	22.79	28.48	107.59	8.20	20.52	24.46	12.74
TopDown+Interpolated	22.77	28.84	106.42	**7.80**	20.72	**25.27**	**12.94**
DiscCap [27]	**21.93**	**27.55**	**112.39**	11.92	**20.32**	23.74	11.84
DiscCap+Unigram	21.56	27.38	110.41	10.88	20.28	24.60	12.00
DiscCap+LSTM	21.64	27.40	111.73	11.34	20.17	23.79	11.87
DiscCap+Interpolated	21.58	27.42	110.90	**10.84**	20.27	**24.52**	**12.02**
AoANet [8]	**27.53**	30.37	**129.12**	10.40	22.77	26.04	13.54
AoANet+Unigram	27.30	**30.43**	128.66	9.52	22.79	26.46	13.75
AoANet+LSTM	27.36	30.26	128.79	10.24	22.71	26.12	13.55
AoANet+Interpolated	27.18	30.39	128.15	**9.28**	**22.81**	**26.53**	**13.80**

Results. Table 3 summarizes the results. For the TopDown baseline, the Top-Down+Interpolated modification improves SPICE-U by an absolute 1.6% over the baseline (from 23.7% to 25.3%) and the geometric mean over all metrics by a relative 2.4% (from 12.6% to 12.9%). For DiscCap model, DiscCap+Interpolated led to an absolute improvement of 0.8% on SPICE-U (from 23.7% to 24.5%) and 1.7% relative on the geometric mean (from 11.8% to 12.0%). For AoANet, AoANet+Interpolated improves SPICE-U by an absolute 0.5% (from 26.0% to 26.5%) and a relative 2.2% improvement on geometric mean.

Figure 4 shows qualitative examples: as expected, the updated captions correspond to more detailed descriptions of the image. The improvements demonstrated here are the result of quite simple algorithmic modification yet propose a promising path forward for improving modern image captioning system.

---

[8] The captioning metrics measure different aspects of the captions and are largely uncorrelated with each other [33]; we use the geometric mean as a simple summary statistic of the overall performance of the models. For CHAIR lower scores are better so we use $\frac{1}{CHAIR}$ in the geometric mean.

| *a bird standing on the water at the water* | *a street sign on the side of a street* | *a person holding a hot dog in a bun with a table* | *a man and a woman sitting on a bench* | *a group of giraffes standing in a field* |
| a bird standing on the water at the beach | a no parking sign on the side of a street | a person holding a hot dog in a paper container | a woman sitting on a bench next a statue | a herd of giraffes standing in a field |

Fig. 4. Captions generated by the AoANet [8] model (in italics) and by our variation AoANet+Interpolated (in regular font). The modification we introduce encourages the model to output more descriptive and accurate captions, such as describing the place ("beach"), the type of the sign ("no parking sign"), the presence of a prominent object ("paper container", "statue") in the first four images. However, there are also some images (like the last one) where despite improvements in SPICE-U the changes are less interesting, such as simply replacing "group" with "herd".

7   Conclusion

State of the art image captioning models produce generic captions, leaving out important image details and misrepresenting facts. In this paper, we quantitatively demonstrated that both modern captioning systems and evaluation metrics tend towards generating and rewarding captions with commonly occurring concepts from the training data. We then introduced a new notion of *uniqueness* and used it to propose a new metric, SPICE-U. Our studies show that SPICE-U correlates better with human judgements compared to SPICE. Finally, we utilized the notion of maximizing mutual information to re-rank captions produced by any captioning system. Our experiments demonstrate that our method results in unique and informative captions, and yields promising improvements over three different state-of-the-art models.

Acknowledgments. This work is partially supported by KAUST under Award No. OSRCRG2017-3405, by Samsung and by the Princeton CSML DataX award. We would like to thank Arjun Mani, Vikram Ramaswamy and Angelina Wang for their helpful feedback on the paper.

References

1. Anderson, P., Fernando, B., Johnson, M., Gould, S.: SPICE: semantic propositional image caption evaluation. In: ECCV (2016)
2. Anderson, P., et al.: Bottom-up and top-down attention for image captioning and visual question answering. In: CVPR (2018)
3. Bahl, L., Brown, P., de Souza, P., Mercer, R.: Maximum mutual information estimation of hidden Markov model parameters for speech recognition. In: ICASSP (1986)

4. Cui, Y., Yang, G., Veit, A., Huang, X., Belongie, S.: Learning to evaluate image captioning. In: CVPR (2018)
5. Datta, D., Varma, S., Chowdary, C.R., Singh, S.K.: Multimodal retrieval using mutual information based textual query reformulation. Expert Syst. Appl. **68**, 81–92 (2017)
6. Dognin, P., Melnyk, I., Mroueh, Y., Ross, J., Sercu, T.: Adversarial semantic alignment for improved image captions. In: CVPR (2019)
7. Henning, C.A., Ewerth, R.: Estimating the information gap between textual and visual representations. In: ICMR (2017)
8. Huang, L., Wang, W., Chen, J., Wei, X.Y.: Attention on attention for image captioning. In: ICCV (2019)
9. Johnson, J., Karpathy, A., Fei-Fei, L.: DenseCap: fully convolutional localization networks for dense captioning. In: CVPR (2016)
10. Johnson, J., et al.: Image retrieval using scene graphs. In: CVPR (2015)
11. Karpathy, A., Fei-Fei, L.: Deep visual-semantic alignments for generating image descriptions. In: CVPR (2015)
12. Kimura, R., Iida, S., Cui, H., Hung, P.H., Utsuro, T., Nagata, M.: Selecting informative context sentence by forced back-translation. In: MT Summit XVII (2019)
13. Krause, J., Johnson, J., Krishna, R., Fei-Fei, L.: A hierarchical approach for generating descriptive image paragraphs. In: CVPR (2017)
14. Krishna, R., et al.: Visual genome: connecting language and vision using crowd-sourced dense image annotations. Int. J. Comput. Vision **123**(1), 32–73 (2017). https://doi.org/10.1007/s11263-016-0981-7
15. Kulkarni, G., et al.: BabyTalk: understanding and generating simple image descriptions. IEEE Trans. Pattern Anal. Mach. Intell. **35**(12), 2891–2903 (2013)
16. Lavie, A., Agarwal, A.: Meteor: an automatic metric for MT evaluation with high levels of correlation with human judgments. In: StatMT (2007)
17. Li, J., Galley, M., Brockett, C., Gao, J., Dolan, B.: A diversity-promoting objective function for neural conversation models. In: NAACL HLT (2016)
18. Li, J., Jurafsky, D.: Mutual Information and Diverse Decoding Improve Neural Machine Translation. arXiv:1601.00372 [cs] (2016). arXiv: 1601.00372
19. Li, W., et al.: Object-driven text-to-image synthesis via adversarial training. In: CVPR (2019)
20. Lin, T.Y., et al.: Microsoft COCO: common objects in context. In: ECCV (2014)
21. Lindh, A., Ross, R.J., Mahalunkar, A., Salton, G., Kelleher, J.D.: Generating diverse and meaningful captions. In: ICANN (2018)
22. Liu, L., Tang, J., Wan, X., Guo, Z.: Generating diverse and descriptive image captions using visual paraphrases. In: ICCV (2019)
23. Liu, S., Zhu, Z., Ye, N., Guadarrama, S., Murphy, K.: Improved image captioning via policy gradient optimization of SPIDEr. In: ICCV (2017)
24. Liu, X., Li, H., Shao, J., Chen, D., Wang, X.: Show, tell and discriminate: image captioning by self-retrieval with partially labeled data. In: ECCV (2018)
25. Lu, D., Whitehead, S., Huang, L., Ji, H., Chang, S.F.: Entity-aware image caption generation. In: EMNLP (2018)
26. Lu, J., Xiong, C., Parikh, D., Socher, R.: knowing when to look: adaptive attention via a visual sentinel for image captioning. In: CVPR (2017)
27. Luo, R., Shakhnarovich, G., Cohen, S., Price, B.: Discriminability objective for training descriptive captions. In: CVPR (2018)
28. Mao, J., Huang, J., Toshev, A., Camburu, O., Yuille, A., Murphy, K.: Generation and comprehension of unambiguous object descriptions. In: CVPR (2016)

29. Melas-Kyriazi, L., Rush, A., Han, G.: Training for diversity in image paragraph captioning. In: EMNLP (2018)
30. Papineni, K., Roukos, S., Ward, T., Zhu, W.J.: BLEU: a method for automatic evaluation of machine translation. In: ACL (2001)
31. Povey, D., Woodland, P.: Minimum phone error and I-smoothing for improved discriminative training. In: ICASSP (2002)
32. Ren, S., He, K., Girshick, R., Sun, J.: Faster R-CNN: towards real-time object detection with region proposal networks. IEEE Trans. Pattern Anal. Mach. Intell. (2017)
33. Rohrbach, A., Hendricks, L.A., Burns, K., Darrell, T., Saenko, K.: Object hallucination in image captioning. In: EMNLP (2018)
34. Shetty, R., Rohrbach, M., Hendricks, L.A., Fritz, M., Schiele, B.: speaking the same language: matching machine to human captions by adversarial training. In: ICCV (2017)
35. Jones, K.S.: A statistical interpretation of term specificity and its application in retrieval. J. Doc. (1972)
36. Tu, Z., Liu, Y., Shang, L., Liu, X., Li, H.: Neural machine translation with reconstruction. In: AAAI (2017)
37. Vedantam, R., Bengio, S., Murphy, K., Parikh, D., Chechik, G.: Context-aware captions from context-agnostic supervision. In: CVPR (2017)
38. Vedantam, R., Zitnick, C.L., Parikh, D.: CIDEr: consensus-based image description evaluation. In: CVPR (2015)
39. Vijayakumar, A.K., et al.: Diverse beam search for improved description of complex scenes. In: AAAI (2018)
40. Vijayakumar, A.K., et al.: Diverse Beam Search: Decoding Diverse Solutions from Neural Sequence Models. arXiv:1610.02424 [cs] (2018). arXiv: 1610.02424
41. Vinyals, O., Toshev, A., Bengio, S., Erhan, D.: Show and tell: a neural image caption generator. In: CVPR (2015)
42. Vinyals, O., Toshev, A., Bengio, S., Erhan, D.: Show and Tell: Lessons Learned from the 2015 MSCOCO Image Captioning Challenge (2017)
43. Wang, Q., Chan, A.B.: Describing like humans: on diversity in image captioning. In: CVPR (2019)
44. Wu, B., Jia, F., Liu, W., Ghanem, B.: Diverse image annotation. In: CVPR (2017)
45. Xu, K., et al.: Show, attend and tell: neural image caption generation with visual attention. In: ICML (2015)
46. Xu, T., et al.: AttnGAN: fine-grained text to image generation with attentional generative adversarial networks. In: CVPR (2018)
47. Yao, T., Mei, T., Ngo, C.W.: Co-reranking by mutual reinforcement for image search. In: CVPR (2010)
48. You, Q., Jin, H., Wang, Z., Fang, C., Luo, J.: Image captioning with semantic attention. In: CVPR (2016)
49. Zhang, H., et al.: StackGAN: text to photo-realistic image synthesis with stacked generative adversarial networks. In: ICCV (2017)
50. Zhang, Y., et al.: Generating informative and diverse conversational responses via adversarial information maximization. In: NeurIPS (2018)

When Does Self-supervision Improve Few-Shot Learning?

Jong-Chyi Su[1]([✉]) [iD], Subhransu Maji[1] [iD], and Bharath Hariharan[2] [iD]

[1] University of Massachusetts Amherst, Amherst, USA
{jcsu,smaji}@cs.umass.edu
[2] Cornell University, Ithaca, USA
bharathh@cs.cornell.edu

Abstract. We investigate the role of self-supervised learning (SSL) in the context of few-shot learning. Although recent research has shown the benefits of SSL on large unlabeled datasets, its utility on small datasets is relatively unexplored. We find that SSL reduces the relative error rate of few-shot meta-learners by 4%–27%, even when the datasets are small and *only* utilizing images within the datasets. The improvements are greater when the training set is smaller or the task is more challenging. Although the benefits of SSL may increase with larger training sets, we observe that SSL can hurt the performance when the distributions of images used for meta-learning and SSL are different. We conduct a systematic study by varying the degree of domain shift and analyzing the performance of several meta-learners on a multitude of domains. Based on this analysis we present a technique that automatically selects images for SSL from a large, generic pool of unlabeled images for a given dataset that provides further improvements.

1 Introduction

Current machine learning algorithms require enormous amounts of training data to learn new tasks. This is an issue for many practical problems across domains such as biology and medicine where labeled data is hard to come by. In contrast, we humans can quickly learn new concepts from limited training data by relying on our past "visual experience". Recent work attempts to emulate this by training a feature representation to classify a training dataset of "base" classes with the hope that the resulting representation generalizes not just to unseen examples of the same classes but also to novel classes, which may have very few training examples (called few-shot learning). However, training for base class classification can force the network to only encode features that are useful for distinguishing between base classes. In the process, it might discard semantic information that is irrelevant for base classes but critical for novel classes.

Electronic supplementary material The online version of this chapter (https://doi.org/10.1007/978-3-030-58571-6_38) contains supplementary material, which is available to authorized users.

A. Vedaldi et al. (Eds.): ECCV 2020, LNCS 12352, pp. 645–666, 2020.
https://doi.org/10.1007/978-3-030-58571-6_38

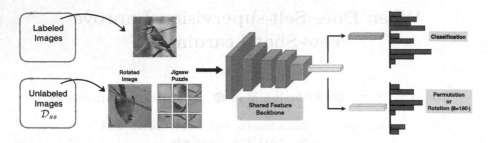

Fig. 1. Combining supervised and self-supervised losses for few-shot learning. Self-supervised tasks such as jigsaw puzzle or rotation prediction act as a data-dependent regularizer for the shared feature backbone. Our work investigates how the performance on the *target task domain* $(\mathcal{D}_s)$ is impacted by the choice of the *domain used for self-supervision* $(\mathcal{D}_{ss})$.

This might be especially true when the base dataset is small or when the class distinctions are challenging.

One way to recover this useful semantic information is to leverage representation learning techniques that do not use class labels, namely, *unsupervised* or *self-supervised learning*. The key idea is to learn about statistical regularities within images, such as the spatial relationship between patches, or its orientation, that might be a cue to semantics. Despite recent advances, these techniques have only been applied to a few domains (*e.g.*, entry-level classes on internet imagery), and under the assumption that large amounts of unlabeled images are available. Their applicability to the general few-shot scenario is unclear. In particular, can these techniques prevent overfitting to base classes and improve performance on novel classes in the few-shot setting? If so, does the benefit generalize across domains and to more challenging tasks? Moreover, can self-supervision boost performance in domains where even unlabeled images are hard to get?

This paper seeks to answer these questions. We show that with *no additional training data*, adding a self-supervised task as an auxiliary task (Fig. 1) improves the performance of existing few-shot techniques on benchmarks across a multitude of domains (Fig. 2), in agreement with conclusions from similar recent work [18]. Intriguingly, we find that the benefits of self-supervision *increase* with the difficulty of the task, for example when training from a smaller base dataset, or with degraded inputs such as low resolution or greyscale images (Fig. 3).

One might surmise that as with traditional SSL, additional unlabeled images might improve performance further. But what unlabeled images should we use for novel problem domains where unlabeled data is not freely available? To answer this, we conduct a series of experiments with additional unlabeled data from different domains. We find that adding more unlabeled images improves performance *only* when the images used for self-supervision are within the *same domain* as the base classes (Fig. 4a); otherwise, they can even *negatively* impact the performance of the few-shot learner (Fig. 4b). Based on this analysis, we present a simple approach that uses a domain classifier to pick similar-domain unlabeled images for self-supervision from a large and generic pool of images (Fig. 5). The resulting method improves over the performance of a model trained with self-supervised learning from images within the dataset (Fig. 6). Taken together, this results in a powerful, general, and practical approach for improving few-shot learning on small datasets in novel domains. Finally, these benefits are also observed in standard classification tasks (Appendix A.3).

2   Related Work

Few-Shot Learning. Few-shot learning aims to learn representations that generalize well to the novel classes where only a few images are available. To this end, several meta-learning approaches have been proposed that evaluate representations by sampling many few-shot tasks within the domain of a *base* dataset. These include optimization-based meta-learners, such as model-agnostic meta-learner (MAML) [16], gradient unrolling [49], closed-form solvers [4], and convex learners [35]. The second class of methods rely on distance-based classifiers such as matching networks [61] and prototypical networks (ProtoNet) [55]. Another class of methods [19,47,48] model the mapping between training data and classifier weights using a feed-forward network.

While the literature is rapidly growing, a recent study by Chen *et al.* [10] has shown that the differences between meta-learners are diminished when deeper networks are used. They develop a strong baseline for few-shot learning and show that the performance of ProtoNet [55] matches or surpasses several recently proposed meta-learners. We build our experiments on top of this work and show that auxiliary self-supervised tasks provide additional benefits across a large array of few-shot benchmarks and across meta-learners.

Self-supervised Learning. Human labels are expensive to collect and hard to scale up. To this end, there has been increasing research interest to investigate learning representations from unlabeled data. In particular, the image itself already contains structural information that can be utilized. One class of methods remove part of the visual data and task the network with predicting what has been removed from the rest in a discriminative manner [34,46,59,68,69]. Another line of works treat each image (and augmentations of itself) as one class and use contrastive learning as self-supervision [3,5,9,15,22,24,25,38,43,65]. Other self-supervised tasks include predicting rotation [20], relative patch location [13], clusters [7,8], and number of objects [42], *etc.*

On top of those SSL tasks, combining different tasks can be beneficial [14], in this work we also see its benefit. Asano *et al.* [2] showed that the representations can be learned with only one image and extreme augmentations. We also investigate SSL on a low-data regime, but use SSL as a regularizer instead of a pre-training task. Goyal *et al.* [21] and Kolesnikov *et al.* [31] compared various SSL tasks at scale and concluded that solving jigsaw puzzles and predicting image rotations are among the most effective, motivating the choice of tasks in our experiments. Note that these two works did not include a comparison with contrastive learning approaches.

In addition to pre-training models, SSL can also be used to improve other tasks. For example, Zhai *et al.* [67] showed that self-supervision can be used to improve recognition in a semi-supervised setting and presented results on a partially labeled version of the ImageNet dataset. Carlucci *et al.* [6] used self-supervision to improve domain generalization. In this work we use SSL to improve few-shot learning where the goal is to generalize to novel classes.

However, the focus of most prior works on SSL is to supplant traditional supervised representation learning with unsupervised learning on large unlabeled datasets for downstream tasks. Crucially in almost all prior works, self-supervised representations consistently lag behind fully-supervised ones trained on the same dataset with the same architecture [21,31]. *In contrast, our work focuses on an important counterexample:* self-supervision can in fact augment standard supervised training for few-shot transfer learning in the low training data regime *without* relying on any external dataset.

The most related work is that of Gidaris *et al.* [18] who also use self-supervision to improve few-shot learning. Although the initial results are similar (Table 3), we further show these benefits on several datasets with harder recognition problems (fine-grained classification) and with deeper models (Sect. 4.1). Moreover, we present a novel analysis of the impact of the domain of unlabeled data (Sect. 4.2). Finally, we propose a new and simple approach to automatically select similar-domain unlabeled data for self-supervision (Sect. 4.3).

Multi-task Learning. Our work is related to multi-task learning, a class of techniques that train on multiple task objectives together to improve each one. Previous works in the computer vision literature have shown moderate benefits by combining tasks such as edge, normal, and saliency estimation for images, or part segmentation and detection for humans [30,37,51]. However, there is significant evidence that training on multiple tasks together often hurts performance on individual tasks [30,37]. Only certain task combinations appear to be mutually beneficial, and sometimes specific architectures are needed. Our key contribution here is showing that self-supervised tasks and few-shot learning are indeed mutually beneficial in this sense.

Domain Selection. On supervised learning, Cui *et al.* [12] used Earth Mover's distance to measure the domain similarity and select the source domain for pre-training. Ngiam *et al.* [39] found more data for pre-training does not always help and proposed to use importance weights to select pre-training data. Task2vec [1] generates a task embedding given a probe network and the target dataset. Such embeddings can help select a better pre-training model from a pool of experts which yields better performance after fine-tuning. Unlike these, we do not assume that the source domain is labeled and rely on self-supervised learning. On self-supervised learning, Goyal *et al.* [21] used two pre-training and target datasets to show the importance of source domain on large-scale self-supervised learning.

Unlike this work, we investigate the performance on few-shot learning across a number of domains, as well as investigate methods for domain selection. A concurrent work [62] also investigates the effect of domain shifts on SSL.

3 Method

We adopt the commonly used setup for few-shot learning where one is provided with labeled training data for a set of *base* classes $\mathcal{D}_b$ and a much smaller training set (typically 1–5 examples per class) for *novel* classes $\mathcal{D}_n$. The goal of the few-shot learner is to learn representations on the base classes that lead to good generalization on novel classes. Although in theory the base classes are assumed to have a large number of labeled examples, in practice this number can be quite small for novel or fine-grained domains, *e.g.* less than 5000 images for the birds dataset [63], making it challenging to learn a generalizable representation.

Our framework, as seen in Fig. 1, combines *meta-learning* approaches for few-shot learning with *self-supervised learning*. Denote a labeled training dataset $\mathcal{D}_s$ as $\{(x_i, y_i)\}_{i=1}^{n}$ consisting of pairs of images $x_i \in \mathcal{X}$ and labels $y_i \in \mathcal{Y}$. A feed-forward convolutional network $f(x)$ maps the input to an embedding space which is then mapped to the label space using a classifier g. The overall mapping from the input to the label can be written as $g \circ f(x) : \mathcal{X} \to \mathcal{Y}$. Learning consists of estimating functions f and g that minimize an empirical loss ℓ over the training data along with suitable regularization $\mathcal{R}$ over the functions f and g. This can be written as:

$$\mathcal{L}_s := \sum_{(x_i, y_i) \in \mathcal{D}_s} \ell\big(g \circ f(x_i), y_i\big) + \mathcal{R}(f, g).$$

A commonly used loss is the cross-entropy loss and a regularizer is the ℓ_2 norm of the parameters of the functions. In a transfer learning setting g is discarded and relearned on training data for novel classes.

We also consider self-supervised losses $\mathcal{L}_{ss}$ based on labeled data $x \to (\hat{x}, \hat{y})$ that can be derived automatically without any human labeling. Figure 1 shows two examples: the *jigsaw task* rearranges the input image and uses the index of the permutation as the target label, while the *rotation task* uses the angle of the rotated image as the target label. A separate function h is used to predict these labels from the shared feature backbone f with a self-supervised loss:

$$\mathcal{L}_{ss} := \sum_{x_i \in \mathcal{D}_{ss}} \ell\big(h \circ f(\hat{x}_i), \hat{y}_i\big).$$

Our final loss combines the two: $\mathcal{L} := \mathcal{L}_s + \mathcal{L}_{ss}$ and thus the self-supervised losses act as a data-dependent regularizer for representation learning. The details of these losses are described in the next sections.

Note that the domain of images used for supervised $\mathcal{D}_s$ and self-supervised $\mathcal{D}_{ss}$ losses need not to be identical. In particular, we would like to use larger sets of images for self-supervised learning from related domains. The key questions we ask are: (1) How effective is SSL when $\mathcal{D}_s = \mathcal{D}_{ss}$ especially when we have a small sample of D_s? (2) How do the domain shifts between $\mathcal{D}_s$ and $\mathcal{D}_{ss}$ affect generalization performance? and (3) How to select images from a large, generic pool to construct an effective $\mathcal{D}_{ss}$ given a target domain $\mathcal{D}_s$?

3.1 Supervised Losses ($\mathcal{L}_s$)

Most of our results are presented using a meta-learner based on prototypical networks [55] that perform episodic training and testing over sampled datasets in stages called meta-training and meta-testing. During meta-training, we randomly sample N classes from the base set $\mathcal{D}_b$, then we select a support set $\mathcal{S}_b$ with K images per class and another query set $\mathcal{Q}_b$ with M images per class. We call this an N-way K-shot classification task. The embeddings are trained to predict the labels of the query set $\mathcal{Q}_b$ conditioned on the support set $\mathcal{S}_b$ using a nearest mean (prototype) classifier. The objective is to minimize the prediction loss on the query set. Once training is complete, given the novel dataset $\mathcal{D}_n$, class prototypes are recomputed for classification and query examples are classified based on the distances to the class prototypes.

Prototypical networks are related to distance-based learners such as matching networks [61] or metric-learning based on label similarity [29]. We also present few-shot classification results using a gradient-based meta-learner called MAML [16], and one trained with a standard cross-entropy loss on all the base classes. We also present standard classification results where the test set contains images from the same base categories in Appendix A.3.

3.2 Self-supervised Losses ($\mathcal{L}_{ss}$)

We consider two losses motivated by a recent large-scale comparison of the effectiveness of self-supervised learning tasks [21] described below:

- *Jigsaw puzzle task loss.* Here the input image x is tiled into 3×3 regions and permuted randomly to obtain an input $\hat{x}$. The target label $\hat{y}$ is the index of the permutation. The index (one of 9!) is reduced to one of 35 following the procedure outlined in [41], which grouped the possible permutations based on the hamming distance to control the difficulty of the task.
- *Rotation task loss.* We follow the method of [20] where the input image x is rotated by an angle $\theta \in \{0°, 90°, 180°, 270°\}$ to obtain $\hat{x}$ and the target label $\hat{y}$ is the index of the angle.

In both cases we use the cross-entropy loss between the target and prediction.

3.3 Stochastic Sampling and Training

When the images used for SSL and meta-learning are identical, *i.e.*, $\mathcal{D}_s = \mathcal{D}_{ss}$, the same batch of images are used for computing both losses $\mathcal{L}_s$ and $\mathcal{L}_{ss}$. For experiments investigating the effect of domain shifts described in Sect. 4.2 and 4.3, where SSL and meta-learner are trained on different domains, *i.e.* $\mathcal{D}_s \neq \mathcal{D}_{ss}$,

Table 1. Example images and dataset statistics. For few-shot learning experiments the classes are split into *base*, *val*, and *novel* set. Image representations learned on *base* set are evaluated on the *novel* set while *val* set is used for cross-validation. These datasets vary in the number of classes but are orders of magnitude smaller than ImageNet dataset.

Setting	Set	Stats	*mini-*ImageNet	*tiered-*ImageNet	Birds	Cars	Aircrafts	Dogs	Flowers
Few-shot transfer	Base	classes	64	351	100	98	50	60	51
		images	38,400	448,695	5885	8162	5000	10337	4129
	Val	classes	16	97	50	49	25	30	26
		images	9,600	124,261	2950	3993	2500	5128	2113
	Novel	classes	20	160	50	49	25	30	25
		images	12,000	206,209	2953	4030	2500	5115	1947

a separate batch of size of 64 is used for computing $\mathcal{L}_{ss}$. After the two forward passes, one for the supervised task and one for the self-supervised task, the two losses are combined and gradient updates are performed. While other techniques exist [11,26,54], simply averaging the two losses performed well.

4 Experiments

We first describe the datasets and experimental details. In Sect. 4.1, we present the results of using SSL to improve few-shot learning on various datasets. In Sect. 4.2, we show the effect of domain shift between labeled and unlabeled data for SSL. Last, we propose a way to select images from a pool for SSL to further improve the performance of few-shot learning in Sect. 4.3.

Datasets and Benchmarks. We experiment with datasets across diverse domains: Caltech-UCSD birds [63], Stanford cars [32], FGVC aircrafts [36], Stanford dogs [27], and Oxford flowers [40]. Each dataset contains between 100 and 200 classes with a few thousands of images. We also experiment with the widely-used *mini*-ImageNet [61] and *tiered*-ImageNet [50] benchmarks for few-shot learning. In *mini*-ImageNet, each class has 600 images, wherein *tiered*-ImageNet each class has 732 to 1300 images.

We split classes within a dataset into three disjoint sets: *base*, *val*, and *novel*. For each class, all the images in the dataset are used in the corresponding set.

A model is trained on the base set of categories, validated on the val set, and tested on the novel set of categories given a few examples per class. For birds, we use the same split as [10], where {*base, val, novel*} sets have {100, 50, 50} classes respectively. The same ratio is used for the other four fine-grained datasets. We follow the original splits for *mini*-ImageNet and *tiered*-ImageNet. The statistics of various datasets used in our experiments are shown in Table 1. Notably, fine-grained datasets are significantly smaller.

We also present results on a setting where the base set is "degraded" either by (1) reducing the resolution, (2) removing color, or (3) reducing the number of training examples. This allows us to study the effectiveness of SSL on even smaller datasets and as a function of the difficulty of the task.

Meta-Learners and Feature Backbone. We follow the best practices and use the codebase for few-shot learning described in [10]. In particular, we use ProtoNet [55] with a ResNet-18 [23] network as the feature backbone. Their experiments found this to be the best performing. We also present experiments with other meta-learners such as MAML [16] and softmax classifiers in Sect. 4.1.

Learning and Optimization. We use 5-way (classes) and 5-shot (examples per-class) with 16 query images for training. For experiments using 20% of labeled data, we use 5 query images for training since the minimum number of images per class is 10. The models are trained with ADAM [28] with a learning rate of 0.001 for 60,000 episodes. We report the mean accuracy and 95% confidence interval over 600 test experiments. In each test episode, N classes are selected from the novel set, and for each class 5 support images and 16 query images are selected. We report results for $N = \{5, 20\}$ classes.

Image Sampling and Data Augmentation. Data augmentation has a significant impact on few-shot learning performance. We follow the data augmentation procedure outlined in [10] which resulted in a strong baseline performance. For label and rotation predictions, images are first resized to 224 pixels for the shorter edge while maintaining the aspect ratio, from which a central crop of 224×224 is obtained. For jigsaw puzzles, we first randomly crop 255×255 region from the original image with random scaling between $[0.5, 1.0]$, then split into 3×3 regions, from which a random crop of size 64×64 is picked. While it might appear that with self-supervision the model effectively sees more images, SSL provides consistent improvements even after extensive data augmentation including cropping, flipping, and color jittering. More experimental details are in Appendix A.5.

Other Experimental Results. In Appendix A.3, we show the benefits of using self-supervision for *standard* classification tasks when training the model *from scratch*. We further visualize these models in Appendix A.4 to show that models trained with self-supervision tend to avoid accidental correlation of background features to class labels.

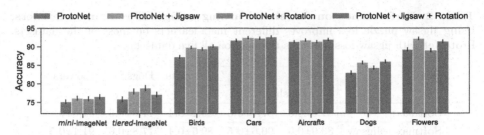

Fig. 2. Benefits of SSL for few-shot learning tasks. We show the accuracy of the ProtoNet baseline of using different SSL tasks. The jigsaw task results in an improvement of the 5-way 5-shot classification accuracy across datasets. Combining SSL tasks can be beneficial for some datasets. Here SSL was performed on images within the base classes only. See Appendix A.1 for a tabular version and results for 20-way 5-shot classification.

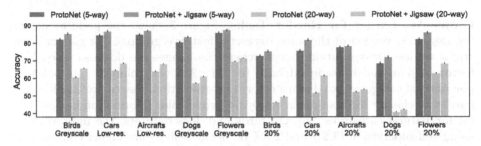

Fig. 3. Benefits of SSL for *harder* few-shot learning tasks. We show the accuracy of using the jigsaw puzzle task over ProtoNet baseline on harder versions of the datasets. We see that SSL is effective even on smaller datasets and the relative benefits are higher.

4.1   Results on Few-Shot Learning

Self-supervised Learning Improves Few-Shot Learning. Figure 2 shows the accuracies of various models on few-shot learning benchmarks. Our ProtoNet baseline matches the results of the *mini*-ImageNet and birds datasets presented in [10] (in their Table A5). Our results show that jigsaw puzzle task improves the ProtoNet baseline on all seven datasets. Specifically, it reduces the *relative error rate* by 4.0%, 8.7%, 19.7%, 8.4%, 4.7%, 15.9%, and 27.8% on *mini*-ImageNet, *tiered*-ImageNet, birds, cars, aircrafts, dogs, and flowers datasets respectively. Predicting rotations also improves the ProtoNet baseline on most of the datasets, except for aircrafts and flowers. We speculate this is because most flower images are symmetrical, and airplanes are usually horizontal, making the rotation task too hard or too trivial respectively to benefit the main task. In addition, combining these two SSL tasks can be beneficial sometimes. A tabular version and the results of 20-way classification are included in Appendix A.1.

Table 2. Performance on few-shot learning using different meta-learners.
Using jigsaw puzzle loss improves different meta-learners on most of the datasets.
ProtoNet with jigsaw loss performs the best on all five datasets.

Loss	Birds	Cars	Aircrafts	Dogs	Flowers
	5-way 5-shot				
Softmax	81.5±0.5	87.7±0.5	89.2±0.4	77.6±0.6	91.0±0.5
Softmax + Jigsaw	83.9±0.5	90.6±0.5	89.6±0.4	77.8±0.6	91.1±0.5
MAML	81.2±0.7	86.9±0.6	88.8±0.5	77.3±0.7	79.0±0.9
MAML + Jigsaw	81.1±0.7	89.0±0.5	89.1±0.5	77.3±0.7	82.6±0.7
ProtoNet	87.3±0.5	91.7±0.4	91.4±0.4	83.0±0.6	89.2±0.6
ProtoNet + Jigsaw	**89.8±0.4**	**92.4±0.4**	**91.8±0.4**	**85.7±0.5**	**92.2±0.4**

Gains Are Larger for Harder Tasks. Figure 3 shows the performance on
the degraded version of the same datasets (first five groups). For cars and aircrafts we use low-resolution images where the images are down-sampled by a
factor of *four* and up-sampled back to 224×224 with bilinear interpolation.
For natural categories we discard color. Low-resolution images are considerably
harder to classify for man-made categories while color information is most useful for natural categories [56]. On birds and dogs datasets, the improvements
using self-supervision (3.2% and 2.9% on 5-way 5-shot) are higher compared to
color images (2.5% and 2.7%), similarly on the cars and aircrafts datasets with
low-resolution images (2.2% and 2.1% vs. 0.7% and 0.4%). We also conduct
an experiment where only 20% of the images in the base categories are used
for both SSL and meta-learning (last five groups in Fig. 3). This results in a
much smaller training set than standard few-shot benchmarks: 20% of the birds
dataset amounts to only roughly 3% of the popular *mini*-ImageNet dataset. We
find larger benefits from SSL in this setting. For example, the gain from the jigsaw puzzle loss for 5-way 5-shot car classification increases from 0.7% (original
dataset) to 7.0% (20% training data).

Improvements Generalize to Other Meta-Learners. We combine SSL
with other meta-learners and find the combination to be effective. In particular,
we use MAML [16] and a standard feature extractor trained with cross-entropy
loss (softmax) as in [10]. Table 2 compares meta-learners based on a ResNet-18
network trained with and without *jigsaw puzzle loss*. We observe that the average
5-way 5-shot accuracies across five fine-grained datasets for softmax, MAML,
and ProtoNet improve from 85.5%, 82.6%, and 88.5% to 86.6%, 83.8%, and
90.4% respectively when combined with the jigsaw puzzle task. Self-supervision
improves performance across different meta-learners and different datasets; however, ProtoNet trained with self-supervision is the best model across all datasets.

Table 3. Comparison with prior works on *mini*-ImageNet. 5-shot 5-way classification accuracies on 600 test episodes are reported. The implementation details including image size, backbone model, and training are different in each paper. *validation classes are used for training. †dropblock [17], label smoothing, and weight decay are used.

Model	Image size	Backbone	SSL	Accuracy (%)
MAML [16]	84 × 84	Conv4-64	-	63.1
ProtoNet [55]		Conv4-64	-	68.2
RelationNet [57]		Conv4-64	-	65.3
LwoF [19]		Conv4-64	-	72.8
PFA [48]*		WRN-28-10	-	73.7
TADAM [44]		ResNet-12	-	76.7
LEO [53]*		WRN-28-10	-	77.6
MetaOptNet-SVM [35]†		ResNet-12	-	78.6
Chen et al. [10]	84 × 84	Conv4-64	-	64.2
(ProtoNet)	224 × 224	ResNet-18	-	73.7
Gidaris et al. [18]	84 × 84	Conv4-64	-	70.0
(ProtoNet)			Rotation	71.7
		Conv4-512	-	71.6
			Rotation	74.0
		WRN-28-10	-	68.7
			Rotation	72.1
Ours	224 × 224	ResNet-18	-	75.2
(ProtoNet)			Rotation	76.0
			Jigsaw	76.2
			Rot.+Jig.	76.6

Self-supervision Alone Is Not Enough. SSL alone significantly lags behind supervised learning in our experiments. For example, a ResNet-18 trained with SSL alone achieve 32.9% (w/ jigsaw) and 33.7% (w/ rotation) 5-way 5-shot accuracy averaged across five fine-grained datasets. While this is better than a random initialization (29.5%), it is dramatically worse than one trained with a simple cross-entropy loss (85.5%) on the labels (details in Table 4 in Appendix A.1). Surprisingly, we also found that initialization with SSL followed by meta-learning did *not* yield improvements over meta-learning starting from random initialization, supporting the view that SSL acts as a feature regularizer.

Few-Shot Learning as an Evaluation for Self-supervised Tasks. The few-shot classification task provides a way of evaluating the effectiveness of self-supervised tasks. For example, on 5-way 5-shot aircrafts classification, training with only jigsaw and rotation task gives 38.8% and 29.5% respectively, suggesting that rotation is not an effective self-supervised task for airplanes. We speculate that it might be because the task is too easy as airplanes are usually horizontal.

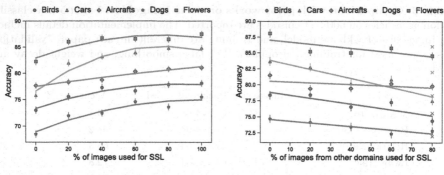

(a) Effect of number of images on SSL.   (b) Effect of domain shift on SSL.

Fig. 4. Effect of size and domain of SSL on 5-way 5-shot classification accuracy. (a) More unlabeled data from the same domain for SSL improves the performance of the meta-learner. **(b)** Replacing a fraction (x-axis) of the images with those from other domains makes SSL less effective.

Comparison with Prior Works. Our results also echo those of [18] who find that the rotation task improves on *mini-* and *tiered*-ImageNet. In addition we show the improvement still holds when using deeper networks, higher resolution images, and in fine-grained domains. We provide a comparison with other few-shot learning methods in Table 3.

4.2 Analyzing the Effect of Domain Shift for Self-supervision

Scaling SSL to massive unlabeled datasets that are readily available for some domains is a promising avenue for improvement. *However, do more unlabeled data always help for a task in hand?* This question hasn't been sufficiently addressed in the literature as most prior works study the effectiveness of SSL on a curated set of images, such as ImageNet, and their transferability to a handful of tasks. We conduct a series of experiments to characterize the effect of size and distribution $\mathcal{D}_{ss}$ of images used for SSL in the context of few-shot learning on domain $\mathcal{D}_s$.

First, we investigate if SSL on unlabeled data from the same domain improves the meta-learner. We use 20% of the images in the base categories for meta-learning identical to the setting in Fig. 3. The labels of the remaining 80% data are withheld and only the images are used for SSL. We systematically vary the number of images used by SSL from 20% to 100%. The results are presented in Fig. 4a. The accuracy improves with the size of the unlabeled set with diminishing returns. Note that 0% corresponds to no SSL and 20% corresponds to using only the labeled images for SSL ($\mathcal{D}_s = \mathcal{D}_{ss}$).

Figure 4b shows an experiment where a fraction of the unlabeled images are replaced with images from other four datasets. For example, 20% along the x-axis for birds indicate that 20% of the images in the base set are replaced by images drawn uniformly at random from other datasets. Since the numbers of

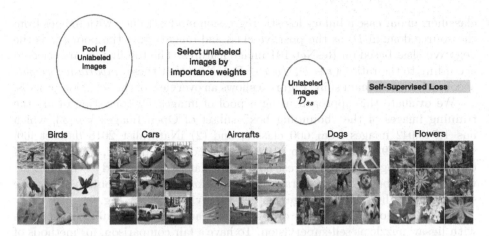

Fig. 5. Overview of domain selection for self-supervision. Top: We first train a domain classifier using $\mathcal{D}_s$ and (a subset of) $\mathcal{D}_p$, then select images using the predictions from the domain classifier for self-supervision. **Bottom:** Selected images of each dataset using importance weights.

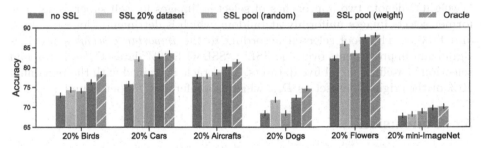

Fig. 6. Effectiveness of selected images for SSL. With random selection, the extra unlabeled data often hurts the performance, while those sampled using the *importance weights* improve performance on all five datasets. A tabular version is shown in Appendix A.2.

images used for SSL is identical, the x-axis from left to right represents increasing amounts of domain shifts between $\mathcal{D}_s$ and $\mathcal{D}_{ss}$. We observe that the effectiveness of SSL decreases as the fraction of out-of-domain images increases. Importantly, training with SSL on the available 20% within domain images (shown as crosses) is often (on 3 out of 5 datasets) better than increasing the set of images by five times to include out of domain images.

4.3 Selecting Images for Self-supervision

Based on the above analysis we propose a simple method to select images for SSL from a large, generic pool of unlabeled images in a dataset dependent manner. We use a "domain weighted" model to select the top images based on a domain classifier, in our case a binary logistic regression model trained with images from the source domain $\mathcal{D}_s$ as the positive class and images from the pool $\mathcal{D}_p$ as the negative class based on ResNet-101 image features. The top images are selected according to the ratio $p(x \in \mathcal{D}_s)/p(x \in \mathcal{D}_p)$. Note that these *importance weights* account for the domain shift. Figure 5 shows an overview of the selection process.

We evaluate this approach using a pool of images $\mathcal{D}_p$ consisting of (1) the training images of the "bounding box" subset of Open Images V5 [33] which has 1,743,042 images from 600 classes, and (2) iNaturalist 2018 dataset [60] which has 461,939 images from 8162 species. For each dataset, we use 20% of the labeled images as $\mathcal{D}_s$. The rest 80% of the data are only used as the "oracle" where the unlabeled data are drawn from the exact same distribution as $\mathcal{D}_s$. We show some of the selected images for self-supervision $\mathcal{D}_{ss}$ in Fig. 5.

Figure 6 shows the results of ProtoNet trained on 20% labeled examples with jigsaw puzzle as self-supervision. To have a fair comparison, for methods of selecting images from the pool, we select the same number (80% of the original labeled dataset size) of images as $\mathcal{D}_{ss}$. We report the mean accuracy of five runs. "SSL with 20% dataset" denotes a baseline of only using $\mathcal{D}_s$ for self-supervision ($\mathcal{D}_s = \mathcal{D}_{ss}$), which is our reference "lower bound". SSL pool "(random)" and "(weight)" denote two approaches of selecting images for self-supervision. The former selects images uniformly at random, which is detrimental for cars, dogs, and flowers. The pool selected according to the *importance weights* provides significant improvements over "no SSL", "SSL with 20% dataset", and "random selection" baselines on all five datasets. The oracle is trained with the remaining 80% of the original dataset as $\mathcal{D}_{ss}$, which is a reference "upper bound".

5   Conclusion

Self-supervision improves the performance on few-shot learning tasks across a range of different domains. Surprisingly, we found that self-supervision is more beneficial for more challenging problems, especially when the number of images used for self-supervision is small, orders of magnitude smaller than previously reported results. This has a practical benefit that the images within small datasets can be used for self-supervision without relying on a large-scale external dataset. We have also shown that additional unlabeled images can improve performance only if they are from the *same or similar* domains. Finally, for domains where unlabeled data is limited, we present a novel, simple approach to automatically identify such similar-domain images from a larger pool.

Future work could investigate if using other self-supervised tasks can also improve few-shot learning, in particular constrastive learning approaches [3,22,24, 38,58]. Future work could also investigate how and when self-supervision improves generalization across self-supervised and supervised tasks empirically [1,66].

Acknowledgement. This project is supported in part by NSF #1749833 and a DARPA LwLL grant. Our experiments were performed on the University of Massachusetts Amherst GPU cluster obtained under the Collaborative Fund managed by the Massachusetts Technology Collaborative.

A Appendix

In Appendix A.1 and Appendix A.2, we provide all the numbers of the figures in Sect. 4.1 and Sect. 4.3 separately. We show that SSL can also improve traditional fine-grained classification in Appendix A.3 and its model visualization in Appendix A.4. Last, we describe the implementation details in Appendix A.5.

A.1 Results on Few-Shot Learning

Table 4 shows the performance of ProtoNet with different self-supervision on seven datasets. We also test the accuracy of the model on novel classes when trained *only* with self-supervision on the base set of images. Compared to the randomly initialized model ("None" rows), training the network to predict rotations gives around 2% to 21% improvements on all datasets, while solving jigsaw puzzles only improves on aircrafts and flowers. However, these numbers are significantly worse than learning with supervised labels on the base set, in line with the current literature.

Table 4. Performance on few-shot learning tasks. The mean accuracy (%) and the 95% confidence interval of 600 randomly chosen test experiments are reported for various combinations of loss functions. The top part shows the accuracy on 5-way 5-shot classification tasks, while the bottom part shows the same on 20-way 5-shot. Adding self-supervised losses to the ProtoNet loss improves the performance on all seven datasets on 5-way classification results. On 20-way classification, the improvements are even larger. The last row indicates results with a randomly initialized network. The top part of this table corresponds to Fig. 2 in Sect. 4.1.

Loss	mini-ImageNet ImageNet	tiered-ImageNet ImageNet	Birds	Cars	Aircrafts	Dogs	Flowers
			5-way 5-shot				
ProtoNet(PN)	75.2±0.6	75.9±0.7	87.3±0.5	91.7±0.4	91.4±0.4	83.0±0.6	89.2±0.6
PN+Jigsaw	76.2±0.6	78.0±0.7	89.8±0.4	92.4±0.4	91.8+0.4	85.7±0.5	**92.2±0.4**
Rel. err. red.	*4.0%*	*8.7%*	*19.7%*	*8.4%*	*4.7%*	*15.9%*	*27.8%*
Jigsaw	25.6±0.5	24.9±0.4	25.7±0.5	25.3±0.5	38.8±0.6	24.3±0.5	50.5±0.7
PN+Rotation	76.0±0.6	**78.9±0.7**	89.4±0.4	92.3±0.4	91.4±0.4	84.3±0.5	89.0±0.5
Rotation	51.4±0.7	50.7±0.8	33.1±0.6	29.4±0.5	29.5±0.5	27.3±0.5	49.4±0.7
PN+Jig.+Rot.	**76.6±0.7**	77.2±0.7	**90.2±0.4**	**92.7±0.4**	**91.9±0.4**	**85.9±0.5**	91.4±0.5
None	31.0±0.5	28.9±0.5	26.7±0.5	25.2±0.5	28.1±0.5	25.3±0.5	42.3±0.8
			20-way 5-shot				
ProtoNet(PN)	46.6±0.3	49.7±0.4	69.3±0.3	78.7±0.3	78.6±0.3	61.6±0.3	75.4±0.3
PN+Jigsaw	47.8±0.3	**52.4±0.4**	73.7±0.3	79.1±0.3	**79.1±0.2**	65.4±0.3	**79.2±0.3**
Jigsaw	9.2±0.2	7.5±0.1	8.1±0.1	7.1±0.1	15.4±0.2	7.1±0.1	25.7±0.2
PN+Rotation	48.2±0.3	**52.4±0.4**	72.9±0.3	**80.0±0.3**	78.4±0.2	63.4±0.3	73.9±0.3
Rotation	27.4±0.2	25.7±0.3	12.9±0.2	9.3±0.2	9.8±0.2	8.8±0.1	26.3±0.2
PN+Jig.+Rot.	**49.0±0.3**	51.2±0.4	**75.0±0.3**	79.8±0.3	79.0±0.2	**66.2±0.3**	78.6±0.3
None	10.8±0.1	11.0±0.2	9.3±0.2	7.5±0.1	8.9±0.1	7.8±0.1	22.6±0.2

Table 5. Performance on *harder* few-shot learning tasks. Accuracies are reported on novel set for 5-way 5-shot and 20-way 5-shot classification with degraded inputs, and with a subset (20%) of the images in the base set. The loss of color or resolution, and the smaller training set size make the tasks more challenging as seen by the drop in the performance of the ProtoNet baseline. However the improvements of using the *jigsaw puzzle loss* are higher in comparison to the results presented in Table 4.

Loss	Birds	Cars	Aircrafts	Dogs	Flowers
	Greyscale	Low-resolution	Low-resolution	Greyscale	Greyscale
5-way 5-shot					
ProtoNet	82.2±0.6	84.8±0.5	85.0±0.5	80.7±0.6	86.1±0.6
ProtoNet + Jigsaw	85.4±0.6	87.0±0.5	87.1±0.5	83.6±0.5	87.6±0.5
20-way 5-shot					
ProtoNet	60.8±0.4	64.7±0.3	64.1±0.3	57.4±0.3	69.7±0.3
ProtoNet + Jigsaw	65.7±0.3	68.6±0.3	68.3±0.3	61.2±0.3	71.6±0.3
Loss	20% Birds	20% Cars	20% Aircrafts	20% Dogs	20% Flowers
5-way 5-shot					
ProtoNet	73.0±0.7	75.8±0.7	77.7±0.6	68.5±0.7	82.2±0.7
ProtoNet + Jigsaw	75.4±0.7	82.8±0.6	78.4±0.6	69.1±0.7	86.0±0.6
20-way 5-shot					
ProtoNet	46.4±0.3	51.8±0.4	52.3±0.3	40.8±0.3	62.8±0.3
ProtoNet + Jigsaw	49.8±0.3	61.5±0.4	53.6±0.3	42.2±0.3	68.5±0.3

Table 5 shows the performance of ProtoNet with *jigsaw puzzle loss* on harder benchmarks. The results on the degraded version of the datasets are shown in the top part, and the bottom part shows the results of using only 20% of the images in the base categories. The gains using SSL are higher in this setting.

A.2   Results on Selecting Images for SSL

Table 6 shows the performance of selecting images for self-supervision, a tabular version of Fig. 5 in Sect. 4.3. "Pool (random)" uniformly samples images proportional to the size of each dataset, while the "pool (weight)" one tends to pick more images from related domains.

Table 6. Performance on selecting images for self-supervision. Adding more unlabeled images selected randomly from a pool often hurts the performance. Selecting similar images by importance weights improves on all five datasets.

Method	20% Birds	20% Cars	20% Aircrafts	20% Dogs	20% Flowers	20% mini-ImageNet
No SSL	73.0±0.7	75.8±0.7	77.7±0.6	68.5±0.7	82.2±0.7	67.81±0.65
SSL 20% dataset	74.4±0.7	82.1±0.6	77.7±0.6	71.8±0.7	85.9±0.6	68.47±0.66
SSL Pool (random)	74.1±0.7	78.4±0.7	78.8±0.6	68.5±0.7	83.5±0.7	68.94±0.68
SSL Pool (weight)	**76.4±0.6**	**82.9±0.6**	**80.2±0.6**	**72.4±0.7**	**87.6±0.6**	**69.81±0.65**
SSL 100% (oracle)	78.4±0.6	83.7±0.6	81.5±0.6	74.7±0.6	88.1±0.6	70.13±0.67

A.3   Results on Standard Fine-Grained Classification

Here we present results on standard fine-grained classification tasks. Different from few-shot transfer learning, all the classes are seen in the training set and the test set contains novel images from the same classes. We use the standard training and test splits provided in the datasets. We investigate if SSL can improve the training of deep networks (*e.g.* ResNet-18 network) when *trained from scratch* (*i.e.* with random initialization) using images and labels in the training set only. The accuracy of using various loss functions are shown in Table 7. Training with self-supervision improves performance across datasets. On birds, cars, and dogs, predicting rotation gives 4.1%, 3.1%, and 3.0% improvements, while on aircrafts and flowers, the *jigsaw puzzle loss* yields 0.9% and 3.6% improvements.

Table 7. Performance on standard fine-grained classification tasks. Per-image accuracy (%) on the test set are reported. Using self-supervision improves the accuracy of a ResNet-18 network trained *from scratch* over the baseline of supervised training with cross-entropy (softmax) loss on all five datasets.

Loss	Birds	Cars	Aircrafts	Dogs	Flowers
Softmax	47.0	72.6	69.9	51.4	72.8
Softmax + Jigsaw	49.2	73.2	**70.8**	53.5	**76.4**
Softmax + Rotation	**51.1**	**75.7**	70.0	**54.4**	73.5

A.4   Visualization of Learned Models

To understand why the representation generalizes, we visualize what pixels contribute the most to the correct classification for various models. In particular, for each image and model, we compute the gradient of the logits (predictions before softmax) for the correct class with respect to the input image. The magnitude of the gradient at each pixel is a proxy for its importance and is visualized as "saliency maps". Figure 7 shows these maps for various images and models

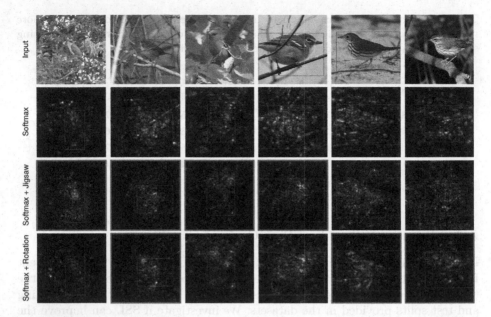

Fig. 7. Saliency maps for various images and models. For each image we visualize the magnitude of the gradient with respect to the correct class for models trained with various loss functions. The magnitudes are scaled to the same range for easier visualization. The models trained with self-supervision often have lower energy on the background regions when there is clutter. We highlight a few examples with blue borders and the bounding-box of the object for each image is shown in red. (Color figure online)

trained with and without self-supervision on the standard classification task. It appears that the self-supervised models tend to focus more on the foreground regions, as seen by the amount of bright pixels within the bounding box. One hypothesis is that self-supervised tasks force the model to rely less on background features, which might be accidentally correlated to the class labels. For fine-grained recognition, localization indeed improves performance when training from few examples (see [64] for a contemporary evaluation of the role of localization for few-shot learning).

A.5   Experimental Details

Optimization Details on Few-Shot Learning. During training, especially for the jigsaw puzzle task, we found it to be beneficial to *not* track the running mean and variance for the batch normalization layer, and instead estimate them for each batch independently. We hypothesize that this is because the inputs contain both full-sized images and small patches, which might have different statistics. At test time we do the same. We found the accuracy goes up as the batch size increases but saturates at a size of 64.

When training with supervised and self-supervised loss, a trade-off term λ between the losses can be used, thus the total loss is $\mathcal{L} = (1 - \lambda)\mathcal{L}_s + \lambda\mathcal{L}_{ss}$. We find that simply use $\lambda = 0.5$ works the best, except for training on *mini-* and *tiered*-ImageNet with jigsaw loss, where we set $\lambda = 0.3$. We suspect that this is because the variation of the image size and the categories are higher, making the self-supervision harder to train with limited data. When both jigsaw and rotation losses are used, we set $\lambda = 0.5$ and the two self-supervised losses are averaged for $\mathcal{L}_{ss}$.

For training meta-learners, we use 16 query images per class for each training episode. When only 20% of labeled data are used, 5 query images per class are used. For MAML, we use 10 query images and the approximation method for backpropagation as proposed in [10] to reduce the GPU memory usage. When training with self-supervised loss, it is added when computing the loss in the outer loop. We use PyTorch [45] for our experiments.

Optimization Details on Domain Classifier. For the domain classifier, we first obtain features from the penultimate-layer (2048 dimensional) from a ResNet-101 model pre-trained on ImageNet [52]. We then train a binary logistic regression model with weight decay using LBFGS for 1000 iterations. The images from the labeled dataset are the positive class and from the pool of unlabeled data are the negative class. A subset of negative images are selected uniformly at random with 10 times the size of positive images. A loss for the positive class is scaled by the inverse of its frequency to account for the significantly larger number of negative examples.

Optimization Details on Standard Classification. For standard classification (Appendix A.3) we train a ResNet-18 network *from scratch*. All the models are trained with ADAM optimizer with a learning rate of 0.001 for 600 epochs with a batch size of 16. We track the running statistics for the batch normalization layer for the softmax baselines following the conventional setting, *i.e.* w/o self-supervised loss, but do not track these statistics when training with self-supervision.

Architectures for Self-supervised Tasks. For jigsaw puzzle task, we follow the architecture of [41] where it was first proposed. The ResNet18 results in a 512-dimensional feature for each input, and we add a fully-connected (fc) layer with 512-units on top. The nine patches give nine 512-dimensional feature vectors, which are concatenated. This is followed by a fc layer, projecting the feature vector from 4608 to 4096 dimensions, and a fc layer with 35-dimensional outputs corresponding to the 35 permutations for the jigsaw task.

For rotation prediction task, the 512-dimensional output of ResNet-18 is passed through three fc layers with {512, 128, 128, 4} units. The predictions correspond to the four rotation angles. Between each fc layer, a ReLU activation and a dropout layer with a dropout probability of 0.5 are added.

References

1. Achille, A., et al.: Task2Vec: task embedding for meta-learning. In: ICCV (2019)
2. Asano, Y.M., Rupprecht, C., Vedaldi, A.: A critical analysis of self-supervision, or what we can learn from a single image. In: ICLR (2020)
3. Bachman, P., Hjelm, R.D., Buchwalter, W.: Learning representations by maximizing mutual information across views. arXiv preprint arXiv:1906.00910 (2019)
4. Bertinetto, L., Henriques, J.F., Torr, P.H., Vedaldi, A.: Meta-learning with differentiable closed-form solvers. In: ICLR (2019)
5. Bojanowski, P., Joulin, A.: Unsupervised learning by predicting noise. In: ICML (2017)
6. Carlucci, F.M., D'Innocente, A., Bucci, S., Caputo, B., Tommasi, T.: Domain generalization by solving jigsaw puzzles. In: CVPR (2019)
7. Caron, M., Bojanowski, P., Joulin, A., Douze, M.: Deep clustering for unsupervised learning of visual features. In: ECCV (2018)
8. Caron, M., Bojanowski, P., Mairal, J., Joulin, A.: Unsupervised pre-training of image features on non-curated data. In: ICCV (2019)
9. Chen, T., Kornblith, S., Norouzi, M., Hinton, G.: A simple framework for contrastive learning of visual representations. In: ICML (2020)
10. Chen, W.Y., Liu, Y.C., Kira, Z., Wang, Y.C., Huang, J.B.: A closer look at few-shot classification. In: ICLR (2019)
11. Chen, Z., Badrinarayanan, V., Lee, C.Y., Rabinovich, A.: Gradnorm: gradient normalization for adaptive loss balancing in deep multitask networks. In: ICML (2018)
12. Cui, Y., Song, Y., Sun, C., Howard, A., Belongie, S.: Large scale fine-grained categorization and domain-specific transfer learning. In: CVPR (2018)
13. Doersch, C., Gupta, A., Efros, A.A.: Unsupervised visual representation learning by context prediction. In: ICCV (2015)
14. Doersch, C., Zisserman, A.: Multi-task self-supervised visual learning. In: ICCV (2017)
15. Dosovitskiy, A., Springenberg, J.T., Riedmiller, M., Brox, T.: Discriminative unsupervised feature learning with convolutional neural networks. In: NeurIPS (2014)
16. Finn, C., Abbeel, P., Levine, S.: Model-agnostic meta-learning for fast adaptation of deep networks. In: ICML (2017)
17. Ghiasi, G., Lin, T.Y., Le, Q.V.: Dropblock: a regularization method for convolutional networks. In: NeurIPS (2018)
18. Gidaris, S., Bursuc, A., Komodakis, N., Pérez, P., Cord, M.: Boosting few-shot visual learning with self-supervision. In: ICCV (2019)
19. Gidaris, S., Komodakis, N.: Dynamic few-shot visual learning without forgetting. In: CVPR (2018)
20. Gidaris, S., Singh, P., Komodakis, N.: Unsupervised representation learning by predicting image rotations. In: ICLR (2018)
21. Goyal, P., Mahajan, D., Gupta, A., Misra, I.: Scaling and benchmarking self-supervised visual representation learning. In: ICCV (2019)
22. He, K., Fan, H., Wu, Y., Xie, S., Girshick, R.: Momentum contrast for unsupervised visual representation learning. In: CVPR (2020)
23. He, K., Zhang, X., Ren, S., Sun, J.: Deep residual learning for image recognition. In: CVPR (2016)
24. Hénaff, O.J., Razavi, A., Doersch, C., Eslami, S., Oord, A.V.D.: Data-efficient image recognition with contrastive predictive coding. arXiv preprint arXiv:1905.09272 (2019)

25. Hjelm, R.D., et al.: Learning deep representations by mutual information estimation and maximization. In: ICLR (2019)
26. Kendall, A., Gal, Y., Cipolla, R.: Multi-task learning using uncertainty to weigh losses for scene geometry and semantics. In: CVPR (2018)
27. Khosla, A., Jayadevaprakash, N., Yao, B., Fei-Fei, L.: Novel dataset for fine-grained image categorization. In: First Workshop on Fine-Grained Visual Categorization, IEEE Conference on Computer Vision and Pattern Recognition (CVPR) (2011)
28. Kingma, D.P., Ba, J.: Adam: a method for stochastic optimization. In: ICLR (2015)
29. Koch, G., Zemel, R., Salakhutdinov, R.: Siamese neural networks for one-shot image recognition. In: ICML Deep Learning Workshop, vol. 2 (2015)
30. Kokkinos, I.: Ubernet: training a universal convolutional neural network for low-, mid-, and high-level vision using diverse datasets and limited memory. In: CVPR (2017)
31. Kolesnikov, A., Zhai, X., Beyer, L.: Revisiting self-supervised visual representation learning. In: CVPR (2019)
32. Krause, J., Stark, M., Deng, J., Fei-Fei, L.: 3D object representations for fine-grained categorization. In: 4th International IEEE Workshop on 3D Representation and Recognition (3DRR), Australia, Sydney (2013)
33. Kuznetsova, A., et al.: The open images dataset V4: unified image classification, object detection, and visual relationship detection at scale. arXiv:1811.00982 (2018)
34. Larsson, G., Maire, M., Shakhnarovich, G.: Learning representations for automatic colorization. In: ECCV (2016)
35. Lee, K., Maji, S., Ravichandran, A., Soatto, S.: Meta-learning with differentiable convex optimization. In: CVPR (2019)
36. Maji, S., Rahtu, E., Kannala, J., Blaschko, M., Vedaldi, A.: Fine-grained visual classification of aircraft. arXiv preprint arXiv:1306.5151 (2013)
37. Maninis, K.K., Radosavovic, I., Kokkinos, I.: Attentive single-tasking of multiple tasks. In: CVPR (2019)
38. Misra, I., van der Maaten, L.: Self-supervised learning of pretext-invariant representations. In: CVPR (2020)
39. Ngiam, J., Peng, D., Vasudevan, V., Kornblith, S., Le, Q.V., Pang, R.: Domain adaptive transfer learning with specialist models. arXiv preprint arXiv:1811.07056 (2018)
40. Nilsback, M.E., Zisserman, A.: A visual vocabulary for flower classification. In: CVPR (2006)
41. Noroozi, M., Favaro, P.: Unsupervised learning of visual representations by solving jigsaw puzzles. In: ECCV (2016)
42. Noroozi, M., Pirsiavash, H., Favaro, P.: Representation learning by learning to count. In: ICCV (2017)
43. Oord, A.V.D., Li, Y., Vinyals, O.: Representation learning with contrastive predictive coding. arXiv preprint arXiv:1807.03748 (2018)
44. Oreshkin, B., López, P.R., Lacoste, A.: Tadam: task dependent adaptive metric for improved few-shot learning. In: NeurIPS (2018)
45. Paszke, A., et al.: PyTorch: an imperative style, high-performance deep learning library. In: NeurIPS (2019)
46. Pathak, D., Krähenbühl, P., Donahue, J., Darrell, T., Efros, A.A.: Context encoders: feature learning by inpainting. In: CVPR (2016)
47. Qi, H., Brown, M., Lowe, D.G.: Low-shot learning with imprinted weights. In: CVPR (2018)

48. Qiao, S., Liu, C., Shen, W., Yuille, A.L.: Few-shot image recognition by predicting parameters from activations. In: CVPR (2018)
49. Ravi, S., Larochelle, H.: Optimization as a model for few-shot learning. In: ICLR (2017)
50. Ren, M., et al.: Meta-learning for semi-supervised few-shot classification. In: ICLR (2018)
51. Ren, Z., Lee, Y.J.: Cross-domain self-supervised multi-task feature learning using synthetic imagery. In: CVPR (2018)
52. Russakovsky, O., et al.: ImageNet large scale visual recognition challenge. Int. J. Comput. Vis. (IJCV) **115**(3), 211–252 (2015)
53. Rusu, A.A., et al.: Meta-learning with latent embedding optimization. arXiv preprint arXiv:1807.05960 (2018)
54. Sener, O., Koltun, V.: Multi-task learning as multi-objective optimization. In: NeurIPS (2018)
55. Snell, J., Swersky, K., Zemel, R.: Prototypical networks for few-shot learning. In: NeurIPS (2017)
56. Su, J.C., Maji, S.: Adapting models to signal degradation using distillation. In: BMVC (2017)
57. Sung, F., Yang, Y., Zhang, L., Xiang, T., Torr, P.H., Hospedales, T.M.: Learning to compare: relation network for few-shot learning. In: CVPR (2018)
58. Tian, Y., Krishnan, D., Isola, P.: Contrastive multiview coding. In: ECCV (2020)
59. Trinh, T.H., Luong, M.T., Le, Q.V.: Selfie: self-supervised pretraining for image embedding. arXiv preprint arXiv:1906.02940 (2019)
60. Van Horn, G., et al.: The iNaturalist species classification and detection dataset. In: CVPR (2018)
61. Vinyals, O., Blundell, C., Lillicrap, T., Wierstra, D., et al.: Matching networks for one shot learning. In: NeurIPS (2016)
62. Wallace, B., Hariharan, B.: Extending and analyzing self-supervised learning across domains. In: ECCV (2020)
63. Welinder, P., et al.: Caltech-UCSD Birds 200. Technical report, CNS-TR-2010-001, California Institute of Technology (2010)
64. Wertheimer, D., Hariharan, B.: Few-shot learning with localization in realistic settings. In: CVPR (2019)
65. Wu, Z., Xiong, Y., Yu, S.X., Lin, D.: Unsupervised feature learning via non-parametric instance discrimination. In: CVPR (2018)
66. Zamir, A.R., Sax, A., Shen, W., Guibas, L.J., Malik, J., Savarese, S.: Taskonomy: disentangling task transfer learning. In: CVPR, pp. 3712–3722 (2018)
67. Zhai, X., Oliver, A., Kolesnikov, A., Beyer, L.: S4L: self-supervised semi-supervised learning. In: ICCV (2019)
68. Zhang, R., Isola, P., Efros, A.A.: Colorful image colorization. In: ECCV (2016)
69. Zhang, R., Isola, P., Efros, A.A.: Split-brain autoencoders: Unsupervised learning by cross-channel prediction. In: CVPR (2017)

Two-Branch Recurrent Network for Isolating Deepfakes in Videos

Iacopo Masi$^{(\boxtimes)}$ ⓘ, Aditya Killekar, Royston Marian Mascarenhas,
Shenoy Pratik Gurudatt, and Wael AbdAlmageed

USC Information Sciences Institute, Marina del Rey, CA, USA
{iacopo,killekar,royston,gurudatt,wamageed}@isi.edu

Abstract. The current spike of hyper-realistic faces artificially generated using *deepfakes* calls for media forensics solutions that are tailored to video streams and work reliably with a low false alarm rate at the video level. We present a method for *deepfake* detection based on a two-branch network structure that isolates digitally manipulated faces by learning to amplify artifacts while suppressing the high-level face content. Unlike current methods that extract spatial frequencies as a preprocessing step, we propose a two-branch structure: one branch propagates the original information, while the other branch suppresses the face content yet amplifies multi-band frequencies using a *Laplacian of Gaussian (LoG)* as a bottleneck layer. To better isolate manipulated faces, we derive a novel cost function that, unlike regular classification, compresses the variability of natural faces and pushes away the unrealistic facial samples in the feature space. Our two novel components show promising results on the FaceForensics++, Celeb-DF, and Facebook's DFDC preview benchmarks, when compared to prior work. We then offer a full, detailed ablation study of our network architecture and cost function. Finally, although the bar is still high to get very remarkable figures at a very low false alarm rate, our study shows that we can achieve good video-level performance when cross-testing in terms of video-level AUC.

Keywords: Deepfake detection · Two-branch recurrent net · Loss function

1 Introduction

Visual misinformation has dramatically increased on social networks and Internet [1]. Nonetheless, image manipulation is not new. Falsification of lithographs or photographs has been used for many years to reinforce political ideas or political characters [21] or to practice censorship by erasing people from pictures. For instance, at the beginning of the twentieth century, political dissidents were assassinated and then erased from photographs through airbrushing during the Great Terror period in the Soviet Union [19].

I. Masi and A. Killekar contributed equally to this paper.

ⓒ Springer Nature Switzerland AG 2020
A. Vedaldi et al. (Eds.): ECCV 2020, LNCS 12352, pp. 667–684, 2020.
https://doi.org/10.1007/978-3-030-58571-6_39

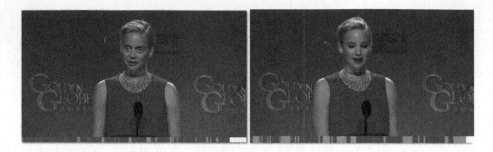

Fig. 1. Deepfake detection in videos. The figure shows our system predictions when trained only on FaceForensics++ for a fake video "in the wild" (left) and its pristine video (right). The heatmap bar below the video indicates the likelihood of the video being fake (red) or unmanipulated (green). (Color figure online)

In the modern era of digital pictures, perpetrators used commercial software and "elbow grease" to create realistic swapping of faces given a pair of still images. Although some of these results look very realistic, they involved a huge amount of manual work (on the order of hours) using a personal computer and an expensive raster graphics editor to produce just a single image [24]. However, the effort required to produce face swaps diminished drastically during the last five years. Democratized artificial intelligence (AI) made it very easy to produce highly realistic face swaps with a few clicks, giving the ability to non-experts to synthesize content with "Hollywood-like" effects just by simply using off-the-shelf applications [47]. The technology was quickly developed to process videos, transferring the identity of a subject from a *source* video into a *target* video. Unlike manual digital editing, face swapping in videos became effective and efficient, reaching hyper-realistic results, thanks to recent advances in data synthesis using Generative Adversarial Networks (GANs) [20], Deep Convolutional Neural Networks (DCNN) [35], and AutoEncoders (AE) [31]. It also became easily available to non-experts through customized applications, such as DeepFaceLab [2], or even mobile applications, such as Zao [4].

Face swapping has been superseded by deepfakes in which the original face is replaced with a victim's face with the intent of showing the victim to be saying something he/she never said. The fake video is usually very realistic so that the viewer believes that the swapped subject is the actual acting person in the video. Although in the beginning, deepfakes were used to entertain users, they became popular to spread political chaos, revenge porn, and defamation. For these reasons, the rapid sharing of deepfakes on the Internet became a threat to society leading to a common perception that *seeing is no longer believing* [1].

A recent report from DeepTrace [3] explains that the rate of increase in these fakes videos is 100% a year. Although deepfakes initially appeared in 2017 on `reddit`, the report estimates that there are currently 14,678 realistic-looking yet fake videos, while the total number available in December 2018 was only 7,964. Given the current progress of AI and deep learning, the prediction is that this number may skyrocket in the near future. In order to mitigate the proliferation of manipulated videos, we propose a deep learning architecture to detect hyper-realistic face manipulations. The paper makes the following contributions:

⋄ A two-branch representation extractor based on densely connected layers [25] that learns to combine information from the color domain and the frequency domain using a multi-scale Laplacian of Gaussian (LoG) operator [10]. The LoG operator suppresses the image content present in the low-level feature maps, acting as a band-pass filter to amplify artifacts.

⋄ A novel loss function that encourages compactness of the representations of natural faces and pushes away manipulated faces for better, wider separation boundaries, which is different than recent methods that use binary cross-entropy for detecting face manipulations [50,52].

⋄ As a minor contribution, we argue that current metrics (accuracy) are improper for this problem, mainly for being very sensitive to class imbalance and failure to capture performance for web-scale applications. Therefore, we follow [33,55] and report True Acceptance Rate (TAR) at low False Acceptance Rates (FAR). Also, besides standard area under receiver operating curve (AUC), we further propose global metrics at a low false alarm rate such as standardized partial AUC (pAUC) [42] and our truncated Area Under the Curve (tAUC).

We optimize our method for better generalization across datasets, reaching a good balance between bias and variance [15,48,59], i.e., performing remarkably on same dataset used for training [50] yet transferring reasonably well across datasets [14,38]. Similar to only few works in literature [21,52], we also use sequential modeling for video-based detection. Our method processes sequences of aligned faces from a video, extracts discriminative features using the backbone, and performs recurrent modeling using bi-directional long short-term memory (LSTM) supervised by our new loss. The entire network is trained end-to-end so that the recurrent model back-propagates to the feature extractor. Figure 1 shows the predictions of our system on face videos downloaded from the web when trained only on FaceForensics++. Our method is summarized in Fig. 2.

2   Prior Work

Face Forensics Datasets and Evaluation. Unlike the proliferation of face recognition datasets [5,22,26,29,32], there has been a lack of large-scale face forensics datasets in the community for both training and evaluation. Although face swapping can be cast as a splicing image forgery technique, and some generic forensics sets contain facial splicing and copy-move forgeries [24], earlier specific face manipulation detection tools [23] have been mainly evaluated on still images. Small-scale benchmarks released for deepfake detection were produced in controlled environments, e.g., DF-TIMIT [33,34] using 32 subjects selected from the VidTIMIT [53] database with the intent of studying the weaknesses of face detection and recognition technology, or UADFV [36] that offers around 50 bona fide and 50 fake videos.

Only recently, Rossler *et al.* proposed several versions of FaceForensics++ [50], a medium-scale collection of manipulated videos counting a total of 1.8 million manipulated frames using four methods: FaceSwap, DeepFakes, Face2Face [57], and NeuralTextures [56]. The same dataset was augmented by Google Research with another set containing deepfake videos, i.e., Google Deepfake Detection (DFD) [16]. At the same time, Facebook and other firms joined efforts to create a competition to detect fakes on the web, releasing a preview dataset "The Deepfake Detection Challenge (DFDC)" [14] along with new metrics for evaluation. With the exception of [37], the interesting novel aspect is that performance is considered at a video-level instead of frame-level, effectively evaluating models at low false alarm rate. Before [14], accuracy was the only metric used to measure fake detection performance with a few exceptions [33,55]. Despite these contributions, the perceived quality of the synthesized videos offered by these sets appears still lower compared to the videos circulating on the web, thus Li *et al.* recently released Celeb-DF [38] to produce hyper-realistic deepfakes, reporting the frame-level AUC as a metric. This benchmark is compelling, offering 5,369 high quality videos for a total of 2.1M frames.

Detection of Face Manipulations. Although image forensics has been widely studied for a long time [17], deepfakes is recent technology and thus several orthogonal works have been proposed lately for solving the problem of detecting face manipulations. Methods for deepfake detection can be roughly categorized in two macroscopic groups—(i) discriminative classifiers that use diverse semantic inconsistencies of the head and face; and (ii) data-driven approaches directly learning a discriminative function from data. Considering the first group, Agarwal *et al.* built person-specific classifiers [7] using one-class support vector machines (SVM) and features computed from Action Units (AU) and 3D head pose movements. Similarly, Li *et al.* [36] used the observation that initial versions of deepfakes were not blinking. Later they extended the work to check for the inconsistency of 3D head poses. They also trained a DCNN though they used as negative samples faces undergoing warping artifacts to simulate the deepfake stitching process [37], while [41] used hand-crafted visual features to amplify artifacts. Regarding the second group, XceptionNet [11] has been widely used [50], while [6] used a variant of Inception module to capture both micro and mesoscopic features. Han *et al.* [23] used a two-branch structure similar to ours, yet, unlike our method, performed late fusion between a RGB branch and steganalysis features, using triplet loss for supervision. Later methods employed multi-task learning [44] with an encoder-decoder similar to [13] and capsule networks [45]. For a complete survey, we refer to [38,46] and the recent work in [58,61].

GAN Synthesis Detection. Finally, a parallel line of related research [13,68,69] [40,60] is detecting entirely GAN-synthesized face images, e.g., using StyleGAN [28]. Our work shares similar traits with the very recent research by Yu *et al.* [68] with some major differences. We focus on detecting deepfakes, while [68]'s interest is in modeling GAN fingerprints. More importantly, our method

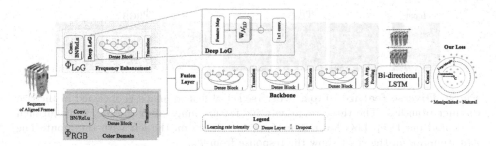

Fig. 2. Our video-based face manipulation detection architecture. A face sequence is processed by two independent DenseBlocks: one subject to a Deep Laplacian of Gaussian (Deep LoG) layer (frequency enhancement) and the second is a branch that works in the color domain. The two feature maps are fused so that a backbone of dense blocks learns a rich representation. The architecture uses dropout after each DenseLayer and a different learning rate per layer to mitigate overfitting. Our architecture ends with a bi-directional LSTM layer supervised using a novel loss formulation. (Color figure online)

is composed of a two-branch structure that fuses RGB information with the frequency domain.

3   Method

The objective is to learn a classifier for the detection of manipulated faces, squishing a set of aligned video frames[1] $\mathbf{I} \in \mathbb{R}^{H \times W \times 3 \times F}$ to an embedding $\Phi(\mathbf{I}) \in \mathbb{R}^D$ so that the representations of natural faces are compact around a reference centroid $\mathbf{c}$ and manipulated faces are spread out, ensuring a large margin between tampered and untamperd faces. In Sect. 3.1 we introduce a two-branch backbone representation extractor $\Phi(\cdot)$ based on densely connected layers [25]. Φ learns to fuse different representations obtained using regular convolutional filters Φ_{RGB} and representations extracted using multi-scale Laplacian of Gaussian [10] kernels Φ_{LoG} (Sect. 3.2). The combined features maps are then fed to the backbone that ends with a bi-directional Long Short-Term Memory (LSTM) for temporal modeling. $\Phi(\mathbf{I})$ indicates the concatenated output from the two bidirectional LSTM streams. The entire recurrent model is supervised through a novel formulation. Unlike recent methods [50,52] that use classification losses for detection, in Sect. 3.3 we introduce a loss function that encourages the compactness of the representations of untampered faces, while distancing the representations of manipulated faces, for wider separation boundaries. At test-time, given an input sequence $\mathbf{I}$, the method obtains the distance $\left\| \Phi(\mathbf{I}) - \mathbf{c} \right\|_2$; the larger the distance the higher the likelihood of the sample being manipulated.

---

[1] Throughout this paper $\mathbf{I}$ indicates a sequence (or window) of aligned faces from video frames of cardinality F.

Input Φ_{LoG} Φ_{RGB}

Fig. 3. Diverse feature maps. A diverse set of feature maps is obtained in the two distinct branches. The three representative feature maps after the first convolutional layer and our Deep LoG layer from Φ_{LoG} are shown on the left with the input. The feature maps on the right show the response from Φ_{RGB}.

3.1   Network Architecture and Optimization

Architecture. The basic network architecture Φ is derived by the recent work in [52] with major modification. The network takes as input RGB faces but consists of two different branches: a regular DenseBlock [25] that learns to process color domain data Φ_{RGB} and another parallel DenseBlock Φ_{LoG} with unshared weights that learns to discard visual face content by applying a Laplacian of Gaussian (LoG) filter to the low-level feature maps. The two feature maps are aligned and have a resolution of 28×28 with 128 planes. These maps are fused together with point-wise convolution with two groups [27] such that each group of convolutional filters independently refines and fuses the information for the three downstream DenseBlocks. All the DenseBlocks end with a Transitional layer except for the one prior the LSTM. We discard the final linear classification layer and reduce the final feature map to a feature vector with dimension 1024 using global average pooling. Dropout with a probability of 0.2 is applied at the end of each DenseLayer to avoid overfitting.

Optimization. Instead of optimizing the entire network with a single learning rate, which may overfit given the large parameter space of DenseNet, we employ a strategy that sets different learning rates per DenseBlock. In particular, given the global learning rate μ, we define a decay for the DenseBlocks so that downstream layers incorporate gradients quickly while upstream layers change less drastically. The learning rate decay is defined as $\mu_L \doteq \mu \cdot 1/(2^L)$ for the entire network with the exception of the DenseBlock of the Deep LoG and the layer in charge of fusing the two-branches. The parameters of fusion layers are updated faster, with the global rate μ, since that they have to be adapted to the frequency domain information. The blue bars in Fig. 2 indicate the intensity of learning rate for each layer. We initialize all the layers from pre-trained weights from ImageNet except those of the LSTM, which are instead initialized from a uniform distribution.

Video-Based Stratified Sampling. Since inter-video variations are stronger than intra-video, we define a "stratified epoch" as the set of sequences obtained by sampling a *random sequence once from all the videos* in the training set. Stratified training ensures that each mini-batch includes a diversified set of training samples, avoiding including similar sequences from the same video within the mini-batch if we use simple random sampling.

3.2   Deep Laplacian of Gaussian

Motivation. Zhang *et al.* [69] show that image manipulations leave medium-and high-frequency traces, and since most of the deepfakes methods reconstruct a face with an average pixel-wise ℓ_2 loss (Mean Square Error (MSE)), producing somewhat blurry (low-frequency) facial features, and because of the up-sampling commonly used in the decoder part. According to these observations, we design a custom layer to propagate multi-band frequency information inside the network with the goal of suppressing high-level face content, thereby amplify artifacts.

Implementation. Without loss of generality, given a feature map $\mathbf{x}$, we apply a Laplacian of Gaussian (LoG) [10] as follows. Input tensor $\mathbf{x}$ (which can be in the first layer the input image alone or directly higher feature maps) is processed by two sets of convolutional filters: fixed, non-learnable filters $\overline{\mathbf{w}}_{\mathcal{N}_{2D}}$, as a 2D Gaussian kernel and a dimensionality reduction filter $\mathbf{w}_{1\times1}$ that maps back the dimensionality to the input expected by the next layer. The layer shares a similar design with [66] although in our case (1) the objective is to suppress global information from the face, not to suppress noise from adversarial samples and (2) the skip-connection is used to *remove* information while [66] used it to ease the training. As described in Eq. (1), the output feature map $\mathbf{x}'$ is then obtained as shown in Eq. (1)

$$\mathbf{x}' = \mathbf{w}_{1\times1}\Big(\mathbf{x} - \mathrm{up}\big(\mathrm{down}(\overline{\mathbf{w}}_{\mathcal{N}_{2D}} \; \mathbf{x})\big)\Big), \tag{1}$$

where $\mathrm{up}(\cdot), \mathrm{down}(\cdot)$ indicate upsampling and downsampling, respectively, of the tensor across multiple scales $S = 3$. Assuming that the LoG is inserted into a layer with K input planes and K' output planes, then internally the tensor depth dimension becomes $K \xrightarrow{\mathrm{LoG}} S\,K \xrightarrow{\mathbf{w}_{1\times1}} K'$. Figure 3 shows the difference in the feature maps between the new LoG branch and the regular RGB branch after the first convolutional layer. All the feature maps are taken from the same filters, so they are aligned across branches. Each map is normalized $\in [0,1]$. We can see that most of the energy in the response for the Φ_{LoG} case is around the edges, the Φ_{RGB} counterpart instead focuses more on the global structure of the face.

3.3   Loss Function to Isolate Manipulated Faces

Motivation. The majority of previous work on face manipulation detection [50,52,69] uses standard cost functions adopted from classification. Cozzolino *et al.* [13] recently made an effort toward representation disentanglement and generalization for face manipulation detection. Unlike previous work summarized in Sect. 2, we propose a new loss for better isolating manipulated faces inspired by recent work on one-class classifiers, such as one-class Deep Support Vector Data Description (Deep SVDD) [51]. The new formulation induces compactness of the embedding space for sequences of unmanipulated faces. However, unlike [51], the proposed loss employs manipulations synthesized by a few generators as negative samples enforcing a larger margin to the natural face sequences.

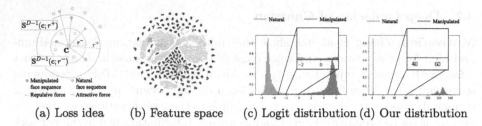

(a) Loss idea   (b) Feature space   (c) Logit distribution (d) Our distribution

Fig. 4. Loss formulation. (a) The loss induces compression of the natural face sequences within a inner hypersphere placing easier samples close to **c** and tougher samples at the boundary; meanwhile it induces a large margin forcing the manipulated face sequences outside the outer hypersphere (b) t-SNE [39] visualization of the feature space on the test set between natural faces (yellow) and deepfakes (violet). The center **c** is shown as an orange cross. (c) Genuine-Impostor distribution of logits with binary cross-entropy and (d) with our loss function: imposing a wider margin induces less confusion in the distribution.

Formulation. More formally, we optimize the entire recurrent network defined in Sect. 3.1 through a cost function that organizes the feature space such that the variability of sequences of natural faces is compacted toward a reference center while the representations of manipulated face sequences are placed far apart at the boundaries of the feature space. Before training, we begin by pre-computing a reference center $\mathbf{c} \in \mathbb{R}^D$ by averaging the encodings of all the natural, unmanipulated face sequences in the training set. The encodings are obtained by taking the responses of our entire architecture with two-branches and the bi-directional LSTM before training. The concatenated bidirectional LSTM features are extracted using the same network that is pre-trained. The two-branches and the backbone are pre-trained on ImageNet. When the training starts, all the features are aligned to this predefined embedding space. Then we define two hyperspheres centered around **c** to constrain the feature space so that natural faces lie within $\mathbb{S}^{D-1}(\mathbf{c}; r^-)$, while manipulated faces are kept outside $\mathbb{S}^{D-1}(\mathbf{c}; r^+)$. The loss induces compression on the regular faces embeddings. However, unlike [51], we avoid reducing all samples to a single high-dimensional point and mitigate overfitting by requiring compression up to an internal inner margin defined by the radius r^- of the first hypersphere. Furthermore, the proposed loss enforces sequences of manipulated faces to be kept outside the second hypersphere defined by the radius r^+. The loss $\mathcal{L}$ given a mini-batch $\Omega \in \mathbb{R}^{H \times W \times 3 \times F \times B}$ of face sequences is defined as shown in Eq. (2):

$$\mathcal{L} = \frac{1}{|\Omega_{\text{nat.}}|} \sum_{i \in \Omega_{\text{nat.}}} \max\left(0, \left\|\Phi(\mathbf{I}_i) - \mathbf{c}\right\|_2 - r^-\right)$$

$$+ \frac{1}{|\Omega_{\text{man.}}|} \sum_{j \in \Omega_{\text{man.}}} \max\left(0, r^+ - \left\|\Phi(\mathbf{I}_j) - \mathbf{c}\right\|_2\right), \quad (2)$$

where $\Omega_{\text{nat.,man.}}$ selects natural and manipulated face samples, respectively. For this loss to be valid, it has to hold that $0 < r^- < r^+$ and the margin imposed between the two classes is $m = r^+ - r^-$. The values of the two radii have to be set according to the dimensionality D of the feature embedding. The loss mitigates the problem of class imbalances by normalizing each term by its cardinality. Further, the second margin r^+ is essential to the loss because the network may chose to lower the cost just by pushing the negative samples indefinitely, without inducing compression on the natural faces.

Figure 4a illustrates the basic idea of the proposed loss, and Fig. 4b demonstrates the feature space of the test set of natural faces vs deepfakes. The features are mapped to $\mathbb{R}^2$ using t-SNE [39] optimizing a plain DenseNet model. Natural faces are compressed while manipulated faces lie at the boundaries. The clusters formed by videos are visible for the manipulated faces. Figure 4c shows the genuine and impostor distribution of the logits at inference time for a model trained for discerning real faces from deepfakes using binary cross-entropy on FaceForensics++ [50]. Although the distribution presents two peaks corresponding to real and deepfakes faces, the variance of those distribution is not minimized, and, more importantly, real face logits are spread out toward the manipulated faces thereby negatively affecting the detection rate at a low false alarm regime. In contrast, Fig. 4d offers the distribution of the distances from the center **c** for the two classes. Using the proposed loss we achieved compression of the natural faces and a clear separation from the manipulated faces, visible when zooming in a highly confusing region.

Interpretation. Equation (2) shares similar traits with the formulation in [51] with a few key differences. First, we have a secondary term for supervision for abnormal cases. Second, we have margins that avoid overfitting and better separate the two classes. The loss function also resembles the classic formulations found in deep metric learning such as contrastive loss functions [65], although in our case the optimization is better constrained since the network is allowed to "move" only $\Phi(\mathbf{I})$ while **c** is kept fixed. Finally, we spare the sampling of pairs or even triplets [54] which significantly reduces training complexity. Our loss differs from recent formulations: [64] uses softmax while we do not; it also sets one center for each class while we have a single center for both classes; finally, unlike us, [64] updates the centers while training. The work in [62] enforces angular margin whereas ours uses radial distance margin; [62] induces compactness in all the classes while ours only on natural face sequences.

4   Experimental Evaluation

Benchmarks and Metrics. Ablation studies and comparisons are conducted on (1) FaceForensics++ [50], (2) Celeb-DF [38], (3) and the Deepfake Detection Challenge (DFDC) Preview Dataset [14]. We report results at the video-level and also at the frame-level. Given that our method works at a sequence level, when comparing to other methods, we made sure that the number of samples prior computing the ROC is the same for all methods when comparing at the frame-level or, at least, that that all methods observed the same quantity of data. Further, we use standard metrics such as True Acceptance Rate (TAR) at low False Acceptance Rates (FAR), similar to [33,55]. Besides standard area under receiver operating curve (AUC), we further use global metrics yet at a low false alarm rate such. These metrics can shed light on performance in realistic operational scenarios, thereby requiring detectors to operate at a very low false alarm rate and raising the bar for the community. We used the standardized partial AUC or pAUC [42] and our tAUC, that is defined as AUC yet taking into consideration only the low false alarm rate up to a cut-off point FAR_τ, thereby ignoring high false alarm rates. tAUC is computed as the ratio between the area of TARs up to a given low FAR_τ normalized by the total area up to the FAR_τ value. Given $\mathcal{F}_\tau = \{0, \ldots, FAR_\tau\}$, then tAUC at an operating point τ is defined as $tAUC_\tau \doteq \frac{\sum_{i \in \mathcal{F}_\tau} TAR_i}{|\mathcal{F}_\tau|}$.

Implementation and Hyper-Parameters. Unless otherwise stated, we used the following settings. The global learning rate μ is 1e–03 using the Adam optimizer and the results are produced with LSTM. The learning rate is decreased three times by a factor of 10. We decrease it every time the validation loss does not decrease after 50 stratified epochs. We used a weight decay of 1e–06. The final global average pooling flattening the spatial dimension gives a descriptor with dimensionality 1024 transformed into $D = 128$ by the LSTM. The final dimensionality considered in the loss is $2D^2$ and the two radii $r^{\{-,+\}} \doteq \{0.042, 1.638\}$ have to be optimized together and cross-validated on a validation set. In high-dimensional space, the volume of the hyper-sphere decreases when the feature descriptor dimension D increases [63]: thus, if D does change, the radii have to be changed accordingly. By increasing the dimensionality D of the final feature, the radii have to be increased as well to compensate for the diminished hyper-volume of the hyper-sphere. The cardinality F of the sequence of aligned frames as input to the recurrent model is 10. Since the sequential modeling is trained on sampled FF++ data, at inference time we take 1 frame over 7 to build the sequence. Faces are aligned with dlib [30]. If alignment fails, we revert back to [9]. In case of multiple detected faces, we select the largest detected face. Since FaceForensics++ has imbalanced labels (1:4), we oversample the natural faces twice and undersample randomly faces for each manipulation with a factor of two to get a proper balance, when training with multiple manipulations. We used average to perform video-level evaluation to aggregate all the scores within a video for all methods. When doing cross-testing, we use always the same model trained on FF++ on the four manipulations on high compression (c40).

4.1   FaceForensics++ (FF++)

Settings. When training and evaluating on FF++, we follow the sampling strategy mentioned in [50] that selects 270 frames/video for the training and 110 frames/video for validation and testing. We evaluated both medium compression (c23) and high compression levels (c40) subsets.

---

[2] The dimensionality is doubled since the results of the bi-directional streams are concatenated.

Table 1. Ablation study on FF++. (a) Testing metrics obtained by training our model under different settings on the FF++ [50] under the highest compression level c40 without LSTM, ablating our optimization and the loss function. (b) Ablation experiments showing the impact of the two branches under the medium compression level c23. (c) Ablation experiments using LSTM on c40.

Deepfakes c40 - wo/ LSTM			
	tAUC$_{1\%}$	tAUC$_{10\%}$	TAR$_{1\%}$
Encoder [52]	57.63	86.61	81.50
+ft,+drop,+loss	76.04	89.91	92.84

(a)

Deepfakes c23 - wo/ LSTM			
	tAUC$_{1\%}$	tAUC$_{10\%}$	TAR$_{1\%}$
Single-Branch	56.78	61.14	99.34
Two-Branch	61.70	70.80	98.34

(b)

Deepfakes c40 - w/ LSTM					
LSTM hid. nodes	LSTM fusion	Φ_{RGB} $\circ$ Φ_{LoG}	f.t. +dropout	tAUC$_{1\%}$	TAR$_{1\%}$
128	cat	conv1x1$_{g=1}$	—	57.21	83.33
128	cat	conv1x1$_{g=1}$	✓	73.58	87.38
128	sum	conv1x1$_{g=2}$	✓	67.49	83.81
256	cat	conv1x1$_{g=2}$	✓	76.35	87.14
128	cat	conv1x1$_{g=2}$	✓	81.53	92.54

(c)

Table 2. Frame-level and Video-level comparison on FF++. Multiple metrics reported for medium compression (c23) and high compression (c40) on FF++ comparing our method with XceptionNet [50] and DSP-FWA [37]. Results are reported on four manipulations.

	HQ (c23)								LQ (c40)							
	Frame Level (~70K samples)				Video Level (700 samples)				Frame Level (~70K samples)				Video Level (700 samples)			
Methods	AUC	pAUC$_{10\%}$	tAUC$_{10\%}$	TAR$_{10\%}$	AUC	pAUC$_{10\%}$	tAUC$_{10\%}$	TAR$_{10\%}$	AUC	pAUC$_{10\%}$	tAUC$_{10\%}$	TAR$_{10\%}$	AUC	pAUC$_{10\%}$	tAUC$_{10\%}$	TAR$_{10\%}$
DSP-FWA [37]	56.89	51.33	7.47	14.60	57.49	51.59	7.48	15.00	59.15	52.04	8.82	17.30	62.34	51.93	9.82	22.14
Xception [50]	92.30	87.71	73.34	81.21	92.50	89.20	58.21	82.85	83.93	74.78	45.92	63.25	86.75	79.10	39.06	68.75
Ours	98.70	97.43	65.29	97.95	99.12	98.41	86.10	98.21	86.59	69.71	40.41	62.48	91.10	76.57	51.18	72.85

Ablation Study, c40. Table 1a shows the ablation study for different building blocks of the proposed pipeline, along with the proposed loss function. These results are reported without the LSTM thereby evaluating only the backbone without stratified sampling. Given that $D = 1024$, the two radii are set $r^{\{-,+\}} \doteq \{2.5, 97.5\}$. We report metrics such as TAR and tAUC at a given FAR value. The cut-off FAR points considered are 1% and 10%. At the top, we report results from [52] re-implementing the method without sequential modeling, thereby using just the DenseNet encoder. All methods evaluated in this table consider only the Φ_{RGB} stream and are trained with a global learning rate of 1e-04. Although [52] reaches compelling result at tAUC$_{10\%}$, the performance degrades at lower FAR. Better performance is obtained by combining minor improvements such as training the network with the optimization mentioned in Sect. 3.1 that assigns a different updating rate per layer (+ft) and dropout (+drop) and by using our new loss function (+loss) proposed in Sect. 3.3. The gain at low false alarm rate is substantial compared to [52] that was trained with binary cross-entropy. In particular, the loss manages to push tAUC$_{1\%}$ up from 57% to 76% by imposing a large margin—see Fig. 4d—while the regular cross-entropy overfits quickly.

Ablation Study, c23. Given the best results obtained in the previous experiment (i.e., +ft,+drop,+loss), we use this configuration as a new baseline to perform other ablations using the FF++ part with medium compression (c23). Table 1b reports experiments showing the difference between a single branch and the two-branch structure.

Table 3. Cross-dataset evaluation on Celeb-DF. (a) Frame- and video-level performance yet computed at a very low false alarm rate. Best competing methods on Celeb-DF are reported. Ours obtains a wide margin in all the low false alarm rate metrics (b) still performs well when tested on just deepfake class (93.18%) AUC on FF++. Results for other methods are from [38].

(a)

Methods	Frame Level				Video Level			
	AUC	pAUC$_{10\%}$	tAUC$_{10\%}$	TAR$_{10\%}$	AUC	pAUC$_{10\%}$	tAUC$_{10\%}$	TAR$_{10\%}$
Xception-c40 [50]	65.86	54.49	12.23	22.97	69.70	57.18	16.85	34.70
DSP-FWA [37]	64.13	52.87	10.18	19.67	69.30	51.40	17.20	32.02
Xception-c23 [50]	66.65	53.05	10.21	19.83	73.04	52.77	9.45	18.82
Ours	**73.41**	**57.42**	**18.18**	**32.22**	**76.65**	**58.70**	**19.73**	**39.70**

(b)

Method	FF++ [50]	Celeb-DF [38]
Two-stream [23]	70.1	53.8
Meso4 [6]	84.7	54.8
MesoInception4	83.0	53.6
HeadPose [67]	47.3	54.6
FWA [37]	80.1	56.9
VA-MLP [41]	66.4	55.0
VA-LogReg	78.0	55.1
Xception-raw [50]	99.7	48.2
Xception-c23	99.7	65.3
Xception-c40	95.5	65.5
Multi-task [44]	76.3	54.3
Capsule [45]	96.6	57.5
DSP-FWA [37]	93.0	64.6
Ours	93.18	**73.41**

Ablation Study Using LSTM, c40. Table 1c shows the ablation experiments when testing the recurrent model. Since adding a recurrent modeling is a drastic change, we verified again that our optimization strategy with different updating rates per layer holds in this case as well. The first two rows in the table support this hypothesis. We further investigate how to fuse the bi-directional outputs from LSTM and optimize its hidden nodes. Our best result is obtained using hidden node size of 128 and concatenating the two bi-directional outputs. Furthermore, when fusing the two branches $\Phi_{RGB} \circ \Phi_{LoG}$ having convolutional filters divided in two groups is beneficial to the performance.

Results. Table 2 shows a thorough comparison on FF++ [50] training and testing with four manipulations types (Deepfakes, FaceSwap, Face2Face, and NeuralTextures) along with the natural faces. Following [50], we trained a model for c23 and another for c40. The table offers multiple evaluations metrics such as AUC, pAUC$_{10\%}$, tAUC$_{10\%}$ and TAR$_{10\%}$. In general, our approach has superior performance compared to Xception. In particular, we improved almost all frame-level performance for the medium compression case (c23), pushing the video-level AUC from 92% to 99%. The result is consistent for the other compression level but in general results are lower due to the low image quality; nevertheless our system improves video-level AUC from 86% to 91% along with other low false alarm video-level metrics. The table also reports the result of a self-supervised method DSP-FWA [37]. Table 4a further shows the binary classification accuracies for several state-of-the-art face manipulation detection methods computed on FF++ [50]. Our approach scores the highest accuracies across manipulations for all the compression levels when trained on the four manipulations. It should be noted that a classifier exploiting the class imbalance here can get an accuracy of 80% by simply predicting all samples as fakes given that we have 140 real and 560 fake videos or similar balance at the frame level.

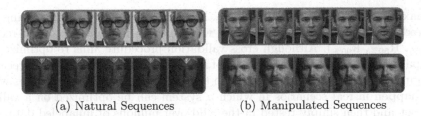

(a) Natural Sequences   (b) Manipulated Sequences

Fig. 5. Qualitative analysis on Celeb-DF. The color indicates correct classification (green) or misclassification (red). (Color figure online)

4.2 Celeb-DF

Results. We evaluate how well our model transfers to Celeb-DF given that it is trained on FF++ with multiple manipulations. We do this with the goal of confirming that we optimized our method for better generalization across datasets, reaching a good balance between bias and variance. Table 3a shows a state-of-the-art evaluation at the frame- and video-level on the 518 test video of Celeb-DF, comparing it to other recent methods. Like other methods [50], we trained the model on FF++ to discern real faces versus four manipulation types at the c40 compression level. Table 3a reports a clear net improvement over the state-of-the-art, even when compared with recent methods that trained the model with self-supervision thereby, in theory, being less prone to overfitting, such as DSP-FWA [37]. Table 3b offers instead the classic evaluation performance in terms of AUC comparing our approach to the very recent method for digital face manipulation detection. We obtained higher AUC when compared to all the other methods on Celeb-DF while keeping an high AUC on FF++ on Deepfakes.

Qualitative Analysis. Figure 5 shows a qualitative analysis performed on the challenging Celeb-DF [38]. Figure 5a shows untampered faces. The method correctly classifies a sequence with good quality although we used FF++ with high compression level (c40) for training. Failure case for the natural faces may be caused by the poor illumination. Figure 5b shows manipulated faces and the method was able to detect a challenging sequence that could be perceived "as real"; the other failure may be due to the presence of strong facial hairs which could be absent in training data.

4.3 The Deepfake Detection Challenge (DFDC) Preview Dataset

We report video-level results on the "The Deepfake Detection Challenge (DFDC) preview set" using the evaluation described in [14]. This dataset contains approximately 5,250 videos of digitally manipulated and bona fide videos. As in [14], we used part of the training for cross validation for the two parameters available in our approach that are the optimal number of sequences and the distance $\|\Phi(\mathbf{I}) - \mathbf{c}\|_2$. We implemented five-fold cross-validation (20% of training retained for validation) and selected the best pair of parameters across the folds required to maximize the log-weighted precision, $\log(\text{wP})$, with $\alpha = 100$, maintaining the desired level of recall. This procedure was repeated for different cutoff recalls ($R_{10\%}$, $R_{50\%}$, $R_{90\%}$). Although cross validation procedure aims to optimize the two parameters to keep a desired level of recall, meeting the same level of recall is not guaranteed when evaluating on the test set. This procedure simulates what can happen in real scenarios in which a system can be optimized on a validation set and then simply tested in the wild over millions of unlabeled data. For this reason, we report $\log(\text{wP})$@recall on the best validation fold under "valid" and the test set with "test-from-valid" using the parameters from validation. Alternatively, we also searched for the best $\log(\text{wP})$ to exactly match the recall value on the test set and report those values under "test". Except for the above parameter selection, our method has not been re-trained on DFDC preview.

Results. Table 4b shows the evaluation results at the video level. Considering our results under "test," our method has slightly worse precision than XceptionNet [50] at $R_{10\%}$. However, if we optimize for high recall ($R_{90\%}$), we obtain a substantial boost in the $\log(\text{wP})$, increasing $\log(\text{wP})$ from -4.041 to -3.548. Moreover, we notice the following if we evaluate with the best hyper-parameters selected on the validation set our method maintains $\log(\text{wP})$ better than other methods (-3.721) with a good recall of 0.943.

Table 4. FF++ Accuracies and DFDC Preview Dataset. (a) Comparison of accuracies on FF++ (b) Video-level $\log(\text{wP})$ for various recall rates.

Methods	HQ (c23)	LQ (c40)
[50] XceptionNet (Full Image)	74.78	70.52
[18] Steg. Features + SVM	70.97	55.98
[12] Cozzolino et al.	78.45	58.69
[8] Bayar and Stamm	82.97	66.84
[49] Rahmouni et al.	79.08	61.18
[6] MesoNet	83.10	70.47
[50] XceptionNet	95.73	81.00
Ours	**96.43**	**86.34**

(a)

Method	$R_{10\%}$	$R_{50\%}$	$R_{90\%}$
TamperNet [14]	-2.796@—	-3.864@—	-4.041@—
XceptionNet [50] (Face)	**-1.999@—**	**-3.012@—**	-4.081@—
XceptionNet [50] (Full)	-3.293@—	-3.835@—	-4.081@—
Ours (test)	-2.564@0.100	-3.152@0.501	**-3.548@0.901**
Ours (valid)	-2.311@0.090	-2.481@0.523	-2.678@0.918
Ours (test-from-valid)	-3.386@0.042	-3.433@0.440	-3.721@0.943

(b)

5   Conclusions and Future Work

We presented a method for video-based deepfake detection that uses a recurrent model to process sequences of aligned faces using a two-branch backbone with a loss function to isolate manipulated face sequences. We have shown results that outperform or are on par with state-of-the-art. However, for practical, web-scale applications, there is significant room for improvement at low false alarm rates. In the short term, we plan to measure the impact of data augmentation and the usage of additional external natural faces [43]. In the long term, we plan to augment our model with an explainability mechanism that does not need any pixel-wise supervision for face manipulations.

Acknowledgment. This work is based on research sponsored by the Defense Advanced Research Projects Agency under agreement number FA8750-16-2-0204. The U.S. Government is authorized to reproduce and distribute reprints for governmental purposes notwithstanding any copyright notation thereon. The views and conclusions contained herein are those of the authors and should not be interpreted as necessarily representing the official policies or endorsements, either expressed or implied, of the Defense Advanced Research Projects Agency or the U.S. Government. The authors would like to thank E. Sabir and A. Jaiswal for the useful discussions and the anonymous reviewers.

References

1. CNN - business - when seeing is no longer believing inside the pentagon's race against deepfake videos. https://www.cnn.com/interactive/2019/01/business/pentagons-race-against-deepfakes/
2. DeepFaceLab. https://github.com/iperov/DeepFaceLab
3. DeepTrace - the antivirus of deepfakes - the state of deepfakes. https://deeptracelabs.com
4. ZAO app. https://apps.apple.com/cn/app/zao/
5. MSR Image Recognition Challenge (IRC) at ACM Multimedia 2016, July 2016
6. Afchar, D., Nozick, V., Yamagishi, J., Echizen, I.: Mesonet: a compact facial video forgery detection network. In: WIFS, pp. 1–7. IEEE (2018)
7. Agarwal, S., Farid, H., Gu, Y., He, M., Nagano, K., Li, H.: Protecting world leaders against deep fakes. In: CVPR Workshops, June 2019
8. Bayar, B., Stamm, M.C.: A deep learning approach to universal image manipulation detection using a new convolutional layer. In: ACM Workshop on Information Hiding and Multimedia Security, pp. 5–10 (2016)
9. Bulat, A., Tzimiropoulos, G.: How far are we from solving the 2D & 3D face alignment problem? (and a dataset of 230,000 3D facial landmarks). In: ICCV (2017)
10. Burt, P., Adelson, E.: The laplacian pyramid as a compact image code. IEEE Trans. Commun. **31**(4), 532–540 (1983)
11. Chollet, F.: Xception: deep learning with depthwise separable convolutions. In: CVPR, pp. 1251–1258 (2017). http://openaccess.thecvf.com/content_cvpr_2017/html/Chollet_Xception_Deep_Learning_CVPR_2017_paper.html
12. Cozzolino, D., Poggi, G., Verdoliva, L.: Recasting residual-based local descriptors as convolutional neural networks: an application to image forgery detection. In: ACM Workshop on Information Hiding and Multimedia Security, pp. 159–164 (2017)
13. Cozzolino, D., Thies, J., Rössler, A., Riess, C., Nießner, M., Verdoliva, L.: Forensictransfer: weakly-supervised domain adaptation for forgery detection. arXiv preprint arXiv:1812.02510 (2018)
14. Dolhansky, B., Howes, R., Pflaum, B., Baram, N., Ferrer, C.C.: The Deepfake Detection Challenge (DFDC) Preview Dataset. arXiv:1910.08854, October 2019. http://arxiv.org/abs/1910.08854, arXiv: 1910.08854
15. Domingos, P.M.: A few useful things to know about machine learning. Commun. ACM **55**(10), 78–87 (2012)
16. Dufour, N., et al.: Deepfakes detection dataset by Google and Jigsaw (2019)
17. Farid, H.: Photo Forensics. MIT Press, Cambridge (2016)

18. Fridrich, J., Kodovsky, J.: Rich models for steganalysis of digital images. TIFS **7**(3), 868–882 (2012)
19. Gellately, R.: Lenin, Stalin, and Hitler: The age of social catastrophe. Alfred a Knopf Incorporated (2007)
20. Goodfellow, I., et al.: Generative adversarial nets. In: NIPS (2014)
21. Güera, D., Delp, E.J.: Deepfake video detection using recurrent neural networks. In: AVSS, pp. 1–6. IEEE (2018)
22. Guo, Y., Zhang, L., Hu, Y., He, X., Gao, J.: MS-Celeb-1M: a dataset and benchmark for large-scale face recognition. In: Leibe, B., Matas, J., Sebe, N., Welling, M. (eds.) ECCV 2016. LNCS, vol. 9907, pp. 87–102. Springer, Cham (2016). https://doi.org/10.1007/978-3-319-46487-9_6
23. Han, X., Morariu, V., Larry Davis, P.I., et al.: Two-stream neural networks for tampered face detection. In: CVPR Workshops, pp. 19–27 (2017)
24. Heller, S., Rossetto, L., Schuldt, H.: The PS-Battles Dataset - an Image Collection for Image Manipulation Detection. CoRR abs/1804.04866 (2018). http://arxiv.org/abs/1804.04866
25. Huang, G., Liu, Z., Van Der Maaten, L., Weinberger, K.Q.: Densely connected convolutional networks. In: CVPR, pp. 4700–4708 (2017)
26. Huang, G.B., Ramesh, M., Berg, T., Learned-Miller, E.: Labeled faces in the wild: a database for studying face recognition in unconstrained environments. Technical report, 07-49, UMass, Amherst, October 2007
27. Ioannou, Y., Robertson, D., Cipolla, R., Criminisi, A.: Deep roots: improving CNN efficiency with hierarchical filter groups. In: CVPR, pp. 1231–1240 (2017)
28. Karras, T., Laine, S., Aila, T.: A style-based generator architecture for generative adversarial networks. In: CVPR, pp. 4401–4410 (2019)
29. Kemelmacher-Shlizerman, I., Seitz, S.M., Miller, D., Brossard, E.: The MegaFace benchmark: 1 million faces for recognition at scale. In: CVPR (2016)
30. King, D.E.: Dlib-ml: a machine learning toolkit. JMLR **10**, 1755–1758 (2009)
31. Kingma, D.P., Welling, M.: Auto-encoding variational bayes. arXiv preprint arXiv:1312.6114 (2013)
32. Klare, B.F., et al.: Pushing the frontiers of unconstrained face detection and recognition: IARPA Janus Benchmark A. In: CVPR, pp. 1931–1939 (2015)
33. Korshunov, P., Marcel, S.: Deepfakes: a new threat to face recognition? assessment and detection. arXiv preprint arXiv:1812.08685 (2018)
34. Korshunov, P., Marcel, S.: Vulnerability assessment and detection of deepfake videos. In: ICB, Crete, Greece, June 2019
35. Krizhevsky, A., Sutskever, I., Hinton, G.E.: Imagenet classification with deep convolutional neural networks. In: NIPS, pp. 1097–1105 (2012)
36. Li, Y., Chang, M.C., Lyu, S.: In ictu oculi: exposing AI created fake videos by detecting eye blinking. In: WIFS, pp. 1–7 (2018)
37. Li, Y., Lyu, S.: Exposing deepfake videos by detecting face warping artifacts. In: CVPR Workshops, June 2019
38. Li, Y., Yang, X., Sun, P., Qi, H., Lyu, S.: Celeb-DF: a large-scale challenging dataset for deepfake forensics. In: CVPR, June 2020
39. Maaten, L.V.D., Hinton, G.: Visualizing data using t-SNE. J. Mach. Learn. Res. **9**(Nov), 2579–2605 (2008)
40. Marra, F., Gragnaniello, D., Verdoliva, L., Poggi, G.: Do GANs leave artificial fingerprints? In: Conference on Multimedia Information Processing and Retrieval (MIPR), pp. 506–511 (2019)
41. Matern, F., Riess, C., Stamminger, M.: Exploiting visual artifacts to expose deepfakes and face manipulations. In: WACV Workshops, pp. 83–92. IEEE (2019)

42. McClish, D.K.: Analyzing a portion of the ROC curve. Med. Decis. Making **9**(3), 190–195 (1989)
43. Nagrani, A., Chung, J.S., Xie, W., Zisserman, A.: Voxceleb: large-scale speaker verification in the wild. Comput. Speech Lang. **60**, 101027 (2020)
44. Nguyen, H.H., Fang, F., Yamagishi, J., Echizen, I.: Multi-task learning for detecting and segmenting manipulated facial images and videos. In: BTAS (2019)
45. Nguyen, H.H., Yamagishi, J., Echizen, I.: Capsule-forensics: using capsule networks to detect forged images and videos. In: ICASSSP, pp. 2307–2311. IEEE (2019)
46. Nguyen, T.T., Nguyen, C.M., Nguyen, D.T., Nguyen, D.T., Nahavandi, S.: Deep learning for deepfakes creation and detection. arXiv preprint arXiv:1909.11573 (2019)
47. Nirkin, Y., Masi, I., Tran, A., Hassner, T., Medioni, G.: On face segmentation, face swapping, and face perception. In: AFGR (2018)
48. Pedro, D.: A unified bias-variance decomposition and its applications. In: 17th International Conference on Machine Learning, pp. 231–238 (2000)
49. Rahmouni, N., Nozick, V., Yamagishi, J., Echizen, I.: Distinguishing computer graphics from natural images using convolution neural networks. In: WIFS, pp. 1–6 (2017)
50. Rössler, A., Cozzolino, D., Verdoliva, L., Riess, C., Thies, J., Nießner, M.: Faceforensics++: learning to detect manipulated facial images. In: ICCV (2019)
51. Ruff, L., et al.: Deep one-class classification. In: ICML, pp. 4393–4402 (2018)
52. Sabir, E., Cheng, J., Jaiswal, A., AbdAlmageed, W., Masi, I., Natarajan, P.: Recurrent convolutional strategies for face manipulation detection in videos. In: CVPR Workshops, pp. 80–87 (2019)
53. Sanderson, C., Lovell, B.C.: Multi-region probabilistic histograms for robust and scalable identity inference. In: Tistarelli, M., Nixon, M.S. (eds.) ICB 2009. LNCS, vol. 5558, pp. 199–208. Springer, Heidelberg (2009). https://doi.org/10.1007/978-3-642-01793-3_21
54. Schroff, F., Kalenichenko, D., Philbin, J.: Facenet: a unified embedding for face recognition and clustering. In: CVPR (2015)
55. Stehouwer, J., Dang, H., Liu, F., Liu, X., Jain, A.: On the detection of digital face manipulation. arXiv preprint arXiv:1910.01717 (2019)
56. Thies, J., Zollhöfer, M., Nießner, M.: Deferred neural rendering: image synthesis using neural textures. ACM Trans. Graph. (TOG) **38**(4), 1–12 (2019)
57. Thies, J., Zollhofer, M., Stamminger, M., Theobalt, C., Nießner, M.: Face2face: real-time face capture and reenactment of RGB videos. In: Proceedings of the IEEE Conference on Computer Vision and Pattern Recognition, pp. 2387–2395 (2016)
58. Tolosana, R., Vera-Rodriguez, R., Fierrez, J., Morales, A., Ortega-Garcia, J.: Deepfakes and beyond: a survey of face manipulation and fake detection. arXiv preprint arXiv:2001.00179 (2020)
59. Valentini, G., Dietterich, T.G.: Bias-variance analysis of support vector machines for the development of SVM-based ensemble methods. JMLR **5**(Jul), 725–775 (2004)
60. Verdoliva, D.C.G.P.L.: Extracting camera-based fingerprints for video forensics (2019)
61. Verdoliva, L.: Media forensics and deepfakes: an overview. IEEE J. Sel. Top. Signal Process. (2020)
62. Wang, F., Cheng, J., Liu, W., Liu, H.: Additive margin softmax for face verification. IEEE Signal Process. Lett. **25**(7), 926–930 (2018)

63. Weisstein, E.W.: Hypersphere (2002)
64. Wen, Y., Zhang, K., Li, Z., Qiao, Yu.: A discriminative feature learning approach for deep face recognition. In: Leibe, B., Matas, J., Sebe, N., Welling, M. (eds.) ECCV 2016. LNCS, vol. 9911, pp. 499–515. Springer, Cham (2016). https://doi.org/10.1007/978-3-319-46478-7_31
65. Wu, C.Y., Manmatha, R., Smola, A.J., Krahenbuhl, P.: Sampling matters in deep embedding learning. In: ICCV, October 2017
66. Xie, C., Wu, Y., Maaten, L.V.D., Yuille, A.L., He, K.: Feature denoising for improving adversarial robustness. In: CVPR, pp. 501–509 (2019)
67. Yang, X., Li, Y., Lyu, S.: Exposing deep fakes using inconsistent head poses. In: ICASSSP, pp. 8261–8265. IEEE (2019)
68. Yu, N., Davis, L.S., Fritz, M.: Attributing fake images to GANs: learning and analyzing GAN fingerprints. In: ICCV, pp. 7556–7566 (2019)
69. Zhang, X., Karaman, S., Chang, S.F.: Detecting and simulating artifacts in GAN fake images. In: WIFS (2019)

Incremental Few-Shot Meta-learning via Indirect Discriminant Alignment

Qing Liu[1], Orchid Majumder[2(✉)], Alessandro Achille[2],
Avinash Ravichandran[2], Rahul Bhotika[2], and Stefano Soatto[2]

[1] Johns Hopkins University, Baltimore, USA
[2] Amazon Web Services, Seattle, USA
orchidmajumder@gmail.com

Abstract. We propose a method to train a model so it can learn new classification tasks while improving with each task solved. This amounts to combining meta-learning with incremental learning. Different tasks can have disjoint classes, so one cannot directly align different classifiers as done in model distillation. On the other hand, simply aligning features shared by all classes does not allow the base model sufficient flexibility to evolve to solve new tasks. We therefore indirectly align features relative to a minimal set of "anchor classes". Such *indirect discriminant alignment* (IDA) adapts a new model to old classes without the need to re-process old data, while leaving maximum flexibility for the model to adapt to new tasks. This process enables incrementally improving the model by processing multiple learning *episodes*, each representing a different learning task, even with few training examples. Experiments on few-shot learning benchmarks show that this incremental approach performs favorably compared to training the model with the entire dataset at once.

1 Introduction

Meta-learning aims to train a model to learn new tasks leveraging knowledge accrued while solving related tasks. Most meta-learning methods do not incorporate experience from learning new tasks to improve the "base" (meta-learned) model. Our goal is to enable such improvement, thus creating a virtuous cycle whereby every new task learned enhances the base model in an incremental fashion, without the need to re-process previously seen data. We call this *incremental meta-learning* (IML).

While visual classification with a large number of training samples per class has reached performance close to human-level, learning from few samples ("shots") remains a challenge, as we discuss in Sect. 4. We explore the hypothesis that incrementally learning a model from many different tasks, each with

Electronic supplementary material The online version of this chapter (https://doi.org/10.1007/978-3-030-58571-6_40) contains supplementary material, which is available to authorized users.

© Springer Nature Switzerland AG 2020
A. Vedaldi et al. (Eds.): ECCV 2020, LNCS 12352, pp. 685–701, 2020.
https://doi.org/10.1007/978-3-030-58571-6_40

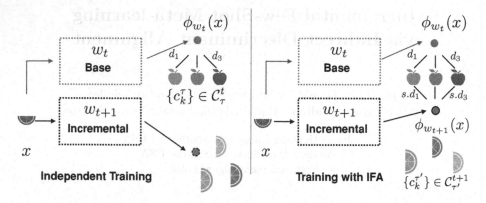

Fig. 1. Indirect Discriminant Alignment (IDA): Before alignment (left), an orange (new input data) processed through a base model backbone yields an embedding that has a different distance-vector to apples (old class anchors) compared with the one processed through the incremental model backbone. After performing alignment, they produce embeddings that have a similar distance-vector signature, while the incremental model can use the remaining degrees of freedom to adapt the embedding to solve new tasks.

few training examples, yields a model comparable to one trained with a large number of images at once. Accordingly, we focus on IML for *few-shot learning*.

IML is not merely meta-training [3,6,19,25,31,35] done by processing the training set in chunks: In IML, the meta-training set keeps changing, and we require both the performance of the model for the new tasks, as well as the base model, to improve. IML is also not just incremental (or continual) learning [4,17,20,21,26,33], which focuses on a *single* model to tackle new tasks while avoiding catastrophic forgetting. In IML, we want to continuously improve the meta-trained model so that, presented with an unseen task, it achieves better performance now that it would have before solving the previous task. Moreover, we want to improve the base learner without the need to re-process old data, since that may no longer be accessible, or it may become too expensive to re-process. However, we also want IML to allow exploiting old data, if that is available. Thus far we have used terms like "training task" or "model" informally. In the next section, we elaborate on these terms and then make them formal in Sect. 2.1.

Nomenclature. We identify a *learning task* with a training set. This dataset, together with a function to be minimized (*loss*) and the set of functions to minimize it (*models*), defines an optimization problem whose solution is *a* trained model that "solves the task." So, a learning task can be identified with both a training set, and a suitably trained model. In Sect. 2.1, we will introduce empirical cross-entropy as a loss, deep neural networks (DNNs) as a set of functions, and stochastic gradient descent (SGD) as an optimization scheme. A model consists of a *feature representation*, or *embedding*, obtained by processing each datum through a *backbone*, which is then used to test each hypothesis, or *class*, using a *discriminant function*. A *discriminant* is a function that maps a feature to the hypothesis space, where its value is used to render a decision. A discriminant vector is the collection of discriminant values associated to each hypothesis or class. A *classifier* is a function that outputs the minimizer (or maximizer) of a discriminant function, which corresponds to a *predicted* class or hypothesis. For instance, the Bayesian discriminant is the posterior density of the classes given the data. The corresponding discriminant vector is the collection of posterior probabilities for each hypothesis. The optimal Bayesian classifier is one that returns the hypothesis with the maximum a-posteriori probability (MAP).

1.1 Key Contribution and Organization

The main contribution of this paper can be more easily understood for the case of metric classifiers, where each class is represented by a prototype, or "center" (Fig. 1), and the discriminant compares features to prototypes, for instance using the Euclidean distance in the embedding space, although our method is not restricted to this case. Each new learning task has a set of classes that is possibly disjoint from those of old tasks. The goal of IML is to update the base model incrementally while solving each new task, without necessarily requiring access to data from old tasks, and despite each new task having only few samples per class. Simply imposing that all tasks use the same features would be too restrictive, as different tasks may require the embedding to change while preserving the old centers. On the other hand, we cannot compare discriminants or classifiers directly since they map to different hypothesis spaces.

Since we cannot compare classifiers directly, and we do not want to restrict the model's freedom to evolve, the **key idea** is to align models for the old and new tasks *indirectly*, by imposing that their discriminants (in the metric case, the vector of distances to the class centers) be aligned *relative to a minimal set of "anchor classes,"* and otherwise leaving the embedding free to adapt to new tasks. The minimal anchor set is represented by the old centers. Thus, *indirect discriminant alignment* (IDA) is performed by mapping the data to old centers, through both the new and the old backbones, and minimizing the misalignment between the two resulting discriminant vectors. Misalignment can be measured in a number of ways, and the process can be conducted by only using new data *incrementally*, resulting in a continuous improvement of the old model. The more general case, which applies to non-metric classifiers, is explained in Sect. 2.2. It results in the **main contribution** of our work, which is to propose what is, to the best of our knowledge, *the first method for incremental few-shot meta-learning.*

We tackle the case of few-shot learning since, in the presence of large amounts of data for the classes of interest, pre-training a large model and fine-tuning it for the task at hand already yields a strong baseline. This is not the case for few-shot learning, where the current state-of-the-art still lags far behind [5]. Our method directly generalizes several meta-learning algorithms [19,25,35], and is applicable to more yet.

In Sect. 2.3 we describe two implementations for performing incremental meta-learning and a number of baselines (Sect. 3.1), which form the basis for empirical evaluation in Sect. 3.3 on few-shot benchmark datasets outlined in Sect. 3.2. We also introduce DomainImageNet in Sect. 3.2 to measure the effect of meta-learning on incremental learning when new classes are both in- and out-of-domain. We highlight some limitations and failure cases in Sect. 3.4. We further discuss related work and future opportunities in Sect. 4.

2 Method

The next section establishes the notation and describes incremental learning and meta-learning in a formalism that will make it easy to describe our key contribution in Sect. 2.2. At that point, it is a small step to incremental meta-learning, as described in Sect. 2.2.

2.1 Preliminaries

A model for a classification task is a parametric approximation $p_w(y|x)$ of the posterior distribution of the class $y \in \{c_1, \ldots, c_K\}$ given the test datum x. For a given class of functions (architecture), the model may be identified with its parameters (*weights*) w. The model is trained by minimizing a loss function L that depends on a dataset $\mathcal{D} = \{(x_i, y_i)\}_{i=1}^{N}$, which defines the task, so that $w_0 \doteq \arg\min_w L(w; \mathcal{D})$.

Incremental learning assumes that an *incremental dataset* $\mathcal{E}$ is provided in addition to $\mathcal{D}$. If the two are disjoint, we can write

$$L(w; \mathcal{D} \cup \mathcal{E}) = L(w; \mathcal{D}) + L(w; \mathcal{E}) \tag{1}$$

If L is differentiable with respect to w and we train until convergence ($\nabla_w L(w_0, \mathcal{D}) = 0$), we can expand L to second-order around the previous parameters w_0 to obtain

$$L(w; \mathcal{D} \cup \mathcal{E}) = L(w; \mathcal{D}) + L(w; \mathcal{E})$$
$$\simeq L(w_0 + \delta w; \mathcal{E}) + L(w_0; \mathcal{D}) + \delta w^T H(w_0; \mathcal{D}) \delta w$$

where $w = w_0 + \delta w$ and $H(w_0; \mathcal{D})$ is the Hessian of the loss $L(w; \mathcal{D})$ computed at w_0. Ignoring the constant term $L(w_0; \mathcal{D})$ yields the derived loss

$$\mathcal{L}(w) = L(w; \mathcal{E}) + \delta w^T H(w_0; \mathcal{D}) \delta w \tag{2}$$

minimizing which corresponds to fine-tuning the base model for the new task while ensuring that the *parameters* change little, using the Hessian as the metric,[1]

---

[1] A metric is a positive semi-definite symmetric bilinear form. Since the Hessian H for deep networks typically may not be, it is often approximated by the Fisher Information Matrix, which is positive semi-definite and easier to compute.

such as in Elastic Weight Consolidation [17]. Note that, even if the incremental set $\mathcal{E}$ is small, there is no guarantee that the weight update δw will be small. Moreover, making δw small in Eq. (2) is unnecessary, since the weights can often change considerably without changing the network behavior.

Distillation is based on approximating the loss *not* by perturbing the weights, $w_0 \to w_0 + \delta w$, but by perturbing the discriminant function, $p_{w_0} \to p_{w_0 + \delta w}$, which can be done by minimizing

$$\mathcal{L}(w) = L(w; \mathcal{E}) + \lambda \mathbb{E}_{x \sim \mathcal{D}} \, \mathrm{KL}(p_{w_0}(y|x) \| p_w(y|x)) \tag{3}$$

where the Kullback-Leibler (KL) divergence measures the perturbation of the new discriminant p_w with respect to the old one p_{w_0} in units λ. The losses in Eq. (2) and Eq. (3) are equivalent up to first-order, meaning that a local first-order optimization would yield the same initial step when minimizing them. Equation (3) may be interpreted as model distillation [2,13] or trust-region optimization [32]. The drawback of this method is that it needs access to old samples to compute the loss, since the KL is averaged over $\mathcal{D}$. Our goal is to extend these ideas to meta-learning where $\mathcal{D}$ may no longer be accessible.

Meta-Learning presents an additional difficulty: A meta-training dataset consists of several tasks, indexed by τ, each learned in a separate training *episode,* represented by a different dataset $\mathcal{D}_\tau$ with possibly different classes $\{c_1^\tau, \ldots, c_K^\tau\} = \mathcal{C}_\tau$. Rather than training a single model to minimize the loss on a single dataset, a meta-learning algorithm aims to produce a task-agnostic model that minimizes the loss across all meta-training tasks. For the case of empirical cross-entropy:

$$L(w; \mathcal{D}) = \frac{1}{N_\tau} \sum_\tau \frac{1}{|\mathcal{D}_\tau|} \sum_{(x_i, y_i) \in \mathcal{D}_\tau} -\log p_w^\tau(y_i|x_i) \tag{4}$$

The first sum ranges over however many *meta-training tasks* $\mathcal{D}_\tau$ are available. To formalize the core idea in the next section, without loss of generality we write the posterior density $p(y|x)$ in terms of a "backbone" function ϕ that maps each sample x to a feature vector: $z = \phi(x)$, and a discriminant "head" f that maps a feature vector to the posterior $p(y|x) = f(y|\phi(x))$.

2.2 Indirect Discriminant Alignment (IDA)

The challenge in extending incremental learning (3) to meta-learning (4) is that each task $\mathcal{D}_\tau$ in the latter has a different discriminant f_τ for a different set of classes $\mathcal{C}_\tau$. Thus, aligning the discriminants directly would be imposing alignment between different classes, which is not meaningful. A naive solution would be to just align the features $\phi_w(x)$ on all inputs, for instance by minimizing their average distance

$$\mathbb{E}_x \| \phi_{w_t}(x) - \phi_{w_{t+1}}(x) \|^2 \tag{5}$$

However, this would be needlessly restrictive: Completely different features can yield the same posterior density, and we want to exploit this flexibility for incremental learning. Moreover, we want our method to only process new data, rather than keep re-processing old data, which would defy the goal of incremental processing. To simplify the notation, we refer to p_{w_τ} as p_{old} and $p_{w_{\tau+1}}$ as p_{new}, and so for the heads f_{old}, f_{new} and the backbones ϕ_{old}, ϕ_{new}. Each can be trained on different tasks, or episodes, τ.

The key idea of this paper is to enable *aligning the old and new discriminants using "class anchors" from the old task* τ, *while processing only data from the new task* τ'. This is done through *indirect discriminative alignment* (IDA), illustrated in Fig. 1, which addresses the challenge that the tasks τ and τ' may not share any classes. IDA uses the classes defined by the old discriminants as "anchors," and imposes that the features processed through the old and new embeddings share the same discriminant relative to these anchor classes. For metric-based classifiers, the classes can be represented by points in latent (feature, or embedding) space, and the anchors are just an under-complete basis of this space, with the discriminant vector represented by the Euclidean distance to each anchor class representative. The under-complete alignment leaves the residual degrees of freedom free for continual learning. However, the method is more general, allowing any discriminant function.

To make the dependency on the anchor classes and episodes explicit, we write the model $p_w^\tau(y|x) = f_w^\tau(y|\phi_w(x))$. Indirect discriminative alignment of the new model to the old one is then performed by minimizing:

$$\text{IDA}_{\mathcal{E}}(\phi_{new}|\phi_{old}; \mathcal{C}_{old}) = \mathbb{E}_{x \sim \mathcal{E}, \tau'} \big[\text{KL}(f_{old}^{\tau'}(y|\phi_{old}(x)) \| f_{old}^{\tau'}(y|\phi_{new}(x))) \big] \quad (6)$$

where $\mathcal{C}_{old}$ is a set of classes obtained after training on the old training set and τ' are tasks sampled from the new dataset $\mathcal{E}$.

Intuitively, we reuse the old class representatives $\mathcal{C}_{old}$ and ask that the new features ϕ_{new} remain compatible with the discriminant f_{old}. Moreover, instead of sampling from the old dataset $\mathcal{D}$ – which we may no longer have access to – we sample from $x \sim \mathcal{E}$. In the case of metric classifiers, this can be interpreted as aligning the new features to a set of anchor points, which in particular are the old class representatives.

Note that f can be any discriminant that can process data generated via a representation function ϕ, where both f and ϕ have their own parameters. Also, the choice of KL-divergence to measure the discrepancy between discriminant vectors is due to the fact that it yields a simple expression for most commonly used models, but IDA is not limited to it and any other divergence measure could be employed instead.

Incremental Meta-Learning. Given (6), incremental meta-learning consists of solving

$$w_{t+1} = \arg\min_{w_{t+1}} L(w_{t+1}; \mathcal{E}) + \lambda \, \text{IDA}_{\mathcal{E}}(\phi_{w_{t+1}}|\phi_{w_t}; \mathcal{C}_t) \quad (7)$$

where the first term corresponds to fine-tuning the base model on the new data, while the second term enforces indirect discriminant alignment relative to the anchors from old classes. In the next section, we describe our implementation and empirical evaluation.

2.3   Implementation

The simplest implementation of our method Eq. (7) is obtained by using a metric classifier as the base meta-learner. This choice limits us to each task having the same number of classes, a choice we will discuss and extend in appendix. We represent a metric-based classifier using a function ψ_w that computes the class representatives, or prototypes, or "centers," $c_k^\tau = \psi_w(\mathcal{D}_\tau)_k$,[2] and a function (metric) $\chi_w(z_i, c_k^\tau)$ that scores the fit of a datum, represented by the feature vector z_i, with an hypothesis corresponding to a class c_k^τ. Each function can be fixed [35] or learned [25]. Note that the backbone ϕ_w is common to all tasks, whereas the metric changes with each few-shot task $\mathcal{D}_\tau$, since $c_k^\tau \in \mathcal{C}_\tau$ and $\mathcal{C}_\tau = \{c_k^\tau = \psi_w(\mathcal{D}_\tau)_k\}_{k=1}^K$. According to this model, the optimal (Bayesian) discriminant for the task $\mathcal{D}_\tau$ is of the form:

$$p(y = k|z) = \frac{e^{\chi_w(z, c_k^\tau)}}{\sum_j e^{\chi_w(z, c_j^\tau)}} \tag{8}$$

where $z = \phi_w(x)$. Note that χ_w and $p(y|x)$ are equivalent discriminants: Maximizing the posterior is equivalent to minimizing the negative log, which yields a loss of the form

$$L(w; \mathcal{D}) = \frac{1}{N_\tau} \sum_\tau \frac{1}{|\mathcal{D}_\tau|} \sum_{(x_i, y_i) \in \mathcal{D}_\tau} -\chi_w(z_i, c_{y_i}^\tau) + \log\left(\sum_{k=1}^K e^{\chi_w(z_i, c_k^\tau)}\right) \tag{9}$$

Our first implementation has a trained backbone ϕ_w but fixes the metric χ to be the L_2 distance and the class representatives to be the means:

$$\chi(z, c) := -\|z - c\|^2,$$
$$\psi(\mathcal{D}_\tau, k) := \frac{1}{|\mathcal{C}_k|} \sum_i \delta_{y_i, k} z_i$$
$$\mathcal{C}_\tau = \psi(\mathcal{D}_\tau, k)_{k=1}^K.$$

The detailed computation of the loss Eq. (9) is described in the appendix. After every training episode, we discard the data used for meta-training and only retain the class anchors $\mathcal{C}_\tau$. Our paragon (oracle), that will be described in Eq. (10), does not retain any class anchors but trains a new meta-learner at every episode, utilizing all data seen thus far. Ideally, the final performance of the two should be similar, which would justify incremental processing of new datasets without the need to re-process old data, which was our working hypothesis and the basis of Eq. (2). Indeed, this is what we observe in Sect. 3.3.

For meta-training, we sample few-shot tasks using episodic sampling i.e., each batch consists of K classes sampled at random. We then sample N_s samples as the support samples and N_q samples as the query samples. The class representations are calculated only using the support samples, while the query samples are used to compute the loss. For training the base model, we sample few-shot

---

[2] We overload the notation c to indicate the classes in $\mathcal{C}$ and the class representation, which are the argument of χ, since both represent the classes.

tasks τ from the old dataset $\mathcal{D}$ and train the model using the loss function in Eq. (4). To train the incremental model we sample a few-shot task τ' from the new dataset $\mathcal{E}$. We then sample K random class anchors (of the old dataset $\mathcal{D}$) from C_τ^t, which are calculated and preserved after the previous training phase. During incremental phase(s), the network is trained by minimizing Eq. (9).

3 Empirical Validation

We compare our simplest method, which is based on a Prototypical Network architecture (PN) [35] as the base meta-learner, with several baselines as well as the paragon model that uses the same architecture but is free to re-process all past data along with new data. In Sect. 3.3 we assess performance on standard few-shot image classification benchmarks (MiniImageNet and TieredImageNet) as well as on a newly curated dataset described in Sect. 3.2. To show that our method is not tied to the specifics of PN, we also perform the same experiments using ECM [25]. That is the basis for extending our simplest method to the case where each task has a different number of classes, described in the appendix.

Implementation Details: We use a ResNet-12 [12] following [23] as our feature extractor ϕ_w. It consists of four residual layers each with 3×3 convolutional layers followed by a max-pooling layer. We use DropBlock regularization [9], a form of structured dropout with a keep-rate of 0.9 after the max-pooling layers. At each round, we train for 200 epochs, each consisting of 800 few-shot training tasks containing 5 (1) support examples per class for 5-shot 5-way (1-shot 5-way). We use 15 query points per class for computing the loss to update the network parameters. Test performance is also measured with 15 query points per class. We use Adam [16] with an initial learning-rate of 0.001 which is reduced by a factor of 0.5 when performance on the validation set does not improve for more than 3 epochs. We use cross-entropy loss with softmax temperature 2.0, following [20]. For IDA, we choose λ to be 1.0 and we show the effect of varying λ in the range of $[0.0, 10.0]$ in the appendix.

3.1 Baselines and Ablation Studies

To evaluate the method quantitatively, we need an upper-bound (oracle) represented by a model that performs meta-training using all the data as well as few other baselines to enable a fair comparison and ablation studies.

No Update (NU) is the simplest baseline, that is a model meta-trained only using the old dataset.

Fine-Tuning (FT) starts with the model meta-trained on old data and performs additional steps of SGD on the new data wit no additional constraint, using the first term of Eq. (7).

Direct Feature Alignment (DFA) adds to the first term of Eq. (7) a penalty for the direct misalignment of features (5) averaged over the new tasks

$$\mathrm{DFA}_{\mathcal{E}}(\phi_{w_{t+1}}|\phi_{w_t}) = \mathbb{E}_{x \sim \mathcal{E}\tau'} \|\phi_{w_{t+1}}(x) - \phi_{w_t}(x)\|_2^2$$

akin to feature distillation.

Exemplar-based incremental meta-learning (EIML) has access to (possibly a subset of) the old data, so we can add an additional term to Eq. (7) to foster tighter alignment via

$$
\begin{aligned}
\mathcal{L}(w_{t+1}) = {} & L(w_{t+1}; \mathcal{E}) \\
& + \lambda \mathbb{E}_{x \in \mathcal{D}_\tau} \left[\mathrm{KL}(f_{w_t}^\tau(y|\phi_{w_t}(x)) \| f_{w_{t+1}}^\tau(y|\phi_{w_{t+1}}(x))) \right] \\
& + \lambda \mathbb{E}_{x \in \mathcal{E}_{\tau'}} \left[\mathrm{KL}(f_{w_t}^\tau(y|\phi_{w_t}(x)) \| f_{w_t}^\tau(y|\phi_{w_{t+1}}(x))) \right]
\end{aligned}
\tag{10}
$$

where $\mathcal{E}_{\tau'}$ is task sampled from the new dataset and $\mathcal{C}_t$ and $\mathcal{C}_{t+1}$ are obtained by re-processing $\mathcal{D}_\tau$ (a task sampled from the old dataset) through the old and the new embeddings respectively. We expect this method to perform best, as it has access to old data. However, it is computationally more expensive than IDA as we need to re-process old data.

Full training paragon (PAR) consists of meta-learning using the union of data from old and new datasets, minimizing the left-hand side of Eq. (1). There is no incremental training, so this method serves as an upper bound for performance.

3.2 Datasets

We test our algorithm on MiniImageNet [38], TieredImageNet [28] and another variant of ImageNet [29] which we call DomainImageNet. MiniImageNet consists of images of size 84×84 sampled from 100 classes of the ILSVRC dataset [29], with 600 images per class. We used the data split outlined in [24], where 64 classes are used for training, 16 classes for validation and 20 for testing. We further split the 64 training classes randomly into 32 for meta-training the base model and the remaining for training the incremental model; 16 validation classes are only used for assessing generalization during meta-training for both the base and incremental models. For a fair measurement of performance on the old data, we also use a separate test set comprising 300 new images per class [10].

TieredImageNet is a larger subset of ILSVRC, with $779,165$ images of size 84×84 representing 608 classes that are hierarchically grouped into 34. This dataset is split to ensure that sub-classes within the 34 groups are not shared among training, validation and test sets. The result is $448,695$ images in 351 classes for training, $124,261$ images in 97 classes for validation, and $206,209$ images in 160 classes for testing. For a fair comparison, we use the same training, validation and testing splits of [28] and use the classes at the lowest level of the hierarchy. Similar to MiniImageNet, we randomly pick 176 classes from the training set for meta-training the base model and use the remaining 175 classes for incremental meta-training. Here we also use a separate test set of about 1000 images per class for measuring old task performance.

To investigate the role of domain gap in IML, we assemble DomainImageNet, along the format of MiniImageNet, with 32 old meta-training classes,

Table 1. Classification accuracy on 3 different sets: tasks sampled from old, new and unseen classes of MiniImageNet using PN [35] and different IML methods.

Model	1-shot 5-way			5-shot 5-way		
	Old classes (32)	New classes (32)	Unseen classes (20)	Old classes (32)	New classes (32)	Unseen classes (20)
NU	73.84 ± 0.50	49.05 ± 0.48	50.55 ± 0.42	91.17 ± 0.18	68.35 ± 0.39	68.60 ± 0.33
FT	60.64 ± 0.49	72.61 ± 0.51	53.60 ± 0.42	82.25 ± 0.26	$\mathbf{89.63 \pm 0.22}$	72.13 ± 0.33
DFA	60.77 ± 0.49	72.23 ± 0.51	53.81 ± 0.42	82.53 ± 0.26	89.32 ± 0.22	72.07 ± 0.33
EIML	$\mathbf{68.95 \pm 0.50}$	71.43 ± 0.52	54.86 ± 0.42	$\mathbf{90.20 \pm 0.20}$	86.91 ± 0.25	74.39 ± 0.50
IDA	66.54 ± 0.49	$\mathbf{71.92 \pm 0.51}$	$\mathbf{55.52 \pm 0.43}$	89.14 ± 0.21	87.32 ± 0.25	$\mathbf{75.11 \pm 0.31}$
PAR	74.65 ± 0.49	75.85 ± 0.50	56.88 ± 0.43	91.77 ± 0.17	92.49 ± 0.17	75.27 ± 0.13

Table 2. Classification accuracy on 3 different sets: tasks sampled from old, new and unseen classes of MiniImageNet using ECM [25] and different IML methods.

Model	1-shot 5-way			5-shot 5-way		
	Old classes (32)	New classes (32)	Unseen classes (20)	Old classes (32)	New classes (32)	Unseen classes (20)
NU	73.82 ± 0.43	53.00 ± 0.43	52.77 ± 0.37	89.38 ± 0.38	71.90 ± 0.36	71.57 ± 0.36
FT	63.71 ± 0.43	75.05 ± 0.43	56.00 ± 0.38	82.90 ± 0.21	89.37 ± 0.21	74.29 ± 0.32
DFA	64.66 ± 0.42	$\mathbf{75.71 \pm 0.43}$	56.68 ± 0.39	83.37 ± 0.21	$\mathbf{89.70 \pm 0.21}$	74.69 ± 0.31
IDA	$\mathbf{72.52 \pm 0.42}$	68.43 ± 0.44	$\mathbf{57.13 \pm 0.39}$	$\mathbf{88.46 \pm 0.27}$	85.45 ± 0.27	$\mathbf{75.55 \pm 0.30}$
PAR	74.40 ± 0.40	75.74 ± 0.42	59.02 ± 0.39	89.68 ± 0.21	89.93 ± 0.21	77.60 ± 0.30

32 new meta-training classes, 16 meta-validation classes and 40 meta-test (unseen) classes. All classes are sampled from the ILSVRC dataset, but old, new and meta-test set have two subdivisions, one sampled from *natural* categories, the other sampled from *man-made* categories. 40 unseen classes consist of 20 classes each of natural and man-made categories. The domain split we use follows [41].

3.3 Quantitative Results

We test IML on each dataset using two common few-shot scenarios: 5-shot 5-way and 1-shot 5-way. We refer to the data used to train the base model as old classes, and that of the incremental model as new classes. We refer to unseen classes as classes that the model has not seen in any training. Final performance of the meta-learner is reported as the mean and 95% confidence interval of the classification accuracy across 2000 episodes or few-shot tasks.

Results of the different methods using PN as a meta-learner are shown in Table 1 for MiniImageNet, Table 3 for TieredImageNet and Table 4 for Domain-ImageNet. Further, we show results using ECM as a meta-learner in Table 2 for MiniImageNet. We also show the results using ECM on DomainImageNet for 5-shot 5-way in Table 5. All results for DomainImageNet are using natural objects as the old domain and man-made objects as the new domain. In the appendix, we show the results for 1-shot 5-way and also for all combinations of

Table 3. Classification accuracy on 3 different sets: tasks sampled from old, new and unseen classes of TieredImageNet using PN [35] and different IML methods.

Model	1-shot 5-way			5-shot 5-way		
	Old classes (176)	New classes (175)	Unseen classes (160)	Old classes (176)	New classes (175)	Unseen classes (160)
NU	73.10 ± 0.52	66.18 ± 0.43	56.82 ± 0.50	89.03 ± 0.27	81.97 ± 0.37	75.78 ± 0.43
FT	71.87 ± 0.52	**71.03 ± 0.52**	58.63 ± 0.50	87.77 ± 0.29	**87.60 ± 0.30**	78.20 ± 0.42
DFA	72.03 ± 0.51	70.83 ± 0.53	**58.81 ± 0.50**	87.82 ± 0.29	87.38 ± 0.30	78.11 ± 0.42
IDA	**72.65 ± 0.51**	70.17 ± 0.53	58.71 ± 0.50	**89.13 ± 0.15**	86.91 ± 0.31	**78.40 ± 0.42**
PAR	78.57 ± 0.51	77.43 ± 0.50	61.87 ± 0.51	91.05 ± 0.24	90.44 ± 0.26	80.58 ± 0.40

shots and meta-learners while using man-made objects as the old domain and natural objects as the new domain.

Catastrophic Forgetting: Tables 1, 2, 3, 4, 5 and 6 show that the classification accuracy on old classes using the incremental model drops significantly when compared with the base model for methods that perform IML without using the old data (i.e., FT and DFA). This holds for both 1-shot 5-way and 5-shot 5-way, both PN and ECM, and across all datasets.

Incremental Meta Learning (IML) with any of the methods described above yields increased performance on both the new classes and the unseen classes. If performance on the old classes is not a priority, any IML method will perform better on the new classes with an added bonus of better performance on unseen classes compared with the base model. Again, these conclusions hold across shots, meta-learners and datasets.

EIML vs IDA: Table 1 shows that the difference in performance of between EIML and IDA is not significant. While we expected EIML to dominate IDA, in some cases EIML performed worse (Table 1: 1-shot 5-way case for MiniImageNet). This illustrates the limited benefit of re-processing old data, justifying IML. We also varied the number of samples we retained from the old dataset in the range of 15 to 120 and noticed that the performance was almost constant (shown in the appendix). Hence, we do not run tests on EIML using ECM. Furthermore, for a class of methods that learn the class anchors such as [19], running EIML is far more expensive as we need to run an additional inner optimization at every step of IML. For completeness, the performance on different datasets using EIML (with PN) is shown in the appendix.

IDA outperforms all baselines for unseen classes across all scenarios shown in this section, except for 1-shot 5-way in Table 3. We further notice better performance compared with FT and DFA for old classes. For new classes, IDA trails FT and DFA but overall it performs best on average, approaching the paragon when new tasks are sampled across old, new and unseen classes.

TieredImageNet: Table 3 shows results using PN [35] as the meta-learner. For this dataset, the improvement from using more classes is relatively small compared with MiniImageNet (Table 1). When the base model is trained with a

Table 4. Results of 5-shot 5-way classification accuracy on different sets of Domain-ImageNet using PN [35] and different IML methods.

Model	Old classes from old domain (32)	New classes from new domain (32)	Unseen classes from old domain (20)	Unseen classes from new domain (20)	Unseen classes from both domains (40)
NU	86.94 ± 0.22	49.14 ± 0.36	57.66 ± 0.38	51.72 ± 0.32	59.59 ± 0.35
FT	64.42 ± 0.35	**84.80 ± 0.28**	50.72 ± 0.38	71.16 ± 0.32	65.44 ± 0.40
DFA	65.12 ± 0.35	83.95 ± 0.29	51.33 ± 0.38	70.46 ± 0.33	65.52 ± 0.40
IDA	**81.26 ± 0.27**	82.06 ± 0.30	**59.32 ± 0.39**	**70.61 ± 0.32**	**70.36 ± 0.36**
PAR	87.44 ± 0.22	88.77 ± 0.25	58.59 ± 0.37	74.46 ± 0.32	74.02 ± 0.37

Table 5. Results of 5-shot 5-way classification accuracy on different sets of Domain-ImageNet using ECM [25] with different IML methods.

Model	Old classes from old domain (32)	New classes from new domain (32)	Unseen classes from old domain (20)	Unseen classes from new domain (20)	Unseen classes from both domains (40)
NU	87.86 ± 0.20	56.71 ± 0.39	63.30 ± 0.38	58.10 ± 0.35	66.09 ± 0.35
FT	67.35 ± 0.34	**89.68 ± 0.20**	55.37 ± 0.38	**74.00 ± 0.31**	69.98 ± 0.39
DFA	69.33 ± 0.33	88.72 ± 0.22	57.06 ± 0.38	73.97 ± 0.31	70.77 ± 0.38
IDA	**86.09 ± 0.22**	81.82 ± 0.28	**64.22 ± 0.38**	69.92 ± 0.33	**72.64 ± 0.33**
PAR	86.83 ± 0.22	88.84 ± 0.21	65.77 ± 0.38	75.98 ± 0.31	77.31 ± 0.33

large number of classes, the generalization ability of the network is already satisfactory, and we observe negligible catastrophic forgetting or increase in meta-learning performance. We also see that IDA is similar to the baselines. This raises the question of what new classes would best improve performance in IML. Our experiments on DomainImageNet address this question.

DomainImageNet: Results for 5-shot 5-way are shown for PN [35] in Table 4 and for ECM [25] in Table 5. The model is first trained using natural classes and then incrementally trained using man-made classes. This helps evaluate the effect of domain shift between old and new training classes. We test on five different sets: seen and unseen classes from natural objects, seen and unseen classes from man-made objects and unseen classes from a mixture of the two.

The tables show that the accuracy on the joint test set improves significantly compared with the baselines. Most of the gain is for the new domain, i.e.,, man-made objects. Also, catastrophic forgetting is significant since there is domain shift between the classes from the old and new domains. This effect is also seen with unseen classes on the same domain. IDA is shows improvement across the board relative to the baselines. The results for 1-shot 5-way and using the reverse domain training (i.e.,, old domain is man-made objects and incremental domain is natural objects) on the three sets for all IML algorithms show similar trends. This suggests that it matters what classes are selected for incremental training.

Table 6. Results of 5-shot 5-way classification accuracy on MiniImageNet using PN [35] with 2 rounds of incremental meta-training, where each round consists of an 16 new classes.

Model	Incremental - Round I			Incremental - Round II		
	Old classes (32)	New classes (16)	Unseen classes (20)	Old classes (32+16)	New classes (16)	Unseen classes (20)
NU	91.17 ± 0.18	65.60 ± 0.39	68.60 ± 0.33	82.25 ± 0.37	71.45 ± 0.38	68.60 ± 0.33
FT	80.70 ± 0.31	87.67 ± 0.37	67.45 ± 0.37	76.03 ± 0.36	90.72 ± 0.23	70.57 ± 0.32
DFA	$\mathbf{87.69 \pm 0.26}$	88.43 ± 0.36	68.20 ± 0.36	80.69 ± 0.38	91.27 ± 0.21	71.19 ± 0.37
IDA	87.30 ± 0.25	$\mathbf{89.56 \pm 0.20}$	$\mathbf{72.08 \pm 0.36}$	$\mathbf{84.21 \pm 0.30}$	$\mathbf{93.25 \pm 0.17}$	$\mathbf{75.15 \pm 0.35}$
PAR	93.94 ± 0.05	93.09 ± 0.06	72.10 ± 0.13	93.03 ± 0.06	95.58 ± 0.05	75.27 ± 0.13

Adding classes with diverse statistics yields maximum advantage. While we can expect this to be the trend for samples belonging to the same class, we find it to be true for samples belonging to unseen classes as well from the same domain. Our method successfully mitigates catastrophic forgetting to a large extent and performs well across different domains.

Multiple Rounds of IML: In the above experiments, our configuration consists of one old and one new dataset. In Table 6, we show the performance of different IML algorithms for a scenario where there are multiple new datasets. We split the new classes of MiniImageNet into two sets each having 16 classes (classes are split randomly) and run IML for a 5-shot 5-way setup using PN. From the table, we can observe that IDA does not incur any performance loss and achieves similar accuracy on the unseen classes compared to a single training with 32 classes. For other methods like DFA and FT, we can observe some performance drop when comparing with Table 1, which shows that IDA scales better beyond single incremental training.

3.4 Limitations and Failure Cases

The implementation we chose, based on [35] and [25], and the tests we performed limit our assessment to tasks that share the same number of classes, $K = 5$, as customary in the literature. While technically not a limitation as one could always build a set of models, each for a different number of classes, and indeed it is not uncommon to train and fine-tune different models for different "ways" as seen in the literature, we use the same model for all tests. It is nonetheless desirable to have a meta-learner that can handle an arbitrary number of classes, different for each training episode. While our general framework Eq. (7) enables it, our simplest implementation described in Eq. (2.3) does not. However, in appendix, we describe a modified implementation that is not subject to this restriction. Since benchmarks in the literature most commonly refer to the cases $K = 1, 5$, we use the simpler model in our experiments.

Further, sampling K classes among many has low probability of yielding hard tasks that can be informative of meta-learning. Even simple classifiers can easily tell 5 random classes from ImageNet apart. *Hard task mining* could be done by selecting tasks using a distance such as [1], by sampling a random class and picking the 4 closest ones in Task2Vec space for a 5-way setup.

Finally, in our experiments we have noticed that there is still a performance gap between IDA and the paragon. The performance is matched for the case of unseen classes, but there is room for improvement in tasks sampled from new/current task distribution across shots, datasets and methods.

4　Discussion and Related Work

The natural occurrence of classes in the world is a long tailed distribution [37,39,42], whereby instances for most classes are rare and instances for few classes are abundant. Deep neural networks trained for classification [12,14,18] do not fare well when trained with small datasets typical of the tail [37], leading to increased interest in few-shot learning. Meta-learning [22,31,36] for few-shot learning [6,10,19,24,25,30,35,38] uses a relatively "meta training" dataset from which several few-shot tasks are sampled to mimic phenomena at the tail. Once meta-trained on the old dataset, these methods cannot take advantage of the new few-shot tasks to update the meta-learner. The obvious fix, to re-train the meta-learner every time a few-shot task arises, is impractical if at all possible, as one may not have access to all past data.

Incremental learning, or continual learning, is typically performed by adapting a neural network model, trained using some dataset, using a new dataset, to arrive at a single model. The main challenge here is to prevent catastrophic forgetting [8]. A few relevant works in this area include [4,17,20,21,26,33]. To learn classifiers in a class-incremental way where new classes are added progressively, [26] proposed to keep exemplars from old classes based on their representation power and the computational budget. [20] used knowledge distillation to preserve the model's capabilities on the old tasks when only new data is accessible. [21] and its extension [4] leveraged a small episodic memory to alleviate forgetting. [17] slowed down learning on the weights that were important for old tasks, while [33] extended it by training a knowledge-base in alternating phases.

Methods that used few-shot incremental sets such as [10] unified the recognition of both new and old classes using attention based few-shot classification. Similarly, [27] used recurrent back-propagation to train a set of new weights to achieve good overall classification on both old and new classes. [34,40] extended this class-incremental framework to other visual recognition tasks like semantic segmentation and attribute recognition. Accordingly, despite being called incremental few-shot learning, these methods are accurately described as incremental learning using few-shot datasets.

On-line meta-learning [7] can be done by exposing an agent to new tasks in a sequential manner. One may see this experimental setup to be similar to ours; however, unlike IML, [7] retains data from all previous tasks and leverages it for meta-training, thus forgoing incremental learning. In our setup, we retain minimal amounts of data from the old training set. [11,15] on the other hand, tackled a continual/online meta-learning setup where an explicit delineation between different tasks is not available, whereas in our experimental setup we are primarily trying to solve new classification tasks with clear task boundaries.

To summarize, there are several approaches to solve IML: One that biases new weights to remain similar to those of the base model (elastic weight consolidation) as in Eq. (2), and one that looks at function space and imposes that the activations remain similar to that of the base model (knowledge distillation), as in Eq. (4). We adopt the latter and empirically test how our general framework performs in the case of two metric-based meta-learners [25,35]. This is a particular instance of the right-hand side of Eq. (1), that was our starting point in Sect. 2.1. It yields empirical performance comparable to meta-learning on the union of the old and new datasets, which is the gold standard. This gives empirical validation to our method, and to the many possible variants that can be explored considering combinations of meta and few-shot set, choices of metrics, classifiers, divergence measures, and a myriad of other ingredients in the IML recipe to minimize Eq. (7). We have tested several options in our experiments and in the appendix, and many more are open for investigation in future work.

References

1. Achille, A., et al.: Task2vec: task embedding for meta-learning. In: Proceedings of the IEEE International Conference on Computer Vision, pp. 6430–6439 (2019)
2. Ba, J., Caruana, R.: Do deep nets really need to be deep? In: Ghahramani, Z., Welling, M., Cortes, C., Lawrence, N.D., Weinberger, K.Q. (eds.) Advances in Neural Information Processing Systems, vol. 27, pp. 2654–2662. Curran Associates, Inc., (2014). http://papers.nips.cc/paper/5484-do-deep-nets-really-need-to-be-deep.pdf
3. Bengio, S., Bengio, Y., Cloutier, J., Gecsei, J.: On the optimization of a synaptic learning rule. In: Preprints Conference Optimality in Artificial and Biological Neural Networks, vol. 2. University of Texas (1992)
4. Chaudhry, A., Ranzato, M., Rohrbach, M., Elhoseiny, M.: Efficient lifelong learning with a-gem. In: International Conference on Learning Representations (2019)
5. Dhillon, G.S., Chaudhari, P., Ravichandran, A., Soatto, S.: A baseline for few-shot image classification. arXiv preprint arXiv:1909.02729 (2019)
6. Finn, C., Abbeel, P., Levine, S.: Model-agnostic meta-learning for fast adaptation of deep networks. In: Proceedings of the 34th International Conference on Machine Learning, vol. 70, pp. 1126–1135. JMLR org (2017)
7. Finn, C., Rajeswaran, A., Kakade, S., Levine, S.: Online meta-learning. arXiv preprint arXiv:1902.08438 (2019)
8. French, R.M.: Catastrophic forgetting in connectionist networks. Trends Cogn. Sci. **3**(4), 128–135 (1999)
9. Ghiasi, G., Lin, T.Y., Le, Q.V.: Dropblock: a regularization method for convolutional networks. In: Advances in Neural Information Processing Systems, pp. 10727–10737 (2018)
10. Gidaris, S., Komodakis, N.: Dynamic few-shot visual learning without forgetting. In: Proceedings of the IEEE Conference on Computer Vision and Pattern Recognition, pp. 4367–4375 (2018)

11. Harrison, J., Sharma, A., Finn, C., Pavone, M.: Continuous meta-learning without tasks. arXiv preprint arXiv:1912.08866 (2019)
12. He, K., Zhang, X., Ren, S., Sun, J.: Deep residual learning for image recognition. In: Proceedings of the IEEE Conference on Computer Vision and Pattern Recognition, pp. 770–778 (2016)
13. Hinton, G., Vinyals, O., Dean, J.: Distilling the knowledge in a neural network. In: NIPS 2014 Deep Learning Workshop (2015)
14. Huang, G., Liu, Z., van der Maaten, L., Weinberger, K.Q.: Densely connected convolutional networks. In: The IEEE Conference on Computer Vision and Pattern Recognition (CVPR), July 2017
15. Jerfel, G., Grant, E., Griffiths, T., Heller, K.A.: Reconciling meta-learning and continual learning with online mixtures of tasks. In: Advances in Neural Information Processing Systems, pp. 9119–9130 (2019)
16. Kingma, D.P., Ba, J.: Adam: A method for stochastic optimization. arXiv preprint arXiv:1412.6980 (2014)
17. Kirkpatrick, J., et al.: Overcoming catastrophic forgetting in neural networks. Proc. Nat. Acad. Sci. **114**(13), 3521–3526 (2017)
18. Krizhevsky, A., Sutskever, I., Hinton, G.E.: Imagenet classification with deep convolutional neural networks. In: Proceedings of the 25th International Conference on Neural Information Processing Systems. NIPS'2012, vol. 1, pp. 1097–1105 (2012)
19. Lee, K., Maji, S., Ravichandran, A., Soatto, S.: Meta-learning with differentiable convex optimization. In: Proceedings of the IEEE Conference on Computer Vision and Pattern Recognition, pp. 10657–10665 (2019)
20. Li, Z., Hoiem, D.: Learning without forgetting. IEEE Trans. Pattern Anal. Mach. Intell. **40**(12), 2935–2947 (2017)
21. Lopez-Paz, D., Ranzato, M.: Gradient episodic memory for continual learning. In: Advances in Neural Information Processing Systems, pp. 6467–6476 (2017)
22. Naik, D.K., Mammone, R.J.: Meta-neural networks that learn by learning. In: Proceedings 1992 IJCNN International Joint Conference on Neural Networks, vol. 1, pp. 437–442. IEEE (1992)
23. Oreshkin, B., López, P.R., Lacoste, A.: Tadam: task dependent adaptive metric for improved few-shot learning. In: Advances in Neural Information Processing Systems, pp. 721–731 (2018)
24. Ravi, S., Larochelle, H.: Optimization as a model for few-shot learning. In: ICLR 2017 (2017)
25. Ravichandran, A., Bhotika, R., Soatto, S.: Few-shot learning with embedded class models and shot-free meta training. In: International Conference on Computer Vision (2019)
26. Rebuffi, S.A., Kolesnikov, A., Sperl, G., Lampert, C.H.: icarl: Incremental classifier and representation learning. In: Proceedings of the IEEE Conference on Computer Vision and Pattern Recognition, pp. 2001–2010 (2017)
27. Ren, M., Liao, R., Fetaya, E., Zemel, R.S.: Incremental few-shot learning with attention attractor networks. arXiv preprint arXiv:1810.07218 (2018)
28. Ren, M., et al.: Meta-learning for semi-supervised few-shot classification. arXiv preprint arXiv:1803.00676 (2018)
29. Russakovsky, O., et al.: Imagenet large scale visual recognition challenge. Int. J. Comput. Vis. **115**(3), 211–252 (2015)
30. Rusu, A.A., et al.: Meta-learning with latent embedding optimization. arXiv preprint arXiv:1807.05960 (2018)

31. Schmidhuber, J.: Evolutionary principles in self referential learning. On learning how to learn: The meta-meta-... hook. Diploma thesis, Institut f. Informatik, Tech. Univ. Munich (1987)
32. Schulman, J., Levine, S., Abbeel, P., Jordan, M., Moritz, P.: Trust region policy optimization. In: International Conference on Machine Learning, pp. 1889–1897 (2015)
33. Schwarz, J., et al.: Progress and compress: a scalable framework for continual learning. In: International Conference on Machine Learning (2018)
34. Siam, M., Oreshkin, B.: Adaptive masked weight imprinting for few-shot segmentation. arXiv preprint arXiv:1902.11123 (2019)
35. Snell, J., Swersky, K., Zemel, R.: Prototypical networks for few-shot learning. In: Advances in Neural Information Processing Systems, pp. 4077–4087 (2017)
36. Thrun, S., Pratt, L.: Learning to Learn. Springer Science & Business Media, New York (2012)
37. Van Horn, G., Perona, P.: The devil is in the tails: Fine-grained classification in the wild. arXiv preprint arXiv:1709.01450 (2017)
38. Vinyals, O., et al.: Matching networks for one shot learning. In: Advances in Neural Information Processing Systems, pp. 3630–3638 (2016)
39. Wang, Y.X., Ramanan, D., Hebert, M.: Learning to model the tail. In: Guyon, I., et al. (eds.) Advances in Neural Information Processing Systems, vol. 30, pp. 7029–7039. Curran Associates, Inc., (2017). http://papers.nips.cc/paper/7278-learning-to-model-the-tail.pdf
40. Xiang, L., Jin, X., Ding, G., Han, J., Li, L.: Incremental few-shot learning for pedestrian attribute recognition. arXiv preprint arXiv:1906.00330 (2019)
41. Yosinski, J., Clune, J., Bengio, Y., Lipson, H.: How transferable are features in deep neural networks? In: Ghahramani, Z., Welling, M., Cortes, C., Lawrence, N.D., Weinberger, K.Q. (eds.) Advances in Neural Information Processing Systems, vol. 27, pp. 3320–3328. Curran Associates, Inc., (2014). http://papers.nips.cc/paper/5347-how-transferable-are-features-in-deep-neural-networks.pdf
42. Zhu, X., Anguelov, D., Ramanan, D.: Capturing long-tail distributions of object subcategories. In: Proceedings of the 2014 IEEE Conference on Computer Vision and Pattern Recognition. CVPR'2014, Washington, DC, USA, pp. 915–922. IEEE Computer Society (2014). https://doi.org/10.1109/CVPR.2014.122, https://doi.org/10.1109/CVPR.2014.122

BigNAS: Scaling up Neural Architecture Search with Big Single-Stage Models

Jiahui Yu[1,2(✉)], Pengchong Jin[1], Hanxiao Liu[1], Gabriel Bender[1],
Pieter-Jan Kindermans[1], Mingxing Tan[1], Thomas Huang[2], Xiaodan Song[1],
Ruoming Pang[1], and Quoc Le[1]

[1] Google Brain, New York, USA
jiahuiyu@google.com
[2] University of Illinois at Urbana-Champaign, Champaign, USA

Abstract. Neural architecture search (NAS) has shown promising results discovering models that are both accurate and fast. For NAS, training a *one-shot model* has become a popular strategy to rank the relative quality of different architectures (*child models*) using a single set of shared weights. However, while one-shot model weights can effectively *rank* different network architectures, the absolute accuracies from these shared weights are typically far below those obtained from stand-alone training. To compensate, existing methods assume that the weights must be retrained, finetuned, or otherwise post-processed after the search is completed. These steps significantly increase the compute requirements and complexity of the architecture search and model deployment. In this work, we propose BigNAS, an approach that challenges the conventional wisdom that post-processing of the weights is necessary to get good prediction accuracies. *Without extra retraining or post-processing steps*, we are able to train a single set of shared weights on ImageNet and use these weights to obtain child models whose sizes range from 200 to 1000 MFLOPs. Our discovered model family, BigNASModels, achieve top-1 accuracies ranging from 76.5% to 80.9%, surpassing state-of-the-art models in this range including EfficientNets and Once-for-All networks without extra retraining or post-processing. We present ablative study and analysis to further understand the proposed BigNASModels.

Keywords: Efficient neural architecture search · AutoML

1 Introduction

Designing network architectures that are both accurate and efficient is crucial for deep learning on edge devices. A single neural network architecture can require more than an order of magnitude more inference time if it is deployed on a slower

Electronic supplementary material The online version of this chapter (https://doi.org/10.1007/978-3-030-58571-6_41) contains supplementary material, which is available to authorized users.

© Springer Nature Switzerland AG 2020
A. Vedaldi et al. (Eds.): ECCV 2020, LNCS 12352, pp. 702–717, 2020.
https://doi.org/10.1007/978-3-030-58571-6_41

device [37]. Furthermore, even two devices which have similar overall speeds (e.g., phone CPUs made by different manufacturers) can favor very different network architectures due to hardware and device driver differences [33]. This makes it appealing to not only search for architectures of varying sizes that are optimized for specific devices, but also ensure that these models can be deployed effectively.

In the past, to optimize network architectures for a single device and latency target [31], Neural Architecture Search (NAS) methods [27,38,39] have shown to be effective. While early NAS methods were prohibitively expensive for most practitioners, recent *efficient* NAS methods based on weight sharing reduce search costs by orders of magnitude [1,22,25,35]. These methods work by training a *super-network* and then identifying a path through the network – a subset of its operations – which gives the best possible accuracy while satisfying a user-specified latency constraint for a specific hardware device. The advantage of this approach is that we can train the super-network and then use it to *rank* many different candidate architectures from a user-defined search space.

However, the *absolute accuracies* of predictions obtained from this super-network are typically much lower than those of models trained from scratch in stand-alone fashion [1]. For this reason, it is commonly assumed that significant post-processing of the super-network's weights is necessary to obtain high-quality accuracies for model deployment. For example, one proposed solution is to retrain a separate model for each device of interest and each latency budget of interest [5,33]. However, this incurs significant overhead, especially if the number of deployment scenarios is large. A second solution would be to post-process the weights after training is finished; for example, using the *progressive shrinking* heuristic proposed for Once-for-All networks [4]. However, this post-processing step complicates the model training pipeline. Moreover, the child models from Once-for-All networks [4] still requires fine-tuning with additional epochs (*e.g.*, 75 epochs on ImageNet) to achieve the best accuracies.

In this work, we reassess the popular belief that the retraining or post-processing of the shared weights is necessary in order to obtain competitive accuracies. We propose several techniques to bridge the gap between the distinct initialization and learning dynamics across small and big child models with shared parameters. With these techniques, we are able to train a *single-stage model*: a single model from which we can directly slice high-quality child models *without any extra post-processing*.

We search over a big *single-stage* model that contains both small child models (~200 MFLOPs, comparable to MobileNetV3) and big child models (~1 GFLOPs, comparable to EfficientNets). Different from existing one-shot methods [1,3,22,25,35], our trained single-stage model offers a much wider coverage of model capacities, and more importantly, all child models are trained in a way such that they simultaneously reach excellent performance at the end of the search phase. Architecture selection can be then carried out via a simple coarse-to-fine selection strategy. Once an architecture is selected, we can obtain a child model by simply slicing the single-stage model for instant deployment

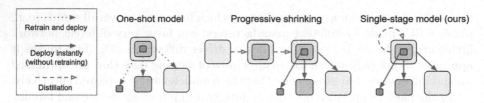

Fig. 1. Comparison with several existing workflows. We use nested squares to denote models with shared weights, and use the size of the square to denote the size of each model. Workflow in the middle refers the concurrent work from [4], where submodels are sequentially induced through progressive distillation and channel sorting. We simultaneously train all child models in a single-stage model with proposed modifications, and deploy them without retraining or finetuning.

w.r.t. the given constraints such as memory footprint and/or runtime latency. The workflow is illustrated in Fig. 1.

The success of simplified BigNAS workflow relies on a single objective: how to train a high-quality single-stage model? This objective is challenging on its own. For example, we find that the training loss explodes if a big single-stage model is not properly initialized; during the training process, big child models start to overfit before small ones plateau; empirically bigger child models tend to overfit more on the training data. To address these challenges, we systematically study and revisit conventional training techniques of stand-alone networks, and adapt them to train weight-sharing single-stage models. With the proposed techniques, we are able train a high-quality single-stage model on ImageNet and obtain a family of child models that simultaneously surpass all the state-of-the-art models in the range of 200 to 1000 MFLOPs, including EfficientNets B0-B2 (1.6% more accurate under 400 MFLOPs), without retraining or finetuning the child models upon the completion of search. For example, one of our child models achieves 80.9% top-1 accuracy at 1G FLOPs (4× less computation than a ResNet-50).

2   Related Work

Earlier NAS methods [20,21,27,38,39] train thousands of candidate architectures from scratch (on a smaller proxy task) and use their validation performance as the feedback to an algorithm that learns to focus on the most promising regions in the search space. More recent works have sought to amortize the cost by training a single over-parameterized *one-shot model*. Each architecture in the search space uses only a subset of the operations in the one-shot model; these *child models* can be efficiently ranked by using the shared weights to estimate their relative accuracies [1,3,5,18,22,25,33–35].

As a complementary direction, resource-aware NAS methods are proposed to simultaneously maximize prediction accuracy and minimize resource requirements such as latency, FLOPs, or memory footprints [2,4,9,30,31,33,35].

All the aforementioned approaches require two-stage training: once the best architectures have been identified (either through the proxy tasks or using a one-shot model), they have to be retrained from scratch to obtain a final model with higher accuracy. In most of these existing works, a single search experiment only targets a single resource budget or a narrow range of resource budgets at a time.

To alleviate these issues, [4] proposed a progressive training approach (OFA) concurrently with our work. The idea is to pre-train a single full network and then progressively distill it to obtain the smaller networks. Moreover, a channel sorting procedure is required to progressively construct the smaller networks. In our proposed BigNAS, however, all the child models in the single-stage model are trained *simultaneously*, allowing the learning of small and big networks to mutually benefit each other. During the training, we always keep lower-index channels in each layer and lower-index layers in each stage for our child models, eliminating the sorting procedure. Our BigNAS is able to handle a wider set of models (from 200 MFLOPs to 1 GFLOPs) and offers a better coverage over diverse deployment scenarios and varied resource budgets.

Our work shares high-level similarities with *slimmable networks* [35–37] in terms of training a single shared set of weights which can be used for many child models. However, while slimmable networks are specialized to vary the number of channels only, we are able to handle a much larger space where many architectural dimensions (kernel and channel sizes, network depths, input resolutions) are searched simultaneously, subsuming and outperforming the manually-designed scaling heuristics in EfficientNets [32].

3   Architecture Search with Single-Stage Models

Our proposed method consists of two steps:

1. We train a big *single-stage model* from which we can directly sample or slice different architectures as *child models* for instant inference and deployment. In contrast to previous works, our training is single-stage. In other words: the trained model weights from a search can be directly used for deployment, without any need to retrain them from scratch (e.g. [1,3,9,22,25,30,35]) or otherwise post-process them (*e.g.*, [4]).
2. Architecture selection using a simple *coarse-to-fine* selection method to find the most accurate model under the given resource constraints (for example, FLOPs, memory footprint and/or runtime latency budgets on different devices).

In the following, we will first systematically study how to train a *high-quality single-stage model* from five aspects: network sampling during training, inplace distillation, network initialization, convergence behavior and regularization. Then we will present a coarse-to-fine approach for efficient resource-aware architecture selection.

3.1 Training a High-Quality Single-Stage Model

Training a high-quality single-stage model is important and highly non-trivial due to the distinct initialization and learning dynamics of small and big child models. In this section, we first generalize two techniques originally introduced by [36] to simultaneously train a set of high-quality networks with different channel numbers, and show that both can be extended to handle a much larger space where the architectural dimensions, including kernel sizes, channel numbers, input resolutions, network depths are jointly searched. We then present three additional techniques to address the distinct initialization and learning dynamics of small and big child models.

Sandwich Rule. In each training step, given a mini-batch of data, the sandwich rule [36] samples the smallest child model, the biggest (full) child model and N randomly sampled child models ($N = 2$ in our experiments). It then aggregates the gradients from all sampled child models before updating the weights of the single-stage model. As multiple architectural dimensions are included in our search space, the "smallest" child model is the one with lowest input resolution, thinnest width, shallowest depth, and smallest kernel size (the kernel of the depthwise convolutions in each inverted residual block [28]). The motivation is to improve all child models in our search space simultaneously, by pushing up both the performance lower bound (the smallest child model) and the performance upper bound (the biggest child model) across all child models.

Inplace Distillation. During the training of a single-stage model, inplace distillation [36] takes the soft labels predicted by the biggest possible child model (full model) to supervise all other child models. The benefit of inplace distillation comes for free in our training setting, as we always have access to the predictions of the largest child model in each gradient update step thanks to the sandwich rule. We note that all child models are only trained with the inplace distillation loss, starting from the first training step to the end of the training. The temperature hyper-parameter or the mixture of distillation/target loss [14] are not used in our experiments for the sake of simplicity.

During training, input images are randomly cropped as a preliminary data augmentation step. When distilling a high-resolution teacher model into a low-resolution student model, we find that it is helpful to feed the same image patches into both the teacher and the student. In our data preparation, we first randomly crop an image with a fixed resolution (on ImageNet we use 224), and then apply bicubic interpolation to the *same patch* to transform it into all target resolutions (*e.g.*, 192, 288, 320, etc.). In this case, soft labels predicted by the biggest child model (the teacher) are more compatible with the inputs seen by other child models (the students). Therefore this can serve as a more accurate distillation signal. Our preliminary results show that this leads to ~0.3% improvement on average top-1 accuracy for child models compared with sampling different patches.

Initialization. When we first tried to train bigger and deeper single-stage models, we found that training was highly unstable, and that the training loss exploded when we used learning rates optimized for training a normal neural network. The training started to work when we reduced the learning rate to 30% of its original value, but this configuration lead to much worse results ($\sim 1.0\%$) top-1 accuracy drop on ImageNet).

While stabilize model training is in general a complex and open-ended problem, we found that in this case a simple change to our setup was sufficient to stabilize training. As all child models in our search space are residual networks, we initialize the output of each residual block (before skip connection) to an all-zeros tensor by setting the learnable scaling coefficient $\gamma = 0$ in the last Batch Normalization [19] layer of each residual block, ensuring identical variance before and after each residual block regardless of the fan-in. This initialization is originally mentioned in [8] which improves accuracy by $\sim 0.2\%$ in their setting, yet is more critical in our setting (improving by $\sim 1.0\%$)). We also additionally add a skip connection in each stage transition when either resolutions or channels differ (using 2×2 average pooling and/or 1×1 convolution if necessary) to explicitly construct an identity mapping [12].

Convergence Behavior. In practice, we find that big child models converge faster while small child models converge slower. Figure 2a shows the typical learning curves during the training of a single-stage model, where we plot the validation accuracies of a small and a big child model over time. This reveals a dilemma: at training step t when the performance of big child models peaks, the small child models are not fully-trained; and at training step t' when the small child models have better performance, the big child models already overfitted.

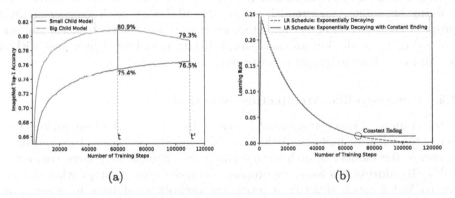

(a)   (b)

Fig. 2. On the left, we show typical accuracy curves during the training process for both small and big child models. It reveals a common dilemma in training big single-stage models: at training step t when the performance of big child models peaks, the small child models are not fully-trained; and at training step t' when the small child models have better performance, the big child models already overfitted. On the right, we plot the simple modified learning rate schedules with constant ending to address this issue.

To address this issue, we put our focus on the learning rate schedule. We first plot the optimized and widely used exponentially decaying learning rate schedule for MobileNet-series [15,16,28], MNasNets [31] and EfficientNets [32] in Fig. 2b. We introduce a simple modification to this learning rate schedule, named *exponentially decaying with constant ending*, which has a constant learning rate at the end of training when it reaches 5% of the initial learning rate (Fig. 2b). It brings two benefits. First, with a slightly larger learning rate at the end, the small child models learn faster. Second, the constant learning rate at the end alleviates the overfitting of big child models as the weights oscillate.

Regularization. Empirically when comparing training/validation losses, we find big child models tend to overfit the training data whereas small child models tend to underfit. In previous work, Bender et al. [1] apply the same weight decay to all child models regardless whether they are small or big. To prevent overfitting of larger networks, For EfficientNets, Tan et al. [32] found it helpful to use larger dropout [29] rates for larger neural networks. This becomes even more complicated in our context of training big single-stage models, due to the interplay among the small child models and big child models with shared parameters. Nevertheless, we introduce a simple rule that is surprisingly effective for this problem: *regularize only the biggest (full) child model* (*i.e.*, the only model that has direct access to the ground truth training labels since other child models are trained with inplace distillation only). We simply apply this rule to both weight decay and dropout, and empirically demonstrate its effectiveness in our experiments.

Batch Norm Calibration. Batch norm statistics are not accumulated when training the single-stage model as they are ill-defined with varying architectures. After the training is completed, we re-calibrate the batch norm statistics (following Yu et al. [36]) for each sampled child model for deployment without retraining or finetuning any network parameters.

3.2 Coarse-to-fine Architecture Selection

After training a single-stage model, one needs to select the best architectures w.r.t. the resource budgets. Although obtaining the accuracy of a child model is cheap, the number of architecture candidates is extremely large (more than 10^{12}). To address this issue, we propose a coarse-to-fine strategy where we first try to find a rough skeleton of promising network candidates in general, and then sample multiple fine-grained variations around each skeleton architecture of interest.

Specifically, in the coarse-grained phase, we define a limited input resolution set, depth set (global depth multipliers), channel set (global width multipliers) and kernel size set, and obtain benchmarks for all child models in this restricted space. This is followed by a fine-grained search phase, where we first pick the best network skeleton satisfying the given resource constraint found in the previous phase, and then randomly mutate its network-wise resolution, stage-wise depth, number of channels and kernel sizes to further discover better network architectures. Finally, we directly use the weights from the single-stage model for the induced child models without any retraining or finetuning. More details will be presented in the experiments.

4   Experiments

In this section, we first present the details of our search space, followed by our main results compared with the previous state-of-the-arts in terms of both accuracy and efficiency. Then we conduct an extensive ablative study to demonstrate the effectiveness of our proposed modifications. Finally, we show the intermediate results of our coarse-to-fine architecture selection.

Table 1. MobileNetV2-based search space.

Stage	Operator	Resolution	#Channels	#Layers	Kernel Sizes
	Conv	192 × 192–320 × 320	32–40	1	3
1	MBConv1	96 × 96–160 × 160	16–24	1–2	3
2	MBConv6	96 × 96–160 × 160	24–32	2–3	3
3	MBConv6	48 × 48–80 × 80	40–48	2–3	3, 5
4	MBConv6	24 × 24–40 × 40	80–88	2–4	3, 5
5	MBConv6	12 × 12–20 × 20	112–128	2–6	3, 5
6	MBConv6	12 × 12–20 × 20	192–216	2–6	3, 5
7	MBConv6	6 × 6–10 × 10	320–352	1–2	3, 5
	Conv	6 × 6–10 × 10	1280–1408	1	1

4.1   Search Space Definition

Following previous resource-aware NAS methods [5,15,31–33], our network architectures consist of a stack with inverted bottleneck residual blocks (MBConv) [28]. We also insert a squeeze-and-excitation module [17] in each block following EfficientNet [32] and MobileNetV3 [15]. The detailed search space is summarized in Table 1. For the input resolution dimension, we sample from set {192, 224, 288, 320}. By training on different input resolutions, we find our trained single-stage model is able to generalize to unseen input resolutions during architecture search or deployment (e.g., 208, 240, 256, 272, 304, 336) after BN calibration. For the depth dimension, our network has seven stages (excluding the first and the last convolution layer). Each stage has multiple choices of the number of layers (e.g., stage 5 can pick any number of layers ranging from 2 to 6). Following slimmable networks [37] that always keep lower-index channels in each layer, we always keep *lower-index layers* in each network stage (and their weights). For weight sharing on the kernel size dimension in the inverted residual blocks, a 3 × 3 depthwise kernel is defined to be the center of a 5 × 5 depth-wise kernel. Both kernel sizes and channel numbers can be adjusted layer-wise. The input resolution is network-wise and the number of layers is a stage-wise configuration in our search space.

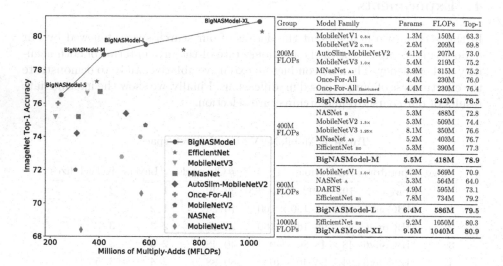

Group	Model Family	Params	FLOPs	Top-1
200M FLOPs	MobileNetV1 0.5×	1.3M	150M	63.3
	MobileNetV2 0.75×	2.6M	209M	69.8
	AutoSlim-MobileNetV2	4.1M	207M	73.0
	MobileNetV3 1.0×	5.4M	219M	75.2
	MNasNet A1	3.9M	315M	75.2
	Once-For-All	4.4M	230M	76.0
	Once-For-All finetuned	4.4M	230M	76.4
	BigNASModel-S	**4.5M**	**242M**	**76.5**
400M FLOPs	NASNet B	5.3M	488M	72.8
	MobileNetV2 1.3×	5.3M	509M	74.4
	MobileNetV3 1.25×	8.1M	350M	76.6
	MNasNet A3	5.2M	403M	76.7
	EfficientNet B0	5.3M	390M	77.3
	BigNASModel-M	**5.5M**	**418M**	**78.9**
600M FLOPs	MobileNetV1 1.0×	4.2M	569M	70.9
	NASNet A	5.3M	564M	64.0
	DARTS	4.9M	595M	73.1
	EfficientNet B1	7.8M	734M	79.2
	BigNASModel-L	**6.4M**	**586M**	**79.5**
1000M FLOPs	EfficientNet B2	9.2M	1050M	80.3
	BigNASModel-XL	**9.5M**	**1040M**	**80.9**

Fig. 3. Main results of BigNASModels on ImageNet.

4.2   Main Results on ImageNet

We train our big single-stage model on ImageNet [7] using same settings following our strongest baseline EfficientNets ([32]: RMSProp optimizer with decay 0.9 and momentum 0.9; batch normalization with post-calibration [36]; weight decaying factor $1e-5$; initial learning rate 0.256 that decays by 0.97 every 2.4 epochs; swish activation [26] and AutoAugment policy [6]. We train our big single-stage model together with all techniques proposed in Sect. 3.1. The learning rate is truncated to a constant value when it reaches 5% of its initial learning rate (*i.e.*, 0.0128) until the training ends. We apply dropout only on training the full network with dropout ratio 0.2, and weight decaying only on full network once in each training iteration. To train the single-stage model, we adopt the sandwich sampling rules and inplace distillation proposed by [36]. After the training, we use a simple coarse-to-fine architecture selection to find the best architecture under each interested resource budgets. We will show the details of coarse-to-fine architecture selection in Sect. 4.4.

We show the performance benchmark of our model family, named BigNAS-Models, in Fig. 3. On the left we show the visualization of FLOPs-Accuracy benchmarks compared with the previous arts including MobileNetV1 [16], NASNet [39], MobileNetV2 [28], AutoSlim-MobileNetV2 [35], MNasNet [31],

MobileNetV3 [15], EfficientNet [32] and concurrent work Once-For-All [4]. We show the detailed benchmark results on the right table. For small-sized models, our BigNASModel-S achieves 76.5% accuracy under only 240 MFLOPs, which is 1.3% better than MobileNetV3 in terms of similar FLOPs, and 0.5% better than ResNet-50 [11] with 17 × fewer FLOPs. For medium-sized models, our BigNASModel-M achieves 1.6% better accuracy than EfficientNet B0. For large-sized models where ImageNet classification accuracy saturates, our BigNASModel-L still has 0.6% improvement compared with EfficientNet B2. Moreover, instead of individually training models of different sizes, our BigNASModel-S, BigNASModel-M and BigNASModel-L are sliced directly from one pretrained single-stage model, without retraining or finetuning.

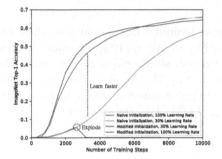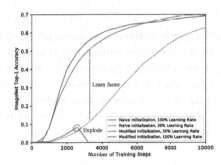

Fig. 4. Focusing on the start of training. Ablation study on different initialization methods. We show the validation accuracy of a small (left) and big (right) child model.

4.3   Ablation Study

Ablation Study on Initialization. Previous weight initialization methods [10] are deduced from fixed neural networks, where the numbers of input units is constant. However, in a single-stage model, the number of input units varies across the different child models. In this part, we start with training a single-stage model using He Initialization [10] designed for fixed neural networks. As shown in Fig. 4, the accuracy of both small (left) and big (right) child models drops to zero after a few thousand training steps during the learning rate warming-up [8]. The single-stage model is able to converge when we reduce the learning rate to the 30% of its original value. If the initialization is modified according to Sect. 3.1, the model learns much faster at the beginning of the training (shown in Fig. 4), and has better performance at the end of the training (shown in Fig. 5). Moreover, we can train the single-stage model with the original learning rate hyper-parameter, which leads to much better performance for both small (Fig. 5, left) and big (Fig. 5, right) child models.

Ablation Study on Convergence Behavior. During the training of a single-stage model, the big child models converge faster and then overfit, while small

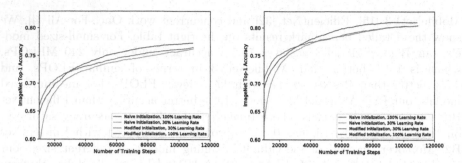

Fig. 5. Focusing on the end of training. Ablation study on different initialization methods. We show the validation accuracy of a small (left) and big (right) child model.

child models converge slower and need more training. In this part, we show the performance after addressing this issue in Fig. 6. We apply the proposed learning rate schedule *exponentially decaying with constant ending* on the right. The detailed learning rate schedules are shown in Fig. 2b. We also tried many other learning rate schedules with an exhaustive hyper-parameter sweep, including linearly decaying [24,36] and cosine decaying [13,23]. But the performances are all worse than exponentially decaying.

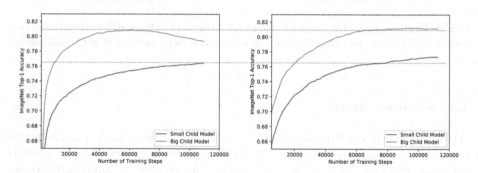

Fig. 6. The validation accuracy curves during the training process for both small and big child models before (left) and after (right) our modifications.

Ablation Study on Regularization. Big child models are prone to overfitting on the training data whereas small child models are prone to underfitting. In this part, we compare the effects of the regularization between two rules: (1) applying regularization on all child models [1], and (2) applying regularization only on the full network. Here the regularization techniques we consider are weight decay with factor $1e - 5$ and dropout with ratio 0.2 (the same hyper-parameters used in training previous state-of-the-art mobile networks). In Fig. 7, we show the performance of both small (left) and big (right) child models using different regularization rules. On the left, the performance of small child models

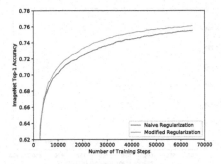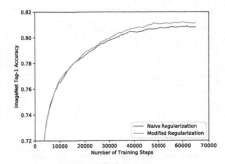

Fig. 7. The validation accuracy of a small (left) and big (right) child model using different regularization rules.

is improved (+0.5 top-1 accuracy) as it has less regularization and more capacity to fit the training data. Meanwhile on the right, we found the performance of the big child model is also improved slightly (+0.2 top-1 accuracy).

4.4 Coarse-to-fine Architecture Selection

After the training of a single-stage model, we use coarse-to-fine architecture selection to find the best architectures under different resource budgets. During the search, the evaluation metrics can be flexible including predictive accuracy, FLOPs, memory footprint, latency on various different devices, and many others. It is noteworthy that we pick the best architectures according to the predictive accuracy on training set, because we used all training data for obtaining our single-stage model (no retraining from scratch), and the validation set of ImageNet [7] is being used as "test set" in the community. In this part, we first show an illustration of our coarse-to-fine architecture selection with the trained big single-stage model in Fig. 8. The search results are based on FLOPs-Accuracy benchmarks (as FLOPs are more reproducible and independent of the software version, hardware version, runtime environments and many other factors).

During the coarse-to-fine architecture selection, we first find rough skeletons of good candidate networks. Specifically, in the coarse selection phase, we pre-define five input resolutions (network-wise, {192, 224, 256, 288, 320}), four depth configurations (stage-wise via global depth multipliers [32]), two channel configurations (stage-wise via global width multipliers [16]) and four kernel size configurations (stage-wise), and obtain all of their benchmarks (shown in Fig. 8 on the left). Then under our interested latency budget, we perform a fine-grained grid search by varying its configurations (shown in Fig. 8 on the right). For example, under FLOPs near 600M we first pick the skeleton of the red dot shown in Fig. 8. We then perform additional fine-grained architecture selection by randomly varying the input resolutions, depths, channels and kernel sizes slightly. We note that the coarse-to-fine architecture selection is flexible and not very exhaustive in our experiments, yet it already discovered fairly good architectures as shown in Fig. 8 on the right. For the FLOPs near 650M, we finally select the child

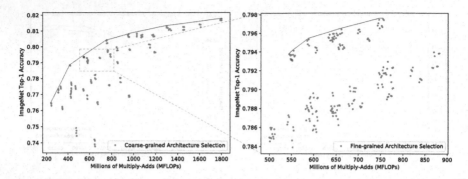

Fig. 8. Benchmark results of coarse-to-fine architecture selection. The red dot in coarse-grained architecture selection is picked and mutated for fine-grained architecture selection.

model with input resolution 256, depth configuration {1:2:2:2:4:4:1}, channel configuration {32:16:24:48:88:128:216:352:1408} and kernel size configuration {3:3:5:3:5:5:3}. After training of the single-stage model, the post-search step is highly parallelizable and independent of training.

5   Analysis of BigNASModel

Finetuning Child Models Sampled from BigNASModel. In previous sections we have reported the accuracies of child models from a single trained BigNASModel without finetuning, what if we do finetune it? To understand whether the trained BigNASModel has reached relatively optimal accuracies, we conduct experiments to finetune these child models (*i.e.*, BigNASModel-S, BigNASModel-M, BigNASModel-L, BigNASModel-XL) for additional 25 epochs under different constant learning rates separately. Table 2 shows that finetuning in our setting no longer improves accuracy significantly.

Table 2. Analysis on Child Models sampled from BigNASModel. We compare the ImageNet validation performance of (1) child model directly sampled from BigNASModel without finetuning (**w/o** Finetuning), (2) child model finetuned with various constant learning rate (**w/** Finetuning at different lr). Blue subscript indicates the performance improvement while Red subscript indicates degradation.

Child Model	w/o Finetuning	w/ Fintuning lr = 0.01	w/ Fintuning lr = 0.001	w/ Fintuning lr = 0.0001
BigNASModel-S	76.5	74.6 (-1.9)	76.4 (-0.1)	76.5 (0.0)
BigNASModel-M	78.9	76.7 (-2.2)	78.8 (-0.1)	78.8 (-0.1)
BigNASModel-L	79.5	77.9 (-1.6)	79.6 $(+0.1)$	79.7 $(+0.2)$
BigNASModel-XL	80.9	79.0 (-1.9)	80.6 (-0.3)	80.8 (-0.1)

Table 3. Analysis on training child architectures from scratch. We compare the ImageNet validation performance of (1) child model directly sampled from BigNASModel without finetuning (**w/o** Finetuning), (2) child architectures trained from scratch without distillation (FromScratch **w/o** distill), and (3) child architectures trained from scratch with two distillation methods A [14] and B [36] (FromScratch **w/** distill (A)/(B)).

Child Architecture	w/o Finetuning	FromScratch w/o distill	FromScratch w/ distill (A)	FromScratch w/ distill (B)
BigNASModel-S	76.5	75.3 (-1.2)	75.3 (-1.2)	76.3 (-0.2)
BigNASModel-M	78.9	77.4 (-1.5)	77.4 (-1.5)	78.6 (-0.3)
BigNASModel-L	79.5	78.2 (-1.3)	77.9 (-1.5)	79.2 (-0.3)
BigNASModel-XL	80.9	79.3 (-1.6)	79.0 (-1.9)	80.4 (-0.5)

Training the Architectures of Child from Scratch. We further study the performance when these selected child models are trained from scratch with or without distillation. We implement two distillation variants. The Distill (A) is a simple distillation [14] without temperature. The teacher network is trained with dropout and label smoothing following our training pipeline. The student network is trained with distillation loss only from soft-predictions of the teacher network. The Distill (B) is inplace distillation [36] where we jointly train a teacher and student network from scratch with weight sharing. The student network is trained with the soft-predictions of the teacher network only. The Distill (B) is most similar to the distillation used in training BigNASModel. We note that although it is commonly believed that distillation can improve regularization, we found that the simple Distill (A) method does not help in EfficientNet-based architectures. Table 3 shows that the accuracies of child models slightly benefit from jointly training a weight-sharing single-stage model, which is consistent to the observations in previous work [36].

6 Conclusion

We presented a novel paradigm for neural architecture search by training a single-stage model, from which high-quality child models of different sizes can be induced for instant deployment without retraining or finetuning. With several proposed techniques, we obtain a family of BigNASModels as slices in a big pre-trained single-stage model. These slices simultaneously surpass all state-of-the-art ImageNet classification models ranging from 200 MFLOPs to 1 GFLOPs. We hope our work can serve to further simplify and scale up neural architecture search.

References

1. Bender, G., Kindermans, P.J., Zoph, B., Vasudevan, V., Le, Q.: Understanding and simplifying one-shot architecture search. In: International Conference on Machine Learning, pp. 549–558 (2018)

2. Berman, M., Pishchulin, L., Xu, N., Blaschko, M.B., Medioni, G.: Aows: adaptive and optimal network width search with latency constraints. In: Proceedings of the IEEE/CVF Conference on Computer Vision and Pattern Recognition (CVPR), June 2020

3. Brock, A., Lim, T., Ritchie, J., Weston, N.: SMASH: one-shot model architecture search through hypernetworks. In: International Conference on Learning Representations (2018). https://openreview.net/forum?id=rydeCEhs-

4. Cai, H., Gan, C., Wang, T., Zhang, Z., Han, S.: Once-for-all: train one network and specialize it for efficient deployment. In: International Conference on Learning Representations (2020). https://openreview.net/forum?id=HylxE1HKwS

5. Cai, H., Zhu, L., Han, S.: ProxylessNAS: direct neural architecture search on target task and hardware. In: International Conference on Learning Representations (2019). https://openreview.net/forum?id=HylVB3AqYm

6. Cubuk, E.D., Zoph, B., Mane, D., Vasudevan, V., Le, Q.V.: Autoaugment: learning augmentation strategies from data. In: Proceedings of the IEEE Conference on Computer vision and Pattern Recognition, pp. 113–123 (2019)

7. Deng, J., Dong, W., Socher, R., Li, L.J., Li, K., Fei-Fei, L.: Imagenet: a large-scale hierarchical image database. In: IEEE Conference on Computer Vision and Pattern Recognition, 2009. CVPR 2009, pp. 248–255. IEEE (2009)

8. Goyal, P., et al.: Accurate, large minibatch SGD: training imagenet in 1 hour. arXiv preprint arXiv:1706.02677 (2017)

9. Guo, Z., et al.: Single path one-shot neural architecture search with uniform sampling. arXiv preprint arXiv:1904.00420 (2019)

10. He, K., Zhang, X., Ren, S., Sun, J.: Delving deep into rectifiers: surpassing human-level performance on imagenet classification. In: Proceedings of the IEEE International Conference on Computer Vision, pp. 1026–1034 (2015)

11. He, K., Zhang, X., Ren, S., Sun, J.: Deep residual learning for image recognition. In: Proceedings of the IEEE Conference on Computer Vision and Pattern Recognition, pp. 770–778 (2016)

12. He, K., Zhang, X., Ren, S., Sun, J.: Identity mappings in deep residual networks. In: Leibe, B., Matas, J., Sebe, N., Welling, M. (eds.) ECCV 2016. LNCS, vol. 9908, pp. 630–645. Springer, Cham (2016). https://doi.org/10.1007/978-3-319-46493-0_38

13. He, T., Zhang, Z., Zhang, H., Zhang, Z., Xie, J., Li, M.: Bag of tricks for image classification with convolutional neural networks. In: Proceedings of the IEEE Conference on Computer Vision and Pattern Recognition, pp. 558–567 (2019)

14. Hinton, G., Vinyals, O., Dean, J.: Distilling the knowledge in a neural network. arXiv preprint arXiv:1503.02531 (2015)

15. Howard, A., et al.: Searching for mobilenetv3. In: Proceedings of the IEEE International Conference on Computer Vision, pp. 1314–1324 (2019)

16. Howard, A.G., et al.: efficient convolutional neural networks for mobile vision applications. arXiv preprint arXiv:1704.04861 (2017)

17. Hu, J., Shen, L., Sun, G.: Squeeze-and-excitation networks. In: Proceedings of the IEEE Conference on Computer Vision and Pattern Recognition, pp. 7132–7141 (2018)

18. Hu, S., et al.: Dsnas: direct neural architecture search without parameter retraining. In: Proceedings of the IEEE/CVF Conference on Computer Vision and Pattern Recognition, pp. 12084–12092 (2020)

19. Ioffe, S., Szegedy, C.: Batch normalization: accelerating deep network training by reducing internal covariate shift. arXiv preprint arXiv:1502.03167 (2015)

20. Liu, C., et al.: Progressive neural architecture search. In: Proceedings of the European Conference on Computer Vision (ECCV), pp. 19–34 (2018)

21. Liu, H., Simonyan, K., Vinyals, O., Fernando, C., Kavukcuoglu, K.: Hierarchical representations for efficient architecture search. In: International Conference on Learning Representations (2018). https://openreview.net/forum?id=BJQRKzbA-
22. Liu, H., Simonyan, K., Yang, Y.: DARTS: differentiable architecture search. In: International Conference on Learning Representations (2019). https://openreview.net/forum?id=S1eYHoC5FX
23. Loshchilov, I., Hutter, F.: SGDR: stochastic gradient descent with warm restarts. arXiv preprint arXiv:1608.03983 (2016)
24. Ma, N., Zhang, X., Zheng, H.T., Sun, J.: Shufflenet v2: practical guidelines for efficient CNN architecture design. In: Proceedings of the European Conference on Computer Vision (ECCV), pp. 116–131 (2018)
25. Pham, H., Guan, M.Y., Zoph, B., Le, Q.V., Dean, J.: Efficient neural architecture search via parameter sharing. In: ICML, pp. 4092–4101 (2018). http://proceedings.mlr.press/v80/pham18a.html
26. Ramachandran, P., Zoph, B., Le, Q.V.: Searching for activation functions (2018). https://openreview.net/forum?id=SkBYYyZRZ
27. Real, E., Aggarwal, A., Huang, Y., Le, Q.V.: Regularized evolution for image classifier architecture search. In: Proceedings of the AAAI Conference on Artificial Intelligence, vol. 33, pp. 4780–4789 (2019)
28. Sandler, M., Howard, A., Zhu, M., Zhmoginov, A., Chen, L.C.: Inverted residuals and linear bottlenecks: mobile networks for classification, detection and segmentation. arXiv preprint arXiv:1801.04381 (2018)
29. Srivastava, N., Hinton, G., Krizhevsky, A., Sutskever, I., Salakhutdinov, R.: Dropout: a simple way to prevent neural networks from overfitting. J. Mach. Learn. Res. 15(1), 1929–1958 (2014)
30. Stamoulis, D., et al.: Single-path NAS: designing hardware-efficient convnets in less than 4 hours. arXiv preprint arXiv:1904.02877 (2019)
31. Tan, M., Chen, B., Pang, R., Vasudevan, V., Le, Q.V.: Mnasnet: platform-aware neural architecture search for mobile. In: Proceedings of the IEEE Conference on Computer Vision and Pattern Recognition (CVPR) (2019)
32. Tan, M., Le, Q.V.: Efficientnet: rethinking model scaling for convolutional neural networks (2019)
33. Wu, B., et al.: FBNET: hardware-aware efficient convnet design via differentiable neural architecture search. In: Proceedings of the IEEE Conference on Computer Vision and Pattern Recognition, pp. 10734–10742 (2019)
34. Yang, Z., et al.: Cars: continuous evolution for efficient neural architecture search. In: The IEEE/CVF Conference on Computer Vision and Pattern Recognition (CVPR), June 2020
35. Yu, J., Huang, T.: Network slimming by slimmable networks: towards one-shot architecture search for channel numbers. arXiv preprint arXiv:1903.11728 (2019)
36. Yu, J., Huang, T.: Universally slimmable networks and improved training techniques. In: 2019 IEEE/CVF International Conference on Computer Vision (ICCV), pp. 1803–1811. IEEE (2019)
37. Yu, J., Yang, L., Xu, N., Yang, J., Huang, T.: Slimmable neural networks. In: International Conference on Learning Representations (2019). https://openreview.net/forum?id=H1gMCsAqY7
38. Zoph, B., Le, Q.V.: Neural architecture search with reinforcement learning. arXiv preprint arXiv:1611.01578 (2016)
39. Zoph, B., Vasudevan, V., Shlens, J., Le, Q.V.: Learning transferable architectures for scalable image recognition. In: Proceedings of the IEEE Conference on Computer Vision and Pattern Recognition, pp. 8697–8710 (2018)

Differentiable Hierarchical Graph Grouping for Multi-person Pose Estimation

Sheng Jin[1,2] , Wentao Liu[2(✉)] , Enze Xie[1], Wenhai Wang[3], Chen Qian[2],
Wanli Ouyang[4], and Ping Luo[1]

[1] The University of Hong Kong, Pok Fu Lam, Hong Kong
pluo@cs.hku.hk
[2] SenseTime Research, Beijing, China
{jinsheng,liuwentao,qianchen}@sensetime.com
[3] Nanjing University, Nanjing, China
[4] The University of Sydney, Sydney, Australia
wanli.ouyang@sydney.edu.au

Abstract. Multi-person pose estimation is challenging because it localizes body keypoints for multiple persons simultaneously. Previous methods can be divided into two streams, *i.e.* top-down and bottom-up methods. The top-down methods localize keypoints after human detection, while the bottom-up methods localize keypoints directly and then cluster/group them for different persons, which are generally more efficient than top-down methods. However, in existing bottom-up methods, the keypoint grouping is usually solved independently from keypoint detection, making them not end-to-end trainable and have sub-optimal performance. In this paper, we investigate a new perspective of human part grouping and reformulate it as a graph clustering task. Especially, we propose a novel differentiable Hierarchical Graph Grouping (HGG) method to learn the graph grouping in bottom-up multi-person pose estimation task. Moreover, HGG is easily embedded into main-stream bottom-up methods. It takes human keypoint candidates as graph nodes and clusters keypoints in a multi-layer graph neural network model. The modules of HGG can be trained end-to-end with the keypoint detection network and is able to supervise the grouping process in a hierarchical manner. To improve the discrimination of the clustering, we add a set of edge discriminators and macro-node discriminators. Extensive experiments on both COCO and OCHuman datasets demonstrate that the proposed method improves the performance of bottom-up pose estimation methods.

Keywords: Human pose estimation · Graph neural network · Grouping

1 Introduction

Multi-person pose estimation aims at localizing 2d keypoints of an unknown number of people in an image. It has attracted much research interest because

© Springer Nature Switzerland AG 2020
A. Vedaldi et al. (Eds.): ECCV 2020, LNCS 12352, pp. 718–734, 2020.
https://doi.org/10.1007/978-3-030-58571-6_42

of its significance in various real-world applications, such as human behavior understanding, human-computer interaction, and action recognition.

Current pose estimation methods perform keypoints detection in two routes. The *top-down* methods [6,16,26,34,38,39,46] first detect human bounding boxes and then estimate keypoints for each person. It performs a single person pose estimation to all human candidates, so it is often time-consuming. Contrarily, *bottom-up* pose estimation approaches [3,22,29,33] follow the keypoints detection-and-grouping pipeline: detecting keypoints at the first stage and grouping them into individuals at the second stage. These methods are more efficient and have gained increasing attention in the industry. Previous works generally treat the grouping stage as post-processing by using integer linear programming [18,19,23,35], heuristic greedy parsing [3,33], or clustering [29,31]. But they are not able to be trained end-to-end, which is in conflict with deep learning's philosophy of learning everything together. Previous bottom-up methods generally learn some substitute indicators which may reflect the grouping accuracy, resulting in sub-optimal solutions. For example, associate embedding (AE) [29] produces the permutation-invariant associative embedding (a vector representation) for each keypoint, and learns by pushing apart the embedding of different people and pulling closer that of the same instance. Although it uses the associative embedding which encodes pairwise relationship to group keypoints, the grouping procedure itself is still offline, and no direct supervision is applied to the grouping results. There is a mismatch between the pairwise loss and the accuracy of the greedy parsing used at inference time. Even though the pairwise loss is low, the parsing results can still be possibly wrong, and vice versa.

A better choice is to directly supervise the grouping process. However, one major challenge is that the previous keypoint grouping procedure is often not differentiable, and thus is hard to be integrated with keypoint detection. Moreover, how to deal with the flexible number of keypoints is still an open problem.

In this paper, we present a simple and elegant solution for bottom-up multi-person pose estimation. In the proposed method, the whole network, composed of a keypoint detection network and a grouping network, is *fully end-to-end trainable*, and able to flexibly deal with the grouping problem of a variable number of human instances. To achieve this, we first reformulate the grouping problem as the graph clustering problem. A graph corresponds to an image, where the nodes denote the keypoint proposals, and edges denote whether the two keypoints belong to the same person. The graph structure is adaptive to different input images instead of constructing a static graph, so it is able to dynamically group various numbers of keypoints into various numbers of human instances. Especially, we propose the Online Hierarchical Graph Clustering (OHGC) algorithm, which makes the process of grouping keypoints learnable and can be easily embedded into main-stream bottom-up methods. The HGG method initializes the graph from the keypoint proposal network and groups pairs of most relative nodes in each iteration through the OHGC algorithm.

In OHGC, keypoints are clustered step-by-step. Each keypoint proposal starts in its own graph node, and the cluster pairs are merged. This forms a pose hierarchy, from small fractions to the whole body. This enables the model to pay more attention to global consistency and learn effective features for predicting the pairwise relation. The group operations are fully differentiable, so OHGC can make the whole network (including keypoint detection and grouping) end-to-end trainable. By directly supervising the grouping results, the grouping loss is back-propagated to the previous keypoint detection network, which will further improve the feature representation ability of the keypoint detection network.

Moreover, we propose the edge discriminator to strengthen the local relationship of keypoints, and the macro-node discriminator to enforce global consistency. It can further increase the discrimination of body-keypoint relational features, leading to better grouping accuracy.

The main contributions of this work are thus three-fold.

- We reformulate the task of multi-person pose estimation as a graph clustering problem and present the first fully end-to-end trainable framework with grouping supervision for bottom-up multi-person pose estimation.
- We propose edge discriminators and macro-node discriminators to learn both local and global pairwise relation features and boost the grouping accuracy.
- The experimental results show that the proposed method outperforms the baseline by a large margin and achieves comparable performance with the state-of-the-art bottom-up pose estimation methods on COCO dataset. Moreover, the proposed method achieves the state of the art performance on the OCHuman datasets (41.8/36.0 mAP for val and test respectively).

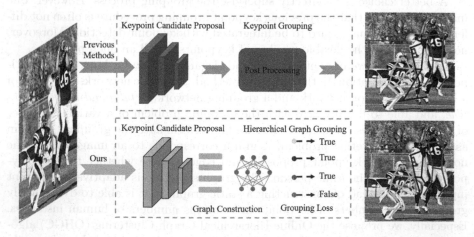

Fig. 1. Hierarchical Graph Grouping embeds grouping procedure with the keypoint candidate proposal network. All modules are differentiable and can be trained end-to-end. Keypoint candidates are grouped in a multi-layer graph neural network, which enables to directly supervise the final grouping results.

2   Related Work

2.1   Multi-person Pose Estimation in Images

Top-down methods [6,12,16,17,26,28,34,38,46] decompose the multi-person pose estimation task into two sub-tasks:(1) Human detection and (2) Pose Estimation in the region of a single human. First, the person detector predicts a bounding box for every human instance in the image. Second, the box is cropped and resized from the image. Third, single-person pose estimation is applied to predict the keypoints for the cropped person. In addition, some work such as Mask R-CNN [16] crop the feature instead of raw images to boost efficiency. In summary, top-down methods are dominant in state-of-the-art methods but they often have higher computational complexity overhead, especially when the number of human instances increases. This is because they need to repeatedly run the single-person pose estimation for every instance. Furthermore, because the pose estimation is dependent on the detection, it is difficult for these methods to recover the pose of an instance if it is missing in the detection results.

Bottom-up approaches [3,18,19,21–23,29,31,33,35] first detect all keypoint candidates in an image, then assemble/group them into full-body keypoints of each instance. Such bottom-up methods are usually efficient, and are capable of achieving real-time performance. To aid the follow-up keypoint association, most bottom-up methods learn descriptors to encode keypoint pairwise relations and to distinguish different instances. PAF [3] learns part-affinity-fields, encoding both the location and orientation of keypoint pairs; GPN [31] learns 2D offset fields, linking keypoints to the corresponding human centers; PersonLab [33] introduces long-range, mid-range and short-range offsets between pairwise keypoints; AE [29] learns the associative embedding for each keypoint and similar embedding indicates higher possibility of belonging to the same person. The grouping process is generally formulated as a post-processing optimization problem and solved by graph partitioning [18,19,21,35], heuristic greedy decoding algorithm [3,33] or spectral clustering [31]. In summary, bottom-up methods can benefit from sharing convolutional computation, as a result, being faster than top-down methods. Nevertheless, the post-processing of grouping is heuristic and involves many hyper-parameters. Since the pose estimation and post-processing are not jointly learned, they cannot collaborate and adapt to each other. Instead of regarding the grouping as a pure post-processing procedure, we propose to train grouping with pose estimation jointly in an end-to-end fashion, enabling the error signals for grouping to be back-propagated.

Single-stage Pose Estimation. With recent advantages of single-shot object detection and instance segmentation [41,47,52], some single-stage pose estimation methods are proposed. CenterNet [52] firstly transfer pose estimation as human center detection and keypoint regression. However, it still needs keypoint detection and projection to improve performance. SPM [32] proposes a structured pose representation to divide the keypoints hierarchically. In this way, it can ease the difficulty of long-range regression. Similarly, DirectPose [40], based on FCOS [41], directly do human center classification and keypoint regression without relying on bounding box. KPAlign is proposed to overcome the feature misalignment between convolutional features and keypoint predictions. However, keypoint regression is not very precise in the above methods, especially under the restriction of High IoU. In comparison, our method retains higher precision, especially under more strict metrics (AP_{75}).

2.2 Graph Representation for Pose Estimation

The graph representation for human pose estimation is not new. For single-person pose estimation, many work [4,5,8,13,14,24,42,49] have been based on various graphical models such as pictorial structure, Mixtures-of-parts, Markov Random Fields (MRF) or Conditional Random Fields (CRF). In these works, the graph nodes represent keypoints and the edges encode the pairwise relationships between keypoints. Since all the keypoints belong to the same human instance, no grouping process is required. Moreover, the number of keypoints of a single person is always fixed, therefore the graph structure, in terms of the number of nodes and the connectivity of edges, is fixed.

Multi-person pose estimation is much more challenging. [18,21,44], the pose estimation problem is cast as a graph partitioning based integer linear programming (ILP) problem. However, the optimization process is offline and very time-consuming. Song *et al.* [37] proposed a method for end-to-end minimum cost multicut problem. Unlike their works which focus on the CRF optimization, we solve the keypoint grouping task by direct graph clustering.

2.3 Graph Neural Networks

This paper reformulates the multi-person pose estimation task using the graph representation and applies graph neural networks to this problem. Graph Neural Networks (GNN) is initially introduced in [15,36] and has become a popular tool for efficient message passing and modeling global relations [7]. Most of GNN models can be categorized into two types: spectral approaches [2,25] and non-spectral approaches [11,45]. This work is related to [45], which efficiently models the edge features. To solve the task of multi-person pose estimation, based on [45] we develop a hierarchical clustering method, which takes the body structure constraints into consideration and models the whole grouping process.

More recently, GNN models have been applied to model the human body structure. Yan *et al.* [48] proposes the spatial-temporal graph convolutional networks for skeleton-based action recognition. Zhang *et al.* [50] proposes to use PGNN to learn the structured representation of keypoints for single-person pose estimation. However, previous works only deal with the single person case, where the structure of the graph is fixed. The multi-person case is more challenging, since the number of keypoints and the number of people vary in different images and even in different grouping stages. We have to develop a dynamic graph interaction model to effectively handle such problems.

3   Method

Overview. An overview of our proposed hierarchical graph grouping (HGG) framework is illustrated in Fig. 2. Our HGG framework consists of two stages, *i.e.* the keypoint candidate proposal stage and the keypoint grouping stage.

In the keypoint candidate proposal stage, all keypoint candidates are detected and corresponding feature maps are extracted. Following AE [29], we use a 4-stacked hourglass [30] as the backbone of the keypoint candidate proposal network. The keypoint proposal network then provides keypoint candidates and raw relational feature embedding for the keypoints grouping module.

In the keypoint grouping stage, we build a graph neural network using the candidates and relational features extracted from the former stage. An online hierarchical graph clustering (OHGC) algorithm is devised to cluster keypoints iteratively. In each iteration, OHGC updates the pairwise relation features and clusters nodes into a *macro-node* by maximizing the weighted edge score. The graph is updated and pruned with respect to the macro-nodes. Contrary to integer linear programming or bipartite matching, the proposed method is fully differentiable and is able to be trained end-to-end with keypoint detection.

We proposed two kinds of the discriminator to strengthen the grouping procedure, the edge discriminator and the macro-node discriminator. In each iteration, the edge discriminator is introduced to classify whether the pair of nodes belong to the same person. The pairwise relation features and the edge scores are updated accordingly. After each iteration of grouping, a macro-node discriminator is applied to each cluster to discriminate between a correctly-clustered macro-node (in which all nodes belong to the same person) and a wrongly-clustered one. In this way, the whole online grouping procedure is fully supervised.

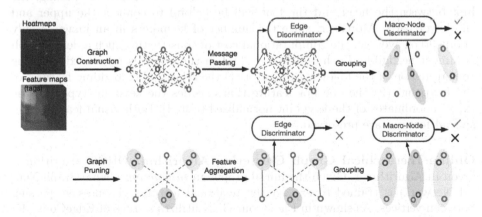

Fig. 2. The keypoint grouping stage of HGG framework. We construct a graph on top of the keypoint candidate proposal network, perform message passing with GNNs, and group the candidates iteratively. Edge discriminators and macro-node discriminators are applied to improve the grouping performance.

3.1   Hierarchical Graph Grouping

Previous work [18,19,21,35] cast the problem of multi-person pose grouping as graph partitioning, and solve it by optimizing an integer linear programming (ILP) problem. However, the optimization process is performed offline and the grouping procedure is not able to be supervised with the keypoint candidate proposal network. In this paper, we rethink this problem from the perspective of graph clustering and solve it with supervised learning. We follow the online agglomerative graph clustering setting. Each keypoint candidate starts with being its own cluster and closest pairs of clusters are merged iteratively. As a result, the keypoint candidates are grouped into several clusters, where each cluster contains all the keypoints of a single person. We are able to directly supervise the final grouping results. In the following sections, we will give a detailed description of the graph construction and hierarchical graph grouping.

Graph Construction. We construct a graph on top of the keypoint candidate proposal network. In the graph $\mathbf{G} = \{\mathbf{V}, \mathbf{E}\}$, the "vertices" $\{\mathbf{V}\} = \{v_i\}_{i=1:N}$ represent keypoint candidates and the "edges" $\{\mathbf{E}\} = \{e_{i_1,i_2}\}_{i_1=1:N,i_2=1:N}$ represent the pairwise relationship between the two candidates (the possibility of belonging to the same person or not). Note that the graph is constructed dynamically, as the graph may have different number of nodes and edges for different images. We choose the fully-connected graph that densely connects every pair of the keypoints with different keypoint types. The keypoints with the same type (both "head"s) are disconnected. Compared to other sparse graph configurations (such as the tree-structure), the fully-connected graph is able to avoid over-segment of a person during occlusion, *i.e.* dividing a single pose into several clusters. For example, when a person's torso is occluded or missing, the link between the head and the foot will be helpful to connect the upper and the lower parts. Moreover, since the number of keypoints in an image is only about 30 on average, the computational cost of constructing such a dense graph is almost negligible. Each vertex $v_i \in \{\mathbf{V}\}$ in the graph is initialized with the concatenation of the following features: (1) the relational embedding features of the keypoint, (2) the one hot feature that encodes the keypoint type, (3) the (x, y) coordinates of the keypoint normalized to $[0, 1]$. Both visual features and spatial features are preserved.

Online Hierarchical Graph Clustering Algorithm. OHGC algorithm is given in Algorithm 1. Given the initial graph, an *interaction GNN* (Graph Neural Network) is trained to extract the relational features via message passing between vertices. As shown in Fig. 3, our GNN utilizes a stack of EdgeConv [45] layers for effective feature learning. In each EdgeConv layer, the edge feature is mapped from the concatenation of features of nodes (linked by the edge) using a fully-connected layer, and the node features are updated by aggregating the features of the associated edges. A three-layer MLP (Multi-layer Perceptron) with Dropout is adopted to further extract high-level node features. As the output, we get representative features of each of the vertex which is used for grouping.

Previous graph clustering algorithms mainly focus on the keypoint-level pairwise relationship, without considering the higher-order term, *i.e.* the relation between two clusters of body parts. We instead propose to model the whole grouping process and design a hierarchical graph clustering algorithm. OHGC repeatedly performs graph feature aggregation, edge proximity update, node clustering and graph pruning, until all the edges are cut.

In each iteration, *feature aggregation* is applied to each of the macro-node (the set of previously grouped nodes) by averaging all features in the set. The proximity score between macro-nodes is measured by the edge discriminator (see Sect. 3.2). After updating the edge weights, we use *graclus clustering* [9] to match each vertex with its neighbors by (approximately) maximizing the edge weights. This finds the most confident pairs and carries out the clustering action. As a result, a group of "low-level" nodes is clustered into a "higher-level" macro-node. The number of clusters is reduced by half. For COCO dataset, the number of keypoint types is $J = 17$, so the grouping will stop in no more than $\lceil \log_2 17 \rceil = 5$ iterations. After that, a macro-node discriminator (see Sect. 3.2) is applied to each cluster to discriminate between a correctly-clustered macro-node (in which all nodes belong to the same person) and a wrongly-clustered one. The grouping procedure should satisfy the following two constraints. 1) A keypoint cannot be assigned to more than one person, *i.e.* two people share a single "head" keypoint. 2) A person cannot have more than one keypoints of the same type, *i.e.* a person containing two "head" keypoints. To avoid infeasible clustering, we perform *graph pruning* to remove infeasible edges after each grouping iteration. If two (macro-)nodes contain the same type of nodes, the edge in between is pruned. This grouping procedure repeats until all edges are pruned.

This grouping procedure naturally forms a hierarchy, from isolated keypoints to a whole body. The model learns to first group easy-to-group parts, then perform cluster in the macro-node level. As the grouping continues, the graph gradually gets coarsened. Finally, the nodes will be clustered into K groups, indicating K human instances. The model learns to group from easy to hard, in a curriculum fashion [1]. Unlike the previous curriculum learning paradigm which requires to manually set curriculum phases, our curriculum tasks are automatically generated during training and well adjusted to the model's current capability.

3.2 Grouping Discriminators

In OHGC, two types of discriminators are introduced to further improve the grouping performance. In each iteration, we utilize the edge discriminator to update proximity scores and the macro-node discriminator to suppress the incorrectly grouped macro-nodes. We use the same discriminators in each clustering loop iteration. The network architectures are demonstrated in Fig. 3. Binary cross-entropy (BCE) loss is used to train.

Edge Discriminator. Edges preserve local but discriminate keypoint-to-keypoint relationship. In order to improve the discrimination ability of the pairwise relation feature, we introduce a *shared* edge discriminator at each iteration.

Algorithm 1. Online Hierarchical Graph Clustering

Input: An RGB image;
Output: Body pose clusters;

Keypoint candidate proposals;
Graph construction: $\mathbf{G} = \{\mathbf{V}, \mathbf{E}\}$;
Relational feature learning with interaction GNN.
repeat
    Feature aggregation via avg-pooling;
    Update the proximity between (macro-)nodes;
    Apply graclus clustering;
    Graph pruning;
until No edges are remained.

The edge discriminator is a two-class discriminator that is used to directly classifying the states of the edges: whether the edge is connected (label 1) or not (label 0). Connected edge means the two keypoints belong to the same person. As shown in Fig. 3, the edge discriminator is implemented as a three-layer MLP (Multi-layer Perceptron) with Dropout. The input is the concatenated features of two linked (macro-)nodes ($2 \times 64 = 128-D$), and the output is the 1-D edge score. Experiments show that the edge discriminator helps to increase the discrimination of body-keypoint relational features, leading to better grouping accuracy.

Macro-Node Discriminator. We propose the macro-node discriminator to directly supervise the grouping procedure. After each grouping iteration, the nodes are clustered into macro-nodes. We apply a *shared* macro-node discriminator to each macro-node to classify whether all keypoint candidates in the group belong to the same person (label 1) or not (label 0). Both the final human-level grouping results and the intermediate part-level grouping results are supervised. This provides denser supervision signals, facilitating the model training. The discriminator takes the aggregated macro-node features (64-D) as input and forwards it into a three-layer MLP to discriminate positive vs negative macro-nodes.

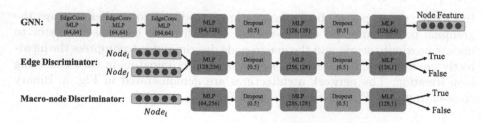

Fig. 3. The network architecture of GNN, the edge discriminator and the macro-edge discriminator. The number of the input/output channels of MLP are given.

3.3 Implementation Details

Keypoint Proposal Network. The keypoint proposal network generates both 2D Gaussian confidence heatmaps as well as the pairwise relational feature maps. 2D Gaussian confidence heatmaps [3,29,31] are used to encode the keypoint locations and the ground truth confidence map for an image is calculated as the maximum of every person. We follow [3,29] to apply keypoint NMS and parse the heatmaps to generate keypoint candidates. The pairwise relational feature maps are learned with push/pull losses, by pushing features of different people apart and pulling together features extracted from the same person.

Training and Inference. We implement OHGC based on AE [29][1]. The input size is set as 512×512 and the output size is 128×128. The keypoint proposal network is first pre-trained and the keypoint proposal network, GNN and the edge/macro-node discriminators are jointly trained in an end-to-end manner. The losses include keypoint detection loss, pairwise pull/push losses, binary cross-entropy (BCE) loss for discriminators. The weights to balance these losses are set as $1 : 1e^{-3} : 1e^{-5}$. We use Adam with an initial learning rate $2e^{-4}$ to train the model. During inference, flip testing and multi-scale testing is adopted. Unlike previous methods [3,29], we do not use single-person refinement.

4 Experiments

4.1 Datasets and Evaluation

To verify the effectiveness of the proposed HGG, we compare it with state-of-the-art methods on two challenging datasets, i.e. MS-COCO [27], and OCHuman [51]. We follow [20] to use Average Percision (AP) to evaluate the methods.

MS-COCO Dataset [27] contains over 200,000 images and 250,000 human instances and 1.7 million labeled keypoints in total, among which 150,000 instances are for training and 80,000 instances are for testing. Our models are trained on the train set only. The ablation studies are reported on the val set and the comparisons with other state-of-the-arts are reported on the test-dev.

OCHuman Dataset [51] is a recently proposed benchmark to examine the limitations of human pose detection in highly challenging scenarios, which does not contain training samples and is intended to be used for evaluating existing models. It consists of 4731 images for validation and 8110 images for testing. The dataset contains only challenging cases of occlusion and the average IoU of the bounding boxes is 67%. Following [51], we train models on the training set of MS-COCO, and report the AP of them.

4.2 Ablation Study

We validate the effectiveness of key modules in HGG by conducting the following ablation studies. For fair comparisons, all models use Hourglass as the backbone network and are trained with the same data augmentation and training schedule.

---

[1] https://github.com/princeton-vl/pose-ae-train.

Table 1. (a) Comparisons with both top-down and bottom-up methods on COCO2017 test-dev dataset. * means using single-person pose refinement. × means using extra segmentation annotation. + means using multi-scale test. Not that our results are obtained without single-person pose refinement.(b) Comparisons with both top-down and bottom-up methods on OCHuman dataset. Our results are obtained without single-person pose refinement.

Method	AP	AP^{50}	AP^{75}	AP^M	AP^L	AR
Top-down methods						
Mask-RCNN [16]	63.1	87.3	68.7	57.8	71.4	−
G-RMI [34]	64.9	85.5	71.3	62.3	70.0	69.7
IPR [39]	67.8	88.2	74.8	63.9	74.0	−
CPN [6]	72.1	91.4	80.0	68.7	77.2	78.5
RMPE [12]	72.3	89.2	79.1	68.0	78.6	−
CFN [17]	72.6	86.1	69.7	78.3	64.1	−
SBL [46]	73.7	91.9	81.1	70.3	80.0	79.0
HRNet-W48 [38]	75.5	92.5	83.3	71.9	81.5	80.5
Bottom-up methods						
OpenPose* [3]	61.8	84.9	67.5	57.1	68.2	66.5
AE*+ [29]	65.5	86.8	72.3	60.6	72.6	70.2
PersonLab+× [33]	68.7	89.0	75.4	64.1	75.5	75.4
Directpose+ [40]	64.8	87.8	71.1	60.4	71.5	−
SPM*+ [32]	66.9	88.5	72.9	62.6	73.1	−
Ours+	67.6	85.1	73.7	62.7	74.6	71.3

(a)

OCHuman	Backbone	Val	Test
Top-down methods			
RMPE [12]	Hourglass	38.8	30.7
SBL [46]	ResNet50	37.8	30.4
SBL [46]	ResNet152	41.0	33.3
Bottom-up methods			
AE [29]	Hourglass	32.1	29.5
AE+ [29]	Hourglass	40.0	32.8
Ours	Hourglass	35.6	34.8
Ours+	Hourglass	**41.8**	**36.0**

(b)

Effectiveness of End-to-End Learning. We compare the performance of the baseline Associate Embedding (AE) model and that with the grouping loss. The grouping loss is provided by the final level macro-node discriminator. As shown in Table 2 #1 and #3, end-to-end learning can increase the AP and the AR of the baseline by 0.6% and 1.3% respectively. #6 uses all these grouping losses to train the models, but uses original post-processing greedy grouping during inference. The improvement of #6 over #1 indicates that the grouping loss and end-to-end learning can improve the capability of Keypoint Proposal Network. Note that under this setting, the grouping module can be removed during inference without adding any additional computation overhead.

Effectiveness of the Edge Discriminator. The edge discriminator can enhance the keypoint relational features, thereby improving the grouping accuracy. To verify this, we compare the performance of models with and without the edge discriminator. As shown in Table 2 #1 and #4, we find that supervising the linkage of the edge will significantly improve the grouping performance by 2.0 mAP, demonstrating the effectiveness of the edge discriminator.

Effectiveness of the Macro-Node Discriminator. We evaluate two kinds of macro-node supervision, intermediate macro-node supervision and final macro-node supervision. As shown in #4 and #5, the final macro-node supervision improves the grouping performance by 0.5 mAP. By performing intermediate supervision to the macro-node, the result is further improved by 0.3 mAP, shown in #5 and #9. In total, the full supervision boosts the performance by 0.8 mAP, showing the importance of supervising the whole grouping process.

Effectiveness of GNN. To evaluate the interaction GNN, we add two baselines for comparison. Ours-GAT uses GAT [43], a popular graph neural network, for replacing EdgeConv. Ours-FC uses the multi-layer perception (dubbed FC for

Table 2. Ablation study of HGG's components on the COCO validation dataset. "FinalM" means the final level macro-node discriminator. "Edge" means edge discriminator. "IntermM" means intermediate macro-node discriminator. "MS" means multi-scale testing.

#	Method	Clustering	FinalM	Edge	IntermM	MS	AP	AP^{50}	AP^{75}	AR	AR^{50}	AR^{75}
1	AE [29]						57.6	79.7	62.6	62.1	81.4	66.1
2	AE [29]					✓	65.6	85.1	71.9	69.1	86.7	74.2
3	Ours	✓	✓				58.2	80.8	63.9	63.4	83.5	68.0
4	Ours	✓		✓			59.6	81.3	65.1	64.2	83.0	69.0
5	Ours	✓		✓	✓		60.1	81.6	66.0	64.5	83.4	69.6
6	Ours		✓	✓	✓		59.6	81.9	65.5	63.9	83.3	68.4
7	Ours-FC	✓	✓	✓	✓		58.3	80.7	63.3	62.5	82.1	66.9
8	Ours-GAT	✓	✓	✓	✓		59.3	81.1	65.5	63.9	82.8	69.0
9	Ours	✓	✓	✓	✓		60.4	83.0	66.2	64.8	84.0	69.8
10	Ours	✓	✓	✓	✓	✓	68.3	86.7	75.8	72.0	88.3	78.0

fully connected layers). For fair comparisons, these models have approximately the same parameter counts. As shown in #7, #8 and #9, both graph-based models perform better than Ours-FC baseline, because of more effective interactive message passing. Moreover, EdgeConv (60.4 AP) performs the best.

Comparisons of Different Graph Configurations. As shown in Fig. 4a, four types of commonly used graph configurations [10] (*i.e.* Tree, Bypass, Extended and Full) are compared. From Tree (the standard tree-structured model) to Full (the fully-connected graph), the graph gets denser. Bypass and Extended model adds some skip connections to the standard tree-structured model. As the complexity of the graph (or the number of connections) increases (Tree-Bypass-Extended-Full), the grouping accuracy increases from 56.1% to 60.4% mAP. In addition, the runtime of different graph configurations is almost the same. Therefore, we choose the fully-connected graph in our implementation.

4.3   Qualitative Analysis

In Fig. 5, we visualize the grouping procedure of OHGC algorithm. We use different colors to denote different clusters and dashed lines to highlight the macro-node merging process. OHGC starts with a set of keypoint candidates, each of which belongs to its own cluster. The grouping is performed iteratively. In each iteration, the most easy-to-group keypoints are merged. We show that the grouping procedure forms a pose hierarchy, from part to whole. Our method benefits from global supervision, which helps improve the grouping performance.

For failure cases, however, the current model is not able to recover false negatives or localization errors. Tiny people in images can lead to false negatives. Severe occlusion and non-typical poses may lead to localization errors. More test-time augmentation such as multi-scale testing, may mitigate these issues.

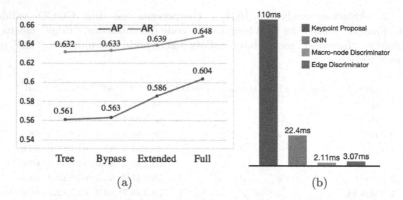

(a)   (b)

Fig. 4. (a) Comparisons of different graph configurations on the COCO val set. Fully-connected graph (Full) performs the best among them. (b) Runtime analysis measured on one GTX-1060 GPU. The grouping module is very efficient compared to the keypoint proposal module.

Fig. 5. The grouping process visualization. We show the grouped keypoint clusters in each iteration. Different colors are used to indicate different clusters.

4.4   Comparisons with the State-of-the-art Methods

We compare our framework with the state-of-the-art methods on two large-scale multi-person pose estimation benchmarks.

Results on MSCOCO Dataset. Table 1(a) shows experimental results on MSCOCO test-dev set. We see that the proposed HGG model achieves overall 67.6 AP. which is slightly lower than the state-of-the-art method PersonLab [33]. However, PersonLab uses extra annotations for instance segmentation. Moreover, we also compare our method with recent single-shot methods (SPM [32] and DirectPose [40]). Surprisingly, although ours are lower than them in AP^{50}, in AP^{75} ours are superior to them. This further indicates that our methods have advantages in scenarios that require high-precision pose estimation.

Results on OCHuman Dataset. To verify the robustness of HGG and other methods, we evaluate the proposed HGG model on the more challenging OCHuman dataset. We can see that our method achieves 41.8% and 36.0% mAP on val and test set, establishing a new state-of-the-art. Especially, HGG even outperforms top-down method SBL with 2.7 AP in test set, which further indicates our method is robust on more challenging scenarios.

4.5   Runtime Analysis

We analyze the time cost of the modules in HGG. Specifically, we evaluate our method on val set of MS-COCO and calculate the average time cost per image as shown in Fig. 4b. The results are tested using PyTorch with a batchsize of 1 on one GTX-1060 GPU in a single thread. We find that the time cost of the grouping module is only a small proportion of the total time cost.

5   Conclusion and Future Work

In this paper, we have reformulated the human pose estimation problem using the graph model and presented a full end-to-end learning framework named HGG. We have shown how we can combine the representative feature learning ability of CNN and the efficient long-range message passing as well as the relational feature learning capability of GNN. The macro-node discriminator and the edge discriminator are introduced to supervise the whole grouping process. We envision that the proposed framework can also be applied to other related problems such as multi-object tracking and instance segmentation. We expect to see more research in this direction in the near future.

Acknowledgement. This work is partially supported by the SenseTime Donation for Research, HKU Seed Fund for Basic Research, Startup Fund, General Research Fund No.27208720, the Australian Research Council Grant DP200103223 and Australian Medical Research Future Fund MRFAI000085.

References

1. Bengio, Y., Louradour, J., Collobert, R., Weston, J.: Curriculum learning. In: International Conference on Machine Learning (ICML) (2009)
2. Bruna, J., Zaremba, W., Szlam, A., LeCun, Y.: Spectral networks and locally connected networks on graphs. arXiv preprint arXiv:1312.6203 (2013)
3. Cao, Z., Simon, T., Wei, S.E., Sheikh, Y.: Realtime multi-person 2d pose estimation using part affinity fields. In: The IEEE Conference on Computer Vision and Pattern Recognition (CVPR) (2017)
4. Chen, X., Mottaghi, R., Liu, X., Fidler, S., Urtasun, R., Yuille, A.: Detect what you can: detecting and representing objects using holistic models and body parts. In: The IEEE Conference on Computer Vision and Pattern Recognition (CVPR) (2014)
5. Chen, X., Yuille, A.L.: Articulated pose estimation by a graphical model with image dependent pairwise relations. In: Advances in Neural Information Processing Systems (NeurIPS) (2014)
6. Chen, Y., Wang, Z., Peng, Y., Zhang, Z., Yu, G., Sun, J.: Cascaded pyramid network for multi-person pose estimation. In: The IEEE Conference on Computer Vision and Pattern Recognition (CVPR) (2018)
7. Chen, Y., Rohrbach, M., Yan, Z., Shuicheng, Y., Feng, J., Kalantidis, Y.: Graph-based global reasoning networks. In: The IEEE Conference on Computer Vision and Pattern Recognition (CVPR) (2019)
8. Chu, X., Ouyang, W., Wang, X., et al.: CRF-CNN: modeling structured information in human pose estimation. In: Advances in Neural Information Processing Systems (NeurIPS) (2016)
9. Dhillon, I.S., Guan, Y., Kulis, B.: Weighted graph cuts without eigenvectors a multilevel approach. IEEE Trans. Pattern Anal. Mach. Intell. (TPAMI) **29**(11), 1944–1957 (2007)
10. Doering, A., Iqbal, U., Gall, J.: Joint flow: temporal flow fields for multi person tracking. arXiv preprint arXiv:1805.04596 (2018)
11. Duvenaud, D.K., et al.: Convolutional networks on graphs for learning molecular fingerprints. In: Advances in Neural Information Processing Systems (NeurIPS) (2015)
12. Fang, H.S., Xie, S., Tai, Y.W., Lu, C.: RMPE: regional multi-person pose estimation. In: The IEEE International Conference on Computer Vision (ICCV) (2017)
13. Felzenszwalb, P.F., Huttenlocher, D.P.: Pictorial structures for object recognition. Int. J. Comput. Vision (IJCV) **61**(1), 55–79 (2005)
14. Fischler, M.A., Elschlager, R.A.: The representation and matching of pictorial structures. IEEE Trans. Comput. **100**(1), 67–92 (1973)
15. Gori, M., Monfardini, G., Scarselli, F.: A new model for learning in graph domains. In: IEEE International Joint Conference on Neural Networks (IJCNN) (2005)
16. He, K., Gkioxari, G., Dollár, P., Girshick, R.: Mask R-CNN. arXiv preprint arXiv:1703.06870 (2017)
17. Huang, S., Gong, M., Tao, D.: A coarse-fine network for keypoint localization. In: The IEEE International Conference on Computer Vision (ICCV) (2017)
18. Insafutdinov, E., et al.: Arttrack: articulated multi-person tracking in the wild. In: The IEEE Conference on Computer Vision and Pattern Recognition (CVPR) (2017)
19. Insafutdinov, E., Pishchulin, L., Andres, B., Andriluka, M., Schiele, B.: Deepercut: a deeper, stronger, and faster multi-person pose estimation model. In: European Conference on Computer Vision (ECCV) (2016)

20. Iqbal, U., Milan, A., Andriluka, M., Ensafutdinov, E., Pishchulin, L., Gall, J.B.S.: PoseTrack: a benchmark for human pose estimation and tracking. In: The IEEE Conference on Computer Vision and Pattern Recognition (CVPR) (2018)
21. Iqbal, U., Milan, A., Gall, J.: Pose-track: joint multi-person pose estimation and tracking. arXiv preprint arXiv:1611.07727 (2016)
22. Jin, S., Liu, W., Ouyang, W., Qian, C.: Multi-person articulated tracking with spatial and temporal embeddings. In: The IEEE Conference on Computer Vision and Pattern Recognition (CVPR) (2019)
23. Jin, S., et al.: Towards multi-person pose tracking: bottom-up and top-down methods. In: ICCV PoseTrack Workshop (2017)
24. Johnson, S., Everingham, M.: Clustered pose and nonlinear appearance models for human pose estimation. In: BMVC (2010)
25. Kipf, T.N., Welling, M.: Semi-supervised classification with graph convolutional networks. arXiv preprint arXiv:1609.02907 (2016)
26. Li, J., Wang, C., Zhu, H., Mao, Y., Fang, H.S., Lu, C.: Crowdpose: efficient crowded scenes pose estimation and a new benchmark. In: The IEEE Conference on Computer Vision and Pattern Recognition (CVPR) (2019)
27. Lin, T.Y., et al.: Microsoft coco: common objects in context. In: European Conference on Computer Vision (ECCV) (2014)
28. Liu, W., Chen, J., Li, C., Qian, C., Chu, X., Hu, X.: A cascaded inception of inception network with attention modulated feature fusion for human pose estimation. In: The Thirty-Second AAAI Conference on Artificial Intelligence (2018)
29. Newell, A., Huang, Z., Deng, J.: Associative embedding: end-to-end learning for joint detection and grouping. In: Advances in Neural Information Processing Systems (NeurIPS) (2017)
30. Newell, A., Yang, K., Deng, J.: Stacked hourglass networks for human pose estimation. In: European Conference on Computer Vision (ECCV) (2016)
31. Nie, X., Feng, J., Xing, J., Yan, S.: Generative partition networks for multi-person pose estimation. arXiv preprint arXiv:1705.07422 (2017)
32. Nie, X., Feng, J., Zhang, J., Yan, S.: Single-stage multi-person pose machines. In: The IEEE International Conference on Computer Vision (ICCV) (2019)
33. Papandreou, G., Zhu, T., Chen, L.C., Gidaris, S., Tompson, J., Murphy, K.: Personlab: person pose estimation and instance segmentation with a bottom-up, part-based, geometric embedding model. arXiv preprint arXiv:1803.08225 (2018)
34. Papandreou, G., et al.: Towards accurate multi-person pose estimation in the wild. arXiv preprint arXiv:1701.01779 (2017)
35. Pishchulin, L., et al.: Deepcut: joint subset partition and labeling for multi person pose estimation. In: The IEEE Conference on Computer Vision and Pattern Recognition (CVPR) (2016)
36. Scarselli, F., Gori, M., Tsoi, A.C., Hagenbuchner, M., Monfardini, G.: The graph neural network model. IEEE Trans. Neural Netw. (TNN) 20(1), 61–80 (2008)
37. Song, J., Andres, B., Black, M.J., Hilliges, O., Tang, S.: End-to-end learning for graph decomposition. In: The IEEE International Conference on Computer Vision (ICCV) (2019)
38. Sun, K., Xiao, B., Liu, D., Wang, J.: Deep high-resolution representation learning for human pose estimation. arXiv preprint arXiv:1902.09212 (2019)
39. Sun, X., Xiao, B., Wei, F., Liang, S., Wei, Y.: Integral human pose regression. In: Proceedings of the European Conference on Computer Vision (ECCV) (2018)
40. Tian, Z., Chen, H., Shen, C.: Directpose: direct end-to-end multi-person pose estimation. arXiv preprint arXiv:1911.07451 (2019)

41. Tian, Z., Shen, C., Chen, H., He, T.: FCOS: fully convolutional one-stage object detection. In: The IEEE International Conference on Computer Vision (ICCV) (2019)
42. Tompson, J.J., Jain, A., LeCun, Y., Bregler, C.: Joint training of a convolutional network and a graphical model for human pose estimation. In: Advances in Neural Information Processing Systems (NeurIPS) (2014)
43. Veličković, P., Cucurull, G., Casanova, A., Romero, A., Lio, P., Bengio, Y.: Graph attention networks (2018)
44. Wang, J., Peng, Z., Lv, P., Sun, J., Zhou, B., Xu, M.: Bi-directional graph structure information model for multi-person pose estimation. arXiv preprint arXiv:1805.00603 (2018)
45. Wang, Y., Sun, Y., Liu, Z., Sarma, S.E., Bronstein, M.M., Solomon, J.M.: Dynamic graph CNN for learning on point clouds. ACM Trans. Graph. (TOG) 38(5), 1–12 (2019)
46. Xiao, B., Wu, H., Wei, Y.: Simple baselines for human pose estimation and tracking. In: European Conference on Computer Vision (ECCV) (2018)
47. Xie, E., et al.: Polarmask: single shot instance segmentation with polar representation. arXiv preprint arXiv:1909.13226 (2019)
48. Yan, S., Xiong, Y., Lin, D.: Spatial temporal graph convolutional networks for skeleton-based action recognition. In: Thirty-Second AAAI Conference on Artificial Intelligence (AAAI) (2018)
49. Yang, Y., Ramanan, D.: Articulated human detection with flexible mixtures of parts. IEEE Trans. Pattern Anal. Mach Intell.(TPAMI) 35(12), 2878–2890 (2012)
50. Zhang, H., et al.: Human pose estimation with spatial contextual information. arXiv preprint arXiv:1901.01760 (2019)
51. Zhang, S.H., et al.: Pose2seg: detection free human instance segmentation. In: The IEEE Conference on Computer Vision and Pattern Recognition (CVPR) (2019)
52. Zhou, X., Wang, D., Krähenbühl, P.: Objects as points. arXiv preprint arXiv:1904.07850 (2019)

Global Distance-Distributions Separation for Unsupervised Person Re-identification

Xin Jin[1,2], Cuiling Lan[2(✉)], Wenjun Zeng[2], and Zhibo Chen[1(✉)]

[1] University of Science and Technology of China, Hefei, China
jinxustc@mail.ustc.edu.cn, chenzhibo@ustc.edu.cn
[2] Microsoft Research Asia, Beijing, China
{culan,wezeng}@microsoft.com

Abstract. Supervised person re-identification (ReID) often has poor scalability and usability in real-world deployments due to domain gaps and the lack of annotations for the target domain data. Unsupervised person ReID through domain adaptation is attractive yet challenging. Existing unsupervised ReID approaches often fail in correctly identifying the positive samples and negative samples through the distance-based matching/ranking. The two distributions of distances for positive sample pairs (Pos-distr) and negative sample pairs (Neg-distr) are often not well separated, having large overlap. To address this problem, we introduce a global distance-distributions separation (GDS) constraint over the two distributions to encourage the clear separation of positive and negative samples from a global view. We model the two global distance distributions as Gaussian distributions and push apart the two distributions while encouraging their sharpness in the unsupervised training process. Particularly, to model the distributions from a global view and facilitate the timely updating of the distributions and the GDS related losses, we leverage a momentum update mechanism for building and maintaining the distribution parameters (mean and variance) and calculate the loss on the fly during the training. Distribution-based hard mining is proposed to further promote the separation of the two distributions. We validate the effectiveness of the GDS constraint in unsupervised ReID networks. Extensive experiments on multiple ReID benchmark datasets show our method leads to significant improvement over the baselines and achieves the state-of-the-art performance.

Keywords: Unsupervised learning · Person re-identification · Global distance-distributions separation · Momentum update · Hard mining

---

This work was done when Xin Jin was an intern at MSRA.

Electronic supplementary material The online version of this chapter (https://doi.org/10.1007/978-3-030-58571-6_43) contains supplementary material, which is available to authorized users.

1   Introduction

Person re-identification aims to identify the same person across images. In recent years, significant progress has been made on fully supervised person re-identification (ReID) [1,11,15,16,18,26,30,31,46,47], where groundtruth labels are accessible for training. However, they often have poor scalability and usability in real-world deployments. First, they typically perform well on the trained dataset but suffer from significant performance degradation when testing on a previously unseen dataset due to the domain gaps. There are usually large style discrepancies across domains/datasets, due to the discrepancy of imaging devices and environments (*e.g.*, lighting conditions, background, viewing angles) [23]. Second, it is costly to annotate images for each newly deployed environment. One popular solution is unsupervised domain adaptation, which transfers the knowledge from the labeled source domain to the unlabeled target domain.

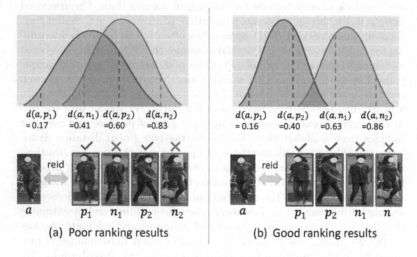

Fig. 1. Illustration of our motivation. The red curves denote the distribution of the distances of positive sample pairs (shorted as Pos-distr) while the green curves denote that of negative sample pairs (shorted as Neg-distr). (a) The two distributions are often not well separated for the current unsupervised ReID models, resulting in poor retrieval/ranking results. (b) Once the two distance distributions are well separated, the positive and negative samples can be well identified based on distance and superior ranking results can be obtained. (Color figure online)

Many efforts have been made to develop unsupervised domain adaptation for person re-identification (UDA-ReID) [7,20,23,25,32,34,38,42–44]. Pseudo label based approaches usually pre-train the network with source domain data and predict pseudo labels for the unlabeled target images, *e.g.*, by clustering, followed by fine-tuning with the pseudo labels [7,9,29,37,40,41,45]. Transfer-based approaches often transfer the labeled source images to have the style of the target domain [5,23,35]. These approaches suffer from either noisy labels or noisy images due to incorrect pseudo labels or unrealisticness of the transferred images

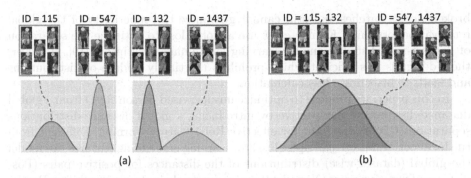

Fig. 2. Local separability is not enough. (a) Within each batch (or subset), the Pos-distr and Neg-distr are well separated. (b) The distributions are inseparable when mixing the two batches together.

[37]. Such distractions lead to serious inseparability of positive and negative samples for ReID.

Person ReID inference/test can be considered as a retrieval task, which aims to identify the images of the same person from a gallery image set by comparing feature distances between the query image and the gallery images [39,49]. Figure 1(a) illustrates the two distributions of distances of positive sample pairs (red curve) and negative sample pairs (green curve). The inseparability of the distance distributions leads to poor retrieval/ranking results. Given an anchor image a, as shown in Fig. 1(a), its distance $(d(a, n_1) = 0.41)$ to the negative sample n_1 is even smaller than its distance $(d(a, p_2) = 0.60)$ to the positive sample p_2. In comparison, when the two distance distributions are better separated as illustrated in Fig. 1(b), the positive samples can be correctly ranked.

Such poor separability is often observed for unsupervised ReID but is unfortunately under-explored. There is a mismatch between the optimization objective design and the ReID purpose. For ReID inference, it is a *global* ranking/retrieval problem (*e.g.*, based on the feature distances to the query image). The separability of the positive and negative global distance distributions is important for this *global* ranking problem. However, most of the current ReID optimizations/losses are designed from a local perspective. Triplet-based losses [13] optimize the embedding space to encourage the distance of the negative pair to be larger than the positive pair. Such constraint is enforced in three instances, *i.e.*, (an anchor sample, a positive sample, and a negative sample). However, as shown in the examples in Fig. 1(a), both the triplets of (a, p_1, n_1), and (a, p_2, n_2) meet the marginal constraints but the identification of positive/negative samples fails when ranking them all together. In practice, it is impossible to optimize over all possible triplets of a dataset within an acceptable duration. We argue that dataset-wise (*i.e.*, global) constraint is imperative to address this problem. Ustinova *et al.* go a step further and propose a Histogram loss for deep embedding to encourage the separation of distributions within each batch [33]. Unfortunately, as illustrated in Fig. 2, being still a local solution, the separation is easily broken across batches and still cannot guarantee the superiority of the global retrieval performance. Kumar *et al.* use a global loss to optimize the separation of dataset-wise distributions for learning local image descriptors [19]. However, their design is less efficient which prohibits the timely update of distributions and leads to inaccurate loss calculation.

In this paper, we propose to optimize unsupervised person ReID from a global distance-distribution perspective by introducing a global distance-distributions separation (GDS) constraint for effective ReID feature learning. Different from the local constraints (*e.g.*, triplet loss) for learning embedding features, we model the global (dataset-wise) distributions of the distances for positive pairs (Pos-distr) and negative pairs (Neg-distr) and promote their clear separability. Particularly, we model the two global distance distributions as Gaussian distributions with *updatable mean and variance*. To model the distributions from a global view and ensure timely updates of the distributions and GDS-related losses, we leverage the momentum update mechanism for building and maintaining the distribution variables and calculate the GDS loss on the fly during the training. The GDS loss helps push away the two distributions while encouraging the sharpness of individual distribution. Moreover, to better separate the Pos-distr and Neg-distr, we introduce a distribution-based hard mining by pushing the right-tail of the Pos-distr and the left-tail of the Neg-distr to have a soft margin. We summarize our main contributions as follows:

- We are the first to propose to optimize unsupervised person ReID from a global distance-distribution perspective by encouraging the global separation of positive and negative samples. We address the problem of inseparability of distance distributions in existing unsupervised ReID models by introducing a global distance-distributions separation (GDS) constraint.
- We maintain and update the distribution variables through a momentum update mechanism, enabling the timely update of the distribution variables and accurate estimation of the loss for each batch.
- To further promote the separation of the Pos-distr and Neg-distr, we introduce a distribution-based hard mining mechanism in GDS.

GDS is simple yet effective and can be potentially used as a plug-and-play tool in many unsupervised ReID frameworks for performance enhancement. We validate the effectiveness of our GDS constraint in two representative UDA-ReID approaches, the clustering-based approach with pseudo labelling, and a style transfer-based approach. Extensive experiments are conducted on multiple ReID benchmark datasets and ours achieves the best performance.

2 Related Work

2.1 Unsupervised Person Re-identification

Unsupervised domain adaptive person ReID aims to learn a ReID model from a labeled source domain and an unlabeled target domain. It is attractive for real-word deployments as it does not require the expensive annotation efforts while exploiting the source domain knowledge. The domain gap between datasets results in poor generalization of a source domain trained model to another domain. Many domain adaptation techniques have been designed for person ReID. They can mainly be grouped into three categories: *style transfer*, *attribute recognition*, and *clustering-based pseudo label estimation*. Style transfer based approaches translate the source labeled images to ones with the style of the target domain by using image style translation techniques (*e.g.*, Cycle-GAN [56]) for adaptation [5,23,35]. Their performance is much inferior to recent clustering-based approaches, since there is still a gap between the generated images and the target domain images [37]. Attribute-based approaches [22,34] aim to share the source domain knowledge with the target domain through learning of some cues, such as person body attributes, to regularize the feature learning. Such external cues rely on manual annotation and thus limit their applicability. Clustering-based approaches are popular with superior performance [7,9,29,37,38,45]. The basic idea is to exploit the similarity of unlabeled samples by feature clustering for predicting pseudo labels and then use them for fine-tuning. Such clustering and training process are usually alternatively performed until the model is stable.

These unsupervised ReID models usually suffer from the interference from noisy pseudo labels or noisy generated images. The inseparability of the distance distributions of positive pairs and negative pairs is serious, there exists undesired small inter-class distances and large intra-class distances (see Fig. 1(a)).

2.2 Metric Learning for Person Re-identification

In person ReID tasks, metric learning aims to make the features of the same identity closer while pushing the features of different identities further apart [14,36,39,49,55]. Loss function designs play the role of metric learning to guide the feature representation learning. For person ReID, there are several widely studied loss functions with their variants. *Identity loss* treats the training process of person ReID as an image classification problem in guiding the feature learning [50]. This enforces a distance/correlation constraint on samples with respect to the "class center" but ignores the direct comparisons between samples. ReID inference is actually a comparison based on the feature similarity/distance between a query image and each image in the gallery set. *Triplet-based loss* and its variants [13] consider the relative ordering of the positive pair distance and negative pair distance by constructing a triplet (an anchor point a, a positive point p, a negative point n). They optimize the features to encourage the distance between the negative pair to be larger than the distance between the positive pair by a hard or soft margin. The relative ordering of positive pairs and negative pairs matches the retrieval purpose better. In recent years, triplet-based loss is popular and has become one of the default losses for most of the ReID networks [9,37–39,45]. However, it only jointly considers the separability among three samples and is far from satisfactory for the global comparison/ranking problem of ReID. Histogram loss [33] goes a step further and encourages the separability of the positive and negative distributions within a batch. As explained in Fig. 2, it is still a local constraint and results in poor separability.

Besides capturing the local structure of data with triplet-based loss, Zhang et al. [45] use global information by appending a changeable classification layer to the model with the number of classes being the number of clusters. This encourages the separability of clustered centers but is less effective in encouraging the separation of distance distributions of positive pairs and negative pairs. Besides, the classification layer needs to be re-trained together with the change of clustering results which may result in a slow and unstable convergence.

To address the poor separability between the distance distributions of the positive pairs and negative pairs observed in existing unsupervised ReID approaches, we introduce a simple yet effective global distributions separation constraint with a momentum updating mechanism. The separation of global distributions has been investigated in learning local image descriptors, with applications in several problems involving the matching of local image patches, such as wide baseline stereo, structure from motion, image classification [19]. Ours is superior to theirs. First, our momentum updating mechanism enables the timely and more accurate updating of losses and networks, leading to optimized performance. In contrast, theirs calculates the distribution statistics from all the samples to obtain the global loss before the next epoch (an epoch means that the entire dataset is passed). This loss is then used for all the mini-batches even though the actual statistics and losses vary with the optimization of each batch. Second, we propose a distribution-based hard mining for effectively promoting the separation. More importantly, we identify one key problem in unsupervised person ReID and address the challenge through a simple yet effective loss design and updating mechanism.

3   Unsupervised ReID with GDS Constraint

We aim at enhancing the performance of unsupervised person ReID, by addressing the inseparability of global distance-distributions of positive pairs and negative pairs. As illustrated in Fig. 1, the inseparability could seriously degrade the ReID performance. We propose a global distance-distributions separation (GDS) constraint powered by a momentum update mechanism, which we also refer to as the GDS algorithm. Conceptually, the GDS algorithm is not limited to any specific unsupervised ReID network and it is general. To facilitate the better understanding of the GDS algorithm, we describe it under the representative and popular clustering-based framework for unsupervised person ReID.

Clustering-based approaches in general consist of three stages with the last two stages executed alternatively for many iterations [7,9,29,37,38,45]. As shown in Fig. 3, the first stage, *model pre-training*, is to pretrain the ReID network with the source domain labeled data for feature learning. The second stage, *clustering stage*, aims at assigning pseudo labels through the clustering results to the unlabeled target domain data. In the third stage of *adaptation*, the pseudo labels are used for the fine-tuning of the network for domain adaptation, where

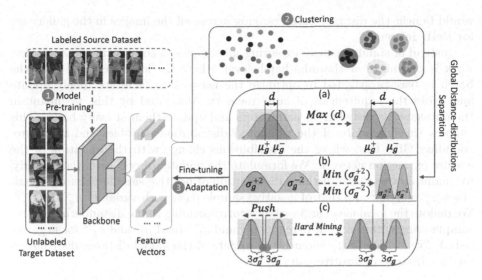

Fig. 3. Flowchart of the clustering-based UDA-ReID framework with our Global Distance-distributions Separation (GDS) constraint. In the third stage for adaptation, our GDS constraint with momentum updating optimizes the feature learning by encouraging the separation of the global Pos-distr (red curve) and Neg-distr (green curve). Particularly, we (a) enlarge the distance of the means of the two distributions; (b) encourage the sharpness of each distribution; and (c) introduce distribution-based hard mining to enforce a soft margin between the right-tail of the Pos-distr and the left-tail of the Neg-distr. (Color figure online)

triplet-based losses are often used for optimization. Triplet-based constraint is enforced on a triplet of instances and cannot assure the correct relative order of the distances for extensive pairs of samples (see Fig. 1(a) for the illustration of the inseparability). We apply our GDS algorithm in the third stage for more effective feature learning. GDS encourages the separation of the global distance-distributions of positive sample pairs and negative sample pairs.

3.1 Global Distance-Distribution Modeling with Momentum Update

We have observed the dataset-wise distance distributions of positive sample pairs and negative sample pairs from ReID models (including unsupervised and supervised methods) and found they exhibit Gaussian-like distributions. Therefore, we model the distance distribution of sample pairs by Gaussian distribution with mean μ and variance σ^2. We denote the distance distribution of positive sample pairs as $\mathcal{N}(\mu^+, \sigma^{+2})$ and that of negative sample pairs as $\mathcal{N}(\mu^-, \sigma^{-2})$. We aim at designing optimization metrics and strategies to encourage the separation of the two dataset-wise (global) distributions in guiding the feature learning, which would benefit the distance-based ranking across all the images in the gallery set for ReID inference.

Instead of simultaneously exploring all samples, a convolutional neural network is optimized at the mini-batch level, where the loss calculated from the batch is back-propagated to optimize the network to facilitate timely update and avoid the requirement of large memory. Motivated by this, we maintain the dataset-wise distribution parameters and update them at every batch. This enables timely update of the estimated distribution variables and the corresponding GDS loss, where the distributions change with the updating of the feature extraction network. We formulate the update process here. Particularly, we maintain the global distance distribution of positive sample pairs with variables μ_g^+ and σ_g^{+2} and that of negative sample pairs with variables μ_g^- and σ_g^{-2}. We denote the local mean and variance corresponding to the distances of positive sample pairs within a local batch as μ_l^+ and σ_l^{+2} (and μ_l^- and σ_l^{-2} for negative pairs). We formulate the momentum update of the global distance-distribution for the distance of positive pairs as

$$\left\{ \begin{array}{l} \mu_g^+ \leftarrow \beta\mu_g^+ + (1-\beta)\mu_l^+ \\ \sigma_g^{+2} \leftarrow \beta\sigma_g^{+2} + (1-\beta)\sigma_l^{+2} \end{array} \right., \text{ with } \left\{ \begin{array}{l} \mu_l^+ = \frac{1}{N^+}\sum_{i=1}^{N^+} d_i^+ \\ \sigma_l^{+2} = \frac{1}{N^+}\sum_{i=1}^{N^+}(d_i^+ - \mu_l^+)^2 \end{array} \right\}\right\} \quad (1)$$

where the hyper-parameter $\beta \in [0, 1)$ is a momentum coefficient, N^+ denotes the number of sampled positive pairs. d_i^+ denotes the Euclidean distance of the ith positive pair, where $d(\mathbf{x}_{i_1}, \mathbf{x}_{i_2}) = \frac{1}{2}||\mathbf{x}_{i_1} - \mathbf{x}_{i_2}|| \in [0, 1]$ for the two normalized feature vectors $\mathbf{x}_{i_1}$ and $\mathbf{x}_{i_2}$ of two samples. The update for negative sample pairs is similar. Please see **Supplementary** for the mathematical analysis of the rationality of our momentum update design.

3.2 Global Distance-Distributions Separation (GDS) Constraint

To encourage the separation of the global distance-distributions of positive sample pairs and negative sample pairs, we design a GDS loss with distribution-based hard mining, i.e., GDS-H loss, which optimizes the network at each mini-batch. The GDS-H loss which consists of the basic GDS loss $\mathcal{L}_{GDS}$ and distribution-based hard mining loss $\mathcal{L}_H$ is defined as

$$\mathcal{L}_{GDS-H} = \mathcal{L}_{GDS} + \lambda_h\mathcal{L}_H, \quad (2)$$

where λ_h is a hyper-parameter that balances their importance.

GDS Loss. $\mathcal{L}_{GDS}$ is defined as

$$\mathcal{L}_{GDS} = \text{Softplus}(\mu_g^+ - \mu_g^-) + \lambda_\sigma(\sigma_g^{+2} + \sigma_g^{-2}), \quad (3)$$

where λ_σ is another hyper-parameter that balances the importance of mean and variance (please see the study on λ_h and λ_σ in the experiment). $\text{Softplus}(\cdot) = \ln(1 + \exp(\cdot))$, as a soft-margin formulation, has similar behavior to the hinge function but it decays exponentially instead of having a hard cut-off [13]. As illustrated in Fig. 3, the first item Softplus($\mu_g^+ - \mu_g^-$) encourages the separation of the centers of the two distributions while the second item ($\sigma_g^{+2} + \sigma_g^{-2}$) encourages the sharpness of the two distributions by minimizing their variances.

Distribution-based Hard Mining. To better promote the separation of the two distributions, as illustrated in Fig. 3(c), we expect the hard samples lying in the potential overlap regions can also be separated. We achieve this by introducing a distribution-based hard mining loss $\mathcal{L}_H$ as

$$\mathcal{L}_H = \text{Softplus}((\mu_g^+ + \kappa\sigma_g^+) - (\mu_g^- - \kappa\sigma_g^-)), \tag{4}$$

where κ is a hyper-parameter which controls the strength of hard mining. The larger of κ, the more areas of the distribution are covered. Motivated by the *three-sigma rule of thumb* which expresses a conventional heuristic that nearly all values (99.7%) are taken to lie within three times of standard deviations of the mean [12], we set κ to 3 and also experimentally found that this results in superior performance. As illustrated in Fig. 3(c), the physical meaning of Eq. (4) is to encourage the right-tail of the Pos-distr to be smaller than the left-tail of the Neg-distr by a soft margin. This enables the relative ordering of the two *distributions* (instead of only ordering of the centers of the distributions).

Differentiability of GDS-H Loss for Optimization. Importantly, the GDS-H loss in Eq. (2) is differentiable w.r.t. the batch-level statistics μ_l and σ_l^2 and thus the batch samples. To facilitate the description, we denote the means of the maintained global distance-distribution of positive sample pairs as μ_g^+ and $\mu_g^{+'}$ before and after the update using the current batch, respectively, where $\mu_g^{+'} = \beta\mu_g^+ + (1-\beta)\mu_l^+$. Similarly, we denote $\sigma_g^{+2'} = \beta\sigma_g^{+2} + (1-\beta)\sigma_l^{+2}$. For ease of presentation, we rewrite the variables $\sigma_g^{+2'}$ and σ_g^{+2} as $\rho_g^{+'}$ and ρ_g^+, respectively. Then $\rho_g^{+'} = \beta\rho_g^+ + (1-\beta)\sigma_l^{+2}$. Similarly, we can define these for the global distance-distribution of negative sample pairs. The gradient of GDS-H loss ($\mathcal{L}_{GDS-H} = \mathcal{L}$) w.r.t. the sample feature $\mathbf{x}_{i_1}$ is as

$$\begin{aligned}
\frac{\partial\mathcal{L}_{GDS-H}}{\partial\mathbf{x}_{i_1}} &= \frac{\partial\mathcal{L}}{\partial\mu_g^{+'}}\frac{\partial\mu_g^{+'}}{\partial\mu_l^+}\frac{\partial\mu_l^+}{\partial d_i^+}\frac{\partial d_i^+}{\partial\mathbf{x}_{i_1}} + \frac{\partial\mathcal{L}}{\partial\rho_g^{+'}}\frac{\partial\rho_g^{+'}}{\partial\sigma_l^+}\frac{\partial\sigma_l^+}{\partial d_i^+}\frac{\partial d_i^+}{\partial\mathbf{x}_{i_1}} \\
&+ \frac{\partial\mathcal{L}}{\partial\mu_g^{-'}}\frac{\partial\mu_g^{-'}}{\partial\mu_l^-}\frac{\partial\mu_l^-}{\partial d_i^-}\frac{\partial d_i^-}{\partial\mathbf{x}_{i_1}} + \frac{\partial\mathcal{L}}{\partial\rho_g^{-'}}\frac{\partial\rho_g^{-'}}{\partial\sigma_l^-}\frac{\partial\sigma_l^-}{\partial d_i^-}\frac{\partial d_i^-}{\partial\mathbf{x}_{i_1}},
\end{aligned} \tag{5}$$

this reveals that our method could enable the batch-level gradient back-propagation for timely update of the network for feature learning.

4   Experiments

4.1   Datasets and Evaluation Metrics

To evaluate the effectiveness of our GDS constraint for unsupervised person ReID and to be consistent with what were done in prior works for performance comparisons, we conduct extensive experiments on the public ReID datasets, including Market1501 [48], DukeMTMC-reID [51], CUHK03 [21], and the large-scale MSMT17 [35]. We denote Market1501 by M, DukeMTMC-reID by Duke or D, and CUHK03 by C for short. Given a labeled source dataset A and an unlabeled target dataset B, we denote this unsupervised ReID setting as A→B.

We follow common practices and use the cumulative matching characteristics (CMC) at Rank-1, and mean average precision (mAP) for evaluation.

4.2 Implementation Details

We build our *Baseline* following the clustering-based pseudo label approach [29], which uses ResNet-50 [2, 24, 29, 37, 46] as the backbone network for feature extraction. In the first stage, we pretrain the network using the source dataset, supervised by classification loss [10, 31] and triplet loss with batch hard mining [13]. In the clustering stage, we perform clustering using DBSCAN [6] based on the extracted features of the target dataset, for the purpose of pseudo label assignment. In the adaptation stage, with the pseudo labels, triplet loss with batch hard mining [13] is used to finetune the network. The second stage and the third stage are executed alternatively for 30 iterations. In our schemes, on top of *Baseline*, we add the proposed GDS losses in the adaptation stage. The input image resolution is 256×128. See **Supplementary** for more training details.

4.3 Ablation Study

We perform most of the ablation studies based on the powerful clustering-based method, *i.e.*, *Baseline*. We follow the popular settings [9, 37, 54] for ablation study, *i.e.*, using Market1501→Duke (M→D), and Duke→Market1501 (D→M).

Effectiveness of Our GDS Constraint. Table 1(a) shows the comparisons. *Direct transfer* denotes the case that the network is only trained on source dataset and is directly tested on the target dataset. *Baseline+GDS* denotes our basic scheme where our proposed GDS loss is added on top of *Baseline*. *Baseline+GDS-H* denotes our final scheme where our GDS-H loss (GDS loss + distribution-based hard-mining loss, with momentum update of distributions) is added on top of *Baseline*. We have the following observations.

1) Thanks to the encouragement of the separation of the global distance distributions, our final scheme *Baseline+GDS-H* significantly outperforms *Baseline* by **6.7%** and **9.1%** in mAP for M→D and D→M, respectively.
2) Our distribution-based hard mining promotes the separation of the two distributions by enabling the relative ordering of the two distributions (instead of only their centers). Such hard mining further brings **2.2%** and **4.1%** improvements in mAP for M→D and D→M (*Baseline+GDS-H* vs. *Baseline+GDS*).
3) *Baseline* which uses a clustering-based approach for adaptation outperforms *Direct transfer* by a large margin, indicating the necessity of the adaptation with target domain data.

Table 1. Effectiveness of the proposed GDS loss and the distribution-based hard mining loss (H).

(a) Study on the clustering-based method.(b) Study on style transfer based method.

Clustering-based	M→D		D→M		Style Transfer based	M→D		D→M	
	mAP	Rank-1	mAP	Rank-1		mAP	Rank-1	mAP	Rank-1
Direct transfer	19.8	35.3	21.8	48.3	SPGAN [5]	22.3	41.1	22.8	51.5
Baseline	48.4	67.1	52.1	74.3					
Baseline+GDS	52.9	71.4	57.1	78.5	SPGAN+GDS	25.3	45.9	25.9	56.4
Baseline+GDS-H	55.1	73.1	61.2	81.1	SPGAN+GDS-H	27.5	47.7	29.4	60.8

Effectiveness Evaluation in Terms of ROC and PR Curves. For some applications of ReID such as people tracking, the determination of whether two person images match or not degrades to a comparison of their feature distance with a pre-defined threshold θ [3,28]. If the distance is smaller than θ, they are judged as the same person. By varying the threshould, we obtain the Receiver Operator Characteristic (ROC) curve [8] and Precision-Recall (PR) curve [4] as shown in Fig. 4. Obviously, our final scheme *Baseline+GDS-H* also significantly outperforms *Baseline* under the threshould-based evaluation metrics.

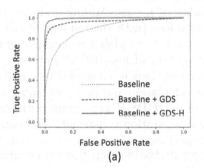
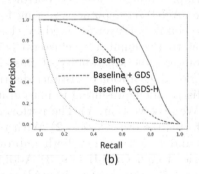

(a)   (b)

Fig. 4. (a) ROC curve and (b) PR curve on the test set of the target dataset Duke (Market1501→Duke) for *Baseline*, *Baseline+GDS* and *Baseline+GDS-H*.

Generality of our GDS Constraint. The GDS constraint is not limited to clustering-based approaches and we also validate its effectiveness under a representative style transfer based ReID approach SPGAN [5]. Table 1(b) shows the results. We observe that **1)** our final scheme *SPGAN+GDS-H* significantly outperforms *SPGAN* by **5.2%** and **6.6%** in mAP for M→D and D→M, respectively; **2)** our distribution-based hard mining brings **2.2%** and **3.5%** improvements in mAP for M→D and D→M, respectively (*SPGAN+GDS-H* vs. *SPGAN+GDS*); **3)** this style transfer based approach *SPGAN* is less effective than the clustering based approach *Baseline* due to the unsatisfactory quality of the transferred images.

Table 2. Performance comparison of different loss designs.

Different losses	M→D		D→M	
	mAP	Rank-1	mAP	Rank-1
Baseline	48.4	67.1	52.1	74.3
Baseline + Histogram loss [33]	50.2	69.4	53.7	76.3
Baseline + F-Statistic loss [27]	51.1	70.3	55.5	76.9
Baseline + Classification loss [45]	49.7	68.9	53.8	75.9
Baseline + Global loss [19]	49.6	68.8	54.3	76.5
Baseline + **GDS-H (Ours)**	**55.1**	**73.1**	**61.2**	**81.1**

Comparison with Other Losses. We compare our GDS constraint with several other losses by implementing them on the same network *Baseline* at its third stage (adaptation stage). Table 2 shows the results. Both Histogram loss [33] and F-Statistic loss [27] explore the local (batch-level) statistics for optimization. Histogram loss [33] estimates the similarity (or distance) distributions of positive sample pairs and negative sample pairs by accumulating the similarity (or distance) values to the bins of two histograms and minimizes their overlap. F-Statistic loss [27] borrows a particular statistic from analysis of variance (ANOVA) hypothesis testing for equality of means. Adding a changeable fully connected layer followed by classification loss (with the number of classes equal to the number of clusters) [45] plays a role of global constraint which encourages the separability of cluster centers. Global loss [19] also encourages the global separation of distance distributions but there is a lack of timely update of distributions, resulting in inaccurate loss calculation and poor optimization.

We observe that: **1)** The performance of our GDS-H loss significantly outperforms the other losses. **2)** With the local separation constraints, Histogram loss and F-Statistic loss both improve the performance over *Baseline* but are inferior to our GDS-H loss. **3)** Adding a global classification loss brings about 1.3%~1.7% improvement in mAP over *Baseline* but are not as effective as ours. **4)** Thanks to the effective momentum update mechanism and distribution-based hard mining, our GDS constraint significantly outperforms [19].

4.4   Design Choices of GDS

Influence of the Momentum Coefficient β. For the distribution update, β controls the contribution ratio of the batch-level statistics to the maintained distributions (Eq. (1)). Figure 5(a) shows its influence. We observe that a relatively larger value (*e.g.*, $\beta = 0.99$) could maintain more stable global distributions and works much better than a smaller value. When β is 0, our GDS loss degrades to a batch-wise (local) distance distribution separation constraint. Such degradation results in a large performance drop in comparison to our GDS ($\beta = 0.99$), from the best 55.1%/61.2% to 51.4%/56.2% in mAP for M→D/D→M, demonstrating the importance of modeling *global* distance distributions.

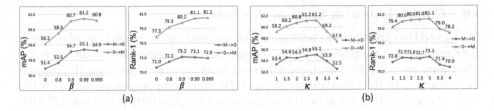

(a)   (b)

Fig. 5. Influence on ReID performance in terms of mAP and Rank-1 accuracy of (a) momentum coefficient β (see Eq. (1) in Subsect. 3.1), and (b) strength κ in the distribution-based hard mining for M→D and D→M settings.

Influence of the Strength κ in the Distribution-based Hard Mining. We compare the cases of adding different width offsets ($\kappa = 1 \sim 4$) over the mean as the "hard" region definition (Eq. (4)). In Fig. 5(b), we observe that $\kappa = 3$ leads to the best performance. Based on *three-sigma rule of thumb*, 99.7% values lie within three times of standard deviations of the mean. This could well cover the entire distribution while excluding the side effects of some extreme outliers.

4.5   Visualization of Dataset-Wise (Global) Distance Distributions

To better understand GDS constraint, we visualize the dataset-wise Pos-distr and Neg-distr in Fig. 6. Thanks to the adaptation on the unlabeled target dataset, the distance distributions of *Baseline* present a much better separability than that of *Direct transfer*. But, there is still a large overlap between the two distributions. By introducing our GDS constraint, our final scheme *Baseline+GDS-H* greatly reduces the overlap of distributions. Besides, our distribution-based hard mining loss is very helpful in promoting the separation ((c) vs. (d)).

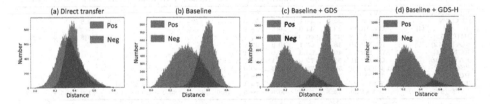

Fig. 6. Histograms of the distances of the positive sample pairs (red) and negative sample pairs (green) on the test set of the target dataset Duke (Market1501→Duke) for schemes of (a) *Direct transfer*, (b) *Baseline*, (c) *Baseline+GDS*, and (d) *Baseline+GDS-H*. Here we use all the 48018 positive sample pairs and 48018 randomly sampled negative sample pairs for visualization. (Color figure online)

4.6   Comparison with State-of-the-Arts

Thanks to the capability of encouraging the separation of the two global distance distributions, our proposed GDS constraint effectively addresses the distance distributions inseparability problem observed in existing unsupervised ReID models. We evaluate the effectiveness of our GDS constraint by comparing with the state-of-the-art approaches on three datasets of Market-1501 (M), DukeMTMC-reID (D) and CUHK03 (C) with six settings in Table 3. More results about the largest dataset MSMT17 can be found in **Supplementary**.

With the effective loss design of GDS, our final scheme *Baseline+GDS-H* achieves the best performance for five dataset settings without any increase in computation complexity in inference. Ours is inferior to *PCB-R-PAST** [45] only for the C→D setting. But we should not look too much into this comparison as it is not a fair one. First, *PCB-R-PAST** applied re-ranking [52] as post-operation but we do not. Second, *PCB-R-PAST** is built on top of a more powerful ReID specific model structure of PCB [31]. Ours uses ResNet-50. Third, the input resolution of *PCB-R-PAST** is 384×128 while ours is 256×128. Our *Baseline+GDS-H* outperforms the second best approach *ACT* [37] on all the settings, achieving 4.6% and 9.9% gain in mAP for D→C and C→D, respectively. Besides, our loss design is simple in implementation and does not require the complicated co-training process used in [37]. Conceptually, our GDS loss is complementary to many approaches like *ACT* [37], *PCB-R-PAST** [45] and could be used to further improve their performance.

Table 3. Performance (%) comparisons with the state-of-the-art approaches for unsupervised person ReID. * means applying a re-ranking method of k-reciprocal encoding [52]. Note that *Baseline* is built following [29] with ResNet-50 backbone and thus has nearly the same performance as *Theory* [29].

Unsupervised ReID	Venue	M→D mAP	M→D Rank-1	D→M mAP	D→M Rank-1	M→C mAP	M→C Rank-1	D→C mAP	D→C Rank-1	C→M mAP	C→M Rank-1	C→D mAP	C→D Rank-1
PTGAN [35]	CVPR'18	–	27.4	–	38.6	–	–	–	–	–	31.5	–	17.6
SPGAN [5]	CVPR'18	22.3	41.1	22.8	51.5	–	–	–	–	19.0	42.8	–	–
TJ-AIDL [34]	CVPR'18	23.0	44.3	26.5	58.2	–	–	–	–	–	–	–	–
HHL [53]	ECCV'18	27.2	46.9	31.4	62.2	–	–	–	–	29.8	56.8	23.4	42.7
MAR [42]	CVPR'19	48.0	67.1	40.0	67.7	–	–	–	–	–	–	–	–
ECN [54]	CVPR'19	40.4	63.3	43.0	75.1	–	–	–	–	–	–	–	–
PAUL [38]	CVPR'19	53.2	72.0	40.1	68.5	–	–	–	–	–	–	–	–
SSG [9]	ICCV'19	53.4	73.0	58.3	80.0	–	–	–	–	–	–	–	–
PCB-R-PAST* [45]	ICCV'19	54.3	72.4	54.6	78.4	–	–	–	–	57.3	79.5	51.8	69.9
Theory [29]	PR'2020	48.4	67.0	52.0	74.1	46.4	47.0	28.8	28.5	51.2	71.4	32.2	49.4
ACT [37]	AAAI'20	54.5	72.4	60.6	80.5	48.9	49.5	30.0	30.6	64.1	81.2	35.4	52.8
Baseline	This work	48.4	67.1	52.1	74.3	46.2	47.0	28.8	28.4	51.2	71.4	32.0	49.4
Baseline+GDS-H	This work	55.1	73.1	61.2	81.1	49.7	50.2	34.6	36.0	66.1	84.2	45.3	64.9
B-SNR[17]	CVPR'20	54.3	72.4	66.1	82.2	47.6	47.5	31.5	33.5	62.4	80.6	45.7	66.7
B-SNR[17]+GDS-H	This work	59.7	76.7	72.5	89.3	50.7	51.4	38.9	41.0	68.3	86.7	51.0	71.5

To further demonstrate the effectiveness of our GDS constraint, we replace the ResNet-50 backbone network of *Baseline* by a more powerful Style Normalization and Restitution (SNR) network [17] (which inserts four light-weight SNR modules to ResNet-50 to tackle the style variation problem for generalizable person ReID) and denote the new baseline scheme as *B-SNR* for simplicity.

In Table 3, the scheme *B-SNR+GDS-H* which adopts our GDS constraint also significantly improves the performance of the strong baseline scheme *B-SNR* and achieves the best performance on all settings.

5   Conclusions

We propose the use of a Global Distance-distributions Separation (GDS) constraint to enhance the unsupervised person ReID performance. We model the global distance-distributions by Gaussian distributions and encourage their separation. Particularly, we exploit a momentum update mechanism to maintain the variables of the global distributions and enable the timely update of the distributions and the GDS-related loss, facilitating the optimization of the network for each batch. Moreover, we propose distribution-based hard mining to better promote the separation of the distributions. Extensive ablation studies demonstrate the effectiveness of our GDS constraint. We achieve the state-of-the-art performance on the bechmark datasets. The GDS design is simple yet effective. It is conceptually complementary to many of the available approaches and can be taken as a plug-and-play tool for ReID performance enhancement.

Acknowledgments. This work was supported in part by NSFC under Grant U1908209, 61632001 and the National Key Research and Development Program of China 2018AAA0101400.

References

1. Ahmed, E., Jones, M., Marks, T.K.: An improved deep learning architecture for person re-identification. In: CVPR (2015)
2. Almazan, J., Gajic, B., Murray, N., Larlus, D.: Re-id done right: towards good practices for person re-identification. arXiv preprint arXiv:1801.05339 (2018)
3. Chen, L., Ai, H., Zhuang, Z., Shang, C.: Real-time multiple people tracking with deeply learned candidate selection and person re-identification. In: ICME, pp. 1–6 (2018)
4. Davis, J., Goadrich, M.: The relationship between precision-recall and roc curves. In: ICML, pp. 233–240 (2006)
5. Deng, W., Zheng, L., Ye, Q., Kang, G., Yang, Y., Jiao, J.: Image-image domain adaptation with preserved self-similarity and domain-dissimilarity for person re-identification. In: CVPR (2018)
6. Ester, M., Kriegel, H.P., Sander, J., Xu, X., et al.: A density-based algorithm for discovering clusters in large spatial databases with noise. Kdd. **96**, 226–231 (1996)
7. Fan, H., Zheng, L., Yan, C., Yang, Y.: Unsupervised person re-identification: clustering and fine-tuning. ACM Trans. Multimedia Comput. Commun. Appl. (TOMM) **14**(4), 1–18 (2018)
8. Fawcett, T.: An introduction to ROC analysis. Pattern Recogn. Lett. **27**(8), 861–874 (2006)
9. Fu, Y., Wei, Y., Wang, G., Zhou, X., Shi, H., Huang, T.S.: Self-similarity grouping: a simple unsupervised cross domain adaptation approach for person re-identification. In: ICCV (2019)

10. Fu, Y., Wei, Y., Zhou, Y., et al.: Horizontal pyramid matching for person re-identification. In: AAAI (2019)
11. Ge, Y., Li, Z., Zhao, H., et al.: FD-GAN: pose-guided feature distilling gan for robust person re-identification. In: NeurIPS (2018)
12. Grafarend, E., Awange, J.: Linear and Nonlinear Models. Springer, Heidelberg (2012). https://doi.org/10.1007/978-3-642-22241-2
13. Hermans, A., Beyer, L., Leibe, B.: In defense of the triplet loss for person re-identification. arXiv preprint arXiv:1703.07737 (2017)
14. Hirzer, M., Roth, P.M., Köstinger, M., Bischof, H.: Relaxed pairwise learned metric for person re-identification. In: Fitzgibbon, A., Lazebnik, S., Perona, P., Sato, Y., Schmid, C. (eds.) ECCV 2012. LNCS, vol. 7577, pp. 780–793. Springer, Heidelberg (2012). https://doi.org/10.1007/978-3-642-33783-3_56
15. Jia, M., Zhai, Y., Lu, S., Ma, S., Zhang, J.: A similarity inference metric for RGB-infrared cross-modality person re-identification. In: IJCAI (2020)
16. Jin, X., Lan, C., Zeng, W., Chen, Z.: Uncertainty-aware multi-shot knowledge distillation for image-based object re-identification. In: AAAI (2020)
17. Jin, X., Lan, C., Zeng, W., Chen, Z., Zhang, L.: Style normalization and restitution for generalizable person re-identification. In: CVPR (2020)
18. Jin, X., Lan, C., Zeng, W., Wei, G., Chen, Z.: Semantics-aligned representation learning for person re-identification. In: AAAI, pp. 11173–11180 (2020)
19. Kumar, B., Carneiro, G., Reid, I., et al.: Learning local image descriptors with deep siamese and triplet convolutional networks by minimising global loss functions. In: CVPR, pp. 5385–5394 (2016)
20. Li, M., Zhu, X., Gong, S.: Unsupervised person re-identification by deep learning tracklet association. In: ECCV (2018)
21. Li, W., Zhao, R., Tian, L., et al.: Deepreid: deep filter pairing neural network for person re-identification. In: CVPR (2014)
22. Lin, S., Li, H., Li, C.T., Kot, A.C.: Multi-task mid-level feature alignment network for unsupervised cross-dataset person re-identification. In: BMVC (2018)
23. D Liu, J., Zha, Z.J., Chen, D., Hong, R., Wang, M.: Adaptive transfer network for cross-domain person re-identification. In: CVPR (2019)
24. Luo, H., Gu, Y., Liao, X., Lai, S., Jiang, W.: Bag of tricks and a strong baseline for deep person re-identification. In: CVPR workshops (2019)
25. Qi, L., Wang, L., Huo, J., Zhou, L., Shi, Y., Gao, Y.: A novel unsupervised camera-aware domain adaptation framework for person re-identification. In: ICCV (2019)
26. Qian, X., Fu, Y., Wang, W., et al.: Pose-normalized image generation for person re-identification. In: ECCV (2018)
27. Ridgeway, K., Mozer, M.C.: Learning deep disentangled embeddings with the f-statistic loss. In: NeurIPS, pp. 185–194 (2018)
28. Ristani, E., Tomasi, C.: Features for multi-target multi-camera tracking and re-identification. In: CVPR, pp. 6036–6046 (2018)
29. Song, L., et al.: Unsupervised domain adaptive re-identification: theory and practice. Pattern Recogn. **102**, 107173 (2020)
30. Su, C., Li, J., Zhang, S., et al.: Pose-driven deep convolutional model for person re-identification. In: ICCV (2017)
31. Sun, Y., Zheng, L., Yang, Y., Tian, Q., Wang, S.: Beyond part models: person retrieval with refined part pooling (and a strong convolutional baseline). In: ECCV, pp. 480–496 (2018)
32. Tang, H., Zhao, Y., Lu, H.: Unsupervised person re-identification with iterative self-supervised domain adaptation. In: CVPR workshops (2019)

33. Ustinova, E., Lempitsky, V.: Learning deep embeddings with histogram loss. In: NeurIPS, pp. 4170–4178 (2016)
34. Wang, J., Zhu, X., Gong, S., Li, W.: Transferable joint attribute-identity deep learning for unsupervised person re-identification. In: CVPR (2018)
35. Wei, L., Zhang, S., Gao, W., Tian, Q.: Person transfer GAN to bridge domain gap for person re-identification. In: CVPR (2018)
36. Wojke, N., Bewley, A.: Deep cosine metric learning for person re-identification. In: WACV, pp. 748–756 (2018)
37. Yang, F., et al.: Asymmetric co-teaching for unsupervised cross domain person re-identification. In: AAAI (2020)
38. Yang, Q., Yu, H.X., Wu, A., Zheng, W.S.: Patch-based discriminative feature learning for unsupervised person re-identification. In: CVPR (2019)
39. Ye, M., Shen, J., Lin, G., Xiang, T., Shao, L., Hoi, S.C.: Deep learning for person re-identification: a survey and outlook. arXiv preprint arXiv:2001.04193 (2020)
40. Yu, H.X., Wu, A., Zheng, W.S.: Cross-view asymmetric metric learning for unsupervised person re-identification. In: ICCV (2017)
41. Yu, H.X., Wu, A., Zheng, W.S.: Unsupervised person re-identification by deep asymmetric metric embedding. In: IEEE TPAMI (2018)
42. Yu, H.X., Zheng, W.S., Wu, A., Guo, X., Gong, S., Lai, J.H.: Unsupervised person re-identification by soft multilabel learning. In: CVPR (2019)
43. Zhai, Y., et al.: Ad-cluster: augmented discriminative clustering for domain adaptive person re-identification. In: CVPR, pp. 9021–9030 (2020)
44. Zhai, Y., Ye, Q., Lu, S., Jia, M., Ji, R., Tian, Y.: Multiple expert brainstorming for domain adaptive person re-identification. In: ECCV (2020)
45. Zhang, X., Cao, J., Shen, C., You, M.: Self-training with progressive augmentation for unsupervised cross-domain person re-identification. In: ICCV (2019)
46. Zhang, Z., Lan, C., Zeng, W., et al.: Densely semantically aligned person re-identification. In: CVPR (2019)
47. Zhao, H., Tian, M., Sun, S., et al.: Spindle net: person re-identification with human body region guided feature decomposition and fusion. In: CVPR (2017)
48. Zheng, L., Shen, L., et al.: Scalable person re-identification: a benchmark. In: ICCV (2015)
49. Zheng, L., Yang, Y., Hauptmann, A.G.: Person re-identification: past, present and future. arXiv preprint arXiv:1610.02984 (2016)
50. Zheng, L., Zhang, H., Sun, S., Chandraker, M., Yang, Y., Tian, Q.: Person re-identification in the wild. In: CVPR, pp. 1367–1376 (2017)
51. Zheng, Z., Zheng, L., Yang, Y.: Unlabeled samples generated by gan improve the person re-identification baseline in vitro. In: ICCV (2017)
52. Zhong, Z., Zheng, L., Cao, D., Li, S.: Re-ranking person re-identification with k-reciprocal encoding. In: CVPR (2017)
53. Zhong, Z., Zheng, L., Li, S., Yang, Y.: Generalizing a person retrieval model hetero- and homogeneously. In: ECCV (2018)
54. Zhong, Z., Zheng, L., Luo, Z., Li, S., Yang, Y.: Invariance matters: exemplar memory for domain adaptive person re-identification. In: CVPR, pp. 598–607 (2019)
55. Zhou, S., Wang, J., Hou, Q., Gong, Y.: Deep ranking model for person re-identification with pairwise similarity comparison. In: Chen, E., Gong, Y., Tie, Y. (eds.) PCM 2016. LNCS, vol. 9917, pp. 84–94. Springer, Cham (2016). https://doi.org/10.1007/978-3-319-48896-7_9
56. Zhu, J.Y., Park, T., Isola, P., et al.: Unpaired image-to-image translation using cycle-consistent adversarial networks. In: ICCV (2017)

I2L-MeshNet: Image-to-Lixel Prediction Network for Accurate 3D Human Pose and Mesh Estimation from a Single RGB Image

Gyeongsik Moon and Kyoung Mu Lee[✉]

ECE & ASRI, Seoul National University, Seoul, Korea
{mks0601,kyoungmu}@snu.ac.kr

Abstract. Most of the previous image-based 3D human pose and mesh estimation methods estimate parameters of the human mesh model from an input image. However, directly regressing the parameters from the input image is a highly non-linear mapping because it breaks the spatial relationship between pixels in the input image. In addition, it cannot model the prediction uncertainty, which can make training harder. To resolve the above issues, we propose I2L-MeshNet, an image-to-lixel (line+pixel) prediction network. The proposed I2L-MeshNet predicts the per-lixel likelihood on 1D heatmaps for each mesh vertex coordinate instead of directly regressing the parameters. Our lixel-based 1D heatmap preserves the spatial relationship in the input image and models the prediction uncertainty. We demonstrate the benefit of the image-to-lixel prediction and show that the proposed I2L-MeshNet outperforms previous methods. The code is publicly available (https://github.com/mks0601/I2L-MeshNet_RELEASE).

1 Introduction

3D human pose and mesh estimation aims to simultaneously recover 3D semantic human joint and 3D human mesh vertex locations. This is a very challenging task because of complicated human articulation and 2D-to-3D ambiguity. It can be used in many applications such as virtual/augmented reality and human action recognition.

SMPL [25] and MANO [39] are the most widely used parametric human body and hand mesh models, respectively, which can represent various human poses and identities. They produce 3D human joint and mesh coordinates from pose and identity parameters. Recent deep convolutional neural network (CNN)-based studies [18, 21, 37] for the 3D human pose and mesh estimation are based on the model-based approach, which trains a network to estimate SMPL/MANO

Electronic supplementary material The online version of this chapter (https://doi.org/10.1007/978-3-030-58571-6_44) contains supplementary material, which is available to authorized users.

Fig. 1. Qualitative results of the proposed I2L-MeshNet on MSCOCO [24] and Frei-HAND [8] datasets.

parameters from an input image. On the other hand, there have been few methods based on model-free approach [9,22], which estimates mesh vertex coordinates directly. They obtain the 3D pose by multiplying a joint regression matrix, included in the human mesh model, to the estimated mesh.

Although the recent deep CNN-based methods perform impressive, when estimating the target (*i.e.*, SMPL/MANO parameters or mesh vertex coordinates), all of the previous 3D human pose and mesh estimation works break the spatial relationship among pixels in the input image because of the fully-connected layers at the output stage. In addition, their target representations cannot model the uncertainty of the prediction. The above limitations can make training harder, and as a result, reduce the test accuracy as addressed in [29,42]. To address the limitations, recent state-of-the-art 3D human pose estimation methods [29,30,41], which localize 3D human joint coordinates without mesh vertex coordinates, utilize the *heatmap* as the target representation of their networks. Each value of one heatmap represents the likelihood of the existence of a human joint at the corresponding pixel positions of the input image and discretized depth value. Therefore, it preserves the spatial relationship between pixels in the input image and models the prediction uncertainty.

Inspired by the recent state-of-the-art heatmap-based 3D human pose estimation methods, we propose I2L-MeshNet, image-to-lixel prediction network that naturally extends heatmap-based 3D human pose to heatmap-based 3D human pose and mesh. Likewise voxel (volume+pixel) is defined as a quantized cell in three-dimensional space, we define *lixel (line+pixel)* as a quantized cell in one-dimensional space. Our I2L-MeshNet estimates per-lixel likelihood on 1D heatmaps for each mesh vertex coordinates, therefore it is based on the model-free approach. The previous state-of-the-art heatmap-based 3D human pose estimation methods predict 3D heatmap of each human joint. Unlike the number of human joints, which is around 20, the number of mesh vertex is much larger (*e.g.*, 6980 for SMPL and 776 for MANO). As a result, predicting 3D heatmaps of all mesh vertices becomes computationally infeasible, which is beyond the limit of modern GPU memory. In contrast, the proposed lixel-based 1D heatmap has an efficient memory complexity, which has a linear relationship with the heatmap resolution. Thus, it allows our system to predict heatmaps with sufficient resolution, which is essential for dense mesh vertex localization.

For more accurate 3D human pose and mesh estimation, we design the I2L-MeshNet as a cascaded network architecture, which consists of PoseNet and MeshNet. The PoseNet predicts the lixel-based 1D heatmaps of each 3D human joint coordinate. Then, the MeshNet utilizes the output of the PoseNet as an additional input along with the image feature to predict the lixel-based 1D heatmaps of each 3D human mesh vertex coordinate. As the locations of the human joints provide coarse but important information about the human mesh vertex locations, utilizing it for 3D mesh estimation is natural and can increase accuracy substantially.

Our I2L-MeshNet outperforms previous 3D human pose and mesh estimation methods on various 3D human pose and mesh benchmark datasets. Figure 1 shows 3D human body and hand mesh estimation results on publicly available datasets.

Our contributions can be summarized as follows.

- We propose I2L-MeshNet, a novel image-to-lixel prediction network for 3D human pose and mesh estimation from a single RGB image. Our system predicts lixel-based 1D heatmap that preserves the spatial relationship in the input image and models the uncertainty of the prediction.
- Our efficient lixel-based 1D heatmap allows our system to predict heatmaps with sufficient resolution, which is essential for dense mesh vertex localization.
- We show that our I2L-MeshNet outperforms previous state-of-the-art methods on various 3D human pose and mesh datasets.

2   Related Works

3D Human Body and Hand Pose and Mesh Estimation. Most of the current 3D human pose and mesh estimation methods are based on the model-based approach, which predict parameters of pre-defined human body and hand mesh models (*i.e.*, SMPL and MANO, respectively). The model-based methods can be trained only from groundtruth human joint coordinates without mesh vertex coordinates because the model parameters are embedded in low dimensional space. Early model-based methods [4] iteratively fit the SMPL parameters to estimated 2D human joint locations. More recent model-based methods regress the body model parameters from an input image using CNN. Kanazawa et al. [18] proposed an end-to-end trainable human mesh recovery (HMR) system that uses the adversarial loss to make their output human shape is anatomically plausible. Pavlakos et al. [37] used 2D joint heatmaps and silhouette as cues for predicting accurate SMPL parameters. Omran et al. [32] proposed a similar system, which

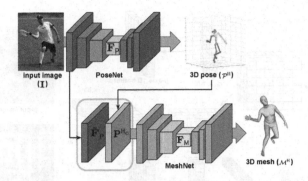

Fig. 2. Overall pipeline of the proposed I2L-MeshNet.

exploits human part segmentation as a cue for regressing SMPL parameters. Xu et al. [45] used differentiable rendering to supervise human mesh in the 2D image space. Pavlakos et al. [35] proposed a system that uses multi-view color consistency to supervise a network using multi-view geometry. Baek et al. [3] trained their network to estimate the MANO parameters using a differentiable renderer. Boukhayma et al. [5] trained their network that takes a single RGB image and estimates MANO parameters by minimizing the distance of the estimated hand joint locations and groundtruth. Kolotouros et al. [21] introduced a self-improving system consists of SMPL parameter regressor and iterative fitting framework [4].

On the other hand, the model-free approach estimates the mesh vertex coordinates directly instead of regressing the model parameters. Due to the recent advancement of the iterative human body and hand model fitting frameworks [4,8,34], pseudo-groundtruth mesh vertex annotation on large-scale datasets [8,14,24,26] became available. Those datasets with mesh vertex annotation motivated several model-free methods that require mesh supervision. Kolotouros et al. [22] designed a graph convolutional human mesh regression system. Their graph convolutional network takes a template human mesh in a rest pose as input and outputs mesh vertex coordinates using image feature from ResNet [12]. Ge et al. [9] proposed a graph convolution-based network which directly estimates vertices of hand mesh. Recently, Choi et al. [7] proposed a graph convolutional network that recovers 3D human pose and mesh from a 2D human pose.

Unlike all the above model-based and model-free 3D human pose and mesh estimation methods, the proposed I2L-MeshNet outputs 3D human pose and mesh by preserving the spatial relationship between pixels in the input image and modeling uncertainty of the prediction. Those two main advantageous are brought by designing the target of our network to the lixel-based 1D heatmap. This can make training much stable, and the system achieves much lower test error.

Heatmap-Based 3D Human Pose Estimation. Most of the recent state-of-the-art 2D and 3D human pose estimation methods use heatmap as a prediction

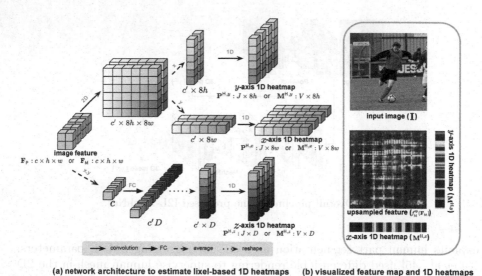

(a) network architecture to estimate lixel-based 1D heatmaps   (b) visualized feature map and 1D heatmaps

Fig. 3. Network architecture to predict lixel-based 1D heatmaps and visualized examples of feature maps and the 1D heatmaps.

target, which preserves the spatial relationship in the input image and models the uncertainty of the prediction. Tompson et al. [42] proposed to estimate the Gaussian heatmap instead of directly regressing coordinates of human body joints. Their heatmap representation helps their model to perform 2D human pose estimation more accurate and motivated many heatmap-based 2D human pose methods [6,31,44]. Pavlakos et al. [36] and Moon et al. [29] firstly proposed to use 3D heatmaps as a prediction target for 3D human body pose and 3D hand pose estimation, respectively. Especially, Moon et al. [29] demonstrated that under the same setting, changing prediction target from coordinates to heatmap significantly improves the 3D hand pose accuracy while requires much less amount of the learnable parameters. Recently, Moon et al. [30] achieved significantly better 3D multi-person pose estimation accuracy using 3D heatmap compared with previous coordinate regression-based methods [38].

3   I2L-MeshNet

Figure 2 shows the overall pipeline of the proposed I2L-MeshNet. I2L-MeshNet consists of PoseNet and MeshNet, which will be described in the following subsections.

3.1   PoseNet

The PoseNet estimates three lixel-based 1D heatmaps of all human joints $\mathcal{P}^H = \{\mathbf{P}^{H,x}, \mathbf{P}^{H,y}, \mathbf{P}^{H,z}\}$ from the input image $\mathbf{I}$. $\mathbf{P}^{H,x}$ and $\mathbf{P}^{H,y}$ are defined in x- and

y-axis of the image space, while $\mathbf{P}^{\mathrm{H},z}$ is defined in root joint (*i.e.*, pelvis or wrist)-relative depth space. For this, PoseNet extracts image feature $\mathbf{F}_{\mathrm{P}} \in \mathbb{R}^{c \times h \times w}$ from the input image by ResNet [12]. Then, three upsampling modules increases the spatial size of $\mathbf{F}_{\mathrm{P}}$ by 8 times, while changing channel dimension from $c = 2048$ to $c' = 256$. Each upsampling module consists of deconvolutional layer, 2D batch normalization layer [13], and ReLU function. The upsampled features are used to compute lixel-based 1D human pose heatmaps, as illustrated in Fig. 3 (a). We obtain x- and y-axis 1D human pose heatmaps as follows:

$$\mathbf{P}^{\mathrm{H},x} = f_{\mathrm{P}}^{\mathrm{1D},x}(\mathrm{avg}^y(f_{\mathrm{P}}^{\mathrm{up}}(\mathbf{F}_{\mathrm{P}}))) \quad \text{and} \quad \mathbf{P}^{\mathrm{H},y} = f_{\mathrm{P}}^{\mathrm{1D},y}(\mathrm{avg}^x(f_{\mathrm{P}}^{\mathrm{up}}(\mathbf{F}_{\mathrm{P}}))), \qquad (1)$$

where $f_{\mathrm{P}}^{\mathrm{up}}$ denotes the three upsampling modules of the PoseNet. avg^i and $f_{\mathrm{P}}^{\mathrm{1D},i}$ denote i-axis marginalization by averaging and a 1-by-1 1D convolution that changes channel dimension from c' to J for i-axis 1D human pose heatmap estimation, respectively.

We obtain z-axis 1D human pose heatmaps as follows:

$$\mathbf{P}^{\mathrm{H},z} = f_{\mathrm{P}}^{\mathrm{1D},z}(\psi(f_{\mathrm{P}}(\mathrm{avg}^{x,y}(\mathbf{F}_{\mathrm{P}})))), \qquad (2)$$

where f_{P} and $\psi \colon \mathbb{R}^{c'D} \to \mathbb{R}^{c' \times D}$ denote a building block and reshape function, respectively. The building block consists of a fully-connected layer, 1D batch normalization layer, and ReLU function, and it changes the activation size from c to $c'D$. D denotes depth discretization size and is equal to $8h = 8w$. We convert the discretized heatmaps of $\mathcal{P}^{\mathrm{H}}$ to continuous coordinates $\mathbf{P}^{\mathrm{C}} = [\mathbf{p}^{\mathrm{C},x}, \mathbf{p}^{\mathrm{C},y}, \mathbf{p}^{\mathrm{C},z}] \in \mathbb{R}^{J \times 3}$ by soft-argmax [41].

3.2   MeshNet

The MeshNet has a similar network architecture with that of the PoseNet. Instead of taking the input image $\mathbf{I}$, MeshNet takes a pre-computed image feature from the PoseNet $\tilde{\mathbf{F}}_{\mathrm{P}}$ and 3D Gaussian heatmap $\mathbf{P}^{\mathrm{H}_{\mathrm{G}}} \in \mathbb{R}^{J \times D \times 8h \times 8w}$. $\tilde{\mathbf{F}}_{\mathrm{P}}$ is the input of the first residual block of the PoseNet whose spatial dimension is $8h \times 8w$. $\mathbf{P}^{\mathrm{H}_{\mathrm{G}}}$ is obtained from $\mathbf{P}^{\mathrm{C}}$ as follows:

$$\mathbf{P}^{\mathrm{H}_{\mathrm{G}}}(j, z, y, x) = \exp\left(-\frac{(x - \mathbf{p}_j^{\mathrm{C},x})^2 + (y - \mathbf{p}_j^{\mathrm{C},y})^2 + (z - \mathbf{p}_j^{\mathrm{C},z})^2}{2\sigma^2}\right), \qquad (3)$$

where $\mathbf{p}_j^{\mathrm{C},x}$, $\mathbf{p}_j^{\mathrm{C},y}$ and $\mathbf{p}_j^{\mathrm{C},z}$ are jth joint x-, y-, and z-axis coordinates from $\mathbf{P}^{\mathrm{C}}$, respectively. σ is set to 2.5.

From $\mathbf{P}^{\mathrm{H}_{\mathrm{G}}}$ and $\tilde{\mathbf{F}}_{\mathrm{P}}$, we obtain image feature $\mathbf{F}_{\mathrm{M}}$ as follows:

$$\mathbf{F}_{\mathrm{M}} = \mathrm{ResNet}_{\mathrm{M}}(f_{\mathrm{M}}(\psi(\mathbf{P}^{\mathrm{H}_{\mathrm{G}}}) \oplus \tilde{\mathbf{F}}_{\mathrm{P}})), \qquad (4)$$

where $\psi \colon \mathbb{R}^{J \times D \times 8h \times 8w} \to \mathbb{R}^{JD \times 8h \times 8w}$ and $\oplus$ denote reshape function and concatenation along the channel dimension, respectively. f_{M} is a convolutional block that consists of a 3-by-3 convolutional layer, 2D batch normalization layer, and

ReLU function. It changes the channel dimension of the input to the input channel dimension of the first residual block of the ResNet. ResNet$_M$ is the ResNet starting from the first residual block.

From the $\mathbf{F}_M$, MeshNet outputs three lixel-based 1D heatmaps of all mesh vertices $\mathcal{M}^H = \{\mathbf{M}^{H,x}, \mathbf{M}^{H,y}, \mathbf{M}^{H,z}\}$ in an exactly the same manner with that of PoseNet, as illustrated in Fig. 3 (a). Likewise heatmaps of PoseNet, $\mathbf{M}^{H,x}$ and $\mathbf{M}^{H,y}$ are defined in x- and y-axis of the image space, while $\mathbf{M}^{H,z}$ is defined in root joint-relative depth space. We obtain x- and y-axis 1D human mesh heatmaps as follows:

$$\mathbf{M}^{H,x} = f_M^{1D,x}(\mathrm{avg}^y(f_M^{up}(\mathbf{F}_M))) \quad \text{and} \quad \mathbf{M}^{H,y} = f_M^{1D,y}(\mathrm{avg}^x(f_M^{up}(\mathbf{F}_M))), \quad (5)$$

where f_M^{up} denotes the three upsampling modules of the MeshNet. $f_M^{1D,i}$ denote a 1-by-1 1D convolution that changes channel dimension from c' to V for i-axis 1D human mesh heatmap estimation, respectively. Figure 3 (b) shows visualized $f_M^{up}(\mathbf{F}_M)$, $\mathbf{M}^{H,x}$, and $\mathbf{M}^{H,y}$.

We obtain z-axis 1D human mesh heatmaps as follows:

$$\mathbf{M}^{H,z} = f_M^{1D,z}(\psi(f_M(\mathrm{avg}^{x,y}(\mathbf{F}_M)))), \quad (6)$$

where f_M and $\psi \colon \mathbb{R}^{c'D} \to \mathbb{R}^{c' \times D}$ denote a building block and reshape function, respectively. The building block consists of a fully-connected layer, 1D batch normalization layer, and ReLU function, and it changes the activation size from c to $c'D$. Likewise we did in the PoseNet, we convert the discretized heatmaps of $\mathcal{M}^H$ to continuous coordinates $\mathbf{M}^C = [\mathbf{m}^{C,x}, \mathbf{m}^{C,y}, \mathbf{m}^{C,z}] \in \mathbb{R}^{V \times 3}$ by soft-argmax [41].

3.3   Final 3D Human Pose and Mesh

The final 3D human mesh $\mathbf{M}$ and pose $\mathbf{P}$ are obtained as follows:

$$\mathbf{M} = \Pi(\mathbf{T}^{-1}\mathbf{M}^C + \mathbf{R}) \quad \text{and} \quad \mathbf{P} = \mathcal{J}\mathbf{M}, \quad (7)$$

where Π, $\mathbf{T}^{-1}$, and $\mathbf{R} \in \mathbb{R}^{1 \times 3}$ denote camera back-projection, inverse affine transformation (i.e., 2D crop and resize), and z-axis offset whose element is a depth of the root joint, respectively. $\mathbf{R}$ is obtained from RootNet [30]. We use normalized camera intrinsic parameters if not available following Moon et al. [30]. $\mathcal{J} \in \mathbb{R}^{J \times V}$ is a joint regression matrix defined in SMPL or MANO model.

3.4   Loss Functions

PoseNet Pose Loss. To train the PoseNet, we use $L1$ loss function defined as follows:

$$L_{\mathrm{pose}}^{\mathrm{PoseNet}} = \|\mathbf{P}^C - \mathbf{P}^{C*}\|_1, \quad (8)$$

where $*$ indicates groundtruth. z-axis loss becomes zero if z-axis groundtruth is unavailable.

MeshNet Pose Loss. To train the MeshNet to predict mesh vertex aligned with body joint locations, we use $L1$ loss function defined as follows:

$$L_{\text{pose}}^{\text{MeshNet}} = \|\mathcal{J}\mathbf{M}^{\text{C}} - \mathbf{P}^{\text{C}*}\|_1, \tag{9}$$

where $*$ indicates groundtruth. z-axis loss becomes zero if z-axis groundtruth is unavailable.

Mesh Vertex Loss. To train the MeshNet to output mesh vertex heatmaps, we use $L1$ loss function defined as follows:

$$L_{\text{vertex}} = \|\mathbf{M}^{\text{C}} - \mathbf{M}^{\text{C}*}\|_1, \tag{10}$$

where $*$ indicates groundtruth. z-axis loss becomes zero if z axis groundtruth is unavailable.

Mesh Normal Vector Loss. Following Wang et al. [43], we supervise normal vector of predicted mesh to get visually pleasing mesh result. The $L1$ loss function for normal vector supervision is defined as follows:

$$L_{\text{normal}} = \sum_f \sum_{\{i,j\}\subset f} \left| \left\langle \frac{\mathbf{m}_i^{\text{C}} - \mathbf{m}_j^{\text{C}}}{\|\mathbf{m}_i^{\text{C}} - \mathbf{m}_j^{\text{C}}\|_2}, n_f^* \right\rangle \right|, \tag{11}$$

where f and n_f indicate a mesh face and unit normal vector of face f, respectively. $\mathbf{m}_i^{\text{C}}$ and $\mathbf{m}_j^{\text{C}}$ denote ith and jth vertex coordinates of $\mathbf{M}^{\text{C}}$, respectively. n_f^* is computed from $\mathbf{M}^{\text{C}*}$, where $*$ denotes groundtruth. The loss becomes zero if groundtruth 3D mesh is unavailable.

Mesh Edge Length Loss. Following Wang et al. [43], we supervise edge length of predicted mesh to get visually pleasing mesh result. The $L1$ loss function for edge length supervision is defined as follows:

$$L_{\text{edge}} = \sum_f \sum_{\{i,j\}\subset f} = |\|\mathbf{m}_i^{\text{C}} - \mathbf{m}_j^{\text{C}}\|_2 - \|\mathbf{m}_i^{\text{C}*} - \mathbf{m}_j^{\text{C}*}\|_2|, \tag{12}$$

where f and $*$ indicate mesh face and groundtruth, respectively. $\mathbf{m}_i^{\text{C}}$ and $\mathbf{m}_j^{\text{C}}$ denote ith and jth vertex coordinates of $\mathbf{M}^{\text{C}}$, respectively. The loss becomes zero if groundtruth 3D mesh is unavailable.

We train our I2L-MeshNet in an end-to-end manner using all the five loss functions as follows:

$$L = L_{\text{pose}}^{\text{PoseNet}} + L_{\text{pose}}^{\text{MeshNet}} + L_{\text{vertex}} + \lambda L_{\text{normal}} + L_{\text{edge}}, \tag{13}$$

where $\lambda = 0.1$ is a weight of L_{normal}. For the stable training, we do not backpropagate gradients before $\mathbf{P}^{\text{HG}}$.

4   Implementation Details

PyTorch [33] is used for implementation. The backbone part is initialized with the publicly released ResNet-50 [12] pre-trained on the ImageNet dataset [40], and the weights of the remaining part are initialized by Gaussian distribution with $\sigma = 0.001$. The weights are updated by the Adam optimizer [20] with a mini-batch size of 48. To crop the human region from the input image, we use groundtruth bounding box in both of training and testing stages following previous works [18,21,22]. When the bounding box is not available in the testing stage, we trained and tested Mask R-CNN [11] to get the bounding box. The cropped human image is resized to 256×256, thus $D = 64$ and $h = w = 8$. Data augmentations including scaling ($\pm 25\%$), rotation ($\pm 60°$), random horizontal flip, and color jittering ($\pm 20\%$) is performed in training. The initial learning rate is set to 10^{-4} and reduced by a factor of 10 at the 10th epoch. We train our model for 12 epochs with three NVIDIA RTX 2080Ti GPUs, which takes 36 h for training. Our I2L-MeshNet runs at a speed of 25 frames per second (fps).

5   Experiment

5.1   Datasets and Evaluation Metrics

Human3.6M. Human3.6M [14] contains 3.6M video frames with 3D joint coordinate annotations. Because of the license problem, previously used groundtruth SMPL parameters of the Human3.6M are inaccessible. Alternatively, we used SMPLify-X [34] to obtain groundtruth SMPL parameters. Please see the supplementary material for a detailed description of SMPL parameters of the Human3.6M. MPJPE and PA MPJPE are used for the evaluation [30], which is Euclidean distance (mm) between predicted and groundtruth 3D joint coordinates after root joint alignment and further rigid alignment, respectively.

3DPW. 3DPW [26] contains 60 video sequences captured mostly in outdoor conditions. We use this dataset only for evaluation on its defined test set following Kolotouros et al. [21]. The same evaluation metrics with Human3.6M (*i.e.*, MPJPE and PA MPJPE) are used, following Kolotouros et al. [21].

FreiHAND. FreiHAND [8] contains real-captured 130K training images and 4K test images with MANO pose and shape parameters. The evaluation is performed at an online server. Following Zimmermann et al. [8], we report PA MPVPE, PA MPJPE, and F-scores.

MSCOCO. MSCOCO [24] contains large-scale in-the-wild images with 2D bounding box and human joint coordinates annotations. We fit SMPL using SMPLify-X [34] on the groundtruth 2D poses, and used the fitted meshes as groundtruth 3D meshes. This dataset is used only for the training.

MuCo-3DHP. MuCo-3DHP [28] is generated by compositing the existing MPI-INF-3DHP 3D [27]. 200K frames are composited, and half of them have augmented backgrounds. We used images of MSCOCO dataset that do not include

Table 1. The MPJPE, the number of parameters, and the GPU memory usage comparison between various target representations on Human3.6M.

Targets	Spatial	Uncertainty	MPJPE	No. param.	GPU mem.
SMPL param.	✗	✗	100.3	91M	4.3 GB
xyz coord	✗	✗	114.3	117M	5.4 GB
xyz lixel hm. wo. spatial	✗	✓	92.6	82M	4.5 GB
xyz lixel hm. (ours)	✓	✓	**86.2**	**73M**	**4.6 GB**

Table 2. The MPJPE and the GPU memory usage comparison between various heatmap representations on Human3.6M.

Targets	Mem. complx.	Resolution	MPJPE	GPU mem.
xyz voxel hm.	$\mathcal{O}(VD^3)$	$8 \times 8 \times 8$	102.8	4.3 GB
		$16 \times 16 \times 16$	-	OOM
xy pixel hm. + z lixel hm.	$\mathcal{O}(VD^2)$	$8 \times 8, 8$	97.9	3.5 GB
		$32 \times 32, 32$	89.4	5.7 GB
		$64 \times 64, 64$	-	OOM
xyz lixel hm. (ours)	$\mathcal{O}(VD)$	$8, 8, 8$	100.2	3.4 GB
		$32, 32, 32$	94.8	4.0 GB
		$64, 64, 64$	**86.2**	**4.6 GB**

humans to augment the backgrounds following Moon et al. [30]. This dataset is used only for the training.

5.2 Ablation Study

All models for the ablation study are trained and tested on Human3.6M. As Human3.6M is the most widely used large-scale benchmark, we believe this dataset is suitable for the ablation study.

Benefit of the Heatmap-Based Mesh Estimation. To demonstrate the benefit of the heatmap-based mesh estimation, we compare models with various target representations of the human mesh, such as SMPL parameters, vertex coordinates, and heatmap. Table 1 shows MPJPE, the number of parameters, and the GPU memory usage comparison between models with different targets. The table shows that our heatmap-based mesh estimation network achieves the lowest errors while using the smallest number of the parameters and consuming small GPU memory.

The superiority of our heatmap-based mesh estimation network is in two folds. First, it can model the uncertainty of the prediction. To validate this, we trained two models that estimate the camera-centered mesh vertex coordinates directly and estimates lixel-based 1D heatmap of the coordinates using two fully-connected layers. Note that the targets of the two models are the same, but

Table 3. The MPJPE and PA MPJPE comparison between various network cascading strategies on Human3.6M.

Settings	3D pose	MPJPE	PA MPJPE
MeshNet	✗	86.2	59.8
PoseNet+MeshNet (ours)	✓	**81.8**	**58.0**
MeshNet	GT	25.5	17.1

their representations are different. As the first network regresses the coordinates directly, it cannot model the uncertainty on the prediction, while the latter one can because of the heatmap target representation. However, both do not preserve the spatial relationship in the input image because of the global average pooling and the fully-connected layers. As the second and third row of the table show, modeling uncertainty on the prediction significantly decreases the errors while using a smaller number of parameters. In addition, it achieves lower errors than the SMPL parameter regression model, which is the most widely used target representation but cannot model the uncertainty.

Second, it preserves the spatial relationship between pixels in the input image. The final model estimates the x- and y-axis heatmaps of each mesh vertex in a fully-convolutional way, thus preserves the spatial relationship. It achieves the best performance with the smallest number of the parameters while consuming similar GPU memory usage compared with SMPL parameter regression method that requires the least amount of GPU memory.

In Table 1, all models have the same network architecture with our I2L-MeshNet except for the final output prediction part. We removed PoseNet from all models, and the remaining MeshNet directly estimates targets from the input image **I**. Except for the last row (ours), all settings output targets using two fully-connected layers. We followed the training details of [18,21] for the SMPL parameter estimation.

Lixel-Based vs. Pixel-Based vs. Voxel-Based Heatmap. To demonstrate the effectiveness of the lixel-based 1D heatmap over other heatmap representations, we train three models that predict lixel-based, pixel-based, and voxel-based heatmap, respectively. We used the same network architecture (*i.e.*, MeshNet of the I2L-MeshNet) for all settings except for the final prediction part. Their networks directly predict the heatmaps from the input image. x-, y-, and z-axis of each heatmap represents the same coordinates. Table 2 shows memory complexity, heatmap resolution, MPJPE and GPU memory usage comparison between models that predict different target representations of human mesh. The table shows that our lixel-based one achieves the lowest error while consuming small GPU memory usage.

Table 4. The MPJPE and PA MPJPE comparison on Human3.6M and 3DPW. All methods are trained on Human3.6M and MSCOCO.

Methods	Human3.6M		3DPW	
	MPJPE	PA MPJPE	MPJPE	PA MPJPE
HMR [18]	153.2	85.5	300.4	137.2
GraphCMR [22]	78.3	59.5	126.5	80.1
SPIN [21]	72.9	51.9	113.1	71.7
I2L-MeshNet (Ours)	**55.7**	**41.7**	**95.4**	**60.8**

Table 5. The MPJPE and PA MPJPE comparison on Human3.6M. Each method is trained on different datasets.

Methods	MPJPE	PA MPJPE
SMPLify [4]	–	82.3
Lassner [23]	–	93.9
HMR [18]	88.0	56.8
NBF [32]	–	59.9
Pavlakos [37]	–	75.9
Kanazawa [19]	–	56.9
GraphCMR [22]	–	50.1
Arnab [2]	77.8	54.3
SPIN [21]	–	41.1
I2L-MeshNet (Ours)	**55.7**	41.7

Table 6. The MPJPE and PA MPJPE comparison on 3DPW. Each method is trained on different datasets.

Methods	MPJPE	PA MPJPE
HMR [18]	–	81.3
Kanazawa [19]	–	72.6
GraphCMR [22]	–	70.2
Arnab [2]	–	72.2
SPIN [21]	–	59.2
I2L-MeshNet (Ours)	**93.2**	**58.6**
I2L-MeshNet (Ours) + SMPL regress	99.6	62.9

Compared with the pixel-based and voxel-based heatmap, our lixel-based one consumes much less amount of GPU memory under the same resolution. The $8 \times 8 \times 8$ voxel-based heatmap requires similar GPU memory usage with that of $64, 64, 64$ lixel-based one, and we found that enlarging the voxel-based heatmap size from it is not allowed in current GPU memory limit (*i.e.*, 12 GB). The pixel-based heatmap is more efficient than the voxel-based one; however still much inefficient than our lixel-based one, which makes enlarging from $32 \times 32, 32$ impossible. This inefficient memory usage limits the heatmap resolution; however, we found that the heatmap resolution is critical for dense mesh vertex localization. On the other hand, the memory complexity of our lixel-based heatmap is a linear function with respect to D; thus, we can predict high-resolution heatmap for each mesh vertex. The memory efficiency will be more important when a high-resolution human mesh model is used.

Under the same resolution, the combination of pixel-based heatmap and lixel-based heatmap achieves the best performance. We think that estimating the voxel-based heatmap involves too many parameters at a single output layer,

Table 7. The PA MPVPE, PA MPJPE, and F-scores comparison between state-of-the-art methods and the proposed I2L-MeshNet on FreiHAND. The checkmark denotes a method use groundtruth information during inference time.

Methods	PA MPVPE	PA MPJPE	F@5 mm	F@15 mm	GT scale
Hasson et al. [10]	13.2	-	0.436	0.908	✓
Boukhayma et al. [5]	13.0	-	0.435	0.898	✓
FreiHAND [8]	10.7	-	0.529	0.935	✓
I2L-MeshNet (Ours)	**7.6**	**7.4**	**0.681**	**0.973**	✗

which makes it produce high errors. In addition, lixel-based heatmap inherently involves spatial ambiguity arises from marginalizing the 2D feature map to 1D, which can be a possible reason for worse performance than the combined one.

Benefit of the Cascaded PoseNet and MeshNet. To demonstrate the benefit of the cascaded PoseNet and MeshNet, we trained and tested three networks using various network cascading strategy. First, we removed PoseNet from the I2L-MeshNet. The remaining MeshNet directly predicts lixel-based 1D heatmap of each mesh vertex from the input image. Second, we trained I2L-MeshNet, which has cascaded PoseNet and MeshNet architecture. Third, to check the upper bound accuracy with respect to the output of the PoseNet, we fed the groundtruth 3D human pose instead of the output of the PoseNet to the MeshNet in both training and testing stage. Table 3 shows utilizing the output of the PoseNet (the second row) achieves better accuracy compared with using only MeshNet (the first row) to estimate the human mesh. Interestingly, passing the groundtruth 3D human pose to the MeshNet (the last row) significantly improves the performance compared with all the other settings. This indicates that improving the 3D human pose estimation network can be one important way to improve 3D human mesh estimation accuracy.

5.3   Comparison with State-of-the-art Methods

Human3.6M and 3DPW. We compare the MPJPE and PA MPJPE of our I2L-MeshNet with previous state-of-the-art 3D human body pose and mesh estimation methods on Human3.6M and 3DPW test set. As each previous work trained their network on different training sets, we report the 3D errors in two ways.

First, we train all methods on Human3.6M and MSCOCO and report the errors in Table 4. The previous state-of-the-art methods [18,21,22] are trained from their officially released codes. The table shows that our I2L-MeshNet significantly outperforms previous methods by a large margin on both datasets.

Second, we report the 3D errors of previous methods from their papers and ours in Table 5 and Table 6. Each network of the previous method is trained on the different combinations of datasets, which include Human3.6M, MSCOCO, MPII [1], LSP [15], LSP-Extended [16], UP [23], and MPI-INF-3DHP [27]. We used MuCo-3DHP for the additional training dataset for the evaluation on 3DPW dataset. We also report the 3D errors from a additional SMPL parameter regression module following Kolotouros et al. [22]. The tables show that the performance gap between ours and the previous state-of-the-art method [21] is significantly reduced.

The reason for the reduced performance gap is that previous model-based state-of-the-art methods [18,21] can get benefit from many in-the-wild 2D human pose datasets [15,16,24] by a 2D pose-based weak supervision. As the human body or hand model assumes a prior distribution between the human model parameters (*i.e.*, 3D joint rotations and identity vector) and 3D joint/mesh coordinates, the 2D pose-based weak supervision can provide gradients in depth axis, calculated from the prior distribution. Although the weak supervision still suffers from the depth ambiguity, utilizing in-the-wild images can be highly beneficial because the images have diverse appearances compared with those of the lab-recorded 3D datasets [14,27,28]. On the other hand, model-free approaches, including the proposed I2L-MeshNet, do not assume any prior distribution, therefore hard to get benefit from the weak supervision. Based on the two comparisons, we can draw two important conclusions.

- The model-free approaches achieve higher accuracy than the model-based ones when trained on the same datasets that provide groundtruth 3D human poses and meshes.
- The model-based approaches can achieve higher accuracy by utilizing additional in-the-wild 2D pose data without requiring the 3D supervisions.

We think that a larger number of accurately aligned in-the-wild image-3D mesh data can significantly boost the accuracy of the model-free approaches. The iterative fitting [4,34], neural network [17], or their combination [21] can be used to obtain more data. This can be an important future research direction, and we leave this as future work.

FreiHAND. We compare MPVPE and F-scores of our I2L-MeshNet with previous state-of-the-art 3D human hand pose and mesh estimation methods [5,8,10]. We trained Mask R-CNN [11] on FreiHAND train images to get the hand bounding box of test images. Table 7 shows that the proposed I2L-MeshNet significantly outperforms all previous works without groundtruth scale information during the inference time. We additionally report MPJPE in the table.

6   Conclusion

We propose a I2L-MeshNet, image-to-lixel prediction network for accurate 3D human pose and mesh estimation from a single RGB image. We convert the output of the network to the lixel-based 1D heatmap, which preserves the spatial relationship in the input image and models uncertainty of the prediction. Our lixel-based 1D heatmap requires much less GPU memory usage under the same heatmap resolution while producing better accuracy compared with a widely used voxel-based 3D heatmap. Our I2L-MeshNet outperforms previous 3D human pose and mesh estimation methods on various 3D human pose and mesh datasets. We hope our method can give useful insight to the following model-free 3D human pose and mesh estimation approaches.

Acknowledgments. This work was supported by IITP grant funded by the Ministry of Science and ICT of Korea (No. 2017-0-01780), and Hyundai Motor Group through HMG-SNU AI Consortium fund (No. 5264-20190101).

References

1. Andriluka, M., Pishchulin, L., Gehler, P., Schiele, B.: 2D human pose estimation: New benchmark and state of the art analysis. In: CVPR (2014)
2. Arnab, A., Doersch, C., Zisserman, A.: Exploiting temporal context for 3D human pose estimation in the wild. In: CVPR (2019)
3. Baek, S., Kim, K.I., Kim, T.K.: Pushing the envelope for RGB-based dense 3D hand pose estimation via neural rendering. In: CVPR (2019)
4. Bogo, F., Kanazawa, A., Lassner, C., Gehler, P., Romero, J., Black, M.J.: Keep it SMPL: automatic estimation of 3D human pose and shape from a single image. In: ECCV (2016)
5. Boukhayma, A., de Bem, R., Torr, P.H.: 3D hand shape and pose from images in the wild. In: CVPR (2019)
6. Chen, Y., Wang, Z., Peng, Y., Zhang, Z., Yu, G., Sun, J.: Cascaded pyramid network for multi-person pose estimation. In: CVPR (2018)
7. Choi, H., Moon, G., Lee, K.M.: Pose2Mesh: graph convolutional network for 3D human pose and mesh recovery from a 2D human pose. In: ECCV (2020)
8. Zimmermann, C., Ceylan, D., Yang, J., Russell, B., Argus, M., Brox, T.: Frei-HAND: a dataset for markerless capture of hand pose and shape from single RGB images. In: ICCV (2019)
9. Ge, L., et al.: 3D hand shape and pose estimation from a single RGB image. In: CVPR (2019)
10. Hasson, Y., et al.: Learning joint reconstruction of hands and manipulated objects. In: CVPR (2019)
11. He, K., Gkioxari, G., Dollár, P., Girshick, R.: Mask R-CNN. In: ICCV (2017)
12. He, K., Zhang, X., Ren, S., Sun, J.: Deep residual learning for image recognition. In: CVPR (2016)
13. Ioffe, S., Szegedy, C.: Batch Normalization: accelerating deep network training by reducing internal covariate shift. In: ICML (2015)
14. Ionescu, C., Papava, D., Olaru, V., Sminchisescu, C.: Human3.6M: large scale datasets and predictive methods for 3D human sensing in natural environments. In: TPAMI (2014)
15. Johnson, S., Everingham, M.: Clustered pose and nonlinear appearance models for human pose estimation. In: BMVC (2010)
16. Johnson, S., Everingham, M.: Learning effective human pose estimation from inaccurate annotation. In: CVPR (2011)
17. Joo, H., Neverova, N., Vedaldi, A.: Exemplar fine-tuning for 3D human pose fitting towards in-the-wild 3D human pose estimation. arXiv preprint arXiv:2004.03686 (2020)

18. Kanazawa, A., Black, M.J., Jacobs, D.W., Malik, J.: End-to-end recovery of human shape and pose. In: CVPR (2018)
19. Kanazawa, A., Zhang, J.Y., Felsen, P., Malik, J.: Learning 3D human dynamics from video. In: CVPR (2019)
20. Kingma, D.P., Ba, J.: Adam: a method for stochastic optimization. In: ICLR (2014)
21. Kolotouros, N., Pavlakos, G., Black, M.J., Daniilidis, K.: Learning to reconstruct 3D human pose and shape via model-fitting in the loop. In: ICCV (2019)
22. Kolotouros, N., Pavlakos, G., Daniilidis, K.: Convolutional mesh regression for single-image human shape reconstruction. In: CVPR (2019)
23. Lassner, C., Romero, J., Kiefel, M., Bogo, F., Black, M.J., Gehler, P.V.: Unite the people: closing the loop between 3D and 2D human representations. In: CVPR (2017)
24. Lin, T.Y., et al.: Microsoft COCO: common objects in context. In: ECCV (2014)
25. Loper, M., Mahmood, N., Romero, J., Pons-Moll, G., Black, M.J.: SMPL: a skinned multi-person linear model. In: ACM TOG (2015)
26. von Marcard, T., Henschel, R., Black, M.J., Rosenhahn, B., Pons-Moll, G.: Recovering accurate 3D human pose in the wild using IMUs and a moving camera. In: ECCV (2018)
27. Mehta, D., et al.: Monocular 3D human pose estimation in the wild using improved CNN supervision. In: 3DV (2017)
28. Mehta, D., et al.: Single-shot multi-person 3D pose estimation from monocular RGB. In: 3DV (2018)
29. Moon, G., Chang, J.Y., Lee, K.M.: V2V-PoseNet: voxel-to-voxel prediction network for accurate 3D hand and human pose estimation from a single depth map. In: CVPR (2018)
30. Moon, G., Chang, J.Y., Lee, K.M.: Camera distance-aware top-down approach for 3D multi-person pose estimation from a single RGB image. In: ICCV (2019)
31. Newell, A., Yang, K., Deng, J.: Stacked hourglass networks for human pose estimation. In: ECCV (2016)
32. Omran, M., Lassner, C., Pons-Moll, G., Gehler, P., Schiele, B.: Neural body fitting: unifying deep learning and model based human pose and shape estimation. In: 3DV. IEEE (2018)
33. Paszke, A., et al.: Automatic differentiation in pytorch (2017)
34. Pavlakos, G., et al.: Expressive body capture: 3D hands, face, and body from a single image. In: CVPR (2019)
35. Pavlakos, G., Kolotouros, N., Daniilidis, K.: TexturePose: supervising human mesh estimation with texture consistency. In: ICCV (2019)
36. Pavlakos, G., Zhou, X., Derpanis, K.G., Daniilidis, K.: Coarse-to-fine volumetric prediction for single-image 3D human pose. In: CVPR (2017)
37. Pavlakos, G., Zhu, L., Zhou, X., Daniilidis, K.: Learning to estimate 3D human pose and shape from a single color image. In: CVPR (2018)
38. Rogez, G., Weinzaepfel, P., Schmid, C.: LCR-Net: localization-classification-regression for human pose. In: CVPR (2017)
39. Romero, J., Tzionas, D., Black, M.J.: Embodied hands: modeling and capturing hands and bodies together. In: ACM TOG (2017)
40. Russakovsky, O., et al.: Imagenet large scale visual recognition challenge. In: IJCV (2015)
41. Sun, X., Xiao, B., Wei, F., Liang, S., Wei, Y.: Integral human pose regression. In: ECCV (2018)
42. Tompson, J.J., Jain, A., LeCun, Y., Bregler, C.: Joint training of a convolutional network and a graphical model for human pose estimation. In: NeurIPS (2014)

43. Wang, N., Zhang, Y., Li, Z., Fu, Y., Liu, W., Jiang, Y.G.: Pixel2Mesh: generating 3D mesh models from single RGB images. In: ECCV (2018)
44. Xiao, B., Wu, H., Wei, Y.: Simple baselines for human pose estimation and tracking. In: ECCV (2018)
45. Xu, Y., Zhu, S.C., Tung, T.: DenseRaC: joint 3D pose and shape estimation by dense render-and-compare. In: ICCV (2019)

Pose2Mesh: Graph Convolutional Network for 3D Human Pose and Mesh Recovery from a 2D Human Pose

Hongsuk Choi, Gyeongsik Moon, and Kyoung Mu Lee[✉]

ECE and ASRI, Seoul National University, Seoul, Korea
{redarknight,mks0601,kyoungmu}@snu.ac.kr

Abstract. Most of the recent deep learning-based 3D human pose and mesh estimation methods regress the pose and shape parameters of human mesh models, such as SMPL and MANO, from an input image. The first weakness of these methods is the overfitting to image appearance, due to the domain gap between the training data captured from controlled settings such as a lab, and in-the-wild data in inference time. The second weakness is that the estimation of the pose parameters is quite challenging due to the representation issues of 3D rotations. To overcome the above weaknesses, we propose Pose2Mesh, a novel graph convolutional neural network (GraphCNN)-based system that estimates the 3D coordinates of human *mesh vertices* directly from the *2D human pose*. The 2D human pose as input provides essential human body articulation information without image appearance. Also, the proposed system avoids the representation issues, while fully exploiting the mesh topology using GraphCNN in a coarse-to-fine manner. We show that our Pose2Mesh significantly outperforms the previous 3D human pose and mesh estimation methods on various benchmark datasets. The codes are publicly available(https://github.com/hongsukchoi/Pose2Mesh_RELEASE).

1 Introduction

3D human pose and mesh estimation aims to recover 3D human joint and mesh vertex locations simultaneously. It is a challenging task due to the depth and scale ambiguity, and the complex human body and hand articulation. There have been diverse approaches to address this problem, and recently, deep learning-based methods have shown noticeable performance improvement.

Most of the deep learning-based methods rely on human mesh models, such as SMPL [32] and MANO [48]. They can be generally categorized into a model-based approach and a model-free approach. The model-based approach trains

H. Choi and G. Moon—Equal contribution.

Electronic supplementary material The online version of this chapter (https://doi.org/10.1007/978-3-030-58571-6_45) contains supplementary material, which is available to authorized users.

A. Vedaldi et al. (Eds.): ECCV 2020, LNCS 12352, pp. 769–787, 2020.
https://doi.org/10.1007/978-3-030-58571-6_45

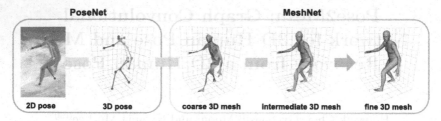

Fig. 1. The overall pipeline of Pose2Mesh.

a network to predict the model parameters and generates a human mesh by decoding them [4–6,23,27,29,41,42,46]. On the contrary, the model-free approach regresses the coordinates of a 3D human mesh directly [13,28]. Both approaches compute the 3D human pose by multiplying the output mesh with a joint regression matrix, which is defined in the human mesh models [32,48].

Although the recent deep learning-based approaches have shown significant improvement, they have two major drawbacks. First, they cannot benefit from the train data of the controlled settings [19,22], which have accurate 3D annotations, without image appearance overfitting. This overfitting occurs because image appearance in the controlled settings, such as monotonous backgrounds and simple clothes of subjects, is quite different from that of in-the-wild images. The second drawback is that the pose parameters of the human mesh models might not be an appropriate regression target, as addressed in Kolotouros et al. [28]. The SMPL pose parameters, for example, represent 3D rotations in an axis-angle, which can suffer from the non-unique problem (*i.e.*, periodicity). While many works [23,29,41] tried to avoid the periodicity by using a rotation matrix as the prediction target, it still has a non-minimal representation issue.

To resolve the above issues, we propose Pose2Mesh, a graph convolutional system that recovers 3D human pose and mesh from the 2D human pose, in a model-free fashion. It has two advantages over existing methods. First, the input 2D human pose makes the proposed system free from the overfitting related to image appearance, while providing essential geometric information on the human articulation. In addition, the 2D human pose can be estimated accurately from in-the-wild images, since many well-performing methods [9,38,52,59] are trained on large-scale in-the-wild 2D human pose datasets [1,30]. The second advantage is that Pose2Mesh avoids the representation issues of the pose parameters, while exploiting the human mesh topology (*i.e.*, face and edge information). It directly regresses the 3D coordinates of mesh vertices using a graph convolutional neural network (GraphCNN) with graphs constructed from the mesh topology.

We designed Pose2Mesh in a cascaded architecture, which consists of PoseNet and MeshNet. PoseNet lifts the 2D human pose to the 3D human pose. MeshNet takes both 2D and 3D human poses to estimate the 3D human mesh in a coarse-to-fine manner. During the forward propagation, the mesh features are initially processed in a coarse resolution and gradually upsampled to a fine resolution. Figure 1 depicts the overall pipeline of the system.

The experimental results show that the proposed Pose2Mesh outperforms the previous state-of-the-art 3D human pose and mesh estimation methods [23, 27, 28] on various publicly available 3D human body and hand datasets [19, 33, 62]. Particularly, our Pose2Mesh provides the state-of-the-art result on in-the-wild dataset [33], even when it is trained only on the controlled setting dataset [19].

We summarize our contributions as follows.

- We propose a novel system, Pose2Mesh, that recovers 3D human pose and mesh from the 2D human pose. It is free from overfitting to image appearance, and thus generalize well on in-the-wild data.
- Our Pose2Mesh directly regresses 3D coordinates of a human mesh using GraphCNN. It avoids representation issues of the model parameters and leverages the pre-defined mesh topology.
- We show that Pose2Mesh outperforms previous 3D human pose and mesh estimation methods on various publicly available datasets.

2 Related Works

3D Human Body Pose Estimation. Current 3D human body pose estimation methods can be categorized into two approaches according to the input type: an image-based approach and a 2D pose-based approach. The image-based approach takes an RGB image as an input for 3D body pose estimation. Sun et al. [53] proposed to use compositional loss, which exploits the joint connection structure. Sun et al. [54] employed soft-argmax operation to regress the 3D coordinates of body joints in a differentiable way. Sharma et al. [50] incorporated a generative model and depth ordering of joints to predict the most reliable 3D pose that corresponds to the estimated 2D pose.

The 2D pose-based approach lifts the 2D human pose to the 3D space. Martinez et al. [34] introduced a simple network that consists of consecutive fully-connected layers, which lifts the 2D human pose to the 3D space. Zhao et al. [60] developed a semantic GraphCNN to use spatial relationships between joint coordinates. Our work follows the 2D pose-based approach, to make the Pose2Mesh more robust to the domain difference between the controlled environment of the training set and in-the-wild environment of the testing set.

3D Human Body and Hand Pose and Mesh Estimation. A model-based approach trains a neural network to estimate the human mesh model parameters [32, 48]. It has been widely used for the 3D human mesh estimation, since it does not necessarily require 3D annotation for mesh supervision. Pavlakos et al. [46] proposed a system that could be only supervised by 2D joint coordinates and silhouette. Omran et al. [41] trained a network with 2D joint coordinates, which takes human part segmentation as input. Kanazawa et al. [23] utilized adversarial loss to regress plausible SMPL parameters. Baek et al. [4]

trained a CNN to estimate parameters of the MANO model using neural renderer [25]. Kolotouros et al. [27] introduced a self-improving system that consists of SMPL parameter regressor and iterative fitting framework [5].

Recently, the advance of fitting frameworks [5,44] has motivated a model-free approach, which estimates human mesh coordinates directly. It enabled researchers to obtain 3D mesh annotation, which is essential for the model-free methods, from in-the-wild data. Kolotouros et al. [28] proposed a GraphCNN, which learns the deformation of the template body mesh to the target body mesh. Ge et al. [13] adopted a GraphCNN to estimate vertices of hand mesh. Moon et al. [40] proposed a new heatmap representation, called lixel, to recover 3D human meshes.

Our Pose2Mesh differs from the above methods, which are image-based, in that it uses the 2D human pose as an input. It can benefit from the data with 3D annotations, which are captured from controlled settings [19,22], without the image appearance overfitting.

GraphCNN for Mesh Processing. Recently, many methods consider a mesh as a graph structure and process it using the GraphCNN, since it can fully exploit mesh topology compared with simple stacked fully-connected layers. Wang et al. [58] adopted a GraphCNN to learn a deformation from an initial ellipsoid mesh to the target object mesh in a coarse-to-fine manner. Verma et al. [56] proposed a novel graph convolution operator and evaluated it on the shape correspondence problem. Ranjan et al. [47] also proposed a GraphCNN-based VAE, which learns a latent space of the human face meshes in a hierarchical manner.

3   PoseNet

3.1   Synthesizing Errors on the Input 2D Pose

PoseNet estimates the root joint-relative 3D pose $\mathbf{P}^{3D} \in \mathbb{R}^{J \times 3}$ from the 2D pose, where J denotes the number of human joints. We define the root joint of the human body and hand as pelvis and wrist, respectively. However, the estimated 2D pose often contains errors [49], especially under severe occlusions or challenging poses. To make PoseNet robust to the errors, we synthesize 2D input poses by adding realistic errors on the ground truth 2D pose, following [38,39], during the training stage. We represent the estimated 2D pose or the synthesized 2D pose as $\mathbf{P}^{2D} \in \mathbb{R}^{J \times 2}$.

3.2   2D Input Pose Normalization

We apply standard normalization to $\mathbf{P}^{2D}$, following [39,57]. For this, we subtract the mean from $\mathbf{P}^{2D}$ and divide it by the standard deviation, which becomes $\bar{\mathbf{P}}^{2D}$. The mean and the standard deviation of $\mathbf{P}^{2D}$ represent the 2D location and scale of the subject, respectively. This normalization is necessary because $\mathbf{P}^{3D}$ is independent of scale and location of the 2D input pose $\mathbf{P}^{2D}$.

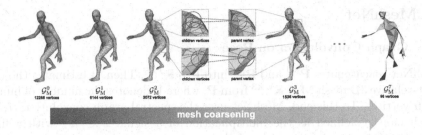

Fig. 2. The coarsening process initially generates multiple coarse graphs from $\mathcal{G}_M$, and adds fake nodes without edges to each graph, following [11]. The numbers of vertices range from 96 to 12288 and from 68 to 1088, for body and hand meshes, respectively.

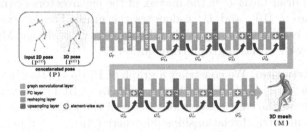

Fig. 3. The network architecture of MeshNet.

3.3 Network Architecture

The architecture of the PoseNet is based on that of [34,39]. The normalized 2D input pose $\bar{\mathbf{P}}^{2D}$ is converted to a 4096-dimensional feature vector through a fully-connected layer. Then, it is fed to the two residual blocks [18]. Finally, the output feature vector of the residual blocks is converted to $(3J)$-dimensional vector, which represents $\mathbf{P}^{3D}$, by a full-connected layer.

3.4 Loss Function

We train the PoseNet by minimizing $L1$ distance between the predicted 3D pose $\mathbf{P}^{3D}$ and groundtruth. The loss function L_{pose} is defined as follows:

$$L_{\text{pose}} = \|\mathbf{P}^{3D} - \mathbf{P}^{3D*}\|_1, \tag{1}$$

where the asterisk indicates the groundtruth.

4   MeshNet

4.1   Graph Convolution on Pose

MeshNet concatenates $\bar{\mathbf{P}}^{2D}$ and $\mathbf{P}^{3D}$ into $\mathbf{P} \in \mathbb{R}^{J \times 5}$. Then, it estimates the root joint-relative 3D mesh $\mathbf{M} \in \mathbb{R}^{V \times 3}$ from $\mathbf{P}$, where V denotes the number of human mesh vertices. To this end, MeshNet uses the spectral graph convolution [7,51], which can be defined as the multiplication of a signal $x \in \mathbb{R}^N$ with a filter $g_\theta = diag(\theta)$ in Fourier domain as follows:

$$g_\theta * x = U g_\theta U^T x, \tag{2}$$

where graph Fourier basis U is the matrix of the eigenvectors of the normalized graph Laplacian L [10], and $U^T x$ denotes the graph Fourier transform of x. Specifically, to reduce the computational complexity, we design MeshNet to be based on Chebysev spectral graph convolution [11].

Graph Construction. We construct a graph of $\mathbf{P}$, $\mathcal{G}_P = (\mathcal{V}_P, A_P)$, where $\mathcal{V}_P = \mathbf{P} = \{\mathbf{p}_i\}_{i=1}^J$ is a set of J human joints, and $A_P \in \{0,1\}^{J \times J}$ is an adjacency matrix. A_P defines the edge connections between the joints based on the human skeleton and symmetrical relationships [8], where $(A_P)_{ij} = 1$ if joints i and j are the same or connected, and $(A_P)_{ij} = 0$ otherwise. The normalized Laplaican is computed as $L_P = I_J - D_P^{-1/2} A_P D_P^{-1/2}$, where I_J is the identity matrix, and D_P is the diagonal matrix which represents the degree of each joint in $\mathcal{V}_P$ as $(D_P)_{ij} = \sum_j (A_P)_{ij}$. The scaled Laplacian is computed as $\tilde{L}_P = 2L_P/\lambda_{max} - I_J$.

Spectral Convolution on Graph. Then, MeshNet performs the spectral graph convolution on $\mathcal{G}_P$, which is defined as follows:

$$F_{out} = \sum_{k=0}^{K-1} T_k(\tilde{L}_P) F_{in} \Theta_k, \tag{3}$$

where $F_{in} \in \mathbb{R}^{J \times f_{in}}$ and $F_{out} \in \mathbb{R}^{J \times f_{out}}$ are the input and output feature maps respectively, $T_k(x) = 2x T_{k-1}(x) - T_{k-2}(x)$ is the Chebysev polynomial [15] of order k, and $\Theta_k \in \mathbb{R}^{f_{in} \times f_{out}}$ is the kth Chebysev coefficient matrix, whose elements are the trainable parameters of the graph convolutional layer. f_{in} and f_{out} are the input and output feature dimensions respectively. The initial input feature map F_{in} is $\mathbf{P}$ in practice, where $f_{in} = 5$. This graph convolution is K-localized, which means at most K-hop neighbor nodes from each node are affected [11,26], since it is a K-order polynomial in the Laplacian. Our MeshNet sets $K = 3$ for all graph convolutional layers following [13].

4.2   Coarse-to-fine Mesh Upsampling

We gradually upsample $\mathcal{G}_P$ to the graph of $\mathbf{M}$, $\mathcal{G}_M = (\mathcal{V}_M, A_M)$, where $\mathcal{V}_M = \mathbf{M} = \{\mathbf{m}_i\}_{i=1}^V$ is a set of V human mesh vertices, and $A_M \in \{0,1\}^{V \times V}$ is an adjacency matrix defining edges of the human mesh. To this end, we apply the graph coarsening [12] technique to $\mathcal{G}_M$, which creates various resolutions of graphs, $\{\mathcal{G}_M^c = (\mathcal{V}_M^c, A_M^c)\}_{c=0}^C$, where C denotes the number of coarsening steps, following Defferrard et al. [11]. Figure 2 shows the coarsening process and a balanced binary tree structure of mesh graphs, where the ith vertex in $\mathcal{G}_M^{c+1}$ is a parent node of the $2i-1$th and $2i$th vertices in $\mathcal{G}_M^c$, and $2|\mathcal{V}_M^{c+1}| = |\mathcal{V}_M^c|$. i starts from 1. The final output of MeshNet is $\mathcal{V}_M$, which is converted from $\mathcal{V}_M^0$ by a pre-defined indices mapping. During the forward propagation, MeshNet first upsamples the $\mathcal{G}_P$ to the coarsest mesh graph $\mathcal{G}_M^C$ by reshaping and a fully-connected layer. Then, it performs the spectral graph convolution on each resolution of mesh graphs as follows:

$$F_{\text{out}} = \sum_{k=0}^{K-1} T_k(\tilde{L}_M^c) F_{\text{in}} \Theta_k, \tag{4}$$

where $\tilde{L}_M^c$ denotes the scaled Laplacian of $\mathcal{G}_M^c$, and the other notations are defined in the same manner as Eq. 3. Following [13], MeshNet performs mesh upsampling by copying features of each parent vertex in $\mathcal{G}_M^{c+1}$ to the corresponding children vertices in $\mathcal{G}_M^c$. The upsampling process is defined as follows:

$$F_c = \psi(F_{c+1}^T)^T, \tag{5}$$

where $F_c \in \mathbb{R}^{\mathcal{V}_M^c \times f_c}$ is the first feature map of $\mathcal{G}_M^c$, $F_{c+1} \in \mathbb{R}^{\mathcal{V}_M^{c+1} \times f_{c+1}}$ is the last feature map of $\mathcal{G}_M^{c+1}$, $\psi \colon \mathbb{R}^{f_{c+1} \times \mathcal{V}_M^{c+1}} \to \mathbb{R}^{f_{c+1} \times \mathcal{V}_M^c}$ denotes a nearest-neighbor upsampling function, and f_c and f_{c+1} are the feature dimensions of vertices in F_c and F_{c+1} respectively. The nearest upsampling function copies the feature of the ith vertex in $\mathcal{G}_M^{c+1}$ to the $2i-1$th and $2i$th vertices in $\mathcal{G}_M^c$. To facilitate the learning process, we additionally incorporate a residual connection between each resolution. Figure 3 shows the overall architecture of MeshNet.

4.3   Loss Function

To train our MeshNet, we use four loss functions.

Vertex Coordinate Loss. We minimize $L1$ distance between the predicted 3D mesh coordinates $\mathbf{M}$ and groundtruth, which is defined as follows:

$$L_{\text{vertex}} = \|\mathbf{M} - \mathbf{M}^*\|_1, \tag{6}$$

where the asterisk indicates the groundtruth.

Joint Coordinate Loss. We use a $L1$ loss function between the groundtruth root-relative 3d pose and the 3D pose regressed from $\mathbf{M}$, to train our MeshNet to estimate mesh vertices aligned with joint locations. The 3D pose is calculated as $\mathcal{J}\mathbf{M}$, where $\mathcal{J} \in \mathbb{R}^{J \times V}$ is a joint regression matrix defined in SMPL or MANO model. The loss function is defined as follows:

$$L_{\text{joint}} = \|\mathcal{J}\mathbf{M} - \mathbf{P}^{3D^*}\|_1, \tag{7}$$

where the asterisk indicates the groundtruth.

Surface Normal Loss. We supervise normal vectors of an output mesh surface to be consistent with groundtruth. This consistency loss improves surface smoothness and local details [58]. Thus, we define the loss function L_{normal} as follows:

$$L_{\text{normal}} = \sum_f \sum_{\{i,j\} \subset f} \left| \left\langle \frac{\mathbf{m}_i - \mathbf{m}_j}{\|\mathbf{m}_i - \mathbf{m}_j\|_2}, n_f^* \right\rangle \right|, \tag{8}$$

where f and n_f^* denote a triangle face in the human mesh and a groundtruth unit normal vector of f, respectively. $\mathbf{m}_i$ and $\mathbf{m}_j$ denote the ith and jth vertices in f.

Surface Edge Loss. We define edge length consistency loss between predicted and groundtruth edges, following [58]. The edge loss is effective in recovering smoothness of hands, feet, and a mouth, which have dense vertices. The loss function L_{edge} is defined as follows:

$$L_{\text{edge}} = \sum_f \sum_{\{i,j\} \subset f} \left| \|\mathbf{m}_i - \mathbf{m}_j\|_2 - \|\mathbf{m}_i^* - \mathbf{m}_j^*\|_2 \right|, \tag{9}$$

where f and the asterisk denote a triangle face in the human mesh and the groundtruth, respectively. $\mathbf{m}_i$ and $\mathbf{m}_j$ denote ith and jth vertex in f.

We define the total loss of our MeshNet, L_{mesh}, as a weighted sum of all four loss functions:

$$L_{\text{mesh}} = \lambda_v L_{\text{vertex}} + \lambda_j L_{\text{joint}} + \lambda_n L_{\text{normal}} + \lambda_e L_{\text{edge}}, \tag{10}$$

where $\lambda_v = 1$, $\lambda_j = 1$, $\lambda_n = 0.1$, and $\lambda_e = 20$.

5 Implementation Details

PyTorch [43] is used for implementation. We first pre-train our PoseNet, and then train the whole network, Pose2Mesh, in an end-to-end manner. Empirically, our two-step training strategy gives better performance than the one-step training. The weights are updated by the Rmsprop optimization [55] with a mini-batch size of 64. We pre-train PoseNet 60 epochs with a learning rate 10^{-3}. The learning rate is reduced by a factor of 10 after the 30th epoch. After integrating the pre-trained PoseNet to Pose2Mesh, we train the whole network 15 epochs with a learning rate 10^{-3}. The learning rate is reduced by a factor of 10 after the 12th epoch. In addition, we set λ_e to 0 until 7 epoch on the second training stage, since it tends to cause local optima at the early training phase. We used four NVIDIA RTX 2080 Ti GPUs for Pose2Mesh training, which took at least a half day and at most two and a half days, depending on the training datasets. In inference time, we use 2D pose outputs from Sun et al. [52] and Xiao et al. [59]. They run at 5 fps and 67 fps respectively, and our Pose2Mesh runs at 37 fps. Thus, the proposed system can process from 4 fps to 22 fps in practice, which shows the applicability to real-time applications.

6 Experiment

6.1 Dataset and Evaluation Metric

Human3.6M. Human3.6M [19] is a large-scale indoor 3D body pose benchmark, which consists of 3.6M video frames. The groundtruth 3D poses are obtained using a motion capture system, but there are no groundtruth 3D meshes. As a result, for 3D mesh supervision, most of the previous 3D pose and mesh estimation works [23,27,28] used pseudo-groundtruth obtained from Mosh [31]. However, because of the license issue, the pseudo-groundtruth from Mosh is not currently publicly accessible. Thus, we generate new pseudo-groundtruth 3D meshes by fitting SMPL parameters to the 3D groundtruth poses using SMPLify-X [44]. For the fair comparison, we trained and tested previous state-of-the-art methods on the obtained groundtruth using their officially released code. Following [23,45], all methods are trained on 5 subjects (S1, S5, S6, S7, S8) and tested on 2 subjects (S9, S11).

We report our performance for the 3D pose using two evaluation metrics. One is mean per joint position error (MPJPE) [19], which measures the Euclidean distance in millimeters between the estimated and groundtruth joint coordinates, after aligning the root joint. The other one is PA-MPJPE, which calculates MPJPE after further alignment (*i.e.*, Procrustes analysis (PA) [14]). $\mathcal{J}\mathbf{M}$ is used for the estimated joint coordinates. We only evaluate 14 joints out of 17 estimated joints following [23,27,28,46].

3DPW. 3DPW [33] is captured from in-the-wild and contains 3D body pose and mesh annotations. It consists of 51K video frames, and IMU sensors are leveraged to acquire the groundtruth 3D pose and mesh. We only use the test set of 3DPW for evaluation following [27]. MPJPE and mean per vertex position error (MPVPE) are used for evaluation. 14 joints from $\mathcal{J}\mathbf{M}$, whose joint set follows that of Human3.6M, are evaluated for MPJPE as above. MPVPE measures the Euclidean distance in millimeters between the estimated and groundtruth vertex coordinates, after aligning the root joint.

COCO. COCO [30] is an in-the-wild dataset with various 2D annotations such as detection and human joints. To exploit this dataset on 3D mesh learning, Kolotouros et al. [27] fitted SMPL parameters to 2D joints using SMPLify [5]. Following them, we use the processed data for training.

MuCo-3DHP. MuCo-3DHP [36] is synthesized from the existing MPI-INF-3DHP 3D single-person pose estimation dataset [35]. It consists of 200K frames, and half of them have augmented backgrounds. For the background augmentation, we use images of COCO that do not include humans to follow Moon et al. [37]. Following them, we use this dataset only for the training.

FreiHAND. FreiHAND [62] is a large-scale 3D hand pose and mesh dataset. It consists of a total of 134K frames for training and testing. Following Zimmermann et al. [62], we report PA-MPVPE, F-scores, and additionally PA-MPJPE of Pose2Mesh. $\mathcal{J}\mathbf{M}$ is evaluated for the joint errors.

Table 1. The performance comparison between four combinations of regression target and network design tested on Human3.6M. 'no. param.' denotes the number of parameters of a network, which estimates SMPL parameters or vertex coordinates from the output of PoseNet.

Target\Network	FC			GraphCNN		
	MPJPE	PA-MPJPE	no. param	MPJPE	PA-MPJPE	no. param
SMPL param	72.8	55.5	17.3M	79.1	59.1	13.5M
Vertex coord	119.6	95.1	37.5M	**64.9**	**48.7**	**8.8M**

6.2   Ablation Study

To analyze each component of the proposed system, we trained different networks on Human3.6M, and evaluated on Human3.6M and 3DPW. The test 2D input poses used in Human3.6M and 3DPW evaluation are outputs from Integral Regression [54] and HRNet [52] respectively, using groundtruth bounding boxes.

Regression Target and Network Design. To demonstrate the effectiveness of regressing the 3D mesh vertex coordinates using GraphCNN, we compare MPJPE and PA-MPJPE of four different combinations of the regression target and the network design in Table 1. First, *vertex-GraphCNN*, our Pose2Mesh, substantially improves the joint errors compared to *vertex-FC*, which regresses vertex coordinates with a network of fully-connected layers. This proves the importance of exploiting the human mesh topology with GraphCNN, when estimating the 3D vertex coordinates. Second, *vertex-GraphCNN* provides better performance than both networks estimating SMPL parameters, while maintaining the considerably smaller number of network parameters. Taken together, the effectiveness of our mesh coordinate regression scheme using GraphCNN is clearly justified.

In this comparison, the same PoseNet and cascaded architecture are employed for all networks. On top of the PoseNet, *vertex-FC* and *param-FC* used a series of fully-connected layers, whereas *param-GraphCNN* added fully-connected layers on top of Pose2Mesh. For the fair comparison, when training *param-FC* and *param-GraphCNN*, we also supervised the reconstructed mesh from the predicted SMPL parameters with L_{vertex} and L_{joint}. The networks estimating SMPL parameters incorporated Zhou et al.'s method [61] for continuous rotations following [27].

Coarse-to-Fine Mesh Upsampling. We compare a coarse-to-fine mesh upsampling scheme and a direct mesh upsampling scheme. The direct upsampling method performs graph convolution on the lowest resolution mesh until the middle layer of MeshNet, and then directly upsamples it to the highest one (*e.g.*, 96 to 12288 for the human body mesh). While it has the same number of graph convolution layers and almost the same number of parameters, our coarse-to-fine model consumes half as much GPU memory and runs 1.5 times

Table 2. The performance comparison on Human3.6M between two upsampling schems. GPU mem. and fps denote the required memory during training and fps in inference time respectively.

Method	GPU mem	fps	MPJPE
Direct	10G	24	65.3
coarse-to-fine	**6G**	**37**	**64.9**

Table 3. The MPJPE comparison between four architectures tested on 3DPW.

Architecture	MPJPE
2D→mesh	101.1
2D→3D→mesh	103.2
2D→3D+2D→mesh	**100.5**

Table 4. The upper bounds of the two different graph convolutional networks that take a 2D pose and a 3D pose. Tested on Human3.6M.

Test input	Architecture	MPJPE	PA-MPJPE
2D pose GT	2D→mesh	55.5	38.4
3D pose from [37]	3D→mesh	56.3	43.2
3D pose GT	**3D→mesh**	**29.0**	**23.0**

faster than the direct upsampling method. It is because graph convolution on the highest resolution takes much more time and memory than graph convolution on lower resolutions. In addition, the coarse-to-fine upsampling method provides a slightly lower joint error, as shown in Table 2. These results confirm the effectiveness of our coarse-to-fine upsampling strategy.

Cascaded Architecture Analysis. We analyze the cascaded architecture of Pose2Mesh to demonstrate its validity in Table 3. To be specific, we construct (a) a GraphCNN that directly takes a 2D pose, (b) a cascaded network that predicts mesh coordinates from a 3D pose from pretrained PoseNet, and (c) our Pose2Mesh. All methods are both trained by synthesized 2D poses. First, (a) outperforms (b), which implies a 3D pose output from PoseNet may lack geometry information in the 2D input pose. If we concatenate the 3D pose output with the 2D input pose as (c), it provides the lowest errors. This explains that depth information in 3D poses could positively affect 3D mesh estimation.

To further verify the superiority of the cascaded architecture, we explore the upper bounds of (a) and (d) a GraphCNN that takes a 3D pose in Table 4. To this end, we fed the groundtruth 2D pose and 3D pose to (a) and (d) as test inputs, respectively. Apparently, since the input 3D pose contains additional depth information, the upper bound of (d) is considerably higher than that of (a). We also fed state-of-the-art 3D pose outputs from [37] to (d), to validate the practical potential for performance improvement. Surprisingly, the performance is comparable to the upper bound of (a). Thus, our Pose2Mesh will substantially outperform (a) a graph convolution network that directly takes a 2D pose, if we can improve the performance of PoseNet.

In summary, the above results prove the validity of our cascaded architecture of Pose2Mesh.

Table 5. The accuracy comparison between state-of-the-art methods and Pose2Mesh on Human3.6M. The dataset names on top are training sets.

Method	Human3.6M		Human3.6M + COCO	
	MPJPE	PA-MPJPE	MPJPE	PA-MPJPE
HMR [23]	184.7	88.4	153.2	85.5
GraphCMR [28]	148.0	104.6	78.3	59.5
SPIN [27]	85.6	55.6	72.9	51.9
Pose2Mesh (Ours)	**64.9**	**48.7**	**67.9**	**49.9**

Table 6. The accuracy comparison between state-of-the-art methods and Pose2Mesh on 3DPW. The dataset names on top are training sets.

Method	Human3.6M			Human3.6M + COCO		
	MPJPE	PA-MPJPE	MPVPE	MPJPE	PA-MPJPE	MPVPE
HMR [23]	377.3	165.7	481.0	300.4	137.2	406.8
GraphCMR [28]	332.5	177.4	380.8	126.5	80.1	144.8
SPIN [27]	313.8	156.0	344.3	113.1	71.7	122.8
Pose2Mesh (Simple [59])	101.8	64.2	119.1	92.3	61.0	110.5
Pose2Mesh (HR [52])	**100.5**	**63.0**	**117.5**	**91.4**	**60.1**	**109.3**

6.3   Comparison with State-of-the-art Methods

Human3.6M. We compare our Pose2Mesh with the previous state-of-the-art 3D body pose and mesh estimation methods on Human3.6M in Table 5. First, when we train all methods only on Human3.6M, our Pose2Mesh significantly outperforms other methods. However, when we train the methods additionally on COCO, the performance of the previous baselines increases, but that of Pose2Mesh slightly decreases. The performance gain of other methods is a well-known phenomenon [54] among image-based methods, which tend to generalize better when trained with diverse images from in-the-wild. Whereas, our Pose2Mesh does not benefit from more images in the same manner, since it only takes the 2D pose. We analyze the reason for the performance drop is that the test set and train set of Human3.6M have similar poses, which are from the same action categories. Thus, overfitting the network to the poses of Human3.6M can lead to better accuracy. Nevertheless, in both cases, our Pose2Mesh outperforms the previous methods in both MPJPE and PA-MPJPE. The test 2D input poses for Pose2Mesh are estimated by the method of Sun et al. [54] trained on MPII dataset [2], using groundtruth bounding boxes.

3DPW. We compare MPJPE, PA-MPJPE, and MPVPE of our Pose2Mesh with the previous state-of-the-art 3D body pose and mesh estimation works on 3DPW, which is an in-the-wild dataset, in Table 6. First, when the image-based methods are trained only on Human3.6M, they give extremely high errors. This is because the image-based methods are overfitted to the image appearance of Human3.6M.

Table 7. The accuracy comparison between state-of-the-art methods and Pose2Mesh on FreiHAND.

Method	PA-MPVPE	PA-MPJPE	F@5 mm	F@15 mm
Hasson et al. [16]	13.2	–	0.436	0.908
Boukhayma et al. [6]	13.0	–	0.435	0.898
FreiHAND [62]	10.7	–	0.529	0.935
Pose2Mesh (Ours)	**7.8**	**7.7**	**0.674**	**0.969**

In fact, since Human3.6M is an indoor dataset from the controlled setting, the image features from it are very different from in-the-wild image features. On the other hand, since our Pose2Mesh takes a 2D human pose as an input, it does not overfit to the particular image appearance. As a result, the proposed system gives far better performance on in-the-wild images from 3DPW, even when it is trained only on Human3.6M while other methods are additionally trained on COCO. By utilizing accurate 3D annotations of the lab-recorded 3D datasets [19] without image appearance overfitting, Pose2Mesh does not require 3D data captured from in-the-wild. This property can reduce data capture burden significantly because capturing 3D data from in-the-wild is very challenging. The test 2D input poses for Pose2Mesh are estimated by HRNet [52] and Simple [59] trained on COCO, using groundtruth bounding boxes. The average precision (AP) of [52] and [59] are 85.1 and 82.8 on 3DPW test set, 72.1 and 70.4 on COCO validation set, respectively.

FreiHAND. We present the comparison between our Pose2Mesh and other state-of-the-art 3D hand pose and mesh estimation works in Table 7. The proposed system outperforms other methods in various metrics, including PA-MPVPE and F-scores. The test 2D input poses for Pose2Mesh are estimated by HRNet [52] trained on FreiHAND [62], using bounding boxes from Mask R-CNN [17] with ResNet-50 backbone [18].

Comparison with Different Train Sets. We report MPJPE and PA-MPJPE of Pose2Mesh trained on Human3.6M, COCO, and MuCo-3DHP, and other methods trained on different train sets in Table 8. The train sets include Human3.6M, COCO, MPII [2] , LSP [20], LSP-Extended [21], UP [29], and MPI-INF-3DHP [35]. Each method is trained on a different subset of them. In the table, the errors of [23,27,28] decrease by a large margin compared to the errors in Table 5 and 6. Although this shows that the image-based methods can improve the generalizability with weak-supervision on in-the-wild 2D pose datasets, Pose2Mesh still provides the lowest errors in 3DPW, which is the in-the-wild benchmark. This suggests that avoiding the image appearance overfitting while benefiting from the accurate 3D annotations from the controlled setting datasets is important. We measured the PA-MPJPE of Pose2Mesh on Human3.6M by testing only on the frontal camera set, following the previous works [23,27,28].

Table 8. The accuracy comparison between state-of-the-art methods and Pose2Mesh on Human3.6M and 3DPW. Different train sets are used.

Method	Human3.6M		3DPW	
	MPJPE	PA-MPJPE	MPJPE	PA-MPJPE
SMPLify [5]	–	82.3	–	–
Lassner et al. [29]	–	93.9	–	–
HMR [23]	88.0	56.8	–	81.3
NBF [41]	–	59.9	–	–
Pavlakos et al. [46]	–	75.9	–	–
Kanazawa et al. [24]	-	56.9	-	72.6
GraphCMR [28]	–	50.1	–	70.2
Arnab et al. [3]	77.8	54.3	–	72.2
SPIN [27]	–	**41.1**	–	59.2
Pose2Mesh (Ours)	**64.9**	47.0	**89.2**	**58.9**

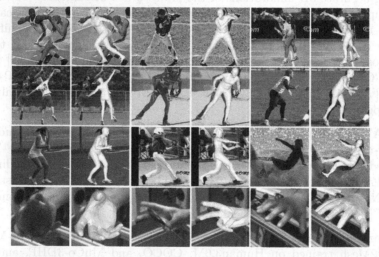

Fig. 4. Qualitative results of the proposed Pose2Mesh. First to third rows: COCO, fourth row: FreiHAND.

Figure 4 shows the qualitative results on COCO validation set and FreiHAND test set. Our Pose2Mesh outputs visually decent human meshes without post-processing, such as model fitting [28]. More qualitative results can be found in the supplementary material.

7   Discussion

Although the proposed system benefits from the image appearance invariant property of the 2D input pose, it could be challenging to recover various 3D *shapes* solely from the pose. While it may be true, we found that the 2D pose still carries necessary information to reason the corresponding 3D shape to some degree. In the literature, SMPLify [5] has experimentally verified that under the canonical body pose, utilizing 2D pose significantly drops the body shape fitting error compared to using the mean body shape. We show that Pose2Mesh can recover various body shapes from the 2D pose in the supplementary material.

8   Conclusion

We propose a novel and general system, Pose2Mesh, for 3D human mesh and pose estimation from a 2D human pose. The 2D input pose enables the system to benefit from the data captured from the controlled settings without the image appearance overfitting. The model-free approach using GraphCNN allows it to fully exploit mesh topology, while avoiding the representation issues of the 3D rotation parameters. We plan to enhance the shape recover capability of Pose2Mesh using denser keypoints or part segmentation, while maintaining the above advantages.

Acknowledgements. This work was supported by IITP grant funded by the Ministry of Science and ICT of Korea (No.2017-0-01780), and Hyundai Motor Group through HMG-SNU AI Consortium fund (No. 5264-20190101).

References

1. Andriluka, M., et al.: Posetrack: a benchmark for human pose estimation and tracking. In: The IEEE Conference on Computer Vision and Pattern Recognition (CVPR) (2018)
2. Andriluka, M., Pishchulin, L., Gehler, P., Schiele, B.: 2D human pose estimation: new benchmark and state of the art analysis. In: The IEEE Conference on Computer Vision and Pattern Recognition (CVPR) (2014)
3. Arnab, A., Doersch, C., Zisserman, A.: Exploiting temporal context for 3D human pose estimation in the wild. In: The IEEE Conference on Computer Vision and Pattern Recognition (CVPR) (2019)
4. Baek, S., In Kim, K., Kim, T.K.: Pushing the envelope for RGB-based dense 3D hand pose estimation via neural rendering. In: The IEEE Conference on Computer Vision and Pattern Recognition (CVPR) (2019)
5. Bogo, F., Kanazawa, A., Lassner, C., Gehler, P., Romero, J., Black, M.J.: Keep it SMPL: automatic estimation of 3D human pose and shape from a single image. In: The European Conference on Computer Vision (ECCV) (2016)
6. Boukhayma, A., de Bem, R., Torr, P.H.: 3D hand shape and pose from images in the wild. In: The IEEE Conference on Computer Vision and Pattern Recognition (CVPR) (2019)

7. Bruna, J., Zaremba, W., Szlam, A., Lecun, Y.: Spectral networks and locally connected networks on graphs. In: The International Conference on Learning Representations (ICLR) (2014)
8. Cai, Y., et al.: Exploiting spatial-temporal relationships for 3D pose estimation via graph convolutional networks. In: The IEEE International Conference on Computer Vision (ICCV) (2019)
9. Chen, Y., Wang, Z., Peng, Y., Zhang, Z., Yu, G., Sun, J.: Cascaded pyramid network for multi-person pose estimation. In: The IEEE Conference on Computer Vision and Pattern Recognition (CVPR) (2018)
10. Chung, F.R.K.: Spectral Graph Theory. American Mathematical Society, Pawtucket (1997)
11. Defferrard, M., Bresson, X., Vandergheynst, P.: Convolutional neural networks on graphs with fast localized spectral filtering. In: Advances in Neural Information Processing Systems (NIPS), vol. 29 (2016)
12. Dhillon, I.S., Guan, Y., Kulis, B.: Weighted graph cuts without eigenvectors a multilevel approach. IEEE Trans. Pattern Anal. Mach. Intell. (TPAMI) **29**, 1944–1957 (2007)
13. Ge, L., et al.: 3D hand shape and pose estimation from a single RGB image. In: The IEEE Conference on Computer Vision and Pattern Recognition (CVPR) (2019)
14. Gower, J.C.: Generalized procrustes analysis. Psychometrika **40**, 33–51 (1975). https://doi.org/10.1007/BF02291478
15. Hammond, D., Vandergheynst, P., Gribonval, R.: Wavelets on graphs via spectral-graph theory. Appl. Comput. Harmonic Anal. **30**, 129–150 (2009)
16. Hasson, Y., et al.: Learning joint reconstruction of hands and manipulated objects. In: The IEEE Conference on Computer Vision and Pattern Recognition (CVPR) (2019)
17. He, K., Gkioxari, G., Dollár, P., Girshick, R.: Mask R-CNN. In: The IEEE International Conference on Computer Vision (ICCV) (2017)
18. He, K., Zhang, X., Ren, S., Sun, J.: Deep residual learning for image recognition. In: The IEEE Conference on Computer Vision and Pattern Recognition (CVPR) (2016)
19. Ionescu, C., Papava, D., Olaru, V., Sminchisescu, C.: Human 3.6m: large scale datasets and predictive methods for 3D human sensing in natural environments. IEEE Trans. Pattern Anal. Mach. Intell. (TPAMI) **36**, 1325–1339 (2014)
20. Johnson, S., Everingham, M.: Clustered pose and nonlinear appearance models for human pose estimation. In: British Machine Vision Conference (BMVC). Citeseer (2010)
21. Johnson, S., Everingham, M.: Learning effective human pose estimation from inaccurate annotation. In: The IEEE Conference on Computer Vision and Pattern Recognition (CVPR) (2011)
22. Joo, H., et al.: Panoptic studio: a massively multiview system for social motion capture. In: The IEEE International Conference on Computer Vision (ICCV) (2015)
23. Kanazawa, A., Black, M.J., Jacobs, D.W., Malik, J.: End-to-end recovery of human shape and pose. In: The IEEE Conference on Computer Vision and Pattern Recognition (CVPR) (2018)
24. Kanazawa, A., Zhang, J.Y., Felsen, P., Malik, J.: Learning 3D human dynamics from video. In: The IEEE Conference on Computer Vision and Pattern Recognition (CVPR) (2019)
25. Kato, H., Ushiku, Y., Harada, T.: Neural 3D mesh renderer. In: The IEEE Conference on Computer Vision and Pattern Recognition (CVPR) (2018)

26. Kipf, T.N., Welling, M.: Semi-supervised classification with graph convolutional networks. In: The International Conference on Learning Representations (ICLR) (2017)

27. Kolotouros, N., Pavlakos, G., Black, M.J., Daniilidis, K.: Learning to reconstruct 3D human pose and shape via model-fitting in the loop. In: The IEEE International Conference on Computer Vision (ICCV) (2019)

28. Kolotouros, N., Pavlakos, G., Daniilidis, K.: Convolutional mesh regression for single-image human shape reconstruction. In: The IEEE Conference on Computer Vision and Pattern Recognition (CVPR) (2019)

29. Lassner, C., Romero, J., Kiefel, M., Bogo, F., Black, M.J., Gehler, P.V.: Unite the people: Closing the loop between 3D and 2D human representations. In: The IEEE Conference on Computer Vision and Pattern Recognition (CVPR) (2017)

30. Lin, T.-Y., et al.: Microsoft coco: common objects in context. In: Fleet, D., Pajdla, T., Schiele, B., Tuytelaars, T. (eds.) ECCV 2014. LNCS, vol. 8693, pp. 740–755. Springer, Cham (2014). https://doi.org/10.1007/978-3-319-10602-1_48

31. Loper, M., Mahmood, N., Black, M.J.: Mosh: motion and shape capture from sparse markers. In: Special Interest Group on Graphics and Interactive Techniques (SIGGRAPH) (2014)

32. Loper, M., Mahmood, N., Romero, J., Pons-Moll, G., Black, M.J.: SMPL: a skinned multi-person linear model. In: Special Interest Group on Graphics and Interactive Techniques (SIGGRAPH) (2015)

33. von Marcard, T., Henschel, R., Black, M., Rosenhahn, B., Pons-Moll, G.: Recovering accurate 3D human pose in the wild using imus and a moving camera. In: European Conference on Computer Vision (ECCV) (2018)

34. Martinez, J., Hossain, R., Romero, J., Little, J.J.: A simple yet effective baseline for 3D human pose estimation. In: The IEEE International Conference on Computer Vision (ICCV) (2017)

35. Mehta, D., et al.: Monocular 3D human pose estimation in the wild using improved CNN supervision. In: International Conference on 3D Vision (3DV) (2017)

36. Mehta, D., et al.: Single-shot multi-person 3D pose estimation from monocular RGB. In: International Conference on 3D Vision (3DV) (2018)

37. Moon, G., Chang, J.Y., Lee, K.M.: Camera distance-aware top-down approach for 3D multi-person pose estimation from a single RGB image. In: The IEEE International Conference on Computer Vision (ICCV) (2019)

38. Moon, G., Chang, J.Y., Lee, K.M.: Posefix: model-agnostic general human pose refinement network. In: The IEEE Conference on Computer Vision and Pattern Recognition (CVPR) (2019)

39. Moon, G., Chang, J.Y., Lee, K.M.: Absposelifter: absolute 3D human pose lifting network from a single noisy 2D human pose. arXiv preprint arXiv:1910.12029 (2020)

40. Moon, G., Lee, K.M.: I2L-MeshNet: image-to-lixel prediction network for accurate 3D human pose and mesh recovery from a single RGB image. In: The European Conference on Computer Vision (ECCV) (2020)

41. Omran, M., Lassner, C., Pons-Moll, G., Gehler, P., Schiele, B.: Neural body fitting: unifying deep learning and model based human pose and shape estimation. In: International Conference on 3D Vision (3DV) (2018)

42. Panteleris, P., Oikonomidis, I., Argyros, A.: Using a single RGB frame for real time 3D hand pose estimation in the wild. In: IEEE Winter Conference on Applications of Computer Vision (WACV) (2018)

43. Paszke, A., et al.: Automatic differentiation in pytorch (2017)

44. Pavlakos, G., et al.: Expressive body capture: 3D hands, face, and body from a single image. In: The IEEE Conference on Computer Vision and Pattern Recognition (CVPR) (2019)
45. Pavlakos, G., Zhou, X., Derpanis, K.G., Daniilidis, K.: Coarse-to-fine volumetric prediction for single-image 3D human pose. In: The IEEE Conference on Computer Vision and Pattern Recognition (CVPR) (2017)
46. Pavlakos, G., Zhu, L., Zhou, X., Daniilidis, K.: Learning to estimate 3D human pose and shape from a single color image. In: The IEEE Conference on Computer Vision and Pattern Recognition (CVPR) (2018)
47. Ranjan, A., Bolkart, T., Sanyal, S., Black, M.J.: Generating 3D faces using convolutional mesh autoencoders. In: The European Conference on Computer Vision (ECCV) (2018)
48. Romero, J., Tzionas, D., Black, M.J.: Embodied hands: modeling and capturing hands and bodies together. In: Special Interest Group on Graphics and Interactive Techniques (SIGGRAPH) (2017)
49. Ruggero Ronchi, M., Perona, P.: Benchmarking and error diagnosis in multi-instance pose estimation. In: The IEEE International Conference on Computer Vision (ICCV) (2017)
50. Sharma, S., Varigonda, P.T., Bindal, P., Sharma, A., Jain, A.: Monocular 3D human pose estimation by generation and ordinal ranking. In: The IEEE International Conference on Computer Vision (ICCV) (2019)
51. Shuman, D.I., Narang, S.K., Frossard, P., Ortega, A., Vandergheynst, P.: The emerging field of signal processing on graphs: extending high-dimensional data analysis to networks and other irregular domains. IEEE Signal Process. Mag. **30**, 83–98 (2013)
52. Sun, K., Xiao, B., Liu, D., Wang, J.: Deep high-resolution representation learning for human pose estimation. In: The IEEE Conference on Computer Vision and Pattern Recognition (CVPR) (2019)
53. Sun, X., Shang, J., Liang, S., Wei, Y.: Compositional human pose regression. In: The IEEE International Conference on Computer Vision (ICCV) (2017)
54. Sun, X., Xiao, B., Wei, F., Liang, S., Wei, Y.: Integral human pose regression. In: The European Conference on Computer Vision (ECCV) (2018)
55. Tieleman, T., Hinton, G.: Lecture 6.5-RMSPROP: Divide the gradient by a running average of its recent magnitude. COURSERA: Neural Networks for Machine Learning (2012)
56. Verma, N., Boyer, E., Verbeek, J.: Feastnet: feature-steered graph convolutions for 3D shape analysis. In: The IEEE Conference on Computer Vision and Pattern Recognition (CVPR) (2018)
57. Wandt, B., Rosenhahn, B.: Repnet: weakly supervised training of an adversarial reprojection network for 3D human pose estimation. In: The IEEE Conference on Computer Vision and Pattern Recognition (CVPR) (2019)
58. Wang, N., Zhang, Y., Li, Z., Fu, Y., Liu, W., Jiang, Y.G.: Pixel2mesh: generating 3D mesh models from single RGB images. In: The European Conference on Computer Vision (ECCV) (2018)
59. Xiao, B., Wu, H., Wei, Y.: Simple baselines for human pose estimation and tracking. In: The European Conference on Computer Vision (ECCV) (2018)
60. Zhao, L., Peng, X., Tian, Y., Kapadia, M., Metaxas, D.N.: Semantic graph convolutional networks for 3D human pose regression. In: The IEEE Conference on Computer Vision and Pattern Recognition (CVPR) (2019)

61. Zhou, Y., Barnes, C., Lu, J., Yang, J., Li, H.: On the continuity of rotation representations in neural networks. In: The IEEE Conference on Computer Vision and Pattern Recognition (CVPR) (2019)
62. Zimmermann, C., Ceylan, D., Yang, J., Russell, B., Argus, M., Brox, T.: Freihand: A dataset for markerless capture of hand pose and shape from single RGB images. In: The IEEE International Conference on Computer Vision (ICCV) (2019)

ALRe: Outlier Detection for Guided Refinement

Mingzhu Zhu[1], Zhang Gao[2], Junzhi Yu[1(✉)], Bingwei He[3], and Jiantao Liu[3]

[1] BIC-ESAT, College of Engineering, Peking University,
Beijing, People's Republic of China
yujunzhi@pku.edu.cn
[2] Institute of Automation, Chinese Academy of Sciences,
Beijing, People's Republic of China
[3] The Department of Mechanical Engineering, Fuzhou University,
Fuzhou, People's Republic of China

Abstract. Guided refinement is a popular procedure of various image post-processing applications. It produces *output image* based on *input* and *guided images*. *Input images* are usually flawed estimates containing kinds of noises and outliers, which undermine the edge consistency between *input* and *guided images*. As improvements, they are refined into *output images* with similar intensities of *input images* and consistent edges of *guided images*. However, outliers are usually untraceable and simply treated as zero-mean noises, limiting the quality of such refinement. In this paper, we propose a general outlier detection method for guided refinement. We assume local linear relationship between *output* and *guided images* to express the expected edge consistency, based on which, the outlier likelihoods of *input* pixels are measured. The metric is termed as ALRe (anchored linear residual) since it is essentially the residual of local linear regression with an equality constraint exerted on the measured pixel. Valuable features of the ALRe are discussed. Its effectiveness is proven by applications and experiment.

Keywords: Anchored linear residual · Outlier detection · Guided refinement · Local linear assumption · Linear regression

1 Introduction

Many computer vision and image processing applications require to calculate *output images* fusing the intensities of *input images* and partial edges of *guided images*, such as matting [1], guided smoothing [2], depth map restoration [3], transmission and disparity refinements [4,5]. The edges of *input images* are expected to be associated with *guided images*. However, it is usually not the case due to theoretical flaws, missing information or noises. As improvements, *output images* are produced based on global optimizations [3,6,7] or local filters [8–10] to ensure both intensity similarity and edge consistency.

© Springer Nature Switzerland AG 2020
A. Vedaldi et al. (Eds.): ECCV 2020, LNCS 12352, pp. 788–802, 2020.
https://doi.org/10.1007/978-3-030-58571-6_46

Edge consistency is commonly described as *"Output image has an edge only if guided image has an edge"* and controlled in two ways: 1) punishing large edge strength ratios between *output* and *guided images* [2,11]; 2) assuming local linear relationship between *output* and *guided images* [12].

Despite a clear purpose, outliers are rarely handled. Except for some applications whose outliers could be traced based on models [13] or hardwares [5], intensity similarities are mostly measured by L2-norms [10,11]. It implies that all the estimates of *input images* are inliers, and the edge consistency is undermined by zero-mean noises only. This obviously wrong simplification limits the quality of guided refinement.

In this paper, we propose a general outlier detection method for guided refinement referred as ALRe (anchored linear residual). It is shown that the outlier likelihoods provided by ALRe could effectively improve the quality of refinement. It is even comparable to model-based and hardware-based detections. ALRe has three advantages: 1) it does not require any prior knowledge of the application; 2) it has the feature of asymmetry, which exactly expresses the concept of edge consistency; 3) its complexity is $O(N)$ where N is the pixel number.

ALRe is based on the local linear assumption between *output* and *guided images*, which has been proven as an effective and general assumption for guided refinement [1,12]. The more the measured pixel against the assumption, the higher its outlier likelihood. The metric is referred as ALRe because it is based on the residual of local linear regression with an equality constraint exerted on the measured pixel. Compared to linear residual, edge strength ratio and SSIM [14], ALRe has important advantages which are especially suitable for its task.

The remaining contents are arranged as follows. Section 2 surveys guided refinement algorithms, applications and existing solutions for outlier detection. Section 3 proposes the method named ALRe. Section 4 analyzes the relations and differences between ALRe and other applicable methods. Section 5 conducts experiments on various applications and Sect. 6 provides quantitative results. Section 7 gives the conclusion.

2   Related Works

Related works are introduced with respect to four guided refinement algorithms, including WLS (weighted least squares) [11], JBF (joint bilateral filter) [2], GF (guided filter) [12] and WMF (weighted median filter) [15].

WLS (weighted least squares) [11] has a straightforward definition following the concept of guided refinement closely. It is defined as

$$E(q) = \sum_i \underset{\triangle}{w_i}(q_i - p_i)^2 + \lambda \sum_{(i,j) \in J} a_{ij}(q_i - q_j)^2, \tag{1}$$

where p is *input image*, q is *output image*, i is pixel index, $(i,j) \in J$ means pixels i and j are adjacent to each other, λ balances the two terms. There are two kinds of weights in Eq. 1. Smooth weight a_{ij} is negatively correlated with the distance between $\mathbf{I}_i$ and $\mathbf{I}_j$, where $\mathbf{I}$ is *guided image*. Data weights w can be calculated based on the inlier fidelities of p. The weights is not defined in the original [11], but can be easily inserted without increasing complexity.

In the field of haze removal, Fattal [16] proposed color-lines model for transmission estimation, whose outlier likelihoods are related to the variances of fitting lines. Berman *et al.* [13] proposed haze-lines model. Its outlier likelihoods are related to the effective lengths of haze-lines. During the refinement, these likelihoods are used to form the data weights w of Eq. 1, which brings out obvious robustness since pixels not following their models affect the results little. Unfortunately, these outlier detection methods are only applicable to these models, thus can not be generalized to other theories or applications.

JBF [2] is an intuitive and easy-to-implement algorithm for guided refinement. It produces *output images* by smoothing *input images*, thus the intensity similarity is guaranteed. Filter kernels are calculated based on *guided images*, as

$$
\begin{cases}
q_i = \sum_{j \in \Omega_i} K_{ij} p_j \\
K_{ij} = \dfrac{1}{Z_i} w_i s_{ij} c_{ij} \\
s_{ij} = exp\left(-\dfrac{||\mathbf{x}_i - \mathbf{x}_j||^2}{\sigma_s^2} \right) \\
c_{ij} = exp\left(-\dfrac{||\mathbf{I}_i - \mathbf{I}_j||^2}{\sigma_c^2} \right),
\end{cases}
\tag{2}
$$

where $\mathbf{x}$ is pixel coordinate, Z_i is normalizing parameter, Ω_i is the local region centered at pixel i. There are three kinds of weights including data weights w, distance weight s and color weight c. The parameters σ_s and σ_c adjust the sensitivities of the spatial and color similarities respectively. Data weights w can be calculated based on the inlier fidelities of p. The weights is not defined in the original [2], but can be easily inserted without increasing complexity.

In the field of disparity estimation, outliers can be detected by cross check [5], which only accepts estimates bidirectionally supported by stereo matching. Pixels have different estimates between left-to-right and right-to-left matchings are considered as outliers, and their w in Eq. 2 are set as zeros. Unfortunately, this method is also not generalizable because specific hardwares are required.

GF [12] is an efficient algorithm for guided refinement. It assumes local linear relationship between *output* and *guided images*, and conducts linear regression to approach *input images*. Therefore, both intensity similarity and edge consistency are considered. It is defined as

$$\begin{cases} q_i = \dfrac{1}{|\Omega|} \sum_{k \in \Omega_i} w_{ik}^a (\mathbf{a}_k^T \mathbf{I}_i + b_k) \\[2ex] (\mathbf{a}_k, b_k) = \arg \min_{\mathbf{a}_k, b_k} \sum_{j \in \Omega_k} \left(R_{jk}(\mathbf{a}_k, b_k) + \epsilon w_k^w \mathbf{a}_k^T \mathbf{a}_k \right) \\[2ex] R_{jk}(\mathbf{a}_k, b_k) = w_j \underset{\triangle}{w_{jk}^t} (\mathbf{a}_k^T \mathbf{I}_j + b_k - p_j)^2, \end{cases} \quad (3)$$

where $\mathbf{a}$ and b are linear parameters, ϵ suppresses large $\mathbf{a}$ for smoothness.

GF are improved in many researches. Anisotropic guided filter [10] introduces the weights w_{ik}^a and weighted guided filter [8] introduces the weights w_k^w. Dai *et al.* [9] relaxed local support region Ω to the entire image domain, and introduced the weights w_{jk}^t based on minimum spanning tree. Additionally, some researches about bidirectional guided filter can be found in [17,18]. These methods introduce various benefits, such as stronger edge-preserving behavior and less halo-effect. However, the inlier fidelities of each p_j is not considered, which should be controlled by the weight w_j.

WMF [15] produces q by picking values from p. It is robust to outliers because unpicked pixels have no impact on the result. WMF is defined as

$$\begin{cases} h(i,v) = \sum_{j \in \Omega_i} w_j w_{i,j} \delta(p_j - v) \\[2ex] q_i = v' \\[2ex] \sum_{v=l}^{v'} h(i,v) \leqslant \dfrac{1}{2} \sum_{v=l}^{u} h(i,v), \quad \sum_{v=l}^{v'+1} h(i,v) > \dfrac{1}{2} \sum_{v=l}^{u} h(i,v), \end{cases} \quad (4)$$

where $\delta(x)$ is 1 if x equals 0, and is 0 otherwise. The weight $w_{i,j}$ depends on the input $\mathbf{I}_i$ and $\mathbf{I}_j$. It can be calculated based on the kernel of any edge-ware filter. Despite the robustness, WMF might fail when filter size is large or some outliers happen to be the medians. This problem can be improved if the fidelity of each single pixel is available. It requires the weight denoted as w_j. It is not originally included in [15], but can be easily realized without increasing complexity.

As introduced, outlier detections for guided refinement are either absent or not generalizable. The weights marked by triangles in Eq. 1, Eq. 2, Eq. 3 and Eq. 4 are only available for specific models and hardwares. We argue that a general outlier detection method should exist since guided refinements have the same purpose whatever the applications. In this paper, we propose ALRe, which to our best knowledge is the first attempt to this problem.

3   Anchored Linear Residual

We assume local linear relationship between *ouput images* q and *guided images* $\mathbf{I}$, which means

$$q_i = \mathbf{a}_k^T \mathbf{I}_i + b_k, \quad i \in \Omega_k, \quad (5)$$

where $(\mathbf{a}_k, b_k)$ are linear parameters, Ω_k is the local region centered at pixel k. If *input images* p are simply q affected by zero-mean noise n, as

$$p = q + n, \tag{6}$$

the optimal q can be solved by linear regression. However, the residual might be large due to outliers, which significantly against the local linear assumption.

The degree of a given pixel k against the local linear assumption is measured on Ω_k by three steps: 1) assume k is an inlier with no noise; 2) find the optimal q_i based on the local linear assumption, where $i \in \Omega_k$; 3) check how well the inlier assumption and local linear assumption are supported. The first step assumes k is an anchored pixel, which means

$$p_k = q_k = \mathbf{a}_k^T \mathbf{I}_k + b_k. \tag{7}$$

The second step means to find the $(\mathbf{a}_k, b_k)$ minimizing

$$e_k = \frac{1}{\sum_{i \in \Omega_k} w_i} \sum_{i \in \Omega_k} w_i (q_i - p_i)^2 = \frac{1}{\sum_{i \in \Omega_k} w_i} \sum_{i \in \Omega_k} w_i (\mathbf{a}_k^T \mathbf{I}_i + b_k - p_i)^2, \tag{8}$$

where w_i is the fidelity of pixel i being an inlier. The last step is implemented based on the residual e_k, as

$$w_k = \frac{\frac{1}{\max(\mathrm{LB}, \min(\mathrm{UB}, \sqrt{e_k}))} - \frac{1}{\mathrm{UB}} + \epsilon}{\frac{1}{\mathrm{LB}} - \frac{1}{\mathrm{UB}} + \epsilon}, \tag{9}$$

where $(\mathrm{LB}, \mathrm{UB})$ are the bounds of $\sqrt{e}$. When e_k is out of the bounds, pixel k is considered as pure inlier and outlier respectively. ϵ is a small number for numerical stability. In this paper, $(\mathrm{LB}, \mathrm{UB}, \epsilon)$ equals $(0.01, 0.3, 0.001)$.

With some algebraic manipulations on Eq. 7 and Eq. 8, it yields

$$\begin{cases} \mathbf{C}_k = \sum_{i \in \Omega_k} w_i (\mathbf{I}_i - \mathbf{I}_k)(\mathbf{I}_i - \mathbf{I}_k)^T \\ \mathbf{a}_k = \mathbf{C}_k^{-1} \sum_{i \in \Omega_k} w_i (p_i - p_k)(\mathbf{I}_i - \mathbf{I}_k) \cdot \\ b_k = p_k - \mathbf{a}_k^T \mathbf{I}_k \end{cases} \tag{10}$$

In programming, it is

$$\begin{cases} \mathbf{C}_k = (\overline{w \mathbf{II}^T})_k + (\overline{w})_k \mathbf{I}_k \mathbf{I}_k^T - (\overline{w \mathbf{I}})_k \mathbf{I}_k^T - \mathbf{I}_k (\overline{w \mathbf{I}^T})_k + \epsilon \\ \mathbf{a}_k = \mathbf{C}_k^{-1} \left((\overline{wp \mathbf{I}})_k - p_k (\overline{w \mathbf{I}})_k - (\overline{wp})_k \mathbf{I}_k + (\overline{w})_k p_k \mathbf{I}_k \right) \\ b_k = p_k - \mathbf{a}_k^T \mathbf{I}_k \\ e_k = \left(\mathbf{a}_k^T (\overline{w \mathbf{II}^T})_k \mathbf{a}_k + (\overline{w})_k b_k^2 + (\overline{wp^2})_k + 2 b_k \mathbf{a}_k^T (\overline{w \mathbf{I}})_k \right. \\ \qquad \left. - 2 \mathbf{a}_k^T (\overline{wp \mathbf{I}})_k - 2 b_k (\overline{wp})_k \right) \Big/ \left((\overline{w})_k + \epsilon \right) \end{cases} \tag{11}$$

where ϵ is a diagonal matrix whose elements all equal ϵ, $(\overline{p})_k$ is the mean value of p in Ω_k, so do the others. The deduction is similar to GF [12], we recommend it to readers who need more details.

Since e and w are interdependent, we use an iteration strategy as $w^t \rightarrow e^{t+1} \rightarrow w^{t+1} \rightarrow ...$, where $w^0 = 1$. The terminal condition is

$$\Delta e^{t+1} = \sum_k |e_k^{t+1} - e_k^t| < \epsilon. \tag{12}$$

In practice, it takes 5–10 iterations. The final ALRe of pixel k, that is e_k, represents its outlier likelihood. In most algorithms, the inlier fidelity w_k is preferred.

Note that, the mean values in Eq. 11 for all the k can be calculated by boxfilter with $O(N)$ complexity, where N is the pixel number. The number of iterations is independent of N. Therefore, the algorithm is $O(N)$ overall.

4   Analysis

4.1   Invariance and Asymmetry

ALRe is invariant to linear transforms on *guided images* and shifts on *input images* because

$$e(\alpha_p p + \beta_p, \alpha_{\mathbf{I}} \mathbf{I} + \beta_{\mathbf{I}}) \equiv \alpha_p^2 e(p, \mathbf{I}), \tag{13}$$

where $(\alpha_p, \alpha_{\mathbf{I}}, \beta_p, \beta_{\mathbf{I}})$ are scalars satisfying $\alpha_{\mathbf{I}}^2 \neq 0$. It can be proven as

$$\begin{cases} \tilde{\mathbf{I}} = \alpha_{\mathbf{I}}^T \mathbf{I} + \beta_{\mathbf{I}} \\ \tilde{p} = \alpha_p p + \beta_p \end{cases} \Rightarrow \tilde{\mathbf{C}} = \alpha_{\mathbf{I}}^2 \mathbf{C} \Rightarrow \begin{cases} \tilde{a} = \dfrac{\alpha_p}{\alpha_{\mathbf{I}}} a \\ \tilde{b} = \alpha_p b \end{cases} \Rightarrow \tilde{e} = \alpha_p^2 e. \tag{14}$$

Equation 13 also reveals the asymmetry of ALRe, which fulfills the concept of edge consistency. Given a pair of *input* and *guided images*, the sharpness can be tuned by α_p and $\alpha_{\mathbf{I}}$. When α_p is large, *input image* has sharp edges, ALRe is small only if *input* and *guided images* closely follow the local linear assumption due to the large a_p^2. This fits the description *"Output image has an edge only if guided image has an edge"*. When α_p is small, *input image* is smooth, ALRe is small because of the small a_p^2. The sharpness of *guided image* is unessential. This fits another fold of the description, as *"Output image can be smooth whether guided image has an edge or not"*. In most applications, *guided image* has more edges than *input image*, but it will not lead to large ALRe because of this asymmetry.

4.2   vs. Linear Residual

Now contemplate the necessity of the iteration framework and equality constraint, without which, the algorithm degenerates to a single linear regression and causes following problems.

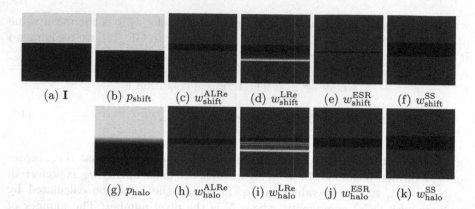

Fig. 1. Comparison of outlier detection methods. Weight maps are displayed in color. Warmer the color, larger the value. The edge of p_{shift} is misaligned with $\mathbf{I}$, and p_{halo} has halo-effect. (Color figure online)

1. If the outlier likelihood of k is investigated based on the linear residual of Ω_k, then the outliers will undermine the fidelities of all its neighbors;
2. If the outlier likelihood of k is investigated based on the distances between p_k and the optimal fitted result of Ω_k, then the residual will be small if $p_k \approx (\bar{p})_k$ and $\mathbf{I}_k \approx (\bar{\mathbf{I}})_k$ even though p_k might be an obvious outlier.

The first problem can be seen in Fig. 1d, where the blue belt is over wide. As a comparison, the belt in Fig. 1c exactly cover the misaligned region. The second problem can be seen in Fig. 1i, where the pixels in the middle of the halo have high fidelities. As shown in Fig. 1h, with the equality constraint, these fake inliers disappear because the result crossing them can not fit other samples well.

4.3   vs. Edge Strength Ratio

The smoothness term of WLS [11] might be the simplest and most straightforward definition of edge consistency. It can be implemented as

$$w_k^{\text{ESR}} = \frac{|G(q_k)| + \epsilon}{|G(\mathbf{I}_k)| + \epsilon},\tag{15}$$

where $|G(x)|$ is the gradient module of x. As shown in Fig. 1, w^{ESR} reveals the misaligned edge in p_{shift} and the halo in p_{halo}. However, the result Fig. 1e can not help guided refinement algorithms to improve edge consistency. As a comparison, w^{ALRe} correctly reveals all the pixels need to be changed.

4.4   vs. SSIM

Structure similarity is one of the three similarity indexes of SSIM [14] defined as

$$w_k^{SS} = 1 - \frac{\sigma_k^{pI} + \epsilon}{\sigma_k^p \sigma_k^I + \epsilon},\tag{16}$$

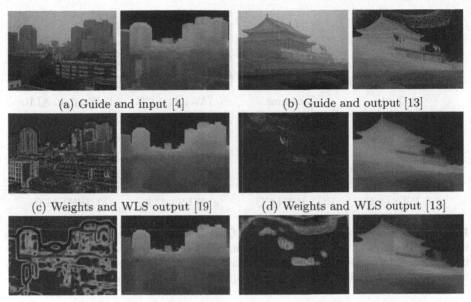

(a) Guide and input [4]   (b) Guide and output [13]

(c) Weights and WLS output [19]   (d) Weights and WLS output [13]

(e) Weights provided by ALRe and corresponding outputs.

Fig. 2. Transmission map refinements. (a,b) Hazy images, and the initial transmission maps based on dark channel prior [4] and haze-line model [13] respectively; (c,d) The weight maps and the refined results based on Zhu *et al.* [19] and Berman *et al.* [13] respectively; (e) The weight maps based on ALRe and corresponding results.

where (σ_k^p, σ_k^I) are standard deviations of p and I (single channel) in Ω_k, σ_k^{pI} is cross-covariance. Despite the outstanding performance in various fields, SSIM is not the right method for detecting outliers of edge consistency. Firstly, it lacks the feature of asymmetry. Secondly, outliers will undermine the SSIM of all its neighbors as shown in Fig. 1f and Fig. 1k, where the blue belts are over wide.

5   Applications

ALRe is tested by four applications. The guided refinement algorithms in Sect. 2 are employed. ALRe improves these algorithms by offering per-pixel inlier fidelities as their data weights w (the ones marked by triangles).

5.1   Transmission Refinement for Haze Removal

In the field of haze removal, hazy images are considered as haze-free images attenuated by atmospheric lights, and transmission maps represent the attenuation ratios. With evenly dispersed haze, attenuation ratios are related to scene depths. Therefore, transmission edges should be consistent with depth edges. Since depth edges mostly happens on color edges, transmission maps are expected to have edge consistency with hazy images.

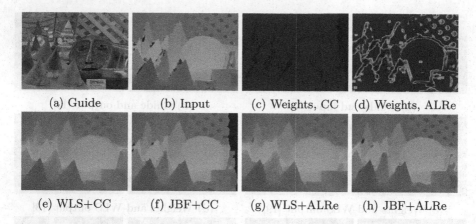

(a) Guide   (b) Input   (c) Weights, CC   (d) Weights, ALRe

(e) WLS+CC   (f) JBF+CC   (g) WLS+ALRe   (h) JBF+ALRe

Fig. 3. Disparity map refinements. (a) Color image; (b,c) The initial disparity map based on Hosni *et al.* [5] and the weight map based on cross check (both require an image from another view); (d) The weight map based on ALRe; (e,f) The refined results based on WLS and JBF with cross check. (g,h) Corresponding results with ALRe.

Limited by existing technologies, transmission maps usually have unsatisfactory edge consistency, thus a refinement guided by hazy images is popular [4,13,16]. In Fig. 2a, the *input image* is produced based on the dark channel prior [4]. It has outliers named block effect, which indicates the over-estimated transmissions in the vicinity of large depth jumps. Zhu *et al.* [19] detects these outliers based on an improved local constant assumption. The result is shown in Fig. 2c. In Fig. 2b, the *input image* is based on the haze-line model [13]. Outliers exist due to short haze-lines, which are traceable as shown in Fig. 2d. Benefiting from the weights, WLS erases these outliers well.

ALRe is able to detect these outliers without any prior knowledge of block effect or haze-line model. In Fig. 2e, ALRe predicts both kinds of outliers correctly. The results are almost the same with Fig. 2c and Fig. 2d.

5.2 Disparity Refinement for Depth Estimation

Disparity refers to the difference in image locations of a point seen by different cameras. Disparity maps are inversely proportional to depth maps, whose edges are mostly consistent with color edges. Therefore, they are also expected to have edge consistency with color images. Disparities can be estimated by stereo matching [5]. However, it might be false or invalid on several pixels due to occlusions. An example of Middlebury dataset 2003 [20] is shown in Fig. 3a. The initial disparity map in Fig. 3b is generated by Hosni *et al.* [5]. Outliers against edge consistency can be seen near the edges. Hosni *et al.* [5] traces them by cross check, which requires the disparity map from another view.

ALRe could detect these outliers without another view. The result is displayed in Fig. 3d, where low weights are in the right positions referring to the binary result of cross check in Fig. 3c. The refined results are similar with each

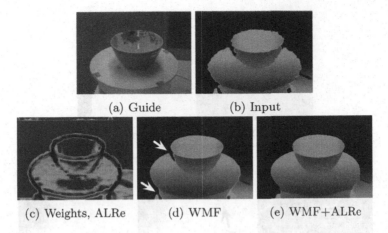

(a) Guide   (b) Input

(c) Weights, ALRe   (d) WMF   (e) WMF+ALRe

Fig. 4. Depth map refinements. (a) Color image; (b) Rough depth map; (c) The weight map based on ALRe; (d) The refined result based on WMF without ALRe; (e) Corresponding result with ALRe.

other. Clearly, cross check is more reliable than ALRe because of the extra information. However, extra information are not always available. For example, RGB-D camera usually provides depth maps with misaligned edges as shown in Fig. 4b. This problem can be solved by WMF. As shown in Fig. 4d, the winding edges are well regularized, but the values of the pointed regions are wrong picked. These regions have zero values because they are invisible to the depth camera, thus should not be considered in median calculation. With the help of ALRe, these regions are trivial in WMF and a more convincing result is achieved.

5.3   Guided Feathering

Guided feathering produces an alpha matte of complex object boundaries based on rough binary mask, which can be obtained manually or from other segmentation methods. GF is an efficient tool for this task but not error-tolerant enough, thus masks with large errors might lead to halo-effects. As shown in Fig. 5d, the result of GF inherits the over-estimated and under-estimated errors marked by A and B. As displayed in Fig. 5c, the weights are all low near the boundaries. Furthermore, phantom of the edges from both images can be observed, and the regions between them have almost zero fidelities. With this message, a more convincing matte is produced as shown in Fig. 8e.

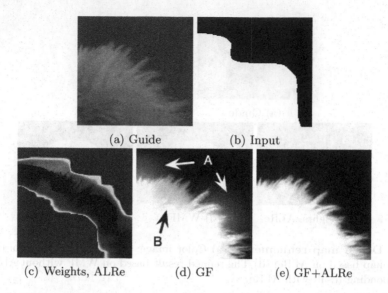

(a) Guide   (b) Input

(c) Weights, ALRe   (d) GF   (e) GF+ALRe

Fig. 5. Feathering. (a) Color image; (b) Rough mask; (c) The weight map based on ALRe; (d) The result based on GF without ALRe; (e) Corresponding result with ALRe.

5.4   Edge-Preserving Smoothing

As an edge-preserving filter, GF has the problem of halo-effects. Various methods have been proposed to solve this problem by introducing weights [8–10], as listed in Eq. 3. In this paper, we address edge-preserving smoothing in the view of guided refinement. The sharp input is firstly smoothed by Gaussian low-pass filter. Then, the smoothed result is refined back by GF in the guidance of the sharp input. Since weak noises are mostly erased by low-pass filter, they are not enhanced in guided refinement. On the other hand, sharp edges are turned into weak edges and halos, leaving clues for GF to enhance them back. ALRe could recognizes these sharp edges based on the halos, as shown in Fig. 6c. The result is shown in Fig. 6e, where the halo-effects are trivial.

6   Experiment

In this section, we compare the outlier detection accuracies of WMF and ALRe on synthetic images. The IoU (intersection over union) of outlier detection result and groundtruth is used for evaluation, as

$$\text{IoU(GT,MASK)} = \frac{|\text{GT} \cap \text{MASK}|}{|\text{GT} \cup \text{MASK}|}. \tag{17}$$

(a) Guide   (b) Input

(c) Weights, ALRe   (d) GF$_{a,a}$ (e) GF$_{b,a}$+ALRe

Fig. 6. Edge preserving filtering. (a) Sharp image; (b) The smoothed image based on Gaussian low-pass filter; (c) The weight map of (b) based on ALRe; (d) The smoothed result of (a) guided by itself based on GF; (e) The enhanced result of (b) guided by (a) based on GF with ALRe.

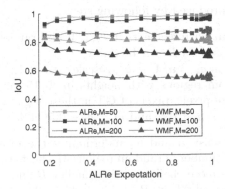

Fig. 7. Outlier detection accuracy.

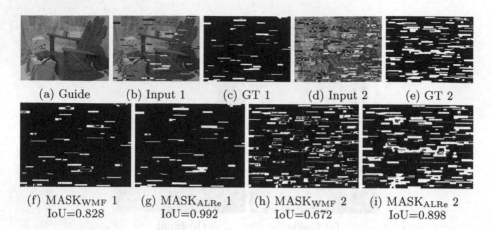

(a) Guide   (b) Input 1   (c) GT 1   (d) Input 2   (e) GT 2

(f) MASK_WMF 1   (g) MASK_ALRe 1   (h) MASK_WMF 2   (i) MASK_ALRe 2
IoU=0.828   IoU=0.992   IoU=0.672   IoU=0.898

Fig. 8. Comparison of ALRe and WMF on outlier detection. (a) Guide image; (b) Contaminated input image ($R = 99, M = 50$); (c,f,g) Corresponding GT, MASK_WMF and MASK_ALRe; (d) Contaminated input image ($R = 15, M = 200$); (e,h,i) Corresponding GT, MASK_WMF and MASK_ALRe;

MASK and GT are binary images, whose pixel x equals 1 if $p(x)$ is asserted as an outlier. The MASK of ALRe is

$$\text{MASK}_{\text{ALRe}}(p, \mathbf{I})_k = \begin{cases} 1, & w(p, \mathbf{I})_k < 0.05 \\ 0, & w(p, \mathbf{I})_k \geqslant 0.05 \end{cases}. \tag{18}$$

The MASK of WMF is produced based on the intuition that pixels greatly changed after filtering are outliers, thus

$$\text{MASK}_{\text{WMF}}(p, \mathbf{I})_k = \begin{cases} 1, & |\text{WMF}(p, \mathbf{I}) - p|_k > 0.3 \\ 0, & |\text{WMF}(p, \mathbf{I}) - p|_k \leqslant 0.3 \end{cases}. \tag{19}$$

Input images $\mathbf{I}$ are provided by Middlebury dataset 2014 [21]. Contaminated input p and GT are produced by following steps.

1. generate random $\mathbf{a}_k$ with elements in $[0, 1/3]$ and random b_k in $[-1, 1]$;
2. smooth $\mathbf{a}$ and b based on $R \times R$ boxfilter;
3. calculate q based on $q_k = \mathbf{a}_k^T \mathbf{I}_k + b_k$, rescale q to $[0, 1]$;
4. generate M random regions with heights in $[0, 15]$ and lengths in $[5, 105]$ centered at random pixels, pixels of GT in these regions equal 1;
5. $p_k = q_k + 0.5\text{GT}$ for $q_k < 0.5$, and $p_k = q_k - 0.5\text{GT}$ for $q_k \geqslant 0.5$.

A small R leads to noisy $\mathbf{a}$ and b, undermining the local linear assumption between q and $\mathbf{I}$. The number of random regions M affects the number of outliers. Therefore, the task is more challenge with smaller R and larger M. We test 22 kinds of R and 3 kinds of M, as $R = [15, 19, 23, ..., 99]$ and $M = [50; 100; 200]$.

The size of Ω for ALRe and WMF is 25×25 (the inputs are 640×480). Larger R leads to better local linear relationship, thus higher $\mathrm{mean}(w_{ALRe}(q, \mathbf{I}))$. It is the basic of ALRe, therefore, we term it as ALRe expectation.

The results are illustrated in Fig. 7. As shown, both ALRe and WMF are barely affected by ALRe expectation, but degraded when M increases. The mean IoUs of ALRe corresponding to the increasing M are 0.978, 0.958 and 0.868, while the ones of WMF are 0.814, 0.727, 0.556. The gap is about 0.2. An example is displayed in Fig. 8. MASK_{ALRe} is almost the same with GT when $R = 99$, $M = 50$. In the case of $R = 15$, $M = 200$, the output is severely contaminated. However, MASK_{ALRe} is still plausible. As a comparison, MASK_{WMF} in both cases contain undesired hollows, where the outliers should be changed by 0.5 but less than 0.3.

7 Conclusion

In this paper, we propose a general outlier detection method for guided refinement, termed ALRe. Different from the traditional model-based and hardware-based detections, ALRe produces meaningful predictions without any prior knowledge. Valuable features such as asymmetry and linear complexity are achieved. The effectiveness of ALRe is verified based on four applications and four guided refinement algorithms. It shows that the weight map provided by ALRe is valuable and even comparable to customized methods. Quantitative comparison reveals that ALRe could detect outliers accurately, even though the image and the local linear relationship are severely contaminated. Its accuracy represented by IoU is about 0.2 higher than weighted median filter.

Acknowledgements. This work was supported in part by the National Key Research and Development Program of China under Grant 2020YFB1312800 and in part by the National Natural Science Foundation of China under Grant U1909206.

References

1. Levin, A., Lischinski, D., Weiss, Y.: A closed-form solution to natural image matting. IEEE Trans. Pattern Anal. Mach. Intell. **30**(2), 228–242 (2008)
2. Petschnigg, G., Szeliski, R., Agrawala, M., Cohen, M., Hoppe, H., Toyama, K.: Digital photography with flash and no-flash image pairs. ACM Trans. Graph. **23**(3), 664–672 (2004)
3. Liu, W., Chen, X., Yang, J., Wu, Q.: Robust color guided depth map restoration. IEEE Trans. Image Process. **26**(1), 315–327 (2016)
4. He, K., Sun, J., Tang, X.: Single image haze removal using dark channel prior. IEEE Trans. Pattern Anal. Mach. Intell. **33**(12), 2341–2353 (2011)
5. Hosni, A., Rhemann, C., Bleyer, M., Rother, C., Gelautz, M.: Fast cost-volume filtering for visual correspondence and beyond. IEEE Trans. Pattern Anal. Mach. Intell. **35**(2), 504–511 (2012)
6. Park, J., Kim, H., Tai, Y.W., Brown, M.S., Kweon, I.: High quality depth map upsampling for 3D-TOF cameras. In: International Conference on Computer Vision, pp. 1623–1630 (2011)

7. Yang, J., Ye, X., Li, K., Hou, C., Wang, Y.: Color-guided depth recovery from RGB-D data using an adaptive autoregressive model. IEEE Trans. Image Process. **23**(8), 3443–3458 (2014)
8. Li, Z., Zheng, J., Zhu, Z., Yao, W., Wu, S.: Weighted guided image filtering. IEEE Trans. Image Process. **24**(1), 120–129 (2014)
9. Dai, L., Yuan, M., Zhang, F., Zhang, X.: Fully connected guided image filtering. In: IEEE International Conference on Computer Vision, pp. 352–360 (2015)
10. Ochotorena, C.N., Yamashita, Y.: Anisotropic guided filtering. IEEE Trans. Image Process. **29**, 1397–1412 (2019)
11. Farbman, Z., Fattal, R., Lischinski, D., Szeliski, R.: Edge-preserving decompositions for multi-scale tone and detail manipulation. ACM Trans. Graph. **27**(3), 1–10 (2008)
12. He, K., Sun, J., Tang, X.: Guided image filtering. IEEE Trans. Pattern Anal. Mach. Intell. **35**(6), 1397–1409 (2013)
13. Berman, D., Avidan, S.: Non-local image dehazing. In: IEEE Conference on Computer Vision and Pattern Recognition, pp. 1674–1682 (2016)
14. Wang, Z., Bovik, A.C., Sheikh, H.R., Simoncelli, E.P.: Image quality assessment: from error visibility to structural similarity. IEEE Trans. Image Process. **13**(4), 600–612 (2004)
15. Ma, Z., He, K., Wei, Y., Sun, J., Wu, E.: Constant time weighted median filtering for stereo matching and beyond. In: IEEE International Conference on Computer Vision, pp. 49–56 (2013)
16. Fattal, R.: Dehazing using color-lines. ACM Trans. Graph. **34**(1), 1–14 (2014)
17. Guo, X., Li, Y., Ma, J., Ling, H.: Mutually guided image filtering. IEEE Trans. Pattern Anal. Mach. Intell. **42**(3), 1283–1290 (2018)
18. Li, Y., Huang, J.B., Ahuja, N., Yang, M.H.: Joint image filtering with deep convolutional networks. IEEE Trans. Pattern Anal. Mach. Intell. **41**(8), 1909–1923 (2019)
19. Zhu, M., He, B., Liu, J., Yu, J.: Boosting dark channel dehazing via weighted local constant assumption. Sig. Process. **171**, 107453 (2020)
20. Scharstein, D., Szeliski, R.: High-accuracy stereo depth maps using structured light. In: IEEE Conference on Computer Vision and Pattern Recognition, p. I (2003)
21. Scharstein, D., et al.: High-resolution stereo datasets with subpixel-accurate ground truth. In: Jiang, X., Hornegger, J., Koch, R. (eds.) GCPR 2014. LNCS, vol. 8753, pp. 31–42. Springer, Cham (2014). https://doi.org/10.1007/978-3-319-11752-2_3

Author Index

Printed in the United States
By Bookmasters